▷LaunchPad PSYCHOLOGY, Third Edition

LaunchPad for PSYCHOLOGY, Third Edition

Available July 2014 at **http://www.worthpublishers.com/launchpad/schacter3e**

Each chapter in ▷LaunchPad for *PSYCHOLOGY,* **Third Edition,** features a collection of activities carefully chosen to help master the major concepts. The site serves students as a comprehensive online study guide, available any time, with opportunities for self-quizzing with instant feedback, exam preparation, and further exploration of topics from the textbook. For instructors, all units and activities can be instantly assigned, and students' results and analytics are collected in the Gradebook.

FOR STUDENTS

- Full e-Book of *PSYCHOLOGY,* Third Edition
- LearningCurve Quizzing
- Student Video Activities
- Interactive Flashcards
- PsychInvestigator
- PsychSim 5.0 by Thomas Ludwig, Hope College
- *Scientific American* Newsfeed

FOR INSTRUCTORS

- Gradebook
- Presentation Slides
- iClicker Questions
- Electronic Figures, Photos, and Tables
- Correlation of *PSYCHOLOGY*, Third Edition, to APA Learning Goals
- Correlation of *PSYCHOLOGY*, Third Edition, to MCAT 2015 Topics

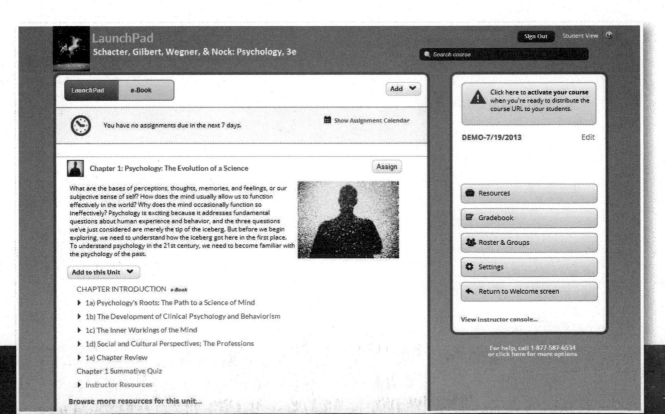

PSYCHOLOGY

RJ Muna

What are these people doing? Dancing? Karate? Levitation? Is the woman in this photo reaching for someone, or pointing to something? And what's up with those guys behind the glass screen? Do they have something to hide? Are they heading in the wrong direction?

Much of what people do can be understood by systematically observing them and testing how they respond in different situations. However, a lot of human thought, emotion, and behavior, and the factors that drive it, occurs in private, outside of the view of others (at least the most interesting parts do). Psychological scientists have developed a wide range of methods that allow them to "peek behind the glass screen," so to speak, and this photo by RJ Muna grabbed us in part because it so nicely captures this theme. This photo also highlights the beauty and excitement of human behavior, which is what drew each of us to psychology in the first place.

PSYCHOLOGY

THIRD EDITION

DANIEL L. SCHACTER
HARVARD UNIVERSITY

DANIEL T. GILBERT
HARVARD UNIVERSITY

DANIEL M. WEGNER
HARVARD UNIVERSITY

MATTHEW K. NOCK
HARVARD UNIVERSITY

WORTH PUBLISHERS

A Macmillan Higher Education Company

Senior Vice President, Editorial and Production: Catherine Woods
Publisher: Kevin Feyen
Senior Acquisitions Editor: Daniel DeBonis
Senior Development Editor: Valerie Raymond
Editorial Assistant: Katie Garrett
Marketing Manager: Lindsay Johnson
Associate Director of Market Research: Carlise Stembridge
Executive Media Editor: Rachel Comerford
Director of Development for Print and Digital Products: Tracey Kuehn
Associate Managing Editor: Lisa Kinne
Project Editor: Robert Errera
Production Manager: Sarah Segal
Photo Editor: Cecilia Varas
Photo Researcher: Elyse Rieder
Chapter Opener Researcher: Lyndall Culbertson
Art Director and Cover Designer: Babs Reingold
Text Designers: Babs Reingold and Lyndall Culbertson
Layout Designer: Paul Lacy
Illustration Coordinator: Matthew McAdams
Illustrations: Evelyn Pence, Jackie Heda, Matthew McAdams, Matt Holt, Christy Krames,
         Don Stewart, and Todd Buck
Cover Photograph: RJ Muna
Composition: MPS Limited
Printing and Binding: RR Donnelley

Chapter Opener Credits: p. xxxiv, Yagi Studio/Getty Images; p. 38, photosindia/Getty Images;
p. 78, Cary Wolinsky/Getty Images; p. 128, Andrew Geiger; p. 176, Chad Baker/Getty Images;
p. 220, David Johnston/Getty Images; p. 264, Gandee Vasan/Getty Images; p. 312, Image
Source/agefotostock; p. 350, Kalium/AgeFotostock; p. 394, Christopher Wilson; p. 424, Tooga/
Getty Images; p. 470, Copyright Karim Parris; p. 506, Tim Macpherson/Getty Images;
p. 548, © Fotosearch/age footstock; p. 582, © easyFotostock/age footstock; p. 626, © 2008 Lívia
Fernandes/Getty Images

Library of Congress Project Control Number: 2013955842

ISBN-13: 978-1-4641-0603-3
ISBN-10: 1-4641-0603-7

Printed in the United States of America

First printing

Worth Publishers
41 Madison Avenue
New York, NY 10010
www.worthpublishers.com

We dedicate this edition to the memory of Dan Wegner, our co-author, colleague, and deeply missed friend.

About the Authors

Daniel Schacter is William R. Kenan, Jr., Professor of Psychology at Harvard University. Dan received his BA degree from the University of North Carolina at Chapel Hill. He subsequently developed a keen interest in amnesic disorders associated with various kinds of brain damage. He continued his research and education at the University of Toronto, where he received his PhD in 1981. He taught on the faculty at Toronto for the next six years before joining the psychology department at the University of Arizona in 1987. In 1991, he joined the faculty at Harvard University. His research explores the relationship between conscious and unconscious forms of memory, the nature of distortions and errors in remembering, and the ways in which we use memory to imagine future events. Many of Schacter's studies are summarized in his 1996 book, *Searching for Memory: The Brain, The Mind, and The Past*, and his 2001 book, *The Seven Sins of Memory: How the Mind Forgets and Remembers*, both winners of the APA's William James Book Award. Schacter has also received a number of awards for teaching and research, including the Harvard-Radcliffe Phi Beta Kappa Teaching Prize, the Warren Medal from the Society of Experimental Psychologists, and the Award for Distinguished Scientific Contributions from the American Psychological Association. In 2013, he was elected to the National Academy of Sciences.

Daniel Wegner was the John Lindsley Professor of Psychology in Memory of William James at Harvard University. He received his BS in 1970 and PhD in 1974, both from Michigan State University. He began his teaching career at Trinity University in San Antonio, TX, before receiving his appointments at the University of Virginia in 1990 and then Harvard University in 2000. He was a Fellow of the American Academy of Arts and Sciences and also the recipient of the William James Award from the Association for Psychological Science, the Award for Distinguished Scientific Contributions from the American Psychological Association, and the Distinguished Scientist Award from the Society of Experimental Social Psychology. His research focused on thought suppression and mental control, transactive memory in relationships and groups, and the experience of conscious will. His work on thought suppression and consciousness served as the basis of two popular books, *White Bears and Other Unwanted Thoughts* and the *Illusion of Conscious Will*, both of which were named *Choice* Outstanding Academic Books. He died in 2013.

Daniel Gilbert is Edgar Pierce Professor of Psychology at Harvard University. Dan received his his BA from the University of Colorado at Denver and his PhD from Princeton University. From 1985 to 1996 he taught at the University of Texas, Austin, and in 1996 he joined the faculty of Harvard University. He has received the American Psychological Association's Distinguished Scientific Award for an Early Career Contribution to Psychology, the Diener Award for Outstanding Contributions to Social Psychology, and has won teaching awards that include the Phi Beta Kappa Teaching Prize and the Harvard College Professorship. His research focuses on how and how well people think about their emotional reactions to future events. He is the author of the international best seller *Stumbling on Happiness*, which won the Royal Society's General Prize for best popular science book of the year, and he is the co-writer and host of the PBS television series, *This Emotional Life*.

Matthew Nock is a Professor of Psychology at Harvard University. Matt received his BA from Boston University (1995) and his PhD from Yale University (2003), and he completed his clinical internship at Bellevue Hospital and the New York University Child Study Center (2003). Matt joined the faculty of Harvard University in 2003 and has been there ever since. While an undergraduate, Matt became very interested in the question of why people do things to intentionally harm themselves, and he has been conducting research aimed at answering this question ever since. His research is multidisciplinary in nature and uses a range of methodological approaches (e.g., epidemiologic surveys, laboratory-based experiments, and clinic-based studies) to better understand how these behaviors develop, how to predict them, and how to prevent their occurrence. He has received multiple teaching awards at Harvard, four early career awards recognizing his research, and in 2011 was named a MacArthur Fellow.

Brief Contents

Contents

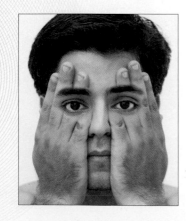

Chapter 3   Neuroscience and Behavior..........79

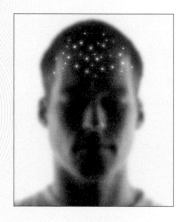

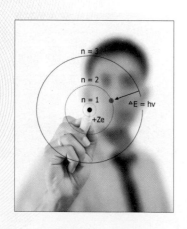

second and somewhat more important reason for bringing out a new edition is that things change. Science changes (psychologists know all sorts of things about the mind and the brain that they didn't know just a few years ago), the world changes (when we wrote the first edition, no one had heard of an iPad or Barack Obama), and we change (our research and reading gave us new perspectives on psychological issues, and our writing and teaching showed us new ways to help students learn). With all of these changes happening around us and to us, we felt that our book should change as well.

Changes in the Third Edition

New focus on critical thinking

As sciences uncover new evidence and develop new theories, scientists change their minds. Some of the facts that students learn in a science course will still be facts a decade later, and others will require qualification or will turn out to have just been plain wrong. That's why students not only need to learn the facts but also how to *think* about facts—how to examine, question, and weigh the evidence that scientists produce. We emphasize this sort of critical thinking throughout our text, of course, but in this edition, we have included a new section dedicated entirely to helping students think about the mistakes human beings make when they try to consider evidence (see "Thinking Critically about Evidence" in Chapter 2: Methods in Psychology, page 66). We hope this section will help students learn how to use empirical evidence to develop well-grounded beliefs—not only about psychological science but also about the stuff of their everyday lives.

New section "Learning in the Classroom"

Like other psychology textbooks, the first two editions of our text provided in-depth coverage of many different kinds of learning, ranging from classical conditioning to observational learning. This edition still does this. But strangely enough, the Learning chapters in most psychology texts, including the previous two editions of this text, haven't said much about the very kind of learning that is most relevant to our readers: learning in the classroom. We think that it is about time to change this puzzling state of affairs, and so we have. Chapter 7 now includes a new section on learning in the classroom that summarizes some of the exciting recent developments in this area, including evaluation of the most effective study techniques, insights into cognitive illusions that can mislead us into studying ineffectively, research on how to improve attention and learning during lectures, and discussion of the prospects for online learning. The Learning chapter should be relevant to the lives of students, and we've done our best to make it so.

New research

A textbook should give students a complete tour of the classics, of course, but it should also take them out dancing on the cutting edge. We want students to realize that psychology is not a museum piece—it is not just a collection of past events but also of current events—and that this young and evolving science has a place for them if they want it. So we've packed the third edition with information about what's happening in the field today. Not only have we included more than 400 new citations, but we've also featured some of the hottest new findings in the "Hot Science" boxes that you'll find in every chapter.

Chapter Number	Hot Science
1	Psychology as a Hub Science, p. 34
2	Do Violent Movies Make Peaceful Streets?, p. 64
3	Epigenetics and the Persisting Effects of Early Experiences, p. 112
4	Taste: From the Top Down, p. 169
5	The Mind Wanders, p. 185
6	Sleep on It, p. 233
7	Dopamine and Reward Learning in Parkinson's Disease, p. 292
8	The Body of Evidence, p. 325
9	Sudden Insight and the Brain, p. 386
10	Dumb and Dumber?, p. 414
11	A Statistician in the Crib, p. 435
11	The End of History Illusion, p. 460
12	Personality on the Surface, p. 479
13	Mouse Over, p. 516
13	The Wedding Planner, p. 538
14	Can Being the Target of Discrimination Cause Stress and Illness?, p. 552
15	Optimal Outcome in Autism Spectrum Disorder, p. 615
16	"Rebooting" Psychological Treatment, p. 642

Fully updated coverage of *DSM-5*

One area where there has been lots of new research—and lots of big changes—is in the study of psychological disorders. As you will learn, psychologists use a manual called the *Diagnostic and Statistical Manual of Mental Disorders* (*DSM*) to make decisions about which behaviors should be formally considered "disordered." For instance, we all get sad from time to time, but when should extreme sadness be classified as a psychological disorder that should be treated? The *DSM* answers questions like this. After nearly 20 years of using the fourth edition of the *DSM* (*DSM-IV*), the field of psychology now has an updated fifth edition (*DSM-5*), which was just published in 2013. Psychologists have learned a lot about psychological disorders over the past 20 years, and this third edition of our book contains updated information about how psychologists think about, define, and classify psychological disorders.

New organization

We've also rearranged our table of contents to better fit our changing sense of how psychology is best taught. Specifically, we've moved the chapter on Stress and Health forward so that it now appears before the chapters on Psychological Disorders and Treatment of Psychological Disorders. We think this change improves the flow of the book in several ways. First, as you will learn, the experience of stress has a lot to do with interpersonal events and how we respond to them, information that you will have just learned about in the chapters on Personality and Social Psychology. Second, current models of psychological disorders view them as resulting from an interaction of some underlying predisposition (e.g., genetic or otherwise) and stressful life events. Such models will be much more intuitive if you first learn about the body's stress response. Third, this chapter has information about health-promoting behaviors that could come in handy during exam season—and so better to tell you about them before the end of the semester!

New Other Voices feature

Long before psychologists appeared on Earth, the human nature business was dominated by poets, playwrights, pundits, philosophers, and several other groups beginning with P. Those folks are still in that business today, and they continue to have deep and original insights into how and why people behave as they do. In this edition, we decided to invite some of them to share their thoughts with you via a new feature that we call "Other Voices." In every chapter, you will find a short essay by someone who has three critical qualities: (a) They think deeply, (b) they write beautifully, and (c) they know things we don't. For example, you will find essays by leading journalists such as David Brooks, Ted Gup, Tina Rosenberg, and David Ewing Duncan; best-selling novelists such as Alice Randall; award-winning educators such as Linda Moore and Robert H. Frank; renowned legal scholars such as Gustin Reichbach and Elyn Saks; and eminent scientists such as biologist Greg Hampikian and computer scientist Daphne Koller. And just to make sure we aren't the only psychologists whose voices you hear, we've included essays by Tim Wilson, Chris Chabris, Daniel Simons, and Charles Fernyhough. Every one of these amazing people has something important to say about human nature, and we are delighted that they've agreed to say it in these pages. Not only do these essays encourage students to think critically about a variety of psychological issues, but they also demonstrate both the relevance of psychology to everyday life and the growing importance of our science in the public forum.

Chapter Number	Other Voices
1	Is Psychology a Science?, p. 17
2	Can We Afford Science?, p. 75
3	Neuromyths, p. 124
4	Hallucinations and the Visual System, p. 173
5	A Judge's Plea for Pot, p. 217
6	Early Memories, p. 261
7	Online Learning, p. 308
8	Fat and Happy, p. 339
9	Americans' Future Has to Be Bilingual, p. 364
10	How Science Can Build a Better You, p. 421
11	Men, Who Needs Them?, p. 429
11	You Are Going to Die, p. 467
12	Does the Study of Personality Lack . . . Personality?, p. 503
13	91% of All Students Read This Box and Love It, p. 531
14	Building a Healthier Society?, p. 579
15	Successful and Schizophrenic, p. 613
16	Diagnosis: Human, p. 653

New Changing Minds questions

What can 784 introductory psychology professors agree about? They can agree that students usually come into their first psychology class with a set of beliefs about the field and that most of these beliefs are wrong. With the help of the wonderful people at Worth Publishers (they made us say that), we conducted a survey of 784 introductory psychology teachers and asked them to name their students' most common misconceptions about psychology. We then created the Changing Minds questions you will see at the end of every chapter. These questions ask you first to think about an everyday situation in which a common misconception might arise, and then to use the science you have just learned to overcome that misconception. We hope these exercises will prepare you to apply what you learn—and maybe even change some minds about psychology (thereby justifying our corny title).

CHANGING MINDS

1. One of the senators from your state is supporting a bill that would impose heavy fines on aggressive drivers who run red lights. One of your classmates thinks this is a good idea. "The textbook taught us a lot about punishment and reward. It's simple. If we punish aggressive driving, its frequency will decline." Is your classmate right? Might the new law backfire? Might another policy be more effective in promoting safe driving?

A Changing Minds question from Chapter 13.

Additional Student Support
Practice

> *Cue questions* encourage critical thinking and help identify the most important concepts in every major section of the text.

> *Bulleted summaries* follow each major section to reinforce key concepts and make it easier to study for the test.

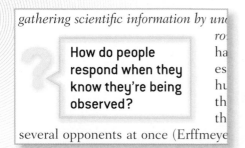

gathering scientific information by un

How do people respond when they know they're being observed?

several opponents at once (Erffmeye

A cue question from Chapter 2.

> *A Key Concept Quiz* at the end of each chapter offers students the opportunity to test what they know.
> *Critical thinking questions* are offered throughout the chapters within a number of the photo captions, offering the opportunity to apply various concepts.

Practical Application

What would the facts and concepts of psychology be without real-world application? Throughout this edition of the text, we provide lots of examples of how the material presented in this book applies to things that you will experience in the real world. For instance, each chapter contains a *Real World* box that applies concepts from inside the book to your life outside the book. (We like this idea so much we even included a box in the Preface! Turn the page to see it.) In addition, because culture influences just about everything we do—from how we perceive lines to how long we'll stand in them—this edition continues to celebrate the rich diversity of human beings both in Culture & Community boxes and throughout the text, as detailed below.

CLEMENT PHILIPPE/ARTERRA PICTURE LIBRARY/ALAMY

According to the theory of natural selection, inherited characteristics that provide a survival advantage tend to spread throughout the population across generations. Why might sensory adaptation have evolved? What survival benefits might it confer to a small animal trying to avoid predators? To a predator trying to hunt prey?

Critical thinking questions in a photo caption from Chapter 4.

Chapter Number	The Real World
1	The Perils of Procrastination, p. 4
1	Improving Study Skills, p. 10
2	Oddsly Enough, p. 61
3	Brain Plasticity and Sensations in Phantom Limbs, p. 104
3	Brain Death and the Vegetative State, p. 123
4	Multitasking, p. 135
4	Music Training: Worth the Time, p. 162
5	Drugs and the Regulation of Consciousness, p. 212
6	Is Google Hurting Our Memories?, p. 248
7	Understanding Drug Overdoses, p. 270
8	Jeet Jet?, p. 337
9	From Zippers to Political Extremism: An Illusion of Understanding, p. 390
10	Look Smart, p. 400
11	Walk This Way, p. 442
12	Are There "Male" and "Female" Personalities?, p. 481
13	Making the Move, p. 519
14	This is Your Brain on Placebos, p. 571
15	How Are Mental Disorders Defined and Diagnosed?, p. 592
16	Types of Psychotherapists, p. 630
16	Treating Severe Mental Disorders, p. 647

Chapter Number	Culture & Community
1	Analytic and Holistic Styles in Western and Eastern Cultures, p. 30
2	Best Place to Fall on Your Face, p. 45
4	Does Culture Influence Change Blindness?, p. 156
5	What Do Dreams Mean to Us around the World?, p. 201
6	Does Culture Affect Childhood Amnesia?, p. 240
7	Are There Cultural Differences in Reinforcers?, p. 281
8	Is It What You Say or How You Say It?, p. 329
9	Does Culture Influence Optimism Bias?, p. 378
12	Does Your Personality Change According to the Language You're Speaking?, p. 492
13	Free Parking, p. 528
14	Land of the Free, Home of the ... Stressed?, p. 566
15	What Do Mental Disorders Look Like in Different Parts of the World?, p. 589
16	Treatment of Psychological Disorders around the World, p. 632

Culture and Multicultural Experience

The Psychology of Men and Women

The Psychology of Men and Women (continued)

THE REAL WORLD

Join the Club!

Once upon a time, Western science was the hobby of wealthy European gentlemen. Fortunately, the face of this field has changed profoundly since its early days and continues to progress even now.

In fact, social changes have led to openness and diversity in psychology more swiftly and completely than in most other fields of study. In 2006, for example, while women were only poorly represented in engineering and the physical sciences, they received more than 71% of all new PhD degrees in psychology (Burrelli, 2008). As you can see in the accompanying figure, although women are earning a growing proportion of PhDs in all fields, they are now a whopping majority in psychology. Meanwhile, psychology PhDs to Hispanic, African American, and Native American students have more than doubled from 1985 to 2005, and those to Asians and Pacific Islanders have tripled (National Science Board, 2008). It is now the future, and in this future, psychology is the science of everyone.

Signs of the openness of psychology are all around. Just take a look at some of the students in undergraduate psychology clubs—or in *Psi Chi* (psychology's undergraduate and graduate student honorary society) or *Psi Beta* (the honorary society for community and junior college psychology students). Psychology students now are far more often women than men (77%; Planty et al., 2008), and there is substantial representation of minority groups in psychology everywhere you look. Like its clubs and honorary societies, the study of psychology is open and welcoming to people of any age, sex, sexual orientation, race, different ability, color, religion, or national or ethnic origin. Please join us!

COURTESY UNIVERSITY OF MISSOURI PSI CHI & PSYCHOLOGY CLUB

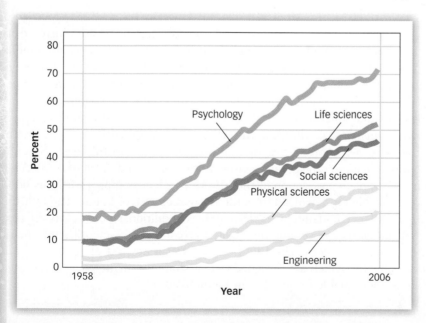

◄ The proportion of new PhDs earned by women has grown faster in psychology than in other fields (Burrelli, 2008).

Focus on Learning Outcomes
Teaching with the APA Learning Goals and Outcomes

In an effort to develop greater consensus on goals and learning outcomes for under-graduate education in psychology, the American Psychological Association (APA) created a task force on Undergraduate Psychology Major Competencies to provide a framework for educators. The task force subsequently published comprehensive recommendations in *The APA Guidelines for the Undergraduate Psychology Major*, recently revised for version 2.0 that was released in May 2013. These revised guidelines present a rigorous standard for what students should gain from foundational courses and from the psychology major as a whole. They comprise five goals relating to the following:

Goal 1: Knowledge Base in Psychology

Goal 2: Scientific Inquiry and Critical Thinking

Goal 3: Ethical and Social Responsibility in a Diverse World

Goal 4: Communication

Goal 5: Professional Development

The intent of the APA Task Force is to provide overarching goals without dictating exactly how students and teachers should achieve them. In that spirit, Worth Publishers offers a wide variety of resources to support students and teachers in achieving the APA outcomes. Most important, a concordance of the content in *Psychology*, Third Edition, to the APA goals is available for download from the Resources area of LaunchPad at http://www.worthpublishers.com/launchpad/schacter3e. To assist with assessment, Worth has tagged all of the items included in the Test Bank accompanying *Psychology*, Third Edition, to the relevant outcomes, and in addition, the Instructor's Resources and LaunchPad learning system feature a variety of activities and additional content items that contribute to the APA goals. All of these resources in combination offer instructors a powerful set of tools for achieving their course outcomes.

Preparing for the MCAT 2015

From 1977 to 2014, the Medical College Admission Test (MCAT) focused on biology, chemistry, and physics, but starting with the test to be administered in 2015, 25% of its questions will cover "Psychological, Social, and Biological Foundations of Behavior," with most of those questions concerning the psychological science taught in introductory psychology courses. According to the *Preview Guide for the MCAT 2015 Exam*, Second Edition, the addition of this content "recognizes the importance of socio-cultural and behavioral determinants of health and health outcomes." The psychology material in the new MCAT covers the breadth of topics in this text, and the table below offers a sample of how the topics in this text's Sensation and Perception chapter correspond precisely to the topics laid out in the MCAT *Preview Guide*. A complete correlation of the MCAT psychology topics with this book's contents is available for download from the Resources area of LaunchPad at http://www. worthpublishers.com/launchpad/schacter3e. In addition, since the MCAT represents a global standard for assessing the ability to reason about scientific information, the Test Bank for *Psychology*, Third Edition, features a new set of data-based questions for each chapter, which are designed to test students' quantitative reasoning. These questions are available for preview in LaunchPad.

MCAT 2015: Categories in Sensation and Perception	SGWN, *Psychology*, Third Edition, Correlations	
Content Category 6A: Sensing the environment	Section Title	Page Number(s)
Sensory Processing	Sensation and Perception	129–173
Sensation	Sensation and Perception	129–173
• Thresholds	Measuring Thresholds	132–133
• Weber's Law	Measuring Thresholds	132–133
• Signal detection theory	Signal Detection	133–134
• Sensory adaptation	Sensory Adaptation	135–136
• Sensory receptors	Sensation and Perception Are Distinct Activities	130–132
• Sensory pathways	The Visual Brain	142–145
	Touch and Pain	163–165
	Body Position, Movement, and Balance	166
	Smell and Taste	167–172
• Types of sensory receptors	Vision I: How the Eyes and the Brain Convert Light Waves to Neural Signals	136–145
	The Human Ear	158–160
	The Body Senses: More Than Skin Deep	163–166
	Smell and Taste	167–172
Vision	Vision I and Vision II	136–156
Structure and function of the eye	The Human Eye	138
Visual processing	Vision I	136–145
• Visual pathways in the brain	From the Eye to the Brain	138–140
• Parallel processing	The Visual Brain	142–145
• Feature detection	Studying the Brain's Electrical Activity	118–119
	The Visual Brain	142–145
Hearing	Audition: More Than Meets the Ear	157–162
Auditory processing	Perceiving Pitch	160
• Auditory pathways in the brain	Perceiving Pitch	160
Sensory reception by hair cells	The Human Ear	158–160
Other Senses	The Body Senses: More Than Skin Deep	163–166
	The Chemical Senses: Adding Flavor	167–173
Somatosensation	Touch	163–164
• Pain perception	Pain	164–165
Taste	Taste	170–173
• Taste buds/chemoreceptors that detect specific chemicals	Taste	170–173
Smell	Smell	167–170
• Olfactory cells/chemoreceptors that detect specific chemicals	Smell	167–168
• Pheromones	Smell	170
• Olfactory pathways in the brain	Smell	167–170
Kinesthetic sense	Body Position, Movement, and Balance	166
Vestibular sense	Body Position, Movement, and Balance	166
Perception	Sensation and Perception	129–173
Perception	Sensation and Perception Are Distinct Activities	130–136
• Bottom-up/Top-down processing	Pain	164–165
	Smell	167–170
• Perceptual organization (e.g., depth, form, motion, constancy)	Vision II: Recognizing What We Perceive	145–157
• Gestalt principles	Principles of Perceptual Organization	148–149

Media and Supplements
LaunchPad with LearningCurve Quizzing

A comprehensive web resource for teaching and learning psychology

LaunchPad combines Worth Publishers' award-winning media with an innovative platform for easy navigation. For students, it is the ultimate online study guide, with rich interactive tutorials and videos, as well as an e-Book and the LearningCurve adaptive quizzing system. For instructors, LaunchPad is a full course space where class documents can be posted, quizzes are easily assigned and graded, and students' progress can be assessed and recorded. Whether you are looking for the most effective study tools or a robust platform for an online course, LaunchPad is a powerful way to enhance your class.

LaunchPad to Accompany *Psychology*, Third Edition, can be previewed and purchased at http://www.worthpublishers.com/launchpad/schacter3e.

Psychology, Third Edition, and LaunchPad can be ordered together with ISBN-10: 1-4641-8945-5 / ISBN-13: 978-1-4641-8945-6.

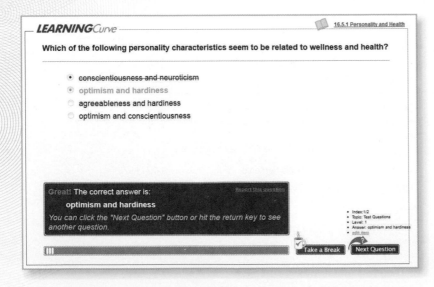

LaunchPad for *Psychology*, Third Edition, includes all the following resources:

> The design of the **LearningCurve** quizzing system is based on the latest findings from learning and memory research. It combines adaptive question selection, immediate and valuable feedback, and a gamelike interface to engage students in a learning experience that is unique to them. Each LearningCurve quiz is fully integrated with other resources in LaunchPad through the Personalized Study Plan, so students will be able to review using Worth's extensive library of videos and activities. And state-of-the-art question analysis reports allow instructors to track the progress of individual students as well as their class as a whole.

> **New!** **Data Visualization Exercises** offer students practice in understanding and reasoning about data. In each activity, students interact with a graph or visual display of data and must think like a scientist to answer the accompanying questions. These activities build quantitative reasoning skills and offer a deeper understanding of how science works.

> **An interactive e-Book** allows students to highlight, bookmark, and scribble in their own notes on the e-Book page, just as they would with a printed textbook. Google-style searching and in-text glossary definitions make the text ready for the digital age.

> **Student Video Activities** include more than 100 engaging video modules that instructors can easily assign and customize for student assessment. Videos cover classic experiments, current news footage, and cutting-edge research, all of which are sure to spark discussion and encourage critical thinking.

> **PsychInvestigator: Laboratory Learning in Introductory Psychology** is a series of activities that model a virtual laboratory and are produced in association with Arthur Kohn, Ph.D, of Dark Blue Morning Productions. Students are introduced to core psychological concepts by a video host and then participate in activities that generate real data and lead to some startling conclusions! Like all activities in LaunchPad, PsychInvestigator activities can be assigned and automatically graded.

> The award-winning tutorials in Tom Ludwig's (Hope College) **PsychSim 5.0** and **Concepts in Action** provide an interactive, step-by-step introduction to key psychological concepts.

> The *Scientific American* **Newsfeed** delivers weekly articles, podcasts, and news briefs on the very latest developments in psychology from the first name in popular science journalism.

Additional Student Supplements

> The **CourseSmart e-Book** offers the complete text of *Psychology*, Third Edition, in an easy-to-use format. Students can choose either to purchase the CourseSmart e-Book as an online subscription or to download it to a personal computer or a portable media player, such as a smart phone or iPad. The CourseSmart e-Book for *Psychology*, Third Edition, can be previewed and purchased at **www.coursesmart.com.**

> *Pursuing Human Strengths: A Positive Psychology Guide* by Martin Bolt of Calvin College is a perfect way to introduce students to both the amazing field of positive psychology as well as their own personal strengths.

> *The Critical Thinking Companion for Introductory Psychology,* by Jane S. Halonen of the University of West Florida and Cynthia Gray of Beloit College, contains both a guide to critical thinking strategies as well as exercises in pattern recognition, practical problem solving, creative

Take advantage of our most popular supplements!

Worth Publishers is pleased to offer cost-saving packages of *Psychology*, Third Edition, with our most popular supplements. Below is a list of some of the most popular combinations available for order through your local bookstore.

Psychology, 3rd Ed. & LaunchPad Access Card
ISBN-10: 1-4641-8945-5 / ISBN-13: 978-1-4641-8945-6

Psychology, 3rd Ed. & iClicker 2
ISBN-10: 1-4641-8990-0 / ISBN-13: 978-1-4641-8990-6

Psychology, 3rd Ed. & *Scientific American* Reader
ISBN-10: 1-4641-8946-3 / ISBN-13: 978-1-4641-8946-3

Psychology, 3rd Ed. & *Psychology and the Real World*
ISBN-10: 1-4641-8944-7 / ISBN-13: 978-1-4641-8944-9

problem solving, scientific problem solving, psychological reasoning, and perspective-taking.

> Worth Publishers is proud to offer several readers of articles taken from the pages of *Scientific American*. Drawing on award-winning science journalism, the ***Scientific American* Reader to Accompany *Psychology*, Third Edition, by Daniel L. Schacter, Daniel T. Gilbert, Daniel M. Wegner, and Matthew K. Nock** features pioneering and cutting-edge research across the fields of psychology. Selected by the authors themselves, this collection provides further insight into the fields of psychology through articles written for a popular audience.

> ***Psychology and the Real World: Essays Illustrating Fundamental Contributions to Society*** is a superb collection of essays by major researchers that describe their landmark studies. Published in association with the not-for-profit FABBS Foundation, this engaging reader includes Elizabeth Loftus's own reflections on her study of false memories, Eliot Aronson on his cooperative classroom study, and Daniel Wegner on his study of thought suppression. A portion of all proceeds is donated to FABBS to support societies of cognitive, psychological, behavioral, and brain sciences.

Course Management

> Worth Publishers supports multiple Course Management Systems with enhanced cartridges for upload into Blackboard, eCollege, Angel, Desire2Learn, Sakai, and Moodle. Cartridges are provided free upon adoption of *Psychology*, Third Edition, and can be downloaded from Worth's online catalog at www.worthpublishers.com.

Assessment

> The **Computerized Test Bank** powered by Diploma includes a full assortment of test items from author Chad Galuska of the College of Charleston. Each chapter features over 200 multiple-choice, true/false, and essay questions to test students at several levels of Bloom's taxonomy. The new edition also features a new set of data-based reasoning questions to test advanced critical thinking skills in a manner similar to the MCAT. All the questions are matched to the outcomes recommended in the 2013 APA Guidelines for the Undergraduate Psychology Major. The accompanying grade book software makes it easy to record students' grades throughout a course, to sort student records, to view detailed analyses of test items, to curve tests, to generate reports, and to add weights to grades.

> The **iClicker** Classroom Response System is a versatile polling system developed by educators for educators that makes class time more efficient and interactive. iClicker allows you to ask questions and instantly record your students' responses, take attendance, and gauge students' understanding and opinions. iClicker is available at a 10% discount when packaged with *Psychology*, Third Edition.

Presentation

> **Interactive Presentation Slides** are another great way to introduce Worth's dynamic media into the classroom without lots of advance preparation. Each presentation covers a major topic in psychology and integrates Worth's high quality videos and animations for an engaging teaching and learning experience. These interactive presentations are complimentary to adopters of *Psychology*, Third Edition, and are perfect for technology novices and experts alike.

> The **Instructor's Resources** by Jeffrey Henriques of The University of Wisconsin-Madison features a variety of materials that are valuable to new and

veteran teachers alike. In addition to background on the chapter reading and suggestions for in-class lectures, the manual is rich with activities to engage students in different modes of learning. The Instructor's Resources can be downloaded at http://www.worthpublishers.com/launchpad/schacter3e.

> **The Worth Video Anthology for Introductory Psychology** includes over 300 unique video clips to bring lectures to life. Provided complimentary to adopters of *Psychology*, Third Edition, this rich collection includes clinical footage, interviews, animations, and news segments that vividly illustrate topics across the psychology curriculum.

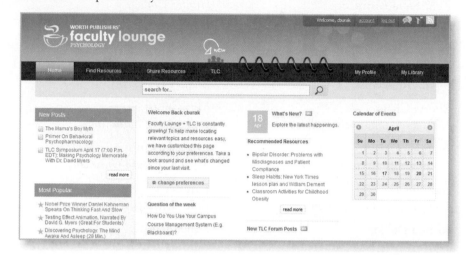

> **Faculty Lounge** is an online forum provided by Worth Publishers where teachers can find and share favorite teaching ideas and materials, including videos, animations, images, PowerPoint slides, news stories, articles, web links, and lecture activities. Sign up to browse the site or upload your favorite materials for teaching psychology at www.worthpublishers.com/facultylounge.

Acknowledgments

Despite what you might guess by looking at our photographs, we all found women who were willing to marry us. We thank Susan McGlynn, Marilynn Oliphant, and Keesha Nock for that particular miracle and also for their love and support during the years when we were busy writing this book.

Although ours are the names on the cover, writing a textbook is a team sport, and we were lucky to have an amazing group of professionals in our dugout. We greatly appreciate the contributions of Martin M. Antony, Mark Baldwin, Michelle A. Butler, Patricia Csank, Denise D. Cummins, Ian J. Deary, Howard Eichenbaum, Sam Gosling, Paul Harris, Catherine Myers, Shigehiro Oishi, Arthur S. Reber, Morgan T. Sammons, Dan Simons, Alan Swinkels, Richard M. Wenzlaff, and Steven Yantis.

We are grateful for the editorial, clerical, and research assistance we received from Molly Evans and Mark Knepley.

In addition, we would like to thank our core supplements authors. They provided insight into the role our book can play in the classroom and adeptly developed the materials to support it. Chad Galuska, Jeff Henriques, and Russ Frohardt, we appreciate your tireless work in the classroom and the experience you brought to the book's supplements.

We would like to thank the faculty who reviewed the manuscript. These teachers showed a level of engagement we have come to expect from our best colleagues:

Eileen Achorn
University of Texas, San Antonio

Jim Allen
SUNY Geneseo

Randy Arnau
University of Southern Mississippi

Benjamin Bennett-Carpenter
Oakland University

Stephen Blessing
University of Tampa

Kristin Biondolillo
Arkansas State University

Jeffrey Blum
Los Angeles City College

Richard Bowen
Loyola University of Chicago

Nicole Bragg
Mt. Hood Community College

Jennifer Breneiser
Valdosta State University

Michele Brumley
Idaho State University

Josh Burk
College of William and Mary

Jennifer Butler
Case Western Reserve University

Richard Cavasina
California University of Pennsylvania

Amber Chenoweth
Kent State University

Stephen Chew
Samford University

Chrisanne Christensen
Southern Arkansas University

Sheryl Civjan
Holyoke Community College

Jennifer Dale
Community College of Aurora

Jennifer Daniels
University of Connecticut

Joshua Dobias
University of New Hampshire

Dale Doty
Monroe Community College

Julie Evey-Johnson
University of Southern Indiana

Valerie Farmer-Dugan
Illinois State University

Diane Feibel
*University of Cincinnati,
Raymond Walters College*

Jocelyn Folk
Kent State University

Chad Galuska
College of Charleston

Afshin Gharib
Dominican University of California

Jeffrey Gibbons
Christopher Newport University

Adam Goodie
University of Georgia

Patricia Grace
Kaplan University Online

Sarah Grison
*University of Illinois at Urbana-
Champaign*

Deletha Hardin
University of Tampa

Jason Hart
Christopher Newport University

Lesley Hathorn
Metropolitan State College of Denver

Mark Hauber
Hunter College

Jacqueline Hembrook
University of New Hampshire

Allen Huffcutt
Bradley University

Mark Hurd
College of Charleston

Linda Jackson
Michigan State University

Jennifer Johnson
Rider University

Lance Jones
Bowling Green State University

Linda Jones
Blinn College

Katherine Judge
Cleveland State University

Don Kates
College of DuPage

Martha Knight-Oakley
Warren Wilson College

Ken Koenigshofer
Chaffey College

Neil Kressel
William Patterson University

Josh Landau
York College of Pennsylvania

Fred Leavitt
California State University, East Bay

Tera Letzring
Idaho State University

Karsten Loepelmann
University of Alberta

Ray Lopez
University of Texas at San Antonio

Jeffrey Love
Penn State University

Greg Loviscky
Penn State, University Park

Lynda Mae
Arizona State University at Tempe

Caitlin Mahy
University of Oregon

Gregory Manley
University of Texas at San Antonio

Karen Marsh
University of Minnesota at Duluth

Robert Mather
University of Central Oklahoma

Wanda McCarthy
*University of Cincinnati
at Clermont College*

Daniel McConnell
University of Central Florida

Robert McNally
Austin Community College

Dawn Melzer
Sacred Heart University

Dennis Miller
University of Missouri

Mignon Montpetit
Miami University

Todd Nelson
California State University at Stanislaus

Margaret Norwood
Community College of Aurora

Aminda O'Hare
University of Kansas

Melissa Pace
Kean University

Brady Phelps
South Dakota State University

Raymond Phinney
Wheaton College

Claire St. Peter Pipkin
West Virginia University, Morgantown

Christy Porter
College of William and Mary

Douglas Pruitt
*West Kentucky Community and Technical
College*

Elizabeth Purcell
Greenville Technical College

Gabriel Radvansky
University of Notre Dame

Celia Reaves
Monroe Community College

Diane Reddy
University of Wisconsin, Milwaukee

Cynthia Shinabarger Reed
Tarrant County College

David Reetz
Hanover College

Tanya Renner
Kapi'olani Community College

Anthony Robertson
Vancouver Island University

Nancy Rogers
University of Cincinnati

Wendy Rote
University of Rochester

Larry Rudiger
University of Vermont

Sharleen Sakai
Michigan State University

Matthew Sanders
Marquette University

Phillip Schatz
Saint Joseph's University

Vann Scott
Armstrong Atlantic State University

Colleen Seifert
University of Michigan at Ann Arbor

Wayne Shebilske
Wright State University

Elisabeth Sherwin
University of Arkansas at Little Rock

Lisa Shin
Tufts University

Kenith Sobel
University of Central Arkansas

Genevieve Stevens
Houston Community College

Mark Stewart
American River College

Holly Straub
University of South Dakota

Mary Strobbe
San Diego Miramar College

William Struthers
Wheaton College

Lisa Thomassen
Indiana University

Jeremy Tost
Valdosta State University

Laura Turiano
Sacred Heart University

Jeffrey Wagman
Illinois State University

Alexander Williams
University of Kansas

John Wright
Washington State University

Dean Yoshizumi
Sierra College

Keith Young
University of Kansas

We are especially grateful to the extraordinary people of Worth Publishers. They include senior vice president Catherine Woods and publisher Kevin Feyen, who provided guidance and encouragement at all stages of the project; our acquisitions editor, Dan DeBonis, who managed the project with intelligence, grace, and good humor; our development editors, Valerie Raymond and Mimi Melek; director of development for print and digital products Tracey Kuehn; project editor Robert Errera; production manager Sarah Segal; and editorial assistant Katie Garrett, who through some remarkable alchemy turned a manuscript into a book; our art director Babs Reingold; layout designer Paul Lacy; photo editor Cecilia Varas; and photo researcher Elyse Rieder, who made that book an aesthetic delight; our media editor Rachel Comerford; and production manager Stacey Alexander, who guided the development and creation of a superb supplements package; our marketing manager Lindsay Johnson; and associate director of market development Carlise Stembridge, who served as tireless public advocates for our vision. Thank you one and all. We look forward to working with you again.

Daniel L. Schacter

Daniel T. Gilbert

Matthew K. Nock

Cambridge, 2014

Psychology: Evolution of a Science

A LOT WAS HAPPENING IN 1860. Abraham Lincoln had just been elected president of the United States, the Pony Express had just begun to deliver mail between Missouri and California, and a woman named Anne Kellogg had just given birth to a child who would one day grow up to invent the cornflake. But none of this mattered very much to William James, a bright, taciturn, 18-year-old who had no idea what to do with his life. He loved to paint and draw, but worried that he wasn't talented enough to become a serious artist. He had enjoyed studying biology in school but doubted that a naturalist's salary would ever allow him to get married and have a family of his own. So, like many young people who are faced with difficult decisions about their futures, William abandoned his dreams and chose to do something in which he had little interest but of which his family heartily approved. Alas, within a few months of arriving at Harvard Medical School, his lack of interest in medicine blossomed into a troubling lack of enthusiasm, and so with a bit of encouragement from the faculty, he put his medical studies on hold to join a biological expedition to the Amazon. The adventure failed to focus his wandering mind (although he learned a great deal about leeches), and when he returned to medical school, both his physical and mental health began to deteriorate. It was clear to everyone that William James was not the sort of person who should be put in charge of a scalpel and a bag of drugs.

Had James become an artist, a biologist, or a physician, we would probably remember nothing about him today. Fortunately for us, he was a deeply confused young man who could speak five languages, and when he became so depressed that he was once again forced to leave medical school, he decided to travel around Europe, where at least he knew how to talk to people. As he talked and listened, he learned about a new science called *psychology* (from a combination of the Greek *psyche* [soul] and *logos* [to study]). He saw that this developing field was taking a modern, scientific approach to

Throughout his youth, William James (1842–1910) seemed seriously mixed up. He began college as a chemistry major, then switched to anatomy, then set sail on a biological expedition to the Amazon, and then traveled to Europe, where he became interested in the new science of psychology. Luckily for us, he stuck with it for a while.

age-old questions about human nature—questions that had become painfully familiar to him during his personal search for meaning, but questions to which only poets and philosophers had ever before offered answers (Bjork, 1983; Simon, 1998). Excited about the new discipline, James returned to America and quickly finished his medical degree. But he never practiced medicine and never intended to do so. Rather, he became a professor at Harvard University and devoted the rest of his life to psychology. His landmark book, *The Principles of Psychology*, is still widely read and remains one of the most influential books ever written on the subject (James, 1890).

A LOT HAS HAPPENED SINCE THEN. Abraham Lincoln has become the face on a penny, the Pony Express has been replaced by e-mail and Twitter, and the Kellogg Company sells about $9 billion worth of cornflakes every year. If William James (1842–1910) were alive today, he would be amazed by all of these things. But he would probably be even more amazed by the intellectual advances that have taken place in the science that he helped create.

Psychology is *the scientific study of mind and behavior*. The **mind** refers to *the private inner experience of perceptions, thoughts, memories, and feelings,* an ever-flowing stream of consciousness. **Behavior** refers to *observable actions of human beings and nonhuman animals,* the things that we do in the world, by ourselves or with others. As you will see in the chapters to come, psychology is an attempt to use scientific methods to address fundamental questions about mind and behavior that have puzzled people for millennia. The answers to these questions would have astonished William James. Let's take a look at three key examples:

1. *What are the bases of perceptions, thoughts, memories, and feelings, or our subjective sense of self?*

For thousands of years, philosophers tried to understand how the objective, physical world of the body was related to the subjective, psychological world of the mind. Today, psychologists know that all of our subjective experiences arise from the electrical and chemical activities of our brains. As you will see throughout this book, some of the most exciting developments in psychological research focus on how our perceptions, thoughts, memories, and feelings are related to activity in the brain. Psychologists and neuroscientists are using new technologies to explore this relationship in ways that would have seemed like science fiction only 20 years ago.

For example, the technique known as *functional magnetic resonance imaging* (fMRI) allows scientists to scan a brain to determine which parts are active when a person reads a word, sees a face, learns a new skill, or remembers a personal experience. In a recent study, the brains of both professional and novice pianists were scanned as they made complex finger movements, like those involved in piano playing. The results showed that professional pianists have *less* activity than novices in the parts of the brain that guide these finger movements (Krings et al., 2000). This suggests that extensive practice at the piano changes the brains of professional pianists and that the regions controlling finger movements operate more efficiently for them than they do for novices. You'll learn more about this in the Memory and Learning chapters and see in the coming chapters how studies using fMRI and related techniques are beginning to transform many different areas of psychology.

Keith Jarrett is a virtuoso who has been playing piano for more than 60 years. Compared to a novice, the brain regions that control Jarrett's fingers are relatively *less* active when he plays.

JACQUES MUNCH/AFP/GETTY IMAGES

2. *How does the mind usually allow us to function effectively in the world?*

Scientists sometimes say that form follows function; that is, if we want to understand *how* something works (e.g., an engine or a thermometer), we need to know what it is working *for* (e.g., powering vehicles or measuring temperature). As William James often noted, "Thinking is for doing," and the function of the mind is to help us do those things that sophisticated animals have to do in order to prosper, such as acquire food, shelter, and mates. Psychological processes are said to be *adaptive,* which means that they promote the welfare and reproduction of organisms that engage in those processes. Perception allows us to recognize our families, see predators before they see us, and avoid stumbling into oncoming traffic. Language allows us to organize our thoughts and communicate them to others, which enables us to form social groups and cooperate. Memory allows us to avoid solving the same problems over again every time we encounter them and to keep in mind what we are doing and why. Emotions allow us to react quickly to events that have life or death significance, and they enable us to form strong social bonds. The list goes on and on.

Given the adaptiveness of psychological processes, it is not surprising that people with deficiencies in these processes often have a pretty tough time. The neurologist Antonio Damasio (1994) described the case of Elliot, a middle-aged husband and father with a good job, whose life was forever changed when surgeons discovered a tumor in the middle of his brain. The surgeons were able to remove the tumor and save his life, and for a while Elliot seemed just fine. But then odd things began to happen. At first, Elliot seemed more likely than usual to make bad decisions (when he could make decisions at all), and as time went on, his bad decisions became truly dreadful ones. He couldn't prioritize tasks at work because he couldn't decide what to do first, and when he did, he got it wrong. Eventually he was fired, so he pursued a series of risky business ventures—all of which failed—and he lost his life's savings. His wife divorced him, he married again, and his second wife divorced him too.

So what ruined Elliot's life? The neurologists who tested Elliot were unable to detect any decrease in his cognitive functioning. His intelligence was intact, and his ability to speak, think, and solve logical problems was every bit as sharp as it ever was. But as they probed further, they made a startling discovery: Elliot was no longer able to experience emotions. For example, Elliot didn't experience any regret or anger when his boss gave him the pink slip and showed him the door, he didn't experience anxiety when he poured his entire bank account into a foolish business venture, and he didn't experience any sorrow when his wives packed up and left him. Most of us have wished from time to time that we could be as stoic and unflappable as that; after all, who needs anxiety, sorrow, regret, and anger? The answer is that we all do.

3. *Why does the mind occasionally function so ineffectively in the world?*

The mind is an amazing machine that can do a great many things quickly. We can drive a car while talking to a passenger while recognizing the street address while remembering the name of the song that just came on the radio. But like all machines, the mind often trades accuracy for speed and versatility. This can produce "bugs" in the system, causing occasional malfunctions in our otherwise efficient mental processing. One of the most fascinating aspects of psychology is that we are *all* prone to a variety of errors and illusions. Indeed, if thoughts, feelings, and actions were error free, then human behavior would be orderly, predictable, and dull, which it clearly is not. Rather, it is endlessly surprising, and its surprises often derive from our ability to do precisely the wrong thing at the wrong time.

Emotions are adaptive. For example, fear leads many animals to freeze so that their enemies can't see them—as it did these young women who were touring a "haunted house" in Niagara Falls.

psychology
The scientific study of mind and behavior.

mind
The private inner experience of perceptions, thoughts, memories, and feelings.

behavior
Observable actions of human beings and nonhuman animals.

Consider a few examples from diaries of people who took part in a study concerning mental errors in everyday life (Reason & Mycielska, 1982, pp. 70–73):

> I meant to get my car out, but as I passed the back porch on my way to the garage, I stopped to put on my boots and gardening jacket as if to work in the yard.

> I put some money into a machine to get a stamp. When the stamp appeared, I took it and said, "Thank you."

> On leaving the room to go to the kitchen, I turned the light off, although several people were there.

If these lapses seem amusing, it is because, in fact, they are. But they are also potentially important as clues to human nature. For example, notice that the person who bought a stamp said, "Thank you," to the machine and not, "How do I find the subway?" In other words, the person did not just do *any* wrong thing; rather, he did something that would have been perfectly correct in a real social interaction. As each of these examples suggests, people often operate on "autopilot," or behave automatically, relying on well-learned habits that they execute without really thinking. When we are not actively focused on what we are saying or doing, these habits may be triggered inappropriately. William James (1890) thought that the influence of habit could help explain the seemingly bizarre actions of "absentminded" people: "Very absent-minded persons," he wrote in *The Principles of Psychology,* "on going into their

The Perils of Procrastination

William James understood that the human mind and behavior are fascinating in part because they are not error free. The mind's mistakes interest us primarily as paths to achieving a better understanding of mental activity and behavior, but they also have practical consequences. Let's consider a malfunction that can have significant consequences in your own life: procrastination.

At one time or another, most of us have avoided carrying out a task or put it off to a later time. The task may be unpleasant, difficult, or just less entertaining than other things we could be doing at the moment. For college students, procrastination can affect a range of academic activities, such as writing a term paper or preparing for a test. Academic procrastination is not uncommon: Over 70% of college students report that they engage in some form of procrastination (Schouwenburg, 1995). Although it's fun to hang out with your friends tonight, it's not so much fun to worry for three days about your impending history exam or try to study at 4:00 a.m. the day of the test. Studying now, or at least a little bit each day, robs procrastination of its power over you.

Some procrastinators defend the practice by claiming that they tend to work best under pressure or by noting that as long as a task gets done, it doesn't matter all that much if it is completed just before the deadline. Is there any merit to such claims, or are they just feeble excuses for counterproductive behavior?

A study of 60 undergraduate psychology college students provided some intriguing answers (Tice & Baumeister, 1997). At the beginning of the semester, the instructor announced a due date for the term paper and told students that if they could not meet the date, they would receive an extension to a later date. About a month later, students completed a scale that mea-

sures tendencies toward procrastination. At that same time, and then again during the last week of class, students recorded health symptoms they had experienced during the past week, the amount of stress they had experienced during that week, and the number of visits they had made to a health care center during the previous month.

Students who scored high on the procrastination scale tended to turn in their papers late. One month into the semester, these procrastinators reported less stress and fewer symptoms of physical illness than did nonprocrastinators. But at the end of the semester, the procrastinators reported more stress and more health symptoms than did the nonprocrastinators, and also reported more visits to the health center. The procrastinators also received lower grades on their papers and on course exams. More recent studies have found that higher levels of procrastination are associated with poorer academic performance (Moon & Illingworth, 2005) and higher levels of psychological distress (Rice, Richardson, & Clark, 2012). Therefore, in addition to making use of the tips provided in the Real World box on increasing study skills (pp. 10–11), it would seem wise to avoid procrastination in this course and others.

bedroom to dress for dinner have been known to take off one garment after another and finally get into bed" (p.115).

James understood that the mind's mistakes are as instructive as they are intriguing, and modern psychology has found it quite useful to study them. Things that are whole and unbroken hum along nicely and do their jobs while leaving no clue about how they do them. Cars gliding down the expressway might as well be magic carpets as long as they are working properly because we have no idea what kind of magic is moving them along. It is only when automobiles break down that we learn about their engines, water pumps, and other fine pieces and processes that normally work together to produce the ride. Breakdowns and errors are not just about destruction and failure, they are pathways to knowledge. (See the Real World box for an example common to us all: procrastination.) In the same way, understanding lapses, errors, mistakes, and the occasionally puzzling nature of human behavior provides a vantage point for understanding the normal operation of mental life and behavior. The story of Elliot, whose behavior broke down after he had brain surgery, is an example that highlights the role that emotions play in guiding normal judgment and behavior.

Psychology is exciting because it addresses fundamental questions about human experience and behavior, and the three questions we've just considered are merely the tip of the iceberg. Think of this book as a guide to exploring the rest of the iceberg. But before we don our parkas and grab our pick axes, we need to understand how the iceberg got here in the first place. To understand psychology in the 21st century, we need to become familiar with the psychology of the past.

Mistakes can teach us a lot about how people think . . . or fail to think, as the case may be.

Psychology's Roots:
The Path to a Science of Mind

When the young William James interrupted his medical studies to travel in Europe during the late 1860s, he wanted to learn about human nature. But he confronted a very different situation than a similarly curious student would confront today, largely because psychology did not yet exist as an independent field of study. As James cheekily wrote, "The first lecture in psychology that I ever heard was the first I ever gave" (quoted in Perry, 1996, p. 228). Of course, that doesn't mean no one had ever thought about human nature before. For 2,000 years, thinkers with scraggly beards and poor dental hygiene had pondered such questions, and in fact, modern psychology acknowledges its deep roots in philosophy. We will begin by examining those roots and then describe some of the early attempts to develop a scientific approach to psychology by relating the mind to the brain. Next, we'll see how psychologists divided into different camps (or schools of thought): *Structuralists* tried to analyze the mind by breaking it down into its basic components, and *functionalists* focused on how mental abilities allow people to adapt to their environments.

Psychology's Ancestors: The Great Philosophers

The desire to understand ourselves is not new. Greek thinkers such as Plato (428 BCE–347 BCE) and Aristotle (384 BCE–322 BCE) were among the first to struggle with fundamental questions about how the mind works (Robinson, 1995). Greek philosophers debated many of the questions that psychologists continue to debate today. For example, are cognitive

How do young children learn about the world? Plato believed that certain kinds of knowledge are innate, whereas Aristotle believed that the mind is a blank slate on which experiences are written.

nativism
The philosophical view that certain kinds of knowledge are innate or inborn.

philosophical empiricism
The view that all knowledge is acquired through experience.

phrenology
A now defunct theory that specific mental abilities and characteristics, ranging from memory to the capacity for happiness, are localized in specific regions of the brain.

physiology
The study of biological processes, especially in the human body.

abilities and knowledge inborn, or are they acquired only through experience? Plato argued in favor of **nativism**, *the philosophical view that certain kinds of knowledge are innate or inborn.* Children in every culture figure out early on that sounds can have meanings that can be arranged into words, which then can be arranged into sentences. Before a child is old enough to poop in the proper place, he or she has already mastered the fundamentals of language without any formal instruction. Is the propensity to learn language "hardwired" (something that children are born with)? Or does the ability to learn language depend on the child's experience? Aristotle believed that the child's mind was a *tabula rasa* (blank slate) on which experiences were written, and he argued for **philosophical empiricism,** *the view that all knowledge is acquired through experience.*

Although few modern psychologists believe that nativism or empiricism is entirely correct, the issue of just how much "nature" and "nurture" explain any given behavior is still a matter of controversy. In some ways, it is quite amazing that ancient philosophers were able to articulate so many of the important questions in psychology and offer many excellent insights into their answers without any access to scientific evidence. Their ideas came from personal observations, intuition, and speculation. Although they were quite good at arguing with one another, they usually found it impossible to settle their disputes because their approach provided no means of testing their theories. As you will see in the Methods chapter, the ability to test a theory is the cornerstone of the scientific approach and the basis for reaching conclusions in modern psychology.

> **?** What fundamental question has puzzled philosophers for millennia?

From the Brain to the Mind: The French Connection

We all know that the brain and the body are physical objects that we can see and touch and that the subjective contents of our minds—our perceptions, thoughts, and feelings—are not. Inner experience is perfectly real, but where in the world is it? French philosopher René Descartes (1596–1650) argued that body and mind are fundamentally different things—that the body is made of a material substance, whereas the mind (or soul) is made of an immaterial or spiritual substance. But if the mind and the body are different things made of different substances, then how do they interact? How does the mind tell the body to put its foot forward, and when the body steps on a rusty nail, why does the mind say "ouch"? This is the problem of *dualism,* or how mental activity can be reconciled and coordinated with physical behavior.

Descartes suggested that the mind influences the body through a tiny structure near the bottom of the brain known as the pineal gland. He was largely alone in this view because other philosophers at the time either rejected his explanation or offered alternative ideas. For example, British philosopher Thomas Hobbes (1588–1679) argued that the mind and body aren't different things at all; rather, the mind *is* what the brain *does*. From Hobbes's perspective, looking for a place in the brain where the mind meets the body is like looking for the place in a television where the picture meets the flat panel display.

> **?** What were early explanations for dualism?

©THOM LANG/CORBIS

Rene Descartes believed that the physical body was a container for the nonphysical thing called the mind. Centuries later, the philosopher Gilbert Ryle (1949) argued that Descartes was wrong, that there is no "ghost in the machine," and that all mental activity is simply the result of the physical activity of the brain. Most modern scientists reject Descartes' "dualism" and embrace Ryle's "scientific materialism."

French physician Franz Joseph Gall (1758–1828) also thought that brains and minds were linked, but by size rather than by glands. He examined the brains of animals and of people who had died of disease, or as healthy adults, or as children, and observed that mental ability often increases with larger brain size and decreases with damage to the brain. These aspects of Gall's findings were generally accepted (and the part about brain damage still is today). But Gall went far beyond his evidence to develop a psychological theory known as **phrenology,** *a now defunct theory that specific* *mental abilities and characteristics, ranging from memory to the capacity for happiness, are localized in specific regions of the brain* (see **FIGURE 1.1**). The idea that different parts of the brain are specialized for specific psychological functions turned out to be right; as you'll learn later in the book, a part of the brain called the *hippocampus* is intimately involved in memory, just as a structure called the *amygdala* is intimately involved in fear. But phrenology took this idea to an absurd extreme. Gall asserted that the size of bumps or indentations on the skull reflected the size of the brain regions beneath them and that by feeling those bumps, one could tell whether a person was friendly, cautious, assertive, idealistic, and so on. What Gall didn't realize was that bumps on the skull do not necessarily reveal anything about the shape of the brain underneath.

Phrenology made for a nice parlor game and gave young people a good excuse for touching each other, but in the end it amounted to a series of strong claims based on weak evidence. Not surprisingly, his critics were galled (so to speak), and they ridiculed many of his proposals. Despite an initially large following, phrenology was quickly discredited (Fancher, 1979).

While Gall was busy playing bumpologist, other French scientists were beginning to link the brain and the mind in a more convincing manner. Biologist Marie Jean Pierre Flourens (1794–1867) was appalled by Gall's far-reaching claims and sloppy methods, so he conducted experiments in which he surgically removed specific parts of the brain from dogs, birds, and other animals and found (not surprisingly!) that their actions and movements differed from those of animals with intact brains.

French surgeon Paul Broca (1824–1880) worked with a patient who had suffered damage to a small part of the left side of the brain (now known as *Broca's area*). The patient, Monsieur Leborgne, was virtually unable to speak and could utter only the single syllable "tan." Yet the patient understood everything that was said to him and was able to communicate using gestures. Broca had the crucial insight that damage to a specific part of the brain impaired a specific mental function, clearly demonstrating that the brain and mind are closely linked. This was important in the 19th century because at that time many people accepted Descartes' idea that the mind is separate from, but interacts with, the brain and the body. Broca and Flourens, then, were the first to demonstrate that the mind is grounded in a material substance, namely, the brain. Their work jump-started the scientific investigation of mental processes.

> **?** How did work involving patients with brain damage help demonstrate the mind–brain connection?

◄ Figure **1.1** **Phrenology** Franz Joseph Gall (1758–1828) developed a theory called phrenology, which suggested that psychological capacities (such as the capacity for friendship) and traits (such as cautiousness and mirth) were located in particular parts of the brain. The more of these capacities and traits a person had, the larger the corresponding bumps on the skull.

MARY EVANS PICTURE LIBRARY/ THE IMAGE WORKS

APIC/GETTY IMAGES

Mr. Leborgne was nicknamed "Tan" because it was the only word he could say. When he died in 1861, Paul Broca dissected his brain and found a lesion in the left hemisphere which, he concluded, had been responsible for Leborgne's loss of speech. Today, Leborgne's brain lives in a jar at the Musée Dupuytren in Paris, France. And to this day, no one knows his first name.

Structuralism: Applying Methods from Physiology to Psychology

In the middle of the 19th century, psychology benefited from the work of German scientists who were trained in the field of **physiology**, *the study of biological processes, especially in the human body.* Physiologists had developed methods that allowed them to measure such things as the speed of nerve impulses, and some of them had begun to use these methods to measure mental abilities. William James was drawn to the work of two such physiologists: Hermann von Helmholtz (1821–1894) and Wilhelm Wundt (1832–1920). "It seems to me that perhaps the time has come for psychology to begin to be a science," wrote James in a letter written in 1867 during his visit to Berlin. "Helmholtz and a man called Wundt at Heidelberg are working at it." What attracted James to the work of these two scientists?

Helmholtz Measures the Speed of Responses

A brilliant experimenter with a background in both physiology and physics, Helmholtz had developed a method for measuring the speed of nerve impulses in a frog's leg, which he then adapted to the study of human beings. Helmholtz trained participants to respond when he applied a **stimulus**—*sensory input from the environment*—to different parts of the leg. He recorded his participants' **reaction time,** or *the amount of time taken to respond to a specific stimulus,* after applying the stimulus. Helmholtz found that people generally took longer to respond when their toe was stimulated than when their thigh was stimulated, and the difference between these reaction times allowed him to estimate how long it took a nerve impulse to travel to the brain. These results were astonishing to 19th-century scientists because, at that time, just about everyone thought that mental processes occurred instantaneously. When you move your hands in front of your eyes, you don't feel your hands move a fraction of a second before you see them. The real world doesn't appear like one of those late-night movies in which the video and the audio are off by just a fraction of a second. Scientists assumed that the neurological processes underlying mental events *must* be instantaneous for everything to be so nicely synchronized, but Helmholtz showed that this wasn't true. In so doing, he also demonstrated that reaction time could be a useful way to study the mind and the brain.

> **What was the useful application of Hemholtz's results?**

HULTON ARCHIVE/GETTY IMAGES

By measuring a person's reaction times to different stimuli, Hermann von Helmholtz (1821–1894) estimated the length of time it takes a nerve impulse to travel to the brain.

Wundt and the Development of Structuralism

Although Helmholtz's contributions were important, historians generally credit the official emergence of psychology to Helmholtz's research assistant, Wilhelm Wundt (1832–1920; Rieber, 1980). In 1867, at the University of Heidelberg, Wundt taught what was probably the first course in physiological psychology, which led to the publication of his book, *Principles of Physiological Psychology,* in 1874. Wundt called the book "an attempt to mark out [psychology] as a new domain of science" (Fancher, 1979, p. 126). In 1879, at the University of Leipzig, Wundt opened the first laboratory exclusively devoted to psychological studies, and this event marked the official birth of psychology as an independent field of study. The new lab was full of graduate students carrying out research on topics assigned by Wundt, and it soon attracted young scholars from all over the world who were eager to learn about the new science that Wundt had developed.

Wundt believed that scientific psychology should focus on analyzing **consciousness,** *a person's subjective experience of the world and the mind.* Consciousness encompasses a broad range of subjective experiences. We may be conscious of sights, sounds, tastes, smells, bodily sensations, thoughts, or feelings. As Wundt tried to figure out a way to study consciousness scientifically, he noted that chemists try to understand the structure of matter by breaking down natural substances into basic elements. So he and his students adopted an approach called **structuralism,** *the analysis of the basic elements that constitute the mind.* This approach involved breaking down consciousness into elemental sensations and feelings, and you can do a bit of structuralism right now without leaving your chair.

> **How did the work of chemists influence early psychology?**

Consider the contents of your own consciousness. At this very moment you may be aware of the meaning of these words, the visual appearance of the letters on the page, the key ring pressing uncomfortably against your thigh, your feelings of excitement or boredom (probably excitement), the smell of curried chicken salad, or the nagging question of whether the War of 1812 really deserves its own overture. At

stimulus
Sensory input from the environment.

reaction time
The amount of time taken to respond to a specific stimulus.

consciousness
A person's subjective experience of the world and the mind.

structuralism
The analysis of the basic elements that constitute the mind.

introspection
The subjective observation of one's own experience.

any given moment, all sorts of things are swimming in the stream of consciousness, and Wundt tried to analyze them in a systematic way using the method of **introspection**, *the subjective observation of one's own experience*. In a typical experiment, observers (usually students) were presented with a stimulus (usually a color or a sound) and then asked to report their introspections. The observers described the brightness of a color or the loudness of a tone. They reported on their "raw" sensory experience, rather than on their interpretations of that experience. For example, an observer presented with this page would not report seeing words on the page (which counts as an interpretation of the experience), but instead might describe a series of black marks, some straight and others curved, against a bright white background. Wundt also attempted to care-

Wilhelm Wundt (1832–1920), far right, founded the first laboratory devoted exclusively to psychology at the University of Leipzig in Germany. He sought to understand consciousness by breaking it down into its basic parts, including individual sensations and feelings.

fully describe the feelings associated with elementary perceptions. For example, when Wundt listened to the clicks produced by a metronome, some of the patterns of sounds were more pleasant than others. By analyzing the relation between feelings and perceptual sensations, Wundt and his students hoped to uncover the basic structure of conscious experience.

Wundt tried to provide objective measurements of conscious processes by using reaction time techniques similar to those first developed by Helmholtz. Wundt used reaction times to examine a distinction between the perception and interpretation of a stimulus. His research participants were instructed to press a button as soon as a tone sounded. Some participants were told to concentrate on perceiving the tone before pressing the button, whereas others were told to concentrate only on pressing the button. Those people who concentrated on the tone responded about one tenth of a second more slowly than those told to concentrate only on pressing the button. Wundt reasoned that both fast and slow participants had to register the tone in consciousness (perception), but only the slower participants also had to interpret the significance of the tone and press the button. The faster research participants, focusing only on the response they were to make, could respond automatically to the tone because they didn't have to engage in the additional step of interpretation (Fancher, 1979). This type of experimentation broke new ground by showing that psychologists could use scientific techniques to disentangle even subtle conscious processes. In fact, as you'll see in later chapters, reaction time procedures have proven extremely useful in modern research.

Titchener Brings Structuralism to the United States

The pioneering efforts of Wundt's laboratory launched psychology as an independent science and profoundly influenced the field for the remainder of the 19th century. Many European and American psychologists journeyed to Leipzig to study with Wundt. Among the most eminent was British-born Edward Titchener (1867–1927), who studied with Wundt for 2 years in the early 1890s. Titchener then came to the United States and set up a psychology laboratory at Cornell University (where, if you'd like to see it, his brain is still on display in the psychology department). Titchener brought some parts of Wundt's approach to America, but he also made some changes (Brock, 1993; Rieber, 1980). For instance, whereas Wundt emphasized the relationship between elements of consciousness, Titchener focused on identifying the basic elements themselves. In his textbook, *An Outline of Psychology* (1896), Titchener put forward a list of more than 44,000 elemental qualities of conscious experience, most of them visual (32,820) or auditory (11,600; Schultz & Schultz, 1987).

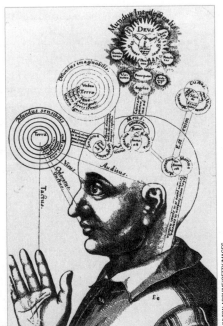

Titchener wasn't the first to try to identify the elements of conscious experience. As this drawing shows, the 17th-century physician and artist, Robert Fludd tried to do the same thing—and was about equally successful.

The influence of the structuralist approach gradually faded, due mostly to the introspective method. Science requires replicable observations; we could never determine the structure of DNA or the life span of a dust mite if every scientist who looked through a microscope saw something different. Alas, even trained observers provided conflicting introspections about their conscious experiences ("I see a cloud that looks like a duck"—"No, *I* think that cloud looks like a horse"), thus making it difficult for different psychologists to agree on the basic elements of conscious experience. Indeed, some psychologists had doubts about whether it was even possible to identify such elements through introspection alone. One of the most prominent skeptics was someone you've already met: a young man with a bad attitude and a useless medical degree named William James.

> **What are the problems with the introspective method?**

James and the Functional Approach

James returned from his European tour inspired by the idea of approaching psychological issues from a scientific perspective. He received a teaching appointment at Harvard (primarily because the president of the university was a neighbor and family friend) and his position at Harvard enabled him to purchase laboratory equipment for classroom experiments. As a result, James taught the first course at an American university to draw on the new experimental psychology developed by Wundt and his German followers (Schultz & Schultz, 1987).

THE REAL WORLD

Improving Study Skills

To get the most out of taking this course, you should begin by doing something that might seem a bit strange: make it hard on yourself. But by making it hard on yourself in the right way, you will end up making the course easier and take away a lot more from it than you would otherwise. What do we mean by making it hard on yourself? Our minds don't work like video cameras, passively recording everything that happens and then faithfully storing the information. In order to retain new information, you need to take an active role in learning, by doing such things as rehearsing, interpreting, and testing yourself. These activities initially might seem difficult, but in fact they are what psychologists call *desirable difficulties* (Bjork & Bjork, 2011): making it more difficult by actively engaging during critical phases of learning will increase your retention and ultimately result in improved performance. Here are some specific suggestions:

- **Rehearse.** One useful type of active manipulation is rehearsal: repeating to-be-learned information to yourself. Psychologists have found that a particularly effective strategy is called spaced rehearsal, where you repeat information to yourself at increasingly long intervals. For example, suppose that you want to learn the name of a person you've just met named Eric. Repeat the name to yourself right away, wait a few seconds and think of it again, wait a bit longer (maybe 30 seconds) and bring the name to mind once more, then rehearse the name again after a minute and once more after 2 or 3 minutes. Making rehearsal gradually more difficult will improve retention; studies show that this type of rehearsal improves long-term learning more than rehearsing the name without any spacing between rehearsals (Landauer & Bjork, 1978). You can apply this technique to names, dates, definitions, and many other kinds of information, including concepts presented in this textbook.

- **Interpret.** Simple rehearsal can be beneficial, but one of the most important lessons from psychological research is that we acquire information most effectively when we think about its meaning and reflect on its significance. In fact, we don't even have to try to remember something if we think deeply enough about what we want to remember; the act of reflection

▲ Anxious feelings about an upcoming exam may be unpleasant, but as you've probably experienced yourself, they can motivate much-needed study.

itself will virtually guarantee good memory. For example, suppose that you want to learn the basic ideas behind Skinner's approach to behaviorism (see page 18). Ask yourself the following kinds of questions: How did behaviorism differ from previous approaches in psychology? How would a behaviorist like Skinner think about psychological issues that interest you, such as whether a mentally disturbed individual should be held responsible for

James agreed with Wundt on some points, including the importance of focusing on immediate experience and the usefulness of introspection as a technique (Bjork, 1983), but he disagreed with Wundt's claim that consciousness could be broken down into separate elements. James believed that trying to isolate and analyze a particular moment of consciousness (as the structuralists did) distorted the essential nature of consciousness. Consciousness, he argued, was more like a flowing stream than a bundle of separate elements. So James decided to approach psychology from a different perspective entirely and developed an approach known as **functionalism**, *the study of the purpose mental processes serve in enabling people to adapt to their environment.* In contrast to structuralism, which examined the structure of mental processes, functionalism set out to understand the functions those mental processes served. (See the Real World box for some strategies to enhance one of those functions—learning.)

> **How does functionalism relate to Darwin's theory of natural selection?**

James's thinking was inspired by the ideas in Charles Darwin's (1809–1882) recently published book on biological evolution, *On the Origin of Species by Means of Natural Selection* (1859). Darwin proposed the principle of **natural selection**: *The features of an organism that help it survive and reproduce are more likely than other features to be passed on to subsequent generations.* From this perspective, James reasoned, mental abilities must have evolved because they were adaptive, that is, because they helped people solve problems and increased their chances of survival. Like other animals, people have always needed to avoid predators, locate food, build shelters,

functionalism
The study of the purpose mental processes serve in enabling people to adapt to their environment.

natural selection
Charles Darwin's theory that the features of an organism that help it survive and reproduce are more likely than other features to be passed on to subsequent generations.

---

committing a crime, or what factors would contribute to your choice of a major subject or career path? In attempting to answer such questions, you will need to review what you've learned about behaviorism and then relate it to other things you already know about. This may seem like a demanding activity, but it is much easier to remember new information when you can relate it to something you already know. The Critical Thinking questions that are sprinkled throughout the text will help you to reflect on and interpret the material, and a happy consequence of that activity is that you will be more likely to remember the information that the questions engage you to think about.

- **Build.** Think about and review the information you have acquired in class on a regular basis. Begin soon after class, and then try to schedule regular "booster" sessions. Don't wait until the last second to cram your review into one sitting; as discussed in the Rehearse section, research shows that spacing out review and repetition leads to longer-lasting recall.

- **Test.** Don't just look at your class notes or this textbook; test yourself on the material as often as you can. As you will learn in the

Memory and Learning chapters, research also shows that actively testing yourself on information you've acquired helps you to later remember that information more than just looking at it again. Testing yourself can also guard against a common pitfall. You may think that you have learned the material because it seems familiar to you after having reviewed it several times, but just because the material seems familiar, that doesn't necessarily mean that you have learned it well enough to answer a test question. Testing yourself will alert you to when you need to study more, even when the information seems familiar. The Cue Questions that you will encounter throughout the text (highlighted by green question marks, as you'll see just above this box) are designed to test you and thereby increase learning and retention. Be sure to use them. The Learning Curve study aid will also help you to test and learn (see the Preface for further discussion of Learning Curve).

- **Hit the main points.** Take some of the load off your memory by developing effective note-taking and outlining skills. Students often scribble down vague and fragmentary notes during lectures, figuring that

the notes will be good enough to jog memory later. But when the time comes to study, they've forgotten so much that their notes are no longer clear. Realize that you can't write down everything an instructor says, and try to focus on making detailed notes about the main ideas, facts, and people mentioned in the lecture.

- **Organize.** The act of organizing an outline in a way that clearly highlights the major concepts will force you to reflect on the information in a way that promotes retention and will also provide you with a helpful study guide to promote self-testing and review. Again, this activity may seem difficult or demanding at first, but it will result in improved retention and ultimately will make learning easier for you.

- **Sleep on it.** We've stressed the importance of making it hard on yourself, but this final item is an easy one: get some sleep. As you'll learn in the Hot Science box in the Memory chapter, research shows that sleep helps to form lasting memories. In fact, research shows that sleep does a particularly good job of increasing memory for important, meaningful material. So be sure to enlist sleep as an ally in studying and test preparation.

You don't have to look at this photo for more than a half-second to know that Vladimir Putin, the President of Russia, is not feeling very happy. William James suggested that your ability to read emotional expressions in an instant serves an important function that promotes your survival and well-being.

G. Stanley Hall believed that as they develop, children retrace the evolutionary history of our species, starting out as "mental cavemen" and ending up as . . . well, us.

and attract mates. Applying Darwin's principle of natural selection, James (1890) reasoned that consciousness must serve an important biological function and the task for psychologists was to understand what those functions are. Wundt and the other structuralists worked in laboratories, and James believed that such work was limited in its ability to tell us how consciousness functioned in the natural environment. Wundt, in turn, believed that James did not focus enough on new findings from the laboratory that he and the structuralists had begun to produce. Commenting on *The Principles of Psychology,* Wundt conceded that James was a topflight writer but disapproved of his approach: "It is literature, it is beautiful, but it is not psychology" (Bjork, 1983, p. 12).

The rest of the world did not agree, and James's functionalist psychology quickly gained followers, especially in North America, where Darwin's ideas were influencing many thinkers. G. Stanley Hall (1844–1924), who studied with both Wundt and James, set up the first psychology research laboratory in North America at Johns Hopkins University in 1881. Hall's work focused on development and education and was strongly influenced by evolutionary thinking (Schultz & Schultz, 1987).

Hall believed that, as children develop, they pass through stages that repeat the evolutionary history of the human race. Thus, the mental capacities of a young child resemble those of our ancient ancestors, and children grow over a lifetime in the same way that a species evolves over aeons. Hall founded the *American Journal of Psychology* in 1887 (the first psychology journal in the United States), and went on to play a key role in founding the American Psychological Association (the first national organization of psychologists in the United States), serving as its first president.

The efforts of James and Hall set the stage for functionalism to develop as a major school of psychological thought in North America. Psychology departments that embraced a functionalist approach started to spring up at many major American universities, and in a struggle for survival that would have made Darwin proud, functionalism became more influential than structuralism had ever been. By the 1920s, functionalism was the dominant approach to psychology in North America.

IN SUMMARY

▶ Philosophers have pondered and debated ideas about human nature for millennia, but given the nature of their approach, they did not provide empirical evidence to support their claims.

▶ Some of the earliest successful efforts to develop a science linking mind and behavior came from the French scientists Marie Jean Pierre Flourens and Paul Broca, who showed that damage to the brain can result in impairments of behavior and mental functions.

▶ Hermann von Helmholtz furthered the science of the mind by developing methods for measuring reaction time.

▶ Wilhelm Wundt is credited with the founding of psychology as a scientific discipline. His structuralist approach focused on analyzing the basic elements of consciousness. Wundt's student, Edward Titchener, brought structuralism to the United States.

▶ William James applied Darwin's theory of natural selection to the study of the mind. His functionalist approach focused on how mental processes serve to enable people to adapt to their environments.

▶ G. Stanley Hall established the first American research laboratory, journal, and professional organization devoted to psychology.

The Development of Clinical Psychology

At about the same time that some psychologists were developing structuralism and functionalism in the laboratory, other psychologists working in the clinic were beginning to study people with psychological disorders. They began to realize that one can often understand how something works by examining how it breaks, and their observations of mental disorders influenced the development of psychology.

The Path to Freud and Psychoanalytic Theory

French physicians Jean-Martin Charcot (1825–1893) and Pierre Janet (1859–1947) reported striking observations when they interviewed patients who had developed a condition known then as **hysteria**, a *temporary loss of cognitive or motor functions, usually as a result of emotionally upsetting experiences.* Hysterical patients became blind, paralyzed, or lost their memories, even though there was no known physical cause of their problems. However, when the patients were put into a trancelike state through the use of hypnosis (an altered state of consciousness characterized by suggestibility), their symptoms disappeared: Blind patients could see, paralyzed patients could walk, and forgetful patients could remember. After coming out of the hypnotic trance, the patients forgot what had happened under hypnosis and again showed their symptoms. The patients behaved like two different people in the waking versus hypnotic states.

These peculiar disorders were ignored by Wundt, Titchener, and other laboratory scientists, who did not consider them a proper subject for scientific psychology (Bjork, 1983). But William James believed they had important implications for understanding the nature of the mind (Taylor, 2001). He thought it was important to capitalize on these mental disruptions as a way of understanding the normal operation of the mind. During our ordinary conscious experience we are only aware of a single "me" or "self," but the aberrations described by Charcot, Janet, and others suggested that the brain can create many conscious selves that are not aware of each other's existence (James, 1890, p. 400). These striking observations also fueled the imagination of a young physician from Vienna, Austria, who studied with Charcot in Paris in 1885. His name was Sigmund Freud (1856–1939).

After his visit to Charcot's clinic in Paris, Freud returned to Vienna, where he continued his work with hysteric patients. (The word *hysteria*, by the way, comes from the Latin word *hyster* [womb]. It was once believed that only women suffered from hysteria, which was thought to be caused by a "wandering womb.") Working with physician Joseph Breuer (1842–1925), Freud began to make his own observations of hysteric patients and develop theories to explain their strange behaviors and symptoms. Freud theorized that many of the patients' problems could be traced to the effects of painful childhood experiences that the person could not remember, and he suggested that the powerful influence of these

How was Freud influenced by work with hysteric patients?

hysteria
A temporary loss of cognitive or motor functions, usually as a result of emotionally upsetting experiences.

unconscious
The part of the mind that operates outside of conscious awareness but influences conscious thoughts, feelings, and actions.

psychoanalytic theory
An approach that emphasizes the importance of unconscious mental processes in shaping feelings, thoughts, and behavior.

In this photograph, Sigmund Freud (1856–1939) sits by the couch reserved for his psychoanalytic patients, where they would be encouraged to recall past experiences and bring unconscious thoughts into awareness.

seemingly lost memories revealed the presence of an unconscious mind. According to Freud, the **unconscious** is *the part of the mind that operates outside of conscious awareness but influences conscious thoughts, feelings, and actions.* This idea led Freud to develop **psychoanalytic theory,** *an approach that emphasizes the importance of unconscious mental processes in shaping feelings, thoughts, and behaviors.* From a psychoanalytic perspective, it is important to uncover a person's early experiences and to illuminate a person's unconscious anxieties, conflicts, and desires. Psychoanalytic theory formed the basis for a therapy that Freud called **psychoanalysis,** which focuses on *bringing unconscious material into conscious awareness to better understand psychological disorders.* During psychoanalysis, patients recalled past experiences ("When I was a toddler, I was frightened by a masked man on a black horse") and related their dreams and fantasies ("Sometimes I close my eyes and imagine not having to pay for this session"). Psychoanalysts used Freud's theoretical approach to interpret what their patients said.

In the early 1900s, Freud and a growing number of followers formed a psychoanalytic movement. Carl Gustav Jung (1875–1961) and Alfred Adler (1870–1937) were prominent in the movement, but both were independent thinkers, and Freud apparently had little tolerance for individuals who challenged his ideas. Soon enough, Freud broke off his relationships with both men so that he could shape the psychoanalytic movement himself (Sulloway, 1992). Psychoanalytic theory became quite controversial (especially in America) because it suggested that understanding a person's thoughts, feelings, and behavior required a thorough exploration of the person's early sexual experiences and unconscious sexual desires. In those days these topics were considered far too racy for scientific discussion.

Most of Freud's followers, like Freud himself, were trained as physicians and did not conduct psychological experiments in the laboratory (although early in his career, Freud did do some nice laboratory work on the sexual organs of eels). By and large, psychoanalysts did not hold positions in universities and developed their ideas in isolation from the research-based approaches of Wundt, Titchener, James, Hall, and others. One of the few times that Freud met with the leading academic psychologists was at a conference that G. Stanley Hall organized at Clark University in 1909. It was there that William James and Sigmund Freud met for the first time. Although James worked in an academic setting and Freud worked with clinical patients, both men believed that mental aberrations provide important clues into the nature of mind.

This famous psychology conference, held in 1909 at Clark University, was organized by G. Stanley Hall and brought together many notable figures, such as William James and Sigmund Freud. Both men are circled, with James on the left.

CORBIS

Influence of Psychoanalysis and the Humanistic Response

Most historians consider Freud to be one of the two or three most influential thinkers of the 20th century, and the psychoanalytic movement influenced everything from literature and history to politics and art. Within psychology, psychoanalysis had its greatest impact on clinical practice, but that influence has been considerably diminished over the past 40 years.

This is partly because Freud's vision of human nature was a dark one, emphasizing limitations and problems rather than possibilities and potentials. He saw people as hostages to their forgotten childhood experiences and primitive sexual impulses, and the inherent pessimism of his perspective frustrated those psychologists who had a more optimistic view of human nature. In America, the years after World War II were positive, invigorating, and upbeat: Poverty and disease were being conquered by technology, the standard of living of ordinary Americans was rising sharply, and people were landing on the moon. The era was characterized by the accomplishments—not the foibles—of the human mind, and Freud's viewpoint was out of step with the spirit of the times.

> **Why are Freud's ideas less influential today?**

©UNITED ARCHIVES GMBH/ALAMY

Humanistic psychology offered a positive view of human nature that matched the zeitgeist of the 1960s.

Freud's ideas were also difficult to test, and a theory that can't be tested is of limited use in psychology or other sciences. Although Freud's emphasis on unconscious processes has had an enduring impact on psychology, psychologists began to have serious misgivings about many aspects of Freud's theory.

It was in these times that psychologists such as Abraham Maslow (1908–1970) and Carl Rogers (1902–1987) pioneered a new movement called **humanistic psychology,** *an approach to understanding human nature that emphasizes the positive potential of human beings.* Humanistic psychologists focused on the highest aspirations that people had for themselves. Rather than viewing people as prisoners of events in their remote pasts, humanistic psychologists viewed people as free agents who have an inherent need to develop, grow, and attain their full potential. This movement reached its peak in the 1960s when a generation of "flower children" found it easy to see psychological life as a kind of blossoming of the spirit. Humanistic therapists sought to help people realize their full potential; in fact, they called them *clients* rather than *patients.* In this relationship, the therapist and the client (unlike the psychoanalyst and the patient) were on equal footing. The development of the humanistic perspective was one more reason why Freud's ideas eventually became less influential.

IN SUMMARY

▶ Psychologists have often focused on patients with psychological disorders as a way of understanding human behavior. Clinicians such as Jean-Martin Charcot and Pierre Janet studied unusual cases in which patients acted like different people while under hypnosis, raising the possibility that each of us has more than one self.

▶ Through his work with hysteric patients, Sigmund Freud developed psychoanalysis, which emphasized the importance of unconscious influences and childhood experiences in shaping thoughts, feelings, and behavior.

▶ Happily, humanistic psychologists offered a more optimistic view of the human condition, suggesting that people are inherently disposed toward growth and can usually reach their full potential with a little help from their friends.

psychoanalysis
A therapeutic approach that focuses on bringing unconscious material into conscious awareness to better understand psychological disorders.

humanistic psychology
An approach to understanding human nature that emphasizes the positive potential of human beings.

behaviorism
An approach that advocates that psychologists restrict themselves to the scientific study of objectively observable behavior.

The Search for Objective Measurement: Behaviorism Takes Center Stage

Our discussion of the development of clinical psychology into the 1960s took us a little ahead of ourselves—we need to turn our attention back a few decades to understand some other important developments.

The schools of psychological thought that had developed by the early 20th century—structuralism, functionalism, and psychoanalysis—differed substantially from one another. But they shared an important similarity: Each tried to understand the inner workings of the mind by examining conscious perceptions, thoughts, memories, and feelings or by trying to elicit previously unconscious material, all of which were reported by participants in experiments or patients in a clinical setting. In each case it proved difficult to establish with much certainty just what was going on in people's minds, due to the unreliable nature of the methodology. As the 20th century unfolded, a new approach developed as psychologists challenged the idea that psychology should focus on mental life at all. This new approach was called **behaviorism**, which *advocated that psychologists restrict themselves* to *the scientific study of objectively observable behavior.* (See Other Voices: Is Psychology a Science? for a modern discussion of the science of psychology.) Behaviorism represented a dramatic departure from previous schools of thought.

Watson and the Emergence of Behaviorism

John Broadus Watson (1878–1958) believed that private experience was too idiosyncratic and vague to be an object of scientific inquiry. Science required replicable, objective measurements of phenomena that were accessible to all observers, and the introspective methods used by structuralists and functionalists were far too subjective for that. So instead of describing conscious experiences, Watson proposed that psychologists focus entirely on the study of behavior—what people *do,* rather than what people *experience*—because behavior can be observed by anyone and it can be measured objectively. Watson thought that a focus on behavior would put a stop to the endless philosophical debates in which psychologists were currently entangled, and it would encourage psychologists to develop practical applications in such areas as business, medicine, law, and education. The goal of scientific psychology, according to Watson, should be to predict and to control behavior in ways that benefit society.

Why would someone want to throw the mind out of psychology? This may seem excessive, until you notice that Watson studied the behavior of animals such as rats and birds. In such studies, inferring a mind is a matter of some debate. Shall we say that dogs have minds, for instance, but leave out pigeons? If we include pigeons, what about worms? Animal behavior specialists staked out claims in this area. In 1908, Margaret Floy Washburn (1871–1939) published *The Animal Mind,* in which she reviewed what was then known about perception, learning, and memory in different animal species. She argued that nonhuman animals, much like human animals, have conscious mental experiences (Scarborough & Furumoto, 1987). Watson reacted to this claim with venom. Because we cannot ask pigeons about their private, inner experiences (well, we can ask, but they never tell us), Watson decided that the only way to understand how animals learn and adapt was to focus solely on their behavior, and he suggested that the study of human beings should proceed on the same basis.

Watson was influenced by the work of Russian physiologist Ivan Pavlov (1849–1936), who carried out pioneering research on the physiology of digestion. In the course

> **How did behaviorism help psychology advance as a science?**

ARCHIVES OF THE HISTORY OF AMERICAN PSYCHOLOGY

In 1894, Margaret Floy Washburn (1871–1939), a student of Edward Titchener at Cornell, became the first woman to receive a PhD degree in psychology. Washburn went on to a highly distinguished career, spent mainly in teaching and research at Vassar College in Poughkeepsie, New York. Washburn wrote an influential book, *The Animal Mind,* developed a theory of consciousness, and contributed to the development of psychology as a profession.

OTHER VOICES

Is Psychology a Science?

Timothy D. Wilson is a professor of psychology at the University of Virginia and the author of several popular books, including *Redirect: The Surprising New Science of Psychological Change* (2011).

PHOTO BY JEN FARIELLO, COURTESY TIMOTHY D. WILSON

Nobody can dispute that you are taking a course in psychology, but are you taking a science course? Some critics maintain that psychology fails to meet accepted criteria for what constitutes a science. Timothy Wilson, a psychology professor at the University of Virginia, took on the critics by drawing from an appropriate source: the scientific literature (Wilson, 2012).

Once, during a meeting at my university, a biologist mentioned that he was the only faculty member present from a science department. When I corrected him, noting that I was from the Department of Psychology, he waved his hand dismissively, as if I were a Little Leaguer telling a member of the New York Yankees that I too played baseball.

There has long been snobbery in the sciences, with the "hard" ones (physics, chemistry, biology) considering themselves to be more legitimate than the "soft" ones (psychology, sociology). It is thus no surprise that many members of the general public feel the same way. But of late, skepticism about the rigors of social science has reached absurd heights. The U.S. House of Representatives recently voted to eliminate funding for political science research through the National Science Foundation. In the wake of that action, an opinion writer for the *Washington Post* suggested that the House didn't go far enough. The NSF should not fund any research in the social sciences, wrote Charles Lane, because "unlike hypotheses in the hard sciences, hypotheses about society usually can't be proven or disproven by experimentation."

Lane's comments echoed ones by Gary Gutting in the Opinionator blog of the *New York Times*. "While the physical sciences produce many detailed and precise predictions," wrote Gutting, "the social sciences do not. The reason is that such predictions almost always require randomized controlled experiments, which are seldom possible when people are involved."

This is news to me and the many other social scientists who have spent their careers doing carefully controlled experiments on human behavior, inside and outside the laboratory. What makes the criticism so galling is that those who voice it, or members of their families, have undoubtedly benefited from research in the disciplines they dismiss.

Most of us know someone who has suffered from depression and sought psychotherapy. He or she probably benefited from therapies such as cognitive behavioral therapy that have been shown to work in randomized clinical trials.

Problems such as child abuse and teenage pregnancy take a huge toll on society. Interventions developed by research psychologists, tested with the experimental method, have been found to lower the incidence of child abuse and reduce the rate of teenage pregnancies.

Ever hear of stereotype threat? It is the double jeopardy that people face when they are at risk of confirming a negative stereotype of their group. When African American students take a difficult test, for example, they are concerned not only about how well they will do but also about the possibility that performing poorly will reflect badly on their entire group. This added worry has been shown time and again, in carefully controlled experiments, to lower academic performance. But fortunately, experiments have also showed promising ways to reduce this threat. One intervention, for example, conducted in a middle school, reduced the achievement gap by 40%.

If you know someone who was unlucky enough to be arrested for a crime he didn't commit, he may have benefited from social psychological experiments that have resulted in fairer lineups and interrogations, making it less likely that innocent people are convicted.

An often-overlooked advantage of the experimental method is that it can demonstrate what doesn't work. Consider three popular programs that research psychologists have debunked: Critical Incident Stress Debriefing, used to prevent post-traumatic stress disorders in first responders and others who have witnessed horrific events; the D.A.R.E. anti-drug program, used in many schools throughout America; and Scared Straight programs designed to prevent at-risk teens from engaging in criminal behavior.

All three of these programs have been shown, with well-designed experimental studies, to be ineffective or, in some cases, to make matters worse. And as a result, the programs have become less popular or have changed their methods. By discovering what doesn't work, social scientists have saved the public billions of dollars.

To be fair to the critics, social scientists have not always taken advantage of the experimental method as much as they could. Too often, for example, educational programs have been implemented widely without being adequately tested. But increasingly, educational researchers are employing better methodologies. For example, in a recent study, researchers randomly assigned teachers to a program called My Teaching Partner, which is designed to improve teaching skills, or to a control group. Students taught by the teachers who participated in the program did significantly better on achievement tests than did students taught by teachers in the control group.

Are the social sciences perfect? Of course not. Human behavior is complex, and it is not possible to conduct experiments to test all aspects of what people do or why. There are entire disciplines devoted to the experimental study of human behavior, however, in tightly controlled, ethically acceptable ways. Many people benefit from the results, including those who, in their ignorance, believe that science is limited to the study of molecules.

Wilson's examples of psychological investigations that have had beneficial effects on society are excellent, but perhaps even more important is his point that much of psychology is based on carefully controlled experimentation using randomization procedures that the critics apparently believe—mistakenly—cannot be applied to the study of human beings. The next chapter in this textbook is devoted to explaining how psychologists apply the scientific method to the study of the mind and behavior. It should come as no surprise to learn that your textbook authors believe that psychology is indeed a science. But what *kind* of science is psychology? (See the Hot Science box, "Psychology as a hub science", for one approach to this question.) Should psychology strive to come up with general laws like those of physics, or try to make precise predictions like those made by so-called hard sciences? Should psychologists focus on laboratory experimentation or spend more effort attempting to study behavior in everyday life? What methods seem most promising to you as tools for psychological investigations? There is room for debate about what kind of science psychology is and should be; we hope that you think about these questions as you read this book.

response
An action or physiological change elicited by a stimulus.

reinforcement
The consequences of a behavior determine whether it will be more or less likely to occur again.

of that work, Pavlov noticed something interesting about the dogs he was studying (Fancher, 1979). Not only did the dogs salivate at the sight of food; they also salivated at the sight of the person who fed them. The feeders were not dressed in Alpo suits, so why should the mere sight of them trigger a basic digestive response in the dogs? To answer this question, Pavlov developed a procedure in which he sounded a tone every time he fed the dogs, and after a while he observed that the dogs would salivate when they heard the tone alone. In Pavlov's experiments, the sound of the tone was a stimulus (sensory input from the environment) that influenced the salivation of the dogs, which was a **response**: *an action or physiological change elicited by a stimulus.* Watson and other behaviorists made these two notions the building blocks of their theories, which is why behaviorism is sometimes called *stimulus–response* (S–R) psychology.

Watson applied Pavlov's techniques to human infants. In a famous and controversial study, Watson and his student Rosalie Rayner taught an infant known as "Little Albert" to have a strong fear of a harmless white rat (and other white furry animals and toys) that he had previously not feared. Why would they do such a thing? You'll learn more about this study in the Learning chapter, but the short answer is this: Watson believed that human behavior is powerfully influenced by the environment, and the experiments with Little Albert provided a chance to demonstrate such influence at the earliest stage of life. Neither Watson nor later behaviorists believed that the environment was the *only* influence on behavior (Todd & Morris, 1992), but they did think it was the most important one. Consistent with that view, Watson became romantically involved with someone prominent in his environment: Rosalie Rayner. He refused to end the affair when confronted by colleagues, and the resulting scandal forced Watson to leave his position at Johns Hopkins University. He found work in a New York advertising agency, where he applied behaviorist principles to marketing and advertising (which certainly involves manipulating the environment to influence behavior!). Watson also wrote popular books that exposed a broad general audience to the behaviorist approach (Watson, 1924, 1928). The result of all these developments (Pavlov's work in the laboratory, Watson and Rayner's applications to humans, and Watson's practical applications to daily life) was that by the 1920s, behaviorism had become a dominant force in scientific psychology.

B. F. Skinner and the Development of Behaviorism

In 1926, Burrhus Frederick Skinner (1904–1990) graduated from Hamilton College. Like William James, Skinner was a young man who couldn't decide what to do with his life. He aspired to become a writer, and his interest in literature led him indirectly to psychology. Skinner wondered whether a novelist could portray a character without understanding why the character behaved as he or she did, and when he came across Watson's books, he knew he had the answer. Skinner completed his PhD studies in psychology at Harvard (Wiener, 1996) and began to develop a new kind of behaviorism. In Pavlov's experiments, the dogs had been passive participants that stood around, listened to tones, and drooled. Skinner recognized that in everyday life, animals don't just stand there—they do something! Animals *act* on their environments in order to find shelter, food, or mates, and Skinner wondered if he could develop behaviorist principles that would explain how they *learned* to act in those situations.

Skinner built what he called a *conditioning chamber* but what the rest of the world would forever call a *Skinner box*. The box has a lever and a food tray, and a hungry rat could get food delivered to the tray by pressing the lever. Skinner observed that when a rat was put in the box, it would wander around, sniffing and exploring, and would usually press the bar by accident, at which point a food pellet would drop into the tray. After that happened, the rate of bar pressing would increase dramatically and remain high until the rat was no longer hungry. Skinner saw evidence for what he called the principle of **reinforcement**, which states that *the consequences of a behavior deter-*

Inspired by Watson's behaviorism, B. F. Skinner (1904–1990) investigated the way an animal learns by interacting with its environment. Here, he demonstrates the Skinner box, in which rats learn to press a lever to receive food: The lever press is the learned behavior and the food is the reinforcement that increases the frequency of future lever pressing.

mine whether it will be more or less likely to occur again. The concept of reinforcement became the foundation for Skinner's new approach to behaviorism (see the Learning chapter), which he formulated in a landmark book, *The Behavior of Organisms: An Experimental Analysis* (Skinner, 1938).

What did Skinner learn by observing the behavior of hungry rats?

Skinner set out to use his ideas about reinforcement to help improve the quality of everyday life. He was visiting his daughter's fourth-grade class when he realized that he might be able to improve classroom instruction by breaking a complicated task into small bits and then using the principle of reinforcement to teach children each bit (Bjork, 1993). He developed automatic devices known as *teaching machines* that did exactly that (Skinner, 1958). The teaching machine asked a series of increasingly difficult questions that built on the students' answers to the simpler ones. To learn a complicated math problem, for instance, students would first be asked an easy question about the simplest part of the problem. They would then be told whether the answer was right or wrong, and if a correct response was made, the machine would move on to a more difficult question. Skinner thought that the satisfaction of knowing they were correct would be reinforcing and help students learn.

If fourth graders and rats could be successfully trained, then why stop there? In the controversial books, *Beyond Freedom and Dignity* (1971) and *Walden II* (1948/1986), Skinner laid out his vision of a utopian society in which behavior was controlled by the judicious application of the principle of reinforcement (Skinner, 1971). In those books he put forth the simple but stunning claim that our subjective sense of free will is an illusion and that when we think we are exercising free will, we are actually responding to present and past patterns of reinforcement. We do things in the present that have been rewarding in the past, and our sense of "choosing" to do them is nothing more than an illusion. In this, Skinner echoed the sentiments of philosopher Benedict Spinoza (1632–1677), who several centuries earlier had noted that "men

Which of Skinner's claims provoked an outcry?

are deceived in thinking themselves free, a belief that consists only in this, that they are conscious of their actions and ignorant of the causes by which they are determined. As to their saying that human actions depend on the will, these are mere words without any corresponding idea" (1677/1982, p. 86).

Skinner argued that his insights could be used to increase human well-being and solve social problems. Not surprisingly, that claim sparked an outcry from critics who believed that Skinner was giving away one of our most cherished attributes—free will—and calling for a repressive society that manipulated people for its own ends. The criticism even extended to *TV Guide,* which featured an interview with Skinner and called his ideas "the taming of mankind through a system of dog obedience schools for all" (Bjork, 1993, p. 201). Given the nature of Skinner's ideas, the critics' attacks were understandable—he had seriously underestimated how much people cherish the idea of free will—but in the sober light of hindsight, they were clearly overblown. Skinner did not want to turn society into a "dog obedience school" or strip people of their personal freedoms. Rather, he argued that an understanding of the principles by which behavior is generated could be used to increase the social welfare, which is precisely what happens when a government launches advertisements to encourage citizens to drink milk or quit smoking. The result of all the controversy, however, was that Skinner's fame reached a level rarely attained by psychologists. A popular magazine that listed the 100 most important people who ever lived ranked Skinner just 39 points below Jesus Christ (Herrnstein, 1977).

Skinner's well-publicized questioning of such cherished notions as free will led to a rumor that he had raised his own daughter in a Skinner box. This urban legend, while untrue, likely originated from the climate-controlled, glass-encased crib that he invented to protect his daughter from the cold Minnesota winter. Skinner marketed the crib under various names, including the "Air-crib" and the "Heir Conditioner," but it failed to catch on with parents.

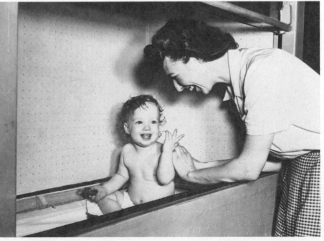

BETTMANN/CORBIS

IN SUMMARY

► Behaviorism advocated the study of observable actions and responses and held that inner mental processes were private events that could not be studied scientifically. Ivan Pavlov and John B. Watson studied the association between a stimulus and a response and emphasized the importance of the environment in shaping behavior.

► Influenced by Watson's behaviorism, B. F. Skinner developed the concept of reinforcement using a Skinner box. He demonstrated that animals and humans repeat behaviors that generate pleasant results and avoid performing those that generate unpleasant results. Skinner extended Watson's contentions about the importance of the environment in shaping behavior by suggesting that free will is an illusion and that the principle of reinforcement can be used to benefit society.

Return of the Mind: Psychology Expands

Watson, Skinner, and the behaviorists dominated psychology from the 1930s to the 1950s. Psychologist Ulric Neisser recalled the atmosphere when he was a student at Swarthmore in the early 1950s:

> Behaviorism was the basic framework for almost all of psychology at the time. It was what you had to learn. That was the age when it was supposed that no psychological phenomenon was real unless you could demonstrate it in a rat. (quoted in Baars, 1986, p. 275)

Behaviorism wouldn't dominate the field for much longer, however, and Neisser himself would play an important role in developing an alternative perspective. Why was behaviorism replaced? Although behaviorism allowed psychologists to measure, predict, and control behavior, it did this by ignoring some important things. First, it ignored the mental processes that had fascinated psychologists such as Wundt and James and, in so doing, found itself unable to explain some very important phenomena, such as how children learn language. Second, it ignored the evolutionary history of the organisms it studied and was thus unable to explain why, for example, a rat could learn to associate nausea with food much more quickly than it could learn to associate nausea with a tone or a light. As we will see, the approaches that ultimately replaced behaviorism met these kinds of problems head-on.

The Pioneers of Cognitive Psychology

Even at the height of behaviorist domination, there were a few revolutionaries whose research and writings were focused on mental processes. German psychologist Max Wertheimer (1880–1943) focused on the study of **illusions**, *errors of perception, memory, or judgment in which subjective experience differs from objective reality.* In one of Wertheimer's experiments, a person was shown two lights that flashed quickly on a screen, one after the other. One light was flashed through a vertical slit, the other through a diagonal slit. When the time between two flashes was relatively long (one fifth of a second or more), an observer would see that it was just two lights flashing in alternation. But when Wertheimer reduced the time between flashes to around one twentieth of a second, observers saw a single flash of light moving back and forth (Fancher, 1979; Sarris, 1989). Wertheimer reasoned that the perceived motion could not be explained in terms of the separate elements that cause the illusion (the two flashing lights) but instead that the moving flash of light is perceived as a *whole* rather than as the sum of its two parts. This unified whole, which in German is called *Gestalt,* makes up

What do you see when you look at this image? Why do you see more than just random markings?

the perceptual experience. Wertheimer's interpretation of the illusion led to the development of **Gestalt psychology,** *a psychological approach that emphasizes that we often perceive the whole rather than the sum of the parts.* In other words, the mind imposes organization on what it perceives, so people don't see what the experimenter actually shows them (two separate lights); instead, they see the elements as a unified whole (one moving light).

> **Why might people not see what an experimenter actually showed them?**

Another pioneer who focused on the mind was Sir Frederic Bartlett (1886–1969), a British psychologist interested in memory. Bartlett was dissatisfied with existing research, especially the research of German psychologist Hermann Ebbinghaus (1850–1909), who had performed groundbreaking experiments on memory in 1885 (described in the Memory chapter). Serving as his own research subject, Ebbinghaus tried to discover how quickly and how well he could memorize and recall meaningless information, such as the three-letter nonsense syllables *dap, kir,* and *sul.* Bartlett believed that it was more important to examine memory for the kinds of information people actually encounter in everyday life, so he gave people stories to remember and carefully observed the kinds of errors they made when they tried to recall them at a later time (Bartlett, 1932). Bartlett discovered many interesting things that Ebbinghaus could never have learned with his nonsense syllables. For example, he found that research participants often remembered what *should* have happened or what they *expected* to happen rather than what actually *did* happen. These and other errors led Bartlett to suggest that memory is not a photographic reproduction of past experience and that our attempts to recall the past are powerfully influenced by our knowledge, beliefs, hopes, aspirations, and desires.

Jean Piaget (1896–1980) was a Swiss psychologist who studied the perceptual and cognitive errors of children in order to gain insight into the nature and development of the human mind. For example, in one of his tasks, Piaget gave a 3-year-old a large and a small mound of clay and told the child to make the two mounds equal. Then Piaget broke one of the clay mounds into smaller pieces and asked the child which mound now had more clay. Although the amount of clay remained the same, of course, 3-year-olds usually said that the mound that was broken into smaller pieces was bigger, but by the age of 6 or 7, they no longer made this error. As you'll see in the Development

illusions
Errors of perception, memory, or judgment in which subjective experience differs from objective reality.

Gestalt psychology
A psychological approach that emphasizes that we often perceive the whole rather than the sum of the parts.

BILL ANDERSON/PHOTO RESEARCHERS, INC.

Jean Piaget (1896–1980) studied and theorized about the developing mental lives of children. How were his methods a marked departure from the methods of the behaviorists?

This 1950s computer was among the first generation of digital computers. How was the computer analogy helpful in the early days of cognitive psychology?

chapter, Piaget theorized that younger children lack a particular cognitive ability that allows older children to appreciate the fact that the mass of an object remains constant even when it is divided. For Piaget, errors such as these provided key insights into the mental world of the child (Piaget & Inhelder, 1969).

German psychologist Kurt Lewin (1890–1947) was also a pioneer in the study of thought at a time when thought had been banished from psychology. Lewin (1936) argued that a person's behavior in the world could be predicted best by understanding the person's subjective experience of the world. A television soap opera is a meaningless series of unrelated physical movements unless one thinks about the characters' experiences (how Karen feels about Bruce; what Van was planning to say to Kathy about Emily; and whether Linda's sister, Nancy, will always hate their mother for meddling in her marriage, etc.). Lewin realized that it was not the stimulus, but rather the person's *construal* of the stimulus, that determined the person's subsequent behavior. A pinch on the cheek can be pleasant or unpleasant depending on who administers it, under what circumstances, and to which set of cheeks. Lewin used a special kind of mathematics called *topology* to model the person's subjective experience, and although his topological theories were not particularly influential, his attempts to model mental life and his insistence that psychologists study how people construe their worlds would have a lasting impact on psychology.

But, aside from a handful of pioneers such as these, psychologists happily ignored mental processes until the 1950s, when something important happened: the computer. The advent of computers had enormous practical impact, of course, but it also had an enormous conceptual impact on psychology. People and computers differ in important ways, but both seem to register, store, and retrieve information, leading psychologists to wonder whether the computer might be useful as a model for the human mind. Computers are information-processing systems, and the flow of information through their circuits is clearly no fairy tale. If psychologists could think of mental events—such as remembering, attending, thinking, believing, evaluating, feeling, and assessing—as the flow of information through the mind, then they might be able to study the mind scientifically after all. The emergence of the computer led to a reemergence of interest in mental processes all across the discipline of psychology, and spawned a new approach called **cognitive psychology**, *the scientific study of mental processes, including perception, thought, memory, and reasoning.*

How did the advent of computers change psychology?

Kurt Lewin argued that people react to the world as they see it and not to the world as it is.

Technology and the Development of Cognitive Psychology

Although the contributions of psychologists such as Wertheimer, Bartlett, Piaget, and Lewin provided early alternatives to behaviorism, they did not depose it. That job required the Army. During World War II, the military turned to psychologists to help understand how soldiers could best learn to use new technologies, such as radar. Radar operators had to pay close attention to their screens for long periods while trying to decide whether blips were friendly aircraft, enemy aircraft, or flocks of wild geese in need of a good chasing (Ashcraft, 1998; Lachman, Lachman, & Butterfield, 1979). How could radar operators be trained to make quicker and more accurate decisions? The answer to this question clearly required more than the swift delivery of pellets to the radar operator's food tray. It required that those who designed the equipment think about and talk about cognitive processes, such as perception, attention, identification, memory, and decision making. Behaviorism solved the problem by denying it, so some psychologists decided to deny behaviorism and forge ahead with a new approach.

British psychologist Donald Broadbent (1926–1993) was among the first to study what happens when people try to pay attention to several things at once. For instance,

> **What did psychologists learn from pilots during World War II?**

Broadbent observed that pilots can't attend to many different instruments at once and must actively move the focus of their attention from one to another (Best, 1992). Broadbent (1958) showed that the limited capacity to handle incoming information is a fundamental feature of human cognition and that this limit could explain many of the errors that pilots (and other people) made. At about the same time, American psychologist George Miller (1956) pointed out a striking consistency in our capacity limitations across a variety of situations: We can pay attention to, and briefly hold in memory, about seven (give or take two) pieces of information. Cognitive psychologists began conducting experiments and devising theories to better understand the mind's limited capacity, a problem that behaviorists had ignored.

As you have already read, the invention of the computer in the 1950s had a profound impact on psychologists' thinking. A computer is made of hardware (e.g., chips and disk drives today; magnetic tapes and vacuum tubes a half century ago) and software (stored on optical disks today; on punch cards a half-century ago). If the brain is roughly analogous to the computer's hardware, then perhaps the mind was roughly analogous to a software program. This line of thinking led cognitive psychologists to begin writing computer programs to see what kinds of software could be made to mimic human speech and behavior (Newell, Shaw, & Simon, 1958).

Ironically, the emergence of cognitive psychology was also energized by the appearance of B. F. Skinner's (1957) book, *Verbal Behavior*, which offered a behaviorist analysis of language. A linguist at the Massachusetts Institute of Technology (MIT), Noam Chomsky (b. 1928), published a devastating critique of the book in which he argued that Skinner's insistence on observable behavior had caused him to miss some of the most important features of language. According to Chomsky, language relies on mental rules that allow people to understand and produce novel words and sentences. The ability of even the youngest child to generate new sentences that he or she had never heard before flew in the face of the behaviorist claim that children learn to use language by reinforcement. Chomsky provided a clever, detailed, and thoroughly cognitive account of language that could explain many of the phenomena that the behaviorist account could not (Chomsky, 1959).

These developments during the 1950s set the stage for an explosion of cognitive studies during the 1960s. Cognitive psychologists did not return to the old introspective procedures used during the 19th century, but instead developed new and ingenious methods that allowed them to study cognitive processes. The excitement of the new approach was summarized in a landmark book, *Cognitive Psychology*, written by someone you met earlier in this chapter, Ulric Neisser. Neisser's (1967) book provided a foundation for the development of cognitive psychology, which grew and thrived in the years that followed.

cognitive psychology
The scientific study of mental processes, including perception, thought, memory, and reasoning.

Noam Chomsky (b. 1928) pointed out that even young children generate sentences they have never heard before, and therefore could not possibly be learning language by reinforcement. This critique of Skinner's theory signaled the end of behaviorism's dominance in psychology and helped spark the development of cognitive psychology.

SHUTTERSTOCK

The Brain Meets the Mind:
The Rise of Cognitive Neuroscience

If cognitive psychologists studied the software of the mind, they had little to say about the hardware of the brain. And yet, as any computer scientist knows, the relationship between software and hardware is crucial: Each element needs the other to get the job done. Our mental activities often seem so natural and effortless—noticing the shape of an object, using words in speech or writing, recognizing a face as familiar—that we fail to appreciate the fact that they depend on intricate operations carried out by the brain. This dependence is revealed by dramatic cases in which damage to a particular part of the brain causes a person to lose a specific cognitive ability. Recall that in the 19th century, French physician Paul Broca described a patient who, after damage to a limited area in the left side of the brain, could not produce words, even though he could understand them perfectly well. As you'll see later in the book, damage to other parts of the brain can also result in syndromes that are characterized by the loss of specific mental abilities (e.g., prosopagnosia, in which the person cannot recognize human faces) or by the emergence of bizarre behavior or beliefs (e.g., Capgras syndrome, in which the person believes that a close family member has been replaced by an imposter). These striking—sometimes startling—cases remind us that even the simplest cognitive processes depend on the brain.

Karl Lashley (1890–1958), a psychologist who studied with John B. Watson, conducted a famous series of studies in which he trained rats to run mazes, surgically removed parts of their brains, and then measured how well they could run the maze again. Lashley hoped to find the precise spot in the brain where *learning* occurred. Alas, no one spot seemed to uniquely and reliably eliminate learning (Lashley, 1960). Rather, Lashley simply found that the more of the rat's brain he removed, the more poorly the rat ran the maze. Lashley was frustrated by his inability to identify a specific site of learning, but his efforts inspired other scientists to take up the challenge. They developed a research area called *physiological psychology.* Today, this area has grown into **behavioral neuroscience,** *an approach to psychology that links psychological processes to activities in the nervous system and other bodily processes.* To learn about the relationship between brain and behavior, behavioral neuroscientists observe animals' responses as the animals perform specially constructed tasks, such as running through a maze to obtain food rewards. The neuroscientists can record electrical or chemical responses in the brain as the task is being performed, or later remove specific parts of the brain to see how performance is affected.

Of course, experimental brain surgery cannot ethically be performed on human beings; thus, psychologists who want to study the human brain often have to rely on nature's cruel and inexact experiments. Birth defects, accidents, and illnesses often cause damage to particular brain regions, and if that damage disrupts a particular ability, then psychologists deduce that the region is involved in producing the ability. For example, in the Memory chapter you'll learn about a patient whose memory was virtually eliminated by damage to a specific part of the brain, and you'll see how this tragedy provided scientists with remarkable clues about how memories are stored (Scoville & Milner, 1957). But in the late 1980s, technological breakthroughs led to the development of noninvasive brain scanning techniques that made it possible for psychologists to watch what happens inside a human brain as a person performs a task such as reading, imagining, listening, and remembering. Brain scanning is an invaluable tool because it allows us to observe the brain in action and to see which parts are involved in which operations (see the Neuroscience and Behavior chapter).

For example, researchers used scanning technology to identify the parts of the brain in the left hemisphere that are involved in specific aspects of language, such as understanding or producing words (Peterson et al., 1989). Later scanning studies showed that people who are deaf from birth, but who learn to communicate using

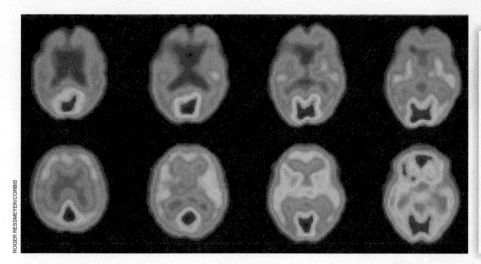

◀ Figure **1.2** **PET Scans of Healthy and Alzheimer's Brains** PET scans are one of a variety of brain imaging technologies that psychologists use to observe the living brain. The four brain images on the top each come from a person suffering from Alzheimer's disease; the four on the bottom each come from a healthy person of similar age. The red and green areas reflect higher levels of brain activity compared to the blue areas, which reflect lower levels of activity. In each image, the front of the brain is on the top and the back of the brain is on the bottom. You can see that the person with Alzheimer's disease, compared with the healthy person, shows more extensive areas of lowered activity toward the front of the brain.

American Sign Language (ASL), rely on regions in the right hemisphere (as well as the left) when using ASL. In contrast, people with normal hearing who learned ASL after puberty seemed to rely only on the left hemisphere when using ASL (Newman et al., 2002). These findings suggest that although both spoken and signed language usually rely on the left hemisphere, the right hemisphere also can become involved—but only for a limited period (perhaps until puberty). The findings also provide a nice example of how psychologists can now use scanning techniques to observe people with various kinds of cognitive capacities and use their observations to unravel the mysteries of the mind and the brain (see **FIGURE 1.2**). In fact, there's a name for this area of research. **Cognitive neuroscience** is the *field of study that attempts to understand the links between cognitive processes and brain activity* (Gazzaniga, 2000).

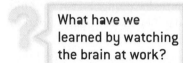

What have we learned by watching the brain at work?

The Adaptive Mind: The Emergence of Evolutionary Psychology

Psychology's renewed interest in mental processes and its growing interest in the brain were two developments that led psychologists away from behaviorism. A third development also pointed them in a different direction. Recall that one of behaviorism's key claims was that organisms are blank slates on which experience writes its lessons, and hence any one lesson should be as easily written as another. But in experiments conducted during the 1960s and 1970s, psychologist John Garcia and his colleagues showed that rats can learn to associate nausea with the smell of food much more quickly than they can learn to associate nausea with a flashing light (Garcia, 1981). Why should this be? In the real world of forests, sewers, and garbage cans, nausea is usually caused by spoiled food and not by lightning, and although these particular rats had been born in a laboratory and had never left their cages, millions of years of evolution had prepared their brains to learn the natural association more quickly than the artificial one. In other words, it was not only the rat's learning history but the rat's *ancestors'* learning histories that determined the rat's ability to learn.

Although that fact was at odds with the behaviorist doctrine, it was the credo for a new kind of psychology. **Evolutionary psychology** *explains mind and behavior in terms of the adaptive value of abilities that are preserved over time by natural selection.* Evolutionary psychology has its roots in Charles Darwin's theory of natural selection, which, as we saw earlier, holds that the features of an organism that help it survive and reproduce are more likely than other features to be passed on to subsequent generations.

behavioral neuroscience
An approach to psychology that links psychological processes to activities in the nervous system and other bodily processes.

cognitive neuroscience
The field of study that attempts to understand the links between cognitive processes and brain activity.

evolutionary psychology
A psychological approach that explains mind and behavior in terms of the adaptive value of abilities that are preserved over time by natural selection.

This theory inspired the functionalist approaches of William James and G. Stanley Hall because it led them to focus on how mental abilities help people to solve problems and therefore increase their chances of survival. But it is only since the publication in 1975 of *Sociobiology,* by the biologist E. O. Wilson, that evolutionary thinking has had an identifiable presence in psychology. That presence is steadily increasing (Buss, 1999; Pinker, 1997a, 1997b; Tooby & Cosmides, 2000). Evolutionary psychologists think of the mind as a collection of specialized "modules" that are designed to solve the human problems our ancestors faced as they attempted to eat, mate, and reproduce over millions of years. According to evolutionary psychology, the brain is not an all-purpose computer that can do or learn one thing just as easily as it can do or learn another; rather, it is a computer that was built to do a few things well and everything else not at all. It is a computer that comes with a small suite of built-in applications that are designed to do the things that previous versions of that computer needed to have done.

Consider, for example, how evolutionary psychology treats the emotion of jealousy. All of us who have been in romantic relationships have experienced jealousy, if only because we noticed our partner noticing someone else. Jealousy can be a powerful, overwhelming emotion that we might wish to avoid, but according to evolutionary psychology, it exists today because it once served an adaptive function. If some of our hominid ancestors experienced jealousy and others did not, then the ones who experienced it might have been more likely to guard their mates and aggress against their rivals and thus may have been more likely to reproduce their "jealous genes" (Buss, 2000, 2007; Buss & Haselton, 2005).

Critics of the evolutionary approach point out that many current traits of people and other animals probably evolved to serve different functions than those they currently serve. For example, biologists believe that the feathers of birds probably evolved initially to perform such functions as regulating body temperature or capturing prey and only later served the entirely different function of flight. Likewise, people are reasonably adept at learning to drive a car, but nobody would argue that such an ability is the result of natural selection; the learning abilities that allow us to become skilled car drivers must have evolved for purposes other than driving cars.

> **What evidence suggests that some traits can be inherited?**

Complications such as these have led the critics to wonder how evolutionary hypotheses can ever be tested (Coyne, 2000; Sterelny & Griffiths, 1999). We don't have a record of our ancestors' thoughts, feelings, and actions, and fossils won't provide much information about the evolution of mind and behavior. Testing ideas about the evolutionary origins of psychological phenomena is indeed a challenging task, but not an impossible one (Buss et al., 1998; Pinker, 1997a, 1997b).

Start with the assumption that evolutionary adaptations should also increase reproductive success. So, if a specific trait or feature has been favored by natural selection, it should be possible to find some evidence of this in the numbers of offspring that are produced by the trait's bearers. Consider, for instance, the hypothesis that men tend to have deep voices because women prefer to mate with baritones rather than sopranos. To investigate this hypothesis, researchers studied a group of modern hunter-gatherers, the Hadza people of Tanzania. Consistent with the evolutionary hypothesis, they found that the pitch of a man's voice did indeed predict how many children he would have, but the pitch of a woman's voice did not (Apicella, Feinberg, & Marlowe, 2007). This kind of study provides evidence that allows evolutionary psychologists to test their ideas. Not every evolutionary hypothesis can be tested, of course, but evolutionary psychologists are becoming increasingly inventive in their attempts.

In 1925, schoolteacher John Scopes was arrested for teaching students about Darwin's theory of evolution. Today, that theory is the centerpiece of modern biology—and of evolutionary psychology.

HULTON ARCHIVE/GETTY IMAGES

©JUNIORS BILDARCHIV GMBH/ALAMY

Behaviorists explain behavior in terms of organisms learning to make particular responses that are paired with reinforcement (and to avoid responses that are paired with punishment). Evolutionary psychology focuses on how abilities are preserved over time if they contribute to an organism's ability to survive and reproduce. How might a proponent of each approach explain the fact that a rat placed in an unfamiliar environment will tend to stay in dark corners and avoid brightly lit open areas?

IN SUMMARY

▶ Psychologists such as Max Wertheimer, Frederic Bartlett, Jean Piaget, and Kurt Lewin defied the behaviorist doctrine and studied the inner workings of the mind. Their efforts, as well as those of later pioneers such as Donald Broadbent, paved the way for cognitive psychology to focus on inner mental processes such as perception, attention, memory, and reasoning.

▶ Cognitive psychology developed as a field due to the invention of the computer, psychologists' efforts to improve the performance of the military, and Noam Chomsky's theories about language.

▶ Cognitive neuroscience attempts to link the brain with the mind by studying individuals with brain damage (connecting the area damaged with the loss of specific abilities) and individuals without brain damage, using brain scanning techniques.

▶ Evolutionary psychology focuses on the adaptive function that minds and brains serve and seeks to understand the nature and origin of psychological processes in terms of natural selection.

Beyond the Individual: Social and Cultural Perspectives

The picture we have painted so far may vaguely suggest a scene from some 1950s science-fiction film in which the protagonist is a living brain that thinks, feels, hopes, and worries while suspended in a vat of pink jelly in a basement laboratory. Although psychologists often do focus on the brain and the mind of the individual, they have not lost sight of the fact that human beings are fundamentally social animals who are part of a vast network of family, friends, teachers, and co-workers. Trying to understand people in the absence of that fact is a bit like trying to understand an ant or a bee without considering the function and influence of the colony or hive. People are the most important and most complex organisms that we ever encounter; thus it is not surprising that our behavior is strongly influenced by their presence—or their absence. The two areas of psychology that most strongly emphasize these facts are social and cultural psychology.

The Development of Social Psychology

Social psychology is *the study of the causes and consequences of sociality.* As this definition suggests, social psychologists address a remarkable variety of topics. Historians trace the birth of social psychology to an experiment conducted in 1895 by psychologist and bicycle enthusiast Norman Triplett, who noticed that cyclists seemed to ride faster when they rode with others. Intrigued by this observation, he conducted an experiment that showed that children reeled in a fishing line faster when tested in the presence of other children than when tested alone. Triplett was not trying to improve the fishing abilities of American children, of course, but rather was trying to show that the mere presence of other people can influence performance on even the most mundane kinds of tasks.

Social psychology's development began in earnest in the 1930s and was driven by several historical events. The rise of Nazism led many of Germany's most talented scientists to immigrate to America, and among them were psychologists such as Solomon Asch (1907–1996) and Kurt Lewin. These psychologists had been strongly influenced by Gestalt psychology, which you'll recall held that "the whole is greater than the sum of its parts," and though the Gestaltists had been talking about the visual

social psychology
The study of the causes and consequences of sociality.

perception of objects, these psychologists felt that the phrase also captured a basic truth about the relationship between social groups and the individuals who constitute them. Philosophers had speculated about the nature of sociality for thousands of years, and political scientists, economists, anthropologists, and sociologists had been studying social life scientifically for some time. But these German refugees were the first to generate theories of social behavior that resembled the theories generated by natural scientists, and more importantly, they were the first to conduct experiments to test their social theories. For example, Lewin (1936) adopted the language of mid-century physics to develop a "field theory" that viewed social behavior as the product of "internal forces" (such as personality, goals, and beliefs) and "external forces" (such as social pressure and culture), whereas Asch (1946) performed laboratory experiments to examine the "mental chemistry" that allows people to combine small bits of information about another person into a full impression of that person's personality.

> **How did historical events influence the development of social psychology?**

Other historical events also shaped social psychology in its early years. For example, the Holocaust brought the problems of conformity and obedience into sharp focus, leading psychologists such as Asch (1956) and others to examine the conditions under which people can influence each other to think and act in inhuman or irrational ways. The civil rights movement and the rising tensions between African Americans and White Americans led psychologists such as Gordon Allport (1897–1967) to study stereotyping, prejudice, and racism and to shock the world of psychology by suggesting that prejudice was the result of a perceptual error that was every bit as natural and unavoidable as an optical illusion (Allport, 1954). Allport argued that the same perceptual processes that allow us to efficiently categorize elements of our social and physical world allow us to erroneously categorize entire groups of people. Social psychologists today study a wider variety of topics (from social memory to social relationships) and use a wider variety of techniques (from opinion polls to neuroimaging) than did their forebears, but this field of psychology remains dedicated to understanding the brain as a social organ, the mind as a social adaptation, and the individual as a social creature.

Social psychology studies how the thoughts, feelings, and behaviors of individuals can be influenced by the presence of others. Members of the Reverend Sun Myung Moon's Unification Church are often married to one another in ceremonies of 10,000 people or more; in some cases couples don't know each other before the wedding begins. Social movements such as this have the power to sway individuals.

The Emergence of Cultural Psychology

North Americans and Western Europeans are sometimes surprised to realize that most of the people on the planet are members of neither culture. Although we're all more alike than we are different, there is nonetheless considerable diversity within the human species in social practices, customs, and ways of living. Culture refers to the values, traditions, and beliefs that are shared by a particular group of people. Although we usually think of culture in terms of nationality and ethnic groups, cultures can also be defined by age (youth culture), sexual orientation (gay culture), religion (Jewish culture), or occupation (academic culture). **Cultural psychology** is *the study of how cultures reflect and shape the psychological processes of their members* (Shweder & Sullivan, 1993). Cultural psychologists study a wide range of phenomena, ranging from visual perception to social interaction, as they seek to understand which of these phenomena are universal and which vary from place to place and time to time.

Perhaps surprisingly, one of the first psychologists to pay attention to the influence of culture was someone recognized today for pioneering the development of experimental psychology, Wilhelm Wundt. He believed that a complete psychology would have to combine a laboratory approach with a broader cultural perspective

(Wundt, 1900–1920). But Wundt's ideas failed to spark much interest from other psychologists, who had their hands full trying to make sense of results from laboratory experiments and formulating general laws of human behavior. Outside of psychology, anthropologists such as Margaret Mead (1901–1978) and Gregory Bateson (1904–1980) attempted to understand the workings of culture by traveling to far-flung regions of the world and carefully observing child-rearing patterns, rituals, religious ceremonies, and the like. Such studies revealed practices—some bizarre from a North American perspective—that served important functions in a culture, such as the painful ritual of violent body mutilation and bloodletting in mountain tribes of New Guinea, which initiates young boys into training to become warriors (Mead, 1935/1968; Read, 1965).

cultural psychology
The study of how cultures reflect and shape the psychological processes of their members.

Yet, at the time, most anthropologists paid as little attention to psychology as psychologists did to anthropology. Cultural psychology only began to emerge as a strong force in psychology during the 1980s and 1990s, when psychologists and anthropologists began to communicate with each other about their ideas and methods (Stigler, Shweder, & Herdt, 1990). It was then that psychologists rediscovered Wundt as an intellectual ancestor of this area of the field (Jahoda, 1993).

How did anthropologists influence psychology in the 1980s?

Physicists assume that $E = mc^2$ whether the m is located in Cleveland, Moscow, or the Orion Nebula. Chemists assume that water is made of hydrogen and oxygen and that it was made of hydrogen and oxygen in 1609 as well. The laws of physics and chemistry are assumed to be universal, and for much of psychology's history, the same assumption was made about the principles that govern human behavior (Shweder, 1991). *Absolutism* holds that culture makes little or no difference for most psychological phenomena, that "honesty is honesty and depression is depression, no matter where one observes it" (Segall, Lonner, & Berry, 1998, p. 1103). And yet, as any world traveler knows, cultures differ in exciting, delicious, and frightening ways, and things that are true of people in one culture are not necessarily true of people in another. *Relativism* holds that psychological phenomena are likely to vary considerably across cultures and should be viewed only in the context of a specific culture (Berry et al., 1992). Although depression is observed in nearly every culture, the symptoms associated with it vary dramatically from one place to another. For example, in Western cultures there is greater emphasis on cognitive symptoms such as worthlessness, whereas in Eastern cultures there is greater focus on somatic symptoms such as fatigue and body aches (Draguns & Tanaka-Matsumi, 2003).

The symptoms of some mental disorders can be reported differently across different cultures. Cultural psychology studies the similarities and differences in psychological processes that arise between people living in different cultures.

Today, most cultural psychologists fall somewhere between these two extremes. Most psychological phenomena can be influenced by culture, some are completely determined by it, and others seem to be entirely unaffected. For example, the age of a person's earliest memory differs dramatically across cultures (MacDonald, Uesiliana, & Hayne, 2000), whereas judgments of facial attractiveness do not (Cunningham et al., 1995). As noted when we discussed evolutionary psychology, it seems likely that the most universal phenomena are those that are closely associated with the basic biology that all human beings share. Conversely, the least universal phenomena are those rooted in the varied socialization practices that different cultures evolve. Of course, the only way to determine whether a phenomenon is variable or constant across cultures is to design research to investigate these possibilities, and

Why are psychological conclusions so often relative to the person, place, or culture described?

CULTURE & COMMUNITY

Analytic and Holistic Styles in Western and Eastern Cultures
The study of cultural influences on mind and behavior has increased dramatically over the past decade. An especially intriguing line of research has revealed differences in how the world is viewed by people from Western cultures such as North America and Europe, and Eastern cultures such as China, Japan, Korea, and other Asian countries. One of the most consistently observed differences is that people from Western cultures tend to adopt an *analytic* style of processing information, focusing on an object or person without paying much attention to the surrounding context, whereas people from Eastern cultures tend to adopt a *holistic* style that emphasizes the relationship between an object or person and the surrounding context (Nisbett & Miyamoto, 2005).

This difference is illustrated nicely by a study in which American and Japanese participants performed a novel task, called the *framed-line test*, which assesses how well an individual incorporates or ignores contextual information when making a judgment about a simple line stimulus (Kitayama et al., 2003). As shown in the accompanying figure, participants saw a line inside a square. They were asked to draw the line again in a new square, either to exactly the same length as the original stimulus (the absolute task), or so that the length of the line in the new square was in the same proportion to the height of its frame as the length of the original line relative to the height of the original frame (the relative task). The absolute task engages analytic processing, whereas the relative task draws on holistic processing. The researchers found that American participants living in the United States were more accurate on the absolute task than on the relative task, whereas Japanese participants living in Japan were more accurate on the relative task than on the absolute task. Interestingly, Americans living in Japan performed more like

Japanese participants, and Japanese living in the United States performed more like American participants. While we don't yet know how long it takes for a culture to produce a shift from an analytic style to a holistic style or vice versa, research on cultural influences continues to develop rapidly and we are even beginning to obtain some clues about how differences between individuals from Eastern and Western cultures are realized in the brain (Kitayama & Uskul, 2011).

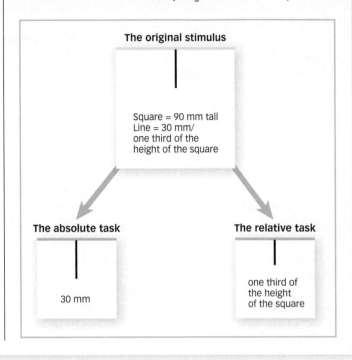

The original stimulus

Square = 90 mm tall
Line = 30 mm/
one third of the
height of the square

The absolute task

30 mm

The relative task

one third of
the height
of the square

cultural psychologists do just that (Cole, 1996; Segall et al., 1998). We'll highlight the work of cultural psychologists throughout the text and in Culture & Community boxes like the one in this section concerning cultural differences in analytic and holistic styles of processing information.

IN SUMMARY

► Social psychology recognizes that people exist as part of a network of other people and examines how individuals influence and interact with one another. Social psychology was pioneered by German émigrés, such as Kurt Lewin, who were motivated by a desire to address social issues and problems.

► Cultural psychology is concerned with the effects of the broader culture on individuals and with similarities and differences among people in different cultures. Within this perspective, absolutists hold that culture has little impact on most psychological phenomena, whereas relativists believe that culture has a powerful effect.

► Together, social and cultural psychology help expand the discipline's horizons beyond just an examination of individuals. These areas of psychology examine behavior within the broader context of human interaction.

The Profession of Psychology: Past and Present

If ever you find yourself on an airplane with an annoying seatmate who refuses to let you read your magazine, there are two things you can do. First, you can turn to the person and say in a calm and friendly voice, "Did you know that I am covered with strange and angry bacteria?" If that seems a bit extreme, you might instead try saying, "Did you know that I am a psychologist, and I'm forming an evaluation of you as you speak?" as this will usually eliminate the problem without getting you arrested. The truth is that most people don't really know what psychology is or what psychologists do, but they do have some vague sense that it isn't wise to talk to one. Now that you've been briefly acquainted with psychology's past, let's consider its present by looking at psychology as a profession. We'll look first at the origins of psychology's professional organizations, next at the contexts in which psychologists tend to work, and finally at the kinds of training required to become a psychologist.

Psychologists Band Together: The American Psychological Association

You'll recall that when we last saw William James, he was wandering around the greater Boston area, expounding the virtues of the new science of psychology. In July 1892, James and five other psychologists traveled to Clark University to attend a meeting called by G. Stanley Hall. Each worked at a large university where they taught psychology courses, performed research, and wrote textbooks. Although they were too few to make up a jury or even a respectable hockey team, these seven men decided that it was time to form an organization that represented psychology as a profession, and on that day the American Psychological Association (APA) was born. The seven psychologists could scarcely have imagined that today their little club would have more than 150,000 members—approximately the population of a decent-sized city in the United States. Although all of the original members were employed by universities or colleges, today academic psychologists make up only 20% of the membership, whereas nearly 70% of the members work in clinical and health-related settings. Because the APA is no longer as focused on academic psychology as it once was, the American Psychological Society (APS) was formed in 1988 by 450 academic psychologists who wanted an organization that focused specifically on the needs of psychologists carrying out scientific research. The APS, renamed the Association for Psychological Science in 2006, grew quickly, attracting 5,000 members within 6 months; today it numbers nearly 12,000 psychologists.

The Growing Role of Women and Minorities

In 1892, the APA had 31 members, all of whom were White and all of whom were male. Today, about half of all APA members are women, and the percentage of non-White members continues to grow. Surveys of recent PhD recipients reveal a picture of increasing diversification in the field. The proportion of women receiving PhDs in psychology increased from only 15% in 1950 to 70% in 2010, and the proportion of racial minorities receiving PhDs in psychology grew from a very small number to 24% during that same period. Clearly, psychology is increasingly reflecting the diversity of American society.

The current involvement of women and minorities in the APA, and psychology more generally, can be traced to early pioneers who blazed a trail that others followed. In 1905, Mary Calkins (1863–1930) became the first woman to serve as president of the APA. Calkins became interested in psychology while teaching Greek at Wellesley College. She studied with William James at Harvard and later became a professor

Mary Whiton Calkins (1863–1930), the first woman elected APA president, suffered from the sex discrimination that was common during her lifetime. Despite academic setbacks (such as Harvard University refusing to grant women an official PhD), Calkins went on to a distinguished career in research and teaching at Wellesley College.

of psychology at Wellesley College, where she worked until retiring in 1929. In her presidential address to the APA, Calkins described her theory of the role of the "self" in psychological function. Arguing against Wundt's and Titchener's structuralist ideas that the mind can be dissected into components, Calkins claimed that the self is a single unit that cannot be broken down into individual parts. Calkins wrote four books and published over 100 articles during her illustrious career (Calkins, 1930; Scarborough & Furumoto, 1987; Stevens & Gardner, 1982). Today, women play leading roles in all areas of psychology. Some of the men who formed the APA might have been surprised by the prominence of women in the field today, but we suspect that William James, a strong supporter of Mary Calkins, would not be one of them.

How has the face of psychology changed as the field has evolved?

Just as there were no women at the first meeting of the APA, there weren't any non-White people either. The first member of a minority group to become president of the APA was Kenneth Clark (1914–2005), who was elected in 1970. Clark worked extensively on the self-image of African American children and argued that segregation of the races creates great psychological harm. Clark's conclusions had a large influence on public policy, and his research contributed to the Supreme Court's 1954 ruling (*Brown v. Board of Education*) to outlaw segregation in public schools (Guthrie, 2000). Clark's interest in psychology was sparked as an undergraduate at Howard University when he took a course from Francis Cecil Sumner (1895–1954), who was the first African American to receive a PhD in psychology (from Clark University in 1920). Sumner's main interest focused on the education of African American youth (Sawyer, 2000).

What Psychologists Do: Research Careers

Before describing what psychologists do, it should be noted that most people who major in psychology do not go on to become psychologists. Psychology has become a major academic, scientific, and professional discipline with links to many other disciplines and career paths (see the Hot Science box). That being said, what should you do if you *do* want to become a psychologist, and what should you fail to do if you desperately want to avoid it? You can become "a psychologist" by a variety of routes, and the people who call themselves psychologists may hold a variety of different degrees. Typically, students finish college and enter graduate school in order to obtain a PhD (or doctor of philosophy) degree in some particular area of psychology (e.g., social, cognitive, developmental). During graduate school, students generally gain exposure to the field by taking classes and learn to conduct research by collaborating with their professors. Although William James was able to master every area of psychology because the areas were so small during his lifetime, today a student can spend the better part of a decade mastering just one.

Kenneth B. Clark (1914–2005) studied the developmental effects of prejudice, discrimination, and segregation on children. In one classic study from the 1950s, he found that African American preschoolers preferred White dolls to Black ones. Clark's research was cited by the U.S. Supreme Court in its decision for the landmark *Brown v. Board of Education* case that ended school segregation.

After receiving a PhD, you can go on for more specialized research training by pursuing a postdoctoral fellowship under the supervision of an established researcher in his or her area, or apply for a faculty position at a college or university or a research position in government

WILLIAM E. SAURO/NEW YORK TIMES CO./GETTY IMAGES

or industry. Academic careers usually involve a combination of teaching and research, whereas careers in government or industry are typically dedicated to research alone.

The Variety of Career Paths

As you saw earlier, research is not the only career option for a psychologist. Most people who call themselves psychologists neither teach nor do research, but rather, they assess or treat people with psychological problems. Most of these *clinical psychologists* work in private practice, often in partnerships with other psychologists or with psychiatrists (who have earned an MD, or medical degree, and are allowed to prescribe medication). Other clinical psychologists work in hospitals or medical schools, some have faculty positions at universities or colleges, and some combine private practice with an academic job. Many clinical psychologists focus on specific problems or disorders, such as depression or anxiety, whereas others focus on specific populations such as children, ethnic minority groups, or older adults (see **FIGURE 1.3**). Just over 10% of APA members are *counseling psychologists,* who assist people in dealing with work or career issues and changes or help people deal with common crises such as divorce, the loss of a job, or the death of a loved one. Counseling psychologists may have a PhD or an MA (master's degree) in counseling psychology or an MSW (Master of Social Work).

Psychologists are also quite active in educational settings. About 5% of APA members are *school psychologists,* who offer guidance to students, parents, and teachers. A similar proportion of APA members, known *as industrial/organizational psychologists,* focus on issues in the workplace. These psychologists typically work in business or industry and may be involved in assessing potential employees, finding ways to improve productivity, or helping staff and management to develop effective planning strategies for coping with change or anticipated future developments. Of course, this brief list doesn't begin to cover all the different career paths that someone with training in psychology might take. For instance, sports psychologists help athletes improve their performance, forensic psychologists assist attorneys and courts, and consumer psychologists help companies develop and advertise new products. Indeed, we can't think of any major enterprise that *doesn't* employ psychologists.

> **? In what ways does psychology contribute to society?**

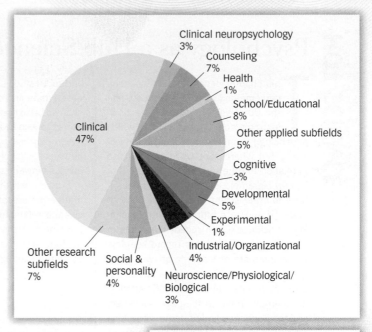

▲ Figure **1.3 The Major Subfields in Psychology** Psychologists are drawn to many different subfields in psychology. Here are the percentages of people receiving PhDs in various subfields. Clinical psychology makes up almost half of the doctorates awarded in psychology.

Source: 2004 Graduate Study in Psychology. Compiled by APA Research Office.

Michael Friedman

Shirley Wang

Betsy Stevens

A person earning a PhD in psychology can go on to a wide range of fields, like these three: a practicing clinical psychologist in New York City, a science and health journalist for a major news outlet, and a behavioral scientist for an international affairs consulting firm.

Psychology as a Hub Science

This chapter describes how psychology emerged as a field of study, and the Other Voices box on page 17 illustrates some of the ways in which psychology is indeed a *scientific* field of study. But where does psychology stand in relation to other areas of science? That is, how big a field is it? What links does it have to other scientific disciplines? What fields (if any) are influenced by psychological science? With recent advances in computing and electronic record keeping, researchers are now able to answer these questions by literally creating maps of science. Information about scientific articles, the journals in which they are published, and the frequency and patterns with which articles in one field are cited by articles in another field, is now fully electronic and available online (in the Science Citation and Social Science Citation Indexes). Researchers can use this information to learn about the interconnectedness of different scientific disciplines.

As an example, in an article called "Mapping the Backbone of Science," Kevin Boyack and his colleagues (2005) used data from more than 1 million articles, with more than 23 million references, published in more than 7,000 journals to create a map showing the similarities and interconnectedness of different areas of science based on how frequently journal articles from different disciplines cite each other. The results are fascinating. As shown in the figure, seven major fields, or "hub sciences," that link with and influence smaller subfields emerged in the data: math, physics, chemistry, earth sciences, medicine, *psychology*, and social science. The organization of the hubs is interesting to note. As you can see in the figure, psychology sits between medicine and social studies, whereas physics sits between math and chemistry. The location of subfields also matches with what you might expect: public health and neurology fall between psychology and medicine, statistics between psychology and math, and economics between social science and math.

Studies like this one provide an informative picture of how different areas of science relate to each other historically (i.e., the citations in that study dated back many years). But science is dynamic and constantly changing and so an important question is: What does the science look like right now (while you are in school and deciding which classes to take and what career path to follow)? Another study used data from more than 6 million citations, found in more than 6,000 journals to create a map of citation patterns focusing only on citations to articles published in a recent 5-year period (in this case from 2000–2004; Rosvall & Bergstrom, 2008). In that analysis, psychology again emerged as a major scientific hub (see the figure on the right). The largest scientific fields,

BOYACK, KEVIN W., KLAVANS, RICHARD, AND BORNER, KATY, MAPPING THE BACKBONE OF SCIENCE. SCIENTOMETRICS, VOL.64, NO.3 (2005) 351–374. ©2005, SPRINGER-VERLAG/AKADEMIAI DIADO

Even this brief and incomplete survey of the APA membership provides a sense of the wide variety of contexts in which psychologists operate. You can think of psychology as an international community of professionals devoted to advancing scientific knowledge; assisting people with psychological problems and disorders; and trying to enhance the quality of life in work, school, and other everyday settings.

IN SUMMARY

▶ The American Psychological Association (APA) has grown dramatically since it was formed in 1892 and now includes over 150,000 members working in clinical, academic, and applied set-in order, are molecular and cell biology, medicine, physics, neuroscience, ecology and evolution, economics, geosciences, psychology, and chemistry. Psychological research has strong links (based on the frequency of citations of work in journals in each field) with neuroscience, psychiatry, education, sociology, business and market-ing, medicine, and ecology and evolution. More recent and larger studies continue to support the overall structure of these maps of science (Börner et al., 2012).

Studies like these are useful to university administrators, funding agencies, and also to students to help them understand the relationships between different academic departments and how the scientific work of one field relates to the scientific field more broadly. They also show the reach of psychology to other disciplines and support the idea that knowledge about psychology has relevance for many related disciplines and career paths. Good thing you are taking this class!

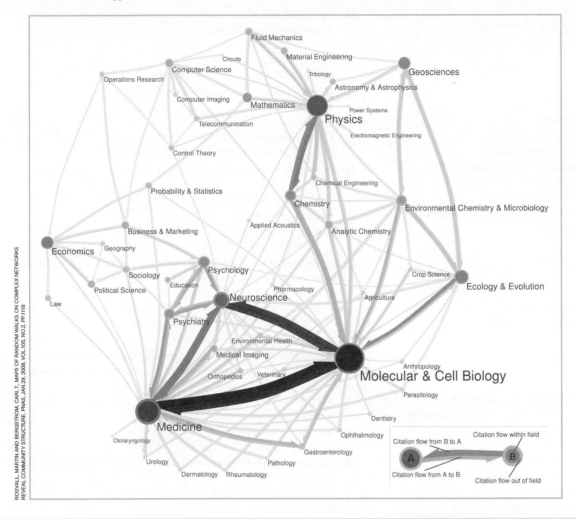

ROSVALL, MARTIN AND BERGSTROM, CARL T., MAPS OF RANDOM WALKS ON COMPLEX NETWORKS REVEAL COMMUNITY STRUCTURE. PNAS, JAN 29, 2008, VOL.105, NO.2, PP.1118

tings. Psychologists are also represented by professional organizations such as the Association for Psychological Science (APS), which focuses on scientific psychology.

▶ Through the efforts of pioneers such as Mary Calkins, women have come to play an increasingly important role in the field and are now as well represented as men. Minority involvement in psychology took longer, but the pioneering efforts of Francis Cecil Sumner, Kenneth B. Clark, and others have led to increased participation of minorities in psychology.

▶ Psychologists prepare for research careers through graduate and postdoctoral training and work in a variety of applied settings, including schools, clinics, and industry.

Chapter Review

KEY CONCEPT QUIZ

1. In the 1800s, French biologist Marie Jean Pierre Flourens and surgeon Paul Broca conducted research that demonstrated a connection between
   a. animals and humans.
   b. the mind and the brain.
   c. brain size and mental ability.
   d. skull indentations and psychological attributes.

2. What was the subject of the famous experiment conducted by Hermann von Helmholtz?
   a. reaction time
   b. childhood learning
   c. phrenology
   d. functions of specific brain areas

3. Wilhelm Wundt is credited with
   a. coining the phrase "philosophical empiricism."
   b. setting the terms for the nature–nurture debate.
   c. the founding of psychology as a scientific discipline.
   d. conducting the first psychological experiment.

4. Wundt and his students sought to analyze the basic elements that constitute the mind, an approach called
   a. consciousness.
   b. introspection.
   c. structuralism.
   d. objectivity.

5. William James and ___ helped establish functionalism as a major school of psychological thought in North America.
   a. G. Stanley Hall
   b. René Descartes
   c. Franz Joseph Gall
   d. Edward Titchener

6. The functional approach to psychology was inspired by
   a. Darwin's *On the Origin of Species by Means of Natural Selection.*
   b. James's *The Principles of Psychology.*
   c. Wundt's *Principles of Physiological Psychology.*
   d. Titchener's *An Outline of Psychology.*

7. To understand human behavior, French physicians Jean-Martin Charcot and Pierre Janet studied people
   a. who appeared to be completely healthy.
   b. with psychological disorders.
   c. with damage in particular areas of the brain.
   d. who had suffered permanent loss of cognitive and motor function.

8. Building on the work of Charcot and Janet, Sigmund Freud developed
   a. psychoanalytic theory.
   b. the theory of hysteria.
   c. humanistic psychology.
   d. physiological psychology.

9. The psychological theory that emphasizes the positive potential of human beings is known as
   a. structuralism.
   b. psychoanalytic theory.
   c. humanistic psychology.
   d. functionalism.

10. Behaviorism involves the study of
    a. observable actions and responses.
    b. the potential for human growth.
    c. unconscious influences and childhood experiences.
    d. human behavior and memory.

11. The experiments of Ivan Pavlov and John Watson centered on
    a. perception and behavior.
    b. stimulus and response.
    c. reward and punishment.
    d. conscious and unconscious behavior.

12. Who developed the concept of reinforcement?
    a. B. F. Skinner
    b. Ivan Pavlov
    c. John Watson
    d. Margaret Floy Washburn

13. The study of mental processes such as perception and memory is called
    a. behavioral determinism.
    b. Gestalt psychology.
    c. social psychology.
    d. cognitive psychology.

14. During World War II, cognitive psychologists discovered that many of the errors pilots make are the result of
    a. computer errors in processing detailed information.
    b. limited human cognitive capacity to handle incoming information.
    c. pilot inattention to incoming information.
    d. lack of behavioral training.

15. The use of scanning techniques to observe the brain in action and to see which parts are involved in which operations helped the development of
    a. evolutionary psychology.
    b. cognitive neuroscience.
    c. cultural psychology.
    d. cognitive accounts of language formation.

16. Central to evolutionary psychology is the ___ function that minds and brains serve.
    a. emotional
    b. adaptive
    c. cultural
    d. physiological

17. Social psychology differs most from other psychological approaches in its emphasis on
    a. human interaction.
    b. behavioral processes.
    c. the individual.
    d. laboratory experimentation.

18. Cultural psychology emphasizes that
    a. all psychological processes are influenced to some extent by culture.
    b. psychological processes are the same across all human beings, regardless of culture.

   c. culture shapes some, but not all psychological phenomena.

   d. insights gained from studying individuals from one culture will only rarely generalize to individuals from other cultures, who have different social identities and rituals.

19. Mary Calkins

   a. studied with Wilhelm Wundt in the first psychology laboratory.

   b. did research on the self-image of African American children.

   c. was present at the first meeting of the APA.

   d. became the first woman president of the APA.

20. Kenneth Clark

   a. did research that influenced the Supreme Court decision to ban segregation in public schools.

   b. was one of the founders of the APA.

   c. was a student of William James.

   d. did research that focused on the education of African American youth.

KEY TERMS

psychology (p. 2)

mind (p. 2)

behavior (p. 2)

nativism (p. 6)

philosophical empiricism (p. 6)

phrenology (p. 6)

physiology (p. 7)

stimulus (p. 8)

reaction time (p. 8)

consciousness (p. 8)

structuralism (p. 8)

introspection (p. 9)

functionalism (p. 11)

natural selection (p. 11)

hysteria (p. 13)

unconscious (p. 13)

psychoanalytic theory (p. 13)

psychoanalysis (p. 14)

humanistic psychology (p. 15)

behaviorism (p. 16)

response (p. 18)

reinforcement (p. 18)

illusions (p. 20)

Gestalt psychology (p. 21)

cognitive psychology (p. 22)

behavioral neuroscience (p. 24)

cognitive neuroscience (p. 25)

evolutionary psychology (p. 25)

social psychology (p. 27)

cultural psychology (p. 28)

CHANGING MINDS

1. One of your classmates says that she's only taking this class because it's required for her education major. "Psychology is all about understanding mental illness and treatment. I don't know why I have to learn this stuff when I'm going to be a teacher, not a psychologist." Why should your friend reconsider her opinion? What subfields of psychology are especially important for a teacher?

2. One of your friends confesses that he really enjoys his psychology courses, but he's decided not to declare a major in psychology. "You have to get a graduate degree to do anything with a psychology major," he says, "and I don't want to stay in school for the rest of my life. I want to get out there and work in the real world." Based on what you've read in this chapter about careers in psychology, what might you tell him?

3. On May 6, you spot a news item announcing that it's the birthday of Sigmund Freud, "the father of psychology." How accurate is it to call Freud the "father of psychology?" Having read about psychology's subfields, are there other people who are as important, or more important than Freud?

4. One of your classmates has flipped ahead in the book, and notices that there is going to be a lot of material—including an entire chapter—on the brain. "I don't see why we have to learn so much biology," he says. "I want to be a school counselor, not a brain surgeon. I don't need to understand the parts of the brain or chemical reactions in order to help people." How are the brain and the mind connected? In what specific ways might knowing about the brain help us to understand the mind?

5. Another classmate is very unsettled after reading about B.F. Skinner's claim that free will is an illusion. "Psychology always tries to treat human beings like lab rats, whose behavior can be manipulated. I have free will, and I decide what I'm going to do next." What would you tell your friend? Does an understanding of the basic principles of psychology allow us to predict every detail of what individual humans will do?

ANSWERS TO KEY CONCEPT QUIZ

1. b; 2. a; 3. c; 4. c; 5. a; 6. a; 7. b; 8. a; 9. c; 10. a; 11. b; 12. a; 13. d; 14. b; 15. b; 16. b; 17. a; 18. c; 19. d; 20. a.

Need more help? Additional resources are located in LaunchPad at:

http://www.worthpublishers.com/launchpad/schacter3e

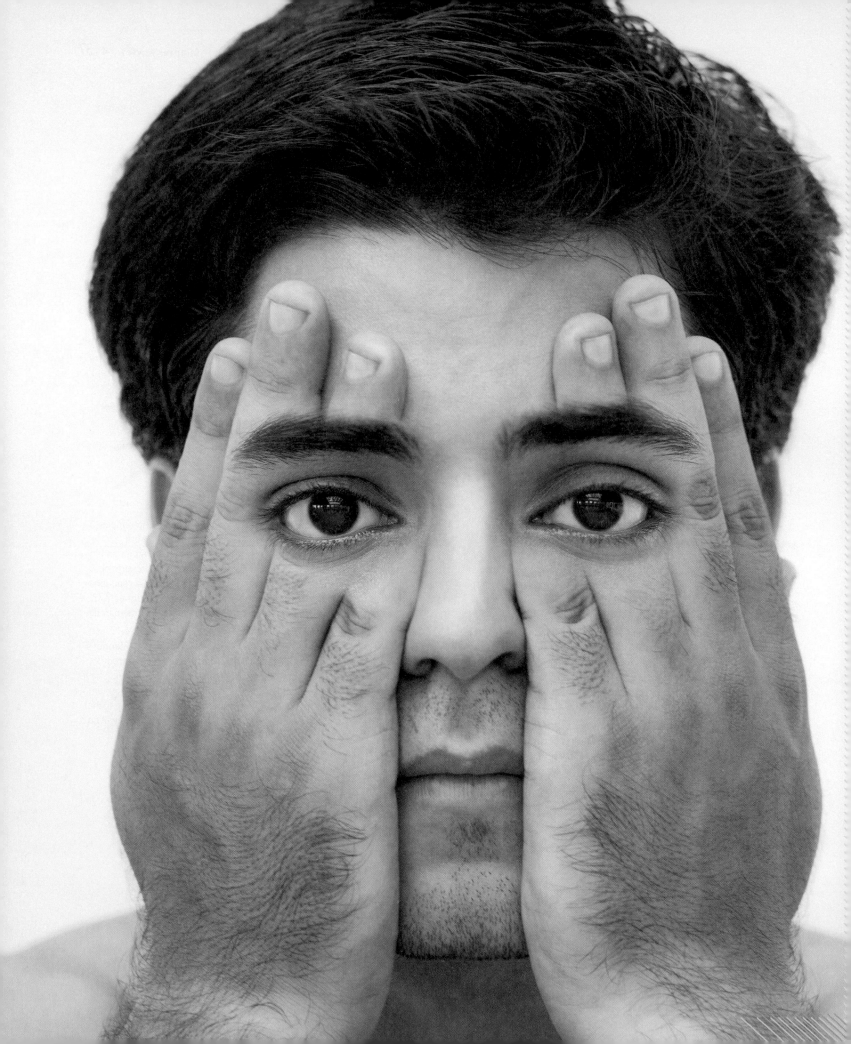

Methods in Psychology

YOU CAN HEAL YOUR LIFE has sold over 35 million copies. Its author, Louise Hay, suggests that everything that happens to us is a result of the thoughts we choose to think. She claims that she cured herself of cancer simply by changing her thoughts, and says that others can learn to do the same by buying her books, CDs, DVDs, and by attending her seminars. In a recent television interview, Hay explained how she knows that her technique is effective.

Interviewer: How do you know what you're saying is right?

Hay: Oh, my inner ding.

Interviewer: Ding?

Hay: My inner ding. It speaks to me. It feels right or it doesn't feel right. Happiness is choosing thoughts that make you feel good. It's really very simple.

Interviewer: But I hear you saying that even if there were no proof for what you believed, or even if there were scientific evidence against it, it wouldn't change.

Hay: Well, I don't believe in scientific evidence, I really don't. Science is fairly new. It hasn't been around that long. We think it's such a big deal, but it's, you know, it's just a way of looking at life.

Louise Hay says she doesn't "believe" in scientific evidence, but what could that possibly mean? After all, if Hay's techniques really do cure cancer, then even she would have to expect cancer victims who practice her techniques to have a higher rate of remission than cancer victims who don't. That isn't "a way of looking at life." It's just plain, old-fashioned, common sense—exactly the kind of common sense that lies at the heart of science.

Science tells us that the only way to know for sure whether a claim is true is to go out and have a look. But that sounds easier than it is. For example, where would you look to see whether Louise Hay's claims are true? Would you go to one of her seminars and ask people in the audience whether or not they'd been healed? Would you examine the medical records of people who had and hadn't bought her books? Would you invite people to sign up for a class that teaches her techniques and then wait to see how many got cancer? All of these things sound reasonable, but the fact is that none of them would be particularly informative. There

Louise Hay says she doesn't believe in scientific evidence and instead trusts her "inner ding."

empiricism
The belief that accurate knowledge can be acquired through observation.

scientific method
A procedure for finding truth by using empirical evidence.

theory
A hypothetical explanation of a natural phenomenon.

hypothesis
A falsifiable prediction made by a theory.

are a few good ways to test claims like Louise Hay's and a whole lot of bad ways, and in this chapter you will learn to tell one from the other. Scientists have developed powerful tools for determining when an inner ding is right and when it is wrong, and it is these tools that make science special. As the philosopher Bertrand Russell (1945, p. 527) wrote, "It is not *what* the man of science believes that distinguishes him, but *how* and *why* he believes it." That, it turns out, goes for women of science too.

WE'LL START BY EXAMINING THE GENERAL PRINCIPLES THAT GUIDE scientific research and distinguish it from every other way of knowing. Next, we'll see that the methods of psychology are meant to answer two basic questions: *what* do people do, and *why* do they do it? Psychologists answer the first question by observing and measuring, and they answer the second question by looking for relationships between the things they measure. We'll see that scientific research allows us to draw certain kinds of conclusions and not others, and we'll see that most people have problems thinking critically about scientific evidence. Finally, we'll consider the unique ethical questions that confront scientists who study people and other animals.

Empiricism: How to Know Stuff

When ancient Greeks sprained their ankles, caught the flu, or accidentally set their togas on fire, they had to choose between two kinds of doctors: dogmatists (from *dogmatikos,* meaning "belief"), who thought that the best way to understand illness was to develop theories about the body's functions, and empiricists (from *empeirikos,* meaning "experience"), who thought that the best way to understand illness was to observe sick people. The rivalry between these two schools of medicine didn't last long because the people who went to see dogmatists tended to die, which was bad for business. Today we use the word *dogmatism* to describe the tendency for people to cling to their assumptions, and the word **empiricism** to describe *the belief that accurate knowledge can be acquired through observation.* The fact that we can answer questions about the natural world by examining it may seem painfully obvious to you, but this painfully obvious fact has only recently gained wide acceptance. For most of human history, people trusted authority to answer important questions, and it is only in the last millennium (and especially in the past three centuries) that people have begun to trust their eyes and ears more than their elders.

BETTMANN/CORBIS

The astronomer Galileo Galilei (1564–1642) was excommunicated and sentenced to prison for sticking to his own observations of the solar system rather than accepting the teachings of the church. In 1597 he wrote to his friend and fellow astronomer Johannes Kepler (1571–1630), "What would you say of the learned here, who, replete with the pertinacity of the asp, have steadfastly refused to cast a glance through the telescope? What shall we make of this? Shall we laugh, or shall we cry?" As it turned out, the answer was *cry.*

The Scientific Method

Empiricism is the essential element of the **scientific method**, which is *a procedure for finding truth by using empirical evidence.* In essence, the scientific method suggests that when we have an idea about the world—about how bats navigate, or where the moon came from, or why people can't forget traumatic events—we should gather empirical evidence relevant to that idea and then modify the idea to fit with the evidence. Scientists usually refer to an idea of this kind as a **theory**, which is *a hypothetical explanation of a natural phenomenon.* We might theorize that bats navigate by making sounds and then listening for the echo, that the moon was formed when a small planet collided with the Earth, or that the brain responds to traumatic events by producing chemicals that facilitate memory. Each of these theories is an explanation of how something in the natural world works.

When scientists set out to develop a theory, they generally follow *the rule of parsimony*, which says that the *simplest* theory that explains all the evidence is the best one. Parsimony comes from the Latin word *parcere,* meaning "to spare," and the rule is often credited to the 14th-century logician William Ockham, who wrote "Plurality should not be posited without necessity." Ockham wasn't suggesting that nature is simple or that complex theories are wrong. He was merely suggesting that it makes sense to *start* with the simplest theory and then make the theory more complicated only if one must. Part of what makes $E = mc^2$ such a lovely theory is that it has exactly three letters and one number.

> **What is the scientific method?**

We want our theories to be as simple as possible, but we also want them to be right. How do we decide if a theory is right? Theories make specific predictions about what we should observe in the world. For example, if bats really do navigate by making sounds and then listening for echoes, then we should observe that deaf bats can't navigate. That "should statement" is technically known as a **hypothesis,** which is *a falsifiable prediction made by a theory*. The word *falsifiable* is a critical part of that definition. Some theories, such as "God created the universe," simply do not specify what we should observe if they are true, and thus no observation can ever falsify them. Because these theories do not give rise to hypotheses, they can never be the subject of scientific investigation. That doesn't mean they're wrong—it just means that we can't evaluate them by using the scientific method.

So what happens when we test a hypothesis? Albert Einstein is reputed to have said that, "No amount of experimentation can ever prove me right, but a single experiment can prove me wrong." Why should that be? Well, just imagine what you could possibly learn about the navigation-by-sound theory if you observed a few bats. If you saw the deaf bats navigating every bit as well as the hearing bats, then the navigation-by-sound theory would instantly be proved wrong; but if you saw the deaf bats navigating more poorly than

> **Why can theories be proven wrong but not right?**

the hearing bats, your observation would be *consistent* with the navigation-by-sound theory but would not prove it. After all, even if you didn't see a deaf bat navigating perfectly today, it is still possible that someone else did, or that you will see one tomorrow. We can't observe every bat that has ever been and will ever be, which means that even if the theory

Classical thinkers like Euclid and Ptolemy believed that our eyes work by emitting rays that travel to the objects we see. Ibn al-Haytham (965–1039) reasoned that if this were true, then when we open our eyes it should take longer to see something far away than something nearby. And guess what? It doesn't. And with that single observation, a centuries-old theory vanished—in the blink of an eye.

SCIENCE SOURCE/
COLORIZATION BY:
MARY MARTIN

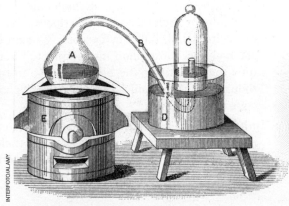

SEFANO BIANCHETTI/CORBIS

INTERFOTO/ALAMY

Scientists once believed that all combustible objects contain an element called *phlogiston* that is released during burning. But in 1779, the chemist Antoine Lavoisier (1734–1794) demonstrated that when metals such as mercury are burned, they don't get lighter, as the phlogiston theory said they must. Lavoisier (*left*) and his theory-killing apparatus (*right*).

wasn't disproved by your observation there always remains some chance that it will be disproved by some other observation. When evidence is consistent with a theory, it increases our confidence in it, but it never makes us completely certain. The next time you see a newspaper headline that says "Scientists prove theory X correct," you are hereby authorized to roll your eyes.

The scientific method suggests that the best way to learn the truth about the world is to develop theories, derive hypotheses from them, test those hypotheses by gathering evidence, and then use that evidence to modify the theories. But what exactly does gathering evidence entail?

The Art of Looking

For centuries, people rode horses. And for centuries when they got off their horses they sat around and argued about whether all four of a horse's feet ever leave the ground at the same time. Some said yes, some said no, and some said they really wished they could talk about something else for a change. In 1877, Eadweard Muybridge invented a technique for taking photographs in rapid succession, and his photos showed that when horses gallop, all four feet do indeed leave the ground. And that was that. Never again did two riders have the pleasure of a flying horse debate because Muybridge had settled the matter, once and for all time.

Frames 2 and 3 of this historic photo by Eadweard Muybridge (1830–1904) show that horses can indeed fly, albeit briefly and only in coach.

But why did it take so long? After all, people had been watching horses gallop for quite a few years, so why did some say that they clearly saw the horse going airborne while others said that they clearly saw at least one hoof on the ground at all times? Because as wonderful as eyes may be, there are a lot of things they cannot see and a lot of things they see incorrectly. We can't see germs but they are very real. The Earth looks perfectly flat but it is imperfectly round. As Muybridge knew, we have to do more than just look if we want to know the truth about the world. Empiricism is the right approach, but to do it properly requires an **empirical method,** which is *a set of rules and techniques for observation.*

In many sciences, the word *method* refers primarily to technologies that enhance the powers of the senses. Biologists use microscopes and astronomers use telescopes because the things they want to observe are invisible to the naked eye. Human behavior, on the other hand, is quite visible, so you might expect psychology's methods to be relatively simple. In fact, the empirical challenges facing psychologists are among the most daunting in all of modern science, thus psychology's empirical methods are among the most sophisticated in all of modern science. These empirical challenges arise because people have three qualities that make them unusually difficult to study:

> *Complexity*: No galaxy, particle, molecule, or machine is as complicated as the human brain. Scientists can describe the birth of a star or the death of a cell in exquisite detail, but they can barely begin to say how the 500 million interconnected neurons that constitute the brain give rise to the thoughts, feelings, and actions that are psychology's core concerns.

What makes human beings especially difficult to study?

> *Variability*: In almost all the ways that matter, one *E. coli* bacterium is pretty much like another. But people are as varied as their fingerprints. No two individuals ever do, say, think, or feel exactly the same thing under exactly the same circumstances, which means that when you've seen one, you've most definitely not seen them all.

empirical method
A set of rules and techniques for observation.

EADWEARD MUYBRIDGE/CORBIS

> ❯ *Reactivity*: An atom of cesium-133 oscillates 9,192,631,770 times per second regardless of whether anyone is watching. But people often think, feel, and act one way when they are being observed and a different way when they are not. When people know they are being studied, they don't always behave as they otherwise would.

The fact that human beings are complex, variable, and reactive presents a major challenge to the scientific study of their behavior, and psychologists have developed two kinds of methods that are designed to meet these challenges head-on: *methods of observation*, which allow them to determine what people do, and *methods of explanation*, which allow them to determine why people do it. We'll examine both of these methods in the sections that follow.

People behave differently when they are and are not being observed. For example, President Obama might have inhibited that neck swivel if he'd realized that a photographer (as well as a rather amused French President Sarkozy) were watching him.

IN SUMMARY

► Empiricism is the belief that the best way to understand the world is to observe it firsthand. It is only in the last few centuries that empiricism has come to prominence.

► Empiricism is at the heart of the scientific method, which suggests that our theories about the world give rise to falsifiable hypotheses, and that we can thus make observations that test those hypotheses. The results of these tests can disprove our theories but cannot prove them.

► Observation doesn't just mean "looking." It requires a method. The methods of psychology are special because, more than most other natural phenomena, human beings are complex, variable, and reactive.

Observation: Discovering What People Do

To *observe* means to use one's senses to learn about the properties of an event (e.g., a storm or a parade) or an object (e.g., an apple or a person). For example, when you observe a round, red apple, your brain is using the pattern of light that is coming into your eyes to draw an inference about the apple's identity, shape, and color. That kind of informal observation is fine for buying fruit but not for doing science. Why? First, casual observations are notoriously unstable. The same apple may appear red in the daylight and crimson at night or spherical to one person and elliptical to another. Second, casual observations can't tell us about all of the properties that might interest us. No matter how long and hard you look, you will never be able to discern an apple's crunchiness or pectin content simply by watching it.

Luckily, scientists have devised techniques that allow them to overcome these problems. In the first section (Measurement), we'll see how psychologists design instruments and then use them to make measurements. In the second section (Description), we'll see what psychologists do with their measurements once they've made them.

Measurement

For most of human history, people had no idea how old they were because there was no simple way to keep track of time—or weight, or volume, or density, or temperature, or anything else for that matter. Today we live in a world of rulers, clocks, calendars, odometers, thermometers, and mass spectrometers. Measurement is not just a basic part of science, it is a basic part of modern life. But what exactly does measurement

What two things does measurement require?

operational definition
A description of a property in concrete, measurable terms.

instrument
Anything that can detect the condition to which an operational definition refers.

validity
The goodness with which a concrete event defines a property.

reliability
The tendency for an instrument to produce the same measurement whenever it is used to measure the same thing.

power
An instrument's ability to detect small magnitudes of the property.

demand characteristics
Those aspects of an observational setting that cause people to behave as they think someone else wants or expects.

naturalistic observation
A technique for gathering scientific information by unobtrusively observing people in their natural environments.

require? Whether we want to measure the intensity of an earthquake, the distance between molecules, or the attitude of a registered voter, we must always do two things—*define* the property we wish to measure and then find a way to *detect* it.

Defining and Detecting

The last time you said, "just give me a second," you probably didn't know you were talking about atomic decay. Every unit of time has an **operational definition,** which is *a description of a property in concrete, measurable terms.* The operational definition of a second is *the duration of 9,192,631,770 cycles of microwave light absorbed or emitted by the hyperfine transition of cesium-133 atoms in their ground state undisturbed by external fields* (which takes roughly 6 seconds just to say). To actually count the cycles of light emitted as cesium-133 decays requires an **instrument,** which is *anything that can detect the condition to which an operational definition refers.* An instrument known as a "cesium clock" can count cycles of light, and when it counts 9,192,631,770 of them, one second has officially passed.

The steps we take to measure a physical property are the same steps we take to measure a psychological property. For example, if we wanted to measure a person's intelligence, or shyness, or happiness, we would have to start by generating an operational definition of that property—that is, by specifying some concrete, measurable event that indicates it. For example, we might define happiness as *the frequency with which a person smiles.* Once we do, we just need a smile-detecting instrument, such as a computer-assisted camera or maybe just a human eye. Having an operational definition that specifies a measurable event and an instrument that measures that event are the keys to scientific measurement.

Validity, Reliability, and Power

There are many ways to define and detect a property such as happiness, so which ways are best? The most important feature of an operational definition is **validity,** *the goodness with which a concrete event defines a property.* For example, the concrete event called *frequency of smiling* is a valid way to define the property called *happiness* because, as we all know, people tend to smile more often when they feel happy. Do they eat more or talk more or spend more money? Well, maybe. But maybe not. And that's why food consumption or verbal output or financial expenditures would probably be regarded by most people as invalid measures of happiness (though perfectly valid measures of something else). Validity is to some extent in the eye of the beholder, but most beholders would agree that the frequency of smiles is a more valid way to operationally define happiness than is frequency of eating, talking, or spending.

What are the properties of a good operational definition and a good instrument?

What then is the most important feature of an instrument? Actually, there are two. First, a good instrument has **reliability,** which is *the tendency for an instrument to produce the same measurement whenever it is used to measure the same thing.* For example, if a person smiles just as much on Tuesday as on Wednesday, then a smile-detecting instrument should produce identical results on those two days. If it produced different results (i.e., if the instrument detected differences that weren't actually there), it would lack reliability. Second, a good instrument has **power,** which is *an instrument's ability to detect small magnitudes of the property.* If a person smiled just *slightly* more often on Tuesday than on Wednesday, then a good smile-detector should produce different results on those two days. If it produced the same result (i.e., if it failed to detect a small difference that was actually there), then it would lack power (see **FIGURE 2.1**).

▼ Figure **2.1** **Measurement** There are two steps in the measurement of a property.

Define the Property		Detect the Property
Generate an operational definition that has validity	→	Design an instrument that has reliability and power

Demand Characteristics

Once we have a valid definition and a reliable and powerful instrument, are we are *finally* ready to measure behavior? Yes, as long as we want to measure the behavior of an amoeba or a raindrop or anything else that doesn't care if we are watching it. But if we want to measure the behavior of a human being, then we still have some work to do, because while we are trying to discover how people normally behave, normal people will be trying to behave as they think we want or expect them to. **Demand characteristics** are *those aspects of an observational setting that cause people to behave as they think someone else wants or expects.* We call these demand characteristics because they seem to "demand" or require that people say and do certain things. When someone you love asks, "Do these jeans make me look fat?" the right answer is always no, and if you've ever been asked this question, then you have experienced demand. Demand characteristics make it hard to measure behavior as it typically unfolds.

REX FEATURES VIA AP PHOTO

Are most people prejudiced against people with disabilities? People rarely admit to being prejudiced when asked, and they generally won't behave in prejudiced ways if someone is watching. So how could you measure prejudice in a way that minimized demand characteristics?

One way that psychologists avoid the problem of demand characteristics is by observing people without their knowledge. **Naturalistic observation** is *a technique for gathering scientific information by unobtrusively observing people in their natural environments.* For example, naturalistic observation has shown that the biggest groups leave the smallest tips in restaurants (Freeman et al., 1975), that hungry shoppers buy the most impulse items at the grocery store (Gilbert, Gill, & Wilson, 2002), that golfers are most likely to cheat when they play several opponents at once (Erffmeyer, 1984), that men do not usually approach the most beautiful woman at a singles' bar (Glenwick, Jason, & Elman, 1978), and that Olympic athletes smile more when they win the bronze medal than the silver medal (Medvec, Madey, & Gilovich, 1995). Each of these conclusions is the result of measurements made by psychologists who observed people who didn't know they were being observed. It seems unlikely that the same observations could have been made if the diners, shoppers, golfers, singles, and athletes had realized that they were being scrutinized.

> How do people respond when they know they're being observed?

Unfortunately, naturalistic observation isn't always a viable solution to the problem of demand characteristics. First, some of the things psychologists want to observe simply don't occur naturally. If we wanted to know whether people who have undergone sensory deprivation perform poorly on motor tasks, we would have to hang around the shopping mall for a very long time before a few dozen blindfolded people with earplugs just happened to wander by and start typing. Second, some of the things that psychologists want to observe can only be gathered from direct interaction with a person, for example, by administering a survey, giving tests, conducting an interview, or hooking someone up to a machine. If we wanted to know how often people worry about dying, how accurately they can remember their high school graduations, how quickly they can solve a logic puzzle, or how much electrical activity their brains produce when they feel jealous, then simply watching them from the bushes won't do.

Luckily, there are other ways to avoid demand characteristics. For instance, people are less likely to be influenced by demand characteristics when they cannot be

CULTURE & COMMUNITY

Best place to fall on your face Robert Levine of California State University–Fresno sent his students to 23 large international cities for an observational study in the field. Their task was to observe helping behaviors in a naturalistic context. In two versions of the experiment, students pretended to be either blind or injured while trying to cross a street, while another student stood by to observe whether anyone would come to help. A third version involved a student dropping a pen to see if anyone would pick it up.

The results showed that people helped in all three events fairly evenly within cities, but there was a wide range of response between cities. Rio de Janeiro, Brazil, came out on top as the most helpful city in the study with an overall helping score of 93%. Kuala Lampur, Malaysia, came in last with a score of 40%, and New York City placed next to last with a score of 45%. On average, Latin American cities ranked as most helpful (Levine, Norenzayan, & Philbrick, 2001).

One way to avoid demand characteristics is to measure behaviors that people are unable or unlikely to control. For example, our pupils contract when we are bored (photo 1) and dilate when we are interested (photo 2), which makes pupillary dilation a useful measure of a person's level of engagement in a task.

identified as the originators of their actions, and psychologists often take advantage of this fact by allowing people to respond privately (e.g., by having them complete questionnaires when they are alone) or anonymously (e.g., by not collecting personal information, such as the person's name or address). Another technique that psychologists often use to avoid demand characteristics is to measure behaviors that cannot easily be demanded. For instance, a person's behavior can't be influenced by demand characteristics if that behavior isn't under the person's voluntary control. You may not want a psychologist to know that you are extremely interested in the celebrity gossip magazine that she's asked you to read, but you can't prevent your pupils from dilating, which is what they do when you are engaged. Behaviors are also unlikely to be influenced by demand characteristics when people don't know that the demand and the behavior are related. For example, you may want the psychologist to believe that you are concentrating hard on the *Wall Street Journal* article that she's asked you to read, but you probably don't realize that your blink rate slows when you are concentrating, thus you probably won't fake a slow blink.

One of the best ways to avoid demand characteristics is to keep the people who are being observed from knowing the true purpose of the observation. When people are "blind" to the purpose of an observation, they can't behave the way they think they should behave because they don't *know* how they should behave. For instance, if you didn't know that a psychologist was studying the effects of music on mood, you wouldn't feel obligated to smile when music was played. This is why psychologists typically don't reveal the true purpose of an observation to the people who are being observed until the study is over.

Why is it important for subjects to be "blind"?

Of course, people are clever and curious, and when psychologists don't tell them the purpose of their observations, people generally try to figure it out for themselves. That's why psychologists sometimes use *cover stories,* or misleading explanations that are meant to keep people from discerning the true purpose of an observation. For example, if a psychologist wanted to know how music influenced your mood, he or she might falsely tell you that the purpose of the study was to determine how quickly people can do logic puzzles while music plays in the background. (We will discuss the ethical implications of deceiving people later in this chapter.) In addition, the psychologist might use *filler items,* or pointless measures that are designed to mislead you about the true purpose of the observation. So, for example, the psychologist might ask you a few questions whose answers are of real interest to him or her (How happy are you right now?), as well as a few questions whose answers are not (Do you like cats more or less than dogs?). This makes it difficult for you to guess the true purpose of the observation from the nature of the questions you were asked.

Observer Bias

The people being observed aren't the only ones who can make measurement a bit tricky. In one study, students in a psychology class were asked to measure the speed with which a rat learned to run through a maze (Rosenthal & Fode, 1963). Some students were told that their rat had been specially bred to be "maze-dull" (i.e., slow to learn a maze) and others were told that their rat had been specially bred to be "maze-bright" (i.e., quick to learn a maze). Although all the rats were actually the same breed, the students who *thought* they were measuring the speed of a maze-dull rat reported that their rats took longer to learn the maze than did the students who *thought* they were measuring the speed of a maze-bright rat. In other words, the measurements revealed precisely what the students expected them to reveal.

Why did this happen? First, *expectations can influence observations.* It is easy to make errors when measuring the speed of a rat, and our expectations often determine the kinds of errors we make. Does putting one paw over the finish line count as learning the maze? If the rat falls asleep, should the stopwatch be left running or should the rat be awakened and given a second chance? If a rat runs a maze in 18.5 seconds, should that number be rounded up or rounded down before it is recorded in the log book? The answers to these questions may depend on whether one thinks the rat is bright or dull. The students who timed the rats probably tried to be honest, vigilant, fair, and objective, but their expectations influenced their observations in subtle ways that they could neither detect nor control. Second, *expectations can influence reality.* Students who expected their rats to learn quickly may have unknowingly done things to help that learning along, for example, by muttering, "Oh no!" when the bright rat looked the wrong direction or by petting the dull rat less affectionately. (We'll discuss both of these phenomena more extensively in the Social Psychology chapter.)

> **?** Why is it important for experimenters to be "blind"?

Observers' expectations, then, can have a powerful influence on both their observations and on the behavior of those whom they observe. Psychologists use many techniques to avoid these influences, and one of the most common is the **double-blind** observation, which is *an observation whose true purpose is hidden from both the observer and the person being observed.* For example, if the students had not been told which rats were bright and which were dull, then they wouldn't have *had* any expectations about their rats, thus their expectations couldn't have influenced their measurements. That's why it is common practice in psychology to keep the observers as blind as the participants. For example, measurements are often made by research assistants who do not know what is being studied or why, and who therefore don't have any expectations about what the people being observed will or should do. Indeed, studies nowadays are often carried out by the world's blindest experimenter—a computer—which can present information to people and measure their responses while having no expectations at all.

People's expectations can cause the phenomena they expect. In 1929, investors who expected the stock market to collapse sold their stocks and thereby caused the very crisis they feared. In this photo, panicked citizens stand outside the New York Stock Exchange the day after the crash, which the *New York Times* attributed to "mob psychology."

Description

You now know how to generate a valid operational definition, how to design a reliable and powerful instrument, and how to use that instrument while avoiding demand characteristics and observer bias. So where does that leave you? With a big page filled with numbers—and if you are like most people, a big page filled with numbers just doesn't seem very informative. Don't worry, most psychologists feel the same way, and that's why they have two techniques for making sense of big pages full of numbers: graphic representations and descriptive statistics.

Graphic Representations

A picture may be worth a thousand words, but it is worth a million digits. As you'll learn in the Sensation and Perception chapter, vision is our most sophisticated sense, and human beings typically find it easier to understand things when they are represented visually than numerically or verbally. Psychologists are people too, and they

double-blind
An observation whose true purpose is hidden from both the observer and the person being observed.

► Figure **2.2** **Frequency Distributions** This graph shows how a hypothetical group of men and women scored on a test of fine motor skills. Test scores are listed along the horizontal axis, and the frequency with which each score was obtained is represented along the vertical axis.

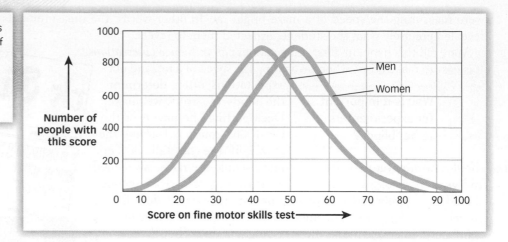

On average, men are taller than women, but there are still many women (like Clare Grant) who are taller than many men (like her husband, Seth Green).

frequency distribution
A graphical representation of measurements arranged by the number of times each measurement was made.

normal distribution
A mathematically defined distribution in which the frequency of measurements is highest in the middle and decreases symmetrically in both directions.

mode
The value of the most frequently observed measurement.

mean
The average value of all the measurements.

median
The value that is in the middle; that is, greater than or equal to half the measurements and less than or equal to half the measurements.

often create graphic representations of the measurements they collect. The most common kind is the **frequency distribution,** which is *a graphic representation of measurements arranged by the number of times each measurement was made*. **FIGURE 2.2** shows a pair of frequency distributions that represent the hypothetical performances of a group of men and women who took a test of fine motor skills (i.e., the ability to manipulate things with their hands). Every possible test score is shown on the horizontal axis. The number of times (or the *frequency with which*) each score was observed is shown on the vertical axis. Although a frequency distribution can have any shape, a common shape is the *bell curve,* which is technically known as the *Gaussian distribution* or the **normal distribution,** which is *a mathematically defined distribution in which the frequency of measurements is highest in the middle and decreases symmetrically in both directions*. The mathematical definition of the normal distribution isn't important. (Well, for you anyway. For statisticians it is slightly more important than breathing.) What is important for you is what you can easily see for yourself: the normal distribution is symmetrical (i.e., the left half is a mirror image of the right half), has a peak in the middle, and trails off at both ends.

> What is a frequency distribution?

The picture in Figure 2.2 reveals in a single optical gulp what a page full of numbers never can. For instance, the shape of the distributions instantly tells you that most people have moderate motor skills, and that only a few have exceptionally good or exceptionally bad motor skills. You can also see that the distribution of men's scores is displaced a bit to the left of the distribution of women's scores, which instantly tells you that women tend to have somewhat better motor skills than men. And finally, you can see that the two distributions have a great deal of overlap, which tells you that although women tend to have better motor skills than men, there are still plenty of men who have better motor skills than plenty of women.

Descriptive Statistics

A frequency distribution depicts every measurement and thus provides a full and complete picture of those measurements. But sometimes a full and complete picture is just TMI.* When we ask a friend how she's been, we don't want her to show us a frequency distribution of her happiness scores on each day of the previous 6 months. We want a brief summary statement that captures the essential information that such a graph would provide (e.g., "I've been doing pretty well," or, "I've been having some ups and downs lately"). In psychology, brief summary statements that capture the

---

* Our editor thinks you need four professors with a combined age of 190 to tell you that this means "too much information." ROFL.

essential information from a frequency distribution are called *descriptive statistics*. There are two important kinds of descriptive statistics: those that describe the *central tendency* of a frequency distribution and those that describe the *variability* in a frequency distribution.

Descriptions of *central tendency* are statements about the value of the measurements that *tend* to lie near the *center* or midpoint of the frequency distribu-

> **What are the two major kinds of descriptive statistics?**

tion. When a friend says that she's been "doing pretty well," she is describing the central tendency (or approximate location of the midpoint) of the frequency distribution of her happiness over time (see **FIGURE 2.3**). The three most common descriptions of central tendency are: the **mode** (*the value of the most frequently observed measurement*); the **mean** (*the average value of all the measurements*); and the **median** (*the value that is in the middle; i.e., greater than or equal to half the measurements and less than or equal to half the measurements*). **FIGURE 2.4** shows how each of these descriptive statistics is calculated. When you hear a descriptive statistic such as "the average American college student sleeps 8.3 hours per day," you are hearing about the central tendency of a frequency distribution (in this case, the mean).

In a normal distribution, the mean, median, and mode all have the same value, but when the distribution is not normal, these three descriptive statistics can differ. For example, imagine that you measured the net worth of 40 college professors, and Mark Zuckerberg. The frequency distribution of your measurements would not be normal, but *positively skewed*. As you can see in **FIGURE 2.5**, the mode and the median of a positively skewed distribution are much lower than the mean because the mean is more strongly influenced by the value of a single extreme measurement (which, in case you've been sleeping for the last few years, would be the net worth of Mark

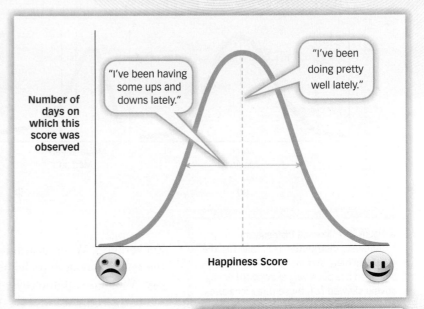

▲ Figure **2.3** **Two Kinds of Descriptive Statistics** Descriptive statistics are used to describe two important features of a frequency distribution: central tendency (where do most of the scores lie?) and variability (how much do the scores differ from one another?).

- Mode = 3 because there are five 3s and only three 2s, two 1s, two 4s, one 5, one 6, and one 7.
- Mean = 3.27 because $(1 + 1 + 2 + 2 + 2 + 3 + 3 + 3 + 3 + 3 + 4 + 4 + 5 + 6 + 7)/15 = 3.27$
- Median = 3 because 10 scores are ≥ 3 and 10 scores are ≤ 3

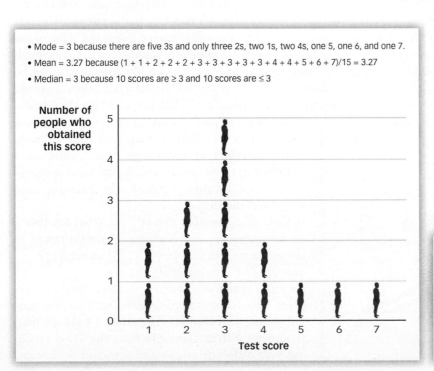

◄ Figure **2.4** **Some Descriptive Statistics** This frequency distribution shows the scores of 15 individuals on a 7-point test. Descriptive statistics include measures of central tendency (such as the mean, median, and mode) and measures of variability (such as the range and the standard deviation).

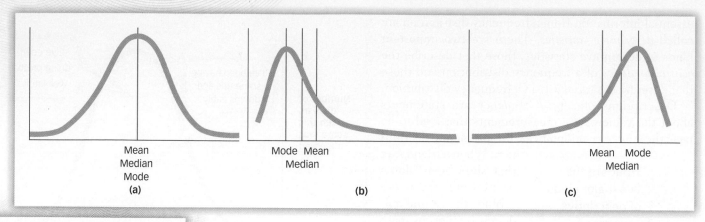

Mean
Median
Mode

(a)

Mode Mean
Median

(b)

Mean Mode
Median

(c)

▲ Figure **2.5** **Skewed Distributions** When a frequency distribution is normal (*a*), the mean, median, and mode are all the same, but when it is positively skewed (*b*) or negatively skewed (*c*), these three measures of central tendency are quite different.

When Mark Zuckerberg walks into a room he dramatically increases the mean income of the people in it, but doesn't much change the median, and does nothing at all to the mode. Facebook is trying to fix that.

AP PHOTO/JEFF CHIU

Zuckerberg). When distributions become skewed, the mean gets dragged off toward the tail, the mode stays home at the hump, and the median goes to live between the two. When distributions are skewed, a single measure of central tendency can paint a misleading picture of the measurements. For example, the average net worth of the people you measured is probably about a billion dollars each, but that statement makes the college professors sound a whole lot richer than they are. You could provide a much better description of the net worth of the people you measured if you also mentioned that the median net worth is $300,000 and that the modal net worth is $288,000. Indeed, you should always be suspicious when you hear some new fact about "the average person" but don't hear anything about the shape of the frequency distribution.

Whereas descriptions of central tendency are statements about the location of the measurements in a frequency distribution, descriptions of variability are statements about the extent to which the measurements differ from each other. When a friend says that she has been "having some ups and downs lately," she is offering a brief summary statement that describes how measurements of her happiness taken at different times tend to differ from one another. The simplest description of variability is the **range,** which is *the value of the largest measurement in a frequency distribution minus the value of the smallest measurement.* When the range is small, the measurements don't vary as much as when the range is large. The range is easy to compute, but like the mean it can be dramatically affected by a single measurement. If you said that the net worth of people you had measured ranged from $40,000 to $14 billion, a listener might get the impression that these people were all remarkably different from each other when, in fact, they were all quite similar save for one very rich guy from California.

Other descriptions of variability aren't quite as susceptible to this problem. For example, the **standard deviation** is *a statistic that describes the average difference between the measurements in a frequency distribution and the mean of that distribution.* In other words, on average, how far are the measurements from the center of the distribution? As **FIGURE 2.6** shows, two frequency distributions can have the same mean, but very different ranges and standard deviations.

What are two measures of variability?

▼ Figure **2.6** **IQ of Men and Women** Men and women have the same average IQ, but men are more variable than women.

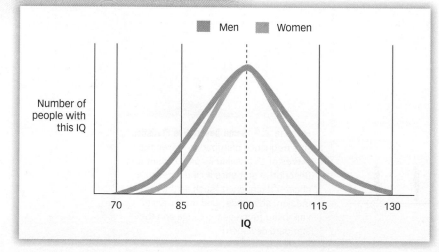

Men Women

Number of people with this IQ

70   85   100   115   130

IQ

For example, studies show that men and women have the same mean IQ, but that men have a larger range and standard deviation, which is to say that a man is more likely than a woman to be much more or much less intelligent than the average person of his or her own gender.

range
The value of the largest measurement in a frequency distribution minus the value of the smallest measurement.

standard deviation
A statistic that describes the average difference between the measurements in a frequency distribution and the mean of that distribution.

IN SUMMARY

▶ Measurement involves defining a property in terms of a concrete condition, and then constructing a measure that can detect that condition. A good measure is valid (the concrete conditions it measures are conceptually related to the property of interest), is reliable (it produces the same measurement whenever it is used to measure the same thing), and is powerful (it can detect the concrete conditions when they actually exist).

▶ When people know they are being observed, they may behave as they think they should. Demand characteristics are features of a setting that suggest to people that they should behave in a particular way. Psychologists try to reduce or eliminate demand characteristics by observing participants in their natural habitats or by hiding their expectations from the participant. Observer bias is the tendency for observers to see what they expect to see or cause others to behave as they expect them to behave. Psychologists try to eliminate observer bias by making double-blind observations.

▶ Psychologists often describe the measurements they make with a graphic representation called a frequency distribution, which often has a special shape known as the normal distribution. They also describe their measurements with descriptive statistics; the most common are descriptions of central tendency (such as the mean, median, and mode) and descriptions of variability (such as the range and the standard deviation).

Explanation: Discovering Why People Do What They Do

It would be interesting to know whether happy people are healthier than unhappy people, but it would be even more interesting to know why. Does happiness make people healthier? Does being healthy make people happier? Does being rich make people healthy and happy? These are the kinds of questions scientists often wish to answer, and scientists have developed some clever ways of using their measurements to do just that. In the first section (Correlation) we'll examine techniques that can tell us whether two things are related. In the second section (Causation), we'll examine techniques that can tell us whether the relationship between two things is one of cause and effect. In the third section (Drawing Conclusions) we'll see what kinds of conclusions these techniques allow us to draw. Finally, in the fourth section, we'll discuss the difficulty that most of us have thinking critically about scientific evidence.

Correlation

How much sleep did you get last night? Okay, now, how many U. S. presidents can you name? If you asked a dozen college students those two questions, you'd probably find that the students who got a good night's sleep are better president namers than are students who pulled an all-nighter. A pattern of responses like the one shown in **TABLE 2.1** would probably lead you to conclude that sleep deprivation causes memory problems. But on what basis did you draw that conclusion? How did you manage to use measurement to tell you not only about *how much* sleeping and remembering had occurred among the students you measured, but also about the *relationship* between sleeping and remembering?

▶ **Table 2.1**

Hypothetical Data Showing the Relationship between Sleep and Memory

Participant	Hours of Sleep	No. of Presidents Named
A	0	11
B	0	17
C	2.7	16
D	3.1	21
E	4.4	17
F	5.5	16
G	7.6	31
H	7.9	41
I	8	40
J	8.1	35
K	8.6	38
L	9	43

Patterns of Variation

Measurements tell us about the properties of objects and events. We can learn about the relationships between those objects and events by comparing the *patterns of variation in a series of measurements*. When you asked college students questions about sleep and presidents, you actually did three things:

> First, you measured a pair of **variables,** which are *properties whose values can vary across individuals or over time.* (When you took your first algebra course you were probably horrified to learn that everything you'd been taught in grade school about the distinction between letters and numbers was a lie, that mathematical equations could contain Xs and Ys as well as 7s and 4s, and that the letters are called *variables* because they can have different values under different circumstances. Same idea here.) You measured one variable (number of hours slept) whose value could vary from 0 to 24, and you measured a second variable (number of presidents named) whose value could vary from 0 to 44.

> | How can we tell if two variables are correlated? |

> Second, you did this again. And then again. And then again. That is, you made a *series* of measurements rather than making just one.

> Third and finally, you tried to discern a pattern in your series of measurements. If you look at the second column of Table 2.1, you will see that it contains values that vary as your eyes move down the column. That column has a particular *pattern of variation.* If you compare the third column with the second, you will notice that the patterns of variation in the two columns are synchronized: in this case, both increase as you move from top to bottom. This synchrony is known as a *pattern of covariation* or a **correlation** (as in "co-relation"). Two variables are said to "covary" or to "be correlated" when *variations in the value of one variable are synchronized with variations in the value of the other.* As the values in the second column vary from small to large, the values in the third column do the same.

By looking for synchronized patterns of variation, we can use measurement to discover the relationships between variables. Indeed, this is the only way anyone has *ever* discovered the relationship between variables, which is why most of the facts you know about the world can be thought of as correlations. For example, you know that people who smoke generally die younger than people who don't, but this is just a shorthand way of saying that as the value of *cigarette consumption* increases, the value of *longevity* decreases. Correlations not only describe the world as it is, they also allow us to predict the world as it will be. For example, given the correlation between smoking and longevity, you can predict with some confidence that a young person who starts smoking today will probably not live as long as a young person who doesn't. In short, when two variables are correlated, knowledge of the value of one variable allows us to make predictions about the value of the other variable.

Measuring the Direction and Strength of a Correlation

If you predict that a sleep-deprived person will have better memory than a well-rested person, you will be right more often than wrong. But you won't be right in every single instance. Statisticians have developed a way to estimate how accurate such predictions are likely to be by measuring the *direction* and *strength* of the correlation on which the predictions are based.

Direction is easy to measure because the direction of a correlation is either positive or negative. A positive correlation exists when two variables have a "more-is-more" or "less-is-less" relationship. So, for example, when we say that *more sleep* is associated with *more memory* or that *less sleep* is associated with *less memory,* we are describing a

THINKSTOCK

Researchers have found a positive correlation between mental illness and smoking. Can you think of three reasons why this correlation might exist?

positive correlation. Conversely, a negative correlation exists when two variables have a "more-is-less" or "less-is-more" relationship. When we say that *more cigarette smoking* is associated with *less longevity* or that *less cigarette smoking* is associated with *more longevity*, we are describing a negative correlation.

The direction of a correlation is easy to measure, but the strength is a little more complicated. The **correlation coefficient** is *a mathematical measure of both the direction and strength of a correlation* and it is symbolized by the letter *r* (as in "relationship"). Like most measures, the correlation coefficient has a limited range. What does that mean? Well, if you were to measure the number of hours of sunshine per day in your hometown, that number

> How can correlations be measured?

could range from 0 to 24. Numbers such as –7 and 36.8 would be meaningless. Similarly, the value of *r* can range from –1 to 1, and numbers outside that range are meaningless. What, then, do the numbers *inside* that range mean?

> If every time the value of one variable increases by a fixed amount the value of the second variable also increases by a fixed amount, then the relationship between the variables is called a *perfect positive correlation* and *r* = 1 (see **FIGURE 2.7a**). For example, if every 30-minute increase in sleep was associated with a 2-president increase in memory, then sleep and memory would be *perfectly positively correlated*.

> If every time the value of one variable increases by a fixed amount the value of the second variable *decreases* by a fixed amount, then the relationship between the variables is called a *perfect negative correlation* and *r* = –1 (see **FIGURE 2.7b**). For example, if every 30-minute increase in sleep was associated with a 2-president decrease in memory, then sleep and memory would be *perfectly negatively correlated*.

> If every time the value of one variable increases by a fixed amount the value of the second variable neither increases nor decreases systematically, then the two variables are said to be *uncorrelated* and *r* = 0 (see **FIGURE 2.7c**). For example, if a 30-minute increase in sleep was sometimes associated with an increase in memory, sometimes associated with a decrease in memory, and sometimes associated with no change in memory at all, then sleep and memory would be uncorrelated.

Perfect correlations are extremely rare. As you'll learn in the Consciousness chapter, sleep really does enhance memory performance, but the relationship is not perfect. It isn't as though every 18 minutes of sleep buys you exactly one third of a remembered president! Sleep and memory are *positively* correlated (i.e., as one increases, the other also increases), but they are *imperfectly* correlated, thus *r* will lie somewhere between 0 and 1. But where? That depends on how many exceptions there are to the "X more

variable
A property whose value can vary across individuals or over time.

correlation
Two variables are said to "be correlated" when variations in the value of one variable are synchronized with variations in the value of the other.

correlation coefficient
A mathematical measure of both the direction and strength of a correlation, which is symbolized by the letter *r*.

▼ Figure **2.7 Three Kinds of Correlations** These figures illustrate correlations between variables. (*a*) a perfect positive correlation (*r* = 1), (*b*) a perfect negative correlation (*r* = –1), and (*c*) no correlation (*r* = 0).

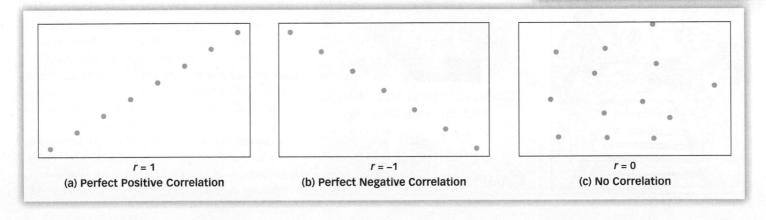

| *r* = 1 | *r* = –1 | *r* = 0 |
| **(a) Perfect Positive Correlation** | **(b) Perfect Negative Correlation** | **(c) No Correlation** |

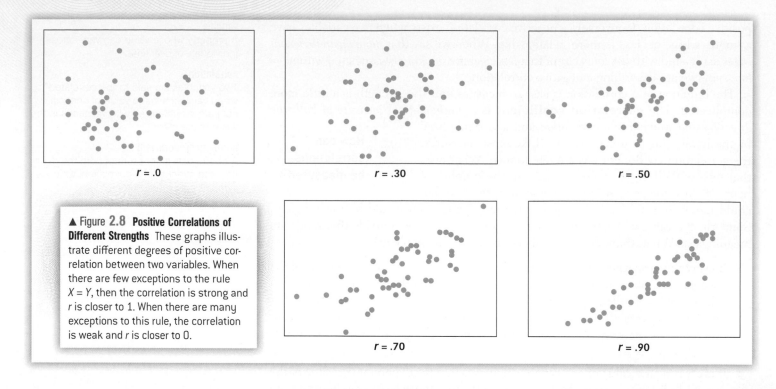

▲ Figure **2.8** **Positive Correlations of Different Strengths** These graphs illustrate different degrees of positive correlation between two variables. When there are few exceptions to the rule $X = Y$, then the correlation is strong and r is closer to 1. When there are many exceptions to this rule, the correlation is weak and r is closer to 0.

minutes of sleep = Y more presidents remembered" rule. If there are only a few exceptions, then r will lie much closer to 1 than to 0. But as the number of exceptions increases, then the value of r will begin to move toward 0.

FIGURE 2.8 shows four cases in which two variables are positively correlated but have different numbers of exceptions, and as you can see, the number of exceptions changes the value of r quite dramatically. Two variables can have a perfect correlation ($r = 1$), a strong correlation (e.g., $r = .90$), a moderate correlation (e.g., $r = .70$), or a weak correlation (e.g., $r = .30$). The correlation coefficient, then, is a measure of both the *direction* and *strength* of the relationship between two variables. The sign of r (plus or minus) tells us the direction of the relationship and the absolute value of r (between 0 and 1) tells us about the number of exceptions and hence about how confident we can be when using the correlation to make predictions.

> **What does it mean for a correlation to be strong?**

Causation

We observe correlations all the time: between automobiles and pollution, between bacon and heart attacks, between sex and pregnancy. **Natural correlations** are *the correlations observed in the world around us,* and although such observations can tell us whether two variables have a relationship, they cannot tell us what *kind* of relationship these variables have. For example, many studies have found a positive correlation between the amount of violence to which a child is exposed through media such as television, movies, and video games (variable X) and the aggressiveness of the child's behavior (variable Y; Anderson & Bushman, 2001; Anderson et al.,

It isn't always easy to detect causal relationships accurately. For centuries, people sacrificed their enemies without realizing that doing so doesn't actually cause rain, and they smoked cigarettes without realizing that doing so actually does cause illness.

THE GRANGER COLLECTION

APIC/GETTY IMAGES

2003; Huesmann et al., 2003). The more media violence a child is exposed to, the more aggressive that child is likely to be. These variables clearly have a relationship—they are imperfectly positively correlated—but why?

The Third-Variable Problem

One possibility is that exposure to media violence (X) causes aggressiveness (Y). For example, media violence may teach children that aggression is a reasonable way to vent anger and solve problems. A second possibility is that aggressiveness (Y) causes children to be exposed to media violence (X). For example, children who are naturally aggressive may be especially likely to seek opportunities to play violent video games

> **What is third-variable correlation?**

or watch violent movies. A third possibility is that a *third variable* (Z) causes children to be aggressive (Y) and to be exposed to media violence (X), neither of which is causally related to the other. For example, lack of adult supervision (Z) may allow children to get away with bullying others and to get away with watching television shows that adults would normally not allow. If so, then being exposed to media violence (X) and behaving aggressively (Y) may not be causally related to each other at all and may instead be the independent effects of a lack of adult supervision (Z). In other words, the relation between aggressiveness and exposure to media violence may be a case of **third-variable correlation,** which means that *two variables are correlated only because each is causally related to a third variable.* **FIGURE 2.9** shows three possible causes of any correlation.

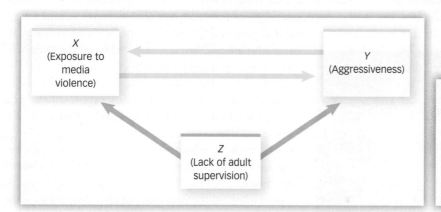

◄ Figure **2.9** **Causes of Correlation** If *X* (exposure to media violence) and *Y* (aggressiveness) are correlated, then there are at least three possible explanations: *X* causes *Y*, *Y* causes *X*, or *Z* (some other factor, such as lack of adult supervision) causes both *Y* and *X*, neither of which causes the other.

How can we determine by simple observation which of these three possibilities best describes the relationship between exposure to media violence and aggressiveness? Take a deep breath. The answer is: *We can't.* When we observe a natural correlation, the possibility of third-variable correlation can never be dismissed. But don't take this claim on faith. Let's try to dismiss the possibility of third-variable correlation and you'll see why such efforts are always doomed to fail.

The most straightforward way to determine whether a third variable, such as lack of adult supervision (Z), causes both exposure to media violence (X) and aggressive behavior (Y) is to eliminate differences in adult supervision (Z) among a group of children and see if the correlation between exposure (X) and aggressiveness (Y) is eliminated too. For example, we could observe children using the **matched samples technique,** which is *a technique whereby the participants in two groups are identical in terms of a third variable* (see **FIGURE 2.10**). For instance, we could measure only children who are supervised by an adult exactly $Q\%$ of the time, thus ensuring that every child who was exposed to media violence had

> **What's the difference between matched samples and matched pairs?**

natural correlation
A correlation observed in the world around us.

third-variable correlation
Two variables are correlated only because each is causally related to a third variable.

matched samples
A technique whereby the participants in two groups are identical in terms of a third variable.

▶ Figure **2.10** **Matched Sample and Pairs** Both the matched samples technique (*left*) and the matched pairs technique (*right*) ensure that children in the exposure and no-exposure groups have the same amount of adult supervision on average, and thus any differences we observe between the groups can't be due to differences in adult supervision.

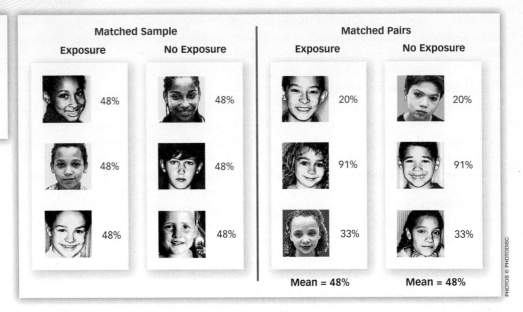

Matched Sample		Matched Pairs	
Exposure	**No Exposure**	**Exposure**	**No Exposure**
48%	48%	20%	20%
48%	48%	91%	91%
48%	48%	33%	33%
		Mean = 48%	**Mean = 48%**

PHOTOS © PHOTODISC

exactly the same amount of adult supervision as every child who was not exposed. Alternatively, we could observe children using the **matched pairs technique,** which is *a technique whereby each participant is identical to one other participant in terms of a third variable.* We could measure children who have different amounts of adult supervision, but we could make sure that for every child we measure who is exposed to media violence and is supervised *Q*% of the time, we also observe a child who is not exposed to media violence and is supervised *Q*% of the time, thus ensuring that chil-

dren who are and are not exposed to media violence have the same amount of adult supervision *on average.* Regardless of which technique we used, we would know that children who were and were not exposed to media violence had equal amounts of adult supervision on average. So if those who were exposed are on average more aggressive than those who were not exposed, we can be sure that lack of adult supervision was not the cause of this difference.

GEORGE MARKS/GETTY IMAGES

BETTMANN/CORBIS

In 1949, Dr. Benjamin Sandler noticed a correlation between the incidence of polio and ice cream consumption, and concluded that sugar made children susceptible to the disease. Public health officials issued warnings. As it turned out, a third variable—warm weather—caused both an increase in disease (viruses become more active in the summer) and an increase in ice cream consumption.

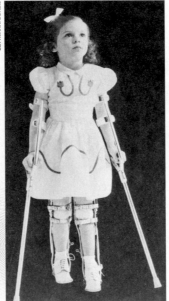

So we solved the problem, right? Well, not exactly. The matched samples technique and the matched pairs technique can be useful, but neither eliminates the possibility of third-variable correlation entirely. Why? Because even if we used these techniques to dismiss a *particular* third variable (such as lack of adult supervision), we would not be able to dismiss *all* third variables. For example, as soon as we finished making these observations, it might suddenly occur to us that emotional instability could cause children to gravitate toward violent television or video games and to behave aggressively. Emotional instability would be a new third variable (Z) and we would have to design a new test to investigate whether it explains the correlation between exposure (X) and aggression (Y). Unfortunately, we could keep dreaming up new third variables all day long without ever breaking a sweat, and every time we dreamed one up, we would have to rush out and do a new test using matched samples or matched pairs to determine whether *this* third variable was the cause of the correlation between exposure and aggressiveness.

Are you starting to see the problem? There are a humongous number of third variables, so there are a humongous number of reasons why X and Y might be correlated.

And because we can't perform a humongous number of studies with matched samples or matched pairs, we cannot be absolutely sure that the correlation we observe between *X* and *Y* is evidence of a causal relationship between them. The **third-variable problem** refers to the fact that *a causal relationship between two variables cannot be inferred from the naturally occurring correlation between them because of the ever-present possibility of third-variable correlation.* In other words, if we care about causality, then naturally occurring correlations just won't tell us what we really want to know. Luckily, another technique will.

Experimentation

The matched pairs and matched samples techniques eliminate a single difference between two groups: for example, the difference in adult supervision between groups of children who were and were not exposed to media violence. The problem is that they only eliminate one difference and a humongous number remain. If we could just find a technique that eliminated *all* of the humongous number of differences then we *could* conclude that exposure and aggression are causally related. If exposed kids were more aggressive than unexposed kids, and if the two groups didn't differ in *any* way except for that exposure, then we could be sure that their level of exposure had caused their level of aggression.

> **What are the two main features of an experiment?**

In fact, scientists have a technique that does exactly that. It is called an **experiment,** which is *a technique for establishing the causal relationship between variables.* The best way to understand how experiments eliminate all the differences between groups is by examining their two key features: *manipulation* and *random assignment.*

Manipulation

The most important thing to know about experiments is that you already know the most important thing about experiments because you've been doing them all your life. Imagine that you are surfing the Web on a laptop when all of a sudden you lose your wireless connection. You suspect that another device—say, your roommate's new cell phone—has somehow bumped you off the network. What would you do to test your suspicion? Observing a natural correlation wouldn't be much help. You could carefully note when you did and didn't have a connection and when your roommate did and didn't use his cell phone, but even if you observed a correlation between these two variables you still couldn't conclude that the cell phone was *causing* you to lose your network connection. After all, if your roommate was afraid of loud noises and called his mommy for comfort whenever there was an electrical storm, and if that storm zapped your router and crashed your wireless network, then the storm (*Z*) would be the cause of both your roommate's cell phone usage (*X*) and your connectivity problem (*Y*).

So how could you test your suspicion? Well, rather than *observing* the correlation between cell phone usage and connectivity, you could try to *create* a correlation by intentionally making a call on your roommate's cell phone, hanging up, making another call, hanging up again, and observing changes in your laptop's connectivity as you did so. If you observed that "laptop connection off" only occurred in conjunction with "cell phone on" then you could conclude that your roommate's cell phone was the *cause* of your failed connection, and you could sell the phone on eBay and then lie about it when asked. The technique you intuitively used to solve the third-variable problem is called **manipulation,** which involves *changing a variable in order to determine its causal power.* Congratulations! You are now officially a manipulator.

(a)   (b)

Where should you put the "sign up" button on a Web page? Developers often create two versions of their Webpages. Some visitors see one version, some see the other, and the developer measures the number of clicks that each version elicits. Developers call this "A/B Testing," but scientists just call it experimentation.

matched pairs
A technique whereby each participant is identical to one other participant in terms of a third variable.

third-variable problem
The fact that a causal relationship between two variables cannot be inferred from the naturally occurring correlation between them because of the ever-present possibility of third-variable correlation.

experiment
A technique for establishing the causal relationship between variables.

manipulation
Changing a variable in order to determine its causal power.

Manipulation is a critical ingredient in experimentation. Until now, we have approached science like polite dinner guests, taking what we were offered and making the best of it. Nature offered us children who differed in how much violence they were exposed to and who differed in how aggressively they behaved, and we dutifully measured the natural patterns of variation in these two variables and computed their correlations. The problem with this approach is that when all was said and done, we still didn't know what we really wanted to know, namely, whether these variables had a causal relationship. No matter how many matched samples or matched pairs we observed, there was always another third variable that we hadn't yet dismissed. Experiments solve this problem. Rather than *measuring* exposure and *measuring* aggression and then computing the correlation between these two naturally occurring variables, experiments require that we *manipulate* exposure in exactly the same way that you manipulated your roommate's cell phone. In essence, we need to systematically switch exposure on and off in a group of children and then watch to see whether aggression goes on and off too.

> How do you determine whether eating 60 hot dogs will make you sick? You eat them one day, don't eat them the next day, and then see which day you barf. *That's manipulation!* BTW, in 2012, world champion Joey Chestnut ate 68 hot dogs in 10 minutes by folding them up. *That's manipulation too!*

AP PHOTO/HENNY RAY ABRAMS

There are many ways to do this. For example, we might ask some children to participate in an experiment, then have half of them play violent video games for an hour and make sure the other half does not. Then, at the end of the hour, we could measure the children's aggression and compare the measurements across the two groups. When we compared these measurements, we would essentially be computing the correlation between a variable that we manipulated (exposure) and a variable that we measured (aggression). Because we *manipulated* rather than *measured* exposure, we would never have to ask whether a third variable (such as lack of adult supervision) caused children to experience different levels of exposure. After all, we already *know* what caused that to happen. *We* did!

Experimentation involves three critical steps (and several ridiculously confusing terms):

independent variable
The variable that is manipulated in an experiment.

experimental group
The group of people who are exposed to a particular manipulation, as compared to the control group, in an experiment.

control group
The group of people who are not exposed to the particular manipulation, as compared to the experimental group, in an experiment.

dependent variable
The variable that is measured in a study.

self-selection
A problem that occurs when anything about a person determines whether he or she will be included in the experimental or control group.

> First, we perform a manipulation. We call *the variable that is manipulated* the **independent variable** because it is under our control, and thus it is "independent" of what the participant says or does. When we manipulate an independent variable (such as exposure to media violence), we create at least two groups of participants: an **experimental group,** which is *the group of people who are exposed to a particular manipulation,* and a **control group,** which is *the group of people who are not exposed to that particular manipulation.*

> Second, having manipulated one variable (exposure), we now measure another variable (aggression). We call *the variable that is measured* the **dependent variable** because its value "depends" on what the person being measured says or does.

> Third and finally, we look to see whether our manipulation of the independent variable produced changes in the dependent variable. **FIGURE 2.11** shows exactly how manipulation works.

> **What are the three main steps in doing an experiment?**

Random Assignment

Once we have manipulated an independent variable and measured a dependent variable, we've done one of the two things that experimentation requires. The second

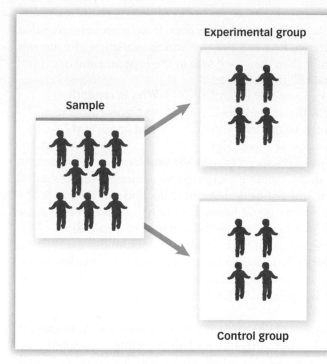

Experimental group

Exposed to media violence?	Aggression
Yes	High
Yes	High
Yes	High
Yes	High

Sample

Exposed to media violence?	Aggression
No	Low
No	Low
No	Low
No	Low

Control group

◄ Figure **2.11** **Manipulation** The independent variable is exposure to media violence and the dependent variable is aggression. Manipulation of the independent variable results in an experimental group and a control group. When we compare the behavior of participants in these two groups, we are actually computing the correlation between the independent variable and the dependent variable.

thing is a little less intuitive but equally important. Imagine that we began our exposure and aggression experiment by finding a group of children and asking each child whether he or she would like to be in the experimental group or the control group. Imagine that half the children said that they'd like to play violent video games and the other half said they would rather not. Imagine that we let the children do what they wanted to do, measured aggression some time later, and found that the children who had played the violent video games were more aggressive than those who had not. Would this experiment allow us to conclude that playing violent video games causes aggression? Definitely not—but *why* not? After all, we switched exposure on and off like a cell phone, and we watched to see whether aggression went on and off too. So where did we go wrong?

We went wrong when we let the children decide for themselves whether or not they would play violent video games. After all, children who ask to play such games

Why can't we allow people to select the condition of the experiment in which they will participate?

are probably different in many ways from those who ask not to. They may be older, or stronger, or smarter—or younger, weaker, or dumber—or less often supervised or more often supervised. The list of possible differences goes on and on. The whole point of doing an experiment was to divide children into two groups that differed *in only one way,* namely, in terms of their exposure to media violence. The moment we let the children decide for themselves whether they would be in the experimental group or the control group, we had two groups that differed in countless ways, and any of those countless differences could have been a third variable that was responsible for any differences we may have observed in their measured aggression. **Self-selection** is *a problem that occurs when anything about a person determines whether he or she will be included in the experimental or control group.* Just as we cannot allow nature to decide which of the children in our study is exposed to media violence, we cannot allow the children to decide either. Okay, then who decides?

There is no evidence that Louise Hay's techniques can cure cancer. But even if cancer victims who bought her books *did* show a higher rate of remission than those who didn't, there would *still* be no evidence because buyers are self-selected and thus may differ from non-buyers in countless ways.

INGRAM PUBLISHING/GETTY IMAGES

ROBERT DALY/GETTY IMAGES

Do strawberries taste better when dipped in chocolate? If you dip the big juicy ones and don't dip the small dry ones, then you won't know if the chocolate is what made the difference. But if you randomly assign some to be dipped and others not to be dipped, and if the dipped ones taste better on average, then you will have demonstrated scientifically what every 3-year-old already knows.

The answer to this question is a bit spooky: *No one does.* If we want to be sure that there is one and only one difference between the children in our study who are and are not exposed to media violence, then their inclusion in the experimental or control groups must be *randomly determined.* If you flipped a coin and a friend asked what had *caused* it to land heads up, you would correctly say that *nothing* had. This is what it means for the outcome of a coin flip to be random. Because the outcome of a coin flip is random, we can put coin flips to work for us to solve the problem that self-selection creates. If we want to be sure that a child's inclusion in the experimental or control group was not caused by nature, was not caused by the child, and was not caused by *any* of the countless third variables we could name if we only had the time to name them, then all we have to do is let it be caused by the outcome of a coin flip—which itself has no cause! For example, we could walk up to each child in our experiment, flip a coin, and, if the coin lands heads up, assign the child to play violent video games. If the coin lands heads down, then we could assign the child to play no violent video games. **Random assignment** is a *procedure that lets chance assign people to the experimental or the control group.*

> **Why is random assignment so useful and important?**

What would happen if we assigned children to groups with a coin flip? As **FIGURE 2.12** shows, the first thing we would expect is that about half the children would be assigned to play violent video games and about half would not. Second—and *much* more important—we could expect the experimental group and the control group to have roughly equal numbers of supervised kids and unsupervised kids, roughly equal numbers of emotionally stable and unstable kids, roughly equal numbers of big kids and small kids, of active kids, fat kids, tall kids, funny kids, and kids with blue hair named Larry McSweeny. In other words, we could expect the two groups to have roughly equal numbers of kids who are anything-you-can-ever-name-and-everything-you-can't! Because the kids in the two groups will be the same *on average* in terms of height, weight, emotional stability, adult supervision, and every other variable in the known universe *except the one we manipulated*, we can be sure that the variable we manipulated (exposure) was the one and only cause of any changes in the variable we measured (aggression). Because exposure was the *only* difference between the two

▶ Figure **2.12 Random Assignment** Children with adult supervision are shown in orange and those without adult supervision are shown in blue. The independent variable is exposure to media violence and the dependent variable is aggression. Random assignment ensures that participants in the experimental and the control groups are on average equal in terms of all possible third variables. In essence, it ensures that there is no correlation between a third variable and the dependent variable.

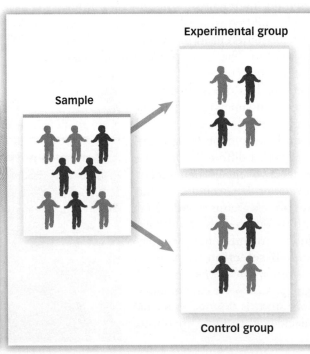

Experimental group

Sample

Exposed to media violence?	Adult supervision?	Aggression
Yes	Yes	High
Yes	No	High
Yes	Yes	High
Yes	No	High

Exposed to media violence?	Adult supervision?	Aggression
No	Yes	Low
No	No	Low
No	Yes	Low
No	No	Low

Control group

groups of children when we started the experiment, it *must* be the cause of any differences in aggression we observe at the end of the experiment.

Significance

Random assignment is a powerful tool, but like a lot of tools, it doesn't work every time you use it. If we randomly assigned children to watch or not watch televised violence, we could expect the two groups to have roughly equal numbers of supervised and unsupervised kids, roughly equal numbers of emotionally stable and unstable kids, and so on. The key word in that sentence is *roughly*. When you flip a coin 100 times, you can expect it to land heads up *roughly* 50 times. But every once in a while, 100 coin flips will produce 80 heads, or 90 heads, or even 100 heads, by sheer chance alone. This does not happen often, of course, but it does happen. Because random assignment is achieved by using a randomizing device such as a coin, every once in a long while the coin will assign more unsupervised, emotionally unstable kids to play violent video games and more supervised, emotionally stable kids to play none. When this happens, random assignment has failed—and when random assignment fails, the third-variable problem rises up out of its grave like a guy with a hockey mask and

random assignment
A procedure that lets chance assign people to the experimental or control group.

THE REAL WORLD

Oddsly Enough

A recent Gallup survey found that 53% of college graduates believe in extrasensory perception, or ESP. Very few psychologists share that belief. What makes them such a skeptical lot is their understanding of the laws of probability.

Consider the case of The Truly Amazing Coincidence. One night you dream that a panda is piloting an airplane over the Indian Ocean, and the next day you tell a friend, who says, "Wow, I had exactly the same dream!" One morning you wake up humming an old Radiohead tune (probably "Paranoid Android") and an hour later you hear it playing in the mall. You and your roommate are sitting around watching television when suddenly you turn to each other and say in perfect unison, "Want pizza?" Coincidences like these might make anyone believe in supernatural mental weirdness.

Well, not anyone. The Nobel laureate Luis Alvarez was reading the newspaper one day and a particular story got him thinking about an old college friend whom he hadn't seen in years. A few minutes later, he turned the page and was shocked to see the very same friend's obituary. But before concluding that he had an acute case of ESP, Alvarez decided to use probability theory to determine just how amazing this coincidence really was.

First he estimated the number of friends an average person has, and then he estimated how often an average person thinks about each of those friends. With these estimates in hand, he did a few simple calculations and determined the likelihood that someone would think about a friend five minutes before learning about that friend's death. The odds were astonishing. In a country the size of the United States, for example, Alvarez predicted that this amazing coincidence should happen to 10 people every day (Alvarez, 1965). Another Nobel laureate disagreed. He put the number closer to 80 people a day (Charpak & Broch, 2004)!

"In 10 years there are 5 million minutes," says statistics professor Irving Jack. "That means each person has plenty of opportunity to have some remarkable coincidences in his life" (quoted in Neimark, 2004). For example, 250 million Americans dream for about two hours every night (that's a half billion hours of dreaming!), so it isn't surprising that two people sometimes have the same dream, or that we sometimes dream about something that actually happens the next day. As mathematics professor John Allen Paulos (quoted in Neimark, 2004) put it, "In reality, the most astonishingly incredible coincidence imaginable would be the complete absence of all coincidence."

If all of this seems surprising to you, then you are not alone. Research shows that people routinely underestimate the likelihood of coincidences happening by chance (Diaconis & Mosteller, 1989; Falk & McGregor, 1983; Hintzman, Asher, & Stern, 1978). If you want to profit from this fact, assemble a group of 24 or more people and bet anyone that at least 2 of the people share a birthday. The odds are in your favor, and the bigger the group, the better the odds. In fact, in a group of 35, the odds are 85%. Happy fleecing!

"Idaho! What a coincidence—I'm from Idaho."

MICHAEL MASLIN ©THE NEW YORKER COLLECTION/WWW.CARTOONBANK.COM

Scientists take a solemn oath to wear this T-shirt under their clothing at all times.

a grudge. When random assignment fails, we cannot conclude that there is a causal relationship between the independent and dependent variables.

How can we tell when random assignment has failed? Unfortunately, we can't tell for sure. But we can calculate the *odds* that random assignment has failed each time we use it. It isn't important for you to know how to do this calculation, but it is important for you to understand how psychologists interpret its results. Psychologists perform this calculation every time they do an experiment, and they do not accept the results of those experiments unless the calculation tells them that if random assignment had failed, then there is less than a 5% chance that they would have seen those particular results.

When there is less than a 5% chance that a result would happen if random assignment had failed, then that result is said to be *statistically significant*. You've already learned about descriptive statistics, such as the mean, median, mode, range, and standard deviation. There is another kind of statistics—called *inferential statistics*—that tells scientists what kinds of conclusions or inferences they can draw from observed differences between the experimental and control groups. For example, p (for "probability") is an inferential statistic that tells psychologists the likelihood that random assignment failed in a particular experiment. When psychologists report that $p < .05$, they are saying that according to the inferential statistics they calculated, the odds that their results would have occurred if random assignment had failed are less than 5%, and given that those results *did* occur, a failure of random assignment is unlikely to have happened. Therefore, differences between the experimental and control groups were unlikely to have been caused by a third variable.

Drawing Conclusions

If we applied all the techniques discussed so far, we could design an experiment that had a very good chance of establishing the causal relationship between two variables. That experiment would have **internal validity,** which is *an attribute of an experiment that allows it to establish causal relationships*. When we say that an experiment is internally valid, we mean that everything *inside* the experiment is working exactly as it must in order for us to draw conclusions about causal relationships. But what exactly are those conclusions? If our imaginary experiment revealed a difference between the aggressiveness of children in the exposed and unexposed groups, then we could conclude that media violence *as we defined it* caused aggression *as we defined it* in the people *whom we studied*. Notice those phrases in italics. Each corresponds to an important restriction on the kinds of conclusions we can draw from an experiment, so let's consider each in turn.

Representative Variables

The results of any experiment depend, in part, on how the independent and dependent variables are defined. For instance, we are more likely to find that exposure to media violence causes aggression when we define exposure as "watching two hours of gory axe murders" rather than "watching 10 minutes of football," or when we define aggression as "interrupting another person" rather than "smacking someone silly with a tire iron." The way we define variables can have a profound influence on what we find, so which of these is the *right* way?

One answer is that we should define variables in an experiment as they are defined in the real world. **External validity** is *an attribute of an experiment in which variables have been defined in a normal, typical, or realistic way*. It seems pretty clear that the kind of aggressive behavior that concerns teachers and parents lies somewhere between an interruption and an assault, and that the kind of media violence to which children are typically exposed

Why isn't external validity necessary?

lies somewhere between sports and torture. If the goal of an experiment is to determine whether the kinds of media violence to which children are typically exposed causes the kinds of aggression with which societies are typically concerned, then external validity is essential. When variables are defined in an experiment as they typically are in the real world, we say that the variables are *representative* of the real world.

External validity sounds like such a good idea that you may be surprised to learn that most psychology experiments are externally *in*valid—and that most psychologists don't mind. The reason for this is that psychologists are rarely trying to learn about the real world by creating tiny replicas of it in their laboratories. Rather, they are usually trying to learn about the real world by using experiments to test hypotheses derived from theories, and externally invalid experiments can often do that quite nicely (Mook, 1983).

Does piercing make a person more or less attractive? The answer, of course, depends entirely on how you operationally define *piercing.*

To see how, consider an example from physics. Physicists have a theory stating that heat is the result of the rapid movement of molecules. This theory gives rise to a hypothesis, namely, that when the molecules that constitute an object are slowed, the object should become cooler. Now imagine that a physicist tested this hypothesis by performing an experiment in which a laser was used to slow the movement of the molecules in a rubber ball, whose temperature was then measured. Would you criticize this experiment by saying, "Sorry, but your experiment teaches us nothing about the real world because in the real world, no one actually uses lasers to slow the movement of the molecules in rubber balls"? Let's hope not. The physicist's theory (molecular motion causes heat) led to a hypothesis about *what would happen in the laboratory* (slowing the molecules in a rubber ball should cool it), and the events that the physicist manipulated and measured in the laboratory served to test the theory. Similarly, a well thought out theory about the causal relationship between exposure to media violence and aggression should lead to hypotheses about how children in a laboratory will behave after watching a violent movie, and thus their reaction to the movie serves to test the theory. If children who watched *Iron Man* 3 were more likely to push and shove each other on their way out of the laboratory, then any theory that says that media violence cannot influence aggression has just been proved wrong.

In short, theories allow us to generate hypotheses about what can, must, or will happen under particular circumstances, and experiments are usually meant to create those circumstances, test the hypotheses, and thereby provide evidence for or against the theories that generated them. Experiments are not usually meant to be miniature versions of everyday life, and thus external invalidity is not necessarily a problem (see the Hot Science box, Do Violent Movies Make Peaceful Streets?).

Representative People

Our imaginary experiment on exposure to media violence and aggression would allow us to conclude that exposure as we defined it caused aggression as we defined it in the people *whom we studied.* That last phrase represents another important restriction on the kinds of conclusions we can draw from experiments.

Who are the people whom psychologists study? Psychologists rarely observe an entire **population,** which is *a complete collection of people,* such as the population of human beings (about 7 billion), the population of Californians (about 38 million), or the population of people with Down syndrome (about 1 million). Rather, they observe

internal validity
An attribute of an experiment that allows it to establish causal relationships.

external validity
An attribute of an experiment in which variables have been defined in a normal, typical, or realistic way.

population
A complete collection of participants who might possibly be measured.

Do Violent Movies Make Peaceful Streets?

In 2000, the American Academy of Pediatrics and five other public health organizations issued a joint statement warning about the risks of exposure to media violence. They cited evidence from psychological experiments in which children and young adults who were exposed to violent movie clips showed a sharp increase in aggressive behavior immediately afterward. They noted that "well over 1,000 studies . . . point overwhelmingly to a causal connection between media violence and aggressive behavior."

Given the laboratory results, we might expect to see a correlation in the real world between the number of people who see violent movies in theaters and the number of violent crimes. When economists Gordon Dahl and Stefano Della Vigna (2009) analyzed crime statistics and box office statistics, they found just such a correlation—except that it was negative! In other words, on eve-

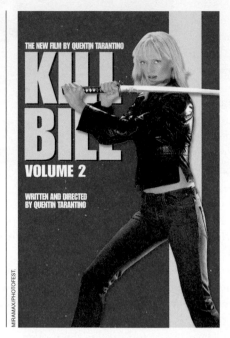

nings when more people went to the theatre to watch violent movies, there were *fewer* violent crimes. Why? The researchers suggested that violent movies are especially appealing to the people who are most likely to commit violent crimes. Because those people are busy watching movies for a few hours, violent crime drops. In other words, blood-and-bullet movies take criminals off the street by luring them to the theater!

Laboratory experiments clearly show that exposure to media violence *can* cause aggression. But as the movie theater data remind us, experiments are a tool for establishing the causal relationships between variables and are not meant to be miniature versions of the real world, where things are ever so much more complex.

◄ One thing we know about the people who went to see the movie *Kill Bill 2* is that for several hours they didn't shoot anybody.

a **sample,** which is *a partial collection of people drawn from a population.* How big can a sample be? The size of a population is signified by the uppercase letter N, the size of a sample is signified by the lowercase letter n, so $0 < n < N$. If you read this as an emoticon it means . . . oh well, never mind.

In most studies n is closer to 0 than to N, and in some cases $n = 1$. For example, sometimes single individuals are so remarkable that they deserve close study, and when psychologists study them they use the **case method,** which is *a procedure for gathering scientific information by studying a single individual.* We can learn a lot about memory by studying someone like Akira Haraguchi, who can recite the first 100,000 digits of pi; about consciousness by studying someone like Henry Molaison, whose ability to look backward and forward in time was destroyed by damage to his brain; about intelligence and creativity by studying someone like 14-year-old Jay Greenburg, whose musical compositions have been recorded by the Julliard String Quartet and the London Symphony Orchestra. Cases such as these are interesting in their own right, but they also provide important insights into how the rest of us work.

Of course, most of the psychological studies you will read about in this book included samples of ten, a hundred, a thousand, or a few thousand people. So how do psychologists decide which people to include in their samples? One way to select a sample from a population is by **random sampling,** which is *a technique for choosing participants that ensures that every member of a population has an equal chance of being included in the sample.* When we randomly sample participants from a population, the sample is said to be *representative* of the population. This allows us to *generalize* from the sample to the population—that is, to conclude that what we observed in our sample would also have been observed if we had measured the entire population. You probably already have solid intuitions about the importance of random sampling. For example, if you stopped at a farm stand to buy a bag of cherries and the farmer offered

What is the difference between a population and a sample?

Jay Greenburg was just 15 years old when his first CD was released—a recording of the London Symphony Orchestra performing his *5th Symphony.*

ULLSTEIN BILD/THE GRANGER COLLECTION

REUTERS/JIM YOUNG

Nonrandom sampling can lead to errors. In the presidential election of 1948, the *Chicago Tribune* mistakenly predicted that Thomas Dewey would beat Harry Truman. Why? Because polling was done by telephone, and Dewey Republicans were more likely to have telephones than were Truman Democrats. In the presidential election of 2004, exit polls mistakenly predicted that John Kerry would beat George Bush. Why? Because polling was done by soliciting voters as they left the polls, and Kerry supporters were more willing to stop and talk.

to let you taste a few that he had handpicked from the bag, you'd be reluctant to generalize from that sample to the population of cherries in the bag. But if the farmer invited you to pull a few cherries from the bag at random, you'd probably be willing to take those cherries as representative of the cherry population.

Random sampling sounds like such a good idea that you might be surprised to learn that most psychological studies involve nonrandom samples—and that most psychologists don't mind. Indeed, virtually every participant in every psychology experiment you will ever read about was a volunteer, and most were college students who were

> **If random sampling is good, why isn't it necessary?**

significantly younger, smarter, healthier, wealthier, and Whiter than the average Earthling. About 96% of the people whom psychologists study come from countries that have just 12% of the world's population, and 70% come from the United States alone (Henrich, Heine, & Norenzayan, 2010).

So why do psychologists sample nonrandomly? They have no choice. Even if there were a computerized list of all the world's human inhabitants from which we could randomly choose our research participants, how would we ever *find* the 72-year-old Bedouin woman whose family roams the desert so that we could measure the electrical activity in her brain while she watched cartoons? How would we convince the 3-week-old infant in New Delhi to complete a lengthy questionnaire about his political beliefs? Most psychology experiments are conducted by professors and graduate students at colleges and universities in the Western hemisphere, and as much as they might *like* to randomly sample the population of the planet, the practical truth is that they are pretty much stuck studying the folks who volunteer for their studies.

> **Why is nonrandom sampling a nonfatal flaw?**

So how can we learn *anything* from psychology experiments? Isn't the failure to sample randomly a fatal flaw? No, it's not, and there are three reasons why. First, sometimes the similarity of a sample and a population doesn't matter. If one pig flew over the Statue of Liberty just one time, it would instantly disprove the traditional theory of porcine locomotion. It wouldn't matter if all pigs flew or if any other pigs flew. If one did, then that's enough. An experimental result can be illuminating even when the sample isn't typical of the population.

Second, when the ability to generalize an experimental result *is* important, psychologists perform new experiments that use the same procedures but on different samples. For example, after measuring how a nonrandomly selected group of American children behaved after playing violent video games, we might try to replicate our

sample
A partial collection of people drawn from a population.

case method
A procedure for gathering scientific information by studying a single individual.

random sampling
A technique for choosing participants that ensures that every member of a population has an equal chance of being included in the sample.

experiment with Japanese children, or with American teenagers, or with deaf adults. In essence, we could treat the attributes of our sample, such as culture and age and ability, as independent variables, and we could do experiments to determine whether these attributes influenced our dependent variable. If the results of our study were replicated in these other samples, then we would be more confident (but never completely confident) that the results describe a basic human tendency. If the results do not replicate, then we would learn something about the influence of culture or age or ability on aggressiveness. Replicating research with new samples drawn from different populations is a win–win strategy: No matter what happens, we learn something interesting.

Third, sometimes the similarity of the sample and the population is simply a reasonable starting assumption. Instead of asking, "Do I have a compelling reason to believe that my sample is representative of the population?" we could instead ask, "Do I have a compelling reason not to?" For example, few of us would be willing to take an experimental medicine if a nonrandom sample of 7 participants took it and died. Indeed, we would probably refuse the medicine even if the 7 participants were mice. Although these nonrandomly sampled participants were different from us in many ways (including tails and whiskers), most of us would be willing to generalize from their experience to ours because we know that even mice share enough of our basic biology to make it a good bet that what harms them can harm us too. By this same reasoning, if a psychology experiment demonstrated that some American children behaved violently after playing violent video games, we might ask whether there is a compelling reason to suspect that Ecuadorian college students or middle-aged Australians would behave any differently. If the answer was yes, then experiments would provide a way for us to investigate that possibility.

Thinking Critically about Evidence

In 1620, Sir Francis Bacon published a book called *Novum Organum* in which he described a new method for discovering the truth about the natural world. Today, his so-called Baconian Method is more simply known as the scientific method, and that method has allowed human beings to learn more in the last four centuries than in all the previous centuries combined.

As you've seen in this chapter, the scientific method allows us to produce empirical evidence. But empirical evidence is only useful if we know how to think about it, and the fact is that most of us don't. Using evidence requires *critical thinking*, which involves asking ourselves tough questions about whether we have interpreted the evidence in an unbiased way, and about whether the evidence tells not just the truth, but the *whole* truth. Research suggests that most people have trouble doing both of these things, and that educational programs designed to teach or improve critical thinking skills are not particularly effective (Willingham, 2007). Why do people have so much trouble thinking critically?

Consider the armadillo. Some animals freeze when threatened, and others duck, run, or growl. Armadillos jump. This natural tendency served armadillos quite well for millennia because for millennia the most common threat to an armadillo's well-being was a rattlesnake. Alas, this natural tendency serves armadillos rather poorly today because when they wander onto a Texas highway and are threatened by a speeding car, they jump up and hit the bumper. This is a mistake no armadillo makes twice.

Human beings also have natural tendencies that once served them well but no longer do. Our natural and intuitive ways of thinking about evidence, for example, worked just fine when we were all hunter-gatherers living in small groups on the African savannah. But now most of us live in large-scale, complex societies, and these natural ways of thinking interfere with our ability to reason in the modern world. Sir Francis Bacon understood this quite well. In the very same book in which he developed the

This mouse died after drinking the green stuff. Want to drink the green stuff? Why not? You're not a mouse, are you?

Sir Francis Bacon (1561–1626) is credited with having devised the scientific method, which he used until he died from pneumonia, which he caught while studying the effects of low temperatures on the preservation of meat.

scientific method, he argued that two ancient and all-too-human tendencies—to see what we expect or want to see and to ignore what we can't see—are the enemies of critical thinking.

We See What We Expect and Want

When two people are presented with the same evidence, they often draw different conclusions. Sir Francis Bacon knew why. "The human understanding, once it has adopted opinions... draws everything else to support and agree with them," thus our "first conclusion colors and brings into conformity with itself all that come after." In other words, our preexisting beliefs color our view of new evidence, causing us to see what we expect to see. As such, evidence often seems to confirm what we believed all along.

This tendency has been widely documented in psychological science. For instance, participants in one study (Darley & Gross, 1983) learned about a little girl named Hannah. One group of participants was told that Hannah came from an affluent family and another group was told that Hannah came from a poor family. All participants were then shown some evidence about Hannah's academic abilities (specifically, they watched a video of Hannah taking a reading test) and were then asked to rate Hannah. Although the video was exactly the same for all participants, those who believed that Hannah was affluent rated her performance more positively than did those who believed that Hannah was poor. What's more, both groups of participants defended their conclusions by citing evidence from the video! Experiments like this one suggest that when we consider evidence, what we see depends on what we *expected* to see.

Our beliefs aren't the only things that color our views of evidence. Those views are also colored by our preferences and prejudices, our ambitions and aversions, our hopes and needs and wants and dreams. As Bacon noted, "The human understanding is not a dry light, but is infused by desire and emotion which give rise to wishful science. For man prefers to believe what he wants to be true."

Research suggests that Bacon was right about this as well. For example, participants in one study (Lord, Ross, & Lepper, 1979) were shown some scientific evidence about the effectiveness of the death penalty. Some of the evidence suggested that the death penalty deterred crime, and some suggested it did not. What did participants make of this mixed bag of evidence? Participants who originally supported the death penalty became even *more* supportive, and participants who originally opposed the death penalty became even *more* opposed. In other words, when presented with exactly the same evidence, participants saw what they *wanted* to see and ended up feeling even more sure about their initial views. Subsequent research has shown that the same pattern emerges when professional scientists are asked to rate the quality of scientific studies that either confirm or disconfirm what they want to believe (Koehler, 1993).

Exactly how do beliefs and desires shape our view of the evidence? People hold different kinds of evidence to different standards. When evidence confirms what we believe or want to believe, we tend to ask ourselves, "*can* I believe it?" and our answer is usually yes; but when evidence disconfirms what we believe or want to believe, we tend to ask ourselves, "*must* I believe it?" and the answer is often no (Gilovich, 1991). *Can* you believe that people with college degrees are happier than people without them? Yes! There are plenty of surveys showing that just such a relation-

> **How do our beliefs and desires shape the way we think about evidence?**

ship exists and a reasonable person who studied the evidence could easily defend this conclusion. Now, *must* you believe it? Well, no. After all, those surveys didn't measure every single person on earth, did they? And if the survey questions had been asked differently they might well have produced different answers, right? A reasonable person who studied the evidence could easily conclude that the relationship between education and happiness is not yet clear enough to warrant an opinion.

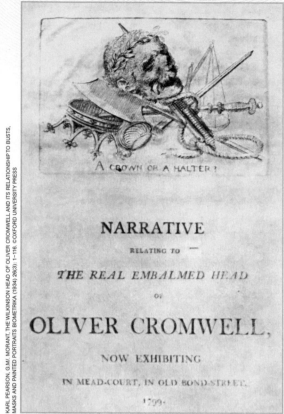

KARL PEARSON, G.M. MORANT, THE WILKINSON HEAD OF OLIVER CROMWELL AND ITS RELATIONSHIP TO BUSTS, MASKS AND PAINTED PORTRAITS BIOMETRIKA (1934) 26(3): 1–116. ©OXFORD UNIVERSITY PRESS

In 1650, the Lord Protector of England, Oliver Cromwell, wrote to the Church of Scotland and said, "I beseech you, in the bowels of Christ, think it possible that you may be mistaken," and his colorful plea is today known as *Cromwell's rule*, which advises us to be less sure than we are, no matter how sure we are! After Cromwell died, his embalmed head (shown in the photo) changed hands for nearly 200 years, and in 1960 was donated to Sidney Sussex College.

Our beliefs and desires also influence *which* evidence we consider in the first place. Most people surround themselves with others who believe what they believe and want what they want, which means that our friends and families are much more likely to validate our beliefs and desires than to challenge them. Studies also show that when given the opportunity to search for evidence, people preferentially search for evidence that confirms their beliefs and fulfills their desires (Hart et al., 2009). What's more, when people find evidence that confirms their beliefs and fulfills their desires, they tend to stop looking, but when they find evidence that does the opposite, they keep searching for more evidence (Kunda, 1990).

What all of these studies suggest is that evidence leaves room for interpretation, and that's the room in which our beliefs and desires spend most of their time. Because it is so easy to see what we expect to see or to see what we want to see, the first step in critical thinking is simply to doubt your own conclusions. One of the best ways to reduce your own certainty is to seek out people who doubt you and listen carefully to what they have to say. Scientists go out of their way to expose themselves to criticism by sending their papers to the colleagues who are most likely to disagree with them or by presenting their findings to audiences full of critics, and they do this in large part so they can achieve a more balanced view of their own conclusions. If you want to be happy, take your friend to lunch; if you want to be right, take your enemy.

We Consider What We See and Ignore What We Don't

In another part of his remarkable book, Sir Francis Bacon recounted an old story about a man who visited a Roman temple. The priest showed the man a portrait of several sailors who had taken religious vows and then miraculously survived a shipwreck, and suggested that this was clear evidence of the power of the gods. The visitor paused a moment and then asked precisely the right question: "But where are the pictures of those who perished after taking their vows?" According to Bacon, most of us never think to ask this kind of question. We consider the evidence we can see and forget about the evidence we can't. Bacon claimed that "little or no attention is paid to things invisible" and he argued that this natural tendency was "the greatest impediment and aberration of the human understanding."

Bacon was right when he claimed that people rarely consider what they can't see. For example, participants in one study (Newman, Wolff, & Hearst, 1980) played a game in which they were shown a set of trigrams, which are three-letter combinations such as *SXY*, *GTR*, *BCG*, and *EVX*. On each trial, the experimenter pointed to one of the trigrams in the set and told the participants that *this* trigram was the special one. The participants' job was to figure out what made the special trigram so special. How many trials did it take before participants figured it out? It depended on the trigram's special feature. For half the participants, the special trigram was always the one that contained the letter *T*, and participants in this condition needed to see about 34 sets of trigrams before they figured out that the presence of *T* was what made the trigram special. But for the other half of the participants, the special trigram was always the one that *lacked* the letter *T*. How many trials did it take before participants figured it out? They *never* figured it out. Never. What this study shows is that we naturally consider the evidence we see and rarely, if ever, consider the evidence we don't.

The tendency to ignore missing evidence can cause us to draw all kinds of erroneous conclusions. Consider a study in which participants were randomly assigned to play one of two roles in a game (Ross, Amabile, & Steinmetz, 1977). The "quizmasters" were asked to make up a series of

Why is it important to consider unseen evidence?

difficult questions, and the "contestants" were asked to answer them. If you give this a quick try, you will discover that it's very easy to generate questions that you can answer but that most other people cannot. For example, think of the last city you visited. Now give someone the name of the hotel you stayed in and ask them what street it's on. Very few will know.

So participants who were cast in the role of quizmaster asked lots of clever-sounding questions and participants who were cast in the role of contestant gave lots of wrong answers. Now comes the interesting part. Quizmasters and contestants played this game while another participant—the observer—watched. After the game was over, the observer was asked to make some guesses about what the players were like in their everyday lives. The results were clear: observers consistently concluded that the quizmaster was a more knowledgeable person than the contestant! Observers *saw* the quizmaster asking sharp questions and *saw* the contestant saying "um, gosh, I don't know," and observers considered this evidence. What they failed to consider was the evidence they did *not* see. Specifically, they failed to consider what would have happened if the person who had been assigned to play the role of quizmaster had instead been assigned to play the role of contestant, and vice versa. If that had happened, then surely the contestant would have been the one asking clever questions and the quizmaster would have been the one struggling to answer them. Bottom line? If the first step in critical thinking is to doubt what you do see, then the second step is to consider what you don't.

No matter how well the contestants perform, Jeopardy host Alex Trebek always seems like the smartest guy on the stage. But would you still get that impression if contestants were given an opportunity to ask him a few questions?

The Skeptical Stance

Winston Churchill once said that democracy is the worst form of government, except for all the others. Similarly, science is not an infallible method for learning about the world; it's just a whole lot less fallible than the other methods. Science is a human enterprise, and humans make mistakes. They see what they expect to see, they see what they want to see, and they rarely consider what they can't see at all.

What makes science different than most other human enterprises is that science actively seeks to discover and remedy its own biases and errors. Scientists are constantly striving to make their observations more accurate and their reasoning more rigorous, and they invite anyone and everyone to examine their evidence and challenge their conclusions. As such, science is the ultimate democracy—one of the only institutions in the world in which the lowliest nobody can triumph over the most celebrated someone. When an unknown Swiss patent clerk named Albert Einstein challenged the greatest physicists of his day, he didn't have a famous name, a fancy degree, powerful friends, or a fat wallet. He just had evidence. And he prevailed for one reason: His evidence was right.

So think of the remaining chapters in this book as a report from the field—a description of the work that psychological scientists have done as they stumble toward knowledge. These chapters tell the story of the men and women who have put their faith in Sir Francis Bacon's method and used it to pry loose small pieces of the truth about who we are, how we work, and what we are all doing here together on the third stone from the sun. Read it with interest, but also with skepticism. Some of the things we are about to tell you simply aren't true; we just don't yet know which things they are. We invite you to think critically about what you read here, and everywhere else. Now, let the doubting begin.

IN SUMMARY

▶ To determine whether two variables are causally related, we must first determine whether they are related at all. This can be done by measuring each variable many times and then comparing the patterns of variation within each series of measurements. If the patterns covary, then the variables are correlated. Correlations allow us to predict the value of one variable from knowledge of the value of the other. The direction and strength of a correlation are measured by the correlation coefficient (r).

▶ Even when we observe a correlation between two variables, we can't conclude that they are causally related because there are an infinite number of third variables that might be causing them both. Experiments solve this third-variable problem by manipulating an independent variable, randomly assigning participants to the experimental and control groups that this manipulation creates, and measuring a dependent variable. These measurements are then compared across groups. If inferential statistics show that if random assignment failed, then the results would only happen 5% of the time, then differences in the measurements across groups are assumed to have been caused by the manipulation.

▶ An internally valid experiment establishes a causal relationship between variables as they were operationally defined and among the participants whom they included. When an experiment mimics the real world, it is externally valid. But most psychology experiments are not attempts to mimic the real world, but to test hypotheses derived from theories.

▶ Thinking critically about evidence is difficult because people have a natural tendency to see what they expect to see, to see what they want to see, and to consider what they see but not what they don't.

The Ethics of Science: First, Do No Harm

Somewhere along the way, someone probably told you that it isn't nice to treat people like objects. And yet, it may seem that psychologists do just that by creating situations that cause people to feel fearful or sad, to do things that are embarrassing or immoral, and to learn things about themselves and others that they might not really want to know. Don't be fooled by appearances. The fact is that psychologists go to great lengths to protect the well-being of their research participants, and they are bound by a code of ethics that is as detailed and demanding as the professional codes that bind physicians, lawyers, and accountants. That code requires that psychologists show respect for people, for animals, and for the truth. Let's examine each of these obligations in turn.

Respecting People

During World War II, Nazi doctors performed truly barbaric experiments on human subjects, such as removing organs or submerging them in ice water just to see how long it would take them to die. When the war ended, the international community developed the Nuremberg Code of 1947 and then the Declaration of Helsinki in 1964, which spelled out rules for the ethical treatment of human subjects. Unfortunately, not everyone obeyed them. For example, from 1932 until 1972, the U.S. Public Health Service conducted the infamous Tuskegee experiment in which 399 African American men with syphilis were denied treatment so that researchers could observe the progression of the disease. As one journalist noted, the government "used human beings as laboratory animals in a long and inefficient study of how long it takes syphilis to kill someone" (Coontz, 2008).

In 1974, the U.S. Congress created the National Commission for the Protection of Human Subjects of Biomedical and Behavioral Research. In 1979, the U.S. Department of Health, Education and Welfare released what came to be known as the Belmont Report, which described three basic principles that all research involving human subjects should follow. First, research should show *respect for persons* and their right to make decisions for and about themselves without undue influence or coercion. Second, research should be *beneficent*, which means that it should attempt to maximize benefits and reduce risks to the participant. Third, research should be *just*, which means that it should distribute benefits and risks equally to participants without prejudice toward particular individuals or groups.

<aside>
What are three features of ethical research?
</aside>

The specific ethical code that psychologists follow incorporates these basic principles and expands them. (You can find the American Psychological Association's *Ethical Principles of Psychologists and Code of Conduct* (2002) at http://www.apa.org/ethics/code/index.aspx.) Here are a few of the most important rules that govern the conduct of psychological research:

> *Informed consent:* Participants may not take part in a psychological study unless they have given **informed consent,** which is *a written agreement to participate in a study made by an adult who has been informed of all the risks that participation may entail.* This doesn't mean that the person must know everything about the study (e.g., the hypothesis), but it does mean that the person must know about anything that might potentially be harmful or painful. If people cannot give informed consent (e.g., because they are minors or are mentally incapable), then informed consent must be obtained from their legal guardians. And even after people give informed consent, they always have the right to withdraw from the study at any time without penalty.

> *Freedom from coercion:* Psychologists may not coerce participation. Coercion not only means physical and psychological coercion but monetary coercion as well. It is unethical to offer people large amounts of money to persuade them to do something that they might otherwise decline to do. College students may be invited to participate in studies as part of their training in psychology, but they are ordinarily offered the option of learning the same things by other means.

> *Protection from harm:* Psychologists must take every possible precaution to protect their research participants from physical or psychological harm. If there are two equally effective ways to study something, the psychologist must use the safer method. If no safe method is available, the psychologist may not perform the study.

> *Risk-benefit analysis:* Although participants may be asked to accept small risks, such as a minor shock or a small embarrassment, they may not even be *asked* to accept large risks, such as severe pain, psychological trauma, or any risk that is greater than the risks they would ordinarily take in their everyday lives. Furthermore, even when participants are asked to take small risks, the psychologist must first demonstrate that these risks are outweighed by the social benefits of the new knowledge that might be gained from the study.

> *Deception:* Psychologists may only use deception when it is justified by the study's scientific, educational, or applied value and when alternative procedures are not feasible. They may never deceive participants about any aspect of a study that could cause them physical or psychological harm or pain.

The man at this bar is upset. He just saw another man slip a drug into a woman's drink and he is alerting the bartender. What he doesn't know is that all the people at the bar are actors and that he is being filmed for the television show *What Would You Do?* Was it ethical for ABC to put this man in such a stressful situation without his consent? And how did men who didn't alert the bartender feel when they turned on their televisions months later and were confronted by their own shameful behavior?

informed consent
A written agreement to participate in a study made by an adult who has been informed of all the risks that participation may entail.

debriefing
A verbal description of the true nature and purpose of a study.

> *Debriefing*: If a participant is deceived in any way before or during a study, the psychologist must provide a **debriefing,** which is *a verbal description of the true nature and purpose of a study.* If the participant was changed in any way (e.g., made to feel sad), the psychologist must attempt to undo that change (e.g., ask the person to do a task that will make him or her happy) and restore the participant to the state he or she was in before the study.

> *Confidentiality*: Psychologists are obligated to keep private and personal information obtained during a study confidential.

These are just some of the rules that psychologists must follow. But how are those rules enforced? Almost all psychology studies are done by psychologists who work at colleges and universities. These institutions have institutional review boards (IRBs) that are composed of instructors and researchers, university staff, and laypeople from the community (e.g., business leaders or members of the clergy). If the research is federally funded (as much research is), then the law requires that the IRB include at least one nonscientist and one person who is not affiliated with the institution. A psychologist may conduct a study only after the IRB has reviewed and approved it.

As you can imagine, the code of ethics and the procedure for approval are so strict that many studies simply cannot be performed anywhere, by anyone, at any time. For example, psychologists would love to know how growing up without exposure to language affects a person's subsequent ability to speak and think, but they cannot ethically manipulate that variable in an experiment. They can only study the natural correlations between language exposure and speaking ability, and so may never be able to firmly establish the causal relationships between these variables. Indeed, there are many questions that psychologists will never be able to answer definitively because doing so would require unethical experiments that violate basic human rights.

Respecting Animals

Not all research participants have human rights because not all research participants are human. Some are chimpanzees, rats, pigeons, or other nonhuman animals. The American Psychological Association's code specifically describes the special rights of these nonhuman participants, and some of the more important ones are these:

> All procedures involving animals must be supervised by psychologists who are trained in research methods and experienced in the care of laboratory animals and who are responsible for ensuring appropriate consideration of the animal's comfort, health, and humane treatment.

> Psychologists must make reasonable efforts to minimize the discomfort, infection, illness, and pain of animals.

What steps must psychologists take to protect nonhuman subjects?

> Psychologists may use a procedure that subjects an animal to pain, stress, or privation only when an alternative procedure is unavailable and when the procedure is justified by the scientific, educational, or applied value of the study.

> Psychologists must perform all surgical procedures under appropriate anesthesia and must minimize an animal's pain during and after surgery.

That's good—but is it good enough? Some people don't think so. For example, philosopher Peter Singer (1975) argued that all creatures capable of feeling pain have the same fundamental rights, and that treating nonhumans differently than humans is a form of speciesism that is every bit as abhorrent as racism or sexism. Singer's philosophy has inspired groups such as People for the Ethical Treatment of Animals to call for an end to all research involving nonhuman animals. Unfortunately, it has also

PAUL MCERLANE/REUTERS/CORBIS

Some people consider it unethical to use animals for clothing or research. Others see an important distinction between these two purposes.

inspired some groups to attack psychologists who legally conduct such research. As two researchers (Ringach & Jentsch, 2009, p. 11417) recently reported:

> We have seen our cars and homes firebombed or flooded, and we have received letters packed with poisoned razors and death threats via e-mail and voicemail. Our families and neighbors have been terrorized by angry mobs of masked protesters who throw rocks, break windows, and chant that "you should stop or be stopped" and that they "know where you sleep at night." Some of the attacks have been cataloged as attempted murder. Adding insult to injury, misguided animal-rights militants openly incite others to violence on the Internet, brag about the resulting crimes, and go as far as to call plots for our assassination "morally justifiable."

Where do most people stand on this issue? The vast majority of Americans consider it morally acceptable to use nonhuman animals in research and say they would reject a governmental ban on such research (Kiefer, 2004; Moore, 2003). Indeed, most Americans eat meat, wear leather, and support the rights of hunters, which is to say that most Americans see a sharp distinction between animal and human rights. Science is not in the business of resolving moral controversies, and every individual must draw his or her own conclusions about this issue. But whatever position you take, it is important to note that only a small percentage of psychological studies involve animals, and only a small percentage of those studies cause animals pain or harm. Psychologists mainly study people, and when they do study animals, they mainly study their behavior.

"What if these guys in white coats who bring us food are, like, studying us and we're part of some kind of big experiment?"

MIKE TWOHY ©THE NEW YORKER COLLECTION

Respecting Truth

Institutional review boards ensure that data are collected ethically. But once the data are collected, who ensures that they are ethically analyzed and reported? No one does. Psychology, like all sciences, works on the honor system. No authority is charged with monitoring what psychologists do with the data they've collected, and no authority is charged with checking to see if the claims they make are true. You may find that a bit odd. After all, we don't use the honor system in stores ("Take the television set home and pay us next time you're in the neighborhood"), banks ("I don't need to look up your account, just tell me how much money you want to withdraw"), or courtrooms ("If you

In 2012, psychologist Diederik Stapel was found to have committed massive fraud over the course of many years. He was fired from his job as a professor and dozens of published scientific articles were retracted.

say you're innocent, well then, that's good enough for me"), so why would we expect it to work in science? Are scientists more honest than everyone else?

Definitely! Okay, we just made that up. But the honor system doesn't depend on scientists being especially honest, but on the fact that science is a community enterprise. When scientists claim to have discovered something important, other scientists don't just applaud, they start studying it too. When physicist Jan Hendrik Schön announced in 2001 that he had produced a molecular-scale transistor, other physicists were deeply impressed—that is, until they tried to replicate his work and discovered that Schön had fabricated his data (Agin, 2007). Schön lost his job and his doctoral degree was revoked, but the important point is that such frauds can't last long because one scientist's conclusion is the next scientist's research question. This doesn't mean that all frauds are uncovered swiftly: psychologist Diederik Stapel lied, cheated, and made up his data for decades before people became suspicious enough to investigate (Levelt Committee, Noort Committee, Drenth Committee, 2012). But it does mean that the *important* frauds are uncovered eventually. The psychologist who fraudulently claims to have shown that chimps are smarter than goldfish may never get caught because no one is likely to follow up on such an obvious finding, but the psychologist who fraudulently claims to have shown the opposite will soon have a lot of explaining to do.

What exactly are psychologists on their honor to do? At least three things. First, when they write reports of their studies and publish them in scientific journals, psychologists are obligated to report truthfully on what they did and what they found. They can't fabricate results (e.g., claiming to have performed studies that they never really performed) or fudge results (e.g., changing records of data that were actually collected), and they can't mislead by omission (e.g., by reporting only the results that confirm their hypothesis and saying nothing about the results that don't). Second, psychologists are obligated to share credit fairly by including as co-authors of their reports the other people who contributed to the work, and by mentioning in their reports the other scientists who have done related work. And third, psychologists are obligated to share their data. The American Psychological Association's code of conduct states that ethical psychologists "do not withhold the data on which their conclusions are based from other competent professionals who seek to verify the substantive claims through reanalysis." The fact that anyone can check up on anyone else is part of why the honor system works as well as it does.

> **What are psychologists expected to do when they report the results of their research?**

IN SUMMARY

▶ Institutional review boards ensure that the rights of human beings who participate in scientific research are based on the principles of respect for persons, beneficence, and justice.

▶ Psychologists are obligated to uphold these principles by getting informed consent from participants, not coercing participation, protecting participants from harm, weighing benefits against risks, avoiding deception, and keeping information confidential.

▶ Psychologists are obligated to respect the rights of animals and treat them humanely. Most people are in favor of using animals in scientific research.

▶ Psychologists are obligated to tell the truth about their studies, to share credit appropriately, and to grant others access to their data.

OTHER VOICES

Can We Afford Science?

David Brooks is a columnist for the New York Times, a commentator on CNN, and the author of several popular books on behavioral science.

PHOTO: ©JOSH HANER/ COURTESY OF THE NEW YORK TIMES

Who pays for all the research described in textbooks like this one? The answer is you. By and large, scientific research is funded by governmental agencies, such as the National Science Foundation, which give scientists grants (also known as money) to do particular research projects that the scientists proposed. Of course, this money could be spent on other things, for example, feeding the poor, housing the homeless, caring for the ill and elderly, and so on. Does it make sense to spend taxpayer dollars on psychological science when some of our fellow citizens are cold and hungry?

Journalist and author David Brooks (2011) argued that research in the behavioral sciences is not an expenditure—it is an investment that pays for itself, and more. Here's what he had to say:

Over the past 50 years, we've seen a number of gigantic policies produce disappointing results—policies to reduce poverty, homelessness, dropout rates, single-parenting and drug addiction. Many of these policies failed because they were based on an overly simplistic view of human nature. They assumed that people responded in straightforward ways to incentives. Often, they assumed that money could cure behavior problems.

Fortunately, today we are in the middle of a golden age of behavioral research. Thousands of researchers are studying the way actual behavior differs from the way we assume people behave. They are coming up with more accurate theories of who we are, and scores of real-world applications. Here's one simple example:

When you renew your driver's license, you have a chance to enroll in an organ donation program. In countries like Germany and the U.S., you have to check a box if you want to opt in. Roughly 14 percent of people do. But behavioral scientists have discovered that how you set the defaults is really important. So in other countries, like Poland or France, you have to check a box if you want to opt out. In these countries, more than 90 percent of people participate.

This is a gigantic behavior difference cued by one tiny and cost-less change in procedure.

Yet in the middle of this golden age of behavioral research, there is a bill working through Congress that would eliminate the National Science Foundation's Directorate for Social, Behavioral and Economic Sciences. This is exactly how budgets should not be balanced—by cutting cheap things that produce enormous future benefits.

Let's say you want to reduce poverty. We have two traditional understandings of poverty. The first presumes people are rational. They are pursuing their goals effectively and don't need much help in changing their behavior. The second presumes that the poor are afflicted by cultural or psychological dysfunctions that sometimes lead them to behave in shortsighted ways. Neither of these theories has produced much in the way of effective policies.

Eldar Shafir of Princeton and Sendhil Mullainathan of Harvard have recently, with federal help, been exploring a third theory, that scarcity produces its own cognitive traits.

A quick question: What is the starting taxi fare in your city? If you are like most upper-middle-class people, you don't know. If you are like many struggling people, you do know. Poorer people have to think hard about a million things that affluent people don't. They have to make complicated trade-offs when buying a carton of milk: If I buy milk, I can't afford orange juice. They have to decide which utility not to pay.

These questions impose enormous cognitive demands. The brain has limited capacities. If you increase demands on one sort of question, it performs less well on other sorts of questions.

Shafir and Mullainathan gave batteries of tests to Indian sugar farmers. After they sell their harvest, they live in relative prosperity. During this season, the farmers do well on the I.Q. and other tests. But before the harvest, they live amid scarcity and have to think hard about a thousand daily decisions. During these seasons, these same farmers do much worse on the tests. They appear to have lower I.Q.'s. They have more trouble controlling their attention. They are more shortsighted. Scarcity creates its own psychology.

Princeton students don't usually face extreme financial scarcity, but they do face time scarcity. In one game, they had to answer questions in a series of timed rounds, but they could borrow time from future rounds. When they were scrambling amid time scarcity, they were quick to borrow time, and they were nearly oblivious to the usurious interest rates the game organizers were charging. These brilliant Princeton kids were rushing to the equivalent of payday lenders, to their own long-term detriment.

Shafir and Mullainathan have a book coming out next year, exploring how scarcity—whether of time, money or calories (while dieting)—affects your psychology. They are also studying how poor people's self-perceptions shape behavior. Many people don't sign up for the welfare benefits because they are intimidated by the forms. Shafir and Mullainathan asked some people at a Trenton soup kitchen to relive a moment when they felt competent and others to recount a neutral experience. Nearly half of the self-affirming group picked up an available benefits package afterward. Only 16 percent of the neutral group did.

People are complicated. We each have multiple selves, which emerge or don't depending on context. If we're going to address problems, we need to understand the contexts and how these tendencies emerge or don't emerge. We need to design policies around that knowledge. Cutting off financing for this sort of research now is like cutting off navigation financing just as Christopher Columbus hit the shoreline of the New World.

What do you think? Is Brooks right? Is psychological science a wise use of public funds, or is it a luxury that we simply can't afford?

Chapter Review

KEY CONCEPT QUIZ

1. The belief that accurate knowledge can be acquired through observation is
   a. parsimony.
   b. dogmatism.
   c. empiricism.
   d. scientific research.

2. Which of the following is the best definition of a hypothesis?
   a. empirical evidence
   b. a scientific investigation
   c. a falsifiable prediction
   d. a theoretical idea

3. The methods of psychological investigation take ____ into account because when people know they are being studied, they don't always behave as they otherwise would.
   a. reactivity
   b. complexity
   c. variability
   d. sophistication

4. When a measure produces the same measurement whenever it is used to measure the same thing, it is said to have
   a. validity.
   b. reliability.
   c. power.
   d. concreteness.

5. Aspects of an observational setting that cause people to behave as they think they should are called
   a. observer biases.
   b. reactive conditions.
   c. natural habitats.
   d. demand characteristics.

6. In a double-blind observation
   a. the participants know what is being measured.
   b. people are observed in their natural environments.
   c. the purpose is hidden from both the observer and the person being observed.
   d. only objective, statistical measures are recorded.

7. Which of the following describes the average value of all the measurements in a particular distribution?
   a. mean
   b. median
   c. mode
   d. range

8. What does a correlation coefficient show?
   a. the value of one specific variable
   b. the direction and strength of a correlation
   c. the efficiency of the relevant research method
   d. the degree of natural correlation

9. When two variables are correlated, what keeps us from concluding that one is the cause and the other is the effect?
   a. the possibility of third-variable correlation
   b. random assignment of control groups
   c. the existence of false-positive correlation
   d. correlation strength is impossible to measure accurately

10. A researcher administers a questionnaire concerning attitudes toward global warming to people of both genders and of all ages who live all across the country. The dependent variable in the study is the ____ of the participants.
    a. age
    b. gender
    c. attitudes toward global warming
    d. geographic location

11. The characteristic of an experiment that allows conclusions about causal relationships to be drawn is called
    a. external validity.
    b. internal validity.
    c. random assignment.
    d. self-selection.

12. An experiment that operationally defines variables in a realistic way is said to be
    a. externally valid.
    b. controlled.
    c. operationally defined.
    d. statistically significant.

13. Research suggests that people are usually
    a. open to seeing both sides of an issue.
    b. able to reason without emotion.
    c. able to arrive at conclusions based solely on facts.
    d. none of the above.

14. When people find evidence that confirms their beliefs, they often
    a. tend to stop looking.
    b. seek evidence that disconfirms their conclusions.
    c. seek evidence that presents both sides.
    d. talk to their colleagues.

15. What are psychologists ethically required to do when reporting research results?
    a. to report findings truthfully
    b. to share credit for research
    c. to make data available for further research
    d. All of the above.

KEY TERMS

empiricism (p. 40)
scientific method (p. 40)
theory (p. 40)
hypothesis (p. 41)
empirical method (p. 42)
operational definition (p. 43)
instrument (p. 44)
validity (p. 44)
reliability (p. 44)
power (p. 44)
demand characteristics (p. 45)

naturalistic observation (p. 45)
double-blind (p. 47)
frequency distribution (p. 48)
normal distribution (p. 48)
mode (p. 49)
mean (p. 49)
median (p. 49)
range (p. 50)
standard deviation (p. 50)
variable (p. 52)
correlation (p. 52)

correlation coefficient (p. 53)
natural correlation (p. 54)
third-variable correlation (p. 55)
matched samples technique (p. 55)
matched pairs technique (p. 56)
third-variable problem (p. 57)
experiment (p. 57)
manipulation (p. 57)
independent variable (p. 58)
experimental group (p. 58)
control group (p. 58)

dependent variable (p. 58)
self-selection (p. 59)
random assignment (p. 60)
internal validity (p. 62)
external validity (p. 62)
population (p. 63)
sample (p. 64)
case method (p. 64)
random sampling (p. 64)
informed consent (p. 71)
debriefing (p. 72)

CHANGING MINDS

1. Back in Psychology: Evolution of a Science, you read about B. F. Skinner, who studied the principle of reinforcement, which states that the consequences of a behavior determine whether it will be more or less likely to occur in the future. So, for example, a rat's rate of lever pressing will increase if it receives food reinforcement after each lever press. When you tell a classmate about this principle, she only shrugs. "That's obvious. Anyone who's ever owned a dog knows how to train animals. If you ask me, psychology is just common sense. You don't have to conduct scientific experiments to test things that everyone already knows are true." How would you explain the value of studying something that seems like "common sense"?

2. You're watching TV with a friend when a news program reports that a research study has found that people in Europe who work longer hours are less happy than those who work shorter hours, but in the United States it's the other way around: Americans who work long hours are happier (Okulicz-Kozaryn, 2011). "That's an interesting experiment," he says. You point out that the news only said it was a research study, not an experiment. What would have to be true for it to be an experiment? Why aren't all research studies experiments? What can't you learn from this study that you *could* learn from an experiment?

3. After the first exam, your professor says she's noticed a strong positive correlation between the location of students' seats and their exam scores: "The closer students sit to the front of the room, the higher their scores on the exam," she says. After class, your friend suggests that the two of you should sit up front for the rest of the semester to improve your grades. Having read about correlation and causation, should you be skeptical? What are some possible reasons for the correlation between seating position and good grades? Could you design an experiment to test whether sitting up front actually causes good grades?

4. A classmate in your criminal justice class suggests that mental illness is a major cause of violent crimes in the United States. As evidence, he mentions a highly publicized murder trial in which the convicted suspect was diagnosed with schizophrenia. What scientific evidence would he need to support this claim?

5. You ask your friend if he wants to go to the gym with you. "No," he says, "I never exercise." You tell him that regular exercise has all kinds of health benefits, including greatly reducing the risk of heart disease. "I don't believe that," he replies, "I had an uncle who got up at 6 a.m. every day of his life to go jogging, and he still died of a heart attack at age 53." What would you tell your friend? Does his uncle's case prove that exercise really doesn't protect against heart disease after all?

ANSWERS TO KEY CONCEPT QUIZ

1. c; 2. c; 3. a; 4. b; 5. d; 6. c; 7. a; 8. b; 9. a; 10. c; 11. b; 12. a; 13. d; 14. a; 15. d.

Need more help? Additional resources are located in LaunchPad at:
http://www.worthpublishers.com/launchpad/schacter3e

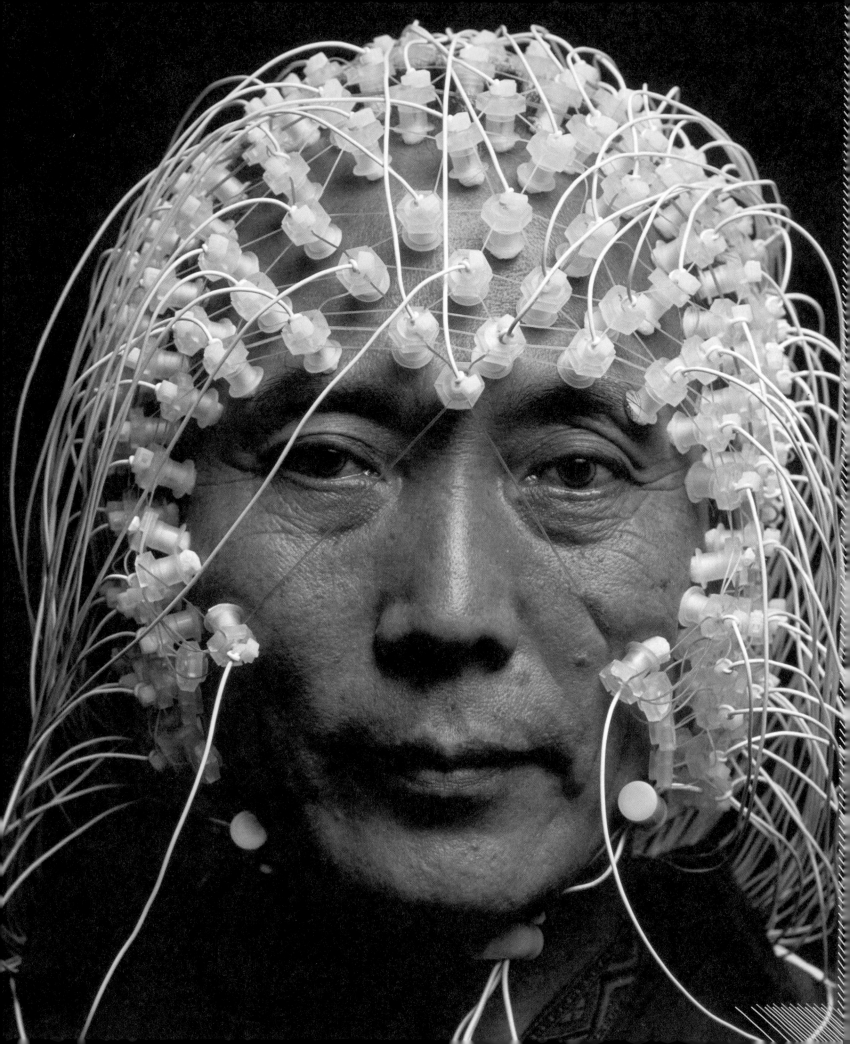

3

Neuroscience and Behavior

RAY EASTERLING AND DAVE DUERSON CAME from different times and places: Easterling, born in 1949, grew up in Richmond, Virginia; Duerson, born in 1960, grew up in Muncie, Indiana. But their lives as young men showed striking parallels. Both loved football and played the position of defensive back well enough to star in college and make it all the way to the National Football League. Easterling played for the Atlanta Falcons during the 1970s, part of the "Gritz Blitz" defense that set an NFL record in 1977 for the fewest points allowed in a season. Duerson played for the Chicago Bears in the 1980s, one of the most fearsome defenses of all time, and contributed importantly to the Bears' Super Bowl win in 1986. Unfortunately, the parallels between Easterling and Duerson continued into their retirement years. Both men suffered from significant cognitive decline and depression, and both ended up taking their own lives: Duerson in 2011, Easterling in 2012. Postmortem analyses of their brains revealed the presence of a condition known as *chronic traumatic encephalopathy* (*CTE*), a form of progressive brain damage that has been linked to repeated concussions (McKee et al., 2012). Duerson and Easterling are just 2 of over 20 former NFL players who have been diagnosed with CTE, and the condition has also been observed after repeated head injuries in boxing, wrestling, hockey, and rugby (Costanza et al., 2011; Daneshvar et al., 2011; Lahkan & Kirchgessner, 2012; McKee et al., 2012).

We don't know whether CTE contributed to the demise of either Easterling or Duerson, but we do know that CTE is associated with an array of cognitive and emotional deficits in afflicted individuals, including inability to concentrate, memory loss, irritability, and depression, usually beginning within a decade after repeated concussions and worsening with time (McKee et al., 2009). CTE isn't confined to aging or retired athletes. A recent study found evidence of CTE in a 17-year-old football player who died as a result of multiple head injuries (McKee et al., 2012). Fortunately, there is growing awareness of CTE and its consequences, which is leading professional sports organizations, as well as colleges, schools, and others involved in youth sports, to take steps to address the problem.

Ray Easterling (*left*) and Dave Duerson (*right*) had similarly outstanding NFL careers and similarly troubled retirements, perhaps associated with brain damage.

neurons
Cells in the nervous system that communicate with one another to perform information-processing tasks.

cell body (or soma)
The part of a neuron that coordinates information-processing tasks and keeps the cell alive.

dendrite
The part of a neuron that receives information from other neurons and relays it to the cell body.

axon
The part of a neuron that carries information to other neurons, muscles, or glands.

The symptoms of CTE, and the havoc they can wreak in the lives of affected individuals and their families, are stark reminders that our psychological, emotional, and social well-being depend critically on the health and integrity of the brain. The consequences of CTE also highlight that understanding neuroscience isn't just an academic exercise confined to scientific laboratories: The more we know about the brain, and the more people who know it, the better our chances of finding solutions to problems such as CTE.

IN THIS CHAPTER, WE'LL CONSIDER HOW THE BRAIN WORKS, what happens when it doesn't, and how both states of affairs determine behavior. First, we'll introduce you to the basic unit of information processing in the brain, the neuron. The electrical and chemical activities of neurons are the starting point of all behavior, thought, and emotion. Next, we'll consider the anatomy of the central nervous system, focusing especially on the brain, including its overall organization, key structures that perform different functions, and its evolutionary development. Finally, we'll discuss methods that allow us to study the brain and clarify our understanding of how it works. These include methods that examine the damaged brain and methods for scanning the living and healthy brain.

Neurons: The Origin of Behavior

An estimated 1 billion people watch the final game of World Cup soccer every 4 years. That's a whole lot of people, but to put it in perspective, it's still only a little over 14% of the estimated 7 billion people currently living on Earth. A more impressive number might be the 30 billion viewers who tune in to watch any of the World Cup action over the course of the tournament. But a really, really big number is inside your skull right now, helping you make sense of these big numbers you're reading about. There are approximately *100 billion* nerve cells in your brain that perform a variety of tasks to allow you to function as a human being.

Humans have thoughts, feelings, and behaviors that are often accompanied by visible signals. Consider how you might feel on your way to meet a good friend. An observer might see a smile on your face or notice how fast you are walking; internally, you might mentally rehearse what you'll say to your friend and feel a surge of happiness as you approach her. All those visible and experiential signs are coordinated by the activity of your brain cells. The anticipation you have, the happiness you feel, and the speed of your feet are the result of information processing in your brain. In a way, all of your thoughts, feelings, and behaviors spring from cells in the brain that take in information and produce some kind of output trillions of times a day. These cells are **neurons,** *cells in the nervous system that communicate with one another to perform information-processing tasks.*

Components of the Neuron

During the 1800s, scientists began to turn their attention from studying the mechanics of limbs, lungs, and livers to studying the harder-to-observe workings of the brain. Philosophers wrote poetically about an "enchanted loom" that mysteriously wove a tapestry of behavior, and many scientists confirmed the metaphor (Corsi, 1991). To those scientists, the brain looked as though it were composed of a continuously connected lattice of fine threads, leading to the conclusion that it was one big woven web of material. However, in the late 1880s, Spanish physician Santiago Ramón y Cajal (1852–1934) learned about a new technique for staining neurons in the brain (DeFelipe & Jones, 1988). The stain highlighted the appearance of entire cells, revealing that they came in different shapes and sizes (see **FIGURE 3.1**).

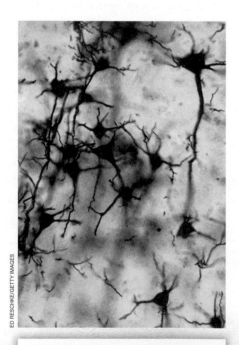

ED RESCHKE/GETTY IMAGES

▲ Figure **3.1 Golgi-Stained Neurons**
Santiago Ramón y Cajal used a Golgi stain (like the one shown here) to highlight the appearance of neurons. He was the first to see that each neuron is composed of a body with many threads extending outward toward other neurons. He also saw that, surprisingly, the threads of each neuron do not actually touch other neurons.

Cajal discovered that neurons are complex structures composed of three basic parts: the cell body, the dendrites, and the axon (see **FIGURE 3.2**). Like cells in all organs of the body, neurons have a **cell body** (also called the *soma*), the largest component of the neuron that *coordinates the information-processing tasks and keeps the cell alive*. Functions such as protein synthesis, energy production, and metabolism take place here. The cell body contains a *nucleus*, which houses chromosomes that contain your DNA, or the genetic blueprint of who you are. The cell body is surrounded by a porous cell membrane that allows some molecules to flow into and out of the cell.

Unlike other cells in the body, neurons have two types of specialized extensions of the cell membrane that allow them to communicate: dendrites and axons. **Dendrites** *receive information from other neurons and relay it to the cell body*. The term *dendrite* comes from the Greek word for "tree"; indeed, most neurons have many dendrites that look like tree branches. The **axon** *carries information to other neurons, muscles, or glands*. Axons can be very long, even stretching up to a meter from the base of the spinal cord down to the big toe.

▼ Figure **3.2** **Components of a Neuron**
A neuron is made up of three parts: a cell body that houses the chromosomes with the organism's DNA and maintains the health of the cell; dendrites that receive information from other neurons; and an axon that transmits information to other neurons, muscles, and glands.

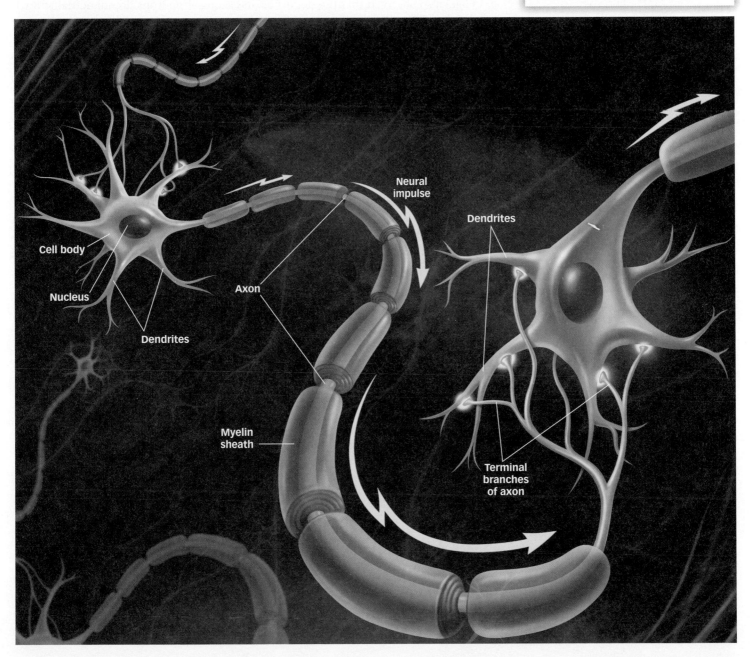

In many neurons, the axon is covered by a **myelin sheath,** *an insulating layer of fatty material.* The myelin sheath is composed of **glial cells** (named for the Greek word for "glue"), which are *support cells found in the nervous system.* Although there are 100 billion neurons busily processing information in your brain, there are 10 to 50 times that many glial cells serving a variety of functions. Some glial cells digest parts of dead neurons, others provide physical and nutritional support for neurons, and others form myelin to help the axon carry information more efficiently. An axon insulated with myelin can more efficiently transmit signals to other neurons, organs, or muscles. In fact, with *demyelinating diseases,* such as multiple sclerosis, the myelin sheath deteriorates, slowing the transmission of information from one neuron to another (Schwartz & Westbrook, 2000). This leads to a variety of problems, including loss of feeling in the limbs, partial blindness, and difficulties in coordinated movement and cognition (Butler, Corboy, & Filley, 2009).

> **Which components of the neuron allow them to communicate?**

Cajal also observed that the dendrites and axons of neurons do not actually touch each other. There's a small gap between the axon of one neuron and the dendrites or cell body of another. This gap is part of the **synapse,** *the junction or region between the axon of one neuron and the dendrites or cell body of another* (see **FIGURE 3.3**). Many of the 100 billion neurons in your brain have a few thousand synaptic junctions, so it should come as no shock that most adults have 100 to 500 trillion synapses. As you'll read shortly, the transmission of information across the synapse is fundamental to communication between neurons, a process that allows us to think, feel, and behave.

Major Types of Neurons

There are three major types of neurons, each performing a distinct function: sensory neurons, motor neurons, and interneurons. **Sensory neurons** *receive information from the external world and convey this information to the brain via the spinal cord.* They have specialized endings on their dendrites that receive signals for light, sound, touch, taste, and smell. For example, sensory neurons' endings in our eyes are sensitive to light. **Motor neurons** *carry signals from the spinal cord to the muscles to produce movement.* These neurons often have long axons that can stretch to muscles at our extremities. However, most of the nervous system is composed of

> **How do the three types of neurons work together to transmit information?**

▼ Figure **3.3** **The Synapse** The synapse is the junction between the dendrites of one neuron and the axon or cell body of another. Notice that neurons do not actually touch one another: There is a small synaptic space between them across which information is transmitted.

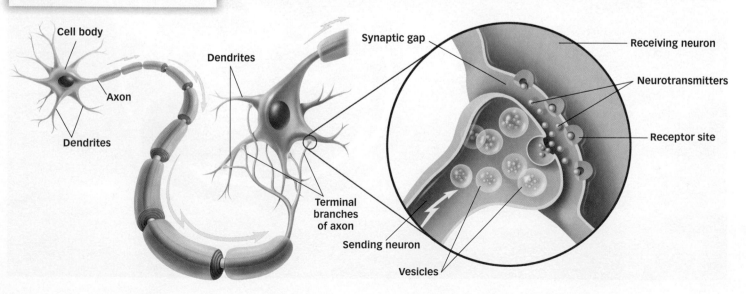

Cell body

Dendrites

Axon

Dendrites

Terminal branches of axon

Sending neuron

Synaptic gap

Receiving neuron

Neurotransmitters

Receptor site

Vesicles

the third type of neuron, **interneurons,** which *connect sensory neurons, motor neurons, or other interneurons.* Some interneurons carry information from sensory neurons into the nervous system, others carry information from the nervous system to motor neurons, and still others perform a variety of information-processing functions within the nervous system. Interneurons work together in small circuits to perform simple tasks, such as identifying the location of a sensory signal, and much more complicated ones, such as recognizing a familiar face.

Neurons Specialized by Location

Besides specialization for sensory, motor, or connective functions, neurons are also somewhat specialized depending on their location (see **FIGURE 3.4**). For example, *Purkinje cells* are a type of interneuron that carries information from the cerebellum to the rest of the brain and spinal cord. These neurons have dense, elaborate dendrites that resemble bushes. *Pyramidal cells*, found in the cerebral cortex, have a triangular cell body and a single, long dendrite among many smaller dendrites. *Bipolar cells*, a type of sensory neuron found in the retinas of the eye, have a single axon and a single dendrite. The brain processes different types of information, so a substantial amount of specialization at the cellular level has evolved to handle these tasks.

myelin sheath
An insulating layer of fatty material.

glial cells
Support cells found in the nervous system.

synapse
The junction or region between the axon of one neuron and the dendrites or cell body of another.

sensory neurons
Neurons that receive information from the external world and convey this information to the brain via the spinal cord.

motor neurons
Neurons that carry signals from the spinal cord to the muscles to produce movement.

interneurons
Neurons that connect sensory neurons, motor neurons, or other interneurons.

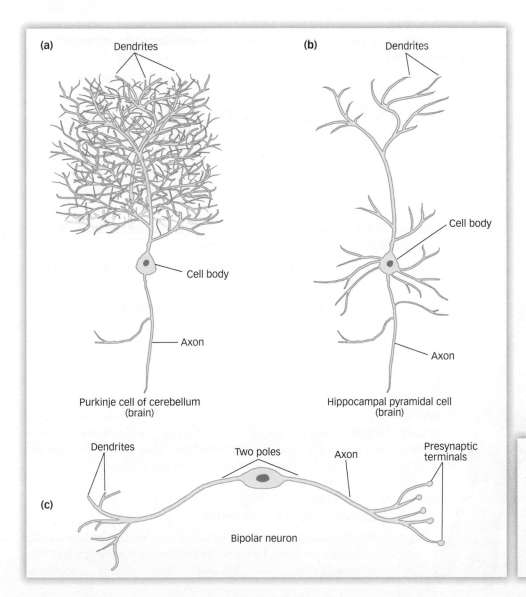

(a) Dendrites — Cell body — Axon

Purkinje cell of cerebellum
(brain)

(b) Dendrites — Cell body — Axon

Hippocampal pyramidal cell
(brain)

(c) Dendrites — Two poles — Axon — Presynaptic terminals

Bipolar neuron

◀ Figure **3.4** **Types of Neurons** Neurons have a cell body, an axon, and at least one dendrite. The size and shape of neurons vary considerably, however. The Purkinje cell has an elaborate treelike assemblage of dendrites (*a*). Pyramidal cells have a triangular cell body and a single, long dendrite with many smaller dendrites (*b*). Bipolar cells have only one dendrite and a single axon (*c*).

IN SUMMARY

► Neurons are the building blocks of the nervous system: They process information received from the outside world, communicate with one another, and send messages to the body's muscles and organs.

► Neurons are composed of three major parts: the cell body, dendrites, and the axon.
  ► The cell body contains the nucleus, which houses the organism's genetic material.
  ► Dendrites receive sensory signals from other neurons and transmit this information to the cell body.
  ► Each axon carries signals from the cell body to other neurons or to muscles and organs in the body.

► Neurons don't actually touch. They are separated by a small gap, which is part of the synapse across which signals are transmitted from one neuron to another.

► Glial cells provide support for neurons, usually in the form of the myelin sheath, which coats the axon to facilitate the transmission of information. In demyelinating diseases, the myelin sheath deteriorates.

► Neurons are differentiated according to the functions they perform. The three major types of neurons include sensory neurons (e.g., bipolar neurons), motor neurons, and interneurons (e.g., Purkinje cells).

The Electrochemical Actions of Neurons: Information Processing

Our thoughts, feelings, and actions depend on neural communication, but how does it happen? The communication of information within and between neurons proceeds in two stages:

> *Conduction* is the movement of an electric signal within neurons, from the dendrites to the cell body, then throughout the axon.

> *Transmission* is movement of electric signals from one neuron to another over the synapse.

Together, these stages are what scientists generally refer to as the *electrochemical action* of neurons.

Electric Signaling: Conducting Information within a Neuron

The neuron's cell membrane has small pores that act as channels to allow small electrically charged molecules, called *ions*, to flow in and out of the cell. It is this flow of ions across the neuron's cell membrane that creates the conduction of an electric signal within the neuron. How does it happen?

The Resting Potential: The Origin of the Neuron's Electrical Properties

Neurons have a natural electric charge called the **resting potential,** *the difference in electric charge between the inside and outside of a neuron's cell membrane* (Kandel, 2000). When first discovered by biologists in

Biologists Alan Hodgkin and Andrew Huxley discovered the resting potential in the summer of 1939, while studying marine invertebrates—sea creatures that lack a spine, such as clams, squid, and lobsters (Stevens, 1971). Hodgkin and Huxley worked with the squid giant axon because it is 100 times larger than the biggest axon in humans. They inserted a thin wire into the squid axon so that it touched the jellylike fluid inside. Then they placed another wire just outside the axon in the watery fluid that surrounds it. They found a substantial difference between the electric charges inside and outside the axon, which they called the resting potential.

MAREVISION/
AGEFOTOSTOCK/
GETTY IMAGES

the 1930s, the resting potential was measured at about about −70 millivolts. This is a much smaller charge than a typical battery; for example, a 9-volt battery has 9,000 millivolts (Klein & Thorne, 2007).

The resting potential arises from the difference in concentrations of ions inside and outside the neuron's cell membrane (see **FIGURE 3.5a**). Ions can carry a positive (+) or a negative (−) charge. In the resting state, there is a high concentration of a positively charged ion, potassium (K^+), as well as negatively charged protein ions (A^-), *inside* the neuron's cell membrane compared to outside it. By contrast, there is a high concentration of positively charged sodium ions (Na^+) and negatively charged chloride ions (Cl^-) *outside* the neuron's cell membrane.

The concentration of K^+ inside and outside a neuron is controlled by channels in the cell membrane that allow K^+ molecules to flow in and out of the neuron. In the resting state, the channels that allow K^+ molecules to flow freely across the cell membrane are open, while channels that allow the flow of Na+ and the other ions noted earlier are generally closed. Because of the naturally higher concentration of K+ molecules *inside* the neuron, some K^+ molecules move out of the neuron through the open channels, leaving the inside of the neuron with a charge of about −70 millivolts relative to the outside. Like the Hoover Dam that holds back the Colorado River until the floodgates are released, resting potential is potential energy, because it creates the environment for a possible electrical impulse.

> **?** What difference between the inside and outside of the neuron's cell membrane creates the resting potential?

resting potential
The difference in electric charge between the inside and outside of a neuron's cell membrane.

▼ Figure **3.5** **The Resting and Action Potentials** Neurons have a natural electric charge called a resting potential. Electric stimulation causes an action potential.

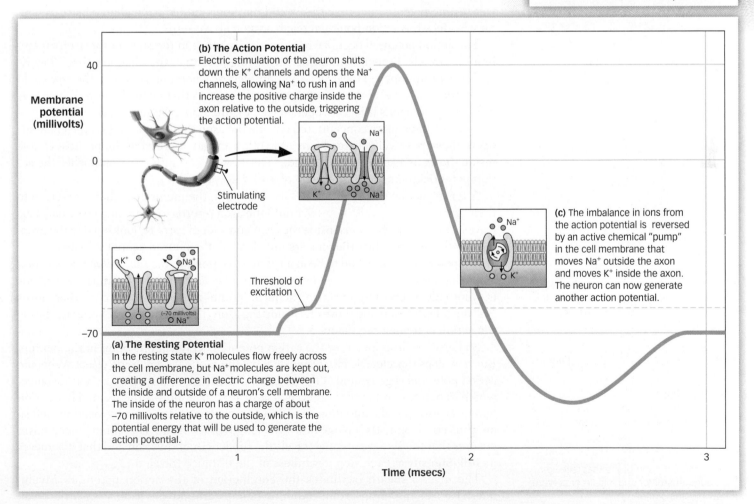

(b) The Action Potential
Electric stimulation of the neuron shuts down the K^+ channels and opens the Na^+ channels, allowing Na^+ to rush in and increase the positive charge inside the axon relative to the outside, triggering the action potential.

Membrane potential (millivolts)

Stimulating electrode

Threshold of excitation

(c) The imbalance in ions from the action potential is reversed by an active chemical "pump" in the cell membrane that moves Na^+ outside the axon and moves K^+ inside the axon. The neuron can now generate another action potential.

(a) The Resting Potential
In the resting state K^+ molecules flow freely across the cell membrane, but Na^+ molecules are kept out, creating a difference in electric charge between the inside and outside of a neuron's cell membrane. The inside of the neuron has a charge of about −70 millivolts relative to the outside, which is the potential energy that will be used to generate the action potential.

Time (msecs)

The Action Potential: Sending Signals across the Neuron

The neuron maintains its resting potential most of the time. However, the biologists working with the giant squid axon (see photo on p. 84) noticed that they could produce a signal by stimulating the axon with a brief electric shock, which resulted in the conduction of an electric impulse down the length of the axon (Hausser, 2000; Hodgkin & Huxley, 1939). This electric impulse is called an **action potential,** *an electric signal that is conducted along the length of a neuron's axon to a synapse.*

Like the flow of electricity when you turn on a light, the action potential is all or none. Either the switch is turned on or the room remains dark. Similarly, either the electrical stimulation in the neuron reaches the threshold to fire an action potential, or it remains at the resting potential.

ISTOCKPHOTO/THINKSTOCK

The action potential occurred only when the electric shock reached a certain level, or *threshold*. When the shock was below this threshold, the researchers recorded only tiny signals, which dissipated rapidly. When the shock reached the threshold, a much larger signal, the action potential, was observed. Interestingly, increases in the electric shock above the threshold did *not* increase the strength of the action potential. The action potential is *all or none*: Electric stimulation below the threshold fails to produce an action potential, whereas electric stimulation at or above the threshold always produces the action potential. The action potential always occurs with exactly the same characteristics and at the same magnitude regardless of whether the stimulus is at or above the threshold.

The biologists working with the giant squid axon observed another surprising property of the action potential: They measured it at a charge of about +40 millivolts, which is well above zero. This suggests that the mechanism driving the action potential could not simply be the loss of the −70 millivolt resting potential because this would have only brought the charge back to zero. So why does the action potential reach a value above zero?

Why is an action potential an all-or-nothing event?

The action potential occurs when there is a change in the state of the axon's membrane channels. Remember, during the resting potential, the channels that allow K⁺ to flow out are open. However, when an electric charge is raised to the threshold value, these channels briefly shut down, and channels that allow the flow of *positively* charged sodium ions (Na⁺) are opened (see Figure 3.5*b*). We've seen already that Na⁺ is typically much more concentrated outside the axon than inside. When the channels open, those positively charged ions (Na⁺) flow inside, increasing the positive charge inside the axon relative to that outside. This flow of Na⁺ into the axon pushes the action potential to its maximum value of +40 millivolts.

After the action potential reaches its maximum, the membrane channels return to their original state, and K⁺ flows out until the axon returns to its resting potential. This leaves a lot of extra Na⁺ ions inside the axon and a lot of extra K⁺ ions outside the axon. During this period when the ions are imbalanced, the neuron cannot initiate another action potential, so it is said to be in a **refractory period,** *the time following an action potential during which a new action potential cannot be initiated.* The imbalance in ions is eventually reversed by an active chemical "pump" in the cell membrane that moves Na⁺ outside the axon and moves K⁺ inside the axon (the pump does not operate during the action potential; see Figure 3.5*c*).

So far we've described how the action potential occurs at one point in the neuron. But how does this electric charge move down the axon? It's a domino effect. When an action potential is generated at the beginning of the axon, it spreads a short distance, which generates an action potential at a nearby location on the axon. That action potential also spreads, initiating an action potential at another nearby location, and so on, thus conducting the charge down the length of the axon. This simple mechanism ensures that the action potential travels the full length of the axon and that it achieves its full intensity at each step, regardless of the distance traveled.

The myelin sheath facilitates the conduction of the action potential. Myelin doesn't cover the entire axon; rather, it clumps around the axon with little break

action potential
An electric signal that is conducted along a neuron's axon to a synapse.

refractory period
The time following an action potential during which a new action potential cannot be initiated.

terminal buttons
Knoblike structures that branch out from an axon.

neurotransmitters
Chemicals that transmit information across the synapse to a receiving neuron's dendrites.

receptors
Parts of the cell membrane that receive the neurotransmitter and initiate or prevent a new electric signal.

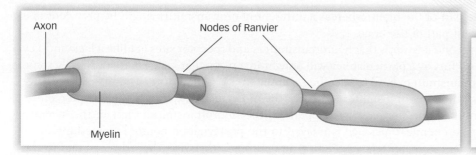

◀ Figure **3.6** **Myelin and Nodes of Ranvier** Myelin is formed by a type of glial cell, and it wraps around a neuron's axon to speed the movement of the action potential along the length of the axon. Breaks in the myelin sheath are called the nodes of Ranvier. The electric impulse jumps from node to node, thereby speeding the conduction of information down the axon.

points between clumps, looking kind of like sausage links. These breakpoints are called the *nodes of Ranvier,* after French pathologist Louis-Antoine Ranvier, who discovered them (see **FIGURE 3.6**). When an electric current passes down the length of a myelinated axon, the charge seems to "jump" from node to node rather than having to traverse the entire axon (Poliak & Peles, 2003). This process is called *saltatory conduction*, and it helps speed the flow of information down the axon.

Chemical Signaling: Transmission between Neurons

When the action potential reaches the end of an axon, you might think that it stops there. After all, the synaptic space between neurons means that the axon of one neuron and the neighboring neuron's dendrites do not actually touch one another. However, the electric charge of the action potential takes a form that can cross the relatively small synaptic gap by relying on a bit of chemistry.

How does a neuron communicate with another neuron?

Axons usually end in **terminal buttons,** *knob-like structures that branch out from an axon.* A terminal button is filled with tiny *vesicles,* or "bags," that contain **neurotransmitters,** *chemicals that transmit information across the synapse to a receiving neuron's dendrites.* The dendrites of the receiving neuron contain **receptors,** *parts of the cell membrane that receive neurotransmitters and either initiate or prevent a new electric signal.*

As K^+ and Na^+ flow across a cell membrane, they move the sending neuron, or *presynaptic neuron,* from a resting potential to an action potential. The action potential travels down the length of the axon to the terminal buttons, where it stimulates the release of neurotransmitters from vesicles into the synapse. These neurotransmitters float across the synapse and bind to receptor sites on a nearby dendrite of the receiving neuron, or *postsynaptic neuron.* A new action potential is initiated in that neuron, and the process continues down that neuron's axon to the next synapse and the next neuron. This electrochemical action, called *synaptic transmission* (see **FIGURE 3.7**), allows neurons to communicate with one another and ultimately underlies your thoughts, emotions, and behavior.

Now that you understand the basic process of how information moves from one neuron to another, let's refine things a bit. You'll recall that a given neuron may make a few thousand synaptic connections with other neurons, so what tells the dendrites which of the neurotransmitters flooding into the synapse to receive? One answer is that neurons tend to form pathways in the brain that are characterized by specific types of neurotransmitters; one neurotransmitter might be prevalent

▼ Figure **3.7** **Synaptic Transmission** (1) The action potential travels down the axon and (2) stimulates the release of neurotransmitters from vesicles. (3) The neurotransmitters are released into the synapse, where they float to bind with receptor sites on a dendrite of a postsynaptic neuron, initiating a new action potential. The neurotransmitters are cleared out of the synapse by (4) reuptake into the sending neuron, (5) being broken down by enzymes in the synapse, or (6) binding to autoreceptors on the sending neuron.

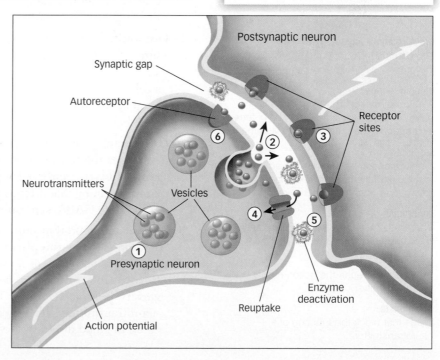

in one part of the brain, whereas a different neurotransmitter might be prevalent in a different part of the brain.

A second answer is that neurotransmitters and receptor sites act like a lock-and-key system. Just as a particular key will only fit in a particular lock, so, too, will only some neurotransmitters bind to specific receptor sites on a dendrite. The molecular structure of the neurotransmitter must "fit" the molecular structure of the receptor site.

Another question is what happens to the neurotransmitters left in the synapse after the chemical message is relayed to the postsynaptic neuron? Something must make neurotransmitters stop acting on neurons; otherwise, there'd be no end to the signals that they send. Neurotransmitters leave the synapse through three processes (see Figure 3.7). First, *reuptake* occurs when neurotransmitters are reabsorbed by the terminal buttons of the presynaptic neuron's axon. Second, neurotransmitters can be destroyed by enzymes in the synapse in a process called *enzyme deactivation*; specific enzymes break down specific neurotransmitters. Finally, neurotransmitters can bind to the receptor sites called *autoreceptors* on the presynaptic neurons. Autoreceptors detect how much of a neurotransmitter has been released into a synapse and signal the neuron to stop releasing the neurotransmitter when an excess is present.

Types and Functions of Neurotransmitters

Given that different kinds of neurotransmitters can activate different kinds of receptors, like a lock and key, you might wonder how many types of neurotransmitters are floating across synapses in your brain right now. Today we know that some 60 chemicals play a role in transmitting information throughout the brain and body and differentially affect thought, feeling, and behavior, but a few major classes seem particularly important. We'll summarize those here, and you'll meet some of these neurotransmitters again in later chapters.

> **Acetylcholine (ACh)** is *a neurotransmitter involved in a number of functions, including voluntary motor control.* Acetylcholine is found in neurons of the brain and in the synapses where axons connect to muscles and body organs, such as the heart. Acetylcholine activates muscles to initiate motor behavior, but it also contributes to the regulation of attention, learning, sleeping, dreaming, and memory (Gais & Born, 2004; Hasselmo, 2006; Wrenn et al., 2006). Alzheimer's disease, a medical condition involving severe memory impairments (Salmon & Bondi, 2009), is associated with the deterioration of ACh-producing neurons.

> **Dopamine** is *a neurotransmitter that regulates motor behavior, motivation, pleasure, and emotional arousal.* Because of its role in basic motivated behaviors, such as seeking pleasure or associating actions with rewards, dopamine plays a role in drug addiction (Baler & Volkow, 2006). High levels of dopamine have been linked to schizophrenia (Winterer & Weinberger, 2004), whereas low levels have been linked to Parkinson's disease.

> **Glutamate** is the *major excitatory neurotransmitter in the brain,* meaning that it enhances the transmission of information between neurons. **GABA (gamma-aminobutyric acid),** in contrast, is *the primary inhibitory neurotransmitter in the brain,* meaning that it tends to stop the firing of neurons. Too much glutamate, or too little GABA, can cause neurons to become overactive, causing seizures.

> Two related neurotransmitters influence mood and arousal: norepinephrine and serotonin. **Norepinephrine** is *particularly involved in states of vigilance, or a heightened awareness of dangers in the environment* (Ressler & Nemeroff, 1999). **Serotonin** is *involved in the regulation of sleep and wakefulness, eating, and aggressive behavior* (Dayan & Huys, 2009; Kroeze & Roth, 1998). Because both neurotransmitters affect mood and arousal, low levels of each have been implicated in mood disorders (Tamminga et al., 2002).

acetylcholine (ACh)
A neurotransmitter involved in a number of functions, including voluntary motor control.

dopamine
A neurotransmitter that regulates motor behavior, motivation, pleasure, and emotional arousal.

glutamate
The major excitatory neurotransmitter in the brain.

GABA (gamma-aminobutyric acid)
The primary inhibitory neurotransmitter in the brain.

norepinephrine
A neurotransmitter that is particularly involved in states of vigilance, or heightened awareness of dangers in the environment.

serotonin
A neurotransmitter that is involved in the regulation of sleep and wakefulness, eating, and aggressive behavior.

endorphins
Chemicals that act within the pain pathways and emotion centers of the brain.

agonists
Drugs that increase the action of a neurotransmitter.

antagonists
Drugs that block the function of a neurotransmitter.

> **Endorphins** *are chemicals that act within the pain pathways and emotion centers of the brain* (Keefe et al., 2001). The term *endorphin* is a contraction of *endogenous* m*orphine,* and that's a pretty apt description. Morphine is a synthetic drug that has a calming and pleasurable effect; an endorphin is an internally produced substance that has similar properties, such as dulling the experience of pain and elevating moods. The "runner's high" experienced by many athletes as they push their bodies to painful limits of endurance can be explained by the release of endorphins in the brain (Boecker et al., 2008).

> **How do neurotransmitters create the feeling of runner's high?**

Sandra Wallenhorst of Germany began a 112-mile bicycle ride, just one part of the 2009 Ironman World Championship in Hawaii. When athletes such as Wallenhorst engage in extreme sports, they may experience subjective highs that result from the release of endorphins—chemical messengers acting in emotion and pain centers that elevate mood and dull the experience of pain.

Each of these neurotransmitters affects thought, feeling, and behavior in different ways, so normal functioning involves a delicate balance of each. Even a slight imbalance—too much of one neurotransmitter or not enough of another—can dramatically affect behavior. These imbalances sometimes occur naturally: The brain doesn't produce enough serotonin, for example, which contributes to depressed or anxious moods. Other times a person may actively seek to cause imbalances. People who smoke, drink alcohol, or take drugs, legal or not, are altering the balance of neurotransmitters in their brains. The drug LSD, for example, is structurally very similar to serotonin, so it binds very easily with serotonin receptors in the brain, producing similar effects on thoughts, feelings, or behavior. In the next section, we'll look at how some drugs are able to "trick" receptor sites in just this way.

How Drugs Mimic Neurotransmitters

Many drugs that affect the nervous system operate by increasing, interfering with, or mimicking the manufacture or function of neurotransmitters (Cooper, Bloom, & Roth, 2003; Sarter, 2006). **Agonists** are *drugs that increase the action of a neurotransmitter.* **Antagonists** are *drugs that block the function of a neurotransmitter.* Some drugs alter a step in the production or release of the neurotransmitter, whereas others have a chemical structure so similar to a neurotransmitter that the drug is able to bind to that neuron's receptor. If, by binding to a receptor, a drug activates the neurotransmitter, it is an agonist; if it blocks the action of the neurotransmitter, it is an antagonist (see **FIGURE 3.8**).

For example, the drug L-dopa was developed to treat Parkinson's disease, a movement disorder characterized by tremors and difficulty initiating movement, caused by the loss of neurons that use the neurotransmitter dopamine. Dopamine is created in neurons by a modification of a common molecule called L-dopa. Ingesting L-dopa will elevate the amount of L-dopa in the brain and spur the surviving neurons to produce more dopamine. In other words, L-dopa acts as an agonist for dopamine. The use of L-dopa has been reasonably successful in the alleviation of Parkinson's disease symptoms (Muenter & Tyce, 1971; Schapira et al., 2009). However, the effectiveness of L-dopa typically decreases when used over a long period of time, so that many longtime users experience some symptoms of the disease. The actor Michael J. Fox,

> **How does L-dopa alleviate symptoms of Parkinson's disease?**

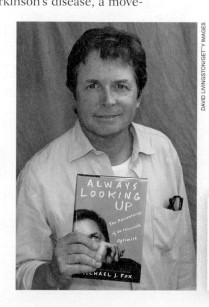

Michael J. Fox vividly described his struggles with Parkinson's disease in his 2009 memoir. Fox's visibility has increased public awareness of the disease and spurred greater efforts toward finding a cure.

who was diagnosed with Parkinson's disease in 1991 and takes L-dopa, described the simple act of trying to brush his teeth in his memoir:

> Grasping the toothpaste is nothing compared to the effort it takes to coordinate the two-handed task of wrangling the toothbrush and strangling out a line of paste onto the bristles. By now, my right hand has started up again, rotating at the wrist in a circular motion, perfect for what I'm about to do. My left hand guides my right hand up to my mouth, and once the back of the Oral-B touches the inside of my upper lip, I let go. It's like releasing the tension on a slingshot and compares favorably to the most powerful state-of-the-art electric toothbrush on the market. With no off switch, stopping means seizing my right wrist with my left hand, forcing it down to the sink basin, and shaking the brush loose as though disarming a knife-wielding attacker. (Fox, 2009, pp. 2–3)

Many other drugs, including some street drugs, alter the actions of neurotransmitters. Let's look at a few more examples.

Amphetamine is a popular drug that stimulates the release of norepinephrine and dopamine. In addition, both amphetamine and *cocaine* prevent the reuptake of norepinephrine and dopamine. The combination of increased release of norepinephrine and dopamine and prevention of their reuptake floods the synapse with those neurotransmitters, resulting in increased activation of their receptors. Both of these drugs therefore are strong agonists, although the psychological effects of the two drugs differ somewhat because of subtle distinctions in where and how they act on the brain. Norepinephrine and dopamine play a critical role in mood control, such that increases in either neurotransmitter result in euphoria, wakefulness, and a burst of energy. However, norepinephrine also increases heart rate. An overdose of amphetamine or cocaine can cause the heart to contract so rapidly that heartbeats do not last long enough to pump blood effectively, leading to fainting and sometimes death.

▼ Figure **3.8** **The Actions of Agonist and Antagonist Drugs** Agonist and antagonist drugs can enhance or interfere with synaptic transmission at every point in the process: in the production of neurotransmitters, in the release of neurotransmitters, at the autoreceptors, in reuptake, in the postsynaptic receptors, and in the synapse itself.

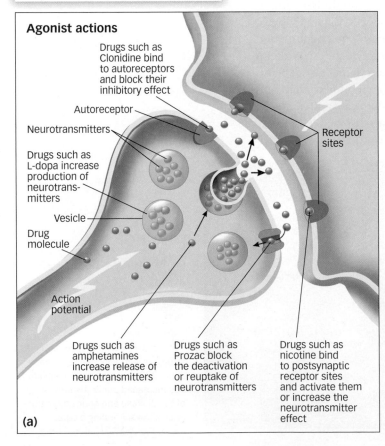

Agonist actions

Drugs such as Clonidine bind to autoreceptors and block their inhibitory effect

Autoreceptor

Neurotransmitters

Receptor sites

Drugs such as L-dopa increase production of neurotransmitters

Vesicle

Drug molecule

Action potential

Drugs such as amphetamines increase release of neurotransmitters

Drugs such as Prozac block the deactivation or reuptake of neurotransmitters

Drugs such as nicotine bind to postsynaptic receptor sites and activate them or increase the neurotransmitter effect

(a)

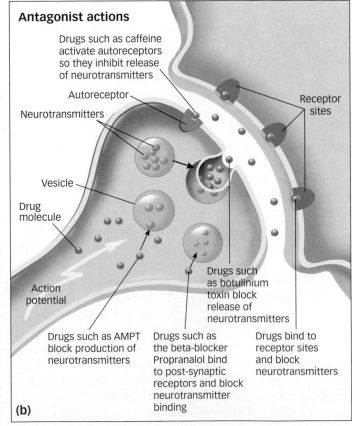

Antagonist actions

Drugs such as caffeine activate autoreceptors so they inhibit release of neurotransmitters

Autoreceptor

Neurotransmitters

Receptor sites

Vesicle

Drug molecule

Action potential

Drugs such as botulinium toxin block release of neurotransmitters

Drugs such as AMPT block production of neurotransmitters

Drugs such as the beta-blocker Propranalol bind to post-synaptic receptors and block neurotransmitter binding

Drugs bind to receptor sites and block neurotransmitters

(b)

Methamphetamine, a variant of amphetamine, affects pathways for dopamine, serotonin, and norepinephrine at the neuron's synapses, making it difficult to interpret exactly how it works. But the combination of its agonist and antagonist effects alters the functions of neurotransmitters that help us perceive and interpret visual images, sometimes resulting in strange hallucinations.

Prozac, a drug commonly used to treat depression, is another example of a neurotransmitter agonist. Prozac blocks the reuptake of the neurotransmitter *serotonin*, making it part of a category of drugs called *selective serotonin reuptake inhibitors*, or *SSRIs* (Wong, Bymaster, & Engelman, 1995). People suffering from clinical depression typically have reduced levels of serotonin in their brains. By blocking reuptake, more of the neurotransmitter remains in the synapse longer and produces greater activation of serotonin receptors. Serotonin elevates mood, which can help relieve depression (Mann, 2005).

An antagonist with important medical implications is a drug called *propranalol*, one of a class of drugs called *beta blockers* that obstruct a receptor site for norepinephrine in the heart. Because norepinephrine cannot bind to these receptors, heart rate slows down, which is helpful for disorders in which the heart beats too fast or irregularly. Beta blockers are also prescribed to reduce the agitation, racing heart, and nervousness associated with stage fright (Mills & Dimsdale, 1991; for additional discussion of antianxiety and antidepression drug treatments, see the Treatment of Psychological Disorders chapter).

IN SUMMARY

▶ The conduction of an electric signal within a neuron happens when the resting potential is reversed by an electric impulse called an action potential.

▶ The neuron's resting potential is due to differences in the potassium (K^+) concentrations inside and outside the cell membrane, resulting from open channels that allow K^+ to flow outside the membrane while closed channels don't allow sodium ions (Na^+) and other ions to flow into the neuron.

▶ If electric signals reach a threshold, this initiates an action potential, an all-or-none signal that moves down the entire length of the axon. The action potential occurs when K^+ channels in the axon membrane close and Na^+ channels open, allowing the Na^+ ions to flow inside the axon. After the action potential has reached its maximum, a chemical pump reverses the imbalance in ions, returning the neuron to its resting potential. For a brief refractory period, the action potential cannot be re-initiated. Once it is initiated, the action potential spreads down the axon, jumping across the nodes of Ranvier to the synapse.

▶ Communication between neurons takes place through synaptic transmission, where an action potential triggers release of neurotransmitters from the terminal buttons of the sending neuron's axon, which travel across the synapse to bind with receptors in the receiving neuron's dendrite.

▶ Neurotransmitters bind to dendrites on specific receptor sites. Neurotransmitters leave the synapse through reuptake, through enzyme deactivation, and by binding to autoreceptors.

▶ Some of the major neurotransmitters are acetylcholine (ACh), dopamine, glutamate, GABA, norepinephrine, serotonin, and endorphins.

▶ Drugs can affect behavior by acting as agonists, that is, by facilitating or increasing the actions of neurotransmitters, or as antagonists by blocking the action of neurotransmitters. Recreational drug use can have an effect on brain function.

nervous system
An interacting network of neurons that conveys electrochemical information throughout the body.

central nervous system (CNS)
The part of the nervous system that is composed of the brain and spinal cord.

peripheral nervous system (PNS)
The part of the nervous system that connects the central nervous system to the body's organs and muscles.

somatic nervous system
A set of nerves that conveys information between voluntary muscles and the central nervous system.

The Organization of the Nervous System

We've seen how individual neurons communicate with each other. What's the bigger picture? Neurons work by forming circuits and pathways in the brain, which in turn influence circuits and pathways in other areas of the body. Without this kind of organization and delegation, neurons would be churning away with little purpose. Neurons are the building blocks that form *nerves*, or bundles of axons and the glial cells that support them. The **nervous system** is *an interacting network of neurons that conveys electrochemical information throughout the body*. In this section, we'll look at the major divisions and components of the nervous system.

Divisions of the Nervous System

There are two major divisions of the nervous system: the central nervous system and the peripheral nervous system (see **FIGURE 3.9**). The **central nervous system (CNS)** is *composed of the brain and spinal cord*. The central nervous system receives sensory information from the external world, processes and coordinates this information, and sends commands to the skeletal and muscular systems for action. At the top of the CNS rests the brain, which contains structures that support the most complex perceptual, motor, emotional, and cognitive functions of the nervous system. The spinal cord branches down from the brain; nerves that process sensory information and relay commands to the body connect to the spinal cord.

The **peripheral nervous system (PNS)** *connects the central nervous system to the body's organs and muscles*. The peripheral nervous system is itself composed of two major subdivisions, the somatic nervous system and the autonomic nervous system. The **somatic nervous system** is *a set of nerves that conveys information between voluntary muscles and the central nervous system*. Humans have conscious control over this system and use it to perceive, think, and coordinate their behaviors. For example, reaching for your morning cup of coffee involves the elegantly orchestrated activities

▼ Figure **3.9** **The Human Nervous System**
The nervous system is organized into the peripheral and central nervous systems. The peripheral nervous system is further divided into the autonomic and somatic nervous systems.

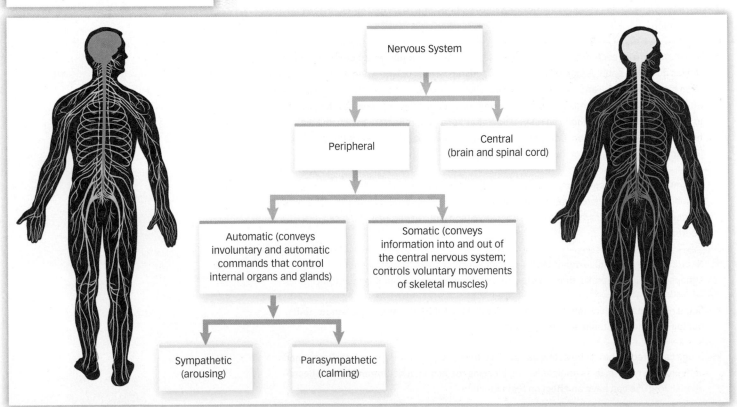

of the somatic nervous system: Information from the receptors in your eyes travels to your brain, registering that a cup is on the table; signals from your brain travel to the muscles in your arm and hand; feedback from those muscles tells your brain that the cup has been grasped, and so on.

In contrast, the **autonomic nervous system (ANS)** is *a set of nerves that carries involuntary and automatic commands that control blood vessels, body organs, and glands.* As suggested by its name, this system works on its own to regulate bodily systems, largely outside of conscious control. The ANS has two major subdivisions, the sympathetic nervous system and the parasympathetic nervous system. Each exerts a different type of control on the body. The **sympathetic nervous system** is *a set of nerves that prepares the body for action in challenging or threatening situations* (see **FIGURE 3.10**). For example, imagine that you are walking alone late at night and frightened by footsteps behind you in a dark alley. Your sympathetic nervous system kicks into action at this point: It dilates your pupils to let in more light, increases your heart rate and respiration to pump more oxygen to muscles, diverts blood flow to your brain and muscles, and activates sweat glands to cool your body. To conserve energy, the sympathetic nervous system inhibits salivation and bowel movements, suppresses the body's immune responses, and suppresses responses to pain and injury. The sum total of these fast, automatic responses is that they increase the likelihood that you can escape.

What triggers the increase in your heart rate when you feel threatened?

autonomic nervous system (ANS)
A set of nerves that carries involuntary and automatic commands that control blood vessels, body organs, and glands.

sympathetic nervous system
A set of nerves that prepares the body for action in challenging or threatening situations.

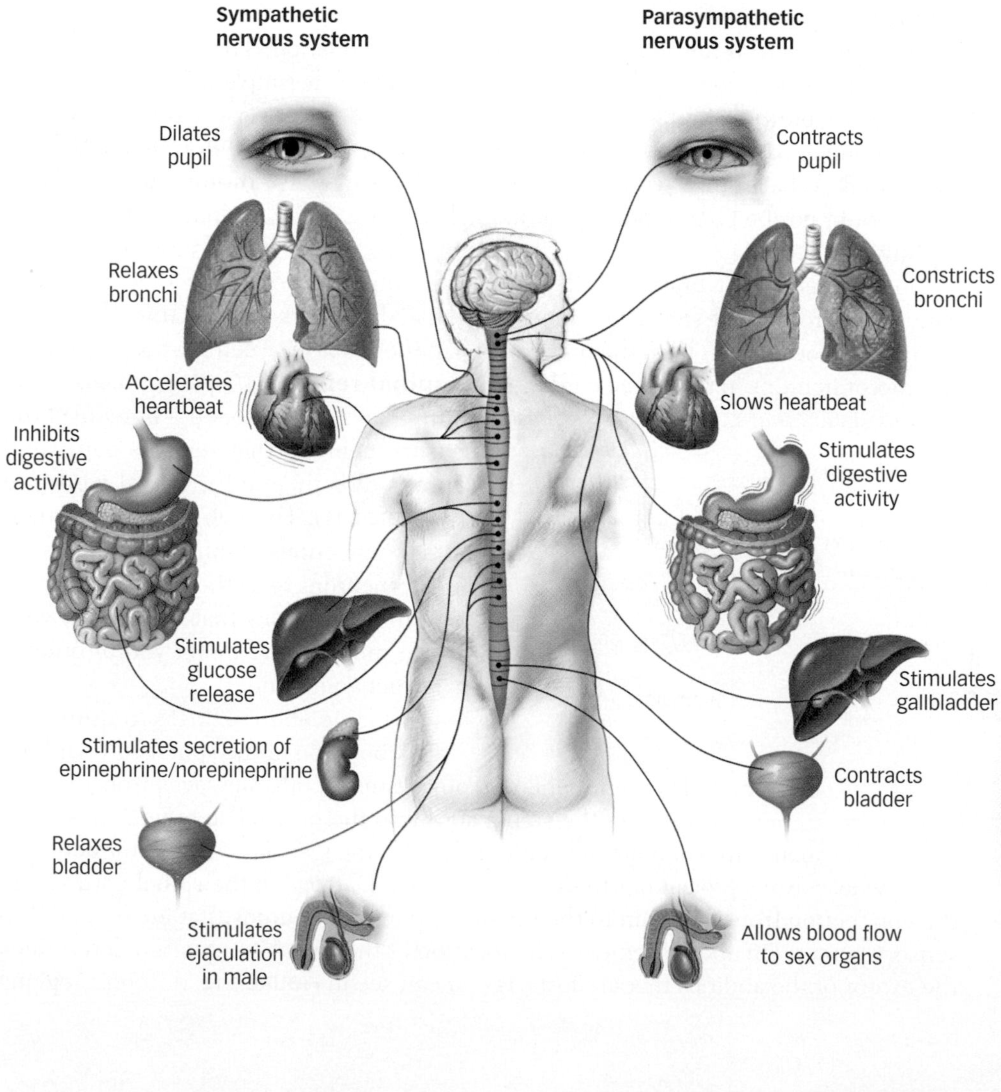

◀ Figure **3.10** **Sympathetic and Parasympathetic Systems** The autonomic nervous system is composed of two subsystems that complement each other. Activation of the sympathetic system serves several aspects of arousal, whereas the parasympathetic nervous system returns the body to its normal resting state.

parasympathetic nervous system
A set of nerves that helps the body return to a normal resting state.

spinal reflexes
Simple pathways in the nervous system that rapidly generate muscle contractions.

The **parasympathetic nervous system** *helps the body return to a normal resting state*. When you're far away from your would-be attacker, your body doesn't need to remain on red alert. Now the parasympathetic nervous system kicks in to reverse the effects of the sympathetic nervous system and return your body to its normal state. The parasympathetic nervous system generally mirrors the connections of the sympathetic nervous system. For example, the parasympathetic nervous system constricts your pupils, slows your heart rate and respiration, diverts blood flow to your digestive system, and decreases activity in your sweat glands.

As you might imagine, the sympathetic and parasympathetic nervous systems coordinate to control many bodily functions. One example is sexual behavior. In men, the parasympathetic nervous system engorges the blood vessels of the penis to produce an erection, but the sympathetic nervous system is responsible for ejaculation. In women, the parasympathetic nervous system produces vaginal lubrication, but the sympathetic nervous system underlies orgasm. In both men and women, a successful sexual experience depends on a delicate balance of these two systems; in fact, anxiety about sexual performance can disrupt this balance. For example, sympathetic nervous system activation caused by anxiety can lead to premature ejaculation in males and lack of lubrication in females.

Components of the Central Nervous System

Compared to the many divisions of the peripheral nervous system, the central nervous system may seem simple. After all, it has only two elements: the brain and the spinal cord. But those two elements are ultimately responsible for most of what we do as humans.

The spinal cord often seems like the brain's poor relation: The brain gets all the glory and the spinal cord just hangs around, doing relatively simple tasks. Those tasks, however, are pretty important: They keep you breathing, respond to pain, and move your muscles, allowing you to walk. What's more, without the spinal cord, the brain would not be able to put any of its higher processing into action.

> **What important functions does the spinal cord perform on its own?**

Do you need your brain to tell you to pull your hand away from a hot stove? For some very basic behaviors such as this, the spinal cord doesn't need input from the brain at all. Connections between the sensory inputs and motor neurons in the spinal cord mediate **spinal reflexes,** *simple pathways in the nervous system that rapidly generate muscle contractions*. If you touch a hot stove, the sensory neurons that register pain send inputs directly into the spinal cord (see **FIGURE 3.11**). Through just a few synaptic connections within the spinal cord, interneurons relay these sensory inputs to motor neurons that connect to your arm muscles and direct you to quickly retract your hand.

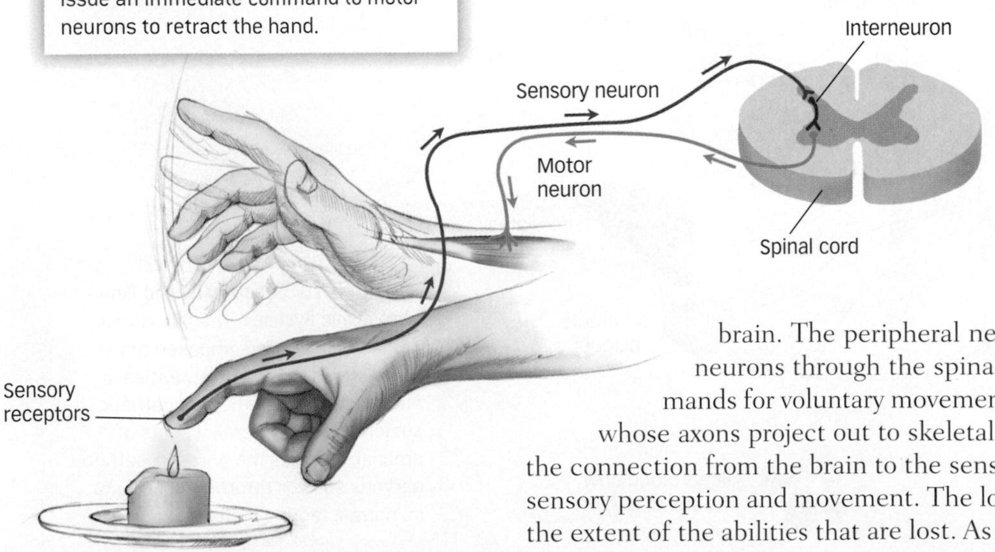

More elaborate tasks require the collaboration of the spinal cord and the brain. The peripheral nervous system sends messages from sensory neurons through the spinal cord into the brain. The brain sends commands for voluntary movement through the spinal cord to motor neurons, whose axons project out to skeletal muscles. Damage to the spinal cord severs the connection from the brain to the sensory and motor neurons that are essential to sensory perception and movement. The location of the spinal injury often determines the extent of the abilities that are lost. As you can see in **FIGURE 3.12**, different regions

▼ Figure **3.11 The Pain Withdrawal Reflex** Many actions of the central nervous system don't require the brain's input. For example, withdrawing from pain is a reflexive activity controlled by the spinal cord. Painful sensations (such as the heat of fire) travel directly to the spinal cord via sensory neurons, which then issue an immediate command to motor neurons to retract the hand.

Interneuron

Sensory neuron

Motor neuron

Spinal cord

Sensory receptors

of the spinal cord control different systems of the body. Individuals with damage at a particular level of the spinal cord lose sensations of touch and pain in body parts below the level of the injury, as well as a loss of motor control of the muscles in the same areas. A spinal injury higher up the cord usually predicts a much poorer prognosis, such as quadriplegia (loss of sensation and motor control over all limbs), breathing through a respirator, and lifelong immobility.

The late actor Christopher Reeve, who starred as Superman in four *Superman* movies, damaged his spinal cord in a horseback riding accident in 1995, resulting in loss of sensation and motor control in all of his body parts below the neck. Despite great efforts over several years, Reeve made only modest gains in his motor control and sensation, highlighting the extent to which we depend on communication from the brain through the spinal cord to the body, and showing how difficult it is to compensate for the loss of these connections (Edgerton et al., 2004). Sadly, Christopher Reeve died at age 52 in 2004 from complications due to his paralysis. On a brighter note, researchers are making progress in understanding the nature of spinal cord injuries and how to treat them by focusing on how the brain changes in response to injury (Blesch & Tuszynski, 2009; Dunlop, 2008), a process that is closely related to the concept of brain plasticity that we will examine later in this chapter.

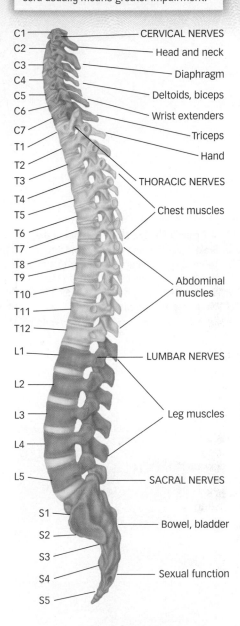

▼ Figure **3.12** **Regions of the Spinal Cord**
The spinal cord is divided into four main sections; each controls different parts of the body. Damage higher on the spinal cord usually means greater impairment.

CERVICAL NERVES
Head and neck
Diaphragm
Deltoids, biceps
Wrist extenders
Triceps
Hand
THORACIC NERVES
Chest muscles
Abdominal muscles
LUMBAR NERVES
Leg muscles
SACRAL NERVES
Bowel, bladder
Sexual function

IN SUMMARY

▶ Neurons make up nerves, which in turn form the human nervous system.

▶ The nervous system is divided into the peripheral and the central nervous systems. The peripheral nervous system connects the central nervous system with the rest of the body, and it is itself divided into the somatic nervous system and the autonomic nervous system.

▶ The somatic nervous system, which conveys information into and out of the central nervous system, controls voluntary muscles, whereas the autonomic nervous system automatically controls the body's organs.

▶ The autonomic nervous system is further divided into the sympathetic and parasympathetic nervous systems, which complement each other in their effects on the body. The sympathetic nervous system prepares the body for action in threatening situations, and the parasympathetic nervous system returns it to its normal state.

▶ The central nervous system is composed of the spinal cord and the brain. The spinal cord can control some basic behaviors such as spinal reflexes without input from the brain.

Structure of the Brain

The human brain, weighing in at about three pounds, is really not much to look at. You already know that its neurons and glial cells are busy humming away, giving you potentially brilliant ideas, consciousness, and feelings. But which neurons in which parts of the brain control which functions? To answer that question, neuroscientists had to find a way of describing the brain that allows researchers to communicate with one another. It can be helpful to talk about areas of the brain from "bottom to top," noting how the different regions are specialized for different kinds of tasks. In general, simpler functions are performed at the "lower levels" of the brain, whereas more complex functions are performed at

OMIKRON/SCIENCE SOURCE

The human brain weighs only three pounds and isn't much to look at, but its accomplishments are staggering.

successively "higher" levels (see **FIGURE 3.13**). Or, as you'll see shortly, the brain can also be approached in a "side-by-side" fashion: Although each side of the brain is roughly analogous, one half of the brain specializes in some tasks that the other half doesn't. Although these divisions make it easier to understand areas of the brain and their functions, keep in mind that none of these structures or areas in the brain can act alone: They are all part of one big, interacting, interdependent whole.

Let's look first at the divisions of the brain, and the responsibilities of each part, moving from the bottom to the top. Using this view, we can divide the brain into three parts: the hindbrain, the midbrain, and the forebrain (see Figure 3.13).

The Hindbrain

If you follow the spinal cord from your tailbone to where it enters your skull, you'll find it difficult to determine where your spinal cord ends and your brain begins. That's because the spinal cord is continuous with the **hindbrain,** *an area of the brain that coordinates information coming into and out of the spinal cord.* The hindbrain looks like a stalk on which the rest of the brain sits, and it controls the most basic functions of life: respiration, alertness, and motor skills. The structures that make up the hindbrain include: the medulla, the reticular formation, the cerebellum, and the pons (see **FIGURE 3.14**).

The **medulla** is *an extension of the spinal cord into the skull that coordinates heart rate, circulation, and respiration.* Beginning inside the medulla and extending upward is a small cluster of neurons called the **reticular formation,** which *regulates sleep, wakefulness, and levels of arousal.* In one early experiment, researchers stimulated the reticular formation of a sleeping cat. This caused the animal to awaken almost instantaneously and remain alert. Conversely, severing the connections between the reticular formation and the rest of the brain caused the animal to lapse into an irreversible coma (Moruzzi & Magoun, 1949). The reticular formation maintains the same delicate balance between alertness and unconsciousness in humans. In fact, many general anesthetics work by reducing activity in the reticular formation, rendering the patient unconscious.

Behind the medulla is the **cerebellum,** *a large structure of the hindbrain that controls fine motor skills.* (*Cerebellum* is Latin for "little brain," and the structure does look like a small replica of the brain.) The cerebellum orchestrates the proper sequence of movements when we ride a bike, play the piano, or maintain balance while walking and running. It contributes to the fine-tuning of behavior: smoothing our actions to allow their graceful execution rather than initiating the actions (Smetacek, 2002). The initiation of behavior

Which part of the brain helps to orchestrate movements that keep you steady on your bike?

involves other areas of the brain; as you'll recall, different brain systems interact and are interdependent with one another.

The last major area of the hindbrain is the **pons,** *a structure that relays information from the cerebellum to the rest of the brain.* (*Pons* means "bridge" in Latin.) Although the detailed functions of the pons remain poorly understood, it essentially acts as a relay station or bridge between the cerebellum and other structures in the brain.

The Midbrain

Sitting on top of the hindbrain is the *midbrain,* which is relatively small in humans. As you can see in **FIGURE 3.15,** the midbrain contains two main structures: the tectum and the tegmentum. The **tectum** *orients an organism in the environment.* The tectum

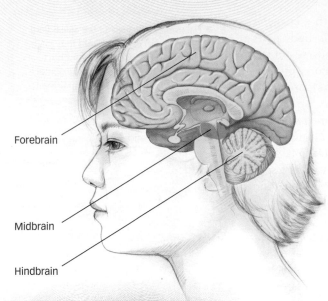

Forebrain

Midbrain

Hindbrain

▲ Figure **3.13 The Major Divisions of the Brain** The brain can be organized into three parts, moving from the bottom to the top, from simpler functions to the more complex: the hindbrain, the midbrain, and the forebrain.

High wire artist Freddy Nock relied on his cerebellum to coordinate the movements necessary to walk on the rope of the Corvatsch cable car from more than 10,000 feet over sea level down to the base station in Silvaplana, Switzerland on January 29, 2011. Nock set a new mark that day for the Guinness World Records.

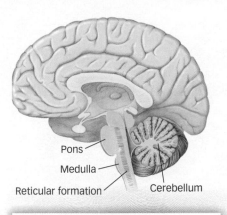

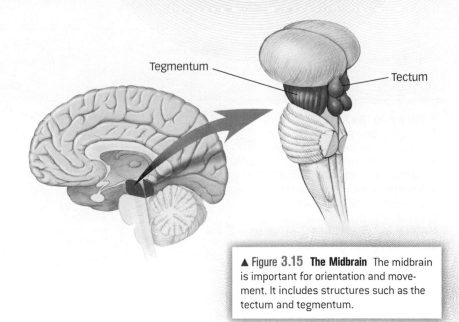

▲ Figure **3.14 The Hindbrain** The hindbrain coordinates information coming into and out of the spinal cord and controls the basic functions of life. It includes the medulla, the reticular formation, the cerebellum, and the pons.

▲ Figure **3.15 The Midbrain** The midbrain is important for orientation and movement. It includes structures such as the tectum and tegmentum.

receives stimulus input from the eyes, ears, and skin and moves the organism in a coordinated way toward the stimulus. For example, when you're studying in a quiet room and you hear a *click* behind and to the right of you, your body will swivel and orient to the direction of the sound; this is your tectum in action.

The **tegmentum** is *involved in movement and arousal*; it also helps to orient an organism toward sensory stimuli. The midbrain may be relatively small, but it is a central location of neurotransmitters involved in arousal, mood, and motivation and the brain structures that rely on them (White, 1996). You could survive if you had only a hindbrain and a midbrain. The structures in the hindbrain would take care of all the bodily functions necessary to sustain life, and the structures in the midbrain would orient you toward or away from pleasurable or threatening stimuli in the environment. But this wouldn't be much of a life. To understand where the abilities that make us fully human come from, we need to consider the last division of the brain.

The Forebrain

When you appreciate the beauty of a poem, detect the sarcasm in a friend's remark, plan to go skiing next winter, or notice the faint glimmer of sadness on a loved one's face, you are enlisting the forebrain. The *forebrain* is the highest level of the brain—literally and figuratively—and controls complex cognitive, emotional, sensory, and motor functions. The forebrain itself is divided into two main sections: the cerebral cortex and the subcortical structures.

The **cerebral cortex** is *the outermost layer of the brain, visible to the naked eye, and divided into two hemispheres*. The **subcortical structures** are *areas of the forebrain housed under the cerebral cortex near the center of the brain* (see **FIGURE 3.16**). We'll have much more to say about the two hemispheres of the cerebral cortex and the functions they serve in the next section, fittingly saving the highest level of the brain for last. First, we'll examine the subcortical structures.

Subcortical Structures

The subcortical (beneath the cortex) structures are nestled deep inside the brain, where they are quite protected. If you imagine sticking an index finger in each of your ears and pushing inward until they touch, that's about where you'd find the thalamus, hypothalamus, pituitary gland, limbic system, and basal ganglia (see Figure 3.16).

hindbrain
An area of the brain that coordinates information coming into and out of the spinal cord.

medulla
An extension of the spinal cord into the skull that coordinates heart rate, circulation, and respiration.

reticular formation
A brain structure that regulates sleep, wakefulness, and levels of arousal.

cerebellum
A large structure of the hindbrain that controls fine motor skills.

pons
A brain structure that relays information from the cerebellum to the rest of the brain.

tectum
A part of the midbrain that orients an organism in the environment.

tegmentum
A part of the midbrain that is involved in movement and arousal.

cerebral cortex
The outermost layer of the brain, visible to the naked eye and divided into two hemispheres.

subcortical structures
Areas of the forebrain housed under the cerebral cortex near the very center of the brain.

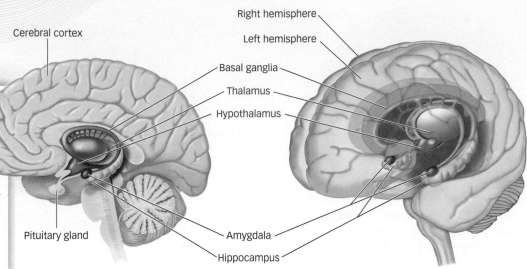

► Figure **3.16** **The Forebrain** The forebrain is the highest level of the brain and is critical for complex cognitive, emotional, sensory, and motor functions. The forebrain is divided into two parts: the cerebral cortex and the underlying subcortical structures. The cerebral cortex, the outermost layer of the brain, is divided into two hemispheres, connected by the corpus callosum (see Figure 3.18). The subcortical structures include the thalamus, hypothalamus, pituitary gland, amygdala, and hippocampus.

Cerebral cortex

Right hemisphere
Left hemisphere
Basal ganglia
Thalamus
Hypothalamus

Pituitary gland

Amygdala

Hippocampus

Each of these subcortical structures plays an important role in relaying information throughout the brain, as well as performing specific tasks that allow us to think, feel, and behave as humans. Here we'll give you a brief introduction to each, and you'll read more about many of these structures in later chapters.

Thalamus, Hypothalamus, and Pituitary Gland. The thalamus, hypothalamus, and pituitary gland, located in the center of the brain, interact closely with several other brain structures. They relay signals to and from these structures and also help to regulate them.

The **thalamus** *relays and filters information from the senses and transmits the information to the cerebral cortex.* The thalamus receives inputs from all the major senses except smell, which has direct connections to the cerebral cortex. The thalamus acts as a kind of computer server in a networked system, taking in multiple inputs and relaying them to a variety of locations (Guillery & Sherman, 2002). However, unlike the mechanical operations of a computer ("send input A to location B"), the thalamus actively filters sensory information, giving more weight to some inputs and less weight to others. The thalamus also closes the pathways of incoming sensations during sleep, providing a valuable function in *not* allowing information to pass to the rest of the brain.

The thalamus receives inputs from all the major senses except smell. You can thank your thalamus when you see the red apple, feel its smoothness in your hand, hear the crunch as you bite into it, and taste its sweetness.

ISTOCKPHOTO/THINKSTOCK

How is the thalamus like a computer?

The **hypothalamus,** located below the thalamus (*hypo-* is Greek for "under"), *regulates body temperature, hunger, thirst, and sexual behavior.* Although the hypothalamus is a tiny area of the brain, clusters of neurons in the hypothalamus oversee a wide range of basic behaviors, keeping body temperature, blood sugar levels, and metabolism within an optimal range for normal human functioning. Lesions to some areas of the hypothalamus result in overeating, whereas lesions to other areas leave an animal with no desire for food at all, highlighting that the hypothalamus plays a key role in regulating food intake (Berthoud & Morrison, 2008). Also, when you think about sex, messages from your cerebral cortex are sent to the hypothalamus to trigger the release of hormones. Finally, electric stimulation of some areas of the hypothalamus in cats can produce hissing and biting, whereas stimulation of other areas in the hypothalamus can produce what appears to be intense pleasure for an animal (Siegel et al., 1999). Researchers James Olds and Peter Milner found that a small electric current delivered to a certain region of a rat's hypothalamus was

thalamus
A subcortical structure that relays and filters information from the senses and transmits the information to the cerebral cortex.

hypothalamus
A subcortical structure that regulates body temperature, hunger, thirst, and sexual behavior.

extremely rewarding for the animal (Olds & Milner, 1954). In fact, when allowed to press a bar attached to the electrode to initiate their own stimulation, rats would do so several thousand times an hour, often to the point of exhaustion!

Located below the hypothalamus is the **pituitary gland,** *the "master gland" of the body's hormone-producing system, which releases hormones that direct the functions of many other glands in the body.* The hypothalamus sends hormonal signals to the pituitary gland, which in turn sends hormonal signals to other glands to control stress, digestive activities, and reproductive processes. For example, when a baby suckles its mother's breast, sensory neurons in her breast send signals to her hypothalamus, which then signals her pituitary gland to release a hormone called *oxytocin* into the bloodstream (McNeilly et al., 1983). Oxytocin, in turn, stimulates the release of milk from reservoirs in the breast. The pituitary gland is also involved in the response to stress. When we sense a threat, sensory neurons send signals to the hypothalamus, which stimulates the release of adrenocorticotropic hormone (ACTH) from the pituitary gland. ACTH, in turn, stimulates the adrenal glands (above the kidneys) to release hormones that activate the sympathetic nervous system (Selye & Fortier, 1950). As you read earlier in this chapter, the sympathetic nervous system prepares the body to either meet the threat head-on or flee from the situation.

The Limbic System. The hypothalamus also is part of the **limbic system,** *a group of forebrain structures including the hypothalamus, the hippocampus, and the amygdala, which are involved in motivation, emotion, learning, and memory* (Maclean, 1970; Papez, 1937). The limbic system is where the subcortical structures meet the cerebral cortex.

The **hippocampus** (from Latin for "sea horse," due to its shape) is *critical for creating new memories and integrating them into a network of knowledge so that they can be stored indefinitely in other parts of the cerebral cortex.* Individuals with damage to the hippocampus can acquire new information and keep it in awareness for a few seconds, but as soon as they are distracted, they forget the information and the experience that produced it (Scoville & Milner, 1957; Squire, 2009). This kind of disruption is limited to everyday memory for facts and events that we can bring to consciousness; memory of learned habitual routines or emotional reactions remains intact (Squire, Knowlton, & Musen, 1993). As an example, people with damage to the hippocampus can remember how to drive and talk, but they cannot recall where they have recently driven or a conversation they have just had. You will read more about the hippocampus and its role in creating, storing, and combining memories in the Memory chapter.

The **amygdala** (from Latin for "almond," also due to its shape), *located at the tip of each horn of the hippocampus, plays a central role in many emotional processes, particularly the formation of emotional memories* (Aggleton, 1992). The amygdala attaches significance to previously neutral events that are associated with fear, punishment, or reward (LeDoux, 1992). As an example, think of the last time something scary or unpleasant happened to you: A car came barreling toward you as you started walking into an intersection or a ferocious dog leaped out of an alley as you passed by. Those stimuli—a car or a dog—are fairly neutral; you don't have a panic attack every time you walk by a used car lot. The emotional significance attached to events involving those stimuli is the work of the amygdala (McGaugh, 2006). When we are in emotionally arousing situations, the amygdala stimulates the hippocampus to remember many details surrounding the situation (Kensinger & Schacter, 2005). For example, people who lived through the terrorist attacks of September 11, 2001 remember vivid details about where they were, what they were doing, and how they felt when they heard the news, even years later (Hirst et al., 2009). In particular, the amygdala seems to be especially involved in encoding events as *fearful* (Adolphs et al., 1995; Sigurdsson et al., 2007). We'll have more to say about the amygdala in the

> **Why are you likely to remember details of a traumatic event?**

pituitary gland
The "master gland" of the body's hormone-producing system, which releases hormones that direct the functions of many other glands in the body.

limbic system
A group of forebrain structures including the hypothalamus, the hippocampus, and the amygdala, which are involved in motivation, emotion, learning, and memory.

hippocampus
A structure critical for creating new memories and integrating them into a network of knowledge so that they can be stored indefinitely in other parts of the cerebral cortex.

amygdala
A part of the limbic system that plays a central role in many emotional processes, particularly the formation of emotional memories.

A haunted house is designed to stimulate your amygdala, but only a little.

basal ganglia
A set of subcortical structures that directs intentional movements.

corpus callosum
A thick band of nerve fibers that connects large areas of the cerebral cortex on each side of the brain and supports communication of information across the hemispheres.

occipital lobe
A region of the cerebral cortex that processes visual information.

parietal lobe
A region of the cerebral cortex whose functions include processing information about touch.

Emotion and Motivation chapter. For now, keep in mind that a group of neurons the size of a lima bean buried deep in your brain help you to laugh, weep, or shriek in fright when the circumstances call for it.

The Basal Ganglia. There are several other structures in the subcortical area, but we'll consider just one more. The **basal ganglia** are *a set of subcortical structures that directs intentional movements*. The basal ganglia are located near the thalamus and hypothalamus; they receive input from the cerebral cortex and send outputs to the motor centers in the brain stem. One part of the basal ganglia, the *striatum*, is involved in the control of posture and movement. As we saw in the excerpt from Michael J. Fox's book, people who suffer from Parkinson's disease typically show symptoms of uncontrollable shaking and sudden jerks of the limbs and are unable to initiate a sequence of movements to achieve a specific goal. This happens because the dopamine-producing neurons in the substantia nigra (found in the tegmentum of the midbrain) have become damaged (Dauer & Przedborski, 2003). The undersupply of dopamine then affects the striatum in the basal ganglia, which in turn leads to the visible behavioral symptoms of Parkinson's.

So, what's the problem in Parkinson's: the jerky movements, the ineffectiveness of the striatum in directing behavior, the botched interplay of the substantia nigra and the striatum, or the underproduction of dopamine at the neuronal level? The answer is all of the above. This unfortunate disease provides a nice illustration of two themes regarding the brain and behavior. First, invisible actions at the level of neurons in the brain can produce substantial effects at the level of behavior. Second, the interaction of hindbrain, midbrain, and forebrain structures shows how the various regions are interdependent.

The Cerebral Cortex

Our tour of the brain has taken us from the very small (neurons) to the somewhat bigger (major divisions of the brain) to the very large: the cerebral cortex. The cortex is the highest level of the brain, and it is responsible for the most complex aspects of perception, emotion, movement, and thought (Fuster, 2003). It sits over the rest of the brain, like a mushroom cap shielding the underside and stem, and it is the wrinkled surface you see when looking at the brain with the naked eye.

The smooth surfaces of the cortex—the raised part—are called *gyri* (*gyrus* if you're talking about just one), and the indentations or fissures are called *sulci* (*sulcus* when singular). Sulci and gyri represent a triumph of evolution. The cerebral cortex occupies roughly the area of a newspaper page. Fitting that much cortex into a human skull is a tough task. But if you crumple a sheet of newspaper, you'll see that the same surface area now fits compactly into a much smaller space. The cortex, with its wrinkles and folds, holds a lot of brainpower in a relatively small package that fits comfortably inside the human skull (see **FIGURE 3.17**). The functions of the cerebral cortex can be understood at three levels: the separation of the cortex into two hemispheres, the functions of each hemisphere, and the role of specific cortical areas.

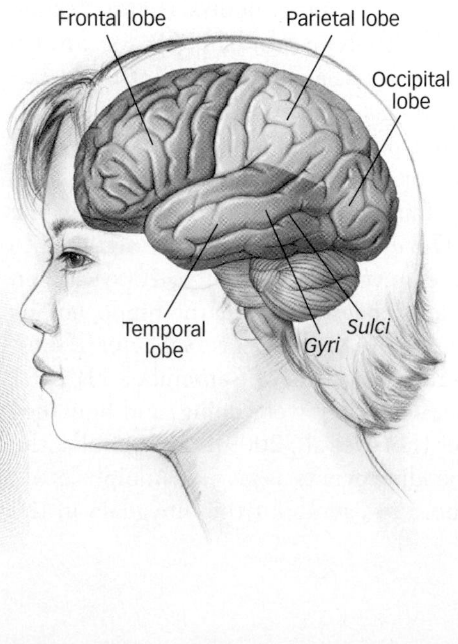

Organization across Hemispheres. The first level of organization divides the cortex into the left and right hemispheres. The two hemispheres are more or less

DONNA RANIERI

Crumpling a newspaper allows the same amount of surface area to fit into a much smaller space, just like the wrinkles and folds in the cortex allow a great deal of brain power to fit inside the human skull.

▶ Figure **3.17** **Cerebral Cortex and Lobes** The four major lobes of the cerebral cortex are the occipital lobe, the parietal lobe, the temporal lobe, and the frontal lobe. The smooth surfaces of the cortex are called gyri and the indentations are called sulci.

symmetrical in their appearance and, to some extent, in their functions. However, each hemisphere controls the functions of the opposite side of the body. This is called *contralateral control*, meaning that your right cerebral hemisphere perceives stimuli from and controls movements on the left side of your body, whereas your left cerebral hemisphere perceives stimuli from and controls movement on the right side of your body.

The cerebral hemispheres are connected to each other by *commissures*, bundles of axons that make possible communication between parallel areas of the cortex in each half. The largest of these commissures is the **corpus callosum,** which *connects large areas of the cerebral cortex on each side of the brain and supports communication of information across the hemispheres* (see **FIGURE 3.18**). This means that information received in the right hemisphere, for example, can pass across the corpus callosum and be registered, virtually instantaneously, in the left hemisphere.

Organization within Hemispheres. The second level of organization in the cerebral cortex distinguishes the functions of the different regions within each hemisphere of the brain. Each hemisphere of the cerebral cortex is divided into four areas, or *lobes*: From back to front, these are the occipital lobe, the parietal lobe, the temporal lobe, and the frontal lobe, as shown in Figure 3.17. We'll examine the functions of these lobes in more detail in later chapters, noting how scientists have used a variety of techniques to understand the operations of the brain. For now, here's a brief overview of the main functions of each lobe.

The **occipital lobe,** located at the back of the cerebral cortex, *processes visual information.* Sensory receptors in the eyes send information to the thalamus, which in turn sends information to the primary areas of the occipital lobe, where simple features of the stimulus are extracted, such as the location and orientation of an object's edges (see the Sensation and Perception chapter for more details). These features are then processed into a more complex "map" of the stimulus onto the occipital cortex, leading to comprehension of what's being seen. As you might imagine, damage to the primary visual areas of the occipital lobe can leave a person with partial or complete blindness. Information still enters the eyes, which work just fine. But without the ability to process and make sense of the information at the level of the cerebral cortex, the information is as good as lost (Zeki, 2001).

The **parietal lobe,** located in front of the occipital lobe, carries out functions that include *processing information about touch.* The parietal lobe contains the *somatosensory cortex*, a strip of brain tissue running from the top of the brain down to the sides (see **FIGURE 3.19**). Within each hemisphere, the somatosensory cortex represents the skin areas on the contralateral surface of the body. Each part of the somatosensory cortex maps onto a particular part of the body. If a body area is more sensitive, a larger part of the somatosensory cortex is devoted to it. For example, the part of the somatosensory cortex that corresponds to the lips and tongue is larger than the area corresponding to the feet. The somatosensory cortex can be illustrated as a distorted figure, called a *homunculus* ("little man"), in which the body parts are rendered according to how much of the somatosensory cortex is devoted to them (Penfield & Rasmussen, 1950). Directly in front of the somatosensory cortex, in the frontal lobe, is a parallel strip of brain tissue called the *motor cortex*. Like the somatosensory cortex, different parts of the motor cortex correspond to different body parts. The motor cortex initiates voluntary movements and sends messages to the basal ganglia, cerebellum, and spinal cord. The motor and somatosensory cortices, then, are like

> Why is the part of the somatosensory cortex relating to the lips bigger than the area corresponding to the feet?

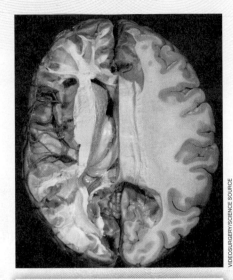

▲ Figure **3.18 Cerebral Hemispheres** The corpus callosum connects the two hemispheres and supports communication between them.

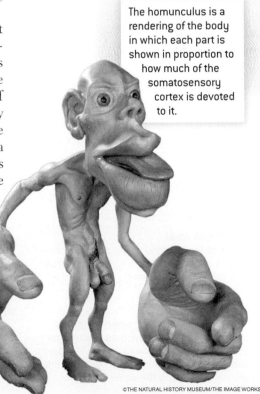

The homunculus is a rendering of the body in which each part is shown in proportion to how much of the somatosensory cortex is devoted to it.

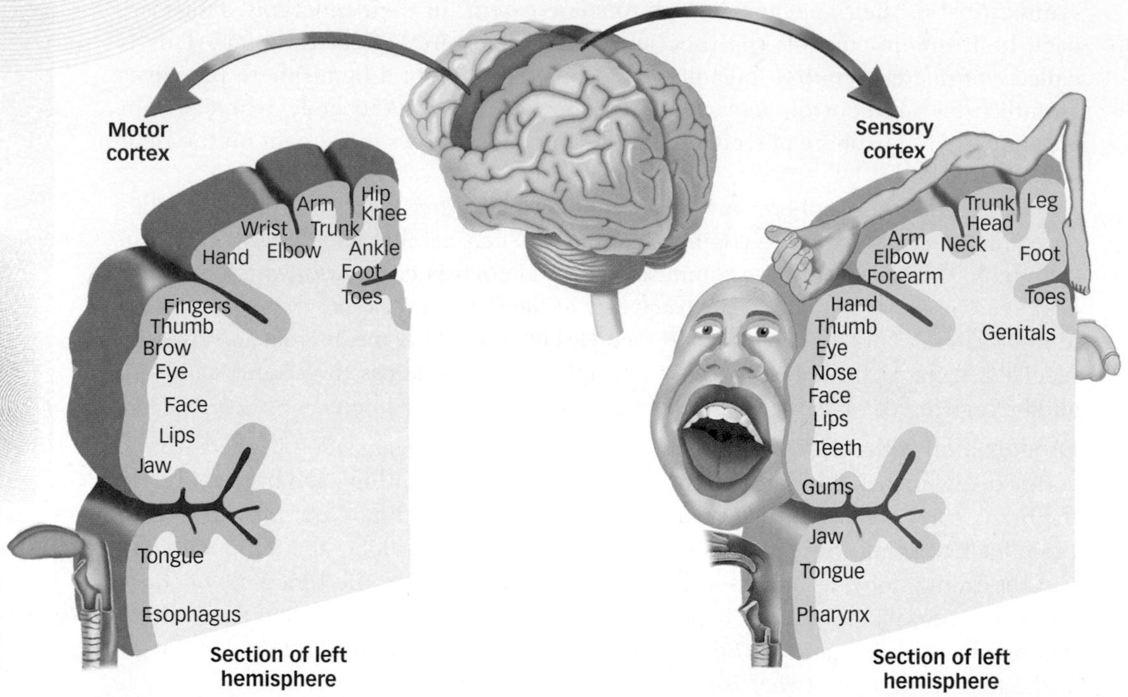

► Figure **3.19** **Somatosensory and Motor Cortices** The motor cortex, a strip of brain tissue in the frontal lobe, represents and controls different skin and body areas on the contralateral side of the body. Directly behind the motor cortex, in the parietal lobe, lies the somatosensory cortex. Like the motor cortex, the somatosensory cortex represents skin areas of particular parts on the contralateral side of the body.

sending and receiving areas of the cerebral cortex, taking in information and sending out commands as the case might be.

The **temporal lobe,** located on the lower side of each hemisphere, is *responsible for hearing and language.* The *primary auditory cortex* in the temporal lobe is analogous to the somatosensory cortex in the parietal lobe and the primary visual areas of the occipital lobe: It receives sensory information from the ears based on the frequencies of sounds (Recanzone & Sutter, 2008). Secondary areas of the temporal lobe then process the information into meaningful units, such as speech and words. The temporal lobe also houses the visual association areas that interpret the meaning of visual stimuli and help us recognize common objects in the environment (Martin, 2007).

The **frontal lobe,** which sits behind the forehead, has *specialized areas for movement, abstract thinking, planning, memory, and judgment.* As you just read, it contains the motor cortex, which coordinates movements of muscle groups throughout the body. Other areas in the frontal lobe coordinate thought processes that help us manipulate information and retrieve memories, which we can use to plan our behaviors and interact socially with others. In short, the frontal cortex allows us to do the kind of thinking, imagining, planning, and anticipating that sets humans apart from most other species (Schoenemann, Sheenan, & Glotzer, 2005; Stuss & Benson, 1986; Suddendorf & Corballis, 2007).

What types of thinking occur in the frontal lobe?

Organization within Specific Lobes. The third level of organization in the cerebral cortex involves the representation of information within specific lobes in the cortex. There is a hierarchy of processing stages from primary areas that handle fine details of information all the way up to **association areas,** which are *composed of neurons that help provide sense and meaning to information registered in the cortex.* For example, neurons in the primary visual cortex are highly specialized: some detect features of the environment that are in a horizontal orientation, others detect movement, and still others process information about human versus nonhuman forms. Secondary areas interpret the information extracted by these primary areas (shape, motion, etc.) to

temporal lobe
A region of the cerebral cortex responsible for hearing and language.

frontal lobe
A region of the cerebral cortex that has specialized areas for movement, abstract thinking, planning, memory, and judgment.

association areas
Areas of the cerebral cortex that are composed of neurons that help provide sense and meaning to information registered in the cortex.

mirror neurons
Neurons that are active when an animal performs a behavior, such as reaching for or manipulating an object, and are also activated when another animal observes that animal performing the same behavior.

make sense of what's being perceived; in this case, perhaps a large cat leaping toward your face. Similarly, neurons in the primary auditory cortex register sound frequencies, but it's the association areas of the temporal lobe that allow you to turn those noises into the meaning of your friend screaming, "Look out for the cat!" Association areas, then, help stitch together the threads of information in the various parts of the cortex to produce a meaningful understanding of what's being registered in the brain.

A striking example of this property of association areas comes from the discovery of the mirror-neuron system. **Mirror neurons** are *active when an animal performs a behavior, such as reaching for or manipulating an object, and are also activated when another animal observes that animal performing the same behavior*. Mirror neurons are found in the frontal lobe (near the motor cortex) and in the parietal lobe (Rizzolatti & Craighero, 2004; Rizzolatti & Sinigaglia, 2010). They have been identified in birds, monkeys, and humans, and their name reflects the function they serve. Neuroimaging studies with humans have shown that mirror neurons are active when people watch someone perform a behavior, such as grasping in midair. But they are more highly activated when that behavior has some purpose or context, such as grasping a cup to take a drink (Iacoboni et al., 2005), and seem to be related to recognizing the goal someone has in carrying out an action and the outcome of the action,

rather than to the particular movements a person makes while performing that action (Hamilton & Grafton, 2006, 2008; Iacoboni, 2009; Rizzolatti & Sinigaglia, 2010). In the Learning chapter we'll find out more about the role of mirror neurons in learning.

Finally, neurons in the association areas are usually less specialized and more flexible than neurons in the primary areas. As such, they can be shaped by learning and experience to do their job more effectively. This kind of shaping of neurons by environmental forces allows the brain flexibility, or plasticity, our next topic.

When one animal observes another engaging in a particular behavior, some of the same neurons become active in the observer as well as in the animal exhibiting the behavior. These mirror neurons seem to play an important role in social behavior.

Brain Plasticity

The cerebral cortex may seem like a fixed structure, one big sheet of neurons designed to help us make sense of our external world. Remarkably, though, sensory cortices are not fixed. They can adapt to changes in sensory inputs, a quality researchers call *plasticity* (i.e., the ability to be molded). As an example, if you lose your middle finger in an accident, the part of the somatosensory area that represents that finger is initially unresponsive (Kaas, 1991). After all, there's no longer any sensory input going from that location to that part of the brain. You might expect the left middle-finger neurons of the somatosensory cortex to wither away. However, over time, that area in the somatosensory cortex becomes responsive to stimulation of the fingers *adjacent* to the missing finger. The brain is plastic: Functions that were assigned to certain areas of the brain may be capable of being reassigned to other areas of the brain to accommodate changing input from the environment (Feldman, 2009). This suggests that sensory inputs "compete" for representation in each cortical area. (See the Real World box for a striking illustration of phantom limbs.)

What does it mean to say that the brain is plastic?

Plasticity doesn't only occur to compensate for missing digits or limbs, however. An extraordinary amount of stimulation of one finger can result in that finger "taking over" the representation of the part of the cortex that usually represents other,

THE REAL WORLD

Brain Plasticity and Sensations in Phantom Limbs

Long after a limb is amputated, many patients continue to experience sensations where the missing limb would be, a phenomenon called *phantom limb syndrome*. Patients can feel their missing limbs moving, even in coordinated gestures such as shaking hands. Some even report feeling pain in their phantom limbs. Why does this happen? Some evidence suggests that phantom limb syndrome may arise in part because of plasticity in the brain.

Researchers stimulated the skin surface in various regions around the face, torso, and arms while monitoring brain activity in amputees and non-amputated volunteers (Ramachandran & Blakeslee, 1998; Ramachandran, Brang, & McGeoch, 2010; Ramachandran, Rodgers-Ramachandran, & Stewart, 1992). Brain imaging techniques displayed the somatosensory cortical areas activated when the skin was stimulated. This allowed the researchers to map how touch is represented in the somatosensory cortex for different areas of the body. For example, when the face was touched, the researchers could determine which areas in the somatosensory cortex were most active; when the torso was stimulated, they could see which areas responded, and so on.

Brain scans of the amputees revealed that stimulating areas of the face and upper arm activated an area in the somatosensory cortex that previously would have been activated by a now-missing hand. The face and arm were represented in the somatosensory cortex in an area adjacent to where the person's hand—now amputated—would have been represented. Stimulating the face or arm produced phantom limb sensations in the amputees; they reported "feeling" a sensation in their missing limbs.

Brain plasticity can explain these results (Pascual-Leone et al., 2005). The cortical representations for the face and the upper arm normally lie on either side of the representation for the hand. The somatosensory areas for the face and upper arm were larger in amputees and had taken over the part of the cortex normally representing the hand. Indeed, the new face and arm representations were now contiguous with each other, filling in the space occupied by the hand representation. Some of these new mappings were quite concise. For example,

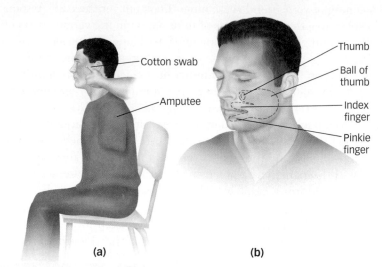

▲ **Mapping Sensations in Phantom Limbs** (*a*) Researchers lightly touch an amputee's face with a cotton swab, eliciting sensations in the "missing" hand. (*b*) Touching different parts of the cheek can even result in sensations in particular fingers or the thumb of the missing hand.

in some amputees, when specific areas of the facial skin were activated, the patient reported sensations in just *one finger* of the phantom hand!

This and related research suggest one explanation for a previously poorly understood phenomenon. How can a person "feel" something that isn't there? Brain plasticity, an adaptive process through which the brain reorganizes itself, offers an answer (Flor, Nikolajsen, & Jensen, 2006). The brain established new mappings that led to novel sensations.

This idea also has practical implications for dealing with the pain that can result from phantom limbs (Ramachandran & Altschuler, 2009). Researchers have used a "mirror box" to teach patients a new mapping to increase voluntary control over their phantom limbs. For example, a patient would place his intact right hand and phantom left hand in the mirror box such that when looking at the mirror, he sees his right hand reflected on the left—where he has placed his phantom—creating the illusion that the phantom has been restored. The phantom hand thus appears to respond to motor commands given by the patient, and with practice the patient can become better at

"moving" the phantom in response to voluntary commands. As a result, when feeling the excruciating pain associated with a clenched phantom hand, the patient can now voluntarily unclench the hand and reduce the pain. This therapeutic approach based on brain plasticity has been applied successfully to a variety of patient populations (Ramachandran & Altschuler, 2009). In one of the most striking applications of this approach, researchers used mirror box therapy with survivors of the destructive 2010 earthquake in Haiti who were experiencing phantom limb pain after amputation of lower limbs (Miller, Seckel, & Ramachandran, 2012). Seventeen of the 18 amputees in that study reported a significant reduction in experienced pain following mirror box therapy.

V. S. RAMACHANDRAN ET AL., 2009

▲ A mirror box creates the illusion that the phantom limb has been restored.

adjacent fingers (Merzenich et al., 1990). For example, concert pianists have highly developed cortical areas for finger control: The continued input from the fingers commands a larger area of representation in the somatosensory cortices in the brain. Consistent with this observation, recent research indicates greater plasticity within the motor cortex of professional musicians compared with nonmusicians, perhaps reflecting an increase in the number of motor synapses as a result of extended practice (Rosenkranz, Williamon, & Rothwell, 2007). Similar findings have been obtained with quilters (who have highly developed areas for the thumb and forefinger, which are critical to their profession) and taxi drivers (who have overdeveloped brain areas in the hippocampus that are used during spatial navigation; Maguire, Woollett, & Spiers, 2006).

Plasticity is also related to a question you might not expect to find in a psychology text: How much exercise have you been getting lately? While we expect that you are spending countless happy hours reading this text, we also hope that you've been finding enough time for physical exercise. A large of number of studies in rats and other nonhuman animals indicate that physical exercise can increase the number of synapses and even promote the development of new neurons in the hippocampus (Hillman, Erickson, & Kramer, 2008; van Praag, 2009). Recent studies with people have begun to document beneficial effects of cardiovascular exercise on aspects of brain function and cognitive performance (Colcombe et al., 2004, 2006). Although these effects tend to be seen most clearly in older adults (okay, so it's time for your textbook authors to get on a treadmill), benefits have also been documented throughout the life span (Hertig & Nagel, 2012; Hillman et al., 2008; Roig et al., 2012). In fact, some researchers believe that this kind of activity-dependent brain plasticity is relevant to treating spinal cord injuries (which, as we saw, have a devastating impact on people's lives), because understanding how to maximize plasticity through exercise and training may help to guide rehabilitation efforts (Dunlop, 2008). It should be clear by now that the plasticity of the brain is not just an interesting theoretical idea; it has potentially important applications to everyday life (Bryck & Fisher, 2012).

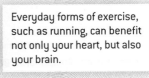

Everyday forms of exercise, such as running, can benefit not only your heart, but also your brain.

MARK ANDERSEN/
GETTY IMAGES

IN SUMMARY

▶ The brain can be divided into the hindbrain, midbrain, and forebrain.

▶ The hindbrain generally coordinates information coming into and out of the spinal cord with structures such as the medulla, the reticular formation, the cerebellum, and the pons. These structures respectively coordinate breathing and heart rate, regulate sleep and arousal levels, coordinate fine motor skills, and communicate this information to the cortex.

▶ The structures of the midbrain, the tectum and tegmentum, generally coordinates functions such as orientation to the environment and movement and arousal toward sensory stimuli.

▶ The forebrain generally coordinates higher-level functions, such as perceiving, feeling, and thinking. The forebrain houses subcortical structures, such as the thalamus, hypothalamus, limbic system (including the hippocampus and amygdala), and basal ganglia; all these structures perform a variety of functions related to motivation and emotion. Also in the forebrain, the cerebral cortex, composed of two hemispheres with four lobes each (occipital, parietal, temporal, and frontal), performs tasks that help make us fully human: thinking, planning, judging, perceiving, and behaving purposefully and voluntarily.

▶ Neurons in the brain can be shaped by experience and the environment, making the human brain amazingly plastic.

The Development and Evolution of Nervous Systems

The human brain is surprisingly imperfect. Why? Far from being a single, elegant machine—the enchanted loom the philosophers wrote so poetically about—the human brain is instead a system comprised of many distinct components that have been added at different times during the course of evolution. The human species has retained what worked best in earlier versions of the brain, then added bits and pieces to get us to our present state through evolution.

To understand the central nervous system, it is helpful to consider two aspects of its development. Prenatal development (growth from conception to birth), reveals how the nervous system develops and changes within each member of a species. Evolutionary development reveals how the nervous system in humans evolved and adapted from other species.

Prenatal Development of the Central Nervous System

The nervous system is the first major bodily system to take form in an embryo (Moore, 1977). It begins to develop within the 3rd week after fertilization, when the embryo is still in the shape of a sphere. Initially, a ridge forms on one side of the sphere and then builds up at its edges to become a deep groove. The ridges fold together and fuse to enclose the groove, forming a structure called the *neural tube*. The tail end of the neural tube will remain a tube, and as the embryo grows larger, it forms the basis of the spinal cord. The tube expands at the opposite end, so that by the 4th week the three basic levels of the brain are visible. During the 5th week, the forebrain and hindbrain further differentiate into subdivisions. During the 7th week and later, the forebrain expands considerably to form the cerebral hemispheres.

> What are the stages of development of the embryonic brain?

As the embryonic brain continues to grow, each subdivision folds onto the next one and begins to form the structures easily visible in the adult brain (see **FIGURE 3.20**). The hindbrain forms the cerebellum and medulla, the midbrain forms the tectum and the tegmentum, and the forebrain subdivides further, separating the thalamus and hypothalamus from the cerebral hemispheres. Over time, the cerebral hemispheres undergo the greatest development, ultimately covering almost all the other subdivisions of the brain.

The *ontogeny* of the brain (how it develops within a given individual) is pretty remarkable. In about half the time it takes you to complete a 15-week semester, the basic structures of the brain are in place and rapidly developing, eventually allowing a newborn to enter the world with a fairly sophisticated set of abilities. In comparison, the *phylogeny* of the brain (how

▼ Figure **3.20** **Prenatal Brain Development** The more primitive parts of the brain, the hindbrain and midbrain, develop first, followed by successively higher levels. The cerebral cortex with its characteristic fissures doesn't develop until the middle of the pregnancy. The cerebral hemispheres undergo most of their development in the final trimester.

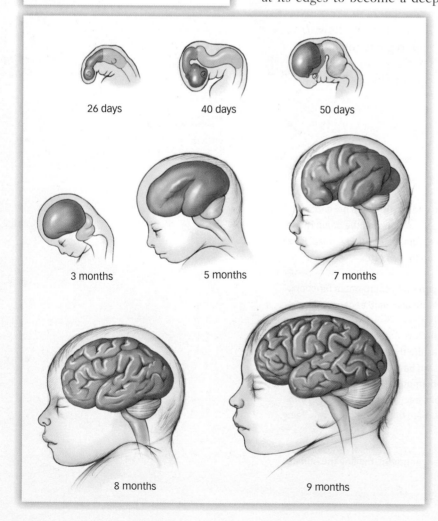

26 days   40 days   50 days

3 months   5 months   7 months

8 months   9 months

it developed within a particular species) is a much slower process. However, it, too, has allowed humans to make the most of the available brain structures, enabling us to perform an incredible array of tasks.

Evolutionary Development of the Central Nervous System

The central nervous system evolved from the very simple one found in simple animals to the elaborate nervous system in humans today. Even the simplest animals have sensory neurons and motor neurons for responding to the environment (Shepherd, 1988). For example, single-celled protozoa have molecules in their cell membrane that are sensitive to food in the water. Those molecules trigger the movement of tiny threads called *cilia,* which help propel the protozoa toward the food source. The first neurons appeared in simple invertebrates, such as jellyfish; the sensory neurons in the jellyfish's tentacles can feel the touch of a potentially dangerous predator, which prompts the jellyfish to swim to safety. If you're a jellyfish, this simple neural system is sufficient to keep you alive. The first central nervous system worthy of the name, though, appeared in flatworms. The flatworm has a collection of neurons in the head—a simple kind of brain— that includes sensory neurons for vision and taste and motor neurons that control feeding behavior. Emerging from the brain is a pair of tracts that form a spinal cord.

Flatworms don't have much of a brain, but then again, they don't need much of a brain. The rudimentary brain areas found in simple invertebrates eventually evolved into the complex brain structures found in humans.

During the course of evolution, a major split in the organization of the nervous system occurred between invertebrate animals (those without a spinal column) and vertebrate animals (those with a spinal column). In all vertebrates, the central nervous system is organized into a hierarchy: The lower levels of the brain and spinal cord execute simpler functions, while the higher levels of the nervous system perform more complex functions. As you saw earlier, in humans, reflexes are accomplished in the spinal cord. At the next level, the midbrain executes the more complex task of orienting toward an important stimulus in the environment. Finally, a more complex task, such as imagining what your life will be like 20 years from now, is performed in the forebrain (Addis, Wong, & Schacter, 2007; Schacter, Addis, et al., 2012; Szpunar, Watson, & McDermott, 2007).

The forebrain undergoes further evolutionary advances in vertebrates. In lower vertebrate species such as amphibians (frogs and newts), the forebrain consists only of small clusters of neurons at the end of the neural tube. In higher vertebrates, including reptiles, birds, and mammals, the forebrain is much larger, and it evolves in two different patterns. Reptiles and birds have almost no cerebral cortex. By contrast, mammals have a highly developed cerebral cortex, which develops multiple areas that serve a broad range of higher mental functions. This forebrain development has reached its peak—so far—in humans (**FIGURE 3.21**).

The human brain, then, is not so much one remarkable thing; rather, it is a succession of extensions from a quite serviceable foundation. Like other species, humans have a hindbrain, and like those species, it performs important tasks to keep us alive. For some species, that's sufficient. All flatworms need to do to ensure their species' survival is eat, reproduce, and stay alive a reasonable length of time. But as the human brain evolved, structures in the midbrain and forebrain developed to handle the increasingly complex demands of the environment. The forebrain of a bullfrog is about as differentiated as

▼ Figure **3.21 Development of the Forebrain** Reptiles and birds have almost no cerebral cortex, whereas mammals such as rats and cats do have a cerebral cortex, but their frontal lobes are proportionately much smaller than the frontal lobes of humans and other primates. How might this explain the fact that only humans have developed complex language, computer technology, and calculus?

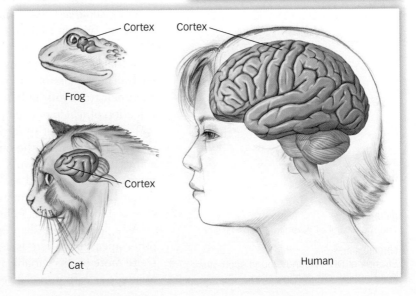

it needs to be to survive in a frog's world. The human forebrain, however, shows substantial refinement, which allows for some remarkable, uniquely human abilities: self-awareness, sophisticated language use, abstract reasoning, and imagining, among others.

There is intriguing evidence that the human brain evolved more quickly than the brains of other species (Dorus et al., 2004). Researchers compared the sequences of 200 brain-related genes in mice, rats, monkeys, and humans and discovered a collection of genes that evolved more rapidly among primates. What's more, they found that primate brains not only evolved quickly compared to those of other species, but the brains of the primates who eventually became humans evolved even more rapidly. These results suggest that in addition to the normal adaptations that occur over the process of evolution, the genes for human brains took particular advantage of a variety of mutations (changes in a gene's DNA) along the evolutionary pathway (Vallender, Mekel-Bobrov, & Lahn, 2008). These results also suggest that the human brain is still evolving—becoming bigger and more adapted to the demands of the environment (Evans et al., 2005; Mekel-Bobrov et al., 2005).

Are our brains still evolving?

Genes may direct the development of the brain on a large, evolutionary scale, but they also guide the development of an individual and, generally, the development of a species. Let's take a brief look at how genes and the environment contribute to the biological bases of behavior.

Genes, Epigenetics, and the Environment

Is it genetics (nature) or the environment (nurture) that reigns supreme in directing a person's behavior? The emerging picture from current research is that both nature *and* nurture play a role in directing behavior, and the focus has shifted to examining the interaction of the two rather than the absolute contributions of either alone (Gottesman & Hanson, 2005; Rutter & Silberg, 2002; Zhang & Meaney, 2010).

What Are Genes?

A **gene** is *the major unit of hereditary transmission.* Historically, the term *gene* has been used to refer to two distinct but related concepts. The initial, relatively abstract concept of a gene referred to units of inheritance that specify traits such as eye color. More recently, genes have been defined as sections on a strand of DNA (deoxyribonucleic acid) that code for the protein molecules that affect traits. Genes are organized into large threads called **chromosomes,** *strands of DNA wound around each other in a double-helix configuration* (see **FIGURE 3.22**). The DNA in our chromosomes produces protein molecules through the action of a molecule known as messenger RNA (ribonucleic acid; mRNA), which communicates a copy of the DNA code to cells that produce proteins. Chromosomes come in pairs, and humans have 23 pairs each. These pairs of chromosomes are similar but not identical: You inherit one of each pair from your father and one from your mother. There's a twist, however: The selection of *which* of each pair is given to you is random.

Perhaps the most striking example of this random distribution is the determination of sex. In mammals, the chromosomes that determine sex are the X and Y chromosomes; females have two X chromosomes, whereas males have one X and one Y chromosome. You inherited an X chromosome from your mother because she has only X chromosomes to give. Your biological sex, therefore, was determined by whether you received an additional X chromosome or a Y chromosome from your father.

As a species, we share about 99% of the same DNA (and almost as much with other apes), but there is a portion of DNA that varies across individuals. Children share more of this variable portion of DNA with their parents than with more distant relatives or with nonrelatives: They share half their genes with each parent, a quarter

gene
The major unit of hereditary transmission.

chromosomes
Strands of DNA wound around each other in a double-helix configuration.

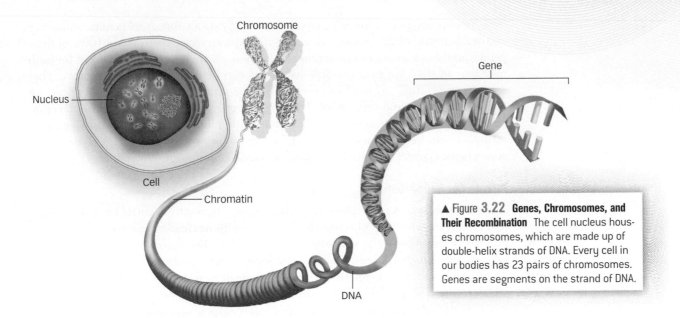

Chromosome

Nucleus

Cell

Chromatin

Gene

DNA

▲ Figure **3.22 Genes, Chromosomes, and Their Recombination** The cell nucleus houses chromosomes, which are made up of double-helix strands of DNA. Every cell in our bodies has 23 pairs of chromosomes. Genes are segments on the strand of DNA.

of their genes with their grandparents, an eighth of their genes with cousins, and so on. The probability of sharing genes is called *degree of relatedness*. The most genetically related people are *monozygotic twins* (also called *identical twins*), who develop from the splitting of a single fertilized egg and therefore share 100% of their genes. *Dizygotic twins* (*fraternal twins*) develop from two separate fertilized eggs and share 50% of their genes, the same as any two siblings born separately.

Many researchers have tried to determine the relative influence of genetics on behavior. One way to do this is to compare a trait shown by monozygotic twins with that same trait among dizygotic twins. This type of research usually enlists twins who were raised in the same household, so that the impact of their environment (their socioeconomic status, access to education, parental child-rearing practices, environmental stressors) remains relatively constant. Finding that monozygotic twins have a higher presence of a specific trait suggests a genetic influence (Boomsma, Busjahn, & Peltonen, 2002).

Why do dizygotic twins share 50% of their genes, just like siblings born separately?

As an example, the likelihood that the dizygotic twin of a person who has schizophrenia (a mental disorder we'll discuss in greater detail in the Psychological Disorders chapter) will *also* develop schizophrenia is 27%. However, this statistic rises to

Monozygotic twins (*left*) share 100% of their genes in common, whereas dizygotic twins (*right*) share 50% of their genes, the same as other siblings. Studies of monozygotic and dizygotic twins help researchers estimate the relative contributions of genes and environmental influences on behavior.

PAUL AVIS/GETTY IMAGES

JBPHOTO1/ALAMY

50% for monozygotic twins. This observation suggests a substantial genetic influence on the likelihood of developing schizophrenia. Monozygotic twins share 100% of their genes, and if one assumes environmental influences are relatively consistent for both members of the twin pair, the 50% likelihood can be traced to genetic factors. That sounds scarily high . . . until you realize that the remaining 50% probability must be due to environmental influences. In short, genetics can contribute to the development, likelihood, or onset of a variety of traits. But a more complete picture of genetic influences on behavior must always take the environmental context into consideration. Genes express themselves within an environment, not in isolation.

A Role for Epigenetics

The idea that genes are expressed within an environment is central to an important and rapidly growing area of research known as **epigenetics:** *environmental influences that determine whether or not genes are expressed, or the degree to which they are expressed, without altering the basic DNA sequences that constitute the genes themselves.* To understand how epigenetic influences work, it is useful to think about DNA as analogous to a script for a play or a movie. The biologist Nessa Carey (2012) offers the example of Shakespeare's *Romeo and Juliet*, which was made into a movie back in 1936 starring classic actors Leslie Howard and Norma Shearer, and in 1996 starring Leonardo DiCaprio and Claire Danes. Shakespeare's script formed the basis of both films, but the directors of the two films used the script in different ways, and the actors in the two films gave different performances. Thus, the final products departed from Shakespeare's script and were different from one another, even though Shakespeare's original script still exists. Something similar happens with epigenetics: depending on the environment, a gene can be expressed or not without altering the underlying DNA code.

The environment can influence gene expression through **epigenetic marks,** *chemical modifications to DNA that can turn genes on or off.* You can think of epigenetic marks as analogous to notes that the movie directors made on Shakespeare's script that determined how the script was used in a particular film. There are two widely studied epigenetic marks:

> **DNA methylation** refers to *adding a methyl group to DNA.* There are special enzymes, referred to as *epigenetic writers,* whose role is to add methyl groups to DNA. Although adding a methyl group doesn't alter the basic DNA sequence, it switches off the methylated gene (see **FIGURE 3.23**). This process is roughly analogous to Claire Danes' director making notes that instruct her to ignore a certain portion of the Shakespeare script. That portion of the script—like the switched off gene—is still there, but its contents are not expressed.

> **Histone modification** involves *adding chemical modifications to proteins called histones that are involved in packaging DNA.* We tend to visualize DNA as the free-floating double helix shown in Figure 3.22, but DNA is actually tightly wrapped around groups of histone proteins, as shown in Figure 3.23. However, whereas DNA methylation serves to switch genes off, histone modification can either switch genes off or turn them on. But just like DNA methylation, histone modifications influence gene expression without altering the underlying DNA sequence (Carey, 2012).

Okay, so now you have learned a lot of strange new terms and may have wondered whether Claire Danes' performance in *Romeo and Juliet* prepared her to play Carrie in *Homeland* (come to think of it, Carrie's relationship with Brody bears some resemblance to Shakespeare's doomed lovers). But what is the relevance of epigenetics to the brain and to psychology? It turns out to be more relevant than anyone suspected until the past decade or so. Experiments with rats and mice have shown that

epigenetics
Environmental influences that determine whether or not genes are expressed, or the degree to which they are expressed, without altering the basic DNA sequences that constitute the genes themselves.

epigenetic marks
Chemical modifications to DNA that can turn genes on or off.

DNA methylation
Adding a methyl group to DNA.

histone modification
Adding chemical modifications to proteins called histones that are involved in packaging DNA.

heritability
A measure of the variability of behavioral traits among individuals that can be accounted for by genetic factors.

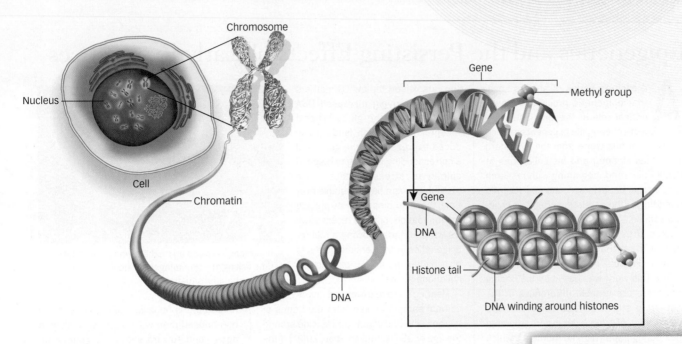

Chromosome

Gene

Methyl group

Nucleus

Cell

Chromatin

Gene

DNA

Histone tail

DNA

DNA winding around histones

▲ Figure **3.23** **Epigenetics** Studies suggest that DNA methylation and histone modification play a key role in the long-lasting effects of early life experiences for both rodents and humans.

epigenetic marks left by DNA methylation and histone modifcation play a role in learning and memory (Bredy et al., 2007; Day & Sweatt, 2011; Levenson, & Sweatt, 2005). Several studies have linked epigenetic changes with responses to stress (Zhang & Meaney, 2010), including recent research with humans. For example, studies of nurses working in high-stress versus low-stress environments found differences between the two groups in DNA methylation (Alasaari et al., 2012). Subjective levels of stress in a sample of 92 Canadian adults, as well as physiological signs of stress, were correlated with levels of DNA methylation (Lam et al., 2012). Another study reported a link between DNA methylation and early life experience, with differences observed between individuals who grew up in relatively affluent households versus those who grew up in poverty, even when controlling for such factors as current socioeconomic status (Lam et al., 2012). Similar findings were reported in a separate study of 40 British adults (Borghol et al., 2012). These observations fit well with an important line of research described in the Hot Science box, showing that DNA methylation and histone modifications play a key role in the long-lasting effects of early experiences for both rats and humans.

The Role of Environmental Factors

Genes set the range of possibilities that can be observed in a population, but the characteristics of any individual within that range are determined by environmental factors and experience. The genetic capabilities that another species might enjoy, such as breathing underwater, are outside the range of *your* possibilities, no matter how much you might desire them.

With these parameters in mind, behavioral geneticists use calculations based on relatedness to compute the heritability of behaviors (Plomin, DeFries, et al., 2001). **Heritability** is *a measure of the variability of behavioral traits among individuals that can be accounted for by genetic factors*. Heritability is calculated as a proportion, and its numerical value (index) ranges from 0 to 1.00. A heritability of 0 means that genes do not contribute to individual differences in the behavioral trait; a heritability of 1.00 means that genes are the *only* reason for the individual differences. As you might guess, scores of 0 or 1.00 occur so infrequently that they serve more as theoretical limits than realistic values; almost nothing in human behavior is completely due to

Epigenetics and the Persisting Effects of Early Experiences

An exciting series of studies show that epigenetic processes play a critical role in the long-lasting effects of early life experiences. Much of this work has come from the laboratory of Michael Meaney and his colleagues at McGill University, beginning with research on maternal behaviors in rats and recently extending to the persisting effects of childhood abuse.

Let's first consider early work from Meaney's lab that provides critical background (Francis et al., 1999; Liu et al., 1997). This work was based on the finding that there are notable differences in the mothering styles of rats: Some mothers spend a lot of time licking and grooming their young pups (high LG mothers), which rat pups greatly enjoy, whereas others spend little time doing so (low LG mothers). The researchers found that pups of high LG mothers are much less fearful as adults when placed in stressful situations than the adult pups of low LG mothers. Perhaps this simply reflects the effects of a genetic profile shared by the mother and her pups? Not so. Meaney and colleagues demonstrated that the same effects are obtained when the offspring of high LG mothers are raised by low LG mothers, and vice versa. These effects were accompanied by physiological changes. When placed in fear-inducing situations, adult rats raised by the high LG mothers showed lower levels of several stress-related hormones than adult rats that had been raised by low LG mothers. There was also increased evidence of hippocampal serotonin in the adult pups of high LG mothers; as you learned earlier in this chapter, increased levels of serotonin are associated with elevated mood. In other words, the high LG pups grow up to become "chilled out" adults. But exactly how did these effects persist from infancy to adulthood? This is where epigenetics come in. The increased serotonin response produced by high LG mothers triggers a decrease in DNA methylation of the glucocorticoid receptor gene (see the Stress & Health chapter for a discussion of glucocorticoids and stress), which leads to greater expression of the gene and a corresponding ability to respond more calmly to stress (Weaver et al., 2004).

The rats raised by low LG mothers showed relatively increased DNA methylation of the glucocorticoid receptor gene, which leads to reduced expression of the gene and a corresponding inability to respond calmly to stress. Because DNA methylation can be very stable over time, these studies with rats provide the foundation for more recent studies with humans showing a role for epigenetics in the persisting effects of a highly disturbing experience: childhood abuse.

Meaney's group examined hippocampal samples taken from the brains of 24 men who had committed suicide around the age of 35 (McGowan et al., 2009). (The hippocampus plays a role in response to stress and has the highest concentration glucocorticoid receptions in the entire brain.) Twelve of those men had a history of childhood abuse and 12 did not. The researchers compared their hippocampal samples to a separate control group of 12 men who had died suddenly at around the same age but had no history of abuse and had not committed suicide. Strikingly, they found evidence for increased levels of DNA methylation at the hippocampal glucocorticoid receptor gene in the 12 men who had suffered childhood abuse and committed suicide compared with the 12 men in the control group. But they found no such differences between the 12 men who committed suicide but had not been abused and the 12 men in the control group. Increased DNA methylation reduced expression of the glucocorticoid receptor gene in the 12 victims of childhood abuse, just as in the adult pups of low LG mothers. Although this research doesn't tell us whether or how differences in DNA methylation were

▲ Rodent pups raised by mothers who spend a lot of time licking and grooming them are less fearful as adults in stressful situations.

related to the behaviors of the abused and non-abused men when they were alive, it does point toward similar epigenetic effects of adverse early experiences in rats and humans.

Studies suggest that the effects of early experience are not restricted to a single gene, but occur more broadly. A more recent study of rats from Meaney's lab demonstrates hundreds of DNA methylation differences in the hippocampus of the offspring of high and low LG mothers (McGowan et al., 2011). New analyses of hippocampal samples from abused suicide victims also reveal widespread DNA methylation differences between the abused sample and a control group of non-abused individuals (Suderman et al., 2012). Although there were also methylation differences between rats and humans that probably reflect a combination of environmental and biological differences between the two species (Suderman et al., 2012), the overall pattern of results suggests a broad role for epigenetic influences in understanding the effects of early experiences on subsequent development and behavior (Meaney & Ferguson-Smith, 2010).

High LG Mother	Low LG Mother
Increased serotonin in the hippocampus Decrease in DNA methylation of glucocorticoid receptor gene (related to stress) Greater expression of the gene	Decreased serotonin in the hippocampus Increase in DNA methylation of glucocorticoid receptor gene (related to stress) Reduced expression of the gene
↓	↓
Pups grow to be "chilled out" adults with better regulated stress response	Pups grow into adults with less ability to respond calmly to stress

the environment or owed *completely* to genetic inheritance. Scores between 0 and 1.00, then, indicate that individual differences are caused by varying degrees of genetic and environmental contributions—a little stronger influence of genetics here, a little stronger influence of the environment there, but each always within the context of the other (Moffitt, 2005; Zhang & Meaney, 2010).

For human behavior, almost all estimates of heritability are in the moderate range, between .30 and .60. For example, a heritability index of .50 for intelligence indicates that half of the variability in intelligence test scores is attributable to genetic influences and the remaining half is due to environmental influences. Smart parents often (but not always) produce smart children; genetics certainly plays a role. But smart and not-so-smart children attend good or not-so-good schools, practice their piano lessons with more or less regularity, study or not study as hard as they might, have good and not-so-good teachers and role models, and so on. Genetics is only half the story in intelligence. Environmental influences also play a significant role in predicting the basis of intelligence (see the Intelligence chapter).

"*The title of my science project is 'My Little Brother: Nature or Nurture.'*"

Heritability has proven to be a theoretically useful and statistically sound concept in helping scientists understand the relative genetic and environmental influences on behavior. However, there are four important points about heritability to bear in mind. First, remember that *heritability is an abstract concept*: It tells us nothing about the *specific* genes that contribute to a trait. Second, *heritability is a population concept*: It tells us nothing about an individual. Heritability provides guidance for understanding differences across individuals in a population rather than abilities within an individual.

> **Are abilities, such as intelligence and memory, inherited through our genes?**

Third, *heritability is dependent on the environment.* Just as behavior occurs within certain contexts, so do genetic influences. For example, intelligence isn't an unchanging quality: People are intelligent within a particular learning context, a social setting, a family environment, a socioeconomic class, and so on. Heritability, therefore, is meaningful only for the environmental conditions in which it was computed, and heritability estimates may change dramatically under other environmental conditions. Finally, *heritability is not fate*. It tells us nothing about the degree to which interventions can change a behavioral trait. Heritability is useful for identifying behavioral traits that are influenced by genes, but it is not useful for determining how individuals will respond to particular environmental conditions or treatments.

IN SUMMARY

▶ Examining the development of the nervous system over the life span of an individual (its ontogeny) and across the time within which a species evolves (its phylogeny) presents further opportunities for understanding the human brain.

▶ The nervous system is the first system that forms in an embryo, starting as a neural tube, which forms the basis of the spinal cord. The neural tube expands on one end to form the hindbrain, midbrain, and forebrain, each of which folds onto the next structure.

▶ Within each of these areas, specific brain structures begin to differentiate. The forebrain shows the greatest differentiation, and in particular, the cerebral cortex is the most developed in humans.

(continued)

▶ Nervous systems evolved from simple collections of sensory and motor neurons in simple animals, such as flatworms, to elaborate centralized nervous systems found in mammals.

　▶ The evolution of the human nervous system can be thought of as a process of refining, elaborating, and expanding structures present in other species.

　▶ Reptiles and birds have almost no cerebral cortex. By contrast, mammals have a highly developed cerebral cortex.

　▶ The human brain appears to have evolved more quickly compared to other species to become adapted to a more complex environment.

▶ The gene, or the unit of hereditary transmission, is built from strands of DNA in a double-helix formation that is organized into chromosomes.

▶ Humans have 23 pairs of chromosomes; half come from each parent.

　▶ A child shares 50% of his or her genes with each parent.

　▶ Monozygotic twins share 100% of their genes, whereas dizygotic twins share 50%, the same as any other siblings. Because of their genetic relatedness, twins are often participants in genetic research.

▶ The study of genetics indicates that both genes and the environment work together to influence behavior. Genes set the range of variation in populations within a given environment, but they do not predict individual characteristics; experience and other environmental factors play a crucial role as well.

▶ Epigenetics refers to environmental influences that determine whether or not genes are expressed, without altering the basic DNA sequences that constitute the genes themselves. Epigenetic marks such as DNA methylation and histone modification influence whether specific genes are switched on or off. Epigenetic influences have been shown to play a critical role in persisting effects of early experiences in rats and humans.

Investigating the Brain

So far, you've read a great deal about the nervous system: how it's organized, how it works, what its components are, and what those components do. But one question remains largely unanswered: *How* do we know all of this? Anatomists can dissect a human brain and identify its structures, but they cannot determine which structures play a role in producing which behaviors by dissecting a nonliving brain.

Scientists use a variety of methods to understand how the brain affects behavior. Let's consider three of the main ones: studying people with brain damage; studying the brain's electrical activity; and using brain imaging to study brain structure and watch the brain in action. Let's examine each of these ways of investigating the brain.

Studying the Damaged Brain

To understand the normal operation of a process better, it is instructive to understand what happens when that process fails. Much research in neuroscience correlates the loss of specific perceptual, motor, emotional, or cognitive functions with specific areas of brain damage (Andrewes, 2001; Kolb & Whishaw, 2003). By studying these instances, neuroscientists can theorize about the functions those brain areas normally perform. The modern history of neuroscience can be dated to the work of Paul Broca (see the Psychology: Evolution of a Science chapter). In 1861,

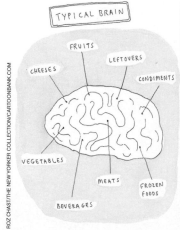

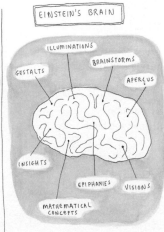

Broca described a patient who had lost the capacity to produce spoken language (but not the ability to understand language) due to damage in a small area in the left frontal lobe. In 1874, Carl Wernicke (1848–1905) described a patient with an impairment in language comprehension (but not the ability to produce speech) associated with damage to an area in the upper-left temporal lobe. These areas were named, respectively, *Broca's area* and *Wernicke's area* (see Figure 9.3 in the Language and Thought chapter), and they provided the earliest evidence that the brain locations for speech production and speech comprehension are separate and that for most people, the left hemisphere is critical to producing and understanding language (Young, 1990).

> **How have brain disorders been central to the study of specific areas of the brain?**

The Emotional Functions of the Frontal Lobes

As you've already seen, the human frontal lobes are a remarkable evolutionary achievement. However, psychology's first glimpse at some functions of the frontal lobes came from a rather unremarkable fellow; so unremarkable, in fact, that a single event in his life defined his place in the annals of psychology's history (Macmillan, 2000). Phineas Gage was a muscular 25-year-old railroad worker. On September 13, 1848, in Cavendish, Vermont, he was packing an explosive charge into a crevice in a rock when the powder exploded, driving a 3-foot, 13-pound iron rod through his head at high speed (Harlow, 1848). As **FIGURE 3.24** shows, the rod entered through his lower left jaw and exited through the middle top of his head. Incredibly, Gage lived to tell the tale. But his personality underwent a significant change.

Before the accident, Gage had been mild mannered, quiet, conscientious, and a hard worker. After the accident, however, he became irritable, irresponsible, indecisive, and given to profanity. The sad decline of Gage's personality and emotional life nonetheless provided an unexpected benefit to psychology. His case study was the first to allow researchers to investigate the hypothesis that the frontal lobe is involved in emotion regulation, planning, and decision making. Furthermore, because the connections between the frontal lobe and the subcortical structures of the limbic system were affected, scientists were able to understand better how the amygdala, hippocampus, and related brain structures interacted with the cerebral cortex (Damasio, 2005).

COLLECTION OF JACK AND BEVERLY WILGUS

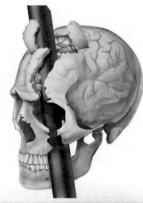

▲ Figure **3.24 Phineas Gage**
Phineas Gage's traumatic accident allowed researchers to investigate the functions of the frontal lobe and its connections with emotion centers in the subcortical structures. The likely path of the metal rod through Gage's skull is reconstructed here.

The Distinct Roles of the Left and Right Hemispheres

You'll recall that the cerebral cortex is divided into two hemispheres, although typically the two hemispheres act as one integrated unit. Sometimes, though, disorders can threaten the ability of the brain to function, and the only way to stop them is with radical methods. This is sometimes the case for people who suffer from severe, intractable epilepsy. Seizures that begin in one hemisphere cross the corpus callosum (the thick band of nerve fibers that allows the two hemispheres to communicate) to the opposite hemisphere and start a feedback loop that results in a kind of firestorm in the brain. To alleviate the severity of the seizures, surgeons can sever the corpus

Roger Wolcott Sperry (1913–1994) received the Nobel Prize in Physiology in 1981 for his pioneering work investigating the independent functions of the cerebral hemispheres.

callosum in a procedure called a *split-brain procedure*. The result is that a seizure that starts in one hemisphere is isolated in that hemisphere because there is no longer a connection to the other side. This procedure helps people with epilepsy, but also produces some unusual, if not unpredictable, behaviors.

Nobel laureate Roger Sperry (1913–1994) was intrigued by the observation that the everyday behavior of people who had their corpus collosum severed did not seem to be affected by the operation. Did this mean that the corpus callosum played no role at all in behavior? Sperry thought that this conclusion was premature, reasoning that casual observations of everyday behaviors could easily fail to detect impairments that might be picked up by sensitive tests. To evaluate this idea experimentally, Sperry and his colleagues first showed that when the corpus callosum was severed in cats, learning was not transferred from one hemisphere to the other (Sperry, 1964). Later, Sperry designed several experiments that investigated the behaviors of people with split brains, and in the process, revealed a great deal about the independent functions of the left and right hemispheres (Sperry, 1964). Normally, any information that initially enters the left hemisphere is also registered in the right hemisphere and vice versa: The information comes in and travels across the corpus callosum, and both hemispheres understand what's going on (see **FIGURE 3.25**). But in a person with a split brain, information entering one hemisphere stays there. Without an intact corpus callosum, there's no way for that information to reach the other hemisphere. Sperry and his colleagues used this understanding of lateralized perception in a series of experiments. For example, they had a person with a split brain look at a spot in the center of a screen and then projected a stimulus either on the left side of the screen (the left visual field) or the right side of the screen (the right visual field), isolating the stimulus to the opposite hemisphere (see Figure 4.10 in the Sensation and Perception chapter for more details about how information from one visual field enters the opposite hemisphere).

What role does the corpus callosum play in behavior?

The hemispheres themselves are specialized for different kinds of tasks. You just learned about Broca's and Wernicke's areas, which revealed that language processing is largely a left-hemisphere activity. So imagine that some information came into the left hemisphere of a person with a split brain, and she was asked to describe verbally what it was. No problem: The left hemisphere has the information, it's the "speaking" hemisphere, so she should have no difficulty verbally describing what she saw. But suppose she were asked to reach behind the screen with her left hand and pick up the object she just saw. Remember that the hemispheres exert contralateral control over the body, meaning that the left hand is controlled by the right hemisphere. But this person's right hemisphere has no clue what the object was because that information was received in the left hemisphere and was unable to travel to the right hemisphere! So, even though she saw the object and could verbally describe it, she would be unable to use the right hemisphere to perform other tasks regarding that object, such as correctly selecting it from a group with her left hand (see Figure 3.25).

Of course, information presented to the right hemisphere would produce complementary deficits. In this case, she might be presented with a familiar object in her left hand (e.g., a key), be able to demonstrate that

▼ Figure **3.25** **Split-Brain Experiment** When a person with a split brain is presented with the picture of a ring on the right and that of a key on the left side of a screen, she can verbalize *ring* but not *key* because the left hemisphere "sees" the ring and language is usually located in the left hemisphere. She would be able to choose a key with her left hand from a set of objects behind a screen. She would not, however, be able to pick out a ring with her left hand because what the left hemisphere "sees" is not communicated to the left side of her body.

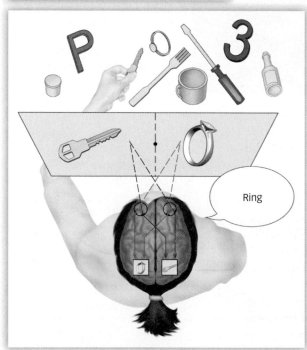

Ring

she knew what it was (by twisting and turning the key in midair), yet be unable to verbally describe what she was holding. In this case, the information in the right hemisphere is unable to travel to the left hemisphere, which controls the production of speech.

Furthermore, suppose a person with a split brain was shown the unusual face in **FIGURE 3.26.** This is called a *chimeric face,* and it is assembled from half-face components of the full faces also shown in the figure. When asked to indicate which face was presented, she would indicate that she saw *both* faces because information about the face on the left is recorded in the right hemisphere and information about the face on the right is recorded in the left hemisphere (Levy, Trevarthen, & Sperry, 1972).

These split-brain studies reveal that the two hemispheres perform different functions and can work together seamlessly as long as the corpus callosum is intact. Without a way to transmit information from one hemisphere to the other, information remains in the hemisphere it initially entered and we become acutely aware of the different functions of each hemisphere. Of course, a person with a split brain can adapt to this by simply moving her eyes a little so that the same information independently enters both hemispheres. Split-brain studies have continued over the past few decades and continue to play an important role in shaping our understanding of how the brain works (Gazzaniga, 2006).

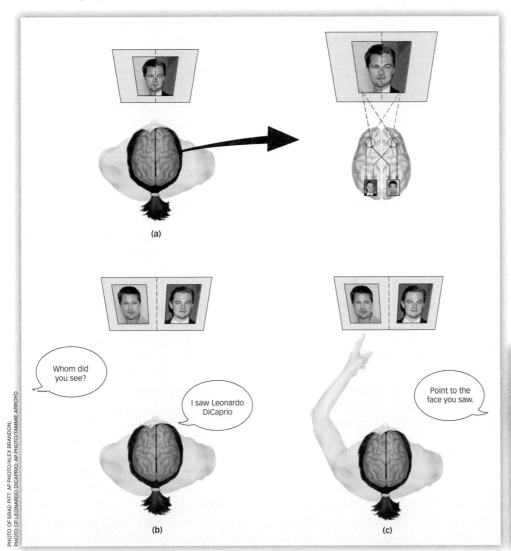

◄ Figure **3.26 Chimeric Faces and the Split Brain** [*a*] When a person with a split brain views a chimeric face of Brad Pitt and Leonardo DiCaprio, her left hemisphere is aware only of Leonardo DiCaprio and her right hemisphere sees only Brad Pitt. [*b*] When asked whom she sees, she answers, "Leonardo DiCaprio," because speech is controlled by the left hemisphere. [*c*] When asked to point to the face she saw with her left hand, she points to Brad Pitt because her right hemisphere is only aware of the left half of the picture.

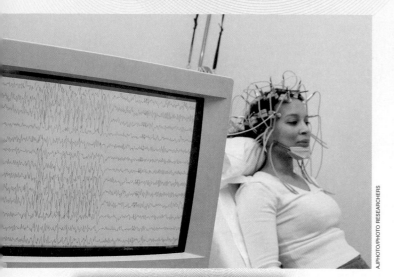

AJ/PHOTO/PHOTO RESEARCHERS

▲ Figure **3.27** **EEG** The electroencephalograph (EEG) records electrical activity in the brain. Many states of consciousness, such as wakefulness and stages of sleep, are characterized by particular types of brain waves.

Studying the Brain's Electrical Activity

A second approach to studying the link between brain structures and behavior involves recording the pattern of electrical activity of neurons. An **electroencephalograph (EEG)** is *a device used to record electrical activity in the brain.* Typically, electrodes are placed on the outside of the head, and even though the source of electrical activity in synapses and action potentials is far removed from these wires, the electric signals can be amplified several thousand times by the EEG. This provides a visual record of the underlying electrical activity, as shown in **FIGURE 3.27**. Using this technique, researchers can determine the amount of brain activity during different states of consciousness. For example, as you'll read in the Consciousness chapter, the brain shows distinctive patterns of electrical activity when awake versus asleep; in fact, there are even different brain-wave patterns associated with different stages of sleep. EEG recordings allow researchers to make these fundamental discoveries about the nature of sleep and wakefulness (Dement, 1978). The EEG can also be used to examine the brain's electrical activity when awake individuals engage in a variety of psychological functions, such as perceiving, learning, and remembering.

> How does the EEG record electrical activity in the brain?

A different approach to recording electrical activity resulted in a more refined understanding of the brain's division of responsibilities, even at a cellular level. Nobel laureates David Hubel and Torsten Wiesel used a technique that inserted electrodes into the occipital lobes of anesthetized cats and observed the patterns of action potentials of individual neurons (Hubel, 1988). Hubel and Wiesel amplified the action potential signals through a loudspeaker so that the signals could be heard as clicks as well as seen on an oscilloscope. While flashing lights in front of the animal's eye, Hubel and Wiesel recorded the resulting activity of neurons in the occipital cortex. What they discovered was not much of anything: Most of the neurons did not respond to this kind of general stimulation. This was frustrating to them. Hubel (1988, p. 69) recalled years later that "we tried everything short of standing on our heads to get it to fire," but then they began to notice something interesting.

Nearing the end of what seemed like a failed set of experiments, they projected a glass slide that contained a black dot in front of the cat's eyes and heard a brisk flurry of clicks as the neurons in the cat's occipital lobe fired away! Observing carefully, they realized that the firing did not have anything to do with the black dot, but instead was produced by a faint but sharp shadow cast by the edge of the glass slide. They discovered that neurons in the primary visual cortex are activated whenever a contrast between light and dark occurs in part of the visual field, seen particularly well when the visual stimulus was a thick line of light against a dark background. In this case, the shadow caused by the edge of the slide provided the kind of contrast that prompted particular neurons to respond. They then found that each neuron responded vigorously only when presented with a contrasting edge at a particular orientation. Since then, many studies have shown that neurons in the primary visual cortex represent particular features of visual stimuli, such as contrast, shape, and color (Zeki, 1993).

These neurons in the visual cortex are known as *feature detectors* because they selectively respond to certain aspects of a visual image. For example, some neurons fire only when detecting a vertical line in the middle of the visual field, other neurons fire when a line at a 45° angle is perceived, and still others in response to wider lines, horizontal lines, lines in the periphery of the visual field, and so on (Livingstone & Hubel, 1988). The discovery of this specialized function for neurons was a huge leap forward in our understanding of how the visual cortex works. Feature detectors iden-

AP PHOTO

David Hubel (*left*, b. 1926) and Torsten Wiesel (*right*, b. 1924) received the Nobel Prize in Physiology in 1981 for their work on mapping the visual cortex.

tify basic dimensions of a stimulus ("slanted line . . . other slanted line . . . horizontal line"); those dimensions are then combined during a later stage of visual processing to allow recognition and perception of a stimulus ("Oh, it's a letter *A*").

Other studies have identified a variety of features that are detected by sensory neurons. For example, some visual processing neurons in the temporal lobe are activated only when detecting faces (Kanwisher, 2000; Perrett, Rolls, & Caan, 1982). Neurons in this area are specialized for processing faces; damage to this area results in an inability to perceive faces. These complementary observations (showing that the type of function that is lost or altered when a brain area is damaged corresponds to the kind of information processed by neurons in that cortical area) provide the most compelling evidence linking the brain to behavior.

Using Brain Imaging to Study Structure and to Watch the Brain in Action

The third major way that neuroscientists can peer into the workings of the human brain has only become possible within the past several decades. EEG readouts give an overall picture of a person's level of consciousness, and single-cell recordings shed light on the actions of particular clumps of neurons. The ideal of neuroscience, however, has been the ability to see the brain in operation during behavior. This goal has been steadily achieved thanks to a wide range of *neuroimaging techniques* that use advanced technology to create images of the living, healthy brain (Posner & Raichle, 1994; Raichle & Mintun, 2006). *Structural brain imaging* provides information about the basic structure of the brain and allows clinicians or researchers to see abnormalities in brain structure. *Functional brain imaging*, in contrast, provides information about the activity of the brain when people perform various kinds of cognitive or motor tasks.

Structural Brain Imaging

One of the first neuroimaging techniques developed was the *computerized axial tomography (CT) scan*. In a CT scan, a scanner rotates a device around a person's head and takes a series of X-ray photographs from different angles. Computer programs then combine these images to provide views from any angle. CT scans show different densities of tissue in the brain. For example, the higher-density skull looks white on a CT scan, the cortex shows up as gray, and the least dense fissures and ventricles in the brain look dark (see **FIGURE 3.28**). CT scans are used to locate lesions or tumors, which typically appear darker because they are less dense than the cortex.

Magnetic resonance imaging (MRI) uses a strong magnetic field to line up the nuclei of specific molecules in the brain tissue. Brief, but powerful, pulses of radio waves cause the nuclei to rotate out of alignment. When a pulse ends, the nuclei snap back

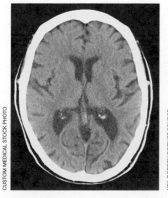 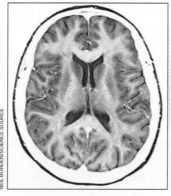

◀ Figure **3.28 Structural Imaging Techniques (CT and MRI)** CT (*left*) and MRI (*right*) scans are used to provide information about the structure of the brain and can help to spot tumors and other kinds of damage. Each scan shown here provides a snapshot of a single slice in the brain. Note that the MRI scan provides a clearer, higher-resolution image than the CT scan (see the text for further discussion of how these images are constructed and what they depict).

in line with the magnetic field and give off a small amount of energy in the process. Different molecules have unique energy signatures when they snap back in line with the magnetic field, so these signatures can be used to reveal brain structures with different molecular compositions. MRI produces pictures of soft tissue at a better resolution than a CT scan, as you can see in Figure 3.28. These techniques give psychologists a clearer picture of the structure of the brain and can help localize brain damage (as when someone suffers a stroke), but they reveal nothing about the functions of the brain.

Diffusion tensor imaging (DTI) is a relatively recently developed type of MRI that is used to visualize white matter pathways, which are fiber bundles that connect both nearby and distant brain regions to one another. DTI measures the rate and direction of diffusion or movement of water molecules along white matter pathways. Because the diffusion of water molecules follows the direction of the pathway, information about the direction in which water molecules diffuse can be used to determine where a white matter pathway goes. Scientists can use measures based on the rate and direction of diffusion to assess the integrity of a white matter pathway, which is very useful in cases of neurological and psychological disorders (Thomason & Thompson, 2011).

Because DTI provides information about pathways that connect brain areas to one another, it is a critical tool in mapping the connectivity of the human brain, and plays a central role in an ambitious undertaking known as the Human Connectome Project. This is a collaborative effort funded by the National Institutes of Health beginning in 2009 that involves a partnership between researchers at Massachusetts General Hospital and UCLA, and another partnership between researchers at Washington University and the University of Minnesota. The main goal of the project is to provide a complete map of the connectivity of neural pathways in the brain: the human connectome (Toga et al., 2012). A unique and exciting feature of the Human Connectome Project is that the researchers have made available some of their results at their Web site (www.humanconnectomeproject.org), which include fascinating colorful images of some of the connection pathways they have discovered.

DTI allows researchers to visualize white matter pathways in the brain, the fiber bundles that play an important role by connecting brain regions to one another.

Functional Brain Imaging

Functional brain imaging techniques show researchers much more than just the structure of the brain by allowing us to watch the brain in action. These techniques rely on the fact that activated brain areas demand more energy for their neurons to work. This energy is supplied through increased blood flow to the activated areas. Functional imaging techniques can detect such changes in blood flow. In *positron emission tomography (PET)*, a harmless radioactive substance is injected into a person's bloodstream. Then the brain is scanned by radiation detectors as the person performs perceptual or cognitive tasks, such as reading or speaking. Areas of the brain that are activated during these tasks demand more energy and greater blood flow, resulting in a higher amount of the radioactivity in that region. The radiation detectors record the level of radioactivity in each region, producing a computerized image of the activated areas (see **FIGURE 3.29**). Note that PET scans differ from CT scans and MRIs in that the image produced shows activity in the brain while the person performs certain tasks. So, for example, a PET scan of a person speaking would show activation in Broca's area in the left frontal lobe.

For psychologists, the most widely used functional brain imaging technique nowadays is *functional magnetic resonance imaging (fMRI)*, which detects the difference between oxygenated hemoglobin and deoxygenated hemoglobin when exposed to magnetic pulses. Hemoglobin is the molecule in the blood that carries oxygen to our tissues, including the brain. When active neurons demand more energy and blood

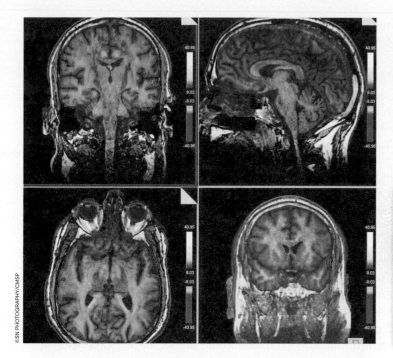

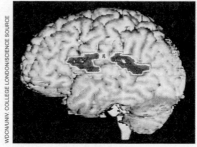

PET scan

▲ Figure 3.29 **Functional Imaging Techniques (PET and fMRI)** PET and fMRI scans provide information about the function of the brain by revealing which brain areas become more or less active in different conditions. The PET scan (*directly above*) shows areas in the left hemisphere (Broca's area, left; lower parietal–upper temporal area, right) that become active when people hold in mind a string of letters for a few seconds. The red areas in the fMRI scans (*all views to the left*) indicate activity in the auditory cortex of a person listening to music.

flow, oxygenated hemoglobin concentrates in the active areas; fMRI detects the oxygenated hemoglobin and provides a picture of the level of activation in each brain area (see Figure 3.29). Just as MRI was a major advance over CT scans, *functional* MRI represents a similar leap in our ability to record the brain's activity during behavior. Both fMRI and PET allow researchers to localize changes in the brain very accurately. However, fMRI has a couple of advantages over PET. First, fMRI does not require any exposure to a radioactive substance. Second, fMRI can localize changes in brain activity across briefer periods than PET, which makes it more useful for analyzing psychological processes that occur extremely quickly, such as reading a word or recognizing a face. With PET, researchers often have to use experimental designs different from those they would use in the psychology laboratory in order to adapt to the limitations of PET technology. With fMRI, researchers can design experiments that more closely resemble the ones they carry out in the psychology laboratory.

What does an fMRI track in an active brain?

Functional MRI can also be used to explore the relationship of brain regions with one another, using a recently developed technique referred to as *resting state functional connectivity*. As implied by the name, this technique does not require participants to perform a task; they simply rest quietly while fMRI measurements are made. Functional connectivity measures the extent to which spontaneous activity in different brain regions is correlated over time; brain regions whose activity is highly correlated are thought to be functionally connected with one another (Lee, Smyser, & Shimony, 2012). Functional connectivity measures have been used extensively in recent years to identify brain *networks*, that is, sets of brain regions that are closely connected to one another (Yeo et al., 2011). For example, functional connectivity helped to identify the *default network* (Gusnard & Raichle, 2001), a group of interconnected regions in the frontal, temporal, and parietal lobes that is involved in internally focused cognitive activities, such as remembering past events, imagining future events, daydreaming, and mind wandering (Andrews-Hanna, 2012; Buckner, Andrews-Hanna, & Schacter, 2008; see chapters on Memory and Consciousness). Functional connectivity, along with DTI (which measures structural connectivity), is used in studies conducted by the Human Connectome Project, and will contribute important information to the map of the human connectome.

Insights from Functional Imaging

PET and fMRI provide remarkable insights into the types of information processing that take place in specific areas of the brain. For example, when a person performs a simple perceptual task, such as looking at a circular checkerboard, the primary visual areas are activated. As you have read, when the checkerboard is presented to the left visual field, the right visual cortex shows activation, and when the checkerboard is presented to the right visual field, the left visual cortex shows activation (Fox et al., 1986). Similarly, when people look at faces, fMRI reveals strong activity in a region located near the border of the temporal and occipital lobes called the *fusiform gyrus* (Kanwisher, McDermott, & Chun, 1997). When this structure is damaged, people experience problems with recognizing faces— even faces of friends and family they've known for years—although they don't have problems with their eyes and can recognize visual objects other than faces (Mestry et al., 2012). Finally, when people perform a task that engages emotional processing (e.g., looking at sad pictures), researchers observe significant activation in the amygdala, which you learned earlier is linked with emotional arousal (Phelps, 2006). There is also increased activation in parts of the frontal lobe that are involved in emotional regulation; in fact, in the same areas that were most likely damaged in the case of Phineas Gage (Wang et al., 2005).

You'll recall from the Methods chapter that at the heart of the scientific method is the relationship between ideas and evidence. There is no statute of limitations on scientific investigation. In this case, these modern brain imaging techniques confirm the theories derived from studies of brain damage from over 100 years ago. When Broca and Wernicke reached their conclusions about language production and language comprehension, they had little more to go on than some isolated cases and good hunches. PET scans have since confirmed that different areas of the brain are activated when a person is listening to spoken language, reading words on a screen, saying words out loud, or thinking of related words. This suggests that different parts of the brain are activated during these related but distinct functions. Similarly, it was pretty clear to the physician who examined Phineas Gage that the location of Gage's injuries played a major role in his drastic change in personality and emotionality. fMRI scans have since confirmed that the frontal lobe plays a central role in regulating emotion. It's always nice when independent methods (in these instances, very old case studies and very recent technology) arrive at the same conclusions. As you'll also see at various points in the text, brain imaging techniques such as fMRI are also revealing new and surprising findings, such as the insights described in the Real World box (Brain Death and the Vegetative State).

Although the insights that we are obtaining from fMRI are exciting, it is important that we don't get too carried away with them, as sometimes happens in media depictions of fMRI results (Marcus, 2012). Consider, as an example, the topic of memory accuracy and distortion. Using experimental paradigms that you'll learn about in the chapter on Memory, fMRI studies have shown that activity in some parts of the brain is greater during the retrieval of accurate rather than inaccurate memories

> **Why should we avoid jumping to conclusions based on fMRI results?**

(Schacter & Loftus, 2013). Does that mean we are ready to use fMRI in the courtroom to determine whether a witness is recounting an accurate memory or an inaccurate memory? Schacter and Loftus argued that the answer to this question is an emphatic no. For example, we don't yet know whether the results of laboratory fMRI studies of memory, which typically use simple materials like words or pictures, generalize to the kinds of complex everyday events that are relevant in the courtroom. Furthermore, evidence that fMRI can distinguish accurate from inaccurate memories

Brain Death and the Vegetative State

In 1981, the President's Commission for the Study of Ethical Problems in Medicine and Biomedical and Behavioral Research defined brain death as the *irreversible loss of all functions of the brain.* Contrary to what you may think, brain death is not the same as being in a coma or being unresponsive to stimulation. Indeed, even a flatline EEG does not indicate that all brain functions have stopped; the reticular formation in the hindbrain, which generates spontaneous respiration and heartbeat, may still be active.

Brain death came to the forefront of national attention in the case of Terri Schiavo, a woman who had been kept alive on a respirator for nearly 15 years in a Florida nursing home. She died on March 31, 2005, after the feeding tube that sustained her was removed. A person like Schiavo is commonly referred to as *brain dead,* but such an individual is more accurately described as being in a *persistent vegetative state.* Does a persistent vegetative state qualify as "life"? Consider this: Neuroimaging research has found evidence that people diagnosed as being in a vegetative state show signs of intentional mental activity (Monti, 2012). In one study, researchers used fMRI to observe the patterns of brain activity in a 25-year-old woman with severe brain injuries as the result of a traffic accident. When the researchers spoke ambiguous sentences ("The creak came from a beam in the ceiling") and unambiguous sentences ("There was milk and sugar in his coffee"), fMRI revealed that the activated areas in the woman's brain were comparable to those areas activated in the brains of normal volunteers (Owen et al., 2006). What's more, when the woman was instructed to imagine playing a game of tennis and then imagine walking through the rooms of her house, the areas of her brain that showed activity were again indistinguishable from those brain areas in normal, healthy volunteers.

The researchers suggested that these findings are evidence for, at least, conscious understanding of spoken commands and, at best, a degree of intentionality in an otherwise vegetative person. The patient's brain activity while "playing tennis" and "walking through her house" revealed that she could both understand the researchers' instructions and willfully complete them. A more recent fMRI study that used these and related mental imagery tasks in a much larger sample found evidence for willful modulation of brain activity in 5 of 54 patients with disorders of consciousness (Monti et al., 2010). Other recent studies have revealed evidence of normal cerebral responses to language and complex sounds in 2 out of 3 patients in a vegetative state (Fernandez-Espejo et al., 2008), stronger emotional responding to familiar than to unfamiliar voices in a single patient (Eickhoff et al., 2008), and willful attempts to execute a command to move a specific hand in another patient (Cruse et al., 2012). Although it's too early to tell how these and other research findings may impact decisions regarding the brain and when life ends (Laureys et al., 2006), scientists and physicians are now engaged in intensive discussions concerning their ethical and clinical implications (Bernat, 2009; Monti, 2012; Monti, Coleman, & Owen, 2009).

comes from studies in which brain activity is averaged across a *group* of participants. But in the courtroom we need to determine whether an *individual* is remembering accurately or not, and there is little evidence yet that fMRI can do so. More generally, it is important to think carefully about how fMRI evidence is obtained before leaping to conclusions about how that evidence can be used in everyday life.

Transcranial Magnetic Stimulation

We noted earlier that scientists have learned a lot about the brain by studying the behavior of people with brain injuries. But, although brain damage may be related to particular patterns of behavior, that relationship may or may not be causal. Experimentation is the premier method for establishing causal relationships between variables, but scientists cannot ethically cause brain damage in human beings, thus they have not been able to establish causal relationships between particular kinds of brain damage and particular patterns of behavior. Functional neuroimaging techniques such as fMRI don't help on this point because they do not provide information about when a particular pattern of brain activity causes a particular behavior.

Happily, scientists have discovered a way to mimic brain damage with a benign technique called *transcranial magnetic stimulation* (TMS; Barker, Jalinous, & Freeston, 1985; Hallett, 2000). If you've ever held a magnet under a piece of paper and used it to drag a pin across the paper's surface, you know that magnetic fields can pass through insulating material. The human skull is no exception. TMS delivers a magnetic pulse that passes through the skull and deactivates neurons in the cerebral cortex for a short period. Researchers can direct TMS

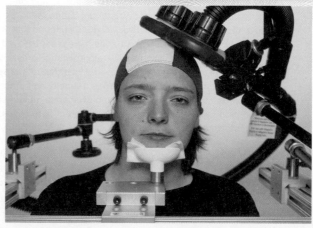

Transcranial magnetic stimulation (TMS) activates and deactivates regions of the brain with a magnetic pulse, temporarily mimicking brain damage.

pulses to particular brain regions (essentially turning them off) and then measure temporary changes in the way a person moves, sees, thinks, remembers, speaks, or feels. By manipulating the state of the brain, scientists can perform experiments that establish causal relationships.

OTHER VOICES

Neuromyths

Christopher Chabris is an associate professor of psychology at Union College and **Daniel Simons** is a professor of psychology at the University of Illinois. Chabris and Simons co-authored *The Invisible Gorilla: And Other Ways Our Intuitions Deceive Us* (2010).

PHOTOS: (*LEFT*) MATT MILLESS;
(*RIGHT*) COURTESY DANIEL S. SIMONS

Y ou've no doubt often heard the phrase "we only use 10% of our brains," and perhaps you've wondered whether there is anything to it. Chabris and Simons (2012) discussed this and other statements about the brain that they believe to be merely myths, based in part, on a recent study by Dekker et al. (2012).

Pop quiz: Which of these statements is false?

1. We use only 10% of our brain.

2. Environments rich in stimuli improve the brains of preschool children.

3. Individuals learn better when they receive information in their preferred learning style, whether auditory, visual, or kinesthetic.

If you picked the first one, congratulations. The idea that we use only 10% of our brain is patently false. Yet it so permeates popular culture that, among psychologists and neuroscientists, it is known as the "10% myth." Contrary to popular belief, the entire brain is put to use—unused neurons die and unused circuits atrophy. Reports of neuroimaging research might perpetuate the myth by showing only a small number of areas "lighting up" in a brain scan, but those are just areas that have more than a base line level of activity; the dark regions aren't dormant or unused.

Did you agree with the other two statements? If so, you fell into our trap. All three statements are false—or at least not substantiated by scientific evidence. Unfortunately, if you got any of them wrong, you're hardly alone.

These "neuromyths," along with others, were presented to 242 primary and secondary school teachers in the Netherlands and the United Kingdom as part of a study by Sanne Dekker and colleagues at VU University Amsterdam and Bristol University, and just published in the journal *Frontiers in Psychology*. They found that 47% of the teachers believed the 10% myth. Even more, 76%, believed that enriching children's environments will strengthen their brains.

This belief might have emerged from evidence that rats raised in cages with amenities like exercise wheels, tunnels, and other rats showed better cognitive abilities and improvements in brain structure compared with rats that grew up isolated in bare cages. But such experiments show only that a truly impoverished and unnatural environment leads to poorer developmental outcomes than a more natural environment with opportunities to play and interact. It follows that growing up locked in a closet or otherwise cut off from human contact will impair a child's brain development. It does not follow that "enriching" a child's environment beyond what is already typical

(e.g., by constant exposure to "Baby Einstein"-type videos) will boost cognitive development.

The myth about learning styles was the most popular: 94% of the teachers believed that students perform better when lessons are delivered in their preferred learning style. Indeed, students do have preferences about how they learn; the problem is that these preferences have little to do with how effectively they learn. . . .

Our own surveys of the U.S. population have found even more widespread belief in myths about the brain. About two-thirds of the public agreed with the 10% myth. Many also believed that memory works like a video recording or that they can tell when someone is staring at the back of their head.

Ironically, in the Dekker group's study, the teachers who knew the most about neuroscience also believed in the most myths. Apparently, teachers who are (admirably) enthusiastic about expanding their knowledge of the mind and brain have trouble separating fact from fiction as they learn. Neuromyths have so much intuitive appeal, and they spread so rapidly in fields like business and self-help, that eradicating them from popular consciousness might be a Sisyphean task. But reducing their influence in the classroom would be a good start.

If for some perverse reason you wanted to annoy the instructor of your psychology course, you probably could do no better than to claim that "we use only 10% of our brains." Even though, as pointed out by Chabris and Simon (2012), a surprisingly high proportion of elementary and secondary schoolteachers in the Netherlands and the United Kingdom subscribe to this myth, we don't know any psychologists teaching courses like the one you are taking who would endorse it, and we hope that there aren't any. How did the myth get started? Nobody really knows. Some think it may have arisen from a quotation by the great psychologist William James ("We are making use of only a small part of our possible mental and physical resources") or that it possibly owes to Albert Einstein's attempt to make sense of his own massive intellect (Boyd, 2008).

The key point for our purposes is that when you hear such bold claims made, say, by a friend who heard it from somebody else, it's time for you to put into action the kinds of critical thinking skills that we are focusing on in this text, and start asking questions: What's the evidence for the claim? Is there a specific study or studies that your friend can name to provide evidence in support of the claim? Are any such studies published in peer-reviewed scientific journals? What kind of sample was used in the study? Is it large enough to support a clear conclusion? Has the finding been replicated? Tall tales like the 10% myth don't stand much chance of surviving for long if claims for their existence are met head on with critical thinking.

COURTESY VICKI GILLIS, COLORADO STATE UNIVERSITY

In the Methods chapter you learned about the difference between correlation and causation, and that even if two events are correlated, it does not necessarily mean that one causes the other. Suppose a researcher designs an experiment in which participants view words on a screen and are asked to pronounce each word aloud, while the researcher uses fMRI to examine brain activity. First, what areas of the brain would you expect to show activity on fMRI while participants complete this task? Second, can the researcher now safely conclude that those brain areas are required for humans to perform word pronunciation?

For example, in an early study using TMS, scientists discovered that magnetic stimulation of the visual cortex temporarily impairs a person's ability to detect the motion of an object without impairing the person's ability to recognize that object (Beckers & Zeki, 1995). This intriguing discovery suggests that motion perception and object recognition are accomplished by different parts of the brain, but moreover, it establishes that activity in the visual cortex *causes* motion perception. More recent research has revealed that applying TMS to the specific part of the visual cortex responsible for motion perception also impairs the accuracy with which people reach for moving objects (Schenk et al., 2005) or for stationary objects when there is motion in the background of a visual scene (Whitney et al., 2007). These findings indicate that the visual motion area plays a crucial role in guiding actions when we're responding to motion in the visual environment.

Rather than relying solely on observational studies of people with brain injuries or the snapshots provided by fMRI or PET scans, researchers can also manipulate brain activity and measure its effects. Scientists have also begun to combine TMS with fMRI, allowing them to localize precisely where in the brain TMS is having its effect (Caparelli, 2007). Studies suggest that TMS has no harmful side effects (Anand & Hotson, 2002; Pascual-Leone et al., 1993), and this new tool has changed the study of how our brains create our thoughts, feelings, and actions.

IN SUMMARY

► There are three major approaches to studying the link between the brain and behavior:

► Observing how perceptual, motor, intellectual, and emotional capacities are affected following brain damage. By carefully relating specific psychological and behavioral disruptions to damage in particular areas of the brain, researchers can better understand how the brain area normally plays a role in producing those behaviors.

► Examining global electrical activity in the brain and the activity patterns of single neurons. The patterns of electrical activity in large brain areas can be examined from outside the skull using the electroencephalograph (EEG). Single-cell recordings taken from specific neurons can be linked to specific perceptual or behavioral events, suggesting that those neurons represent particular kinds of stimuli or control particular aspects of behavior.

► Using brain imaging to scan the brain as people perform different perceptual or intellectual tasks. Correlating energy consumption in particular brain areas with specific cognitive and behavioral events suggests that those brain areas are involved in specific types of perceptual, motor, cognitive, or emotional processing.

Chapter Review

KEY CONCEPT QUIZ

1. Which of the following is NOT a function of a neuron?
   a. processing information
   b. communicating with other neurons
   c. nutritional provision
   d. sending messages to body organs and muscles

2. Signals from other neurons are received and relayed to the cell body by
   a. the nucleus.
   b. dendrites.
   c. axons.
   d. glands.

3. Signals are transmitted from one neuron to another
   a. across a synapse.
   b. through a glial cell.
   c. by the myelin sheath.
   d. in the cell body.

4. Which type of neuron receives information from the external world and conveys this information to the brain via the spinal cord?
   a. sensory neuron
   b. motor neuron
   c. interneuron
   d. axon

5. An electric signal that is conducted along the length of a neuron's axon to the synapse is called
   a. a resting potential.
   b. an action potential.
   c. a node of Ranvier.
   d. an ion.

6. The chemicals that transmit information across the synapse to a receiving neuron's dendrites are called
   a. vesicles.
   b. terminal buttons.
   c. postsynaptic neurons.
   d. neurotransmitters.

7. The _____ automatically controls the organs of the body.
   a. autonomic nervous system
   b. parasympathetic nervous system
   c. sympathetic nervous system
   d. somatic nervous system

8. Which part of the hindbrain coordinates fine motor skills?
   a. the medulla
   b. the cerebellum
   c. the pons
   d. the tegmentum

9. What part of the brain is involved in movement and arousal?
   a. the hindbrain
   b. the midbrain
   c. the forebrain
   d. the reticular formation

10. The _____ regulates body temperature, hunger, thirst, and sexual behavior.
    a. cerebral cortex
    b. pituitary gland
    c. hypothalamus
    d. hippocampus

11. What explains the apparent beneficial effects of cardiovascular exercise on aspects of brain function and cognitive performance?
    a. the different sizes of the somatosensory cortices
    b. the position of the cerebral cortex
    c. specialization of association areas
    d. neuron plasticity

12. During the course of embryonic brain growth, the _____ undergoes the greatest development.
    a. cerebral cortex
    b. cerebellum
    c. tectum
    d. thalamus

13. The first true central nervous system appeared in
    a. flatworms.
    b. jellyfish.
    c. protozoa.
    d. early primates.

14. Genes set the _____ in populations within a given environment.
    a. individual characteristics
    b. range of variation
    c. environmental possibilities
    d. behavioral standards

15. Identifying the brain areas that are involved in specific types of motor, cognitive, or emotional processing is best achieved through
    a. recording patterns of electrical activity.
    b. observing psychological disorders.
    c. psychosurgery.
    d. brain imaging.

KEY TERMS

neurons (p. 80)

cell body (or soma) (p. 81)

dendrite (p. 81)

axon (p. 81)

myelin sheath (p. 82)

glial cells (p. 82)

synapse (p. 82)

sensory neurons (p. 82)

motor neurons (p. 82)

interneurons (p. 83)

resting potential (p. 84)

action potential (p. 86)

refractory period (p. 86)

terminal buttons (p. 87)

neurotransmitters (p. 87)

receptors (p. 87)

acetylcholine (ACh) (p. 88)

dopamine (p. 88)

glutamate (p. 88)

GABA (gamma-aminobutyric acid)
(p. 88)

norepinephrine (p. 88)

serotonin (p. 88)

endorphins (p. 88)

agonists (p. 88)

antagonists (p. 88)

nervous system (p. 92)

central nervous system
(CNS) (p. 92)

peripheral nervous system
(PNS) (p. 92)

somatic nervous system (p. 92)

autonomic nervous system
(ANS) (p. 93)

sympathetic nervous system
(p. 93)

parasympathetic nervous system
(p. 94)

spinal reflexes (p. 94)

hindbrain (p. 96)

medulla (p. 96)

reticular formation (p. 96)

cerebellum (p. 96)

pons (p. 96)

tectum (p. 96)

tegmentum (p. 97)

cerebral cortex (p. 97)

subcortical structures (p. 97)

thalamus (p. 98)

hypothalamus (p. 99)

pituitary gland (p. 99)

limbic system (p. 99)

hippocampus (p. 99)

amygdala (p. 99)

basal ganglia (p. 100)

corpus callosum (p. 101)

occipital lobe (p. 101)

parietal lobe (p. 101)

temporal lobe (p. 102)

frontal lobe (p. 102)

association areas (p. 102)

mirror neurons (p. 103)

gene (p. 108)

chromosomes (p. 108)

epigenetics (p. 110)

epigenetic marks (p. 110)

DNA methylation (p. 110)

histone modification (p. 110)

heritability (p. 111)

electroencephalograph
(EEG) (p. 118)

CHANGING MINDS

1. While watching late-night TV, you come across an infomercial for all-natural BrainGro. "It's a well-known fact that most people use only 10% of their brain," the spokesman promises, "but with BrainGro you can increase that number from 10% to 99%!" Why should you be skeptical of the claim that we use only 10% of our brains? What would happen if a drug actually increased neuronal activity by ten-fold?

2. Your friend has been feeling depressed and has gone to a psychiatrist for help. "He prescribed a medication that's supposed to increase serotonin in my brain. But my feelings depend on me, not on a bunch of chemicals in my head," she said. What examples could you give your friend to convince her that hormones and neurotransmitters really do influence our cognition, mood, and behavior?

3. A classmate has read the section in this chapter about the evolution of the central nervous system. "Evolution is just a theory," he says. "Not everyone believes in it. And, even if it's true that we're all descended from monkeys, that doesn't have anything to do with the psychology of humans alive today." What is your friend misunderstanding about evolution? How would you explain to him the relevance of evolution to modern psychology?

4. A news program reports on a study (Hölzel et al., 2011) in which people who practiced meditation for about 30 minutes a day for 8 weeks showed changes in their brains, including increases in the size of the hippocampus and the amygdala. You tell a friend, who's skeptical. "The brain doesn't change like that. Basically, the brain you're born with is the brain you're stuck with for the rest of your life." Why is your friend's statement wrong? What are several specific ways in which the brain does change over time?

5. A friend of yours announces that he's figured out why he's bad at math. "I read it in a book," he says. "Left-brained people are analytical and logical, but right-brained people are creative and artistic. I'm an art major, so I must be right-brained, and that's why I'm not good at math." Why is your friend's view too simplistic?

ANSWERS TO KEY CONCEPT QUIZ

1. c; 2. b; 3. a; 4. a; 5. b; 6. d; 7. a; 8. b; 9. b; 10. c; 11. d; 12. a; 13. a; 14. b; 15. d.

Need more help? Additional resources are located in LaunchPad at:
http://www.worthpublishers.com/launchpad/schacter3e

Sensation and Perception

N THE 1930S, A YOUNG ARCHITECT and designer named Donald Deskey won a competition to design the interiors for Radio City Music Hall in New York City. His design was met with immediate acclaim and enabled Deskey to create his own graphic design firm. In 1946, he helped to create the box design for Procter & Gamble's revolutionary new laundry detergent, Tide, which used, for the first time, synthetic compounds rather than plain old soap (Hine, 1995). Although extremely familiar to us today, in 1946 the bold, blue lettered "Tide" emblazoned on bull's-eye rings of yellow and orange marked the first use of eye-catching Day-Glo colors on a commercial product, and this mix of type and graphics was unlike any product design that anyone had seen before. The product would be impossible to miss on the shelves of a store, and as admirers of the design observed, "it was the box itself that most dynamically conveyed the new product's extraordinary power" (Dyer, Dalzell, & Olegario, 2004). Tide went to market in 1949 and Procter & Gamble never looked back.

Nowadays we're used to seeing advertisements that feature exciting, provocative, or even sexual images to sell products. In television commercials these images are accompanied by popular music that advertisers hope will evoke an overall mood favorable to the product. The notion is that the sight and sound of exciting things will become associated with what might be an otherwise drab product. This form of advertising is known as *sensory branding* (Lindstrom, 2005). The idea is to exploit all the senses to promote a product or a brand. Sensory branding goes beyond sight and sound by enlisting smell, taste, and touch as well as vision and hearing. That new-car smell you anticipate while you take a test drive? It's a manufactured fragrance sprayed into the car, carefully tested to evoke positive feelings among potential buyers. Bang and Olufsen, a Danish high-end stereo manufacturer, carefully designed its remote control units to have a certain distinctive "feel" in a user's hand. Singapore Airlines, which has consistently been rated "the world's best airline," has actually patented the smell of their airplane cabins (it's called Stefan Floridian Waters).

These companies, just like Procter & Gamble back in 1946, recognize the power of sensation and perception to shape human experience and behavior.

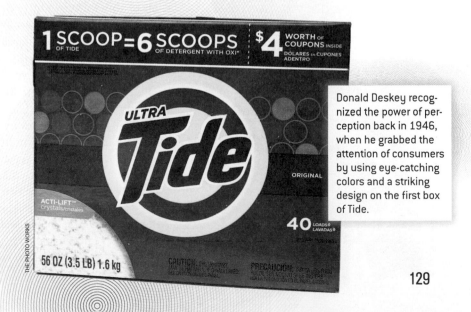

Donald Deskey recognized the power of perception back in 1946, when he grabbed the attention of consumers by using eye-catching colors and a striking design on the first box of Tide.

IN THIS CHAPTER WE'LL EXPLORE KEY INSIGHTS into the nature of sensation and perception. These experiences are basic to survival and reproduction; we wouldn't last long without the ability to accurately make sense of the world around us. Indeed, research on sensation and perception is the basis for much of psychology, a pathway toward understanding more complex cognition and behavior such as memory, emotion, motivation, or decision making. Yet sensation and perception also sometimes reveal various kinds of illusions that you might see at a science fair or in a novelty shop: reminders that the act of perceiving the world is not as simple or straightforward as it might seem.

We'll look at how physical energy in the world around us is encoded by our senses, sent to the brain, and enters conscious awareness. Vision is predominant among our senses; correspondingly, we'll devote a fair amount of space to understanding how the visual system works. Then we'll discuss how we perceive sound waves as words or music or noise, followed by the body senses, emphasizing touch, pain, and balance. We'll end with the chemical senses of smell and taste, which together allow you to savor the foods you eat. But before doing any of that, we will provide a foundation for examining all of the sensory systems by reviewing how psychologists measure sensation and perception in the first place.

Sensation and Perception Are Distinct Activities

To us, sensation and perception appear to be one seamless event. However, they are two distinct activities.

> **Sensation** is *simple stimulation of a sense organ*. It is the basic registration of light, sound, pressure, odor, or taste as parts of your body interact with the physical world.

> After a sensation registers in your central nervous system, **perception** takes place at the level of your brain: *the organization, identification, and interpretation of a sensation in order to form a mental representation*.

As an example, your eyes are coursing across these sentences right now. The sensory receptors in your eyeballs are registering different patterns of light reflecting off the page. Your brain, however, is integrating and processing that light information into the meaningful perception of words, such as *meaningful*, *perception*, and *words*. Your eyes—the sensory organ—aren't really seeing words; they're simply encoding different lines and curves on a page. Your brain—the perceptual organ—is transforming those lines and curves into a coherent mental representation of words and concepts.

If all of this sounds a little peculiar, it's because, from the vantage point of your conscious experience, it *seems* as if you're reading words directly. If you think of the discussion of brain damage in the Neuroscience and Behavior chapter, you'll recall that sometimes a person's eyes can work just fine, yet the individual is still "blind" to faces she has seen for many years (p. 122). Damage to the visual processing centers in the brain can interfere with the interpretation of information coming from the eyes: The senses are intact, but perceptual ability is compromised. Sensation and perception are related—but separate—events.

How do sensory receptors communicate with the brain? It all depends on the process of **transduction,** which occurs *when many sensors in the body convert physical signals from the environment into encoded neural signals sent to the central nervous system*. In vision, light reflected from surfaces provides the eyes with information about the

You can enjoy a tempting ice cream sundae even if you do not know that its sweet taste depends on a complex process of transduction, in which molecules dissolved in saliva are converted to neural signals processed by the brain.

FOTOFLARE/ISTOCKPHOTO

What role does the brain play in what we see and hear?

shape, color, and position of objects. In audition, vibrations (from vocal cords or a guitar string, perhaps) cause changes in air pressure that propagate through space to a listener's ears. In touch, the pressure of a surface against the skin signals its shape, texture, and temperature. In taste and smell, molecules dispersed in the air or dissolved in saliva reveal the identity of substances that we may or may not want to eat. In each case physical energy from the world is converted to neural energy inside the central nervous system (see **TABLE 4.1**). We'll discuss in more detail how transduction works with each of the five primary senses—vision, hearing, touch, taste, and smell—in separate sections later in this chapter.

Psychophysics

Knowing that perception takes place in the brain, you might wonder if two people see the same colors in the sunset when looking at the evening sky. It's intriguing to consider the possibility that our basic perceptions of sights or sounds might differ fundamentally from those of other people. How can we measure such a thing objectively? Measuring the physical energy of a stimulus, such as the wavelength of a light, is easy

sensation
Simple stimulation of a sense organ.

perception
The organization, identification, and interpretation of a sensation in order to form a mental representation.

transduction
What takes place when many sensors in the body convert physical signals from the environment into encoded neural signals sent to the central nervous system.

Table 4.1		
Transduction		
The five senses convert physical energy from the world into neural energy, which is sent to the brain.		
Sense	**Sensory Input**	**Conversion into Neural Energy**

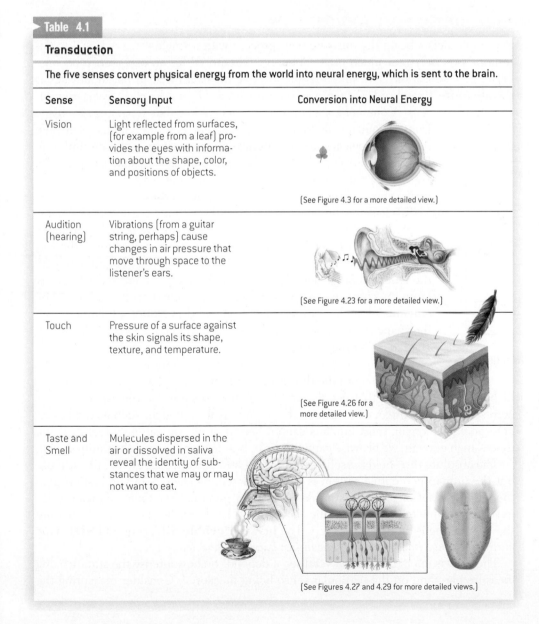

Vision	Light reflected from surfaces, (for example from a leaf) provides the eyes with information about the shape, color, and positions of objects.	(See Figure 4.3 for a more detailed view.)
Audition (hearing)	Vibrations (from a guitar string, perhaps) cause changes in air pressure that move through space to the listener's ears.	(See Figure 4.23 for a more detailed view.)
Touch	Pressure of a surface against the skin signals its shape, texture, and temperature.	(See Figure 4.26 for a more detailed view.)
Taste and Smell	Molecules dispersed in the air or dissolved in saliva reveal the identity of substances that we may or may not want to eat.	(See Figures 4.27 and 4.29 for more detailed views.)

psychophysics
Methods that measure the strength of a stimulus and the observer's sensitivity to that stimulus.

absolute threshold
The minimal intensity needed to just barely detect a stimulus in 50% of the trials.

just noticeable difference (JND)
The minimal change in a stimulus that can just barely be detected.

Weber's law
The just noticeable difference of a stimulus is a constant proportion despite variations in intensity.

enough: You can probably buy the necessary instruments online to do that yourself. But how do you quantify a person's private, subjective *perception* of that light?

The structuralists, led by Wilhelm Wundt and Edward Titchener, tried using introspection to measure perceptual experiences (see the Psychology: Evolution of a Science chapter). They failed miserably at this task. After all, two people may both describe their experience of the sunset in the same words ("orange" and "beautiful"), but neither can directly perceive the other's experience of the same event. In the mid-1800s, German scientist and philosopher Gustav Fechner (1801–1887) developed a new approach to measuring sensation and perception called **psychophysics:** *methods that measure the strength of a stimulus and the observer's sensitivity to that stimulus* (Fechner, 1860/1966). In a typical psychophysics experiment, researchers ask people to make a simple judgment—whether or not they saw a flash of light, for example. The psychophysicist then relates the measured stimulus, such as the brightness of the light flash, to each observer's yes-or-no response.

> **Why isn't it enough for a psychophysicist to measure only the strength of a stimulus?**

Measuring Thresholds

Psychophysicists begin the measurement process with a single sensory signal to determine precisely how much physical energy is required for an observer to become aware of a sensation. The simplest quantitative measurement in psychophysics is the **absolute threshold,** *the minimal intensity needed to just barely detect a stimulus in 50% of the trials.* A *threshold* is a boundary. The doorway that separates the inside from the outside of a house is a threshold, as is the boundary between two psychological states (awareness and unawareness, for example). In finding the absolute threshold for sensation, the two states in question are *sensing* and *not sensing* some stimulus. **TABLE 4.2** lists the approximate sensory thresholds for each of the five senses.

To measure the absolute threshold for detecting a sound, for example, an observer sits in a soundproof room wearing headphones linked to a computer. The experimenter presents a pure tone (the sort of sound made by striking a tuning fork) using the computer to vary the loudness or the length of time each tone lasts and recording how often the observer reports hearing that tone under each condition. The outcome of such an experiment is graphed in **FIGURE 4.1.** Notice from the shape of the curve that the transition from *not hearing* to *hearing* is gradual rather than abrupt.

If we repeat this experiment for many different tones, we can observe and record the thresholds for tones ranging from very low to very high pitch. It turns out that people tend to be most sensitive to the range of tones corresponding to human conversation. If the tone is low enough, such as the lowest note on a pipe organ, most humans cannot hear it at all; we can only feel it. If the tone is high enough, we likewise cannot hear it, but dogs and many other animals can.

The absolute threshold is useful for assessing how sensitive we are to faint stimuli, but the human perceptual system is better at detecting *changes* in stimulation than the simple onset or offset of stimulation. When parents hear their infant's cry, it's useful to be able to differentiate the "I'm hungry" cry from the "I'm cranky" cry from the "something is biting my toes" cry. The **just noticeable difference (JND)** is *the minimal change in a stimulus that can just barely be detected.*

The JND is not a fixed quantity; rather, it depends on how intense the stimuli being measured are and on the particular sense being measured. Consider measuring the

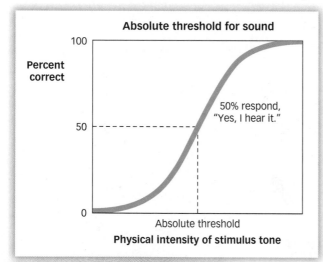

▲ Figure **4.1 Absolute Threshold** Some of us are more sensitive than others, and we may even detect sensory stimulation below our own absolute threshold. Absolute threshold is graphed here as the point where the increasing intensity of the stimulus enables an observer to detect it on 50% of the trials. As its intensity gradually increases, we detect the stimulation more frequently.

JND for a bright light. An observer in a dark room is shown a light of fixed intensity, called the *standard* (S), next to a comparison light that is slightly brighter or dimmer than the standard. When S is very dim, observers can see even a very small difference in brightness between the two lights: The JND is small. But if S is bright, a much larger increment is needed to detect the difference: The JND is larger.

When calculating a difference threshold, it is the proportion between stimuli that is important. This relationship was first noticed in 1834 by German physiologist Ernst Weber (Watson, 1978). Fechner applied Weber's insight directly to psychophysics, resulting in a formal relationship called **Weber's law:** *The just noticeable difference of a stimulus is a constant proportion despite variations in intensity.* As an example, if you picked up a 1-ounce envelope, then a 2-ounce envelope, you'd probably notice the difference between them. But if you picked up a 20-pound package, then a 20-pound, 1-ounce package, you'd probably detect no difference at all between them.

> **What is the importance of proportion to the measurement of *just noticeable difference*?**

Signal Detection

Measuring absolute and difference thresholds requires a critical assumption: that a threshold exists! But much of what scientists know about biology suggests that such a discrete, all-or-none change in the brain is unlikely. Humans don't suddenly and rapidly switch between perceiving and not perceiving; in fact, recall that the transition from *not sensing* to *sensing* is gradual (see Figure 4.1). The very same physical stimulus, such as a dim light or a quiet tone, presented on several different occasions, may be perceived by the same person on some occasions but not on others. Remember, an absolute threshold is operationalized as perceiving the stimulus 50% of the time, which means the other 50% of the time it might go undetected.

Our accurate perception of a sensory stimulus, then, can be somewhat haphazard. Whether in the psychophysics lab or out in the world, sensory signals face a lot of competition, or *noise,* which refers to all the other stimuli coming from the internal and external environment. Memories, moods, and motives intertwine with what you are seeing, hearing, and smelling at any given time. This internal "noise" competes with your ability to detect a stimulus with perfect, focused attention. Other sights, sounds, and smells in the world at large also compete for attention; you rarely have the luxury of attending to just one stimulus apart from everything else. As a consequence of noise, you may not perceive everything that you sense, and you may even perceive things that you haven't sensed. Think of the last time you had a hearing test. You no doubt missed some of the quiet beeps that were presented, but you also probably said you heard beeps that weren't really there.

> **How accurate and complete are our perceptions of the world?**

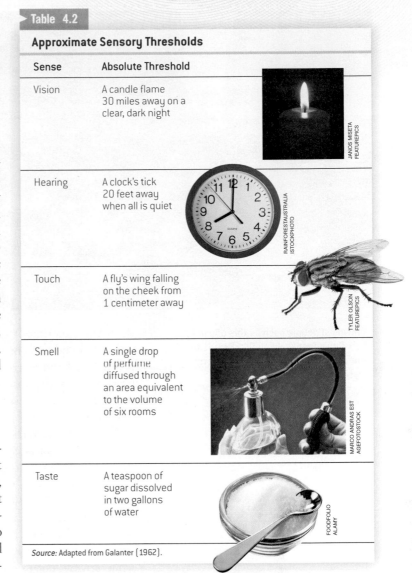

Table 4.2

Approximate Sensory Thresholds

Sense	Absolute Threshold	
Vision	A candle flame 30 miles away on a clear, dark night	JANOS MISETA FEATUREPICS
Hearing	A clock's tick 20 feet away when all is quiet	RAINFORESTAUSTRALIA ISTOCKPHOTO
Touch	A fly's wing falling on the cheek from 1 centimeter away	TYLER OLSON FEATUREPICS
Smell	A single drop of perfume diffused through an area equivalent to the volume of six rooms	MARCO ANDRAS EST AGEFOTOSTOCK
Taste	A teaspoon of sugar dissolved in two gallons of water	FOODFOLIO ALAMY

Source: Adapted from Galanter (1962).

Crowds of people such as this one in New York City's Thanksgiving Day Parade present our visual system with a challenging signal detection task.

BLICKWINKEL/ALAMY

An approach to psychophysics called **signal detection theory** holds that *the response to a stimulus depends both on a person's sensitivity to the stimulus in the presence of noise and on a person's decision criterion.* That is, observers consider the sensory evidence evoked by the stimulus and compare it to an internal decision criterion (Green & Swets, 1966; Macmillan & Creelman, 2005). If the sensory evidence exceeds the criterion, the observer responds by saying, "Yes, I detected the stimulus," and if it falls short of the criterion, the observer responds by saying, "No, I did not detect the stimulus."

Signal detection theory allows researchers to quantify an observer's response in the presence of noise. In a signal detection experiment, a stimulus, such as a dim light, is randomly presented or not. If you've ever taken an eye exam that checks your peripheral vision, you have an idea about this kind of setup: Lights of varying intensity are flashed at various places in the visual field, and your task is to respond anytime you see one. Observers in a signal detection experiment must decide whether they saw the light or not. If the light is presented and the observer correctly responds yes, the outcome is a *hit*. If the light is presented and the observer says no, the result is a *miss*. However, if the light is *not* presented and the observer nonetheless says it was, a *false alarm* has occurred. Finally, if the light is *not* presented and the observer responds no, a *correct rejection* has occurred: The observer accurately detected the absence of the stimulus.

Signal detection theory proposes a way to measure *perceptual sensitivity* (how effectively the perceptual system represents sensory events) separately from the observer's decision-making strategy. It explicitly takes into account observers' response tendencies, such as liberally saying yes when there is any hint of a stimulus or conservatively reserving identifications only for obvious instances of the stimulus. Even when one person says yes much more often than another, both may be equally accurate in distinguishing between the presence or absence of a stimulus.

Signal detection theory has practical applications at home, school, work, and even while driving. For example, a radiologist may have to decide whether a mammogram shows that a woman has breast cancer. The radiologist knows that certain features, such as a mass of a particular size and shape, are associated with the presence of cancer. But noncancerous features can have a very similar appearance to cancerous ones. The radiologist may decide on a strictly liberal criterion and check every possible case of cancer with a biopsy. This decision strategy minimizes the possibility of missing a true cancer but leads to many unnecessary biopsies. A strictly conservative criterion will cut down on unnecessary biopsies but will miss some treatable cancers.

As another example, imagine that police are on the lookout for a suspected felon who they have reason to believe will be at a crowded soccer match. Although the law enforcement agency provided a fairly good description (6 feet tall, sandy brown hair, beard, glasses) there are still thousands of people to scan. Rounding up all men between 5'5" and 6'5" would probably produce a hit (the felon is caught) but at the expense of an extraordinary number of false alarms (many innocent people are detained and questioned).

These different types of errors have to be weighed against one another in setting the decision criterion. Signal detection theory offers a practical way to choose among criteria that permit decision makers to take into account the consequences of hits, misses, false alarms, and correct rejections (McFall & Treat, 1999; Swets, Dawes, & Monahan, 2000). For an example of a common everyday task that can interfere with signal detection, see the Real World box.

signal detection theory
The response to a stimulus depends both on a person's sensitivity to the stimulus in the presence of noise and on a person's response criterion.

sensory adaptation
Sensitivity to prolonged stimulation tends to decline over time as an organism adapts to current conditions.

THE REAL WORLD

Multitasking

By one estimate, using a cell phone while driving makes having an accident four times more likely (McEvoy et al., 2005). In response to highway safety experts and statistics such as this, state legislatures are passing laws that restrict, and sometimes ban, using mobile phones while driving. You might think that's a fine idea . . . for everyone else on the road. But surely *you* can manage to punch in a number on a phone, carry on a conversation, or maybe even text-message while simultaneously driving in a safe and courteous manner. Right? In a word, *wrong*.

The issue here is *selective attention,* or perceiving only what's currently relevant to you. Perception is an active, moment-to-moment exploration for relevant or interesting information, not a passive receptacle for whatever happens to come along. Talking on a cell phone while driving demands that you juggle two independent sources of sensory input—vision and audition—at the same time. This is problematic because research has found that when attention is directed to audition, activity in visual areas decreases (Shomstein & Yantis, 2004).

This kind of *multitasking* creates problems when you need to react suddenly while driving. Researchers have tested experienced drivers in a highly realistic driving simulator, measuring their response times to brake lights and stop signs while they listened to the radio or carried on phone conversations about a political issue, among other tasks (Strayer, Drews, & Johnston, 2003). These experienced drivers reacted significantly more slowly during phone conversations than during

the other tasks. This is because a phone conversation requires memory retrieval, deliberation, and planning what to say and often carries an emotional stake in the conversation topic. Tasks such as listening to the radio require far less attention.

The tested drivers became so engaged in their conversations that their minds no longer seemed to be in the car. Their slower braking response translated into an increased stopping distance that, depending on the driver's speed, would have resulted in a rear-end collision. Whether the phone was handheld or hands-free made little difference, and similar results have been obtained in field studies of actual driving (Horrey & Wickens, 2006). This suggests that laws requiring drivers to use hands-free phones may have little effect on reducing accidents. Even after extensive practice at driving while using a hands-free cell phone in a simulator, the distruptive effects of cell phone use were still observed (Cooper & Strayer, 2008). The situation is even worse when text messaging is involved: Compared with a no-texting control condition, when either sending or receiving a text message in the simulator, drivers spent dramatically less time looking at the road, had a much harder time staying in their lane, missed numerous lane changes, and had greater difficulty maintaining an appropriate distance behind the car ahead of them (Hosking, Young, & Regan, 2009). A recent review concluded

that the impairing effect of texting while driving is comparable to that of alcohol consumption and greater than that of smoking marijuana (Pascual-Ferrá, Liu, & Beatty, 2012).

Interestingly, people who report that they multitask frequently in everyday life have difficulty in laboratory tasks that require focusing attention in the face of distractions compared with individuals who do not multitask much in daily life (Ophir, Nass, & Wagner, 2009). So how well do we multitask in several thousand pounds of metal hurtling down the highway? Unless you have two heads with one brain each—one to talk and one to concentrate on driving—you would do well to keep your eyes on the road and not on the phone.

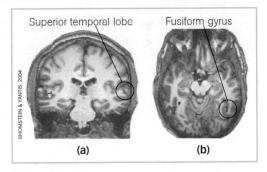

▲ **Shifting Attention** Participants received fMRI scans as they performed tasks that required them to shift their attention between visual and auditory information. (*a*) When focusing on auditory information, a region in the superior (upper) temporal lobe involved in auditory processing showed increased activity (yellow/orange). (*b*) In striking contrast, a visual region, the fusiform gyrus, showed decreased activity when participants focused on auditory information (blue).

Sensory Adaptation

When you walk into a bakery, the aroma of freshly baked bread overwhelms you, but after a few minutes the smell fades. If you dive into cold water, the temperature is shocking at first, but after a few minutes you get used to it. When you wake up in the middle of the night for a drink of water, the bathroom light blinds you, but after a few minutes you no longer squint. These are all examples of **sensory adaptation:** *Sensitivity to prolonged stimulation tends to decline over time as an organism adapts to current conditions.*

Sensory adaptation is a useful process for most organisms. Imagine what your sensory and perceptual world would be like without it. When you put on your jeans in the morning, the feeling of rough

What conditions have you already adapted to today? Sounds? Smells?

cloth against your bare skin would be as noticeable hours later as it was in the first few minutes. The stink of garbage in your apartment when you first walk in would never dissipate. If you had to be constantly aware of how your tongue feels while it is resting in your mouth, you'd be driven to distraction. Our sensory systems respond more strongly to changes in stimulation than to constant stimulation. A stimulus that doesn't change usually doesn't require any action; your car probably emits a certain hum all the time that you've gotten used to. But a change in stimulation often signals a need for action. If your car starts making different kinds of noises, you're not only more likely to notice them, but you're also more likely to do something about it.

According to the theory of natural selection, inherited characteristics that provide a survival advantage tend to spread throughout the population across generations. Why might sensory adaptation have evolved? What survival benefits might it confer to a small animal trying to avoid predators? To a predator trying to hunt prey?

IN SUMMARY

▶ Sensation and perception are critical to survival. Sensation is the simple stimulation of a sense organ, whereas perception organizes, identifies, and interprets sensation at the level of the brain.

▶ All of our senses depend on the process of transduction, which converts physical signals from the environment into neural signals carried by sensory neurons into the central nervous system.

▶ In the 19th century, researchers developed psychophysics, an approach to studying perception that measures the strength of a stimulus and an observer's sensitivity to that stimulus. Psychophysicists have developed procedures for measuring an observer's absolute threshold, or the smallest intensity needed to just barely detect a stimulus, and the just noticeable difference (JND), or the smallest change in a stimulus that can just barely be detected.

▶ Signal detection theory allows researchers to distinguish between an observer's perceptual sensitivity to a stimulus and criteria for making decisions about the stimulus.

▶ Sensory adaptation occurs because sensitivity to lengthy stimulation tends to decline over time.

Vision I: How the Eyes and the Brain Convert Light Waves to Neural Signals

You might be proud of your 20/20 vision, even if it is corrected by glasses or contact lenses. 20/20 refers to a measurement associated with a Snellen chart, named after Hermann Snellen (1834–1908), the Dutch ophthalmologist who developed it as a means of assessing **visual acuity,** *the ability to see fine detail;* it is the smallest line of letters that a typical person can read from a distance of 20 feet. But if you dropped into the Birds of Prey Ophthalmologic Office, your visual pride would wither. Hawks, eagles, owls, and other raptors have much greater visual acuity than humans: in many cases, about 8 times greater, or the equivalent of 20/2 vision (meaning that what the normal human can just see from 2 feet away can be seen by these birds at a distance of 20 feet away). Your sophisticated visual system has evolved to transduce visual energy in the world into neural signals in the brain. Humans have sensory receptors in their eyes that respond to wavelengths of light energy. When we look at people, places, and things, patterns of light and color give us information about where one surface stops

Though controversial for other reasons, research has shown that action-shooter games improve attention and even basic visual acuity (Green & Bavelier, 2007; Li et al., 2009).

and another begins. The array of light reflected from those surfaces preserves their shapes and enables us to form a mental representation of a scene (Rodieck, 1998). Understanding vision, then, starts with understanding light.

Sensing Light

Visible light is simply the portion of the electromagnetic spectrum that we can see, and it is an extremely small slice (see **FIGURE 4.2**). You can think about light as waves of energy. Like ocean waves, light waves vary in height and in the distance between their peaks, or *wavelengths*. There are three properties of light waves, each of which has a physical dimension that produces a corresponding psychological dimension (see **TABLE 4.3**). In other words, light doesn't need a human to have the properties it does: Length, amplitude, and purity are properties of the light waves themselves. What humans perceive from those properties are color, brightness, and saturation.

> The *length* of a light wave determines its hue, or what humans perceive as color.

> The intensity or *amplitude* of a light wave—how high the peaks are—determines what we perceive as the brightness of light.

> *Purity* is the number of distinct wavelengths that make up the light. Purity corresponds to what humans perceive as saturation, or the richness of colors.

visual acuity
The ability to see fine detail.

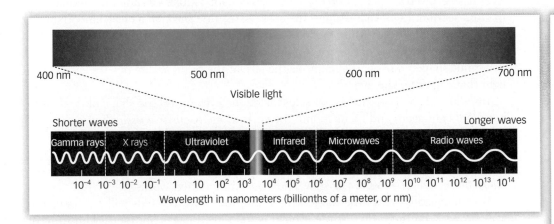

◀ Figure **4.2** **Electromagnetic Spectrum** The sliver of light waves visible to humans as a rainbow of colors from violet-blue to red is bounded on the short end by ultraviolet rays, which honeybees can see, and on the long end by infrared waves, upon which night-vision equipment operates. Someone wearing night-vision goggles, for example, can detect another person's body heat in complete darkness. Light waves are minute, but the scale along the bottom of this chart offers a glimpse of their varying lengths, measured in nanometers (nm; 1 nm = 1 billionth of a meter).

Table 4.3

Properties of Light Waves

Physical Dimension		Psychological Dimension
Length		Hue or what we perceive as color
Amplitude		Brightness
Purity saturated desaturated		Saturation or richness of color

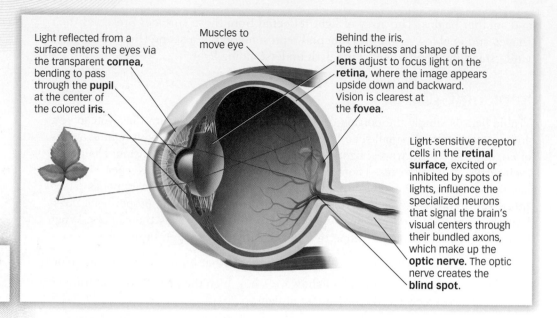

Light reflected from a surface enters the eyes via the transparent **cornea**, bending to pass through the **pupil** at the center of the colored **iris**.

Muscles to move eye

Behind the iris, the thickness and shape of the **lens** adjust to focus light on the **retina**, where the image appears upside down and backward. Vision is clearest at the **fovea**.

Light-sensitive receptor cells in the **retinal surface**, excited or inhibited by spots of lights, influence the specialized neurons that signal the brain's visual centers through their bundled axons, which make up the **optic nerve**. The optic nerve creates the **blind spot**.

▶ Figure **4.3 Anatomy of the Human Eye** Specialized organs of the eye evolved to detect light.

The Human Eye

Eyes have evolved as specialized organs to detect light. **FIGURE 4.3** shows the human eye in cross-section. Light that reaches the eyes passes first through a clear, smooth outer tissue called the *cornea,* which bends the light wave and sends it through the *pupil,* a hole in the colored part of the eye. This colored part is the *iris,* which is a translucent, doughnut-shaped muscle that controls the size of the pupil and hence the amount of light that can enter the eye.

Immediately behind the iris, muscles inside the eye control the shape of the *lens* to bend the light again and focus it onto the **retina**, *light-sensitive tissue lining the back of the eyeball.* The muscles change the shape of the lens to focus objects at different distances, making the lens flatter for objects that are far away or rounder for nearby objects. This is called **accommodation,** *the process by which the eye maintains a clear image on the retina.* **FIGURE 4.4a** shows how accommodation works.

If your eyeballs are a little too long or a little too short, the lens will not focus images properly on the retina. If the eyeball is too long, images are focused in front of the retina, leading to nearsightedness (*myopia*), which is shown in **FIGURE 4.4b.** If the eyeball is too short, images are focused behind the retina, and the result is farsightedness (*hyperopia*), as shown in **FIGURE 4.4c.** Eyeglasses, contact lenses, and surgical procedures can correct either condition. For example, eyeglasses and contacts both provide an additional lens to help focus light more appropriately, and procedures such as LASIK physically reshape the eye's existing lens.

How do eyeglasses actually correct vision?

From the Eye to the Brain

How does a wavelength of light become a meaningful image? The retina is the interface between the world of light outside the body and the world of vision inside the central nervous system. Two types of *photoreceptor cells* in the retina contain light-sensitive pigments that transduce light into neural impulses. **Cones** *detect color, operate under normal daylight conditions, and allow us to focus on fine detail.* **Rods** *become active under low-light conditions for night vision* (see **FIGURE 4.5**).

Rods are much more sensitive photoreceptors than cones, but this sensitivity comes at a cost. Because all rods contain the same photopigment, they provide no information about color and sense only shades of gray. Think about this the next time you wake up in the middle of the night and make your way to the bathroom for a drink

retina
Light-sensitive tissue lining the back of the eyeball.

accommodation
The process by which the eye maintains a clear image on the retina.

cones
Photoreceptors that detect color, operate under normal daylight conditions, and allow us to focus on fine detail.

rods
Photoreceptors that become active under low-light conditions for night vision.

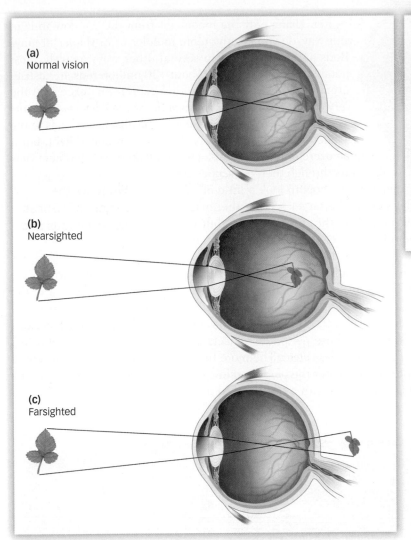

(a) Normal vision

(b) Nearsighted

(c) Farsighted

◄ Figure **4.4** **Accommodation** Inside the eye, the lens changes shape to focus nearby or faraway objects on the retina. (*a*) People with normal vision focus the image on the retina at the back of the eye, both for near and far objects. (*b*) Nearsighted people see clearly what's nearby, but distant objects are blurry because light from them is focused in front of the retina, a condition called *myopia*. (*c*) Farsighted people have the opposite problem: Distant objects are clear, but those nearby are blurry because their point of focus falls beyond the surface of the retina, a condition called *hyperopia*.

▼ Figure **4.5** **Close-up of the Retina** The surface of the retina is composed of photoreceptor cells, the rods and cones, beneath a layer of transparent neurons, the bipolar and retinal ganglion cells (RGCs), connected in sequence. The axon of a retinal ganglion cell joins with all other RGC axons to form the optic nerve. Viewed close up in this cross-sectional diagram is the area of greatest visual acuity, the fovea, where most color-sensitive cones are concentrated, allowing us to see fine detail as well as color. Rods, the predominant photoreceptors activated in low-light conditions, are distributed everywhere else on the retina.

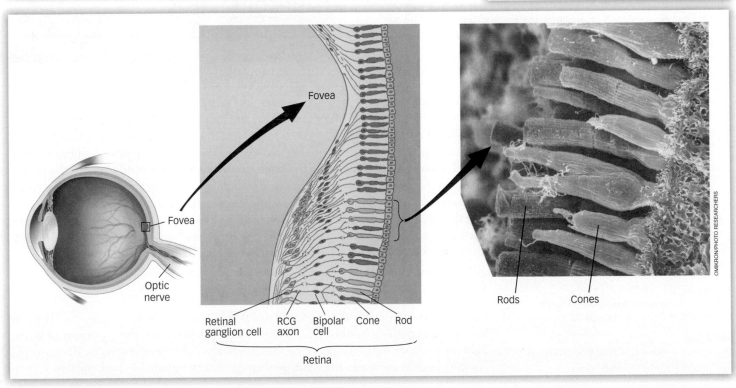

Fovea

Fovea

Optic nerve

Retinal ganglion cell

RCG axon

Bipolar cell

Cone

Rod

Retina

Rods

Cones

OMIKRON/PHOTO RESEARCHERS

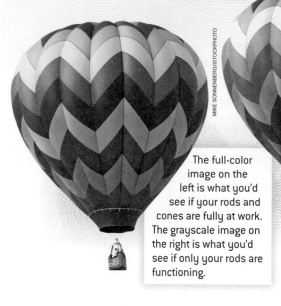

MIKE SONNENBERG/ISTOCKPHOTO

The full-color image on the left is what you'd see if your rods and cones are fully at work. The grayscale image on the right is what you'd see if only your rods are functioning.

of water. Using only the moonlight from the window to light your way, do you see the room in color or in shades of gray? Rods and cones differ in several other ways as well, most notably in their numbers. About 120 million rods are distributed more or less evenly around each retina except in the very center, the **fovea**, *an area of the retina where vision is the clearest and there are no rods at all.* The absence of rods in the fovea decreases the sharpness of vision in reduced light, but it can be overcome. For example, when amateur astronomers view dim stars through their telescopes at night, they know to look a little off to the side of the target so that the image will not fall on the rod-free fovea, but on some other part of the retina that contains many highly sensitive rods.

> **What are the major differences between rods and cones?**

In contrast to rods, each retina contains only about 6 million cones, which are densely packed in the fovea and much more sparsely distributed over the rest of the retina, as you can see in Figure 4.5. This distribution of cones directly affects visual acuity and explains why objects off to the side, in your *peripheral vision,* aren't so clear. The light reflecting from those peripheral objects is less likely to land in the fovea, making the resulting image less clear. The more fine detail encoded and represented in the visual system, the clearer the perceived image. The process is analogous to the quality of photographs taken with a 6-megapixel digital camera versus a 2-megapixel camera.

The image on the left was taken at a higher resolution than the image on the right. The difference in quality is analogous to light falling on the fovea versus the periphery of the retina.

THINKSTOCK

The retina is thick with cells. As seen in Figure 4.5, the photoreceptor cells (rods and cones) form the innermost layer. They are beneath a layer of transparent neurons, the bipolar and retinal ganglion cells. The *bipolar cells* collect neural signals from the rods and cones and transmit them to the outermost layer of the retina, where neurons called *retinal ganglion cells* (*RGCs*) organize the signals and send them to the brain.

The bundled RGC axons—about 1.5 million per eye—form the *optic nerve,* which leaves the eye through a hole in the retina. Because it contains neither rods nor cones and therefore has no mechanism to sense light, this hole in the retina creates a **blind spot,** *a location in the visual field that produces no sensation on the retina.* Try the demonstration in **FIGURE 4.6** to find the blind spot in each of your own eyes.

fovea
An area of the retina where vision is the clearest and there are no rods at all.

blind spot
A location in the visual field that produces no sensation on the retina.

Perceiving Color

Sir Isaac Newton pointed out around 1670 that color is not something "in" light. In fact, color is nothing but our perception of wavelengths from the spectrum of visible light (see Figure 4.2). We perceive the shortest visible wavelengths as deep purple. As wavelengths increase, the color perceived changes gradually and continuously to

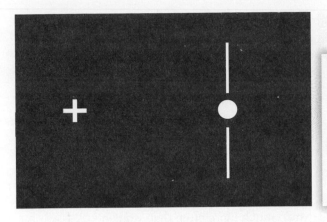

◄ Figure **4.6** **Blind Spot Demonstration** To find your blind spot, close your left eye and stare at the cross with your right eye. Hold the book 6 to 12 inches (15 to 30 centimeters) away from your eyes and move it slowly toward and away from you until the dot disappears. The dot is now in your blind spot and not visible. At this point the vertical lines may appear as one continuous line because the visual system fills in the area occupied by the missing dot. To test your left eye's blind spot, turn the book upside down and repeat with your right eye closed.

blue, then green, yellow, orange, and, with the longest visible wavelengths, red. This rainbow of hues and accompanying wavelengths is called the *visible spectrum*, illustrated in **FIGURE 4.7**.

You'll recall that all rods are ideal for low-light vision but bad for distinguishing colors. Cones, by contrast, come in three types; each type is especially sensitive to either red (long-wavelength), green (medium-wavelength), or blue (short-wavelength)

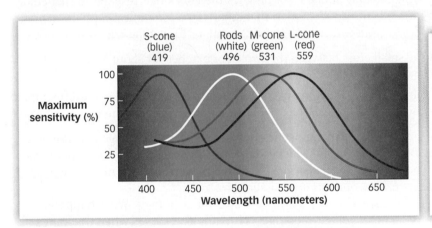

◄ Figure **4.7** **Seeing in Color** We perceive a spectrum of color because objects selectively absorb some wavelengths of light and reflect others. Color perception corresponds to the summed activity of the three types of cones. Each type is most sensitive to a narrow range of wavelengths in the visible spectrum—short (bluish light), medium (greenish light), or long (reddish light). Rods, represented by the white curve, are most sensitive to the medium wavelengths of visible light but do not contribute to color perception.

light. Red, green, and blue are the primary colors of light; color perception results from different combinations of the three basic elements in the retina that respond to the wavelengths corresponding to the three primary colors of light. For example, lighting designers add primary colors of light together, such as shining red and green spotlights on a surface to create a yellow light, as shown in **FIGURE 4.8**. Notice that in the center of the figure, where the red, green, and blue lights overlap, the surface looks white. This demonstrates that a white surface really is reflecting all visible wavelengths of light.

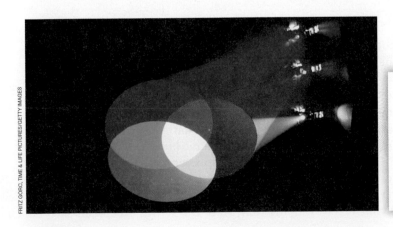

FRITZ GORO, TIME & LIFE PICTURES/GETTY IMAGES

◄ Figure **4.8** **Color Mixing** The millions of shades of color that humans can perceive are products not only of a light's wavelength, but also of the mixture of wavelengths a stimulus absorbs or reflects. Colored spotlights work by causing the surface to reflect light of a particular wavelength, which stimulates the red, blue, or green photopigments in the cones. When all visible wavelengths are present, we see white.

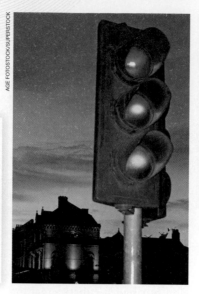

Many people (including about 5% of all males) inherit conditions in which either the "red" or the "green" photoreceptors do not transduce light properly. Such people have difficulty distinguishing hues that to typical individuals appear as red or green. Unfortunately, in the United States, traffic signals use red and green lights to indicate whether cars should stop or go through an intersection. Why do drivers with red–green blindness not risk auto accidents every time they approach an intersection?

The fact that three types of cones in the retina respond preferentially to different wavelengths (corresponding to blue, green, or red light) means that the pattern of responding across the three types of cones provides a unique code for each color. In fact, researchers can "read out" the wavelength of the light entering the eye by working backward from the relative firing rates of the three types of cones (Gegenfurtner & Kiper, 2003). A genetic disorder in which one of the cone types is missing—and, in some very rare cases, two or all three—causes a *color deficiency*. This trait is sex-linked, affecting men much more often than women.

Color deficiency is often referred to as *color blindness,* but in fact, people missing only one type of cone can still distinguish many colors, just not as many as someone who has the full complement of three cone types. You can create a kind of temporary color deficiency by exploiting the idea of sensory adaptation. Just like the rest of your body, cones need an occasional break too. Staring too long at one color fatigues the cones that respond to that color, producing a form of sensory adaptation that results in a *color afterimage*. To demonstrate this effect for yourself, follow these instructions for **FIGURE 4.9:**

> Stare at the small cross between the two color patches for about 1 minute. Try to keep your eyes as still as possible.

> After a minute, look at the lower cross. You should see a vivid color aftereffect that lasts for a minute or more. Pay particular attention to the colors in the afterimage.

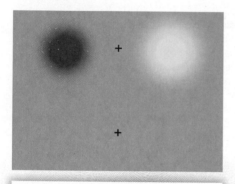

▲ Figure **4.9** **Color Afterimage Demonstration** Follow the accompanying instructions in the text, and sensory adaptation will do the rest. When the afterimage fades, you can get back to reading the chapter.

Were you puzzled that the red patch produces a green afterimage and the green patch produces a red afterimage? This result reveals something important about color perception. The explanation stems from the **color-opponent system,** where *pairs of visual neurons work in opposition:* red-sensitive cells against green-sensitive (as in Figure 4.9) and blue-sensitive cells against yellow-sensitive (Hurvich & Jameson, 1957). The color-opponent system explains color aftereffects. When you view a color, let's say, green, the cones that respond most strongly to green become fatigued over time. Now, when you stare at a white or gray patch, which reflects all the colors equally, the green-sensitive cones respond only weakly compared with the still-fresh red-sensitive cones, which fire strongly. The result? You perceive the patch as tinted red.

What happens when the cones in your eyes get fatigued?

The Visual Brain

Streams of action potentials containing information encoded by the retina (neural impulses) travel to the brain along the optic nerve. Half of the axons in the optic nerve

What is the relationship between the right and left eyes, and the right and left visual fields?

that leave each eye come from retinal ganglion cells (RGCs) that code information in the right visual field, whereas the other half code information in the left visual field. These two nerve bundles link to the left and right hemispheres of the brain, respectively (see **FIGURE 4.10**). The optic nerve travels from each eye to the *lateral geniculate nucleus* (*LGN*), located in the thalamus. As you will recall from the Neuroscience and Behavior chapter, the thalamus receives inputs from all of the senses except smell. From

color-opponent system
Pairs of visual neurons that work in opposition.

area V1
The part of the occipital lobe that contains the primary visual cortex.

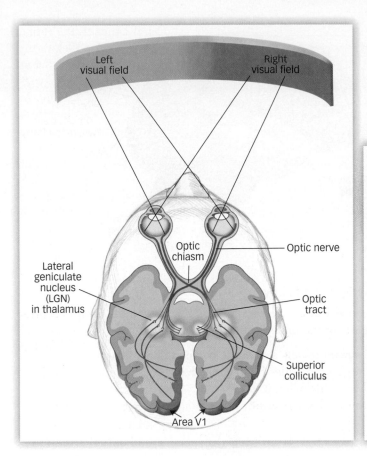

◀ Figure **4.10** **Visual Pathway from Eye through Brain** Objects in the right visual field stimulate the left half of each retina, and objects in the left visual field stimulate the right half of each retina. The optic nerves, one exiting each eye, are formed by the axons of retinal ganglion cells emerging from the retina. Just before they enter the brain at the optic chiasm, about half the nerve fibers from each eye cross. The left half of each optic nerve (representing the right visual field) runs through the brain's left hemisphere via the thalamus, and the right half of each optic nerve (representing the left visual field) travels this route through the right hemisphere. So, information from the right visual field ends up in the left hemisphere and information from the left visual field ends up in the right hemisphere.

there, the visual signal travels to the back of the brain, to a location called **area V1,** the *part of the occipital lobe that contains the primary visual cortex.* Here the information is systematically mapped into a representation of the visual scene.

Neural Systems for Perceiving Shape

One of the most important functions of vision involves perceiving the shapes of objects; our day-to-day lives would be a mess if we couldn't distinguish individual shapes from one another. Imagine not being able to reliably differentiate between a warm doughnut with glazed icing and a straight stalk of celery and you'll get the idea; breakfast could become a traumatic experience if you couldn't distinguish shapes. Perceiving shape depends on the location and orientation of an object's edges. It is not surprising, then, that area V1 is specialized for encoding edge orientation. As you also read in the Neuroscience and Behavior chapter, neurons in the visual cortex selectively respond to bars and edges in specific orientations in space (Hubel & Weisel, 1962, 1998). In effect, area V1 contains populations of neurons, each "tuned" to respond to edges oriented at each position in the visual field. This means that some neurons fire when an object in a vertical orientation is perceived, other neurons fire when an object in a horizontal orientation is perceived, still other neurons fire when objects in a diagonal orientation of 45° are perceived, and so on (see **FIGURE 4.11**). The outcome of the coordinated response of all these feature detectors contributes to a sophisticated visual system that can detect where a doughnut ends and celery begins.

▼ Figure **4.11** **Single-Neuron Feature Detectors** Area V1 contains neurons that respond to specific orientations of edges. Here a single neuron's responses are recorded (*left*) as the monkey views bars at different orientations (*right*). This neuron fires continuously when the bar is pointing to the right at 45°, less often when it is vertical, and not at all when it is pointing to the left at 45°.

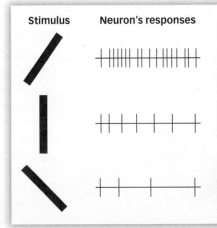

FRITZ GORO/TIME & LIFE PICTURES/GETTY IMAGES

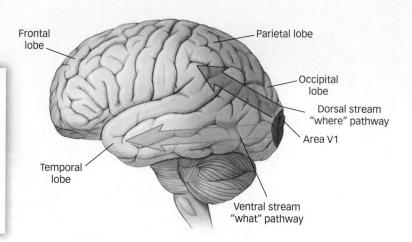

▼ Figure **4.12** **Visual Streaming** One interconnected visual system forms a pathway that courses from the occipital visual regions into the lower temporal lobe. This ventral pathway enables us to identify what we see. Another interconnected pathway travels from the occipital lobe through the upper regions of the temporal lobe into the parietal regions. This dorsal pathway allows us to locate objects, to track their movements, and to move in relation to them.

Pathways for What, Where, and How

Two functionally distinct pathways, or *visual streams,* project from the occipital cortex to visual areas in other parts of the brain (see **FIGURE 4.12**):

> The *ventral* (below) *stream* travels across the occipital lobe into the lower levels of the temporal lobes and includes brain areas that represent an object's shape and identity, in other words, what it is, essentially a "what" pathway (Kravtiz et al., 2013; Ungerleider & Mishkin, 1982).

> The *dorsal* (above) *stream* travels up from the occipital lobe to the parietal lobes (including some of the middle and upper levels of the temporal lobes), connecting with brain areas that identify the location and motion of an object, in other words, where it is (Kravtiz et al., 2011). Because the dorsal stream allows us to perceive spatial relations, researchers originally dubbed it the "where" pathway (Ungerleider & Mishkin, 1982). Neuroscientists later argued that because the dorsal stream is crucial for guiding movements, such as aiming, reaching, or tracking with the eyes, the "where" pathway should more appropriately be called the "how" pathway (Milner & Goodale, 1995).

What are the main jobs of the ventral and dorsal streams?

How do we know there are two pathways? The most dramatic evidence comes from studying the impairments that result from brain injuries to each of the areas.

For example, a woman known as D.F. suffered permanent damage to a large region of the lateral occipital cortex, an area in the ventral stream (Goodale et al., 1991). Her ability to recognize objects by sight was greatly impaired, although her ability to recognize objects by touch was normal. This suggests that her *visual representation* of objects, and not her *memory* for objects, was damaged. D.F.'s brain damage belongs to a category called **visual form agnosia,** *the inability to recognize objects by sight* (Goodale & Milner, 1992, 2004). Oddly, although D.F. could not recognize objects visually, she could accurately *guide* her actions by sight, as demonstrated in **FIGURE 4.13**. When D.F. was scanned with fMRI, researchers found that she showed normal activation of regions within the dorsal stream during guided movement (James et al., 2003).

Conversely, other people with brain damage to the parietal lobe, a section of the dorsal stream, have difficulty using vision to guide their reaching and grasping movements (Perenin & Vighetto, 1988). However, their ventral streams are intact, meaning they recognize what objects are.

▼ Figure **4.13** **Testing Visual Form Agnosia** (*left*) When researchers asked D.F. to orient her hand to match the angle of the slot in the testing apparatus, she was unable to comply. (*right*) However, when asked to insert a card into the slot at various angles, D.F. accomplished the task virtually to perfection.

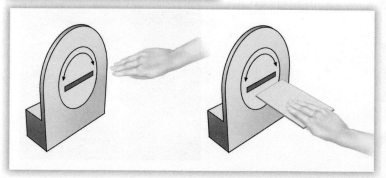

We can conclude from these two patterns of impairment that the ventral and dorsal visual streams are functionally distinct; it is possible to damage one while leaving the other intact. Still, the two streams must work together during visual perception in order to integrate "what" and "where," and researchers are starting to examine how they interact. One intriguing possibility is suggested by recent fMRI research indicating that some regions within the dorsal stream are sensitive to properties of an object's identity, responding differently, for example, to line drawings of the same object in different sizes or viewed from different vantage points (Konen & Kastner, 2008; Sakuraba et al., 2012). This may be what allows the dorsal and ventral streams to exchange information and thus integrate the "what" and "where" (Farivar, 2009; Konen & Kastner, 2008).

visual form agnosia
The inability to recognize objects by sight.

IN SUMMARY

▶ Light passes through several layers in the eye to reach the retina. Two types of photoreceptor cells in the retina transduce light into neural impulses: cones, which operate under normal daylight conditions and sense color; and rods, which are active under low-light conditions for night vision. The neural impulses are sent along the optic nerve to the brain.

▶ The retina contains several layers, and the outermost consists of retinal ganglion cells (RGCs) that collect and send signals to the brain. Bundles of RGCs form the optic nerve.

▶ Light striking the retina causes a specific pattern of response in each of three cone types that are critical to color perception: short-wavelength (bluish) light, medium-wavelength (greenish) light, and long-wavelength (reddish) light. The overall pattern of response across the three cone types results in a unique code for each color.

▶ Information encoded by the retina travels to the brain along the optic nerve, which connects to the lateral geniculate nucleus in the thalamus and then to the primary visual cortex, area V1, in the occipital lobe.

▶ Two functionally distinct pathways project from the occipital lobe to visual areas in other parts of the brain. The ventral stream travels into the lower levels of the temporal lobes and includes brain areas that represent an object's shape and identity. The dorsal stream goes from the occipital lobes to the parietal lobes, connecting with brain areas that identify the location and motion of an object.

Vision II: Recognizing What We Perceive

Our journey into the visual system has already revealed how it accomplishes some pretty astonishing feats. But the system needs to do much more in order for us to be able to interact effectively with our visual worlds. Let's now consider how the system links together individual visual features into whole objects, allows us to recognize what those objects are, organizes objects into visual scenes, and detects motion and change in those scenes. Along the way we'll see that studying visual errors and illusions provides key insights into how these processes work.

Attention: The "Glue" That Binds Individual Features into a Whole

Specialized feature detectors in different parts of the visual system analyze each of the multiple features of a visible object: orientation, color, size, shape, and so forth. But how are different features combined into single, unified objects? What allows us to perceive so easily and correctly that the young man in the photo is wearing a red shirt

We correctly combine features into unified objects; so, for example, we see that the young man is wearing a red shirt and the young woman is wearing a yellow shirt.

FUSE/PUNCHSTOCK

and the young woman is wearing a yellow shirt? Why don't we see free-floating patches of red and yellow, or even incorrect combinations, such as the young man wearing a yellow shirt and the young woman wearing a red shirt? These questions refer to what researchers call the **binding problem** in perception, *how features are linked together so that we see unified objects in our visual world rather than free-floating or miscombined features* (Treisman, 1998, 2006).

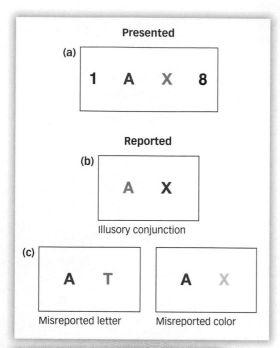

Presented

(a)

1   A   X   8

Reported

(b)

A   X

Illusory conjunction

(c)

A   T   A   X

Misreported letter   Misreported color

▲ Figure **4.14 Illusory Conjunctions** Illusory conjunctions occur when features such as color and shape are combined incorrectly. For example, when participants are shown a red *A* and blue *X*, they sometimes report seeing a blue *A* and red *X*. Other kinds of errors, such as a misreported letter (e.g., reporting *T* when no *T* was presented) or misreported color (reporting green when no green was presented) occur rarely, indicating that illusory conjunctions are not the result of guessing (based on Robertson, 2003).

Illusory Conjunctions: Perceptual Mistakes

In everyday life, we correctly combine features into unified objects so automatically and effortlessly that it may be difficult to appreciate that binding is ever a problem at all. However, researchers have discovered errors in binding that reveal important clues about how the process works. One such error is known as an **illusory conjunction,** *a perceptual mistake where features from multiple objects are incorrectly combined.* In a pioneering study of illusory conjunctions, Anne Treisman and Hilary Schmidt (1982) briefly showed study participants visual displays in which black digits flanked colored letters, then instructed them first to report the black digits and second to describe the colored letters. Participants frequently reported illusory conjunctions, claiming to have seen, for example, a blue *A* or a red *X* instead of the red *A* and the blue *X* that had actually been shown (see **FIGURE 4.14a** and **b**). These illusory conjunctions were not just the result of guessing; they occurred more frequently than other kinds of errors, such as reporting a letter or color that was not present in the display (see **FIGURE 4.14c**). Illusory conjunctions look real to the participants, who were just as confident they had seen them as they were about the actual colored letters they perceived correctly.

> How does the study of illusory conjunctions help us understand the role of attention in feature binding?

Why do illusory conjunctions occur? Treisman and her colleagues have tried to explain them by proposing a **feature-integration theory** (Treisman, 1998, 2006; Treisman & Gelade, 1980; Treisman & Schmidt, 1982), which holds that *focused attention is not required to detect the individual features that comprise a stimulus, such as the color, shape, size, and location of letters, but is required to bind those individual features together.* From this perspective, attention provides the "glue" necessary to bind features together, and illusory conjunctions occur when it is difficult for participants to pay full attention to the features that need to be glued together. For example, in the experiments we just considered, participants were required to process the digits that flank the colored letters, thereby reducing attention to the letters and allowing illusory conjunctions to occur. When experimental conditions are changed so that participants can pay full attention to the colored letters, and they are able to correctly bind their features together, illusory conjunctions disappear (Treisman, 1998; Treisman & Schmidt, 1982).

The Role of the Parietal Lobe

The binding process makes use of feature information processed by structures within the ventral visual stream, the "what" pathway (Seymour et al., 2010; see Figure 4.12). But because binding involves linking together features processed in distinct parts of the ventral stream at a particular spatial location, it also depends critically on the parietal lobe in the dorsal stream, the "where" pathway (Robertson, 1999). For example, Treisman and others studied R.M., who had suffered strokes that destroyed both his left and right parietal lobes. Although many aspects of his visual function were intact, he had severe problems attending to spatially distinct objects. When presented with stimuli such as those in Figure 4.14, R.M. perceived an abnormally large number of

binding problem
How features are linked together so that we see unified objects in our visual world rather than free-floating or miscombined features.

illusory conjunction
A perceptual mistake where features from multiple objects are incorrectly combined.

feature-integration theory
The idea that focused attention is not required to detect the individual features that comprise a stimulus, but is required to bind those individual features together.

illusory conjunctions, even when he was given as long as 10 seconds to look at the displays (Friedman-Hill, Robertson, & Treisman, 1995; Robertson, 2003). More recent studies of persons with similar brain injuries suggest that damage to the upper and posterior portions of the parietal lobe is likely to produce similar problems (Braet & Humphreys, 2009; McCrea, Buxbaum, & Coslett, 2006). These same parietal regions are activated in healthy individuals when they perform the kind of visual feature binding that persons with parietal lobe damage are unable to perform (Shafritz, Gore, & Marois, 2002), as well as when they search for conjunction features (Corbetta et al., 1995; Donner et al., 2002).

Recognizing Objects by Sight

Take a quick look at the letters in the accompanying illustration. Even though they're quite different from one another, you probably effortlessly recognized them as all being examples of the letter G. Now consider the same kind of demonstration using your best friend's face. Your friend might have long hair, but one day she decides to get it cut dramatically short. Suppose one day your friend gets a dramatic new haircut—or adds glasses, hair dye, or a nose ring. Even though your friend now looks strikingly different, you still recognize that person with ease. Just like the variability in Gs, you somehow are able to extract the underlying features of the face that allow you to accurately identify your friend.

This thought exercise may seem trivial, but it's no small perceptual feat. If the visual system were somehow stumped each time a minor variation occurred in an object being perceived, the inefficiency of it all would be overwhelming. We'd have to process information effortfully just to perceive our friend as the same person from one meeting to another, not to mention laboring through the process of knowing when a G is really a G. In general, though, object recognition proceeds fairly smoothly, in large part due to the operation of the feature detectors we discussed earlier.

How do feature detectors help the visual system get from a spatial array of light hitting the eye to the accurate perception of an object in different circumstances, such as your friend's face? Some researchers argue for a *modular view*, that specialized brain areas, or modules, detect and represent faces or houses or even body parts. Using fMRI to examine visual processing in healthy young adults, researchers found a subregion in the temporal lobe that responds most strongly to faces compared to just about any other object category, whereas a nearby area responds most strongly to buildings and landscapes (Kanwisher, McDermott, & Chun, 1997). This view suggests we not only have feature detectors to aid in visual perception but also "face detectors," "building detectors," and possibly other types of neurons specialized for particular types of object perception (Downing et al., 2006; Kanwisher & Yovel, 2006). Other researchers argue for a more *distributed representation* of object categories. In this view, it is the pattern of activity across multiple brain regions that identifies any viewed object,

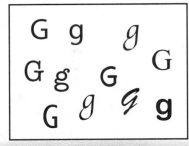

A quick glance and you recognize all these letters as *G*, but their varying sizes, shapes, angles, and orientations ought to make this recognition task difficult. What is it about the process of object recognition that allows us to perform this task effortlessly?

Our visual systems allow us to identify people as the same individual even when they change such features as hair style and skin color. Despite the extreme changes in these two photos, you can probably tell that they both portray Johnny Depp.

perceptual constancy
A perceptual principle stating that even as aspects of sensory signals change, perception remains consistent.

including faces (Haxby et al., 2001). Each of these views explains some data better than the other one, and researchers continue to debate their relative merits.

Another perspective on this issue is provided by experiments designed to measure precisely where seizures originate; these experiments have also provided insights on how single neurons in the human brain respond to objects and faces (Suthana & Fried, 2012). For example, in a study by Quiroga et al. (2005), electrodes were placed in the temporal lobes of people who suffer from epilepsy. Then the volunteers were shown photographs of faces and objects as the researchers recorded their neural responses. The researchers found that neurons in the temporal lobe respond to specific objects viewed from multiple angles and to people wearing different clothing and facial expressions and photographed from various angles. In some cases, the neurons also respond to the words for these same objects. For example, a neuron that responded to photographs of the Sydney Opera House also responded when the words *Sydney Opera* were displayed, but not when the words *Eiffel Tower* were displayed.

Taken together, these experiments demonstrate the principle of **perceptual constancy:** *Even as aspects of sensory signals change, perception remains consistent.* Think

How do we recognize our friends, even when they're hidden behind sunglasses?

back once again to our discussion of difference thresholds early in this chapter. Our perceptual systems are sensitive to relative differences in changing stimulation and make allowances for varying sensory input. This general principle helps explain why you still recognize your friend despite changes in hair color or style or the addition of facial jewelry. It's not as though your visual perceptual system responds to a change with, "Here's a new and unfamiliar face to perceive." Rather, it's as though it responds with, "Interesting . . . here's a deviation from the way this face usually looks." Perception is sensitive to changes in stimuli, but perceptual constancies allow us to notice the differences in the first place.

Principles of Perceptual Organization

Before object recognition can even kick in, the visual system must perform another important task: grouping the image regions that belong together into a representation of an object. The idea that we tend to perceive a unified, whole object rather than a collection of separate parts is the foundation of Gestalt psychology, which you read about in Chapter 1. Gestalt principles characterize many aspects of human perception. Among the foremost are the Gestalt *perceptual grouping rules,* which govern how the features and regions of things fit together (Koffka, 1935). Here's a sampling:

> *Simplicity:* A basic rule in science is that the simplest explanation is usually the best so, when confronted with two or more possible interpretations of an object's shape, the visual system tends to select the simplest or most likely interpretation. In **FIGURE 4.15a** we see an arrow.

> *Closure:* We tend to fill in missing elements of a visual scene, allowing us to perceive edges that are separated by gaps as belonging to complete objects. In **FIGURE 4.15b** we see an arrow despite the gaps.

> *Continuity:* Edges or contours that have the same orientation have what the Gestalt psychologists called *good continuation,* and we tend to group them together perceptually. In **FIGURE 4.15c** we perceive two crossing lines instead of two V shapes.

> *Similarity:* Regions that are similar in color, lightness, shape, or texture are perceived as belonging to the same object. In **FIGURE 4.15d** we perceive three columns—a column of circles flanked by two columns of triangles.

> *Proximity:* Objects that are close together tend to be grouped together. In **FIGURE 4.15e** we perceive three groups or "clumps" of 5 or 6 dots each, not just 16 dots.

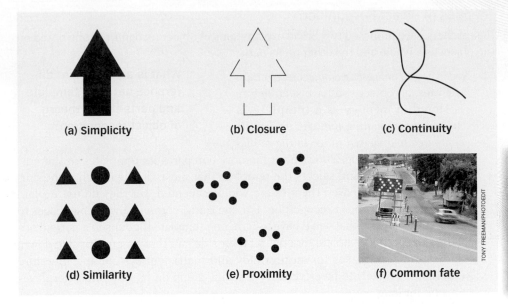

(a) Simplicity   (b) Closure   (c) Continuity

(d) Similarity   (e) Proximity   (f) Common fate

TONY FREEMAN/PHOTOEDIT

◄ Figure **4.15** **Perceptual Grouping Rules**
Principles first identified by Gestalt psychologists and now supported by experimental evidence demonstrate that the brain is predisposed to impose order on incoming sensations. One neural strategy for perception involves responding to patterns among stimuli and grouping like patterns together.

> *Common fate:* Elements of a visual image that move together are perceived as parts of a single moving object. In **FIGURE 4.15f** the series of flashing lights in the road sign are perceived as a moving arrowhead.

Separating Figure from Ground

Perceptual grouping is a powerful aid to our ability to recognize objects by sight. Grouping involves visually separating an object from its surroundings. In Gestalt terms, this means identifying a *figure* apart from the (back)*ground* in which it resides. For example, the words on this page are perceived as figural: They stand out from the ground of the sheet of paper on which they're printed. Similarly, your instructor is perceived as the figure against the backdrop of all the other elements in your classroom. You certainly can perceive these elements differently, of course: The words *and* the paper are all part of a thing called *a page*, and your instructor *and* the classroom can all be perceived as *your learning environment*. Typically, though, our perceptual systems focus attention on some objects as distinct from their environments.

Size provides one clue to what's figure and what's ground: Smaller regions are likely to be figures, such as tiny letters on a big sheet of paper. Movement also helps: Your instructor is (we hope) a dynamic lecturer, moving around in a static environment. Another critical step toward object recognition is *edge assignment*. Given an edge, or boundary, between figure and ground, which region does that edge belong to? If the edge belongs to the figure, it helps define the object's shape, and the background continues behind the edge. Sometimes, though, it's not easy to tell which is which.

Edgar Rubin (1886–1951), a Danish psychologist, capitalized on this ambiguity and developed a famous illusion called the *Rubin vase* or, more generally, a *reversible figure–ground relationship*. You can view this "face–vase" illusion in **FIGURE 4.16** in two ways, either as a vase on a black background or as a pair of silhouettes facing each other. Your visual system settles on one or the other interpretation and fluctuates between them every few seconds. This happens because the edge that would normally separate figure from ground is really part of neither: It equally defines the contours of the vase as it does the contours of the faces. Evidence from fMRIs shows, quite nicely, that when people are seeing the Rubin image as faces, there is greater activity in the face-selective region of the temporal lobe we discussed earlier than when they are seeing it as a vase (Hasson et al., 2001).

▲ Figure **4.16** **Ambiguous Edges**
Here's how Rubin's classic reversible figure–ground illusion works: Fixate your eyes on the center of the image and your perception will alternate between a vase and facing silhouettes, even as the sensory stimulation remains constant.

template
A mental representation that can be directly compared to a viewed shape in the retinal image.

monocular depth cues
Aspects of a scene that yield information about depth when viewed with only one eye.

Theories of Object Recognition

Researchers have proposed two broad explanations of object recognition, one based on the object as a whole and the other on its parts.

> According to *image-based object recognition* theories, an object you have seen before is stored in memory as a **template,** *a mental representation that can be directly compared to a viewed shape in the retinal image* (Tarr & Vuong, 2002). Your memory compares its templates to the current retinal image and selects the template that most closely matches the current image. Image-based theories are widely accepted, yet they do not explain everything about object recognition. For one thing, correctly matching images to templates suggests that you'd have to have one template for cups in a normal orientation, another template for cups on their side, another for cups upside down, and so on. This makes for an unwieldy and inefficient system and therefore one that is unlikely to be effective, yet seeing a cup on its side rarely perplexes anyone for long.

> *Parts-based object recognition* theories propose instead that the brain deconstructs viewed objects into a collection of parts (Marr & Nishihara, 1978). One important parts-based theory contends that objects are stored in memory as structural descriptions: mental inventories of object parts along with the spatial relations among those parts (Biederman, 1987). The parts inventories act as a sort of "alphabet" of geometric elements called *geons* that can be combined to make objects, just as letters are combined to form words (see **FIGURE 4.17**). Parts-based object recognition does not require a template for every view of every object, and so avoids some of the pitfalls of image-based theories. But parts-based object recognition does have major limitations. Most importantly, it allows for object recognition only at the level of categories and not at the level of the individual object. Parts-based theories offer an explanation for recognizing an object such as a face, for example, but are less effective at explaining how you distinguish between your best friend's face and a stranger's face.

Each set of theories has strengths and weaknesses, making object recognition an active area of study in psychology. Researchers are developing hybrid theories that attempt to exploit the strengths of each approach (Peissig & Tarr, 2007).

> **What is an important difference between template and parts-based theory of object recognition?**

Perceiving Depth and Size

Objects in the world are arranged in three dimensions—length, width, and depth—but the retinal image contains only two dimensions, length and width. How does the brain process a flat, 2-D retinal image so that we perceive the depth of an object and how far away it is? The answer lies in a collection of *depth cues* that change as you move through space. Monocular and binocular depth cues all help visual perception (Howard, 2002).

Monocular Depth Cues

Monocular depth cues are *aspects of a scene that yield information about depth when viewed with only one eye.* These cues rely on the relationship between distance and size. Even with one eye closed, the retinal image of an object you're focused on grows smaller as that object moves farther away, and larger as it moves closer. Our brains routinely use these dif-

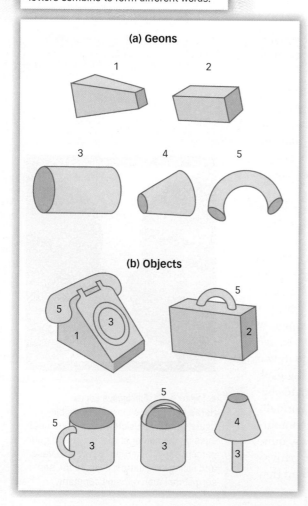

▼ Figure 4.17 **An Alphabet of Geometric Elements** Parts-based theory holds that objects such as those shown in (b) are made up of simpler 3-D components called *geons*, shown in (a), much as letters combine to form different words.

(a) Geons

(b) Objects

ferences in retinal image size, or *relative size,* to perceive distance.

This works particularly well in a monocular depth cue called *familiar size.* Most adults, for example, fall within a familiar range of heights (perhaps 5–7 feet tall), so retinal image size alone is usually a reliable cue to how far away they are. Our visual system automatically corrects for size differences and attributes them to differences in distance. **FIGURE 4.18** demonstrates how strong this mental correction for familiar size is.

In addition to relative size and familiar size, there are several more monocular depth cues, such as

> Linear perspective, which describes the phenomenon that parallel lines seem to converge as they recede into the distance (see **FIGURE 4.19a**).

> *Texture gradient,* which arises when you view a more or less uniformly patterned surface because the size of the pattern elements, as well as the distance between them, grows smaller as the surface recedes from the observer (see **FIGURE 4.19b**).

> *Interposition,* which occurs when one object partly blocks another (see **FIGURE 4.19c**). You can infer that the blocking object is closer than the block*ed* object. However, interposition by itself cannot provide information about how far apart the two objects are.

> *Relative height in the image* depends on your field of vision (see **FIGURE 4.19d**). Objects that are closer to you are lower in your visual field, whereas faraway objects are higher.

▲ Figure **4.18** **Familiar Size and Relative Size** When you view images of people, such as the people in the left-hand photo, or of things you know well, the object you perceive as smaller appears farther away. With a little image manipulation, you can see in the right-hand photo that the relative size difference projected on your retinas is far greater than you perceive. The image of the person in the blue vest is exactly the same size in both photos.

(a)

(b)

(c)

(d)

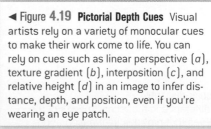

◀ Figure **4.19** **Pictorial Depth Cues** Visual artists rely on a variety of monocular cues to make their work come to life. You can rely on cues such as linear perspective (*a*), texture gradient (*b*), interposition (*c*), and relative height (*d*) in an image to infer distance, depth, and position, even if you're wearing an eye patch.

Binocular Depth Cues

We can also obtain depth information through **binocular disparity,** *the difference in the retinal images of the two eyes that provides information about depth.* Because our eyes are slightly separated, each registers a slightly different view of the world. Your brain computes the disparity between the two retinal images to perceive how far away objects are, as shown in **FIGURE 4.20**. Viewed from above in the figure, the images of the more distant square and the closer circle each fall at different points on each retina.

Binocular disparity as a cue to depth perception was first discussed by Sir Charles Wheatstone in 1838. Wheatstone went on to invent the stereoscope, essentially a holder for a pair of photographs or drawings taken from two horizontally displaced locations. (Wheatstone did not lack for original ideas; he also invented the accordion and an early telegraph and coined the term *microphone.*) When viewed, one by each eye, the pairs of images evoked a vivid sense of depth. The View-Master toy is the modern successor to Wheatstone's invention, and 3-D movies are based on this same idea.

► Figure **4.20 Binocular Disparity** We see the world in three dimensions because our eyes are a distance apart and the image of an object falls on the retinas of each eye at a slightly different place. In this two-object scene, the images of the square and the circle fall on different points of the retina in each eye. The disparity in the positions of the circle's retinal images provides a compelling cue to depth.

The View-Master has been a popular toy for decades. It is based on the principle of binocular disparity: Two images taken from slightly different angles produce a stereoscopic effect.

Illusions of Depth and Size

We all are vulnerable to *illusions,* which, as you'll remember from the Psychology: Evolution of a Science chapter, are errors of perception, memory, or judgment in which subjective experience differs from objective reality (Wade, 2005). The relation between size and distance has been used to create elaborate illusions that depend on fooling the visual system about how far away objects are. All these illusions depend on the same principle: When you view two objects that project the same retinal image size, the object you perceive as farther away will be perceived as larger. One of the most famous illusions is the *Ames room,* constructed by the American ophthalmologist Adelbert Ames in 1946. The room is trapezoidal in shape rather than square: Only two sides are parallel (see **FIGURE 4.21a**). A person standing in one corner of an Ames room is physically twice as far away from the viewer as a person standing in the other corner. But when viewed with one eye through the small peephole placed in one wall, the Ames room looks square because the shapes of the windows and the flooring tiles are carefully crafted to *look* square from the viewing port (Ittelson, 1952).

The visual system perceives the far wall as perpendicular to the line of sight so that people standing at different positions along that wall appear to be at the same

binocular disparity
The difference in the retinal images of the two eyes that provides information about depth.

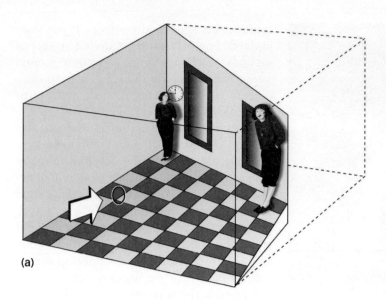

(a)

(b)

▲ Figure 4.21 The Amazing Ames Room
(a) A diagram showing the actual proportions of the Ames room reveals its secrets. The sides of the room form a trapezoid with parallel sides but a back wall that's way off square. The uneven floor makes the room's height in the far back corner shorter than the other. Add misleading cues such as specially designed windows and flooring and position the room's occupants in each far corner and you're ready to lure an unsuspecting observer. (b) Looking into the Ames room through the viewing port with only one eye, the observer infers a normal size–distance relationship—that both people are the same distance away. But the different image sizes they project on the retina leads the viewer to conclude, based on the monocular cue of familiar size, that one person is very small and the other is very large.

distance, and the viewer's judgments of their sizes are based directly on retinal image size. As a result, a person standing in the right corner appears to be much larger than a person standing in the left corner (see **FIGURE 4.21b**).

Perceiving Motion and Change

You should now have a good sense of how we see what and where objects are, a process made substantially easier when the objects stay in one place. But real life, of course, is full of moving targets. Objects change position over time: Birds fly and horses gallop; rain and snow fall; and trees bend in the wind. Understanding how we perceive motion and why we sometimes fail to perceive change can bring us closer to appreciating how visual perception works in everyday life.

Motion Perception

To sense motion, the visual system must encode information about both space and time. The simplest case to consider is an observer who does not move trying to perceive an object that does.

As an object moves across an observer's stationary visual field, it first stimulates one location on the retina, and then a little later it stimulates another location on the retina. Neural circuits in the brain can detect this change in position over time and respond to specific speeds and directions of motion (Emerson, Bergen, & Adelson, 1992). A region in the middle of the temporal lobe referred to as *MT* (part of the dorsal stream we discussed earlier) is specialized for the visual perception of motion (Born & Bradley, 2005; Newsome & Paré, 1988), and brain damage in this area leads to a deficit in normal motion perception (Zihl, von Cramon, & Mai, 1983).

Of course, in the real world, rarely are you a stationary observer. As you move around, your head and eyes move all the time, and motion perception is not as simple. The motion-perception system must take into account the position and movement of your eyes, and ultimately of your head and body, in order to perceive the motions of objects correctly and allow you to approach or avoid them. The brain accomplishes this by monitoring your eye and head movements and "subtracting" them from the motion in the retinal image.

Motion perception, like color perception, operates in part on opponent processes and is subject to sensory adaptation. A motion aftereffect called the *waterfall illusion*

YURIY BRYKAYLO/ALAMY

Color perception and motion perception both rely partially on opponent processing, which is why we fall prey to illusions such as color aftereffects and the waterfall illusion.

is analogous to color aftereffects. If you stare at the downward rush of a waterfall for several seconds, you'll experience an upward motion aftereffect when you then look at stationary objects near the waterfall such as trees or rocks. What's going on here?

The process is similar to seeing green after staring at a patch of red. Motion-sensitive neurons are connected to motion detector cells in the brain that encode motion in opposite directions. A sense of motion comes from the difference in the strength of these two opposing sensors. If one set of motion detector cells is fatigued through adaptation to motion in one direction, then the opposing sensor will take over. The net result is that motion is perceived in the opposite direction. Evidence from fMRIs indicates that when people experience the waterfall illusion while viewing a stationary stimulus, there is increased activity in region MT, which plays a key role in motion perception (Tootell et al., 1995).

The movement of objects in the world is not the only event that can evoke the perception of motion. The successively flashing lights of a Las Vegas casino sign can evoke a strong sense of motion because people perceive a series of flashing lights as a whole, moving object (see Figure 4.15*f*). This *perception of movement as a result of alternating signals appearing in rapid succession in different locations* is called **apparent motion.**

> **How can flashing lights on a casino sign give the impression of movement?**

Video technology and animation depend on apparent motion. Motion pictures flash 24 still frames per second (fps). A slower rate would produce a much choppier sense of motion; a faster rate would be a waste of resources because we would not perceive the motion as any smoother than it appears at 24 fps.

Change Blindness and Inattentional Blindness

Motion involves a change in an object's position over time, but objects in the visual environment can change in ways that do not involve motion (Rensink, 2002). You might walk by the same clothing store window every day and notice when a new suit or dress is on display or register surprise when you see a friend's new haircut. Intuitively, we feel that we can easily detect changes to our visual environment. However, our comfortable intuitions have been challenged by experimental demonstrations of **change blindness,** which occurs *when people fail to detect changes to the visual details of a scene* (Rensink, 2002; Simons & Rensink, 2005). Strikingly, change blindness occurs even when major details of a scene are changed—changes that we incorrectly believe that we could not miss (Beek, Levin, & Angelone, 2007). For example, participants in one study were shown a movie in which a young blond man sits at a desk, gets up and walks away from the desk, and exits from the room (Levin and Simons, 1997). The scene then shifted outside the room, where the young man made a phone call. This all sounds straightforward, but unknown to the participants, the man sitting at the desk was not the same person as the man who made the phone call. Although both are young, blond, and wearing glasses, they were clearly different people. Still, two-thirds of the participants failed to notice the change.

It's one thing to create change blindness by splicing a film, but does change blindness also occur in live interactions? Another study tested this idea by having

apparent motion
The perception of movement as a result of alternating signals appearing in rapid succession in different locations.

change blindness
When people fail to detect changes to the visual details of a scene.

inattentional blindness
A failure to perceive objects that are not the focus of attention.

(a) (b) (c)

an experimenter ask a person on a college campus for directions (Simons & Levin, 1998). While they were talking, two men walked between them holding a door that hid a second experimenter (see **FIGURE 4.22**). Behind the door, the two experimenters traded places, so that when the men carrying the door moved on, a different person was asking for directions than the one who had been there just a second or two earlier. Remarkably, only 7 of 15 participants reported noticing this change.

Although it is surprising that people can be blind to such dramatic changes, these findings once again illustrate the importance of focused attention for visual perception (see the discussion of feature-integration theory, p. 146). Just as focused attention is critical for binding together the features of objects, it is also necessary for detecting changes to objects and scenes (Rensink, 2002; Simons & Rensink, 2005). Change

> **How can a failure of focused attention explain change blindness?**

blindness is most likely to occur when people fail to focus attention on the changed object (even though the object is registered by the visual system) and is least likely to occur for items that draw attention to themselves (Rensink, O'Regan, & Clark, 1997).

The role of focused attention in conscious visual experience is also dramatically illustrated by the closely related phenomenon of **inattentional blindness,** *a failure to perceive objects that are not the focus of attention.* Imagine the following scenario. You are watching a circle of people passing around a basketball, somebody dressed in a gorilla costume walks through the circle, and the gorilla stops to beat his chest before moving on. It seems inconceivable that you would fail to notice the gorilla, right? Think again. Simons and Chabris (1999) filmed such a scene, using two teams of three players each who passed the ball to one another as the costumed gorilla made his entrance and exit. Participants watched the film and were asked to track the movement of the ball by counting the number of passes made by one of the teams. With their attention focused on the moving ball, approximately half the participants failed to notice the chest-beating gorilla.

This has interesting implications for a world in which many of us are busy texting and talking on our cell phones while carrying on other kinds of everyday business. We've already seen that using cell phones has negative effects on driving (see The Real World: Multitasking). Ira Hyman and colleagues (2010) asked whether cell phone use contributes to inattentional blindness in everyday life. They recruited a clown to ride a unicycle in the middle of a large square in the middle of the campus at Western

▲ Figure **4.22 Change Blindness** The white-haired man was giving directions to one experimenter (*a*), who disappeared behind the moving door (*b*), only to be replaced by another experimenter (*c*). Like many other people, the man failed to detect a seemingly obvious change.

After Simons, D. J., & Levin, D. T. (1998). Failure to detect changes to people during a real-world interaction. *Psychonomic Bulletin & Review, 5*(4), 644–649.

College students who were using their cell phones while walking through campus failed to notice the unicycling clown more frequently than students who were not using their cell phones.

HYMAN ET AL, 2010

CULTURE & COMMUNITY

Does culture influence change blindness? The experiments discussed in this section of the chapter show that change blindness is dramatic and occurs across a range of situations. But the evidence for change blindness that we've considered comes from studies using participants from Western cultures, mainly Americans. Would change blindness occur in individuals from other cultures? If so, is there any reason to suspect that it would work differently across cultures? Think back to the Culture & Community box from the Psychology: Evolution of a Science chapter, where we discussed evidence showing that people from Western cultures rely on an *analytic* style of processing information (i.e., they tend to focus on an object without paying much attention to the surrounding context), whereas people from Eastern cultures tend to adopt a *holistic* style (i.e., they tend to focus on the relationship between an object and the surrounding context: Kitayama et al., 2003; Nisbett & Miyamoto, 2005).

With this distinction in mind, Masuda and Nisbett (2006) noted that previous studies of change blindness, using mainly American participants, had shown that participants are more likely to detect changes in the main or focal object in a scene, and less likely to detect changes in surrounding context. They hypothesized that individuals from an Eastern culture would be more focused on, and therefore likely to notice, changes in surrounding context than individuals from a Western culture. To test their prediction, they conducted three experiments examining change detection in American (University of Michigan) and Japanese (Kyoto University) college students using still photos and brief movie-type vignettes (Masuda & Nisbett, 2006). In each experiment, they made changes either to the main or focal object in a scene, or to the surrounding context (e.g., objects in the background of a scene).

The results of the experiments were consistent with predictions: Japanese students detected more changes to contextual information than did American students, whereas American students detected more changes to focal objects than did Japanese students. These findings extend earlier reports that people from Eastern and Western cultures see the world differently, with Easterners focusing more on the context in which an object appears and Westerners focusing more on the object itself.

Washington University. On a pleasant afternoon, the researchers asked 151 students who had just walked through the square whether they saw the clown. Seventy-five percent of the students who were using cell phones failed to notice the clown, compared with less than 50% who were not using cell phones. Using cell phones draws on focused attention, resulting in increased inattentional blindness and emphasizing again that our conscious experience of the visual environment is restricted to those features or objects selected by focused attention.

IN SUMMARY

▶ Illusory conjunctions occur when features from separate objects are mistakenly combined. According to feature-integration theory, attention provides the glue necessary to bind features together. The parietal lobe is important for attention and contributes to feature binding.

▶ Some regions in the occipital and temporal lobes respond selectively to specific object categories, supporting the modular view that specialized brain areas represent particular classes of objects such as faces or houses or body parts.

▶ The principle of perceptual constancy holds that even as sensory signals change, perception remains consistent. Gestalt principles of perceptual grouping, such as simplicity, closure, and continuity, govern how the features and regions of things fit together.

- ▶ Image-based and parts-based theories each explain some, but not all, features of object recognition.

- ▶ Depth perception depends on: monocular cues, such as familiar size and linear perspective; binocular cues, such as retinal disparity; and motion-based cues, which are based on the movement of the head over time.

- ▶ We experience a sense of motion through the differences in the strengths of output from motion-sensitive neurons. These processes can give rise to illusions such as apparent motion.

- ▶ Change blindness and inattentional blindness occur when we fail to notice visible and even salient features of our environment, emphasizing that our conscious visual experience depends on focused attention.

pitch
How high or low a sound is.

loudness
A sound's intensity.

Audition: More Than Meets the Ear

Vision is based on the spatial pattern of light waves on the retina. The sense of hearing, by contrast, is all about *sound waves*: changes in air pressure unfolding over time. Plenty of things produce sound waves: the collision of a tree hitting the forest floor, the impact of two hands clapping, the vibration of vocal cords during a stirring speech, the resonance of a bass guitar string during a thrash metal concert. Understanding auditory experience requires understanding how we transform changes in air pressure into perceived sounds.

Sensing Sound

Striking a tuning fork produces a *pure tone,* a simple sound wave that first increases air pressure and then creates a relative vacuum. This cycle repeats hundreds or thousands of times per second as sound waves travel outward in all directions from the source. Just as there are three dimensions of light waves corresponding to three dimensions of visual perception, so, too, there are three physical dimensions of a sound wave. Frequency, amplitude, and complexity determine what we hear as the pitch, loudness, and quality of a sound (see **TABLE 4.4**).

> Hear the World Foundation advocates for the over 630,000,000 people globally who are affected by hearing loss, which has a profound impact on their daily lives and reminds us of how important hearing is for our everyday activities.

- ❯ The *frequency* of the sound wave, or its wavelength, depends on how often the peak in air pressure passes the ear or a microphone, measured in cycles per second, or hertz (Hz). Changes in the physical frequency of a sound wave are perceived by humans as changes in **pitch,** *how high or low a sound is.*

- ❯ The *amplitude* of a sound wave refers to its height, relative to the threshold for human hearing (which is set at zero decibels, or dBs). Amplitude corresponds to **loudness,** or *a sound's intensity.* To give you an idea of amplitude and intensity, the rustling of leaves in a soft breeze is about 20 dB, normal conversation is measured at about 40 dB, shouting produces 70 dB, a Slayer concert is about 130 dB, and the sound of the space shuttle taking off 1 mile away registers at 160 dB or more. That's loud enough to cause permanent damage to the auditory system and is well above the pain threshold; in fact, any sounds above 85 dB can be enough to cause hearing damage, depending on the length and type of exposure.

timbre
A listener's experience of sound quality or resonance.

cochlea
A fluid-filled tube that is the organ of auditory transduction.

basilar membrane
A structure in the inner ear that undulates when vibrations from the ossicles reach the cochlear fluid.

hair cells
Specialized auditory receptor neurons embedded in the basilar membrane.

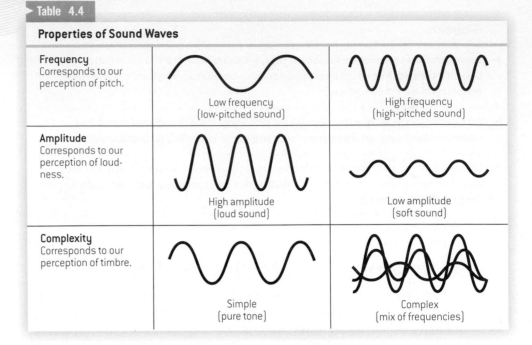

▶ **Table 4.4**

Properties of Sound Waves

Frequency Corresponds to our perception of pitch.	Low frequency (low-pitched sound)	High frequency (high-pitched sound)
Amplitude Corresponds to our perception of loudness.	High amplitude (loud sound)	Low amplitude (soft sound)
Complexity Corresponds to our perception of timbre.	Simple (pure tone)	Complex (mix of frequencies)

"The ringing in your ears—I think I can help."

> Differences in the *complexity* of sound waves, or their mix of frequencies, correspond to **timbre,** *a listener's experience of sound quality or resonance.* Timbre (pronounced "TAM-ber") offers us information about the nature of sound. The same note played at the same loudness produces a perceptually different experience depending on whether it was played on a flute versus a trumpet, a phenomenon due entirely to timbre. Many natural sounds also illustrate the complexity of wavelengths, such as the sound of bees buzzing, the tonalities of speech, or the babbling of a brook. Unlike the purity of a tuning fork's hum, the drone of cicadas is a clamor of many different sound frequencies.

> **Why does one note sound so different on a flute and a trumpet?**

Most sounds—such as voices, music, the sound of wind in trees, the screech of brakes, the purring of a cat—are composed of not one, but many different frequency components. Although you perceive the mixture (the cat's purr, for example, not the 206 Hz component in the purr) the first thing the ear does to a sound is to break it down—to analyze it—into its separate component frequencies. The psychological attributes of pitch, loudness, and timbre are then "built up" by the brain from the separate frequency components that are represented in the inner ear, just like visual perceptions are "built up" from the spatial pattern of activity on the retina. The focus in our discussion of hearing, then, is on how the auditory system encodes and represents sound frequency (Kubovy, 1981).

The Human Ear

How does the auditory system convert sound waves into neural signals? The process is very different from the visual system, which is not surprising, given that light is a form of electromagnetic radiation, whereas sound is a physical change in air pressure over time: Different forms of energy require different processes of transduction. The human ear is divided into three distinct parts, as shown in **FIGURE 4.23.** The *outer ear*

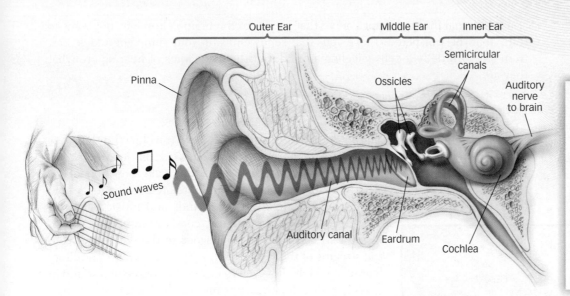

◄ Figure **4.23 Anatomy of the Human Ear** The pinna funnels sound waves into the auditory canal to vibrate the eardrum at a rate that corresponds to the sound's constituent frequencies. In the middle ear, the ossicles pick up the eardrum vibrations, amplify them, and pass them along by vibrating a membrane at the surface of the fluid-filled cochlea in the inner ear. Here fluid carries the wave energy to the auditory receptors that transduce it into electrochemical activity, exciting the neurons that form the auditory nerve, leading to the brain.

collects sound waves and funnels them toward the *middle ear,* which transmits the vibrations to the *inner ear,* embedded in the skull, where they are transduced into neural impulses.

The outer ear consists of the visible part on the outside of the head (called the *pinna*); the auditory canal; and the eardrum, an airtight flap of skin that vibrates in response to sound waves gathered by the pinna and channeled into the canal. The middle ear, a tiny, air-filled chamber behind the eardrum, contains the three smallest bones in the body, called *ossicles.* Named for their appearance as hammer, anvil, and stirrup, the ossicles fit together into a lever that mechanically transmits and intensifies vibrations from the eardrum to the inner ear.

How do hair cells in the ear enable us to hear?

The inner ear contains the spiral-shaped **cochlea** (Latin for "snail"), *a fluid-filled tube that is the organ of auditory transduction.* The cochlea is divided along its length by the **basilar membrane,** *a structure in the inner ear that undulates when vibrations from the ossicles reach the cochlear fluid* (see **FIGURE 4.24**). Its wavelike movement stimulates thousands of tiny **hair cells,** *specialized auditory receptor neurons embedded in the basilar membrane.* The hair cells then release neurotransmitter molecules, initiating

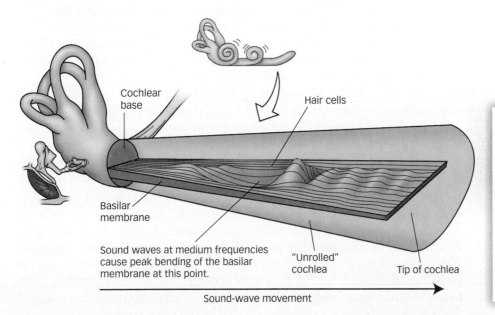

◄ Figure **4.24 Auditory Transduction** Inside the cochlea (shown here as though it were uncoiling) the basilar membrane undulates in response to wave energy in the cochlear fluid. Waves of differing frequencies ripple varying locations along the membrane, from low frequencies at its tip to high frequencies at the base, and bend the embedded hair cell receptors at those locations. The hair cell motion generates impulses in the auditory neurons, whose axons form the auditory nerve that emerges from the cochlea.

a neural signal in the auditory nerve that travels to the brain. You might not want to think that the whispered "I love you" that sends chills up your spine got a kick start from lots of little hair cells wiggling around, but the mechanics of hearing are what they are!

Perceiving Pitch

From the inner ear, action potentials in the auditory nerve travel to the thalamus and ultimately to an area of the cerebral cortex called **area A1,** *a portion of the temporal lobe that contains the primary auditory cortex* (see **FIGURE 4.25**). For most of us, the auditory areas in the left hemisphere analyze sounds related to language and those in the right hemisphere specialize in rhythmic sounds and music. There is also evidence that the auditory cortex is composed of two distinct streams, roughly analogous to the dorsal and ventral streams of the visual system. Spatial ("where") auditory features, which allow you to locate the source of a sound in space, are handled by areas toward the back (caudal) part of the auditory cortex, whereas nonspatial ("what") features, which allow you to identify the sound, are handled by areas in the lower (ventral) part of the auditory cortex (Recanzone & Sutter, 2008).

Neurons in area A1 respond well to simple tones, and successive auditory areas in the brain process sounds of increasing complexity (see Figure 4.25, inset; Rauschecker & Scott, 2009; Schreiner, Read, & Sutter, 2000; Schreiner & Winer, 2007). The human ear is most sensitive to frequencies around 1,000 to 3,500 Hz. But how is the frequency of a sound wave encoded in a neural signal? Our ears have evolved two mechanisms to encode sound-wave frequency, one for high frequencies and one for low frequencies.

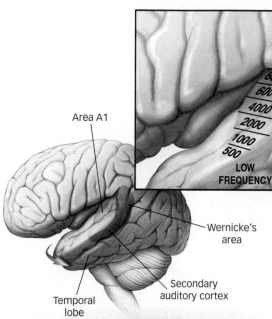

Area A1

HIGH
FREQUENCY

8000
6000
4000
2000
1000
500

LOW
FREQUENCY

Wernicke's
area

Secondary
auditory cortex

Temporal
lobe

▲ Figure **4.25** **Primary Auditory Cortex**
Area A1 is folded into the temporal lobe beneath the lateral fissure in each hemisphere. The left hemisphere auditory areas govern speech in most people. A1 cortex has a topographic organization (*inset*), with lower frequencies mapping toward the front of the brain and higher frequencies toward the back, mirroring the organization of the basilar membrane along the cochlea (see Figure 4.24).

> The **place code,** used mainly for high frequencies, refers to the process by which *different frequencies stimulate neural signals at specific places along the basilar membrane.* In a series of experiments carried out from the 1930s to the 1950s, Nobel laureate Georg von Békésy (1899–1972) used a microscope to observe the basilar membrane in the inner ear of cadavers that had been donated for medical research (Békésy, 1960). Békésy found that the movement of the basilar membrane resembles a traveling wave (see Figure 4.24). The frequency of the stimulating sound determines the wave's shape. When the frequency is low, the wide, floppy tip (*apex*) of the basilar membrane moves the most; when the frequency is high, the narrow, stiff end (*base*) of the membrane moves the most. The movement of the basilar membrane causes hair cells to bend, initiating a neural signal in the auditory nerve. Axons fire the strongest in the hair cells along the area of the basilar membrane that moves the most, and the brain uses information about which axons are the most active to help determining the pitch you "hear."

How does the frequency of a sound wave relate to what we hear?

> A complementary process handles lower frequencies. A **temporal code** *registers relatively low frequencies (up to about 5000 Hz) via the firing rate of action potentials entering the auditory nerve.* Action potentials from the hair cells are synchronized in time with the peaks of the incoming sound waves (Johnson, 1980). If you imagine the rhythmic *boom-boom-boom* of a bass drum, you can probably also imagine the *fire-fire-fire* of action potentials corresponding to the beats. This process provides the brain with very precise information about pitch that supplements the information provided by the place code.

Localizing Sound Sources

Just as the differing positions of our eyes give us stereoscopic vision, the placement of our ears on opposite sides of the head gives us stereophonic hearing. The sound arriving at the ear closer to the sound source is louder than the sound in the farther ear, mainly because the listener's head partially blocks sound energy. This loudness difference decreases as the sound source moves from a position directly to one side (maximal difference) to straight ahead (no difference).

Another cue to a sound's location arises from timing: Sound waves arrive a little sooner at the near ear than at the far ear. The timing difference can be as brief as a few microseconds, but together with the intensity difference, it is sufficient to allow us to perceive the location of a sound. When the sound source is ambiguous, you may find yourself turning your head from side to side to localize it. By doing this, you are changing the relative intensity and timing of sound waves arriving in your ears and collecting better information about the likely source of the sound. Turning your head also allows you to use your eyes to locate the source of the sound—and your visual system is much better at pinpointing the location of things than your auditory system is.

Hearing Loss

Broadly speaking, hearing loss has two main causes. *Conductive hearing loss* arises because the eardrum or ossicles are damaged to the point that they cannot conduct sound waves effectively to the cochlea. The cochlea itself, however, is normal, making this a kind of "mechanical problem" with the moving parts of the ear: the hammer, anvil, stirrup, or eardrum. In many cases, medication or surgery can correct the problem. Sound amplification from a hearing aid also can improve hearing through conduction via the bones around the ear directly to the cochlea.

Sound amplification helps in the case of which type of hearing loss?

Sensorineural hearing loss is caused by damage to the cochlea, the hair cells, or the auditory nerve, and it happens to almost all of us as we age. Sensorineural hearing loss can be heightened in people regularly exposed to high noise levels (such as rock musicians or jet mechanics). Simply amplifying the sound does not help because the hair cells can no longer transduce sound waves. In these cases a *cochlear implant* may offer some relief.

A cochlear implant is an electronic device that replaces the function of the hair cells (Waltzman, 2006). The external parts of the device include a microphone and speech processor, about the size of a USB key, worn behind the ear, and a small, flat, external transmitter that sits on the scalp behind the ear. The implanted parts include a receiver just inside the skull and a thin wire containing electrodes inserted into the cochlea to stimulate the auditory nerve. Sound picked up by the microphone is transformed into electric signals by the speech processor, which is essentially a small computer. The signal is transmitted to the implanted receiver, which activates the electrodes in the cochlea. Cochlear implants are now in routine use and can improve hearing to the point where speech can be understood.

Marked hearing loss is commonly experienced by people as they grow older, but is rare in an infant. However, infants who have not yet learned to speak are especially vulnerable because they may miss the critical period for language learning (see the Learning chapter). Without auditory feedback during this time, normal speech is nearly impossible to achieve, but early use of cochlear implants has been associated with improved speech and language skills for deaf children (Hay-McCutcheon et al., 2008). Efforts are under way to introduce cochlear implants to children as young as 12 months old or younger to maximize their chances of normal language development (DesJardin, Eisenberg, & Hodapp, 2006; Holman et al., 2013). (For research on the importance of music and brain development, see the Real World box).

area A1
A portion of the temporal lobe that contains the primary auditory cortex.

place code
The process by which different frequencies stimulate neural signals at specific places along the basilar membrane, from which the brain determines pitch.

temporal code
The cochlea registers low frequencies via the firing rate of action potentials entering the auditory nerve.

A cochlear implant works when a microphone picks up sounds and sends them to a small speech-processing computer worn on the user's belt or behind the ear. The electric signals from the speech processor are transmitted to an implanted receiver, which sends the signals via electrodes to the cochlea, where the signals directly stimulate the auditory nerve.

AP PHOTO/ROCHESTER POST-BULLETIN, JERRY OLSON

THE REAL WORLD

Music Training: Worth the Time

Did you learn to play an instrument when you were younger? Maybe for you, music was its own reward (or maybe not). For anyone who practiced mostly to keep Mom and Dad happy, there's good news. Musical training has a range of benefits. Let's start with the brain. Musicians have greater plasticity in the motor cortex compared with nonmusicians (Rosenkranz et al., 2007); they have increased grey matter in motor and auditory brain regions compared with nonmusicians (Gaser & Schlaug, 2003; Hannon & Trainor, 2007); and they show differences in brain responses to musical stimuli compared with nonmusicians (Pantev et al., 1998). But musical training also extends to auditory processing in nonmusical domains (Kraus & Chandrasekaran, 2010). Musicians, for example, show enhanced brain responses when listening to speech compared with nonmusicians (Parbery-Clark et al., 2012). Musicians also exhibit an improved ability to detect speech when it is presented in a noisy background (Parbery-Clark, Skoe, & Kraus, 2009). This effect has been demonstrated in children, young adults, and even older adults, who typically have serious problems perceiving speech in a noisy environment (Parbery-Clark et al., 2011)

Remembering to be careful not to confuse correlation with causation, you may ask: Do differences between musicians and nonmusicians reflect the effects of musical training, or do they reflect individual differences, perhaps genetic ones, that lead some people to become musicians in the first place? Maybe people blessed with enhanced brain responses to musical or other auditory stimuli decide to become musicians *because* of their natural abilities. Recent experiments support a causal role for

THINKSTOCK

musical training. One study demonstrated structural brain differences in auditory and motor areas of elementary schoolchildren after 15 months of musical training (learning to play piano), compared with children who did not receive musical training (Hyde et al., 2009). Furthermore, brain changes in the trained group were associated with improvements in motor and auditory skills. Another study compared two groups of 8-year-old children, one group with 6 months of musical training and the other with 6 months of painting training. Musical training produced changes in the brain's electrical responses to musical and speech stimuli, and those changes were correlated with enhanced performance on both musical and speech perception tasks (Moreno et al., 2009). More recent musical training studies have also documented benefits for speech perception (François et al., 2013), and indicate that neural changes produced by musical training in childhood persist into adulthood (Skoe & Kraus, 2012).

We don't yet know all the reasons why musical training has such broad effects on auditory processing, but one likely contributor is that learning to play an instrument demands attention to precise details of sounds (Kraus & Chandrasekaran, 2010). Future studies will no doubt pinpoint additional factors, but the research to date leaves little room for doubt that your hours of practice were indeed worth the time.

IN SUMMARY

▶ Perceiving sound depends on three physical dimensions of a sound wave: The frequency of the sound wave determines the pitch; the amplitude determines the loudness; and differences in the complexity, or mix, of frequencies determines the sound quality or timbre.

▶ Auditory pitch perception begins in the ear, which consists of an outer ear that funnels sound waves toward the middle ear, which in turn sends the vibrations to the inner ear, which contains the cochlea. Action potentials from the inner ear travel along an auditory pathway through the thalamus to the primary auditory cortex (area A1) in the temporal lobe.

▶ Auditory perception depends on both a place code and a temporal code. Our ability to localize sound sources depends critically on the placement of our ears on opposite sides of the head.

▶ Some hearing loss can be overcome with hearing aids that amplify sound. When hair cells are damaged, a cochlear implant is a possible solution.

The Body Senses: More Than Skin Deep

Vision and audition provide information about the world at a distance. By responding to light and sound energy in the environment, these "distance" senses allow us to identify and locate the objects and people around us. In comparison, the body senses, also called *somatosenses* (*soma* from the Greek for "body"), are up close and personal. **Haptic perception** is the *active exploration of the environment by touching and grasping objects with our hands*. We use sensory receptors in our muscles, tendons, and joints as well as a variety of receptors in our skin to get a feel for the world around us (see **FIGURE 4.26**).

Touch

Touch begins with the transduction of skin sensations into neural signals. Four types of receptors located under the skin's surface enable us to sense pressure, texture, pattern, or vibration against the skin (see Figure 4.26). The receptive fields of these specialized cells work together to provide a rich tactile (from Latin, "to touch") experience when you explore an object by feeling it or attempting to grasp it. In addition, *thermoreceptors*, nerve fibers that sense cold and warmth, respond when your skin temperature changes. All these sensations blend seamlessly together in perception, of course, but detailed physiological studies have successfully isolated the parts of the touch system (Hollins, 2010; Johnson, 2002).

There are three important principles regarding the neural representation of the body's surface. First, the left half of the body is represented in the right half of the brain and vice versa. Second, just as more of the visual brain is devoted to foveal vision where acuity is greatest, more of the tactile brain is devoted to parts of the skin surface that have greater spatial resolution. Regions such as the fingertips and lips are very good at discriminating fine spatial detail, whereas areas such as the lower back are quite poor at that task. Think back to the homunculus you read about in the Neuroscience and Behavior chapter; you'll recall that different locations on the body project sensory signals to different locations in the somatosensory cortex in the parietal lobe. Third, there is mounting evidence for a distinction between "what" and "where" pathways in touch analogous to similar distinctions we've already considered for vision and audition. The "what"

? Why might discriminating spatial detail be important for fingertips and lips?

This rather unimposing geodesic dome sits on the floor of the Exploratorium, a world-renowned science museum in San Francisco. Called the Tactile Dome, it was created in 1971 by August Coppola (brother of director Francis Ford Coppola and father of actor Nicolas Cage) and Carl Day, who wanted to create an environment in which only haptic perception could be used. The inside of the dome is pitch black; visitors must crawl, wiggle, slide, and otherwise navigate the unfamiliar terrain using only their sense of touch. How would you feel being in that environment for an hour or so?

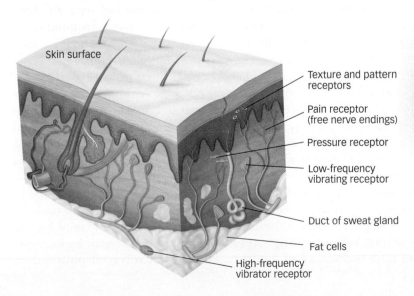

Skin surface

Texture and pattern receptors

Pain receptor (free nerve endings)

Pressure receptor

Low-frequency vibrating receptor

Duct of sweat gland

Fat cells

High-frequency vibrator receptor

◀ Figure **4.26** **Touch Receptors** Specialized sensory neurons form distinct groups of haptic receptors that detect pressure, temperature, and vibrations against the skin. Touch receptors respond to stimulation within their receptive fields, and their long axons enter the brain via the spinal or cranial nerves. Pain receptors populate all body tissues that feel pain; they are distributed around bones and within muscles and internal organs as well as under the skin surface. Both types of pain receptors (the fibers that transmit immediate, sharp pain sensations quickly and those that signal slow, dull pain that lasts and lasts) are free nerve endings.

CKOJ/CORBIS

Be warned for your next shopping trip: Touching the merchandise can lead you to value it more highly than just looking at it.

system for touch provides information about the properties of surfaces and objects; the "where" system provides information about a location in external space that is being touched or a location on the body that is being stimulated (Lederman & Klatzky, 2009). fMRI evidence suggests that the "what" and "where" touch pathways involve areas in the lower and upper parts of the parietal lobe, respectively (Reed, Klatzky, & Halgren, 2005).

Touch information can have a powerful effect on our decisions and judgments. For example, recent research has shown that merely touching an object that we don't already own can increase our feeling of ownership and lead us to value the object more highly than when we view it but don't touch it (Peck & Shu, 2009); the longer we touch an object, the more highly we value it (Wolf, Arkes, & Muhanna, 2008). You might keep this "mere touch" effect in mind next time you are in a shop and considering buying an expensive item. Retailers are probably aware of this effect: During the 2003 holiday shopping season the office of the Illinois state attorney general warned shoppers to be cautious in stores that encouraged them to touch the merchandise (Peck & Shu, 2009).

Pain

Does the possibility of a life free from pain seem appealing? Although pain is arguably the least pleasant of sensations, this aspect of touch is among the most important for survival: Pain indicates damage or potential damage to the body. Without the ability to feel pain, we might ignore infections, broken bones, or serious burns. Congenital insensitivity to pain, a rare inherited disorder that specifically impairs pain perception, is more of a curse than a blessing: Children who experience this disorder often mutilate themselves (e.g., biting into their tongues or gouging their skin while scratching) and are at increased risk of dying during childhood (Nagasako, Oaklander, & Dworkin, 2003).

Tissue damage is transduced by pain receptors, the free nerve endings shown in Figure 4.26. Researchers have distinguished between fast-acting *A-delta fibers,* which transmit the initial sharp pain one might feel right away from a sudden injury, and slower *C fibers,* which transmit the longer-lasting, duller pain that persists after the initial injury. If you were running barefoot outside and stubbed your toe against a rock, you would first feel a sudden stinging pain transmitted by A-delta fibers that would die down quickly, only to be replaced by the throbbing but longer-lasting pain carried by C fibers. Both the A-delta and C fibers are impaired in cases of congenital insensitivity to pain, which is one reason why the disorder can be life threatening.

As you'll remember from the chapter on Neuroscience and Behavior, the pain withdrawal reflex is coordinated by the spinal cord. No brainpower is required when you touch a hot stove; you retract your hand almost instantaneously. But neural signals for pain—such as wrenching your elbow as you brace yourself from falling—travel to two distinct areas in the brain and evoke two distinct psychological experiences (Treede et al., 1999). One pain pathway sends signals to the somatosensory cortex, identifying where the pain is occurring and what sort of pain it is (sharp, burning, dull). The second pain pathway sends signals to the motivational and emotional centers of the brain, such as the hypothalamus and amygdala, and to the frontal lobe. This is the aspect of pain that is unpleasant and motivates us to escape from or relieve the pain.

Pain typically feels as if it comes from the site of the tissue damage that caused it. If you burn your finger, you will perceive the pain as originating there. But we have pain receptors in many areas besides the skin: around bones and within muscles and internal organs as well. When pain originates internally, in a body organ, for example, we actually feel it on the surface of the body. This kind of **referred pain** occurs when *sensory information from internal and external areas converges on the same nerve cells in the spinal cord.* One common example is a heart attack: Victims often feel pain radiating from the left arm rather than from inside the chest.

Pain intensity cannot always be predicted solely from the extent of the injury that causes the pain (Keefe, Abernathy, & Campbell, 2005). For example, *turf toe* sounds like the mildest of ailments; it is pain at the base of the big toe as a result of bending or pushing off repeatedly, as a runner or football player might do during a sporting event. This small-sounding injury in a small area of the body can nonetheless sideline an athlete for a month with considerable pain. On the other hand, you've probably heard a story or two about someone treading bone-chilling water for hours on end, or dragging their shattered legs a mile down a country road to seek help after a tractor accident, or performing some other incredible feat despite searing pain and extensive tissue damage. Pain type and pain intensity show a less-than-perfect correlation, a fact that has researchers intrigued.

Some recent evidence indicates subjective pain intensity may differ among ethnic groups (Campbell & Edwards, 2012). For example, a study that examined responses to various kinds of experimentally induced pain, including heat pain and cold pain, found that compared to White young adults, African American young adults had a lower tolerance for several kinds of pain and rated the same pain stimuli as more intense and unpleasant (Campbell, Edwards, & Fillingim, 2005).

One influential account of pain perception is known as **gate-control theory of pain,** which holds that *signals arriving from pain receptors in the body can be stopped, or gated, by interneurons in the spinal cord via feedback from two directions* (Melzack & Wall, 1965). Pain can be gated by the skin receptors, for example, by rubbing the affected area. Rubbing your stubbed toe activates neurons that "close the gate" to stop pain signals from traveling to the brain. Pain can also be gated from the brain by modulating the activity of pain-transmission neurons. This neural feedback is elicited not by the pain itself, but rather by activity deep within the thalamus.

> **?** Why does rubbing an injured area sometimes help alleviate pain?

The neural feedback comes from a region in the midbrain called the *periaqueductal gray* (PAG). Under extreme conditions, such as high stress, naturally occurring endorphins can activate the PAG to send inhibitory signals to neurons in the spinal cord that then suppress pain signals to the brain, thereby modulating the experience of pain. The PAG is also activated through the action of opiate drugs, such as morphine.

A different kind of feedback signal can *increase* the sensation of pain. This system is activated by events such as infection and learned danger signals. When we are quite ill, what might otherwise be experienced as mild discomfort can feel quite painful. This pain facilitation signal presumably evolved to motivate people who are ill to rest and avoid strenuous activity, allowing their energy to be devoted to healing.

Although some details of the gate-control theory of pain have been challenged, a key concept underlying the theory—that perception is a two-way street—has broad implications. The senses feed information such as pain sensations to the brain, a pattern termed *bottom-up control* by perceptual psychologists. The brain processes this sensory data into perceptual information at successive levels to support movement, object recognition, and eventually more complex cognitive tasks, such as memory and planning. But there is ample evidence that the brain exerts plenty of control over what we sense as well. Visual illusions and the gestalt principles of filling in, shaping up, and rounding out what isn't really there provide some examples. This kind of *top-down control* also explains how the brain influences the experience of touch and pain.

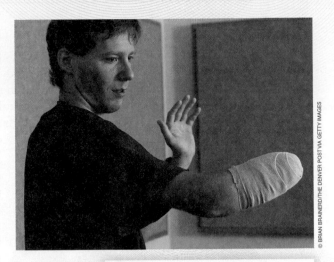

© BRIAN BRAINERD/THE DENVER POST VIA GETTY IMAGES

Aron Ralston was hiking in a remote canyon in Utah when tragedy struck. A 1,000-pound boulder pinned him in a 3-foot-wide space for 5 days, eventually leaving him no choice but to amputate his own arm with a pocketknife. He then applied a tourniquet, rappelled down the canyon, and hiked out to safety. These and similar stories illustrate that the extent of an injury is not perfectly correlated with the amount of pain felt. Although self-amputation is undoubtedly excruciating, luckily in this case it was not debilitating.

referred pain
Feeling of pain when sensory information from internal and external areas converges on the same nerve cells in the spinal cord.

gate-control theory of pain
A theory of pain perception based on the idea that signals arriving from pain receptors in the body can be stopped, or *gated*, by interneurons in the spinal cord via feedback from two directions.

Body Position, Movement, and Balance

It may sound odd, but one aspect of sensation and perception is knowing where parts of your body are at any given moment. Your body needs some way to sense its position in physical space other than moving your eyes constantly to visually check the location of your limbs. Sensations related to position, movement, and balance depend on stimulation produced within our bodies. Receptors in the muscles, tendons, and joints signal the position of the body in space, whereas information about balance and head movement originates in the inner ear.

Sensory receptors provide the information we need to perceive the position and movement of our limbs, head, and body. These receptors also provide feedback about whether we are performing a desired movement correctly and how resistance from held objects may be influencing the movement. For example, when you swing a baseball bat, the weight of the bat affects how your muscles move your arm as well as the change in sensation when the bat hits the ball. Muscle, joint, and tendon feedback about how your arms actually moved can be used to improve performance through learning.

Maintaining balance depends primarily on the **vestibular system,** *the three fluid-filled semicircular canals and adjacent organs located next to the cochlea in each inner ear* (see Figure 4.23). The semicircular canals are arranged in three perpendicular orientations and studded with hair cells that detect movement of the fluid when the head moves or accelerates. The bending of the hair cells generates activity in the vestibular nerve which is then conveyed to the brain. This detected motion enables us to maintain our balance, or the position of our bodies relative to gravity (Lackner & DiZio, 2005).

Vision also helps us keep our balance. If you see that you are swaying relative to a vertical orientation, such as the contours of a room, you move your legs and feet to keep from falling over. Psychologists have experimented with this visual aspect of balance by placing people in rooms that can be tilted forward and backward (Bertenthal, Rose, & Bai, 1997; Lee & Aronson, 1974). If the room tilts enough—

> **Why is it so hard to stand on one foot with your eyes closed?**

particularly when small children are tested—people will topple over as they try to compensate for what their visual system is telling them. When a mismatch between the information provided by visual cues and vestibular feedback occurs, motion sickness can result. Remember this discrepancy the next time you try reading in the back seat of a moving car!

AP PHOTO/RICK RYCROFT

Hitting a ball with a bat or racket provides feedback as to where your arms and body are in space, as well as how the resistance of these objects affects your movement and balance. Successful athletes, such as Serena Williams, have particularly well-developed body senses.

IN SUMMARY

▶ Sensory receptors on the body send neural signals to locations in the somatosensory cortex, a part of the parietal lobe, which the brain translates as the sensation of touch.

▶ The experience of pain depends on signals that travel along two distinct pathways. One sends signals to the somatosensory cortex to indicate the location and type of pain, and another sends signals to the emotional centers of the brain that result in unpleasant feelings that we wish to escape. The experience of pain varies across individuals, which is explained by bottom-up and top-down aspects of the gate-control theory of pain.

▶ Balance and acceleration depend primarily on the vestibular system, but are also influenced by vision.

The Chemical Senses: Adding Flavor

Somatosensation is all about physical changes in or on the body: Vision and audition sense energetic states of the world—light and sound waves—and touch is activated by physical changes in or on the body surface. The last set of senses we'll consider share a chemical basis to combine aspects of distance and proximity. The chemical senses of *olfaction* (smell) and *gustation* (taste) respond to the molecular structure of substances floating into the nasal cavity as you inhale or dissolving in saliva. Smell and taste combine to produce the perceptual experience we call *flavor*.

Smell

Olfaction is the least understood sense and the only one directly connected to the forebrain, with pathways into the frontal lobe, amygdala, and other forebrain structures (recall from the Neuroscience and Behavior chapter that the other senses connect first to the thalamus). This mapping indicates that smell has a close relationship with areas involved in emotional and social behavior. Smell seems to have evolved in animals as a signaling sense for the familiar: a friendly creature, an edible food, or a sexually receptive mate.

Countless substances release odors into the air, and some of their *odorant molecules* make their way into our noses, drifting in on the air we breathe. Situated along the top of the nasal cavity shown in **FIGURE 4.27** is a mucous membrane called the *olfactory epithelium*, which contains about 10 million **olfactory receptor neurons (ORNs)**, *receptor cells that initiate the sense of smell*. Odorant molecules bind to sites on these specialized receptors, and if enough bindings occur, the ORNs send action potentials into the olfactory nerve (Dalton, 2003).

vestibular system
The three fluid-filled semicircular canals and adjacent organs located next to the cochlea in each inner ear.

olfactory receptor neurons (ORNs)
Receptor cells that initiate the sense of smell.

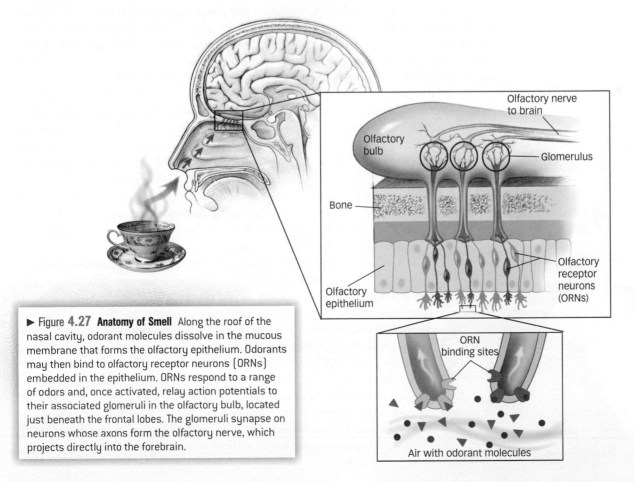

▶ Figure **4.27** **Anatomy of Smell** Along the roof of the nasal cavity, odorant molecules dissolve in the mucous membrane that forms the olfactory epithelium. Odorants may then bind to olfactory receptor neurons (ORNs) embedded in the epithelium. ORNs respond to a range of odors and, once activated, relay action potentials to their associated glomeruli in the olfactory bulb, located just beneath the frontal lobes. The glomeruli synapse on neurons whose axons form the olfactory nerve, which projects directly into the forebrain.

olfactory bulb
A brain structure located above the nasal cavity beneath the frontal lobes.

Each olfactory neuron has receptors that bind to some odorants but not to others, as if the receptor is a lock and the odorant is the key (see Figure 4.27). Groups of ORNs send their axons from the olfactory epithelium into the **olfactory bulb,** *a brain structure located above the nasal cavity beneath the frontal lobes.* Humans possess about 350 different ORN types that permit us to discriminate among some 10,000 different odorants through the unique patterns of neural activity each odorant evokes. This setup is similar to our ability to see a vast range of colors based on only a small number of retinal receptor cell types or to feel a range of skin sensations based on only a handful of touch receptor cell types.

How many scents can humans smell?

Some dogs have as many as 100 times more ORNs than humans do, producing a correspondingly sharpened ability to detect and discriminate among millions of odors. Nevertheless, humans are sensitive to the smells of some substances in extremely small concentrations. For example, a chemical compound that is added to natural gas to help detect gas leaks can be sensed at a concentration of just 0.0003 part per million. By contrast, acetone (nail polish remover), something most people regard as pungent, can be detected only if its concentration is 15 parts per million or greater.

The olfactory bulb sends outputs to various centers in the brain, including the parts that are responsible for controlling basic drives, emotions, and memories. Odor perception includes both information about the identity of an odor, which involves relating olfactory inputs to information stored in memory (Stevenson & Boakes, 2003), as well as our emotional response to whether it is pleasant or unpleasant (Khan et al., 2007). Which of these processes occurs first? When you walk into a house and encounter the wonderful smell of freshly baked chocolate chip cookies, does your positive emotional response come before you identify the smell or vice versa? According to the *object-centered approach*, information about the identity of the "odor object" is quickly accessed from memory and then triggers an emotional response (Stevenson & Wilson, 2007). According to the *valence-centered approach*, the emotional response comes first and provides a basis for determining the identity of the odor (Yeshrun & Sobel, 2010). Recent attempts to distinguish between these two views support that odor perception is guided first by memory and then by emotion (Olofsson et al., 2012).

The relationship between smell and emotion explains why smells can have immediate, strongly positive or negative effects on us. If the slightest whiff of an apple pie baking brings back fond memories of childhood or the unexpected sniff of vomit mentally returns you to a particularly bad party you once attended, you've got the idea. Thankfully, sensory adaptation is at work when it comes to smell, just as it is with the other senses. Whether the associations are good or bad, after just a few minutes the smell fades. Smell adaptation makes sense: It allows us to detect new odors that may require us to act, but after that initial evaluation has occurred, it may be best to reduce our sensitivity to allow us to detect other smells.

Our experience of smell is determined not only by bottom-up influences, such as odorant molecules binding to sites on ORNs, but also by top-down influences, such as our previous experiences with an odor (Gottfried, 2008). Consistent with this idea, people rate the identical odor as more pleasant when it is paired with an appealing verbal label such as *cheddar cheese* rather than an unappealing one such as *body odor* (de Araujo et al., 2005; Herz & von Clef, 2001). fMRI evidence indicates that brain regions involved in coding the pleasantness of an experience, such as the orbiotofrontal cortex, respond more strongly to the identical odor when people think it is cheddar cheese than when they think it is a body odor (de Araujo et al., 2005; see the Hot Science box, Taste for the Top Down, for a related finding concerning taste perception).

Taste and smell both contribute to what we perceive as flavor. This is why smelling the bouquet of a wine is an essential part of the wine-tasting ritual. The experience of wine tasting is also influenced by cognitive factors, such as knowledge of a wine's price.

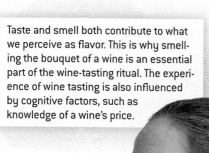

ALUMA IMAGES/
MASTERFILE/
RADIUS IMAGES

Taste: From the Top Down

In 2008, the publication of a book titled *The Wine Trials* (Goldstein & Herschkowitsch, 2008) ruffled the feathers of more than a few wine connoisseurs. The book was based on an article in which the authors and several colleagues analyzed the results of 6,175 observations gathered during 17 blind wine tastings involving wines of varying prices, organized by lead author and food critic Robin Goldstein (Goldstein, Almenberg, Dreber, Emerson, Herschkowitsch, & Katz, 2008). The results suggested that, if anything, tasters liked the more expensive wines slightly *less* than the more inexpensive ones.

Although these findings will not encourage ordinary wine drinkers to spend a large amount of money on their next wine purchase, they leave open the question of whether knowing a wine's price affects enjoyment of it. Similar to olfaction, our experience of taste is partly determined by bottom-up influences, such as the patterns of activity in the five taste receptor types that are evoked by food molecules, but it is also influenced by top-down factors, such as knowing what brand we are eating or drinking.

To investigate the effects of a top-down influence (price knowledge) on the enjoyment of wine and associated brain activity, researchers used fMRI to scan 20 participants while they drank different wines or a control solution (Plassman et al., 2008). The participants were told that they would be sampling five different cabernet sauvignons, that the different wines would be identified by their price, and that they should rate how much they liked each wine. The participants did not know, however, that only three different wines were actually presented, and that two critical wines were presented twice. One critical wine was presented once at its actual price ($5) and once marked-up to a high price ($45); the other critical wine was also presented once at its actual price ($90) and once at a marked-down price ($10). This design allowed the researchers to compare ratings and brain activity for the identical wine when participants thought it was expensive or cheap.

Results revealed that during scanning, participants reported liking both wines better when they were accompanied by a high price than by a low price. For the fMRI analysis, the researchers focused on the activity of the medial orbitofrontal cortex (mOFC), a part of the brain located deep inside the frontal lobe that is known to be involved in coding the pleasantness of an experience (Kuhn & Gallinat, 2012). The level of mOFC activity was closely correlated with subjective ratings of taste pleasantness in a previous fMRI study (Kringelbach et al., 2003). As shown in the accompanying figure, there was greater mOFC activity for both wines in the high price condition than in the low price condition.

These results demonstrate clearly that taste experience and associated neural activity can be affected by top-down influences such as price knowledge. Related work has shown that other top-down influences, such as expectations, can also affect both taste experience and brain responses (Nitschke et al., 2006). Consider a recent fMRI study in which researchers manipulated whether participants expected that a liquid they were about to taste would be sweet or tasteless (Veldhuizen et al., 2011). On most trials, the participants' expectations were met: They were cued to expect a sweet or a tasteless liquid and then received the type of liquid indicated by the cue. On some trials, though, their expectations were violated: They were cued to expect a sweet or a tasteless liquid and then received the opposite. When expectations were violated either by receiving a sweet or a tasteless stimulus, activity in a number of brain regions showed increased activity, reflecting in part a general "surprise" response. However, a part of the brain's taste system known as the *anterior insula* showed the most activity when the unexpected stimulus contained the sweet taste, thus indicating that top-down influences can affect a part of the brain known to be involved in the experience of taste.

The results of these studies should provide some comfort to wine drinkers who are willing to pay for expensive brands. Even if they can't tell the difference from cheaper brands under blind tasting conditions, just knowing that they're drinking an expensive wine should make for an enjoyable experience.

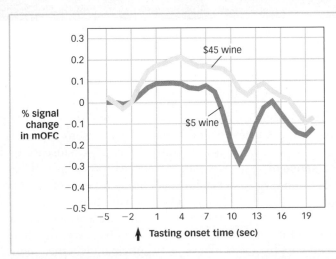

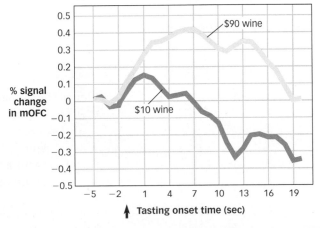

pheromones
Biochemical odorants emitted by other members of its species that can affect an animal's behavior or physiology.

taste buds
The organ of taste transduction.

Smell may also play a role in social behavior. Humans and other animals can detect odors from **pheromones,** *biochemical odorants emitted by other members of its species that can affect the animal's behavior or physiology.* Parents can distinguish the smell of their own children from other people's children. An infant can identify the smell of its mother's breast from the smell of other mothers. Pheromones also play a role in reproductive behavior in insects and in several mammalian species, including mice, dogs, and primates (Brennan & Zufall, 2006). Can the same thing be said of human reproductive behavior?

Studies of people's preference for the odors of individuals of the opposite sex have produced mixed results, with no consistent tendency for people to prefer them over other pleasant odors. Recent research, however, has provided a link between sexual orientation and responses to odors that may constitute human pheromones. Researchers used positron emission tomography (PET) scans to study the brain's response to two odors, one related to testosterone, which is produced in men's sweat, and the other related to estrogen, which is found in women's urine. The testosterone-based odor activated the hypothalamus (a part of the brain that controls sexual behavior; see the Neuroscience and Behavior chapter) in heterosexual women but not in heterosexual men, whereas the estrogen-based odor activated the hypothalamus in heterosexual men but not in women. Strikingly, homosexual men responded to the two chemicals in the same way as women did: The hypothalamus was activated by the testosterone-but not estrogen-based odor (Savic, Berglund, & Lindstrom, 2005; see **FIGURE 4.28**). Other common odors unrelated to sexual arousal were processed similarly by all three groups. A follow-up study with lesbian women showed that their responses to the testosterone- and estrogen-based odors were largely similar to those of heterosexual men (Berglund, Lindstrom, & Savic, 2006). Taken together, the two studies suggest that some human pheromones are related to sexual orientation.

▶ Figure **4.28 Smell and Social Behavior** In a PET study, heterosexual women, homosexual men, and heterosexual men were scanned as they were presented with each of several odors. During the presentation of a testosterone-based odor (referred to in the figure as AND), there was significant activation in the hypothalamus for heterosexual women (*left*) and homosexual men (*center*) but not for (*right*) heterosexual men (Savic et al., 2005).

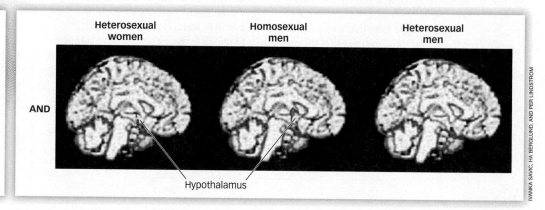

IVANKA SAVIC, HA BERGLUND, AND PER LINDSTROM

Taste

One of the primary responsibilities of the chemical sense of taste is identifying things that are bad for you—as in poisonous and lethal. Many poisons are bitter, and we avoid eating things that nauseate us for good reason, so taste aversions have a clear adaptive significance. Some aspects of taste perception are genetic, such as an aversion to extreme bitterness, and some are learned, such as an aversion to a particular food that once caused nausea. In either case, the direct contact between a tongue and possible foods allows us to anticipate whether something will be harmful or palatable.

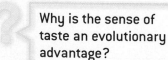

Why is the sense of taste an evolutionary advantage?

The tongue is covered with thousands of small bumps, called *papillae,* which are easily visible to the naked eye. Within each papilla are hundreds of **taste buds,** *the organ of taste transduction* (see **FIGURE 4.29**). The mouth contains 5,000 to 10,000 taste buds fairly evenly distributed over the tongue, roof of the mouth, and upper throat (Bartoshuk & Beauchamp, 1994; Halpern, 2002). Each taste bud contains 50 to 100 taste receptor cells. Taste perception fades with age (Methven et al., 2012): On average, people lose half their taste receptors by the time they turn 20. This may help to explain why young children seem to be "fussy eaters," since their greater number of taste buds brings with it a greater range of taste sensations.

The human eye contains millions of rods and cones, the human nose contains some 350 different types of olfactory receptors, but the taste system contains just five main types of taste receptors, corresponding to five primary taste sensations: salt, sour, bitter, sweet, and umami (savory). The first four are quite familiar, but *umami* may not be. In fact, perception researchers are still debating its existence. The umami receptor was discovered by Japanese scientists who attributed it to the tastes evoked by foods containing a high concentration of protein, such as meats and cheeses (Yamaguchi, 1998). If you're a meat eater and you savor the feel of a steak topped with butter or a cheeseburger as it sits in your mouth, you've got an idea of the umami sensation.

Each taste bud contains several types of taste receptor cells whose tips, called *microvilli,* react with *tastant molecules* in food. Salt taste receptors are most strongly activated by sodium chloride (table salt). Sour receptor cells respond to acids, such as vinegar or lime juice. Bitter and sweet taste receptors are more complex. Some 50 to 80 distinct binding sites in bitter receptors are activated by an equal number of different bitter-tasting chemicals. Sweet receptor cells likewise can be activated by a wide range of substances in addition to sugars.

Although umami receptor cells are the least well understood, researchers are homing in on their key features (Chandrashekar et al., 2006). They respond most strongly to glutamate, an amino acid in many protein-containing foods. Recall from the

Fussy eater or just too many taste buds? Our taste perception declines with age: We lose about half of our taste receptors by the time we're 20 years old. That can make childhood a time of either savory delight or a sensory overload of taste.

▼ Figure **4.29** **A Taste Bud** Taste buds stud the bumps (papillae) on the tongue, shown here, as well as the back, sides, and roof of the mouth (*a*). Each taste bud contains a range of receptor cells that respond to varying chemical components of foods called *tastants* (*b*). Tastant molecules dissolve in saliva and stimulate the microvilli that form the tips of the taste receptor cells (*c*). Each taste bud contacts the branch of a cranial nerve at its base.

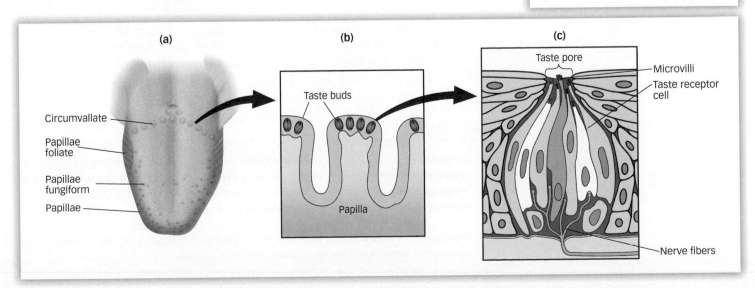

Neuroscience and Behavior chapter, glutamate acts as a neurotransmitter; in fact, it's a major excitatory neurotransmitter. The food additive *monosodium glutamate* (MSG), which is often used to flavor Asian foods, particularly activates umami receptors. Some people develop headaches or allergic reactions after eating MSG.

Of course, the variety of taste experiences greatly exceeds the five basic receptors discussed here. Any food molecules dissolved in saliva evoke specific, combined patterns of activity in the five taste receptor types. Although we often think of taste as the primary source for flavor, in fact, taste and smell collaborate to produce this complex perception. As any wine connoisseur will attest, the full experience of a wine's flavor cannot be appreciated without a finely trained sense of smell. Odorants from substances outside your mouth enter the nasal cavity via the nostrils, and odorants in the mouth enter through the back of the throat. This is why wine aficionados are taught to pull air in over wine held in the mouth: It allows the wine's odorant molecules to enter the nasal cavity through this "back door." (The taste of wine can also be influenced by cognitive factors, as illustrated in the Hot Science box.)

You can easily demonstrate the contribution of smell to flavor by tasting a few different foods while holding your nose, preventing the olfactory system from detecting their odors. If you have a head cold, you probably already know how this turns out. Your favorite spicy burrito or zesty pasta probably tastes as bland as can be.

Taste experiences also vary widely across individuals. About 50% of people report a mildly bitter taste in caffeine, saccharine, certain green vegetables, and other substances, whereas roughly 25% report no bitter taste. Members of the first group are called *tasters* and members of the second group are called *nontasters*. The remaining 25% of people are *supertasters*, who report that such substances, especially dark green vegetables, are extremely bitter, to the point of being inedible (Bartoshuk, 2000). Children start out as tasters or supertasters, which could help explain their early tendency toward fussiness in food preference. However, some children grow up to become nontasters. Because supertasters tend to avoid fruits and vegetables that contain tastes they experience as extremely bitter, they may be at increased health risk for diseases such as colon cancer. On the other hand, because they also tend to avoid fatty, creamy foods, they tend to be thinner and may have decreased risk of cardiovascular disease (Bartoshuk, 2000). There is evidence that genetic factors contribute to individual differences in taste perception (Kim et al., 2003), but much remains to be learned about the specific genes that are involved (Hayes et al., 2008; Reed, 2008).

SAM GROSS/THE NEW YORKER COLLECTION/CARTOONBANK.COM

"We would like to be genetically modified to taste like Brussels sprouts."

IN SUMMARY

► Our experience of smell, or olfaction, is associated with odorant molecules binding to sites on specialized olfactory receptors, which converge at the glomerulus within the olfactory bulb. The olfactory bulb in turn sends signals to parts of the brain that control drives, emotions, and memories, which helps to explain why smells can have immediate and powerful effects on us.

► Smell is also involved in social behavior, as illustrated by pheromones, which are related to reproductive behavior and sexual responses in several species.

▶ Sensations of taste depend on taste buds, which are distributed across the tongue, roof of the mouth, and upper throat and on taste receptors that correspond to the five primary taste sensations of salt, sour, bitter, sweet, and umami.

▶ Taste experiences vary widely across individuals and, like olfactory experiences, depend in part on cognitive influences.

OTHER VOICES

Hallucinations and the Visual System

We rely on our perceptual systems to provide reliable information about the world around us. Yet we've already seen that perception is prone to various kinds of illusions. Even more striking, our perceptual systems are capable of creating hallucinations: perceptions of sights, sounds, or other sensory experiences that don't exist in the world outside us. As discussed by the by perceptual psychologist V.S. Ramachandran in an interview with the *New York Times*, reported in an article written by Susan Kruglinski, vivid visual hallucinations can even occur in low vision or even blind individuals with severe damage to their retinas.

One day a few years ago, Doris Stowens saw the monsters from Maurice Sendak's "Where the Wild Things Are" stomping into her bedroom. Then the creatures morphed into traditional Thai dancers with long brass fingernails, whose furious dance took them from the floor to the walls to the ceiling.

Although shocked to witness such a spectacle, Ms. Stowens, 85, was aware that she was having hallucinations, and she was certain that they had something to do with the fact that she suffered from the eye disease macular degeneration.

"I knew instantly that something was going on between my brain and my eyes," she said.

Ms. Stowens says that ever since she developed partial vision loss, she has been seeing pink walls and early American quilts floating through the blind spots in her eyes several times each week.

In fact, Ms. Stowens's hallucinations are a result of Charles Bonnet syndrome, a strange but relatively common disorder found in people who have vision problems. Because the overwhelming majority of people with vision problems are more than 70 years old, the syndrome, named after its 18th-century Swiss discoverer, is mostly found among the elderly. And because older people are more susceptible to cognitive deterioration, which can include hallucinations or delusions, Charles Bonnet (pronounced bon-NAY) is easily misdiagnosed as mental illness.

Many patients who have it never consult a doctor, out of fear that they will be labeled mentally ill.

"It is not a rare disorder," said Dr. V. S. Ramachandran, a neurologist at the University of California at San Diego, who has written about the syndrome. "It's quite common. It's just that people don't want to talk about it when they have it."

Researchers estimate that 10 to 15 percent of people whose eyesight is worse than 20/60 develop the disorder. Any eye disease that causes blind spots or low vision can be the source, including cataracts, glaucoma, diabetic retinopathy and, most commonly, macular degeneration. The hallucinations can vary from simple patches of color or patterns to lifelike images of people or landscapes to phantasms straight out of dreams. The hallucinations are usually brief and nonthreatening, and people who have the syndrome usually understand that what they are seeing is not real....

In some ways, researchers say, the hallucinations that define the syndrome are similar to the phenomenon of phantom limbs, where patients still vividly feel limbs that have been amputated, or phantom hearing, where a person hears music or other sounds while going deaf. In all three cases, the perceptions are caused by a loss of the sensory information that normally flows unceasingly into the brain.

In the case of sight, the primary visual cortex is responsible for taking in information, and also for forming remembered or imagined images. This dual function, Dr. Ramachandran and other experts say, suggests that normal vision is in fact a fusion of incoming sensory information with internally generated sensory input, the brain filling in the visual field with what it is used to seeing or expects to see. If you expect the person sitting next to you to be wearing a blue shirt, for example, you might, in a quick sideways glance, mistakenly perceive a red shirt as blue. A more direct gaze allows for more external information to correct the misperception.

"In a sense, we are all hallucinating all the time," Dr. Ramachandran said. "What we call normal vision is our selecting the hallucination that best fits reality."

With extensive vision loss, less external information is available to adjust and guide the brain's tendency to fill in sensory gaps. The results may be Thai dancers or monsters from a children's book....

Charles Bonnet syndrome was first described over 250 years ago by Bonnet, a Swiss scientist whose own blind grandfather experienced hallucinations like those reported by Ms. Stowens. However, neurologists and others have only recently begun to study the syndrome. Can you make some sense of this syndrome based on what you have learned about the visual system? How can someone who sees poorly or cannot see at all have intense visual experiences? What brain processes could be responsible for these kinds of visual hallucinations? Some clues come from neuroimaging studies of people who experience visual hallucinations, which have shown that specific types of hallucinations are accompanied by activity in parts of the brain responsible for the particular content of the hallucinations (Allen, Larøi, McGuire, & Aleman, 2008). For example, facial hallucinations are accompanied by activity in a part of the temporal lobe known to be involved in face processing. Our understanding of the visual system beyond the retina can provide some insight into how and why blind individuals experience visual hallucinations.

Chapter Review

KEY CONCEPT QUIZ

1. Sensation involves _____ , whereas perception involves _____.
   a. organization; coordination
   b. stimulation; interpretation
   c. identification; translation
   d. comprehension; information

2. What process converts physical signals from the environment into neural signals carried by sensory neurons into the central nervous system?
   a. representation
   b. identification
   c. propagation
   d. transduction

3. The smallest intensity needed to just barely detect a stimulus is called
   a. proportional magnitude.
   b. absolute threshold.
   c. just noticeable difference.
   d. Weber's law.

4. The world of light outside the body is linked to the world of vision inside the central nervous system by the
   a. cornea.
   b. lens.
   c. retina.
   d. optic nerve.

5. Light striking the retina, causing a specific pattern of response in the three cone types, leads to our ability to see
   a. motion.
   b. colors.
   c. depth.
   d. shadows.

6. In which part of the brain is the primary visual cortex, where encoded information is systematically mapped into a representation of the visual scene?
   a. the thalamus
   b. the lateral geniculate nucleus
   c. the fovea
   d. area V1

7. Our ability to visually combine details so that we perceive unified objects is explained by
   a. feature-integration theory.
   b. illusory conjunction.
   c. synesthesia.
   d. ventral and dorsal streaming.

8. The idea that specialized brain areas represent particular classes of objects is
   a. the modular view.
   b. attentional processing.

   c. distributed representation.
   d. neuron response.

9. The principle of _____ holds that even as sensory signals change, perception remains consistent.
   a. apparent motion
   b. signal detection
   c. perceptual constancy
   d. closure

10. Image-based and parts-based theories both involve the problem of
    a. motion detection.
    b. object identification.
    c. separating figure from ground.
    d. judging proximity.

11. What kind of cues are relative size and linear perspective?
    a. motion-based
    b. binocular
    c. monocular
    d. template

12. What does the frequency of a sound wave determine?
    a. pitch
    b. loudness
    c. sound quality
    d. timbre

13. The placement of our ears on opposite sides of the head is crucial to our ability to
    a. localize sound sources.
    b. determine pitch.
    c. judge intensity.
    d. recognize complexity.

14. The location and type of pain we experience is indicated by signals sent to
    a. the amygdala.
    b. the spinal cord.
    c. pain receptors.
    d. the somatosensory cortex.

15. What best explains why smells can have immediate and powerful effects?
    a. the involvement in smell of brain centers for emotions and memories
    b. the vast number of olfactory receptor neurons we have
    c. our ability to detect odors from pheromones
    d. the fact that different odorant molecules produce varied patterns of activity

KEY TERMS

sensation (p. 131)
perception (p. 131)
transduction (p. 131)
psychophysics (p. 132)
absolute threshold (p. 132)
just noticeable difference (JND) (p. 132)
Weber's law (p. 132)
signal detection theory (p. 134)
sensory adaptation (p. 134)
visual acuity (p. 137)
retina (p. 138)

accommodation (p. 138)
cones (p. 138)
rods (p. 138)
fovea (p. 140)
blind spot (p. 140)
color-opponent system (p. 142)
area V1 (p. 143)
visual form agnosia (p. 144)
binding problem (p. 146)
illusory conjunction (p. 146)
feature-integration theory (p. 146)
perceptual constancy (p. 148)

template (p. 150)
monocular depth cues (p. 150)
binocular disparity (p. 152)
apparent motion (p. 154)
change blindness (p. 154)
inattentional blindness (p. 155)
pitch (p. 157)
loudness (p. 157)
timbre (p. 158)
cochlea (p. 159)
basilar membrane (p. 159)
hair cells (p. 159)

area A1 (p. 160)
place code (p. 160)
temporal code (p. 160)
haptic perception (p. 163)
referred pain (p. 164)
gate-control theory of pain (p. 165)
vestibular system (p. 166)
olfactory receptor neurons (ORNs) (p. 167)
olfactory bulb (p. 168)
pheromones (p. 170)
taste buds (p. 171)

CHANGING MINDS

1. A friend of yours is taking a class in medical ethics. "We discussed a tough case today," she says. "It has to do with a patient who's been in a vegetative state for several years, and the family has to decide whether to take him off life support. The doctors say he has no awareness of himself or his environment, and he is never expected to recover. But when light is shined in his eyes, his pupils contract. That shows he can sense light, so he has to have some ability to perceive his surroundings, doesn't he?" Without knowing any of the details of this particular case, how would you explain to your friend that a patient might be able to sense light but not perceive it? What other examples from the chapter could you use to illustrate the difference between sensation and perception?

2. In your philosophy class, the professor discusses the proposition that "perception is reality." From the point of view of philosophy, reality is the state of things that actually exists, whereas perception is how they appear to the observer. What does psychophysics have to say about this issue? What are three ways in which sensory transduction can alter perception, causing perceptions that may differ from absolute reality?

3. A friend comes across the story of an American soldier, Leroy Petry, who received the Medal of Honor for saving the lives of two of his men. The soldiers were in a firefight in Afghanistan when a live grenade landed at their feet; Petry picked up the grenade and tried to toss it away from the others, but it exploded, destroying his right hand. According to the news report, Petry didn't initially feel any pain; instead, he set about applying a tourniquet to his own arm while continuing to shout orders to his men as the firefight continued. "That's amazingly heroic," your friend says, "but that bit about not feeling the pain—that's crazy. He must just be so tough that he kept going despite the pain." What would you tell your friend? How can the perception of pain be altered?

ANSWERS TO KEY CONCEPT QUIZ

1. b; 2. d; 3. b; 4. c; 5. b; 6. d; 7. a; 8. a; 9. c; 10. b; 11. c; 12. a; 13. a; 14. d; 15. a.

Need more help? Additional resources are located in LaunchPad at:
http://www.worthpublishers.com/launchpad/schacter3e

Consciousness

UNCONSCIOUSNESS IS SOMETHING YOU DON'T REALLY appreciate until you need it. Belle Riskin needed it one day on an operating table, when she awoke just as doctors were pushing a breathing tube down her throat. She felt she was choking, but she couldn't see, breathe, scream, or move. Unable even to blink an eye, she couldn't signal to the surgeons that she was conscious. "I was terrified. Why is this happening to me? Why can't I feel my arms? I could feel my heart pounding in my head. It was like being buried alive, but with somebody shoving something down your throat," she explained later. "I knew I was conscious, that something was going on during the surgery. I had just enough awareness to know I was being intubated" (Groves, 2004).

How could this happen? Anesthesia for surgery is supposed to leave the patient unconscious, "feeling no pain," and yet in this case—and in about one in every 1,000–2,000 surgeries (Sandin et al., 2000)—the patient regains consciousness at some point and even remembers the experience. Some patients remember pain; others remember the clink of surgical instruments in a pan or the conversations of doctors and nurses. This is not how modern surgery is supposed to go, but the problem arises because muscle-relaxing drugs are used to keep the patient from moving involuntarily and making unhelpful contributions to the operation. Then, when the drugs that are given to induce unconsciousness fail to do the job, the patient with extremely relaxed muscles is unable to show or tell doctors that there is a problem.

Waking up in surgery sounds pretty rough all by itself, but this could cause additional complications. The conscious patient could become alarmed and emotional during the operation, spiking blood pressure and heart rate to dangerous levels. Awareness also might lead to later emotional problems. Fortunately, new methods of monitoring wakefulness by measuring the electrical activity of the brain are being developed. One system uses sensors attached to the patient's head and gives readings on a scale from 0 (*no electrical activity in the brain*) to 100 (*fully alert*), providing a kind of "consciousness

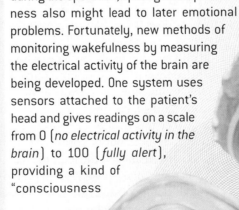

MASTERFILE

When it's time for surgery,
it's great to be unconscious.

meter." Anesthesiologists using this index deliver anesthetics to keep the patient in the recommended range of 40–60 for general anesthesia during surgery; they have found that this system reduces postsurgical reports of consciousness and memory of the surgical experience (Myles et al., 2004), and that letting patients fall below 45 on this index for prolonged periods increases the risk of negative postoperative outcomes, including death (Kertai et al., 2010). One of these devices in the operating room might have helped Belle Riskin settle into the unconsciousness she so dearly needed.

MOST OF THE TIME, OF COURSE, CONSCIOUSNESS IS SOMETHING we cherish. How else could we experience a favorite work of art, the familiar lyrics of an old song, the taste of a sweet, juicy peach, or the touch of a loved one's hand? **Consciousness** is *a person's subjective experience of the world and the mind.* Although you might think of consciousness as simply "being awake," the defining feature of consciousness is *experience,* which you have when you're awake or when having a vivid dream. Conscious experience is essential to what it means to be human. The anesthesiologist's dilemma in trying to monitor Belle Riskin's consciousness is a stark reminder, though, that it is impossible for one person to experience another's consciousness. Your consciousness is utterly private, a world of personal experience that only you can know.

How can this private world be studied? We'll begin by examining consciousness directly, trying to understand what it is like and how it compares with the mind's *unconscious* processes. Then we'll examine its departures from normal by exploring altered states: sleep and dreams, intoxication with alcohol and other drugs, and hypnosis and meditation. Like the traveler who learns the meaning of *home* by roaming far away, we can learn the meaning of *consciousness* by exploring its exotic variations.

Conscious and Unconscious: The Mind's Eye, Open and Closed

What does it feel like to be you right now? It probably feels as though you are somewhere inside your head, looking out at the world through your eyes. You can feel your hands on this book, perhaps, and notice the position of your body or the sounds in the room when you orient yourself toward them. If you shut your eyes, you may be able to imagine things in your mind, even though all the while thoughts and feelings come and go, passing through your imagination. But where are "you," really? And how is it that this theater of consciousness gives you a view of some things in your world and your mind but not others? The theater in your mind doesn't have seating for more than one, making it difficult to share what's on your mental screen with your friends, a researcher, or even yourself in precisely the same way a second time. We'll look first at the difficulty of studying consciousness directly, examine the nature of consciousness (what it is that can be seen in this mental theater), and then explore the unconscious mind (what is *not* visible to the mind's eye).

The Mysteries of Consciousness

Other sciences, such as physics, chemistry, and biology, have the great luxury of studying *objects,* things that we all can see. Psychology studies objects, too, looking at people and their brains and behaviors, but it has the unique challenge of also trying to make sense of *subjects.* A physicist is not concerned with what it is like to be a neutron, but psychologists hope to understand what it is like to be a human; that is, they seek to understand the subjective perspectives of the people whom they study.

consciousness
A person's subjective experience of the world and the mind.

phenomenology
How things seem to the conscious person.

problem of other minds
The fundamental difficulty we have in perceiving the consciousness of others.

Psychologists hope to include an understanding of **phenomenology,** *how things seem to the conscious person,* in their understanding of mind and behavior. After all, consciousness is an extraordinary human property. But including phenomenology in psychology brings up mysteries pondered by great thinkers almost since the beginning of thinking. Let's look at two of the more vexing mysteries of consciousness: the problem of other minds and the mind–body problem.

What are the great mysteries of consciousness?

The Problem of Other Minds

One great mystery is called the **problem of other minds,** *the fundamental difficulty we have in perceiving the consciousness of others.* How do you know that anyone else is conscious? They tell you that they are conscious, of course, and are often willing to describe in depth how they feel, how they think, what they are experiencing, and how good or how bad it all is. But perhaps they are just *saying* these things. There is no clear way to distinguish a conscious person from someone who might do and say all the same things as a conscious person but who is *not* conscious. Philosophers have called this hypothetical nonconscious person a *zombie,* in reference to the living-yet-dead creatures of horror films (Chalmers, 1996). A philosopher's zombie could talk about experiences ("The lights are so bright!") and even seem to react to them (wincing and turning away) but might not be having any inner experience at all. No one knows whether there could be such a zombie, but then again, because of the problem of other minds, none of us will ever know for sure that another person is *not* a zombie.

Luckily these zombies have the standard zombie look. But how do you know those around you are really conscious the same way that you are?

Even the consciousness meter used by anesthesiologists falls short. It certainly doesn't give the anesthesiologist any special insight into what it is like to be the patient on the operating table; it only predicts whether patients will *say* they were conscious. We simply lack the ability to directly perceive the consciousness of others. In short, *you* are the only thing in the universe you will ever truly know what it is like to be.

The problem of other minds also means there is no way you can tell if another person's experience of anything is at all like yours. Although you know what the color red looks like to you, for instance, you cannot know whether it looks the same to other people. Maybe they're seeing what you see as blue and just calling it red in a consistent way. If their inner experience "looks" blue, but they say it looks hot and is the color of a tomato, you'll never be able to tell that their experience differs from yours. Of course, most people have come to trust each other in describing their inner lives, reaching the general assumption that other human minds are pretty much like their own. But they don't know this for a fact, and they can't know it directly.

How do people perceive other minds? Researchers conducting a large online survey asked people to compare the minds of 13 different targets, such as a baby, chimp, robot, man, and woman, on 18 different mental capacities, such as feeling pain, pleasure, hunger, and consciousness (see **FIGURE 5.1**; Gray, Gray, & Wegner, 2007). Respondents who were judging the mental capacity to feel pain, for example, compared pairs of targets: Is a frog or a dog more able to feel pain? Is a baby or a robot more able to feel pain? When the researchers examined all the comparisons on the different mental capacities with the computational technique of factor analysis (see the Intelligence chapter), they found two dimensions of mind perception. People judge minds according to the capacity for *experience* (such as the ability to feel pain, pleasure, hunger, consciousness, anger, or fear) and the capacity for *agency* (such as the ability for self-control, planning, memory,

How do people perceive other minds?

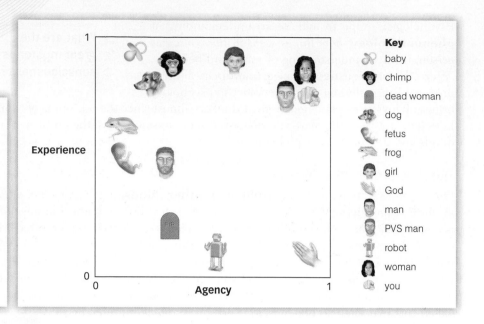

▶ Figure **5.1** **Dimensions of Mind Perception** When participants judged the mental capacities of 13 targets, two dimensions of mind perception were discovered (Gray et al., 2007). Participants perceived minds as varying in the capacity for experience (such as abilities to feel pain or pleasure) and in the capacity for agency (such as abilities to plan or exert self-control). They perceived normal adult humans (male, female, or "you," the respondent) to have minds on both dimensions, whereas other targets were perceived to have reduced experience or agency. The man in a persistent vegetative state ("PVS man"), for example, was judged to have only some experience and very little agency.

or thought). As shown in Figure 5.1, respondents rated some targets as having little experience or agency (the dead woman), others as having experiences but little agency (the baby), and yet others as having both experience and agency (adult humans). Still others were perceived to have agency without experiences (the robot, God). The perception of minds, then, involves more than just whether something has a mind. People appreciate that minds both have experiences and lead us to perform actions.

> **How does the capacity for experience differ from the capacity for agency?**

Ultimately, the problem of other minds is a problem for psychological science. As you'll remember from the Methods chapter, the scientific method requires that any observation made by one scientist should, in principle, be available for observation by any other scientist. But if other minds aren't observable, how can consciousness be a topic of scientific study? One radical solution is to eliminate consciousness from psychology entirely and follow the other sciences into total objectivity by renouncing the study of *anything* mental. This was the solution offered by behaviorism, and it turned out to have its own shortcomings, as you saw in the Psychology: Evolution of a Science chapter. Despite the problem of other minds, modern psychology has embraced the study of consciousness. The astonishing richness of mental life simply cannot be ignored.

The Mind–Body Problem

▼ Figure **5.2** **Seat of the Soul** Descartes imagined that the seat of the soul—and consciousness—might reside in the pineal gland located in the ventricles of the brain. This original drawing from Descartes (1662) shows the pineal gland (H) nicely situated for a soul, right in the middle of the brain.

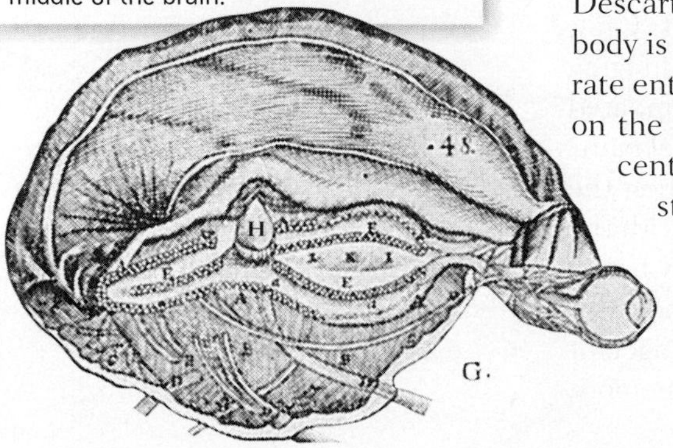

Another mystery of consciousness is the **mind–body problem,** *the issue of how the mind is related to the brain and body.* French philosopher and mathematician René Descartes (1596–1650) is famous for proposing, among other things, that the human body is a machine made of physical matter but that the human mind or soul is a separate entity made of a "thinking substance." He suggested that the mind has its effects on the brain and body through the pineal gland, a small structure located near the center of the brain (see **FIGURE 5.2**). In fact, the pineal gland is not even a nerve structure but rather is an endocrine gland, and so is poorly equipped to serve as a center of human consciousness. We now know that, far from the tiny connection between mind and brain in the pineal gland that was proposed by Descartes, the mind and brain are connected everywhere to each other. In other words, "the mind is what the brain does" (Minsky, 1986, p. 287).

But Descartes was right in pointing out the difficulty of reconciling the physical body with the mind. Most psychologists assume that mental events are intimately tied to brain events, such that every thought, perception, or feeling is associated with a particular pattern of activation of neurons in the brain (see the Neuroscience & Behavior chapter). Thinking about a particular person, for instance, occurs with a unique array of neural connections and activations. If the neurons repeat that pattern, then you must be thinking of the same person; conversely, if you think of the person, the brain activity occurs in that pattern.

One telling set of studies, however, suggests that the brain's activities *precede* the activities of the conscious mind. The electrical activity in the brains of volunteers was measured using sensors placed on their scalps as they repeatedly decided when to move a hand (Libet, 1985). Participants were also asked to indicate exactly when they consciously chose to move by reporting the position of a dot moving rapidly around the face of a clock just at the point of the decision (**FIGURE 5.3a**). As a rule, the brain begins to show electrical activity around half a second before a voluntary action (535 milliseconds, to be exact). This makes sense because brain activity certainly seems to be necessary to get an action started.

mind–body problem
The issue of how the mind is related to the brain and body.

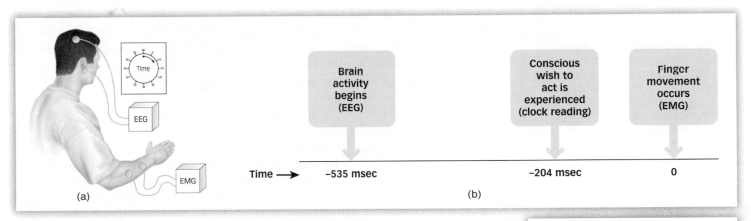

Brain activity begins (EEG) | **Conscious wish to act is experienced (clock reading)** | **Finger movement occurs (EMG)**

Time →   −535 msec   −204 msec   0

(a)   (b)

What this experiment revealed, though, was that the brain also started to show electrical activity before the person's conscious decision to move. As shown in **FIGURE 5.3b**, these studies found that the brain becomes active more than 300 milliseconds before participants report that they are consciously trying to move. The feeling that you are consciously willing your actions, it seems, may be a result rather than a cause of your brain activity. Although your personal intuition is that you *think* of an action and *then* do it, these experiments suggest that your brain is getting started before *either* the thinking or the doing, preparing the way for both thought and action. Quite simply, it may appear to us that our minds are leading our brains and bodies, but the order of events may be the other way around (Haggard & Tsakiris, 2009; Wegner, 2002).

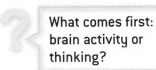

What comes first: brain activity or thinking?

▲ Figure **5.3 The Timing of Conscious Will**
(*a*) In Benjamin Libet's experiments, the participant was asked to move fingers at will while watching a dot move around the face of a clock to mark the moment at which the action was consciously willed. Meanwhile, EEG sensors timed the onset of brain activation and EMG sensors timed the muscle movement. (*b*) The experiment showed that brain activity (EEG) precedes the willed movement of the finger (EMG), but that the reported time of consciously willing the finger to move follows the brain activity.

Consciousness has its mysteries, but psychologists like a challenge. Although researchers may not be able to see the consciousness of others or know exactly how consciousness arises from the brain, this does not prevent them from collecting people's reports of conscious experiences and learning how these reports reveal the nature of consciousness.

The Nature of Consciousness

How would you describe your own consciousness? Researchers examining people's descriptions suggest that consciousness has four basic properties (intentionality, unity, selectivity, and transience), that it occurs on different levels, and that it includes a range of different contents. Let's examine each of these points in turn.

NORTH CAROLINA MUSEUM OF ART/CORBIS

▲ Figure **5.4 Bellotto's Dresden and Closeup** (*left*) The people on the bridge in the distance look very finely detailed in *View of Dresden with the Frauenkirche* by Bernardo Bellotto (1720–1780). However, when you examine the detail closely (*right*), you discover that the people are made of brushstrokes merely *suggesting* people—an arm here, a torso there. Consciousness produces a similar impression of "filling in," as it seems to consist of extreme detail even in areas that are peripheral (Dennett, 1991).

Four Basic Properties

The first property of consciousness is *intentionality*, the quality of being directed toward an object. Consciousness is always *about* something. Psychologists have tried to measure the relationship between consciousness and its objects, examining the size and duration of the relationship. How long can consciousness be directed toward an object, and how many objects can it take on at one time? Researchers have found that conscious attention is limited. Despite all the lush detail you see in your mind's eye, the kaleidoscope of sights and sounds and feelings and thoughts, the object of your consciousness at any one moment is just a small part of all of this (see **FIGURE 5.4**). To describe how this limitation works, psychologists refer to three other properties of consciousness: unity, selectivity, and transience.

The second basic property of consciousness is *unity*, which is resistance to division, or the ability to integrate information from all of the body's senses into one coherent whole. As you read this book, your five senses are taking in a great deal of information. Your eyes are scanning lots of black squiggles on a page (or screen) while also sensing an enormous array of shapes, colors, depths, and textures in your periphery; your hands are gripping a heavy book (or computer); your butt and feet may sense pressure from gravity pulling you against a chair or floor; and you may be listening to music or talking in another room, while smelling the odor of freshly made popcorn (or your roommate's dirty laundry). Although your body is constantly sensing an enormous amount of information from the world around you, your brain—amazingly—integrates all of this information into the experience of one unified consciousness (or two in the case of the split-brain patients described in the Neuroscience & Behavior chapter).

The third property of consciousness is *selectivity*, the capacity to include some objects but not others. While binding the many sensations around you into a coherent whole, your mind must make decisions about which pieces of information to include, and which to exclude. This property is shown through studies of **dichotic listening,** *in which people wearing headphones hear different messages in each ear.* Research participants were instructed to repeat aloud the words they heard in one ear while a different message was presented to the other ear (Cherry, 1953). As a result of focusing on the words they were supposed to repeat, participants noticed little of the second message, often not even realizing that at some point it changed from English to German! So, consciousness *filters out* some information. At the same time, participants did notice when the voice in the unattended ear changed from a man's to a woman's, suggesting that the selectivity of consciousness can also work to *tune in* other information.

How does consciousness decide what to filter in and what to tune out? The conscious system is most inclined to select information of special interest to the person. For example, in what has come to be known as the **cocktail-party phenomenon,** *people tune in one message even while they filter out others nearby.* In the dichotic

Participants in a dichotic listening experiment hear different messages played to the right and left ears and may be asked to "shadow" one of the messages by repeating it aloud.

IMAGE SOURCE PLUS/ALAMY

listening situation, for example, research participants are especially likely to notice if their own name is spoken into the unattended ear (Moray, 1959). Perhaps you, too, have noticed how abruptly your attention is diverted from whatever conversation you are having when someone else within earshot at the party mentions your name. Selectivity is not only a property of waking consciousness: the mind works this way in other states. People are more sensitive to their own name than others' names, for example, even during sleep (Oswald, Taylor, & Triesman, 1960). This is why, when you are trying to wake someone, it is best to use the person's name.

> How does your mind know which information to allow into consciousness, and which to filter out?

dichotic listening
A task in which people wearing headphones hear different messages presented to each ear.

cocktail-party phenomenon
A phenomenon in which people tune in one message even while they filter out others nearby.

The fourth and final basic property of consciousness is *transience,* or the tendency to change. Consciousness wiggles and fidgets like a toddler in the seat behind you on an airplane. The mind wanders not just sometimes, but incessantly, from one "right now" to the next "right now" and then on to the next (Wegner, 1997). William James, whom you met way back in the Psychology: Evolution of a Science chapter, famously described consciousness as a stream: "Consciousness . . . does not appear to itself chopped up in bits. Such words as 'chain' or 'train' do not describe it. . . . It is nothing jointed; it flows. A 'river' or a 'stream' are the metaphors by which it is most naturally described" (James, 1890, Vol. 1, p. 239). Books written in the "stream of consciousness" style, such as James Joyce's *Ulysses,* illustrate the whirling, chaotic, and constantly changing flow of consciousness. Here's an excerpt:

> I wished I could have picked every morsel of that chicken out of my fingers it was so tasty and browned and as tender as anything only for I didn't want to eat everything on my plate those forks and fishslicers were hallmarked silver too I wish I had some I could easily have slipped a couple into my muff when I was playing with them then always hanging out of them for money in a restaurant for the bit you put down your throat we have to be thankful for our mangy cup of tea itself as a great compliment to be noticed the way the world is divided in any case if its going to go on I want at least two other good chemises for one thing and but I don't know what kind of drawers he likes none at all I think didn't he say yes and half the girls in Gibraltar never wore them either naked as God made them that Andalusian singing her Manola she didn't make much secret of what she hadnt yes and the second pair of silkette stockings is laddered after one days wear I could have brought them back to Lewers this morning and kicked up a row and made that one change them only not to upset myself and run the risk of walking into him and ruining the whole thing and one of those kidfitting corsets Id want advertised cheap in the Gentlewoman with elastic gores on the hips he saved the one I have but thats no good what did they say they give a delightful figure line 11/6 obviating that unsightly broad appearance across the lower back to reduce flesh my belly is a bit too big Ill have to knock off the stout at dinner or am I getting too fond of it (1922/1994, p. 741)

The stream of consciousness may flow in this way partly because of the limited capacity of the conscious mind. We humans can hold only so much information in mind, after all, so when more information is selected, some of what is currently there must disappear. As a result, our focus of attention keeps changing. The stream of consciousness flows so inevitably that it even changes our perspective when we view a constant object like a Necker cube (see **FIGURE 5.5**).

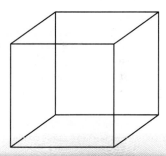

▲ Figure **5.5 The Necker Cube** This cube has the property of reversible perspective in that you can bring one or the other of its two square faces to the front in your mind's eye. Although it may take a while to reverse the figure at first, once people have learned to do it, they can reverse it regularly, about once every 3 seconds (Gomez et al., 1995). The stream of consciousness flows even when the target is a constant object.

Levels of Consciousness

Consciousness can also be understood as having levels, ranging from minimal consciousness to full consciousness to self-consciousness. These levels of consciousness would probably all register as "conscious" on that wakefulness meter for surgery patients you read about at the beginning of the chapter. The levels of consciousness that psychologists distinguish among are not a matter of degree of overall brain activity but instead involve different qualities of awareness of the world and of the self.

PHOTOMONDO/PHOTODISC/GETTY IMAGES

Full consciousness involves a consciousness of oneself, such as thinking about the act of driving while driving a car. How is this different from self-consciousness?

minimal consciousness
A low-level kind of sensory awareness and responsiveness that occurs when the mind inputs sensations and may output behavior.

full consciousness
Consciousness in which you know and are able to report your mental state.

self-consciousness
A distinct level of consciousness in which the person's attention is drawn to the self as an object.

Self-consciousness is a curse and a blessing. Looking in a mirror can make people evaluate themselves on deeper attributes such as honesty as well as superficial ones such as looks.

CULTURA CREATIVE/ALMY

In its minimal form, consciousness is just a connection between the person and the world. When you sense the sun coming in through the window, for example, you might turn toward the light. Such **minimal consciousness** is *a low-level kind of sensory awareness and responsiveness that occurs when the mind inputs sensations and may output behavior* (Armstrong, 1980). This kind of sensory awareness and responsiveness could even happen when someone pokes you during sleep and you turn over. Something seems to register in your mind, at least in the sense that you experience it, but you may not think at all about having had the experience. It could be that animals or, for that matter, even plants can have this minimal level of consciousness. But because of the problem of other minds and the notorious reluctance of animals and plants to talk to us, we can't know for sure that they *experience* the things that make them respond. At least in the case of humans, we can safely assume that there is something it "feels like" to be them and that when they're awake, they are at least minimally conscious.

Human consciousness is often more than minimal, of course, but what exactly gets added? Consider the glorious feeling of waking up on a spring morning as rays of sun stream across your pillow. It's not just that you are having this experience: Being fully conscious means that you are also *aware* that you are having this experience. The critical ingredient that accompanies **full consciousness** is that you *know and are able to report your mental state*. That's a subtle distinction: Being fully conscious means that you are aware of having a mental state while you are experiencing the mental state itself. When you have a hurt leg and mindlessly rub it, for instance, your pain may be minimally conscious. After all, you seem to be experiencing pain because you have acted and are indeed rubbing your leg.

> What factor of full consciousness distinguishes it from minimal consciousness?"

It is only when you realize that it hurts, though, that the pain becomes fully conscious. Have you ever been driving a car and suddenly realized that you don't remember the past 15 minutes of driving? Chances are that you were not unconscious, but instead minimally conscious. When you are completely aware and thinking about your driving, you have moved into the realm of full consciousness. Full consciousness involves not only thinking about things but also thinking about the fact that you are thinking about things (Jaynes, 1976; see the Hot Science box).

Full consciousness involves a certain consciousness of oneself; the person notices the self in a particular mental state ("Here I am, reading this sentence."). However, this is not quite the same thing as *self*-consciousness. Sometimes consciousness is entirely flooded with the self ("Not only am I reading this sentence, but I have a blemish on the end of my nose today that makes me feel like guiding a sleigh."). Self-consciousness focuses on the self to the exclusion of almost everything else. William James (1890) and other theorists have suggested that **self-consciousness** is yet another *distinct level of consciousness in which the person's attention is drawn to the self as an object* (Morin, 2006). Most people report experiencing such self-consciousness when they are embarrassed; when they find themselves the focus of attention in a group; when someone focuses a camera on them; or when they are deeply introspective about their thoughts, feelings, or personal qualities.

Self-consciousness brings with it a tendency to evaluate yourself and notice your shortcomings. Looking in a mirror, for example, is all it takes to make people evaluate themselves—thinking not just about their looks, but also about whether they are good or bad in other ways. People go out of their way to avoid mirrors when they've done something they are ashamed of (Duval & Wicklund, 1972). Self-consciousness can certainly spoil a good mood, so much so that a tendency to be chronically self-conscious is associated with depression (Pyszczynski, Holt, & Greenberg, 1987). However, because it makes people self-critical, the self-consciousness that results when

> When do people go out of their way to avoid mirrors?

HOT SCIENCE

The Mind Wanders

Yes, the mind wanders. Ideally, it doesn't wander so much that it can't finish this paragraph. But it does tend to come and go over time, not only changing topics as it goes, but sometimes simply "zoning out." You've no doubt had experiences of reading and suddenly realizing that you have not even been processing what you've read. Even while your eyes are dutifully following the lines of print, at some point you begin to think about something else—and only later catch yourself having wandered, perhaps thinking, where was I? Or, why did I come into this room?

Mind wandering, or the experience of "stimulus-independent thoughts," occurs most often when we are engaged in repetitive, undemanding tasks (Buckner, Andrews-Hanna, & Schacter, 2008). This happens a lot. A recent study revealed that we engage in mind wandering during nearly half of our daily activities (46.9%), regardless of what we are doing (Killingsworth & Gilbert, 2010). Indeed, mind wandering occurred at least 30% of the time in every activity recorded (with the one exception being making love, during which it is apparently rare to have stimulus-independent thoughts). Although the mind often wanders, this study found

COURTESY OF THE LEO BAECK INSTITUTE, NEW YORK

◀ New research suggests that mind wandering can improve creative problem-solving. As a real-world example of this, Einstein is said to have come up with some of his greatest breakthroughs not while sitting at his desk, but while going for walks. Here he is hard at work.

that people are significantly less happy when mind wandering compared to when they are thinking about what they are currently doing.

Learning about the connection between mind wandering and unhappiness might lead you to feel... unhappy. But don't wander off before reading to the end of this box! As it turns out, mind wandering may also have its benefits. For thousands of years some of the world's greatest thinkers have noted that their most important breakthroughs came during periods of daydreaming or mind wandering. For instance, Einstein is said to have made

major breakthroughs in his relativity theory while going for a walk (rather than sitting at his desk). New research suggests that mind wandering may indeed help to improve our creative problem solving. In one recent study, researchers tested this idea by having participants complete a creative problem-solving test in which they were asked to generate as many uses as they could for everyday objects (e.g., brick, feather) both before and after engaging in either a demanding or undemanding task (Baird et al., 2012). The authors hypothesized, and found, that engagement in the undemanding task would facilitate higher levels of mind wandering (which it did), and would in turn lead to improvements in their performance on the previously worked-on tests (which it did), but not new tests (correct again). These findings suggest that allowing our minds to wander, while remaining active, can enhance our ability to think creatively and solve difficult problems.

people see their own mirror images can make them briefly more helpful, more cooperative, and less aggressive (Gibbons, 1990). Perhaps everyone would be a bit more civilized if mirrors were held up for them to see themselves as objects of their own scrutiny.

Most animals can't follow this path to civilization. The typical dog, cat, or bird seems mystified by a mirror, ignoring it or acting as though there is some other critter back there. However, chimpanzees that have spent time with mirrors sometimes behave in ways that suggest they recognize themselves in a mirror. To examine this, researchers painted an odorless red dye over the eyebrow of an anesthetized chimp and then watched when the awakened chimp was presented with a mirror (Gallup, 1977). If the chimp interpreted the mirror image as a representation of some other chimp with an unusual approach to cosmetics, we would expect it just to look at the mirror or perhaps to reach toward it. But the chimp reached toward its *own eye* as it looked into the mirror—not the mirror image—suggesting that it recognized the image as a reflection of itself.

Versions of this experiment have now been repeated with many different animals, and it turns out that, like humans, animals such as chimpanzees and orangutans (Gallup, 1997), possibly dolphins (Reiss & Marino, 2001), and maybe even elephants (Plotnik, de Waal, & Reiss, 2006) and magpies (Prior, Schwartz, & Güntürkün, 2008) recognize their own mirror images. Dogs, cats, crows, monkeys, and gorillas have been tested, too, but don't seem to know they are looking at themselves. Even humans don't have self-recognition right away. Infants don't recognize themselves in mirrors until

A chimpanzee tried to wipe off the red dye on its eyebrow in the Gallup experiment. This suggests that some animals recognize themselves in the mirror.

DR. DANIEL POVINELLI/MONKEY IMAGES

Dilbert

OKAY, LET ME THINK ALOUD FOR A MINUTE.

THE COST WILL BE $3,000...LOSING FOCUS...MONKEYS ARE FUNNY...MY TONGUE IS DIGESTING IN MY MOUTH.

THAT DIDN'T HELP AS MUCH AS I HAD HOPED.

they've reached about 18 months of age (Lewis & Brooks-Gunn, 1979). The experience of self-consciousness, as measured by self-recognition in mirrors, is limited to a few animals and to humans only after a certain stage of development.

Conscious Contents

What's on your mind? For that matter, what's on everybody's mind? One way to learn what is on people's minds is to ask them, and much research has called on people simply to *think aloud.* A more systematic approach is the *experience-sampling technique,* in which people are asked to report their conscious experiences at particular times. Equipped with electronic beepers or called on cell phones, for example, participants are asked to record their current thoughts when asked at random times throughout the day (Bolger, Davis, & Rafaeli, 2003).

Experience-sampling studies show that consciousness is dominated by the immediate environment—what is seen, felt, heard, tasted, and smelled—all are at the forefront of the mind. Much of consciousness beyond this orientation to the environment turns to the person's *current concerns,* or what the person is thinking about repeatedly (Klinger, 1975). **TABLE 5.1** shows the results of a Minnesota study where 175 college students were asked to report their current concerns (Goetzman, Hughes, & Klinger,

▶ Table 5.1

What's on Your Mind? College Students' Current Concerns

Current Concern Category	Example	Frequency of Students Who Mentioned the Concern
Family	Gain better relations with immediate family	40%
Roommate	Change attitude or behavior of roommate	29%
Household	Clean room	52%
Friends	Make new friends	42%
Dating	Desire to date a certain person	24%
Sexual intimacy	Abstaining from sex	16%
Health	Diet and exercise	85%
Employment	Get a summer job	33%
Education	Go to graduate school	43%
Social activities	Gain acceptance into a campus organization	34%
Religious	Attend church more	51%
Financial	Pay rent or bills	8%
Government	Change government policy	14%

From Goetzman, E. S., Hughes, T., & Klinger, E. (1994). *Current concerns of college students in a midwestern sample.* University of Minnesota, Morris.

1994). The researchers sorted the concerns into the categories shown in the table. Keep in mind that these concerns are ones the students didn't mind reporting to psychologists; their private preoccupations may have been different and probably far more interesting.

Think for a moment about your own current concerns. What topics have been on your mind the most in the past day or two? Your mental "to do" list may include things you want to get, keep, avoid, work on, remember, and so on (Little, 1993). Items on the list often pop into mind, sometimes even with an emotional punch ("The test in this class is tomorrow!"). People in one study had their skin conductance level (SCL) measured to assess their emotional responses (Nikula, Klinger, & Larson-Gutman, 1993). SCL sensors attached to their fingers indicated when sweat appeared on their skin—a good indication that they were thinking about something distressing. Once in a while, SCL would rise spontaneously, and at these times the researchers quizzed the participants about their conscious thoughts. These emotional moments, compared to those when SCL was normal, often corresponded with a current concern popping into mind. Thoughts that are not emotional all by themselves can still come to mind with an emotional bang when they are topics of current concern.

One concern on many students' minds is diet and exercise to keep in shape.

How do researchers study subjective experience?

We discussed thinking about our current concerns before, but what is our subjective experience when actually carrying out the events of our daily lives? We each, of course, are engaged in our daily lives, but rarely examine what our moment-by-moment experiences are like, or make cross-experience comparisons. Researchers are now using experience-sampling methods to record the emotions people experience during everyday activities with interesting results. One recent study collected data from over 900 working women by asking them to reflect on the events of the past day and record how they felt while engaging in each activity (Kahneman et al., 2004). Some of the results are as expected. For instance, as shown in **TABLE 5.2**, people score lowest on positive affect when commuting, working, and doing housework, and unfortunately this is how we spend a large part of our day. The women in this study reported having the most positive affect while being intimate with another person, although they only did this for 12 minutes of the day. Some less intuitive findings are the activities that fell in between the two. In survey studies parents often report that they are happiest when spending time with their children, but when asked about actual events of the prior day, being with one's children ranked just two ticks above housework and well below other activities like shopping, watching TV, and making more children.

Daydreaming. Current concerns do not seem all that concerning, however, during *daydreaming*, a state of consciousness in which a seemingly purposeless flow of thoughts comes to mind. When thoughts drift along this way, it may seem as if you are just wasting time. The brain, however, is active even when there is no specific task at hand. This mental work done in daydreaming was examined in an fMRI study of people resting in the scanner (Mason et al., 2007). Usually, people in brain scanning studies don't have time to daydream much because they are kept busy

Table 5.2

How Was Your Day? Women's Ratings of Level of Positive Affect and Amount of Time in Daily Activities

Activities	Mean Affect Rating Positive Affect	Mean Hours/Day
Intimate relations	5.1	0.2
Socializing	4.59	2.3
Relaxing	4.42	2.2
Pray/worship/meditate	4.35	0.4
Eating	4.34	2.2
Exercising	4.31	0.2
Watching TV	4.19	2.2
Shopping	3.95	0.4
Preparing food	3.93	1.1
On the phone	3.92	2.5
Napping	3.87	0.9
Taking care of my children	3.86	1.1
Computer/e-mail/Internet	3.81	1.9
Housework	3.73	1.1
Working	3.62	6.9
Commuting	3.45	1.6

From Kahneman, D., Krueger, A. B., Schkade, D. A., Schwartz, N., & Stone, A. A. (2004). A survey method for characterizing daily life experience: The day reconstruction method (Table 1). *Science, 306,* 1776–1780.

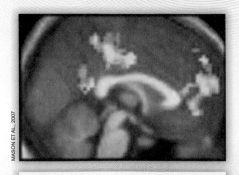

▲ Figure **5.6 The Default Network Activated during Daydreaming** An fMRI scan shows that many areas, known as the default network, are active when the person is not given a specific mental task to perform during the scan (Mason et al., 2007).

with mental tasks—scans cost money and researchers want to get as much data as possible for their bucks. But when people are *not* busy, they still show a widespread pattern of activation in many areas of the brain—now known as the *default network* (Gusnard & Raichle, 2001). The study by Mason et al. revealed that this network became activated whenever people worked on a mental task that they knew so well that they could daydream while doing it (see **FIGURE 5.6**). The areas of the default network are known to be involved in thinking about social life, about the self, and about the past and future—all the usual haunts of the daydreaming mind (Mitchell, 2006).

What part of the brain is active during daydreaming?

Thought Suppression. The current concerns that populate consciousness can sometimes get the upper hand, transforming daydreams or everyday thoughts into rumination and worry. Thoughts that return again and again, or problem-solving attempts that never seem to succeed, can come to dominate consciousness. When this happens, people may exert **mental control,** *the attempt to change conscious states of mind.* For example, someone troubled by a recurring worry about the future ("What if I can't get a decent job when I graduate?") might choose to try *not* to think about this because it causes too much anxiety and uncertainty. Whenever this thought comes to mind, the person engages in **thought suppression,** the *conscious avoidance of a thought.* This may seem like a perfectly sensible strategy because it eliminates the worry and allows the person to move on to think about something else.

Or does it? The great Russian novelist, Fyodor Dostoyevsky (1863/1988, p. 49), remarked on the difficulty of thought suppression: "Try to pose for yourself this task: not to think of a polar bear, and you will see that the cursed thing will come to mind every minute." Inspired by this observation, Daniel Wegner and his colleagues (1987) gave people this exact task in the laboratory. Participants were asked to try not to think about a white bear for 5 minutes while they recorded all their thoughts aloud into a tape recorder. In addition, they were asked to ring a bell if the thought of a white bear came to mind. On average, they mentioned the white bear or rang the bell (indicating the thought) more than once per minute. Thought suppression simply didn't work and instead produced a flurry of returns of the unwanted thought. What's more, when some research participants later were specifically asked to change tasks and deliberately *think* about a white bear, they became oddly preoccupied with it. A graph of their bell rings in **FIGURE 5.7** shows that these participants had the white bear come to mind far more often than did people who had only been asked

Go ahead, look away from the book for a minute and try not to think about a white bear.

▶ Figure **5.7 Rebound Effect** Research participants were first asked to try not to think about a white bear, and then they were asked to think about it and to ring a bell whenever it came to mind. Compared to those who were simply asked to think about a bear without prior suppression, those people who *first* suppressed the thought showed a rebound of increased thinking (Wegner et al., 1987).

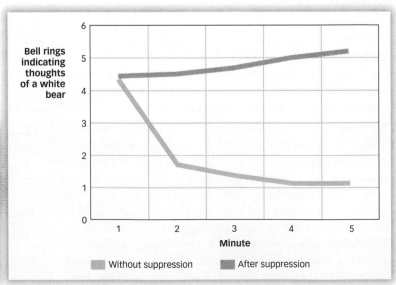

to think about the bear from the outset, with no prior suppression. This **rebound effect of thought suppression,** *the tendency of a thought to return to consciousness with greater frequency following suppression,* suggests that attempts at mental control may be difficult indeed. The act of trying to suppress a thought may itself cause that thought to return to consciousness in a robust way.

The Ironic Monitor. Similar to thought suppression, other attempts to steer consciousness in any direction can result in mental states that are precisely the opposite of those desired. How ironic: Trying to consciously achieve one task may produce precisely the opposite outcome! These ironic effects seem most likely to occur when the person is distracted or under stress. People who are distracted while they are trying to get into a good mood, for example, tend to become sad (Wegner, Erber, & Zanakos, 1993), and those who are distracted while trying to relax actually become more anxious than those who are not trying to relax (Wegner, Broome, & Blumberg, 1997). Likewise, an attempt not to overshoot a golf putt, undertaken during distraction, often yields the unwanted overshot (Wegner, Ansfield, & Pilloff, 1998). The theory of **ironic processes of mental control** proposes that such *ironic errors occur because the mental process that monitors errors can itself produce them* (Wegner, 1994a, 2009). In the attempt not to think of a white bear, for instance, a small part of the mind is ironically *searching* for the white bear.

This ironic monitoring process is not present in consciousness. After all, trying *not* to think of something would be useless if monitoring the progress of suppression required keeping that target in consciousness. For example, if trying not to think of a white bear meant that you consciously kept repeating to yourself, "No white bear! No white bear!" then you've failed before you've begun: That thought is present in consciousness even as you strive to eliminate it. Rather, the ironic monitor is

> **Is consciously avoiding a worrisome thought a sensible strategy?**

a process of the mind that works *outside* of consciousness, making us sensitive to all the things we do not want to think, feel, or do so that we can notice and consciously take steps to regain control if these things come back to mind. As this unconscious monitoring whirs along in the background, it unfortunately increases the person's sensitivity to the very thought that is unwanted. Ironic processes are mental functions that are needed for effective mental control—they help in the process of banishing a thought from consciousness—but they can sometimes yield the very failure they seem designed to overcome. Ironic effects of mental control arise from processes that work outside of consciousness, so they remind us that much of the mind's machinery may be hidden from our view, lying outside the fringes of our experience.

The Unconscious Mind

Many mental processes are unconscious, in the sense that they occur without our experience of them. When we speak, for instance, "We are not really conscious either of the search for words, or of putting the words together into phrases, or of putting the phrases into sentences. . . . The actual process of thinking . . . is not conscious at all . . . only its preparation, its materials, and its end result are consciously perceived" (Jaynes, 1976, p. 41). Just to put the role of consciousness in perspective, think for a moment about the mental processes involved in simple addition. What happens in consciousness between hearing a problem (what's four plus five?) and thinking of the answer (nine)? Probably nothing—the answer just appears in the mind. But this is a piece of calculation that must take at least a bit of thinking. After all, at a very young age you may have had to solve such problems by counting on your fingers. Now that you don't have to do that anymore (please tell me you don't have to do that

mental control
The attempt to change conscious states of mind.

thought suppression
The conscious avoidance of a thought.

rebound effect of thought suppression
The tendency of a thought to return to consciousness with greater frequency following suppression.

ironic processes of mental control
Mental processes that can produce ironic errors because monitoring for errors can itself produce them.

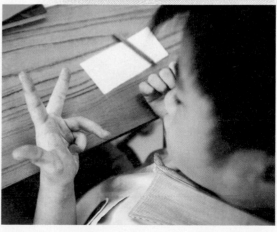

There are no conscious steps between hearing an easy problem (what's four plus five?) and thinking of the answer—unless you have to count on your fingers.

FUSE/GETTY IMAGES

dynamic unconscious
An active system encompassing a lifetime of hidden memories, the person's deepest instincts and desires, and the person's inner struggle to control these forces.

repression
A mental process that removes unacceptable thoughts and memories from consciousness and keeps them in the unconscious.

cognitive unconscious
All the mental processes that give rise to a person's thoughts, choices, emotions, and behavior even though they are not experienced by the person.

subliminal perception
Thought or behavior that is influenced by stimuli that a person cannot consciously report perceiving.

anymore), the answer seems to pop into your head automatically, by virtue of a process that doesn't require you to be aware of any underlying steps and, for that matter, doesn't even *allow* you to be aware of the steps. The answer just suddenly appears.

In the early part of the 20th century, when structuralist psychologists, such as Wilhelm Wundt, believed that introspection was the best method of research (see the Psychology: Evolution of a Science chapter), research volunteers trained in describing their thoughts tried to discern what happens when a simple problem brings to mind a simple answer (e.g., Watt, 1905). They drew the same blank you probably did. Nothing conscious seems to bridge this gap, but the answer comes from somewhere, and this emptiness points to the unconscious mind. To explore these hidden recesses, we can look at the classical theory of the unconscious introduced by Sigmund Freud and then at the modern cognitive psychology of unconscious mental processes.

Freudian Unconscious

The true champion of the unconscious mind was Sigmund Freud. As you read in the Psychology: Evolution of a Science chapter, Freud's psychoanalytic theory viewed conscious thought as the surface of a much deeper mind made up of unconscious processes. Far more than just a collection of hidden processes, Freud described a **dynamic unconscious**—*an active system encompassing a lifetime of hidden memories, the person's deepest instincts and desires, and the person's inner struggle to control these forces.* The dynamic unconscious might contain hidden sexual thoughts about one's parents, for example, or destructive urges aimed at a helpless infant—the kinds of thoughts people keep secret from others and may not even acknowledge to themselves. According to Freud's theory, the unconscious is a force to be held in check by **repression,** *a mental process that removes unacceptable thoughts and memories from consciousness and keeps them in the unconscious.* Without repression, a person might think, do, or say every unconscious impulse or animal urge, no matter how selfish or immoral. With repression, these desires are held in the recesses of the dynamic unconscious.

Freud looked for evidence of the unconscious mind in speech errors and lapses of consciousness, or what are commonly called *Freudian slips.* Forgetting the name of someone you dislike, for example, is a slip that seems to have special meaning. Freud believed that errors are not random and instead have some surplus meaning that may appear to have been created by an intelligent unconscious mind, even though

> **What do Freudian slips tell us about the unconscious mind?**

the person consciously disavows them. For example, when reporting on the news that members of the U.S. military had killed Osama bin Laden, several reporters and commentators at Fox News, a conservative news outlet, independently reported that *Obama* bin Laden was dead. This slip even appeared as a printed announcement on one of its news shows.

Did the Fox News slip mean anything? One experiment revealed that slips of speech can indeed be prompted by a person's pressing concerns (Motley & Baars, 1979). Research participants in one group were told they might receive minor electric shocks, whereas those in another group heard no mention of this. Each person was then asked to read quickly through a series of word pairs, including *shad bock.* Those in the group warned about shock more often slipped in pronouncing this pair, blurting out *bad shock.*

Unlike errors created in experiments such as this one, many of the meaningful errors Freud attributed to the dynamic unconscious were not predicted in advance and so seem to depend on clever after-the-fact interpretations. Such interpretations can be wrong. Suggesting a pattern to a series of random events is not the same as scientifically predicting

After the death of Osama bin Laden, several staff members at the conservative Fox News channel slipped and reported on the death of *Obama* bin Laden.

NBC NEWS SPECIAL REPORT
PRES. OBAMA ANNOUNCES
OSAMA BIN LADEN KILLED

NEWSIES MEDIA/ALAMY

and explaining when and why an event should happen. Anyone can offer a reasonable, compelling explanation for an event after it has already happened, but the true work of science is to offer testable hypotheses that are evaluated based on reliable evidence. Freud's (1901/1938) book, *The Psychopathology of Everyday Life*, suggests not so much that the dynamic unconscious produces errors but that Freud himself was a master at finding meaning in errors that might otherwise have seemed random.

A Modern View of the Cognitive Unconscious

Modern psychologists share Freud's interest in the impact of unconscious mental processes on consciousness and on behavior. However, rather than Freud's vision of the unconscious as a teeming menagerie of animal urges and repressed thoughts, the current study of the unconscious mind views it as the factory that builds the products of conscious thought and behavior (Kihlstrom, 1987; Wilson, 2002). The **cognitive unconscious** includes *all the mental processes that give rise to a person's thoughts, choices, emotions, and behavior even though they are not experienced by the person.*

One indication of the cognitive unconscious at work is when a person's thoughts or behaviors are changed by exposure to information outside of consciousness. This happens in **subliminal perception,** when *thought or behavior is influenced by stimuli that a person cannot consciously report perceiving.* Worries about the potential of subliminal influence were first provoked in 1957, when a marketer, James Vicary, claimed he had increased concession sales at a New Jersey theater by flashing the words "Eat Popcorn" and "Drink Coke" briefly on-screen during movies. It turns out his story was a hoax, and many attempts to increase sales using similar methods have failed. But the very idea of influencing behavior outside of consciousness created a wave of alarm about insidious "subliminal persuasion" that still concerns people (Epley, Savitsky, & Kachelski, 1999; Pratkanis, 1992).

Although the story above was a hoax, factors outside our conscious awareness can indeed influence our behavior. For example, one classic study reported that exposure to information about getting old can make a person walk more slowly. John Bargh and his colleagues had college students complete a survey that called for them to make sentences with various words (1996). The students were not informed that most of the words were commonly associated with aging (*Florida, gray, wrinkled*), and even afterward they didn't report being aware of this trend. In this case, the "aging" idea wasn't presented subliminally, just not very noticeably. As these research participants left the experiment, they were clocked as they walked down the hall. Compared with those not exposed to the aging-related words, the participants walked more slowly! Just as with subliminal perception, a passing exposure to ideas can influence actions without conscious awareness.

The unconscious mind can be a kind of "mental butler," taking over background tasks that are too tedious, subtle, or bothersome for consciousness to trifle with (Bargh & Chartrand, 1999; Bargh & Morsella, 2008; Bower, 1999). Psychologists have long debated just how smart this mental butler might be. Freud attributed great intelligence to the unconscious, believing that it harbors complex motives and inner conflicts and that it expresses these in an astonishing array of thoughts and emotions, as well as psychological disorders (see the Disorders chapter). Contemporary cognitive psychologists wonder whether the unconscious is so smart, however, and point out that some unconscious processes even seem downright "dumb" (Loftus & Klinger, 1992). For example, the unconscious processes that underlie the perception of subliminal visual stimuli do not seem able to understand the combined meaning of word pairs, although they can understand single words. To the *conscious* mind, for example, a word pair such as *enemy loses* is somewhat positive—it is good to have your enemy lose. However, subliminal presentations of this word pair make people

Do people in a movie theater need any subliminal messages to get them to eat popcorn? Probably not. Would subliminal messages make them more likely to eat popcorn? Maybe, but not much.

Choosing a roommate can be like playing the lottery: You win some, you lose some, and then you lose some more.

think of negative things, as though the unconscious mind is simply adding together the unpleasantness of the single words *enemy* and *loses* (Greenwald, 1992). Perhaps the mental butler is not all that bright.

In some cases, however, the unconscious mind can make better decisions than the conscious mind. Participants in an experiment were asked to choose which of three hypothetical people with many different qualities they would prefer to have as a roommate (Dijksterhuis, 2004). One candidate was objectively better, with more positive qualities, and participants who were given 4 minutes to make a *conscious decision* tended to choose that one. A second group was asked for an *immediate decision* as soon as the information display was over, and a third group was encouraged to reach an *unconscious decision*. This group was also given 4 minutes after the display ended to give their answer (as the conscious group had been given), but during this interval their conscious minds were occupied with solving a set of anagrams. As you can see in **FIGURE 5.8**, the unconscious decision group showed a stronger preference for the good roommate than did the immediate decision or conscious decision groups. Unconscious minds seemed *better able* than conscious minds to sort out the complex information and arrive at the best choice. You sometimes can end up more satisfied with decisions you make after just going with your gut than with the decisions you consciously agonize over.

> **What evidence shows the unconscious mind is a good decision maker?**

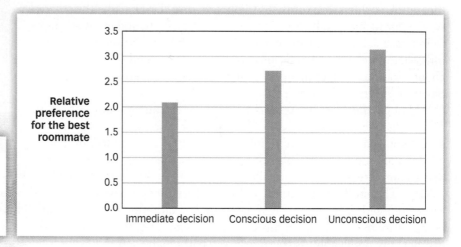

▶ Figure **5.8 Decisions** People making roommate decisions who had some time for unconscious deliberation chose better roommates than those who thought about the choice consciously or those who made snap decisions (Dijksterhuis, 2004).

IN SUMMARY

▶ Consciousness is a mystery of psychology because other people's minds cannot be perceived directly and because the relationship between mind and body is perplexing.

▶ Consciousness has four basic properties: intentionality, unity, selectivity, and transience. It can also be understood in terms of levels: minimal consciousness, full consciousness, and self-consciousness.

▶ Conscious contents can include current concerns, daydreams, and unwanted thoughts.

▶ Unconscious processes are sometimes understood as expressions of the Freudian dynamic unconscious, but they are more commonly viewed as processes of the cognitive unconscious that create our conscious thought and behavior.

▶ The cognitive unconscious is at work when subliminal perception and unconscious decision processes influence thought or behavior without the person's awareness.

Sleep and Dreaming: Good Night, Mind

What's it like to be asleep? Sometimes it's like nothing at all. Sleep can produce a state of unconsciousness in which the mind and brain apparently turn off the functions that create experience: The theater in your mind is closed. But this is an oversimplification because the theater actually seems to reopen during the night for special shows of bizarre cult films—in other words, dreams. Dream consciousness involves a transformation of experience that is so radical it is commonly considered an **altered state of consciousness:** *a form of experience that departs significantly from the normal subjective experience of the world and the mind.* Such altered states can be accompanied by changes in thinking, disturbances in the sense of time, feelings of the loss of control, changes in emotional expression, alterations in body image and sense of self, perceptual distortions, and changes in meaning or significance (Ludwig, 1966). The world of sleep and dreams, the two topics in this section, provides two unique perspectives on consciousness: a view of the mind without consciousness and a view of consciousness in an altered state.

> **?** Why are dreams considered an altered state of consciousness?

Sleep

Consider a typical night. As you begin to fall asleep, the busy, task-oriented thoughts of the waking mind are replaced by wandering thoughts and images and odd juxtapositions, some of them almost dreamlike. This presleep consciousness is called the *hypnagogic state*. On some rare nights you might experience a *hypnic jerk,* a sudden quiver or sensation of dropping, as though missing a step on a staircase. No one is quite sure why these happen. Eventually, your presence of mind goes away entirely. Time and experience stop, you are unconscious, and in fact there seems to be no "you" there to have experiences. But then come dreams, whole vistas of a vivid and surrealistic consciousness you just don't get during the day, a set of experiences that occur with the odd prerequisite that there is nothing "out there" you are actually experiencing. More patches of unconsciousness may occur, with more dreams here and there. And finally, the glimmerings of waking consciousness return again in a foggy and imprecise form as you enter postsleep consciousness (the *hypnopompic state*) and then awake, often with bad hair.

Dreamers, **by Albert Joseph Moore (1879/1882)** Although their bodies are in the same room, their minds are probably worlds apart.

MOORE, ALBERT JOSEPH/BIRMINGHAM MUSEUMS AND ART GALLERY/THE BRIDGEMAN ART LIBRARY

Sleep Cycle

The sequence of events that occurs during a night of sleep is part of one of the major rhythms of human life, the cycle of sleep and waking. This **circadian rhythm** is *a naturally occurring 24-hour cycle*, from the Latin *circa* (about) and *dies* (day). Even people sequestered in underground buildings without clocks ("time-free environments") who are allowed to sleep when they want tend to have a rest–activity cycle of about 25.1 hours (Aschoff, 1965). This slight deviation from 24 hours is not easily explained (Lavie, 2001), but it seems to underlie the tendency many people have to want to stay up a little later each night and wake up a little later each day. We're 25.1-hour people living in a 24-hour world.

The sleep cycle is far more than a simple on–off routine, however, as many bodily and psychological processes ebb and flow in this rhythm. In 1929 researchers made EEG (electroencephalograph) recordings of the human brain for the first time (Berger, 1929; see the Neuroscience & Behavior chapter). Before this, many people

altered state of consciousness
A form of experience that departs significantly from the normal subjective experience of the world and the mind.

circadian rhythm
A naturally occurring 24-hour cycle.

REM sleep
A stage of sleep characterized by rapid eye movements and a high level of brain activity.

electrooculograph (EOG)
An instrument that measures eye movements.

had offered descriptions of their nighttime experiences, and researchers knew that there are deeper and lighter periods of sleep, as well as dream periods. But no one had been able to measure much of anything about sleep without waking up the sleeper and ruining it. The EEG recordings revealed a regular pattern of changes in electrical activity in the brain accompanying the circadian cycle. During waking, these changes involve alternation between high-frequency activity (*beta waves*) during alertness and lower-frequency activity (*alpha waves*) during relaxation.

The largest changes in EEG occur during sleep. These changes show a regular pattern over the course of the night that allowed sleep researchers to identify five sleep stages (see **FIGURE 5.9**). In the first stage of sleep, the EEG moves to frequency patterns even lower than alpha waves (*theta waves*). In the second stage of sleep, these patterns are interrupted by short bursts of activity called *sleep spindles* and *K complexes,* and the sleeper becomes somewhat more difficult to awaken. The deepest stages of sleep are stages 3 and 4, known as slow-wave sleep, in which the EEG patterns show activity called *delta waves*.

> **What do EEG recordings tell us about sleep?**

During the fifth sleep stage, **REM sleep,** *a stage of sleep characterized by rapid eye movements and a high level of brain activity,* EEG patterns become high-frequency sawtooth waves, similar to beta waves, suggesting that the mind at this time is as active as it is during waking (see Figure 5.9). Using an **electrooculograph (EOG)**—*an instrument that measures eye movements*—during sleep, researchers found that sleepers wakened during REM periods reported having dreams much more often than

▶ Figure **5.9** **EEG Patterns during the Stages of Sleep**
The waking brain shows high-frequency beta wave activity, which changes during drowsiness and relaxation to lower-frequency alpha waves. Stage 1 sleep shows lower-frequency theta waves, which are accompanied in stage 2 by irregular patterns called sleep spindles and K complexes. Stages 3 and 4 are marked by the lowest frequencies, delta waves. During REM sleep, EEG patterns return to higher-frequency sawtooth waves that resemble the beta waves of waking.

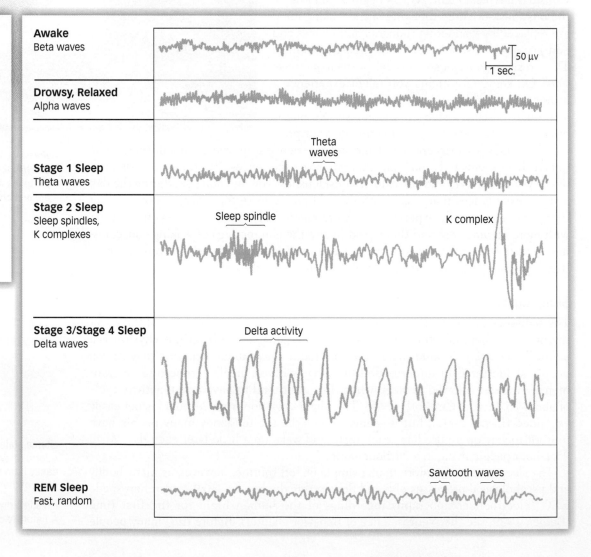

those wakened during non-REM periods (Aserinsky & Kleitman, 1953). During REM sleep, the pulse quickens, blood pressure rises, and there are telltale signs of sexual arousal. At the same time, measurements of muscle movements indicate that the sleeper is very still, except for a rapid side-to-side movement of the eyes. (Watch someone sleeping and you may be able to see the REMs through their closed eyelids. But be careful doing this with strangers down at the bus station.)

Although many people believe that they don't dream much (if at all), some 80% of people awakened during REM sleep report dreams. If you've ever wondered whether dreams actually take place in an instant or whether they take as long to happen as the events they portray might take, the analysis of REM sleep offers an answer. Sleep researchers William Dement and Nathaniel Kleitman (1957) woke volunteers either 5 minutes or 15 minutes after the onset of REM sleep and asked them to judge, on the basis of the events in the remembered dream, how long they had been dreaming. Sleepers in 92 of 111 cases were correct, suggesting that dreaming occurs in "real time." The discovery of REM sleep has offered many insights into dreaming, but not all dreams occur in REM periods. Some dreams are also reported in other sleep stages, but not as many—and the dreams that occur at those times are described as less wild than REM dreams and more like normal thinking.

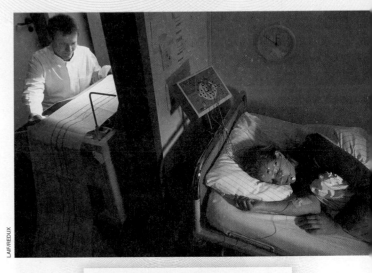

Psychologists learn about what happens when we sleep by collecting EOG, EEG, and other measurements from research volunteers while they sleep in sleep laboratories, like this one.

Putting EEG and REM data together produces a picture of how a typical night's sleep progresses through cycles of sleep stages (see **FIGURE 5.10**). In the first hour of the night, you fall all the way from waking to the fourth and deepest stage of sleep, the stage marked by delta waves. These slow waves indicate a general synchronization of neural firing, as though the brain is doing one thing at this time rather than many:

What are the stages in a typical night's sleep?

the neuronal equivalent of "the wave" moving through the crowd at a stadium as lots of individuals move together in synchrony. You then return to lighter sleep stages, eventually reaching REM and dreamland. Note that although REM sleep is lighter than that of lower stages, it is deep enough that you may be difficult to awaken. You then continue to cycle between REM and slow-wave sleep stages every 90 minutes or so throughout the night. Periods of REM last longer as the night goes on, and lighter sleep stages predominate between these periods, with the deeper slow-wave stages 3 and 4 disappearing halfway through the night. Although you're either unconscious or dream-conscious at the time, your brain and mind cycle through a remarkable array of different states each time you have a night's sleep.

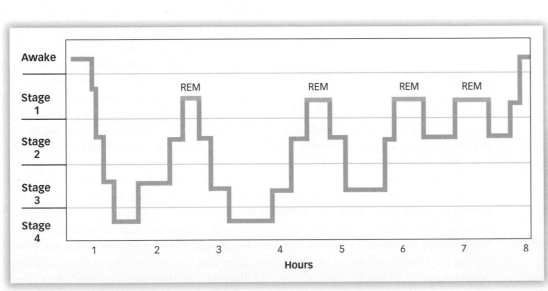

◄ Figure **5.10** **Stages of Sleep during the Night** Over the course of the typical night, sleep cycles into deeper stages early on and then more shallow stages later. REM periods become longer in later cycles, and the deeper slow-wave sleep of stages 3 and 4 disappears halfway through the night.

Sleep Needs and Deprivation

How much do people sleep? The answer depends on the age of the sleeper (Dement, 1999). Newborns will sleep 6 to 8 times in 24 hours, often totaling more than 16 hours. Their napping cycle gets consolidated into "sleeping through the night," usually sometime between 9 and 18 months, but occasionally even later. The typical 6-year-old child might need 11 or 12 hours of sleep, and the progression to less sleep then continues into adulthood, when the average is about 7 to 7.5 hours per night. With aging, people can get along with even a bit less sleep than that. Over a whole lifetime, we get about 1 hour of sleep for every 2 hours we are awake.

This is a lot of sleeping. Could we tolerate less? Monitored by William Dement, Randy Gardner stayed up for 264 hours and 12 minutes in 1965 for a science project. When 17-year-old Randy finally did go to sleep, he slept only 14 hours and 40 minutes and awakened essentially recovered (Dement, 1978).

Feats like this one suggest that sleep might be expendable. This is the theory behind the classic all-nighter that you may have tried on the way to a rough exam. But it turns out that this theory is mistaken. Robert Stickgold and his colleagues (2000) found that when people learning a difficult perceptual task are kept up all night after they have finished practicing the task, their learning of the task is wiped out. Even after two nights of catch-up sleep, they show little indication of their initial training on the task. Sleep following learning appears to be essential for memory consolidation (see Hot Science: Sleep on It, p. 233 in the Memory chapter). It is as though memories normally deteriorate unless sleep occurs to help keep them in place. Studying all night may help you cram for the exam, but it won't make the material stick, which pretty much defeats the whole point.

> **What is the relationship between sleep and learning?**

Sleep turns out to be a necessity rather than a luxury in other ways as well. At the extreme, sleep loss can be fatal. When rats are forced to break Randy Gardner's human waking record and stay awake even longer, they have trouble regulating their body temperature and lose weight although they eat much more than normal. Their bodily systems break down and they die, on average, in 21 days (Rechtshaffen et al., 1983). Shakespeare called sleep "nature's soft nurse," and it is clear that even for healthy young humans, a few hours of sleep deprivation each night can have a cumulative detrimental effect: reducing mental acuity and reaction time, increasing irritability and depression, and increasing the risk of accidents and injury (Coren, 1997).

Some studies have deprived people of different sleep stages selectively by waking them whenever certain stages are detected. Studies of REM sleep deprivation indicate that this part of sleep is important psychologically. Memory problems and excessive aggression are observed in both humans and rats after only a few days of being wakened whenever REM activity starts (Ellman et al., 1991). The brain must value something about REM sleep because REM deprivation causes a rebound of more REM sleep the next night (Brunner et al., 1990). Deprivation from slow-wave sleep (in stages 3 and 4), in turn, has more physical effects, with just a few nights of deprivation leaving people feeling tired, fatigued, and hypersensitive to muscle and bone pain (Lentz et al., 1999).

It's clearly dangerous to neglect the need for sleep. But why would we have such a need in the first place? All animals appear to sleep, although the amount of sleep required varies quite a bit (see **FIGURE 5.11**). Giraffes sleep less than 2 hours daily, whereas brown bats snooze for almost 20 hours. These variations in sleep needs, and the very existence of a need, are hard to explain. Is the restoration that happens during the unconsciousness of sleep something that simply can't be achieved during consciousness? Sleep is, after all, potentially costly in the course of evolution. The

SONDA DAWES/THE IMAGE WORKS

Sleep following learning is essential for memory consolidation. Sleep during class, on the other hand, not so much.

insomnia
Difficulty in falling asleep or staying asleep.

AVERAGE DAILY SLEEP TOTALS

BOTTLENOSE DOLPHIN
BROWN BAT
GIRAFFE
HUMAN
ELEPHANT
CHIMPANZEE   RABBIT   GERBIL   TIGER

HOURS
0   5   10   15   20
1.9 3.5   8.0   9.7 10.4 11.4   13.1   15.8   19.9

◄ Figure **5.11** All animals and insects seem to require sleep, although in differing amounts. Next time you oversleep and someone accuses you of "sleeping like a baby," you might tell them that instead that you were sleeping like a tiger, or a brown bat.

sleeping animal is easy prey, so the habit of sleep would not seem to have developed so widely across species unless it had significant benefits that made up for this vulnerability. Theories of sleep have not yet determined why the brain and body have evolved to need these recurring episodes of unconsciousness.

Sleep Disorders

In answer to the question, "Did you sleep well?," comedian Stephen Wright said, "No, I made a couple of mistakes." Sleeping well is something everyone would love to do, but for many people, sleep disorders are deeply troubling. The most common disorders that plague sleep include insomnia, sleep apnea, and somnambulism.

Insomnia, *difficulty in falling asleep or staying asleep,* is perhaps the most common sleep disorder. About 30–48% of people report symptoms of insomnia, 9–15% report insomnia severe enough to lead to daytime complaints, and 6% of people meet criteria for a diagnosis of insomnia, which requires persistent and impairing sleep problems (Bootzin & Epstein, 2011; Ohayon, 2002). Unfortunately, insomnia often is a persistent problem and most people with insomnia experience it for at least a year (Morin et al., 2009).

There are many potential causes of insomnia. In some instances it results from lifestyle choices such as working night shifts (self-induced insomnia), whereas in other cases it occurs in response to depression, anxiety, or some other condition (secondary insomnia), and in other cases there are no obvious causal factors (primary insomnia). Regardless of type, insomnia can be exacerbated by worrying about insomnia (Borkevec, 1982). No doubt you've experienced some nights when sleeping was a high priority, such as before a class presentation or an important interview, and you've found that you were unable to fall asleep. The desire to sleep initiates an ironic process of mental control—a heightened sensitivity to signs of sleeplessness—and this sensitivity interferes with sleep. In fact, participants in an experiment who were instructed to go to sleep quickly became hypersensitive and had more difficulty sleeping than those who were not instructed to hurry (Ansfield, Wegner, & Bowser, 1996). The paradoxical solution for insomnia in some cases, then, may be to give up the pursuit of sleep and instead find something else to do.

Giving up on trying so hard to sleep is probably better than another common remedy—the use of sleeping pills. Although sedatives can be

INSOMNIA JEOPARDY

WAYS IN WHICH PEOPLE HAVE WRONGED ME	STRANGE NOISES	DISEASES I PROBABLY HAVE	MONEY TROUBLES	WHY DID I SAY/DO THAT?	IDEAS FOR A SCREENPLAY
$10	$10	$10	$10	$10	$10
$20	$20	$20	$20	$20	$20
$30	$30	$30	$30	$30	$30
$40	$40	$40	$40	$40	$40
$50	$50	$50	$50	$50	$50

R. Chast

useful for brief sleep problems associated with emotional events, their long-term use is not effective. To begin with, most sleeping pills are addictive. People become dependent on the pills to sleep and may need to increase the dose over time to achieve the same effect. Even in short-term use, sedatives can interfere with the normal sleep cycle. Although they promote sleep, they can reduce the proportion of time spent in REM and slow-wave sleep (Qureshi & Lee-Chiong, 2004), robbing people of dreams and their deepest sleep stages. As a result, the quality of sleep achieved with pills may not be as high as without, and there may be side effects such as grogginess and irritability during the day. Finally, stopping the use of sleeping pills suddenly can produce insomnia that is worse than before.

What are some problems caused by sleeping pills?

Sleep apnea is *a disorder in which the person stops breathing for brief periods while asleep.* A person with apnea usually snores because apnea involves an involuntary obstruction of the breathing passage. When episodes of apnea occur for over 10 seconds at a time and recur many times during the night, they may cause many awakenings and sleep loss or insomnia. Apnea occurs most often in middle-age overweight men (Punjabi, 2008) and may go undiagnosed because it is not easy for the sleeper to notice. Bed partners may be the ones who finally get tired of the snoring and noisy gasping for air when the sleeper's breathing restarts, or the sleeper may eventually seek treatment because of excessive sleepiness during the day. Therapies involving weight loss, drugs, sleep masks that push air into the nasal passage, or surgery may solve the problem.

Somnambulism (or **sleepwalking**), occurs when *a person arises and walks around while asleep.* Sleepwalking is more common in children, peaking between the ages of 4 and 8 years, with 15–40% of children experiencing at least one episode (Bhargava, 2011). Sleepwalking tends to happen early in the night, usually in slow-wave sleep, and sleepwalkers may awaken during their walk or return to bed without waking, in which case they will probably not remember the episode in the morning. The sleepwalker's eyes are usually open in a glassy stare. Walking with hands outstretched is uncommon except in cartoons. Sleepwalking is not usually linked to any additional problems and is only problematic in that sleepwalkers sometimes engage in strange or unwise behaviors such as urinating in places other than the toilet and leaving the house while still sleeping. People who walk while they are sleeping do not tend to be very coordinated and can trip over furniture or fall down stairs. After all, they're sleeping. Contrary to popular belief, it is safe to wake sleepwalkers or lead them back to bed (but best to wait until after they finish their business).

Is it safe to wake a sleepwalker?

There are other sleep disorders that are less common. **Narcolepsy** is *a disorder in which sudden sleep attacks occur in the middle of waking activities.* Narcolepsy involves the intrusion of a dreaming state of sleep (with REM) into waking and is often accompanied by unrelenting excessive sleepiness and uncontrollable sleep attacks lasting from 30 seconds to 30 minutes. This disorder appears to have a genetic basis, as it runs in families, and can be treated effectively with medication. **Sleep paralysis** is *the experience of waking up unable to move* and is sometimes associated with narcolepsy. This eerie experience usually happens as you are awakening from REM sleep but before you have regained motor control. This period typically lasts only a few seconds or minutes and can be accompanied by hypnopompic (when awakening) or hypnagogic (when falling asleep) hallucinations in which dream content may appear to occur in the waking world. A very clever series of recent studies suggests that sleep paralysis accompanied by hypnopompic hallucinations of figures being in one's bedroom seems to explain many perceived instances of alien abductions and recovered memories of sexual abuse (aided by therapists who used hypnosis to help the sleepers

Sleepwalkers in cartoons have their arms outstretched and eyes closed, but that's just for cartoons. A real-life sleepwalker usually walks normally with eyes open, sometimes with a glassy look.

ESTHALTO/MATTHIEU SPOHN/GETTY IMAGES

[incorrectly] piece it all together; McNally & Clancy, 2005). **Night terrors** (or **sleep terrors**) are *abrupt awakenings with panic and intense emotional arousal.* These terrors, which occur most often in children and in only about 2% of adults (Ohayon, Guilleminault, & Priest, 1999), happen most often in non-REM sleep early in the sleep cycle and do not usually have dream content the sleeper can report.

To sum up, there is a lot going on when we close our eyes for the night. Humans follow a pretty regular sleep cycle, going through the five stages of sleep during the night. Disruptions to that cycle, either from sleep deprivation or sleep disorders, can produce consequences for waking consciousness. But something else happens during a night's sleep that affects our consciousness, both while asleep and when we wake up.

Dreams

Pioneering sleep researcher William C. Dement (1959) said, "Dreaming permits each and every one of us to be quietly and safely insane every night of our lives." Indeed, dreams do seem to have a touch of insanity about them. We experience crazy things in dreams, but even more bizarre is the fact that we are the writers, producers, and directors of the crazy things we experience. Just what are these experiences, and how can they be explained?

Dream Consciousness

Dreams depart dramatically from reality. You may dream of being naked in public, of falling from a great height, of sleeping through an important appointment, of your teeth being loose and falling out, or of being chased (Holloway, 2001). These things don't happen much in reality unless you're having a very bad life. The quality of consciousness in dreaming is also altered significantly from waking consciousness. There are five major characteristics of dream consciousness that distinguish it from the waking state (Hobson, 1988).

> **What distinguishes dream consciousness from the waking state?**

> We intensely feel *emotion,* whether it is bliss or terror or love or awe.
> Dream *thought* is illogical: The continuities of time, place, and person don't apply. You may find you are in one place and then another, for example, without any travel in between—or people may change identity from one dream scene to the next.
> *Sensation* is fully formed and meaningful; visual sensation is predominant, and you may also deeply experience sound, touch, and movement (although pain is very uncommon).
> Dreaming occurs with *uncritical acceptance,* as though the images and events are perfectly normal rather than bizarre.
> We have *difficulty remembering* the dream after it is over. People often remember dreams only if they are awakened during the dream and even then may lose recall for the dream within just a few minutes of waking. If waking memory were this bad, you'd be standing around half-naked in the street much of the time, having forgotten your destination, clothes, and lunch money.

Not all of our dreams are fantastic and surreal, however. Far from the adventures in nighttime insanity storied by Freud, dreams are often ordinary (Domhoff, 2007). We often dream about mundane topics that reflect prior waking experiences or "day residue." Current conscious concerns pop up (Nikles et al., 1998), along with images from the recent past. A dream may even incorporate sensations experienced during sleep, as when

sleep apnea
A disorder in which the person stops breathing for brief periods while asleep.

somnambulism (or sleepwalking)
Occurs when a person arises and walks around while asleep.

narcolepsy
A disorder in which sudden sleep attacks occur in the middle of waking activities.

sleep paralysis
The experience of waking up unable to move.

night terrors (or sleep terrors)
Abrupt awakenings with panic and intense emotional arousal.

Dreams often are quite intense, vivid, and illogical. This can lead to very cool experiences, such as that depicted in this scene from the movie *Inception.*

WARNER BROS/THE KOBAL COLLECTION/ART RESOURCE

GOETHE HOUSE AND MUSEUM/SNARK/ART RESOURCE, NY

The Nightmare, by Henry Fuseli (1790). Fuseli depicts not only a mare in this painting but also an incubus—an imp perched on the dreamer's chest that is traditionally associated with especially horrifying nightmares.

sleepers in one study were led to dream of water when drops were sprayed on their faces during REM sleep (Dement & Wolpert, 1958). The day residue does not usually include episodic memories, that is, complete daytime events replayed in the mind. Rather, dreams that reflect the day's experience tend to single out sensory experiences or objects from waking life. Rather than simply being a replay of that event, dreams often consist of "interleaved fragments of experience" from different times and places that our mind weaves together into a single story (Wamsley & Stickgold, 2011). For instance, after a fun day at the beach with your roommates, your dream that night might include cameo appearances by bouncing beach balls or a flock of seagulls. One study had research participants play the computer game Tetris and found that participants often reported dreaming about the Tetris geometrical figures falling down—even though they seldom reported dreams about being in the experiment or playing the game (Stickgold et al., 2001). Even severely amnesic individuals who couldn't recall playing the game at all reported Tetris-like images appearing in their dreams (Stickgold et al., 2000). The content of dreams takes snapshots from the day rather than retelling the stories of what you have done or seen. This means that dreams often come without clear plots or story lines, so they may not make a lot of sense.

Some of the most memorable dreams are nightmares, and these frightening dreams can wake up the dreamer (Levin & Nielsen, 2009). One set of daily dream logs from college undergraduates suggested that the average student has about 24 nightmares per year (Wood & Bootzin, 1990), although some people may have them as often as every night. Children have more nightmares than adults, and people who have experienced traumatic events are inclined to have nightmares that relive those events. Following the 1989 earthquake in the San Francisco Bay area, for example, college students who had experienced the quake reported more nightmares than those who had not and often reported that the dreams were about the quake (Wood et al., 1992). This effect of trauma may not only produce dreams of the traumatic event: When police officers experience "critical incidents" of conflict and danger, they tend to have more nightmares in general (Neylan et al., 2002).

Dream Theories

Dreams are puzzles that cry out to be solved. How could you not want to make sense out of these experiences? Although dreams may be fantastic and confusing, they are emotionally riveting, filled with vivid images from your own life, and they seem very real. The search for dream meaning goes all the way back to biblical figures, who interpreted dreams and looked for prophecies in them. In the Old Testament, the prophet Daniel (a favorite of three of the authors of this book) curried favor with King Nebuchadnezzar of Babylon by interpreting the king's dream. The question of what dreams mean has been burning since antiquity, mainly because the meaning of dreams is usually far from obvious.

In the first psychological theory of dreams, Freud (1900/1965) proposed that dreams are confusing and obscure because the dynamic unconscious creates them precisely *to be* confusing and obscure. According to Freud's theory, dreams represent wishes, and some of these wishes are so unacceptable, taboo, and anxiety producing that the mind can only express them in disguised form. Freud believed that many of the most unacceptable wishes are sexual. For instance, he would interpret a dream of a train going into a tunnel as symbolic of sexual intercourse. According to Freud, the **manifest content** of a dream, *a dream's apparent topic or superficial meaning,* is a smoke screen for its **latent content,** *a dream's true underlying meaning.* For example, a dream about a tree burning down in the park across the street from where a friend once lived (the manifest content) might represent a camouflaged wish for the death of the friend (the latent content). In this case, wishing for the death of a friend is unacceptable, so it is disguised as a tree on fire. The problem with Freud's approach is that there is an infinite number of potential interpretations of any dream and finding the correct one is a matter of guesswork—and of convincing the dreamer that one interpretation is superior to the others.

Although dreams may not represent elaborately hidden wishes, there is evidence that they do feature the return of suppressed thoughts. Researchers asked volunteers to think of a personal acquaintance and then to spend five minutes before going to bed writing down whatever came to mind (Wegner, Wenzlaff, & Kozak, 2004). Some participants were asked to suppress thoughts of this person as they wrote, others were asked to focus on thoughts of the person, and yet others were asked just to write freely about anything. The next morning, participants wrote dream reports. Overall, all participants mentioned dreaming more about the person they had named than about other people. But they most often dreamed of the person they named if they were in the group that had been assigned to suppress thoughts of the person the night before. This finding suggests that Freud was right to suspect that dreams harbor unwanted thoughts. Perhaps this is why actors dream of forgetting their lines, travelers dream of getting lost, and football players dream of fumbling the ball.

> **What is the evidence that we dream about our suppressed thoughts?**

Another key theory of dreaming is the **activation–synthesis model** (Hobson & McCarley, 1977). This theory proposes that *dreams are produced when the brain attempts to make sense of random neural activity that occurs during sleep.* During waking consciousness, the mind is devoted to interpreting lots of information that arrives

manifest content
A dream's apparent topic or superficial meaning.

latent content
A dream's true underlying meaning.

activation–synthesis model
The theory that dreams are produced when the brain attempts to make sense of random neural activity that occurs during sleep.

CULTURE & COMMUNITY

What Do Dreams Mean to Us around the World? A recent study (Morewedge & Norton, 2009) assessed how people from three different cultures evaluate their dreams. Participants were asked to rate different theories of dreaming on a scale of 1 (*do not agree at all*) to 7 (*agree completely*). A significant majority of students from the United States, South Korea, and India agreed with the Freudian theory that dreams have meanings. Only small percentages believed the other options, that dreams provide a means to solve problems, promote learning, or are by-products of unrelated brain activity. The accompanying figure illustrates the findings across all three cultural groups. It appears that in many parts of the world, people have an intuition that dreams contain something deep and relevant.

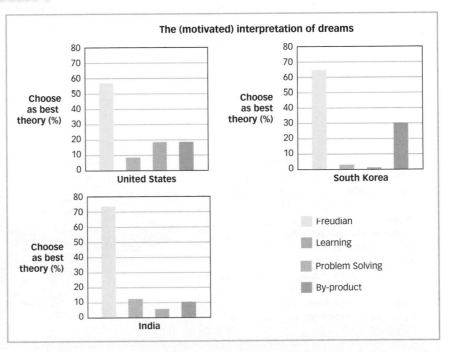

The (motivated) interpretation of dreams

Freudian
Learning
Problem Solving
By-product

BARBARA L. SALISBURY/THE WASHINGTON TIMES/LANDOV

Freud theorized that dreams represent unacceptable wishes that the mind can only express in disguised form. The activation-synthesis model proposes that dreams are produced when the mind attempts to make sense of random neural activity that occurs during sleep. Suppose a man is expecting a visit from his mother-in-law; the night before her arrival, he dreams that a bus is driven through the living room window of his house. How might Freud have interpreted such a dream? How might the activation-synthesis model interpret such a dream?

through the senses. You figure out that the odd noise you're hearing during class is your cell phone vibrating, for example, or you realize that the strange smell in the hall outside your room must be from burned popcorn. In the dream state, the mind doesn't have access to external sensations, but it keeps on doing what it usually does: interpreting information. Because that information now comes from neural activations that occur without the continuity provided by the perception of reality, the brain's interpretive mechanisms can run free. This might be why, for example, a person in a dream can sometimes change into someone else. There is no actual person being perceived to help the mind keep a stable view. In the mind's effort to perceive and give meaning to brain activation, the person you view in a dream about a grocery store might seem to be a clerk but then change to be your favorite teacher when the dream scene moves to your school. The great interest people have in interpreting their dreams the next morning may be an extension of the interpretive activity they've been doing all night.

The Freudian theory and the activation–synthesis theory differ in the significance they place on the meaning of dreams. In Freud's theory, dreams begin with meaning, whereas in the activation–synthesis theory, dreams begin randomly—but meaning can be added as the mind lends interpretations in the process of dreaming. Dream research has not yet sorted out whether one of these theories or yet another might be the best account of the meaning of dreams.

The Dreaming Brain

What happens in the brain when we dream? Several studies have made fMRI scans of people's brains during sleep, focusing on the areas of the brain that show changes in activation during REM periods. These studies show that the brain changes that occur during REM sleep correspond clearly with certain alterations of consciousness that occur in dreaming. **FIGURE 5.12** shows some of the patterns of activation and deactivation found in the dreaming brain (Nir & Tononi, 2010; Schwartz & Maquet, 2002).

In dreams there are heights to look down from, dangerous people lurking, the occasional monster, some minor worries, and at least once in a while that major exam you've forgotten about until you walk into class. These themes suggest that the brain areas responsible for fear or emotion somehow work overtime in dreams, and it turns out that this is clearly visible in fMRI scans. The amygdala is involved in responses

▶ Figure 5.12 **Brain Activation and Deactivation during REM Sleep** Brain areas shaded red are activated during REM sleep; those shaded blue are deactivated. (a) The medial view shows activation of the amygdala, the visual association areas, the motor cortex, and the brain stem and deactivation of the prefrontal cortex. (b) The ventral view shows activation of other visual association areas and deactivation of the prefrontal cortex (Schwartz & Maquet, 2002).

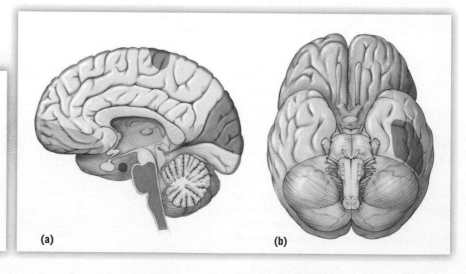

(a)   (b)

to threatening or stressful events, and indeed the amygdala is quite active during REM sleep.

The typical dream is also a visual wonderland, with visual events present in almost all dreams. However, there are fewer auditory sensations, even fewer tactile sensations, and almost no smells or tastes. This dream "picture show" doesn't involve actual perception, of course, just the imagination of visual events. It turns out that the areas of the brain responsible for visual perception are *not* activated during dreaming, whereas the visual association areas in the occipital lobe that are responsible for visual imagery *do* show activation (Braun et al., 1998). Your brain is smart enough to realize that it's not really seeing bizarre images but acts instead as though it's imagining bizarre images.

During REM sleep, the prefrontal cortex shows relatively less arousal than it usually does during waking consciousness. What does this mean for the dreamer? As a rule, the prefrontal areas are associated with planning and executing actions, and often dreams seem to be unplanned and rambling. Perhaps this is why dreams often don't have very sensible story lines—they've been scripted by an author whose ability to plan is inactive.

> **What do fMRIs tell us about why dreams don't have coherent story lines?**

Another odd fact of dreaming is that while the eyes are moving rapidly, the body is otherwise very still. During REM sleep, the motor cortex is activated, but spinal neurons running through the brain stem inhibit the expression of this motor activation (Lai & Siegal, 1999). This turns out to be a useful property of brain activation in dreaming; otherwise, you might get up and act out every dream! Individuals suffering from one rare sleep disorder, in fact, lose the normal muscular inhibition accompanying REM sleep and so act out their dreams, thrashing around in bed or stalking around the bedroom (Mahowald & Schenck, 2000). However, most people who are moving during sleep are probably not dreaming. The brain specifically inhibits movement during dreams, perhaps to keep us from hurting ourselves.

IN SUMMARY

▶ Sleeping and dreaming present a view of the mind in an altered state of consciousness.

▶ During a night's sleep, the brain passes in and out of five stages of sleep; most dreaming occurs in the REM sleep stage.

▶ Sleep needs decrease over the life span, but being deprived of sleep and dreams has psychological and physical costs.

▶ Sleep can be disrupted through disorders that include insomnia, sleep apnea, somnambulism, narcolepsy, sleep paralysis, and night terrors.

▶ In dreaming, the dreamer uncritically accepts changes in emotion, thought, and sensation but poorly remembers the dream on awakening.

▶ Theories of dreaming include Freud's psychoanalytic theory and the activation–synthesis model.

▶ fMRI studies of the brain in dreaming reveal activations associated with visual imagery, reductions of other sensations, increased sensitivity to emotions such as fear, lessened capacities for planning, and the prevention of movement.

Drugs and Consciousness: Artificial Inspiration

The author of the dystopian novel *Brave New World,* Aldous Huxley (1932), once wrote of his experiences with the drug mescaline. *The Doors of Perception* described the intense experience that accompanied his departure from normal consciousness. He described "a world where everything shone with the Inner Light, and was infinite in its significance. The legs, for example, of a chair—how miraculous their tubularity, how supernatural their polished smoothness! I spent several minutes—or was it several centuries?—not merely gazing at those bamboo legs, but actually *being* them" (Huxley, 1954, p. 22).

Being the legs of a chair? This probably is better than being the seat of a chair, but it still sounds like an odd experience. Still, many people seek out such experiences, often through using drugs. **Psychoactive drugs** are *chemicals that influence consciousness or behavior by altering the brain's chemical message system.* You read about several such drugs in the Neuroscience and Behavior chapter when we explored the brain's system of neurotransmitters. And you will read about them in a different light when we turn to their role in the treatment of psychological disorders in the Treatment chapter. Whether these drugs are used for entertainment, for treatment, or for other reasons, they each exert their influence by increasing the activity of a neurotransmitter (the agonists) or decreasing its activity (the antagonists).

Some of the most common neurotransmitters are serotonin, dopamine, gamma-aminobutyric acid (GABA), and acetylcholine. Drugs alter the functioning of neurotransmitters by preventing them from bonding to sites on the postsynaptic neuron, by inhibiting their reuptake to the presynaptic neuron, or by enhancing their bonding and transmission. Different drugs can intensify or dull transmission patterns, creating changes in brain electrical activities that mimic natural operations of the brain. For example, a drug such as Valium (benzodiazepine) induces sleep but prevents dreaming and so creates a state similar to slow-wave sleep, that is, what the brain naturally develops several times each night. Other drugs prompt patterns of brain activity that do not occur naturally, however, and their influence on consciousness can be dramatic. Like Huxley experiencing himself becoming the legs of a chair, people using drugs can have experiences unlike any they might find in normal waking consciousness or even in dreams. To understand these altered states, let's explore how people use and abuse drugs, and examine the major categories of psychoactive drugs.

Why do kids enjoy spinning around until they get so dizzy that they fall down? Even from a young age, there seems to be something enjoyable about altering states of consciousness.

MATTHEW NOCK

Drug Use and Abuse

Why do children sometimes spin around until they get dizzy and fall down? There is something strangely attractive about states of consciousness that depart from the norm, and people throughout history have sought out these altered states by dancing, fasting, chanting, meditating, and ingesting a bizarre assortment of chemicals to intoxicate themselves (Tart, 1969). People pursue altered consciousness even when there are costs, from the nausea that accompanies dizziness to the life-wrecking obsession with a drug that can come with addiction. In this regard, the pursuit of altered consciousness can be a fatal attraction.

Often, drug-induced changes in consciousness begin as pleasant and spark an initial attraction. Researchers have measured the attractiveness of psychoactive drugs by seeing how hard laboratory animals will work to get them. In one study researchers allowed rats to administer cocaine to themselves intravenously by pressing

What is the allure of altered consciousness?

a lever (Bozarth & Wise, 1985). Rats given free access to cocaine increased their use over the course of the 30-day study. They not only continued to self-administer at a high rate but also occasionally binged to the point of giving themselves convulsions. They stopped grooming themselves and eating until they lost on average almost a third of their body weight. About 90% of the rats died by the end of the study. Rats do show more attraction to sweets such as sugar or saccharine than they do to cocaine (Lenoir et al., 2007), but their interest in cocaine is deadly serious.

Rats are not tiny little humans, of course, so such research is not a firm basis for understanding human responses to cocaine. But these results do make it clear that cocaine is addictive and that the consequences of such addiction can be dire. Studies of self-administration of drugs in laboratory animals show that animals will work to obtain not only cocaine but also alcohol, amphetamines, barbiturates, caffeine, opiates (such as morphine and heroin), nicotine, phencyclidine (PCP), MDMA (Ecstasy), and THC (tetrahydrocannabinol, the active ingredient in marijuana). There are some psychoactive drugs that animals won't work for (such as mescaline or the antipsychotic drug phenothiazine), suggesting that these drugs have less potential for causing addiction (Bozarth, 1987).

People usually do not become addicted to a psychoactive drug the first time they use it. They may experiment a few times, then try again, and eventually find that their tendency to use the drug increases over time due to several factors, such as drug tolerance, physical dependence, and psychological dependence. **Drug tolerance** is *the tendency for larger drug doses to be required over time to achieve the same effect.* Physicians who prescribe morphine to control pain in their patients are faced with tolerance problems because steadily greater amounts of the drug may be needed to dampen the same pain. With increased tolerance comes the danger of drug overdose; recreational users find they need to use more and more of a drug to produce the same high. But then, if a new batch of heroin or cocaine is more concentrated than usual, the "normal" amount the user takes to achieve the same high can be fatal.

Self-administration of addictive drugs can also be prompted by withdrawal symptoms, which result when drug use is discontinued. Some withdrawal symptoms signal *physical dependence,* when pain, convulsions, hallucinations, or other unpleasant symptoms accompany withdrawal. People who suffer from physical dependence seek to continue drug use to avoid becoming physically ill. A common example is the "caffeine headache" some people complain of when they haven't had their daily jolt of java. Other withdrawal symptoms result from *psychological dependence,* a strong desire to return to the drug even when physical withdrawal symptoms are gone. Drugs can create an emotional need over time that continues to prey on the mind, particularly in circumstances that are reminders of the drug. Some ex-smokers report longing wistfully for an after-dinner smoke, for example, even years after they've successfully quit the habit.

What problems can arise in drug withdrawal?

Drug addiction reveals a human frailty: our inability to look past the immediate consequences of our behavior to see and appreciate the long-term consequences. Although we would like to think that our behavior is guided by a rational analysis of future consequences, more typically occasions when we "play first, pay later" lead directly to "let's just play a lot right now." There is something intensely inviting about the prospect of a soon-to-be-had pleasure and something pale, hazy, and distant about the costs this act might bring at some future time. For example, given the choice of receiving $1 today or $2 a week later, most people will take the $1 today. However, if the same choice is to be made for some date a year in the future (when the immediate pleasure of today's windfall is not so strong), people choose to wait and get the $2 (Ainslie, 2001). The immediate satisfaction associated with taking most drugs may outweigh a rational analysis of the later consequences that can result from taking those drugs, such as drug addiction.

psychoactive drugs
Chemicals that influence consciousness or behavior by altering the brain's chemical message system.

drug tolerance
The tendency for larger doses of a drug to be required over time to achieve the same effect.

Many soldiers serving in Vietnam became addicted to heroin while there. Robins and colleagues (1980) found that after returning home to the United States, the vast majority left their drug habit behind and were no longer addicted.

The psychological and social problems stemming from drug addiction are major. For many people, drug addiction becomes a way of life, and for some, it is a cause of death. Like the cocaine-addicted rats in the study noted earlier (Bozarth & Wise, 1985), some people become so attached to a drug that their lives are ruled by it. However, this is not always the end of the story. This ending is most well-known because the addict becomes a recurrent, visible social problem, "publicized" through repeated crime and repeated appearances in prisons and treatment programs. But a life of addiction is not the only possible end point of drug use. Stanley Schachter (1982) suggested that the visibility of addiction is misleading and that in fact many people overcome addictions. He found that 64% of a sample of people who had a history of cigarette smoking had quit successfully, although many had to try again and again to achieve their success. Indeed, large-scale studies conducted in the 1980s, 1990s, and 2000s consistently show that approximately 75% of those with substance use disorders overcome their addiction, with the biggest drop in use occurring between ages 20–30 (Heyman, 2009). One classic study of soldiers who became addicted to heroin in Vietnam found that, years after their return, only 12% remained addicted (Robins et al., 1980). The return to the attractions and obligations of normal life, as well as the absence of the familiar places and faces associated with their old drug habit, made it possible for returning soldiers to successfully quit. Although addiction is dangerous, it is not necessarily incurable.

What are the statistics on overcoming addiction?

It may not be accurate to view all recreational drug use under the umbrella of "addiction." Many people at this point in the history of Western society, for example, would not call the repeated use of caffeine an addiction, and some do not label the use of alcohol, tobacco, or marijuana in this way. In other times and places, however, each of these has been considered a terrifying addiction worthy of prohibition and public censure. In the early 17th century, for example, tobacco use was punishable by death in Germany, by castration in Russia, and by decapitation in China (Corti, 1931). Not a good time to be a smoker. By contrast, cocaine, heroin, marijuana, and amphetamines have each been popular and even recommended as medicines at several points throughout history, each without any stigma of addiction attached (Inciardi, 2001).

Although "addiction" as a concept is familiar to most of us, there is no standard clinical definition of what an addiction actually is. The concept of addiction has been extended to many human pursuits, giving rise to such terms as *sex addict*, *gambling addict*, *workaholic*, and, of course, *chocoholic*. Societies react differently at different times, with some uses of drugs ignored, other uses encouraged, others simply taxed, and yet others subjected to intense prohibition (see the Real World box on p. 212). Rather than viewing *all* drug use as a problem, it is important to consider the costs and benefits of such use and to establish ways to help people choose behaviors that are informed by this knowledge (Parrott et al., 2005).

"Hi, my name is Barry, and I check my E-mail two to three hundred times a day."

Types of Psychoactive Drugs

Four in five North Americans use caffeine in some form every day, but not all psychoactive drugs are this familiar. To learn how both the well-known and lesser-known drugs influence the mind, let's consider several broad categories of drugs: depressants, stimulants, narcotics, hallucinogens, and marijuana. **TABLE 5.3** summarizes what is known about the potential dangers of these different types of drugs.

Depressants

Depressants are *substances that reduce the activity of the central nervous system*. The most commonly used depressant is alcohol, and others include barbiturates, benzodiazepines, and toxic inhalants (such as glue or gasoline). Depressants have a sedative or calming effect, tend to induce sleep in high doses, and can arrest breathing in extremely high doses. Depressants can produce both physical and psychological dependence.

Alcohol. Alcohol is king of the depressants, with its worldwide use beginning in prehistory, its easy availability in most cultures, and its widespread acceptance as a socially approved substance. Fifty-two percent of Americans over 12 years of age report having had a drink in the past month, and 24% have binged on alcohol (over five drinks in succession) in that time. Young adults (ages 18–25) have even higher rates, with 62% reporting a drink the previous month and 42% reporting a binge (National Center for Health Statistics, 2012).

Alcohol's initial effects, euphoria and reduced anxiety, feel pretty positive. As it is consumed in greater quantities, drunkenness results, bringing slowed reactions, slurred speech, poor judgment, and other reductions in the effectiveness of thought and action. The exact way in which alcohol influences neural mechanisms is still not understood, but like other depressants, alcohol increases activity of the neurotransmitter GABA (De Witte, 1996). As you read in the Neuroscience and Behavior chapter, GABA normally inhibits the transmission of neural impulses, and so one effect of alcohol is as an inhibitor—a chemical that stops the firing of other neurons. But there are many contradictions. Some people using alcohol become loud and aggressive, others become emotional and weepy, others become sullen, and

depressants
Substances that reduce the activity of the central nervous system.

> Table 5.3

Dangers of Drugs

Drug	Dangers		
	Overdose (Can taking too much cause death or injury?)	Physical Dependence (Will stopping use make you sick?)	Psychological Dependence (Will you crave it when you stop using it?)
Depressants			
Alcohol	X	X	X
Benzodiazepines/Barbiturates	X	X	X
Toxic inhalants	X	X	X
Stimulants			
Amphetamines	X	X	X
MDMA (Ecstasy)	X		?
Nicotine	X	X	X
Cocaine	X	X	X
Narcotics (opium, heroin, morphine, methadone, codeine)	X	X	X
Hallucinogens (LSD, mescaline, psilocybin, PCP, ketamine)	X		?
Marijuana		?	?

expectancy theory
The idea that alcohol effects can be produced by people's expectations of how alcohol will influence them in particular situations.

balanced placebo design
A study design in which behavior is observed following the presence or absence of an actual stimulus and also following the presence or absence of a placebo stimulus.

alcohol myopia
A condition that results when alcohol hampers attention, leading people to respond in simple ways to complex situations.

stimulants
Substances that excite the central nervous system, heightening arousal and activity levels.

still others turn giddy—and the same person can experience each of these effects in different circumstances. How can one drug do this? Two theories have been offered to account for these variable effects: *expectancy theory* and *alcohol myopia*.

Why do people experience being drunk differently?

Expectancy theory suggests that *alcohol effects can be produced by people's expectations of how alcohol will influence them in particular situations* (Marlatt & Rohsenow, 1980). So, for instance, if you've watched friends or family drink at weddings and notice that this often produces hilarity and gregariousness, you could well experience these effects yourself should you drink alcohol on a similarly festive occasion. Seeing people getting drunk and fighting in bars, in turn, might lead to aggression after drinking.

The expectancy theory has been tested in studies that examine the effects of actual alcohol ingestion independent of the *perception* of alcohol ingestion. In experiments using a **balanced placebo design,** *behavior is observed following the presence or absence of an actual stimulus and also following the presence or absence of a placebo stimulus.* In such a study, participants are given drinks containing alcohol or a substitute liquid, and some people in each group are led to believe they had alcohol and others are led to believe they did not. People told they are drinking alcohol when they are not, for instance, might get a touch of vodka on the plastic lid of a cup to give it the right odor when the drink inside is merely tonic water. These experiments often show that the belief that one has had alcohol can influence behavior as strongly as the ingestion of alcohol itself (Goldman, Brown, & Christiansen, 1987). You may have seen people at parties getting rowdy after only one beer—perhaps because they expected this effect rather than because the beer actually had this influence.

Another approach to the varied effects of alcohol is the theory of **alcohol myopia,** which proposes that *alcohol hampers attention, leading people to respond in simple ways to complex situations* (Steele & Josephs, 1990). This theory recognizes that life is filled with complicated pushes and pulls, and our behavior is often a balancing act. Imagine that you are really attracted to someone who is dating your friend. Do you make your feelings known or focus on your friendship? The myopia theory holds that when you drink alcohol, your fine judgment is impaired. It becomes hard to appreciate the subtlety of these different options, and the inappropriate response is to veer full tilt one way or the other. So, alcohol might lead you to make a wild pass at your friend's

Which theory, expectancy theory or alcohol myopia, views a person's response to alcohol as being (at least partially) learned, through a process similar to observational learning?

date or perhaps just cry in your beer over your timidity—depending on which way you happened to tilt in your myopic state.

In one study on the alcohol myopia theory, men (half of whom were drinking alcohol) watched a video showing an unfriendly woman and then were asked how acceptable it would be for a man to act sexually aggressive toward a woman (Johnson, Noel, & Sutter-Hernandez, 2000). The unfriendly woman seemed to remind them that sex was out of the question, and indeed, men who were drinking alcohol and had seen this video were no more likely to think sexual advances were acceptable than men who were sober. However, when the same question was asked of a group of men who had seen a video of a *friendly* woman, those who were drinking were more inclined to recommend sexual overtures than those who were not, even when these overtures might be unwanted. Apparently, alcohol makes the complicated decisions involved in relationships seem simple ("Gee, she was so friendly")—and potentially open to serious misjudgments.

Both the expectancy and myopia theories suggest that people using alcohol will often go to extremes (Cooper, 2006). In fact, it seems that drinking is a major contributing factor to social problems that result from extreme behavior. Drinking while driving is a main cause of auto accidents. Twenty-two percent of drivers involved in fatal car crashes in 2009 had a blood alcohol level of .08% or higher (U.S. Census Bureau, 2012). A survey of undergraduate women revealed that alcohol contributes to approximately 76% of cases of incapacitated rape (rape after the victim is incapacitated by self-induced intoxication) and 72% of drug- or alcohol-facilitated rapes (in which the perpetrator deliberately intoxicates the victim prior to rape; McCauley et al., 2009).

Barbiturates, Benzodiazepines, and Toxic Inhalants. Compared to alcohol, the other depressants are much less popular but still are widely used and abused. Barbiturates such as Seconal or Nembutal are prescribed as sleep aids and as anesthetics before surgery. Benzodiazepines such as Valium and Xanax are also called minor tranquilizers and are prescribed as antianxiety drugs. These drugs are prescribed by physicians to treat anxiety or sleep problems, but they are dangerous when used in combination with alcohol because they can cause respiratory depression. Physical dependence is possible because withdrawal from long-term use can produce severe symptoms (including convulsions), and psychological dependence is common as well. Finally, toxic inhalants are perhaps the most alarming substances in this category (Ridenour & Howard, 2012). These drugs are easily accessible even to children in the vapors of household products such as glue, hair spray, nail polish remover, or gasoline. Sniffing or "huffing" vapors from these products can promote temporary effects that resemble drunkenness, but overdoses can be lethal, and continued use holds the potential for permanent neurological damage (Howard et al., 2011).

People will often endure significant inconveniences to maintain their addictions.

Stimulants

Stimulants are *substances that excite the central nervous system, heightening arousal and activity levels.* They include caffeine, amphetamines, nicotine, cocaine, modafinil, and Ecstasy, and sometimes have a legitimate pharmaceutical purpose. Amphetamines (also called *speed*), for example, were originally prepared for medicinal uses and as diet drugs; however, amphetamines such as Methedrine and Dexedrine are widely abused, causing insomnia, aggression, and paranoia with long-term use. Stimulants increase the levels of dopamine and norepinephrine in the brain, thereby inducing higher levels of activity in the brain circuits that depend on these neurotransmitters. As a result, they increase alertness and energy in the user, often producing a euphoric sense of confidence and a kind of agitated motivation to get things done. Stimulants produce physical and psychological dependence, and their withdrawal symptoms involve depressive effects such as fatigue and negative emotions.

? Do stimulants create dependency?

Ecstasy (also known as MDMA, "X," or "E"), an amphetamine derivative, is a stimulant but it has added effects somewhat like those of hallucinogens (we'll talk about those shortly). Ecstasy is particularly known for making users feel empathic and close to those around them. It is used often as a party drug to enhance the group feeling at dance clubs or raves, but it has unpleasant side effects such as causing jaw clenching and interfering with the regulation of body temperature. The rave culture has popularized pacifiers and juices as remedies for these problems, but users remain highly susceptible to heatstroke and exhaustion. Although Ecstasy is not as likely as some other drugs to cause physical or psychological dependence, it nonetheless can lead to some dependence. What's more, the impurities sometimes found in street pills are also dangerous (Parrott, 2001). Ecstasy's potentially toxic effect on serotonin neurons in the human brain is under debate, although mounting evidence from animal and human studies suggests that sustained use is associated with damage to serotonergic neurons and potentially associated problems with mood, attention and memory, and impulse control (Kish et al., 2010; Urban et al., 2012).

Cocaine is derived from leaves of the coca plant, which has been cultivated by indigenous peoples of the Andes for millennia and chewed as a medication. Yes, the urban legend is true: Coca-Cola contained cocaine until 1903 and still may use coca leaves (with cocaine removed) as a flavoring—although the company's not telling (Pepsi-Cola never contained cocaine and is probably made from something brown). Sigmund Freud tried cocaine and wrote effusively about it for a while. Cocaine (usually snorted) and crack cocaine (smoked) produce exhilaration and euphoria and are seriously addictive, both for humans and the rats you read about earlier in this chapter. Withdrawal takes the form of an unpleasant crash, and dangerous side effects of cocaine use include both psychological problems such as insomnia, depres-

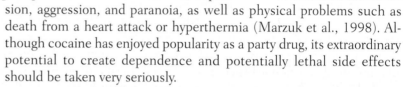

What are some of the dangerous side effects of cocaine use?

sion, aggression, and paranoia, as well as physical problems such as death from a heart attack or hyperthermia (Marzuk et al., 1998). Although cocaine has enjoyed popularity as a party drug, its extraordinary potential to create dependence and potentially lethal side effects should be taken very seriously.

Nicotine is something of a puzzle. This is a drug with almost nothing to recommend it to the newcomer. It usually involves inhaling smoke that doesn't smell that great, at least at first, and there's not much in the way of a high either—at best, some dizziness or a queasy feeling. So why do people do it? Tobacco use is motivated far more by the unpleasantness of quitting than by the pleasantness of using. The positive effects people report from smoking—relaxation and improved concentration, for example—come chiefly from relief from withdrawal symptoms (Baker, Brandon, & Chassin, 2004). The best approach to nicotine is to never get started.

IMAGEBROKER.NET/SUPERSTOCK

Smoking tobacco can be very difficult to quit. NPR recently reported one interesting strategy being tried in Japan is filling ashtrays with soap and encouraging people to blow bubbles rather than smoke cigarettes.

Narcotics

Opium, which comes from poppy seeds, and its derivatives heroin, morphine, methadone, and codeine (as well as prescription drugs such as Demerol and Oxycontin), are known as **narcotics** (or **opiates**), *highly addictive drugs derived from opium that relieve pain.* Narcotics induce a feeling of well-being and relaxation that is enjoyable but can also induce stupor and lethargy. The addictive properties of narcotics are powerful, and long-term use produces both tolerance and dependence. Because these drugs are often administered with hypodermic syringes, they also introduce the danger of diseases such as HIV when users share syringes. Unfortunately, these drugs are especially alluring because they mimic the brain's own internal relaxation and well-being system.

Why are narcotics especially alluring?

The brain produces endogenous opioids or endorphins, which are neurotransmitters closely related to opiates. As you learned in the Neuroscience & Behavior chapter, endorphins play a role in how the brain copes internally with pain and stress. These substances reduce the experience of pain naturally. When you exercise for a while and start to feel your muscles burning, for example, you may also find that there comes a time when the pain eases—sometimes even *during* exercise. Endorphins are secreted in the pituitary gland and other brain sites as a response to injury or exertion, creating a kind of natural remedy (like the so-called runner's high) that subsequently reduces pain and increases feelings of well-being. When people use narcotics, the brain's endorphin receptors are artificially flooded, however, reducing receptor effectiveness and possibly also depressing the production of endorphins. When external administration of narcotics stops, withdrawal symptoms are likely to occur.

Hallucinogens

The drugs that produce the most extreme alterations of consciousness are the **hallucinogens,** *drugs that alter sensation and perception, and often cause visual and auditory hallucinations.* These include LSD (lysergic acid diethylamide, or acid), mescaline, psilocybin, PCP (phencyclidine), and ketamine (an animal anesthetic). Some of these drugs are derived from plants (mescaline from peyote cactus, psilocybin or "shrooms" from mushrooms) and have been used by people since ancient times. For example, the ingestion of peyote plays a prominent role in some Native American religious practices. The other hallucinogens are largely synthetic. LSD was first made by chemist Albert Hofman in 1938, leading to a rash of experimentation that influenced popular culture in the 1960s. Timothy Leary, at the time a lecturer in the Department of Psychology at Harvard, championed the use of LSD to "turn on, tune in, and drop out"; the Beatles sang of "*Lucy in the Sky with Diamonds*" (denying, of course, that this might be a reference to LSD); and the wave of interest led many people to experiment with hallucinogens.

The experiment was not a great success. These drugs produce profound changes in perception. Sensations may seem unusually intense, stationary objects may seem to move or change, patterns or colors may appear, and these perceptions may be accompanied by exaggerated emotions ranging from blissful transcendence to abject terror. These are the "I've-become-the-legs-of-a-chair!" drugs. But the effects of hallucinogens are dramatic and unpredictable, creating a psychological roller-coaster ride that some people find intriguing and others find deeply disturbing. Hallucinogens are the main class of drugs that animals won't work to self-administer, so it is not surprising that in humans these drugs are unlikely to be addictive. Hallucinogens do not induce significant tolerance or dependence, and overdose deaths are rare. Although hallucinogens still enjoy a marginal popularity with people interested in experimenting with their perceptions, they have been more a cultural trend than a dangerous attraction.

What are the effects of hallucinogens?

Marijuana

Marijuana (or **cannabis**) *is a plant whose leaves and buds contain a psychoactive drug called tetrahydrocannabinol (THC).* When smoked or eaten, either as is or in concentrated form as *hashish,* this drug produces an intoxication that is mildly hallucinogenic. Users describe the experience as euphoric, with heightened senses of sight and sound and the perception of a rush of ideas. Marijuana affects judgment and short-term memory, and impairs motor skills and coordination—making driving a car or operating heavy equipment a poor choice during its use ("Dude, where's my bulldozer?"). Researchers have found that receptors in the brain that respond to THC (Stephens, 1999) are normally activated by a neurotransmitter called *anandamide* that is naturally produced in the brain (Wiley, 1999). Anandamide is involved in the regulation of mood, memory, appetite, and pain perception and has been found temporarily to stimulate overeating in laboratory animals, much as marijuana does in humans (Williams & Kirkham, 1999). Some chemicals found in dark chocolate also mimic anandamide, although very weakly, perhaps accounting for the well-being some people claim they enjoy after a "dose" of chocolate.

The addiction potential of marijuana is not strong, as tolerance does not seem to develop, and physical withdrawal symptoms are minimal. Psychological dependence is possible, however, and some people do become chronic users. Marijuana use has been

Psychedelic art and music of the 1960s were inspired by some visual and auditory effects of drugs such as LSD.

narcotics (or opiates)
Highly addictive drugs derived from opium that relieve pain.

hallucinogens
Drugs that alter sensation and perception and often cause visual and auditory hallucinations.

marijuana
The leaves and buds of the hemp plant, which contain a psychoactive drug called tetrahydrocannabinol (THC).

widespread throughout the world for recorded history, both as a medicine for pain and/or nausea and as a recreational drug, but its use remains controversial. Marijuana abuse and dependence have been linked with increased risk of depression, anxiety, and other forms of psychopathology. Many people also are concerned that marijuana (along with alcohol and tobacco) is a **gateway drug,** *a drug whose use increases the risk of the subsequent use of more harmful drugs.* The gateway theory has gained mixed support, with recent studies challenging this theory and suggesting that early-onset drug use in general, regard-

> **What are the risks of marijuana use?**

less of type of drug, increases the risk of later drug problems (Degenhardt et al., 2010). Because of the harm attributed to marijuana use, the U.S. government classifies marijuana as a Schedule I Controlled Substance, recognizing no medical use and maintaining that marijuana has the same high potential for abuse as other drugs like heroin. Despite the federal laws against the use of marijuana, approximately 42% of adults in the United States reported using it at some point in their lives—a rate much higher than that observed in most other countries (Degenhardt et al., 2008). Perhaps due to the perceived acceptability of marijuana among the general public, several states recently have taken steps to permit the sale of marijuana for medical purposes, decriminalize possession of marijuana (so violators pay a fine rather than

THE REAL WORLD

Drugs and the Regulation of Consciousness

Everyone has an opinion about drug use. Given that it's not possible to perceive what happens in anyone else's mind, why does it matter to us what people do to their own consciousness? Is consciousness something that governments should be able to legislate? Or should people be free to choose their own conscious states (McWilliams, 1993)? After all, how can a "free society" justify regulating what people do inside their own heads?

Individuals and governments alike answer these questions by pointing to the costs of drug addiction, both to the addict and to the society that must "carry" unproductive people, pay for their welfare, and often even take care of their children. Drug users appear to be troublemakers and criminals, the culprits behind all those drug-related shootings, knifings, and robberies you see in the news every day. Widespread anger about the drug problem surfaced in the form of the War on Drugs, a federal government program born in the Nixon years that focused on drug use as a criminal offense and attempted to stop drug use through the imprisonment of users.

Drug use did not stop with 40 years of the War on Drugs though, and instead, prisons filled with people arrested for drug use. From 1990 to 2007, the number of drug offenders in state and federal prisons increased from 179,070 to 348,736—a jump of 94% (Bureau of Justice Statistics, 2008)—not because of a measurable increase in drug use, but because of the rapidly increasing use of imprisonment for drug offenses. Many people who were being prevented from ruining their lives with drugs were instead having their lives ruined by prison. Like the failed policy of alcohol Prohibition from 1920 to 1933

▲ There are many reasons that U.S. prisons are overcrowded—this country has the highest incarceration rate in the world. Treating drug abuse as a crime that requires imprisonment is one of the reasons.

going to jail), or to legalize its sale and possession outright. The debate about the legal status of marijuana will likely take years to resolve. In the meantime, depending on where you live, the greatest risk of marijuana use may be incarceration (see The Real World: Drugs and the Regulation of Consciousness).

gateway drug
A drug whose use increases the risk of the subsequent use of more harmful drugs.

harm reduction approach
A response to high-risk behaviors that focuses on reducing the harm such behaviors have on people's lives.

IN SUMMARY

▶ Psychoactive drugs influence consciousness by altering the brain's chemical messaging system and intensifying or dulling the effects of neurotransmitters.

▶ Drug tolerance can result in overdose, and physical and psychological dependence can lead to addiction.

▶ Major types of psychoactive drugs include depressants, stimulants, narcotics, hallucinogens, and marijuana.

▶ The varying effects of alcohol, a depressant, are explained by theories of alcohol expectancy and alcohol myopia.

(Trebach & Zeese, 1992), the policy of the drug war seemed to be causing more harm than it was preventing.

What can be done? The policy of the Obama administration is to wind down the war mentality and instead focus on reducing the harm that drugs cause (Fields, 2009). This **harm reduction approach** is *a response to high-risk behaviors that focuses on reducing the harm such behaviors have on people's lives* (Marlatt & Witkiewitz, 2010). Harm reduction originated in the Netherlands and England with tactics such as eliminating criminal penalties for some drug use or providing intravenous drug users with sterile syringes to help them avoid contracting HIV and other infections from shared needles (Des Jarlais et al., 2009). Harm reduction may even involve providing drugs for addicts to reduce the risks of poisoning and overdose they face when they get impure drugs of unknown dosage from criminal suppliers. A harm reduction idea for alcoholics, in turn, is to meet people where they are (in terms of their current level of drinking), and not to condemn their drinking behavior but to allow moderate drinking while minimizing the harmful effects of heavy drinking (Marlatt & Witkiewitz, 2010). Harm reduction strategies do not always find public

IAN CUMMING/AXIOM/AURORA PHOTOS

◀ In the Netherlands, marijuana use is not prosecuted. The drug is sold in "coffee shops" to those over 18.

support because they challenge the popular idea that the solution to drug and alcohol problems must always be prohibition: stopping use entirely.

There appears to be increasing support for the idea that people should be free to decide whether they want to use substances to alter their consciousness, especially when use of the substance carries a medical benefit, such as decreased nausea, decreased insomnia, and increased appetite. Since 1996, 18 states and the District of Columbia have enacted laws to legalize the use of marijuana for medical purposes. On

November 6, 2012, Colorado and Washington became the first two states to legalize marijuana for purely recreational purposes. The fact that marijuana continues to be a Schedule I Controlled Substance under federal law complicates matters and it may take years before the legal issues involved are fully resolved. Indeed, upon learning of the passing of the legalization initiative, Colorado Governor John Hickenlooper warned citizens of Colorado: "Federal law still says marijuana is an illegal drug so don't break out the Cheetos or Goldfish too quickly."

Hypnosis: Open to Suggestion

You may have never been hypnotized, but you have probably heard or read about it. Its wonders are often described with an air of amazement, and demonstrations of stage hypnosis make it seem very powerful and mysterious. When you think of hypnosis, you may envision people completely under the power of a hypnotist, who is ordering them to dance like a chicken or perhaps "regress" to early childhood and talk in childlike voices. Many common beliefs about hypnosis are false. **Hypnosis** refers to *a social interaction in which one person (the hypnotist) makes suggestions that lead to a change in another person's (the subject's) subjective experience of the world* (Kirsch et al., 2011). The essence of hypnosis is in leading people to expect that certain things will happen to them that are outside their conscious will (Wegner, 2002).

Induction and Susceptibility

To induce hypnosis, a hypnotist may ask the person to be hypnotized to sit quietly and focus on some item, such as a spot on the wall (or a swinging pocket watch), and then make suggestions to the person about what effects hypnosis will have (e.g., "your eyelids are slowly closing" or "your arms are getting heavy"). Even without hypnosis, some suggested behaviors might commonly happen just because a person is concentrating on them—just thinking about their eyelids slowly closing, for instance, may make many people shut their eyes briefly or at least blink. In hypnosis, however, suggestions may be made—and followed by people in a susceptible state of mind—for very unusual behavior that most people would not normally do, such as flapping their arms and making loud clucking sounds

Not everyone is equally hypnotizable. Susceptibility varies greatly. Some highly suggestible people are very easily hypnotized, most people are only moderately influenced, and some people are entirely unaffected by attempts at hypnosis. Susceptibility is not easily predicted by a person's personality traits. A hypnotist will typically test someone's hypnotic susceptibility with a series of suggestions designed to put a person into a more easily influenced

> **What makes someone easy to hypnotize?**

state of mind. One of the best indicators of a person's susceptibility is the person's own judgment. So, if you think you might be hypnotizable, you may well be (Hilgard, 1965). People with active, vivid imaginations, or who are easily absorbed in activities such as watching a movie, are also somewhat more prone to be good candidates for hypnosis (Sheehan, 1979; Tellegen & Atkinson, 1974).

Hypnotic Effects

From watching stage hypnotism, you might think that the major effect of hypnosis is making people do peculiar things. So what do we actually know to be true about hypnosis? There are some impressive demonstrations that suggest real changes occur in those under hypnosis. At the 1849 festivities for Prince Albert of England's birthday, for example, a hypnotized guest was asked to ignore any loud noises and then didn't even flinch when a pistol was fired near his face. These days, hypnotists are discouraged from using firearms during stage shows, but they often have volunteers perform other impressive feats. One common claim for superhuman strength under hypnosis involves asking a hypnotized person to become "stiff as a board" and lie unsupported with shoulders on one chair and feet on another while the hypnotist stands on the hypnotized person's body.

Studies have demonstrated that hypnosis can undermine memory, but with important limitations. People susceptible to hypnosis can be led to experience **posthypnotic amnesia,** *the failure to retrieve memories following hypnotic suggestions to forget.* Ernest Hilgard (1986) taught a hypnotized person the populations of some

hypnosis
A social interaction in which one person (the hypnotist) makes suggestions that lead to a change in another person's (the subject's) subjective experience of the world.

posthypnotic amnesia
The failure to retrieve memories following hypnotic suggestions to forget.

hypnotic analgesia
The reduction of pain through hypnosis in people who are susceptible to hypnosis.

remote cities, for example, and then suggested that the participant forget the study session; the person was quite surprised after the session at being able to give the census figures correctly. Asked how he knew the answers, the individual decided he might have learned them from a TV program. Such amnesia can then be reversed in subsequent hypnosis.

Importantly, research has found that only memories that were lost under hypnosis can be retrieved through hypnosis. The false claim that hypnosis helps people to unearth memories that they are not able to retrieve in normal consciousness seems to have surfaced because hypnotized people often make up memories to satisfy the hypnotist's suggestions. For example, Paul Ingram, a sheriff's deputy accused of sexual abuse by his daughters in the 1980s, was asked by interrogators in session after session to relax and imagine having committed the crimes. He emerged from these sessions having confessed to dozens of horrendous acts of "satanic ritual abuse." These confessions were called into question, however, when independent investigator Richard Ofshe used the same technique to ask Ingram about a crime that Ofshe had simply made up out of thin air, something of which Ingram had never been accused. Ingram produced a three-page handwritten confession, complete with dialogue (Ofshe, 1992). Still, prosecutors in the case accepted Ingram's guilty plea, and he was only released in 2003 after a public outcry and years of work on his defense. After a person claims to remember something, even under hypnosis, it is difficult to convince others that the memory was false (Loftus & Ketchum, 1994).

Hypnosis can lead to measurable physical and behavioral changes in the body. One well-established effect is **hypnotic analgesia,** *the reduction of pain through hypnosis in people who are susceptible to hypnosis.* For example, one study (see **FIGURE 5.13**) found that for pain induced in volunteers in the laboratory, hypnosis was more effective than morphine, diazepam (Valium), aspirin, acupuncture, or placebos (Stern et al., 1977). For people who are hypnotically susceptible, hypnosis can be used to control pain in surgeries and dental procedures, in some cases more effectively than any form of anesthesia (Druckman & Bjork, 1994; Kihlstrom, 1985).

> **What evidence supports the idea that hypnosis leads to observable changes in the body?**

Stage hypnotists often perform an induction on the whole audience and then bring some of the more susceptible members on stage for further demonstrations.

PHOTOGRAPHER: MENELAOS PROKOS (WWW.ATHOUSANDCLICKS.COM)
HYPNOTIST: ERIC WALDEN (HTTPS://WWW.FACEBOOK.COM/HYPNOTISTERIC)

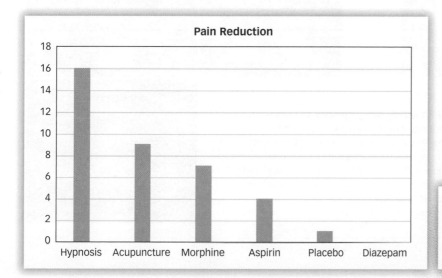

◄ Figure **5.13 Hypnotic Analgesia** The degree of pain reduction reported by people using different techniques for the treatment of laboratory-induced pain. Hypnosis wins (Stern et al., 1977).

Hypnosis also has been shown to enable people to control mental processes previously believed to be beyond conscious control. For instance, the Stroop task (Stroop, 1935) is a classic psychological test in which a person is asked to name the color of words on a page (appearing in ink that is red, blue, green, etc.). This is a simple task. However, sometimes the words themselves are the names of colors, but are printed in a different color of the ink. It turns out that people are significantly slower, and make more errors, when naming ink colors that don't match the content of the word (e.g., when the word "green" is written in red ink) than if the content is neutral or congruent (e.g., if the word "desk" or "red" is written in red ink). This effect is present no matter how hard we try. Amazingly, the effect is completely eliminated when highly suggestible people are hypnotized and told to respond to all words the same way (Raz et al., 2002). Importantly, though, follow-up studies have revealed that hypnotic induction is not required to eliminate the Stroop effect. It turns out that simply suggesting to highly suggestible people that they should respond to all words the same has the same effect as hypnosis (Lifshitz, et al., 2013). This suggests that hypnotic effects may be the result of highly suggestible people complying with the suggestions of others.

Nevertheless, people under hypnotic suggestion are not merely telling the hypnotist what they want to hear. Instead, they seem to be experiencing what they have been asked to experience. Under hypnotic suggestion, for example, regions of the brain responsible for color vision are activated in highly hypnotizable people when they are asked to perceive color, even when they are really shown gray stimuli (Kosslyn et al., 2000). While engaged in the Stroop task, people who can eliminate the Stroop effect under suggestion show decreased activity in the anterior cingulate cortex (ACC), the part of the brain involved in conflict monitoring (**FIGURE 5.14**; Raz, Fan, & Posner 2005), consistent with the lack of conflict perceived between the color name and ink. Overall, hypnotic suggestion appears to change the subjective perception of those experiencing it, as reflected by changes in their self-report, behavior, and brain activity.

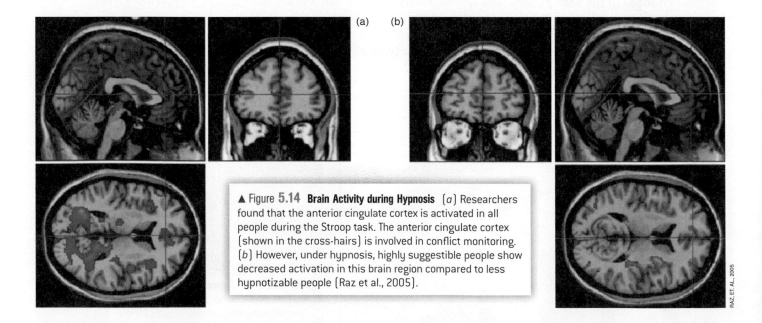

(a)   (b)

▲ Figure **5.14 Brain Activity during Hypnosis** (a) Researchers found that the anterior cingulate cortex is activated in all people during the Stroop task. The anterior cingulate cortex (shown in the cross-hairs) is involved in conflict monitoring. (b) However, under hypnosis, highly suggestible people show decreased activation in this brain region compared to less hypnotizable people (Raz et al., 2005).

RAZ, ET. AL., 2005

IN SUMMARY

▶ Hypnosis is an altered state of consciousness characterized by suggestibility.

▶ Although many claims for hypnosis overstate its effects, hypnosis can create the experience that one's actions are occurring involuntarily, create analgesia, and even change brain activations in ways that suggest that hypnotic experiences are more than imagination.

OTHER VOICES

A Judge's Plea for Pot

The Honorable Gustin L. Reichbach served as a New York State Supreme Court Justice from 1999 until 2012. He died of pancreatic cancer in July 2012.

PHOTO: © RICK KOPSTEIN

Should all drugs be illegal? Where should we draw the line between acceptable chemical alteration of one's own consciousness and criminal or pathological behavior? Let's take a specific example—think for a minute about where you stand on the legalization of marijuana. The Honorable Gustin L. Reichbach (2012, p. A27), a New York State Supreme Court Justice, recently wrote a strongly worded piece (slightly condensed here) on this issue, although his position surprised many people.

Three and a half years ago, on my 62nd birthday, doctors discovered a mass on my pancreas. It turned out to be Stage 3 pancreatic cancer. I was told I would be dead in four to six months. Today I am in that rare coterie of people who have survived this long with the disease. But I did not foresee that after having dedicated myself for 40 years to a life of the law, including more than two decades as a New York State judge, my quest for ameliorative and palliative care would lead me to marijuana.

My survival has demanded an enormous price, including months of chemotherapy, radiation hell and brutal surgery. For about a year, my cancer disappeared, only to return. About a month ago, I started a new and even more debilitating course of treatment. Every other week, after receiving an IV booster of chemotherapy drugs that takes three hours, I wear a pump that slowly injects more of the drugs over the next 48 hours.

Nausea and pain are constant companions. One struggles to eat enough to stave off the dramatic weight loss that is part of this disease. Eating, one of the great pleasures of life, has now become a daily battle, with each forkful a small victory. Every drug prescribed to treat one problem leads to one or two more drugs to offset its side effects. Pain medication leads to loss of appetite and constipation. Anti-nausea medication raises glucose levels, a serious problem for me with my pancreas so compromised. Sleep, which might bring respite from the miseries of the day, becomes increasingly elusive.

Inhaled marijuana is the only medicine that gives me some relief from nausea, stimulates my appetite, and makes it easier to fall asleep. The oral synthetic substitute, Marinol, prescribed by my doctors, was useless. Rather than watch the agony of my suffering, friends have chosen, at some personal risk, to provide the substance. I find a few puffs of marijuana before dinner gives me ammunition in the battle to eat. A few more puffs at bedtime permits desperately needed sleep.

This is not a law-and-order issue; it is a medical and a human rights issue. Being treated at Memorial Sloan Kettering Cancer Center, I am receiving the absolute gold standard of medical care. But doctors cannot be expected to do what the law prohibits, even when they know it is in the best interests of their patients. When palliative care is understood as a fundamental human and medical right, marijuana for medical use should be beyond controversy. . . .

Cancer is a nonpartisan disease, so ubiquitous that it's impossible to imagine that there are legislators whose families have not also been touched by this scourge. It is to help all who have been affected by cancer, and those who will come after, that I now speak. Given my position as a sitting judge still hearing cases, well-meaning friends question the wisdom of my coming out on this issue. But I recognize that fellow cancer sufferers may be unable, for a host of reasons, to give voice to our plight. It is another heartbreaking aporia in the world of cancer that the one drug that gives relief without deleterious side effects remains classified as a narcotic with no medicinal value.

Because criminalizing an effective medical technique affects the fair administration of justice, I feel obliged to speak out as both a judge and a cancer patient suffering with a fatal disease. . . . Medical science has not yet found a cure, but it is barbaric to deny us access to one substance that has proved to ameliorate our suffering.

How should we decide which consciousness-altering substances are OK for members of our society to use, and which should be made illegal? What criteria would you propose? Should this decision be based on negative health consequences associated with use of the substance? What weight should be given to positive consequences, such as those described by Justice Reichbach? Research described in this chapter tested, and failed to support, the gateway theory of drug use. If you had the opportunity to design and conduct one study to answer a key question in this area, what would you do?

Chapter Review

KEY CONCEPT QUIZ

1. Which of the following is NOT a basic property of consciousness?
   a. intentionality
   b. disunity
   c. selectivity
   d. transience

2. Currently, unconscious processes are understood as
   a. a concentrated pattern of thought suppression.
   b. a hidden system of memories, instincts, and desires.
   c. a blank slate.
   d. unexperienced mental processes that give rise to thoughts and behavior.

3. The _____ unconscious is at work when subliminal and unconscious processes influence thought and behavior.
   a. minimal
   b. repressive
   c. dynamic
   d. cognitive

4. The cycle of sleep and waking is one of the major patterns of human life called
   a. the circadian rhythm.
   b. the sleep stages.
   c. the altered state of consciousness.
   d. subliminal perception.

5. Sleep needs _____ over the life span.
   a. decrease
   b. increase
   c. fluctuate
   d. remain the same

6. During dreaming, the dreamer _____ changes in emotion, thought, and sensation.
   a. is skeptical of
   b. is completely unconscious of
   c. uncritically accepts
   d. views objectively

7. Which explanation of dreams proposes that they are produced when the mind attempts to make sense of random neural activity that occurs in the brain during sleep?
   a. Freud's psychoanalytic theory
   b. the activation–synthesis model
   c. the cognitive unconscious model
   d. the manifest content framework

8. fMRI studies of the dreaming brain reveal all of the following EXCEPT
   a. increased sensitivity to emotions.
   b. activations associated with visual activity.
   c. increased capacity for planning.
   d. prevention of movement.

9. Psychoactive drugs influence consciousness by altering the effects of
   a. agonists.
   b. neurotransmitters.
   c. amphetamines.
   d. spinal neurons.

10. Tolerance for drugs involves
    a. larger doses being required over time to achieve the same effect.
    b. openness to new experiences.
    c. the initial attraction of drug use.
    d. the lessening of the painful symptoms that accompany withdrawal.

11. Drugs that heighten arousal and activity levels by affecting the central nervous system are
    a. depressants.
    b. stimulants.
    c. narcotics.
    d. hallucinogens.

12. Alcohol expectancy refers to
    a. alcohol's initial effects of euphoria and reduced anxiety.
    b. the widespread acceptance of alcohol as a socially approved substance.
    c. alcohol leading people to respond in simple ways to complex situations.
    d. people's beliefs about how alcohol will influence them in particular situations.

13. Hypnosis has been proven to have
    a. an effect on physical strength.
    b. a positive effect on memory retrieval.
    c. an analgesic effect.
    d. an age-regression effect.

14. Which of the following four individuals is LEAST likely to be a good candidate for hypnosis?
    a. Jake, who spends lots of time watching movies
    b. Ava, who is convinced she is easily hypnotizable
    c. Evan, who has an active, vivid imagination
    d. Isabel, who loves to play sports

KEY TERMS

consciousness (p. 178)
phenomenology (p. 179)
problem of other minds (p. 179)
mind–body problem (p. 180)

dichotic listening (p. 182)
cocktail-party phenomenon (p. 182)
minimal consciousness (p. 184)
full consciousness (p. 184)

self-consciousness (p. 184)
mental control (p. 188)
thought suppression (p. 188)

rebound effect of thought suppression (p. 189)
ironic processes of mental control (p. 189)

dynamic unconscious (p. 190)

repression (p. 190)

cognitive unconscious (p. 191)

subliminal perception (p. 191)

altered state of consciousness (p. 193)

circadian rhythm (p. 193)

REM sleep (p. 194)

electrooculograph (EOG) (p. 194)

insomnia (p. 197)

sleep apnea (p. 198)

somnambulism (or sleepwalking) (p. 198)

narcolepsy (p. 198)

sleep paralysis (p. 198)

night terrors (or sleep terrors) (p. 199)

manifest content (p. 200)

latent content (p. 200)

activation–synthesis model (p. 201)

psychoactive drugs (p. 204)

drug tolerance (p. 205)

depressants (p. 207)

expectancy theory (p. 208)

balanced placebo design (p. 208)

alcohol myopia (p. 208)

stimulants (p. 209)

narcotics (or opiates) (p. 210)

hallucinogens (p. 211)

marijuana (or cannabis) (p. 211)

gateway drug (p. 212)

harm reduction approach (p. 213)

hypnosis (p. 214)

posthypnotic amnesia (p. 214)

hypnotic analgesia (p. 215)

CHANGING MINDS

1. "I had a really weird dream last night," your friend tells you. "I dreamed that I was trying to fly like a bird but I kept flying into clotheslines. I looked it up online, and dreams where you're struggling to fly mean that there is someone in your life who's standing in your way and preventing you from moving forward. I suppose that has to be my boyfriend, so maybe I'd better break up with him." Based on what you've read in this chapter, what would you tell your friend about the reliability of dream interpretation?

2. During an early-morning class, you notice your friend yawning, and you ask if he slept well the night before. "On weekdays, I'm in class all day, and I work the night shift," he says. "So I don't sleep much during the week. But I figure it's okay because I make up for it by sleeping in late on Saturday mornings." Is it realistic for your friend to assume

that he can balance regular sleep deprivation with rebound sleep on the weekends?

3. You and a friend are watching the 2010 movie *Inception*, starring Leonardo DiCaprio as a corporate spy. DiCaprio's character is hired by a businessman named Saito to plant an idea in the unconscious mind of a competitor while he sleeps. According to the plan, when the competitor awakens, he'll be compelled to act on the idea, to the secret benefit of Saito's company. "It's a cool idea," your friend says, "but it's pure science fiction. There's no such thing as an unconscious mind, and no way that unconscious ideas could influence the way you act when you're conscious." What would you tell your friend? What evidence do we have that the unconscious mind exists and can influence conscious behavior?

ANSWERS TO KEY CONCEPT QUIZ

1. b; 2. d; 3. d; 4. a; 5. a; 6. c; 7. b; 8. c; 9. b; 10. a; 11. b; 12. d; 13. c; 14. d

Need more help? Additional resources are located in LaunchPad at:
http://www.worthpublishers.com/launchpad/schacter3e

Memory

Jill Price was 12 years old when she began to suspect that she possessed an unusually good memory. Studying for a seventh-grade science final on May 30th, her mind drifted and she became aware that she could recall vividly everything she had been doing on May 30th of the previous year. A month later, something similar happened: Enjoying vanilla custards at Paradise Cove near Los Angeles with her friend Kathy, Jill recalled that they had done the same thing precisely a year earlier. Expecting that Kathy would recall the episode as easily as she did, Jill was surprised when Kathy replied blankly: "We did?"

Remembering specifics of events that occurred a year ago may not seem so extraordinary—you can probably recall what you did for your last birthday, or where you spent last Thanksgiving—but can you recall the details of what you did exactly 1 year ago today? Or what you did a week, a month, 6 months, or 6 years before that day? Probably not, but Jill Price can.

As she grew older, Jill's memory flashes became even more frequent. Now in her late 40s, Jill can recall clearly and in great detail what has happened to her *every single day since early 1980* (Price & Davis, 2008). This is not just Jill's subjective impression. Dr. James McGaugh, a well-known memory researcher based at the University of California–Irvine, and his colleagues tested Jill's memory over a period of a few years and came up with some shocking results (Parker, Cahill, & McGaugh, 2006). For example, they asked Jill to recall the dates of each Easter from 1980 to 2003, which is a pretty tough task considering that Easter can fall on any day between March 22nd and April 15th. Even though she had no idea that she would be asked this question, Jill recalled the correct dates quickly and easily; nobody else the researchers tested came close. When Jill was asked about the dates of public events that had occurred years earlier (Rodney King beating? O. J. Simpson verdict? Bombing at Atlanta Olympics?), she rattled off the correct answers without a hitch (March 3, 1991; October 3, 1995; July 26, 1996). The researchers also asked Jill about the details of what she had been doing on various randomly chosen dates, and they checked Jill's recall against her personal diary. Again,

Jill Price can accurately remember just about everything that has happened to her during the past 30 years, as confirmed by her diary, but Jill's extraordinary memory is more of a curse than a blessing.

DAN TUFFS CONTRIBUTOR, GETTY IMAGES

memory
The ability to store and retrieve information over time.

encoding
The process of transforming what we perceive, think, or feel into an enduring memory.

storage
The process of maintaining information in memory over time.

retrieval
The process of bringing to mind information that has been previously encoded and stored.

Jill answered quickly and accurately: *July 1, 1986?*—"I see it all, that day, that month, that summer. Tuesday. Went with (friend's name) to (restaurant name)." *October 3, 1987?*—"That was a Saturday. Hung out at the apartment all weekend, wearing a sling—hurt my elbow." *April 27, 1994?*—"That was Wednesday. That was easy for me because I knew where I was exactly. I was down in Florida. I was summoned to come down and to say goodbye to my grandmother who they all thought was dying but she ended up living" (Parker et al., 2006, pp. 39–40).

Jill's memory is a gift we'd all love to have—right? Not necessarily. Here's what Jill has to say about her ability: "Most have called it a gift but I call it a burden. I run my entire life through my head every day and it drives me crazy!!!" (Parker et al., 2006, p. 35).

Researchers still don't understand all the reasons why Jill Price can remember her past so much more fully than the rest of us, but it turns out that Jill is not alone. Jill's extraordinary memory abilities became widely known after a *60 Minutes* story that featured her and Dr. McGaugh. That story elicited a flurry of inquiries to Dr. McGaugh from other people around the world who thought that they, too, possessed the spectacular memory abilities demonstrated by Jill. Although most of them did not, McGaugh and his colleagues identified 11 other individuals with "highly superior autobiographical memory" abilities that resemble those they had seen in Jill Price (LePort et al., 2012). The researchers discovered differences in the structure of several brain regions known to be involved in memory in the superior autobiographical memory group compared with a control group, suggesting that further study of these unusual individuals might help to understand the nature of memory more generally.

MEMORY *IS THE ABILITY TO STORE AND RETRIEVE INFORMATION OVER TIME.* Even though few of us possess the extraordinary memory abilities of Jill Price and the handful of others with highly superior autobiographical memory, each of us has a unique identity that is intricately tied to the things we have thought, felt, done, and experienced. Memories are the residue of those events, the enduring changes that experience makes in our brains and leaves behind when it passes. If an experience passes without leaving a trace, it might just as well not have happened. But as Jill's story suggests, remembering all that has happened is not necessarily a good thing, either—a point we'll explore more fully later in the chapter.

The ease with which someone like Jill can instantly remember her past shouldn't blind us from appreciating how complex that act of remembering really is. Because memory is so remarkably complex, it is also remarkably fragile (Schacter, 1996). We all have had the experience of forgetting something we desperately wanted to remember or of remembering something that never really happened. Why does memory serve us so well in some situations and play such cruel tricks on us in other cases? When can we trust our memories and when should we view them skeptically? Is there just one kind of memory, or are there many? These are among the questions that psychologists have asked and answered.

As you've seen in other chapters, the mind's mistakes provide key insights into its fundamental operation, and there is no better illustration of this than in the realm of memory. In this chapter, we will consider the three key functions of memory: **encoding,** *the process of transforming what we perceive, think, or feel into an enduring memory;* **storage,** *the process of maintaining information in memory over time;* and **retrieval,** *the process of bringing to mind information that has been previously encoded and stored.* We'll then examine several different kinds of memory and focus on the ways in which errors, distortions, and imperfections can reveal the nature of memory itself.

Encoding: Transforming Perceptions into Memories

Bubbles P., a professional gambler with no formal education, who spent most of his time shooting craps at local clubs or playing high-stakes poker, had no difficulty rattling off 20 numbers, in either forward or backward order, after just a single glance (Ceci, DeSimone, & Johnson, 1992). Most people can listen to a list of numbers and then repeat them from memory—as long as the list is no more than about seven items long (try it for yourself using **FIGURE 6.1**).

How did Bubbles accomplish his astounding feats of memory? For at least 2,000 years, people have thought of memory as a recording device that makes exact copies of information that comes in through our senses, and then stores those copies for later use. This idea is simple and intuitive. It is also completely incorrect. Memories are made by combining information we *already* have in our brains with new information that comes in through our senses. In this way memory is like cooking; starting from a recipe but improvising along the way, we add old information to new information, mix, shake, bake, and out pops a memory. Memories are *constructed,* not recorded, and encoding is the process by which we transform what we perceive, think, or feel into an enduring memory. Let's look at three types of encoding processes—semantic encoding, visual imagery encoding, and organizational encoding—and then consider the possible survival value of encoding for our ancestors.

> **How is making a memory like following a recipe?**

```
            2 8
           6 9 1
          0 4 7 3
         8 7 4 5 4
        9 0 2 4 8 1
       5 7 4 2 2 9 6
      6 4 7 1 9 3 0 4
     3 5 6 7 1 8 4 8 5
    1 0 2 8 8 3 4 7 2 9
   4 7 2 0 8 2 7 4 2 6 4
  7 3 1 0 9 3 4 3 5 1 3 8
```

◄ Figure **6.1** **Digit Memory Test** How many digits can you remember? Start on the first row and cover the rows below it with a piece of paper. Study the numbers in the row for 1 second and then cover that row back up again. After a couple of seconds, try to repeat the numbers. Then uncover the row to see if you were correct. If so, continue down to the next row, using the same instructions, until you can't recall all the numbers in a row. The number of digits in the last row you can remember correctly is your digit span. Bubbles P. could remember 20 random numbers, or about five rows deep. How did you do?

Semantic Encoding

Memories are a combination of old and new information, so the nature of any particular memory depends as much on the old information already in our memories as it does on the new information coming in through our senses. In other words, how we remember something depends on how we think about it at the time. For example, as a professional gambler, Bubbles found numbers unusually meaningful, so when he saw a string of digits, he tended to think about their meanings. He might have thought about how they related to his latest bet at the racetrack or to his winnings after a long night at the poker table. Whereas you might try to memorize the string 22061823 by saying it over and over, Bubbles would think about betting $220 at 6-to-1 odds on horse number 8 to place 2nd in the 3rd race. Indeed, when Bubbles was tested with materials other than numbers—faces, words, objects, or locations—his memory performance was no better than average.

In one study, researchers presented participants with a series of words and asked them to make one of three types of judgments (Craik & Tulving, 1975): *semantic judgments* required the participants to think about the meaning of the words (Is *hat* a type of clothing?); *rhyme judgments* required the participants to think about the sound of the words (Does *hat* rhyme with *cat*?); and

> Have you ever wondered why you can remember 20 experiences (your favorite camping trip, your 16th birthday party, your first day at college, etc.) but not 20 digits? One reason is that we often think about the meaning behind our experiences, so we semantically encode them without even trying (Craik & Tulving, 1975).

ISTOCKPHOTO/THINKSTOCK

semantic encoding
The process of relating new information in a meaningful way to knowledge that is already stored in memory.

visual imagery encoding
The process of storing new information by converting it into mental pictures.

organizational encoding
The process of categorizing information according to the relationships among a series of items.

visual judgments required the participants to think about the appearance of the words (Is *HAT* written uppercase or lowercase?). The type of judgment task influenced how participants thought about each word—what old information they combined with the new—and had a powerful impact on their memories. Those participants who made semantic judgments (i.e., had thought about the meaning of the words) had much better memory for the words than did participants who thought about how the word looked or sounded. The results of these and many other studies have shown that long-term retention is greatly enhanced by **semantic encoding,** *the process of relating new information in a meaningful way to knowledge that is already stored in memory* (Brown & Craik, 2000).

> **Which is most effective, semantic, rhyme, or visual judgment, and why?**

So where does this semantic encoding take place? What's going on in the brain when this type of information processing occurs? Studies reveal that semantic encoding is uniquely associated with increased activity in the lower left part of the frontal lobe and the inner part of the left temporal lobe (**FIGURE 6.2a**; Demb et al., 1995; Kapur et al., 1994; Wagner et al., 1998). In fact, the amount of activity in each of these two regions during encoding is directly related to whether people later remember an item. The more activity there is in these areas, the more likely the person will remember the information.

Visual Imagery Encoding

In Athens in 477 BCE, the Greek poet Simonides had just left a banquet when the ceiling collapsed and killed all the people inside. Simonides was able to name every one of the dead simply by visualizing each chair around the banquet table and recalling the person who had been sitting there. Simonides wasn't the first, but he was among the most proficient, to use **visual imagery encoding,** *the process of storing new information by converting it into mental pictures.*

If you wanted to use Simonides' method to create an enduring memory, you could simply convert the information that you wanted to remember into a visual image and then store it in a familiar location. For instance, if you were going to the grocery store and wanted to remember to buy Coke, popcorn, and cheese dip, you could use the rooms in your house as locations and imagine your living room flooded in Coke, your bedroom pillows stuffed with popcorn, and your bathtub as a greasy pond of cheese dip. When you arrived at the store, you could then take a mental walk around your house and "look" into each room to remember the items you needed to purchase.

Semantic encoding involves relating new information in a meaningful way to facts you already know; visual imagery encoding involves storing new information by converting it into mental pictures. How might you use both kinds of encoding to help store a new fact, such as the date of a friend's birthday that falls on, say, November 24th?

RADIUS IMAGES/ALAMY

Numerous experiments have shown that visual imagery encoding can substantially improve memory. In one experiment, participants who studied lists of words by creating visual images of them later recalled twice as many items as participants who just mentally repeated the words (Schnorr & Atkinson, 1969). Why does visual imagery encoding work so well? First, visual imagery encoding does some of the same things that semantic encoding does: When you create a visual image, you relate incoming information to knowledge already in memory. For example, a visual image of a parked car might help you create a link to your memory of your first kiss.

> **How does visual encoding influence memory?**

Second, when you use visual imagery to encode words and other verbal information, you end up with two different mental *placeholders* for the items—a visual one and a verbal one—which gives you more ways to remember them than just a verbal

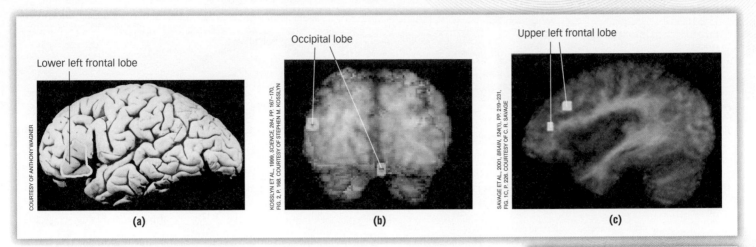

Lower left frontal lobe

COURTESY OF ANTHONY WAGNER

(a)

Occipital lobe

KOSSLYN ET AL., 1999, SCIENCE, 284, PP. 167–170, FIG. 2, P. 168. COURTESY OF STEPHEN M. KOSSLYN

(b)

Upper left frontal lobe

SAVAGE ET AL., 2001, BRAIN, 124(1), PP. 219–231, FIG. 1C, P. 226. COURTESY OF C. R. SAVAGE

(c)

placeholder alone (Paivio, 1971, 1986). Visual imagery encoding activates visual processing regions in the occipital lobe (see **FIGURE 6.2b**), which suggests that people actually enlist the visual system when forming memories based on mental images (Kosslyn et al., 1993).

Organizational Encoding

Have you ever ordered dinner with a group of friends and watched in amazement as your server took the order without writing anything down? To find out how this is done, one researcher spent 3 months working in a restaurant where servers routinely wrote down orders but then left the check at the customer's table before proceeding to the kitchen and *telling* the cooks what to make (Stevens, 1988). The researcher wired the servers with microphones and asked them to think aloud, that is, to say what they were thinking as they walked around all day doing their jobs. The researcher found that as soon as the server left a customer's table, he or she immediately began *grouping* or *categorizing* the orders into hot drinks, cold drinks, hot foods, and cold foods. The servers grouped the items into a sequence that matched the layout of the kitchen, first placing drink orders, then hot food orders, and finally cold food orders. The servers remembered their orders by relying on **organizational encoding,** *the process of categorizing information according to the relationships among a series of items.*

For example, suppose you had to memorize the words *peach, cow, chair, apple, table, cherry, lion, couch, horse, desk.* The task seems difficult, but if you organize the items into three categories—fruit (*peach, apple, cherry*), animals (*cow, lion, horse*), and furniture (*chair, table, couch, desk*)—the task becomes much easier. Studies have shown that instructing people to sort items into categories like this is an effective way to enhance their subsequent recall of those items (Mandler, 1967). Even more complex organizational schemes have been used, such as the hierarchy in **FIGURE 6.3** (Bower et al., 1969). People can improve their recall of individual items by organizing them into multiple-level categories, all the way from a general category such as *animals*, through intermediate categories such as *birds* and *songbirds*, down to specific examples such as *wren* and *sparrow*.

> **Why might mentally organizing the material for an exam enhance your retrieval of that material?**

▲ Figure **6.2 Brain Activity during Different Types of Judgments** fMRI studies reveal that different parts of the brain are active during different types of judgments: (*a*) During semantic judgments, the lower left frontal lobe is active; (*b*) during visual judgments, the occipital lobe is active; and (*c*) during organizational judgments, the upper left frontal lobe is active.

Ever wonder how a server remembers who ordered the pizza and who ordered the fries without writing anything down? Some have figured out how to use organizational encoding.

JEFF GREENBERG/ALAMY

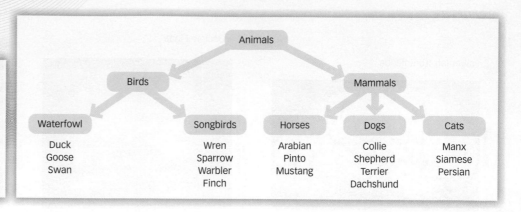

► Figure **6.3** **Organizing Words into a Hierarchy** Organizing words into conceptual groups and relating them to one another—such as in this example of a hierarchy—makes it easier to reconstruct the items from memory later (Bower et al., 1969). Keeping track of the 17 items in this example can be facilitated by remembering the hierarchical groupings they fall under.

Just as semantic and visual imagery encoding activates distinct regions of the brain, so, too, does organizational encoding. As you can see in **FIGURE 6.2c**, organizational encoding activates the upper surface of the left frontal lobe (Fletcher, Shallice, & Dolan, 1998; Savage et al., 2001). Different types of encoding strategies appear to rely on different areas of brain activation.

Encoding of Survival-Related Information

Encoding new information is critical to many aspects of everyday life—prospects for attaining your degree would be pretty slim without this ability—and the survival of our ancestors likely depended on encoding and later remembering such things as the sources of food and water or where a predator appeared (Nairne & Pandeirada, 2008; Sherry & Schacter, 1987).

Recent experiments have addressed these ideas by examining encoding of survival-related information. The experiments were motivated by an evolutionary perspective based on Darwin's principle of natural selection: The features of an organism that help it survive and reproduce are more likely than other features to be passed on to subsequent generations (see the Psychology: Evolution of a Science chapter). Therefore, memory mechanisms that help us to survive and reproduce should be preserved by natural selection, and our memory systems should be built in a way that allows us to remember especially well encoded information that is relevant to our survival.

To test this idea, the researchers gave participants three different encoding tasks (Nairne, Thompson, & Pandeirada, 2007). In the survival-encoding condition, participants were asked to imagine that they were stranded in the grasslands of a foreign land without any survival materials and that over the next few months they would need supplies of food and water and also need to protect themselves from predators. The researchers then showed participants randomly chosen words (e.g., *stone, meadow, chair*) and asked them to rate on a 1–5 scale how relevant each item would be to survival in the hypothetical situation. In the moving-encoding condition, a second group of participants was asked to imagine that they were planning to move to a new home in a foreign land, and to rate on a 1–5 scale how useful each item might be in helping them to set up a new home. Finally, in the pleasantness-encoding condition, a third group was shown the same words and asked to rate on a 1–5 scale the pleasantness of each word.

The findings, displayed in **FIGURE 6.4**, show that participants recalled more words after the survival-encoding task than after either the moving or pleasantness tasks. In later studies, the researchers found that survival encoding resulted in higher levels of recall than several other non-survival-encoding tasks involving semantic encoding, imagery encoding, or organizational encoding (Nairne, Pandeirada, & Thompson, 2008). Exactly what about survival encoding produces such high levels of memory?

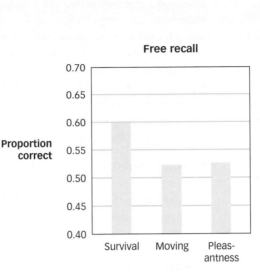

◄ Figure **6.4** **Survival Encoding Enhances Later Recall** What does a pouncing cougar that may threaten our survival have to do with recall? People recall more words after survival encoding (Nairne et al., 2007).

Survival encoding draws on elements of semantic, visual imagery, and organizational encoding, which may give it an advantage over any one of the other three (Burns, Hwang, & Burns, 2011). Also, survival encoding encourages participants to engage in extensive planning, which in turn benefits memory and may account for much of the benefit of survival encoding. For example, when participants imagine scenarios in which they are stranded in grasslands without food, and encode a series of words with respect to their survival relevance, survival scenarios that *do* involve planning produce superior subsequent memory compared with survival scenarios that do *not* involve planning. Critically, superior recall is also observed for scenarios that *involve planning but not survival*, such as planning a dinner party (Klein, Robertson, & Delton, 2011). Of course, planning for the future is itself critical for our long-term survival, so these findings are still broadly consistent with an evolutionary perspective in which memory is built to support planning and related forms of thinking about the future that enhance our chances of survival (Klein et al., 2011; Schacter, 2012; Suddendorf & Corballis, 2007).

IN SUMMARY

▶ Encoding is the process of transforming into a lasting memory the information our senses take in. Most instances of spectacular memory performance reflect the skillful use of encoding strategies rather than so-called photographic memory. Memory is influenced by the type of encoding we perform regardless of whether we consciously intend to remember an event or a fact.

▶ Semantic encoding, visual imagery encoding, and organizational encoding all increase memory, but they use different parts of the brain to accomplish that.

▶ Encoding information with respect to its survival value is a particularly effective method for increasing subsequent recall, perhaps because our memory systems have evolved in a way that allows us to remember especially well information that is relevant to our survival.

sensory memory
A type of storage that holds sensory information for a few seconds or less.

iconic memory
A fast-decaying store of visual information.

echoic memory
A fast-decaying store of auditory information.

Storage: Maintaining Memories over Time

Encoding is the process of turning perceptions into memories. But one of the hallmarks of a memory is that you can bring it to mind on Tuesday, not on Wednesday, and then bring it to mind again on Thursday. So where are our memories when we aren't using them? Clearly, those memories are stored in some form in your brain. As pointed out earlier, *storage is the process of maintaining information in memory over time*. There are three major kinds of memory storage: sensory, short-term, and long-term. As these names suggest, the three kinds of storage are distinguished primarily by the amount of time over which a memory is retained.

Sensory Storage

Sensory memory is *a type of storage that holds sensory information for a few seconds or less*. In a series of classic experiments, research participants were asked to remember rows of letters (Sperling, 1960). In one version of the procedure, participants viewed three rows of four letters each, as shown in **FIGURE 6.5**. The researcher flashed the letters on a screen for just 1/20th of a second. When asked to remember all 12 of the letters they had just seen, participants recalled fewer than half. There were two possible explanations for this: Either people simply couldn't encode all the letters in such a brief period of time, or they had encoded the letters but forgotten them while trying to recall everything they had seen.

To test the two ideas, the researcher relied on a clever trick. Just after the letters disappeared from the screen, a tone sounded that cued the participants to report the letters in a particular row. A *high* tone cued participants to report the contents of the top row, a *medium* tone cued participants to report the contents of the middle row, and a *low* tone cued participants to report the contents of the bottom row. When asked to report only a single row, people recalled almost all of the letters in that row! Because the tone sounded after the letters disappeared from the screen, the researchers concluded that people could have recalled the same number of letters from any of the rows, had they been asked. Participants had no way of knowing which of the three rows would be cued, so the researcher inferred that virtually all the letters had been encoded. In fact, if the tone was substantially delayed, participants couldn't perform the task because the information had slipped away from their sensory memories. Like the after image of a flashlight, the 12 letters flashed on a screen are visual icons, a lingering trace stored in memory for a very short period.

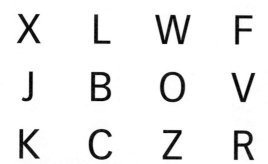

▲ Figure **6.5** **Iconic Memory Test** When a grid of letters is flashed on screen for only 1/20th of a second, it is difficult to recall individual letters. But if prompted to remember a particular row immediately after the grid is shown, research participants will do so with high accuracy. Sperling used this procedure to demonstrate that although iconic memory stores the whole grid, the information fades away too quickly for a person to recall everything (Sperling, 1960).

Because we have more than one sense, we have more than one kind of sensory memory. **Iconic memory** is *a fast-decaying store of visual information*. A similar storage area serves as a temporary warehouse for sounds. **Echoic memory** is *a fast-decaying store of auditory information*. When you have difficulty understanding what someone has just said, you probably find yourself replaying the last few words—listening to them echo in your "mind's ear," so to speak. When you do that, you are accessing information that is being held in your echoic memory store. The hallmark of both the iconic and echoic memory stores is that they hold information for a very short time. Iconic memories usually decay in about 1 second or less, and echoic memories usually decay in about 5 seconds (Darwin, Turvey, & Crowder, 1972). These two sensory memory stores are a bit like doughnut shops: The products come in, they sit briefly on the shelf, and then they are discarded. If you want one, you have to grab it fast.

> ? How long is information held in iconic and echoic memory before it decays?

Short-Term Storage and Working Memory

A second kind of memory storage is **short-term memory,** which *holds nonsensory information for more than a few seconds but less than a minute*. For example, if someone tells you a telephone number, you can usually repeat it back with ease—but only for a few seconds. In one study, research participants were given consonant strings to remember, such as DBX and HLM. After seeing each string, participants were asked to count backward from 100 by 3 for varying amounts of time and were then asked to recall the strings (Peterson & Peterson, 1959). As shown in **FIGURE 6.6**, memory for the consonant strings declined rapidly, from approximately 80% after a 3-second delay to less than 20% after a 20-second delay. These results suggest that information can be held in the short-term memory store for about 15 to 20 seconds.

What if 15 to 20 seconds isn't enough time? What if we need the information for a while longer? We can use a trick that allows us to get around the natural limitations of our short-term memories. **Rehearsal** is *the process of keeping information in short-term memory by mentally repeating it*. If someone gives you a telephone number and you can't put it immediately into your cell phone or write it down, you say it over and over to yourself until you can. Each time you repeat the number, you are reentering it into short-term memory, giving it another 15 to 20 seconds of shelf life.

> **Why is it helpful to repeat a telephone number you're trying to remember?**

Short-term memory is limited in how *long* it can hold information, and also limited in how *much* information it can hold. Not only can most people keep approximately seven numbers in short-term memory, but if they put more new numbers in, then old numbers begin to fall out (Miller, 1956). Short-term memory isn't limited to numbers, of course. It can also hold about seven letters or seven words—even though those seven words contain many more than seven letters. In fact, short-term memory can hold about seven *meaningful items* at once (Miller, 1956). Therefore, one way to increase storage is to group several letters into a single meaningful item. **Chunking** involves *combining small pieces of information into larger clusters or chunks that are more easily held in short-term memory*. Waitresses who use organizational encoding (p. xxx) to organize customer orders into groups are essentially chunking the information, giving themselves less to remember.

Short-term memory was originally conceived of as a kind of "place" where information is kept for a limited amount of time. More recently, researchers developed and refined a more dynamic model of a limited-capacity memory system, **working memory,** which refers to *active maintenance of information in short-term storage* (Baddeley & Hitch, 1974). Working memory includes subsystems that store and manipulate visual images or verbal information, as well as a central executive that coordinates the subsystems (Baddeley, 2001). If you wanted to keep the arrangement of pieces on a chessboard in mind as you contemplated your next move, you'd be relying on working memory. Working memory includes the visual representation of the positions of the pieces, your mental manipulation of the possible moves, and your awareness of the flow of information into and out of memory, all stored for a limited amount of time. In short, the working memory model acknowledges both the limited nature of this kind of memory storage and the activities that are commonly associated with it.

Research conducted in the context of this model has taught us that working memory plays an important role in many aspects of our cognitive lives. For example, studies

short-term memory
A type of storage that holds nonsensory information for more than a few seconds but less than a minute.

rehearsal
The process of keeping information in short-term memory by mentally repeating it.

chunking
Combining small pieces of information into larger clusters or chunks that are more easily held in short-term memory.

working memory
Active maintenance of information in short-term storage.

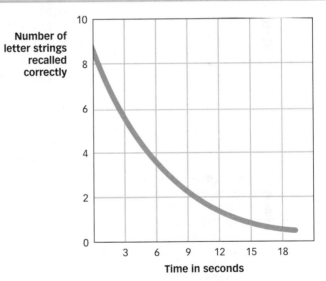

▲ Figure **6.6** **The Decline of Short-Term Memory** A 1959 experiment showed how quickly short-term memory fades without rehearsal. On a test for memory of three-letter strings, research participants were highly accurate when tested a few seconds after exposure to each string, but if the test was delayed another 15 seconds, people barely recalled the strings at all (Peterson & Peterson, 1959).

long-term memory
A type of storage that holds information for hours, days, weeks, or years.

of individuals with neurological damage to the verbal subsystem of working memory reveal that, not only do they have problems holding onto strings of digits and letters for a few seconds, they also have difficulty learning novel words. This suggests a link between this part of the working memory system and the ability to learn language (Baddeley, 2001; Gathercole, 2008).

Brain imaging studies indicate that the central executive component of working memory depends on regions within the frontal lobe that are important for controlling and manipulating information on a wide range of cognitive tasks (Baddeley, 2001). Children who score low on working memory tasks have difficulty learning new information and performing well in the classroom (Alloway et al., 2009). Can working memory skills can be trained, and can such training enhance cognitive functioning? This question has become a hot research topic over the past few years (Klingberg, 2010; Shipstead, Redick, & Engle, 2012).

In typical studies, participants are first given extensive practice performing working memory tasks that require the maintenance and manipulation of visual or verbal information. They are then tested on new working memory tasks that have not been specifically trained, as well as on other cognitive tasks that tap such capacities as reasoning, comprehension, or paying sustained attention. Some encouraging results have been reported. For example, elementary school students trained on several working memory tasks (about 35 minutes/day for at least 20 days over a 5- to 7-week time period) showed improvement on other working memory tasks when compared with untrained low working memory children (Holmes, Gathercole, & Dunning, 2009). These gains were evident even when the children were tested 6 months after training. There was also some evidence of improvement on math tasks. However, working memory training studies typically compare a working memory training group with control groups that do not perform any kind of training, or perform less challenging training tasks than the working memory group performs, so it is not clear whether working memory training in particular is responsible for the effects that are observed (Slagter, 2012). Indeed, a recent study that used a control condition involving active processing (a visual search task) found that working memory training improved performance on the working memory task that was trained, but did not result in improvements on other cognitive tasks (Redick et al., 2013). More research will be needed to determine whether working memory training produces any general improvements in cognitive performance (Shipstead et al., 2012).

Long-Term Storage

The artist Franco Magnani was born in Pontito, Italy, in 1934. In 1958, he left his village to see the rest of the world and settled in San Francisco in the 1960s. Soon after arriving, Magnani began to suffer from a strange illness. Every night he experienced feverish dreams of Pontito, in which he recalled the village in vivid detail. The dreams soon penetrated his waking life in the form of overpowering recollections, and Magnani decided that the only way to rid himself of these images was to capture them on canvas. For the next 20 years, he devoted much of his time to painting, in exquisite detail, his memories of his beloved village. Many years later, photographer Susan Schwartzenberg went to Pontito, armed with a collection of Magnani's paintings, and photographed each scene from the perspective of the paintings. As you can see in the images, the correspondence between the paintings and the photographs was striking (Sacks, 1995; Schacter, 1996).

Even years after leaving home in Pontito, Italy, painter Franco Magnani was able to create a near-perfect reproduction of what he'd seen there. Magnani's painting (*left*), based on a memory of a place he hadn't seen for years, is remarkably similar to the photograph (*right*) Susan Schwartzenberg took of the actual scene.

© FRANCO MAGNANI

SUSAN SCHWARTZENBERG. © EXPLORATORIUM, WWW.EXPLORATORIUM.EDU

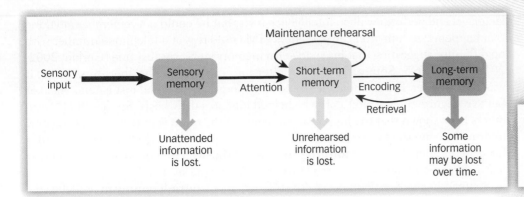

◀ Figure **6.7 The Flow of Information through the Memory System** Information moves through several stages of memory as it gets encoded, stored, and made available for later retrieval.

Many years intervened between Magnani's visual perception and artistic reconstruction of the village, suggesting that very detailed information can sometimes be stored for a very long time. In contrast to the time-limited sensory memory and short-term memory stores, **long-term memory** is *a type of storage that holds information for hours, days, weeks, or years*. In contrast to both sensory and short-term memory, long-term memory has no known capacity limits (see **FIGURE 6.7**). For example, most people can recall 10,000 to 15,000 words in their native language, tens of thousands of facts (The capital of France is Paris and 3 × 3 = 9), and an untold number of personal experiences. Just think of all the song lyrics you can recite by heart, and you'll understand that you've got a lot of information tucked away in long-term memory!

Amazingly, people can recall items from long-term memory even if they haven't thought of them for years. For example, researchers have found that even 50 years after graduation, people can accurately recognize about 90% of their high school classmates from yearbook photographs (Bahrick, 2000). The feat is more remarkable when you consider that most of this information had probably not been accessed for years before the experiment.

The Role of the Hippocampus as Index

Where is long-term memory located in the brain? The clues to answering this question come from individuals who are unable to store long-term memories. Not everyone has the same ability to encode information into long-term memory. In 1953, a 27-year-old man, known then by the initials HM, suffered from intractable epilepsy (Scoville & Milner, 1957). In a desperate attempt to stop the seizures, HM's doctors removed parts of his temporal lobes, including the hippocampus and some surrounding regions (**FIGURE 6.8**). After the operation, HM could converse easily, use and understand

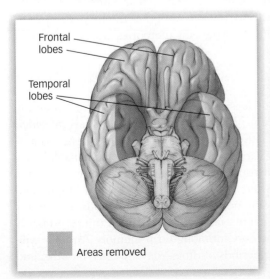

Frontal lobes

Temporal lobes

Areas removed

◀ Figure **6.8 The Hippocampus Patient** HM had his hippocampus and adjacent structures of the medial temporal lobe (indicated by the shaded area) surgically removed to stop his epileptic seizures (left). As a result, he could not remember things that happened after the surgery. Henry Molaison (right), better known to the world as patient HM, passed away on December 2, 2008, at the age of 82 at a nursing home near Hartford, Connecticut. Henry participated in countless memory experiments after he became amnesic in 1953, and in so doing made fundamental contributions to our understanding of memory and the brain.

anterograde amnesia
The inability to transfer new information from the short-term store into the long-term store.

retrograde amnesia
The inability to retrieve information that was acquired before a particular date, usually the date of an injury or surgery.

consolidation
The process by which memories become stable in the brain.

reconsolidation
Memories can become vulnerable to disruption when they are recalled, requiring them to become consolidated again.

language, and perform well on intelligence tests, but he could not remember anything that happened to him after the operation. HM could repeat a telephone number with no difficulty, suggesting that his short-term memory store was just fine (Corkin, 2002, 2013; Hilts, 1995; Squire, 2009). But after information left the short-term store, it was gone forever. For example, he would often forget that he had just eaten a meal or fail to recognize the hospital staff who helped him on a daily basis. Studies of HM and others have shown that the hippocampal region of the brain is critical for putting new information into the long-term store. When this region is damaged, individuals suffer from a condition known as **anterograde amnesia,** which is *the inability to transfer new information from the short-term store into the long-term store.*

Some individuals with amnesia also suffer from **retrograde amnesia,** which is *the inability to retrieve information that was acquired before a particular date, usually the date of an injury or surgery.* The fact that HM had much worse anterograde than retrograde amnesia suggests that the hippocampal region is not the site of long-term memory. Indeed, research has shown that different aspects of a single memory—its sights, sounds, smells, emotional content—are stored in different places in the cortex (Damasio, 1989; Schacter, 1996; Squire & Kandel, 1999). Some psychologists have argued that the hippocampal region acts as a kind of "index" that links together all of these otherwise separate bits and pieces so that we remember them as one memory (Schacter, 1996; Squire, 1992; Teyler & DiScenna, 1986). Over time, this index may become less necessary.

> **How is using the hippocampal region index like learning a recipe?**

Going back to our cooking analogy, you can think of the hippocampal region index like a printed recipe. The first time you make a pie, you need the recipe to help you retrieve all the ingredients and then mix them together in the right amounts. As you bake more and more pies, though, you don't need to rely on the printed recipe anymore. Similarly, although the hippocampal region index is critical when a new memory is first formed, it may become less important as the memory ages. Another possibility is that the hippocampal index remains involved over long periods of time with some memories (highly detailed recollections of personal experiences, the kinds of memories that give us the feeling that we are almost reliving a past experience), but does not stay involved in less detailed, more general memories (Harand et al., 2012; Winocur, Moscovitch, & Bontempi, 2010). In terms of the cooking analogy, you might need to rely on a recipe each time you cook a complex meal with many details, but not when you cook a simpler meal with a less detailed recipe. Scientists are still debating the extent to which the hippocampal region helps us to remember details of our old memories (Bayley, Gold, et al., 2005; Kirwan et al., 2008; Moscovitch et al., 2006; Squire & Wixted, 2011; Winocur et al., 2010), but the notion of the hippocampus as an index explains why people like HM cannot make new memories and why they can remember old ones.

Memory Consolidation

The idea that the hippocampus becomes less important over time for maintaining memories is closely related to the concept of **consolidation,** *the process by which memories become stable in the brain* (McGaugh, 2000). Shortly after encoding, memories exist in a fragile state in which they can be easily disrupted; once consolidation has occurred, they are more resistant to disruption. One type of consolidation operates over seconds or minutes. For example, when someone experiences a head injury in a car crash and later cannot recall what happened during the few seconds or minutes before the crash—but can recall other events normally—the head injury probably prevented consolidation of short-term memory into long-term memory. Another type of consolidation occurs over much longer periods of time—days, weeks, months, and years—and likely involves transfer of information from the hippocampus to more permanent storage sites in the cortex. The operation of this longer-term consolidation process is why individuals with retrograde amnesia with hippocampal damage can recall memories from childhood relatively normally, but are impaired when recalling experiences that occurred just a few years prior to the time they became amnesic (Kirwan et al., 2008; Squire & Wixted, 2011).

How does a memory become consolidated? The act of recalling a memory, thinking about it, and talking about it with others probably contributes to consolidation (Moscovitch et al., 2006). And though you may not be aware of it, consolidation gets a boost from something that you do effortlessly every night: sleep. As explained in the Hot Science box (p. xxx), mounting evidence gathered during the past decade indicates that sleep plays an important role in memory consolidation.

HOT SCIENCE

Sleep on It

Thinking about pulling an all-nighter before your next big test? Here's a reason to reconsider: Our minds don't simply shut off when we sleep (see the Consciousness chapter), and in fact, sleep may be as important to our memories as wakefulness.

Nearly a century ago, Jenkins and Dallenbach (1924) reported that recall of recently learned information is greater immediately after sleeping than after the same amount of time spent awake. But Jenkins and Dallenbach did not think that sleep played an active role in strengthening or consolidating memory. They argued instead that being asleep passively protects us from encountering information that interferes with our ability to remember. As is explained by retroactive interference (p. 250), that's a valid argument. However, during the past few years, evidence has accumulated that sleep plays an active role in memory consolidation, doing more than simply protecting us from waking interference (Diekelman & Born, 2010; Ellenbogen, Payne, & Stickgold, 2006). Sleep selectively enhances the consolidation of memories that reflect the meaning or gist of an experience (Payne et al., 2009), as well as emotionally important memories (Payne et al., 2008), suggesting that sleep helps us to remember what's important and to discard what's trivial.

This idea is reinforced by recent evidence which shows that the beneficial effects of sleep on subsequent memory are observed only when people expect to be tested. In one study, Wilhelm et al. (2011) found that after studying a list of word pairs, participants who were informed that their memory would be tested later showed improved recall after sleep compared with an equivalent period of wakefulness. But a separate group that had not been informed of the memory test (and did not suspect it) showed no improvement in recall after sleep compared with wakefulness.

In an additional study (van Dongen et al., 2012), participants studied pictures of either buildings or furniture that were each associated with a particular location on a slide (see below). Soon after, participants received a memory test for the picture–location associations. They were then instructed that they would be retested 14 hours later for either the building pictures or the furniture pictures (the relevant category) and would not be retested on the other type of picture (the irrelevant category). Half of the participants were tested after sleep (initial learning was in the afternoon for these individuals) and half after remaining awake (initial learning was in the morning for these individuals). On the retest, there was less forgetting for the relevant than irrelevant categories in the sleep group, but there was no such difference in the awake group. Furthermore, for participants in the sleep group, the amount of time spent sleeping was correlated with retention of relevant information but not with retention of irrelevant information; those participants who slept longer retained more of the relevant information.

So, when you find yourself nodding off after hours of studying for your exam, the science is on the side of a good night's sleep.

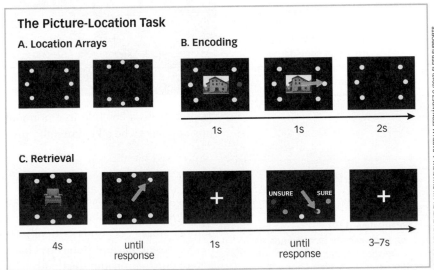

The Picture-Location Task

A. Location Arrays

B. Encoding

1s   1s   2s

C. Retrieval

UNSURE   SURE

4s   until response   1s   until response   3–7s

VAN DONGEN EV, THIELEN J-W, TAKASHIMA A, BARTH M, FERNANDEZ G (2012) SLEEP SUPPORTS SELECTIVE RETENTION OF ASSOCIATIVE MEMORIES BASED ON RELEVANCE FOR FUTURE UTILIZATION. PLOS ONE 7(8): E43426. DOI:10.1371/JOURNAL.PONE.0043426. © VAN DONGEN ET AL.

Many researchers have long believed that a fully consolidated memory becomes a permanent fixture in the brain, more difficult to get rid of than a computer virus. But another line of research that has developed rapidly in recent years suggests that things are not so simple. Experiments have shown that even seemingly consolidated *memories can become vulnerable to disruption when they are recalled, thus requiring them to be consolidated again.* This process is called **reconsolidation** (Dudai, 2012; Nader & Hardt, 2009). Evidence for reconsolidation mainly comes from experiments with rats showing that when animals are cued to retrieve a new memory that was acquired a day earlier, giving the animal a drug (or an electrical shock) that prevents initial consolidation will cause forgetting (Nader, Shafe, & LeDoux, 2000; Sara, 2000). Critically, if the animal is not actively retrieving the memory, the same drug (or shock) has no effect when given a day after initial encoding.

This finding is surprising because it was once thought that when memories are consolidated, drugs or shock that prevent initial consolidation no longer have any impact. To the contrary, it appears that each time they are retrieved, memories become vulnerable to disruption and have to be reconsolidated.

> **When is a consolidated memory vulnerable to disruption?**

Might it be possible one day to eliminate painful memories by disrupting reconsolidation? Recent research with traumatized individuals suggests it could be: When a traumatic event was reactivated after administration of a drug that reduces anxiety, there was a subsequent reduction in traumatic symptoms (Brunet et al., 2008, 2011).

Has seeing too many shark movies left your afraid to swim in the ocean? What evidence is there that someday we might be able to erase painful memories?

Other research with nontraumatized individuals has shown that something like this happens, without the use of drugs, as a result of reactivating a fear memory (being shocked in the presence of a particular object) a day after the memory was acquired. Adding non-fearful information to the reactivated memory (re-presenting the object without shock) a few minutes later—when the memory is vulnerable to reconsolidation—resulted in long-lasting reduction of fear responses to the object, whereas adding nonfearful information to the reactivated memory 6 hours later—when the memory is no longer vulnerable to reconsolidation—did not have a long-lasting effect (Schiller et al., 2010). Related work indicates that disrupting reconsolidation can seemingly eliminate a conditioned fear memory in a part of the brain called the *amygdala*, which we will learn, later in this chapter, plays a key role in emotional memory (Agren et al., 2012). Reconsolidation thus appears to be a key memory process with many important implications.

Memories, Neurons, and Synapses

We've already discussed parts of the brain that are related to memory storage, but we haven't said much about how or where memories are stored. Research suggests that memory storage depends critically on the *spaces* between neurons. You'll recall from the Neuroscience and Behavior chapter that a *synapse* is the small space between the axon of one neuron and the dendrite of another, and neurons communicate by sending neurotransmitters across these synapses. As it turns out, sending a neurotransmitter

long-term potentiation (LTP)
A process whereby communication across the synapse between neurons strengthens the connection, making further communication easier.

across a synapse isn't like sending a toy boat across a pond because the act of sending actually *changes* the synapse. Specifically, it strengthens the connection between the two neurons, making it easier for them to transmit to each other the next time. This is why researchers sometimes say, "cells that fire together wire together" (Hebb, 1949).

The idea that the connections between neurons are strengthened by their communication, making communication easier the next time, provides the neurological basis for long-term memory, and much of what we know about this comes from the tiny sea slug *Aplysia*. The story of *Aplysia* and memory is closely linked with the work of neuroscientist Eric Kandel, who won the Nobel Prize in 2000 for his work with the creature. When Kandel first became interested in *Aplysia* back in the late 1950s, there were only two researchers in the entire world studying the tiny slug. But *Aplysia* was attractive to Kandel because it is relatively uncomplicated and has an extremely simple nervous system consisting of only 20,000 neurons (compared to roughly 100 billion in the human brain), so Kandel followed his intuition and studied *Aplysia* (Kandel, 2006).

When an experimenter stimulates *Aplysia*'s tail with a mild electric shock, the slug immediately withdraws its gill, and if the experimenter does it again a moment later, *Aplysia* withdraws its gill even more quickly. If the experimenter comes back an hour later and shocks *Aplysia,* the withdrawal of the gill happens as slowly as it did the first time, as if *Aplysia* can't "remember" what happened an hour earlier (Abel et al., 1995). But if the experimenter shocks *Aplysia* over and over, it does develop an enduring "memory" that can last for days or even weeks. Research suggests that this long-term storage involves the growth of new synaptic connections between neurons (Abel et al., 1995; Kandel, 2006; Squire & Kandel, 1999). So, learning in *Aplysia* is based on changes involving the synapses for both short-term storage (enhanced neurotransmitter release) and long-term storage (growth of new synapses). Any experience that results in memory produces physical changes in the nervous system—even if you are a slug.

If you're something more complex than a slug—say, a chimpanzee or your roommate—a similar process of synaptic strengthening happens in the hippocampus, which

Nobel Prize–winning neuroscientist Eric Kandel took a risk and studied the tiny sea slug *Aplysia* based in part on a lesson he had learned from his wife regarding their recent marriage, which encouraged him to trust his intuition: "Denise was confident that our marriage would work, so I took a leap of faith and went ahead. I learned from that experience that there are many situations in which one cannot decide on the basis of cold facts alone—because the facts are often insufficient. One ultimately has to trust one's unconscious, one's instincts, one's creative urge. I did this again in choosing *Aplysia*" (Kandel, 2006, p. 149).

How does building a memory produce a physical change in the nervous system?

we've seen is an area crucial for storing new long-term memories. In the early 1970s, researchers applied a brief electrical stimulus to a neural pathway in a rat's hippocampus (Bliss & Lømo, 1973). They found that the electrical current produced a stronger connection between synapses that lay along the pathway and that the strengthening lasted for hours or even weeks. They called this **long-term potentiation** (more commonly known as **LTP**), *a process whereby communication across the synapse between neurons strengthens the connection, making further communication easier.* Long-term potentiation has a number of properties that indicate to researchers that it plays an important role in long-term memory storage: It occurs in several pathways within the hippocampus; it can be induced rapidly; and it can last for a long time. In fact, drugs that block LTP can turn rats into rodent versions of patient HM: The animals have great difficulty remembering where they've been recently and become easily lost in a maze (Bliss, 1999; Morris et al., 1986).

By studying the sea slug *Aplysia californica's* extremely simple nervous system, researchers were able to determine that long-term memory storage depends on the growth of new synaptic connections between neurons.

▶ There are several different types of memory storage:

Sensory memory holds information for a second or two.

Short-term or working memory retains information for about 15 to 20 seconds.

Long-term memory stores information anywhere from minutes to years or decades.

▶ The hippocampus and nearby structures play an important role in long-term memory storage, as shown by the severe amnesia of individuals such as HM. The hippocampus also is important for memory consolidation, the process that makes memories increasingly resistant to disruption over time. Sleep contributes importantly to memory consolidation.

▶ Memory storage depends on changes in synapses, and long-term potentiation (LTP) increases synaptic connections.

Retrieval: Bringing Memories to Mind

There is something fiendishly frustrating about piggy banks. You can put money in them, you can shake them around to assure yourself that the money is there, but you can't easily get the money out. If memories were like pennies in a piggy bank, stored but inaccessible, what would be the point of saving them in the first place? Retrieval is the process of bringing to mind information that has been previously encoded and stored, and it is perhaps the most important of all memory processes (Roediger, 2000; Schacter, 2001a).

Retrieval Cues: Reinstating the Past

One of the best ways to retrieve information from *inside* your head is to encounter information *outside* your head that is somehow connected to it. The information outside your head is called a **retrieval cue,** *external information that is associated with stored information and helps bring it to mind.* Retrieval cues can be incredibly effective. How many times have you said something like, "I *know* who starred in *Trouble with the Curve,* but I just can't remember her name ?", only to have a friend give you a hint ("Wasn't she in *Julie & Julia*?"), which instantly brings the answer to mind ("Amy Adams!").

In one experiment, undergraduates studied lists of words, such as *table, peach, bed, apple, chair, grape,* and *desk* (Tulving & Pearlstone, 1966). Later, the students were asked to write down all the words from the list that they could remember. When they were absolutely sure that they had emptied their memory stores of every last word that was in them, the experimenters again asked the students to remember the words on the list, but this time, the experimenters provided retrieval cues, such as "furniture" or "fruit." The students who were sure that they had done all the remembering they possibly could were suddenly able to remember more words. These results suggest that information is sometimes *available* in memory even when it is momentarily *inaccessible*, and that retrieval cues help us bring inaccessible information to mind.

Hints are one kind of retrieval cue, but they are not the only kind. The **encoding specificity principle** states that *a retrieval cue can serve as an effective reminder when it helps re-create the specific way in which information was initially encoded* (Tulving & Thomson, 1973). External contexts often make powerful retrieval cues (Hockley, 2008). For example, in one study divers learned some words on land and some other words underwater; they recalled the words best when they were tested in the same dry or

Retrieval cues are hints that help bring stored information to mind. How does this explain the fact that most students prefer multiple-choice exams to fill-in-the-blank exams?

AP PHOTO/POCONO RECORD, ADAM RICH

What is an example of a retrieval cue you have used?

wet environment in which they had initially learned them because the environment itself served as a retrieval cue (Godden & Baddeley, 1975). Recovering alcoholics often experience a renewed urge to drink when visiting places in which they once drank because those places serve as retrieval cues. There may even be some wisdom to finding a seat in a classroom, sitting in it every day, and then sitting in it again when you take the test because the feel of the chair and the sights you see may help you remember the information you learned while you sat there.

Retrieval cues need not be external contexts—they can also be inner states. **State-dependent retrieval** is *the tendency for information to be better recalled when the person is in the same state during encoding and retrieval.* For example, retrieving information when you are in a sad or happy mood increases the likelihood that you will retrieve sad or happy episodes (Eich, 1995), which is part of the reason it is so hard to "look on the bright side" when you're feeling low. Similarly, you'd probably expect a fellow student who studied for an exam while drunk to perform poorly, and you would probably be right—but only if he made the mistake of taking the exam while sober! Studies of state-dependent retrieval suggest that if the student studied while drunk, he would probably perform poorly the next day, but he'd perform better if he'd had a six-pack instead of Cheerios for breakfast (Eich, 1980; Weissenborn, 2000). Why should that be? Because a person's physiological or psychological state at the time of encoding is associated with the information that is encoded. For example, being in a good mood affects patterns of electrical activity in parts of the brain responsible for semantic processing, suggesting that mood has a direct influence on semantic encoding (Kiefer et al., 2007). If the person's state at the time of retrieval matches the person's state at the time of encoding, the state itself serves as a retrieval cue—a bridge that connects the moment at which we experience something to the moment at which we remember it. Retrieval cues can even be thoughts themselves, as when one thought calls to mind another, related thought (Anderson et al., 1976).

The encoding specificity principle makes some unusual predictions. For example, you learned earlier that making semantic judgments about a word (e.g., What does *brain* mean?) usually produces more durable memory for the word than does making rhyme judgments (e.g., What rhymes with *brain*?). So if you were shown a cue card of the word "brain," and your friend was asked to think about what *brain* means while you were asked to think of a word that rhymes with *brain*, we would expect your friend to remember the word better the next day if we simply asked you both, "Hey, what was that word you saw yesterday?" However, if instead of asking that question, we asked you both, "What was that word that rhymed with *train*?" the retrieval cue would match your encoding context better than your friend's, and we would expect you to remember it better than your friend did (Fisher & Craik, 1977). This is a fairly astounding finding. The principle of **transfer-appropriate processing** is *the idea that memory is likely to transfer from one situation to another when the encoding and retrieval contexts of the situations match* (Morris, Bransford, & Franks, 1977; Roediger, Weldon, & Challis, 1989).

Consequences of Retrieval

Human memory differs substantially from computer memory. Simply retrieving a file from my computer doesn't have any effect on the likelihood that the file will open again in the future. Not so with human memory. Retrieval doesn't merely provide a readout of what is in memory, it also changes the state of the memory system in important ways.

Retrieval Can Improve Subsequent Memory
Psychologists have known for some time that the act of retrieval can strengthen a retrieved memory, making it easier to remember that information at a later time (Bjork, 1975). Does this finding surprise you? Probably not. Repeating an item usually

retrieval cue
External information that is associated with stored information and helps bring it to mind.

encoding specificity principle
The idea that a retrieval cue can serve as an effective reminder when it helps re-create the specific way in which information was initially encoded.

state-dependent retrieval
The tendency for information to be better recalled when the person is in the same state during encoding and retrieval.

transfer-appropriate processing
The idea that memory is likely to transfer from one situation to another when the encoding and retrieval contexts of the situations match.

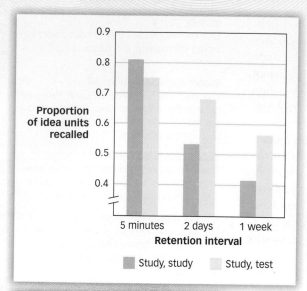

▲ Figure **6.9 Memory Testing Benefits Long-Term Retention** With a 5-minute retention interval, the study–study condition results in slightly higher recall. But the results change dramatically with retention intervals of 2 days and 1 week: at these longer delays, the study–test condition yields much higher levels of recall than does the study–study condition (Roediger & Karpicke, 2006).

improves memory for that item, so the act of retrieval might boost subsequent memory simply because the information is repeated, resulting in the same benefit you would receive from studying the information twice instead of once. Makes sense, right? Wrong. It turns out that retrieving information from memory has different effects than studying it again. This point was made dramatically in an experiment where participants studied brief stories and then either studied them again or were given a test that required retrieving the stories (Roediger & Karpicke, 2006). Participants were then given a final recall test for the stories either 5 minutes, 2 days, or 1 week later. As shown in **FIGURE 6.9**, at the 5-minute delay, studying the stories twice resulted in slightly higher recall than studying and retrieving them. Critically, the opposite occurred at the 2-day and 1-week delays: Retrieval produced much higher levels of recall than did an extra study exposure. A subsequent experiment using foreign vocabulary items also revealed that retrieval of the items produced a much bigger benefit on a delayed vocabulary test than did further study (Karpicke & Roediger, 2008). These findings have potentially important implications for learning in educational contexts (Karpicke, 2012), which we will explore further in the Learning chapter (p. xxx).

> **Should students spend more time testing themselves on material (retrieval), or studying it over and over?**

Retrieval Can Impair Subsequent Memory

As much as retrieval can help memory, that's not always the case. **Retrieval-induced forgetting** is *a process by which retrieving an item from long-term memory impairs subsequent recall of related items* (Anderson, 2003; Anderson, Bjork, & Bjork, 1994).

Let's see how a typical experiment on retrieval-induced forgetting works (Anderson et al., 1994). Participants first studied word pairs consisting of a category name and an example from that category (e.g., *fruit–orange, fruit–apple, tree–elm, tree–birch*). Then they practiced recalling some of the items from a few of the studied categories by retrieving the target in response to a category cue and the initial letters of the target. As an example, for the fruit category participants would practice recalling *orange* to the cue "fruit or ____," but would not practice recalling *apple*. The general idea is that while they are practicing recall of *orange*, participants are trying to suppress the competitor *apple*. For other categories (e.g., *trees*), no retrieval practice was given for any of the studied pairs. Later, the participants were given a final test for all the words they initially studied. Not surprisingly, on the final test participants remembered words that they practiced (e.g., *orange*) better than words from categories that they did not practice (e.g., *elm*). But what happened on the final test to the items such as *apple*, which were not practiced, and which participants presumably had to suppress while they practiced recall of related items? Those items were recalled most poorly of all, indicating that retrieving the similar target items (e.g., *orange*) caused subsequent forgetting of the related but suppressed items (e.g., *apple*). In fact, even if you don't successfully retrieve the target, the act of suppressing the competitors while you attempt to retrieve the target still reduces your ability to retrieve the competitors at a later time (Storm et al., 2006).

Can you think of any examples of how retrieval-induced forgetting could impact memory in everyday life? Here are two. First, retrieval-induced forgetting can occur during conversations: When a speaker selectively talks about some aspects of memories shared with a listener and doesn't mention related information, the listener later has a harder time remembering the omitted events, as does the speaker (Cuc, Koppel, & Hirst,

> **How can retrieval-induced forgetting occur during conversations?**

retrieval-induced forgetting
A process by which retrieving an item from long-term memory impairs subsequent recall of related items.

2007; Hirst & Echterhoff, 2012). This effect occurs even for memories as important as the events of September 11, 2001 (Coman, Manier, & Hirst, 2009). Second, retrieval-induced forgetting can affect eyewitness memory. When witnesses to a staged crime are questioned about some details of the crime scene, their ability to later recall related details that they were not asked about is impaired compared with witnesses who were not questioned at all initially (MacLeod, 2002; Shaw, Bjork, & Handal, 1995). These findings suggest that initial interviews with eyewitnesses should be as complete as possible in order to avoid potential retrieval-induced forgetting of significant details that are not probed during an interview (MacLeod & Saunders, 2008).

Retrieval Can Change Subsequent Memory

In addition to improving and impairing subsequent memory, the act of retrieval can also change what we remember from an experience. Consider a recent experiment in which participants went on a tour of a museum, where they took some time to view designated exhibits, each of which contained several different stops (St. Jacques & Schacter, in press). The participants took the tour while wearing a camera that, every 15 seconds, automatically took pictures of what was in from of them. Two days later, participants visited the memory laboratory (in a separate building) for a "reactivation session." After memories of some of the stops were reactivated by looking at photos of them, participants were asked to rate, on a 1–5 scale, how vividly they reexperienced what had happened at each stop. Next, the participants were shown novel photos of *unvisited* stops within the exhibit, then were asked to judge how closely these novel photos were related to the photos of the stops that they had actually seen in that exhibit. Finally, the participants were given a memory test 2 days after the reactivation session.

Participants sometimes incorrectly remembered that the stop shown in the novel photo had been part of the original tour. Most importantly, participants who tended to make this mistake also tended to have more vivid recollections during the reactivation session. In other words, retrieving and vividly reexperiencing memories of what participants actually did see at the museum led them to incorporate into their memory information that was not part of their original experience. This finding may be related to the phenomenon of reconsolidation that we discussed earlier (p.xxx), where reactivating a memory temporarily makes it vulnerable to disruption and change. At the very least, this finding reinforces the idea that retrieving a memory involves far more than a simple readout of information.

As part of a recent experiment, participants wore cameras that took pictures every 15 seconds as they toured a museum.

Separating the Components of Retrieval

Before leaving the topic of retrieval, let's look at how the process actually works. There is reason to believe that *trying* to recall an incident and *successfully* recalling one are fundamentally different processes that occur in different parts of the brain (Moscovitch, 1994; Schacter, 1996). For example, regions in the left frontal lobe show heightened activity when people *try* to retrieve information that was presented to them earlier (Oztekin, Curtis, & McElree, 2009; Tulving et al., 1994). This activity may reflect the mental effort of struggling to dredge up the past event (Lepage et al., 2000). However, *successfully* remembering a past experience tends to be accompanied by activity in the hippocampal region (see **FIGURE 6.10**; Eldridge et al., 2000; Giovanello, Schnyer, & Verfaellie, 2004; Schacter, Alpert, et al., 1996). Furthermore, successful recall also activates parts of the brain that play a role in processing the sensory features of an

How is brain activity different when *trying* to recall versus *successfully* recalling?

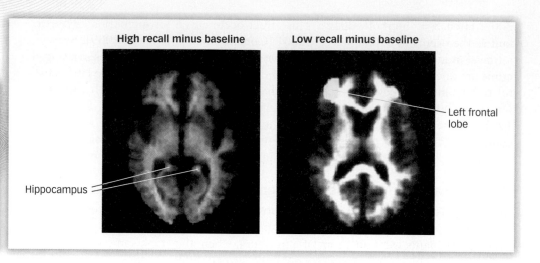

High recall minus baseline Low recall minus baseline

▶ Figure **6.10** **PET Scans of Successful and Unsuccessful Recall** When people successfully remembered words they saw earlier in an experiment (achieving high levels of recall on a test), the hippocampus showed increased activity. When people tried but failed to recall words they had seen earlier (achieving low levels of recall on a test), the left frontal lobe showed increased activity (Schacter, Alpert, et al., 1996).

experience. For instance, recall of previously heard sounds is accompanied by activity in the auditory cortex (the upper part of the temporal lobe), whereas recall of previously seen pictures is accompanied by activity in the visual cortex (in the occipital lobe; Wheeler, Petersen, & Buckner, 2000). Although retrieval may seem like a single process, brain studies suggest that separately identifiable processes are at work.

This sheds some light on the phenomena we just discussed: retrieval-induced forgetting. Recent fMRI evidence indicates that during memory retrieval, regions within the frontal lobe that are involved in retrieval effort play a role in suppressing competitors (Benoit & Anderson, 2012; Kuhl et al., 2007; Wimber et al., 2009). When hippocampal activity during retrieval practice signals successful recall of an unwanted competitor, frontal lobe mechanisms are recruited that help to suppress the competitor. Once the competitor is suppressed, the frontal lobe no longer has to work as hard at controlling retrieval, ultimately making it easier to recall the target

CULTURE & COMMUNITY

Does culture affect childhood amnesia? You can easily recall many experiences from different times in your life. But you probably have few or no memories from the first few years of your life, which is called *childhood amnesia* or *infantile amnesia*. On average, an individual's first memory dates to about 3 to 3 ½ years of age (Dudycha & Dudycha, 1933; Waldfogel, 1948), with women reporting slightly earlier first memories (3.07 years of age) than men (3.4 years) (Howes, Siegel, & Brown, 1993). But these estimates are based on individuals from Western (i.e., North American and European) cultures, which emphasize talking about the past. First memories are seen at later ages in Asian cultures that place less emphasis on talking about the past, such as Korea and China (MacDonald, Uesiliana, & Hayne, 2000; Mullen, 1994; Peterson, Wang, & Hou, 2009). A comparison of Canadian and Chinese children showed that first memories of 8-year-old children in both cultures come from younger ages than the first memories of 14-year-old children, suggesting that early memories fade or disappear as children age (Peterson et al., 2009). Critically, the first memories of the 14-year-old Chinese children came from a later age than did the first memories of the 14-year-old Canadians. In fact, the onset of childhood amnesia in the Chinese 14-year-olds was identical to that of North American adults. Culture thus has a significant impact on even our earliest memories.

▲ First memories are seen later in cultures that place less emphasis on talking about the past.

item (Kuhl et al., 2007). In addition, successful suppression of an unwanted memory causes reduced activity in the hippocampus (Anderson et al., 2004). These findings make sense once we understand the specific roles played by particular brain regions in the retrieval process.

IN SUMMARY

▶ Whether we remember a past experience depends on whether retrieval cues are available to trigger recall. Retrieval cues are effective when they are given in the same context as when we encoded an experience. Moods and inner states can serve as retrieval cues.

▶ Retrieving information from memory has consequences for later remembering. Retrieval improves subsequent memory of the retrieved information, as exemplified by the beneficial effect of testing on later recall. However, retrieval can impair subsequent remembering of related information that is not retrieved. It can also change subsequent remembering when novel information is associated with vivid recollections.

▶ Retrieval can be separated into the effort we make while trying to remember what happened in the past and the successful recovery of stored information. Neuroimaging studies suggest that trying to remember activates the left frontal lobe, whereas successful recovery of stored information activates the hippocampus and regions in the brain related to sensory aspects of an experience.

Multiple Forms of Memory: How the Past Returns

In 1977, neurologist Oliver Sacks interviewed a young man named Greg who had a tumor in his brain that wiped out his ability to remember day-to-day events. One thing Greg could remember was his life during the 1960s in New York's Greenwich Village, years before the tumor formed, when Greg's primary occupation seemed to be attending rock concerts by his favorite band, The Grateful Dead. Greg's memories of those Dead concerts stuck with him over the following years, when he was living in a long-term care hospital and interviewed regularly by Dr. Sacks. In 1991, Dr. Sacks took Greg to a Dead concert at New York's Madison Square Garden, wondering whether such a momentous event might jolt his memory into action. "That was fantastic," Greg told Dr. Sacks as they left the concert. "I will always remember it. I had the time of my life." But when Dr. Sacks saw Greg the next morning and asked him whether he recalled the previous night's Dead concert at the Garden, Greg drew a blank: "No, I've never been to the Garden" (Sacks, 1995, pp. 76–77).

Although Greg was unable to make new memories, some of the new things that happened to him seemed to leave a mark. For example, Greg did not recall learning that his father had died, but he did seem sad and withdrawn for years after hearing the news. Similarly, HM could not make new memories after his surgery, but if he played a game in which he had to track a moving target, his performance gradually improved with each round (Milner, 1962). Greg could not consciously remember hearing about his father's death, and HM could not consciously remember playing the tracking game, but both showed clear signs of having been permanently changed by experiences that they so rapidly forgot. In other words, they *behaved* as though they were remembering things while claiming to remember nothing at all. This suggests that there must be several kinds of memory, some that are accessible to conscious recall, and some that we cannot consciously access (Eichenbaum & Cohen, 2001; Schacter & Tulving, 1994; Schacter, Wagner, & Buckner, 2000; Squire & Kandel, 1999).

Explicit and Implicit Memory

The fact that people can be changed by past experiences without having any awareness of those experiences suggests that there must be at least two different classes of memory (**FIGURE 6.11**). **Explicit memory** occurs *when people consciously or intentionally retrieve past experiences.* Recalling last summer's vacation, incidents from a novel you just read, or facts you studied for a test all involve explicit memory. Indeed, anytime you start a sentence with "I remember . . . ," you are talking about an explicit memory. **Implicit memory** occurs when *past experiences influence later behavior and performance, even without an effort to remember them or an awareness of the recollection* (Graf & Schacter, 1985; Schacter, 1987). Implicit memories are not consciously recalled, but their presence is "implied" by our actions. Greg's persistent sadness after his father's death, even though he had no conscious knowledge of the event, is an example of implicit memory. So is HM's improved performance on a tracking task that he didn't consciously remember doing. So is the ability to ride a bike or tie your shoelaces or play guitar: You may know how to do these things, but you probably can't describe how to do them. Such knowledge reflects a particular kind of implicit memory called **procedural memory,** which refers to *the gradual acquisition of skills as a result of practice, or "knowing how" to do things.*

> **What type of memory is it when you just "know how" to do something?**

One of the hallmarks of procedural memory is that the things you remember are automatically translated into actions. Sometimes you can explain how it is done (put one finger on the third fret of the E string, one finger . . .) and sometimes you can't (get on the bike and . . . well, uh . . . just balance). The fact that people who have amnesia can acquire new procedural memories suggests that the hippocampal structures that are usually damaged in these individuals may be necessary for explicit memory, but they aren't needed for implicit procedural memory. In fact, it appears that brain regions outside the hippocampal area (including areas in the motor cortex) are involved in procedural memory. The Learning chapter discusses this evidence further, where you will also see that procedural memory is crucial for learning various kinds of motor, perceptual, and cognitive skills.

Not all implicit memories are procedural or "how to" memories. For example, in one experiment, college students were asked to study a long list of words, including items such as *avocado, mystery, climate, octopus,* and *assassin* (Tulving, Schacter, & Stark, 1982). Later, explicit memory was tested by showing participants some of these

Guitarists such as Jack White rely heavily on procedural memory to acquire and use the skills needed to play their music at a high level.

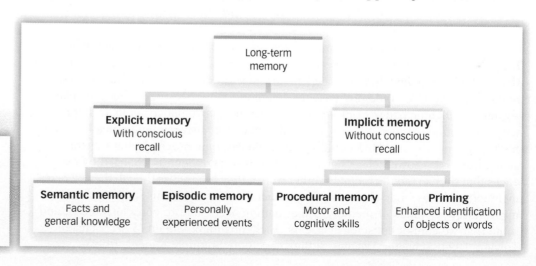

▶ Figure **6.11 Multiple Forms of Memory** Explicit and implicit memories are distinct from each other. Thus, a person with amnesia may lose explicit memory, yet display implicit memory for material that she or he cannot consciously recall learning.

Long-term memory

Explicit memory
With conscious recall

Implicit memory
Without conscious recall

Semantic memory
Facts and general knowledge

Episodic memory
Personally experienced events

Procedural memory
Motor and cognitive skills

Priming
Enhanced identification of objects or words

DAVID WOLFF PATRICK/WIREIMAGE/GETTY IMAGES

words along with new ones they hadn't seen and asking them which words were on the list. To test implicit memory, participants received word fragments and were asked to come up with a word that fit the fragment. Try the test yourself:

ch – – – – nk   o – t – p – –   – og – y – – –   – l – m – te

You probably had difficulty coming up with the answers for the first and third fragments (*chipmunk, bogeyman*) but had little problem coming up with answers for the second and fourth (*octopus, climate*). Seeing *octopus* and *climate* on the original list made those words more accessible later, during

> **How does priming make memory more efficient?**

the fill-in-the-blanks test. This is an example of **priming,** which refers to *an enhanced ability to think of a stimulus, such as a word or object, as a result of a recent exposure to the stimulus* (Tulving & Schacter, 1990). Just as priming a pump makes water flow more easily, priming the memory system makes some information more accessible. In the fill-in-the-blanks experiment, people showed priming for studied words even when they failed to consciously remember that they had seen them earlier. This suggests that priming is an example of implicit, not explicit, memory.

A truly stunning example of this point comes from a study by Mitchell (2006) in which participants first studied black-and-white line drawings depicting everyday objects. Later, the participants were shown fragmented versions of the drawings that are difficult to identify; some of them depicted objects that had been studied earlier in the experiment, whereas others depicted new objects that had not been studied. Mitchell found that participants correctly identified more fragmented drawings of studied than new objects, and identified more studied objects than did participants in a control group who had never seen the pictures—a clear demonstration of priming (see **FIGURE 6.12**). Here's the stunning part: The fragmented drawing test was given 17 years after presentation of the study list! By that time, participants had little or no explicit memory of having seen the drawings,

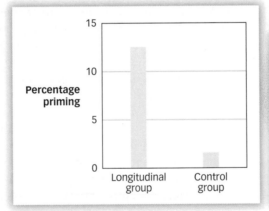

and some had no recollection that they had ever participated in the experiment! "I'm sorry—I really don't remember this experiment at all," said one 36-year-old man who showed a strong priming effect. A 36-year-old woman who showed even more priming stated simply, "Don't remember anything about it" (Mitchell, 2006, p. 929). These observations confirm that priming is an example of implicit memory, and also that priming can persist over very long periods of time.

As such, you'd expect amnesic individuals such as HM and Greg to show priming. In fact, many experiments have shown that amnesic individuals can show substantial priming effects—often as large as healthy, nonamnesic individuals—even though they have no explicit memory for the items they studied. These and other similar results suggest that priming, like procedural memory, does not require the hippocampal structures that are damaged in cases of amnesia (Schacter & Curran, 2000).

If the hippocampal region isn't required for procedural memory and priming, what parts of the brain are involved? Experiments have revealed that priming is associated with *reduced* activity in various regions of the cortex that are activated when people perform an unprimed task. For instance, when research participants are shown the word stem *mot___* or *tab___* and are asked to provide the first word that comes to mind, parts of the occipital lobe involved in visual processing and parts of the frontal lobe involved in word retrieval become active. But if people perform the same task

explicit memory
The act of consciously or intentionally retrieving past experiences.

implicit memory
The influence of past experiences on later behavior and performance, even without an effort to remember them or an awareness of the recollection.

procedural memory
The gradual acquisition of skills as a result of practice, or "knowing how" to do things.

priming
An enhanced ability to think of a stimulus, such as a word or object, as a result of a recent exposure to the stimulus.

◄ Figure **6.12** **Long-Term Priming of Visual Objects** Participants who viewed drawings of common objects, and 17 years later were given a test in which they tried to identify the objects from fragmented drawings (longitudinal group), showed a strong priming effect; by contrast, participants who had not seen the drawings 17 years earlier (control group) showed nonsignificant priming (Mitchell, 2006).

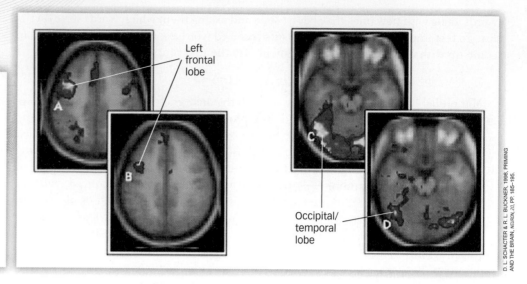

D. L. SCHACTER & R. L. BUCKNER, 1998, PRIMING AND THE BRAIN, *NEURON, 20,* PP. 185–195.

► Figure **6.13** **Primed and Unprimed Processing of Stimuli** Priming is associated with reduced levels of activation in the cortex on a number of different tasks. In each pair of fMRIs, the images on the upper left (A, C) show brain regions in the frontal lobe (A) and occipital/temporal lobe (C) that are active during an unprimed task (in this case, providing a word response to a visual word cue). The images on the lower right within each pair (B, D) show reduced activity in the same regions during the primed version of the same task.

after being primed by seeing *motel* and *table,* there's less activity in these same regions (Buckner et al., 1995; Schott et al., 2005). Something similar happens when people see pictures of everyday objects on two different occasions. On the second exposure to a picture, there's less activity in parts of the visual cortex that were activated by seeing the picture initially. Priming seems to make it easier for parts of the cortex that are involved in perceiving a word or object to identify the item after a recent exposure to it (Schacter, Dobbins, & Schnyer, 2004; Wiggs & Martin, 1998). This suggests that the brain saves a bit of processing time after priming (see **FIGURE 6.13**).

Neuroimaging studies also indicate that different brain systems are involved in two distinct forms of priming: *perceptual priming,* which reflects implicit memory for the sensory features of an item (e.g., the visual characteristics of a word or picture), and *conceptual priming,* which reflects implicit memory for the meaning of a word or how you would use an object. Studies using fMRI indicate that perceptual priming depends primarily on regions toward the back of the brain, such as the visual cortex, whereas conceptual priming depends more on regions toward the front of the brain, such as the frontal lobes (Wig, Buckner, & Schacter, 2009). There is also some evidence that perceptual priming is associated primarily with the right cerebral hemisphere, whereas conceptual priming is associated with the left hemisphere (Schacter, Wig, & Stevens, 2007).

Semantic and Episodic Memory

Consider these two questions: (1) Why do we celebrate on July 4th? and (2) What is the most spectacular Fourth of July celebration you've ever seen? Every American knows the answer to the first question (we celebrate the signing of the Declaration of Independence on July 4, 1776), but we all have our own answers to the second. Although both of these questions require you to search your long-term memory and explicitly retrieve information that is stored there, one requires you to dredge up a fact that every American schoolchild knows and that is not part of your personal autobiography, and one requires you to revisit a particular time and place—or episode—from your personal past. These memories are called *semantic* and *episodic* memories, respectively (Tulving, 1972, 1983, 1998). **Semantic memory** is *a network of associated facts and concepts that make up our general knowledge of the world,* whereas **episodic memory** is *the collection of past personal experiences that occurred at a particular time and place.*

Episodic memory is special because it is the only form of memory that allows us to engage in mental time travel, projecting ourselves into the past and revisiting events

semantic memory
A network of associated facts and concepts that make up our general knowledge of the world.

episodic memory
The collection of past personal experiences that occurred at a particular time and place.

These new Americans are taking the Oath of Allegiance after passing a citizenship test that would have required them to use their semantic memories.

that have happened to us. This ability allows us to connect our pasts and our presents and construct a cohesive story of our lives. People who have amnesia can usually travel

What form of memory uses mental time travel?

back in time and revisit episodes that occurred before they became amnesic, but they are unable to revisit episodes that happened later. For example, Greg couldn't travel back to any time after 1969 because that's when he stopped being able to create new episodic memories. But can people with amnesia create new semantic memories?

Researchers have studied three young adults who suffered damage to the hippocampus during birth as a result of difficult deliveries that interrupted oxygen supply to the brain (Brandt et al., 2009; Vargha-Khadem et al., 1997). Their parents noticed that the children could not recall what happened during a typical day, had to be constantly reminded of appointments, and often became lost and disoriented. In view of their hippocampal damage, you might also expect that each of the three would perform poorly in school and might even be classified as learning disabled. Remarkably, however, all three children learned to read, write, and spell, developed normal vocabularies, and acquired other kinds of semantic knowledge that allowed them to perform well in school. Based on this evidence, researchers have concluded that the hippocampus is not necessary for acquiring new *semantic* memories.

Episodic Memory and Imagining the Future

We've already seen that episodic memory allows us to travel backward in time, but it turns out that episodic memory also plays a role in allowing to us to travel forward in time. An amnesic man known by the initials K.C. provided an early clue. K.C. could not recollect any specific episodes from his past, and when asked to imagine a future episode such as what he might do tomorrow—he reported a complete "blank" (Tulving, 1985). Consistent with this observation, more recent findings from individuals with hippocampal amnesia reveal that some of them have difficulty imagining new experiences, such as sunbathing on a sandy beach (Hassabis et al., 2007), or events that might happen in their everyday lives (Race, Keane, & Verfaellie, 2011). Something similar happens with aging. When asked either to recall episodes that actually occurred in their pasts or imagine new episodes that might occur in their futures, older adults provided fewer details about what happened, or what might happen, than did college students (Addis, Wong, & Schacter, 2008; Schacter, Gaesser, & Addis, 2012). Consistent with these findings, neuroimaging studies reveal that a network of brain regions known to be involved in episodic memory—including the hippocampus—shows

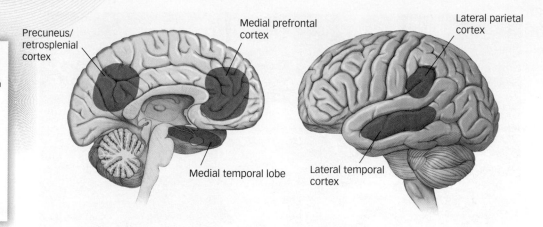

Precuneus/retrosplenial cortex

Medial prefrontal cortex

Lateral parietal cortex

Medial temporal lobe

Lateral temporal cortex

► Figure **6.14** **Remembering the Past and Imagining the Future Depend on a Common Network of Brain Regions** A common brain network is activated when people re-member episodes that actually occurred in their personal pasts and when they imagine episodes that might occur in their personal futures. This network includes the hippocampus, a part of the medial temporal lobe long known to play an important role in episodic memory (Schacter, Addis, & Buckner, 2007).

similarly increased activity when people remember the past and imagine the future (Addis, Wong, & Schacter, 2007; Okuda et al., 2003; Schacter, Addis, et al., 2012; Szpunar, Watson, & McDermott, 2007; see **FIGURE 6.14**).

Taken together, these observations strongly suggest that we rely heavily on episodic memory to envision our personal futures (Schacter, Addis, & Buckner, 2008; Szpunar, 2010). Episodic memory is well-suited to the task, because it is a flexible system that allows us to recombine elements of past experience in new ways, so that we can men-tally try out different versions of what might happen (Schacter, 2012; Schacter & Addis, 2007; Sudden-dorf & Corballis, 2007). For example, when you imagine having a difficult conversation with a friend that will take place in a couple of days, you can draw on past experiences to envisage different ways in which the conversation might un-fold, and hopefully avoid saying things that, based on past experience, are likely to make the situation worse. As we'll discuss later, however, this flexibility of episodic memory might also be responsible for some kinds of memory errors (see p. xxx).

How does episodic memory help us imagine our futures?

Social Influences on Remembering: Collaborative Memory

So far we've focused mainly on memory in individuals functioning on their own. But this is an incomplete picture that is missing something important: other people. Re-membering serves important social functions. Getting together with friends or family to talk about memories of shared experiences is a familiar and enjoyable activity for most of us. When we post photos of parties or vacations on Facebook, we are effectively sharing memories with our friends. And we are quick to communicate our memories to others: In a diary study where college students recorded a memorable event each day for a week, they disclosed 62% of these events to others before the end of the day on which the event occurred (Pasupathi, McLean, & Weeks, 2009). Sharing memories with others can strengthen them (Hirst & Echterhoff, 2012), but we've already seen that talking about some aspects of a memory but omitting other related events, can also produce retrieval-induced forgetting (see p. xxx; Coman et al., 2009; Cue et al., 2007). Psychologists have become increasingly interested in how people remember in groups, which is now referred to as *collaborative memory* (Rajaram, 2011).

In a typical collaborative memory experiment, participants first encode a set of tar-get materials, such as a list of words, on their own (just like in the traditional memory experiments that we've already considered). Things start to get interesting at the time of retrieval, when participants work together in small groups (usually two or three participants) to try to remember the target items. The number of items recalled by this group can then be compared with the number of items recalled by individuals who are trying to recall items on their own, without any help from others. The collaborative group typically recalls more target items than any individual (Hirst & Echterhoff, 2012; Weldon, 2001), suggesting that collaboration benefits memory. That makes a lot of sense and generally fits with our intuitions about what should happen in such a situation (Rajaram, 2011). For example, Tim might recall an item that Emily forgot, and Eric might remember items that neither Tim nor Emily recalled, so the sum total of the group will exceed what any one person can recall.

But things get really interesting when we compare the performance of the collaborative group to the performance of what is called a *nominal group*: the combined recall of several individuals recalling target items on their own. Let's consider a nominal group of three compared with a collaborative group of three. In the nominal group, let's assume that after studying a list of eight words, Tim recalls items 1, 2, and 8, Emily recalls items 1, 4, and 7, and Eric recalls items 1, 5, 6, and 8. Functioning on their own, Tim, Emily, and Eric recalled in combination seven of the eight items that were presented (nobody recalled item 3). The surprising finding now reported by many studies is that the collaborative group typically recalls fewer items than the nominal group; that is, when they remember together, Tim, Emily, and Eric will come up with fewer total items than when they remember on their own (Basden et al., 1997; Hirst & Echterhoff, 2012; Rajaram, 2011; Rajaram & Pereira-Pasarin, 2010; Weldon, 2001). This negative effect of group recall on memory is known as *collaborative inhibition*: the same number of individuals working together recall fewer items than they would on their own.

What's going on here? Most people believe that, based on intuition, working together should increase rather than decrease recall (Rajaram, 2011). Why does it turn out otherwise? One possibility is that in a group, some individuals are prone to "social loafing": they let others do the work and don't pull their own weight. Although social loafing is well known to occur in groups (Karau & Williams, 1993), memory researchers have tested this account of collaborative

> **Why does a collaborative group typically recall fewer items than a nominal group?**

inhibition and rejected it (Barber, Rajaram, & Fox, 2012). A more likely account is that when recalling items together, the retrieval strategies used by individual members of the group disrupt those used by others (Basden et al., 1997; Hirst & Echterhoff, 2012; Rajaram, 2011). For example, suppose that Tim goes first and recalls items in the order that they were presented. This retrieval strategy may be disruptive to Emily, who prefers to recall the last item first and then work backward through the list.

But collaborative recall has other benefits. When individuals recall information together in a group, they are exposed to items recalled by others they may not recall themselves, which improves their memory when they are retested at a later time (Blumen & Rajaram, 2008). And when group members discuss what they have recalled, they can help each other to correct and reduce memory errors (Ross, Blatz, & Schryer, 2008). These observations fit with earlier work showing that couples in close relationships often rely on collaborative remembering (also called *transactive memory*; Wegner, Erber, & Raymond, 1991), where each member of the couple remembers certain kinds of information that they can share with the other. (Can you rely on your computer for collaborative remembering? See The Real World: Is Google Hurting our Memories?) So, next time you are sharing memories of a past activity with friends, you will be shaping your memories for both better and worse.

Remembering as a collaborative group leads to greater recall than would be achieved by any single member of the group, but less than that produced by a nominal group of individuals remembering on their own.

THE REAL WORLD

Is Google Hurting our Memories?

Take some time to try to answer a simple question before returning to reading this box: What country has a national flag that is not rectangular? Now let's discuss what went through your mind as you searched for an answer (the correct one is Nepal). Did you start thinking about the shapes of national flags? Take a mental walk through a map of the world? Or did you think instead about computers — more specifically, about typing the question into Google? There was probably a time not too long ago when most people would have tried to conjure up images of national flags or take a mental world tour, but recent research conducted in the lab of one of your textbook authors indicates that nowadays, most of us think about computers and Google searches when confronted with questions of this kind (Sparrow, Liu, & Wegner, 2011).

Sparrow et al. found that people were slower to name the color in which a computer word (e.g., Google, internet, Yahoo) was printed than the color in which a non-computer word (e.g., Nike, table, Yoplait) was printed after they were given difficult general knowledge questions (like the one about nonrectangular flags) than after they were given easy questions to which they knew the answers. The slow color naming to computer words suggests that people were thinking about things related

to computers after being given difficult questions, which interfered with their ability to name the color in which the word was printed. The researchers concluded that we are now so used to searching for information on Google when we don't immediately know the answer to a question that we immediately think of computers, rather than searching our memories. Thinking about computers when faced with a tough question makes sense: We will probably come up with the answer more quickly if we do a Google search than if we think about what different flags look like. But this result also raises troubling questions: Is reliance on computers and the internet having an adverse effect on human memory? If we rely

HA PHOTOS/ALAMY

▲ What does your computer remember for you?

on Google for answers, are we unknowingly making our memories obsolete?

Sparrow et al. conducted additional experiments aimed at addressing these kinds of questions. In one of them, they found that participants had a harder time remembering bits of trivia ("An ostrich's eye is bigger than its brain") that they typed into a computer when they were told that the computer would save their answers than when they were told that the answers would be erased. But in later experiments, they found that when people saved information to one of several folders on a computer, they were often able to remember where they saved it even when they did not remember the information itself. People seemed to be using the computer in an efficient way to help remember facts, while relying on their own memories to recall where those facts could be found. Sparrow and colleagues suggested that people may be adapting their memories to the demands of new technology, relying on computers in a way that is similar to how we sometimes rely on other people (friends, family members, or colleagues) to remember things that we may not remember ourselves. This is similar to what we discussed as *collaborative memory*, and just as collaborative remembering with other people has both helpful and harmful effects, so does collaborative remembering with our computers.

IN SUMMARY

▶ Long-term memory consists of several different forms. Explicit memory is the act of consciously or intentionally retrieving past experiences, whereas implicit memory refers to the unconscious influence of past experiences on later behavior and performance, such as procedural memory and priming. Procedural memory involves the acquisition of skills as a result of practice, and priming is a change in the ability to recognize or identify an object or a word as the result of past exposure to it.

▶ People who have amnesia are able to retain implicit memory, including procedural memory and priming, but they lack explicit memory.

▶ Episodic memory is the collection of personal experiences from a particular time and place; it allows us both to recollect the past and imagine the future. Semantic memory is a networked, general, impersonal knowledge of facts, associations, and concepts.

▶ Collaborative memory refers to remembering in groups. Collaborative remembering can both impair memory (collaborative inhibition) and enhance it by exposing people to new information and helping to correct errors.

Memory Failures:
The Seven Sins of Memory

You probably haven't given much thought to breathing today, and the reason is that from the moment you woke up, you've been doing it effortlessly and well. But the moment breathing fails, you are reminded of just how important it is. Memory is like that. Every time we see, think, notice, imagine, or wonder, we are drawing on our ability to use information stored in our brains, but it isn't until this ability fails that we become acutely aware of just how much we should treasure it. We've seen in other contexts how an understanding of foibles and errors of human thought and action reveals the normal operation of various behaviors. Such memory errors—the "seven sins" of memory—cast similar illumination on how memory normally operates and how often it operates well (Schacter, 1999, 2001b). We'll discuss each of the seven sins in detail below.

transience
Forgetting what occurs with the passage of time.

1. Transience

On March 6, 2007, I. Lewis "Scooter" Libby, former Chief of Staff to Vice President Dick Cheney, was convicted of perjury, making false statements, and obstruction of justice during an FBI investigation into whether members of the Bush administration had unlawfully disclosed the identity of a CIA agent to the media a couple of years earlier. According to Libby's defense team, any misstatements he might have made in response to FBI questioning were the result of faulty memory, not an intention to deceive. Libby's case received massive media attention and resulted in a national debate: How could Libby forget such important events? Subsequent research has shown that people sometimes mistake the factors that influence forgetting of important events (Kassam et al., 2009). Despite the controversy over forgetting in the Libby case, one thing is certain: Memories can and do degrade with time. The culprit here is **transience:** *forgetting what occurs with the passage of time.*

Transience occurs during the storage phase of memory, after an experience has been encoded and before it is retrieved. You've already seen the workings of transience—rapid forgetting—in sensory storage and short-term storage. Transience also occurs in long-term storage, as was first illustrated in the late 1870s by Hermann Ebbinghaus, a German philosopher who measured his own memory for lists of nonsense syllables at different delays after studying them (Ebbinghaus, 1885/1964). Ebbinghaus charted his recall of nonsense syllables over time, creating the forgetting curve shown in **FIGURE 6.15**. Ebbinghaus noted a rapid drop-off in retention during the first few tests, followed by a slower rate of forgetting on later tests—a general pattern

I. Lewis "Scooter" Libby was convicted of perjury and obstructing justice, but claimed that forgetting and related memory problems were responsible for any misstatements he made.

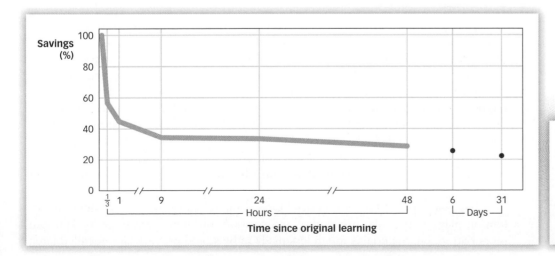

◄ Figure **6.15** **The Curve of Forgetting** Hermann Ebbinghaus measured his retention at various delay intervals after he studied lists of nonsense syllables. Retention was measured in percent savings, that is, the percentage of time needed to relearn the list compared to the time needed to learn it initially.

retroactive interference
Situations in which information learned later impairs memory for information acquired earlier.

proactive interference
Situations in which information learned earlier impairs memory for information acquired later.

absentmindedness
A lapse in attention that results in memory failure.

prospective memory
Remembering to do things in the future.

confirmed by many subsequent memory researchers (Wixted & Ebbensen, 1991). So, for example, when English speakers were tested for memory of Spanish vocabulary acquired during high school or college courses 1 to 50 years previously, there was a rapid drop-off in memory during the first 3 years after the students' last class, followed by tiny losses in later years (Bahrick, 1984, 2000). In all these studies, memories didn't fade at a constant rate as time passed; most forgetting happened soon after an event occurred, with increasingly less forgetting as more time passed.

Not only do we forget memories with the passage of time, the quality of our memories also changes. At early time points on the forgetting curve—minutes, hours, and days—memory preserves a relatively detailed record, allowing us to reproduce the past with reasonable if not perfect accuracy. But with the passing of time, we increasingly rely on our general memories for what usually happens and attempt to reconstruct the details by inference and even sheer guesswork. Transience involves a gradual switch from specific to more general memories (Brewer, 1996; Eldridge, Barnard, & Bekerian, 1994; Thompson et al., 1996). In one early study, British research participants read a brief Native American folktale that had odd imagery and unfamiliar plots in it, and then recounted it as best they could after a delay (Bartlett, 1932). The readers made interesting but understandable errors, often eliminating details that didn't make sense to them or adding elements to make the story more coherent. As the specifics of the story slipped away, the general meaning of the events stayed in memory but usually with elaborations and embellishments that were consistent with the readers' worldview. Because the story was unfamiliar to the readers, they raided their stores of general information and patched together a reasonable recollection of what *probably* happened.

> How might general memories come to distort specific memories?

Yet another way that memories can be distorted is by interference from other memories. For example, if you carry out the same activities at work each day, by the time Friday rolls around, it may be difficult to remember what you did on Monday because later activities blend in with earlier ones. This is an example of **retroactive interference,** *situations in which later learning impairs memory for information acquired earlier* (Postman & Underwood, 1973). **Proactive interference,** in contrast, refers to *situations in which earlier learning impairs memory for information acquired later*. If you use the same parking lot each day at work or at school, you've probably gone out to find your car and then stood there confused by the memories of having parked it on previous days.

CHARLES LIVINGSTON BULL / LIBRARY OF CONGRESS PRINTS AND PHOTOGRAPHS DIVISION [CAI-BULL, NO. 6 (CSIZE) [P&P]

As an example of transience, when there is a delay between the hearing and retelling of the story, someone unfamiliar with Native American legends would more likely recount the general gist than the specific details. This image by Charles Livingston Bull is titled, *Hawk made a light by striking the flints together, and set fire to the ball.*

2. Absentmindedness

The great cellist Yo-Yo Ma put his treasured $2.5 million instrument in the trunk of a taxicab in Manhattan and then rode to his destination. After a 10-minute trip, he paid the driver and left the cab, forgetting his cello. Minutes later, Ma realized what he had done and called the police. Fortunately, they tracked down the taxi and recovered the instrument within hours (Finkelstein, 1999). But how had the celebrated cellist forgotten about something so important that had occurred only 10 minutes earlier? Transience is not a likely culprit. As soon as Mr. Ma realized what he'd done with his instrument, he recalled where he had put it. This information had not disappeared from his memory (which is why he was able to tell the police where the cello was). Instead, Yo-Yo Ma was a victim of **absentmindedness**, *a lapse in attention that results in memory failure*.

What makes people absentminded? One common cause is lack of attention. Attention plays a vital role in encoding information into long-term memory. Without proper attention, material is much less likely to be stored properly and recalled later.

In studies of divided attention, research participants are given materials to remember, such as a list of words, a story, or a series of pictures. At the same time, they are required to perform an additional task that draws their attention away from the material. For example, in one study, participants listened to lists of 15 words for a later memory test (Craik et al., 1996). They were allowed to pay full attention to some of the lists, but while they heard other lists, they simultaneously viewed a visual display containing four boxes and pressed different keys to indicate where an asterisk was appearing and disappearing. On a later test, participants recalled far fewer words from the list they had heard while their attention was divided.

What happens in the brain when attention is divided? In one study, volunteers tried to learn a list of word pairs while researchers scanned their brains with positron emission tomography (PET; Shallice et al., 1994). Some people simultaneously performed a task that took little attention (they moved a bar the same way over and over), whereas other people simultaneously performed a task that took a great deal of attention (they moved a bar over and over but in a novel, unpredictable way each time). The researchers observed less activity in the participants' lower left frontal lobe when their attention was divided. As you saw earlier, greater activity in the lower left frontal region during encoding is associated with better memory. Dividing attention, then, prevents the lower left frontal lobe from playing its normal role in semantic encoding, and the result is absentminded forgetting. More recent research using fMRI has shown that divided attention also leads to less hippocampal involvement in encoding (Kensinger, Clarke, & Corkin, 2003; Uncapher & Rugg, 2008). Given the importance of the hippocampus to episodic memory, this finding may help to explain why absentminded forgetting is sometimes so extreme, as when we forget where we put our keys or glasses only moments earlier.

How is memory affected for someone whose attention is divided?

Yo-Yo Ma with his $2.5 million cello. The famous cellist lost it when he absentmindedly forgot that he'd placed the instrument in a taxicab's trunk minutes earlier.

Another common cause of absentmindedness is forgetting to carry out actions that we planned to do in the future. On any given day, you need to remember the times and places that your classes meet, you need to remember with whom and where you are having lunch, you need to remember which grocery items to pick up for dinner, and you need to remember which page of this book you were on when you fell asleep. In other words, you have to remember to remember, and this is called **prospective memory**, *remembering to do things in the future* (Einstein & McDaniel, 1990, 2005).

Failures of prospective memory are a major source of absentmindedness. Avoiding these problems often requires having a cue available at the moment you need to remember to carry out an action. For example, air traffic controllers must sometimes postpone an action, such as granting a pilot's request to change altitude, but remember to carry out that action a few minutes later when conditions change. In a simulated air traffic control experiment, researchers provided controllers with electronic signals to remind them to carry out a deferred request 1 minute later. The reminders were made available either during the 1-minute waiting period or at the time the controller needed to act on the deferred request. The controllers' memory for the deferred action improved only when the reminder was available at the time needed for retrieval. Providing the reminder during the waiting period did not help (Vortac, Edwards, & Manning, 1995). An early reminder, then, is no reminder at all.

Talking on a cell phone while driving is a common occurrence of divided attention in everyday life; texting is even worse. This can be dangerous, and an increasing number of states have banned the practice.

3. Blocking

Have you ever tried to recall the name of a famous movie actor or a book you've read—and felt that the answer was on the tip of your tongue, rolling around in your head *somewhere* but just out of reach at the moment? This tip-of-the-tongue experience is a classic example of **blocking**, *a failure to retrieve information that is available in memory even though you are trying to produce it*. The sought-after information has been encoded and stored, and a cue is available that would ordinarily trigger recall of it. The information has not faded from memory, and you aren't forgetting to retrieve it. Rather, you are experiencing a full-blown retrieval failure, which makes this memory breakdown especially frustrating. It seems absolutely clear that you should be able to produce the information you seek, but the fact of the matter is that you can't. Researchers have described the tip-of-the-tongue state, in particular, as "a mild torment, something like [being] on the brink of a sneeze" (Brown & McNeill, 1966, p. 326).

Studies have found that when people are in tip-of-the-tongue states, they often know something about the item they can't recall, such as the meaning of a word (Schwartz, 2002). When experimenters induced tip-of-the-tongue states by playing participants theme songs from 1950s and 1960s television shows and asking for the names of the shows, people who were blocked on *The Munsters* often came up with another comically ghoulish sitcom, *The Addams Family* (Riefer, Kevari, & Kramer, 1995).

Blocking occurs especially often for the names of people and places (Cohen, 1990; Semenza, 2009; Valentine, Brennen, & Brédart, 1996). Why? Because their links to related concepts and knowledge are weaker than for common names. That somebody's last name is Baker doesn't tell us much about the person, but saying that he *is* a baker does. To illustrate this point, researchers showed people pictures of cartoon and comic strip characters, some with descriptive names that highlight key features of the character (e.g., Grumpy, Snow White, Scrooge) and others with arbitrary names (e.g., Aladdin, Mary Poppins, Pinocchio; Brédart & Valentine, 1998). Even though the two types of names were equally familiar to participants in the experiment, they blocked less often on the descriptive names than on the arbitrary names.

Why is Snow White's name easier to remember than Mary Poppins?

Although it's frustrating when it occurs, blocking is a relatively infrequent event for most of us. However, it occurs more often as we grow older, and it is a very common complaint among people in their 60s and 70s (Burke et al., 1991; Schwartz, 2002). Even more striking, some individuals with brain damage live in a nearly perpetual tip-of-the-tongue state (Semenza, 2009). One such individual could recall the names of only 2 of 40 famous people when she saw their photographs, compared to 25 of 40 for healthy volunteers in the control group (Semenza & Zettin, 1989). Yet she could still recall correctly the occupations of 32 of these people—the same number as healthy people could recall. This case and similar ones have given researchers important clues about what parts of the brain are involved in retrieving proper names. Name blocking usually results from damage to parts of the left temporal lobe on the surface of the cortex, most often as a result of a stroke. In fact, studies that show strong activation of regions within the temporal lobe when people recall proper names support this idea (Damasio et al., 1996; Gorno-Tempini et al., 1998).

4. Memory Misattribution

Shortly after the devastating 1995 bombing of the federal building in Oklahoma City, police set about searching for two suspects they called John Doe 1 and John Doe 2. John Doe 1 turned out to be Timothy McVeigh, who was quickly apprehended and

Suppose that, mentally consumed by planning for a psychology test the next day, you place your keys in an unusual spot, and later forget where you put them. Is this more likely to reflect the memory sin of transience, absentmindedness, or blocking?

later convicted of the crime and sentenced to death. John Doe 2, who had supposedly accompanied McVeigh when he rented a van from Elliott's Body Shop two days before the bombing, was never found. In fact, John Doe 2 had never existed; he was a product of the memory of Tom Kessinger, a mechanic at Elliott's Body Shop who was present when McVeigh rented the van. The day after, two other men had also rented a van in Kessinger's presence. The first man, like McVeigh, was tall and fair. The second man was shorter and stockier, was dark-haired, wore a blue and white cap, and had a tattoo beneath his left sleeve—a match to the description of John Doe 2. Tom Kessinger had confused his recollections of men he had seen on separate days in the same place. He was a victim of **memory misattribution**, *assigning a recollection or an idea to the wrong source* (see **FIGURE 6.16**).

Memory misattribution errors are some of the primary causes of eyewitness misidentifications. The memory researcher Donald Thomson was accused of rape based on the victim's detailed recollection of his face, but he was eventually cleared when it turned out he had an airtight alibi. At the time of the rape, Thomson was giving a live television interview on the subject of distorted memories! The victim had been watching the show just before she was assaulted and misattributed her memory of Thomson's face to the rapist (Schacter, 1996; Thomson, 1988). Thomson's case, though dramatic, is not an isolated occurrence: Faulty eyewitness memory was a factor in more than 75% of the first 250 cases in which individuals were shown to be innocent by DNA evidence after conviction for crimes they did not commit (Garrett, 2011).

Part of memory is knowing where our memories came from. This is known as **source memory**, *recall of when, where, and how information was acquired* (Johnson, Hashtroudi, & Lindsay, 1993; Mitchell & Johnson, 2009; Schacter, Harbluk, & McLachlan, 1984). People sometimes correctly recall a fact they learned earlier or accurately recognize a person or object they have seen before but misattribute the source of this knowledge—just as happened to Tom Kessinger and the rape victim in the Donald Thomson incident (Davies, 1988). Such misattribution could be the cause of déjà vu experiences, where you suddenly feel that you have been in a situation before even though you can't recall any details. A present situation that is similar to a past experience may trigger a general sense of familiarity that is mistakenly attributed to having been in the exact situation previously (Brown, 2004; Reed, 1988).

> **What can explain a déjà vu experience?**

Individuals with damage to the frontal lobes are especially prone to memory misattribution errors (Schacter et al., 1984; Shimamura & Squire, 1987). This is probably because the frontal lobes play a significant role in effortful retrieval processes, which are required to dredge up the correct source of a memory. These individuals sometimes produce bizarre misattributions. In 1991, a British photographer in his mid-40s known as MR was overcome with feelings of familiarity about people he didn't know. He kept asking his wife whether each new passing stranger was "somebody"—a screen actor, television newsperson, or local celebrity. MR's feelings were so intense that he often could not resist approaching strangers and asking whether they were indeed famous celebrities. When given formal tests, MR recognized the faces of actual celebrities as accurately as did healthy volunteers in the control group. But MR also "recognized" more than 75% of unfamiliar faces, whereas healthy volunteers hardly ever

▲ Figure **6.16** **Memory Misattribution** In 1995 the Murrah Federal Building in Oklahoma City was bombed in an act of terrorism. The police sketch shows John Doe 2, who was originally thought to have been culprit Timothy McVeigh's partner in the bombing. It was later determined that the witness had confused his memories of different men whom he had encountered at Elliott's Body Shop on different days.

blocking
A failure to retrieve information that is available in memory even though you are trying to produce it.

memory misattribution
Assigning a recollection or an idea to the wrong source.

source memory
Recall of when, where, and how information was acquired.

Table 6.1

False Recognition

Sour	Thread
Candy	Pin
Sugar	Eye
Bitter	Sewing
Good	Sharp
Taste	Point
Tooth	Prick
Nice	Thimble
Honey	Haystack
Soda	Pain
Chocolate	Hurt
Heart	Injection
Cake	Syringe
Tart	Cloth
Pie	Knitting

▼ Figure **6.17 Hippocampal Activity during True and False Recognition** Many brain regions show similar activation during true and false recognition, including the hippocampus. The figure shows results from an fMRI study of true and false recognition of visual shapes (Slotnick & Schacter, 2004). (*a*) A plot showing the activity level in the strength of the fMRI signal from the hippocampus over time. This shows that after a few seconds, there is comparable activation for true recognition of previously studied shapes (red line) and false recognition of similar shapes that were not presented (yellow line). Both true and false recognition show increased hippocampal activity compared with correctly classifying unrelated shapes as new (purple line). (*b*) A region of the left hippocampus.

did. Neurological exams revealed that MR suffered from multiple sclerosis, which had caused damage to his frontal lobes (Ward et al., 1999). Psychologists call the type of memory misattribution made by MR **false recognition**, *a feeling of familiarity about something that hasn't been encountered before.*

The subjective experience for MR, as in everyday déjà vu experiences, is characterized by a strong sense of familiarity without any recall of associated details. Other individuals with neurological damage exhibit a recently discovered type of memory misattribution called déjà vécu: They feel strongly—but mistakenly—that they have already lived through an experience and remember the details of what happened (Moulin et al., 2005). For example, when watching television, one such individual was certain that he recalled seeing each show before, even when he was watching an entirely new episode. When he went shopping, he constantly thought it was unnecessary to buy needed items because he remembered having done so already. Although the basis of this strange disorder is not well understood, it probably involves disruption to parts of the temporal lobe that normally generate a subjective feeling of remembering (Moulin et al., 2005).

But we are all vulnerable to memory misattribution. Take the following test and there is a good chance that you will experience false recognition for yourself. First, study the two lists of words presented in **TABLE 6.1** by reading each word for about 1 second. When you are done, return to this paragraph for more instructions, but don't look back at the table! Now try to recognize which of the following words appeared on the list you just studied: *taste, bread, needle, king, sweet, thread.* If you think that *taste* and *thread* were on the lists you studied, you're right. And if you think that *bread* and *king* weren't on those lists, you're also right. But if you think that *needle* or *sweet* appeared on the lists, you're dead wrong.

Most people make exactly the same mistake, claiming with confidence that they saw *needle* and *sweet* on the list. This occurs because all the words in the lists are associated with *needle* or *sweet*. Seeing each word in the study list activates related words. Because *needle* and *sweet* are related to all of the associates, they become more activated than other words—so highly activated that only minutes later, people swear that they actually studied the words (Deese, 1959; Gallo, 2006, 2010; Roediger & McDermott, 1995, 2000). In fact, brain scanning studies using PET and fMRI show that many of the same brain regions are active during false recognition and true recognition, including the hippocampus (Cabeza et al., 2001; Schacter, Reiman, et al., 1996; see **FIGURE 6.17**). Similar results are obtained when people view a series of common objects (e.g., cars, umbrellas) and then are later shown a new object that looks

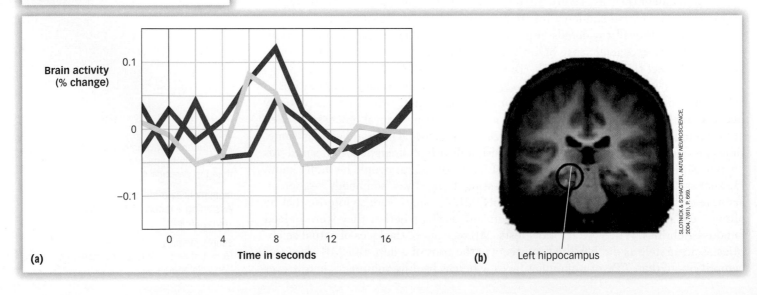

Brain activity (% change)

0.1

0

−0.1

0 4 8 12 16

Time in seconds

(a)

(b) Left hippocampus

SLOTNICK & SCHACTER, *NATURE NEUROSCIENCE*, 2004, 7(6), P. 669.

like one they saw earlier: They often falsely recognize the similar new item, and many of the same brain regions become active during this kind of false recognition (Gutchess & Schacter, 2012; Slotnick & Schacter, 2004).

However, false recognition can be reduced (Schacter, Israel, & Racine, 1999). For example, recent evidence shows that when participants are given a choice between an object that they actually saw (e.g., a car) and a visually similar new object (a different car that looks like the one they saw), they almost always choose the car that they actually saw and thus avoid making a false recognition error (Guerin et al., 2012a, 2012b). This finding suggests that false recognition occurs, at least in part, because when presented with a similar new object on its own, participants don't recollect specific details about the object they actually studied, but these details need to be retrieved in order to correctly indicate that the similar object is new. Yet this information is available in memory, as shown by the ability of participants to correctly choose between the studied object and the visually similar new object. When people experience a strong sense of familiarity about a person, object, or event but lack specific recollections, a potentially dangerous recipe for memory misattribution is in place, both in the laboratory and also in real-world situations involving eyewitness memory. Understanding this point may be a key to reducing the dangerous consequences of misattribution in eyewitness testimony.

5. Suggestibility

On October 4, 1992, an El Al cargo plane crashed into an apartment building in a southern suburb of Amsterdam, killing 39 residents and all 4 members of the airline crew. The disaster dominated news in the Netherlands for days as people viewed footage of the crash scene and read about the catastrophe. Ten months later, Dutch psychologists

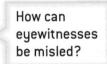

How can eyewitnesses be misled?

asked a simple question of university students: "Did you see the television film of the moment the plane hit the apartment building?" Fifty-five percent answered yes (Crombag, Wagenaar, & Van Koppen, 1996). All of this might seem perfectly normal except for one key fact: There was no television film of the moment when the plane actually crashed. The researchers had asked a suggestive question that implied that television film of the crash had been shown. Respondents may have viewed television film of the post-crash scene, and they may have read, imagined, or talked about what might have happened when the plane hit the building, but they most definitely did not see it. The suggestive question led participants to misattribute information from these or other sources to a film that did not exist. **Suggestibility** is the *tendency to incorporate misleading information from external sources into personal recollections.*

If misleading details can be implanted in people's memories, is it also possible to suggest entire episodes that never occurred? The answer seems to be yes (Loftus, 1993, 2003). In one study, the research participant, a teenager named Chris, was asked by his older brother, Jim, to try to remember the time Chris had been lost in a shopping mall at age 5. He initially recalled nothing, but after several days, Chris produced a detailed recollection of the event. He recalled that he "felt so scared I would never see my family again" and remembered that a kindly old man wearing a flannel shirt found him crying (Loftus, 1993, p. 532). But according to Jim and other family members, Chris was never lost in a shopping mall. Of 24 participants in a larger study

In 1992, an El Al cargo plane crashed into an apartment building in a suburb of Amsterdam. When Dutch psychologists asked students if they had seen the television film of the plane crashing, a majority said they had. In fact, no such footage exists (Crombag et al., 1996).

false recognition
A feeling of familiarity about something that hasn't been encountered before.

suggestibility
The tendency to incorporate misleading information from external sources into personal recollections.

on implanted memories, approximately 25% falsely remembered being lost as a child in a shopping mall or in a similar public place (Loftus & Pickrell, 1995).

People develop false memories in response to suggestions for some of the same reasons memory misattribution occurs. We do not store all the details of our experiences in memory, making us vulnerable to accepting suggestions about what might have happened or should have happened. In addition, visual imagery plays an important role in constructing false memories (Goff & Roediger, 1998). Asking people to imagine an event like spilling punch all over the bride's parents at a wedding increases the likelihood that they will develop a false memory of it (Hyman & Pentland, 1996).

> **Why can childhood memories be influenced by suggestion?**

Suggestibility played an important role in a controversy that arose during the 1980s and 1990s concerning the accuracy of childhood memories that people recalled during psychotherapy. One highly publicized example involved a woman named Diana Halbrooks (Schacter, 1996). After a few months in psychotherapy, she began recalling disturbing incidents from her childhood, for example, that her mother had tried to kill her and that her father had abused her sexually. Although her parents denied that these events had ever occurred, her therapist encouraged her to believe in the reality of her memories. Eventually Diana Halbrooks stopped therapy and came to realize that the "memories" she had recovered were inaccurate.

How could this happen? A number of the techniques used by psychotherapists to try to pull up forgotten childhood memories are clearly suggestive (Poole et al., 1995). Specifically, research has shown that imagining past events and hypnosis can help create false memories (Garry et al., 1996; Hyman & Pentland, 1996; McConkey, Barnier, & Sheehan, 1998). More recent studies show that memories that people remember spontaneously on their own are corroborated by other people at about the same rate as the memories of individuals who never forgot their abuse, whereas memories recovered in response to suggestive therapeutic techniques are virtually never corroborated by others (McNally & Geraerts, 2009).

6. Bias

In 2000, the outcome of a very close presidential race between George W. Bush and Al Gore was decided by the Supreme Court 5 weeks after the election had taken place. The day after the election (when the result was still in doubt), supporters of Bush and Gore were asked to predict how happy they would be after the outcome of the election was determined (Wilson, Meyers, & Gilbert, 2003). These same respondents reported how happy they felt with the outcome on the day after Al Gore conceded. And 4 months later, the participants recalled how happy they had been right after the election was decided.

How happy do you think you'd be if the candidate you supported won an election? Do you think you'd accurately remember your level of happiness if you recalled it several months later? Chances are good that bias in the memory process would alter your recollection of your previous happiness. Indeed, 4 months after they heard the outcome of the 2000 presidential election, Bush supporters overestimated how happy they were, whereas Gore supporters underestimated how happy they were.

Bush supporters, who eventually enjoyed a positive result (their candidate took office), were understandably happy the day after the Supreme Court's decision. However, their retrospective accounts *over*estimated how happy they were at the time. Conversely, Gore supporters were not pleased with the outcome. But when polled 4 months after the election was decided, Gore supporters *under*estimated how happy they actually were at the time of the result. In both groups, recollections of happiness were at odds with existing reports of their actual happiness at the time (Wilson et al., 2003).

These results illustrate the problem of **bias**, *the distorting influences of present knowledge, beliefs, and feelings on recollection of previous experiences.* Sometimes what people remember from their

PAUL J. RICHARDS/AFP/GETTY IMAGES

DOUG MILLS/AP PHOTO

pasts says less about what actually happened than about what they think, feel, or believe now. Researchers have also found that our current moods can bias our recall of past experiences (Bower, 1981; Buchanan, 2007; Eich, 1995). So, in addition to helping you recall actual sad memories (as you saw earlier in this chapter), a sad mood can also bias your recollections of experiences that may not have been so sad. *Consistency bias* is the bias to reconstruct the past to fit the present. One researcher asked people in 1973 to rate their attitudes toward a variety of controversial social issues, including legalization of marijuana, women's rights, and aid to minorities (Marcus, 1986). They were asked to make the same rating again in 1982 and also to indicate what their attitudes had been in 1973. Researchers found that participants' recollections of their 1973 attitudes in 1982 were more closely related to what they believed in 1982 than to what they had actually said in 1973.

> **How does your current outlook color your memory of a past event?**

bias
The distorting influences of present knowledge, beliefs, and feelings on recollection of previous experiences.

Whereas consistency bias exaggerates the similarity between past and present, *change bias* is the tendency to exaggerate differences between what we feel or believe now and what we felt or believed in the past. In other words, *change biases* also occur. For example, most of us would like to believe that our romantic attachments grow stronger over time. In one study, dating couples were asked, once a year for 4 years, to assess the present quality of their relationships and to recall how they felt in past years (Sprecher, 1999). Couples who stayed together for the 4 years recalled that the strength of their love had increased since they last reported on it. Yet their actual ratings at the time did not show any increases in love and attachment. Objectively, the couples did not love each other more today than yesterday. But they did from the subjective perspective of memory.

A special case of change bias is *egocentric bias,* the tendency to exaggerate the change between present and past in order to make ourselves look good in retrospect. For example, students sometimes remember feeling more anxious before taking an exam than they actually reported at the time (Keuler & Safer, 1998), and blood donors sometimes recall being more nervous about giving blood than they actually were (Breckler, 1994). In both cases, change biases color memory and make people feel that they behaved more bravely or courageously than they actually did. Similarly, when college students tried to remember high school grades and their memories were checked against actual transcripts, they were highly accurate for grades of A (89% correct) and extremely inaccurate for grades of D (29% correct; Bahrick, Hall, & Berger, 1996). The same kind of egocentric bias occurs with memory for college grades: 81% of errors inflated the actual grade, and this bias was evident even when participants were asked about their grades soon after graduation (Bahrick, Hall, & DaCosta, 2008). People were remembering the past as they wanted it to be rather than the way it was.

The way each member of this happy couple recalls earlier feelings toward the other depends on how each currently views their relationship.

7. Persistence

The artist Melinda Stickney-Gibson awoke in her apartment to the smell of smoke. She jumped out of bed and saw black plumes rising through cracks in the floor. Raging flames had engulfed the entire building, and there was no chance to escape except by jumping from her third-floor window. Shortly after she crashed to the ground, the building exploded into a brilliant fireball. Although she survived the fire and the fall, Melinda became overwhelmed by memories of the fire. When Melinda sat down in front of a blank canvas to start a new painting, her memories of that awful night intruded. Her paintings, which were previously bright, colorful abstractions, became dark meditations that included only black, orange, and ochre—the colors of the fire (Schacter, 1996).

ANDERSEN ROSS/
PHOTOLIBRARY

persistence
The intrusive recollection of events that we wish we could forget.

flashbulb memories
Detailed recollections of when and where we heard about shocking events.

Melinda Stickney-Gibson's experiences illustrate memory's seventh and most deadly sin, **persistence**: *the intrusive recollection of events that we wish we could forget.* Melinda's experience is far from unique; persistence frequently occurs after disturbing or traumatic incidents, such as the fire that destroyed her home. Although being able to recall memories quickly is usually considered a good thing, in the case of persistence, that ability mutates into an unwelcome burden.

Controlled laboratory studies have revealed that emotional experiences tend to be better remembered than nonemotional ones. For instance, memory for unpleasant pictures, such as mutilated bodies, or pleasant ones, such as attractive men and women, is more accurate than for emotionally neutral pictures, such as household objects (Ochsner, 2000). Emotional arousal seems to focus our attention on the central features of an event. In one experiment, people who viewed an emotionally arousing sequence of slides involving a bloody car accident remembered more of the central themes and fewer peripheral details than people who viewed a nonemotional sequence (Christianson & Loftus, 1987).

Intrusive memories are undesirable consequences of emotional experiences because emotional experiences generally lead to more vivid and enduring recollections than nonemotional experiences do. One line of evidence comes from the study of **flashbulb memories**, which are *detailed recollections of when and where we heard about shocking events* (Brown & Kulick, 1977). For example, most Americans can recall exactly where they were and how they heard about the September 11, 2001, terrorist attacks on the World Trade Center and the Pentagon—almost as if a mental flashbulb had gone off automatically and recorded the event in long-lasting and vivid detail (Kvavilashvili et al., 2009). Several studies have shown that flashbulb memories are not always entirely accurate, but they are generally better remembered than mundane news events from the same time (Larsen, 1992; Neisser & Harsch, 1992). Enhanced retention of flashbulb memories is partly attributable to the emotional arousal elicited by events such as the 9/11 terrorist attacks, and partly attributable to the fact that we tend to talk and think a lot about these experiences. Recall that semantic encoding enhances memory: When we talk about flashbulb experiences, we elaborate on them and thus further increase the memorability of those aspects of the experience that we discuss (Hirst et al., 2009).

> **How does emotional trauma affect memory?**

Some events are so emotionally charged, such as President Kennedy's assassination and the terrorist attack on the World Trade Center, that we form unusually detailed memories of when and where we heard about them. These flashbulb memories generally persist much longer than memories for more ordinary events.

Why do our brains succumb to persistence? A key player in the brain's response to emotional events is a small, almond-shaped structure called the *amygdala*, shown in **FIGURE 6.18.** The amygdala influences hormonal systems that kick into high gear when we experience an arousing event; these stress-related hormones, such as adrenaline and cortisol, mobilize the body in the face of threat—and they also enhance memory for the experience. Damage to the amygdala does not result in a general memory deficit. Individuals with amygdala damage, however, do not remember emotional events any better than nonemotional events (Cahill & McGaugh, 1998).

For example, consider what happened when people viewed a series of photographic slides that began with a mother walking her child to school and later included an emotionally arousing event: the child being hit by a car. When tested later, the research participants remembered the arousing event better than the mundane ones. But individuals with amygdala damage remembered the mundane and emotionally arousing events equally well (Cahill & McGaugh, 1998). PET and fMRI scans show that when healthy people view a slide sequence that includes an emotionally arousing event, the level of activity in the amygdala at the time they see it is a good predictor of their subsequent memory for the slide. When there is heightened activity in the amygdala as people watch emotional events, there's a better chance that they will recall those events on a later test (Cahill et al., 1996; Kensinger & Schacter, 2005, 2006). And when people are given a drug that interferes with the amygdala-mediated release of stress hormones, their memory for the emotional sections is no better than their memory for the mundane sections.

In many cases, there are clear benefits to forming strong memories for highly emotional events, particularly those that are life-threatening. In the case of persistence, though, such memories may be too strong—strong enough to interfere with other aspects of daily life.

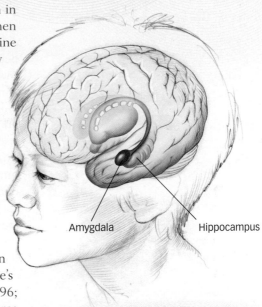

▲ Figure **6.18 The Amygdala's Influence on Memory** The amygdala, located next to the hippocampus, responds strongly to emotional events. Individuals with amygdala damage are unable to remember emotional events any better than nonemotional ones (Cahill & McGaugh, 1998).

Are the Seven Sins Vices or Virtues?

You may have concluded that evolution has burdened us with an extremely inefficient memory system that is so prone to error that it often jeopardizes our well-being. Not so. The seven sins are the price we pay for the many benefits that memory provides, the occasional result of the normally efficient operation of the human memory system (Schacter, 2001b).

Consider transience, for example. Wouldn't it be great to remember all the details of every incident in your life, no matter how much time had passed? Not necessarily. Do you remember Jill Price, the woman we described earlier in this chapter, who has this ability and said it drives her crazy (see p. xxx)?

It's helpful and sometimes important to forget information that isn't current, like an old phone number. If we didn't gradually forget information over time, our minds would be cluttered with details that we no longer need (Bjork, 2011; Bjork & Bjork, 1988). Information that is used infrequently is less likely to be needed in the future than information that is used more frequently over the same period (Anderson & Schooler, 1991, 2000). Memory, in essence, makes a bet that when we haven't used information recently, we probably won't need it in the future. We win this bet more often than we lose it, making transience an adaptive property of memory. But we are acutely aware of the losses—the frustrations of forgetting—and are never aware of the wins. This is why people are often quick to complain about their memories: The drawbacks of forgetting are painfully evident, but the benefits of forgetting are hidden.

How are we better off with imperfect memories?

Similarly, absentmindedness and blocking can be frustrating, but they are side effects of our memory's usually successful attempt to sort through incoming information, preserving details that are worthy of attention and recall, and discarding those that are less worthy.

Memory misattribution and suggestibility both occur because we often fail to recall the details of exactly when and where we saw a face or learned a fact. This is because memory is adapted to retain information that is most likely to be needed in the environment in which it operates. We seldom need to remember all the precise contextual details of every experience. Our memories carefully record such details only when we think they may be needed later, and most of the time we are better off for it. Furthermore, we often use memories to anticipate possible future events. As discussed earlier, memory is flexible, allowing us to recombine elements of past experience in new ways, so that we can mentally try out different versions of what might happen. But this very flexibility—a strength of memory—may sometimes produce misattribution errors in which elements of past experience are miscombined (Schacter & Addis, 2007; Schacter, Guerin, & St. Jacques, 2011). Bias skews our memories so that we depict ourselves in an overly favorable light, but it can produce the benefit of contributing to our overall sense of contentment. Holding positive illusions about ourselves can lead to greater psychological well-being (Taylor, 1989). Although persistence can cause us to be haunted by traumas that we'd be better off forgetting, overall, it is probably adaptive to remember threatening or traumatic events that could pose a threat to survival.

Although each of the seven sins can cause trouble in our lives, they have an adaptive side as well. You can think of the seven sins as costs we pay for benefits that allow memory to work as well as it does most of the time.

IN SUMMARY

▶ Memory's mistakes can be classified into seven sins.

▶ Transience is reflected by a rapid decline in memory followed by more gradual forgetting. With the passing of time, memory switches from detailed to general. Both decay and interference contribute to transience. Absentmindedness results from failures of attention, shallow encoding, and the influence of automatic behaviors, and is often associated with forgetting to do things in the future. Blocking occurs when stored information is temporarily inaccessible, as when information is on the tip of the tongue.

▶ Memory misattribution happens when we experience a sense of familiarity but don't recall, or mistakenly recall, the specifics of when and where an experience occurred. Misattribution can result in eyewitness misidentification or false recognition. Individuals suffering from frontal lobe damage are especially susceptible to false recognition. Suggestibility gives rise to implanted memories of small details or entire episodes. Suggestive techniques such as hypnosis or visualization can promote vivid recall of suggested events, and therapists' use of suggestive techniques may be responsible for some individuals' false memories of childhood traumas. Bias reflects the influence of current knowledge, beliefs, and feelings on memory or past experiences. Bias can lead us to make the past consistent with the present, exaggerate changes between past and present, or remember the past in a way that makes us look good.

▶ Persistence reflects the fact that emotional arousal generally leads to enhanced memory, whether we want to remember an experience or not. Persistence is partly attributable to the operation of hormonal systems influenced by the amygdala. Although each of the seven sins can cause trouble in our lives, they have an adaptive side as well.

▶ You can think of the seven sins as costs we pay for benefits that allow memory to work as well as it does most of the time.

OTHER VOICES

Early Memories

Charles Fernyhough is a psychologist at Durham University in England, and the author of several books, including *The Baby in the Mirror: A Child's World from Birth to Three* (2008).

PHOTO: LANN

In this eloquent passage from his recent book about memory, *Pieces of Light*, psychologist Charles Fernyhough (2012, pp. 1–2) described his attempt to remember the first fish that he ever caught. He comes up with what he thinks may be the answer, but how does he really know?

"Can you remember?"

It starts with a question from my 7-year-old son. We are in the grounds of our rented cottage in the Baixa Alentejo, killing time before we head to the Algarve coast for a boat trip. With his holiday money, Isaac has bought himself a hand-held toy that fires little foam rockets prodigious distances up into the air, and he has lost one of them on the graveled ground behind the swimming pool. As we search, he has been chattering away about how he wants to go fishing with me when we get home from Portugal. I have told him that I used to go fishing, as a child of about his age, with my uncle in the lake in the grounds of my grandparents' house in Essex. Then, out of the blue, he asks the question:

"Can you remember the first fish you ever caught?"

I stand straight and look out at the farmland that slopes away from our hillside vantage point. I have not been fishing in thirty-five years, but my thoughts have occasionally returned to my outings with my uncle. When they do, certain images rise out of the past. I can picture the greenish lake with its little island in the middle, how mysterious and unreachable that weeping willowed outcrop looked to my small-scale imaginings. I can sense my jocular young uncle next to me, his stretches of silence punctuated with kindly teasing. I remember the feel of the crustless bits of white bread soaked in pond water that we used to squidge on to the fish-hooks as bait, and the excitement (for a keen young amateur naturalist) of an afternoon visitation from a stoat, scurrying along by the bullrushes with its black-tipped tail bobbing. I remember the weird, faintly gruesome exercise of extracting the hook from a rudd's mouth and then throwing the muscular sliver back into the lake to restart its perforated life. But I have never thought about the moment of feeling the tug on the line, the thrill that prefigured the landing of a fish. And I have certainly not had the question framed like this, narrowing my remembering down to the first time it ever happened.

"I don't know," I reply. "I *think* so."

What accounts for my uncertainty?

Try to recall your own earliest memory of a specific event from your life: How do you know when your recollection took place? How do you know that what you are remembering is the actual event? What kind of evidence would you require to be convinced that your memory is valid? Can you think of an experiment that might be conducted to provide that evidence?

One way to address this problem is to ask people about memories for events that have clearly definable dates, such as the birth of a younger sibling, the death of a loved one, or a family move. For example, one study found that individuals can recall events surrounding the birth of a sibling that occurred when they were about 2.4 years old (Eacott & Crawley, 1998).

Do you think that firm conclusions can be drawn from these kinds of studies? Isn't it still possible that memories of these early events are based on family conversations that took place long after the events occurred? An adult or a child who remembers having ice cream in the hospital as a 3-year-old when his baby sister was born may be recalling what his parents told him after the event (see the Culture & Community box). Carefully designed studies may bring us closer to answering the kinds of questions raised by Charles Fernyhough's response to his son's innocent question, but we still have a long way to go before we can provide convincing answers to the mysteries posed by our earliest memories.

Chapter Review

KEY CONCEPT QUIZ

1. Encoding is the process
   a. by which we transform what we perceive, think, or feel into an enduring memory.
   b. of maintaining information in memory over time.
   c. of bringing to mind information that has been previously stored.
   d. through which we recall information previously learned but forgotten.

2. What is the process of relating new information in a meaningful way to knowledge that is already in memory?
   a. spontaneous encoding
   b. organization encoding
   c. semantic encoding
   d. visual imagery encoding

3. Our human ancestors depended on the encoding of
   a. organizational information.
   b. reproductive mechanisms.
   c. survival-related information.
   d. pleasantness conditions.

4. What kind of memory storage holds information for a second or two?
   a. retrograde memory
   b. working memory
   c. short-term memory
   d. sensory memory

5. The process by which memories become stable in the brain is called
   a. consolidation.
   b. long-term memory.
   c. iconic memory.
   d. hippocampal indexing.

6. Long-term potentiation occurs through
   a. the interruption of communication between neurons.
   b. the strengthening of synaptic connections.
   c. the reconsolidation of disrupted memories.
   d. sleep.

7. The increased likelihood of recalling a sad memory when you are in a sad mood is an illustration of
   a. the encoding specificity principle.
   b. state-dependent retrieval.
   c. transfer-appropriate processing.
   d. memory accessibility.

8. Which of the following statements regarding the consequences of memory retrieval is false?
   a. Retrieval-induced forgetting can affect eyewitness memory.
   b. The act of retrieval can strengthen a retrieved memory.
   c. Retrieval can impair subsequent memory.
   d. Retrieval boosts subsequent memory through the repetition of information.

9. Neuroimaging studies suggest that *trying* to remember activates the
   a. left frontal lobe.
   b. hippocampal region.

   c. occipital lobe.
   d. upper temporal lobe.

10. The act of consciously or intentionally retrieving past experiences is
   a. priming.
   b. procedural memory.
   c. implicit memory.
   d. explicit memory.

11. People who have amnesia are able to retain all of the following except
   a. explicit memory.
   b. implicit memory.
   c. procedural memory.
   d. priming.

12. Remembering a family reunion that you attended as a child illustrates
   a. semantic memory.
   b. procedural memory.
   c. episodic memory.
   d. perceptual priming.

13. The rapid decline in memory, followed by more gradual forgetting, is reflected by
   a. chunking.
   b. blocking.
   c. absentmindedness.
   d. transience.

14. Eyewitness misidentification or false recognition is most likely a result of
   a. memory misattribution.
   b. suggestibility.
   c. bias.
   d. retroactive interference.

15. The fact that emotional arousal generally leads to enhanced memory is supported by
   a. egocentric bias.
   b. persistence.
   c. proactive interference.
   d. source memory.

KEY TERMS

memory (p. 222)
encoding (p. 222)
storage (p. 222)
retrieval (p. 222)
semantic encoding (p. 224)
visual imagery encoding (p. 224)
organizational encoding (p. 224)
sensory memory (p. 228)
iconic memory (p. 228)
echoic memory (p. 228)
short-term memory (p. 229)
rehearsal (p. 229)

chunking (p. 229)
working memory (p. 229)
long-term memory (p. 230)
anterograde amnesia (p. 232)
retrograde amnesia (p. 232)
consolidation (p. 232)
reconsolidation (p. 232)
long-term potentiation (LTP) (p. 234)
retrieval cue (p. 237)
encoding specificity principle (p. 237)

state-dependent retrieval (p. 237)
transfer-appropriate processing (p. 237)
retrieval-induced forgetting (p. 238)
explicit memory (p. 243)
implicit memory (p. 243)
procedural memory (p. 243)
priming (p. 243)
semantic memory (p. 244)
episodic memory (p. 244)
transience (p. 249)
retroactive interference (p. 250)

proactive interference (p. 250)
absentmindedness (p. 250)
prospective memory (p. 250)
blocking (p. 253)
memory misattribution (p. 253)
source memory (p. 253)
false recognition (p. 255)
suggestibility (p. 255)
bias (p. 257)
persistence (p. 258)
flashbulb memories (p. 258)

CHANGING MINDS

1. A friend of yours lost her father to cancer when she was a very young child. "I really wish I remembered him better," she says. "I know all the memories are locked in my head. I'm thinking of trying hypnotism to unlock some of those memories." You explain that we don't, in fact, have stored memories of everything that ever happened to us locked in our heads. What examples could you give of ways in which memories can be lost over time?

2. Another friend of yours has a very vivid memory of sitting with his parents in the living room on September 11, 2001, watching live TV as the Twin Towers fell during the terrorist attacks. "I remember my mother was crying," he says, "and that scared me more than the pictures on the TV." Later, he goes home for a visit and discusses the events of 9/11 with his mother—and is stunned when she assures him that he was actually in school on the morning of the attacks and was only sent home at lunchtime, after the towers had fallen. "I don't understand," he tells you afterward. "I think she must be confused, because I have a perfect memory of that morning." Assuming your friend's mother is recalling events correctly, how would you explain to your friend the ways in which his snapshot memory could be wrong? What memory sin might be at fault?

3. You ask one of your psychology classmates if she wants to form a study group to prepare for an upcoming exam. "No offense," she says, "but I can study the material best by just reading the chapter eight or nine times, and I can do that without a study group." What's wrong with your classmate's study plan? In what ways might the members of a study group help one another learn more effectively?

4. You and a friend go to a party on campus where you meet a lot of new people. After the party, your friend says, "I liked a lot of the people we met, but I'll never remember all their names. Some people just have a good memory, and some don't, and there's nothing I can do about it." What advice could you give your friend to help him remember the names of people he meets at the next party?

5. A friend of yours who is taking a criminal justice class reads about a case in which the conviction of an accused murderer was later overturned, based on DNA evidence. "It's a travesty of justice," she says. "An eyewitness clearly identified the man by picking him out of a lineup and then identified him again in court during the trial. No results from a chemistry lab should count more than eyewitness testimony." What is your friend failing to appreciate about eyewitness testimony? What sin of memory could lead an eyewitness to honestly believe she is identifying the correct man when she is actually making a false identification?

ANSWERS TO KEY CONCEPT QUIZ

1. a; 2. c; 3. c; 4. d; 5. a; 6. b; 7. b; 8. d; 9. a; 10. d; 11. a; 12. c; 13. d; 14. a; 15. b.

Need more help? Additional resources are located in LaunchPad at:
http://www.worthpublishers.com/launchpad/schacter3e

Learning

JENNIFER, A 45-YEAR-OLD CAREER MILITARY NURSE, lived quietly in a rural area of the United States with her spouse of 21 years and their two children before she served 19 months abroad during the Iraq war. In Iraq, she provided care to American and international soldiers as well as to Iraqi civilians, prisoners, and militant extremists.

Jennifer served 4 months of her assignment in a hospital near Baghdad, where she witnessed many horrifying events. The prison was the target of relentless mortar fire, resulting in numerous deaths and serious casualties, including bloody injuries and loss of limbs. Jennifer worked 12- to 14-hour shifts, trying to avoid incoming fire while tending to some of the most gruesomely wounded cases. She frequently encountered the smell of burnt flesh and the sight of "young, mangled bodies" as part of her daily duties (Feczer & Bjorklund, 2009, p. 285).

This repetitive trauma took a toll on Jennifer, and when she returned home, it became evident that she had not left behind her war experiences. Jennifer thought about them repeatedly and they profoundly influenced her reactions to many aspects of everyday life. The sight of blood or the smell of cooking meat made her sick to her stomach, to the point that she had to stop eating meat. The previously innocent sound of a helicopter approaching, which in Iraq signaled that new wounded bodies were about to arrive, now created in Jennifer heightened feelings of fear and anxiety. She regularly awoke from nightmares concerning the most troubling aspects of her Iraq experiences, such as tending to soldiers with multiple amputations. In the words of the authors who described her case, Jennifer was "forever changed" by her Iraq experiences (Feczer & Bjorklund, 2009). And that is one reason why Jennifer's story is a compelling, though disturbing, introduction to the topic of learning.

Much of what happened to Jennifer after she returned home reflects the operation of a kind of learning based on association. Sights, sounds, and smells in Iraq had become associated with negative emotions in a way that created an enduring bond, so that encountering similar sights, sounds, and smells at home elicited similarly intense negative feelings.

During the 4 months that she served at a prison hospital near Baghdad during the Iraq war, Jennifer learned to associate the sound of an arriving helicopter with wounded bodies. That learned association had a long-lasting influence on her.

AP PHOTO/JOHN MOORE

LEARNING IS SHORTHAND FOR A COLLECTION OF DIFFERENT TECHNIQUES, procedures, and outcomes that produce changes in an organism's behavior. Learning psychologists have identified and studied as many as 40 different kinds of learning. However, there is a basic principle at the core of all of them. **Learning** involves *the acquisition of new knowledge, skills, or responses from experience that results in a relatively permanent change in the state of the learner.* This definition emphasizes these key ideas:

> Learning is based on experience.
> Learning produces changes in the organism.
> These changes are relatively permanent.

Think about Jennifer's time in Iraq and you'll see all of these elements: Experiences such as the association between the sound of an approaching helicopter and the arrival of wounded bodies changed the way Jennifer responded to certain situations in a way that lasted for years.

Learning can also occur in much simpler, nonassociative forms. You are probably familiar with the phenomenon of **habituation,** *a general process in which repeated or prolonged exposure to a stimulus results in a gradual reduction in responding.* If you've ever lived under the flight path of your local airport, near railroad tracks, or by a busy highway, you've probably noticed the deafening roar as a Boeing 737 made its way toward the landing strip, the clatter of a train speeding down the track, or the sound of traffic when you first moved in. You probably also noticed that, after a while, the roar wasn't quite so deafening anymore and that eventually you ignored the sounds of the planes, trains, or automobiles in your vicinity. This welcome reduction in responding reflects the operation of habituation.

Habituation occurs even in the simplest organisms. For example, in the Memory chapter you learned about the tiny sea slug *Aplysia,* studied in detail by Nobel Prize winner Eric Kandel (2006). Kandel and his colleagues showed clearly that *Aplysia* exhibits habituation: When lightly touched, the sea slug initially withdraws its gill, but the response gradually weakens after repeated light touches. In addition, *Aplysia* also exhibits another simple form of learning known as **sensitization,** which occurs when *presentation of a stimulus leads to an increased response to a later stimulus.* For example, Kandel found that after receiving a strong shock, *Aplysia* showed an increased gill withdrawal response to a light touch. In a similar manner, people whose houses have been broken into may later become hypersensitive to late-night sounds that wouldn't have bothered them previously.

Although these simple kinds of learning are important, in this chapter we'll focus on more complex kinds of learning that psychologists have studied intensively. As you'll recall from the Psychology: Evolution of a Science chapter, a sizable chunk of psychology's history was devoted to behaviorism, with its insistence on measuring only observable, quantifiable behavior and its dismissal of mental activity as irrelevant and unknowable. Behaviorism was the major outlook of most psychologists working from the 1930s through the 1950s, the period during which most of the fundamental work on learning theory took place.

You might find the intersection of behaviorism and learning theory a bit surprising. After all, at one level learning seems abstract: Something intangible happens to you, and you think or behave differently thereafter. It seems logical that you'd need to explain that transformation in terms of a change in mental outlook. However, most behaviorists argued that learning's "permanent change in experience" could be demonstrated equally well in almost any organism: rats, dogs, pigeons, mice, pigs, or humans. From this perspective, behaviorists viewed learning as a purely behavioral activity requiring no mental activity.

In many ways the behaviorists were right. Much of what we know about how organisms learn comes directly from the behaviorists' observations of behaviors.

How might psychologists use the concept of habituation to explain the fact that today's action movies tend to show much more graphic violence than movies of the 1980s, which in turn tended to show more graphic violence than movies of the 1950s?

However, they also overstated their case. There are some important cognitive considerations (i.e., elements of mental activity) that need to be addressed in order to understand the learning process. In the first two sections of this chapter, we'll discuss the development and basic principles of two major approaches to learning: classical conditioning and operant conditioning. We'll then move on to see that some important kinds of learning occur simply by watching others, and that such observational learning plays an important role in the cultural transmission of behavior. Next, we'll discover that some kinds of learning can occur entirely outside of awareness. Finally, we'll discuss learning in a context that should matter a lot to you: the classroom.

Classical Conditioning: One Thing Leads to Another

American psychologist John B. Watson kick-started the behaviorist movement, arguing that psychologists should "never use the terms *consciousness, mental states, mind, content, introspectively verifiable, imagery,* and the like" (Watson, 1913, p. 166). Watson's firebrand stance was fueled in large part by the work of a Russian physiologist, Ivan Pavlov (1849–1936).

Pavlov was awarded the Nobel Prize in Physiology in 1904 for his work on the salivation of dogs. Pavlov studied the digestive processes of laboratory animals by surgically implanting test tubes into the cheeks of dogs to measure their salivary responses to different kinds of foods. Serendipitously, his explorations into spit and drool revealed the mechanics of one form of learning, which came to be called classical conditioning. **Classical conditioning** occurs *when a neutral stimulus produces a response after being paired with a stimulus that naturally produces a response*. In his classic experiments, Pavlov showed that dogs learned to salivate to neutral stimuli such as a bell or a tone after that stimulus had been associated with another stimulus that naturally evokes salivation, such as food.

The Development of Classical Conditioning: Pavlov's Experiments

Pavlov's basic experimental setup involved cradling dogs in a harness to administer the foods and to measure the salivary response, as shown in **FIGURE 7.1**. He noticed that dogs that had previously been in the experiment began to produce a kind of "anticipatory" salivary response as soon as they were put in the harness, before any food was presented. Pavlov and his colleagues regarded these responses as annoyances at first because they interfered with collecting naturally occurring salivary secretions. In reality, the dogs were behaving in line with the four basic elements of classical conditioning:

> When the dogs were initially presented with a plate of food, they began to salivate. No surprise here—placing food in front of most animals will launch the salivary process. Pavlov called the presentation of food an **unconditioned stimulus (US)**, *something that reliably produces a naturally occurring reaction in an organism.*

> He called the dogs' salivation an **unconditioned response (UR)**, *a reflexive reaction that is reliably produced by an unconditioned stimulus.*

learning
The acquisition of new knowledge, skills, or responses from experience that results in a relatively permanent change in the state of the learner.

habituation
A general process in which repeated or prolonged exposure to a stimulus results in a gradual reduction in responding.

sensitization
A simple form of learning that occurs when presentation of a stimulus leads to an increased response to a later stimulus.

classical conditioning
A type of learning that occurs when a neutral stimulus produces a response after being paired with a stimulus that naturally produces a response.

unconditioned stimulus (US)
Something that reliably produces a naturally occurring reaction in an organism.

unconditioned response (UR)
A reflexive reaction that is reliably produced by an unconditioned stimulus.

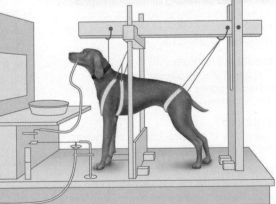

▼ Figure 7.1 **Pavlov's Apparatus for Studying Classical Conditioning** Pavlov presented auditory stimuli to the animals using a bell or a tuning fork. Visual stimuli could be presented on the screen.

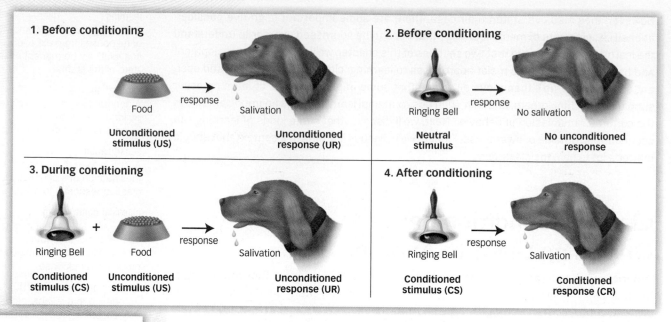

1. Before conditioning

Food

response →

Salivation

Unconditioned stimulus (US) | **Unconditioned response (UR)**

2. Before conditioning

Ringing Bell

response →

No salivation

Neutral stimulus | **No unconditioned response**

3. During conditioning

Ringing Bell + Food

response →

Salivation

Conditioned stimulus (CS) | **Unconditioned stimulus (US)** | **Unconditioned response (UR)**

4. After conditioning

Ringing Bell

response →

Salivation

Conditioned stimulus (CS) | **Conditioned response (CR)**

▲ Figure **7.2 The Elements of Classical Conditioning** In classical conditioning, a previously neutral stimulus (such as the sound of a bell) is paired with an unconditioned stimulus (such as the presentation of food). After several trials associating the two, the conditioned stimulus (the sound) alone can produce a conditioned response.

> Pavlov soon discovered that he could make the dogs salivate to neutral stimuli, things that don't usually make animals salivate such as the ringing of a bell. In various experiments, Pavlov paired the presentation of food with the sound of a bell, the ticking of a metronome, the humming of a tuning fork, or the flash of a light (Pavlov, 1927). Sure enough, he found that the dogs salivated to these sounds and flashes, each of which had become a **conditioned stimulus (CS),** *a previously neutral stimulus that produces a reliable response in an organism after being paired with a US* (see **FIGURE 7.2**).

> Nothing in nature would make a dog salivate to the sound of a bell. However, when the CS (the sound of a bell) is paired over time with the US (the food), the animal will learn to associate food with the sound and eventually the CS is sufficient to produce a response, or salivation. This response resembles the UR, but Pavlov called it the **conditioned response (CR),** *a reaction that resembles an unconditioned response but is produced by a conditioned stimulus.* In this example, the dogs' salivation (CR) was eventually prompted by the sound of the bell (CS) alone because the sound of the bell and the food (US) had been associated so often in the past.

Consider your own dog (or cat). Does your dog always know when dinner's coming, preparing just short of pulling up a chair and tucking a napkin into her collar? It's as though she has one eye on the clock every day, waiting for the dinner hour. Alas, your dog is no clock-watching wonder hound. Instead, the presentation of food (the US) has become associated with a complex CS—your getting up, moving into the kitchen, opening the cabinet, working the can opener—such that the CS alone signals to your dog that food is on the way and therefore initiates the CR of her getting ready to eat.

Why do some dogs seem to know when it's dinnertime?

The Basic Principles of Classical Conditioning

When Pavlov's findings first appeared in the scientific and popular literature (Pavlov, 1923a, 1923b), they produced a flurry of excitement because psychologists now had demonstrable evidence of how conditioning produced learned behaviors. This was the kind of behaviorist psychology John B. Watson was proposing: An organism experiences events or stimuli that are observable and measurable, and changes in that

conditioned stimulus (CS)
A previously neutral stimulus that produces a reliable response in an organism after being paired with a US.

conditioned response (CR)
A reaction that resembles an unconditioned response but is produced by a conditioned stimulus.

acquisition
The phase of classical conditioning when the CS and the US are presented together.

second-order conditioning
Conditioning where a CS is paired with a stimulus that became associated with the US in an earlier procedure.

organism can be directly observed and measured. Dogs learned to salivate to the sound of a buzzer, and there was no need to resort to explanations about why it had happened, what the dog wanted, or how the animal thought about the situation. In other words, there was no need to consider the mind in this classical conditioning paradigm, which appealed to Watson and the behaviorists. Pavlov also appreciated the significance of his discovery and embarked on a systematic investigation of the mechanisms of classical conditioning. Let's take a closer look at some of these principles. (As the Real World box shows, these principles help explain how drug overdoses occur.)

"I THINK MOM'S USING THE CAN OPENER."

Acquisition

Remember when you first got your dog? Chances are she didn't seem too smart, especially the way she stared at you vacantly as you went into the kitchen, not anticipating that food was on the way. That's because learning through classical conditioning requires some period of association between the CS and US. This period is called **acquisition,** *the phase of classical conditioning when the CS and the US are presented together.* During the initial phase of classical conditioning, typically there is a gradual increase in learning: It starts low, rises rapidly, and then slowly tapers off, as shown on the left side of **FIGURE 7.3.** Pavlov's dogs gradually increased their amount of salivation over several trials of pairing a tone with the presentation of food, and similarly, your dog eventually learned to associate your kitchen preparations with the subsequent appearance of food. After learning has been established, the CS by itself will reliably elicit the CR.

Second-Order Conditioning

After conditioning has been established, a phenomenon called **second-order conditioning** can be demonstrated: *conditioning where a CS is paired with a stimulus that became associated with the US in an earlier procedure.* For example, in an early study Pavlov repeatedly paired a new CS, a black square, with the now reliable tone. After a number of training trials, his dogs produced a salivary response to the black square even though the square itself had never been directly associated with the food. Second-order conditioning helps explain why some people desire money to the point

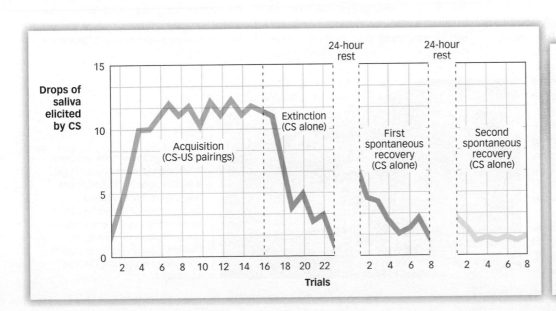

◀ Figure **7.3** **Acquisition, Extinction, and Spontaneous Recovery** In classical conditioning, the CS is originally neutral and produces no specific response. After several trials pairing the CS with the US, the CS alone comes to elicit the salivary response (the CR). Learning tends to take place fairly rapidly and then levels off as stable responding develops. In extinction, the CR diminishes quickly until it no longer occurs. A rest period, however, is typically followed by spontaneous recovery of the CR. In fact, a well-learned CR may show spontaneous recovery after more than one rest period even though there have been no additional learning trials.

that they hoard it and value it even more than the objects it purchases. Money is initially used to purchase objects that produce gratifying outcomes, such as an expensive car. Although money is not directly associated with the thrill of a drive in a new sports car, through second-order conditioning, money can become linked with this type of desirable quality.

Extinction and Spontaneous Recovery

After Pavlov and his colleagues had explored the process of acquisition extensively, they turned to the next logical question: What would happen if they continued to present the CS (tone) but stopped presenting the US (food)? Repeatedly presenting

THE REAL WORLD

Understanding Drug Overdoses

All too often, police are confronted with a perplexing problem: the sudden death of addicts from a drug overdose. These deaths are puzzling for at least three reasons: The victims are often experienced drug users; the dose taken is usually not larger than what they usually take; and the deaths tend to occur in unusual settings. Experienced drug users are just that: experienced! So, you'd think that the chances of an overdose would be lower than usual.

Classical conditioning provides some insight into how these deaths occur. First, when classical conditioning takes place, the CS is more than a simple bell or tone: It also includes the overall *context* within which the conditioning takes place. Indeed, Pavlov's dogs often began to salivate even as they approached the experimental apparatus. Second, many CRs are compensatory reactions to the US. Heroin, for example, slows down a person's breathing rate, so the body responds with a compensatory reaction that speeds up breathing in order to maintain a state of balance or homeostasis, a critically important CR.

These two finer points of classical conditioning help explain the seeming paradox of fatal heroin overdoses in experienced drug users (Siegel, 1984, 2005). When the drug is injected, the entire setting (the drug paraphernalia, the room, the lighting, the addict's usual companions) functions as the CS, and the addict's brain reacts to the heroin by secreting neurotransmitters that counteract its effects. Over time, this protective physiological response becomes part of the CR, and like all CRs, it occurs in the presence of the CS but prior to the actual administration of the drug. These compensatory physiological reactions are also what make drug abusers take increasingly larger doses to achieve the same effect. Ultimately, these reactions produce *drug tolerance*, discussed in the Consciousness chapter.

Based on these principles of classical conditioning, taking drugs in a new environment can be fatal for a longtime drug user. If an addict injects the usual dose in a setting that is sufficiently novel or where heroin has never been taken before, the CS is now altered, so that the physiological compensatory CR that usually serves a protective function either does not occur or is substantially decreased (Siegel et al., 2000). As a result, the addict's usual dose becomes an overdose and death often results. Intuitively, addicts may stick with the crack houses, opium dens, or "shooting galleries" with which they're familiar for just this reason. This effect has also been shown experimentally: Rats that have had extensive experience with morphine in one setting were much more likely to survive dose increases in that same setting than

in a novel one (Siegel, 1976; Siegel et al., 2000). This same basic effect occurs with a variety of drugs. For example, college students show less tolerance for the intoxicating effects of alcohol when they consume it in the presence of a novel cue (a peppermint-flavored drink) than a familiar one (a beer-flavored drink; Siegel, 2005).

Understanding these principles has also led to treatments for drug addicts. For example, the brain's compensatory response to a drug, when elicited by the familiar contextual cues ordinarily associated with drug taking that constitute the CS, can be experienced by the addict as withdrawal symptoms. In *cue exposure therapies*, an addict is exposed to drug-related cues without being given the usual dose of the drug itself, eventually resulting in extinction of the association between the contextual cues and the effects of the drug. After such treatment, encountering familiar drug-related cues will no longer result in the compensatory response linked to withdrawal symptoms, thereby making it easier for a recovering addict to remain abstinent (Siegel, 2005).

◄ Although opium dens and crack houses may be considered blight, it is often safer for addicts to use drugs there. The environment becomes part of the addict's CS, so ironically, busting crack houses may contribute to more deaths from drug overdoses when addicts are pushed to use drugs in new situations.

AP PHOTO/CHRIS GARDNER

the CS without the US produces exactly the result you might imagine. As shown on the right side of the first panel in Figure 7.3, behavior declines abruptly and continues to drop until eventually the dog ceases to salivate to the sound of the tone. This process is called **extinction,** *the gradual elimination of a learned response that occurs when the CS is repeatedly presented without the US.* The term was introduced because the conditioned response is "extinguished" and no longer observed.

> **How does conditioned behavior change when the unconditioned stimulus is removed?**

Having established that he could produce learning through conditioning and then extinguish it, Pavlov wondered if this elimination of conditioned behavior was permanent. Is a single session of extinction sufficient to knock out the CR completely, or is there some residual change in the dog's behavior so that the CR might reappear? To explore this question, Pavlov extinguished the classically conditioned salivation response and then allowed the dogs to have a short rest period. When they were brought back to the lab and presented with the CS again, they displayed **spontaneous recovery,** *the tendency of a learned behavior to recover from extinction after a rest period.* This phenomenon is shown in the middle panel in Figure 7.3. Notice that this recovery takes place even though there have not been any additional associations between the CS and US. Some spontaneous recovery of the conditioned response even takes place in what is essentially a second extinction session after another period of rest (see the right-hand panel in Figure 7.3). Clearly, extinction had not completely erased the learning that had been acquired. The ability of the CS to elicit the CR was weakened, but it was not eliminated.

Generalization and Discrimination

Do you think your dog will be stumped, unable to anticipate the presentation of her food, if you get a new can opener? Will a whole new round of conditioning need to be established with this modified CS?

Probably not. It wouldn't be very adaptive for an organism if each little change in the CS–US pairing required an

> **How can a change in can opener affect a conditioned dog's response?**

extensive regimen of new learning. Rather, the phenomenon of **generalization** tends to take place: *The CR is observed even though the CS is slightly different from the CS used during acquisition.* This means that the conditioning generalizes to stimuli that are similar to the CS used during the original training. As you might expect, the more the new stimulus changes, the less conditioned responding is observed. If you replaced a manual can opener with an electric can opener, your dog would probably show a much weaker conditioned response (Pearce, 1987; Rescorla, 2006).

When an organism generalizes to a new stimulus, two things are happening. First, by responding to the new stimulus used during generalization testing, the organism demonstrates that it recognizes the similarity between the original CS and the new stimulus. Second, by displaying *diminished* responding to that new stimulus, it also tells us that it notices a difference between the two stimuli. In the second case, the organism shows **discrimination,** *the capacity to distinguish between similar but distinct stimuli.* Generalization and discrimination are two sides of the same coin. The more organisms show one, the less they show the other, and training can modify the balance between the two.

extinction
The gradual elimination of a learned response that occurs when the CS is repeatedly presented without the US.

spontaneous recovery
The tendency of a learned behavior to recover from extinction after a rest period.

generalization
The CR is observed even though the CS is slightly different from the CS used during acquisition.

discrimination
The capacity to distinguish between similar but distinct stimuli.

> Your first electric can opener may cause your dog some confusion, but likely only for a little while.

GVICTORIA/SHUTTERSTOCK

Conditioned Emotional Responses: The Case of Little Albert

Before you conclude that classical conditioning is merely a sophisticated way to train your dog, let's revisit the larger principles of Pavlov's work. Classical conditioning demonstrates that durable, substantial changes in behavior can be achieved simply by setting up the proper conditions. It was this kind of simplicity that appealed to behaviorists. In fact, Watson and his followers thought that it was possible to develop general explanations of pretty much *any* behavior of *any* organism based on classical conditioning principles. As a step in that direction, Watson embarked on a controversial study with his research assistant Rosalie Rayner (Watson & Rayner, 1920). To support his contention that even complex behaviors were the result of conditioning, Watson enlisted the assistance of 9-month-old "Little Albert." Albert was a healthy, well-developed child, and, by Watson's assessment, "stolid and unemotional" (Watson & Rayner, 1920, p. 1). Watson wanted to see if such a child could be classically conditioned to experience a strong emotional reaction, namely, fear.

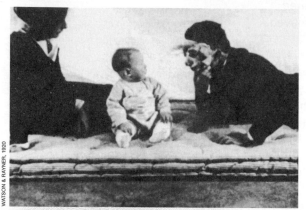

WATSON & RAYNER, 1920

John Watson and Rosalie Rayner show Little Albert an unusual bunny mask. Why doesn't the mere presence of these experimenters serve as a conditioned stimulus in itself?

Watson presented Little Albert with a variety of stimuli: a white rat, a dog, a rabbit, various masks, and a burning newspaper. Albert's reactions in most cases were curiosity or indifference, and he showed no fear of any of the items. Watson also established that something *could* make him afraid. While Albert was watching Rayner, Watson unexpectedly struck a large steel bar with a hammer, producing a loud noise. Predictably, this caused Albert to cry, tremble, and be generally displeased.

Watson and Rayner then led Little Albert through the acquisition phase of classical conditioning. Albert was presented with a white rat. As soon as he reached out to touch it, the steel bar was struck. This pairing occurred again and again over several trials. Eventually, the sight of the rat alone caused Albert to recoil in terror, crying and clamoring to get away from it. In this situation, a US (the loud sound) was paired with a CS (the presence of the rat) such that the CS all by itself was sufficient to produce the CR (a fearful reaction). Little Albert also showed stimulus generalization. The sight of a white rabbit, a seal-fur coat, and a Santa Claus mask produced the same kinds of fear reactions in the infant.

Why did Albert fear the rat?

What was Watson's goal in all this? First, he wanted to show that a relatively complex reaction could be conditioned using Pavlovian techniques. Second, he wanted to show that emotional responses such as fear and anxiety could be produced by classical conditioning and therefore need not be the product of deeper unconscious processes or early life experiences as Freud and his followers had argued (see the Psychology: Evolution of a Science chapter). Instead, Watson proposed that fears could be learned, just like any other behavior. Third, Watson wanted to confirm that conditioning could be applied to humans as well as to other animals. This study was controversial in its cavalier treatment of a young child, especially given that Watson and Rayner did not follow up with Albert or his mother during the ensuing years (Harris, 1979). Modern ethical guidelines that govern the treatment of research participants make sure that this kind of study could not be conducted today. At the time, however, it was consistent with a behaviorist view of psychology.

What response do you think the advertisers of Budweiser are looking for when they feature a Clydesdale horse in an ad?

AP PHOTO/KYLE ERICSON

The kind of conditioned fear responses that were at work in Little Albert's case were also important in the chapter-opening case of Jennifer, who experienced fear and anxiety when hearing the previously innocent sound of an approaching helicopter as a result of her experiences in Iraq. Indeed, a therapy that has proven effective in dealing with such trauma-induced fears is based directly on principles of classical conditioning: Individuals are repeatedly exposed to conditioned stimuli associated with their trauma in a safe setting in an attempt to extinguish the conditioned fear response (Bouton, 1988; Rothbaum & Schwartz, 2002). However, conditioned emotional responses include much more than just fear and anxiety responses. Advertisers, for example, understand that conditioned emotional responses can include various kinds of positive emotions that they would like potential customers to associate with their products, which may be why attractive women are commonly involved in ads for products geared toward young males, including beer and sports cars. Even the warm and fuzzy feeling that envelopes you when hearing a song on the radio that you used to listen to with a former boyfriend or girlfriend represents a type of conditioned emotional response.

A Deeper Understanding of Classical Conditioning

As a form of learning, classical conditioning could be reliably produced: It had a simple set of principles and applications to real-life situations. In short, classical conditioning offered a good deal of utility for psychologists who sought to understand the mechanisms underlying learning, and it continues to do so today.

Like a lot of strong starters, though, classical conditioning has been subjected to deeper scrutiny in order to understand exactly how, when, and why it works. Let's examine three areas that give us a closer look at the mechanisms of classical conditioning: the cognitive, neural, and evolutionary elements.

The Cognitive Elements of Classical Conditioning

As we've seen, Pavlov's work was a behaviorist's dream come true. In this view, conditioning is something that *happens* to a dog, a rat, or a person, apart from what the organism thinks about the conditioning situation. However, although the dogs salivated when their feeders approached (see Psychology: Evolution of a Science), they did not salivate when Pavlov did. Eventually someone was bound to ask an important question: *Why not?* After all, Pavlov also delivered the food to the dogs, so why didn't he become a CS? Indeed, if Watson was present whenever the unpleasant US was sounded, why didn't Little Albert come to fear *him*?

Somehow, Pavlov's dogs were sensitive to the fact that Pavlov was not a *reliable* indicator of the arrival of food. Pavlov was linked with the arrival of food, but he was also linked with other activities that had nothing to do with food, including checking on the apparatus, bringing the dog from the kennel to the laboratory, and standing around and talking with his assistants.

Robert Rescorla and Allan Wagner (1972) were the first to theorize that classical conditioning occurs when an animal has learned to set up an *expectation*. The sound of a bell, because of its systematic pairing with food, served to set up this cognitive state for the laboratory dogs; Pavlov, because of the lack of any reliable link with food, did not. In fact, in situations such as this, many responses are actually being conditioned. When the bell sounds, the dogs also wag their tails, make begging sounds, and look toward the food source (Jenkins et al., 1978). In short, what is really happening is something like the situation shown in **FIGURE 7.4.**

▼ Figure **7.4 Expectation in Classical Conditioning** In the Rescorla–Wagner model of classical conditioning, a CS serves to set up an expectation. The expectation in turn leads to an array of behaviors associated with the presence of the CS.

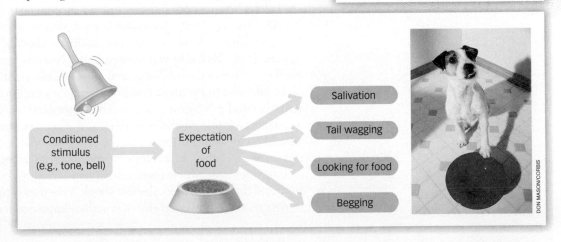

The Rescorla–Wagner model introduced a cognitive component that accounted for a variety of classical conditioning phenomena that were difficult to understand from a simple behaviorist point of view. For example, the model predicted that conditioning

> **How does the role of expectation in conditioning challenge behaviorist ideas?**

would be easier when the CS was an *unfamiliar* event than when it was familiar. The reason is that familiar events, being familiar, already have expectations associated with them, making new conditioning difficult. In short, classical conditioning might appear to be a primitive process, but it is actually quite sophisticated and incorporates a significant cognitive element.

One issue that arises from this cognitive view of classical conditioning concerns the role of consciousness. In the Rescorla–Wagner model, the cognitive elements are not necessarily conscious. Rather, they likely reflect the operation of nonconscious associative mechanisms that do more than just record co-occurrences of events: They link those co-occurrences to prior experiences, generating an expectation. Studies of classical conditioning in humans indicate that conditioning can occur without conscious awareness of the relationship between the CS and US, except when special conditioning procedures are used in which a brief time interval is inserted between the CS and the US. Under these circumstances, consciousness of the relationship between the CS and US appears to be necessary for conditioning to occur (Clark, Manns, & Squire, 2002; Clark & Squire, 1998). However, even the tiny sea slug *Aplysia* exhibits some evidence for this kind of conditioning, and scientists do not believe that *Aplysia* is capable of consciousness. After all, conditioning in *Aplysia* involves just a few neurons, as opposed to millions of neurons and complex brain systems in humans (Bekinschtein et al., 2011). This observation reminds us that even though there are many cross-species similarities in classical conditioning, there are also differences.

The Neural Elements of Classical Conditioning

Pavlov saw his research as providing insights into how the brain works. After all, he was trained in medicine, not psychology, and was a bit surprised when psychologists became excited by his findings. Recent research has clarified some of what Pavlov hoped to understand about conditioning and the brain.

A series of pioneering experiments conducted across several decades by Richard Thompson and his colleagues focused on classical conditioning of eyeblink responses in the rabbit. In the most basic type of eyeblink conditioning, the CS (a tone) is immediately followed by the US (a puff of air), which elicits a reflexive eyeblink response. After many CS–US pairings, the eyeblink response occurs in response to the CS alone. Thompson and colleagues showed convincingly that the cerebellum is critical for the occurrence of eyeblink conditioning (Thompson, 2005). Studies of people with lesions to the cerebellum supported these findings by demonstrating impaired eyeblink conditioning (Daum et al., 1993). Rounding out the picture, more recent neuroimaging findings in healthy young adults show activation in the cerebellum during the eyeblink conditioning (Cheng et al., 2008). As you learned in the Neuroscience and Behavior chapter, the cerebellum is part of the hindbrain and plays an important role in motor skills and learning.

In addition to eyeblink conditioning, fear conditioning has been extensively studied. Also in the Neuroscience and Behavior chapter, you saw that the amygdala plays an important role in the experience of emotion, including fear and anxiety. So, it should come as no surprise that the amygdala, particularly an area known as the *central nucleus*, is also critical for emotional conditioning.

Consider a rat who is conditioned to a series of CS–US pairings where the CS is a tone and the US is a mild electric shock. When rats experience sudden painful stimuli in nature, they show a defensive reaction, known as *freezing*, where they crouch down and sit motionless. In addition, their autonomic nervous systems go to work: Heart rate and blood pressure increase, and various hormones associated with stress are released. When fear conditioning takes place, these two components—one behavioral and one physiological—occur, except that now they are elicited by the CS.

The central nucleus of the amygdala plays a role in producing both of these outcomes through two distinct connections with other parts of the brain. If connections linking the amygdala to the midbrain are disrupted, the rat does not exhibit the behavioral freezing response. If the connections between the amygdala and the hypothalamus are severed, the autonomic responses associated with fear cease (LeDoux et al., 1988). Hence, the action of the amygdala is an essential element in fear conditioning, and its links with other areas of the brain are responsible for producing specific features of conditioning. The amygdala is involved in fear conditioning in people as well as rats and other animals (Olsson & Phelps, 2007; Phelps & LeDoux, 2005).

What is the role of the amygdala in fear conditioning?

The Evolutionary Elements of Classical Conditioning

In addition to this cognitive component, evolutionary mechanisms also play an important role in classical conditioning. As you learned in the Psychology: Evolution of a Science chapter, evolution and natural selection go hand in hand with adaptiveness: Behaviors that are adaptive allow an organism to survive and thrive in its environment. In the case of classical conditioning, psychologists began to appreciate how this type of learning could have adaptive value. Much research exploring this adaptiveness has focused on conditioned food aversions.

Consider this example: A psychology professor was once on a job interview in Southern California, and his hosts took him to lunch at a Middle Eastern restaurant. Suffering from a case of bad hummus, he was up all night long, and developed a lifelong aversion to hummus.

On the face of it, this looks like a case of classical conditioning, but there are several peculiar aspects to this case. The hummus was the CS, a bacterium or some other source of toxicity was the US, and the resulting nausea was the UR. The UR (the nausea) became linked to the once-neutral CS (the hummus) and became a CR (an aversion to hummus). However, all of the psychologist's hosts also ate the hummus, yet none of them reported feeling ill. It's not clear, then, what the US was; it couldn't have been anything that was actually in the food. What's more, the time between the hummus and the distress was several hours; usually, a response follows a stimulus fairly quickly. Most baffling, this aversion was cemented with a single acquisition trial. Usually it takes several pairings of a CS and US to establish learning.

These peculiarities are not so peculiar from an evolutionary perspective. Any species that forages or consumes a variety of foods needs to develop a mechanism by which it can learn to avoid any food that once made it ill. To have adaptive value, this mechanism should have several properties:

> There should be rapid learning that occurs in perhaps one or two trials. If learning takes more trials than this, the animal could die from eating a toxic substance.

> Conditioning should be able to take place over very long intervals, perhaps up to several hours. Toxic substances often don't cause illness immediately, so the organism would need to form an association between the food and the illness over a longer term.

> The organism should develop the aversion to the smell or taste of the food rather than its ingestion. It's more adaptive to reject a potentially toxic substance based on smell alone than it is to ingest it.

© PAUL COWAN DREAMSTIME.COM

Under certain conditions, people may develop food aversions. This serving of hummus looks inviting and probably tastes delicious, but at least one psychologist avoids it like the plague.

> Learned aversions should occur more often with novel foods than familiar ones. It is not adaptive for an animal to develop an aversion to everything it has eaten on the particular day it got sick. Our psychologist friend didn't develop an aversion to the Coke he drank with lunch or the scrambled eggs he had for breakfast that day; however, the sight and smell of hummus do make him uneasy.

John Garcia and his colleagues illustrated the adaptiveness of classical conditioning in a series of studies with rats (Garcia & Koelling, 1966). They used a variety of CSs (visual, auditory, tactile, taste, and smell) and several different USs (injection of a toxic substance, radiation) that caused nausea and vomiting hours later. The researchers found weak or no conditioning when the CS was a visual, auditory, or tactile stimulus, but a strong food aversion developed with stimuli that have a distinct taste and smell.

This research had an interesting application. It led to the development of a technique for dealing with an unanticipated side effect of radiation and chemotherapy: Cancer patients who experience nausea from their treatments often develop aversions to foods they ate before the therapy. Broberg and Bernstein (1987) reasoned that, if the findings with rats generalized to humans, a simple technique should minimize the negative consequences of this effect. They gave their patients an unusual food (coconut- or root-beer–flavored candy) at the end of the last meal before undergoing treatment. Sure enough, the conditioned food aversions that the patients developed were overwhelmingly for one of the unusual flavors and not for any of the other foods in the meal. Other than any root beer or coconut fanatics among the sample, patients were spared developing aversions to common foods that they were more likely to eat.

How has cancer patients' discomfort been eased by our understanding of food aversions?

Studies such as these suggest that evolution has provided each species with a kind of **biological preparedness,** *a propensity for learning particular kinds of associations over others,* so that some behaviors are relatively easy to condition in some species but not others. For example, the taste and smell stimuli that produce food aversions in rats do not work with most species of birds. Birds depend primarily on visual cues for finding food and are relatively insensitive to taste and smell. However, as you might guess, it is relatively easy to produce a food aversion in birds using an unfamiliar visual stimulus as the CS, such as a brightly colored food (Wilcoxon, Dragoin, & Kral, 1971). Indeed, most researchers agree that conditioning works best with stimuli that are biologically relevant to the organism (Domjan, 2005).

Rats can be difficult to poison because of learned taste aversions, which are an evolutionarily adaptive element of classical conditioning. Here a worker tries his best in the sewers of Paris.

BOYER/ROGER VIOLLET/GETTY IMAGES

IN SUMMARY

► Classical conditioning can be thought of as an exercise in pairing a neutral stimulus with a meaningful event or stimulus. Ivan Pavlov's initial work paired a neutral tone (a conditioned stimulus) with a meaningful act: the presentation of food to a hungry animal (an unconditioned stimulus). As he and others demonstrated, the pairing of a CS and US during the acquisition phase of classical conditioning eventually allows the CS, all by itself, to elicit a response called a conditioned response (CR).

► Classical conditioning was embraced by behaviorists such as John B. Watson, who viewed it as providing a foundation for a model of human behavior. As a behaviorist, Watson believed that no higher-level functions, such as thinking or awareness, needed to be invoked to understand behavior.

► Later researchers showed, however, the underlying mechanism of classical conditioning turned out to be more complex (and more interesting) than the simple association between a CS and a US. Classical conditioning involves setting up expectations and is sensitive to the degree to which the CS functions as a genuine predictor of the US, indicating that classical conditioning can involve some degree of cognition.

▶ The cerebellum plays an important role in eyeblink conditioning, whereas the amygdala is important for fear conditioning.

▶ The evolutionary aspects of classical conditioning show that each species is biologically predisposed to acquire particular CS–US associations based on its evolutionary history. In short, classical conditioning is not an arbitrary mechanism that merely forms associations. Rather, it is a sophisticated mechanism that evolved precisely because it has adaptive value.

biological preparedness
A propensity for learning particular kinds of associations over others.

operant conditioning
A type of learning in which the consequences of an organism's behavior determine whether it will be repeated in the future.

Operant Conditioning: Reinforcements from the Environment

The study of classical conditioning is the study of behaviors that are *reactive*. Most animals don't voluntarily salivate or feel spasms of anxiety; rather, these animals exhibit these responses involuntarily during the conditioning process. Involuntary behaviors make up only a small portion of our behavioral repertoires. The remainder are behaviors that we voluntarily perform. We engage in these voluntary behaviors in order to obtain rewards and avoid punishment; understanding them is essential to developing a complete picture of learning. Because classical conditioning has little to say about these voluntary behaviors, we turn now to a different form of learning: **operant conditioning,** *a type of learning in which the consequences of an organism's behavior determine whether it will be repeated in the future.* The study of operant conditioning is the exploration of behaviors that are *active*.

The Development of Operant Conditioning: The Law of Effect

The study of how active behavior affects the environment began at about the same time as classical conditioning. In fact, Edward L. Thorndike (1874–1949) first examined active behaviors back in the 1890s, before Pavlov published his findings. Thorndike's research focused on *instrumental behaviors*, that is, behavior that required an organism to *do* something, solve a problem, or otherwise manipulate elements of its environment (Thorndike, 1898). For example, Thorndike completed several experiments using a puzzle box, which was a wooden crate with a door that would open when a concealed lever was moved in the right way (see **FIGURE 7.5**). A hungry cat placed in a puzzle box would try various behaviors to get out—scratching at the door, meowing loudly, sniffing the inside of the box, putting its paw through the openings—but only one behavior opened the door and led to food: tripping the lever in just the right way. After this happened, Thorndike placed the cat back in the box for another round. Don't get the wrong idea. Thorndike probably *really liked* cats. Far from teasing them, he was after an important behavioral principle.

Fairly quickly, the cats became quite skilled at triggering the lever for their release. Notice what's going on. At first, the cat enacts any number of likely (but ultimately ineffective) behaviors, but only one behavior leads to freedom and food. Over time, the ineffective behaviors become less and less frequent, and the one instrumental behavior (going right for the latch) becomes more frequent (see

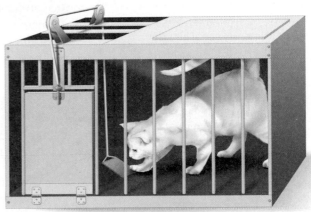

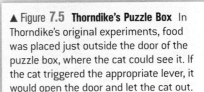

▲ Figure **7.5 Thorndike's Puzzle Box** In Thorndike's original experiments, food was placed just outside the door of the puzzle box, where the cat could see it. If the cat triggered the appropriate lever, it would open the door and let the cat out.

What is the relationship between behavior and reward?

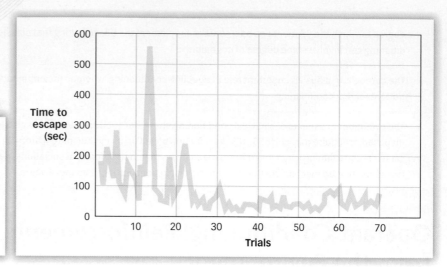

▶ Figure **7.6 The Law of Effect** Thorndike's cats displayed trial-and-error behavior when trying to escape from the puzzle box. They made lots of irrelevant movements and actions until, over time, they discovered the solution. Once they figured out what behavior was instrumental in opening the latch, they stopped all other ineffective behaviors and escaped from the box faster and faster.

FIGURE 7.6). From these observations, Thorndike developed the **law of effect:** *Behaviors that are followed by a "satisfying state of affairs" tend to be repeated and those that produce an "unpleasant state of affairs" are less likely to be repeated.*

The circumstances that Thorndike used to study learning were very different from those in studies of classical conditioning. Remember that in classical conditioning experiments, the US occurred on every training trial no matter what the animal did. Pavlov delivered food to the dog whether it salivated or not. But in Thorndike's work, the behavior of the animal determined what happened next. If the behavior was "correct" (i.e., the latch was triggered), the animal was rewarded with food. Incorrect behaviors produced no results and the animal was stuck in the box until it performed the correct behavior. Although different from classical conditioning, Thorndike's work resonated with most behaviorists at the time: It was still observable, quantifiable, and free from explanations involving the mind (Galef, 1998).

B. F. Skinner with one of his many research participants.

B. F. Skinner: The Role of Reinforcement and Punishment

Several decades after Thorndike's work, B. F. Skinner (1904–1990) coined the term **operant behavior** to refer to *behavior that an organism produces that has some impact on the environment.* In Skinner's system, all of these emitted behaviors "operated" on the environment in some manner, and the environment responded by providing events that either strengthened those behaviors (i.e., they *reinforced* them) or made them less likely to occur (i.e., they *punished* them). Skinner's elegantly simple observation was that most organisms do *not* behave like a dog in a harness, passively waiting to receive food no matter what the circumstances. Rather, most organisms are like cats in a box, actively engaging the environment in which they find themselves to reap rewards (Skinner, 1938, 1953).

In order to study operant behavior scientifically, Skinner developed a variation on Thorndike's puzzle box. The *operant conditioning chamber,* or *Skinner box,* as it is commonly called (shown in **FIGURE 7.7**), allows a researcher to study the behavior of small organisms in a controlled environment.

Skinner's approach to the study of learning focused on *reinforcement* and *punishment.* These terms, which have commonsense connotations, turned out to be rather difficult to define. For example, some people love roller coasters, whereas others find them horrifying; the chance to go on one will be reinforcing for one group but punishing for another. Dogs can be trained with praise and a good belly rub—procedures that are nearly useless for most cats. Skinner settled on a neutral definition that would characterize each term by its effect on behavior. Therefore, a **reinforcer** is *any stimulus or event that functions to increase the likelihood of the behavior that led to it*, whereas a **punisher** is *any stimulus or event that functions to decrease the likelihood of the behavior that led to it*.

Whether a particular stimulus acts as a reinforcer or a punisher depends in part on whether it increases or decreases the likelihood of a behavior. Presenting food is usually reinforcing and produces an increase in the behavior that led to it; removing food is often punishing and leads to a decrease in the behavior. Turning on an electric shock is typically punishing (and decreases the behavior that led to it); turning it off is rewarding (and increases the behavior that led to it).

To keep these possibilities distinct, Skinner used the term *positive* for situations in which a stimulus was presented and *negative* for situations in which it was removed. Consequently, there is *positive reinforcement* (where a rewarding stimulus is presented) and *negative reinforcement* (where an unpleasant stimulus is removed), as well as *positive punishment* (where an unpleasant stimulus is administered) and *negative punishment* (where a rewarding stimulus is removed). Here the words *positive* and *negative* mean, respectively, something that is *added* or something that is *taken away*, but do not mean "good" or "bad" as they do in everyday speech. As you can see from **TABLE 7.1**, positive and negative reinforcement increase the likelihood of the behavior; positive and negative punishment decrease the likelihood of the behavior.

▲ Figure **7.7** **Skinner Box** In a typical Skinner box, or *operant conditioning chamber*, a rat, pigeon, or other suitably sized animal is placed in this environment and observed during learning trials that use operant conditioning principles.

▸ Table **7.1**

Reinforcement and Punishment

	Increases the Likelihood of Behavior	Decreases the Likelihood of Behavior
Stimulus is presented	Positive reinforcement	Positive punishment
Stimulus is removed	Negative reinforcement	Negative punishment

These distinctions can be confusing at first; after all, "negative reinforcement" and "punishment" both sound like they should be "bad" and produce the same type of behavior. However, negative reinforcement, for example, involves something pleasant; it's the *removal* of something unpleasant, like a shock, and the absence of a shock is indeed pleasant.

Reinforcement is generally more effective than punishment in promoting learning. There are many reasons (Gershoff, 2002), but one reason is this: Punishment signals that an unacceptable behavior has occurred, but it doesn't specify what should be done instead. Spanking a young child for starting to run into a busy street certainly stops the behavior, but it doesn't promote any kind of learning about the *desired* behavior.

> **?** Why is reinforcement more constructive than punishment in learning desired behavior?

Primary and Secondary Reinforcement and Punishment

Reinforcers and punishers often gain their functions from basic biological mechanisms. A pigeon that pecks at a target in a Skinner box is usually reinforced with food pellets, just as an animal who learns to escape a mild electric shock has avoided the punishment of tingly paws. Food, comfort, shelter, or warmth are examples of

law of effect
Behaviors that are followed by a "satisfying state of affairs" tend to be repeated and those that produce an "unpleasant state of affairs" are less likely to be repeated.

operant behavior
Behavior that an organism produces that has some impact on the environment.

reinforcer
Any stimulus or event that functions to increase the likelihood of the behavior that led to it.

punisher
Any stimulus or event that functions to decrease the likelihood of the behavior that led to it.

Negative reinforcement involves the removal of something unpleasant from the environment. When Daddy stops the car, he gets a reward: His little monster stops screaming. However, from the perspective of the child, this is positive reinforcement. The child's tantrum results in something positive added to the environment—stopping for a snack.

©MICHELLE SELESNICK/FLICKR VISION

primary reinforcers because they help satisfy biological needs. However, the vast majority of reinforcers or punishers in our daily lives have little to do with biology: Verbal approval, a bronze trophy, or money all serve powerful reinforcing functions, yet none of them taste very good or help keep you warm at night. The point is, we learn to perform a lot of behaviors based on reinforcements that have little or nothing to do with biological satisfaction.

These *secondary reinforcers* derive their effectiveness from their associations with primary reinforcers through classical conditioning. For example, money starts out as a neutral CS that, through its association with primary USs like acquiring food or shelter, takes on a conditioned emotional element. Flashing lights, originally a neutral CS, acquire powerful negative elements through association with a speeding ticket and a fine.

Immediate versus Delayed Reinforcement and Punishment

A key determinant of the effectiveness of a reinforcer is the amount of time between the occurrence of a behavior and the reinforcer: The more time that elapses, the less effective the reinforcer (Lattal, 2010; Renner, 1964). This was dramatically illustrated in experiments with hungry rats in which food reinforcers were given at varying times after the rat pressed the lever (Dickinson, Watt, & Griffiths, 1992). Delaying reinforcement by even a few seconds led to a reduction in the number of times the rat subsequently pressed the lever, and extending the delay to a minute rendered the food reinforcer completely ineffective (see **FIGURE 7.8**). The most likely explanation for this effect is that delaying the reinforcer made it difficult for the rats to figure out exactly what behavior they needed to perform in order to obtain it. In the same way, parents who wish to reinforce their children for playing quietly with a piece of candy should provide the candy while the child is still playing quietly; waiting until later when the child may be engaging in other behaviors—perhaps making a racket with pots and pans—will make it more difficult for the child to link the reinforcer with the behavior of playing quietly (Powell et al., 2009).

The greater potency of immediate versus delayed reinforcers may help us to appreciate why it can be difficult to engage in behaviors that have long-term benefits. The smoker who desperately wants to quit smoking will be reinforced immediately by the feeling of relaxation that results from lighting up, but may have to wait years to be reinforced with better health that results from

> **How does the concept of delayed reinforcement relate to difficulties with quitting smoking?**

quitting; the dieter who sincerely wants to lose weight may easily succumb to the temptation of a chocolate sundae that provides reinforcement now, rather than waiting weeks or months for the reinforcement (looking and feeling better) that would be associated with losing weight.

Similar considerations apply to punishment: As a general rule, the longer the delay between a behavior and the administration of punishment, the less effective the punishment will

▼ Figure **7.8 Delay of Reinforcement** Rats pressed a lever in order to obtain a food reward. Researchers varied the amount of time between the lever press and the delivery of food reinforcement. The number of lever presses declined substantially with longer delays.

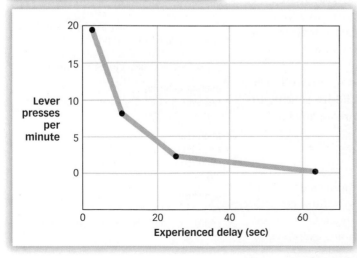

Lever presses per minute

Experienced delay (sec)

CULTURE & COMMUNITY

Are there cultural differences in reinforcers? Reinforcers play a critical role in operant conditioning, and operant approaches that use positive reinforcement have been applied extensively in everyday settings such as behavior therapy (see Treatment of Psychological Disorders, pp. 626–663). Surveys designed to assess what kinds of reinforcers are rewarding to individuals have revealed that there can be wide differences among various groups (Dewhurst, & Cautela, 1980; Houlihan et al., 1991).

Recently, 750 high school students from America, Australia, Tanzania, Denmark, Honduras, Korea, and Spain were surveyed in order to evaluate possible cross-cultural differences among reinforcers (Homan et al., 2012). The survey asked students to rate on a 5-point scale how rewarding they found a range of activities, including listening to music, playing music, various kinds of sports, shopping, reading, spending time with friends, and so on. The researchers hypothesized that American high school students would differ most strongly from high school students in the third-world countries of Tanzania and Honduras, and that's what they found. The differences between American and Korean students were nearly as large, and somewhat surprisingly, so were the differences between American and Spanish students. There were much smaller differences between Americans and their Australian or Danish counterparts.

These results should be taken with a grain of salt because the researchers did not control for variables other than culture that could influence their results, such as economic status. Nonetheless, they suggest that cultural differences should be considered in the design of programs or interventions that rely on the use of reinforcers to influence the behavior of individuals who come from different cultures.

be in suppressing the targeted behavior (Kamin, 1959; Lerman & Vorndran, 2002). The reduced effectiveness of delayed punishment can be a serious problem in non-laboratory settings, because in everyday life it is often difficult to administer punishment immediately or even soon after a problem behavior has occurred (Meindl & Casey, 2012). For example, a parent whose child misbehaves at a shopping mall may be unable to punish the child immediately with a time-out because it is impractical in the mall setting. Some problem behaviors, such as cheating, can be difficult to detect immediately and therefore punishment is necessarily delayed. Research in both the laboratory and everyday settings suggests several strategies for increasing the effectiveness of delayed punishment, including increasing the severity of the punishment or attempting to bridge the gap between the behavior and the punishment with verbal instructions (Meindl & Casey, 2012). The parent in the shopping mall, for example, might tell the misbehaving child exactly when and where a later time-out will occur.

Suppose you are the mayor of a suburban town and you want to institute some new policies to decrease the number of drivers who speed on residential streets. How might you use punishment to decrease the behavior you desire (speeding)? How might you use reinforcement to increase the behavior you desire (safe driving)? Based on the principles of operant conditioning you read about in this section, which approach do you think might be most fruitful?

The Basic Principles of Operant Conditioning

After establishing how reinforcement and punishment produced learned behavior, Skinner and other scientists began to expand the parameters of operant conditioning. This took the form of investigating some phenomena that were well known in classical conditioning (such as discrimination, generalization, and extinction) as well as some practical applications, such as how best to administer reinforcement or how to produce complex learned behaviors in an organism. Let's look at some of these basic principles of operant conditioning.

Discrimination, Generalization, and the Importance of Context

We all take off our clothes at least once a day, but usually not in public. We scream at rock concerts, but not in libraries. We say, "Please pass the gravy," at the dinner table, but not in a classroom. Although these observations may seem like nothing more than common sense, Thorndike was the first to recognize the underlying message: Learning takes place *in contexts*, not in the free range of any plausible situation. As Skinner rephrased it later, most behavior is under *stimulus control*, which develops when a particular response only occurs when an appropriate *discriminative stimulus*, a stimulus that indicates that a response will be reinforced, is present. Skinner (1972) discussed this process in terms of a "three-term contingency": In the presence of a *discriminative stimulus* (classmates drinking coffee together in Starbucks), a *response* (joking comments about a psychology professor's increasing waistline and receding hairline) produces a *reinforcer* (laughter among classmates). The same response in a different context—the professor's office—would most likely produce a very different outcome.

> **What does it mean to say that learning takes place in contexts?**

Stimulus control, perhaps not surprisingly, shows both discrimination and generalization effects similar to those we saw with classical conditioning. To demonstrate this, researchers used either a painting by the French Impressionist Claude Monet or one of Pablo Picasso's paintings from his Cubist period for the discriminative stimulus (Watanabe, Sakamoto, & Wakita, 1995). Participants in the experiment were only reinforced if they responded when the appropriate painting was presented. After training, the participants discriminated appropriately; those trained with the Monet

In research on stimulus control, participants trained with Picasso paintings, such as the one on the left, responded to other paintings by Picasso or even to paintings by other Cubists. Participants trained with Monet paintings, such as the one on the right, responded to other paintings by Monet or by other French Impressionists. Interestingly, the participants in this study were pigeons.

TATE GALLERY, LONDON/ART RESOURCE, NY

TATE GALLERY, LONDON/ART RESOURCE, NY

painting responded when other paintings by Monet were presented and those trained with a Picasso painting reacted when other Cubist paintings by Picasso were shown. And as you might expect, Monet-trained participants did not react to Picassos and Picasso-trained participants did not respond to Monets. What's more, the research participants showed that they could generalize *across* painters as long as they were from the same artistic tradition. Those trained with Monet responded appropriately when shown paintings by Auguste Renoir (another French Impressionist), and the Picasso-trained participants responded to artwork by Cubist painter Henri Matisse, despite never having seen those paintings before. If these results don't seem particularly startling to you, it might help to know that the research participants were pigeons who were trained to key-peck to these various works of art. Stimulus control, and its ability to foster stimulus discrimination and stimulus generalization, is effective even if the stimulus has no meaning to the respondent.

Extinction

As in classical conditioning, operant behavior undergoes extinction when the reinforcements stop. Pigeons cease pecking at a key if food is no longer presented following the behavior. You wouldn't put more money into a vending machine if it failed to give you its promised candy bar or soda. Warm smiles that are greeted with scowls and frowns will quickly disappear. On the surface, extinction of operant behavior looks like that of classical conditioning: The response rate drops off fairly rapidly and, if a rest period is provided, spontaneous recovery is typically seen.

However, there is an important difference. As noted, in classical conditioning, the US occurs on every trial no matter what the organism does. In operant conditioning, the reinforcements only occur when the proper response has been made, and they don't always occur even then. Not every trip into the forest produces nuts for a squirrel, auto salespeople don't sell to everyone who takes a test drive, and researchers run many experiments that do not work out and never get published. Yet these behaviors don't weaken and gradually extinguish. In fact, they typically become stronger and more resilient. Curiously, then, extinction is a bit more complicated in operant conditioning than in classical conditioning because it depends, in part, on how often reinforcement is received. In fact, this principle is an important cornerstone of operant conditioning that we'll examine next.

Schedules of Reinforcement

Skinner was intrigued by the apparent paradox surrounding extinction, and in his autobiography, he described how he began studying it (Skinner, 1979). He was laboriously rolling ground rat meal and water to make food pellets to reinforce the rats in his early experiments. It occurred to him that perhaps he could save time and effort

How is the concept of extinction different in operant conditioning versus classical conditioning?

by not giving his rats a pellet for every bar press but instead delivering food on some intermittent schedule. The results of this hunch were dramatic. Not only did the rats continue bar pressing, but they also shifted the rate and pattern of bar pressing depending on the timing and frequency of the presentation of the reinforcers. Unlike classical conditioning, where the sheer *number* of learning trials was important, in operant conditioning the *pattern* with which reinforcements appeared was crucial.

Skinner explored dozens of what came to be known as *schedules of reinforcement* (Ferster & Skinner, 1957; see **FIGURE 7.9**). The two most important are *interval schedules*, based on the time intervals between reinforcements, and *ratio schedules*, based on the ratio of responses to reinforcements.

Students cramming for an exam often show the same kind of behavior as pigeons being reinforced under a fixed-interval schedule.

Interval Schedules. Under a **fixed-interval schedule (FI),** *reinforcers are presented at fixed-time periods, provided that the appropriate response is made.* For example, on a 2-minute fixed-interval schedule, a response will be reinforced, but only after 2 minutes have expired since the last reinforcement. Rats and pigeons in Skinner boxes produce predictable patterns of behavior under these schedules. They show little responding right after the presentation of the reinforcement, but as the next time interval draws to a close, they show a burst of responding. Many undergraduates behave exactly like this. They do relatively little work until just before the upcoming exam, then engage in a burst of reading and studying.

Under a **variable-interval schedule (VI),** *a behavior is reinforced based on an average time that has expired since the last reinforcement.* For example, on a 2-minute variable-interval schedule, responses will be reinforced every 2 minutes *on average* but not after each 2-minute period. Variable-interval schedules typically produce steady, consistent responding because the time until the next reinforcement is less predictable. Variable-interval schedules are not encountered that often in real life, although one example might

> **How does a radio station use scheduled reinforcements to keep you listening?**

Radio station promotions and giveaways often follow a variable-interval schedule of reinforcement.

be radio promotional giveaways, such as tickets to rock concerts. The reinforcement—getting the tickets—might average out to once an hour across the span of the broadcasting day, but the presentation of the reinforcement is variable: It might come early in the 10:00 o'clock hour, later in the 11:00 o'clock hour, immediately into the 12:00 o'clock hour, and so on.

Both fixed-interval schedules and variable-interval schedules tend to produce slow, methodical responding because the reinforcements follow a time scale that is independent of how many responses occur. It doesn't matter if a rat on a fixed-interval schedule presses a bar 1 time during a 2-minute period or 100 times: The reinforcing food pellet won't drop out of the shoot until 2 minutes have elapsed, regardless of the number of responses.

▶ Figure **7.9 Reinforcement Schedules** Different schedules of reinforcement produce different rates of responding. These lines represent the amount of responding that occurs under each type of reinforcement. The black slash marks indicate when reinforcement was administered. Notice that ratio schedules tend to produce higher rates of responding than do interval schedules, as shown by the steeper lines for fixed-ratio and variable-ratio reinforcement.

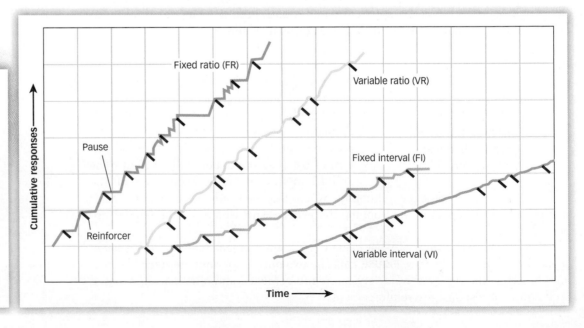

Ratio Schedules. Under a **fixed-ratio schedule (FR),** *reinforcement is delivered after a specific number of responses have been made.* One schedule might present reinforcement after every fourth response, a different schedule might present reinforcement after every 20 responses; the special case of presenting reinforcement after *each* response is called *continuous reinforcement,* and it's what drove Skinner to investigate these schedules in the first place. Notice that, in each example, the ratio of reinforcements to responses, once set, remains fixed.

There are many situations in which people, sometimes unknowingly, find themselves being reinforced on a fixed-ratio schedule: Book clubs often give you a freebie after a set number of regular purchases; pieceworkers get paid after making a fixed

> **How do ratio schedules work to keep you spending your money?**

number of products; and some credit card companies return to their customers a percentage of the amount charged. When a fixed-ratio schedule is operating, it is possible, in principle, to know exactly when the next reinforcer is due. A laundry pieceworker on a 10-response, fixed-ratio schedule who has just washed and ironed the ninth shirt knows that payment is coming after the next shirt is done.

Under a **variable-ratio schedule (VR),** *the delivery of reinforcement is based on a particular average number of responses.* For example, if a laundry worker was following a 10-response variable-ratio schedule instead of a fixed-ratio schedule, she or he would still be paid, on average, for every ten shirts washed and ironed but not for *each* 10th shirt. Slot machines in a modern casino pay off on variable-ratio schedules that are determined by the random number generator that controls the play of the machines. A casino might advertise that they pay off on "every 100 pulls on average," which could be true. However, one player might hit a jackpot after 3 pulls on a slot machine, whereas another player might not hit a jackpot until after 80 pulls. The ratio of responses to reinforcements is variable, which probably helps casinos stay in business.

Not surprisingly, variable-ratio schedules produce slightly higher rates of responding than fixed-ratio schedules primarily because the organism never knows when the next reinforcement is going to appear. What's more, the higher the ratio, the higher the response rate tends to be; a 20-response variable-ratio schedule will produce considerably more responding than a 2-response variable-ratio schedule. When schedules of reinforcement provide **intermittent reinforcement,** *when only some of the responses made are followed by reinforcement,* they produce behavior that is much more resistant to extinction than a continuous reinforcement schedule. One way to think about this effect is to recognize that the more irregular and intermittent a schedule is, the more difficult it becomes for an organism to detect when it has actually been placed on extinction.

For example, if you've just put a dollar into a soda machine that, unbeknownst to you, is broken, no soda comes out. Because you're used to getting your sodas on a continuous reinforcement schedule—one dollar produces one soda—this abrupt change in the environment is easily noticed and you are unlikely to put additional money into the machine: You'd quickly show extinction. However, if you've put your dollar into a slot machine that, unbeknownst to you, is broken, do you stop after one or two plays? Almost certainly not. If you're a regular slot player, you're used to going for many plays in a row without winning anything, so it's difficult to tell that anything is

These pieceworkers in a textile factory get paid following a fixed-ratio schedule: They receive payment after some set number of shirts have been sewn.

JEFF HOLT/BLOOMBERG VIA GETTY IMAGES

©MBI/ALAMY

Slot machines in casinos pay out following a variable-ratio schedule. This helps explain why some gamblers feel incredibly lucky, whereas others (like this chap) can't believe they can play a machine for so long without winning a thing.

fixed-interval schedule (FI)
An operant conditioning principle in which reinforcers are presented at fixed-time periods, provided that the appropriate response is made.

variable-interval schedule (VI)
An operant conditioning principle in which behavior is reinforced based on an average time that has expired since the last reinforcement.

fixed-ratio schedule (FR)
An operant conditioning principle in which reinforcement is delivered after a specific number of responses have been made.

variable-ratio schedule (VR)
An operant conditioning principle in which the delivery of reinforcement is based on a particular average number of responses.

Imagine you own an insurance company and you want to encourage your salespeople to sell as many policies as possible. You decide to give them bonuses, based on the number of policies sold. How might you set up a system of bonuses using an FR schedule? Using a VR schedule? Which system do you think would encourage your salespeople to work harder, in terms of making more sales?

out of the ordinary. Under conditions of intermittent reinforcement, all organisms will show considerable resistance to extinction and continue for many trials before they stop responding. This effect has even been observed in infants (Weir et al., 2005).

This relationship between intermittent reinforcement schedules and the robustness of the behavior they produce is called the **intermittent reinforcement effect,** *the fact that operant behaviors that are maintained under intermittent reinforcement schedules resist extinction better than those maintained under continuous reinforcement.* In one extreme case, Skinner gradually extended a variable-ratio schedule until he managed to get a pigeon to make an astonishing 10,000 pecks at an illuminated key for one food reinforcer! Behavior maintained under a schedule like this is virtually immune to extinction.

Shaping through Successive Approximations

Have you ever been to AquaLand and wondered how the dolphins learn to jump up in the air, twist around, splash back down, do a somersault, and then jump through a hoop, all in one smooth motion? Well, they don't. Wait—of course they do—you've seen them. It's just that they don't learn to do all those complex aquabatics in *one* smooth motion. Rather, elements of their behavior are shaped over time until the final product looks like one smooth motion.

Skinner noted that the trial-by-trial experiments of Pavlov and Thorndike were rather artificial. Behavior rarely occurs in fixed frameworks where a stimulus is presented and then an organism has to engage in some activity or another. We are continuously acting and behaving, and the world around us reacts in response to our actions. Most of our behaviors, then, are the result of **shaping,** *learning that results from the reinforcement of successive steps to a final desired behavior.* The outcomes of one set of behaviors shape the next set of behaviors, whose outcomes shape the next set of behaviors, and so on.

> How can operant conditioning produce complex behaviors?

Skinner realized the potential power of shaping one day in 1943 when he was working on a wartime project sponsored by General Mills in a lab on the top floor of a flour mill where pigeons frequently visited (Peterson, 2004). In a lighthearted moment, Skinner and his colleagues decided to see whether they could teach the pigeons to "bowl" by swiping with their beaks at a ball that Skinner had placed in a box along with some pins. Nothing worked until Skinner decided to reinforce any response even remotely related to a swipe, such as merely looking at the ball. "The result amazed us," Skinner recalled. "In a few minutes the ball was caroming off the walls of the box as if the pigeon had been a champion squash player" (Skinner, 1958, p. 974). Skinner applied this insight in his later laboratory research. For example, he noted

B. F. Skinner shaping a dog named Agnes. In the span of 20 minutes, Skinner was able to use reinforcement of successive approximations to shape Agnes's behavior. The result was a pretty neat trick: to wander in, stand on hind legs, and jump.

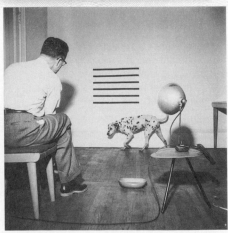

1 Minute

4 Minutes

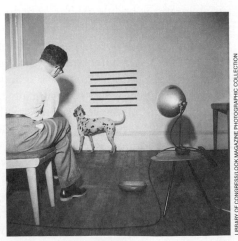

8 Minutes

that if you put a rat in a Skinner box and wait for it to press the bar, you could end up waiting a very long time: Bar pressing just isn't very high in a rat's natural hierarchy of responses. However, it is relatively easy to shape bar pressing. Watch the rat closely: If it turns in the direction of the bar, deliver a food reward. This will reinforce turning toward the bar, making such a movement more likely. Now wait for the rat to take a step toward the bar before delivering food; this will reinforce moving toward the bar. After the rat walks closer to the bar, wait until it touches the bar before presenting the food. Notice that none of these behaviors is the final desired behavior (reliably pressing the bar). Rather, each behavior is a *successive approximation* to the final product, or a behavior that gets incrementally closer to the overall desired behavior. In the dolphin example—and indeed, in many instances of animal training in which relatively simple animals seem to perform astoundingly complex behaviors—you can think through how each smaller behavior is reinforced until the overall sequence of behavior is performed reliably.

Superstitious Behavior

Everything we've discussed so far suggests that one of the keys to establishing reliable operant behavior is the correlation between an organism's response and the occurrence of reinforcement. In the case of continuous reinforcement, when every response is followed by the presentation of a reinforcer, there is a one-to-one, or perfect, correlation. In the case of intermittent reinforcement, the correlation is weaker (i.e., not every response is met with the delivery of reinforcement), but it's not zero. As you read in the Methods in Psychology chapter, however, just because two things are correlated (i.e., they tend to occur together in time and space) doesn't imply that there is causality (i.e., the presence of one reliably causes the other to occur).

Skinner (1948) designed an experiment that illustrates this distinction. He put several pigeons in Skinner boxes, set the food dispenser to deliver food every 15 seconds, and left the birds to their own devices. Later he returned and found the birds engaging in odd, idiosyncratic behaviors, such as pecking aimlessly in a corner or turning in circles. He referred to these behaviors as "superstitious" and offered a behaviorist analysis of their occurrence. The pigeons, he argued, were simply repeating behaviors that had been accidentally reinforced. A pigeon that just happened to have pecked randomly in the corner when the food showed up had connected the delivery of food to that behavior. Because this pecking behavior was reinforced by the delivery of food, the pigeon was likely to repeat it. Now pecking in the corner was more likely to occur, and it was more likely to be reinforced 15 seconds later when the food appeared again. For each pigeon, the behavior reinforced would most likely be

> **How would a behaviorist explain superstitions?**

intermittent reinforcement
An operant conditioning principle in which only some of the responses made are followed by reinforcement.

intermittent reinforcement effect
The fact that operant behaviors that are maintained under intermittent reinforcement schedules resist extinction better than those maintained under continuous reinforcement.

shaping
Learning that results from the reinforcement of successive steps to a final desired behavior.

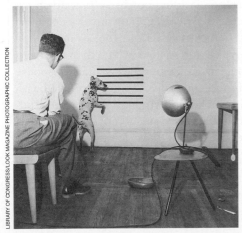

12 Minutes

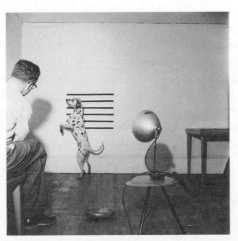

16 Minutes

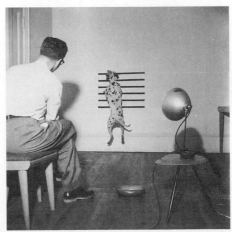

20 Minutes

People believe in many different superstitions and engage in all kinds of superstitious behaviors. Baseball players and coaches are notoriously superstitious. When the Detroit Tigers went on a winning streak in the summer of 2011, Tigers' manager Jim Leyland refused to change his underwear, wearing them to the park every day until the winning streak ended. Skinner thought superstitions resulted from the unintended reinforcement of inconsequential behavior.

whatever the pigeon happened to be doing when the food was first delivered. Skinner's pigeons acted as though there was a causal relationship between their behaviors and the appearance of food when it was merely an accidental correlation.

Although some researchers questioned Skinner's characterization of these behaviors as superstitious (Staddon & Simmelhag, 1971), later studies have shown that reinforcing adults or children using schedules in which reinforcement is not contingent on their responses can produce seemingly superstitious behavior. It seems that people, like pigeons, behave as though there's a correlation between their responses and reward when in fact the connection is merely accidental (Bloom et al., 2007; Mellon, 2009; Ono, 1987; Wagner & Morris, 1987). Such findings should not be surprising to sports fans. Baseball players who enjoy several home runs on a day when they happened not to have showered are likely to continue that tradition, laboring under the belief that the accidental correlation between poor personal hygiene and a good day at bat is somehow causal. This "stench causes home runs" hypothesis is just one of many examples of human superstitions (Gilbert et al., 2000; Radford & Radford, 1949).

A Deeper Understanding of Operant Conditioning

Like classical conditioning, operant conditioning also quickly proved to be a powerful approach to learning. But B. F. Skinner, like Watson before him, was satisfied to observe an organism perform a learned behavior; he didn't look for a deeper explanation of mental processes (Skinner, 1950). In this view, an organism behaved in a certain way as a response to stimuli in the environment, not because there was any wanting, wishing, or willing by the animal in question. However, some research on operant conditioning digs deeper into the underlying mechanisms that produce the familiar outcomes of reinforcement. Like we did earlier in the chapter with classical conditioning, let's examine three elements that expand our view of operant conditioning: the cognitive, neural, and evolutionary elements of operant conditioning.

The Cognitive Elements of Operant Conditioning

Edward Chace Tolman (1886–1959) was one of the first researchers to question Skinner's strictly behaviorist interpretation of learning, and was the strongest early advocate of a cognitive approach to operant learning. Tolman argued that there was more to learning than just knowing the circumstances in the environment (the properties of the stimulus) and being able to observe a particular outcome (the reinforced response). Instead, Tolman proposed that an animal established a means–ends relationship. That is, the conditioning experience produced knowledge or a belief that, in this particular situation, a specific reward (the end state) will appear if a specific response (the means to that end) is made.

Tolman's means–ends relationship may remind you of the Rescorla–Wagner model of classical conditioning. Rescorla argued that the CS functions by setting up an expectation about the arrival of a US, and "expectations" most certainly involve cognitive processes. In both Rescorla's and Tolman's theories, the stimulus does not directly evoke a response; rather, it establishes an internal cognitive state, which then produces the behavior. These cognitive theories of learning focus less on the stimulus–response (SR) connection and more on what happens in the organism's mind when faced with the stimulus. During the 1930s and 1940s, Tolman and his students conducted studies that focused on *latent learning* and *cognitive maps*, two phenomena that strongly suggest that simple S–R interpretations of operant learning behavior are inadequate.

Edward Chace Tolman advocated a cognitive approach to operant learning and provided evidence that in maze-learning experiments, rats develop a mental picture of the maze, which he called a cognitive map.

Latent Learning and Cognitive Maps. In **latent learning,** *something is learned, but it is not manifested as a behavioral change until sometime in the future.* Latent learning can easily be established in rats and occurs without any obvious reinforcement, a finding that posed a direct challenge to the then-dominant behaviorist position that all learning required some form of reinforcement (Tolman & Honzik, 1930a).

Tolman gave three groups of rats access to a complex maze every day for over 2 weeks. The control group never received any reinforcement for navigating the maze. They were simply allowed to run around until they reached the goal box at the end of the maze. In **FIGURE 7.10** you can see that over the 2 weeks of the study, the control group (in green) got a little better at finding their way through the maze, but not by much. A second group of rats received regular reinforcements; when they reached the goal box, they found a small food reward there. Not surprisingly, these rats showed clear learning, as can be seen in blue in Figure 7.10. A third group was treated exactly like the control group for the first 10 days and then rewarded for the last 7 days. This group's behavior (in orange) was quite striking. For the first 10 days, they behaved like the rats in the control group. However, during the final 7 days, they behaved a lot like the rats in the second group that had been reinforced every day. Clearly, the rats in this third group had learned a lot about the maze and the location of the goal box during those first 10 days even though they had not received any reinforcements for their behavior. In other words, they showed evidence of latent learning.

These results suggested to Tolman that beyond simply learning "start here, end here," his rats had developed a sophisticated mental picture of the maze. Tolman called this a **cognitive map,** *a mental representation of the physical features of the environment*. Tolman thought that the rats had developed a mental picture of the maze, along the lines of "make two lefts, then a right, then a quick left at the corner," and he devised several experiments to test that idea (Tolman & Honzik, 1930b; Tolman, Ritchie, & Kalish, 1946).

> **What are cognitive maps and why are they a challenge to behaviorism?**

Further Support for Cognitive Explanations. One simple experiment provided support for Tolman's theories and wreaked havoc with the noncognitive explanations offered by staunch behaviorists. Tolman trained a group of rats in the maze shown in **FIGURE 7.11a.** As you can see, rats run down a straightaway, take a left, a right, a long right, and then end up in the goal box at the end of the maze. Because we're looking at it from above, we can see that the rat's position at the end of the maze, relative to the starting point, is "diagonal to the upper right." Of course, all the rat in the maze sees are the next set of walls and turns until it eventually reaches the goal box. Nonetheless, rats learned to navigate this maze without error or hesitation after about four nights. Clever rats. But they were more clever than you think.

After they had mastered the maze, Tolman changed things around a bit and put them in the maze shown in **FIGURE 7.11b.** The goal box was still in the same place relative to the start box. However, many alternative paths now spoked off the main platform, and the main straightaway that the rats had learned to use was blocked. Most behaviorists would predict that the rats in this situation—running down a familiar path only to find it blocked—would show stimulus generalization and pick the next closest path, such as one immediately adjacent to the straightaway. This was not what Tolman observed. When faced with the blocked path, the rats instead ran all the way down the path that led directly to the goal box. The rats had formed a sophisticated cognitive map of their environment and behaved in a way that suggested they were successfully following that map after the conditions had changed. Latent learning and cognitive maps suggest that operant conditioning involves much more than an animal

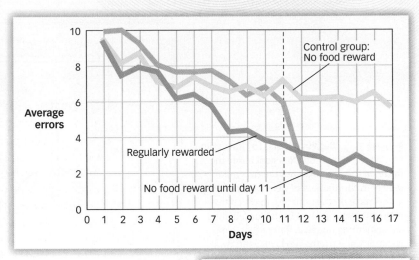

▲ Figure **7.10** **Latent Learning** Rats in a control group that never received any reinforcement (in green) improved at finding their way through the maze over 17 days but not by much. Rats that received regular reinforcements (in blue) showed fairly clear learning; their error rate decreased steadily over time. Rats in the latent learning group (in orange) were treated exactly like the control group rats for the first 10 days and then like the regularly rewarded group for the last 7 days. Their dramatic improvement on day 12 shows that these rats had learned a lot about the maze and the location of the goal box even though they had never received reinforcements. Notice, also, that on the last 7 days, these latent learners actually seem to make *fewer* errors than their regularly rewarded counterparts.

latent learning
Something is learned, but it is not manifested as a behavioral change until sometime in the future.

cognitive map
A mental representation of the physical features of the environment.

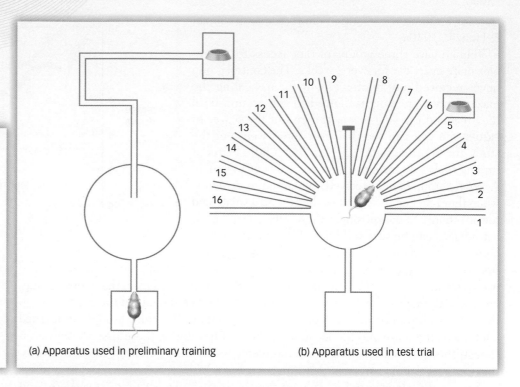

► Figure **7.11 Cognitive Maps** (*a*) Rats trained to run from a start box to a goal box in the maze on the left mastered the task quite readily. When those rats were then placed in the maze on the right (*b*), in which the main straightaway had been blocked, they did something unusual. Rather than simply backtrack and try the next closest runway (i.e., those labeled 8 or 9 in the figure), which would be predicted by stimulus generalization, the rats typically chose runway 5, which led most directly to where the goal box had been during their training. The rats had formed a cognitive map of their environment and knew where they needed to end up spatially, compared to where they began.

(a) Apparatus used in preliminary training

(b) Apparatus used in test trial

responding to a stimulus. Tolman's experiments strongly suggest that there is a cognitive component, even in rats, to operant learning.

Learning to Trust: For Better or Worse. Cognitive factors also played a key role in an experiment examining learning and brain activity (using fMRI) in people who played a "trust" game with a fictional partner (Delgado, Frank, & Phelps, 2005). On each trial, a participant could either keep a $1 reward or transfer the reward to a partner, who would receive $3. The partner could then either keep the $3 or share half of it with the participant. When playing with a partner who was willing to share the reward, the participant would be better off transferring the money, but when playing with a partner who did not share, the participant would be better off keeping the reward in the first place. Participants in such experiments typically find out who is trustworthy on the basis of trial-and-error learning during the game, transferring more money to partners who reinforce them by sharing.

In the study by Delgado et al., participants were given detailed descriptions of their partners that either portrayed the partners as trustworthy, neutral, or suspect. Even though during the game itself the sharing behavior of the three types of partners did not differ—they each reinforced participants to the same extent through sharing—the participants' cognitions about their partners had powerful effects. Participants transferred more money to the trustworthy partner than to the others, essentially ignoring the trial-by-trial feedback that would ordinarily shape their playing behavior, thus reducing the amount of reward they received. Highlighting the power of the cognitive effect, signals in a part of the brain that ordinarily distinguishes between positive and negative feedback were evident only when participants played with the neutral partner; these feedback signals were absent when participants played with the trustworthy partner and reduced when participants played with the suspect partner.

These kinds of effects might help us to understand otherwise perplexing real-life cases such as that of con artist Bernard Madoff, who in March 2009 pleaded guilty to swindling numerous investors out of billions of dollars in a highly publicized case that attracted worldwide attention. Madoff

Why might cognitive factors have been a factor in people's trust of Bernie Madoff?

Although this evidence implies that there is a cultural influence on the cognitive processes that support observational learning, the researchers noted that the effects on observational learning could be attributed to any number of influences on the human-reared monkeys, including more experience with tools, more attention to a model's behavior, or as originally suggested by Tomasello et al. (1993), increased sensitivity to the intentions of others. Thus, more work is needed to understand the exact nature of those processes (Bering, 2004; Tomasello & Call, 2004).

Neural Elements of Observational Learning

Observational learning involves a neural component as well. As you read in the Neuroscience and Behavior chapter, *mirror neurons* are a type of cell found in the brains of primates (including humans). Mirror neurons fire when an animal performs an action, such as when a monkey reaches for a food item. More importantly, however, mirror neurons also fire when an animal watches someone *else* perform the same specific task (Rizzolatti & Craighero, 2004). Although this "someone else" is usually a fellow member of the same species, some research suggests that mirror neurons in monkeys also fire when they observe humans performing an action (Fogassi et al., 2005). For example, monkeys' mirror neurons fired when they observed humans grasping for a piece of food, either to eat it or to place it in a container.

Mirror neurons, then, may play a critical role in the imitation of behavior as well as the prediction of future behavior (Rizzolatti, 2004). Mirror neurons are thought to be represented in specific subregions in the frontal and parietal lobes, and there is evidence that individual subregions respond most strongly to observing certain kinds of actions (see **FIGURE 7.17**). If appropriate neurons fire when another organism is seen performing an action, it could indicate an awareness of intentionality, or that the animal is anticipating a likely course of future actions. Although the exact functions of mirror neurons continue to be debated (Hickok, 2009), both of these elements—rote imitation of well-understood behaviors and an awareness of how behavior is likely to unfold—contribute to observational learning.

? What do mirror neurons do?

Studies of observational learning in healthy adults have shown that watching someone else perform a task engages some of the same brain regions that are activated when people actually perform the task themselves. Do you consider yourself a good dancer? Have you ever watched someone who is a good dancer—a friend or maybe a celebrity on *Dancing with the Stars*—in the hopes of improving your own dance floor moves? In a recent fMRI study, participants performed two tasks for several days prior to scanning: practicing dance sequences to unfamiliar techno-dance songs, and watching music videos containing other dance sequences accompanied by unfamiliar techno-dance songs (Cross et al., 2009). They were then scanned while viewing videos of sequences that they had previously danced or watched, as well as videos of untrained sequences.

Analysis of the fMRI data revealed that in comparison with the untrained sequences, viewing the previously danced or watched sequences recruited a largely similar brain network, including regions considered to be part of the mirror neuron system, as well as a couple of brain regions that showed more activity for previously danced than watched videos. The results of a surprise dancing test given to participants after the conclusion of scanning showed that performance was better on sequences previously watched than on the untrained sequences, demonstrating significant observational learning, but was best of all on the previously danced sequences (Cross et al., 2009). So, while watching *Dancing in the Stars* might indeed improve your dancing skills, practicing on the dance floor should help even more.

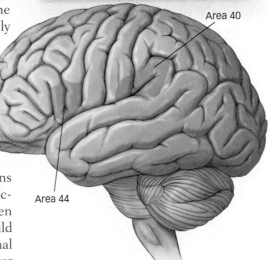

▼ Figure **7.17** **Mirror Neuron System** Regions in the frontal lobe (area 44) and parietal lobe (area 40) are thought to be part of the mirror neuron system in humans.

Area 40

Area 44

Observing skilled dancers, such as Sugar Ray Leonard and Anna Trebunsyaya on *Dancing with the Stars*, engages many of the same brain regions as does actual dance practice, and can produce significant learning.

Related evidence indicates that observational learning of some motor skills relies on the motor cortex, which is known to be critical for motor learning. For example, when participants watch another individual engage in a task that involves making a complex reaching movement, significant observational learning occurs (Mattar & Gribble, 2005). To examine whether the observational learning depends on the motor cortex, researchers applied transcranial magnetic stimulation (TMS) to the motor cortex just after participants observed performance of the reaching movement (as you learned in the Neuroscience and Behavior chapter, TMS results in a temporary disruption in the function of the brain region to which it is applied). Strikingly, applying TMS to the motor cortex greatly reduced the amount of observational learning, whereas applying TMS to a control region outside the motor cortex had no effect on observational learning (Brown, Wilson, & Gribble, 2009).

These findings indicate that some kinds of observational learning are grounded in brain regions that are essential for action. When one organism patterns its actions on another organism's behaviors, learning is speeded up and potentially dangerous errors (think of Margie, who won't burn her hand on the stove) are prevented.

IN SUMMARY

▶ Observational learning is based on cognitive mechanisms such as attention, perception, memory, or reasoning. But observational learning also has roots in evolutionary biology and for the most basic of reasons: It has survival value. Observational learning is an important process by which species gather information about the world around them.

▶ Observational learning has important social and cultural consequences, as it appears to be well suited for transmission of novel behaviors across individuals. Chimpanzees and monkeys can benefit from observational learning, especially those reared in settings that include humans.

▶ The mirror neuron system becomes active during observational learning, and many of the same brain regions are active during observation and performance of a skill. Observational learning is closely tied to parts of the brain that are involved in action.

Implicit Learning: Under the Wires

It's safe to assume that people are sensitive to the patterns of events that occur in the world around them. Most people don't stumble through life thoroughly unaware of what's going on. Okay, maybe your roommate does. But people usually are attuned to linguistic, social, emotional, or sensorimotor events in the world around them so much so that they gradually build up internal representations of those patterns that were acquired without explicit awareness. This process is often called **implicit learning,** or *learning that takes place largely independent of awareness of both the process and the products of information acquisition.* Because it occurs without awareness, implicit learning is knowledge that sneaks in "under the wires."

Habituation, which we discussed at the outset of the chapter, is a very simple kind of implicit learning where repeated exposure to a stimulus results in a reduced response. Habituation occurs even in a simple organism such as *Aplysia*, which lacks the brain structures necessary for explicit learning, such as the hippocampus (Eichenbaum, 2008; Squire & Kandel, 1999). In

> **How can you learn something without being aware of it?**

Ten years ago, no one knew how to type using thumbs; now just about all teenagers do it automatically.

AP PHOTO/MARY ALTAFFER

contrast, some forms of learning start out explicitly but become more implicit over time. When you first learned to drive a car, for example, you probably devoted a lot of attention to the many movements and sequences that needed to be carried out simultaneously ("step lightly on the accelerator while you push the turn indicator and look in the rearview mirror while you turn the steering wheel"). That complex interplay of motions is now probably quite effortless and automatic for you. Explicit learning has become implicit over time.

How are learning and memory linked?

implicit learning
Learning that takes place largely independent of awareness of both the process and the products of information acquisition.

These distinctions in learning might remind you of similar distinctions in memory and for good reason. In the Memory chapter, you read about the differences between *implicit* and *explicit* memories. Do implicit and explicit learning mirror implicit and explicit memory? It's not that simple, but it is true that learning and memory are inextricably linked. Learning produces memories, and conversely, the existence of memories implies that knowledge was acquired, that experience was registered and recorded in the brain, or that learning has taken place.

Cognitive Approaches to Implicit Learning

Interest in implicit learning among psychologists was sparked when researchers began to investigate how children learned language and social conduct (Reber, 1967). Most children, by the time they are 6 or 7 years old, are linguistically and socially fairly sophisticated. Yet most children reach this state with very little explicit awareness that they have learned something, and with equally little awareness of what it was they have actually learned. As an example, although children are often given explicit rules of social conduct ("Don't chew with your mouth open"), they learn how to behave in a civilized way through experience. They're probably not aware of when or how they learned a particular course of action and may not even be able to state the general principle underlying their behavior. Yet most kids have learned not to eat with their feet, to listen when they are spoken to, and not to kick the dog.

To investigate implicit learning in the laboratory, early studies showed research participants 15 or 20 letter strings and asked them to memorize them. The letter strings, which at first glance look like nonsense syllables, were actually formed using a complex set of rules called an *artificial grammar* (see **FIGURE 7.18**). Participants were not told anything about the rules, but with experience, they gradually developed a vague, intuitive sense of the "correctness" of particular letter groupings. These letter groups became familiar to the participants and they processed them more rapidly and efficiently than the "incorrect" letter groupings (Reber, 1967, 1996).

Grammatical Strings	Nongrammatical Strings
VXJJ	VXTJJ
XXVT	XVTVVJ
VJTVXJ	VJTTVTV
VJTVTV	VJTXXVJ
XXXXVX	XXXVTJJ

◄ Figure **7.18 Artificial Grammar and Implicit Learning** These are examples of letter strings formed by an artificial grammar. Research participants are exposed to the rules of the grammar and are later tested on new letter strings. Participants show reliable accuracy at distinguishing the valid, grammatical strings from the invalid, nongrammatical strings even though they usually can't explicitly state the rule they are following when making such judgments. Using an artificial grammar is one way of studying implicit learning (Reber, 1996)

Take a look at the letter strings shown in Figure 7.18. The ones on the left are correct and follow the rules of the artificial grammar; the ones on the right all violated the rules. The differences are pretty subtle, and if you haven't been through the learning phase of the experiment, both sets look a lot alike. In fact, each nongrammatical string only has a single letter violation. Research participants are asked to classify new letter strings based on whether they follow the rules of the grammar. People turn out to be quite good at this task (usually they get 60–70% correct), but they are unable to provide much in the way of explicit awareness of the rules and regularities that they are using. The experience is similar to coming across a sentence with a grammatical error. You are immediately aware that something is wrong and you can certainly make the sentence grammatical, but unless you are a trained linguist, you'll probably find it difficult to articulate which rules of English grammar were violated or which rules you used to repair the sentence.

Other studies of implicit learning have used a *serial reaction time* task (Nissen & Bullemer, 1987). Here research participants are presented with five small boxes on a computer screen. Each box lights up briefly, and when it does, the participant is asked to press the button that is just underneath that box as quickly as possible. Like the artificial grammar task, the sequence of lights appears to be random, but in fact it follows a pattern. Research participants eventually get faster with practice as they learn to anticipate which box is most likely to light up next. But, if asked, they are generally unaware that there is a pattern to the lights.

Why are tasks learned implicitly difficult to explain to others?

Implicit learning has some characteristics that distinguish it from explicit learning. For example, when asked to carry out implicit tasks, people differ relatively little from one another, but on explicit tasks (such as conscious problem solving), they show large individual-to-individual differences (Reber, Walkenfeld, & Hernstadt, 1991). Implicit learning also seems to be unrelated to IQ: People with high scores on standard intelligence tests are no better at implicit learning tasks, on average, than those whose scores are more modest (Reber & Allen, 2000). Implicit learning changes little across the life span. Researchers discovered well-developed implicit learning of complex, rule-governed auditory patterns in 8-month-old infants (Saffran, Aslin, & Newport, 1996). Infants heard streams of speech that contained experimenter-defined nonsense words. For example, the infants might hear a sequence such as "bidakupadotigolabubidaku," which contains the nonsense word *bida*. The infants weren't given any explicit clues as to which sounds were "words" and which were not, but after several repetitions, the infants showed signs that they had learned the novel words. Infants tend to prefer novel information, and they spent more time listening to novel nonsense words that had not been presented earlier than to the nonsense words such as *bida* that had been presented. Remarkably, the infants in this study were as good at learning these sequences as college students. At the other end of the life span, researchers have found that implicit learning abilities extend well into old age and that they decline more slowly than explicit learning abilities (Howard & Howard, 1997).

STEVE SMITH/PURESTOCK

Implicit learning, which is involved in acquiring and retaining the skills needed to ride a bicycle, tends to be less affected by age than explicit learning.

Implicit learning is remarkably resistant to various disorders that are known to affect explicit learning. A group of patients suffering from various psychoses were so severely impaired that they could not solve simple problems that college students had little difficulty with. Yet those patients were able to solve an artificial grammar learning task about as well as college students (Abrams & Reber, 1988). Other studies have found that profoundly amnesic patients not only show normal implicit memories, but also display virtually normal implicit learning of artificial grammar (Knowlton, Ramus, & Squire, 1992). In fact, they made accurate judgments about novel letter strings even though they had essentially no explicit memory of having been in the learning phase of the experiment! In contrast, several studies have shown that dyslexic children, who fail to acquire reading skills despite normal intelligence and good educational opportunities, exhibit deficits in implicit learning of artificial grammars (Pavlidou, Williams, & Kelly, 2009) and motor and spatial sequences on the serial reaction time task (Bennett et al., 2008; Orban, Lungu, & Doyon, 2008; Stoodley et al., 2008). These findings suggest that problems with implicit learning play an important role in developmental dyslexia and need to be taken into account when developing remedial programs (Stoodley et al., 2008).

Implicit and Explicit Learning Use Distinct Neural Pathways

The fact that individuals suffering amnesia show intact implicit learning strongly suggests that the brain structures that underlie implicit learning are distinct from those that underlie explicit learning. As we learned in the Memory chapter, amnesic individuals are characterized by lesions to the hippocampus and nearby structures in the medial temporal lobe; accordingly, these regions are not necessary for implicit learning (Bayley, Frascino, & Squire, 2005). What's more, it appears that distinct regions of the brain may be activated depending on how people approach a task.

For example, in one study, participants saw a series of dot patterns, each of which looked like an array of stars in the night sky (Reber et al., 2003). Actually, all the stimuli were constructed to conform to an underlying prototypical dot pattern. The dots, however, varied so much that it was virtually impossible for a viewer to guess that they all had this common structure. Before the experiment began, half of the participants were told about the existence of the prototype; in other words, they were given instructions that encouraged explicit processing. The others were given standard implicit learning instructions: They were told nothing other than to attend to the dot patterns.

The participants were then scanned as they made decisions about new dot patterns, attempting to categorize them into those that conformed to the prototype and those that did not. Interestingly, both groups performed equally well on this task, correctly classifying about 65% of the new dot patterns. However, the brain scans revealed that the two groups were making these decisions using very different parts of their brains (see **FIGURE 7.19**). Participants who were given the explicit instructions showed *increased* brain activity in the prefrontal cortex, parietal cortex, hippocampus, and a variety of other areas known to be associated with the processing of explicit memories. Those given the implicit instructions showed *decreased* brain activation primarily in the occipital region, which is involved in visual processing. This finding suggests that participants recruited distinct brain structures in different ways depending on whether they were approaching the task using explicit or implicit learning.

> **What technology shows that implicit and explicit learning are associated with separate structures of the brain?**

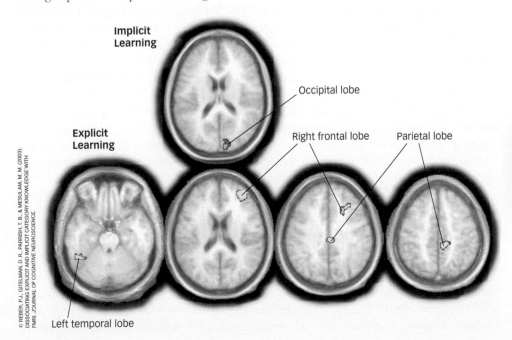

Implicit Learning

Explicit Learning

Occipital lobe

Right frontal lobe

Parietal lobe

Left temporal lobe

© REBER, P.J., GITELMAN, D. R., PARRISH, T. B., & MESULAM, M. M. (2003). DISSOCIATING EXPLICIT AND IMPLICIT CATEGORY KNOWLEDGE WITH FMRI *JOURNAL OF COGNITIVE NEUROSCIENCE*

◀ Figure **7.19 Implicit and Explicit Learning Activate Different Brain Areas** Research participants were scanned with fMRI while engaged in either implicit or explicit learning about the categorization of dot patterns. The occipital region (in blue) showed decreased brain activity after implicit learning. The areas in yellow, orange, and red showed increased brain activity during explicit learning, including the left temporal lobe (*far left*), right frontal lobe (*second from left and second from right*), and parietal lobe (*second from right and far right*; Reber et al., 2003).

Other studies have begun to pinpoint the brain regions that are involved in two of the most commonly used implicit learning tasks: artificial grammar learning and sequence learning on the serial reaction time task. Several fMRI studies have shown that Broca's area—which, as you learned in the Neuroscience and Behavior chapter, plays a key role in language production—is turned on during artificial grammar learning (Forkstam et al., 2006; Petersson, Forkstam, & Ingvar, 2004). Furthermore, activating Broca's area by applying electrical stimulation to the nearby scalp enhances implicit learning of artificial grammar, most likely by facilitating acquisition of grammatical rules (De Vries et al., 2010). In contrast, the motor cortex appears critical for sequence learning on the serial reaction time task. When the motor cortex was temporarily disabled by the application of a recently developed type of TMS that lasts for a long time (so that participants could perform the task without having TMS constantly applied while they are doing so), sequence learning was abolished (Wilkinson et al., 2010).

IN SUMMARY

▶ Implicit learning is a process that detects, learns, and stores patterns without the application of explicit awareness on the part of the learner.

▶ Simple behaviors such as habituation can reflect implicit learning, but complex behaviors, such as language use or socialization, can also be learned through an implicit process.

▶ Tasks that have been used to document implicit learning include artificial grammar and serial reaction time tasks.

▶ Implicit and explicit learning differ from each other in a number of ways: There are fewer individual differences in implicit than explicit learning; psychotic and amnesic patients with explicit learning problems can exhibit intact implicit learning; and neuroimaging studies indicate that implicit and explicit learning recruit distinct brain structures, sometimes in different ways.

Learning in the Classroom

In this chapter we've considered several different types of learning from behavioral, cognitive, evolutionary, and neural perspectives. Yet it may seem strange to you that we haven't discussed the kind of learning to which you are currently devoting much of your life: learning in educational settings such as the classroom. Way back in the first chapter of this book (Psychology: Evolution of a Science), we reviewed some techniques that we think are useful for studying the material in this course and others (see The Real World, Improving Study Skills, pp. 10–11). But, we didn't say much about the actual research that supports these suggestions. During the past several years, psychologists have published a great deal of work specifically focused on enhancing learning in educational settings. Let's consider what some of this research says about learning techniques, and then turn to the equally important topic of exerting control over learning processes.

Techniques for Learning

Students use a wide variety of study techniques in attempts to increase learning. Popular techniques—ones that you might use yourself—include highlighting and underlining, rereading, summarizing, and visual imagery mnemonics (Annis & Annis, 1982; Wade, Trathen, & Schraw, 1990). How effective are these and other techniques? A team of psychologists that specialize in learning recently published a comprehensive analysis of research concerning 10 learning techniques that are used to by students

(Dunlosky et al., 2013). They considered the usefulness of each technique across four main variables: learning conditions (e.g., how often and in what context the technique is used), to-be-learned materials (e.g., texts, math problems, concepts), student characteristics (e.g., age and ability level), and outcome measures (e.g., rote retention, comprehension, problem solving). Based on the picture that emerged across these four variables, Dunlosky et al. evaluated the overall usefulness of each technique and classified it as high, moderate, or low utility. **TABLE 7.2** provides a brief description of each of the 10 techniques and the overall utility assessment for each one.

Despite their popularity, highlighting, rereading, summarizing, and visual imagery mnemonics all received a low utility assessment. That doesn't mean that these techniques have no value whatsoever for improving learning, but it does indicate that each one has significant limitations and that time could be better spent using other approaches—a reason why none of these techniques appeared in the Improving Study Skills box. The Improving Study Skills box did review strategies that roughly correspond to two of the techniques in Table 7.2 that received a moderate utility assessment—elaboration interrogation and self-explanation—and we also discussed some material related to these techniques in the Memory chapter (pp. 220–263). Furthermore, the Improving Study Skills box highlighted both of the techniques that received high utility assessments: distributed practice and practice testing. Let's take a deeper look at some of the research that supports the beneficial effects of these two effective techniques, which have been intensively investigated during the past few years.

Distributed Practice

Cramming for exams (neglecting to study for an extended period of time and then studying intensively just before an exam; Vacha & McBride, 1993) is a common occurrence in educational life. Surveys of undergraduates across a range of colleges and universities indicate that anywhere from about 25% to as many as 50% of students report relying on cramming (McIntyre & Munson, 2008). Though cramming is better than not studying at all, when students cram for an exam, they repeatedly study the to-be-learned information with little or no time between repetitions, a procedure

> **Table 7.2**

Rating the Effectiveness of Study Techniques

Technique	Description	Utility
Elaborative interrogation	Generating an explanation for why an explicitly stated fact or concept is true	Moderate
Self-explanation	Explaining how new information is related to known information, or explaining steps taken during problem solving	Moderate
Summarization	Writing summaries (of various lengths) of to-be-learned texts	Low
Highlighting/underlining	Marking potentially important portions of to-be-learned material while reading	Low
Keyword mnemonic	Using keywords and mental images of text materials while reading or listening	Low
Imagery for text	Attempting to form mental images of text materials while reading or listening	Low
Rereading	Restudying text material again after an initial reading	Low
Practice testing	Self-testing or taking practice tests over to-be-learned material	High
Distributed practice	Implementing a schedule of practice that spreads out study activities over time	High
Interleaved practice	Implementing a schedule of practice that mixes different kinds of problems, or a schedule of study that mixes different kinds of material, within a single study session	Moderate

Studying well in advance of an exam, so that you can take breaks and distribute study time, will generally produce a better outcome than cramming at the last minute.

known as *massed practice*. Such students are thus denying themselves the benefits of distributed practice, which involves spreading out study activities so that more time intervenes between repetitions of the to-be-learned information (and students who rely on cramming are also inviting some of the health and performance problems associated with procrastination that we outlined in The Real World box on p. 270).

The benefits of distributed practice relative to massed practice have been known for a long time; in fact, they were first reported in the classic studies of Ebbinghaus (1885/1964) concerning retention of nonsense syllables (see the Memory chapter). What's most impressive is just how widespread the benefits of distributed practice are: They have been observed for numerous different kinds of materials, including foreign vocabulary, definitions, and face–name pairs, and have been demonstrated not only in undergraduates, but also in children, older adults, and individuals with memory problems due to brain damage (Dunlosky et al., 2013). A review of 254 separate studies involving more than 14,000 participants concluded that, on average, participants retained 47% of studied information after distributed practice compared with 37% after massed practice (Cepeda et al., 2006).

Despite all the evidence indicating that distributed practice is an effective learning strategy, we still don't fully understand why that is so. One promising idea is that when engaging in massed practice, retrieving recently studied information is relatively easy, whereas during distributed practice, it is more difficult to retrieve information that was studied less recently. More difficult retrievals benefit subsequent learning more than easy retrievals, in line with idea of "desirable difficulties" (Bjork & Bjork, 2011) introduced in the Improving Study Skills box. Whatever the explanation for the effects of distributed practice, there is no denying its benefits for students.

Practice Testing

Practice testing, like distributed practice, has proven useful across a wide range of materials, including learning of stories, facts, vocabulary, and lectures (Dunlosky et al., 2013; Karpicke, 2012; see also the LearningCurve system associated with this

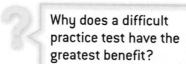

Why does a difficult practice test have the greatest benefit?

text, which uses practice testing). As you learned in the Memory chapter, practice testing is effective, in part, because actively retrieving an item from memory on a test improves subsequent retention of that item more than simply studying it again (Roediger & Karpicke, 2006). Yet when asked about their preferred study strategies, students indicated by a wide margin that they prefer rereading materials to testing themselves (Karpicke, 2012). The benefits of testing tend to be greatest when the test is difficult and requires considerable retrieval effort (Pyc & Rawson, 2009), also consistent with the desirable difficulties hypothesis (Bjork & Bjork, 2011). Not only does testing increase verbatim learning of the exact material that is tested, it also enhances the *transfer* of learning from one situation to another (Carpenter, 2012). For example, if you are given practice tests with short-answer questions, such testing improves later performance on both short-answer and multiple-choice questions more than restudying (Kang, McDermott, & Roediger, 2007). Testing also improves the ability to draw conclusions from the studied material, which is an important part of learning and often critical to performing well in the classroom (Karpicke & Blunt, 2011).

Testing Aids Attention

Recent research conducted in the laboratory of one of your textbook authors highlights yet another benefit of testing: including brief tests during a lecture can improve learning by reducing the tendency to mind wander (Szpunar, Khan, & Schacter, 2013). How often have you found your mind wandering—thinking about your evening plans, recalling a scene from a movie, or texting a friend—in the midst of a lecture that you know that you ought to be attending to carefully? It's probably happened more than once. Research indicates that students' minds wander frequently during classroom lectures (Bunce, Flens, & Neiles, 2011; Lindquist & McLean, 2011; Wilson & Korn, 2007). Critically, such mind wandering impairs learning of the lecture material (Risko et al., 2012). In the study by Szpunar et al. (2013), participants watched a videotaped statistics lecture that was divided into four segments. All of the participants were told that they might or might not be tested after each segment; they were also encouraged to take notes during the lectures.

> Participants in the *tested* group received brief tests on each segment.

> Participants in the *nontested* group did not receive a test until after the final segment (they worked on arithmetic problems after each of the earlier segments).

> Participants in a *re-study* group were shown, but not tested on, the same material as the tested group after each segment.

At random times during the lectures, participants in all groups were probed about whether they were paying attention to the lecture or mind wandering off to other topics. Participants in the nontested and re-study groups indicated that they were mind wandering in response to about 40% of the probes, but the incidence of mind wandering was cut in to half, to about 20%, in the tested group. Participants in the tested group took significantly more notes during the lectures, and retained significantly more information from the lecture on a final test than did than participants in the other two groups, who performed similarly. Participants in the tested group were also less anxious about the final test than those in the other groups. These results indicate that part of the value of testing comes from encouraging people to sustain attention to a lecture in a way that discourages task-irrelevant activities such as mind wandering and encourages task-relevant activities such as note taking. Because these benefits of testing were observed in response to a videotaped lecture, they apply most directly to online learning, where taped lectures are the norm (see Other Voices: Online Learning), but there is every reason to believe that the results would apply in live classroom settings as well.

How does taking practice tests help focus a wandering mind?

Control of Learning

It's the night before the final exam in your introductory psychology course. You've put in a lot of time reviewing your course notes and the material in this textbook, and you feel that you have learned most of it pretty well. You are coming down the home stretch with little time left, and you've got to decide whether to devote those precious remaining minutes to studying psychological disorders or social psychology. How do you make that decision? What are its potential consequences? An important part of learning involves assessing how well we know something and how much more time we need to devote to studying it.

Recent research has shown that people's judgments about what they have learned play a critical role in guiding further study and learning (Dunlosky & Thiede, 2013; Metcalfe, 2009). Experimental evidence reveals that these subjective assessments, which psychologists refer to as *judgments of learning* (JOLs), have a casual influence on learning: People typically devote more time to studying items that they judge they have not learned well (Metcalfe & Finn, 2008; Son & Metcalfe, 2000).

The finding that JOLs are causally related to decisions about how much to study a particular item is important because JOLs are sometimes inaccurate (Castel, McCabe, & Roediger, 2007). For example, after reading and rereading a chapter or article in preparation for a test, the material will likely feel quite familiar, and that feeling may convince you that you've learned the material well enough that you don't need to study it further. However, the feeling of familiarity can be misleading: It may be the result of a low-level process such as perceptual priming (see the Memory chapter) and not the kind of learning that will be required to perform well on an exam (Bjork & Bjork, 2011). Similarly, recent research has shown that students are sometimes overconfident in judging how well they have learned definitions of new terms, and fail to study them effectively (Dunlosky & Rawson, 2012). One way to avoid being fooled by such misleading subjective impressions is to test yourself from time to time when studying for an exam under exam-like conditions, and in the case of learning definitions, carefully compare your answers to the actual definitions.

> **In what ways can JOLs be misleading?**

So, if you are preparing for the final exam in this course and need to decide whether to devote more time to studying psychological disorders or social psychology, try to exert control over learning by testing yourself on material from the two chapters; you can use the results of those tests to help you decide which chapter requires further work. Heed the conclusion from researchers (Bjork, Dunlosky, and Kornell, 2013) that becoming

OTHER VOICES

Online Learning

Daphne Koller is a professor of computer science at Stanford University.

PHOTO BY HECTOR GARCIA-MOLINA

Online learning has become a hot topic recently as a result of new online initiatives from a number of leading brick-and-mortar colleges and universities. Daphne Koller, a professor of computer science at Stanford University, is one of the founders of the popular online learning platform, Coursera. She wrote the following article several months before the launch of Coursera in April 2012.

Our education system is in a state of crisis. Among developed countries, the United States is 55th in quality rankings of elementary math and science education, 20th in high school completion rate and 27th in the fraction of college students receiving undergraduate degrees in science or engineering.

As a society, we can and should invest more money in education. But that is only part of the solution. The high costs of high-quality education put it off limits to large parts of the population, both in the United States and abroad, and threaten the school's place in society as a whole. We need to significantly reduce those costs while at the same time improving quality.

If these goals seem contradictory, let's consider an example from history. In the 19th century, 60 percent of the American work force was in agriculture, and there were frequent food shortages. Today, agriculture accounts for less than 2 percent of the work force, and there are food surpluses.

The key to this transition was the use of technology—from crop rotation strategies to GPS-guided farm machinery—which greatly increased productivity. By contrast, our approach to education has remained largely unchanged since the Renaissance: From middle school through college, most teaching is done by an instructor lecturing to a room full of students, only some of them paying attention.

How can we improve performance in education, while cutting costs at the same time? In 1984, Benjamin Bloom showed that individual tutoring had a huge advantage over standard lecture environments: The average tutored student performed better than 98 percent of the students in the standard class.

Until now, it has been hard to see how to make individualized education affordable. But I argue that technology may provide a path to this goal.

Consider the success of the Khan Academy, which began when Salman Khan tried to teach math remotely to his young cousins. He recorded short videos with explanations and placed them on the Web, augmenting them with automatically graded exercises. This simple approach was so compelling that by now, more than 700 million videos have been watched by millions of viewers.

At Stanford, we recently placed three computer science courses online, using a similar format. Remarkably, in the first four weeks, 300,000 students registered for these courses, with millions of video views and hundreds of thousands of submitted assignments.

What can we learn from these successes? First, we see that video content is engaging to students—many of whom grew up on YouTube—and easy for instructors to produce.

Second, presenting content in short, bite-size chunks, rather than monolithic hour-long lectures, is better suited to students' attention spans, and provides the flexibility to tailor instruction to individual students. Those with less preparation can dwell longer on background material without feeling uncomfortable about how they might be perceived by classmates or the instructor.

Conversely, students with an aptitude for the topic can move ahead rapidly, avoiding boredom and disengagement. In short, everyone has access to a personalized experience that resembles individual tutoring.

Watching passively is not enough. Engagement through exercises and assessments is a critical component of learning. These exercises are designed not just to evaluate the student's learning, but also, more a more sophisticated and effective learner requires understanding: (a) key features of learning and memory; (b) effective learning techniques; (c) how to monitor and control one's own learning; and (d) biases that can undermine judgments of learning.

IN SUMMARY

▶ Research on learning techniques indicates that some popular study methods such as highlighting, underlining, and rereading have low utility, whereas other techniques such as practice testing and distributed practice have high utility.

▶ Practice testing improves retention and transfer of learning and can also enhance learning and reduce mind wandering during lectures.

▶ Judgments of learning play a causal role in determining what material to study, but they can be misleading.

important, to enhance understanding by prompting recall and placing ideas in context.

Moreover, testing allows students to move ahead when they master a concept, rather than when they have spent a stipulated amount of time staring at the teacher who is explaining it.

For many types of questions, we now have methods to automatically assess students' work, allowing them to practice while receiving instant feedback about their performance. With some effort in technology development, our ability to check answers for many types of questions will get closer and closer to that of human graders.

Of course, these student–computer interactions can leave many gaps. Students need to be able to ask questions and discuss the material. How do we scale the human interaction to tens of thousands of students?

Our Stanford courses provide a forum in which students can vote on questions and answers, allowing the most important questions to be answered quickly—often by another student. In the future, we can adapt Web technology to support even more interactive formats, like real-time group discussions, affordably and at large scale.

More broadly, the online format gives us the ability to identify what works. Until now, many education studies have been based on populations of a few dozen students. Online technology can capture every click: what students watched more than once, where they paused, what mistakes they made. This mass of data is an invaluable resource for understanding the learning process and figuring out which strategies really serve students best.

Some argue that online education can't teach creative problem-solving and critical-thinking skills. But to practice problem-solving, a student must first master certain concepts. By providing a cost-effective solution for this first step, we can focus precious classroom time on more interactive problem-solving activities that achieve deeper understanding—and foster creativity.

In this format, which we call the flipped classroom, teachers have time to interact with students, motivate them and challenge them. Though attendance in my Stanford class is optional, it is considerably higher than in many standard lecture-based classes. And after the Los Altos school district in Northern California adopted this blended approach, using the Khan Academy, seventh graders in a remedial math class sharply improved their performance, with 41 percent reaching advanced or proficient levels, up from 23 percent.

A 2010 analysis from the Department of Education, based on 45 studies, showed that online learning is as effective as face-to-face learning, and that blended learning is considerably more effective than either.

Online education, then, can serve two goals. For students lucky enough to have access to great teachers, blended learning can mean even better outcomes at the same or lower cost. And for the millions here and abroad who lack access to good, in-person education, online learning can open doors that would otherwise remain closed.

Nelson Mandela said, "Education is the most powerful weapon which you can use to change the world." By using technology in the service of education, we can change the world in our lifetime.

Koller makes a strong positive case for online learning, and the rapid spread of online courses since the publication of this article indicates that others agree with her. Furthermore, Koller's comments about the delivery of information in "bite-sized chunks" and the use of testing are generally consistent with the recent findings of Szpunar et al. (2013) discussed in the main text showing that intermittent testing can reduce mind wandering during online lectures. But online learning is not without its critics. For example, in a *New York Times* op-ed article written some 6 months after Koller's column, when Harvard and MIT announced their own online plans, David Brooks (2012a) raised some important questions: "If a few star professors can lecture to millions, what happens to the rest of the faculty? Will academic standards be as rigorous? What happens to the students who don't have enough intrinsic motivation to stay glued to their laptop hour after hour? How much communication is lost—gesture, mood, eye contact—when you are not actually in a room with a passionate teacher and students?"

What do you see as the major challenges for online learning? How important is face-to-face interaction in your own educational experience? What kind of research would you like to see done to further the effectiveness of online learning?

Chapter Review

KEY CONCEPT QUIZ

1. In classical conditioning, a conditioned stimulus is paired with an unconditioned stimulus to produce
   a. a neutral stimulus.
   b. a conditioned response.
   c. an unconditioned response.
   d. another conditioned stimulus.

2. What occurs when a conditioned stimulus is no longer paired with an unconditioned stimulus?
   a. generalization
   b. spontaneous recovery
   c. extinction
   d. acquisition

3. What did Watson and Rayner seek to demonstrate about behaviorism through the Little Albert experiment?
   a. Conditioning involves a degree of cognition.
   b. Classical conditioning has an evolutionary component.
   c. Behaviorism alone cannot explain human behavior.
   d. Even sophisticated behaviors such as emotion are subject to classical conditioning.

4. Which part of the brain is involved in the classical conditioning of fear?
   a. the amygdala
   b. the cerebellum
   c. the hippocampus
   d. the hypothalamus

5. After having a bad experience with a particular type of food, people can develop a lifelong aversion to the food. This suggests that conditioning has a(n) _____ aspect.
   a. cognitive
   b. evolutionary
   c. neural
   d. behavioral

6. Which of the following is NOT an accurate statement concerning operant conditioning?
   a. Actions and outcomes are critical to operant conditioning.
   b. Operant conditioning involves the reinforcement of behavior.
   c. Complex behaviors cannot be accounted for by operant conditioning.
   d. Operant conditioning has associative mechanisms with roots in evolutionary behavior.

7. Which of the following mechanisms have no role in Skinner's approach to behavior?
   a. cognitive
   b. neural
   c. evolutionary
   d. all of the above

8. Latent learning provides evidence for a cognitive element in operant conditioning because
   a. it occurs without any obvious reinforcement.
   b. it requires both positive and negative reinforcement.
   c. it points toward the operation of a neural reward center.
   d. it depends on a stimulus–response relationship.

9. Activity of neurons in the _____ contributes to the process of reinforcement.
   a. hippocampus
   b. pituitary gland
   c. medial forebrain bundle
   d. parietal lobe

10. Which of the following mechanisms does NOT help form the basis of observational learning?
    a. attention
    b. perception
    c. punishment
    d. memory

11. Neural research indicates that observational learning is closely tied to brain areas that are involved in
    a. memory.
    b. vision.
    c. action.
    d. emotion.

12. What kind of learning takes place largely independent of awareness of both the process and the products of information acquisition?
    a. latent learning
    b. implicit learning
    c. observational learning
    d. conscious learning

13. The process in which repeated or prolonged exposure to a stimulus results in a gradual reduction in responding is called
    a. habituation.
    b. explicit learning.
    c. serial reaction time.
    d. delay conditioning.

14. Which of the following statements about implicit learning is inaccurate?
    a. Some forms of learning start out explicitly but become more implicit over time.
    b. Implicit learning occurs even in the simplest organisms.
    c. People with high scores on intelligence tests are more adept at implicit learning tasks.
    d. Children learn language and social conduct largely through implicit learning.

15. Responding to implicit instructions results in decreased brain activation in which part of the brain?
    a. the hippocampus
    b. the parietal cortex
    c. the prefrontal cortex
    d. the occipital region

16. Which study strategy has been shown to be the most effective?
    a. highlighting text
    b. rereading
    c. summarizing
    d. taking practice tests

KEY TERMS

learning (p. 266)
habituation (p. 266)
sensitization (p. 266)
classical conditioning (p. 267)
unconditioned stimulus (US) (p. 267)
unconditioned response (UR) (p. 267)
conditioned stimulus (CS) (p. 268)
conditioned response (CR) (p. 268)

acquisition (p. 269)
second-order conditioning (p. 269)
extinction (p. 271)
spontaneous recovery (p. 271)
generalization (p. 271)
discrimination (p. 271)
biological preparedness (p. 276)
operant conditioning (p. 277)
law of effect (p. 278)
operant behavior (p. 278)

reinforcer (p. 279)
punisher (p. 279)
fixed-interval schedule (FI) (p. 284)
variable-interval schedule (VI) (p. 284)
fixed-ratio schedule (FR) (p. 285)
variable-ratio schedule (VR) (p. 285)
intermittent reinforcement (p. 285)
intermittent reinforcement effect (p. 286)

shaping (p. 286)
latent learning (p. 288)
cognitive map (p. 289)
observational learning (p. 295)
diffusion chain (p. 296)
implicit learning (p. 300)

CHANGING MINDS

1. A friend is taking a class in childhood education. "Back in the old days," she says, "teachers used physical punishment, but of course that's not allowed any more. Now, a good teacher should only use reinforcement. When children behave, teachers should provide positive reinforcement, like praise. When children misbehave, teachers should provide negative reinforcement, like scolding or withholding privileges." What is your friend misunderstanding about reinforcement? Can you give better examples of how negative reinforcement could be productively applied in an elementary school classroom?

2. A friend of your family is trying to train her daughter to make her bed every morning. You suggest she tries positive reinforcement. A month later, the woman reports back to you. "It's not working very well," she says. "Every time she makes her bed, I put a gold star on the calendar, and at the end of the week, if there are seven gold stars, I give Vicky a reward—a piece of licorice. But so far, she's only earned the licorice twice." How could you explain why the desired behavior—bed-making—might not increase as a result of this reinforcement procedure?

3. While studying for the exam, you ask your study partner to provide a definition of classical conditioning. "In classical conditioning," she says, "there's a stimulus—the CS—that predicts an upcoming event, the US. Usually, it's something bad, like an electric shock, nausea, or a frightening loud noise. The learner makes a response, the CR, in order to prevent the US. Sometimes, the US is good, like food for Pavlov's dogs, and then the learner makes the response in order to earn the US." What's wrong with this definition?

4. One of your classmates announces that he liked the last chapter (on memory) better than the current chapter on learning. "I want to be a psychiatrist," he says, "so I mostly care about human learning. Conditioning might be a really powerful way to train animals to push levers or perform tricks, but it really doesn't have much relevance to how humans learn things." How similar is learning in humans and other animals? What real-world examples can you provide to show that conditioning does occur in humans?

ANSWERS TO KEY CONCEPT QUIZ

1. b; 2. c; 3. d; 4. a; 5. b; 6. c; 7. d; 8. a; 9. c; 10. c; 11. c; 12. b; 13. a; 14. c; 15. D; 16. d.

Emotion and Motivation

Leonardo is 5 years old and cute as a button. He can do many of the things that other 5-year-olds can do: solve puzzles, build towers of blocks, and play guessing games with grown-ups. But unlike other 5-year-olds, Leonardo has never been proud of his abilities, angry at his mother, or bored with his lessons. That's because Leonardo has a condition that makes him unable to experience emotions of any kind. He has never felt joy or sorrow, delight or despair, shame, envy, annoyance, excitement, gratitude, or regret. He has never laughed or cried.

Leonardo's condition has had a profound impact on his life. For example, because he doesn't experience emotions, he isn't motivated to do things that bring most children pleasure, such as eating cookies or playing hide-and-seek or watching Saturday morning cartoons. And because he doesn't feel, he doesn't have any intuitions about what others are feeling, which can make social interaction a challenge. His mother has spent years teaching him how to make the facial expressions that indicate emotions such as surprise and sadness, and how to detect those facial expressions in others. Leonardo now knows that he should smile when someone says something nice to him and that he should raise his eyebrow once in a while to show interest in what people are saying. Leonardo is a quick learner, and he's gotten so good at this that when strangers interact with him they find it hard to believe that deep down inside he is feeling nothing at all.

So when Leonardo's mother smiles at him, he always smiles back. And yet, she is keenly aware that Leonardo is merely making the faces he was taught to make and that he doesn't really love her.

A typical 5-year-old can experience emotions such as pride, anger, and boredom.

Leonardo and his "mom," MIT Professor Cynthia Breazeal.

"I never realized they had feelings."

But that's okay. Although Leonardo cannot return her affection, Dr. Cynthia Breazeal still considers him one of the greatest robots she's ever designed (Breazeal, 2009).

YES, LEONARDO IS A MACHINE. HE CAN SEE AND HEAR, he can remember and reason. But despite his adorable smile and knowing wink, he can't feel a thing, and that makes him infinitely different than us. Our ability to love and to hate, to be amused and annoyed, to feel elated and devastated, is an essential element of our humanity, and a person who could not feel these things would seem a lot like a robot to the rest of us. But what exactly are these things we call emotions and why are they so essential? In this chapter we will explore these questions. We'll start by discussing the nature of emotions and seeing how they relate to the states of our bodies and our brains. Next we'll see how people express their emotions, and how they use those expressions to communicate with each other. Finally, we'll examine the essential role that emotions play in motivation—how they inform us, and how they compel us do everything from making war to making love.

It is almost impossible not to feel something when you look at this photograph, and it is almost impossible to say exactly what you are feeling.

Emotional Experience: The Feeling Machine

Leonardo doesn't know what love feels like and there's no way to teach him, because trying to describe the feeling of love to someone who has never experienced it is a bit like trying to describe the color green to someone who was born blind. We could tell Leonardo what causes the feeling ("It happens whenever I see Marilynn") and we could tell him about its consequences ("I breathe hard and say goofy stuff"), but in the end these descriptions would miss the point because the essential feature of love—like the essential feature of all emotions—is the *experience*. It *feels* like something to love, and what it feels like is love's defining attribute (Heavey, Hurlburt, & Lefforge, 2012).

What Is Emotion?

How can we study something whose defining attribute defies description? Psychologists have developed a clever technique that capitalizes on the fact that although people can't always say what an emotional experience feels like ("Love is . . . um . . . uh . . ."), they usually can say how similar one experience is to another ("Love is more like happiness than like anger"). By asking people to rate the similarity of dozens of emotional experiences, psychologists have been able to use a technique known as *multidimensional scaling* to create a map of those experiences. The mathematics behind this technique is complex, but the logic is simple. If you drew up a list of the distances between a half-dozen U.S. cities, handed the list to a friend, and challenged her to turn those distances into a map, your friend would have to draw a map of the United States (see **FIGURE 8.1**). Why? Because there is no other map that allows every city to appear at precisely the right distance from every other.

The same technique can be used to generate a map of the emotional landscape. If you listed the similarity of a large number of emotional experiences (assigning smaller distances to those that feel similar and larger distances to those that feel dissimilar) and then challenged a friend to incorporate them into a map, your

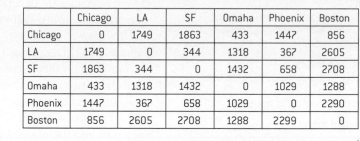

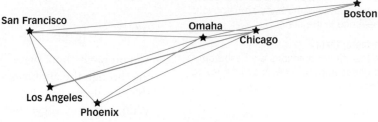

> **Why do psychologists use multidimensional scaling?**

friend would be forced to draw a map like the one shown in **FIGURE 8.2**. This is the unique map that allows every emotional experience to be precisely the right distance from every other. What good is this map? As it turns out, maps don't just show how close things are to each other. They also reveal the *dimensions* on which those things vary. For example, the map in Figure 8.2 reveals that emotional experiences differ on two dimensions called *valence* (how positive or negative the experience is) and *arousal* (how active or passive the experience is). Research shows that all emotional

▲ Figure **8.1** **From Distances to Maps**
Knowing the distances between things—like cities, for example—allows us to draw a map that reveals the dimensions on which they vary.

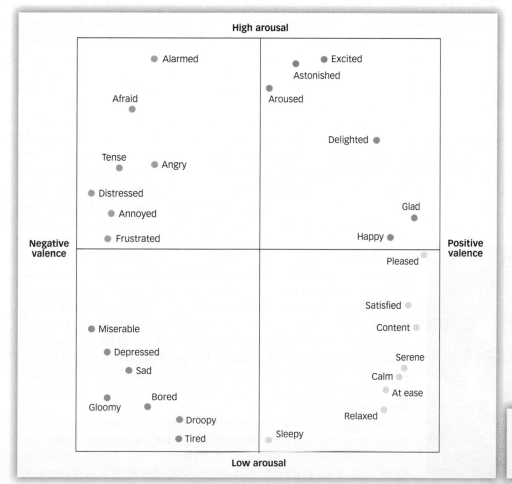

◄ Figure **8.2** **Two Dimensions of Emotion**
Just as cities can be mapped by their longitude and latitude, emotions can be mapped by their arousal and valence.

emotion
A positive or negative experience that is associated with a particular pattern of physiological activity.

James–Lange theory
The theory that a stimulus triggers activity in the body, which in turn produces an emotional experience in the brain.

Cannon–Bard theory
The theory that a stimulus simultaneously triggers activity in the body and emotional experience in the brain.

two-factor theory
The theory that emotions are based on inferences about the causes of physiological arousal.

experiences can be described by their unique coordinates on this two-dimensional map (Russell, 1980; Watson & Tellegen, 1985; Yik, Russell, & Steiger, 2011).

This map of emotional experience suggests that any definition of emotion must include two things: first, the fact that emotional experiences are good or bad; and second, the fact that these experiences are have characteristic levels of bodily arousal. With these two facts in mind, we can define **emotion** as *a positive or negative experience that is associated with a particular pattern of physiological activity.* As you are about to see, the first step in understanding emotion involves understanding how the experience part and the physiological activity part of this definition are related.

The Emotional Body

You probably think that if you walked into your kitchen right now and saw a bear nosing through the cupboards, you would feel fear, your heart would start to pound, and the muscles in your legs would prepare you for running. But in the late 19th century, William James suggested that the events that produce an emotion might actually happen in the opposite order: First you see the bear, then your heart starts pounding and your leg muscles contract, and *then* you experience fear, which is nothing more than your experience of your body's response. As James (1884, pp. 189–190) wrote, "Bodily changes follow directly the perception of the exciting fact. . . . And feeling of the same changes as they occur *is* the emotion." For James, each unique emotional experience was the result of a unique pattern of physiological responses, and he suggested that without all the heart pounding and muscle clenching, there would be no experience of emotion at all. Psychologist Carl Lange suggested something similar at about the same time, so the idea, now known as the **James–Lange theory** of emotion, is that a *stimulus triggers activity in the body, which in turn produces an emotional experience in the brain.* According to this theory, emotional experience is the consequence—not the cause—of our physiological reactions to objects and events in the world.

James's former student, Walter Cannon, didn't like this idea very much, and so together with *his* student, Philip Bard, he proposed an alternative. The **Cannon–Bard theory** of emotion is the theory that *a stimulus simultaneously triggers activity in the body and emotional experience in the brain* (Bard, 1934; Cannon, 1927). Cannon claimed that his theory was better than the James–Lange theory for several reasons. First, he noted, emotions happen quickly even though the body often reacts slowly. For example, a blush is a bodily response to embarrassment that takes 15 to 30 seconds to occur, and yet, people feel embarrassed within seconds of noticing that, oh say, their pants have fallen off in public. So how could the blush be the cause of the feeling? Second, people often have difficulty accurately detecting bodily responses, such as changes in their heart rates. If people cannot detect changes in their heart rates, then how can they experience those changes as an emotion? Third, nonemotional stimuli—such as an increase in room temperature—can cause the same bodily response as emotional stimuli do. So why don't people feel afraid when they get a fever? Finally, Cannon noted that there simply weren't enough unique patterns of bodily activity to account for all the unique emotional experiences people have. If many different emotional experiences are associated with the same pattern of bodily activity, then how could that pattern of activity be the sole determinant of the emotional experience?

These are all good questions, and about 30 years after Cannon asked them, psychologists Stanley Schachter and Jerome Singer supplied some answers (Schachter & Singer, 1962). James and Lange were right, they claimed, to equate emotion with the perception of

Did Princess Kate make Prince William blush by embarrassing him, or did she embarrass him by making him blush? The experience of embarrassment precedes blushing by up to 30 seconds, so it is unlikely that blushing is the cause of the emotional experience.

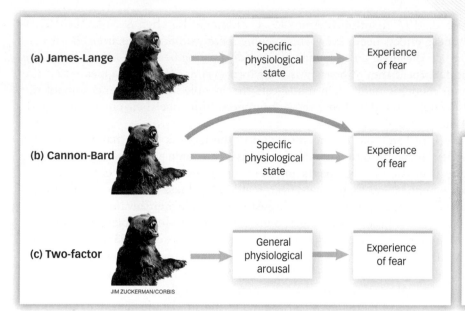

(a) James-Lange → Specific physiological state → Experience of fear

(b) Cannon-Bard → Specific physiological state → Experience of fear

(c) Two-factor → General physiological arousal → Experience of fear

JIM ZUCKERMAN/CORBIS

◄ Figure **8.3** **Classic Theories of Emotion** Classic theories make different claims about the origins of emotion. The James–Lange theory suggests that stimuli trigger specific physiological states, which are then experienced as emotions (*a*). The Cannon–Bard theory suggests that stimuli trigger both specific physiological states and emotional experiences independently (*b*). The two-factor theory suggests that stimuli trigger general physiological arousal whose cause the brain interprets, and this interpretation leads to emotional experience (*c*).

one's bodily reactions. But Cannon and Bard were right, they claimed, to note that there are not nearly enough distinct bodily reactions to account for the wide variety of emotions that human beings can experience. Whereas James and Lange had suggested that different emotions are *different experiences* of *different patterns* of bodily activity, Schachter and Singer claimed that different emotions are merely *different interpretations* of *a single pattern* of bodily activity, which they called "undifferentiated physiological arousal" (see **FIGURE 8.3**).

Schachter and Singer's **two-factor theory** of emotion is the theory that *emotions are based on inferences about the causes of physiological arousal*. When you see a bear in your kitchen, your heart begins to pound. Your brain quickly scans the environment, looking for a reasonable explanation for all that pounding, and notices, of all things, a bear. Having noticed both a bear and a pounding heart, your brain then does what brains do so well: It puts two and two together, makes a logical inference, and interprets your arousal as fear. In other words, when you are physiologically aroused in the presence of something that you think should scare you, you label that arousal as *fear*. But if you have precisely the same bodily response in the presence of something that you think should delight you, then you might label that arousal as *excitement*. According to Schachter and Singer, people have the same physiological reaction to all emotional stimuli, but they interpret that reaction differently on different occasions.

> **How did the two-factor theory of emotion expand on earlier theories?**

How has the two-factor model fared in the last half century? One of the model's claims has fared very well. For instance, participants in one study (Schachter & Singer, 1962) were injected with epinephrine, which causes physiological arousal, and then exposed to either a goofy or a nasty confederate. Just as the two-factor theory predicted, when the confederate acted goofy, participants concluded that they were feeling *happy*, but when the confederate acted nasty, participants concluded that they were feeling *angry*. Subsequent research has shown that when people are aroused in other ways—say, by having them ride an exercise bike in the laboratory—they subsequently find attractive people more attractive, annoying people more annoying, and funny cartoons funnier, as if they were interpreting their exercise-induced arousal as attraction, annoyance, or amusement

The fact that people can mistake physical arousal for romantic attraction may help explain why so many first dates involve roller coasters. This couple—reality television stars Spencer Pratt and Heidi Montag—ended up getting married a few years after this photo was taken. Since then, they've had some ups and downs.

ANDREW SHAWAF/PACIFICCOASTNEWS/NEWSCOM

appraisal
An evaluation of the emotion-relevant aspects of a stimulus.

(Byrne et al., 1975; Dutton & Aron, 1974; Zillmann, Katcher, & Milavsky, 1972). In fact, these effects occur even when people merely *think* they're aroused—for example, when they hear an audiotape of a rapidly beating heart and are led to believe that the heartbeat they're hearing is their own (Valins, 1966). It appears that the two-factor model is right when it suggests that people make inferences about the causes of their arousal and that those inferences influence their emotional experience (Lindquist & Barrett, 2008).

However, research has not been so kind to the model's claim that all emotional experiences are merely different interpretations of the same bodily state. For example, researchers measured participants' physiological reactions as they experienced six different emotions and found that anger, fear, and sadness each produced a higher heart rate than disgust; that fear and disgust produced higher galvanic skin response (sweating) than did sadness or anger; and that anger produced a larger increase in finger temperature than did fear (Ekman, Levenson, & Friesen, 1983; see **FIGURE 8.4**). These findings have been replicated across different age groups, professions, genders, and cultures (Levenson, Ekman, & Friesen, 1990; Levenson et al., 1991, 1992). In fact, some physiological responses seem unique to a single emotion. For example, a blush is the result of increased blood volume in the subcutaneous capillaries in the face, neck, and chest, and research suggests that people blush when they feel embarrassment but not when they feel any other emotion (Leary et al., 1992). Similarly, certain patterns of activity in the parasympathetic branch of the autonomic nervous system (which is responsible for slowing and calming rather than speeding and exciting) seem uniquely related to prosocial emotions such as compassion (Oately, Keltner, & Jenkins, 2006).

So which of these duos was right? James and Lange were right when they suggested that patterns of physiological response are not the same for all emotions. But Cannon and Bard were right when they suggested that people are not perfectly sensitive to these patterns of response, which is why people must sometimes make inferences about what they are feeling. Our bodily activity and our mental activity are both the causes and the consequences of our emotional experience. The precise nature of their interplay is not yet fully understood, but as you are about to see, much progress has been made over last few decades by following the trail of emotion from the beating heart to the living brain.

▼ Figure **8.4 The Physiology of Emotion** Contrary to the claims of the two-factor theory, different emotions do seem to have different underlying patterns of physiological arousal. Anger, fear, and sadness all produce higher heart rates compared to happiness, surprise, and disgust (*a*). Anger produces a much larger increase in finger temperature than any other emotion (*b*).

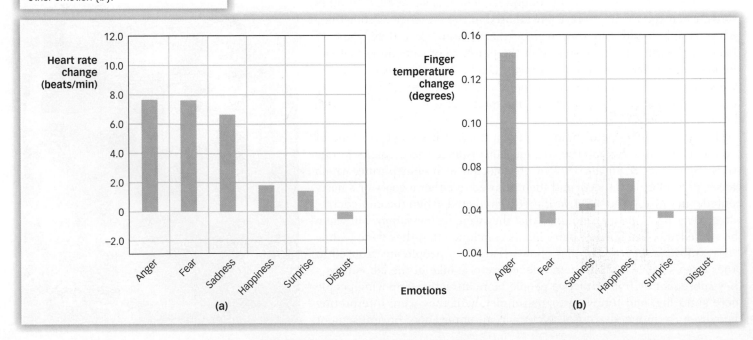

The Emotional Brain

In the late 1930s, psychologist Heinrich Klüver and physician Paul Bucy made an accidental discovery. A few days after performing brain surgery on a monkey named Aurora, they noticed that she was acting strangely. First, Aurora would eat just about anything and have sex with just about anyone—as though she could no longer distinguish between good and bad food, or between good and bad mates. Second, Aurora seemed absolutely fearless and unflappable, remaining calm when she was handled by experimenters, and even when she was confronted by snakes (Klüver & Bucy, 1937, 1939). What had happened to her? As it turned out, during the surgery, Klüver and Bucy had accidentally damaged a structure in Aurora's brain called the *amygdala*. Subsequent studies confirmed that the amygdala plays a special role in producing emotions such as fear. For example, in one study, researchers performed an operation so that information entering a monkey's left eye was transmitted to its amygdala, but information entering the monkey's right eye was not (Downer, 1961). When the monkey was allowed to see a threatening stimulus with only its left eye, it responded with fear and alarm, but when it was allowed to see the threatening stimulus with only its right eye, it was calm and unruffled. Research with humans shows much the same thing. For example, people normally have superior memory for emotionally evocative words such as *death* or *vomit*, but people whose amygdalae are damaged (LaBar & Phelps, 1998) or who take drugs that temporarily impair neurotransmission in the amygdala (van Stegeren et al., 1998) do not (see **FIGURE 8.5**). Interestingly, although people with amygdala damage often don't feel fear when they *see* a threat, they do feel fear when they *experience* a threat, for example, when they suddenly find they can't breathe (Feinstein et al., 2013).

The tourist and the tiger have something in common: each has an amygdala that is working at lightning speed to decide whether the other is a threat. Why did nature design the brain to make this particular decision so quickly?

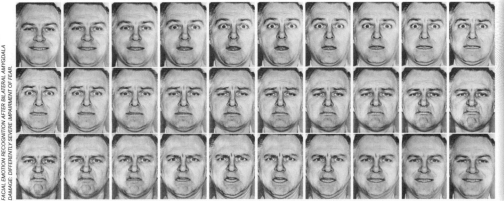

◀ Figure **8.5** **Emotion Recognition and the Amygdala** Facial expressions of emotion were morphed into a continuum that ran from happiness to surprise to fear to sadness to disgust to anger and back to happiness. This sequence was shown to a patient with bilateral amygdala damage and to a control group of 10 people without brain damage. Although the patient's recognition of happiness, sadness, and surprise was generally in line with that of the control group, her recognition of anger, disgust, and fear was impaired (Calder et al., 1996).

What exactly does the amygdala do? Is it some sort of "fear center"? Not exactly (Cunningham & Brosch, 2012). Before an animal can feel fear, its brain must first decide that there is something to be afraid of. This decision is called an **appraisal,** which is *an evaluation of the emotion-relevant aspects of a stimulus* (Arnold, 1960; Ellsworth & Scherer, 2003; Lazarus, 1984; Roseman, 1984; Roseman & Smith, 2001; Scherer, 1999, 2001). The amygdala is critical to making these appraisals. In essence, the amygdala is an extremely fast and sensitive threat detector (Whalen et al., 1998). Psychologist Joseph LeDoux (2000) mapped the route that information about a stimulus takes through the brain and found that it is transmitted simultaneously along two distinct routes: the "fast pathway," which goes from the thalamus directly to the amygdala, and the "slow pathway," which goes from the thalamus to

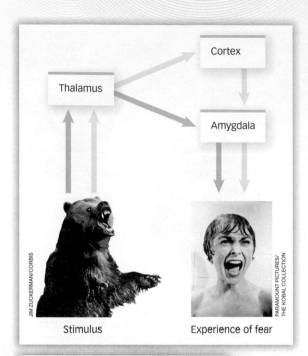

Stimulus   Experience of fear

▲ Figure **8.6 The Fast and Slow Pathways of Fear** According to Joseph LeDoux (2000), information about a stimulus takes two routes simultaneously: the "fast pathway" (shown in pink), which goes from the thalamus directly to the amygdala, and the "slow pathway" (shown in green), which goes from the thalamus to the cortex and then to the amygdala. Because the amygdala receives information from the thalamus before it receives information from the cortex, people can be afraid of something before they know what it is.

the cortex and *then* to the amygdala (see **FIGURE 8.6**). This means that while the cortex is slowly using the information to conduct a full-scale investigation of the stimulus's identity and importance ("This seems to be an animal . . . probably a mammal . . . perhaps a member of the genus *Ursus* . . ."), the amygdala has already received the information directly from the thalamus and is making one very fast and very simple decision: "Is this a threat?" If the amygdala's answer to that question is yes, it initiates the neural processes that ultimately produce the bodily reactions and conscious experience that we call fear.

The cortex takes much longer to process this information, but when it finally does, it sends a signal to the amygdala. That signal can tell the amygdala to maintain the state of fear ("We've now analyzed all the data up here, and sure enough, that thing is a bear—and bears bite!") or decrease it ("Relax, it's just some guy in a bear costume"). When experimental subjects are instructed to *experience* emotions such as sadness, fear, and anger, they show increased activity in the amygdala and decreased activity in the cortex (Damasio et al., 2000), but when they are asked to *inhibit* these emotions, they show increased cortical activity and decreased amygdala activity (Ochsner et al., 2002). In a sense, the amygdala presses the emotional gas pedal and the cortex then hits the brakes. That's why both adults with cortical damage and children (whose cortices are not well developed) have difficulty inhibiting their emotions (Stuss & Benson, 1986).

Studies of the brain suggest that emotion is part of a primitive system that prepares us to react rapidly and on the basis of little information to things that are relevant to our survival and well-being. While our new cortex identifies a stimulus, considers what it knows about it, and carefully plans a response, our ancient amygdala does what it has done so well for all those millennia before the cortex evolved: It makes a split-second decision about the significance of the objects and events in our environment and, when necessary, prepares our hearts and our legs to get our butts out of the woods.

> How do the limbic system and cortex interact to produce emotion?

The Regulation of Emotion

You may or may not care about hedgehogs, earwax, or the War of 1812, but if you are human, you almost certainly care about what you are feeling. **Emotion regulation** refers to *the strategies people use to influence their own emotional experience,* and although people occasionally want to experience negative emotions rather than positive emotions (Erber, Wegner, & Therriault, 1996; Michaela et al., 2009; Parrott, 1993; Tamir & Ford, 2012), most of the time people would rather feel good than bad.

Nine out of 10 people report that they attempt to regulate their emotional experience at least once a day (Gross, 1998), and they describe more than a thousand different strategies for doing so (Parkinson & Totterdell, 1999). Some of these are behavioral strategies (e.g., avoiding situations that trigger unwanted emotions) and some are cognitive strategies (e.g., recruiting memories that trigger the desired emotion; Webb, Miles, & Sheeran, 2012). Research shows that people don't always know which strategies will be most effective. For example, people tend to think that *suppression,* which involves inhibiting the outward signs of an emotion, is an effective strategy. But by and large, it isn't (Gross, 2002). Conversely, people tend to think that *affect labeling,* which involves putting one's feelings into words, will have little impact on their emotions, when in fact, it is generally effective in reducing the intensity of emotional states (Lieberman et al., 2011).

One of the best strategies for emotion regulation is **reappraisal**, which involves *changing one's emotional experience by changing the way one thinks about the emotion-*

eliciting stimulus (Ochsner et al., 2009). For example, participants in one study who watched a video of a circumcision that was described as a joyous religious ritual had slower heart rates and reported less distress than did participants who watched the same video but did not hear the same description (Lazarus & Alfert, 1964). In another study, participants' brains were scanned as they saw photos that induced negative emotions, such as a photo of a woman crying during a funeral.

> **How, and how well, does reappraisal work?**

Some participants were then asked to reappraise the picture, for example, by imagining that the woman in the photo was at a wedding rather than a funeral. The results showed that when participants initially saw the photo, their amygdalae became active. But as they reappraised the picture, several key areas of the cortex became active, and moments later, their amygdalae were deactivated (Ochsner et al., 2002). In other words, participants were able to turn down the activity of their own amygdalae simply by thinking about the photo in a different way.

Reappraisal is an important skill. Some people are better at it than others (Malooly, Genet, & Siemer, 2013), and the ability to reappraise is associated with both mental and physical health (Davidson, Putnam, & Larson, 2000; Gross & Munoz, 1995). Indeed, as you will learn in the Stress and Health chapter, therapists often attempt to alleviate depression and distress by teaching people how to reappraise key events in their lives (Jamieson, Mendes, & Nock, 2013). On the other hand, this ability can allow us to be less compassionate toward those who are suffering (Cameron & Payne, 2011). About two thousand years ago, Roman emperor Marcus Aurelius wrote: "If you are distressed by anything external, the pain is not due to the thing itself, but to your estimate of it; and this you have the power to revoke at any moment." Modern science suggests that the emperor was on to something.

Emotion regulation can be difficult. In 2011, the city of Portland, Oregon flushed 8 million gallons of drinking water simply because a man was seen urinating in this reservoir. Although the miniscule amount of urine posed no health threat, it made people feel disgusted—and the inability to regulate that emotion cost the citizens of Portland nearly $30,000.

AP PHOTO/RICK BOWMER

IN SUMMARY

▶ Emotional experiences are difficult to describe, but psychologists have identified their two underlying dimensions: arousal and valence.

▶ Psychologists have spent more than a century trying to understand how emotional experience and physiological activity are related. The James–Lange theory suggests that a stimulus causes a physiological reaction, which leads to an emotional experience; the Cannon–Bard theory suggests that a stimulus causes both an emotional experience and a physiological reaction simultaneously; and Schachter and Singer's two-factor theory suggests that a stimulus causes undifferentiated physiological arousal about which people draw inferences. None of these theories are entirely right, but each has elements that are supported by research.

▶ Emotions are produced by the complex interaction of limbic and cortical structures (see Figure 3.16 on p. 98). Information about a stimulus is sent simultaneously to the amygdala (which makes a quick appraisal of the stimulus's goodness or badness) and the cortex (which does a slower and more comprehensive analysis of the stimulus). In some instances, the amygdala will trigger an emotional experience that the cortex later inhibits.

▶ People care about their emotional experiences and use many strategies to regulate them. Reappraisal involves changing the way one thinks about an object or event, and is one of the most effective strategies for emotion regulation.

emotion regulation
The strategies people use to influence their own emotional experience.

reappraisal
Changing one's emotional experience by changing the way one thinks about the emotion-eliciting stimulus.

emotional expression
An observable sign of an emotional state.

universality hypothesis
Emotional expressions have the same meaning for everyone.

Emotional Communication: Msgs w/o Wrds

Leonardo the robot may not be able to feel, but he sure can smile. And wink. And nod. Indeed, one of the reasons why people who interact with Leonardo find it so hard to think of him as a machine is that Leonardo *expresses* emotions that he doesn't actually have. An **emotional expression** is *an observable sign of an emotional state*, and while robots can be taught to exhibit them, human beings seem to do it quite naturally.

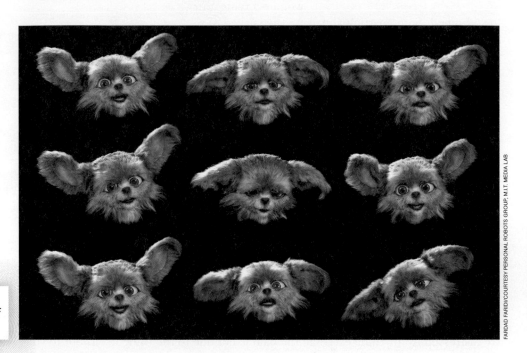

Leonardo's face is capable of expressing a wide range of emotions (Breazeal, 2003).

FARDAD FARIDI/COURTESY PERSONAL ROBOTS GROUP, M.I.T. MEDIA LAB

Our emotional states express themselves in a wide variety of ways. For example, they change the way we talk—from our intonation and inflection to the loudness and duration of our speech—and research shows that listeners can infer emotional states from vocal cues alone with better-than-chance accuracy (Banse & Scherer, 1996; Frick, 1985). Observers can also estimate emotional states from the direction of a person's gaze, the rhythm of their gait, or even from a brief touch on the arm (Dael, Mortillaro, & Scherer, 2012; Dittrich et al., 1996; Hertenstein et al., 2009; Keltner & Shiota, 2003; Wallbott, 1998). In some sense, we are walking, talking advertisements for what's going on inside us.

Why are we "walking, talking advertisements" of our inner states?

Of course, no part of your body is more exquisitely designed for communicating emotion than your face. Underneath your face lie 43 muscles that are capable of creating more than 10,000 unique configurations, which enable you to convey information about your emotional state with an astonishing degree of subtlety and specificity (Ekman, 1965). Psychologists Paul Ekman and Wallace Friesen (1971) spent years cataloguing the muscle movements of which the human face is capable. They isolated 46 unique movements, which they called *action units*, and they gave each one a number and a name, such as "cheek puffer," "dimpler," and "nasolabial deepener" (which, coincidentally enough, are also the names of heavy metal bands). Research has shown that combinations of these action units are reliably related to specific emotional states (Davidson et al., 1990). For example, when we feel happy, our

SCOTT FAHLMAN—COURTESY OF SCOTT FAHLMAN

On September 19, 1982, Scott Fahlman posted a message to an Internet user's group that read, "I propose the following character sequence for joke markers: :-) Read it sideways." And so the emoticon was born. Fahlman's smile (above right) is a sign of happiness, whereas his emoticon is a symbol.

zygomatic major (a muscle that pulls our lip corners up) and our *obicularis oculi* (a muscle that crinkles the outside edges of our eyes) produce a unique facial expression that psychologists describe as "action units 6 and 12" and that the rest of us simply call smiling (Ekman & Friesen, 1982; Frank, Ekman, & Friesen, 1993; Steiner, 1986).

Communicative Expression

Why are our emotions written all over our faces? In 1872, Charles Darwin published *The Expression of the Emotions in Man and Animals*, in which he speculated about the evolutionary significance of emotional expression. Darwin noticed that human and nonhuman animals share certain facial and postural expressions, and he suggested that these expressions were meant to communicate information about internal states. It's not hard to see how such communications could be useful (Shariff & Tracy, 2011). For example, if a dominant animal can bare its teeth and communicate the message, "I am angry at you," and if a subordinate animal can lower its head and communicate the message, "I am afraid of you," then the two can establish a pecking order without actually spilling any blood. Darwin suggested that emotional expressions are a convenient way for one animal to let another animal know how it is feeling and therefore how it is prepared to act. In this sense, emotional expressions are a bit like the words of a nonverbal language.

According to Charles Darwin (1872/1998), both human and nonhuman animals use facial expressions to communicate information about their internal states.

The Universality of Expression

Of course, a language only works if everybody speaks the same one, which is why Darwin advanced the **universality hypothesis,** which suggests that *emotional expressions have the same meaning for everyone.* In other words, every human being naturally expresses happiness with a smile, and every human being naturally understands that a smile signifies happiness.

There is some evidence for Darwin's hypothesis. For example, people who have never seen a human face make the same facial expressions as those who have. Congenitally blind people smile when they are happy (Galati, Scherer, & Ricci-Bitt, 1997; Matsumoto & Willingham, 2009), and 2-day-old infants make a disgust face when bitter chemicals are put in their mouths (Steiner, 1973, 1979). In addition, people are fairly accurate when judging the emotional expressions of members of other cultures (Ekman & Friesen, 1971; Elfenbein & Ambady, 2002; Frank & Stennet, 2001; Haidt & Keltner, 1999). Not only do Chileans, Americans, and Japanese all recognize a smile as a sign of happiness and a frown as a sign of sadness, but so do members of preliterate cultures. In the 1950s, researchers took photographs of Westerners expressing anger, disgust, fear, happiness, sadness, and surprise (see **FIGURE 8.7**) and showed them to members of the South Fore, a people who lived a Stone Age existence in the highlands of Papua New Guinea and who at that point had had little contact with the modern world. Researchers asked these participants to match each photograph to a word (such as "happy" or "afraid") and discovered that the South Fore made matches that were essentially the same as those made by Americans. (The one exception to this rule was

> ? **What evidence suggests that facial expressions are universal?**

▼ Figure **8.7** **Six Basic Emotions** Humans all over the globe generally agree that these six faces are displaying anger, disgust, fear, happiness, sadness, and surprise. What might account for this widespread agreement? Adapted from Arellano, Varona, & Perales, 2008.

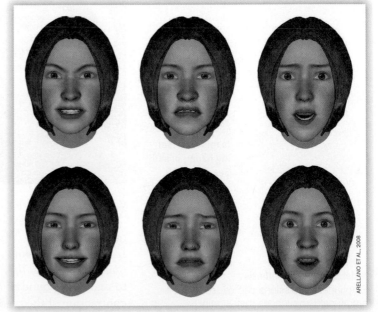

In 2013, Nobuyuki Tsujii won the prestigious Van Cliburn International Piano competition. Although he was born blind and has never seen a facial expression, winning a million dollar prize immediately gave rise to a million dollar smile.

that the Fore had trouble distinguishing expressions of surprise from expressions of fear, perhaps because for people who live in the wild, surprises are rarely pleasant.) Evidence of this sort has convinced many psychologists that facial displays of at least six emotions—*anger, disgust, fear, happiness, sadness,* and *surprise*—are universal. And a few other emotions—*embarrassment, amusement, guilt, shame,* and *pride*—may have universal patterns of facial expression as well (Keltner, 1995; Keltner & Buswell, 1996; Keltner & Haidt, 1999; Keltner & Harker, 1998; Tracy et al., 2013).

But not all psychologists are convinced. For example, recent research (Gendron et al., in press) shows that like the South Fore, members of an isolated tribe called the Himba can match faces to emotion words just as Americans do. But when the Himba are instead asked to match faces that are "feeling the same way" to each other, they produce matches that are quite unlike those produced by their American counterparts. Studies such as these suggest that the universality hypothesis may be stated too strongly. At present, we can say with confidence that there is considerable agreement among all humans about the emotional meaning of many facial expressions, but that this agreement is not perfect.

The Cause and Effect of Expression

Members of different cultures express many emotions in the same ways, but why? After all, they don't speak the same languages, so why do they smile the same smiles and frown the same frowns? The answer is that words are *symbols*, but facial expressions are *signs*. Symbols are arbitrary designations that have no causal relationship with the things they symbolize. English speakers use the word *cat* to indicate a particular animal, but there is nothing about felines that actually causes this particular sound to pop out of our mouths, and we aren't surprised when other human beings make different sounds—such as *popoki* or *gatto*—to indicate the same thing. In contrast, facial expressions are not arbitrary symbols of emotion. They are signs of emotion because signs are *caused* by the things they signify. The feeling of happiness *causes* the contraction of the zygomatic major; thus that contraction is a sign of that feeling in the same way a footprint in the snow is a sign that someone walked there.

Of course, just as a symbol (*bat*) can have more than one meaning (wooden club or flying mammal), so, too, can a sign. Is the man in the photo at left feeling joy or

Is this man feeling happy or sad? See page 329.

sorrow? In fact, these two emotions often produce rather similar facial expressions, so how do we tell them apart? Research suggests that one answer is *context*. When someone says, "The centerfielder hit the ball with the bat," the sentence provides a context that tells us that *bat* means "club" and not "mammal." Similarly, the context in which a facial expression occurs often tells us what that expression means (Aviezer et al., 2008; Barrett, Mesquita, & Gendron, 2011; Meeren, Heijnsbergen, & de Gelder, 2005). It is difficult to tell what the man in the photo to the left is feeling. But if you turn to page 329 and see the photo in context, you will have no trouble. Indeed, when you return to this page, you may well wonder how you could *ever* have had any trouble.

Our emotional experiences cause our emotional expressions, but it also works the other way around. The **facial feedback hypothesis** (Adelmann & Zajonc, 1989; Izard, 1971; Tomkins, 1981) suggests that *emotional expressions can cause the emotional experiences they signify*. For instance, people feel happier when they are asked to make the sound of a long *e* or to hold a pencil in their teeth (both of which cause contraction of the zygomatic major) than when they are asked to make the sound of a

facial feedback hypothesis
Emotional expressions can cause the emotional experiences they signify.

The Body of Evidence

What can you tell from a face? Much less than you realize. Aviezer, Trope, and Todorov (2012) showed participants faces taken from pictures of tennis players who had either just won a point (Faces 2, 3, and 5 in the figure shown here) or lost a point (Faces 1, 4, and 6) and asked them to guess whether the athlete was experiencing a positive or negative emotion. As the leftmost bars of the graph show, participants couldn't tell. They guessed that the "winning faces" and the "losing faces" were experiencing equal amounts of somewhat negative emotion.

Next, the researchers showed a new group of participants bodies (without faces) taken from pictures of tennis players who had either just won a point (Body 1 in the figure) or lost a point (Body 2), and asked them to make the same judgment. As the middle bars show, participants were quite good at this. Participants guessed that "winning bodies" were experiencing positive emotions and that "losing bodies" were experiencing negative emotions.

Finally, the researchers showed a new group of participants the athletes' bodies *and* faces together. As the rightmost bars show, participants' ratings of the body–face combinations were identical to their ratings of the bodies alone, suggesting that when participants made their guesses, they relied entirely on the athletes' bodies and not on their faces. And yet, when they were later asked which information they had relied on most, more than half the participants said they had relied on the faces!

It seems that facial expressions of emotion are more ambiguous than most of us realize. When we see people expressing anger, fear, or joy, we are using information from their bodies, their voices, and their physical and social contexts to figure out what they are feeling. Yet, we mistakenly believe that we are getting most of our information from their facial expression.

The moral of the story? Next time you want to know how a losing athlete feels, concentrate more on defeat than deface. (Sorry).

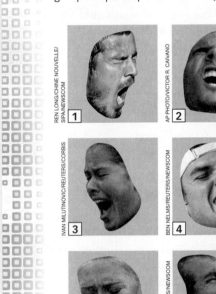

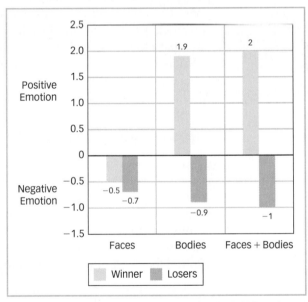

Hillel Aviezer, Yaacov Trope, and Alexander Todorov. Body Cues, Not Facial Expressions, Discriminate Between Intense Positive and Negative Emotions. *Science, 30,* November 2012: Vol. 338, no. 6111, pp. 1225–1229. DOI: 10.1126/science.1224313

---

long *u* or to hold a pencil in their lips (Strack, Martin, & Stepper, 1988; Zajonc, 1989; see **FIGURE 8.8** on the next page). Similarly, when people are instructed to arch their brows they find facts more surprising, and when instructed to wrinkle their noses they find odors less pleasant (Lewis, 2012). These things happen because facial expressions and emotional states become strongly associated with each other over time (remember Pavlov?), and eventually each can bring about the other. These effects are not limited to the face. For example, people feel more assertive when instructed to make a fist (Schubert & Koole, 2009) and rate others as more hostile when instructed to extend their middle fingers (Chandler & Schwarz, 2009).

Why do emotional expressions cause emotional experience?

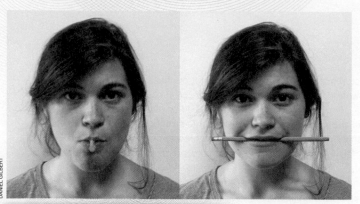

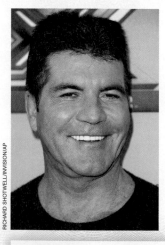

▲ Figure **8.8** **The Facial Feedback Hypothesis** Research shows that people who hold a pen with their teeth feel happier than those who hold a pen with their lips. These two postures cause contraction of the muscles associated with smiling and frowning, respectively.

A popular form of cosmetic surgery is the Botox injection, which paralyzes certain facial muscles. Former *American Idol* judge Simon Cowell (quoted in Davis, 2008) gets them regularly and says, "Botox is no more unusual than toothpaste. . . . It works, you do it once a year—who cares?" Well, maybe he should. Some evidence suggests that Botox injections can impair both the experience of emotion (Davis et al., 2010) and the ability to process emotional information (Havas et al., 2010). What phenomenon have you learned about so far that might explain how this could happen?

The fact that emotional expressions can cause the emotional experiences they signify may help explain why people are generally so good at recognizing the emotional expressions of others. Many studies show that people unconsciously mimic other people's body postures and facial expressions (Chartrand & Bargh, 1999; Dimberg, 1982). When we see someone smile (or even when we read about someone smiling), our zygomatic major contracts ever so slightly—as yours almost surely is right now (Foroni & Semin, 2009). (By the way, the tendency to ape the facial expressions of our interaction partners is so natural that, yes, even apes do it; Davila Ross, Menzler, & Zimmermann, 2008.) Because facial expressions can cause the emotions they signify, mimicking another person's facial expression allows us to feel what they are feeling and therefore identify their emotions.

What's the evidence for this? First, people find it difficult to identify other people's emotions when they are unable to make facial expressions of our own, for example, if their facial muscles are paralyzed with Botox (Niedenthal et al., 2005). People also find it difficult to identify other people's emotions when they are unable to *experience* emotions of their own (Hussey & Safford, 2009; Pitcher et al., 2008). For example, people with amygdala damage don't normally feel fear and anger, and are typically poor at recognizing the expressions of those emotions in others (Adolphs, Russell, & Tranel, 1999). On the flip side, people who are naturally quite good at figuring out what others are feeling tend to be natural mimics (Sonnby-Borgstrom, Jonsson, & Svensson, 2003), and their mimicry seems to pay off: Negotiators who mimic the facial expressions of their opponents earn more money than those who don't (Maddux, Mullen, & Galinsky, 2008).

Deceptive Expression

Our emotional expressions can communicate our feelings truthfully—or not. When a friend makes a sarcastic remark about our haircut, we truthfully express our contempt with an arched brow and a reinforcing hand gesture; but when our boss makes the same remark, we swallow hard and fake a pained smile. Our knowledge that it is permissible to show contempt for a peer but not a superior is a **display rule,** which is a *norm for the appropriate expression of emotion* (Ekman, 1972; Ekman & Friesen, 1968). Obeying a display rule requires several techniques:

> *Intensification* involves exaggerating the expression of one's emotion, as when a person pretends to be more surprised by a gift than she really is.

> *Deintensification* involves muting the expression of one's emotion, as when the loser of a contest tries to look less distressed than he really is.

> *Masking* involves expressing one emotion while feeling another, as when a poker player tries to look distressed rather than delighted as she examines a hand with four aces.

> *Neutralizing* involves feeling an emotion but displaying no expression, as when a judge tries not to betray his leanings while lawyers are making their arguments (see **FIGURE 8.9**).

Although people in different cultures use many of the same techniques, they use them in the service of different display rules. For example, in one study, Japanese and American college students watched an unpleasant video of car accidents and amputations (Ekman, 1972; Friesen, 1972). When the students didn't know that the experimenters were observing them, Japanese

> **How does emotional expression differ across cultures?**

and American students made similar expressions of disgust, but when they realized that they were being observed, the Japanese students (but not the American students) masked their disgust with pleasant expressions. In many Asian countries it is considered rude to display negative emotions in the presence of a respected person, and so citizens of these countries tend to mask or neutralize their expressions. The fact that different cultures have different display rules may also help explain the fact that people are better at recognizing the facial expressions of people from their own cultures (Elfenbein & Ambady, 2002).

◄ Figure **8.9** **Neutralizing** Can you tell what this man is feeling? He sure hopes not. Doyle Brunson is a champion poker player who knows how to keep a "poker face," which is a neutral expression that provides little information about his emotional state.

Our attempts to obey our culture's display rules don't always work out so well. Darwin (1899/2007) noted that "those muscles of the face which are least obedient to the will, will sometimes alone betray a slight and passing emotion" (p. 64). Anyone who has ever watched the loser of a beauty pageant congratulate the winner knows that voices, bodies, and faces are "leaky" instruments that often betray a person's emotional state. Even when people smile bravely to mask their disappointment, for example, their faces tend to express small bursts of disappointment that last just 1/5 to 1/25 of a second (Porter & ten Brinke, 2008). These *micro-expressions* happen so quickly that they are almost impossible to detect with the naked eye. Four other features that are more readily observable seem to distinguish between sincere and insincere facial expressions (Ekman, 2003).

◄ Figure **8.10** **Crinkle Eyes** Can you tell which of the two finalists in the 1986 Miss America pageant just won? Check out their eyes. Only one woman is showing the telltale "corner crinkle" that signifies genuine happiness. The winner is on the right, but don't feel too bad for the loser on the left. Her name is Halle Berry and she went on to have a pretty good acting career.

> *Morphology*: Certain facial muscles tend to resist conscious control, and for a trained observer, these so-called *reliable muscles* are quite revealing. For example, the zygomatic major raises the corners of the mouth, and this happens when people smile spontaneously or when they force themselves to smile. But only a genuine, spontaneous smile engages the obicularis oculi, which crinkles the corners of the eyes (see **FIGURE 8.10**).

> *Symmetry*: Sincere expressions are a bit more symmetrical than insincere expressions. A slightly lopsided smile is less likely to be genuine than is a perfectly even one.

> *Duration*: Sincere expressions tend to last between a half second and 5 seconds, and expressions that last for shorter or longer periods are more likely to be insincere.

> *Temporal patterning*: Sincere expressions appear and disappear smoothly over a few seconds, whereas insincere expressions tend to have more abrupt onsets and offsets.

Our emotions don't just leak on our faces: They leak all over the place. Research has shown that many aspects of our verbal and nonverbal behavior are altered when we tell a lie (DePaulo et al., 2003). For example, liars speak more slowly, take longer to respond to questions, and respond in less detail than do those who are telling the truth. Liars are also less fluent, less engaging, more uncertain, more tense, and less pleasant than truth-tellers. Oddly enough, one of the telltale signs of a liar is that his or her performances tend to be just a bit too good. A liar's speech lacks the little

display rule
A norm for the appropriate expression of emotion.

Speaker of the House John Boehner wipes away tears he shed at a ceremony to award the Congressional Gold Medal. Crying is very difficult to control and thus provides reliable information about the intensity of a person's emotions.

imperfections that are typical of truthful speech, such as superfluous detail ("I noticed that the robber was wearing the same shoes that I saw on sale last week at Bloomingdale's and I found myself wondering what he paid for them"), spontaneous correction ("He was six feet tall . . . well, no, actually more like six-two"), and expressions of self-doubt ("I think he had blue eyes, but I'm really not sure").

Given the reliable differences between sincere and insincere expressions, you might think that people would be quite good at telling one from the other. In fact, studies show that people are dreadful at this, and under most circumstances perform barely better than chance (DePaulo, Stone, & Lassiter, 1985; Ekman, 1992; Zuckerman, DePaulo, & Rosenthal, 1981; Zuckerman & Driver, 1985). One reason for this is that people have a strong bias toward believing that others are sincere, which explains why people tend to mistake liars for truth-tellers more often than they mistake truth-tellers for liars (Gilbert, 1991). A second reason is that people don't seem to know what they should attend to and what they should ignore (Vrij et al., 2011). For instance, people think that fast talking is a sign of lying when actually it isn't, and that slow talking is not a sign of lying when actually it is. People are bad lie detectors who don't even know how bad they are: The correlation between a person's ability to detect lies and the person's confidence in that ability is essentially zero (DePaulo et al., 1997).

When people can't do something well (e.g., adding numbers or picking up 10-ton rocks), they typically turn the job over to machines (see **FIGURE 8.11**). Can machines detect lies better than we can? The answer is yes, but that's not saying very much. The most widely used lie detection machine is the *polygraph*, which measures a variety of physiological responses that are associated with stress, which people often feel when they are afraid of being caught in a lie. A polygraph can detect lies at a rate that is significantly better than chance, but its error rate is still too high to make it a reliable lie detector. For example, let's imagine that 10 of the 10,000 people coming through a particular airport are terrorists and that when hooked up to a polygraph, they all claim to be innocent. A polygraph that was set to *maximum* sensitivity would catch 8 of the 10 terrorists lying, but it would also mistakenly catch 1,598 innocent people. A poly-

What is the problem with lie-detecting machines?

▶ Figure **8.11 Lie Detection Machines** Some researchers hope to replace the polygraph with accurate machines that measure changes in blood flow in the brain and the face. As the top panel shows, some areas of the brain are more active when people tell lies than when they tell the truth (shown in red), and some are more active when people tell the truth than when they tell lies (shown in blue; Langleben et al., 2005). The bottom panel shows images taken by a thermal camera that detects the heat caused by blood flow to different parts of the face. The images show a person's face before (*left*) and after (*right*) telling a lie (Pavlidis, Eberhardt, & Levine, 2002). Although neither of these new techniques is extremely accurate, that could soon change.

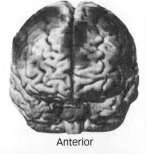

Right side   Left side   Anterior

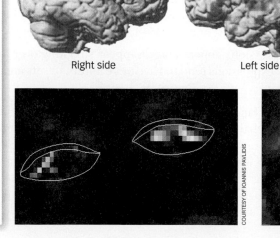

CULTURE & COMMUNITY

Is it what you say or how you say it? We can learn a lot about people by paying attention both to what they say and to how they say it. But recent evidence (Ishii, Reyes, & Kitayama, 2003) suggests that some cultures place more emphasis on one of these than on the other.

Research participants heard a voice pronouncing pleasant or unpleasant words (such as *pretty* or *complaint*) in either a pleasant or an unpleasant tone of voice. On some trials, they were told to ignore the word and to classify the pleasantness of the voice; on other trials, they were told to ignore the voice and classify the pleasantness of the word.

Which of these kinds of information was more difficult to ignore? It depended on the participant's nationality. American participants found it relatively easy to ignore the speaker's tone of voice, but relatively difficult to ignore the pleasantness of the word being spoken. Japanese participants, on the other hand, found it relatively easy to ignore the pleasantness of the word, but relatively difficult to ignore the speaker's tone of voice. It seems that, in America, what you say matters more than how you say it, but in Japan, just the opposite is true.

graph set to *minimum* sensitivity would mistakenly catch just 39 innocent people, but would only catch 2 of the 10 real terrorists. And these numbers assume that terrorists don't know how to fool a polygraph, which is something that people can, in fact, be trained to do. No wonder the National Research Council (2003) warned, "Given its level of accuracy, achieving a high probability of identifying individuals who pose major security risks in a population with a very low proportion of such individuals would require setting the test to be so sensitive that hundreds, or even thousands, of innocent individuals would be implicated for every major security violator correctly identified" (p. 6). In short, neither people nor machines are particularly good at lie detection, which is why lying remains such a popular sport.

This Pakistani man is being led away from the scene of a suicide bombing that killed his father.

IN SUMMARY

► The voice, the body, and the face all communicate information about a person's emotional state.

► Darwin suggested that these emotional expressions are the same for all people and are universally understood, and research suggests that this is generally true.

► Emotions cause expressions, but expressions can also cause emotions.

► Emotional mimicry allows people to experience and hence identify the emotions of others.

► Not all emotional expressions are sincere because people use display rules to help them decide which emotions to express.

► Different cultures have different display rules, but people enact those rules using the same techniques.

► There are reliable differences between sincere and insincere emotional expressions and between truthful and untruthful utterances, but people are generally poor at determining when an expression is sincere or an utterance is truthful. The polygraph can distinguish true from false utterances with better-than-chance accuracy, but its error rate is troublingly high.

motivation
The purpose for or psychological cause of an action.

hedonic principle
The claim that people are motivated to experience pleasure and avoid pain.

Motivation: Getting Moved

Leonardo is a robot, so he does what he is programmed to do, but nothing more. Because he doesn't have wants and urges—doesn't crave friendship or desire chocolate or hate homework—he doesn't initiate his own behavior. He can learn, but he cannot yearn, and thus he isn't motivated to act in the same way that we are. **Motivation** refers to *the purpose for or psychological cause of an action*, and it is no coincidence that the words *emotion* and *motivation* share a common linguistic root that means "to move." Unlike robots, human beings act because their emotions move them, and emotions do this in two different ways: First, emotions provide people with *information* about the world; and second, emotions are the *objectives* toward which people strive. Let's examine each of these in turn.

The Function of Emotion

In the old sci-fi film *Invasion of the Body Snatchers*, a young couple suspects that most of the people they know have been kidnapped by aliens and replaced with replicas. This sort of bizarre belief is a common story device in bad movies, but it is also the primary symptom of Capgras syndrome (see **FIGURE 8.12**). People who suffer from this syndrome typically believe that one or more of their family members are imposters. As one Capgras sufferer told her doctor, "He looks exactly like my father, but he really isn't. He's a nice guy, but he isn't my father. . . . Maybe my father employed him to take care of me, paid him some money so he could pay my bills" (Hirstein & Ramachandran, 1997, p. 438).

This woman's dad had not been body-snatched, of course, nor had he hired his own stunt double. Rather, this woman sustained damage to the neural connections between her temporal lobe (where faces are identified) and her limbic system (where emotions are generated). As a result, when she saw her father's face, she recognized it, but because this information was not transmitted to her limbic system, she didn't feel the warm emotions that her father's face should have produced. Her father "looked right" but didn't "feel right," so she concluded that the man before her was an imposter (see Figure 8.12).

People with Capgras syndrome use their emotional experience as information about the world, and as it turns out, so do the rest of us. For example, people report having better lives when they are asked about their lives on a sunny day rather than a rainy day. Why? Because people naturally feel happier on sunny days, and they use their happiness as information about the quality of their lives (Schwarz & Clore, 1983). People who are in good moods believe that they have a higher probability of winning a lottery than do people who are in bad moods. Why? Because people use their moods as information about the likelihood of succeeding at a task (Isen & Patrick, 1983). We all know that satisfying lives and bright futures make us feel good—so when we feel good, we conclude that our lives must be satisfying and our futures must be bright. Because the world influences our emotions, our emotions can provide information about the world (Schwarz, Mannheim, & Clore, 1988). Indeed, recent research

COURTESY EVERETT COLLECTION

In 1956's *Invasion of the Body Snatchers*, little Jimmy Grimaldi tells the nurse and the doctor that his mother has been replaced by a replica. Their response? Chill him out with drugs and send him home to be eaten by aliens.

► Figure **8.12** **Capgras Syndrome** This graph shows the emotional responses (as measured by skin conductance) of a patient with Capgras syndrome and a group of control participants to a set of familiar and unfamiliar faces. Although the controls have stronger emotional responses to the familiar than to the unfamiliar faces, the Capgras patient has similar emotional responses to both (Hirstein & Ramachandran, 1997).

Strength of emotional response

50
40
30
20
10
0

| | Capgras patient | Normal controls |
| Familiar faces | Unfamiliar faces |

suggests that people who trust their feelings to provide this kind of information tend to make more accurate predictions and better decisions than people who don't (Mikels, Maglio, Reed, & Kaplowitz, 2011; Pham, Lee, & Stephen, 2012).

The information we get from our emotions is so useful that we can actually be lost without it. When neurologist Antonio Damasio was asked to examine a patient with an unusual form of brain damage, he asked the patient to choose between two dates for an appointment. It sounds like a simple decision, but for the next half hour, the patient enumerated reasons for and against each of the two possible dates, completely unable to decide in favor of one option or the other (Damasio, 1994). The problem wasn't any impairment of the patient's ability to think or reason. On the contrary, he could think and reason all too well. What he couldn't do was feel. The patient's injury had left him unable to experience emotion, so when he entertained one option ("If I come next Tuesday, I'll have to cancel my lunch with Fred"), he didn't feel any better or any worse than when he entertained another ("If I come next Wednesday, I'll have to get up early to catch the bus"). And because he *felt* nothing when he thought about his options, he couldn't decide which one was best. Studies show that when individuals with this particular form of brain damage are given the opportunity to gamble, they make a lot of reckless bets because they don't feel the twinge of anxiety that tells them they are about to do something stupid. On the other hand, under certain conditions, such individuals make excellent investors, precisely because they are willing to take risks that most of us would not (Shiv et al., 2005).

> **?** How might emotions help us make decisions?

If the first function of emotion is to provide us with information about the world, then the second function is to tell us what to do with that information. The **hedonic principle** is *the claim that people are motivated to experience pleasure and avoid pain*, and this claim has a long history. The ancient Greek philosopher Aristotle (350 BCE/1998) argued that the hedonic principle explained everything there was to know about human motivation: "It is for the sake of this that we all do all that we do." We want many things, from peace and prosperity to health and security, but we want them for just one reason, and that is that they make us feel good. "Are these things good for any other reason except that they end in pleasure, and get rid of and avert pain?" asked Plato (380 BCE/1956). "Are you looking to any other standard but pleasure and pain when you call them good?" Plato and Aristotle were suggesting that pleasure isn't just good: It is what good *means*.

According to the hedonic principle, then, our emotional experience can be thought of as a gauge that ranges from bad to good, and our primary motivation—perhaps even our *sole* motivation—is to keep the needle on the gauge as close to *good* as possible. Even when we voluntarily do things that tilt the needle in the opposite direction, such as letting the dentist drill our teeth or waking up early for a boring class, we are doing these things because we believe that they will nudge the needle toward *good* in the future and keep it there longer.

STEVE/JASON/OBI/NATIONAL PHOTO GROUP

When we try to make a decision, we often ask how we "feel" about it. If we couldn't feel, then we wouldn't know which alternative to choose. Without emotions, Rihanna would just stand there until someone gave her a Grammy for Best Hot Pink Stiletto.

Instincts and Drives

If our primary motivation is to keep the needle on *good*, then which things push the needle in that direction and which things push it away? And where do these things get the power to push our needle around, and exactly how do they do the pushing? The answers to such questions lie in two concepts that have played an unusually important role in the history of psychology: *instincts* and *drives*.

Instincts

When a newborn baby is given a drop of sugar water, it smiles, and when it is given a check for $10,000, it acts like it couldn't care less. By the time the baby goes to

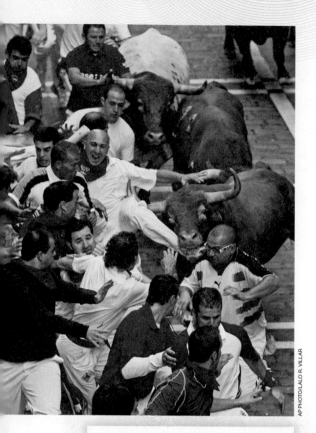

All animals are born with instincts. In the annual running of the bulls in Pamplona, Spain, no one has to teach the bulls to chase the runners, and no one has to teach the runners to flee.

AP PHOTO/ILALO R. VILLAR

college, these responses pretty much reverse. It seems clear that nature endows us with certain motivations and that experience endows us with others. William James (1890) called the natural tendency to seek a particular goal an *instinct*, which he defined as "the faculty of acting in such a way as to produce certain ends, without foresight of the ends, and without previous education in the performance" (p. 383). According to James, nature hardwired penguins, parrots, puppies, and people to want certain things without training and to execute the behaviors that produce these things without thinking. He and other psychologists of his time tried to make a list of what those things were.

Unfortunately, they were quite successful, and in just a few decades their list of instincts had grown preposterously long and included some rather exotic entries, such as "the instinct to be secretive" and "the instinct to grind one's teeth." By 1924, sociologist Luther Bernard counted 5,759 instincts and concluded that after three decades of list making, the term seemed to be suffering from "a great variety of usage and the almost universal lack of critical standards" (Bernard, 1924, p. 21). Furthermore, some psychologists began to worry that attributing the tendency for people to befriend each other to an "affiliation instinct" was more of a description than an explanation (Ayres, 1921; Dunlap, 1919; Field, 1921).

> Does an *instinct* explain behavior, or just name it?

By 1930, the concept of instinct had fallen out of fashion. Not only did it fail to explain anything, but it also flew in the face of American psychology's hot new trend: behaviorism. Behaviorists rejected the concept of instinct on two grounds. First, they believed that behavior should be explained by the external stimuli that evoke it and not by the hypothetical internal states on which it presumably depends. John Watson (1913) had written that "the time seems to have come when psychology must discard all reference to consciousness" (p. 163), and behaviorists saw instincts as just the sort of unnecessary "mind blather" that Watson forbade. Second, behaviorists wanted nothing to do with the notion of inherited behavior because they believed that all complex behavior was learned. Because instincts were inherited tendencies that resided inside the organism, behaviorists considered them doubly repugnant.

Drives

But within a few decades, some of Watson's younger followers began to realize that the strict prohibition against the mention of internal states made certain phenomena difficult to explain. For example, if all behavior is a response to an external stimulus, then why does a rat that is sitting still in its cage at 9:00 a.m. start wandering around and looking for food by noon? Nothing in the cage has changed, so why has the rat's behavior changed? What visible, measurable, external stimulus is the wandering rat responding to? The obvious answer is that the rat is responding to something inside itself, which meant that Watson's young followers (the "new behaviorists" as they called themselves) were forced to look inside the rat to explain its wandering. How could they do that without talking about the "thoughts" and "feelings" that Watson had forbidden them to mention?

They began by noting that bodies are a bit like thermostats. When thermostats detect that the room is too cold, they send signals that initiate corrective actions such as turning on a furnace. Similarly, when bodies detect that they are underfed, they send signals that initiate corrective actions such as eating. **Homeostasis** is *the tendency for a system to take action to keep itself in a particular state*, and two of the new behaviorists, Clark Hull and Kenneth Spence, suggested that rats, people, and thermostats are all homeostatic mechanisms. To survive, an organism needs to

> In what ways is the human body like a thermostat?

homeostasis
The tendency for a system to take action to keep itself in a particular state.

drive
An internal state caused by physiological needs.

maintain precise levels of nutrition, warmth, and so on, and when these levels depart from an optimal point, the organism receives a signal to take corrective action. That signal is called a **drive,** which is *an internal state caused by physiological needs.* According to Hull and Spence, it isn't food per se that organisms find rewarding; it is the reduction of the drive for food. Hunger is a drive, a drive is an internal state, and when organisms eat, they are attempting to change their internal state.

Although the words *instinct* and *drive* are no longer widely used in psychology, both concepts have something to teach us. The concept of instinct reminds us that nature endows organisms with a tendency to seek certain things, and the concept of drive reminds us that this seeking is initiated by an internal state. The psychologist William McDougall (1930) called the study of motivation *hormic psychology,* which is a term derived from the Greek word for "urge," and people clearly do have urges—some of which they acquire through experience and some of which they do not—that motivate them to take certain actions. What kinds of urges do we have, and what kinds of actions do we take to satisfy them?

VISIONS OF AMERICA, LLC/ALAMY

Aristotle claimed that water had "gravity" and fire had "levity" and that these properties made them go downward and upward, respectively. It now seems obvious that Aristotle was merely describing the motion of these elements and not really explaining it—much as William James did when he attributed behavior to instinct. By the way, that's Plato and Aristotle standing together under the arch in Raphael's 1509 masterpiece *The School of Athens.*

What the Body Wants

Abraham Maslow (1954) attempted to organize the list of human urges (or, as he called them, *needs*) in a meaningful way (see **FIGURE 8.13**). He noted that some needs

> **Why do some motivations take precedence over others?**

(such as the need to eat) must be satisfied before others (such as the need to have friends), and he built a hierarchy of needs that had the most immediate needs at the bottom and the most deferrable needs at the top. Maslow suggested that, as a rule, people are more likely to experience a need when the needs below it are met. So when people are hungry or thirsty or exhausted, they are less likely to seek intellectual fulfillment or moral clarity (see **FIGURE 8.14**). According to Maslow, the needs that take precedence are typically those we share with other animals. For example, because all animals must survive and reproduce, all animals need to eat and mate. Human beings have these needs as well, but as you are about to see, they are more powerful and more complicated than most of us imagine (Kenrick et al., 2010).

Survival: The Motivation for Food

Animals convert matter into energy by eating, and they are driven to do this by an internal state called *hunger.* But what is hunger and where does it come from? At every moment, your body is sending signals to your brain about its current energy state. If your body needs energy, it sends an *orexigenic* signal to tell your brain to switch hunger on, and if your body has sufficient energy, it sends an *anorexigenic* signal to tell your brain to switch hunger off (Gropp et al., 2005). No one knows precisely what these signals are or how they are sent and received, but research has identified a variety of candidates.

For example, *ghrelin* is a hormone that is produced in the stomach and appears to be a signal that tells the

▼ Figure **8.13** **Maslow's Hierarchy of Needs** Human beings are motivated to satisfy a variety of needs. Psychologist Abraham Maslow thought these needs formed a hierarchy, with physiological needs forming a base and self-actualization needs forming a pinnacle. He suggested that people don't experience higher needs until the needs below them have been met.

Need for self-actualization

Esteem needs

Belongingness and love needs

Safety and security needs

Physiological needs

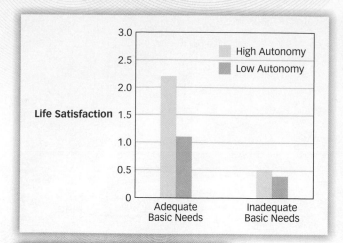

▲ Figure **8.14 When Do Higher Needs Matter?** Maslow was right. A recent study of 77,000 people in the world's 51 poorest nations (Martin & Hill, 2012) showed that if people have their basic needs met, then autonomy (i.e., freedom to make their own decisions) increases their satisfaction with their lives. But when people do not have their basic needs met, autonomy makes little difference.

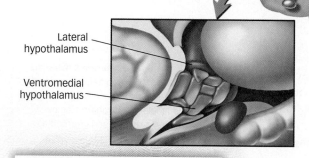

▲ Figure **8.15 Hunger, Satiety, and the Hypothalamus** The hypothalamus comprises many parts. In general, the lateral hypothalamus receives the signals that turn hunger on and the ventromedial hypothalamus receives the signals that turn hunger off.

bulimia nervosa
An eating disorder characterized by binge eating followed by purging.

anorexia nervosa
An eating disorder characterized by an intense fear of being fat and severe restriction of food intake.

brain to switch hunger on (Inui, 2001; Nakazato et al., 2001). When people are injected with ghrelin, they become intensely hungry and eat about 30% more than usual (Wren et al., 2001). Interestingly, ghrelin also binds to neurons in the hippocampus and temporarily improves learning and memory (Diano et al., 2006) so that we become just a little bit better at locating food when our bodies need it most. *Leptin* is a chemical secreted by fat cells, and it appears to be a signal that tells the brain to switch hunger off. It seems to do this by making food less rewarding (Farooqi et al., 2007). People who are born with a leptin deficiency have trouble controlling their appetites (Montague et al., 1997). For example, in 2002, medical researchers reported on the case of a 9-year-old girl who weighed 200 pounds, but after just a few leptin injections, she reduced her food intake by 84% and attained normal weight (Farooqi et al., 2002). Some researchers think the idea that chemicals turn hunger on and off is far too simple, and they argue that there is no general state called *hunger*, but rather that there are many different hungers, each of which is a response to a unique nutritional deficit and each of which is switched on by a unique chemical messenger (Rozin & Kalat, 1971). For example, rats that are deprived of protein will seek proteins while turning down fats and carbohydrates, suggesting that they are experiencing a specific "protein hunger" and not a general hunger (Rozin, 1968).

> **What purpose does hunger serve?**

Whether hunger is one signal or many, the primary receiver of these signals is the hypothalamus. Different parts of the hypothalamus receive different signals (see **FIGURE 8.15**). The *lateral hypothalamus* receives orexigenic signals, and when it is destroyed, animals sitting in a cage full of food will starve themselves to death. The *ventromedial hypothalamus* receives anorexigenic signals, and when it is destroyed, animals will gorge themselves to the point of illness and obesity (Miller, 1960; Steinbaum & Miller, 1965). These two structures were once thought to be the "hunger center" and "satiety center" of the brain, but it turns out that this view is far too simple (Woods et al., 1998). Hypothalamic structures play an important role in turning hunger on and off, but the precise way in which they execute these functions is complex and poorly understood (Stellar & Stellar, 1985).

Eating Disorders

Feelings of hunger tell us when to eat and when to stop. But for the 10 to 30 million Americans who have eating disorders, eating is a much more complicated affair (Hoek & van Hoeken, 2003). For instance, **bulimia nervosa** is *an eating disorder characterized by binge eating followed by purging*. People with bulimia typically ingest large quantities of food in a relatively short period and then take laxatives or induce vomiting to purge the food from their bodies. These people are caught in a cycle: They eat to ease negative emotions such as sadness and anxiety, but then concern about weight gain leads them to experience negative emotions such as guilt and self-loathing, and these emotions then lead them to purge (Sherry & Hall, 2009; cf. Haedt-Matt & Keel, 2011).

Anorexia nervosa is *an eating disorder characterized by an intense fear of being fat and severe restriction of food intake*. People with anorexia tend to have a distorted body image that leads them to believe they are fat when they are actually emaciated, and they tend to be high-achieving perfectionists who see their severe control of eating as a triumph of will over impulse. Contrary to what you might expect, people with anorexia have extremely *high* levels of ghrelin in their blood, which suggests that their bodies are trying desperately to switch hunger on but that hunger's call is being suppressed, ignored, or overridden (Ariyasu et al., 2001). Like most eating disorders, anorexia strikes more women than men, and 40% of newly identified cases of anorexia are among women 15 to 19 years old.

Anorexia may have both cultural and biological causes (Klump & Culbert, 2007). For example, women with anorexia typically believe that thinness equals beauty, and it isn't hard to understand why. The average American woman is 5′4″ tall and weighs

What causes anorexia?

140 pounds, but the average American fashion model is 5′11″ tall and weighs 117 pounds. Indeed, most college-age women report wanting to be thinner than they are (Rozin, Trachtenberg, & Cohen, 2001), and nearly 1 in 5 reports being *embarrassed* to be seen buying a chocolate bar (Rozin, Bauer, & Catanese, 2003). But anorexia is not just "vanity run amok" (Striegel-Moore & Bulik, 2007). Many researchers believe that there are as-yet-undiscovered biological and/or genetic components to the illness as well. For example, although anorexia primarily affects women, men have a sharply increased risk of becoming anorexic if they have a female twin who has the disorder (Procopio & Marriott, 2007), suggesting that anorexia may have something to do with prenatal exposure to female hormones.

Bulimia and anorexia are problems for many people. But America's most pervasive eating-related problem is obesity. Since 1999, Americans have collectively gained more than a billion pounds (Kolbert, 2009). The average American man is now 17 pounds heavier and the average American woman is now 19 pounds heavier than they were in the 1970s. The proportion of overweight children has doubled, the proportion of overweight teens has tripled, and a full 40% of American women are now too heavy to enlist in the military. In 1991, no state had an obesity rate higher than 20%. In 2012, only one state (Colorado) had an obesity rate lower than 20% (see **FIGURE 8.16**).

Obesity is defined as having a body mass index (BMI) of 30 or greater. **TABLE 8.1** allows you to compute your BMI, and the odds are that you won't like what you learn. Although BMI is a better predictor of mortality for some people than for others (Romero-Corral et al., 2006; van Dis et al., 2009), most researchers agree that an extremely high BMI is unhealthy. Every year, obesity-related illnesses cost our nation about $147 billion (Finkelstein et al., 2009) and about 3 million lives (Allison et al., 1999). In addition to these physical risks, obese people tend to be viewed negatively by others, have lower self-esteem, and have a lower quality of life (Hebl & Heatherton, 1997; Kolotkin, Meter, & Williams, 2001). Obese women earn about 7% less than

Bar Refaeli is Israel's best known supermodel. In 2012, Israel enacted a law banning models whose body mass index is under 18.5 from appearing in advertisements. So a 5′ 8″ model must weigh at least 119 pounds.

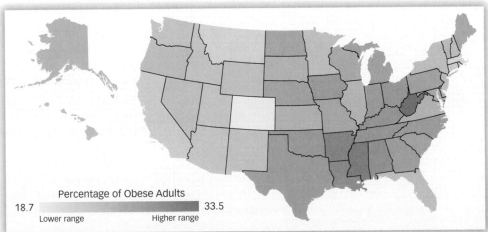

Percentage of Obese Adults

18.7   33.5
Lower range   Higher range

◄ Figure **8.16** **The Geography of Obesity**
This 2013 map of U.S. obesity rates shows that obesity is a problem everywhere, but especially in the Southeast.

"If You Want To Be Popular... YOU CAN'T AFFORD TO BE SKINNY!"

WATE-ON AT DRUG COUNTERS EVERYWHERE

JORDAN L. SMITH COLLECTION

Times have changed. People today are often astonished to see that ads once promised to help young women *gain* weight to become popular.

their non-obese counterparts (Lempert, 2007), and the stigma of obesity is so powerful that average-weight people are viewed negatively if they even have a relationship with someone who is obese (Hebl & Mannix, 2003). All of this is terribly unfair, of course. As one scientist noted, we need to declare "a war on obesity, not the obese" (Friedman, 2003).

Obesity has many causes. For example, obesity is highly heritable (Allison et al., 1996) and may have a genetic component, which may explain why a disproportionate amount of the weight gained by Americans in the past few decades has been gained by those who were already the heaviest (Flegal & Troiano, 2000). Some studies suggest that "obesogenic" toxins in the environment can disrupt the functioning of the endocrine system and predispose people to obesity (Grün & Blumberg, 2006; Newbold et al., 2005), whereas other studies suggest that obesity can be caused by a dearth of "good bacteria" in the gut (Liou et al., 2013). Whatever the cause, obese people are often leptin-resistant (i.e., their brains do not respond to the chemical message that shuts hunger off) and even leptin injections don't seem to help (Friedman & Halaas, 1998; Heymsfield et al., 1999).

Genes, pollutants, and bacteria have all been implicated in the tendency toward obesity. But in most cases the cause of obesity isn't such a mystery: We simply eat too much. We eat when we are hungry, of course, but we also eat when we are sad or anxious, or when everyone else is eating (Herman, Roth, & Polivy, 2003). Sometimes we eat simply because the clock tells us to, which is why people with amnesia will happily eat a second lunch shortly after finishing an unremembered first one (Rozin et al., 1998; see the Real World box). Why does this happen? After all, most of us don't breathe ourselves sick or sleep ourselves sick, so why do we eat ourselves sick?

Blame the design. Hundreds of thousands of years ago, the main food-related problem facing our ancestors was starvation, and humans evolved two strategies to avoid

Why do people overeat?

► Table 8.1

Body Mass Index Table

Height (Inches)	Normal						Overweight					Obese										Extreme Obesity															
BMI	19	20	21	22	23	24	25	26	27	28	29	30	31	32	33	34	35	36	37	38	39	40	41	42	43	44	45	46	47	48	49	50	51	52	53	54
	Body Weight (pounds)																																			
58	91	96	100	105	110	115	119	124	129	134	138	143	148	153	158	162	167	172	177	181	186	191	196	201	205	210	215	220	224	229	234	239	244	248	253	258
59	94	99	104	109	114	119	124	128	133	138	143	148	153	158	163	169	173	178	183	188	193	198	203	308	212	217	222	227	232	237	242	247	252	257	262	267
60	97	102	107	112	116	123	128	133	138	143	148	153	156	163	168	174	179	184	189	194	199	204	209	215	220	225	230	235	240	245	250	256	261	266	271	278
61	100	108	111	116	122	127	132	137	143	148	153	156	164	169	174	180	186	190	195	201	206	211	217	222	227	232	238	243	248	254	259	264	269	275	280	285
62	104	109	115	120	126	131	138	142	147	153	158	164	169	175	180	186	191	196	202	207	213	218	224	229	235	240	248	251	256	262	267	273	278	264	289	295
63	107	113	118	124	130	135	141	148	152	158	163	169	175	180	188	191	197	203	208	214	220	225	231	237	242	248	254	260	265	270	278	282	287	293	299	304
64	110	118	122	128	134	140	145	151	157	163	169	174	180	188	192	197	204	209	215	221	227	232	238	244	250	258	262	267	273	279	285	291	298	302	308	314
65	114	120	128	132	138	144	150	156	162	168	174	180	186	192	193	204	210	218	222	228	234	240	246	252	258	264	270	278	282	288	294	300	308	312	318	324
66	118	124	130	138	142	148	155	161	167	173	179	186	192	198	204	210	216	223	229	235	241	247	253	260	266	272	278	284	291	297	303	309	315	322	328	334
67	121	127	134	140	146	153	159	166	172	178	185	191	198	204	211	217	223	230	238	242	249	256	261	268	274	280	287	293	299	308	312	319	325	331	338	344
68	125	131	138	144	151	158	164	171	177	184	190	197	203	210	216	223	230	236	243	249	256	262	269	278	282	289	295	302	303	315	322	328	335	341	348	354
69	128	135	142	149	155	162	169	178	182	189	195	203	209	218	223	230	236	243	250	257	263	270	277	284	291	297	304	311	318	324	331	338	345	351	358	365
70	132	139	146	153	160	167	174	181	188	195	202	209	216	222	229	236	243	250	257	264	271	278	285	292	299	308	313	320	327	334	341	348	355	362	369	378
71	138	143	150	157	166	172	179	186	193	200	208	215	222	229	235	243	250	257	265	272	279	288	293	301	308	315	322	329	338	343	351	358	365	372	379	388
72	140	147	154	162	169	177	184	191	199	208	213	221	228	235	242	250	258	265	272	279	287	294	302	309	316	324	331	338	346	353	361	368	375	383	390	397
73	144	151	159	166	174	182	189	197	204	212	219	227	236	242	250	257	266	272	280	288	295	302	310	318	326	333	340	348	355	363	371	378	388	393	401	408
74	148	155	163	171	179	188	194	202	210	218	225	233	241	249	256	264	272	280	287	295	303	311	319	328	334	342	350	358	365	373	381	389	398	404	412	420
75	152	160	168	178	184	192	200	208	216	224	232	240	248	256	264	272	279	287	295	303	311	319	327	335	343	351	359	367	375	383	391	399	407	415	423	431
76	158	164	172	180	189	197	205	213	221	230	238	246	254	263	271	279	287	295	304	312	320	328	338	344	353	361	369	377	385	394	402	410	418	428	436	443

Source: Adapted from National Institutes of Health, 1998, *Clinical Guidelines on the Identification, Evaluation, and Treatment of Overweight and Obesity in Adults: The Evidence Report.* This and other information about overweight and obesity can be found at www.nhlbi.nih.gov/guidelines/obesity/ob_home.htm.

THE REAL WORLD

Jeet Jet?

n 1923, a reporter for the *New York Times* asked the British mountaineer George Leigh Mallory why he wanted to climb Mount Everest. Mallory replied: "Because it's there."

Apparently, that's also the reason why we eat. Brian Wansink and colleagues (2005) wondered whether the amount of food people eat is influenced by the amount of food they see in front of them. So they invited participants to their laboratory, sat them down in front of a large bowl of tomato soup, and told them to eat as much as they wanted. In one condition of the study, a server came to the table and refilled the participant's bowl whenever it got down to about a quarter full. In another condition, the bowl was not refilled by a server. Rather, unbeknownst to the participants, the bottom of the bowl was connected by a long tube to a large vat of soup, so whenever the participant ate from

BOB FILA/CHICAGO TRIBUNE/NEWSCOM

▲ Researcher Brian Wansink and his bottomless bowl of soup.

the bowl it would slowly and almost imperceptibly refill itself.

What the researchers found was sobering. Participants who unknowingly ate from

a "bottomless bowl" consumed a whopping 73% more soup than those who ate from normal bowls—and yet, they didn't think they had consumed more and they didn't report feeling any more full.

It seems that we find it easier to keep track of what we are eating than how much, and this can cause us to overeat even when we are trying our best to do just the opposite. For instance, one study showed that diners at an Italian restaurant often chose to eat butter on their bread rather than dipping it in olive oil because they thought that doing so would reduce the number of calories per slice. And they were right. What they didn't realize, however, is that they would unconsciously compensate for this reduction in calories by eating 23% more bread during the meal (Wansink & Linder, 2003).

This and other research suggests that one of the best ways to reduce our waists is simply to count our bites.

---

it. First, we developed a strong attraction to foods that provide large amounts of energy per bite (in other words, foods that are calorically rich), which is why most of us prefer hamburgers and milkshakes to celery and water. Second, we developed an ability to store excess food energy in the form of fat, which enabled us to eat more than we needed when food was plentiful and then live off our reserves when food was scarce. We are beautifully engineered for a world in which high calorie foods are scarce, and the problem is that we don't live in that world anymore. Instead, we live in a world in which the fatty miracles of modern technology—from chocolate cupcakes to sausage pizzas—are inexpensive and readily available. As two researchers recently wrote, "We evolved on the savannahs of Africa; we now live in Candyland" (Power & Schulkin, 2009). To make matters worse, many of Candyland's foods tend to be high in saturated fat, which has the paradoxical effect of making the brain *less* sensitive to some of the chemical messengers that tell us to stop eating (Benoit et al., 2009).

It is all too easy to overeat and become overweight or obese, and it is all too difficult to reverse course. The human body resists weight loss in two

Why is dieting so difficult and ineffective?

ways. First, when we gain weight, we experience an increase in both the size and the number of fat cells in our bodies (usually in our abdomens if we are male and in our thighs and buttocks if we are female). But when we lose weight, we experience a decrease in the size of our fat cells but no decrease in their number. Once our bodies have added a fat cell, that cell is pretty much there to stay. It may become thinner when we diet, but it is unlikely to die.

Idris Lewis and his wife both fit into the pants he used to wear in 2009 when he weighed 364 pounds. Unfortunately, dieting rarely works. Most people who lose significant amounts of weight regain most or all of it within a year (Polivy & Herman, 2002).

BEN BIRCHALL/PA WIRE URN: 7606032
(PRESS ASSOCIATION VIA AP IMAGES)

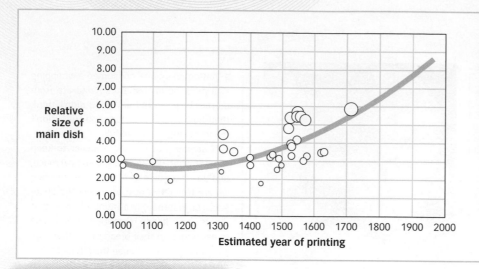

One reason why obesity rates are rising is that "normal portions" keep getting larger. When researchers analyzed 52 depictions of *The Last Supper* that were painted between the years 1000 and 1800, they found that the average plate size increased by 66% (Wansink & Wansink, 2010).

Second, our bodies respond to dieting by decreasing our **metabolism,** which is *the rate at which energy is used by the body.* When our bodies sense that we are living through a famine (which is what they conclude when we refuse to feed them), they find more efficient ways to turn food into fat: a great trick for our ancestors but a real nuisance for us. Indeed, when rats are overfed, then put on diets, then overfed again and put on diets again, they gain weight faster and lose it more slowly the second time around, which suggests that with each round of dieting, their bodies become increasingly efficient at converting food to fat (Brownell et al., 1986). The bottom line is that avoiding obesity is easier than overcoming it (Casazza et al., 2013).

And avoiding it isn't as difficult as you might think. For instance, just by placing hard-boiled eggs 10 inches away from the more healthful ingredients in a salad bar, researchers reduced the number of eggs that customers ate by about 10% (Rozin et al., 2011). Replacing the serving spoons with tongs reduced the amount by about 16%. In one study, snacking students ate fewer Pringles when every seventh chip was colored red, presumably because the color coding allowed them to keep track of how much they were eating (Geier, Wansink, & Rozin, 2012). In another study, people ate 22% less pasta with tomato sauce when they used a white plate instead of a red plate, presumably because the white plate provided a stark contrast that allowed them to see what they were eating (van Ittersum & Wansink, 2012). These and dozens of other studies show that small changes in our environments can prevent big changes in our waistlines.

Reproduction: The Motivation for Sex

Food motivates us because it is essential to our survival. But sex is also essential to our survival (at least to the survival of our DNA) which is why evolution has ensured that a desire for sex is wired deep into the brain of almost every one of us. In some ways, that wiring scheme is simple: Glands secrete hormones that travel through the blood to the brain and stimulate sexual desire. But which hormones, which parts of the brain, and what triggers the launch in the first place?

The hormone dihydroepiandosterone (DHEA) seems to be involved in the initial onset of sexual desire. Both boys and girls begin producing this slow-acting hormone at about the age of 6, which may explain why boys and girls both experience their initial sexual interest at about the age of 10, despite the fact that

"Come back, young man. He needs a booster shot."

OTHER VOICES

Fat and Happy

Alice Randall is a novelist whose books include The Wind Done Gone, Pushkin and the Queen of Spades, Rebel Yell, and Ada's Rules.

PHOTO: ©SARA KRULWICH/ THE NEW YORK TIMES/REDUX PICTURES

Nobody *wants* to be fat. At least that's what you might think. But as the novelist Alice Randall noted, in some cultures being heavy isn't just acceptable—it is desirable.

Four out of five black women are seriously overweight. One out of four middle-aged black women has diabetes. With $174 billion a year spent on diabetes-related illness in America and obesity quickly overtaking smoking as a cause of cancer deaths, it is past time to try something new.

What we need is a body-culture revolution in black America. Why? Because too many experts who are involved in the discussion of obesity don't understand something crucial about black women and fat: many black women are fat because we want to be.

The black poet Lucille Clifton's 1987 poem "Homage to My Hips" begins with the boast, "These hips are big hips." She establishes big black hips as something a woman would want to have and a man would desire. She wasn't the first or the only one to reflect this community knowledge. Twenty years before, in 1967, Joe Tex, a black Texan, dominated the radio airwaves across black America with a song he wrote and recorded, "Skinny Legs and All." One of his lines haunts me to this day: "some man, somewhere who'll take you baby, skinny legs and all." For me, it still seems almost an impossibility.

Chemically, in its ability to promote disease, black fat may be the same as white fat. Culturally it is not.

How many white girls in the '60s grew up praying for fat thighs? I know I did. I asked God to give me big thighs like my dancing teacher, Diane. There was no way I wanted to look like Twiggy, the white model whose boy-like build was the dream of white girls. Not with Joe Tex ringing in my ears.

How many middle-aged white women fear their husbands will find them less attractive if their weight drops to less than 200 pounds? I have yet to meet one.

But I know many black women whose sane, handsome, successful husbands worry when their women start losing weight. My lawyer husband is one.

Another friend, a woman of color who is a tenured professor, told me that her husband, also a tenured professor and of color, begged her not to lose "the sugar down below" when she embarked on a weight-loss program. . . .

I live in Nashville. There is an ongoing rivalry between Nashville and Memphis. In black Nashville, we like to think of ourselves as the squeaky-clean brown town best known for our colleges and churches. In contrast, black Memphis is known for its music and bars and churches. We often tease the city up the road by saying that in Nashville we have a church on every corner and in Memphis they have a church and a liquor store on every corner. Only now the saying goes, there's a church, a liquor store and a dialysis center on every corner in black Memphis.

The billions that we are spending to treat diabetes is money that we don't have for education reform or retirement benefits, and what's worse, it's estimated that the total cost of America's obesity epidemic could reach almost $1 trillion by 2030 if we keep on doing what we have been doing.

We have to change. . . .

Randall suggests that if we really want to solve the obesity problem, we must first understand why some people don't see it as a problem at all. Do you agree?

boys reach puberty much later than girls. Two other hormones have more gender-specific effects. Both males and females produce testosterone and estrogen, but males produce more of the former and females produce more of the latter. As you will learn in the Development chapter, these two hormones are largely responsible for the physical and psychological changes that characterize puberty. But are they also responsible for the waxing and waning of sexual desire in adults?

The answer appears to be yes—as long as those adults are rats. Testosterone increases the sexual desire of male rats by acting on a particular area of the hypothalamus, and estrogen increases the sexual desire of female rats by acting on a different area of the hypothalamus. Lesions to these areas reduce sexual motivation in the respective genders, and when testosterone or estrogen is applied to these areas, sexual motivation increases. In short, testosterone regulates sexual desire in male rats and estrogen regulates both sexual desire and fertility in female rats.

The story for human beings is far more interesting. The females of most mammalian species (e.g., dogs, cats, and rats) have little or no interest in sex except when their estrogen levels are high, which happens when they are ovulating (i.e., when they

metabolism
The rate at which energy is used by the body.

The red coloration on the female gelada's chest (*left*) indicates that she is in estrus and amenable to sex. The sexual interest of a female human being (*right*) is not limited to a particular time in her monthly cycle.

are "in estrus" or "in heat"). In other words, estrogen regulates both ovulation and sexual interest in these mammals. But female human beings can be interested in sex at any point in their monthly cycles. Although the level of estrogen in a woman's body changes dramatically over the course of her monthly menstrual cycle, studies suggest that sexual desire changes little, if at all. Somewhere in the course of our evolution, it seems, women's sexual interest became independent of their ovulation.

Some theorists have speculated that the advantage of this independence was that it made it more difficult for males to know whether a female was in the fertile phase of her monthly cycle. Male mammals often guard their mates jealously when their mates are ovulating, but go off in search of other females when their mates are not. If a male cannot use his mate's sexual receptivity to tell when she is ovulating, then he has no choice but to stay around and guard her all the time. For females who are trying to keep their mates at home so that they will contribute to the rearing of children, sexual interest that is continuous and independent of fertility may be an excellent strategy.

Why don't female humans show clear signs of ovulation?

If estrogen is not the hormonal basis of women's sex drives, then what is? Two pieces of evidence suggest that the answer is testosterone—the same hormone that drives male sexuality. First, when women are given testosterone, their sex drives increase. Second, men naturally have more testosterone than women do, and they generally have stronger sex drives. Men are more likely than women to think about sex, have sexual fantasies, seek sex and sexual variety (whether positions or partners), masturbate, want sex at an early point in a relationship, sacrifice other things for sex, have permissive attitudes toward sex, and complain about low sex drive in their partners (Baumeister, Cantanese, & Vohs, 2001). All of this suggests that testosterone may be the hormonal basis of sex drive in both men and women.

Sexual Activity

Men and women may have different levels of sexual drive, but their physiological responses during sex are fairly similar. Prior to the 1960s, data on human sexual behavior consisted primarily of people's answers to questions about their sex lives (and you may have noticed that this is a topic about which people don't always tell the truth). William Masters and Virginia Johnson changed all that by conducting groundbreaking studies in which they actually measured the physical responses of hundreds of volunteers as they masturbated or had sex in the laboratory (Masters & Johnson, 1966). Their work led to a deeper understanding of the **human sexual response cycle,** which refers to *the stages of physiological arousal during sexual activity* (see **FIGURE 8.17**). Human sexual response has four phases:

human sexual response cycle
The stages of physiological arousal during sexual activity.

> During the *excitement phase*, muscle tension and blood flow increase in and around the sexual organs, heart and respiration rates increase, and blood pressure rises. Both men and women may experience erect nipples and a "sex flush" on the skin of the upper body and face. A man's penis typically becomes erect or partially erect and his testicles draw upward, while a woman's vagina typically becomes lubricated and her clitoris becomes swollen.

> During the *plateau phase*, heart rate and muscle tension increase further. A man's urinary bladder closes to prevent urine from mixing with semen, and muscles

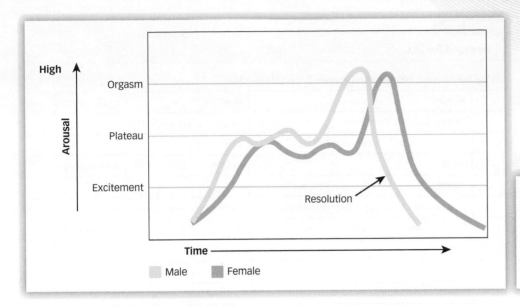

◄ Figure **8.17 The Human Sexual Response Cycle** The pattern of the sexual response cycle is quite similar for men and for women. Both men and women go through the excitement, plateau, orgasm, and resolution phases, though the timing of their response may differ.

at the base of his penis begin a steady rhythmic contraction. A man's Cowper gland may secrete a small amount of lubricating fluid (which, by the way, often contains enough sperm to cause pregnancy). A woman's clitoris may withdraw slightly, and her vagina may become more lubricated. Her outer vagina may swell, and her muscles may tighten and reduce the diameter of the opening of the vagina.

> During the *orgasm* phase, breathing becomes extremely rapid and the pelvic muscles begin a series of rhythmic contractions. Both men and women experience quick cycles of muscle contraction of the anus and lower pelvic muscles, and women often experience uterine and vaginal contractions as well. During this phase, men ejaculate about two to five milliliters of semen (depending on how long it has been since their last orgasm and how long they were aroused prior to ejaculation). Ninety-five percent of heterosexual men and 69% of heterosexual women reported having an orgasm during their last sexual encounter (Richters et al., 2006), although roughly 15% of women never experience orgasm, less than half experience orgasm from intercourse alone, and roughly half report having "faked" an orgasm at least once (Wiederman, 1997). The frequency with which women have orgasms seems to have a genetic component (Dawood et al., 2005). And it goes without saying that when men and women have orgasms, they typically experience them as intensely pleasurable.

> During the *resolution phase*, muscles relax, blood pressure drops, and the body returns to its resting state. Most men and women experience a *refractory period*, during which further stimulation does not produce excitement. This period may last from minutes to days and is typically longer for men than for women.

Although sex is typically a prerequisite for reproduction, the vast majority of sexual acts are not meant to produce babies. College students, for example, are rarely aiming to get pregnant, but they do have sex because of *physical attraction* ("The person had beautiful eyes"), as a *means to an end* ("I wanted to be popular"), to increase *emotional connection* ("I wanted to communicate at a deeper level"), and to *alleviate insecurity* ("It was the only way my partner would spend time with me"; Meston & Buss, 2007). Although men are more likely than women to report having sex for purely physical reasons, **TABLE 8.2** shows that men and women don't differ dramatically in their most frequent responses. It is worth noting that not all sex is motivated by reasons like these: About half of college-age women

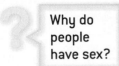

Why do people have sex?

> **Table 8.2**

Reasons for Sex

Top Ten Reasons Why Men and Women Report Having Sex

	Women	Men
1	I was attracted to the person.	I was attracted to the person.
2	I wanted to experience the physical pleasure.	It feels good.
3	It feels good.	I wanted to experience the physical pleasure.
4	I wanted to show my affection to the person.	It's fun.
5	I wanted to express my love for the person.	I wanted to show my affection to the person.
6	I was sexually aroused and wanted the release.	I was sexually aroused and wanted the release.
7	I was "horny."	I was "horny."
8	It's fun.	I wanted to express my love for the person.
9	I realized I was in love.	I wanted to achieve an orgasm.
10	I was "in the heat of the moment."	I wanted to please my partner.

Source: Meston & Buss, 2007.

and a quarter of college-age men report having unwanted sexual activity in a dating relationship (O'Sullivan & Allegeier, 1998). We will have much more to say about sexual attraction and relationships in the Social Psychology chapter.

What the Mind Wants

Survival and reproduction are every animal's first order of business, so it is no surprise that we are strongly motivated by food and sex. But we are motivated by other things too. We crave kisses of both the chocolate and romantic variety, but we also crave friendship and respect, security and certainty, wisdom and meaning, and a whole lot more. Our psychological motivations can be every bit as powerful as our biological motivations, but they differ in two ways.

First, although we share our biological motivations with most other animals, our psychological motivations are relatively unique. Chimps and rabbits and robins and turtles are all motivated to have sex, but only human beings seem motivated to imbue the act with meaning. Second, although our biological motivations are few—food, sex, oxygen, sleep, and a handful of other things—our psychological motivations are virtually limitless. The things we care about feeling and thinking, knowing and believing, having and being are so numerous and varied that no psychologist has ever been able to make a complete list (Hofmann, Vohs, & Baumeister, 2012). Nonetheless, even if you looked at an incomplete list, you'd quickly notice that psychological motivations vary on three key dimensions: extrinsic versus intrinsic, conscious versus unconscious, and approach versus avoidance. Let's examine each of these.

Intrinsic vs. Extrinsic

Taking a psychology exam and eating a French fry are different in many ways. One makes you tired and the other makes you chubby, one requires that you move your lips and the other requires that you don't, and so on. But the key difference between these activities is that one is a means to an end and one is an end in itself. An **intrinsic motivation** is *a motivation to take actions that are themselves rewarding*. When we eat a French fry because it tastes good, exercise

Mohamed Bouazizi was a fruit seller. In 2010 he set himself on fire to protest his treatment by the Tunisian government, and his dramatic suicide ignited the revolution that came to be known as "Arab Spring." Clearly, psychological needs—such as the need for justice—can be even more powerful than biological needs.

FETHI BELAID/AFP/GETTY IMAGES

because it feels good, or listen to music because it sounds good, we are intrinsically motivated. These activities don't *have* a payoff: They *are* a payoff. Conversely, an **extrinsic motivation** is *a motivation to take actions that lead to reward*. When we floss our teeth so we can avoid gum disease (and get dates), when we work hard for money so we can pay our rent (and get dates), and when we take an exam so we can get a college degree (and get money to get dates), we are extrinsically motivated. None of these things directly bring pleasure, but all may lead to pleasure in the long run.

Extrinsic motivation gets a bad rap. Americans tend to believe that people should "follow their hearts" and "do what they love," and we feel sorry for students who choose courses just to please their parents and for parents who choose jobs just to earn a pile of money. But the fact is that our ability to engage in behaviors that are

> **Why should people delay gratification?**

unrewarding in the present because we believe they will bring greater rewards in the future is one of our species' most significant talents, and no other species can do it quite as well as we can (Gilbert, 2006). In research on the ability to delay gratification (Ayduk et al., 2007; Mischel et al., 2004), people are typically faced with a choice between getting something they want right now (e.g., a scoop of ice cream) or waiting and getting more of what they want later (e.g., two scoops of ice cream). Waiting for ice cream is a lot like taking an exam or flossing: It isn't much fun, but you do it because you know you will reap greater rewards in the end. Studies show that 4-year-old children who can delay gratification are judged to be more intelligent and socially competent 10 years later and have higher SAT scores when they enter college (Mischel, Shoda, & Rodriguez, 1989). In fact, the ability to delay gratification is a better predictor of a child's grades in school than is the child's IQ (Duckworth & Seligman, 2005). Apparently there is something to be said for extrinsic motivation.

There is a lot to be said for intrinsic motivation too (Patall, Cooper, & Robinson, 2008). People work harder when they are intrinsically motivated, they enjoy what they do more, and they do it more creatively. Both kinds of motivation have advantages, which is why many of us try to build lives in which we are both intrinsically and extrinsically motivated by the same activity—lives in which we are paid the big bucks for doing exactly what we like to do

> **Why do rewards sometimes backfire?**

best. Who hasn't fantasized about becoming an artist or an athlete or Kanye's personal party planner? Alas, research suggests that it is difficult to get paid for doing what you love and still end up loving what you do because extrinsic rewards can undermine intrinsic interest (Deci, Koestner, & Ryan, 1999; Henderlong & Lepper, 2002). For example, in one study, college students who were intrinsically interested in a puzzle either were paid to complete it or completed it for free, and those who were paid were less likely to play with the puzzle later on (Deci, 1971). In a similar study, children who enjoyed drawing with Magic Markers were either promised or not promised an award for using them, and those who were promised the award were less likely to use the markers later (Lepper, Greene, & Nisbett, 1973). It appears that under some circumstances people take rewards to indicate that an activity isn't inherently pleasurable ("If they had to pay me to do that puzzle, it couldn't have been a very fun one"); thus rewards can cause people to lose their intrinsic motivation.

Just as rewards can undermine intrinsic motivation, punishments can create it. In one study, children who had no intrinsic interest in playing with a toy suddenly gained an interest when the experimenter threatened to punish them if they touched it (Aronson, 1963). College students who had no intrinsic motivation to cheat on a test were more likely to do so if the experimenter explicitly warned against it (Wilson & Lassiter, 1982). Threats can suggest that a forbidden activity is desirable, and they can also have the paradoxical consequence of promoting the very behaviors they are meant to discourage. For example, when a group of day care centers got fed up with

In most elections, only about a third of the eligible voters in Arizona bother to cast a ballot. That's what made Mark Osterloh (above) propose the Arizona Voter Reward Act which would award $1 million to a randomly selected voter in every election. Given what you know about intrinsic and extrinstic motivation, what consequences might such an act have?

intrinsic motivation
A motivation to take actions that are themselves rewarding.

extrinsic motivation
A motivation to take actions that lead to reward.

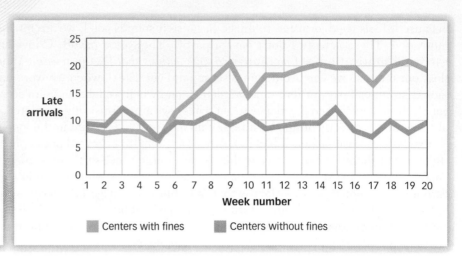

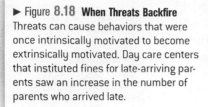

► Figure **8.18 When Threats Backfire**
Threats can cause behaviors that were once intrinsically motivated to become extrinsically motivated. Day care centers that instituted fines for late-arriving parents saw an increase in the number of parents who arrived late.

parents who arrived late to pick up their children, some of them instituted a financial penalty for tardiness. As **FIGURE 8.18** shows, the financial penalty caused an *increase* in late arrivals (Gneezy & Rustichini, 2000). Why? Because parents are intrinsically motivated to fetch their kids and they generally do their best to be on time. But when the day care centers imposed a fine for late arrival, the parents became extrinsically motivated to fetch their children—and because the fine wasn't particularly large, they decided to pay a small financial penalty in order to leave their children in day care for an extra hour. When threats and rewards change intrinsic motivation into extrinsic motivation, unexpected consequences can follow.

Conscious versus Unconscious

When prizewinning artists or scientists are asked to explain their achievements, they typically say things like, "I wanted to liberate color from form" or "I wanted to cure diabetes." They almost never say, "I wanted to exceed my father's accomplishments, thereby proving to my mother that I was worthy of her love." People clearly have **conscious motivations,** which are *motivations of which people are aware*, but they also have **unconscious motivations,** which are *motivations of which people are not aware* (Aarts, Custers, & Marien, 2008; Bargh et al., 2001; Hassin, Bargh, & Zimerman, 2009).

For example, psychologists David McClelland and John Atkinson argued that people vary in their **need for achievement,** which is *the motivation to solve worthwhile problems* (McClelland et al., 1953). They argued that this basic motivation is unconscious and thus must be measured with special techniques such as the Thematic Apperception Test, which presents people with a series of drawings and asks them to tell stories about them. The amount of "achievement-related imagery" in the person's story ostensibly reveals the person's unconscious need for achievement. (You'll learn more about these sorts of tests in the Personality chapter.) Although there has been much controversy about the validity and reliability of measures such as these (Lilienfeld, Wood, & Garb, 2000; Tuerlinckx, De Boeck, & Lens, 2002), research shows that a person's responses on this test reliably predict the person's behavior in certain circumstances. For example, they can predict a child's grades in school (Khalid, 1991). Research also suggests that this motivation can be "primed" in much the same way that thoughts and feelings can be primed. For example, when words such as *achievement* are presented on a computer screen so rapidly that people cannot consciously perceive them, those people will work especially hard to solve a puzzle (Bargh et al., 2001) and will feel especially unhappy if they fail (Chartrand & Kay, 2006).

What determines whether we are conscious of our motivations? Most actions have more than one motivation, and Robin Vallacher and Daniel Wegner (1985, 1987) have

conscious motivations
Motivations of which people are aware.

unconscious motivations
Motivations of which people are not aware.

need for achievement
The motivation to solve worthwhile problems.

approach motivation
A motivation to experience a positive outcome.

avoidance motivation
A motivation not to experience a negative outcome.

suggested that the ease or difficulty of performing the action determines which of these motivations we will be aware of. When actions are easy (e.g., screwing in a light bulb), we are aware of our most *general motivations* (e.g., to be helpful), but when actions are difficult (e.g., wrestling with a light bulb

> **What makes people conscious of their motivations?**

that is stuck in its socket), we are aware of our more *specific motivations* (e.g., to get the threads aligned). Vallacher and Wegner argued that people are usually aware of the general motivations for their behavior and only become aware of their more specific motivations when they encounter problems. For example, participants in an experiment drank coffee either from a normal mug or from a mug that had a heavy weight attached to the bottom, which made the mug difficult to manipulate. When asked what they were doing, those who were drinking from the normal mug explained that they were "satisfying needs," whereas those who were drinking from the weighted mug explained that they were "swallowing" (Wegner et al., 1984). The ease with which we can execute an action is one of many factors that determine whether we are or are not conscious of our motivations.

Michael Phelps is clearly high—in need for achievement, that is—which is one of the reasons why he ultimately became the most decorated Olympic athlete of all time.

Approach versus Avoidance

The poet James Thurber (1956) wrote: "All men should strive to learn before they die/ What they are running from, and to, and why." The hedonic principle describes two conceptually distinct motivations: a motivation to "run to" pleasure and a motivation to "run from" pain. These motivations are what psychologists call an **approach motivation,** which is *a motivation to experience a positive outcome*, and an **avoidance motivation,** which is *a motivation not to experience a negative outcome*. Pleasure is not just the lack of pain, and pain is not just the lack of pleasure. They are independent experiences that occur in different parts of the brain (Davidson et al., 1990; Gray, 1990).

Research suggests that, all else being equal, avoidance motivations tend to be more powerful than approach motivations. Most people will turn down a chance to bet on a coin flip that would pay them $10 if it came up heads but would require them to pay $8 if it came up tails, because they believe that the pain of losing $8 will be more intense than the pleasure of winning $10 (Kahneman & Tversky, 1979). Because people expect losses to have more powerful emotional consequences than equal-size gains, they will take more risks to avoid a loss than to achieve a gain. When participants are told that a disease is expected to kill 600 people and are asked to choose between administering Vaccine A, which will save exactly 200 people, or Vaccine B, which has a one-third chance of saving everybody and a two-thirds chance of saving nobody, about three-quarters of them decide to play it safe and select Vaccine A. Yet, when people are given a choice between Vaccine C, which will allow exactly 400 people to die, or Vaccine D which has a one-third chance of allowing no one to die and a two-thirds chance of allowing everyone to die, about three quarters of them decide to take the gamble and select Vaccine D (Tversky & Kahneman, 1981). Now, if you do the math you will quickly see that Vaccine A and Vaccine C are identical, as are Vaccine B and Vaccine D. The descriptions of the identical vaccines are just two ways of saying the same thing. And yet, when vaccines are described in terms of the number of lives lost (as C and D are) instead of the number of lives gained (as A and B are), most people are ready to take a big risk. It is interesting to note that monkeys show the same tendency (Lakshminarayanan, Chen, & Santos, 2011).

On average, avoidance motivation is stronger than approach motivation, but the relative strength of these two tendencies does differ somewhat from person to person. **TABLE 8.3** on the next page shows a series of questions that have been used to measure the relative strength of a person's approach and avoidance tendencies (Carver & White, 1994). Research shows that people who are described by the high-approach items are happier when rewarded than those who are not, and that those who are described by the high-avoidance items are more anxious when threatened than those who are not (Carver, 2006). Just as some people seem to be more responsive to rewards than to punishments (and vice versa), some people tend to think about their behavior as attempts to get reward rather than to avoid punishment (and vice versa). People who have a *promotion focus* tend to think in terms of achieving gains whereas people who have a *prevention focus* tend to think in terms of avoiding losses (Higgins, 1997). In one study, participants were given an anagram task. Some were told that they would be paid $4 for the experiment, but they could earn an extra dollar by finding 90% or more of all the possible words. Others were told that they would be paid $5 for the experiment, but they could avoid losing a dollar by not missing more than 10% of all the possible words. People who had a promotion focus performed better in the first case than in the second, but people who had a prevention focus performed better in the second case than in the first (Shah, Higgins, & Friedman, 1998). Similarly, people with a high need for achievement tend to be somewhat more motivated by their hope for success, whereas people with a low need for achievement tend to be somewhat more motivated by their fear of failure.

> **What is the difference between being motivated to avoid and being motivated to approach?**

> **Table 8.3**

Scale for Measuring the Behavioral Inhibition System and Behavioral Activation System

To what extent do each of these items describe you? The items in red measure the strength of your avoidance tendency and the items in green measure the strength of your approach tendency.

- Even if something bad is about to happen to me, I rarely experience fear or nervousness. (LOW AVOIDANCE)
- I go out of my way to get things I want. (HIGH APPROACH)
- When I'm doing well at something, I love to keep at it. (HIGH APPROACH)
- I'm always willing to try something new if I think it will be fun. (HIGH APPROACH)
- When I get something I want, I feel excited and energized. (HIGH APPROACH)
- Criticism or scolding hurts me quite a bit. (HIGH AVOIDANCE)
- When I want something, I usually go all-out to get it. (HIGH APPROACH)
- I will often do things for no other reason than that they might be fun. (HIGH APPROACH)
- If I see a chance to get something I want, I move on it right away. (HIGH APPROACH)
- I feel pretty worried or upset when I think or know somebody is angry at me. (HIGH AVOIDANCE)
- When I see an opportunity for something I like, I get excited right away. (HIGH APPROACH)
- I often act on the spur of the moment. (HIGH APPROACH)
- If I think something unpleasant is going to happen, I usually get pretty "worked up." (HIGH AVOIDANCE)
- When good things happen to me, it affects me strongly. (HIGH APPROACH)
- I feel worried when I think I have done poorly at something important. (HIGH AVOIDANCE)
- I crave excitement and new sensations. (HIGH APPROACH)
- When I go after something, I use a "no holds barred" approach. (HIGH APPROACH)
- I have very few fears compared to my friends. (LOW AVOIDANCE)
- It would excite me to win a contest. (HIGH APPROACH)
- I worry about making mistakes. (HIGH AVOIDANCE)

Source: Carver & White, 1994.

And what is probably the biggest thing that people want to avoid? All animals strive to stay alive, but only human beings realize that this striving is ultimately in vain and that death is life's inevitable end. Some psychologists have suggested that the motivation to avoid the anxiety associated with death creates a sense of "existential terror" and that much of our behavior is merely an attempt to manage it. **Terror Management Theory** is *a theory about how people respond to knowledge of their own mortality,* and it suggests that one of the ways that people cope with their existential terror is by developing a "cultural worldview"—a shared set of beliefs about what is good and right and true (Greenberg, Solomon, & Arndt, 2008; Solomon et al., 2004). These beliefs allow people to see themselves as more than mortal animals because they inhabit a world of meaning in which they can achieve symbolic immortality (e.g., by leaving a great legacy or having children) and perhaps even literal immortality (e.g., by being pious and earning a spot in the afterlife). According to this theory, our cultural worldview is a shield that buffers us against the anxiety that the knowledge of our own mortality creates.

A "credit card surcharge" and a "cash discount" are precisely the same thing. But they sure don't feel that way! RyanAir customers were outraged in 2012 when the airline imposed a 2% surcharge on customers who paid with credit cards. Would the airline have been wiser to raise their ticket prices by 2% and then offer a 2% discount to customers who paid with cash?

Terror management theory gives rise to the *mortality-salience hypothesis*, which is the prediction that people who are reminded of their own mortality will work to reinforce their cultural worldviews. In the last 20 years, this hypothesis has been supported by nearly 400 studies. The results show that when people are reminded of death (often in very subtle ways, such as by flashing the word "death" for just a few milliseconds in a laboratory, or by stopping people on a street corner that happens to be near a graveyard), they are more likely to praise and reward those who share their cultural worldviews, derogate and punish those who don't, value their spouses and defend their countries, feel disgusted by "animalistic" behaviors such as breastfeeding, and so on. All of these responses are presumably ways of shoring up one's cultural worldview and thereby defending against the anxiety that reminders of one's own mortality naturally elicit.

> **How do people deal with knowledge of death?**

IN SUMMARY

▶ Emotions motivate us indirectly by providing information about the world, but they also motivate us directly.

▶ The hedonic principle suggests that people approach pleasure and avoid pain and that this basic motivation underlies all others. All organisms are born with some motivations and acquire others through experience.

▶ When the body experiences a deficit, we experience a drive to remedy it. Biological motivations generally take precedence over psychological motivations. An example of a biological motivation is hunger, which is the result of a complex system of physiological processes, and problems with this system can lead to eating disorders and obesity, both of which are difficult to overcome. Another example of a biological motivation is sexual interest. Men and women experience roughly the same sequence of physiological events during sex, they engage in sex for most of the same reasons, and both have sex drives that are regulated by testosterone.

▶ People have many psychological motivations that vary on three key dimensions. Intrinsic motivations can be undermined by extrinsic rewards and punishments. People tend to be conscious of their more general motivations unless difficulty with the production of action forces them to become conscious of more specific motivations that are typically unconscious. Avoidance motivations are generally more powerful than approach motivations, although this is truer for some people than for others.

terror management theory
The theory that people cope with their existential terror by developing a "cultural worldview."

Chapter Review

KEY CONCEPT QUIZ

1. Emotions can be described by their location on the two dimensions of
   a. motivation and scaling.
   b. arousal and valence.
   c. stimulus and reaction.
   d. pain and pleasure.

2. Which theorists claimed that that a stimulus simultaneously causes both an emotional experience and a physiological reaction?
   a. Cannon and Bard
   b. James and Lange
   c. Schacter and Singer
   d. Klüver and Bucy

3. Which brain structure is most directly involved in the rapid appraisal of whether a stimulus is good or bad?
   a. the cortex
   b. the hypothalamus
   c. the amygdala
   d. the thalamus

4. Through _____, we change an emotional experience by changing the meaning of the emotion-eliciting stimulus.
   a. deactivation
   b. appraisal
   c. valence
   d. reappraisal

5. Which of the following does NOT provide any support for the universality hypothesis?
   a. Congenitally blind people make the facial expressions associated with the basic emotions.
   b. Infants only days old react to bitter tastes with expressions of disgust.
   c. Robots have been engineered to exhibit emotional expressions.
   d. Researchers have discovered that isolated people living a Stone Age existence with little contact with the outside world recognize the emotional expressions of Westerners.

6. _____ is the idea that emotional expressions can cause emotional experiences.
   a. A display rule
   b. Expressional deception
   c. The universality hypothesis
   d. The facial feedback hypothesis

7. Two friends have asked you to help them settle a disagreement. You hear each side of the story and have an emotional response to one viewpoint, but you don't express it. This is an example of which display rule?
   a. deintensification
   b. masking
   c. neutralizing
   d. intensification

8. Which of the following does NOT distinguish sincere from insincere expressions?
   a. temporal patterning
   b. duration

   c. symmetry
   d. levity

9. Which of the following statements is inaccurate?
   a. Certain facial muscles are reliably engaged by sincere facial expressions.
   b. Even when people smile bravely to mask disappointment, their faces tend to express small bursts of disappointment.
   c. Studies show that human lie detection ability is extremely good.
   d. Polygraph machines detect lies at a rate better than chance, but their error rate is still quite high.

10. The hedonic principle states that
    a. emotions provide people with information.
    b. people are motivated to experience pleasure and avoid pain.
    c. people use their moods as information about the likelihood of succeeding at a task.
    d. motivations are acquired solely through experience.

11. According to the early psychologists, an unlearned tendency to seek a particular goal is called
    a. an instinct.
    b. a drive.
    c. a motivation.
    d. a corrective action.

12. According to Maslow, our most basic needs are
    a. self-actualization and self-esteem.
    b. biological.
    c. unimportant until other needs are met.
    d. belongingness and love.

13. Which of the following is NOT a dimension on which psychological motivations vary?
    a. intrinsic–extrinsic
    b. conscious–unconscious
    c. avoid–approach
    d. appraisal–reappraisal

14. Which of the following statements is true?
    a. Men and women engage in sex for many of the same reasons.
    b. Boys and girls experience initial sexual interest at different ages.
    c. The sequence of physiological arousal for men and women differs dramatically.
    d. The human male sex drive is regulated by testosterone while the human female sex drive is regulated by estrogen.

15. Which of the following activities is most likely the result of extrinsic motivation?
    a. completing a crossword puzzle
    b. pursuing a career as a musician
    c. having ice cream for dessert
    d. flossing one's teeth

KEY TERMS

emotion (p. 316)
James–Lange theory (p. 316)
Cannon–Bard theory (p. 316)
two-factor theory (p. 317)
appraisal (p. 319)
emotion regulation (p. 320)
reappraisal (p. 321)
emotional expression (p. 322)

universality hypothesis (p. 323)
facial feedback hypothesis (p. 324)
display rules (p. 327)
motivation (p. 330)
hedonic principle (p. 331)
homeostasis (p. 332)
drive (p. 333)
bulimia nervosa (p. 334)

anorexia nervosa (p. 334)
metabolism (p. 338)
human sexual response cycle (p. 340)
intrinsic motivation (p. 342)
extrinsic motivation (p. 343)
conscious motivation (p. 344)
unconscious motivation (p. 344)

need for achievement (p. 344)
approach motivation (p. 345)
avoidance motivation (p. 345)
terror management theory (p. 347)

CHANGING MINDS

1. A friend is nearing graduation and has received a couple of job offers. "I went on the first interview," she says, "and I really liked the company, but I know you shouldn't go with your first impressions on difficult decisions. You should be completely rational and not let your emotions get in the way." Are emotions always barriers to rational decision making? In what ways can emotions help guide our decisions?

2. While watching TV, you and a friend hear about a celebrity who punched a fan in a restaurant. "I just lost it," the celebrity said. "I saw what I was doing, but I just couldn't control myself." According to the TV report, the celebrity was sentenced to anger management classes. "I'm not excusing the violence," your friend says, "but I'm not sure anger management classes are any use either. You can't control your emotions; you just feel them." What example could you give your friend of ways in which we can attempt to control our emotions?

3. One of your friends has just been dumped by her boyfriend, and she's devastated. She's spent days in her room, crying and refusing to go out. You and your roommate decide to keep a close eye on her during this tough time. "Negative emotions are so destructive," your roommate says. "We'd all be better off without them." What would you tell your roommate? In what ways are negative emotions critical for our survival and success?

4. A friend is majoring in education. "We learned today about several cities, including New York and Chicago, that tried giving cash rewards to students who passed their classes or did well on achievement tests. That's bribing kids to get good grades, and as soon as you stop paying them, they'll stop studying." Your friend is assuming that extrinsic motivation undermines intrinsic motivation. In what ways is the picture more complicated?

5. One of your friends is a gym rat who spends all his free time working out and is very proud of his ripped abs. His roommate, though, is very overweight. "I keep telling him to diet and exercise," your friend says, "but he never loses any weight. If he just had a little more willpower, he could succeed." What would you tell your friend? When an individual has difficulty losing weight, what factors may contribute to this difficulty?

ANSWERS TO KEY CONCEPT QUIZ

1. b; 2. a; 3. c; 4. d; 5. c; 6. d; 7. c; 8. a; 9. c; 10. b; 11. a; 12. b; 13. d; 14. a; 15. d.

Need more help? Additional resources are located in LaunchPad at:
http://www.worthpublishers.com/launchpad/schacter3e

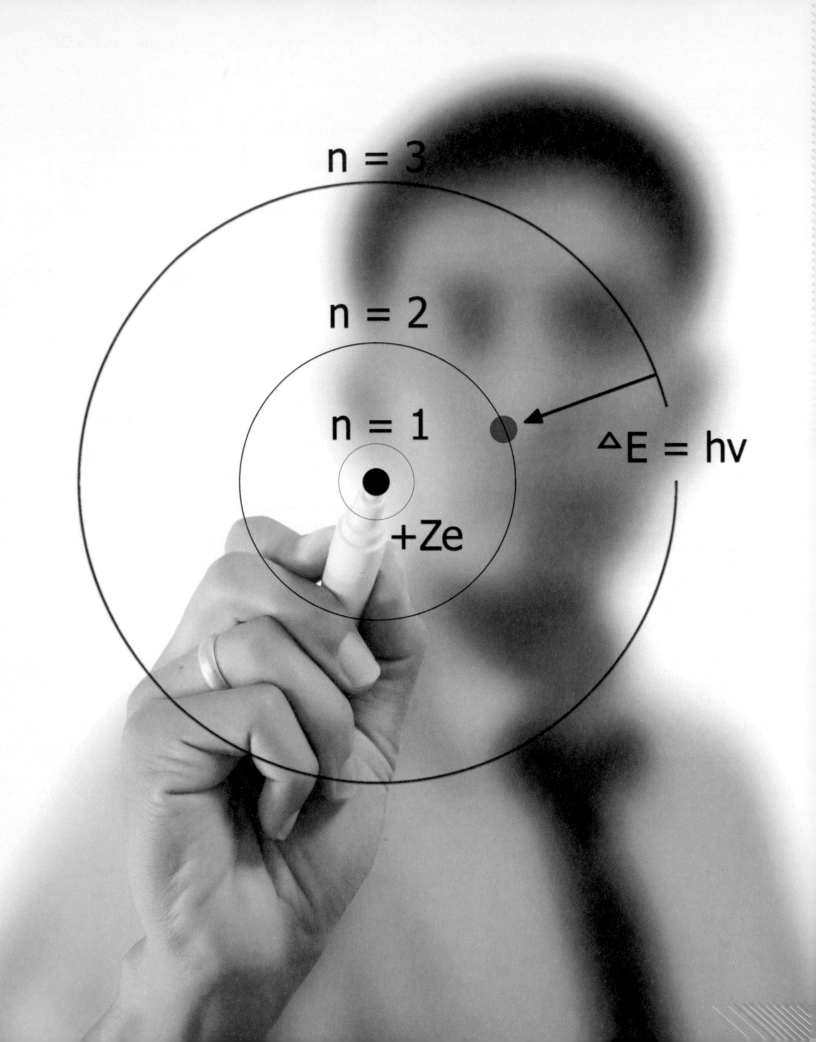

9

Language and Thought

AN ENGLISH BOY NAMED CHRISTOPHER showed an amazing talent for languages. By the age of 6, he had learned French from his sister's schoolbooks; he acquired Greek from a textbook in only 3 months. His talent was so prodigious that grown-up Christopher could converse fluently in 16 languages. When tested on English–French translations, he scored as well as a native French speaker. Presented with a made-up language, he figured out the complex rules easily, even though advanced language students found them virtually impossible to decipher (Smith & Tsimpli, 1995).

If you've concluded that Christopher is extremely smart, perhaps even a genius, you're wrong. His scores on standard intelligence tests are far below normal. He fails simple cognitive tests that 4-year-old children pass with ease, and he cannot even learn the rules for simple games like tic-tac-toe. Despite his dazzling talent, Christopher lives in a halfway house because he does not have the cognitive capacity to make decisions, reason, or solve problems in a way that would allow him to live independently.

Christopher absorbed languages quickly from textbooks, yet he completely failed simple tests of other cognitive abilities.

CHRISTOPHER'S STRENGTHS AND WEAKNESSES offer compelling evidence that cognition is composed of distinct abilities. People who learn languages with lightning speed are not necessarily gifted at decision making or problem solving. People who excel at reasoning may have no special ability to master languages. In this chapter, you will learn about five key higher cognitive functions: acquiring and using language, forming concepts and categories, making decisions, solving problems, and reasoning. We excel at these functions compared with other animals, and they help define who we are as a species. We'll learn about each of these abilities by examining evidence that reveals their unique psychological characteristics, and we'll learn about their distinct neural underpinnings by considering individuals with brain lesions as well as neuroimaging studies. But despite clear differences among them, these five cognitive abilities share something important in common: They are critical to our functioning in just about all aspects of our everyday existence—including work, school, and personal relationships—and as we've already seen with Christopher, impairment of these cognitive abilities can result in major and lasting disruptions to our lives.

Language and Communication: From Rules to Meaning

DON FARRALL/GETTY IMAGES

Most social species have systems of communication that allow them to transmit messages to each other. Honeybees communicate the location of food sources by means of a "waggle dance" that indicates both the direction and distance of the food source from the hive (Kirchner & Towne, 1994; Von Frisch, 1974). Vervet monkeys have three different warning calls that uniquely signal the presence of their main predators: a leopard, an eagle, and a snake (Cheney & Seyfarth, 1990). A leopard call provokes them to climb higher into a tree; an eagle call makes them look up into the sky. Each different warning call conveys a particular meaning and functions like a word in a simple language.

Language is *a system for communicating with others using signals that are combined according to rules of grammar and convey meaning.* **Grammar** is *a set of rules that specify how the units of language can be combined to produce meaningful messages.* Language allows individuals to exchange information about the world, coordinate group action, and form strong social bonds.

Human language may have evolved from signaling systems used by other species. However, three striking differences distinguish human language from vervet monkey yelps, for example. First, the complex structure of human language distinguishes it from simpler signaling systems. Most humans can express a wide range of ideas and concepts as well as generate an essentially infinite number of novel sentences. Second, humans use words to refer to intangible things, such as *unicorn* or *democracy.* These words could not have originated as simple alarm calls. Third, we use language to name, categorize, and describe things to ourselves when we think, which influences how knowledge is organized in our brains. It's doubtful that honeybees consciously think, "I'll fly north today to find more honey so the queen will be impressed!"

> **What are the distinctions between human language and animal communication?**

In this section, we'll examine the elements of human language that contribute to its complex structure, the ease with which we acquire language despite this complexity, and how both biological and environmental influences shape language acquisition

Honeybees communicate with each other about the location of food by doing a waggle dance that indicates the direction and distance of food from the hive.

MEDIA BAKERY

and use. We'll also look at startling disorders that reveal how language is organized in the brain and at researchers' attempts to teach apes human language. Finally, we'll consider the longstanding puzzle of how language and thought are related.

The Complex Structure of Human Language

Compared with other forms of communication, human language is a relatively recent evolutionary phenomenon, emerging as a spoken system no more than 1 to 3 million years ago and as a written system as little as 6,000 years ago. There are approximately 4,000 human languages, which linguists have grouped into about 50 language families (Nadasdy, 1995). Despite their differences, all of these languages share a basic structure involving a set of sounds and rules for combining those sounds to produce meanings.

What do all languages have in common?

Basic Characteristics

The smallest units of sound that are recognizable as speech rather than as random noise are **phonemes.** These building blocks of spoken language differ in how they are produced. For example, when you say *ba,* your vocal cords start to vibrate as soon as you begin the sound, but when you say *pa,* there is a 60-millisecond lag between the time you start the *p* sound and the time your vocal cords start to vibrate. *B* and *p* are classified as separate phonemes in English because they differ in the way they are produced by the human speaker.

Every language has **phonological rules** that *indicate how phonemes can be combined to produce speech sounds.* For example, the initial sound *ts* is acceptable in German but not in English. Typically, people learn these phonological rules without instruction, and if the rules are violated, the resulting speech sounds so odd that we describe it as speaking with an accent.

Phonemes are combined to make **morphemes,** *the smallest meaningful units of language* (see **FIGURE 9.1**). For example, your brain recognizes the *pe* sound you make at the beginning of *pat* as a speech *sound,* but it carries no particular meaning. The morpheme *pat,* on the other hand, is recognized as an element of speech that carries meaning.

All languages have grammar rules that generally fall into two categories: rules of morphology and rules of syntax. **Morphological rules** *indicate how morphemes can be combined to form words.* Some morphemes—content morphemes and function morphemes—can stand alone as words. *Content morphemes* refer to things and events

language
A system for communicating with others using signals that are combined according to rules of grammar and convey meaning.

grammar
A set of rules that specify how the units of language can be combined to produce meaningful messages.

phoneme
The smallest unit of sound that is recognizable as speech rather than as random noise.

phonological rules
A set of rules that indicate how phonemes can be combined to produce speech sounds.

morphemes
The smallest meaningful units of language.

morphological rules
A set of rules that indicate how morphemes can be combined to form words.

▼ Figure **9.1 Units of Language** A sentence —the largest unit of language—can be broken down into progressively smaller units: phrases, morphemes, and phonemes. In all languages, phonemes and morphemes form words, which can be combined into phrases and ultimately into sentences.

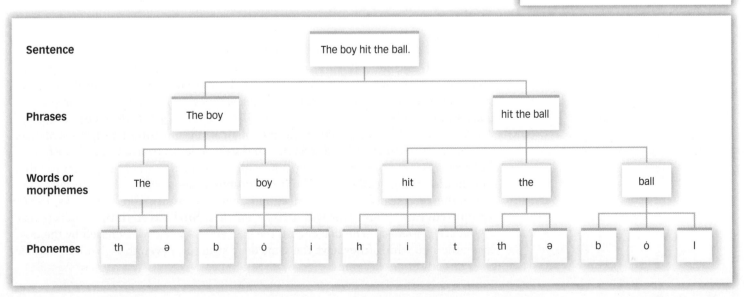

(e.g., "cat," "dog," "take"). *Function morphemes* serve grammatical functions, such as tying sentences together ("and," "or," "but") or indicating time ("when"). About half of the morphemes in human languages are function morphemes, and it is the function morphemes that make human language grammatically complex enough to permit us to express abstract ideas rather than simply to point verbally to real objects in the here and now.

Content and function morphemes can be combined and recombined to form an infinite number of new sentences, which are governed by syntax. **Syntactical rules** *indicate how words can be combined to form phrases and sentences.* A simple syntactical rule in English is that every sentence must contain one or more nouns, which may be combined with adjectives or articles to create noun phrases (see **FIGURE 9.2**). A sentence also must contain one or more verbs, which may be combined with adverbs or articles to create verb phrases. So, the utterance "dogs bark" is a full sentence, but "the big gray dog over by the building" is not.

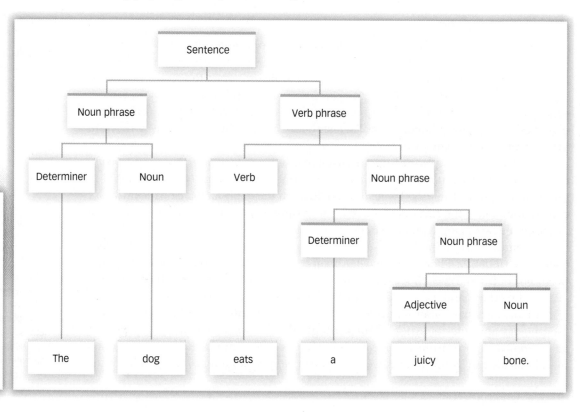

► Figure **9.2 Syntactical Rules** Syntactical rules indicate how words can be combined to form sentences. Every sentence must contain one or more nouns, which may be combined with adjectives or articles to create a noun phrase. A sentence also must contain one or more verbs, which may be combined with noun phrases, adverbs, or articles to create a verb phrase.

Meaning: Deep Structure versus Surface Structure

Sounds and rules are critical ingredients of human language that allow us to convey meaning. A sentence can be constructed in a way that obeys syntactical and other rules, yet be entirely lacking in meaning or *semantics,* as in the famous example provided by linguist Noam Chomsky (1957, p. 15), "Colorless green ideas sleep furiously." Though we wouldn't be breaking any grammatical rules by uttering such a sentence, we could expect to elicit head scratches and strange looks from any nearby listeners. Language usually conveys meaning quite well, but everyday experience shows us that misunderstandings can occur. These errors sometimes result from differences between the deep structure of sentences and their surface structure (Chomsky, 1957). **Deep structure** refers to *the meaning of a sentence.* **Surface structure** refers to *how a sentence is worded.* "The dog chased the cat" and "The cat was chased by the dog" mean the same thing (they have the same deep structure) even though on the surface their structures are different.

To generate a sentence, you begin with a deep structure (the meaning of the sentence) and create a surface structure (the particular words) to convey that meaning. When you comprehend a sentence, you do the reverse, processing the surface structure in order to extract the deep structure. After the deep structure is extracted, the surface structure is usually forgotten (Jarvella, 1970, 1971). In one study, researchers played tape-recorded stories to volunteers and then asked them to pick the sentences they had heard (Sachs, 1967). Participants frequently confused sentences they heard with sentences that had the same deep structure but a different surface structure. For example, if they heard the sentence "He struck John on the shoulder," they often mistakenly claimed they had heard "John was struck on the shoulder by him." In contrast, they rarely misidentified "John struck him on the shoulder" because this sentence has a different deep structure from the original sentence.

> **Is the meaning or wording of a sentence typically more memorable?**

Why are we able to communicate effectively when we quickly forget the surface structure of sentences? Why might this be an evolutionary benefit?

Language Development

Language is a complex cognitive skill, yet we can carry on complex conversations with playmates and family before we begin school. Three characteristics of language development are worth bearing in mind. First, children learn language at an astonishingly rapid rate. The average 1-year-old has a vocabulary of 10 words. This tiny vocabulary expands to over *10,000* words in the next 4 years, requiring the child to learn, on average, about 6 or 7 new words *every day*. Second, children make few errors while learning to speak, and as we'll see shortly, the errors they do make usually result from applying, but overgeneralizing, grammatical rules they've learned. This is an extraordinary feat. There are over 3 *million* ways to rearrange the words in any 10-word sentence, but only a few of these arrangements will be both grammatically correct and meaningful (Bickerton, 1990). Third, children's *passive mastery* of language develops faster than their *active mastery*. At every stage of language development, children understand language better than they speak.

Distinguishing Speech Sounds

At birth, infants can distinguish among all of the contrasting sounds that occur in all human languages. Within the first 6 months of life, they lose this ability, and, like their parents, can only distinguish among the contrasting sounds in the language they hear being spoken around them. For example, two distinct sounds in English are the *l* sound and the *r* sound, as in *lead* and *read*. These sounds are not distinguished in Japanese; instead, the *l* and *r* sounds fall within the same phoneme. Japanese adults cannot hear the difference between these two phonemes, but American adults can distinguish between them easily—and so can Japanese infants.

> **What language ability do infants have that adults do not?**

In one study, researchers constructed a tape of a voice saying "la-la-la" or "ra-ra-ra" repeatedly (Eimas et al., 1971). They rigged a pacifier so that whenever an infant sucked on it, a tape player that broadcast the *la-la* tape was activated. When the *la-la* sound began playing in response to their sucking, the infants were delighted and kept sucking on the pacifier to keep the *la-la* sound playing. After a while, they began to lose interest, and sucking frequency declined to about half of its initial rate. At this point, the experimenters switched the tape so that *ra-ra* was repeatedly broadcast. The Japanese infants began sucking again with vigor, indicating that they could hear the difference between the old, boring *la* sound and the new, interesting *ra* sound.

syntactical rules
A set of rules that indicate how words can be combined to form phrases and sentences.

deep structure
The meaning of a sentence.

surface structure
How a sentence is worded.

In this videotaped test, the infant watches an animated toy animal while a single speech sound is repeated. After a few repetitions, the sound changes and then the display changes, and then they both change again. If the infant switches her attention when the sound changes, she is anticipating the new display, which demonstrates that she can discriminate between the sounds.

Deaf infants who learn sign language from their parents start babbling with their hands around the same time that hearing infants babble vocally.

Infants can distinguish among speech sounds, but they cannot produce them reliably, relying mostly on cooing (i.e, simple vowel-like sounds, such as *ah-ah*), cries, laughs, and other vocalizations to communicate. Between the ages of about 4 and 6 months, they begin to babble speech sounds. Babbling involves combinations of vowels and consonants that sound like real syllables but are meaningless. Regardless of the language they hear spoken, all infants go through the same babbling sequence. For example, *d* and *t* appear in infant babbling before *m* and *n*. Even deaf infants babble sounds they've never heard, and they do so in the same order as hearing infants do (Ollers & Eilers, 1988). This is evidence that infants aren't simply imitating the sounds they hear and suggests that babbling is a natural part of the language development process. Recent research has shown that babbling serves as a signal that the infant is in a state of focused attention and ready to learn (Goldstein et al., 2010). Deaf infants don't babble as much, however, and their babbling is delayed relative to hearing infants (11 months rather than 6 months).

In order for vocal babbling to continue, however, infants must be able to hear themselves. In fact, delayed babbling or the cessation of babbling merits testing for possible hearing difficulties. Babbling problems can lead to speech impairments, but they do not necessarily prevent language acquisition. Deaf infants whose parents communicate using American Sign Language (ASL) begin to babble with their hands at the same age that hearing children begin to babble vocally—between 4 and 6 months (Petitto & Marentette, 1991). Their babbling consists of sign language syllables that are the fundamental components of ASL.

Language Milestones

At about 10 to 12 months of age, infants begin to utter (or sign) their first words. By 18 months, they can say about 50 words and can understand several times more than that. Toddlers generally learn nouns before verbs, and the nouns they learn first are names for everyday, concrete objects (e.g., chair, table, milk) (see **TABLE 9.1**). At about this time, their vocabularies undergo explosive growth. By the time the average child begins school, a vocabulary of 10,000 words is not unusual. By fifth grade, the average child knows the meanings of 40,000 words. By college, the average student's vocabulary is about 200,000 words. **Fast mapping,** in which *children map a word onto an underlying concept after only a single exposure,* enables them to learn at this rapid pace (Kan & Kohnert, 2008; Mervis & Bertrand, 1994). This astonishingly easy process contrasts dramatically with the effort required later to learn other concepts and skills, such as arithmetic or writing.

Around 24 months, children begin to form two-word sentences, such as "more milk" or "throw ball." Such sentences are referred to as **telegraphic speech** because

Table 9.1

Language Milestones

Average Age	Language Milestones
0–4 months	Can tell the difference between speech sounds (phonemes). Cooing, especially in response to speech.
4–6 months	Babbles consonants.
6–10 months	Understands some words and simple requests.
10–12 months	Begins to use single words.
12–18 months	Vocabulary of 30–50 words (simple nouns, adjectives, and action words).
18–24 months	Two-word phrases ordered according to syntactic rules. Vocabulary of 50–200 words. Understands rules.
24–36 months	Vocabulary of about 1,000 words. Production of phrases and incomplete sentences.
36–60 months	Vocabulary grows to more than 10,000 words; production of full sentences; mastery of grammatical morphemes (such as -*ed* for past tense) and function words (such as *the, and, but*). Can form questions and negations.

they are *devoid of function morphemes and consist mostly of content words.* Yet despite the absence of function words, such as prepositions or articles, these two word sentences tend to be grammatical; the words are ordered in a manner consistent with the syntactical rules of the language children are learning to speak. So, for example, toddlers will say "throw ball" rather than "ball throw" when they want you to throw the ball to them, and "more milk" rather than "milk more" when they want you to give them more milk. With these seemingly primitive expressions, 2-year-olds show that they have already acquired an appreciation of the syntactical rules of the language they are learning.

In what way do 2-year-olds show a basic understanding of language rules?

The Emergence of Grammatical Rules

Evidence of the ease with which children acquire grammatical rules comes from some interesting errors that children make while forming sentences. If you listen to average 2- or 3-year-old children speaking, you may notice that they use the correct past-tense versions of common verbs, as in the expressions "I ran" and "you ate." By the age of 4 or 5, the same children will be using incorrect forms of these verbs, saying such things as "I runned" or "you eated," forms most children are unlikely to have ever heard (Prasada & Pinker, 1993). The reason is that very young children memorize the particular sounds (i.e., words) that express what they want to communicate. But as children acquire the grammatical rules of their language, they tend to *overgeneralize.* For example, if a child overgeneralizes the rule that past tense is indicated by -*ed,* then *run* becomes *runned* or even *ranned* instead of *ran.*

Why is it unlikely that children are using imitation to pick up language?

These errors show that language acquisition is not simply a matter of imitating adult speech. Instead, children acquire grammatical rules by listening to the speech around them and using the rules to create verbal forms they've never heard. They manage this without explicit awareness of the grammatical rules they've learned. In fact, few children or adults can articulate the grammatical rules of their native language, yet the speech they produce obeys these rules.

By about 3 years of age, children begin to generate complete simple sentences that include function words (e.g., "Give me *the* ball" and "That belongs *to* me"). The

fast mapping
The fact that children can map a word onto an underlying concept after only a single exposure.

telegraphic speech
Speech that is devoid of function morphemes and consists mostly of content words.

sentences increase in complexity over the next 2 years. By 4 to 5 years of age, many aspects of the language acquisition process are complete. As children continue to mature, their language skills become more refined, with added appreciation of subtler communicative uses of language, such as humor, sarcasm, or irony.

Language Development and Cognitive Development

Language development typically unfolds as a sequence of steps in which one milestone is achieved before moving on to the next. Nearly all infants begin with one-word utterances before moving on to telegraphic speech and then to simple sentences that include function morphemes. It's hard to find solid evidence of infants launching immediately into speaking in sentences—even though you may occasionally hear reports of such feats from proud parents, including possibly your own! This orderly progression could result from general cognitive development that is unrelated to experience with a specific language (Shore, 1986; Wexler, 1999). For example, perhaps infants begin with one- and then two-word utterances because their short-term memories are so limited that initially they can only hold in mind a word or two; additional cognitive development might be necessary before they have the capacity to put together a simple sentence. By contrast, the orderly progression might depend on experience with a specific language, reflecting a child's emerging knowledge of that language (Bates & Goodman, 1997; Gillette et al., 1999).

These two possibilities are difficult to tease apart, but recent research has begun to do so using a novel strategy: examining the acquisition of English by internationally adopted children who did not know any English prior to adoption (Snedeker, Geren, & Shafto, 2007, 2012). According to government statistics, there were just over 8,600 international adoptions to the United States in 2012 (U.S. Department of State, 2013). Although most of those adoptees are infants or toddlers, a significant proportion is composed of preschoolers. Studying the acquisition of English in such an older population provides a unique opportunity to explore the relationship between language development and cognitive development. If the orderly sequence of milestones that characterizes the acquisition of English by infants is a by-product of general cognitive development, then different patterns should be observed in older internationally adopted children, who are more advanced cognitively than infants. However, if the milestones of language development are critically dependent on experience with a specific language—English—then language learning in older adopted children should show the same orderly progression as seen in infants.

> **Why are studies of internationally adopted children especially useful?**

Snedeker et al. (2007) examined preschoolers ranging from 2½ to 5½ years old, 3 to 18 months after they were adopted from China. They did so by mailing materials to parents, who periodically recorded language samples in their homes and also completed questionnaires concerning specific features of language observed in their children. These data were compared to similar data obtained from monolingual infants. The main result was clear-cut: Language acquisition in preschool-aged adopted children showed the same orderly progression of milestones that characterizes infants. These children began with one-word utterances before moving on to simple word combinations. Furthermore, their vocabulary, just like that of infants, was initially dominated by nouns and they produced few function morphemes.

These results indicate that some of the key milestones of language development depend on experience with English. However, the adopted children did add new words to their vocabularies more quickly than infants did, perhaps reflecting an influence of general cognitive development. Overall, though, the main message from this study is that observed shifts in early language development reflect specific characteristics of language learning rather than

Chinese preschoolers who are adopted by English-speaking parents progress through the same sequence of linguistic milestones as do infants born into English-speaking families, suggesting that these milestones reflect experience with English rather than general cognitive development.

general limitations of cognitive development. A later study by Snedeker et al. (2012) provided additional support for this general conclusion, but also produced new evidence for a role of cognitive development in specific aspects of language. For example, adopted preschoolers acquire words that refer to the past or the future, such as *tomorrow*, *yesterday*, *before*, or *after*, much more quickly than do infants, perhaps reflecting that infants have difficulty representing these abstract concepts and therefore take longer to learn the words than more cognitively sophisticated preschoolers.

Theories of Language Development

We know a good deal about how language develops, but what underlies the process? The language acquisition process has been the subject of considerable controversy and (at times) angry exchanges among scientists coming from three different approaches: behaviorist, nativist, and interactionist.

Behaviorist Explanations

According to B. F. Skinner's behaviorist explanation of language learning, we learn to talk in the same way we learn any other skill: through reinforcement, shaping, extinction, and the other basic principles of operant conditioning that you learned about in the Learning chapter (Skinner, 1957). As infants mature, they begin to vocalize. Those vocalizations that are not reinforced gradually diminish, and those that are reinforced remain in the developing child's repertoire. So, for example, when an infant gurgles "prah," most parents are pretty indifferent. However, a sound that even remotely resembles "da-da" is likely to be reinforced with smiles, whoops, and cackles of "Goooood baaaaaby!" by doting parents. Maturing children also imitate the speech patterns they hear. Then parents or other adults shape those speech patterns by reinforcing those that are grammatical and ignoring or punishing those that are ungrammatical. "I no want milk" is likely to be squelched by parental clucks and titters, whereas "No milk for me, thanks" will probably be reinforced.

The behavioral explanation is attractive because it offers a simple account of language development, but the theory cannot account for many fundamental characteristics of language development (Chomsky, 1986; Pinker, 1994; Pinker & Bloom, 1990).

> **To a behaviorist, why will an infant repeat "da-da" and not "prah"?**

> First, parents don't spend much time teaching their children to speak grammatically. In one well-documented study, researchers found that parents typically respond more to the truth content of their children's statements than to the grammar (Brown & Hanlon, 1970). So, for example, when a child expresses a sentiment such as "Nobody like me," his or her mother will respond with something like "Why do you think that?" or "I like you!" rather than "Now, listen carefully and repeat after me: Nobody likes me."

> Second, children generate many more grammatical sentences than they ever hear. This shows that children don't just imitate, they learn the rules for generating sentences. You'll recall that the same deep structure can generate a multitude of surface structures. It's highly unlikely that each of those separate surface structures was heard, reinforced, and learned by the developing child; it's much more likely that children simply acquire the ability to generate grammatical sentences.

> Third, as you read earlier in this chapter, the errors children make when learning to speak tend to be overgeneralizations of grammatical rules. The behaviorist explanation would not predict these overgeneralizations if children were learning through trial and error or simply imitating what they hear. That is, it would be difficult to overgeneralize if language development consisted solely of reinforced individual sentences or phrases.

Nativist Explanations

The study of language and cognition underwent an enormous change in the 1950s, when linguist Noam Chomsky (1957, 1959) published a blistering reply to the behaviorist approach. According to Chomsky, language-learning capacities are built into the brain, which is specialized to acquire language rapidly through simple exposure to speech. Chomsky and others have argued that humans have a particular ability for language that is separate from general intelligence. This **nativist theory** holds that *language development is best explained as an innate, biological capacity.* According to Chomsky, the human brain is equipped with a **language acquisition device (LAD),** *a collection of processes that facilitate language learning.* Language processes naturally emerge as the infant matures, provided the infant receives adequate input to maintain the acquisition process.

Christopher's story is consistent with the nativist view of language development: His genius for language acquisition, despite his low overall intelligence, indicates that language capacity can be distinct from other mental capacities. Other individuals show the opposite pattern: People with normal or nearly normal intelligence can find certain aspects of human language difficult or impossible to learn. This condition is known as **genetic dysphasia,** *a syndrome characterized by an inability to learn the grammatical structure of language despite having otherwise normal intelligence.* Genetic dysphasia tends to run in families, and a single dominant gene has been implicated in its transmission (Gontier, 2008; Gopnik, 1990a, 1990b; Vargha-Khadem et al., 2005). Consider some sentences generated by children with the disorder:

She remembered when she hurts herself the other day.

Carol is cry in the church.

Notice that the ideas these children are trying to communicate are intelligent. Their problems with grammatical rules persist even if they receive special language training. When asked to describe what she did over the weekend, one child wrote, "On Saturday I watch TV." Her teacher corrected the sentence to "On Saturday, I watch*ed* TV," drawing attention to the *-ed* rule for describing past events. The following week, the child was asked to write another account of what she did over the weekend. She wrote, "On Saturday I wash myself and I watched TV and I went to bed." Notice that although she had memorized the past-tense forms *watched* and *went,* she could not generalize the rule to form the past tense of another word (*washed*).

As predicted by the nativist view, studies of people with genetic dysphasia suggest that normal children learn the grammatical rules of human language with ease in part because they are "wired" to do so. This biological predisposition to acquire language explains why newborn infants can make contrasts among phonemes that occur in all human languages—even phonemes they've never heard spoken. If we learned language through imitation, as behaviorists theorized, infants would only distinguish the phonemes they'd actually heard. The nativist theory also explains why deaf infants babble speech sounds they have never heard and why the pattern of language development is similar in children throughout the world. These characteristics of language development are just what would be expected if our biological heritage provided us with the broad mechanics of human language.

> **How would a nativist explain why deaf infants babble?**

Also consistent with the nativist view is evidence that language can be acquired only during a restricted period of development, as has been observed with songbirds. If young songbirds are prevented from hearing adult birds sing during a particular period in their early lives, they do not learn to sing. A similar mechanism seems to affect human language learning, as illustrated by the tragic case of Genie (Curtiss, 1977). At the age of 20 months, Genie was tied to a chair by her parents and kept in virtual isolation. Her father forbade Genie's mother and brother to speak to her, and he himself

"GOT IDEA. TALK BETTER. COMBINE WORDS, MAKE SENTENCES."

nativist theory
The view that language development is best explained as an innate, biological capacity.

language acquisition device (LAD)
A collection of processes that facilitate language learning.

genetic dysphasia
A syndrome characterized by an inability to learn the grammatical structure of language despite having otherwise normal intelligence.

only growled and barked at her. She remained in this brutal state until the age of 13. Genie's life improved substantially and she received years of language instruction, but it was too late. Her language skills remained extremely primitive. She developed a basic vocabulary and could communicate her ideas, but she could not grasp the grammatical rules of English.

Similar cases have been reported, with a common theme: Once puberty is reached, acquiring language becomes extremely difficult (Brown, 1958). Data from studies of language acquisition in immigrants support this conclusion. In one study, researchers found that the proficiency with which immigrants spoke English depended not on how long they'd lived in the United States, but on their age at immigration (Johnson & Newport, 1989). Those who arrived as children were the most proficient, whereas among those who immigrated after puberty, proficiency showed a significant decline regardless of the number of years in their new country. More recent work using fMRI shows that acquiring a second language early in childhood (between 1 and 5 years of age) results in very different representation of that language in the brain than does acquiring that language much later (after 9 years of age; Bloch et al., 2009).

Immigrants who learn English as a second language are more proficient if they start to learn English before puberty rather than after.

Interactionist Explanations

Nativist theories are often criticized because they do not explain *how* language develops; they merely explain why. A complete theory of language acquisition requires an explanation of the processes by which the innate, biological capacity for language combines with environmental experience. The interactionist approach is that although infants are born with an innate ability to acquire language, social interactions play a crucial role in language. Interactionists point out that parents tailor their verbal interactions with children in ways that simplify the language acquisition process: They speak slowly, enunciate clearly, and use simpler sentences than they do when speaking with adults (Bruner, 1983; Farrar, 1990).

How does the interactionist theory of language acquisition differ from behaviorist and nativist theories?

Further evidence of the interaction of biology and experience comes from a fascinating study of deaf children's creation of a new language (Senghas, Kita, & Ozyurek, 2004). Prior to about 1980, deaf children in Nicaragua stayed at home and usually had little contact with other deaf individuals. In 1981, some deaf children began to attend a new vocational school. At first, the school did not teach a formal sign language, and none of the children had learned to sign at home, but the children gradually began to communicate using hand signals that they invented.

Over the past 30 years, their sign language has developed considerably (Pyers et al., 2010), and researchers have studied this new language for the telltale characteristics of languages that have evolved over much longer periods. For instance, mature languages typically break down experience into separate components. When we describe something in motion, such as a rock rolling down a hill, our language separates the type of movement (rolling) and the direction of movement (down). If we simply made a gesture, however, we would use a single continuous downward movement to indicate this motion. This is exactly what the first children to develop the Nicaraguan sign

How does the evolution of the Nicaraguan deaf children's sign language support the interactionist explanation of language development?

language did. But younger groups of children, who have developed the sign language further, use separate signs to describe the direction and the type of movement—a defining characteristic of mature languages. That the younger children did not merely copy the signs from the older users suggests that a predisposition exists to use language to dissect our experiences. Thus, their acts of creation nicely illustrate the interplay of nativism (the predisposition to use language) and experience (growing up in an insulated deaf culture).

Language Development and the Brain

As the brain matures, specialization of specific neurological structures takes place, and this allows language to develop (Kuhl, 2010; Kuhl & Rivera-Gaxiola, 2008). Where, then, are the language centers of the brain?

Broca's Area and Wernicke's Area of the Brain

In early infancy, language processing is distributed across many areas of the brain. But language processing gradually becomes more and more concentrated in two areas, Broca's area and Wernicke's area, sometimes referred to as the language centers of the brain. As the brain matures, these areas become increasingly specialized for language, so much so that damage to them results in a serious condition called **aphasia,** *difficulty in producing or comprehending language.*

> **How does language processing change in the brain as the child matures?**

Broca's area is located in the left frontal cortex and is involved in the production of the sequential patterns in vocal and sign languages (see **FIGURE 9.3**). As you saw in the Psychology: Evolution of a Science chapter, Broca's area is named after French physician Paul Broca, who first reported on speech problems resulting from damage to a specific area of the left frontal cortex (Broca, 1861, 1863). Individuals with this damage, resulting in *Broca's aphasia,* understand language relatively well, although they have increasing comprehension difficulty as grammatical structures get more complex. But their real struggle is with speech production. Typically, they speak in short, staccato phrases that consist mostly of content morphemes (e.g., *cat, dog*). Function morphemes (e.g., *and, but*) are usually missing and grammatical structure is impaired. A person with the condition might say something like "Ah, Monday, uh, Casey park. Two, uh, friends, and, uh, 30 minutes."

Wernicke's area, located in the left temporal cortex, is involved in language comprehension (whether spoken or signed). German neurologist Carl Wernicke first described the area that bears his name after observing speech difficulty in patients who had sustained damage to the left posterior temporal cortex (Wernicke, 1874). Individuals with *Wernicke's aphasia* differ from those with Broca's aphasia in two ways: They can produce grammatical speech, but it tends to be meaningless, and they have considerable difficulty comprehending language. A person suffering from Wernicke's aphasia might say something like, "Feel very well. In other words, I used to be able to work cigarettes. I don't know how. Things I couldn't hear from are here."

In normal language processing, Wernicke's area is highly active when we make judgments about word meaning, and damage to this area impairs comprehension of spoken and signed language, although the ability to identify nonlanguage sounds is unimpaired. For example, Japanese can be written using symbols that, like the English alphabet, represent speech sounds, or by using pictographs that, like Chinese pictographs, represent ideas. Japanese persons who suffer from Wernicke's aphasia encounter difficulties in writing and understanding the symbols that represent speech sounds but not pictographs (Sasanuma, 1975).

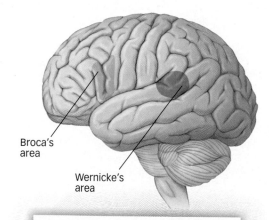

Broca's area

Wernicke's area

▲ Figure **9.3 Broca's and Wernicke's Areas**
Neuroscientists study people with brain damage in order to better understand how the brain normally operates. When Broca's area is damaged, people have a hard time producing sentences. When Wernicke's area is damaged, people can produce sentences, but they tend to be meaningless.

aphasia
Difficulty in producing or comprehending language.

Involvement of the Right Cerebral Hemisphere

As important as Broca's and Wernicke's areas are for language, they are not the entire story. Four kinds of evidence indicate that the right cerebral hemisphere also contributes to language processing, especially to language comprehension (Jung-Beeman, 2005). First, when words are presented to the right hemisphere of healthy participants using divided visual field techniques (see the Neuroscience chapter), the right hemisphere shows some capacity for processing meaning. Second, individuals with damage to the right hemisphere sometimes have subtle problems with language comprehension. Third, a number of neuroimaging studies have revealed evidence of right-hemisphere activation during language tasks. Fourth, and most directly related to language development, some children who have had their entire left hemispheres removed during adolescence as a treatment for epilepsy can recover many of their language abilities.

Japanese individuals who suffer from Wernicke's aphasia can still understand pictographs like this one, even though they have difficulty understanding speech sounds.

Bilingualism and the Brain

Early studies of bilingual children seemed to suggest that bilingualism slows or interferes with normal cognitive development. When compared with monolingual children, bilingual children performed more slowly when processing language, and their IQ scores were lower. A reexamination of these studies, however, revealed several crucial flaws. First, the tests were given in English even when that was not the child's primary language. Second, the bilingual participants were often first- or second-generation immigrants whose parents were not proficient in English. Finally, the bilingual children came from lower socioeconomic backgrounds than the monolingual children (Andrews, 1982).

Later studies controlled for these factors, revealing a very different picture of bilingual children's cognitive skills. The available evidence concerning language acquisition indicates that bilingual and monolingual children do not differ significantly in the course and rate of many aspects of their language development (Nicoladis & Genesee, 1997). In fact, middle-class children who are fluent in two languages have been found to score higher than monolingual children on several measures of cognitive functioning, including executive control capacities such as the ability to prioritize information and flexibly focus attention (Bialystok, 1999, 2009; Bialystok, Craik, & Luk, 2012). The idea here is that bilingual individuals benefit from exerting executive control in their daily lives when they attempt to suppress the language that they don't want to use. Recent evidence indicates that bilingualism also has benefits much later in life: Bilingual individuals tend to have a later onset of Alzheimer's disease than monolingual individuals, perhaps reflecting that during their lives they have built up a greater amount of back-up cognitive ability or "cognitive reserve" (Schweizer et al., 2012; this finding and some other benefits of bilingualism are noted in the Other Voices box). These findings are consistent with research showing that learning a second language produces lasting changes in the brain (Mechelli et al., 2004; Stein et al., 2009). For example, the gray matter in a part of the left parietal lobe that is involved in language is denser in bilingual than in monolingual individuals, and the increased density is most pronounced in those who are most proficient in using their second language (Mechelli et al., 2004; see **FIGURE 9.4**).

▼ Figure **9.4** **Bilingualism Alters Brain Structure** Learning a second language early in life increases the density of gray matter in the brain. A view of the lower left parietal region, which has denser gray matter in bilingual relative to monolingual individuals (*a*). As proficiency in a second language increases, so does the density of gray matter in the lower parietal region (*b*). People who acquired a second language earlier in life were also found to have denser gray matter in this region. Interestingly, this area corresponds to the same area that is activated during verbal fluency tasks (Mechelli et al., 2004).

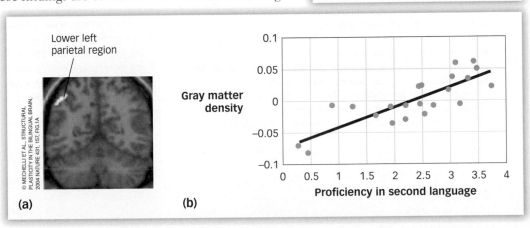

OTHER VOICES

Americans' Future Has to Be Bilingual

Linda Moore is the founder and executive director of the Elsie Whitlow Stokes Community Freedom Public Charter School in Washington, DC.

© SATSUN PHOTOGRAPHY/
BEVERLIE LORD

We discuss in the text some benefits of bilingualism that have been documented in recent research. Linda Moore (2012) noted several such benefits in the following article from *The Washington Diplomat* and argued that the American educational system should teach students foreign languages earlier than is commonly done.

We Americans must confront a stark disadvantage we face when it comes to the global economy. Some eight in 10 Americans speak only English, and the number of schools teaching a foreign language is in decline, according to a new study by the Council on Foreign Relations. But the opposite is true among our economic competitors.

While some 200 million Chinese students are learning English, only 24,000 Americans are studying Chinese, U.S. Department of Education statistics say. Foreign language degrees account for only 1 percent of all U.S. undergraduate degrees. And fewer than 2 percent of U.S. undergraduates study abroad in a given year, the Education Department says.

Our nation is largely monolingual but is entering an increasingly multilingual world. More than half of European Union citizens speak a language other than their mother tongue, and more than a quarter speak at least three languages. This is because additional languages are studied in European primary and secondary schools, and are taken up by European college students in much larger numbers than in the United States.

The Council on Foreign Relations-sponsored task force report, headed by former New York City Schools Chancellor Joel Klein and former Secretary of State Condoleezza Rice, concluded: "Education failure puts the United States' future economic prosperity, global position, and physical safety at risk." It warned that the country "will not be able to keep pace—much less lead—globally unless it moves to fix the problems it has allowed to fester for too long."

For decades, our children were deprived of bilingual or multilingual education out of a mistaken belief that it took time away from other subjects, hindering students' academic development. But recent research has shown that learning another language is a wise investment, rather than a waste. Research from the University of Georgia found that bilingual school children perform better on standardized tests including the Scholastic Aptitude Test (SAT) than their monolingual peers. A George Mason University study discovered that younger students who had enrolled in a second language immersion program outperformed those who did not in coursework, as well as on standardized tests, throughout their scholastic careers.

Educators now conclude that learning additional languages improves one's ability to focus, plan and solve problems. Among other benefits, this means that such students are better able to move efficiently from one subject to another. The D.C.-based Center for Applied Linguistics has ascertained that the earlier we learn a foreign language, the greater the benefits. Moreover, these benefits can last a lifetime. Learning another language can help people stave off the effects of aging, including preventing the onset of dementia and other age-related conditions like Alzheimer's, according to research done by University of California neuroscientists.

I believe that teaching students foreign languages in pre-kindergarten to sixth-grade classes is a worthwhile investment. Our school educates 350 students in Northeast Washington, D.C., to think, speak, read, write and learn in two languages, either English and French, or English and Spanish.

Exposure to a new language and the skills it helps develop is a key reason that our school, where 80 percent of our students come from low-income households, was ranked as high performing by D.C.'s Public Charter School Board in December. The ranking system was based on several factors, including test scores, attendance and re-enrollment rates.

The benefits of learning a new language go beyond the classroom. When students graduate, being fluent in a second language improves their career prospects. The Bureau of Labor Statistics reports that a number of emerging occupations need workers who can speak and write in more than one language. A University of Florida study revealed that in large, linguistically diverse cities such as Miami and San Antonio, the ability to speak a second language translates into more than $7,000 of increased annual income. We want our students to have access to these opportunities and more.

The economic importance of being bilingual is highlighted by the fact that 31 percent of company executives can speak at least two languages, according to international executive search firm Korn/Ferry.

Using multilingualism, we are expanding the scope of children's learning at a time when public policy limits school accountability to math and reading. Most policymakers want their children to have global skill sets but do not encourage this in our public schools.

Other countries have learned this lesson and have made the necessary commitments to teach their students additional languages. Their students' exposure to additional languages is paying dividends. I would like to see the U.S. Department of Education encourage local education authorities to invest in bilingual and multilingual education. Given the global competition for good jobs, this is not a luxury, but a necessity. It will help our children, and our nation, to succeed in the economy of tomorrow.

Are you convinced by Moore's argument? If not, why not? And if so, how far do you think that the educational system should go in promoting multilingual education? What about the possible impact of devoting more time in early grades to teaching languages on other subjects? What kinds of research would you want to see done to evaluate the effects of early instruction in foreign languages?

Some studies have revealed disadvantages, however. Bilingual children tend to have a smaller vocabulary in each language than their monolingual peers (Portocarrero, Burright, & Donovick, 2007); they also process language more slowly than monolingual children and can sometimes take longer to formulate sentences (Bialystok, 2009; Taylor & Lambert, 1990). Thus, learning a second language produces a number of benefits along with some costs.

Can Other Species Learn Human Language?

The human vocal tract and the extremely nimble human hand are better suited to human language than are the throats and paws of other species. Nonetheless, attempts have been made to teach nonhuman animals, particularly apes, to communicate using human language.

Early attempts to teach apes to speak failed dismally because their vocal tracts cannot accommodate the sounds used in human languages (Hayes & Hayes, 1951). Later attempts to teach apes human language have met with more success, including teaching them to use American Sign Language and computer-monitored keyboards that display geometric symbols that represent words. Allen and Beatrix Gardner were the first to use ASL with apes (Gardner & Gardner, 1969). The Gardners worked with a young female chimpanzee named Washoe as though she were a deaf child, signing to her regularly, rewarding her correct efforts at signing, and assisting her acquisition of signs by manipulating her hands in a process referred to as *molding*. In 4 years, Washoe learned approximately 160 words and could construct simple sentences, such as "More fruit." She also formed novel word constructions such as "water bird" for "duck." After a fight with a rhesus monkey, she signed, "dirty monkey!" This constituted a creative use of the term because she had only been taught the use of *dirty* to refer to soiled objects.

Allen and Beatrix Gardner used sign language to teach the female chimpanzee Washoe about 160 words. Washoe could also construct simple sentences and combine words in novel ways.

Other chimpanzees were immersed in ASL in a similar fashion, and Washoe and her companions were soon signing to each other, creating a learning environment conducive to language acquisition. One of Washoe's cohorts, a chimpanzee named Lucy, learned to sign "drink fruit" for watermelon. When Washoe's second infant died, her caretakers arranged for her to adopt an infant chimpanzee named Loulis.

In a few months, young Loulis, who was not exposed to human signers, learned 68 signs simply by watching Washoe communicate with the other chimpanzees. People who have observed these interactions and are themselves fluent in ASL report little difficulty in following the conversations (Fouts & Bodamer, 1987). One such observer, a *New York Times* reporter who spent some time with Washoe, reported, "Suddenly I realized I was conversing with a member of another species in my native tongue."

Other researchers have taught bonobo chimpanzees to communicate using a geometric keyboard system (Savage-Rumbaugh, Shanker, & Taylor, 1998). Their star pupil, Kanzi, learned the keyboard system by watching researchers try to teach his mother. Like Loulis, young Kanzi picked up the language relatively easily (his mother never did learn the system), suggesting that like humans, birds, and other species, apes experience a critical period for acquiring communicative systems.

Kanzi has learned hundreds of words and has combined them to form thousands of word combinations. Also like human children, his passive mastery of language appears to exceed his ability to produce language. In one study, researchers tested 9-year-old Kanzi's understanding of 660 spoken sentences. The grammatically complex sentences asked him to perform simple actions, such as "Go get the balloon that's in the microwave" and "Pour the Perrier into the Coke." Some sentences were also potentially misleading, such as "Get the pine needles that are in the refrigerator,"

Kanzi, a young male chimpanzee, learned hundreds of words and word combinations through a keyboard system as he watched researchers try to teach his mother.

when there were pine needles in clear view on the floor. Impressively, Kanzi correctly carried out 72% of the 660 requests (Savage-Rumbaugh & Lewin, 1996).

These results indicate that apes can acquire sizable vocabularies, string words together to form short sentences, and process sentences that are grammatically complex. Their skills are especially impressive because human language is hardly their normal means of communication. Research with apes also suggests that the neurological "wiring" that allows us to learn language overlaps to some degree with theirs (and perhaps with other species').

> **What do studies of apes and language teach us about humans and language?**

Equally informative are the limitations apes exhibit when learning, comprehending, and using human language. The first limitation is the size of the vocabularies they acquire. As mentioned, Washoe's and Kanzi's vocabularies number in the hundreds, but an average 4-year-old human child has a vocabulary of approximately 10,000 words. The second limitation is the type of words they can master, primarily names for concrete objects and simple actions. Apes (and several other species) have the ability to map arbitrary sounds or symbols onto objects and actions, but learning, say, the meaning of the word *economics* would be difficult for Washoe or Kanzi. In other words, apes can learn signs for concepts they understand, but their conceptual repertoire is smaller and simpler than that of humans.

The third and perhaps most important limitation is the complexity of grammar that apes can use and comprehend. Apes can string signs together, but their constructions rarely exceed three or four words, and when they do, they are rarely grammatical. Comparing the grammatical structures produced by apes with those produced by human children highlights the complexity of human language as well as the ease and speed with which we generate and comprehend it.

TOM CHALKLEY/THE NEW YORKER COLLECTION/CARTOONBANK.COM

"He says he wants a lawyer."

IN SUMMARY

▶ Human language is characterized by a complex organization—from phonemes to morphemes to phrases and finally to sentences.

▶ Each of these levels of human language is constructed and understood according to grammatical rules that are acquired early in development, even without being taught explicitly. Instead, children appear to be biologically predisposed to process language in ways that allow them to extract these grammatical rules from the language they hear.

▶ Our abilities to produce and comprehend language depend on distinct regions of the brain, with Broca's area critical for language production and Wernicke's area critical for comprehension.

▶ Bilingual and monolingual children show similar rates of language development. However, some bilingual children show greater executive control capacities, such as the ability to prioritize information and flexibly focus attention, and they tend to have a later onset of Alzheimer's disease.

▶ Nonhuman primates can learn new vocabulary and construct simple sentences, but there are significant limitations on the size of their vocabularies and the grammatical complexity they can handle.

linguistic relativity hypothesis
The proposal that language shapes the nature of thought.

Language and Thought: How Are They Related?

Language is such a dominant feature of our mental world that it is tempting to equate language with thought. Some theorists have even argued that language is simply a means of expressing thought. The **linguistic relativity hypothesis** maintains that *language shapes the nature of thought*. This idea was championed by Benjamin Whorf (1956), an engineer who studied language in his spare time and was especially interested in Native American languages. The most frequently cited example of linguistic relativity comes from the Inuit in Canada. Their language has many different terms for frozen white flakes of precipitation, for which we use the word *snow*. Whorf believed that because they have so many terms for snow, the Inuit perceive and think about snow differently than do English speakers.

The Inuit in Canada use many different terms for snow, leading Benjamin Whorf (1956) to propose that they think about snow differently than do English speakers.

Language and Color Processing

Whorf has been criticized for the anecdotal nature of his observations (Pinker, 1994), and some controlled research has cast doubt on Whorf's hypothesis. Eleanor Rosch (1973) studied the Dani, an isolated agricultural tribe living in New Guinea. They have only two terms for colors that roughly refer to "dark" and "light." If Whorf's hypothesis were correct, you would expect the Dani to have problems perceiving and learning different shades of color. But in Rosch's experiments, they learned shades of color just as well as people who have many more color terms in their first language. However, more recent evidence shows that language may indeed influence color processing (Roberson et al., 2004). Researchers compared English children with African children from a cattle-herding tribe in Namibia known as the Himba. The English have 11 basic color terms, but the Himba, who are largely isolated from the outside world, have only five. For example, they use the term *serandu* to refer to what English speakers would call red, pink, or orange.

> **How does language influence our understanding of color?**

Researchers showed a series of colored tiles to each child and then asked the child to choose that color from an array of 22 different colors. The youngest children, both English and Himba, who knew few or no color names, tended to confuse similar colors. But as the children grew and acquired more names for colors, their choices increasingly reflected the color terms they had learned. English children made fewer errors matching tiles that had English color names; Himba children made fewer errors for tiles with color names in Himba. These results reveal that language can indeed influence how children think about colors.

Similar effects have been observed in adults. Consider the 20 blue rectangles shown in **FIGURE 9.5**, which you'll easily see change gradually from lightest blue on the left to darkest blue on the right. What you might not know is that in Russian, there are different words for light blue (*goluboy*) and dark blue (*siniy*). Researchers investigated whether Russian speakers would respond differently to patches of blue when they fell into different linguistic categories rather than into the same linguistic category (Winawer et al., 2007). Both Russian and English speakers on

▼ Figure **9.5 Language Affects How We Think About Color** Unlike English, the Russian language has different words for light blue and dark blue. Russian speakers asked to pick which of the two bottom squares matched the color of the single square above responded more quickly when one of the bottom squares was called *goluboy* (light blue) and the other was called *siniy* (dark blue) than when both were referred to by the same name. English speakers took about the same amount of time.

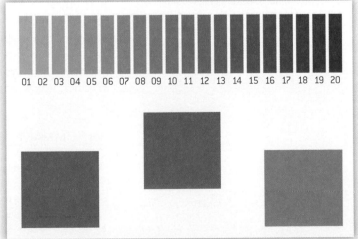

average classified rectangles 1–8 as light blue and 9–20 as dark blue, but only Russian speakers use different words to refer to the two classes of blue. In the experimental task, participants were shown three blue squares, as in the lower part of Figure 9.5, and were asked to pick which of the two bottom squares matched the colors of the top square. Russian speakers responded more quickly when one of the bottom squares was *goluboy* and the other was *siniy* than when both bottom squares were *goluboy* or both were *siniy*, whereas English speakers took about the same amount of time to respond in the two conditions (Winawer et al., 2007). As with children, language can affect how adults think about colors.

Language and the Concept of Time

In another study exploring the relationship between language and thought, researchers looked at the way people think about time. In English, we often use spatial terms: We look *forward* to a promising future or move a meeting *back* to fit our schedule (Casasanto & Boroditsky, 2008). We also use these terms to describe horizontal spatial relations, such as taking three steps *forward* or two steps *back* (Boroditsky, 2001). In contrast, speakers of Mandarin (Chinese) often describe time using terms that refer to a vertical spatial dimension: Earlier events are referred to as *up*, and later events as *down*. To test the effect of this difference, researchers showed English speakers and Mandarin speakers either a horizontal or vertical display of objects and then asked them to make a judgment involving time, such as whether March comes before April (Boroditsky, 2001). English speakers were faster to make the time judgments after seeing a horizontal display, whereas for Mandarin speakers the opposite was true. When English speakers learned to use Mandarin spatial terms, their time judgments were also faster after seeing the vertical display! This result nicely shows another way in which language can influence thought.

> **How does a horizontal concept of time contrast with a vertical concept of time?**

Bear in mind, though, that either thought or language ability can be severely impaired while the capacity for the other is spared, as illustrated by the dramatic case of Christopher that you read earlier in this chapter—and as we'll see again in the next section. These kinds of observations have led some researchers to suggest that Whorf was only "half right" in his claims about the effect of language on thought (Regier & Kay, 2009). Consistent with this idea, others suggest that it is overly simplistic to talk in general terms about whether language influences thought, and that researchers need to be more specific about the exact ways in which language influences thought. For example, Wolff & Holmes (2011) rejected the idea that language entirely determines thought. But they also pointed out that there is considerable evidence that language can influence thought both by highlighting specific properties of concepts and by allowing us to formulate verbal rules that help to solve problems. Thus, recent research has started to clarify the ways in which the linguistic relativity hypothesis is right and the ways in which it is wrong.

Westerners talk about moving a meeting *forward* or *back* a few days, a horizontal concept of time. Speakers of Mandarin talk about the same meeting as moving *up* or *down*, a vertical concept of time.

AP PHOTO/MARCIO JOSE SANCHEZ

IN SUMMARY

► The linguistic relativity hypothesis maintains that language shapes the nature of thought.

► Recent studies on color processing and time judgments point to an influence of language on thought. However, it is also clear that language and thought are to some extent separate.

Concepts and Categories: How We Think

In October 2000, a 69-year old man known by the initials JB went for a neurological assessment because he was having difficulty understanding the meaning of words, even though he still performed well on many other perceptual and cognitive tasks. In 2002, as his problems worsened, he began participating in a research project concerned with the role of language in naming, recognizing, and classifying colors (Haslam et al., 2007). As the researchers observed JB over the next 15 months, they documented that his color language deteriorated dramatically; he had great difficulty naming colors and could not even match objects with their typical colors (e.g., strawberry and red, banana and yellow). Yet even as his language deteriorated, JB could still classify colors normally, sorting color patches into groups of green, yellow, red, and blue in the exact same manner that healthy participants did. JB retained an intact concept of colors despite the decline of his language ability—a finding that suggests that we need to look at factors in addition to language in order to understand concepts (Haslam et al., 2007).

Concept refers to a *mental representation that groups or categorizes shared features of related objects, events, or other stimuli.* A concept is an abstract representation, description, or definition that serves to designate a class or category of things. The brain organizes our concepts about the world, classifying them into categories based on shared similarities. Our category for *dog* may be something like "small, four footed animal with fur that wags its tail and barks." Our category for *bird* may be something like "small, winged, beaked creature that flies." We form these categories in large part by noticing similarities among objects and events that we experience in everyday life. For example, your concept of a chair might include such features as sturdiness, relative flatness, and an object that you can sit on. That set of attributes defines a category of objects in the world—desk chairs, recliner chairs, flat rocks, bar stools, and so on—that can all be described in that way.

Concepts are fundamental to our ability to think and make sense of the world. We'll first compare various theories that explain the formation of concepts and then consider studies that link the formation and organization of concepts to the brain. As with other aspects of cognition, we can gain insight into how concepts are organized by looking at some instances in which they are rather disorganized. We'll encounter some unusual disorders that help us understand how concepts are organized in the brain.

? Why are concepts useful to us?

concept
A mental representation that groups or categorizes shared features of related objects, events, or other stimuli.

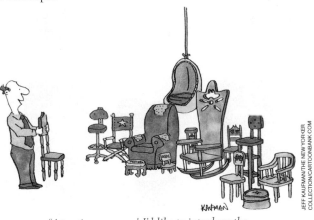

"Attention everyone! I'd like to introduce the newest member of our family."

JEFF KAUFMAN/THE NEW YORKER COLLECTION/CARTOONBANK.COM

There is family resemblance between family members despite the fact that there is no defining feature that they all have in common. Instead, there are shared common features. Someone who also shares some of those features may be categorized as belonging to the family.

Psychological Theories of Concepts and Categories

Early psychological theories described concepts as rules that specify the necessary and sufficient conditions for membership in a particular category. A *necessary condition* is something that must be true of the object in order for it to belong to the category. For example, suppose you were trying to determine whether an unfamiliar animal was a dog. It is necessary that the creature be a mammal; otherwise it doesn't belong to the category *dog* because all dogs are mammals. A *sufficient condition* is something that, if it is true of the object, proves that it belongs to the category. Suppose someone told you that the creature was a German shepherd and you know that a German shepherd is a type of dog. *German shepherd* is a sufficient condition for membership in the category *dog*.

BLEND IMAGES/SUPERSTOCK

▲ Figure **9.6 Family Resemblance Theory**
The family resemblance here is unmistakable, even though no two Smith brothers share all the family features. The prototype is brother 9. He has it all: brown hair, large ears, large nose, mustache, and glasses.

Most natural categories, however, cannot be so easily defined in terms of this classical approach of necessary and sufficient conditions. For example, what is your definition of *dog*? Can you come up with a rule of "dogship" that includes all dogs and excludes all non-dogs? Most people can't, but they still use the term *dog* intelligently, easily classifying objects as dogs or non-dogs. Three theories seek to explain how people perform these acts of categorization.

Family Resemblance Theory

Eleanor Rosch put aside necessity and sufficiency to develop a theory of concepts based on **family resemblance**, that is, *features that appear to be characteristic of category members but may not be possessed by every member* (Rosch, 1973, 1975; Rosch & Mervis, 1975; Wittgenstein, 1953/1999). For example, you and your brother may have your mother's eyes, although you and your sister may have your father's high cheekbones. There is a strong family resemblance between you, your parents, and your siblings despite the fact that there is no necessarily defining feature that you all have in common. Similarly, many members of the *bird* category have feathers and wings, so these are the characteristic features. Anything that has these features is likely to be classified as a bird because of this "family resemblance" to other members of the *bird* category. **FIGURE 9.6** illustrates family resemblance theory.

Prototype Theory

Building on the idea of family resemblance, Rosch also proposed that psychological categories (those that we form naturally) are best described as organized around a **prototype,** *the "best" or "most typical" member of a category.* A prototype possesses most (or all) of the most characteristic features of the category. For North Americans, the prototype of the *bird* category would be something like a wren: a small animal with feathers and wings that flies through the air, lays eggs, and migrates (see **FIGURE 9.7**). If you lived in Antarctica, your prototype of a bird might be a penguin: a small animal that has flippers, swims, and lays eggs. According to *prototype theory,* if your prototypical bird is a robin, then a canary would be considered a better example of a bird than would an ostrich because a canary has more features in common with a robin than an ostrich does. People make category judgments by comparing new instances to the category's prototype. This contrasts with the classical approach to concepts in which something either is or is not an example of a concept (i.e., it either does or does not belong in the category *dog* or *bird*).

► Figure **9.7 Critical Features of a Category**
We tend to think of a generic bird as possessing a number of critical features, but not every bird possesses all of those features. In North America, a wren is a better example of a bird than a penguin or an ostrich.

Properties	Generic bird	Wren	Blue heron	Golden eagle	Domestic goose	Penguin
Flies regularly	✓	✓	✓	✓		
Sings	✓	✓	✓			
Lays eggs	✓	✓	✓	✓	✓	✓
is small	✓	✓				
Nests in trees	✓	✓				

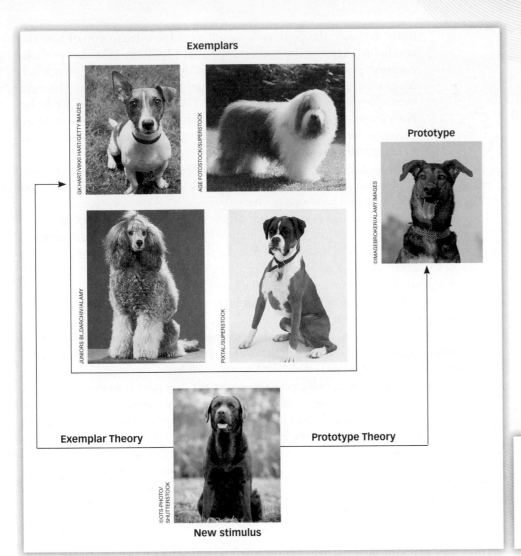

Exemplars

Prototype

Exemplar Theory

Prototype Theory

New stimulus

◀ Figure **9.8 Prototype Theory and Exemplar Theory** According to prototype theory, we classify new objects by comparing them to the "prototype" (or most typical) member of a category. According to exemplar theory, we classify new objects by comparing them to all category members.

Exemplar Theory

In contrast to prototype theory, **exemplar theory** holds that *we make category judgments by comparing a new instance with stored memories for other instances of the category* (Medin & Schaffer, 1978). Imagine that you're out walking in the woods, and from the corner of your eye you spot a four-legged animal that might be a wolf or a coyote but that reminds you of your cousin's German shepherd. You figure it must be a dog and continue to enjoy your walk rather than fleeing in a panic. You probably categorized this new animal as a dog because it bore a striking resemblance to other dogs you've encountered; in other words, it was a good example (or an *exemplar*) of the category *dog*. Exemplar theory does a better job than prototype theory in accounting for certain aspects of categorization, especially in that we recall not only what a *prototypical* dog looks like but also what *specific* dogs look like. **FIGURE 9.8** illustrates the difference between prototype theory and exemplar theory.

Concepts, Categories, and the Brain

Studies that have attempted to link concepts and categories to the brain have helped to make sense of the theories we just considered. For example, in one set of studies (Marsolek, 1995), participants classified prototypes faster when the stimuli were presented to the right visual field, meaning that the left hemisphere received the

family resemblance theory
Members of a category have features that appear to be characteristic of category members but may not be possessed by every member.

prototype
The "best" or "most typical" member of a category.

exemplar theory
A theory of categorization that argues that we make category judgments by comparing a new instance with stored memories for other instances of the category.

"Don't panic. It's only a prototype."

input first (see the Neuroscience chapter for a discussion of how the two hemispheres of the brain receive input from the outside world). In contrast, participants classified previously seen exemplars faster when images were presented to the left visual field (meaning that the right hemisphere received the input first). These results suggest a role for both exemplars and prototypes: The left hemisphere is primarily involved in forming prototypes and the right hemisphere is mainly active in recognizing exemplars.

More recently, researchers using neuroimaging techniques have also concluded that we use both prototypes and exemplars when forming concepts and categories. The visual cortex is involved in forming prototypes, whereas the prefrontal cortex and basal ganglia are involved in learning exemplars (Ashby & Ell, 2001; Ashby & O'Brien, 2005). This evidence suggests that exemplar-based learning involves analysis and decision making (prefrontal cortex), whereas prototype formation is a more holistic process involving image processing (visual cortex).

How do prototypes and exemplars relate to each other?

Some of the most striking evidence linking concepts and categories with the brain originated in a pioneering study conducted over 30 years ago. Two neuropsychologists (Warrington & McCarthy, 1983) described a man with brain damage who could not recognize a variety of human-made objects or retrieve any information about them, but his knowledge of living things and foods was perfectly normal. In the following year, neuropsychologists (Warrington & Shallice, 1984) reported on four individuals with brain damage who exhibited the reverse pattern: They could recognize information about human-made objects, but their ability to recognize information about living things and foods was severely impaired. Over 100 similar cases have since been reported (Martin & Caramazza, 2003). These unusual cases became the basis for a syndrome called **category-specific deficit,** *an inability to recognize objects that belong to a particular category, although the ability to recognize objects outside the category is undisturbed.*

Category-specific deficits like these have been observed even when the brain trauma that produces them occurs shortly after birth. Two researchers reported the case of Adam, a 16-year-old boy who suffered a stroke a day after he was born (Farah & Rabinowitz, 2003). Adam has severe difficulty recognizing faces and other biological objects. When shown a picture of a cherry, he identified it as "a Chinese yo-yo." When shown a picture of a mouse, he identified it as an owl. He made errors like these on 79% of the animal pictures and 54% of the plant pictures he was shown. In contrast, he made errors only 15% of the time when identifying pictures of nonliving things, such as spatulas, brooms, and cigars. What's so important about this case? The fact that 16-year-old Adam exhibited category-specific deficits despite suffering a stroke when he was only 1 day old strongly suggests that the brain is "prewired" to organize perceptual and sensory inputs into broad-based categories, such as living and nonliving things.

The type of category-specific deficit suffered depends on where the brain is damaged. Deficits usually result when an individual suffers a stroke or other trauma to areas in the left hemisphere of the cerebral cortex (Mahon & Caramazza, 2009). Damage to the front part of the left temporal lobe results in difficulty identifying humans; damage to the lower left temporal lobe results in difficulty identifying animals; and damage to the region where the temporal lobe meets the occipital and parietal lobes impairs the ability to retrieve names of tools (Damasio et al., 1996). Similarly, when healthy people undertake the same task, imaging studies have demonstrated that the same regions of the brain are more active during naming of tools than animals and vice versa, as shown in **FIGURE 9.9** (Martin, 2007; Martin & Chao, 2001).

category-specific deficit
A neurological syndrome that is characterized by an inability to recognize objects that belong to a particular category, although the ability to recognize objects outside the category is undisturbed.

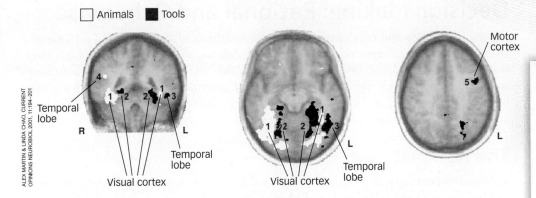

ALEX MARTIN & LINDA CHAO, CURRENT OPINIONS NEUROBIOL 2001, 11:194–201

◄ Figure **9.9 Brain Areas Involved in Category-Specific Processing** Participants were asked to silently name pictures of animals and tools while they were scanned with fMRI. The fMRIs revealed greater activity in the areas in white when participants named animals, and areas in black showed greater activity when participants named tools. Specific regions indicated by numbers include areas within the visual cortex (1, 2), parts of the temporal lobe (3, 4), and the motor cortex (5). Note that the images are left/right reversed.

How do particular brain regions develop category preferences for objects such as tools or animals? One possibility is that these preferences develop from the specific visual experiences that individuals have during the course of their lives. An alternative possibility is suggested by the study of Adam that we just considered: The brain may be prewired such that particular regions respond more strongly to some categories than others. A recent study tested these ideas by examining the activity of category-preferential regions in adults who have been blind since birth (Mahon et al., 2009).

What is the role of vision in category-specific organization?

While in the fMRI scanner, blind and sighted individuals each heard a series of words, including some words that referred to animals and others that referred to tools. For each word, participants made a judgment about the size of the corresponding object. The critical finding was that category-preferential regions showed highly similar patterns of activity in the blind and sighted individuals. In both groups, for example, regions in the visual cortex and temporal lobe responded to animals and tools in much the same manner as shown in Figure 9.9.

These results provide compelling evidence that category-specific organization of visual regions does not depend on an individual's visual experience. The category-specific organization could conceivably have arisen from interactions with objects that blind individuals have had involving senses other than vision, such as touch (Peelen & Kastner, 2009). However, when combined with the observations of Adam, the simplest explanation may be that category-specific brain organization is innately determined (Bedny & Saxe, 2012; Mahon et al., 2009).

IN SUMMARY

► We organize knowledge about objects, events, or other stimuli by creating concepts, prototypes, and exemplars.

► We acquire concepts using three theories: family resemblance theory, which states that items in the same category share certain features, if not all; prototype theory, which uses the most typical member of a category to assess new items; and exemplar theory, which states that we compare new items with stored memories of other members of the category.

► Neuroimaging studies have shown that prototypes and exemplars are processed in different parts of the brain.

► Studies of people with cognitive and visual deficits have shown that the brain organizes concepts into distinct categories, such as living things and human-made things, and also suggest that visual experience is not necessary for the development of such categories.

Decision Making: Rational and Otherwise

We use categories and concepts to guide the hundreds of decisions and judgments we make during the course of an average day. Some decisions are easy (what to wear, what to eat for breakfast, and whether to walk, ride a bicycle, or drive to class) and some are more difficult (which car to buy, which apartment to rent, who to hang out with on Friday night, and even which job to take after graduation). Some decisions are made based on sound judgments. Others are not.

The Rational Ideal

Economists contend that if we are rational and are free to make our own decisions, we will behave as predicted by **rational choice theory:** *We make decisions by determining how likely something is to happen, judging the value of the outcome, and then multiplying the two* (Edwards, 1955). This means that our judgments will vary depending on the value we assign to the possible outcomes. Suppose, for example, you were asked to choose between a 10% chance of gaining $500 and a 20% chance of gaining $2,000. The rational person would choose the second alternative because the expected payoff is $400 ($2,000 × 20%), whereas the first offers an expected gain of only $50 ($500 × 10%). Selecting the option with the highest expected value seems so straightforward that many economists accept the basic ideas in rational choice theory. But how well does this theory describe decision making in our everyday lives? In many cases, the answer is not very well.

The Irrational Reality

Is the ability to classify new events and objects into categories always a useful skill? Alas, no. These strengths of human decision making can turn into weaknesses when certain tasks inadvertently activate these skills. In other words, the same principles that allow cognition to occur easily and accurately can pop up to bedevil our decision making.

Judging Frequencies and Probabilities

Consider the following list of words:

> *block table block pen telephone block disk glass table block telephone block watch table candy*

You probably noticed that the words *block* and *table* occurred more frequently than the other words did. In fact, studies have shown that people are quite good at estimating *frequency*, or simply the number of times something will happen. This skill matters quite a bit when it comes to decision making. In contrast, we perform poorly on tasks that require us to think in terms of *probabilities*, or the likelihood that something will happen.

Even with probabilities, however, performance varies depending on how the problem is described. In one experiment, 100 physicians were asked to predict the incidence of breast cancer among women whose mammogram screening tests showed possible evidence of breast cancer. The physicians were told to take into consideration the rarity of breast cancer (1% of the population at the time the study was done) and radiologists' record in diagnosing the condition (correctly recognized only 79% of the time and falsely diagnosed almost 10% of the time). Of the 100 physicians, 95 estimated the probability that cancer was present to be about 75%! The correct answer was 8%. The physicians apparently experienced dif-

> Why is a better decision more likely when considering frequency, versus likelihood, that something will happen?

People don't always make rational choices. When a lottery jackpot is larger than usual, more people will buy lottery tickets, thinking that they might well win big. However, more people buying lottery tickets reduces the likelihood of any one person winning the lottery. Ironically, people have a better chance at winning a lottery with a relatively small jackpot.

SANTA ROSA PRESS DEMOCRAT/ZUMAPRESS.COM/ALAMY

ficulty taking so much information into account when making their decision (Eddy, 1982). Similar dismal results have been reported with a number of medical screening tests (Hoffrage & Gigerenzer, 1996; Windeler & Kobberling, 1986).

However, dramatically different results were obtained when the study was repeated using *frequency* information instead of *probability* information. Stating the problem as "10 out of every 1,000 women actually have breast cancer" instead of "1% of women actually have breast cancer" led 46% of the physicians to derive the right answer, compared to only 8% who came up with the right answer when the problem was presented using probabilities (Hoffrage & Gigerenzer, 1998). This finding suggests, at a minimum, that when seeking advice (even from a highly skilled decision maker), make sure your problem is described using frequencies rather than probabilities.

Availability Bias

Take a look at the list of names in **FIGURE 9.10.** Now look away from the book and estimate the number of male names and female names in the figure. Did you notice that some of the women on the list are famous and none of the men are? Was your estimate off because you thought the list contained more women's than men's names (Tversky & Kahneman, 1973, 1974)? The reverse would have been true if you had looked at a list with the names of famous men and unknown women because people typically fall prey to **availability bias**: *Items that are more readily available in memory are judged as having occurred more frequently.*

The availability bias affects our estimates because memory strength and frequency of occurrence are directly related. Frequently occurring items are remembered more easily than *infrequently* occurring items, so you naturally conclude that items for which you have better memory must also have been more frequent. Unfortunately, better memory in this case was not due to greater *frequency,* but to greater *familiarity.*

> **How are memory strength and frequency of occurrence related?**

Shortcuts such as the availability bias are sometimes referred to as **heuristics**, *fast and efficient strategies that may facilitate decision making but do not guarantee that a solution will be reached.* Heuristics are mental shortcuts, or "rules of thumb," that are often—but not always—effective when approaching a problem (Swinkels, 2003). In contrast, an **algorithm** is *a well-defined sequence of procedures or rules that guarantees a solution to a problem.* Consider, for example, two approaches to constructing a Power-Point presentation involving features you rarely use, such as inserting movies and complex animations: (1) You try to remember what you did the last time you tried to do a similar presentation; (2) You follow a set of step-by-step directions that you wrote down the last time you did something similar, which tells you exactly how to insert movies and build complex animations.

The first procedure is an intelligent heuristic that may be successful, but you could continue searching your memory until you finally run out of time or patience. The second strategy is a series of well-defined steps that, if properly executed, will guarantee a solution.

The Conjunction Fallacy

The availability bias illustrates a potential source of error in human cognition. Unfortunately, it's not the only one. Consider the following description:

> Linda is 31 years old, single, outspoken, and very bright. In college, she majored in philosophy. As a student, she was deeply concerned with issues of discrimination and social justice and also participated in antinuclear demonstrations.
>
> Which state of affairs is more probable?
>
> **a.** Linda is a bank teller.
> **b.** Linda is a bank teller and is active in the feminist movement.

Jennifer Aniston	Robert Kingston
Judy Smith	Gilbert Chapman
Frank Carson	Gwyneth Paltrow
Elizabeth Taylor	Martin Mitchell
Daniel Hunt	Thomas Hughes
Henry Vaughan	Michael Drayton
Agatha Christie	Julia Roberts
Arthur Hutchinson	Hillary Clinton
Jennifer Lopez	Jack Lindsay
Allan Nevins	Richard Gilder
Jane Austen	George Nathan
Joseph Litton	Britney Spears

▲ Figure **9.10** **Availability Bias** Looking at this list of names, estimate the number of women's and men's names.

rational choice theory
The classical view that we make decisions by determining how likely something is to happen, judging the value of the outcome, and then multiplying the two.

availability bias
Items that are more readily available in memory are judged as having occurred more frequently.

heuristic
A fast and efficient strategy that may facilitate decision making but does not guarantee that a solution will be reached.

algorithm
A well-defined sequence of procedures or rules that guarantees a solution to a problem.

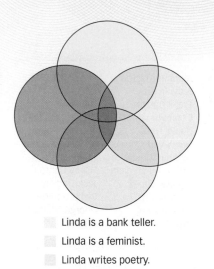

Linda is a bank teller.

Linda is a feminist.

Linda writes poetry.

Linda has endorsed a fair-housing petition.

▲ Figure **9.11 The Conjunction Fallacy** People often think that with each additional bit of information, the probability that all the facts are simultaneously true of a person increases. In fact, the probability decreases dramatically. Notice how the intersection of all these possibilities is much smaller than the area of any one possibility alone.

conjunction fallacy
When people think that two events are more likely to occur together than either individual event.

representativeness heuristic
A mental shortcut that involves making a probability judgment by comparing an object or event to a prototype of the object or event.

framing effects
When people give different answers to the same problem depending on how the problem is phrased (or framed).

sunk-cost fallacy
A framing effect in which people make decisions about a current situation based on what they have previously invested in the situation.

In one study, 89% of participants rated option **b** as more probable than option **a** (Tversky & Kahneman, 1983), although that's logically impossible. Let's say there's a 20% chance that Linda is a bank teller; after all, there are plenty of occupations she might hold. Independently, let's say there's also a 20% chance that she's active in the feminist movement; she probably has lots of interests. The joint probability that *both* things are true simultaneously is the product of their separate probabilities. In other words, the 20% chance that she's a teller multiplied by the 20% chance that she's in the feminist movement produces a 4% chance that both things are true at the same time (.20 × .20 = .04, or 4%). The combined probability of events is always less than the independent probability of each event; therefore, it's always *more* probable that any one state of affairs is true than is a set of events simultaneously.

This is called the **conjunction fallacy** because *people think that two events are more likely to occur together than either individual event*. The fallacy is that with more and more pieces of information, people think there's a higher probability that all are true. Actually, the probability diminishes rapidly. Based on her description, do you think Linda also voted for the liberal candidate in the last election? Do you think she also writes poetry? Do you think she's also signed her name to fair-housing petitions? With each additional bit of information, you probably think you're getting a better and better description of Linda, but as you can see in **FIGURE 9.11**, the likelihood of all those events being true *at the same time* is very small.

> **How can more information sometimes lead people to wrong conclusions?**

Representativeness Heuristic

Think about the following situation:

> A panel of psychologists wrote 100 descriptions based on interviews with engineers and lawyers. THE DESCRIPTIONS CAME FROM 70 ENGINEERS AND 30 LAWYERS. You will be shown a random selection of these descriptions. Read each and then pause and decide if it is more likely that the person is an engineer or a lawyer. Note your decision and read on.
>
> 1. Jack enjoys reading books on social and political issues. During the interview, he displayed particular skill at argument.
> 2. Tom is a loner who enjoys working on mathematical puzzles during his spare time. During the interview, his speech remained fairly abstract and his emotions were well controlled.
> 3. Harry is a bright man and an avid racquetball player. During the interview, he asked many insightful questions and was very well spoken.

Research participants were shown a series of descriptions like these and asked after each one to judge the likelihood that the person described was a lawyer or an engineer (Kahneman & Tversky, 1973). Remember, of the descriptions, 70 were engineers and 30 were lawyers. If participants took this proportion into consideration, their judgments should have reflected the fact that there were more than twice as many engineers as lawyers. But researchers found that people didn't use this information and based their judgments solely on how closely the description matched their concepts of lawyers and engineers. So, the majority of participants thought descriptions such as 1 were more likely to be lawyers, those like 2 were more likely to be engineers, and those like 3 could be either.

Consider participants' judgments about Harry. His description doesn't sound like a lawyer's or an engineer's, so most people said he was *equally likely* to hold either occupation. But the pool contains more than twice as many engineers as lawyers, so it is far *more* likely that Harry is an engineer. People seem to ignore information about *base rate,* or the existing probability of an event, basing their judgments on similarities to categories. Researchers call this the **representativeness heuristic**: *making a probability judgment by comparing an object or event to a prototype of the object or event* (Kahneman & Tversky, 1973). Thus, the probability judgments were skewed toward the participants' prototypes of lawyer and engineer. The greater the similarity, the more likely they were judged to be members of that category despite the existence of much more useful base rates.

> **What can cause people to ignore the *base rate* of an event?**

Heuristics such as availability, representativeness, or the conjunction fallacy highlight both the strengths and weaknesses of the way we think. We are very good at forming categories based on prototypes and making classification judgments on the basis of similarity to prototypes. Judging probabilities is not our strong suit. As we saw earlier in this chapter, the human brain easily processes frequency information, and decision-making performance can usually be improved if probability problems are reframed using frequencies.

Framing Effects

You've seen that, according to rational choice theory, our judgments will vary depending on the value we place on the expected outcome. So how effective are we at assigning value to our choices? Studies show that **framing effects,** which occur when *people give different answers to the same problem depending on how the problem is phrased (or framed),* can influence the assignment of value.

> **Is a 70% success rate better than a 30% failure rate?**

For example, if people are told that a particular drug has a 70% effectiveness rate, they're usually pretty impressed: 70% of the time the drug cures what ails you sounds like a good deal. Tell them instead that a drug has a 30% failure rate—30% of the time it does no good—and they typically perceive it as risky, potentially harmful, and something to be avoided. Notice that the information is the same: A 70% effectiveness rate means that 30% of the time, it's ineffective. The way the information is framed, however, leads to substantially different conclusions (Tversky & Kahneman, 1981).

One of the most striking framing effects is the **sunk-cost fallacy**, which occurs when *people make decisions about a current situation based on what they have previously invested in the situation.* Imagine waiting in line for 3 hours, paying $100 for a ticket to the Warped Tour to see your favorite bands, and waking on the day of the outdoor concert to find that it's bitterly cold and rainy. If you go, you'll feel miserable. But you go anyway, reasoning that the $100 you paid for the ticket and the time you spent in line will have been wasted if you stay home.

Notice that you have two choices: (1) Spend $100 and stay comfortably at home or (2) spend $100 and endure many uncomfortable hours in the rain. The $100 is gone in either case: It's a sunk cost, irretrievable at the moment of your decision. But the way you framed the problem created a problem: Because you invested time and money, you feel obligated to follow through, even though it's something you no longer want. If you can turn off this feeling and ask, would I rather spend $100 to be comfortable or spend it to be miserable? the smart choice is clear: Stay home and listen to the podcast!

Even the National Basketball Association (NBA) is guilty of a sunk-cost fallacy. Coaches should play their most productive players and keep them on the team longer, but they don't. The most *expensive* players are given more time on court and are kept on the team longer than cheaper players, even if the costly players are not performing up to par (Staw & Hoang, 1995). Coaches act to justify their team's investment in an expensive player rather than recognize the loss. Framing effects can be costly!

AP PHOTO/TONY GUTIERREZ

Worth the cost? Sports teams sometimes try to justify their investment in an expensive player who is underperforming, an example of a sunk-cost effect. Hedo Turkoglu is a highly paid basketball player, but his recent performance has not lived up to his salary.

CULTURE & COMMUNITY

Does culture influence optimism bias? In addition to heuristics and biases described in this chapter, human decision making often reflects the effects of *optimism bias*: People believe that they are more likely to experience positive events and less likely to experience negative events in the future, compared with other people (Sharot, 2011; Weinstein, 1980). Several studies have found that optimism bias is greater in North Americans than in individuals from eastern cultures such as Japan (Heine & Lehman, 1995; Klein & Helwig-Larsen, 2002). One recent study examined optimism bias concerning the risk of natural disasters and terrorist attacks in American, Japanese, and Argentinean mental health workers who had received training in responding to such events (Gierlach, Blesher, & Beutler, 2010). Evidence for optimism bias was evident to some degree in all three samples: Participants in each country judged that they were at lower risk of experiencing a disaster than others in their country. However, optimism bias was strongest in the American sample. This bias was most clearly evident in responses across cultures to questions regarding vulnerability to terrorist attacks. Despite America's recent experience with terrorist attacks, Americans judged themselves to be at lower risk of a terrorist attack than did Japanese or Argentineans.

Findings such as these may ultimately be helpful in attempting to understand *why* the optimism bias occurs. Although many possibilities have been suggested (Sharot, 2011), researchers haven't yet come up with a theory that explains all the relevant evidence. Focusing on cultural similarities and differences in optimism bias may help to achieve that goal, although we shouldn't be unrealistically optimistic that we will achieve it anytime soon!

Why Do We Make Decision-Making Errors?

As you have seen, everyday decision making seems riddled with errors and short-comings. Our decisions vary wildly depending on how a problem is presented (e.g., frequencies vs. probabilities or framed in terms of losses rather than savings), and we seem to be prone to fallacies, such as the sunk-cost fallacy or the conjunction fallacy. Psychologists have developed several explanations for why everyday decision making suffers from these failings. We'll review two of the most influential theories: prospect theory and the frequency format hypothesis.

Prospect Theory

According to a totally rational model of inference, people should make decisions that maximize value; in other words, they should seek to increase what psychologists and economists call *expected utility*. We face decisions like this every day. If you are making a decision that involves money and money is what you value, then you should choose the outcome that is likely to bring you the most money. When deciding which of two apartments to rent, you'd compare the monthly expenses for each and choose the one that leaves more money in your pocket.

Why will most people take more risks to avoid losses than to make gains?

As you have seen, however, people often make decisions that are inconsistent with this simple principle. The question is, why? To explain these effects, Amos Tversky and Daniel Kahneman (1992) developed **prospect theory**: *People choose to take on risk when evaluating potential losses and avoid risks when evaluating potential gains.* These decision processes take place in two phases.

> First, people simplify available information. So, in a task like choosing an apartment, they tend to ignore a lot of potentially useful information because apartments differ in so many ways (the closeness of restaurants, the presence of a swimming pool, the color of the carpet, and so forth). Comparing each apartment

on each factor is simply too much work; focusing only on differences that matter is more efficient.

> In the second phase, people choose the prospect that they believe offers the best value. This value is personal and may differ from an objective measure of "best value." For example, you might choose the apartment with higher rent because you can walk to eight great bars and restaurants.

Prospect theory makes other assumptions that account for people's choice patterns. One assumption, called the *certainty effect*, suggests that when making decisions, people give greater weight to outcomes that are a sure thing. When deciding between playing a lottery with an 80% chance of winning $4,000 or receiving $3,000 outright, most people choose the $3,000, even though the expected value of the first choice is $200 more ($4,000 × 80% = $3,200)! Apparently, people weigh certainty much more heavily than expected payoffs when making choices.

Prospect theory also assumes that in evaluating choices, people compare them to a reference point. For example, suppose you're still torn between two apartments. The $400 monthly rent for apartment A is discounted $10 if you pay before the fifth of the month. A $10 surcharge is tacked onto the $390 per month rent for apartment B if you pay after the fifth of the month. Although the apartments are objectively identical in terms of cost, different reference points may make apartment A seem psychologically more appealing than apartment B.

Prospect theory also assumes that people are more willing to take risks to avoid losses than to achieve gains. Given a choice between a definite $300 rebate on your first month's rent or spinning a wheel that offers an 80% chance of getting a $400 rebate, you'll most likely choose the lower sure payoff over the higher potential payoff ($400 × 80% = $320). However, given a choice between a sure fine of $300 for damaging an apartment or spinning a wheel that has an 80% chance of a $400 fine, most people will choose the higher potential loss over the sure loss. This asymmetry in risk preferences shows that we are willing to take on risk if we think it will ward off a loss, but we're risk-averse if we expect to lose some benefits.

prospect theory
People choose to take on risk when evaluating potential losses and avoid risks when evaluating potential gains.

frequency format hypothesis
The proposal that our minds evolved to notice how frequently things occur, not how likely they are to occur.

RON SACHS/PICTURE-ALLIANCE/DPA/AP IMAGES
Marco Rubio

AP PHOTO/MEL EVANS, FILE
Chris Christie

AP PHOTO/HARRY HAMBURG
Harry Reid

ZUMA PRESS/ALAMY
Elizabeth Warren

Frequency Format Hypothesis

According to the **frequency format hypothesis,** *our minds evolved to notice how frequently things occur, not how likely they are to occur* (Gigerenzer, 1996; Gigerenzer & Hoffrage, 1995). Thus, we interpret, process, and manipulate information about frequency with comparative ease because that's the way quantitative information usually occurs in natural circumstances. For example, the 20 men, 15 women, 5 dogs, 13 cars, and 2 bicycle accidents you encountered on the way to class came in the form of frequencies, not probabilities or percentages.

? **Why are we better at estimating frequencies than probabilities?**

According to rational choice theory, people evaluate all options when making a decision and choose the alternative with the greatest benefit to them. However, psychological research shows us that this is not always the case. How might some political candidates use the conjunction fallacy, framing effects, or prospect theory to influence voters' evaluations of their opponents or their opponents' views?

Probabilities and percentages are, evolutionarily speaking, recent developments, emerging in the mid-17th century (Hacking, 1975). Millennia passed before humans developed these cultural notions, and years of schooling are needed to use them competently as everyday cognitive tools. Thus, our susceptibility to errors when dealing with probabilities is not surprising.

In contrast, people can track frequencies virtually effortlessly and flawlessly (Hasher & Zacks, 1984). We are also remarkably good at recognizing how often two events occur together (Mandel & Lehman, 1998; Spellman, 1996; Waldmann, 2000). Infants as young as 6 months of age can tell the difference between displays that differ in the number of items present (Starkey, Spelke, & Gelman, 1983, 1990). Frequency monitoring is a basic biological capacity rather than a skill learned through formal instruction. According to the frequency format hypothesis, presenting statistical information in frequency format rather than probability format results in improved performance because it capitalizes on our evolutionary strengths (Gigerenzer & Hoffrage, 1995; Hertwig & Gigerenzer, 1999).

Decision Making and the Brain

A man identified as Elliot (whom you met briefly in the Psychology: Evolution of a Science chapter) was a successful businessman, husband, and father prior to developing a brain tumor. After surgery, his intellectual abilities seemed intact, but he was unable to differentiate between important and unimportant activities and would spend hours at mundane tasks. He lost his job and got involved in several risky financial ventures that bankrupted him. He had no difficulty discussing what had happened, but his descriptions were so detached and dispassionate that it seemed as though his abstract intellectual functions had become dissociated from his social and emotional abilities.

Research confirms that this interpretation of Elliot's downfall is right on track. In one study, researchers looked at how healthy volunteers differed from people with prefrontal lobe damage on a gambling task that involves risky decision making (Bechara et al., 1994, 1997). Four decks of cards were placed face down, and participants were required to make 100 selections of cards that specified an amount of play money they could win or lose. Two of the decks usually provided large payoffs or large losses, whereas the other two provided smaller payoffs and losses. While playing the game, the participants' galvanic skin responses (GSRs) were recorded to measure heightened emotional reactions.

The performance of players with prefrontal lobe damage mirrored Elliot's real-life problems: They selected cards equally from the riskier and the safer decks, leading most to eventually go bankrupt. At first, the healthy volunteers also selected from each deck equally, but they gradually shifted to choosing primarily from the safer decks. This difference in strategy occurred even though both groups showed strong emotional reactions to big gains and losses, as measured by their comparable GSR scores. The two groups differed in one important way. As the game progressed, the healthy participants began to show anticipatory emotional reactions when they even *considered* choosing a card from the risky deck. Their GSR scores jumped dramatically even before they were able to say that some decks were riskier than others (Bechara et al., 1997). The participants with prefrontal damage didn't show these anticipatory feelings when they were thinking about selecting a card from the risky deck. Apparently, their emotional reactions did not guide their thinking, so they continued to make risky decisions, as shown in **FIGURE 9.12**.

> **What is the relationship of the prefrontal cortex to risky behavior?**

Further studies of the participants with prefrontal damage suggest that their risky decision making grows out of insensitivity to the future consequences of their behavior (Naqvi, Shiv, & Bechara, 2006). Unable to think beyond immediate consequences,

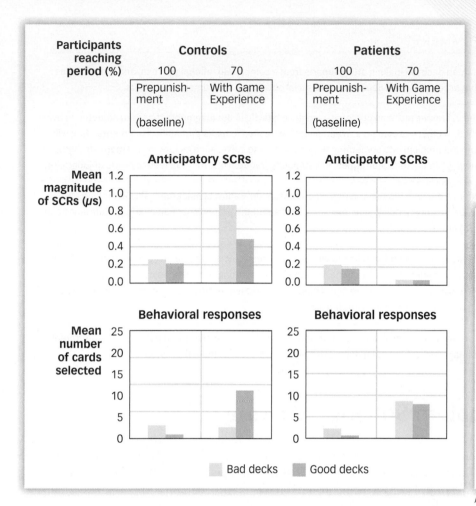

◄ Figure **9.12** **The Neuroscience of Risky Decision Making** In a study of risky decision making, researchers compared healthy controls' choices to those made by people with damage to the prefrontal cortex. Participants played a game in which they selected a card from one of four decks. Two of the decks were made up of riskier cards, that is, cards that provided large payoffs or large losses. The other two contained safer cards—those with much smaller payoffs and losses. At the beginning of the game, both groups chose cards from the two decks with equal frequency. Over the course of the game, the healthy controls avoided the bad decks and showed large emotional responses (SCRs, or skin conductance responses) when they even considered choosing a card from a risky deck. Participants with prefrontal brain damage, on the other hand, continued to choose cards from the two decks with equal frequency and showed no evidence of emotional learning and eventually went bankrupt.

After Bechara et al., 1997.

they could not shift their choices in response to a rising rate of losses or a declining rate of rewards (Bechara, Tranel, & Damasio, 2000). Interestingly, substance-dependent individuals, such as alcoholics and cocaine addicts, act the same way. Most perform as poorly on the gambling task as do individuals with prefrontal damage (Bechara et al., 2001). More recent work has extended these impairments on the gambling task across cultures to Chinese adolescents with binge-drinking problems (Johnson, Xiao, et al., 2008). These findings have potentially important implications for such everyday issues as road safety. A recent study focused on people who had been convicted of driving while impaired with alcohol (DWI). Offenders who performed poorly on the gambling task were much more likely to commit repeated DWI offenses than those who performed well on the gambling task (Bouchard, Brown, & Nadeau, 2012). Related recent work has documented gambling task impairments in binge eaters, another group in which there is an insensitivity to the future consequences of behavior (Danner et al., 2012)

Neuroimaging studies of healthy individuals have provided evidence that fits well with the earlier studies of individuals with damage to the prefrontal cortex: When performing the gambling task, an area in the prefrontal cortex is activated when participants need to make risky decisions as compared to safe decisions. Indeed, the activated region is in the part of the prefrontal cortex that is typically damaged in participants who perform poorly on the gambling task, and greater activation in this region is correlated with better task performance in healthy individuals (Fukui et al., 2005; Lawrence et al., 2009). Taken together, the neuroimaging and lesion studies show clearly that aspects of risky decision making depend critically on the contributions of the prefrontal cortex.

IN SUMMARY

▶ Human decision making often departs from a completely rational process, and the mistakes that accompany this departure tell us a lot about how the human mind works.

▶ The values we place on outcomes weigh so heavily in our judgments that they sometimes overshadow objective evidence. When people are asked to make probability judgments, they will turn the problem into something they know how to solve, such as judging memory strength, judging similarity to prototypes, or estimating frequencies. This can lead to errors of judgment.

▶ When a problem fits their mental algorithms, people show considerable skill at making appropriate judgments. In making a judgment about the probability of an event, performance can vary dramatically.

▶ Because we feel that avoiding losses is more important than achieving gains, framing effects can affect our choices. Emotional information also strongly influences our decision making, even when we are not aware of it. Although this influence can lead us astray, it often is crucial for making decisions in everyday life.

▶ The prefrontal cortex plays an important role in decision making, and patients with prefrontal damage make more risky decisions than do non-brain-damaged indiviuals.

Problem Solving: Working It Out

You have a problem when you find yourself in a place where you don't want to be. In such circumstances, you try to find a way to change the situation so that you end up in a situation you *do* want. Let's say that it's the night before a test, and you are trying to study but just can't settle down and focus on the material. This is a situation you don't want. So, you try to think of ways to help yourself focus. You might begin with the material that most interests you, or provide yourself with rewards, such as a music break or trip to the refrigerator. If these activities enable you to get down to work, your problem is solved.

Two major types of problems complicate our daily lives. The first and most frequent is the *ill-defined problem,* one that does not have a clear goal or well-defined solution paths. Your study block is an ill-defined problem: Your goal isn't clearly defined (i.e., somehow get focused), and the solution path for achieving the goal is even less clear (i.e., there are many ways to gain focus). Most everyday problems (being a better person, finding that special someone, achieving success) are ill defined. In contrast, a *well-defined problem* is one with clearly specified goals and clearly defined solution paths. Examples include following a clear set of directions to get to school, solving simple algebra problems, or playing a game of chess.

Means–Ends Analysis

In 1945, German psychologist Karl Duncker reported some important studies of the problem-solving process. He presented people with ill-defined problems and asked them to "think aloud" while solving them (Duncker, 1945). Based on what people said about how they solve problems, Duncker described problem solving in terms of **means–ends analysis**, *a process of searching for the means or steps to reduce the differences between the current situation and the desired goal.* This process usually took the following steps:

1. Analyze the goal state (i.e., the desired outcome you want to attain).
2. Analyze the current state (i.e., your starting point, or the current situation).

CORBIS COLLECTION/ALAMY

Even though it may not be easy to put together this Lego model, having instructions for assembly makes it a well-defined problem.

3. List the differences between the current state and the goal state.

4. Reduce the list of differences by
   - Direct means (a procedure that solves the problem without intermediate steps).
   - Generating a subgoal (an intermediate step on the way to solving the problem).
   - Finding a similar problem that has a known solution.

Consider, for example, one of Duncker's problems:

> A patient has an inoperable tumor in his abdomen. The tumor is inoperable because it is surrounded by healthy but fragile tissue that would be severely damaged during surgery. How can the patient be saved?

The *goal state* is a patient without the tumor and with undamaged surrounding tissue. The *current state* is a patient with an inoperable tumor surrounded by fragile tissue. The *difference* between these two states is the tumor. A *direct-means solution* would be to destroy the tumor with X-rays, but the required X-ray dose would destroy the fragile surrounding tissue and possibly kill the patient. A *subgoal* would be to modify the X-ray machine to deliver a weaker dose. After this subgoal is achieved, a direct-means solution could be to deliver the weaker dose to the patient's abdomen. But this solution won't work either: The weaker dose wouldn't damage the healthy tissue but also wouldn't kill the tumor. So, what to do? Find a similar problem that has a known solution. Let's see how this can be done.

Analogical Problem Solving

When we engage in **analogical problem solving,** we attempt to *solve a problem by finding a similar problem with a known solution and applying that solution to the current problem.* Consider the following story:

> An island surrounded by bridges is the site of an enemy fortress. The massive fortification is so strongly defended that only a very large army could overtake it. Unfortunately, the bridges would collapse under the weight of such a huge force. So, a clever general divides the army into several smaller units and sends the units over different bridges, timing the crossings so that the many streams of soldiers converge on the fortress at the same time and the fortress is taken.

Does this story suggest a solution to the tumor problem? It should. Removing a tumor and attacking a fortress are very different problems, but the two problems are analogous because they share a common structure: The *goal state* is a conquered fortress with undamaged surrounding bridges. The *current state* is an occupied fortress surrounded by fragile bridges. The *difference* between the two states is the occupying enemy. The *solution* is to divide the required force into smaller units that are light enough to spare the fragile bridges and send them down the bridges simultaneously so that they converge on the fortress. The combined units will form an army strong enough to take the fortress (see **FIGURE 9.13**).

This analogous problem of the island fortress suggests the following direct-means solution to the tumor problem:

> Surround the patient with X-ray machines and simultaneously send weaker doses that converge on the tumor. The combined strength of the weaker X-ray doses will be sufficient to destroy the tumor, but the individual doses will be weak enough to spare the surrounding healthy tissue.

Did this solution occur to you after reading the fortress story? In studies that have used the tumor problem, only 10% of participants spontaneously generated the correct solution. This percentage rose to 30% if participants read the island fortress problem or other analogous story. However, the success climbed dramatically to 75%

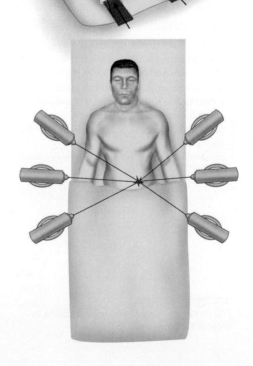

▼ Figure **9.13 Analogical Problem Solving**
Just as smaller, lighter battalions can reach the fortress without damaging the bridges, many small X-ray doses can destroy the tumor without harming the delicate surrounding tissue. In both cases, the additive strength achieves the objective.

among participants who had a chance to read more than one analogous problem or were given a deliberate hint to use the solution to the fortress story (Gick & Holyoak, 1980).

Why was the fortress problem so ineffective by it-self? Problem solving is strongly affected by superficial similarities between problems, and the relationship between the tumor and fortress problems lies deep in their structure (Catrambone, 2002).

> **Why are analogies useful in problem solving?**

Creativity and Insight

Analogical problem solving shows us that successfully solving a problem often depends on learning the principles underlying a particular type of problem and also that solving lots of problems improves our ability to recognize certain problem types and generate effective solutions. Some problem solving, however, seems to involve brilliant flashes of insight and creative solutions that have never before been tried. Creative and insightful solutions often rely on restructuring a problem so that it turns into a problem you already know how to solve (Cummins, 2012).

Genius and Insight

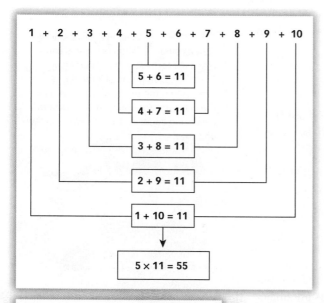

▲ Figure **9.14 Genius and Insight** Young Friedrich Gauss imagined the scheme shown here and quickly reduced a laborious addition problem to an easy multiplication task. Gauss's early insight led him to realize later an intriguing truth: This simple solution generalizes to number series of any length.

After Wertheimer, 1945/1982.

Consider the exceptional mind of the mathematician Friedrich Gauss (1777–1855). One day, Gauss's elementary schoolteacher asked the class to add up the numbers 1 through 10. While his classmates laboriously worked their sums, Gauss had a flash of insight that caused the answer to occur to him immediately. Gauss imagined the numbers 1 through 10 as weights lined up on a balance beam, as shown in **FIGURE 9.14**. Starting at the left, each "weight" increases by 1. In order for the beam to balance, each weight on the left must be paired with a weight on the right. You can see this by starting at the middle and noticing that $5 + 6 = 11$, then moving outward, $4 + 7 = 11$, $3 + 8 = 11$, and so on. This produces five number pairs that add up to 11. Now the problem is easy. Multiply. Gauss's genius lay in restructuring the problem in a way that allowed him to notice a very simple and elegant solution to an otherwise tedious task—a procedure, by the way, that generalizes to series of any length.

According to Gestalt psychologists, insights such as these reflect a spontaneous restructuring of a problem. A sudden flash of insight contrasts with incremental problem-solving procedures in which one gradually gets closer and closer to a solution. Early researchers studying insight found that people were more likely to solve a non-insight problem if they felt they were gradually getting "warmer" (incremen-

> **What is the role of the unconscious in flashes of insight?**

tally closer to the solution). But whether someone felt warm did not predict the likelihood of their solving an insight problem (Metcalfe & Wiebe, 1987). The solution for an insight problem seemed to appear out of the blue, regardless of what the participant felt.

Later research, however, suggests that sudden insightful solutions may actually result from unconscious incremental processes (Bowers et al., 1990). In one study, research participants were shown paired, three-word series like those in **FIGURE 9.15** and asked to find a fourth word that was associated with the three words in each series. However, only one series in each pair had a common associate. Solvable series were termed *coherent,* whereas those with no solution were called *incoherent.*

Even if participants couldn't find a solution, they could reliably decide, more than by chance alone, which of the pairs was coherent. However, if insightful solutions actually occur in a sudden, all-or-nothing manner, their performance should have been no better than chance. Thus, the findings suggest that even insightful problem solv-

functional fixedness
The tendency to perceive the functions of objects as fixed.

ing is an incremental process—one that occurs outside of conscious awareness. The process works something like this: The pattern of clues that constitute a problem unconsciously activates relevant information in memory. Activation then spreads through the memory network, recruiting additional relevant information (Bowers et al., 1990). When sufficient information has been activated, it crosses the threshold of awareness and we experience a sudden flash of insight into the problem's solution.

Finding a connection between the words *strawberry* and *traffic* might take some time, even for someone motivated to figure out how they are related. But if the word *strawberry* activates *jam* in long-term memory (see the Memory chapter) and the activation spreads from *strawberry* to *traffic,* the solution to the puzzle may suddenly spring into awareness without the thinker knowing how it got there. What would seem like a sudden insight would really result from an incremental process that consists of activation spreading through memory, adding new information as more knowledge is activated. Nonetheless, studies of brain activity during problem solving reveal striking differences between problems solved by sudden insight and those solved by using more deliberate strategies (see the Hot Science box).

Coherent	Incoherent
Playing	Still
Credit	Pages
Report	Music
Blank	Light
White	Folk
Lines	Head
ticket	Town
Shop	Root
Broker	Car
Magic	House
Plush	Lion
Floor	Butter
Base	Swan
Snow	Army
Dance	Mask
Gold	Noise
Stool	Foam
Tender	Shade

Solutions: Card, paper, pawn, carpet, ball, bar

▲ Figure **9.15 Insightful Solutions Are Really Incremental** Participants were asked to find a fourth word that was associated with the other three words in each series. Even if they couldn't find a solution, they could reliably choose which series of three words were solvable and which were not. Try to solve these.

After Bowers et al., 1990.

Functional Fixedness

If insight is a simple incremental process, why isn't its occurrence more frequent? In the research discussed previously, participants produced insightful solutions only 25% of the time. Insight is rare because problem solving (like decision making) suffers from framing effects. In problem solving, framing tends to limit the types of solutions that occur to us. **Functional fixedness**—*the tendency to perceive the functions of objects as fixed*—is a process that constricts our thinking. Look at **FIGURES 9.16** and **9.17** and see if you can solve the problems before reading on. In Figure 9.16, your task is to illuminate a dark room using the following objects: some thumbtacks, a box of matches, and a candle. In Figure 9.17, your task is to use the items on the table to find a way to hold on to a string hanging from the ceiling and at the same time reach a second string that is too far away to grasp.

▲ Figure **9.16 Functional Fixedness and the Candle Problem** How can you use these objects—a box of matches, thumbtacks, and a candle—to mount the candle on the wall so that it illuminates the room? Give this problem some thought before you check the answer in Figure 9.19 on page 388.

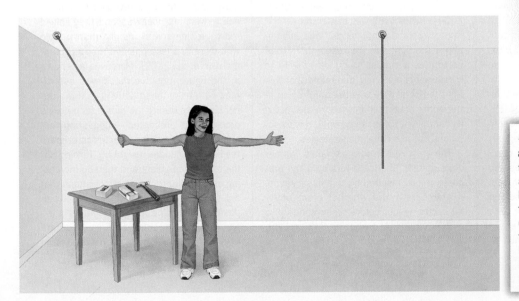

◀ Figure **9.17 Functional Fixedness and the String Problem** The strings hung from hooks on either side of the ceiling are long enough to be tied together, but they are positioned too far apart to reach one while holding on to the other. Using the tools shown on the table (nails, matches and a hammer), how can you accomplish the task? Compare your answer to that in Figure 9.20 on page 389.

▲ Figure **9.18 The Nine-Dot Problem** Connect all nine dots with four straight lines without lifting your pencil from the paper. Compare your answer to those in Figure 9.21 on page 391.

Difficulty solving these problems derives from our tendency to think of the objects only in terms of their normal, typical, or "fixed" functions. We don't think to use the matchbox for a candleholder because boxes typically hold matches, not candles. Similarly, using the hammer as a pendulum weight doesn't spring to mind because hammers are typically used to pound things. Did functional fixedness prevent you from solving these problems? (The solutions are shown in **FIGURES 9.19** and **9.20**.)

Sometimes framing limits our ability to generate a solution. Before reading on, look at **FIGURE 9.18**. Without lifting your pencil from the page, try to connect all nine dots with only four straight lines. To solve this problem, you must allow the lines you draw to extend outside the imaginary box that surrounds the dots (see **FIGURE 9.21**). This constraint does not reside in the problem but in the mind of the problem solver (Kershaw & Ohlsson, 2004). Despite the apparent sudden flash of insight that seems to yield a solution to problems of this type, research indicates that the thought processes people use when solving even this type of insight problem are best described as an incremental, means–ends analysis (MacGregor, Ormerod, & Chronicle, 2001).

Sudden Insight and the Brain

HOT SCIENCE

The "aha!" moment that accompanies a sudden flash of insight is a compelling experience, one that highlights that solving a problem based on insight *feels* radically different from solving it through step-by-step analysis or trial and error. This difference in subjective experience suggests that something different is going on in the brain when we solve a problem using insight instead of analytic strategies (Kounios & Beeman, 2009).

To examine brain activity associated with insight, researchers used a procedure called *compound remote associates* that is similar in some respects to the three-word problems displayed in Figure 9.15. Each compound remote associates problem consists of three words, such as *crab*, *pine*, and *sauce*. Sometimes people solve these problems with a flash of insight: The solution word (*apple!*) suddenly pops into their minds, seemingly out of nowhere. Other times, people solve the problem by using analytic strategies that involve trying out different alternatives generating a compound word for *crab* and then assessing whether they fit *pine* and *sauce*. *Crabgrass*, works, but grass doesn't work with *pine* and *sauce*. *Crabapple?* Problem solved.

Participants are instructed to press a button the moment a solution comes to mind, then describe whether they arrived at the solution via insight or through an analytic strategy. In an initial study, researchers used the electroencephalograph (EEG; see the Neuroscience chapter) to measure brain electrical activity as participants attempted to solve the problems. What they observed was striking: Beginning about one-third of a second before participants came up with a solution, there was a sudden and dramatic burst of high-frequency electrical activity (40 cycles per second or gamma band) for problems solved via insight as compared with problems solved via analytic strategies (Jung-Beeman et al., 2004). This activity was centered over the front part of the right temporal lobe, slightly above the right ear. The researchers then performed a similar study using fMRI to measure brain activity, and found that this right temporal area was the only region in the entire brain that showed greater activity for insight solutions compared with solutions based on analytic strategies.

The great French scientist Louis Pasteur once stated: "Chance favors only the prepared mind." Inspired by this observation, researchers asked whether brain activity occurring just before presentation of a problem influenced whether that problem was solved via insight or analytic strategies (Kounios et al., 2006). It did. In the moments before a problem was solved with an insight solution, there was increased activity deep in the frontal lobes, in a part of the brain known as the anterior cingulate, which controls cognitive processes such as the ability to switch attention from one thing to another. The researchers suggested that this increased activity in the anterior cingulate allowed participants to attend to and detect associations that were only weakly activated, perhaps at a subconscious level, and that facilitate sudden insight.

A related study with the compound remote associates task revealed that when people were in a positive mood, they solved more problems with insight than people who were in a less positive mood (Subramaniam et al., 2009). Moreover, as shown in the figure, positive mood was associated with heightened activity in the anterior cingulate during the moments before a problem was presented—suggesting that being in a positive mood helps to prepare the brain for sudden insight by "turning on" the anterior cingulate and thereby increasing one's ability to detect associations that aid problem solution. This link between positive mood and insight might help explain a striking recent finding: Moderate levels of alcohol intoxication resulted in

IN SUMMARY

▶ Like concept formation and decision making, problem solving is a process in which new inputs (in this case, problems) are interpreted in terms of old knowledge. Problems may be ill defined or well defined, leading to more or less obvious solutions.

▶ The solutions we generate depend as much on the organization of our knowledge as they do on the objective characteristics of the problems. Means–ends analysis and analogical problem solving offer pathways to effective solutions, although we often frame things in terms of what we already know and already understand.

▶ Sometimes, as in the case of functional fixedness, that knowledge can restrict our problem-solving processes, making it difficult to find solutions that should be easy to find.

enhanced performance on the remote associates task, and also produced a stronger feeling that problem solutions are the result of sudden insight (Jarosz, Colflesh, & Wiley, 2012). Alternatively, the beneficial effects of alcohol could be attributable to a reduction in controlled, focused processing, which frees up the ability to generate distant associations.

Brain activity prior to problem solving provides clues about which individuals are more likely to rely on insight over analytic strategies to solve compound remote associates (Kounios et al., 2008). Using EEG to measure resting brain activity, researchers found that insight problem solvers showed more resting activity in the right cerebral hemisphere than did analytic problem solvers, which is consistent with other research linking creativity with right-hemisphere activity (Folley & Park, 2005; Howard-Jones et al., 2005).

The results of these studies suggest that the familiar image of a light bulb going off in your head when you experience an "aha!" moment is on the mark: Those moments are indeed accompanied by something like an electrical power surge in the brain, and are preceded by specific types of electrical activity patterns. It seems likely that future research will tell us much more about how to turn on the mental light bulb and keep it burning bright.

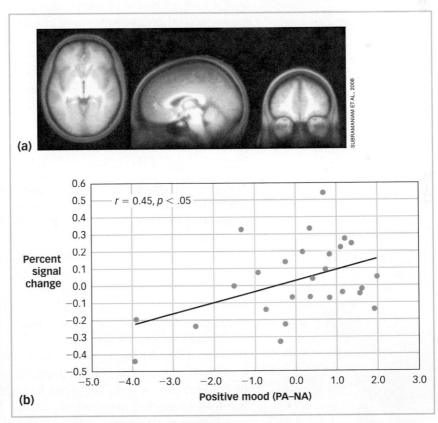

(a)

(b)

▲ (a) Being in a positive mood was associated with increased activity in the anterior cingulate (yellow area) in the moments before people solved a problem via sudden insight. (b) Positive mood (Positive Affect–Negative Affect) is associated with heightened activity in the anterior cingulate, suggesting an increase in one's ability to create associations needed for problem solving.

Transforming Information: How We Reach Conclusions

Reasoning is *a mental activity that consists of organizing information or beliefs into a series of steps in order to reach conclusions.* Not surprisingly, sometimes our reasoning seems sensible and straightforward, and other times it seems a little off. Consider some reasons offered by people who filed actual insurance accident claims (www. swapmeetdave.com):

> "I left for work this morning at 7:00 a.m. as usual when I collided straight into a bus. The bus was 5 minutes early."

> "Coming home, I drove into the wrong house and collided with a tree I don't have."

> "My car was legally parked as it backed into another vehicle."

> "The indirect cause of the accident was a little guy in a small car with a big mouth."

> "Windshield broke. Cause unknown. Probably voodoo."

When people like these hapless drivers argue with you in a way that seems inconsistent or poorly thought out, you may accuse them of being "illogical." Logic is a system of rules that specifies which conclusions follow from a set of statements. To put it another way, if you know that a given set of statements is true, logic will tell you which other statements *must* also be true. If the statement "Jack and Jill went up the hill" is true, then according to the rules of logic, the statement "Jill went up the hill" must also be true. To accept the truth of the first statement while denying the truth of the second statement would be a contradiction. Logic is a tool for evaluating reasoning, but it should not be confused with the process of reasoning itself. Equating logic and reasoning would be like equating carpenter's tools (logic) with building a house (reasoning).

Practical, Theoretical, and Syllogistic Reasoning

Earlier in the chapter, we discussed decision making, which often depends on reasoning with probabilities. Practical reasoning and theoretical reasoning also allow us to make decisions (Walton, 1990). **Practical reasoning** is *figuring out what to do, or reasoning directed toward action.* Means–ends analysis is one kind of practical reasoning. An example is figuring out how to get to a concert across town if you don't have a car. In contrast, **theoretical reasoning** (also called *discursive reasoning*) is *reasoning directed toward arriving at a belief.* We use theoretical reasoning when we try to determine which beliefs follow logically from other beliefs.

Suppose you asked your friend Bruce to take you to a concert, and he said that his car wasn't working. You'd undoubtedly find another way to get to the concert. If you then spied him driving into the concert parking lot, you might reason: "Bruce told me his car wasn't working. He just drove into the parking lot. If his car wasn't working, he couldn't drive it here. So, either he suddenly fixed it, or he was lying to me. If he was lying to me, he's not much of a friend." Notice the absence of an action-oriented goal. Theoretical reasoning is just a series of inferences concluding in a belief—in this case, about your so-called friend's unfriendliness!

If you concluded from these examples that we are equally adept at both types of reasoning, experimental evidence suggests you're wrong. People generally find figuring out what to do easier than deciding which beliefs follow logically from other beliefs. In cross-cultural studies, this tendency to respond practically when theoretical reasoning is sought has been demonstrated in individuals without schooling. Consider, for

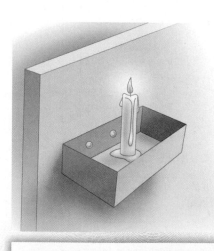

▲ Figure **9.19 The Solution to the Candle Problem** What makes this problem difficult is that the usual function of the box (to hold matches) interferes with recognizing that it can be tacked to the wall to serve as a candleholder.

example, this dialogue between a Nigerian rice farmer, a member of the preliterate Kpelle people, and an American researcher (Scribner, 1975, p. 155):

Experimenter: All Kpelle men are rice farmers. Mr. Smith (this is a Western name) is not a rice farmer. Is he a Kpelle man?

Farmer: I don't know the man in person. I have not laid eyes on the man himself.

Experimenter: Just think about the statement.

Farmer: If I know him in person, I can answer that question, but since I do not know him in person, I cannot answer that question.

Experimenter: Try and answer from your Kpelle sense.

Farmer: If you know a person, if a question comes up about him, you are able to answer. But if you do not know a person, if a question comes up about him, it's hard for you to answer it.

As this excerpt shows, the farmer does not seem to understand that the problem can be resolved with theoretical reasoning. Instead, he is concerned with retrieving and verifying facts, a strategy that does not work for this type of task.

A very different picture emerges when members of preliterate cultures are given tasks that require practical reasoning. One well-known study of rural Kenyans illustrates a typical result (Harkness, Edwards, & Super, 1981). The problem describes a dilemma in which a boy must decide whether to obey his father and give the family some of the money he has earned, even though his father previously promised that the boy could keep it all. After hearing the dilemma, the participants were asked what the boy should do. Here is a typical response from a villager:

> A child has to give you what you ask for just in the same way as when he asks for anything you give it to him. Why then should he be selfish with what he has? A parent loves his child and maybe the son refused without knowing the need of helping his father. . . . By showing respect to one another, friendship between us is assured, and as a result this will increase the prosperity of our family.

This preliterate individual had little difficulty understanding this practical problem. His response is intelligent, insightful, and well reasoned. A principal finding from this kind

What have cross-cultural studies shown us about reasoning tests?

of cross-cultural research is that the appearance of competency on reasoning tests depends more on whether the task makes sense to participants than on their problem-solving ability.

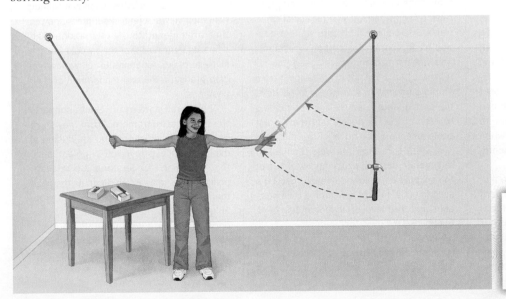

◄ Figure **9.20 The Solution to the String Problem** The usual function of the hammer (to pound things) interferes with recognizing that it can also serve as a weighted pendulum to swing the string into the person's grasp.

reasoning
A mental activity that consists of organizing information or beliefs into a series of steps in order to reach conclusions.

practical reasoning
Figuring out what to do, or reasoning directed toward action.

theoretical reasoning (or **discursive reasoning**) Reasoning directed toward arriving at a belief.

belief bias
People's judgments about whether to accept conclusions depend more on how believable the conclusions are than on whether the arguments are logically valid.

syllogistic reasoning
Determining whether a conclusion follows from two statements that are assumed to be true.

Educated individuals in industrial societies are prone to similar failures in reasoning, as illustrated by **belief bias:** *People's judgments about whether to accept conclusions depend more on how believable the conclusions are than on whether the arguments are logically valid* (Evans, Barston, & Pollard, 1983; see also The Real World Box). For example, in **syllogistic reasoning** assesses *whether a conclusion follows from two statements that are assumed to be true.* Consider the two following syllogisms, evaluate the argument, and ask yourself whether or not the conclusions must be true if the statements are true:

Syllogism 1

Statement 1: No cigarettes are inexpensive.

Statement 2: Some addictive things are inexpensive.

Conclusion: Some addictive things are not cigarettes.

From Zippers to Political Extremism: An Illusion of Understanding

Zippers are extremely helpful objects and we have all used them more times than we could possibly recall. Most of us also think that we have a pretty good understanding of how a zipper works—at least until we are asked to provide a step-by-step explanation. In experiments by Rozenblit and Keil (2002), participants initially rated the depth of their understanding of various everyday objects (e.g., zippers, flush toilets, sewing machines) or procedures (e.g., how to make chocolate cookies from scratch), tried to provide detailed, step-by-step explanations, viewed expert descriptions and diagrams, and then re-rated their depth of understanding. The second set of ratings was significantly lower than the first. Attempting to explain the workings of the objects and procedures, and then seeing the much more detailed expert description, led participants to realize that they had greatly overestimated the depth of their understanding, which Rozenblit and Keil referred to as *the illusion of explanatory depth.* Additional experiments revealed that the illusion of explanatory depth can occur as a consequence of attempting to generate detailed explanations even when expert descriptions are not subsequently provided.

Recent research suggests that the illusion of explanatory depth applies to a very different domain of everyday life: political extremism. Many pressing issues of our times, such as climate change and health care, share two features: They involve complex policies and tend to generate extreme

STEVE MILLER/SUPERSTOCK

views at either end of the political spectrum. Fernbach et al. (2013) asked whether polarized views occur because people think that they understand the relevant policies in greater depth than they actually do. To investigate this hypothesis, the researchers asked participants to rate their positions regarding six contemporary political policies (sanctions on Iran for its nuclear program, raising the retirement age for social security, single-payer health care system, cap-and-trade system for carbon emissions, national flat tax, and merit-based pay for teachers) on a 7-point scale ranging from *strongly against* to *strongly in favor.* Next, the participants rated their understanding of each of the six policies on the 7-point scale used previously by Rozenblit and Keil (2002). Participants were then asked to generate detailed explanations of two of the six policies, followed in each case by a second set of ratings concerning their positions and their level of understanding of all the policies.

Fernbach et al. (in press) found that after attempting to generate detailed explanations, participants provided lower ratings of

understanding and less extreme positions concerning all six policies than they had previously. Furthermore, those participants who exhibited the largest decreases in their pre- versus post-explanation understanding ratings also exhibited the greatest moderation of their positions as a result of explaining them. Were these changes simply a result of thinking more deeply about the policies, or were they specifically attributable to generating explanations? To address this issue, the researchers conducted an additional experiment in which some participants provided explanations of policies, whereas others listed reasons why they held their positions. Once again, generating explanations led to lower understanding ratings and less extreme positions. However, no such changes were observed in participants who listed reasons why they held their views. A final experiment showed that after generating explanations, participants indicated that they would be less likely to make donations to relevant advocate groups, reflecting moderation of their positions.

The overall pattern of results supports the idea that extreme political views are enabled, at least in part, by an illusion of explanatory depth: Once people realize that they don't understand the relevant policy issues in as much depth as they had thought, their views moderate. There probably aren't too many psychological phenomena that are well-illustrated by both political policies and the workings of zippers, but the illusion of explanatory depth is one of them.

Syllogism 2

Statement 1: No addictive things are inexpensive.

Statement 2: Some cigarettes are inexpensive.

Conclusion: Some cigarettes are not addictive.

If you're like most people, you probably concluded that the reasoning is valid in Syllogism 1 but flawed in Syllogism 2. Indeed, researchers found that nearly 100% of participants accepted the first conclusion as valid, but fewer than half accepted the second (Evans, Barston, & Pollard, 1983). But notice that the syllogisms are in exactly the same form. This form of syllogism is valid, so both conclusions are valid. Evidently, the believability of the conclusions influences people's judgments.

Reasoning and the Brain

Research using fMRI provides novel insights into belief biases on reasoning tasks. In *belief-laden* trials, participants were scanned while they reasoned about syllogisms that could be influenced by knowledge affecting the believability of the conclusions. In *belief-neutral* trials, syllogisms contained obscure terms whose meanings were unknown to participants, as in the following example:

Syllogism 3

Statement 1: No codes are highly complex.

Statement 2: Some quipu are highly complex.

Conclusion: No quipu are codes.

Belief-neutral reasoning activated different brain regions than did belief-laden reasoning (as shown in **FIGURE 9.22**). Activity in a part of the left temporal lobe involved in retrieving and selecting facts from long-term memory increased during belief-laden reasoning. In contrast, that part of the brain showed little activity and parts of the parietal lobe involved in mathematical reasoning and spatial representation showed greater activity during belief-neutral reasoning (Goel & Dolan, 2003). This evidence suggests that participants took different approaches to the two types of reasoning tasks, relying on previously encoded memories in belief-laden reasoning and on more abstract thought processes in belief-neutral reasoning. These findings fit with other results from neuroimaging studies indicating that there is no single reasoning center in the brain; different types of reasoning tasks call on distinct processes that are associated with different brain regions (Goel, 2007).

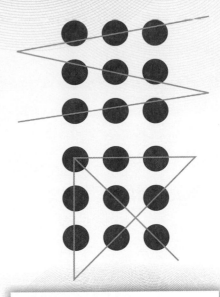

▲ Figure **9.21 Two Solutions to the Nine-Dot Problem** Solving this problem requires "thinking outside the box," that is, going outside the imaginary box implied by the dot arrangement. The limiting box isn't really there; it is imposed by the problem solver's perceptual set.

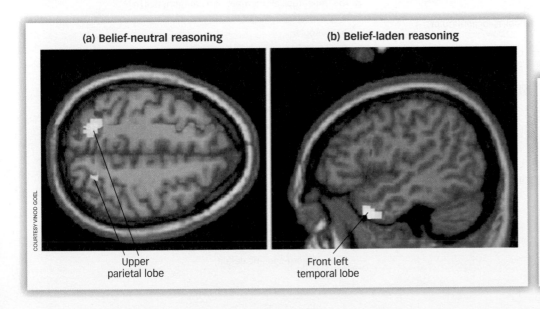

(a) Belief-neutral reasoning   (b) Belief-laden reasoning

Upper parietal lobe

Front left temporal lobe

COURTESY VINOD GOEL

◀ Figure **9.22 Active Brain Regions in Reasoning** These images from an fMRI study show that different types of reasoning activate different brain regions. Areas within the parietal lobe (*a*) were especially active during logical reasoning that is not influenced by prior beliefs (belief-neutral reasoning), whereas (*b*) shows an area within the left temporal lobe showed enhanced activity during reasoning that was influenced by prior beliefs (belief-laden reasoning). This suggests that people approach each type of reasoning problem in a different way.

IN SUMMARY

► The success of human reasoning depends on the content of the argument or scenario under consideration. People seem to excel at practical reasoning while stumbling when theoretical reasoning requires evaluation of the truth of a set of arguments.

► Belief bias describes a distortion of judgments about conclusions of arguments, causing people to focus on the believability of the conclusions rather than on the logical connections between the premises.

► Neuroimaging provides evidence that different brain regions are associated with different types of reasoning.

► We can see here and elsewhere in the chapter that some of the same strategies that earlier helped us to understand perception, memory, and learning—carefully examining errors and trying to integrate information about the brain into our psychological analyses—are equally helpful in understanding thought and language.

Chapter Review

KEY CONCEPT QUIZ

1. The combining of words to form phrases and sentences is governed by
   a. phonological rules.
   b. morphological rules.
   c. structural rules.
   d. syntactical rules.

2. Which of the following statements about language development is inaccurate?
   a. Language acquisition is largely a matter of children imitating adult speech.
   b. Deep structure refers to the meaning of a sentence, while surface structure refers to how it is constructed.
   c. By the time the average child begins school, a vocabulary of 10,000 words is not unusual.
   d. Children's passive mastery of language develops faster than their active mastery.

3. Language development as an innate, biological capacity is explained by
   a. fast mapping.
   b. behaviorism.
   c. nativist theory.
   d. interactionist explanations.

4. A collection of processes that facilitate language learning is referred to as
   a. phonological rules.
   b. dysphasia.
   c. a language acquisition device.
   d. grammatical generalizations.

5. Damage to the brain region called Broca's area results in
   a. failure to comprehend language.
   b. difficulty in producing grammatical speech.
   c. the reintroduction of infant babbling.
   d. difficulties in writing.

6. The linguistic relativity hypothesis maintains that
   a. language and thought are separate cognitive phenomena.
   b. words have different meanings to different cultures.
   c. human language is too complex for nonhuman animals to acquire.
   d. language shapes the nature of thought.

7. The "most typical" member of a category is a(n)
   a. prototype.
   b. exemplar.
   c. concept.
   d. definition.

8. Which theory of how we form concepts is based on our judgment of features that appear to be characteristic of category members but may not be possessed by every member?
   a. prototype theory
   b. family resemblance theory
   c. exemplar theory
   d. heuristic theory

9. The inability to recognize objects that belong to a particular category, athough the ability to recognize objects outside the category is undisturbed is called
   a. category-preferential organization.
   b. cognitive-visual deficit.
   c. a category-specific deficit.
   d. aphasia.

10. Making use of which of the following would most likely lead to a solution to a problem?
    a. rational choice theory
    b. probability
    c. a heuristic
    d. an algorithm

11. People give different answers to the same problem depending on how the problem is phrased because of
    a. the availability bias.
    b. the conjunction fallacy.
    c. the representativeness heuristic.
    d. framing effects.

12. The view that people choose to take on risk when evaluating potential losses and avoid risks when evaluating potential gains describes
    a. expected utility.
    b. the frequency format hypothesis.
    c. prospect theory.
    d. the sunk-cost fallacy.

13. People with damage to the prefrontal cortex are prone to
    a. heightened anticipatory emotional reactions.
    b. risky decision making.
    c. galvanic skin response.
    d. extreme sensitivity to behavioral consequences.

14. Miranda decides on a goal, analyzes her current situation, lists the differences between her current situation and her goal, then settles on strategies to reduce those differences. Miranda is engaging in
    a. means–ends analysis.
    b. analogical problem solving.
    c. capitalizing on insight.
    d. functional fixedness.

15. What kind of reasoning is aimed at deciding on a course of action?
    a. theoretical
    b. belief
    c. syllogistic
    d. practical

KEY TERMS

language (p. 352)
grammar (p. 352)
phoneme (p. 353)
phonological rules (p. 353)
morphemes (p. 353)
morphological rules (p. 353)
syntactical rules (p. 354)
deep structure (p. 354)
surface structure (p. 354)
fast mapping (p. 356)
telegraphic speech (p. 357)

nativist theory (p. 360)
language acquisition device (LAD)
    (p. 360)
genetic dysphasia (p. 360)
aphasia (p. 362)
linguistic relativity hypothesis
    (p. 367)
concept (p. 369)
family resemblance theory (p. 370)
prototype (p. 370)
exemplar theory (p. 371)

category-specific deficit (p. 372)
rational choice theory (p. 374)
availability bias (p. 375)
heuristic (p. 375)
algorithm (p. 375)
conjunction fallacy (p. 376)
representativeness heuristic
    (p. 377)
framing effects (p. 377)
sunk-cost fallacy (p. 377)
prospect theory (p. 378)

frequency format hypothesis
    (p. 379)
means–ends analysis (p. 382)
analogical problem solving (p. 383)
functional fixedness (p. 385)
reasoning (p. 388)
practical reasoning (p. 388)
theoretical reasoning (or discursive
    reasoning) (p. 388)
belief bias (p. 390)
syllogistic reasoning (p. 390)

CHANGING MINDS

1. You mention to a friend that you've just learned that the primary language we learn can shape the way that we think. You're friend says that people are people everywhere, and that this can't be true. What evidence could you describe to support your point?

2. In September, 2011, *Wired* magazine ran an article discussing the fourth-down decisions of NFL coaches. On fourth down, a coach can choose to play aggressively and go for a first down (or even a touchdown), or the coach can settle for a punt or a field goal, which are

safer options but result in fewer points than a touchdown. Statistically, the riskier play results in greater point gain, on average, than playing it safe. But in reality, coaches choose the safer plays over 90% of the time. Reading this article, one of your friends is incredulous. "Coaches aren't stupid, and they want to win," he says. "Why would they always make the wrong decision?" Your friend is assuming that humans are rational decision makers. In what ways is your friend wrong? What might be causing the irrational decision making by football coaches?

ANSWERS TO KEY CONCEPT QUIZ

1. d; 2. a; 3. c; 4. c; 5. b; 6. d; 7. a; 8. b; 9. c; 10. d; 11. d; 12. c;
13. b; 14. a; 15. d.

Need more help? Additional resources are located in LaunchPad at:
http://www.worthpublishers.com/launchpad/ schacter3e

Intelligence

WHEN ANNE MCGARRAH DIED at the age of 57, she had lived more years than she could count. That's because Anne couldn't count at all. Like most people with Williams syndrome, she couldn't add 3 and 7, couldn't make change for a dollar, and couldn't distinguish right from left. Her disability was so severe that she was unable to care for herself or hold a full-time job. So what did she do with her time?

I love to read. Biographies, fiction, novels, different articles in newspapers, articles in magazines, just about anything. I just read a book about a young girl—she was born in Scotland—and her family who lived on a farm. . . . I love listening to music. I like a little bit of Beethoven, but I specifically like Mozart and Chopin and Bach. I like the way they develop their music—it's very light, it's very airy, and it's very cheerful music. I find Beethoven depressing. (Finn, 1991, p. 54)

Although people with Williams syndrome are often unable to tie their own shoes or make their own beds, they typically have gifts for music and language. Williams syndrome is caused by the absence of 20 genes on chromosome 7. No one knows why this tiny genetic glitch so profoundly impairs people's general cognitive abilities, yet leaves them with a few special talents.

People with Williams syndrome have a distinct "elfin" facial appearance and diminished cognitive abilities, but they often have unusual gifts for music and language.

intelligence
The ability to direct one's thinking, adapt to one's circumstances, and learn from one's experiences.

WAS ANNE MCGARRAH INTELLIGENT? IT SEEMS ODD TO SAY that someone is intelligent when she can't do simple addition. But it seems equally odd to say that someone is unintelligent when she can articulate the difference between baroque counterpoint and 19th-century romanticism. In a world of Albert Einsteins and Homer Simpsons, we'd have no trouble distinguishing the geniuses from the dullards. But ours is a world of people like Anne McGarrah and people like us: people who are sometimes brilliant, often bright, usually competent, and occasionally dimmer than broccoli. Which forces us to ask the hard question: What exactly *is* intelligence? About 20 years ago, 52 scientific experts came together to answer this very question, and they concluded that **intelligence** is *the ability to direct one's thinking, adapt to one's circumstances, and learn from one's experiences* (Gottfredson, 1997). As you will see, that definition captures much of what scientists and laypeople mean when they use that term.

For more than a century, psychologists have been asking four questions about intelligence: *How* can it be measured? *What* exactly is it? *Where* does it come from? *Who* has it and who doesn't? As you'll see, intelligence is a set of abilities that can be measured quite accurately, it is the product of both genes and experience, and it is something that some people and some groups have more of than others.

How Can Intelligence Be Measured?

Few things are more dangerous than a man with a mission. In the 1920s, psychologist Henry Goddard administered intelligence tests to arriving immigrants at Ellis Island and concluded that the overwhelming majority of Jews, Hungarians, Italians, and Russians were "feebleminded." Goddard also used his tests to identify feebleminded American families (whom, he claimed, were largely responsible for the nation's social problems) and suggested that the government should segregate them in isolated colonies and "take away from these people the power of procreation" (Goddard, 1913, p. 107). The United States subsequently passed laws restricting the immigration of people from Southern and Eastern Europe, and 27 states passed laws requiring the sterilization of "mental defectives."

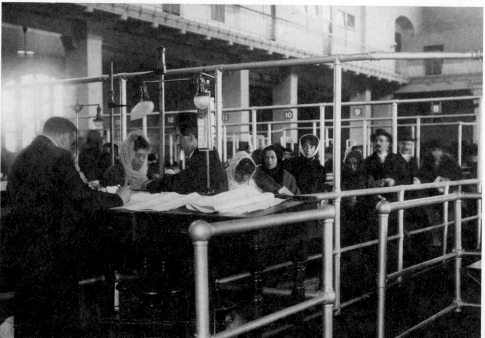

When immigrants arrived at Ellis Island in the 1920s, they were given intelligence tests, which supposedly revealed whether they were "feebleminded."

©BETTMANN/CORBIS

From Goddard's day to our own, intelligence tests have been used to rationalize prejudice and discrimination against people of different races, religions, and nationalities. Although intelligence testing has achieved many notable successes, its history is marred by more than its share of fraud and disgrace (Chorover, 1980; Lewontin, Rose, & Kamin, 1984). The fact that intelligence tests have occasionally been used to further detestable ends is especially ironic because, as you are about to see, such tests were originally developed for the most noble of purposes: to help underprivileged children succeed in school.

The Intelligence Quotient

At the end of the 19th century, France instituted a sweeping set of education reforms that made a primary school education available to children of every social class, and suddenly French classrooms were filled with a diverse mix of children who differed dramatically in their readiness to learn. The French government called on Alfred Binet and Theodore Simon to create a test that would allow educators to develop remedial programs for those children who lagged behind their peers (Siegler, 1992).

Why were intelligence tests originally developed?

"Before these children could be educated," Binet (1909) wrote, "they had to be selected. How could this be done?"

Binet and Simon worried that if teachers were allowed to do the selecting, then the remedial classrooms would be filled with poor children, and that if parents were allowed to do the selecting, then the remedial classrooms would be empty. So they set out to develop an objective test that would provide an unbiased measure of a child's ability. They began, sensibly enough, by looking for tasks that the best students in a class could perform and that the worst students could not—in other words, tasks that could distinguish the best and worst students and thus predict a future child's success in school. The tasks they tried included solving logic problems, remembering words, copying pictures, distinguishing edible and inedible foods, making rhymes, and answering questions such as, "When anyone has offended you and asks you to excuse him, what ought you to do?" Binet and Simon settled on 30 of these tasks and assembled them into a test that they claimed could measure a child's "natural intelligence." What did they mean by that phrase?

Alfred Binet (1857–1911; *left*) and Theodore Simon (1872–1961; *right*) developed the first intelligence test to identify children who needed remedial education.

> We here separate natural intelligence and instruction . . . by disregarding, insofar as possible, the degree of instruction which the subject possesses. . . . We give him nothing to read, nothing to write, and submit him to no test in which he might succeed by means of rote learning. In fact, we do not even notice his inability to read if a case occurs. It is simply the level of his natural intelligence that is taken into account. (Binet, 1905)

Binet and Simon designed their test to measure a child's *aptitude* for learning independent of the child's prior educational *achievement,* and it was in this sense that they called theirs a test of natural intelligence. They suggested that teachers could use their test to estimate a particular child's "mental level" simply by computing the average test score of many children in different age groups and then finding the age group whose average test score was most like that of the particular child's. For example, a child who was 10 years old but whose score was about the same as the score of the average 8-year-old was considered to have the mental level of an 8-year-old and thus to need remedial education.

The magazine columnist Marilyn vos Savant is said to have the world's highest measured IQ. The relatively stupid guy standing next to her is her husband, Dr. Robert Jarvik, who was one of the early inventors of the artificial heart.

German psychologist William Stern (1914) suggested that this mental level could be thought of as a child's *mental age* and that the best way to determine whether a child was developing normally was to examine the ratio of the child's mental age to the child's physical age. American psychologist Lewis Terman (1916) formalized this comparison by developing a statistic called *the intelligence quotient* or *IQ score*. There are two ways to compute an IQ score, each of which has a unique problem.

> **How do the two kinds of intelligence quotients differ?**

> ▶ **Ratio IQ** *is a statistic obtained by dividing a person's mental age by the person's physical age and then multiplying the quotient by 100.* According to this formula, a 10-year-old child whose test score was about the same as the average 10-year-old child's test score would have a ratio IQ of 100 because $(10/10) \times 100 = 100$. But a 10-year-old child whose test score was about the same as the average 8-year-old child's test score would have a ratio IQ of 80 because $(8/10) \times 100 = 80$. So what's the problem? Well, a 7-year-old who performs like the average 14-year-old has a ratio IQ of 200, and that high score seems reasonable because a 7-year-old who can do algebra is obviously pretty smart. But a 20-year-old who performs like the average 40-year-old will also have a ratio IQ of 200, and that doesn't seem very reasonable at all.

> ▶ **Deviation IQ** is a *statistic obtained by dividing a person's test score by the average test score of people in the same age group and then multiplying the quotient by 100.* According to this formula, a person who scored the same as the average person his or her age would have a deviation IQ of 100. The deviation IQ overcomes the problem with the ratio IQ inasmuch as a 20-year-old who scores like the average 40-year-old is not mistakenly labeled a genius. Alas, the deviation IQ has a different problem: It does not allow us to compare people of different ages. A 5-year-old and a 65-year-old might both have a deviation IQ of 100 because they both scored the same as their average peer, but that does not mean that the 5-year-old and 65-year-old are equally intelligent. Which one is smarter? We can't tell by comparing deviation IQs.

Each of the methods for computing IQ has a problem—but luckily, each has a different problem so they can be used in combination. Psychologists typically compute ratio IQ when testing children and compute deviation IQ when testing adults.

The Intelligence Test

Most modern intelligence tests have their roots in the test developed more than a century ago by Binet and Simon. For instance, the *Stanford–Binet Intelligence Scale* is based on Binet and Simon's original test and was initially updated by Lewis Terman and his colleagues at Stanford University. Probably the most widely used modern intelligence test is the *Wechsler Adult Intelligence Scale* (WAIS), named after its originator, psychologist David Wechsler. Like Binet and Simon's original test, it measures intelligence by asking respondents to answer questions and solve problems. Respondents are required to see similarities and differences between ideas and objects, to draw inferences from evidence, to work out and apply rules, to remember and manipulate material, to construct shapes, to articulate the meaning of words, to recall general knowledge, to explain practical actions in everyday life, to use numbers, to attend to details, and so forth. In the spirit of Binet and Simon's early test, none of the tests require writing words. Some sample problems from the WAIS are shown in **TABLE 10.1**.

These sample problems may look to you like fun and games (perhaps minus the fun part), but decades of research show that a person's performance on tests like the WAIS predict a wide variety of important life outcomes (Deary, Batty, & Gale, 2008; Deary, Batty, Pattie, & Gale, 2008; Der, Batty, & Deary, 2009; Gottfredson & Deary,

ratio IQ
A statistic obtained by dividing a person's mental age by the person's physical age and then multiplying the quotient by 100 (see *deviation IQ*).

deviation IQ
A statistic obtained by dividing a person's test score by the average test score of people in the same age group and then multiplying the quotient by 100 (see *ratio IQ*).

Table 10.1

The Tests and Core Subtests of the Wechsler Adult Intelligence Scale IV

WAIS-IV Test	Core Subtest	Questions and Tasks
Verbal Comprehension Test	Vocabulary	The test taker is asked to tell the examiner what certain words mean. For example: *chair* (easy), *hesitant* (medium), and *presumptuous* (hard).
	Similarities	The test taker is asked what 19 pairs of words have in common. For example: In what way are an apple and a pear alike? In what way are a painting and a symphony alike?
	Information	The test taker is asked several general knowledge questions. These cover people, places, and events. For example: How many days are in a week? What is the capital of France? Name three oceans. Who wrote *The Inferno*?
Perceptual Reasoning Test	Block Design	The test taker is shown 2-D patterns made up of red and white squares and triangles and is asked to reproduce these patterns using cubes with red and white faces.
	Matrix Reasoning	The test taker is asked to add a missing element to a pattern so that it progresses logically. For example: Which of the four symbols at the bottom goes in the empty cell of the table?
	Visual Puzzles	The test taker is asked to complete visual puzzles like this one: "Which three of these pictures go together to make this puzzle?"
Working Memory Test	Digit Span	The test taker is asked to repeat a sequence of numbers. Sequences run from two to nine numbers in length. In the second part of this test, the sequences must be repeated in reversed order. An easy example is to repeat 3-7-4. A harder one is 3-9-1-7-4-5-3-9.
	Arithmetic	The test taker is asked to solve arithmetic problems, progressing from easy to difficult ones.
Processing Speed Test	Symbol Search	The test taker is asked to indicate whether one of a pair of abstract symbols is contained in a list of abstract symbols. There are many of these lists, and the test taker does as many as he or she can in 2 minutes.
	Coding	The test taker is asked to write down the number that corresponds to a code for a given symbol (e.g., a cross, a circle, and an upside-down T) and does as many as he or she can in 90 seconds.

2004; Leon et al., 2009; Richards et al., 2009; Rushton & Templer, 2009; Whalley & Deary, 2001). For example, intelligence test scores are excellent predictors of income. One study compared siblings who had significantly different IQs and found that the less intelligent sibling earned roughly half of what the more intelligent sibling earned over the course of their lifetimes (Murray, 2002; see **FIGURE 10.1**).

What important life outcomes do intelligence test scores predict?

One reason for this is that intelligent people have a variety of traits that promote economic success. For example, they are more patient, they are better at calculating risk, and they are better at predicting how other people will act and how they should respond (Burks et al., 2009). But the main reason why intelligent people earn much more money than their less intelligent counterparts (or siblings!) is that they get more education (Deary et al., 2005; Nyborg & Jensen, 2001). In fact, a person's IQ is

In 2012, 4-year old Heidi Hankins became one of the youngest people every admitted to Mensa, an organization for people with unusually high IQs. Heidi's IQ is 159—about the same as Albert Einstein's.

SOLENT NEWS/REX FEATURES/AP PHOTO

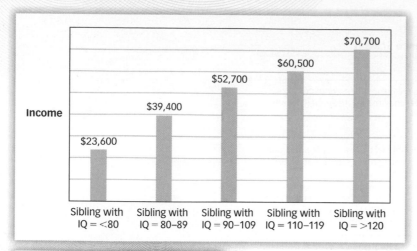

▲ Figure **10.1** **Income and Intelligence among Siblings** This graph shows the average annual salary of a person who has an IQ of 90–109 (shown in pink) and of his or her siblings who have higher or lower IQs (shown in blue).

a better predictor of the amount of education he or she will receive than is the person's social class (Deary, 2012; Deary et al., 2005). Intelligent people spend more time in school and perform better when they're there: The correlation between IQ and academic performance is roughly $r = .50$ across a wide range of people and situations. This continues after school ends. Intelligent people perform so much better at their jobs (Hunter & Hunter, 1984) that one pair of researchers concluded that "for hiring employees without previous experience in the job, the most valid measure of future performance and learning is general mental ability" (Schmidt & Hunter, 1998, p. 262; see the Real World box).

Intelligent people aren't just wealthier, they are healthier as well. Researchers who have followed millions of people over decades have found a strong correlation between intelligence and both health and longevity. Intelligent people are less likely to smoke and drink alcohol, and are more likely to exercise and eat well (Batty et al., 2007; Weiser et al., 2010). Not surprisingly, they also live longer. In fact, every 15 point increase in a young person's IQ is associated with a 24% decrease in his or her ultimate risk of death from a wide variety of causes, including cardiovascular disease, suicide, homicide, and accidents (Calvin et al., 2010). Health and wealth are related, of course, and some data

THE REAL WORLD

Look Smart

Your interview is in 30 minutes. You've checked your hair twice, eaten your weight in breath mints, combed your résumé for typos, and rehearsed your answers to all the standard questions. Now you have to dazzle them with your intelligence whether you've got it or not. Because intelligence is one of the most valued of all human traits, we are often in the business of trying to make others think we're smart regardless of whether that's true. So we make clever jokes and drop the names of some of the longer books we've read in the hope that prospective employers, prospective dates, prospective customers, and prospective in-laws will be appropriately impressed.

But are we doing the right things, and if so, are we getting the credit we deserve? Research shows that ordinary people are, in fact, reasonably good judges of other people's intelligence (Borkenau & Liebler, 1995). For example, observers can look at a pair of photographs and reliably determine which of the two people in them is smarter (Zebrowitz et al., 2002). When observers watch 1-minute videotapes of different people engaged in social interactions, they can accurately estimate which

person has the highest IQ—even if they see the videos without sound (Murphy, Hall, & Colvin, 2003).

People base their judgments of intelligence on a wide range of cues, from physical features (being tall and attractive) to dress (being well groomed and wearing glasses) to behavior (walking and talking quickly). And yet, none of these cues is

AP PHOTO/TIM JOHNSON

actually a reliable indicator of a person's intelligence. The reason why people are such good judges of intelligence is that in addition to all these useless cues, they also take into account one very useful cue: eye gaze. As it turns out, intelligent people hold the gaze of their conversation partners both when they are speaking and when they are listening, and observers know this, which is what enables them to estimate a person's intelligence accurately, despite their mythical beliefs about the informational value of spectacles and neckties (Murphy et al., 2003). All of this is especially true when the observers are women (who tend to be better judges of intelligence) and the people being observed are men (whose intelligence tends to be easier to judge).

The bottom line? Breath mints are fine and a little gel on the cowlick certainly can't hurt, but when you get to the interview, don't forget to stare.

◄ Wahad Mehood is interviewing for a job as a petroleum engineer with EPC Global. Studies show that when a job candidate holds an interviewer's gaze, the interviewer is more likely to consider the candidate to be intelligent. And the interviewer is right!

suggest that intelligence promotes longevity by allowing people to succeed in school, which allows them to get better jobs, which allows them to earn more money, which allows them to avoid illnesses such as cardiovascular disease (Deary, Weiss, & Batty, 2011). However it happens, the bottom line is clear: Intelligence matters.

Intelligence is highly correlated with income. Ken Jennings has won more money on television game shows than any other human being—over three million dollars. He was defeated just twice on *Jeopardy*: in 2004 by Nancy Zerg, and in 2011 by an IBM computer named Watson. (In response to being beaten by a machine Jennings graciously said, "I for one welcome our new computer overlords").

IN SUMMARY

▶ *Intelligence* is a mental ability that enables people to direct their thinking, adapt to their circumstances, and learn from their experiences.

▶ Intelligence tests produce a score known as an *intelligence quotient* or IQ. *Ratio IQ* is the ratio of a person's mental to physical age and *deviation IQ* is the deviation of a person's test score from the average score of his or her peers.

▶ Intelligence test scores predict a variety of important life outcomes, such as scholastic performance, job performance, health, and wealth.

What Is Intelligence?

During the 1990s, Michael Jordan won the National Basketball Association's Most Valuable Player award five times, led the Chicago Bulls to six league championships, and had the highest regular season scoring average in the history of the game. The Associated Press named him the second-greatest athlete of the century, and ESPN named him the first. So when Jordan quit professional basketball in 1993 to join professional baseball, he was as surprised as anyone to find that he—well, there's really no way to say this nicely—sucked. One of his teammates lamented that Jordan "couldn't hit a curveball with an ironing board," and a major-league manager called him "a disgrace to the game" (Wulf, 1994). Given his lackluster performance, it's no wonder that Jordan gave up baseball after just one season and returned to basketball, where he led his team to three consecutive championships.

Michael Jordan's brilliance on the basketball court and his mediocrity on the baseball field proved beyond all doubt that these two sports require different abilities that are not necessarily possessed by the same individual. But if basketball and baseball require different abilities, then what does it mean to say that someone is the greatest athlete of the century? Is *athleticism* a meaningless abstraction? The science of intelligence has grappled with a similar question for more than a hundred years. As we have seen, intelligence test scores predict important outcomes, from academic success to longevity. But is that because they measure a real property of the human mind, or is intelligence just a meaningless abstraction?

Michael Jordan was an extraordinary basketball player and a mediocre baseball player. So was he or wasn't he a great athlete?

A Hierarchy of Abilities

Charles Spearman was a student of Wilhelm Wundt (who founded the first experimental psychology laboratory), and he set out to answer precisely this question. Spearman invented a technique known as **factor analysis**, which is *a statistical technique that explains a large number of correlations in terms of a small number of underlying factors*. (We'll get into a bit more detail about this in the next section.) Although Spearman's technique was complex, his reasoning was simple: If there really is a single, general ability called *intelligence* that enables people to perform a variety of intelligent behaviors, then those who have this ability should do well at just about everything

factor analysis
A statistical technique that explains a large number of correlations in terms of a small number of underlying factors.

two-factor theory of intelligence
Spearman's theory suggesting that every task requires a combination of a general ability (which he called *g*) and skills that are specific to the task (which he called *s*).

COURTESY CHRIS QUEEN

Dr. Jennifer Richeson received a so-called genius award from the MacArthur Foundation for her research in social psychology. Spearman's notion of general ability suggests that because she's *really* good at science, then she's probably at least *pretty* good at many other things, such as dancing. And in fact, she is!

and those who lack it should do well at just about nothing. In other words, if intelligence is a single, general ability, then there should be a very strong positive correlation between people's performances on all kinds of tests.

To find out if there was, Spearman (1904) measured how well school-age children could discriminate small differences in color, auditory pitch, and weight, and he then correlated these scores with the children's grades in different academic subjects as well as with their teachers' estimates of their intellectual ability. His research revealed two things. First, it revealed that most of these measures were indeed positively correlated: Children who scored high on one measure (e.g., distinguishing the musical note C-sharp from D) tended to score high on the other measures (e.g., solving algebraic equations). Some psychologists have called this finding "the most replicated result in all of psychology" (Deary, 2000, p. 6), and in fact, even *mice* show a strong positive correlation between performances on different kinds of cognitive tests (Matzel et al., 2003). Second, Spearman's research revealed that although different measures were positively correlated, they were not perfectly correlated: The child who had the very highest score on one measure didn't necessarily have the very highest score on *every* measure. Spearman combined these two facts into a **two-factor theory of intelligence**, which suggested that *every task requires a combination of a general ability* (g) *and skills that are specific to the task* (s).

As sensible as Spearman's conclusions were, not everyone agreed with them. Louis Thurstone (1938) noticed that, although scores on most tests were indeed positively correlated, scores on one kind of verbal test were more highly correlated with scores on another kind of verbal test than they were with scores on perceptual tests. Thurstone took this "clustering of correlations" to mean that there was actually no such thing as *g* and that there were, instead, a few stable and independent mental abilities such as perceptual ability, verbal ability, and numerical ability, which he called the *primary mental abilities*. These primary mental abilities were neither general like *g* (e.g., a person might have strong verbal abilities and weak numerical abilities), nor specific like *s* (e.g., a person who had strong verbal abilities tended both to speak and read well). In essence, Thurstone argued that just as we have games called *baseball* and *basketball* but no game called *athletics,* so we have abilities such as verbal ability and perceptual ability but no general ability called intelligence. **TABLE 10.2** shows the primary mental abilities that Thurstone identified.

The debate among Spearman, Thurstone, and other mathematical giants was quite technical, and it raged for half a century as psychologists debated the existence of *g*. But in the 1980s, a new mathematical technique called *confirmatory factor analysis* brought the debate to a quiet close by revealing that Spearman and Thurstone had each been right in his own way. Specifically, this new technique showed that the

> **Table 10.2**

Thurstone's Primary Mental Abilities

Primary Mental Ability	Description
Word Fluency	Ability to solve anagrams and to find rhymes, etc.
Verbal Comprehension	Ability to understand words and sentences
Numerical Ability	Ability to make mental and other numerical computations
Spatial Visualization	Ability to visualize a complex shape in various orientations
Associative Memory	Ability to recall verbal material, learn pairs of unrelated words, etc.
Perceptual Speed	Ability to detect visual details quickly
Reasoning	Ability to induce a general rule from a few instances

correlations between scores on different mental ability tests are best described by a three-level hierarchy (see **FIGURE 10.2**) with a *general factor* (like Spearman's g) at the top, *specific factors* (like Spearman's s) at the bottom, and a set of factors called *group*

> **How was the debate between Spearman and Thurstone resolved?**

factors (like Thurstone's *primary mental abilities*) in the middle (Gustafsson, 1984). A reanalysis of massive amounts of data collected over 60 years from more than 130,000 healthy adults, schoolchildren, infants, college students, people with learning disabilities, and people with mental and

physical illnesses has shown that almost every study done over the past half century results in a three-level hierarchy of this kind (Carroll, 1993). This hierarchy suggests that people have a very general ability called intelligence, which is made up of a small set of middle-level abilities, which are made up of a large set of specific abilities that are unique to particular tasks. Although this resolution to a hundred years of disagreement is not particularly exciting, it appears to have the compensatory benefit of being true.

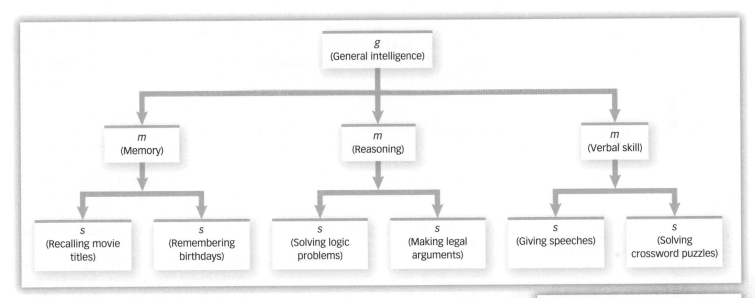

▲ Figure 10.2 **A Three-Level Hierarchy** Most intelligence test data are best described by a three-level hierarchy with general intelligence (g) at the top, specific abilities (s) at the bottom, and a small number of middle-level abilities (m) (sometimes called group factors) in the middle.

The Middle-Level Abilities

Michael Jordan played basketball much better than baseball, but he played both sports much better than most people can. His specific abilities allowed him to be more successful at one sport than another, but his general ability allowed him to outperform 99.9% of the world's population on both the court and the field. It is easy to see that Michael Jordan had both specific abilities (dribbling) and a general ability (athleticism), but it is not so easy to say precisely what his middle-level abilities were. Should we draw a distinction between speed and power, between guile and patience, or between the ability to work with a team or perform as an individual? Should we describe his athleticism as a function of 3 middle-level abilities or 4? or 6? or 92?

Similar questions arise when we consider intelligence. Most psychologists agree that there are very specific mental abilities as well as a very general mental ability and that one of the important challenges is to describe the middle-level abilities that lie between them. Some psychologists have taken a *data-based approach* to this problem by starting with people's responses on intelligence tests and then looking to see what kinds of independent clusters these responses form. Other psychologists have taken a *theory-based approach* to this problem by starting with a broad survey of human

fluid intelligence
The ability to see abstract relationships and draw logical inferences.

crystallized intelligence
The ability to retain and use knowledge that was acquired through experience.

abilities and then looking to see which of these abilities intelligence tests measure—or fail to measure. These approaches have led to rather different suggestions about the best way to describe the middle-level abilities that constitute intelligence.

The Data-Based Approach

One way to determine the nature of the middle-level abilities is to start with the data and go where they lead us. Just as Spearman and Thurstone did, we could compute the correlations between the performances of a large number of people on a large number of tests and then see how those correlations cluster. For example, imagine that we tested how quickly and well a large group of people could (a) balance teacups, (b) understand Shakespeare, (c) swat flies, and (d) sum the whole numbers between 1 and 1,000. Now imagine that we computed the correlation between scores on each of these tests and observed a pattern of correlations like the one shown in **FIGURE 10.3a**. What would this pattern tell us?

This pattern suggests that a person who can swat flies well can also balance teacups well and that a person who can understand Shakespeare well can also sum numbers well, but that a person who can swat flies well and balance teacups well may or may not be able to sum numbers or understand Shakespeare well. From this pattern, we could conclude that there are two middle-level abilities (shown in **FIGURE 10.3b**), which we might call *physical coordination* (the ability that allows people to swat flies and balance teacups) and *academic skill* (the ability that allows people to understand Shakespeare and sum numbers). This pattern suggests that different specific abilities such as fly swatting and teacup balancing are made possible by a single middle-level ability called physical coordination, and that this middle-level ability is unrelated to the other middle-level ability, academic skill, which enables people to sum numbers and understand Shakespeare. As this example reveals, simply by examining the pattern of correlations between different tests, we can divine the nature and number of the middle-level abilities.

In the real world, of course, there are more than four tests. So what kinds of patterns do we observe when we calculate the correlations between the tests of mental ability that psychologists actually use? This is precisely what psychologist John Carroll (1993) set out to discover in his landmark analysis of intelligence test scores

> **How do patterns of correlation reveal the middle-level abilities?**

▼ Figure **10.3** **Patterns of Correlation Can Reveal Middle-Level Abilities**. The pattern of correlations shown in (a) suggests that these four specific abilities can be thought of as instances of the two middle-level abilities, as shown in (b) physical coordination and academic skill.

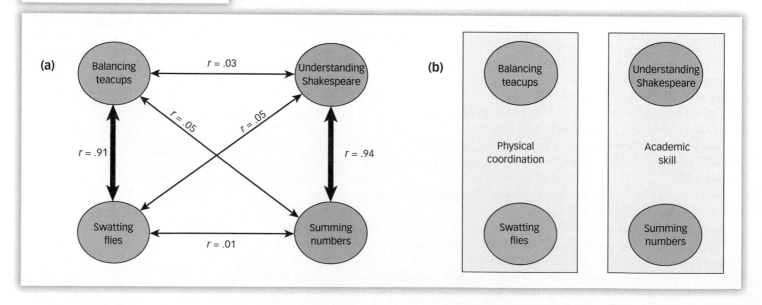

from nearly 500 studies conducted over a half century. Carroll found that the pattern of correlations among these tests suggested the existence of eight independent middle-level abilities: *memory and learning, visual perception, auditory perception, retrieval ability, cognitive speediness, processing speed, crystallized intelligence,* and *fluid intelligence.*

Although most of the abilities on this list are self-explanatory, the last two are not. **Fluid intelligence** is *the ability to see abstract relationships and draw logical inferences;* **crystallized intelligence** is *the ability to retain and use knowledge that was acquired through experience* (Horn & Cattell, 1966). If we think of the brain as an information-processing device, then crystallized intelligence refers to the "information" part and fluid intelligence refers to the "processing" part (Salthouse, 2000). Whereas crystallized intelligence is generally assessed by tests of vocabulary, factual information, and so on, fluid intelligence is generally assessed by tests that pose novel, abstract problems that must be solved under time pressure, such as Raven's Progressive Matrices Test (shown in **FIGURE 10.4**). The distinction between these two kinds of intelligence is not just conceptual; it is neural. Tests of fluid intelligence and crystallized intelligence seem to activate different regions of the brain, which may explain why impairment of one kind of intelligence does not necessitate impairment of the other. For example, autism and Alzheimer's disease both impair crystallized intelligence, but leave fluid intelligence virtually intact, whereas damage to the prefrontal cortex (whether through accident or normal aging) does the opposite (Blair, 2006).

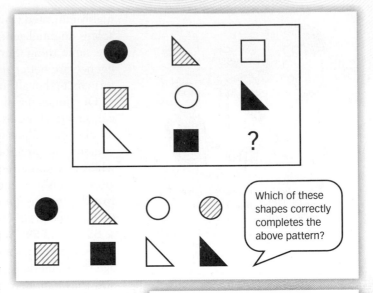

Which of these shapes correctly completes the above pattern?

▲ Figure **10.4** **Raven's Progressive Matrices Test** This item from Raven's Progressive Matrices Test measures nonverbal reasoning abilities and is unlikely to be culturally biased.

The Theory-Based Approach

The data-based approach attempts to discover the middle-level abilities by analyzing people's responses to questions on intelligence tests. The good thing about this approach is that its conclusions are based on hard evidence. But the bad thing about this approach is that it is incapable of discovering any middle-level ability that the intelligence tests it uses didn't already measure (Stanovich, 2009). For example, no intelligence test asks people to find three new uses for an origami fish or to answer the question, "What is the question you thought you'd be asked but weren't?" As a result, the scores from these tests may be incapable of revealing the middle-level abilities such as imagination or creativity. Are there middle-level abilities to which the data-based approach is blind?

What are the advantages of a theory-based approach to intelligence?

Psychologist Robert Sternberg (1999) has argued that, in fact, there are three kinds of intelligence, only one of which is measured by standard intelligence tests. *Analytic intelligence* is the ability to identify and define problems and to find strategies for solving them; *practical intelligence* is the ability to apply and implement these solutions in everyday settings; and *creative intelligence* is the ability to generate solutions that other people do not. According to Sternberg, standard intelligence tests typically confront people with clearly defined problems that have one right answer and then supply all the information needed to solve them. These kinds of problems measure analytic intelligence. But everyday life confronts people with situations in which they must formulate the *problem,* find the information needed to solve it, and then choose among multiple acceptable solutions. These situations require practical and creative intelligence. Some studies suggest that these different kinds of intelligence are independent. For example, workers at milk-processing plants develop complex strategies for efficiently combining partially filled cases of milk, and not only do they outperform

Ten years after being diagnosed with Alzheimer's disease, psychology professor Richard Taylor has become a leading advocate for people who have the disease. Although Alzheimer's impairs crystallized intelligence, it leaves fluid intelligence relatively intact (Matsuda & Saito, 1998).

DAVID SIPRESS/THE NEW YORKER COLLECTION/CARTOONBANK.COM

"I don't have to be smart, because someday I'll just hire lots of smart people to work for me."

highly educated white-collar workers, but their performance is also unrelated to their scores on intelligence tests, suggesting that practical and analytic intelligence are not the same thing (Scribner, 1984). Sternberg has argued that tests of practical intelligence are better than tests of analytic intelligence at predicting a person's job performance, though such claims have been criticized (Brody, 2003; Gottfredson, 2003).

Of course, not all of the problems that intelligence enables us to solve are analytical, practical, or creative. For instance, how do you tell a friend that she talks too much without hurting her feelings? How do you cheer yourself up after failing a test? How do you know whether you are feeling anxious or angry? Psychologists John Mayer and Peter Salovey define **emotional intelligence** as *the ability to reason about emotions and to use emotions to enhance reasoning* (Mayer, Roberts, & Barsade, 2008; Salovey & Grewal, 2005). Emotionally intelligent people know what kinds of emotions a particular event will trigger, they can identify, describe, and manage their emotions, they know how to use their emotions to improve their decisions, and they can identify other people's emotions from facial expressions and tones of voice. Furthermore, they do all this quite easily, which is why emotionally intelligent people show *less* neural activity when solving emotional problems than emotionally unintelligent people do (Jausovec & Jausovec, 2005; Jausovec, Jausovec, & Gerlic, 2001). These skills are also quite important for social relationships. Emotionally intelligent people have better social skills and more friends (Eisenberg et al., 2000; Mestre et al., 2006; Schultz, Izard, & Bear, 2004), they are judged to be more competent in their interactions (Brackett et al., 2006), and they have better romantic relationships (Brackett, Warner, & Bosco, 2005) and workplace relationships (Elfenbein et al., 2007; Lopes et al., 2006). Given all this, it isn't surprising that emotionally intelligent people tend to be happier (Brackett & Mayer, 2003; Brackett et al., 2006) and more satisfied with their lives (Ciarrochi, Chan, & Caputi, 2000; Mayer, Caruso, & Salovey, 1999).

> **What skills are particularly strong in emotionally intelligent people?**

1.

COURTESY OF DANIEL GILBERT

Emotion	Select one:
a. Happy	○
b. Angry	○
c. Fearful	○
d. Sad	○

2.

Tom felt worried when he thought about all the work he needed to do. He believed he could handle it—if only he had the time. When his supervisor brought him an additional project, he felt _____. (Select the best choice.)

Emotion	Select one:
a. Frustrated and anxious	○
b. Content and calm	○
c. Ashamed and accepting	○
d. Sad and guilty	○

Two items from a test of emotional intelligence. Item 1 measures the accuracy with which a person can read emotional expressions (*left*). Item 2 measures the ability to predict emotional responses to external events (*right*). The correct answer to both questions is A.

From Mayer, Roberts, & Barsade, 2008.

The data-based approach is also blind to middle-level abilities that are valued in cultures where intelligence tests are not common. For instance, Westerners regard people as intelligent when they speak quickly and often, but Africans regard people as intelligent when they are deliberate and quiet (Irvine, 1978). The Confucian tradition emphasizes the ability to behave properly, the Taoist tradition emphasizes humility and self-knowledge, and the Buddhist tradition emphasizes determination and mental effort (Yang & Sternberg, 1997). Unlike Western societies, many African and Asian societies conceive of intelligence as including social responsibility and cooperativeness (Azuma & Kashiwagi, 1987; Serpell, 1974; White & Kirkpatrick, 1985), and the word for *intelligence* in Zimbabwe, *ngware*, means to be wise in social relationships. Definitions of intelligence may even differ within a culture: Californians of Latino ancestry are more likely to equate intelligence with social competence, whereas Californians of Asian ancestry are more likely to equate it with cognitive skill (Okagaki & Sternberg, 1993). Some researchers take all this to mean that different cultures have radically different conceptualizations of intelligence, but

> **How does the concept of intelligence differ across cultures?**

emotional intelligence
The ability to reason about emotions and to use emotions to enhance reasoning.

others are convinced that what appear to be differences in the conceptualization of intelligence are really just differences in language. They argue that every culture values the ability to solve important problems and that what really distinguishes cultures is the *kinds* of problems that are considered to be important.

IN SUMMARY

▶ People who score well on one test of mental ability *usually* score well on others, which suggests that there is a property called *g* (general intelligence).

▶ People who score well on one test of mental ability don't *always* score well on others, which suggests that there are properties called *s* (specific abilities).

▶ Research reveals that between *g* and *s* are several *middle-level abilities*.

▶ The *data-based approach* suggests that there are eight middle-level abilities.

▶ The *theory-based approach* suggests that there may be middle-level abilities that standard intelligence tests don't measure, such as practical, creative, and emotional intelligence. Non-Western cultures may include measures of social responsibility and cooperation in their definitions of intelligence.

Africans tend to think of intelligent people as deliberate and quiet. *Thought is hallowed in the lean oil of solitude,* wrote Nigerian poet Wole Soyinka, who spent nearly 2 years in solitary confinement for his radical writing. A decade later he won the Nobel Prize in Literature.

Where Does Intelligence Come From?

No one is born knowing calculus and no one has to be taught how to blink. Some things are learned, others are not. But almost all of the really *interesting* things about people are a joint product of the innate characteristics with which their genes have endowed them and of the experiences they have in the world. Intelligence is one of those really interesting things that is influenced both by nature and by nurture. Let's start with nature.

Genetic Influences on Intelligence

The notion that intelligence is "in the blood" has been with us for a long time. For example, in *The Republic,* the philosopher Plato suggested that some people are born to rule, others to be soldiers, and others to be tradesmen. But it wasn't until late in the 19th century that this suggestion became the subject of scientific inquiry. Sir Francis Galton was a half cousin of Charles Darwin, and his contributions to science ranged from meteorology to fingerprinting. Late in life, Galton (1869) became interested in the origins of intelligence. He did careful genealogical studies of eminent families and collected measurements from over 12,000 people that ranged from head size to the ability to discriminate tones. As the title of his book *Hereditary Genius* suggests, he concluded that intelligence was inherited. Was he right?

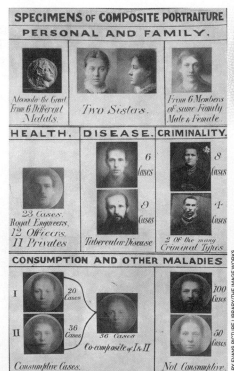

Sir Francis Galton (1822–1911) studied the physical and psychological traits that appeared to run in families. In his book *Hereditary Genius,* he concluded that intelligence was largely inherited.

Small genetic differences can make a big difference. A single gene on chromosome 15 determines whether a dog will be too small for your pocket or too large for your garage.

fraternal twins (or dizygotic twins)
Twins who develop from two different eggs that were fertilized by two different sperm (see *identical twins*).

identical twins (or monozygotic twins)
Twins who develop from the splitting of a single egg that was fertilized by a single sperm (see *fraternal twins*).

heritability coefficient
A statistic (commonly denoted as h^2) that describes the proportion of the difference between people's scores that can be explained by differences in their genes.

Studying Relatives

The fact that intelligence appears to "run in families" isn't very good evidence of this genetic influence. After all, brothers and sisters share genes, but they share many other things as well. They typically grow up in the same house, go to the same schools, read many of the same books, and have many of the same friends. Members of a family may have similar levels of intelligence because they share genes, environments, or both. To separate the influence of genes and environments, we need to examine the intelligence test scores of people who share genes but not environments (e.g., biological siblings who are separated at birth and raised by different families), people who share environments but not genes (e.g., adopted siblings who are raised together), and people who share both (e.g., biological siblings who are raised together).

> **Why are the intelligence test scores of relatives so similar?**

There are several kinds of siblings with different degrees of genetic relatedness. When siblings have the same biological parents but different birthdays, they share on average 50% of their genes. **Fraternal twins** (or **dizygotic twins**) *develop from two different eggs that were fertilized by two different sperm*, and although they happen to have the same birthday, they are merely siblings who shared a womb and they, too, share on average 50% of their genes. **Identical twins** (or **monozygotic twins**) *develop from the splitting of a single egg that was fertilized by a single sperm*, and unlike other siblings, they are genetic copies of each other, sharing 100% of their genes.

These different degrees of genetic relatedness allow psychologists to assess the influence that genes have on intelligence. Studies show that the IQs of identical twins are strongly correlated when the twins are raised in the same household ($r = .86$), but they are also strongly correlated when the twins are separated at birth and raised in different households ($r = .78$). In fact, as you'll notice from **TABLE 10.3**, identical twins who are raised apart have more similar IQs than do fraternal twins who are raised together.

What this means is that people who share all their genes have similar IQs regardless of whether they share their environments. Indeed, the correlation between the intelligence test scores of identical twins who have never met is about the same as the correlation between the intelligence test scores of a single person who has taken the test twice! By comparison, the intelligence test scores of unrelated people raised in the same household (e.g., two siblings, one or both of whom were adopted) are correlated only modestly, about $r = .26$ (Bouchard & McGue, 2003). These patterns of correlation suggest that genes play an important role in determining intelligence. This shouldn't surprise us. Intelligence is, in part, a function of how the brain works,

These photos, taken from the "Genetic Portraits" series by artist Ulric Collette, were made by blending the face of a 32-year old woman with the face of her mother (*left*) and the face of her father (*right*). Because physical appearance is highly heritable, the resemblance between family members can often be quite striking.

> **Table 10.3**

Intelligence Test Correlations between People with Different Relationships

Relationship	Shared Home?	Shared Genes (%)	Correlation between Intelligence Test Scores (r)
Twins			
Identical twins (n = 4,672)	yes	100	.86
Identical twins (n = 93)	no	100	.78
Fraternal twins (n = 5,533)	yes	50	.60
Parents and Children			
Parent–biological child (n = 8,433)	yes	50	.42
Parent–biological child (n = 720)	no	50	.24
Nonbiological parent–adopted child (n = 1,491)	yes	0	.19
Siblings			
Biological siblings (2 parents in common) (n = 26,473)	yes	50	.47
Nonbiological siblings (no parents in common) (n = 714)	yes	0	.32
Biological siblings (2 parents in common) (n = 203)	no	50	.24

Source: Plomin, DeFries, et al., 2001a, p. 168.

and given that brains are designed by genes, it would be quite remarkable if genes *didn't* play a role in determining a person's intelligence. Indeed, a mere 20 genes on a single chromosome are all that separates you from a person with Williams syndrome. Clearly, genes influence intelligence.

Heritability

But exactly how powerful is that influence? The **heritability coefficient** (commonly denoted as h^2) is *a statistic that describes the proportion of the difference between people's scores that can be explained by differences in their genes.* When the data from numerous studies of children and adults are analyzed together, the heritability of intelligence is roughly .5, which is to say that about 50% of the difference between people's intelligence test scores is due to genetic differences between them (Plomin & Spinath, 2004; Plomin et al., 2013; cf. Chabris et al., 2012).

This fact may tempt you to conclude that half your intelligence is due to your genes and half is due to your experiences, but that's not right. To understand why, consider the rectangles in **FIGURE 10.5**. These rectangles clearly differ in size, and if you were asked to say what percentage of that difference was due to differences in the rectangles' heights and what percentage was due to differences in the rectangles' widths, you would correctly say that 100% of the difference in their sizes was due to differences in their widths and 0% was due to differences in their heights (which are, after all, identical). Good answer. Now, if you were asked to say how much of rectangle A's size was due to its height and how much was due to its width, you would correctly say, "That's a silly question." It is a silly question because a rectangle's size is a product of *both* its height and its width and it can't be "due" to one more or less than the other.

Tamara Rabi and Adriana Scott were 20 years old when they met in a McDonald's parking lot in New York. "I'm just standing there looking at her," Adriana recalled. "It was a shock. I saw me" (Gootman, 2003). The two soon discovered that they were twins who had been separated at birth and adopted by different families.

◄ Figure **10.5** **How to Ask a Silly Question** These four rectangles differ in size. How much of the difference in their sizes is due to differences in their widths and how much is due to differences in their heights? Answer: 100% and 0%, respectively. Now, how much of rectangle A's size is due to width and how much is due to height? Answer: That's a silly question.

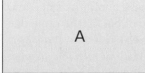   

Research shows that intelligence is more heritable in wealthy neighborhoods than in poor ones.

Similarly, if you measured the intelligence of all the people at a basketball game and were then asked to say what percentage of the difference in their intelligences was due to differences in their genes and what percentage was due to differences in their experiences, you could reasonably guess that about 50% of the difference was due to each of these factors. That's what the heritability coefficient of .5 suggests. But if you were next asked to say how much of the intelligence of the annoying guy with the bad haircut in Row 17, Seat 4 was due to his genes and how much was due to his experiences, you could only reply, "That's a silly question." It is a silly question because the intelligence of a particular person is a joint product of both genes and experience—just like the size of a particular rectangle is a joint product of both its height and width—and cannot be "due" to one of these things more than another.

The heritability coefficient tells us why people in a particular group differ from one another; thus its value can change depending on the particular group of people we measure. For example, the heritability of intelligence among wealthy children is about .72 and among poor children about .10 (Turkheimer et al., 2003). How can that be? Well, if we assume that wealthy children have fairly similar environments—that is, if they all have nice homes with books, plenty of free time, ample nutrition, and so on—then all the differences in their intelligence must be due to the one

> **Why is *h*² higher among wealthy people than among poor people?**

and only factor that distinguishes them from each other, namely, their genes. Conversely, if we assume that poor children have fairly different environments—that is, some have books and free time and ample nutrition while others have little or none of these—then the difference in their intelligences may be due to either of the factors that distinguish them, namely, their genes and their environments (Tucker-Drob et al., 2010). The value of the heritability coefficient also depends on the age of the people being measured and is typically larger among adults than among children (see **FIGURE 10.6**), which suggests that the environments of any pair of 65-year-olds tend to be more similar than the environments of any pair of 3-year-olds. In short, when people have identical experiences, then the difference in their intelligences must be due to the difference in their genes, and when people have identical genes, then the difference in their intelligences must be due to the difference in their experiences. It may seem paradoxical, but in a science-fictional world of perfect clones, the heritability of intelligence (and of everything else) would be zero.

Does this imply that in a science-fictional world of individuals who lived in exactly the same kinds of houses and received exactly the same kinds of meals, educations, parental care, and so on, the heritability coefficient would be 1.00? Not likely. Two unrelated people who live in the same household will have *some* but not *all* of their experiences in common. The **shared environment** refers to *those environmental factors that are experienced by all relevant members of a household*. For example, siblings raised in the same household have about the same level of affluence, the same number and type of books, the same diet, and so on. The **nonshared environment** refers to *those environmental factors that are not experienced by all relevant members of a household*. Siblings raised in the same household may have

▼ Figure **10.6** **Age and Heritability of Intelligence** The heritability of intelligence generally increases with the age of the sample measured.

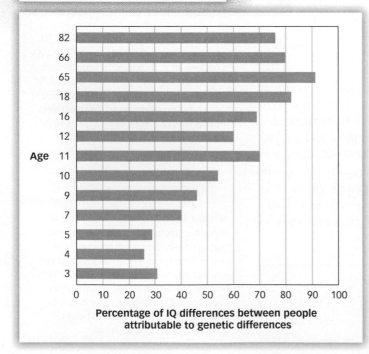

Percentage of IQ differences between people attributable to genetic differences

First-born children tend to be more intelligent than their later-born siblings. But when a first-born child dies in infancy and the second-born child becomes the oldest child in the family, that second-born child ends up being just as intelligent as the average first-born child (Kristensen & Bjerkedal, 2007). This suggests that first-borns are smarter than their siblings because they experience a different family environment. So if Joe and Nick murdered Paul . . . um, never mind.

different friends and teachers and may contract different illnesses. This may be why the correlation between the IQ scores of siblings is greater when they are close in age (Sundet, Eriksen, & Tambs, 2008). Being raised in the same household is only a rough measure of the similarity of two people's experiences (Turkheimer & Waldron, 2000); thus, studies of twins may overestimate the influence of genes and underestimate the influence of experiences (Nisbett, 2009). As psychologist Eric Turkheimer (2000, p. 162) noted:,

> The appropriate conclusion [to draw from twin studies] is not so much that the family environment does not matter for development, but rather that the part of the family environment that is shared by siblings does not matter. What does matter is the individual environments of children, their peers, and the aspects of their parenting that they do not share.

Environmental Influences on Intelligence

Americans believe that every individual should have an equal chance to succeed in life, and one of the reasons why we bristle when we hear about genetic influences on intelligence is that we mistakenly believe that our genes are our destinies—that

In what ways is intelligence like height?

"genetic" is a synonym for "unchangeable" (Pinker, 2003). In fact, traits that are strongly influenced by genes may also be strongly influenced by the environment. Height is a heritable trait, which is why tall parents tend to have tall children; and yet, the average height of Korean boys has increased by more than 7 inches in the last 50 years simply because of changes in nutrition (Nisbett, 2009). In 1848, 25% of all Dutch men were rejected by the military because they were less than 5′ 2″ tall, but today the average Dutch man is over 6′ tall (Max, 2006). Genes may explain why two people who have the same diet differ in height—that is, why Chang-sun is taller than Kwan-ho and why Thijs is taller than Daan—but they do not dictate how tall any of these boys will actually grow up to be.

Is intelligence like height in this regard? Alfred Binet (1909) thought so:

> A few modern philosophers . . . assert that an individual's intelligence is a fixed quantity that cannot be increased. We must protest and react against this brutal pessimism. . . . With practice, training, and above all method, we manage to increase our attention, our memory, our judgment, and literally to become more intelligent than we were before.

It turns out that Binet was right. As **FIGURE 10.7** shows, intelligence changes over time (Owens, 1966; Schaie, 1996, 2005; Schwartzman, Gold, & Andres, 1987). For

At 7′, Pieter Gijselaar is taller than most of his friends—but not *that* much taller. The Dutch government recently adjusted building codes so that doors must now be 7′ 6.5″ high.

shared environment
Those environmental factors that are experienced by all relevant members of a household (see *nonshared environment*).

nonshared environment
Those environmental factors that are not experienced by all relevant members of a household (see *shared environment*).

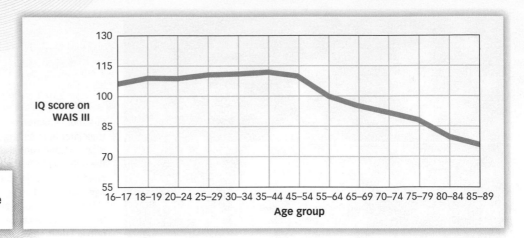

▶ Figure **10.7**
Absolute Intelligence Changes Over Time
Data from Kaufman, 2001.

most people, intelligence increases between adolescence and middle age and then declines thereafter. The sharpest decline occurs in old age (Kaufman, 2001; Salthouse, 1996a, 2000; Schaie, 2005), and may be due to a general slowing of the brain's processing speed (Salthouse, 1996b; Zimprich & Martin, 2002). Age-related declines are more evident in some domains than in others. For example, on tests that measure vocabulary, general information, and verbal reasoning, people show only small changes from the ages of 18 to 70, but on tests that are timed, have abstract material, involve making new memories, or require reasoning about spatial relationships, most people show marked declines in performance after middle age (Avolio & Waldman, 1994; Lindenberger & Baltes, 1997; Rabbitt et al., 2004; Salthouse, 2001).

Not only does intelligence change over the life span, but it also changes over generations. The *Flynn effect* refers to the accidental discovery by James Flynn that the average IQ score is 30 points higher than it was about a century ago (Dickens & Flynn, 2001; Flynn, 2012; cf. Lynn, 2013). The average person today is smarter than 95% of the people who were living in 1900! Why is each generation scoring higher than the one before it? Some researchers give the credit to improved nutrition, schooling, and parenting (Lynn, 2009; Neisser, 1998), and some suggest that the least intelligent people are being left out of the mating game (Mingroni, 2007). But most (and that includes Flynn himself) believe that the industrial and technological revolutions have changed the nature of daily living such that people now spend more and more time solving precisely the kinds of abstract problems that intelligence tests include—and as we all know, practice makes perfect (Flynn, 2012). In other words, you are likely to score higher on an IQ test than your grandparents did because your daily life is more like an IQ test than theirs was!

105-year-old Khatijah (front row, second from right) sits with five generations of her family. The Flynn Effect suggests that intelligence is increasing across generations.

Now, here is a fact that is almost sure to confuse you: Although intelligence changes over the lifetime, there is a strong correlation between an individual's performance on intelligence tests that are taken at two different times (Deary, 2000; Deary et al., 2004; Deary, Batty, & Gale, 2008; Deary, Batty, Pattie, & Gale, 2008). **TABLE 10.4** shows the results of several studies that demonstrate this fact. How can that be? If intelligence changes over time, then why is there such a strong correlation between tests taken in childhood and tests taken in old age? The answer is that intelligence does change over time, but it changes in much the same way for everyone. The large correlations between tests administered at different times merely tell us that the people who got the best (or worst) scores when the test was administered the first time also tended to get the best (or worst) scores when it was administered the second time. You already know that the same thing happens with height. People get taller as they go from childhood to adulthood, and yet, the tallest child is likely to be among the tallest adults. Like height, a person's absolute level of intelligence changes over time, but his or her level of intelligence *relative to others* stays about the same.

The fact that intelligence changes over the life span and across generations shows that it is not "a fixed quantity that cannot be increased." Our genes may determine the *range* in which our IQ is likely to fall, but our experiences determine the exact *point* in that range at which it does fall (Hunt, 2011; see **FIGURE 10.8**). Two of the most powerful experiential factors are economics and education.

> **Table 10.4**

The Correlation Between Scores on Intelligence Tests Taken Over Time

Study	Mean Initial Age (years)	Mean Follow-up Age (years)	Correlation (r)
1	2	9	.56
2	14	42	.68
3	19	61	.78
4	25	65	.78
5	30	43	.64–.79
6	50	70	.90

Source: Adapted from Deary, 2000.

Economics

Maybe money can't buy love, but it sure appears to buy intelligence. One of the best predictors of a person's intelligence is the material wealth of the family in which he or she was raised—what scientists call *socioeconomic status* (SES). Studies suggest that being raised in a high-SES family rather than a low-SES family is worth between 12 and 18 IQ points (Nisbett, 2009; van Ijzendoorn, Juffer, & Klein Poelhuis, 2005). For example, one study compared pairs of siblings who were born to low-SES parents. In each case, one of the siblings was raised by his or her low-SES parents and the other was adopted and raised by a high-SES family. On average, the child who had been raised by high-SES parents had an IQ that was 14 points higher than his or her sibling (Schiff et al., 1978). Although these siblings had similar genes, they ended up with dramatically different IQs simply because one was raised by wealthier parents.

Exactly how does SES influence intelligence? One way is by influencing the brain itself. Low-SES children have poorer nutrition and medical care, they experience greater daily stress, and they are more likely to be exposed to environmental toxins such as air pollution and lead—all of which can impair brain development (Chen, Cohen, & Miller, 2010; Evans, 2004; Hackman & Farah, 2008). The fact that low SES can impair a child's brain development may explain why children who experience poverty in early childhood are less intelligent than those who experience poverty in middle or late childhood (Duncan et al., 1998).

Why are wealthier people more intelligent?

SES affects the brain, and it also affects the environment in which that brain lives and learns. Intellectual stimulation increases intelligence (Nelson et al., 2007), and research shows that high-SES parents are more likely to provide it (Nisbett, 2009). For instance, high-SES parents are more likely to read to their children and to connect what they are reading to the outside world ("Billy has a rubber ducky. Who do you know who has a rubber ducky?"; Heath, 1983; Lareau, 2003). When high-SES parents talk to their children, they tend to ask stimulating questions ("Do you think a ducky likes to eat grass?"), whereas low-SES parents tend to give instructions ("Please put your ducky away"; Hart & Risley, 1995). By the age of 3, the average high-SES child has heard 30 million different words, while the average low-SES child has heard only 10 million different words, and as a result, the high-SES child knows 50% more words than his or her low-SES counterpart. These differences in the intellectual richness of the home environment may explain why children from low-SES families show

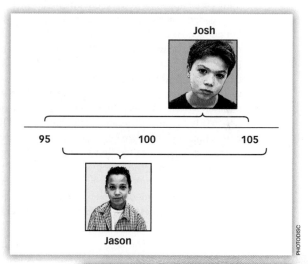

▲ Figure **10.8 Genes and Environment**
Genes may establish the range in which a person's intelligence *may* fall, but environment determines the point in that range at which the person's intelligence *will* fall. Although Jason's genes give him a better chance to be smart than Josh's genes do, differences in their diets could easily cause Josh to have a higher IQ than Jason.

Dumb and Dumber?

For most of human history, the smartest people had the most children, and our species reaped the benefits. But in the middle of the 19th century, this effect began to reverse and the smartest people began having fewer children, a trend that scientists call *dysgenic fertility*. That trend continues today.

But wait. If the smartest people are having the fewest children, and if IQ is largely heritable, then why—as James Flynn showed—is IQ rising over generations?

Some researchers suspect that two things are happening at once: Our inherited intelligence is going down over generations, but our acquired intelligence is going up! In other words, we were all born with a *slightly* less capable brain than our parents had, but this small effect is masked because we were born into a world that *greatly* boosted our intelligence with everything from nutrition to video games! How can we tell whether this hypothesis is right?

Francis Galton was the first to suggest that reaction time (the speed with which a person can respond to a stimulus) is a basic indicator of mental ability, and his suggestion has been confirmed by mod-

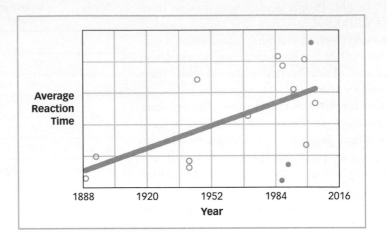

ern research (Deary, Der, & Ford, 2001). Recently, a group of researchers (Woodley, te Nijenhuis, & Murphy, 2013) went back and analyzed all available data on human reaction time collected between 1884 and 2004 (including data collected by Galton himself) and what they found was striking: The average reaction time has gotten slower since the Victorian era! The figure above shows the average reaction time of people in different studies conducted in different years.

Does this mean that we are innately less clever and that this fact is being obscured by the big IQ boost we get from our environments? Maybe, but maybe not. There are problems with using old data that were collected under unknown circumstances, and the participants in older studies were probably not representative of the entire population. Nonetheless, the finding is provocative because it suggests that modern life may be an even more powerful cognitive enhancer than we realize.

a decrease in intelligence during the summer when school is not in session, whereas children from high-SES families do not (Burkham et al., 2004; Cooper et al., 1996). Clearly, poverty is the enemy of intelligence (Evans & Kim, 2012).

Education

Alfred Binet believed that if poverty was intelligence's enemy, then education was its friend. And he was right about that too. The correlation between the amount of formal education a person receives and his or her intelligence is quite large, somewhere in the range of $r = .55$ to .90 (Ceci, 1991; Neisser et al., 1996). One reason why this correlation is so large is that smart people tend to stay in school, but the other reason is that school makes people smarter (Ceci & Williams, 1997). When schooling is delayed because of war, political strife, or the simple lack of qualified teachers, children show a measurable decline in intelligence (Nisbett, 2009). Indeed, children born in the first 9 months of a calendar year typically start school an entire year earlier than those born in the last 3 months of the same year, and sure enough, people with late birthdays tend to have lower intelligence test scores than people with early birthdays (Baltes & Reinert, 1969).

Does this mean that anyone can become a genius just by showing up for class? Unfortunately not. Although education reliably increases intelligence, its impact is small, and some studies suggest that it tends to enhance test-taking ability more than general cognitive ability and that its effects vanish within a few years (Perkins & Grotzer,

1997). In other words, education seems to produce increases in intelligence that are smaller, narrower, and shorter-lived than we would like. That might mean that education just can't change intelligence all that much, or it might mean that education is potentially very powerful, but that modern schools aren't very good at providing it. Researchers lean toward the latter conclusion. Although most experiments in education—from magnet schools and charter schools to voucher systems and Head Start programs—have failed to produce substantial intellectual gains for students, a few have been quite successful (Nisbett, 2009), which shows that education *can* substantially increase intelligence even if it doesn't *usually* do so. No one knows just how big the impact of an optimal education could be, but it seems clear that our current educational system is less than optimal.

Education increases intelligence. But not everyone is in favor of that. In Afghanistan, for example, the Taliban attack young girls with acid, guns, and poison to keep them from attending school.

Genes and Environments

Both genes and environment influence intelligence. But that shouldn't lead you to think of genes and environments as two separate ingredients that are somehow blended together like flour and sugar in a recipe for IQ. The fact is that genes and environments interact in complex ways that make the distinction between them a bit murky.

For example, imagine a gene that made people enjoy the smell of library dust or that made them unusually sensitive to the glare produced by television sets. People who had such a gene might well read more books and thus end up being smarter. Would their increased intelligence be due to their genes or to their environments? Well, if they hadn't had those genes, then they wouldn't have gone to the library, but if they hadn't gone to the library, then they wouldn't have gotten smarter. The fact is that genes can exert some of their most powerful influences not by changing the structure of a person's brain, but by changing the person's environment (Dickens & Flynn, 2001; Nisbett, 2009; Plomin, DeFries, et al., 2001). A gene that made someone sociable might lead her to have good relationships with peers, which might lead her to stay in school longer, which might lead her to become smarter. Would we call such a gene a "sociability gene" or an "intelligence gene" (Posthuma & de Geus, 2006)? Would we attribute that person's intelligence to her genes or to the environment that her genes enabled her to create? As these questions suggest, genes and environments are not independent influences on intelligence, and the clear difference between nature and nurture is not as clear as it might first appear.

How might genes exert their influence on intelligence?

Roundworms that have a gene called NPR-1 dislike low-oxygen environments, which just so happen to be where the bacteria hang out. As a result, these roundworms get fewer infections. Is NPR-1 a health gene?

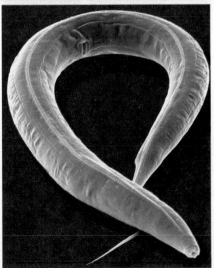

IN SUMMARY

▶ Both genes and environments influence intelligence.

▶ The heritability coefficient (h^2) tells us what portion of the difference between the intelligence scores of different people is attributable to differences in their genes.

▶ Relative intelligence is generally stable over time, but absolute intelligence changes.

▶ SES has a powerful influence on intelligence, and education has a moderate influence.

Who Is Most Intelligent?

If everyone in the world were equally intelligent, we probably wouldn't even have a word for it. What makes intelligence such an interesting and important topic is that some individuals—and some groups of individuals—have more of it than others.

Individual Differences in Intelligence

The average IQ is 100, and the vast majority of us—about 70% in fact—have IQs between 85 and 115 (see **FIGURE 10.9**). The people who score well above this large middle range are said to be *intellectually gifted*, and the people who score well below it are said to be *intellectually disabled*. The people who live at opposite ends of this continuum have one thing in common: They are more likely to be male than female. Although males and females have the same average IQ, the distribution of males' IQ scores is more variable than the distribution of females' IQ scores, which means that there are more males than females at both the very top and the very bottom of the IQ range (Hedges & Nowell, 1995; Lakin, 2013; Wai, Putallaz, & Makel, 2012). Some of this difference is surely due to the different ways in which boys and girls are socialized. Whether some of this difference is also due to innate biological differences between males and females remains a hotly debated issue in psychology (Ceci, Williams, & Barnett, 2009; Nisbett et al., 2012; Spelke, 2005).

▶ Figure **10.9** **The Normal Curve of Intelligence** Deviation IQ scores produce a normal curve. This graph shows the percentage of people who score in each range of IQ.

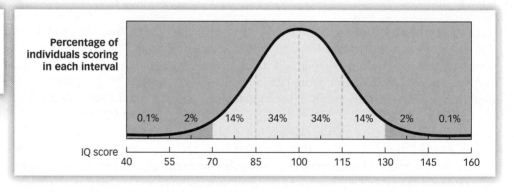

The artist Vincent van Gogh was the iconic "tortured genius." But data suggest that it is low intelligence, and not high intelligence, that is most strongly associated with mental illness.

Those of us who occupy the large middle of the intelligence spectrum often embrace a number of myths about those who live at the extremes. For example, movies typically portray the "tortured genius" as a person (usually a male person) who is brilliant, creative, misunderstood, despondent, and more than a little bit weird. Although some psychologists do think there is a link between creative genius and certain forms of psychopathology (Gale et al., 2012; Jamison, 1993; cf. Schlesinger, 2012), for the most part Hollywood has the relationship between intelligence and mental illness backwards: People with very high intelligence are *less* prone to mental illness than are people with very low intelligence (Dekker & Koot, 2003; Didden et al., 2012; Walker et al., 2002). Indeed, a 15 point *decrease* in IQ at age 20 is associated with a 50% *increase* in the risk of later hospitalization for schizophrenia, mood disorder, and alcohol-related disorders (Gale et al., 2010) as well as for personality disorders (Moran et al., 2009). Just as intelligence seems to buffer people against physical illness, it seems to buffer people against mental illness as well.

Another staple of Hollywood's vivid imagination is the "maladjusted child braniac." In fact, research suggests that very high IQ children are about as well-adjusted as their peers, and any special social or emotional problems they have seem to stem largely from a lack of appropriate scholastic opportunities (Garland & Zigler, 1999; Neihart, 1999). Being intellectually gifted doesn't necessarily make a child's life worse, but it also doesn't necessarily make it better. For instance, profoundly gifted children are no more likely than moderately intelligent children to become major contributors to the fields in which they work (Richert, 1997; Terman & Oden, 1959). No one knows why the gifts of childhood don't always ripen into the fruits of adulthood: Perhaps there is a natural limit on how much intelligence can improve one's outcomes, or perhaps the educational system fails to help gifted children make the best use of their talents (Robinson & Clinkenbeard, 1998; Winner, 2000).

It is worth noting that gifted children are rarely gifted in all departments, but instead have gifts in a single domain such as math, language, or music. More than 95% of gifted children show a sharp disparity between their mathematical and verbal abilities (Achter, Lubinski, & Benbow, 1996). Because gifted children tend to be "single-gifted," they also tend to be single-minded, displaying a "rage to master" the domain in which they excel. As one expert noted, "one cannot tear these children away from activities in their area of giftedness, whether they involve an instrument, a computer, a sketch pad, or a math book. These children . . . can focus so intently on work in this domain that they lose sense of the outside world" (Winner, 2000, p. 162). Indeed, some research suggests that the one thing that most clearly distinguishes gifted children from their less gifted peers is the sheer amount of time they spend engaged in their domain of excellence (Ericsson & Charness, 1999). A large part of nature's gift may be the capacity for passionate devotion to a single activity (Mayer et al., 1989; cf. Hambrick et al., 2013).

> **What one thing most clearly distinguishes gifted children?**

On the other end of the intelligence spectrum are people with intellectual disabilities, which can range from mild (50 < IQ < 69) to moderate (35 < IQ < 49) to severe (20 < IQ < 34) to profound (IQ < 20). About 70% of people with IQs in this range are male. Two of the most common causes of intellectual disability are *Down syndrome* (caused by the presence of a third copy of chromosome 21) and *fetal alcohol syndrome* (caused by a mother's alcohol use during pregnancy). These intellectual disabilities are quite general, and people who have them typically show impaired performance on most or all cognitive tasks. Myths about people with intellectual disabilities abound. For example, many people think the intellectually disabled are mentally ill, but in fact, their rate of mental illness is similar to that found in the general population (Deb, Thomas, & Bright, 2001). Another myth about the intellectually disabled is that they are unhappy. A recent survey of people with Down syndrome (Skotko, Levine, & Goldstein, 2011) revealed that more than 96% are happy with their lives, like who they are, and like how they look. People with intellectual disabilities face many challenges, and being misunderstood is one of the most difficult.

Dustin Bean has Down Syndrome, but that didn't prevent him from earning a black belt in Kung Fu (or from showing off several swaggy moves to Bruce Lee's widow).

Group Differences in Intelligence

In the early 1900s, Stanford professor Lewis Terman improved on Binet and Simon's work and produced the intelligence test now known as the Stanford–Binet Intelligence Scale. Among the things his test revealed was that Whites performed better than non-Whites. "Are the inferior races really inferior, or are they merely unfortunate in their lack of opportunity to learn?" he asked, and then answered unequivocally: "Their dullness seems to be racial, or at least inherent in the family stocks from which they come." He went on to suggest that "children of this group should be segregated into separate classes . . . [because] they cannot master abstractions but they can often be made into efficient workers" (Terman, 1916, pp. 91–92).

A century later, these sentences make most of us cringe. Terman appeared to be making three claims: First, that intelligence is influenced by genes; second, that members of some racial groups score better than others on intelligence tests; and third,

Research suggests that men tend to out-perform women in abstract mathematical and scientific domains and women tend to outperform men on production and comprehension of complex prose. Sonya Kovalevskaya (1850–1891), who was regarded as one of the greatest mathematicians of her time, wrote: "It seems to me that the poet must see what others do not see, must look deeper than others look. And the mathematician must do the same thing. As for myself, all my life I have been unable to decide for which I had the greater inclination, mathematics or literature" (Kovalevskaya, 1978, p. 35).

that the difference in scores is due to a difference in genes. Virtually all modern scientists agree that Terman's first two claims are true: Intelligence *is* influenced by genes and some groups *do* perform better than others on intelligence tests. However, Terman's third claim—that differences in genes are the *reason* why some groups outperform others—is not a fact. Indeed, it is a provocative conjecture that has been the subject of both passionate and acrimonious debate. What does science have to tell us about it?

Before answering that question we should be clear about one thing: Between-group differences in intelligence are not inherently troubling. No one is troubled by the possibility that Nobel laureates are on average more intelligent than shoe salesmen, and that includes the shoe salesmen. On the other hand, most of us *are* troubled by the possibility that people of one gender, race, or nationality may be more intelligent than people of another because intelligence is a valuable commodity and it doesn't seem fair for a few groups to corner the market by accidents of birth or geography.

But fair or not, they do. Whites routinely outscore Latinos, who routinely outscore Blacks (Neisser et al., 1996; Rushton, 1995). Women routinely outscore men on tests that require rapid access to and use of semantic information, production and comprehension of complex prose, fine motor skills, and perceptual speed of verbal intelligence, and men routinely outscore women on tests that require transformations in visual or spatial memory, certain motor skills, spatiotemporal responding, and fluid reasoning in abstract mathematical and scientific domains (Halpern, 1997; Halpern et al., 2007). Indeed, group differences in performance on intelligence tests "are among the most thoroughly documented findings in psychology" (Suzuki & Valencia, 1997, p. 1104). Although the average difference between groups is considerably less than the average difference within groups, Terman was right when he noted that some groups perform better than others on intelligence tests. The question is why?

Tests and Test Takers

One possibility is that there is something wrong with the tests. In fact, there is now little doubt that the earliest intelligence tests asked questions whose answers were more likely to be known by members of one group (usually White Europeans) than by members of another. For example, when Binet and Simon asked students, "When anyone has offended you and asks you to excuse him, what ought you to do?," they were looking for answers such as "accept the apology graciously." Answers such as "demand three goats" would have been counted as wrong. But intelligence tests have come a long way in a century, and one would have to look hard to find questions on a modern intelligence test that have the same blatant cultural bias that Binet and Simon's test did (Suzuki & Valencia, 1997). Moreover, group differences emerge even on those portions of intelligence tests that measure nonverbal skills, such as Raven's Progressive Matrices Test (see Figure 10.4). It would be difficult to argue that the large differences between the average scores of different groups is due entirely—or even largely—to a cultural bias in IQ tests.

Of course, even when test *questions* are unbiased, testing *situations* may not be. For example, studies show that African American students perform more poorly on tests if they are asked to report their race at the top of the answer sheet, because doing so causes them to feel anxious about confirming racial stereotypes (Steele & Aronson, 1995) and anxiety naturally interferes with test performance (Reeve, Heggestad, & Lievens, 2009). European American students do not show the same effect when asked to report their race. When Asian American women are reminded of their gender, they perform unusually poorly on tests of mathematical skill, presumably because they are aware of stereotypes suggesting that women can't do math. But when the same women are instead reminded of their

> **How can the testing situation affect a person's performance on an IQ test?**

"I don't know anything about the bell curve, but I say heredity is everything."

ethnicity, they perform unusually *well* on such tests, presumably because they are aware of stereotypes suggesting that Asians are especially good at math (Shih, Pittinsky, & Ambady, 1999). Indeed, when women read an essay suggesting that mathematical ability is strongly influenced by genes, they perform more poorly on subsequent math tests (Dar-Nimrod & Heine, 2006). Findings such as these remind us that the situation in which intelligence tests are administered can affect members of different groups differently and may cause group differences in performance that do not reflect group differences in actual intelligence.

These high school juniors in South Carolina are taking the SAT. When people are anxious about the possibility of confirming a racial or gender stereotype, their test performance can suffer.

Environments and Genes

Biases in the testing situation may explain some of the between-group differences in intelligence test scores, but probably not all. If we assume that some of these differences reflect real differences in the abilities that intelligence tests are meant to measure, then what accounts for these ability differences?

There is broad agreement among scientists that environment plays a major role. For example, African American children have lower birth weights, poorer diets, higher rates of chronic illness, poorer medical care, attend worse schools, and are three times more likely than European American children to live in single-parent households (Acevedo-Garcia et al., 2007; National Center for Health Statistics, 2004). Given the vast differences between the SES of European Americans and African Americans, it isn't very surprising that African Americans score on average 10 points lower on IQ tests than do European Americans. Do genes play any role in this difference? So far, scientists have not found a single fact that requires such a conclusion, but they have found several facts that make such a conclusion difficult to accept. For example, the average African American has about 20% European genes, but those who have more are no smarter than those who have fewer, which is not what we'd expect if European genes made people smart (Loehlin, 1973; Scarr et al., 1977). Similarly, African American children and mixed-race children have different amounts of European genes, and yet, when they are adopted into middle-class families, their IQs don't differ (Moore, 1986). These facts do not rule out the possibility that between-group differences in intelligence are caused by genetic differences, but they do make that possibility unlikely.

> **How can environmental factors help explain between-group differences in intelligence?**

What would it take to prove that behavioral and psychological differences between groups have a genetic origin? It would take the kind of evidence that scientists often find when they study the *physical* differences between groups. For example, people who have hepatitis C are often given a prescription for antiviral drugs, and European Americans typically benefit more from this treatment than African Americans do. Although physicians once thought this was because European Americans were more likely to *take* the medicine they were given, scientists have recently discovered a gene that makes people unresponsive to these antiviral drugs—and guess what? African Americans are much more likely than European Americans to have that gene (Ge et al., 2009). This kind of clear-cut evidence of genetic differences between groups is exactly what's lacking in the debate on the causes of between-group differences in intelligence. As one researcher recently noted, "No individual genetic variants are conclusively related to intelligence or its change with age in healthy individuals" (Deary, 2012, p. 463). This may mean that intelligence is influenced by many very tiny genetic effects rather than by a few major "intelligence genes" (Davies et al., 2011). Until researchers can locate such genes, and until they can show that those genes are more prevalent in one group than another, most psychologists are unlikely to be persuaded by genetic explanations of between-group differences in intelligence. Indeed, some experts, such as psychologist Richard Nisbett, believe the debate is all but over: "Genes account for none of the difference in IQ between blacks and whites; measurable environmental factors plausibly account for all of it" (Nisbett, 2009, p. 118).

Improving Intelligence

Intelligence can be improved—by money, for example, and by education. But most people can't just snap their fingers and become wealthier, and education takes time. Is there anything that the average parent can do to raise their child's IQ? Researchers recently analyzed the data from all the high-quality scientific studies on this question that have been performed over the last few decades (Protzko, Aronson, & Blair, 2013), and they found that four things reliably raise a child's intelligence. First, supplementing the diets of pregnant women and neonates with long-chain polyunsaturated fatty acids (a substance found in breast milk) raises children's IQ by about 4 points. Second, enrolling low-SES infants in so-called early educational interventions raises their IQ by about 6 points (though surprisingly, enrolling them at a younger age seems to be no better than enrolling them at an older age). Third, reading to children in an interactive manner raises their IQ by about 6 points (and in this case, the earlier the parent starts reading the better). Fourth and finally, sending children to preschool raises their IQ by about 6 points. Clearly, there are some things that parents can do to make their kids smarter.

Perhaps all this will be simpler in the future. *Cognitive enhancers* are drugs that produce improvements in the psychological processes that underlie intelligent behavior. For example, stimulants such as Ritalin (methylphenidate) and Adderall (mixed amphetamine salts) can enhance cognitive performance (Elliott et al., 1997; Halliday et al., 1994; McKetin et al., 1999), which is why there has been an increase in their use by healthy students over the past few years. Surveys suggest that almost 7% of students in U. S. universities have used prescription stimulants for cognitive enhancement, and that on some campuses the number is as high as 25% (McCabe et al., 2005). These drugs improve people's ability to focus attention, manipulate information in working memory, and flexibly control responses (Sahakian & Morein-Zamir, 2007). Cognitive performance can also be enhanced by a class of drugs called ampakines (Ingvar et al., 1997). Modafinil is one such drug, and it has been shown to improve short-term memory and planning abilities in healthy, young volunteers (Turner et al., 2003).

We should of course be worried about the abuse of these drugs. Nonetheless, the distinction between enhancing cognition by taking drugs and enhancing it by other means is not cut and dried. As one distinguished group of scientists (Greely et al., 2008, p. 703) recently concluded, "Drugs may seem distinctive among enhancements in that they bring about their effects by altering brain function, but in reality so does any intervention that enhances cognition. Recent research has identified beneficial neural changes engendered by exercise, nutrition and sleep, as well as instruction and reading." In other words, if both drugs and exercise enhance cognition by altering the way the brain functions, then what exactly is the difference between them? Other scientists believe this question will soon be

How might your children enhance their intelligence?

Millionaire Robert Graham opened the Repository for Germinal Choice in 1980 to collect sperm from Nobel laureates and mathematical prodigies and allow healthy young women to be inseminated with it. His so-called "genius factory" produced more than 200 children but closed after his death in 1999.

ERIC MYER PHOTOGRAPHY INC.

moot because cognitive enhancement will be achieved not by altering the brain's chemistry in college, but by altering its basic structure at birth. By manipulating the genes that guide hippocampal development, scientists have created a strain of "smart mice" that have extraordinary memory and learning abilities, leading the researchers to conclude that "genetic enhancement of mental and cognitive attributes such as intelligence and memory in mammals is feasible" (Tang et al., 1999, p. 64). Although no one has yet developed a safe and powerful "smart pill" or "smart gene therapy," many experts believe that this will happen in the next few years (Farah et al., 2004; Rose, 2002; Turner & Sahakian, 2006). When it does, we will need a whole lot of wisdom to know how to handle it.

OTHER VOICES

How Science Can Build a Better You

David Ewing Duncan is an award-winning author and journalist whose most recent book is *When I'm 164: The new science of radical life extension, and what happens if it succeeds.*

CHRIS HARDY PHOTOGRAPHY

ntelligence is a highly prized commodity that buys people a lot of the good things in life. It can be increased by a solid education and a healthy diet, and everyone's in favor of those things. But it can also be increased by drugs— and there is little doubt that in the near future it will be increased by other even more powerful technologies. Is this a bad idea or a moral imperative? How will we decide who gets to use these technologies and who gets left behind? Author David Ewing Duncan thinks that these are critically important questions that we must answer now—*before* the "Age of Enhancement" begins. The following is an abridged version of his article that appeared in *The New York Times*.

... Over the last couple of years during talks and lectures, I have asked thousands of people a hypothetical question that goes like this: "If I could offer you a pill that allowed your child to increase his or her memory by 25 percent, would you give it to them?"

The show of hands in this informal poll has been overwhelming, with 80 percent or more voting no.

Then I asked a follow-up question. "What if this pill was safe and increased your kid's grades from a B average to an A average?" People tittered nervously, looked around to see how others were voting as nearly half said yes. (Many didn't vote at all.)

"And what if all of the other kids are taking the pill?" I asked. The tittering stopped and nearly everyone voted yes.

No pill now exists that can boost memory by 25 percent. Yet neuroscientists tell me that pharmaceutical companies are testing compounds in early stage human trials that may enable patients with dementia and other memory-stealing diseases to have better recall. No one knows if these will work to improve healthy people, but it's possible that one will work in the future.

More intriguing is the notion that a supermemory or attention pill might be used someday by those with critical jobs like pilots, surgeons, police officers—or the chief executive of the United States. In fact, we may demand that they use them, said the bioethicist Thomas H. Murray. "It might actually be immoral for a surgeon not to take a drug that was safe and steadied his hand," said Mr. Murray, the former president of the Hastings Center, a bioethics research group. "That would be like using a scalpel that wasn't sterile." ...

For years, scientists have been manipulating genes in animals to make improvements in neural performance, strength and agility, among other augmentations. Directly altering human DNA using "gene therapy" in humans remains dangerous and fraught with ethical challenges. But it may be possible to develop drugs that alter enzymes and other proteins associated with genes for, say, speed and endurance or dopamine levels in the brain connected to improved neural performance.

Synthetic biologists contend that re-engineering cells and DNA may one day allow us to eliminate diseases; a few believe we will be able to build tailor-made people. Others are convinced that stem cells might one day be used to grow fresh brain, heart or liver cells to augment or improve cells in these and other organs.

Not all enhancements are high-tech or invasive. Neuroscientists are seeing boosts from neuro-feedback and video games designed to teach and develop cognition and from meditation and improvements in diet, exercise and sleep. "We may see a convergence of several of these technologies," said the neurologist Adam Gazzaley of the University of California at San Francisco. He is developing brain-boosting games with developers and engineers who once worked for Lucas Arts, founded by the "Star Wars" director George Lucas. ...

Ethical challenges for the coming Age of Enhancement include, besides basic safety questions, the issue of who would get the enhancements, how much they would cost, and who would gain an advantage over others by using them. In a society that is already seeing a widening gap between the very rich and the rest of us, the question of a democracy of equals could face a critical test if the well-off also could afford a physical, genetic or bionic advantage. It also may challenge what it means to be human.

Still, the enhancements are coming, and they will be hard to resist. The real issue is what we do with them once they become irresistible.

IN SUMMARY

▶ Some groups outscore others on intelligence tests because (a) testing situations impair the performance of some groups more than others, and (b) some groups live in less healthful and stimulating environments.

▶ There is no compelling evidence to suggest that between-group differences in intelligence are due to genetic differences.

▶ The distinction between genetic and environmental influences on intelligence can be murky. For example, genes can influence an organism's behavior by determining which environments it is drawn to.

▶ Intelligence is correlated with mental health, and gifted children are as well-adjusted as their peers.

▶ Human intelligence can be temporarily increased by cognitive enhancers such as Ritalin and Adderall, and nonhuman intelligence has been permanently increased by genetic manipulation.

Chapter Review

KEY CONCEPT QUIZ

1. Which of the following abilities is not an accepted feature of intelligence?
   a. the ability to direct one's thinking
   b. the ability to adapt to one's circumstances
   c. the ability to care for oneself
   d. the ability to learn from one's experiences

2. Intelligence tests
   a. were first developed to help children who lagged behind their peers.
   b. were developed to measure aptitude rather than educational achievement.
   c. have been used for detestable ends.
   d. all of the above

3. Intelligence tests have been shown to be predictors of
   a. academic performance.
   b. mental health.
   c. physical health.
   d. all of the above.

4. People who score well on one test of mental ability usually score well on others, suggesting that
   a. tests of mental ability are perfectly correlated.
   b. intelligence cannot be measured meaningfully.
   c. there is a general ability called intelligence.
   d. intelligence is genetic.

5. The two-factor theory suggests that intelligence is a combination of general ability and
   a. factor analysis.
   b. specific abilities.
   c. primary mental abilities.
   d. creative intelligence.

6. Most scientists now believe that intelligence is best described
   a. as a set of group factors.
   b. by a two-factor framework.
   c. as a single, general ability.
   d. by a three-level hierarchy.

7. Standard intelligence tests typically measure
   a. analytic intelligence.
   b. practical intelligence.
   c. creative intelligence.
   d. all of the above.

8. Intelligence is influenced by
   a. genes alone.
   b. genes and environment.
   c. environment alone.
   d. neither genes nor environment.

9. The heritability coefficient is a statistic that describes how much of the difference between different people's intelligence scores can be explained by
   a. the nature of the specific test.
   b. differences in their environment.
   c. differences in their genes.
   d. their age at the time of testing.

10. Intelligence changes
    a. over the life span and across generations.
    b. over the life span but not across generations.
    c. across generations but not over the life span.
    d. neither across generations nor over the life span.

11. A person's socioeconomic status has a(n) ____ effect on intelligence.
    a. powerful
    b. negligible
    c. unsubstantiated
    d. unknown

12. Which of the following statements is false?
    a. Modern intelligence tests have a very strong cultural bias.
    b. Testing situations can impair the performance of some groups more than others.
    c. Test performance can suffer if the test taker is concerned about confirming a racial or gender stereotype.
    d. Some ethnic groups perform better than others on intelligence tests.

13. On which of the following does broad agreement exist among scientists?
    a. Differences in the intelligence test scores of different ethnic groups are clearly due to genetic differences between those groups.
    b. Differences in the intelligence test scores of different ethnic groups are caused in part by factors such as low birth weight and poor diet that are more prevalent in some groups than in others.
    c. Differences in the intelligence test scores of different ethnic groups always reflect real differences in intelligence.
    d. Genes that are strongly associated with intelligence have been found to be more prevalent in some ethnic groups than in others.

14. Gifted children tend to
    a. be equally gifted in several domains.
    b. be gifted in a single domain.
    c. lose their special talent in adulthood.
    d. change the focus of their interests relatively quickly.

KEY TERMS

intelligence (p. 396)
ratio IQ (p. 398)
deviation IQ (p. 398)
factor analysis (p. 401)

two-factor theory of intelligence (p. 402)
fluid intelligence (p. 405)
crystallized intelligence (p. 405)

emotional intelligence (p. 406)
fraternal twins (or dizygotic twins) (p. 408)
identical twins (or monozygotic twins) (p. 408)

heritability coefficient (p. 409)
shared environment (p. 410)
nonshared environment (p. 410)

CHANGING MINDS

1. In biology class, the topic turns to genetics. The professor describes the "Doogie" mouse, named after a 1990s TV show starring Neil Patrick Harris as a child genius named Doogie Howser. Doogie mice have a genetic manipulation that makes them smarter than other, genetically normal mice. Your classmate turns to you. "I knew it," she said. "There's a 'smart gene' after all—some people have it, and some people don't, and that's why some people are intelligent and some people aren't." What would you tell her about the role genetics play in intelligence? What other factors, besides genes, play an important role in determining an individual's intelligence?

2. One of your friends tells you about his sister. "We're very competitive," he says. "But she's smarter. We both took IQ tests when we were kids, and she scored 104 but I only scored 102." What would you tell your friend about the relationship between IQ scores and intelligence? What do IQ scores really measure?

3. A speaker visiting your university notes that there are still gender differences in academia; for example, in math departments across the country, women make up only about 26% of assistant professors and 10% of full professors. One of your classmates notes that the statistic isn't surprising: "Girls don't do as well as boys at math," he says. "So it's not surprising that fewer girls choose math-related careers." Based on what you've read in the text about group differences in intelligence, why might women perform more poorly then men on tests of math or science, even if the groups actually have similar ability?

4. One of your cousins has a young son, and she's very proud of the boy's accomplishments. "He's very smart," she says. "I know this because he has a great memory: He gets 100% on all his vocabulary tests." What kind of skills do vocabulary tests measure? Although these skills are important for intelligence, what other abilities contribute to an individual's overall intelligence?

ANSWERS TO KEY CONCEPT QUIZ

1. c; 2. d; 3. d; 4. c; 5. b; 6. d; 7. a; 8. b; 9. c; 10. a; 11. a; 12. a; 13. b; 14. b.

Need more help? Additional resources are located in LaunchPad at:
http://www.worthpublishers.com/launchpad/ schacter3e

Development

His mother called him Adi and showered him with affection, but his father was not so kind. As his sister later recalled, "Adi challenged my father to extreme harshness and got his sound thrashing every day. . . . How often on the other hand did my mother caress him and try to obtain with her kindness where the father could not succeed with harshness." Although his father wanted him to become a civil servant, Adi's true love was art, and his mother quietly encouraged that gentler interest. Adi was just 18 years old when his mother was diagnosed with terminal cancer, and he was heartbroken when she died.

But Adi had little time for grieving. As he later wrote, "Poverty and hard reality compelled me to make a quick decision. I was faced with the problem of somehow making my own living." Adi resolved to make that living as an artist. He applied to art school but he was flatly rejected. Motherless and penniless, Adi wandered the city streets for 5 long years, sleeping on park benches, living in homeless shelters, and eating in soup kitchens, while trying desperately to sell his sketches and watercolors.

In just 10 years, Adi had achieved the fame he desired, and more. Today his paintings are sought by collectors, who pay significant sums to acquire them. The largest collection of Adi's work is owned by the U.S. government, which keeps the pieces locked in a room in Washington, DC. The curator of the collection, Marylou Gjernes, once remarked, "I often looked at them and wondered, 'what if? What if he had been accepted into art school? Would World War II have happened?'" The curator's question makes sense because while the artist's mother called him Adi, the rest of us know him as Adolf Hitler.

Adi painted in many styles, including the precise and well-structured watercolor shown here. In 2013, one of his paintings sold at auction for $40,000.

INTERFOTO/ALAMY

MAKSYM BONDACHUK/SHUTTERSTOCK

WHY IS IT SO DIFFICULT TO IMAGINE THE GREATEST mass murderer of the 20th century as a gentle child who loved to draw, as a compassionate adolescent who cared for his ailing mother, or as a dedicated young adult who endured cold and hunger for the sake of art? After all, *you* didn't begin as the person you are today, and odds are that you aren't yet in finished form. From birth to infancy, from childhood to adolescence, from young adulthood to old age, human beings change over time. Their development includes both dramatic transformations and striking consistencies in the way they look, think, feel, and act. **Developmental psychology** is *the study of continuity and change across the life span,* and in the last century, developmental psychologists have discovered some truly amazing things about this metamorphosis.

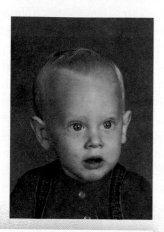   

From infancy to childhood to adolescence to adulthood, people exhibit both continuity and change.

Let's start where *you* started. We'll first examine the 9-month period between conception and birth and see how prenatal events set the stage for everything to come. Then we'll examine childhood, during which children must learn how to think about the world and their relationship to it, to understand and bond with others, and to tell the difference between right and wrong. Next, we'll examine a relatively new invention called adolescence, which is the stage at which children become both independent and sexual. Finally, we'll examine adulthood, the stage at which people typically leave their parents, find mates, and have children.

developmental psychology
The study of continuity and change across the life span.

zygote
A fertilized egg that contains chromosomes from both a sperm and an egg.

germinal stage
The 2-week period of prenatal development that begins at conception.

embryonic stage
The period of prenatal development that lasts from the 2nd week until about the 8th week.

Prenatality: A Womb with a View

You probably calculate your age by counting your birthdays. But the fact is that on the day you were born, you were already 9 months old. The *prenatal stage* of development ends with birth and begins 9 months earlier when about 200 million sperm make the journey from a woman's vagina, through her uterus, and on to her fallopian tubes. That journey is a perilous one. Many of the sperm have defects that prevent them from swimming vigorously enough to make any progress, and others get stuck in the spermatazoidal equivalent of a traffic jam in which too many sperm are headed in the same direction at the same time. Of those that do manage to make their way through the uterus, many will take a wrong turn and end up in the fallopian tube that does not contain an egg. In fact, a mere 200 or so of the original 200 million sperm will manage to find the correct fallopian tube and get close enough to an egg to release digestive enzymes that erode the egg's protective outer layer. The moment the first sperm manages to penetrate the egg's coating, the egg will release a chemical that seals the coating and keeps all the other sperm from entering. After triumphing over 199,999,999 of its closest friends, this single successful sperm will shed its tail and fertilize the egg. About 12 hours later, the egg will merge with the nuclei of the sperm, and the prenatal development of a unique human being will begin.

Prenatal Development

A **zygote** is *a fertilized egg that contains chromosomes from both an egg and a sperm*. From the first moment of its existence, a zygote has one thing in common with the person it will someday become: sex. Each human sperm and each human egg contain 23 *chromosomes*. One of these chromosomes (the 23rd) comes in two varieties known as X and Y. An egg always has an X chromosome, but a sperm can have either an X or a Y chromosome. If the egg is fertilized by a sperm that has a Y chromosome, then the zygote is male (XY), and if it is fertilized by a sperm that has an X chromosome, then the zygote is female (XX).

The **germinal stage** is *the 2-week period that begins at conception*. During this stage, the one-celled zygote divides into two cells that then divide into four cells that then divide into eight, and so on. By the time an infant is born, its body contains trillions of cells, each of which came from the original zygote, and each of which contains exactly one set of 23 chromosomes from the sperm and one set of 23 chromosomes from the egg. During the germinal stage, the zygote migrates back down the fallopian tube and implants itself in the wall of the uterus. This too is a difficult journey, and about half of zygotes do not complete it, either because they are defective or because they implant themselves in an inhospitable part of the uterus. Male zygotes are especially unlikely to complete this journey and no one understands why (though several comedians have suggested that it's because male zygotes are especially unwilling to stop and ask for directions).

> **?** What are the three prenatal stages?

If the zygote successfully implants itself in the uterine wall, it earns the right to be called an *embryo* and a new stage of development begins. The **embryonic stage** is *a period that lasts from the 2nd week until about the 8th week* (see **FIGURE 11.1**). During this stage, the embryo continues to divide and its cells begin to differentiate. Merely 1 inch long, the embryo already has a beating heart and other body parts, such as arms and legs. Embryos that have XY chromosomes begin to produce a hormone called testosterone, which masculinizes their reproductive organs.

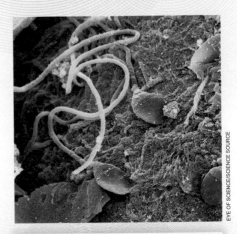

EYE OF SCIENCE/SCIENCE SOURCE

This electron micrograph shows several human sperm, one of which is fertilizing an egg. Contrary to what many people think, fertilization does not happen right away. It typically happens 1 to 2 days after intercourse, but can happen as much as 5 days later.

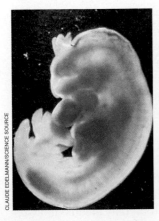
CLAUDE EDELMANN/SCIENCE SOURCE

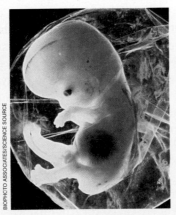
BIOPHOTO ASSOCIATES/SCIENCE SOURCE

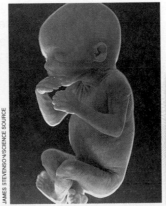
JAMES STEVENSON/SCIENCE SOURCE

◀ Figure 11.1 Human beings undergo amazing development in the 9 months of prenatal development. These images show an embryo at 30 days (about the size of a poppy seed), an embryo at 8 to 9 weeks (about the size of an olive), and a fetus at 5 months (about the size of a pomegranate).

At about 9 weeks, the embryo gets a new name: *fetus*. The **fetal stage** is *a period that lasts from the 9th week until birth*. The fetus has a skeleton and muscles that make it capable of movement. It develops a layer of insulating fat beneath its skin, and its digestive and respiratory systems mature. The cells that will ultimately become the brain divide very quickly around the 3rd and 4th week after conception, and this process is more or less complete by 24 weeks. During the fetal stage, brain cells begin to generate axons and dendrites (which permit communication with other brain cells). They also begin to undergo a process (described in the Neuroscience and Behavior chapter) known as **myelination,** which is *the formation of a fatty sheath around the axons of a neuron.* Just as plastic sheathing insulates a wire, myelin insulates a brain cell and prevents the leakage of neural signals that travel along the axon. This process starts during the fetal stage but doesn't end for years; the myelination of the cortex, for example, continues into adulthood.

Although the brain undergoes rapid and complex growth during the fetal period, at birth it is nowhere near its adult size. Whereas a newborn chimpanzee's brain is nearly 60% of its adult size, a newborn human's brain is only 25% of its adult size, which is to say that 75% of a human's brain development occurs outside the womb. Why are humans born with such underdeveloped brains?

First, adult humans have huge heads. If a newborn human's head were 60% of its adult size—like a newborn chimp's head is—then that human would never be newborn because it could never pass through its mother's birth canal. Second, one of our species' greatest talents is its ability to adapt to a wide range of novel environments that differ in climate, social structure, and so on. Rather than arriving in the world with a fully developed brain that may or may not meet the requirements of its environment, human beings arrive with brains that do much of their developing *within* the very environments in which they ultimately must function. The fact that our underdeveloped brains are specifically shaped by the unique social and physical environment into which we are born is one of the main reasons why we are so adaptable.

> **Why are human beings born with underdeveloped brains?**

KAREN HUNT/CORBIS

This chimp and boy share a deep interest in dirt, bugs, and leaves. But one big difference between them is that the chimp was born with a nearly adult-sized brain, whereas the boy was born with a brain that will ultimately triple in size.

Prenatal Environment

The womb is an environment that has a powerful impact on development (Coe & Lubach, 2008; Glynn & Sandman, 2011; Wadhwa, Sandman, & Garite, 2001). For example, the *placenta* is the organ that physically links the bloodstreams of the mother and the embryo or fetus and permits the exchange of certain chemicals. That's why the foods a woman eats during pregnancy can affect her unborn child. The children of mothers who receive insufficient nutrition during pregnancy often have physical problems (Stein et al., 1975) and psychological problems, most notably an increased risk of schizophrenia and antisocial personality disorder (Neugebauer, Hoek, & Susser, 1999; Susser, Brown, & Matte, 1999). The foods a woman eats during pregnancy can also shape her child's food preferences: Studies show that infants tend to like the foods and spices that their mothers ate while they were in utero (Mennella, Johnson, & Beauchamp, 1995).

> **How does the uterine environment affect the unborn child?**

But it isn't just food that affects the fetus. Almost anything a woman eats, drinks, inhales, injects, sniffs, snorts, or rubs on her skin can pass through the placenta. *Agents that impair development* are called **teratogens,** which literally means "monster

fetal stage
The period of prenatal development that lasts from the 9th week until birth.

myelination
The formation of a fatty sheath around the axons of a neuron.

teratogens
Agents that damage the process of development, such as drugs and viruses.

fetal alcohol syndrome (FAS)
A developmental disorder that stems from heavy alcohol use by the mother during pregnancy.

OTHER VOICES

Men, Who Needs Them?

Greg Hampikian is a professor of biology and criminal justice at Boise State University and the director of the Idaho Innocence Project.
PHOTO COURTESY OF GREG HAMPIKIAN

All of the authors of this book are men, so we're very much in favor of their continued existence. But in this only-slightly-tongue-in-cheek essay, biologist Greg Hampikian (2012) does a nice job of explaining just how biologically unimportant men are to the perpetuation of our species.

. . . With expanding reproductive choices, we can expect to see more women choose to reproduce without men entirely. Fortunately, the data for children raised by only females is encouraging. As the Princeton sociologist Sara S. McLanahan has shown, poverty is what hurts children, not the number or gender of parents.

That's good, since women are both necessary and sufficient for reproduction, and men are neither. From the production of the first cell (egg) to the development of the fetus and the birth and breastfeeding of the child, fathers can be absent. They can be at work, at home, in prison or at war, living or dead.

Think about your own history. Your life as an egg actually started in your mother's developing ovary, before she was born; you were wrapped in your mother's fetal body as it developed within your grandmother.

After the two of you left Grandma's womb, you enjoyed the protection of your mother's prepubescent ovary. Then, sometime between 12 and 50 years after the two of you left your grandmother, you burst forth and were sucked by her fimbriae into the fallopian tube. You glided along the oviduct, surviving happily on the stored nutrients and genetic messages that Mom packed for you.

Then, at some point, your father spent a few minutes close by, but then left. A little while later, you encountered some very odd tiny cells that he had shed. They did not merge with you, or give you any cell membranes or nutrients—just an infinitesimally small packet of DNA, less than one-millionth of your mass.

Over the next nine months, you stole minerals from your mother's bones and oxygen from her blood, and you received all your nutrition, energy and immune protection from her. By the time you were born your mother had contributed six to eight pounds of your weight. Then as a parting gift, she swathed you in billions of bacteria from her birth canal and groin that continue to protect your skin, digestive system and general health. In contrast, your father's 3.3 picograms of DNA comes out to less than one pound of male contribution since the beginning of Homo sapiens 107 billion babies ago.

And while birth seems like a separation, for us mammals it's just a new form of attachment to our female parent. If your mother breast-

fed you, as our species has done for nearly our entire existence, then you suckled from her all your water, protein, sugar, fats and even immune protection. She sampled your diseases by holding you close and kissing you, just as your father might have done; but unlike your father, she responded to your infections by making antibodies that she passed to you in breast milk.

I don't dismiss the years I put in as a doting father, or my year at home as a house husband with two young kids. And I credit my own father as the more influential parent in my life. Fathers are of great benefit. But that is a far cry from "necessary and sufficient" for reproduction.

If a woman wants to have a baby without a man, she just needs to secure sperm (fresh or frozen) from a donor (living or dead). The only technology the self-impregnating woman needs is a straw or turkey baster, and the basic technique hasn't changed much since Talmudic scholars debated the religious implications of insemination without sex in the fifth century. If all the men on earth died tonight, the species could continue on frozen sperm. If the women disappear, it's extinction.

Ultimately the question is, does "mankind" really need men? With human cloning technology just around the corner and enough frozen sperm in the world to already populate many generations, perhaps we should perform a cost–benefit analysis.

It's true that men have traditionally been the breadwinners. But women have been a majority of college graduates since the 1980s, and their numbers are growing. It's also true that men have, on average, a bit more muscle mass than women. But in the age of ubiquitous weapons, the one with the better firepower (and knowledge of the law) triumphs.

Meanwhile women live longer, are healthier and are far less likely to commit a violent offense. If men were cars, who would buy the model that doesn't last as long, is given to lethal incidents and ends up impounded more often?

Recently, the geneticist J. Craig Venter showed that the entire genetic material of an organism can be synthesized by a machine and then put into what he called an "artificial cell." This was actually a bit of press-release hyperbole: Mr. Venter started with a fully functional cell, then swapped out its DNA. In doing so, he unwittingly demonstrated that the female component of sexual reproduction, the egg cell, cannot be manufactured, but the male can.

When I explained this to a female colleague and asked her if she thought that there was yet anything irreplaceable about men, she answered, "They're entertaining."

Gentlemen, let's hope that's enough.

makers." Teratogens include environmental poisons such as lead in the water, paint dust in the air, or mercury in fish, but the most common teratogens can be purchased at 7-Eleven. **Fetal alcohol syndrome (FAS)** is *a developmental disorder that stems from heavy alcohol use by the mother during pregnancy,* and children with FAS have a variety of brain abnormalities and cognitive deficits (Carmichael Olson et al., 1997;

This child has some of the telltale facial features associated with FAS: short eye openings, a flat midface, a flat ridge under the nose, a thin upper lip, and an underdeveloped jaw.

Streissguth et al., 1999). Some studies suggest that light drinking does not harm the fetus, but there is little consensus about how much drinking is light (Warren & Hewitt, 2009). However, everyone agrees that "none" is a perfectly safe amount.

Tobacco is the other common teratogen, and there is no debate about its effects. About 20% of American mothers admit to smoking during pregnancy (Substance Abuse and Mental Health Services Administration, 2005). The half-million infants to which they annually give birth are smaller (Horta et al., 1997) and more likely to have perceptual and attentional problems in childhood (Espy et al., 2011; Fried & Watkinson, 2000). Even secondhand smoke can lead to reduced birth weight and deficits in attention and learning (Makin, Fried, & Watkinson, 1991; Windham, Eaton, & Hopkins, 1999). The embryo is more vulnerable to teratogens than is the fetus, but structures such as the central nervous system remain vulnerable throughout the entire prenatal period. Some researchers estimate that if all pregnant women in America quit smoking, there would be an 11% reduction in stillbirths and a 5% reduction in newborn deaths (March of Dimes, 2010).

The prenatal environment is rich with chemicals, and it is also rich with information. Unlike an automobile, which operates only after it has been fully assembled, the human brain is operating while it is being built, and research shows that the developing fetus can sense stimulation and learn from it. Wombs are dark because only the brightest light can filter through the mother's abdomen, but they are not quiet. The

What can a fetus hear?

fetus can hear its mother's heartbeat, the gastrointestinal sounds associated with her digestion, and her voice. How do we know? Newborns will suck a nipple more vigorously when they hear the sound of their mother's voice than when they hear the voice of a female stranger (Querleu et al., 1984), demonstrating that they are more familiar with the former. Similarly, newborns whose mothers read aloud from *The Cat in the Hat* during their pregnancies react as though the story is familiar (DeCasper & Spence, 1986). Newborns who are presented with words from two languages prefer hearing their mother's native language—unless their mother is bilingual—in which case they are just as happy to hear both languages (Byers-Heinlein, Burns, & Werker, 2010). What newborns hear even influences the sounds they make at birth: French newborns cry with a rising melody and German newborns with a falling melody, mimicking the cadence of their mother's native tongue (Mampe et al., 2009). Clearly, the fetus is listening.

IN SUMMARY

► Developmental psychology studies continuity and change across the life span.

► The prenatal stage of development begins when a sperm fertilizes an egg, producing a zygote. The zygote, which contains chromosomes from both the egg and the sperm, develops into an embryo at 2 weeks and then into a fetus at 8 weeks.

► The fetal environment has important physical and psychological influences on the fetus. In addition to the food a pregnant woman eats, teratogens, or agents that impair fetal development, can affect the fetus. Some of the most common teratogens are tobacco and alcohol.

► Although the fetus cannot see much in the womb, it can hear sounds and become familiar with those it hears often, such as its mother's voice.

Infancy and Childhood: Becoming a Person

Newborns may appear to be capable of little more than squalling and squirming, but in the last decade, researchers have discovered that they are much more sophisticated than they appear. **Infancy** is *the stage of development that begins at birth and lasts between 18 and 24 months,* and as you will see, a lot more happens during this stage than meets the untrained eye.

Perceptual and Motor Development

New parents like to stand around the crib and make goofy faces at the baby because they think the baby will be amused. In fact, newborns have a rather limited range of vision. The level of detail that a newborn can see at a distance of 20 feet is roughly equivalent to the level of detail that an adult can see at 600 feet (Banks & Salapatek,

> **What do newborns see?**

1983), which is to say that they are missing out on a lot of the cribside shenanigans. On the other hand, when stimuli are 8 to 12 inches away (about the distance between a nursing infant's eyes and its mother's face), newborns are visually quite responsive. How do we know what newborns are seeing? In one study, newborns were shown a circle with diagonal stripes over and over again. The infants stared a lot at first, and then less and less on each subsequent presentation. Recall from the Learning chapter that *habituation* is the tendency for organisms to respond less intensely to a stimulus as the frequency of exposure to that stimulus increases, and infants habituate just like the rest of us do. So what happened when the researchers rotated the circle 90°? The newborns once again stared intently, indicating that they had noticed the change in the circle's orientation (Slater, Morison, & Somers, 1988).

Newborns are especially attentive to social stimuli. For example, newborns in one study were shown a circle, a circle with scrambled facial features, or a circle with a regular face. When the circle was moved across their fields of vision, the newborns tracked the circle by moving their heads and eyes—but they tracked the circle with the regular face longer than they tracked the others (Johnson et al., 1991). Newborns do more than simply track social stimuli. Researchers in one study stood close to some newborns while sticking out their tongues and stood close to other newborns while pursing their lips. Newborns in the first group stuck out their own tongues more often than those in the second group did, and newborns in the second group pursed their lips more often than those in the first group did (Meltzoff & Moore, 1977). Indeed, newborns have been shown to mimic facial expressions in their very first *hour* of life (Reissland, 1988) and to mimic speech sounds as early as 12 weeks (Kuhl & Meltzoff, 1996).

Although infants can use their eyes right away, they must spend considerably more time learning how to use their other parts. **Motor development** is *the emergence of the ability to execute physical actions* such as reaching, grasping, crawling, and walking. Infants are born with a small set of **reflexes,** which are *specific patterns of motor response that are triggered by specific patterns of sensory stimulation.* For example, the *rooting reflex* is the tendency for

> **Why are infants born with reflexes?**

infants to move their mouths toward any object that touches their cheek, and the *sucking reflex* is the tendency to suck any object that enters their mouths. These two reflexes allow newborns to find their mother's nipple and begin feeding—a behavior so vitally important that nature took no chances and hardwired it into every one of us. Interestingly, these and other reflexes that are present at birth seem to disappear in the first few months as infants learn to execute more sophisticated motor behavior.

Infants mimic the facial expressions of adults—and vice versa, of course!

infancy
The stage of development that begins at birth and lasts between 18 and 24 months.

motor development
The emergence of the ability to execute physical action.

reflexes
Specific patterns of motor response that are triggered by specific patterns of sensory stimulation.

cephalocaudal rule
The "top-to-bottom" rule that describes the tendency for motor skills to emerge in sequence from the head to the feet.

proximodistal rule
The "inside-to-outside" rule that describes the tendency for motor skills to emerge in sequence from the center to the periphery.

The development of these more sophisticated behaviors tends to obey two general rules. The first is the **cephalocaudal rule** (or the "top-to-bottom" rule), which describes *the tendency for motor skills to emerge in sequence from the head to the feet*. Infants tend to gain control over their heads first, their arms and trunks next, and their legs last. A young infant who is placed on her stomach may lift her head and her chest by using her arms for support, but she typically has little control over her legs. The second rule is the **proximodistal rule** (or the "inside-to-outside" rule), which describes *the tendency for motor skills to emerge in sequence from the center to the periphery*. Infants learn to control their trunks before their elbows and knees, which they learn to control before their hands and feet (see **FIGURE 11.2**).

> In what order do infants learn to use parts of their bodies?

Motor skills generally emerge in an orderly sequence but not on a strict timetable. Rather, the timing of these skills is influenced by many factors, such as the infant's incentive for reaching, body weight, muscular development, and general level of activity. In one study, infants who had visually stimulating mobiles hanging above their cribs began reaching for objects 6 weeks earlier than infants who did not (White & Held, 1966). Furthermore, different infants seem to acquire the same skill in different ways. By closely following the development of four infants, one study examined how children learn to reach (Thelen et al., 1993). Two of the infants were especially energetic and initially produced large circular movements of both arms. To reach accurately, these infants had to learn to dampen these large circular movements by holding their arms rigid at the elbow and swiping at an object. The other two infants were less energetic and did not produce large, circular movements. Thus, their first step in learning to reach involved learning to lift their arms against the force of gravity and extend them forward. Detailed observations such as these suggest that, although most infants learn how to reach, different infants learn in different ways (Adolph & Avoilio, 2000).

KAYTE DEIOMA/PHOTO EDIT

Motor skills develop through practice. In just 1 hour in a playroom, the average 12- to 19-month-old infant takes 2,368 steps, travels 0.4 miles, and falls 17 times (Adolph et al., 2012).

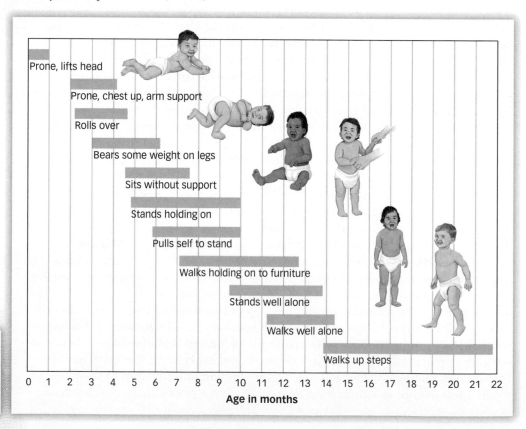

▶ Figure **11.2 Motor Development** Infants learn to control their bodies from head to feet and from center to periphery. These skills do not emerge on a strict timetable, but they do emerge in a strict sequence.

Prone, lifts head
Prone, chest up, arm support
Rolls over
Bears some weight on legs
Sits without support
Stands holding on
Pulls self to stand
Walks holding on to furniture
Stands well alone
Walks well alone
Walks up steps

0 1 2 3 4 5 6 7 8 9 10 11 12 13 14 15 16 17 18 19 20 21 22
Age in months

Cognitive Development

Infants can hear and see and move their bodies. But can they think? In the first half of the 20th century, a Swiss biologist named Jean Piaget became interested in this question. He noticed that when confronted with difficult problems (Does the big glass have more liquid in it than the small glass? Can Billy see what you see?), children of the same age made roughly the same mistakes. And as they aged, they stopped making these mistakes at about the same time. This led Piaget to suggest that children move through discrete stages of **cognitive development,** which is *the emergence of the ability to think and understand.* Between infancy and adulthood, children must come to understand three important things: (a) how the physical world works, (b) how their minds represent the world, and (c) how other minds represent the world. Let's see how children accomplish these three essential tasks.

> **What are the three essential tasks of cognitive development?**

Discovering the World

Piaget (1954) suggested that cognitive development occurs in four stages: the *sensorimotor* stage, the *preoperational* stage, the *concrete operational* stage, and the *formal operational* stage (see **TABLE 11.1**). The **sensorimotor stage** is *a period of development that begins at birth and lasts through infancy.* As the word *sensorimotor* suggests, infants at this stage are mainly busy using their ability to *sense* and their ability to *move* to acquire information about the world. By actively exploring their environments with their eyes, mouths, and fingers, infants begin to construct **schemas,** which are *theories about the way the world works.*

cognitive development
The emergence of the ability to think and understand.

sensorimotor stage
A stage of development that begins at birth and lasts through infancy in which infants acquire information about the world by sensing it and moving around within it.

schemas
Theories about the way the world works.

assimilation
The process by which infants apply their schemas in novel situations.

Jean Piaget (1896–1980) was the father of modern developmental psychology, as well as the last man to look good in a beret.

> **Table 11.1**

Piaget's Four Stages of Cognitive Development

Stage	Characteristic
Sensorimotor (Birth–2 years)	Infant experiences world through movement and senses, develops schemas, begins to act intentionally, and shows evidence of understanding object permanence.
Preoperational (2–6 years)	Child acquires motor skills but does not understand conservation of physical properties. Child begins this stage by thinking egocentrically but ends with a basic understanding of other minds.
Concrete operational (6–11 years)	Child can think logically about physical objects and events and understands conservation of physical properties.
Formal operational (11 years and up)	Child can think logically about abstract propositions and hypotheticals.

As every scientist knows, the key advantage of having a theory is that one can use it to predict and control what will happen in novel situations. If an infant learns that tugging at a stuffed animal causes the toy to come closer, then that observation is incorporated into the infant's theory about how physical objects behave, and the infant can later use that theory when he or she wants a different object to come closer, such as a rattle or a ball. Piaget called this **assimilation,** which happens when *infants apply their schemas in novel situations.* Of course, if the infant tugs the tail of the family cat, the cat is likely to sprint in the opposite direction. Infants' theories about the world ("Things come closer if I pull them") are occasionally disconfirmed, and so infants must occasionally adjust their schemas in light of

> **What happens at the sensorimotor stage?**

During the sensorimotor stage, infants explore with their hands and mouths, learning important lessons about the physical world such as, "If you whack Jell-O hard enough, you can actually wear it."

accommodation
The process by which infants revise their schemas in light of new information.

object permanence
The belief that objects continue to exist even when they are not visible.

childhood
The stage of development that begins at about 18 to 24 months and lasts until adolescence, which begins between 11 and 14 years.

preoperational stage
The stage of cognitive development that begins at about 2 years and ends at about 6 years, during which children develop a preliminary understanding of the physical world.

their new experiences ("Aha! Only *inanimate* things come closer when I pull them"). Piaget called this **accommodation,** which happens when *infants revise their schemas in light of new information.*

What kinds of schemas do infants develop, apply, and adjust? Piaget suggested that infants lack some very basic understandings about the physical world and therefore must acquire them through experience. For example, when you put your shoes in the closet, you know that they exist even after you close the closet door, and you would be rather surprised if you opened the door a moment later and found the closet empty. But according to Piaget, this wouldn't surprise an infant because infants do not have a theory of **object permanence,** which is *the belief that objects exist even when they are not visible.* Piaget noted that in the first few months of life, infants act as though objects stop existing the moment they are out of sight. For instance, he observed that a 2-month-old infant will track a moving object with her eyes, but once the object leaves her visual field, she will not search for it. Put the shoes in the closet and—poof!—they are gone!

> **?** When do children acquire a theory of object permanence?

Was Piaget right? As a general rule, when infants demonstrate an ability, then they definitely have it, but when they fail to demonstrate an ability, they may lack the ability *or* the test may not be sensitive enough to reveal it. Modern research shows that when other tests are used, infants can demonstrate their sense of object permanence much earlier than Piaget realized (Shinskey & Munakata, 2005). For instance, in one study, infants were shown a miniature drawbridge that flipped up and down (see **FIGURE 11.3**). Once the infants got used to this, they watched as a box was placed behind the drawbridge—in its path but out of their sight. Some infants then saw a *possible* event: The drawbridge began to flip and then suddenly stopped, as if impeded by the box that the infants could not see. Other infants saw an *impossible* event: The drawbridge began to flip and then continued, as if unimpeded by the box. What did infants do? Four-month-old infants stared longer at the impossible event than at the possible event, suggesting that they were puzzled by it (Baillargeon, Spelke, & Wasserman, 1985). The only thing that could have made it puzzling, of course, was the fact that the unseen box was not stopping the progress of the drawbridge (Fantz, 1964).

Studies such as these suggest that infants do indeed have some understanding of object permanence by the time they are just 4 months old. For example, what do

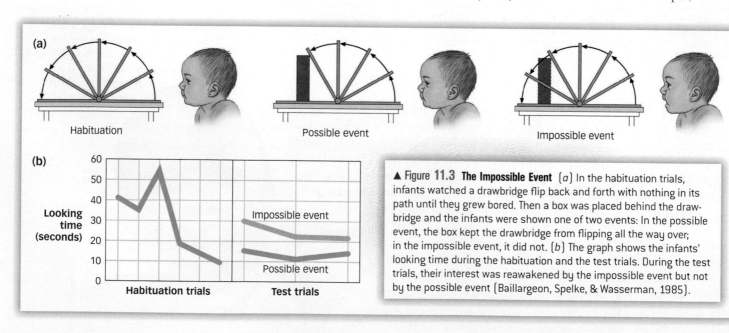

(a)

Habituation   Possible event   Impossible event

(b) Looking time (seconds)

▲ Figure **11.3** **The Impossible Event** [*a*] In the habituation trials, infants watched a drawbridge flip back and forth with nothing in its path until they grew bored. Then a box was placed behind the drawbridge and the infants were shown one of two events: In the possible event, the box kept the drawbridge from flipping all the way over; in the impossible event, it did not. [*b*] The graph shows the infants' looking time during the habituation and test trials. During the test trials, their interest was reawakened by the impossible event but not by the possible event (Baillargeon, Spelke, & Wasserman, 1985).

infants see when they look at the line labeled A in **FIGURE 11.4**? Adults see a continuous blue line that is being obstructed by the solid orange block in front of it. Do infants see line A as continuous and obstructed, or do they see it as two blue objects on either side of an orange object? Studies show that when infants are allowed to become familiar with line A, they are subsequently more surprised by line C than by line B, despite the fact that line C actually *looks* more like line A than does line B (Kellman & Spelke, 1983). This suggests that infants see line A as a continuous line. Infants clearly do not think of the world only in terms of its visible parts, and at a very early age they seem to "know" that objects continue to exist even when they are out of sight (Wang & Baillargeon, 2008).

Piaget (1927/1977, p. 199) wrote: "The child's first year of life is unfortunately still an abyss of mysteries for the psychologist. If only we could know what is going on in a baby's mind while observing him in action, we could certainly understand everything there is to psychology." Although the mystery of the infant mind is still far from solved, it is no longer an abyss. Research has taught us a great deal about what infants do and do not know, and the general conclusion is that they know much more than Piaget (or their parents) ever suspected (Gopnik, 2012).

Discovering the Mind

The long period following infancy is called **childhood,** which is *the period that begins at about 18 to 24 months and lasts until about 11 to 14 years.* According to Piaget, children enter childhood at one stage of cognitive development and leave at another. They enter in the **preoperational stage,** which is *the stage of cognitive development that begins at about 2 years and ends at about 6 years, during which children develop a preliminary understanding of the physical world.* They exit at the

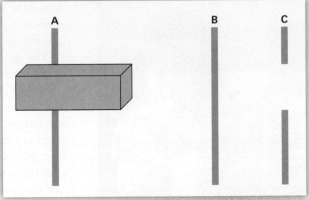

▲ Figure **11.4 Object Permanence**
Do infants see line A as continuous or broken? Infants who are shown line A are subsequently more interested when they are shown line C than line B. This indicates that they consider C more novel than B, which suggests that the infants saw line A as continuous and not broken (Kellman & Spelke, 1983).

A Statistician in the Crib

A magician asks you to shuffle a deck of cards and then name your favorite. He then dons a blindfold, reaches out his hand, and pulls your favorite card from the deck. You are astonished—and the reason you are astonished is that you know that when a magician reaches into a deck of 52 cards, the odds that he will pick your favorite by sheer chance alone is rather small.

Would that trick astonish an infant? That's pretty hard to imagine. After all, to appreciate the trick, one has to understand a basic rule of statistics, namely, that random samples look roughly like the populations from which they are drawn. But recent research (Denison, Reed, & Xu, 2013) suggests that infants as young as 24 weeks understand just that.

In one study, researchers showed infants two boxes: one had mostly pink balls and just a few yellows; the other had mostly yellow balls with a few pinks. The infants then watched as an experimenter closed her eyes and reached into the mostly pink box, pulled out some balls, and deposited them in a little container in front of the infant. Sometimes she deposited four pinks and a yellow, and sometimes she deposited four yellows and a pink. What did the infants do?

When the experimenter pulled mainly pink balls from a mainly pink box, the infants glanced and then looked away. But when she pulled mainly yellow balls from a mainly pink box, they stared like bystanders at a train wreck. The fact that infants looked longer at the improbable sample than at the probable sample suggests that they found the former more astonishing; in other words, they had some basic understanding of how random sampling works.

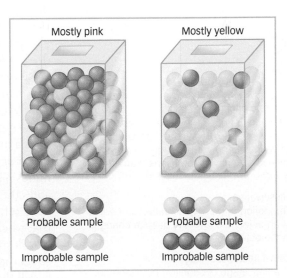

Mostly pink   Mostly yellow

Probable sample   Probable sample

Improbable sample   Improbable sample

This study—like so many in developmental psychology—teaches us that infants know a lot more than anyone could guess from casual observation of their behavior.

When preoperational children are shown two equal-size glasses filled with equal amounts of liquid, they correctly say that neither glass "has more." But when the contents of one glass are poured into a taller, thinner glass, they incorrectly say that the taller glass now "has more." Concrete operational children don't make this mistake because they recognize that operations such as pouring change the appearance of the liquid but not its actual volume.

concrete operational stage
The stage of cognitive development that begins at about 6 years and ends at about 11 years, during which children learn how various actions or "operations" can affect or transform "concrete" objects.

conservation
The notion that the quantitative properties of an object are invariant despite changes in the object's appearance.

formal operational stage
The final stage of cognitive development that begins around the age of 11, during which children learn to reason about abstract concepts.

egocentrism
The failure to understand that the world appears differently to different people.

concrete operational stage, which is *the stage of cognitive development that begins at about 6 years and ends at about 11 years, during which children learn how actions or "operations" can transform the "concrete" objects of the physical world.*

The difference between these stages is nicely illustrated by one of Piaget's clever experiments in which he showed children a row of cups and asked them to place an egg in each. Preoperational children were able to do this, and afterward they readily agreed that there were just as many eggs as there were cups. Then Piaget removed the eggs and spread them out in a long line that extended beyond the row of cups. Preoperational children incorrectly claimed that there were now more eggs than cups, pointing out that the row of eggs was longer than the row of cups and hence must be more of them. Concrete operational children, on the other hand, correctly reported that the number of eggs did not change when they were spread out in a longer line. They understood that *quantity* is a property of a set of concrete objects that does not change when an operation such as *spreading out* alters the set's appearance (Piaget, 1954). Piaget called the child's insight **conservation,** which is *the notion that the quantitative properties of an object are invariant despite changes in the object's appearance.*

> What distinguishes the preoperational and concrete operational stages?

Why don't preoperational children seem to grasp the notion of conservation? Piaget suggested that children have several tendencies that explain this mistake. For instance, *centration* is the tendency to focus on just one property of an object to the exclusion of all others. Whereas adults can consider several properties at once, children focus on the length of the line of eggs without simultaneously considering the amount of space between each egg. Piaget also suggested that children fail to think about *reversibility.* That is, they do not consider the fact that the operation that made the line of eggs longer could be reversed: The eggs could be repositioned more closely together, and the line would become shorter. Both of these tendencies make it difficult for the preoperational child to recognize that a *longer line of eggs* doesn't necessarily mean *more eggs.*

But there is an even deeper reason why preoperational children do not fully grasp the notion of conservation: They do not fully grasp the fact that they have *minds* and that these minds contain *mental representations* of the world! As adults, we naturally distinguish between the subjective and the objective, between appearances and realities, between things in the mind and things in the world. We realize that things aren't always as they seem: A wagon can *be* red but *look* gray at dusk, and a highway can *be* dry but *look* wet in the heat. We make a distinction between the way things *are* and the way we *see* them. Visual illusions delight us precisely because we know that they look like *this* but are really like *that.* Preoperational children don't make this distinction. When something *looks* gray or wet, they assume it *is* gray or wet.

As children move from the preoperational to the concrete operational stage, they have a major epiphany that will stay with them for the rest of their lives: The way the world *appears* is not necessarily the way the world really *is.* They realize that their minds represent—and hence can misrepresent—the objects in the world, and this enables them to solve problems that require them to ignore an object's subjective appearance (cf. Deák, 2006). For instance, concrete operational children can understand that when a ball of clay is rolled, stretched, or flattened, it is still the same amount of clay despite the fact that it looks larger in one form than in another. They can understand that when water is poured from a short, wide beaker into a tall, thin cylinder, it is still the same amount of water despite the fact that the water level in the cylinder is higher. They can understand that when a sponge is painted gray to look like a rock, it is still a sponge despite its appearance. Once children can make a distinction between objects and their mental representations of those objects, they begin to understand that certain operations—such as squishing, pouring, and spreading out—can change what an object *looks* like without changing what the object *is* like.

Once children are at the concrete operational stage, they can readily solve physical problems involving egg-spreading and clay-squishing. They learn to solve nonphysical problems with equal ease at the **formal operational stage,** which is *the final stage of cognitive development that begins around the age of 11, during which children learn to reason about abstract concepts.* Childhood ends when formal operations begin, and people who move on to this stage (and Piaget believed that some people never did) are able to reason systematically about abstract concepts such as *liberty* and *love* and about hypotheticals and counterfactuals—about events that have not yet happened, and about events that might have happened but didn't. There are no concrete objects in the world to which words such as *liberating* or *loving* refer, and yet people at the formal operational stage can think and reason about such concepts in the same way that a concrete operational child can think and reason about squishing and folding. The ability to generate, consider, reason about, or mentally "operate on" abstract objects, is the hallmark of formal operations.

> **What is the essential feature of the formal operational stage?**

People who reach the formal operational stage can reason about abstract concepts such as freedom and justice. These two protesters are taking part in a demonstration in front of the White House, calling for the closing of the U.S. military prison at Guantanamo Bay, Cuba.

Discovering Other Minds

As children develop, they discover their own minds, but they also discover the minds of others. Because preoperational children don't fully grasp the fact that they have minds that mentally represent objects, they also don't fully grasp the fact that other people have minds that may mentally represent the same objects in different ways. As such, preoperational children generally expect others to see the world as they do. When 3-year-old children are asked what a person on the opposite side of a table is seeing, they typically claim that the other person sees what they see. **Egocentrism** is *the failure to understand that the world appears differently to different people.* Egocentrism is a hallmark of the preoperational stage and it reveals itself in a variety of interesting ways.

Perceptions and Beliefs. Just as 3-year-old children don't realize that other people don't see what they see, they also don't realize that other people don't know what they know. This fact has been demonstrated in hundreds of studies using *the false-belief task* (Wimmer & Perner, 1983). In the standard version of this task, children see a puppet named Maxi deposit some chocolate in a cupboard and then leave the room. A second puppet arrives a moment later, finds the chocolate, and moves it to a different cupboard. The children are then asked where Maxi will look for the chocolate when he returns: in the first cupboard where he initially put it, or in the second cupboard where the children know it currently is. Most 5-year-olds realize that Maxi will search the first cupboard because Maxi did not see what the children saw, namely, that the chocolate was moved. But 3-year-olds typically claim that Maxi will look in the second cupboard. Why? Because that's where *the children* know the chocolate to be—and what they know, everyone knows! Children are able to do the false-belief task somewhere between the ages of 4 to 6 (Callaghan et al., 2005), and children in some cultures are able to do it earlier than children in others (Liu et al., 2008).

> **What does the false-belief task show?**

When small children are told to hide, they sometimes cover their eyes. Because they can't see you, they assume that you can't see them (Russell, Gee, & Bullard, 2012).

Some researchers believe that the false-belief task, like Piaget's test for object permanence, doesn't allow very young children to demonstrate their true abilities, and several recent studies have shown that much younger

theory of mind
The understanding that human behavior is guided by mental representations.

children can indeed do modified versions of the false-belief task (Baillargeon, Scott, & He, 2010; Onishi & Baillargeon, 2005; Rubin-Fernandez & Geurts, 2012; Senju et al., 2011; Southgate, Senju, & Csibra, 2007). But it isn't clear that very young children do these tasks the same way that older children do, namely, by truly understanding that other people can have beliefs that differ from their own (Apperly & Butterfill, 2009; Low & Watts, 2013). But whatever very young children are doing, their performances are impressive, and it seems clear that children begin to understand the nature of other minds much earlier than Piaget suspected.

Just as egocentrism affects children's understandings of others' minds, so does it affect their understanding of their own minds. Researchers showed young children an M&M's box and then opened it, revealing that it contained pencils instead of candy. Then the researchers closed the box and asked, "When I first showed you the box all closed up like this, what did you think was inside?" Although most 5-year-olds said M&M's, most 3-year-olds said pencils (Gopnik & Astington, 1988). For the 3-year-old child, a past self is like another person, and so the past self must have known what the child now knows.

Desires and Emotions. Different people have different perceptions and beliefs. They also have different desires and emotions. Do children understand that these aspects of other people's mental lives may also differ from their own? Surprisingly, even very young children who do not yet fully understand that others have different perceptions or beliefs do seem to understand that other people have different desires. For example, a 2-year-old who likes dogs can understand that other children don't like dogs, and can correctly predict that other children will avoid dogs that the child herself would approach. When 18-month-old toddlers see an adult express disgust while eating a food that the toddlers enjoy, they hand the adult a different food, as if they understand that different people have different tastes (Repacholi & Gopnik, 1997). Interestingly, young children understand other people's desires best when their own desires have already been fulfilled and are not competing for their attention (Atance, Bélanger, & Meltzoff, 2010).

> Do children understand emotions better than beliefs?

In contrast, children take a much longer time to understand that other people may have emotional reactions unlike their own. When 5-year-olds hear a story in which Little Red Riding Hood knocks on her grandmother's door, unaware that a wolf is inside waiting to devour her, they realize that Little Red Riding Hood does not know what they know; nonetheless, they expect Little Red Riding Hood to feel what they feel, namely, fear (Bradmetz & Schneider, 2004; DeRosnay et al., 2004; Harris et al., 1989). When asked where Maxi will look for the chocolate that was moved while Maxi was out of the room, they correctly say that Maxi will look in the original location, but they incorrectly say that Maxi feels sad. It is only at about 6 years of age that children come to understand that because they and others have different knowledge, they and others may also experience different emotions in the same situation.

Theory of Mind. Clearly, children have a whole lot to learn about how the mind works—and most of them eventually do. The vast majority of children ultimately come to understand that they and others have minds and that these minds represent the world in different ways. Once children understand these things, they are said to have acquired a **theory of mind,** which is *the understanding that other people's mental representations guide their behavior.*

"You're five. How could you possibly understand the problems of a five-and-a-half-year-old?"

Most of us eventually acquire a theory of mind, but two groups of people are somewhat slower to do so. Children with *autism* (a disorder we'll cover in more depth in the Disorders chapter) typically have difficulty communicating with other people and making friends, and some psychologists have suggested that this is because they have

Which children have special difficulty acquiring a theory of mind?

trouble acquiring a theory of mind (Frith, 2003). Although children with autism are typically normal on most intellectual dimensions—and sometimes far better than normal—they have difficulty understanding the inner lives of other people (Dawson et al., 2007). They do not seem to understand that other people can have false beliefs (Baron-Cohen, Leslie, & Frith, 1985; Senju et al., 2009), and they have special trouble understanding belief-based emotions such as embarrassment and shame (Baron-Cohen, 1991; Heerey, Keltner, & Capps, 2003). Interestingly, until children acquire a theory of mind they are generally not susceptible to the phenomenon of "contagious yawning" (Platek et al., 2003), and in fact, people with autism are also less likely to "catch a yawn" (Senju et al., 2007).

The second group of children who lag behind their peers in acquiring a theory of mind are deaf children whose parents do not know sign language. These children are slow to learn to communicate because they do not have ready access to any form of conventional language, and this restriction seems to slow the development of their understanding of other minds. Like children with autism, they display difficulties in understanding false beliefs even at 5 or 6 years of age (DeVilliers, 2005; Peterson & Siegal, 1999). Just as learning a spoken language seems to help hearing children acquire a theory of mind, so does learning a sign language help deaf children do the same (Pyers & Senghas, 2009).

The age at which children acquire a theory of mind appears to be influenced by a variety of other factors, such as the number of siblings the child has, the frequency with which the child engages in pretend play, whether the child has an imaginary companion, and the socioeconomic status of the child's family. But of all the factors researchers have studied, language seems to be the most important (Astington & Baird, 2005). Children's language skills are an excellent predictor of how well they perform on false-belief tasks (Happé, 1995). The way that caregivers talk to children is also a good predictor of how well children do these tasks. Perhaps not surprisingly, children whose caregivers frequently talk about thoughts and feelings tend to be good at understanding beliefs and belief-based emotions. Some psychologists speculate that children benefit from hearing psychological words such as *want, think, know,* and *sad;* others suggest that children benefit from the grammatically complex sentences that typically contain these psychological words; and some believe that caregivers who use psychological words are also more effective in getting children to reflect on mental states. Whatever the explanation, it is clear that language—and especially language about thoughts and feelings—is an important tool for helping children make sense of their own and others' minds (Harris, de Rosnay, & Pons, 2005).

People with autism often have an unusual ability to concentrate on small details, words, and numbers for extended periods of time. Thorkil Sonne (*right*) started a company called Specialisterne.com, which places people with autism—like his son Lars (*left*)—at jobs that they can do better than more "neurotypical" people can.

Piaget Remixed. Cognitive development is an amazing and complex journey, and Piaget's ideas about it were nothing short of groundbreaking. Few psychologists have had such a profound impact on the field. Many of these ideas have held up quite well, but in the last few decades, psychologists have discovered two general ways in which Piaget got it wrong. First, Piaget thought that children graduated from one stage to another in the same way that they graduated from kindergarten to first grade: a child

ISTOCKPHOTO/THINKSTOCK

Development is not the step-like progression that Piaget imagined. Children who are transitioning between stages may act more mature one day and less mature the next.

is in kindergarten *or* first grade, he is never in both, and there is an exact moment of transition to which everyone with a clock or a calendar can point. Modern psychologists see development as more fluid and continuous: a less step-like progression than Piaget believed. Children who are transitioning between stages may perform more mature behaviors one day and less mature behaviors the next. Cognitive development is more like the change of seasons than it is like graduation.

The second thing about which Piaget was mistaken was the ages at which these transitions occur. By and large, they happen *earlier* than he realized (Gopnik, 2012).

What did Piaget get wrong?

For example, Piaget suggested that infants had no sense of object permanence because they did not actively search for objects that were moved out of their sight. But when researchers use experimental procedures that allow infants to "show what they know," even 4-month-olds display a sense of object permanence. Piaget suggested that it takes many years until children can overcome their egocentrism enough to realize that others do not know what they know, but new experimental procedures have detected some evidence of this understanding in 13-month-old infants (Baillargeon et al., 2010). Every year, clever researchers find new ways of testing infants and children, and every year, textbook authors must lower the age at which cognitive milestones are achieved.

Discovering Our Cultures

Piaget saw the child as a lone scientist who made observations, developed theories, and then revised those theories in light of new observations. And yet, most scientists don't start from scratch. Rather, they receive training from more experienced scientists and they inherit the theories and methods of their disciplines. According to Russian psychologist Lev Vygotsky, children do much the same thing. Vygotsky was born in 1896, the same year as Piaget, but unlike Piaget, he believed that cognitive development was largely the result of the child's interaction with members of his or her own culture rather than his or her interaction with concrete objects. Vygotsky noted that cultural tools, such as language and counting systems, exert a strong influence on cognitive development (Vygotsky, 1978).

Children are not lone explorers who discover the world for themselves but members of families, communities, and societies that teach them much of what they need to know.

For example, in English, the numbers beyond 20 are named by a decade (twenty) that is followed by a digit (one) and their names follow a logical pattern (twenty-one, twenty-two, twenty-three, etc.). In Chinese, the numbers from 11 to 19 are similarly constructed (ten-one, ten-two, ten-three . . .). But in English, the names of the numbers between 11 and 19 either reverse the order of the decade and the digit (sixteen, seventeen) or are entirely arbitrary (eleven, twelve). The difference in the regularity of these two systems

How does culture affect cognitive development?

makes a big difference to the children who must learn them. It is obvious to a Chinese child that 12—which is called "ten-two"—can be decomposed into 10 and 2, but it is not so obvious to an English-speaking child, who calls the number "twelve" (see **FIGURE 11.5**). In one study, children from many countries were asked to hand an experimenter a certain number of bricks. Some of the bricks were single, and some were glued together in strips of 10. When Asian children were asked to hand the experimenter 26 bricks, they tended to hand over two strips of 10 plus six singles. Non-Asian children tended to use the clumsier strategy of counting out 26 single bricks (Miura et al., 1994). Results such as these suggest that the regularity of the counting system that children inherit can promote or discourage their discovery of the fact that two-digit numbers can be decomposed (Gordon, 2004; Imbo & LeFevre, 2009).

Of course, if you've ever tried to train a pet snake, you already know that not all species are well prepared to learn from others. Human beings are the

DANIEL GILBERT

champions in this regard, because they have three skills that make them nature's most exceptional students (Meltzoff et al., 2009; Striano & Reid, 2006).

> If an adult turns her head to the left, young infants (3 months) and older infants (9 months) will look to the left. But if the adult first closes her eyes and then looks to the left, the young infant will look to the left but the older infant will not (Brooks & Meltzoff, 2002). This suggests that older infants are not following the adult's head movements, but rather, they are following her gaze: They are trying to see what they think she is seeing. If older infants can hear but not see an adult, they will use auditory cues to determine which way the adult must be looking and will then look in that direction (Rossano, Carpenter, & Tomasello, 2012). The ability to focus on what another person is focused on is known as *joint attention* and it is a prerequisite for learning what others have to teach (see **FIGURE 11.6**).

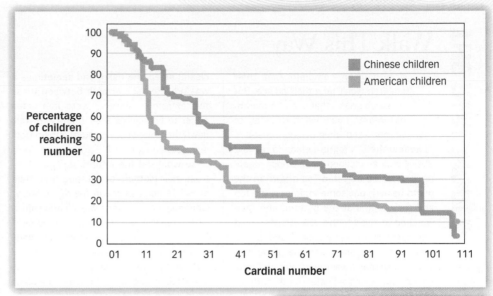

▲ Figure **11.5** **Twelve or Two-Teen?** As this graph shows, the percentage of American children who can count through the cardinal numbers drops off suddenly when they hit the number 11, whereas the percentage of Chinese children shows a more gradual decline (Miller, Smith, & Zhu, 1995).

> Infants are natural mimics who often do what they see adults do (Jones, 2007). But very early on, infants begin to mimic adults' *intentions* rather than their actions per se. When an 18-month-old sees an adult's hand slip as the adult tries to pull the lid off a jar, the infant won't copy the slip, but will instead perform the *intended* action by removing the lid (Meltzoff, 1995, 2007). The tendency to do what an adult does—or what an adult meant to do—is known as *imitation*. By the age of 3, children begin to copy adults so precisely that they will even copy parts of actions that they know to be pointless, a phenomenon called *overimitation* (Lyons, Young, & Keil, 2007; Simpson & Riggs, 2011).

> An infant who approaches a new toy will often stop and look back at his or her mother, examining her face for cues about whether mom thinks the toy is or isn't dangerous. The ability to use another person's reactions as information about how we should think about the world is known as *social referencing* (Kim, Walden, & Knieps, 2010; Walden & Ogan, 1988). (You'll learn a lot more about how adults continue to use this skill when we discuss *informational influence* in the Social Psychology chapter).

▼ Figure **11.6** **Joint Attention**
Joint attention allows children to learn from others. When a 12-month-old infant interacts with an adult (*a*) who then looks at an object (*b*), the infant will typically look at the same object (*c*)—but only when the adult's eyes are open (Meltzoff et al., 2009).

Joint attention ("I see what you see"), imitation ("I do what you do"), and social referencing ("I think what you think") are the three basic abilities that allow infants to learn from other members of their species.

(a)

(b)

(c)

A.N. MELTZOFF, P.K. KUHL, T.J. SEJNOWSKI, & J. MOVELLAN. "FOUNDATIONS FOR A NEW SCIENCE OF LEARNING" PUBLISHED IN SCIENCE, 2009, VOL. 325, JULY 17, PP. 284–288

Walk This Way

Parents often complain that their children won't take their advice. But research shows that even 18-month-old infants know when to listen to their parents—and when to ignore them.

Researchers (Tamis-LeMonda et al., 2008) built an inclined plane whose steepness could be adjusted (as shown in the photo below), put some infants at the top and their moms at the bottom, and then watched to see whether the infants would attempt to walk down the plane and toward their mothers. Sometimes the plane was adjusted so that it was clearly flat and safe, sometimes it was adjusted so that it was

clearly steep and risky, and sometimes it was adjusted somewhere between these two extremes. Mothers were instructed either to encourage their infants to walk down the plane or to discourage them from doing so.

So what did the infants do? Did they trust their mothers or did they trust their eyes? As you can see in the figure below, when the inclined plane was clearly safe or clearly risky, infants ignored their mothers. They typically trotted down the flat plane even when mom advised against it and refused to try the risky plane even when mom said it was okay. But when the plane

was somewhere between safe and risky, the infants tended to follow mom's advice.

These data show that infants use social information in a very sophisticated way. When their senses provide unambiguous information about the world, they ignore what people tell them. But when their senses leave them unsure about what to do, they readily accept parental advice. It appears that from the moment children start to walk, they know when to listen to their parents and when to shake their heads, roll their eyes, and do what they darn well please.

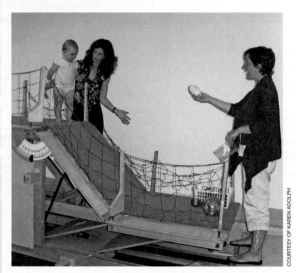

COURTESY OF KAREN ADOLPH

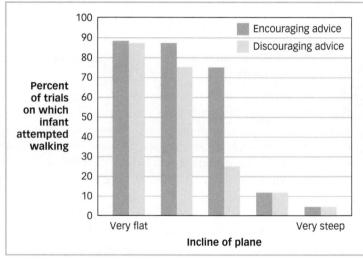

Social Development

Unlike baby turtles, baby humans cannot survive without their caregivers. But what exactly do caregivers provide? Some obvious answers are warmth, safety, and food, and those obvious answers are right. But caregivers also provide something that is far less obvious but every bit as essential to an infant's development.

During World War II, psychologists studied infants who were living in orphanages while awaiting adoption. Although these children were warm, safe, and well fed, many were developmentally impaired, both physically and psychologically, and nearly 40% died before they could be adopted (Spitz, 1949). A few years later, psychologist Harry Harlow (1958; Harlow & Harlow, 1965) discovered that infant rhesus monkeys that were warm, safe, and well fed, but were not allowed any social contact for the first 6 months of their lives, developed a variety of behavioral abnormalities. They compulsively rocked back and forth while biting themselves, and if they were introduced to other monkeys, they avoided them entirely. These socially isolated monkeys turned out to be incapable of communicating with or learning from others of their kind, and when the females matured and became mothers, they ignored, rejected, and sometimes even attacked their own infants. Harlow also discovered that when socially isolated monkeys were put in a cage with two "artificial mothers"—one that was made of

Harlow's monkeys preferred the comfort and warmth of a soft cloth mother (*left*) to the wire mother (*right*) even when the wire mother was associated with food.

wire and dispensed food and one that was made of cloth and dispensed no food—they spent most of their time clinging to the soft cloth mother despite the fact that the wire mother was the source of their nourishment. Clearly, infants of all these species require something more from their caregivers than mere sustenance. But what?

Becoming Attached

When Konrad Lorenz was a child he became the proud owner of a duck, and he quickly noticed something very interesting. Several decades later, the thing he had noticed helped him win the Nobel Prize. As he explained in his acceptance speech, "From a neighbor, I got a one-day-old duckling and found, to my intense joy, that it transferred its following response to my person." Ducklings normally follow their mother everywhere she goes, and what Lorenz discovered as a child (and then proved scientifically as an adult) is that new hatchlings will faithfully follow the first moving object to which they are exposed. If that object is a human being or a tennis ball, then the hatchling will ignore its mother and follow that object instead. Lorenz theorized that nature designed birds so that the first moving object they saw was *imprinted* on their brains as "the thing I must always stay near" (Lorenz, 1952).

Psychiatrist John Bowlby was fascinated by Lorenz's work, as well as by Harlow's studies of rhesus monkeys reared in isolation and the work on children reared in orphanages, and he sought to understand how human infants form attachments to their caregivers (Bowlby, 1969, 1973, 1980). Bowlby began by noting that from the moment they are born, ducks waddle after their mothers and monkeys cling to their mothers' furry chests because the newborns of both species must stay close to their caregivers to survive. Human infants, he suggested, have a similar need, but they are much less physically developed than ducks or monkeys and therefore can neither waddle nor cling. What they can do is smile and cry. Because they do not have webbed feet or furry hands that allow them to stay close to their caregivers, they use what they do have to keep their caregivers close to them. When an infant cries, gurgles, coos, makes eye contact, or smiles, most adults reflexively move toward the infant, and Bowlby suggested that this is *why* infants have been designed to emit these signals.

> **?** How does an infant identify the primary caregiver?

According to Bowlby, infants initially send these signals to anyone within visual or auditory range. For the first 6 months or so, they keep a "mental tally" of who responds most often and most promptly to their signals, and soon they begin to target the best and fastest responder, also known as the *primary caregiver*. This person quickly becomes the emotional center of the infant's universe. Infants feel secure in the primary caregiver's presence and will happily crawl around, exploring their environments with their eyes, ears, fingers, and mouths. But if their primary caregiver gets too far away,

Like hatchlings, human infants need to stay close to their mothers to survive. Unlike hatchlings, human infants know how to get their mothers to come to them rather than the other way around.

Children are naturally social creatures who readily develop relationships with caregivers and peers. Toddlers who spend time with a responsive robot will begin to treat it like a classmate instead of like a toy (Tanaka, Cicourel, & Movellan, 2007).

infants begin to feel insecure, and they take action to decrease the distance between themselves and their primary caregiver, perhaps by crawling toward their caregiver or perhaps by crying until their caregiver moves toward them. Bowlby believed that all of this happens because evolution has equipped human infants with a social reflex that is every bit as basic as the physical reflexes that cause them to suck and to grasp. Human infants, Bowlby suggested, are predisposed to form an **attachment**—that is, *an emotional bond*—with a primary caregiver.

Infants who are deprived of the opportunity to become attached experience a variety of negative consequences (Gillespie & Nemeroff, 2007; O'Connor & Rutter, 2000; Rutter, O'Connor, & the English and Romanian Adoptees Study Team, 2004). But even when attachment does happen, it can happen more or less successfully (Ainsworth et al., 1978). Psychologist Mary Ainsworth developed a way to measure this: **Strange Situation** is *a behavioral test used to determine a child's attachment style.* The test involves bringing a child and his or her primary caregiver (usually the child's mother) to a laboratory room and then staging a series of episodes, including ones in which the primary caregiver briefly leaves the room and then returns, while psychologists monitor the infant's reaction. Research shows that those reactions tend to fall into one of four patterns known as *attachment styles*.

> **How is attachment assessed?**

> About 60% of American infants have a *secure* attachment style. When the caregiver leaves, the infant may or may not be distressed. When she returns, non-distressed infants will acknowledge her with a glance or greeting, and distressed infants will go to her and are calmed by her presence.

> About 20% of American infants have an *avoidant* attachment style. When the caregiver leaves, the infant will not be distressed, and when she returns the infant will not acknowledge her.

> About 15% of American infants have an *ambivalent* attachment style. When the caregiver leaves the infant will be distressed, and when she returns the infant will rebuff her, refusing any attempt at calming while arching his or her back and squirming to get away.

> About 5% or fewer American infants have a *disorganized* attachment style. These infants show no consistent pattern of response to their caregiver's leaving and returning.

It doesn't take a psychologist to see that this child is securely attached.

Research has shown that a child's behavior in the Strange Situation in the laboratory correlates fairly well with his or her behavior at home (Solomon & George, 1999; see **FIGURE 11.7**). Nonetheless, it is not unusual for a child's attachment style to change over time (Lamb, Sternberg, & Prodromidis, 1992). And although some aspects of attachment styles appear to be stable across cultures—secure attachment is the most common style all over the world (van IJzendoorn & Kroonenberg, 1988)—other aspects of attachment styles vary across cultures. For example, German children (whose parents tend to foster independence) are more likely to have avoidant than ambivalent attachment styles, whereas Japanese children (whose mothers typically stay home and do not leave them in the care of others) are more likely to have ambivalent than avoidant attachment styles (Takahashi, 1986).

▶ Figure **11.7 Attachment Style and Memory** We often remember best those events that fit with our view of the world. Researchers assessed 1-year-old children's attachment styles with the Strange Situation task. Two years later, the same group of children were shown a puppet show in which some happy events (e.g., the puppet got a present) or unhappy events (e.g., the puppet spilled his juice) occurred. Securely attached children later remembered more of the happy events than the unhappy ones, but insecurely attached children showed the opposite pattern (Belsky, Spritz, & Crnic, 1996).

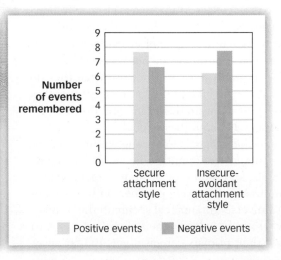

Number of events remembered (y-axis: 0–9)

Secure attachment style | Insecure-avoidant attachment style

Positive events | Negative events

Where Do Attachment Styles Come From?

A child's attachment style is determined in part by the child's biology. Different children are born with different **temperaments,** or *characteristic patterns of emotional reactivity* (Thomas & Chess, 1977). Whether measured by parents' reports or by physiological indices such as heart rate or cerebral blood flow, very young children vary in their tendency toward fearfulness, irritability, activity, positive affect, and other emotional traits (Rothbart & Bates, 1998). These differences are unusually stable over time. For example, infants who react fearfully to novel stimuli—such as sudden movements, loud sounds, or unfamiliar people—tend to be more subdued, less social, and less positive at 4 years old (Kagan, 1997). These temperamental differences among infants appear to result from innate biological differences (Baker et al., 2013). For example, 10 to 15% of infants have a highly reactive limbic system (which, you may recall from the Neuroscience and Behavior chapter, is a collection of brain regions including the amygdala that play an important role in emotional reaction). These infants thrash and cry when shown a new toy or a new person, and they become children who tend to avoid novel people, objects, and situations, and then adults who are quiet, cautious, and shy (Schwartz et al., 2003).

The infant's biologically based temperament plays a role in determining his or her attachment style, but for the most part, attachment style is determined by the infant's social interactions with his or her caregiver. Studies have shown that mothers of securely attached infants tend to be especially sensitive to signs of their child's emotional state, especially good at detecting their infant's "request" for reassurance, and especially responsive to that request (Ainsworth et al., 1978; De Wolff & van IJzendoorn, 1997). Mothers of infants with an ambivalent attachment style tend to respond inconsistently, only sometimes attending to their infants when they show signs of distress. Mothers of infants with an avoidant attachment style are typically indifferent to their child's need for reassurance and may even reject their attempts at physical closeness (Isabelle, 1993). As a result of all this, infants develop an **internal working model of relationships,** which is *a set of beliefs about the self, the primary caregiver, and the relationship between them* (Bretherton & Munholland, 1999). Infants with different attachment styles appear to have different working models of relationships (see **FIGURE 11.8**). Specifically, infants with a secure attachment style act as though they are *certain that their primary caregiver will respond* when they feel insecure; infants with an avoidant attachment style act as though they are *certain that their primary caregiver will not respond*; and infants with an ambivalent attachment style act as though they are *uncertain about whether their primary caregiver will respond*. Infants with a disorganized attachment style seem to be confused about their caregivers, which has led some psychologists to speculate that this style primarily characterizes children who have been abused (Carolson, 1998; Cicchetti & Toth, 1998).

If the caregiver's responsiveness determines (in large part) the child's working model, and if the child's working model determines (in large part) the child's attachment style, then what determines the caregiver's responsiveness (see **FIGURE 11.9**)? Differences in how caregivers respond are probably due (in large part) to

attachment
The emotional bond that forms between newborns and their primary caregivers.

Strange Situation
A behavioral test developed by Mary Ainsworth that is used to determine a child's attachment style.

temperaments
Characteristic patterns of emotional reactivity.

internal working model of relationships
A set of beliefs about the self, the primary caregiver, and the relationship between them.

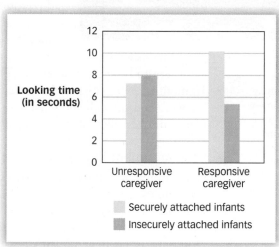

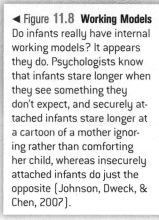

◀ Figure **11.8** **Working Models**
Do infants really have internal working models? It appears they do. Psychologists know that infants stare longer when they see something they don't expect, and securely attached infants stare longer at a cartoon of a mother ignoring rather than comforting her child, whereas insecurely attached infants do just the opposite (Johnson, Dweck, & Chen, 2007).

▶ Figure **11.9** **Parents' Attachment Styles**
Attachment is an interaction between two people, and both of them—the primary caregiver and the child—play a role in determining the nature of the child's working model. Studies show that securely attached infants tend to have parents who themselves have secure working models of attachment (van IJzendoorn, 1995). Why might that be?

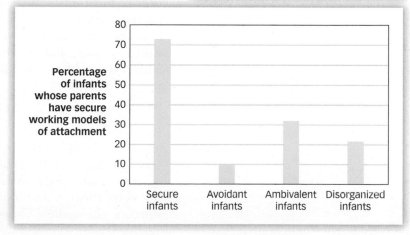

DAVID GROSSMAN/ALAMY

Does spending time in day care impair the attachment process? A massive long-term study by the National Institute for Child Health and Human Development showed that attachment style is strongly influenced by maternal sensitivity and responsiveness, but not by the quality, amount, stability, or type of day care (Friedman & Boyle, 2008).

differences in their ability to read their infant's emotional states. Caregivers who are highly sensitive to these signs are almost twice as likely to have a securely attached child as are mothers who are less sensitive (van Ijzendoorn & Sagi, 1999). Mothers who think of their infants as unique individuals with emotional lives and not just as creatures with urgent physical needs are more likely to have infants who are securely attached (Meins, 2003; Meins et al., 2001). Although such data are merely correlational, there is reason to suspect that a mother's sensitivity and responsiveness are a *cause* of the infant's attachment style. For instance, researchers studied a group of young mothers whose infants were particularly irritable or difficult. When the infants were about 6 months old, half the mothers participated in a training program designed to sensitize them to their infants' emotional signals and to encourage them to be more responsive. The results showed that when the children were 18 months, 24 months, and 3 years old, those whose mothers had received the training were considerably more likely to have a secure attachment style than were those whose mothers did not receive the training (van den Boom, 1994, 1995).

> **How do caregivers influence an infant's attachment style?**

Do Attachment Styles Matter?

Does an infant's attachment style have any influence on his or her subsequent development? Children who were securely attached as infants do better than children who were not securely attached on a wide variety of measures, from their psychological well-being (Madigan et al., 2013) to their academic achievement (Jacobson & Hoffman, 1997) to the quality of their relationships (McElwain, Booth-LaForce, & Wu, 2011; Schneider, Atkinson, & Tardif, 2001; Simpson, Collins, & Salvatore, 2011; Steele et al., 1999; Vondra et al., 2001).

For example, in one study that tracked people from infancy to adulthood, researchers found that 1-year-old infants who displayed insecure attachment during the Strange Situation experienced more negative emotions when trying to resolve major relationship conflicts with their romantic partners at age 21 (Simpson et al., 2007). And 1-year-old infants who displayed secure attachment styles in the Strange Situation went on to become adults who rebounded more quickly from conflicts with their romantic partners (Salvatore et al., 2011). Some psychologists have suggested that people apply the working models they developed as infants to their later relationships with teachers, friends, and lovers: In other words, attachment styles cause infants to become more or less successful adults (Sroufe, Egeland, & Kruetzer, 1990). But other psychologists argue that an infant's attachment style is correlated with subsequent outcomes only because both of these are caused by the same environment: In other words, sensitive and responsive caregivers cause both the infant's attachment style and his or her later adult outcomes (Lamb et al., 1985).

Moral Development

From the moment of birth, human beings can make one distinction quickly and well, and that's the distinction between pleasure and pain. Before their bottoms hit their very first diapers, infants can tell when something feels good or bad, and can demonstrate to anyone within earshot that they strongly prefer the former. Over the next few years, they begin to notice that their pleasures ("Throwing food is fun") are often someone else's pains ("Throwing food makes Mom mad"), which is a bit of a problem because infants need these other people to survive. So they start to learn how to balance their needs and the needs of those around them, and they do this in part by developing a distinction between *right* and *wrong*.

Knowing What's Right

How do children think about right and wrong? Piaget had something to say about this too. He spent time playing games with children and quizzing them about how they came to know the rules of these games and what they thought should happen to children who broke those rules. By listening carefully to what children said, Piaget concluded that the child's moral thinking develops in three important ways (Piaget, 1932/1965).

> **According to Piaget, what three shifts characterize moral development?**

> ❯ First, Piaget noticed that children's moral thinking tends to shift *from realism to relativism.* Very young children regard moral rules as real, inviolable truths about the world. For the young child, right and wrong are like day and night: They exist in the world and do not depend on what people think or say. That's why young children generally don't think that a bad action (such as hitting someone) can ever be good, even if everyone agreed to allow it. As they mature, children begin to realize that some moral rules (e.g., wives should obey their husbands) are inventions and not discoveries and that people can therefore agree to adopt them, change them, or abandon them entirely.

> ❯ Second, Piaget noticed that children's moral thinking tends to shift *from prescriptions to principles.* Young children think of moral rules as guidelines for specific actions in specific situations ("Each child can play with the iPad for 5 minutes and must then pass it to the child sitting to their left"). As they mature, children come to see that rules are expressions of more general principles, such as fairness and equity, which means that specific rules can be abandoned or modified when they fail to uphold the general principle ("If Jason missed his turn with the iPad, then he should get two turns now").

> ❯ Third and finally, Piaget noticed that children's moral thinking tends to shift from *outcomes* to *intentions.* For the young child, an unintentional action that causes great harm ("Josh accidentally broke Dad's iPad") seems "more wrong" than an intentional action that causes slight harm ("Josh got mad and broke Dad's pencil") because young children tend to judge the morality of an action by its outcome rather than by the actor's intentions. As they mature, children begin to see that the morality of an action is critically dependent on the actor's state of mind.

Piaget's observations about the development of moral thinking have generally held up quite well, although he once again seemed to overestimate the ages at which some of these transitions take place. For example, research shows that children as young as 3 years old do sometimes consider people's intentions when judging the morality of their actions (Yuill & Perner, 1988). Psychologist Lawrence Kohlberg used Piaget's insights to produce a detailed theory of

HOANG DINH NAM/AFP/GETTY IMAGES

According to Piaget, young children do not realize that moral rules can vary across persons and cultures. For instance, most Americans think it is immoral to eat a dog, but most Vietnamese disagree.

©GODONG/ROBERT HARDING/NEWSCOM

During WWII, many Albanian Muslims shielded their Jewish neighbors from the Nazis. Baba Haxhi Dede Reshatbardhi (pictured) was one of those who saved so many Jewish lives.

preconventional stage
A stage of moral development in which the morality of an action is primarily determined by its consequences for the actor.

conventional stage
A stage of moral development in which the morality of an action is primarily determined by the extent to which it conforms to social rules.

postconventional stage
A stage of moral development in which the morality of an action is determined by a set of general principles that reflect core values.

the development of moral reasoning (Kohlberg, 1963, 1986). According to Kohlberg, moral reasoning proceeds through three basic stages. Kohlberg (1958) based his theory on people's responses to a series of dilemmas such as this one:

> A woman was near death from a special kind of cancer. There was one drug that the doctors thought might save her. It was a form of radium that a druggist in the same town had recently discovered. The drug was expensive to make, but the druggist was charging ten times what the drug cost him to make. He paid $200 for the radium and charged $2,000 for a small dose of the drug. The sick woman's husband, Heinz, went to everyone he knew to borrow the money, but he could only get together about $1,000, which is half of what it cost. He told the druggist that his wife was dying and asked him to sell it cheaper or let him pay later. But the druggist said: "No, I discovered the drug and I'm going to make money from it." So Heinz got desperate and broke into the man's store to steal the drug for his wife. Should the husband have done that?

On the basis of their responses, Kohlberg concluded that most children are at the **preconventional stage,** which is *a stage of moral development in which the morality of an action is primarily determined by its consequences for the actor.* Immoral actions are simply those for which one is punished, and the appropriate resolution to any moral dilemma is to choose the behavior with the least likelihood of punishment. For example, children at this stage often base their moral judgment of Heinz on the relative costs of one decision ("It would be bad if he got blamed for his wife's death") and another ("It would be bad if he went to jail for stealing").

What are Kohlberg's three stages of moral development?

Kohlberg argued that children are preconventional, but somewhere around adolescence they move to the **conventional stage,** which is *a stage of moral development in which the morality of an action is primarily determined by the extent to which it conforms to social rules.* People at this stage believe that everyone should uphold the generally accepted norms of their cultures, obey the laws of society, and fulfill their civic duties and familial obligations. They argue that Heinz must weigh the dishonor he will bring upon himself and his family by stealing (i.e., breaking a law) against the guilt he will feel if he allows his wife to die (i.e., failing to fulfill a duty). People at this stage are concerned not just about spankings and prison sentences but also about the approval of others. Immoral actions are those for which one is condemned.

Finally, Kohlberg believed that in adulthood, some adults (but not all) move to the **postconventional stage,** which is *a stage of moral development in which the morality of an action is determined by a set of general principles that reflect core values,* such as the right to life, liberty, and the pursuit of happiness. When a behavior violates these principles, it is immoral, and if a law requires these principles to be violated, then it should be disobeyed. For a person who has reached the postconventional stage, a woman's life is always more important than a shopkeeper's profits and so stealing the drug is not only a moral behavior, it is a moral obligation.

W.B. PARK/CARTOONSTOCK

"You've been circling three days, and your prey won't die—what's your position, ethically speaking?"

Research supports Kohlberg's general claim that moral reasoning shifts from an emphasis on punishment to an emphasis on social rules and finally to an emphasis on ethical principles (Walker, 1988). But research also suggests that these stages are not quite as discrete as Kohlberg thought. For instance, a single person may use preconventional, conventional, and postconventional thinking in different circumstances, which suggests that the developing person does not "reach a stage" so much as he "acquires a skill" that he may or may not use on a particular occasion.

What was Kohlberg right about and wrong about?

The use of the male pronoun here is intentional. Because Kohlberg developed his theory by studying a sample of American boys, some critics have suggested that it does not describe the development of moral thinking in girls (Gilligan, 1982) or in non-Westerners (Simpson, 1974). The first of these criticisms has received little scientific support (Jaffee & Hyde, 2000; Turiel, 1998), but the second has. For example, some non-Western societies value obedience and community over liberty and individuality; thus, the moral reasoning of people in those societies may *appear* to reflect a conventional devotion to social norms when it *actually* reflects a postconventional consideration of ethical principles. Other critics have noted that, although a child's level of moral reasoning is positively correlated with his or her moral behavior (Blasi, 1980), the correlation is not strong, and this is particularly true when the moral behavior involves doing a good deed rather than refraining from doing a bad deed (Haidt, 2001; Thoma et al., 1999). These critics suggest that how people reason about morality may be interesting in and of itself, but doesn't tell us very much about how people will behave in their everyday lives. But if moral reasoning doesn't determine moral behavior, then what does?

Feeling What's Right

Research on moral reasoning suggests that people are like judges in a court of law, using rational analysis—sometimes simple and sometimes sophisticated—to distinguish between right and wrong. But moral dilemmas don't just make us think; they also make us *feel*. Consider this one:

> You are standing on a bridge. Below you can see a runaway trolley hurtling down the track toward five people who will be killed if it remains on its present course. You are sure that you can save these people by flipping a lever that will switch the trolley onto a different track, where it will kill just one person instead of five. Is it morally permissible to divert the trolley and prevent five deaths at the cost of one?

Now consider a slightly different version of this problem:

> You and a large man are standing on a bridge. Below you can see a runaway trolley hurtling down the track toward five people who will be killed if it remains on its present course. You are sure that you can save these people by pushing the large man onto the track, where his body will be caught up in the trolley's wheels and stop it before it kills the five people. Is it morally permissible to push the large man and prevent five deaths at the cost of one?

These scenarios are illustrated in **FIGURE 11.10**. If you are like most people, you concluded that is morally permissible to pull a switch but not to push a man (Greene et al., 2001). In both cases you had to decide whether to sacrifice one human life in order to save five, and in one case you said yes and in another you said no. How can

▼ Figure **11.10** **The Trolley Problem** Why does it seem permissible to trade one life for five lives by pulling a switch but not by pushing a man from a bridge? Research suggests that the scenario shown in (*b*) elicits a more negative emotional response than does the scenario shown in (*a*), and this emotional response may be the basis for our moral intuitions.

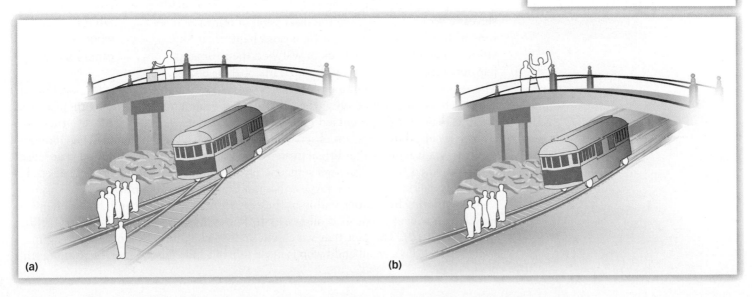

(a)   (b)

moral reasoning yield such inconsistent conclusions? It can't, and the odds are that you didn't reach these conclusions by moral reasoning at all. Rather, you simply had a strong negative emotional reaction to the thought of pushing another human being into the path of an oncoming trolley and watching him get sliced and diced, and that reaction instantly led you to conclude that pushing him was wrong. Sure, you may have come up with a few good arguments to support this conclusion ("What if he turned around and bit me?" or "I'd hate to get spleen on my new shoes"), but those arguments probably followed rather than preceded your conclusion (Greene, 2013).

The way people respond to cases such as these has convinced some psychologists that moral judgments are the consequences—and not the causes—of emotional reactions (Haidt, 2001). According to this *moral intuitionist* perspective, we have evolved to react emotionally to a small family of events that are particularly relevant to reproduction and survival, and we have developed the distinction between right and wrong as a way of labeling and explaining these emotional reactions (Hamlin, Wynn, & Bloom, 2007). For instance, most of us think that incest disgusts us because it is wrong, but another possibility is that we consider it wrong because it disgusts us. Incest is a poor method for producing genetically viable offspring, and so nature may have selected for people who are disgusted by it. Our reasoning about the immorality of incest may be the *consequence* of that disgust and not its *cause*.

> **Do moral judgments come before or after emotional reactions?**

Some research supports the moral intuitionist perspective. For example, in one study, people who had brain damage that prevented them from experiencing normal emotions treated the two situations shown in Figure 11.10 identically, choosing in both cases to sacrifice one life to save five (Koenigs et al., 2007). In another study (Wheatley & Haidt, 2005), participants were hypnotized and told that whenever they heard the word *take,* they would experience "a brief pang of disgust . . . a sickening feeling in your stomach." After they came out of the hypnotic state, the participants were asked to rate the morality of several actions. Sometimes the description of the action contained the word *take* ("How immoral is it for a police officer to *take* a bribe") and sometimes it did not ("How immoral is it for a police officer to *accept* a bribe?"). Participants rated the action as less moral when it contained the word *take,* suggesting that their negative feelings were causing—rather than being caused by—their moral reasoning.

All of this suggests that we consider it immoral to push someone onto the tracks simply because the idea of watching someone suffer makes us feel bad (Greene et al., 2001). In fact, research has shown that watching someone suffer activates the very same brain regions that are activated when we suffer ourselves (Carr et al., 2003; see the discussion of mirror neurons in the Neuroscience and Behavior chapter). In one study, women received a shock or watched their romantic partners receive a shock on different parts of their bodies.

> **What happens when we see others suffer?**

The regions of the women's brains that processed information about the location of the shock were activated only when the women experienced the shock themselves, but the regions that processed emotional information were activated whether the women received the shock or observed it (Singer et al., 2004). Similarly, the emotion-relevant brain regions that are activated when a person smells a foul odor are also activated when the person sees someone else smelling the foul odor (Wicker et al., 2003). Studies such as these suggest that our brains respond to other people's *expressions* of suffering by creating within us the *experience* of suffering, and this mechanism may have evolved because it allows us to know instantly what others are feeling (de Waal, 2012). The fact that we can actually *feel* another person's suffering may explain why even a small child who is incapable of sophisticated moral reasoning still considers it wrong when someone hurts someone else, especially when the person being hurt is similar to the child (Hamlin et al., 2013).

This may also explain why our aversion to watching others suffer begins so early in childhood (Warneken & Tomasello, 2009). When adults pretend to hit their thumbs with a hammer, even very young children seem alarmed and will attempt to comfort them (Zahn-Waxler et al., 1992). Indeed, even very young children distinguish between actions that are wrong because they violate a social rule and actions that are wrong because they cause suffering. When asked whether it would be okay to leave toys on the floor in a school that allowed such behavior, young children tend to say it would. But when asked whether it would be okay to hit another child in a school that allowed such behavior, young children tend to say it would not (Smetana, 1981; Smetana & Braeges, 1990). Young children say that hitting is wrong even when an adult instructs someone to do it (Laupa & Turiel, 1986). It appears that from a very early age, other people's suffering can become our suffering, and this leads us to conclude that the actions that caused the suffering are immoral.

CREASOURCE/CORBIS

Most people are upset by the suffering of others, and research suggests that even young children have this response, which may be the basis of their emerging morality.

IN SUMMARY

▶ Infants have a limited range of vision, but they can see and remember objects that appear within it. They learn to control their bodies from the top down and from the center out.

▶ Infants slowly develop theories about how the world works. Piaget believed that these theories developed through four stages, in which children learn basic facts about the world, such as the fact that objects continue to exist even when they are out of sight, and the fact that objects have enduring properties that are not changed by superficial transformations. Children also learn that their minds represent objects; hence objects may not be as they appear, and others may not see them as the child does.

▶ Cognitive development also comes about through social interactions in which children are given tools for understanding that have been developed over millennia by members of their cultures.

▶ At a very early age, human beings develop strong emotional ties to their primary caregivers. The quality of these ties is determined both by the caregiver's behavior and the child's temperament.

▶ People get along with each other by learning and obeying moral principles.

▶ Children's reasoning about right and wrong is initially based on an action's consequences, but as they mature, children begin to consider the actor's intentions as well as the extent to which the action obeys abstract moral principles.

▶ Moral judgments may be caused by our emotional reactions to the suffering of others.

Adolescence: Minding the Gap

Between childhood and adulthood is an extended developmental stage that may not qualify for a "hood" of its own, but that is clearly distinct from the stages that come before and after. **Adolescence** is *the period of development that begins with the onset of sexual maturity (about 11 to 14 years of age) and lasts until the beginning of adulthood (about 18 to 21 years of age)*. Unlike the transition from embryo to fetus or from infant to child, this transition is sudden and clearly marked. In just 3 or 4 years, the

adolescence
The period of development that begins with the onset of sexual maturity (about 11 to 14 years of age) and lasts until the beginning of adulthood (about 18 to 21 years of age).

Adolescents are often described as gawky because different parts of their faces and bodies mature at different rates. But as musician Justin Timberlake can attest, the gawkiness generally clears up.

average adolescent gains about 40 pounds and grows about 10 inches. For girls, all this growing starts at about the age of 10 and ends when they reach their full heights at about the age of 15.5. For boys it starts at about the age of 12 and ends at about the age of 17.5.

The beginnings of this growth spurt signals the onset of **puberty**, which refers to *the bodily changes associated with sexual maturity.* These changes involve **primary sex characteristics,** which are *bodily structures that are directly involved in reproduction,* for example, the onset of menstruation in girls and the enlargement of the testes, scrotum, and penis and the emergence of the capacity for ejaculation in boys. They also involve **secondary sex characteristics,** which are *bodily structures that change dramatically with sexual maturity but that are not directly involved in reproduction,* for example, the enlargement of the breasts and the widening of the hips in girls and the appearance of facial hair, pubic hair, underarm hair, and the lowering of the voice in both genders. This pattern of changes is caused by increased production of estrogen in girls and testosterone in boys.

Just as the body changes during adolescence, so too does the brain. For example, there is a marked increase in the growth rate of tissue connecting different regions of the brain just before puberty (Thompson et al., 2000). Between the ages of 6 and 13, the connections between the temporal lobe (the brain region specialized for language) and the parietal lobe (the brain region specialized for understanding spatial relations) multiply rapidly and then stop—just about the time that the critical period for learning a language ends (see **FIGURE 11.11**).

How does the brain change at puberty?

But the most important neural changes occur in the prefrontal cortex. An infant's brain forms many more new synapses than it actually needs, and by the time children are 2 years old they have about 15,000 synapses per neuron, which is roughly twice as many as the average adult (Huttenlocher, 1979). This early period of *synaptic proliferation* is followed by a period of *synaptic pruning* in which the connections that are not frequently used are eliminated. This is a clever system that allows the brain's wiring to be determined in part by its experience in the world. Scientists used to think that this process ended early in life, but recent evidence suggests that the prefrontal cortex undergoes a second wave of synaptic proliferation just before puberty, and a second round of synaptic pruning during adolescence (Giedd et al., 1999). Clearly, the adolescent brain is a work in progress.

puberty
The bodily changes associated with sexual maturity.

primary sex characteristics
Bodily structures that are directly involved in reproduction.

secondary sex characteristics
Bodily structures that change dramatically with sexual maturity but that are not directly involved in reproduction.

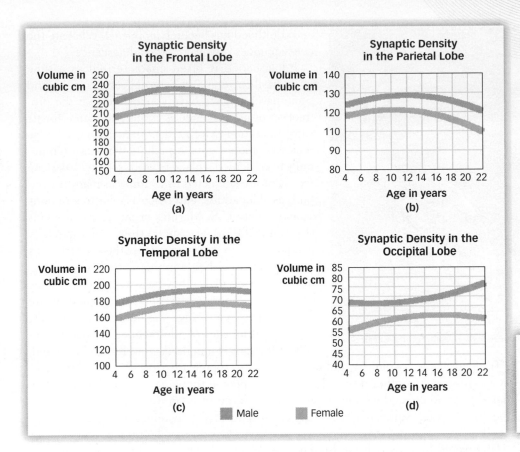

◄ Figure **11.11** **Your Brain on Puberty**
The development of neurons peaks in the frontal and parietal lobes at about age 12 (*a, b*), in the temporal lobe at about age 16 (*c*), and continues to increase in the occipital lobe through age 20 (*d*).

The Protraction of Adolescence

The age at which puberty begins varies across individuals (e.g., people tend to reach puberty at about the same age as their same-sexed parent did) and across cultures (e.g., African American girls tend to reach puberty before European American girls do). It also varies across generations (Malina, Bouchard, & Beunen, 1988). For example, in Scandinavia, the United Kingdom, and the United States, the age of first menstruation was between 16 and 17 years in the 19th century but was approximately 13 years in 1960. A more recent study found that the average age of breast development for Danish girls has decreased by an entire year since 1992 alone (Aksglaede et al., 2009). The average age at which American boys begin puberty has now fallen to between 9 and 10 years old (Herman-Giddens et al., 2012). Why so much earlier now than just a few decades ago? Puberty is accelerated by body fat (Kim & Smith, 1998), and the decrease in the age of the onset is largely due to improved diet and health (Ellis & Garber, 2000). But puberty in girls can also be hastened by exposure to environmental toxins that mimic estrogen (Buck Louis et al., 2008) or by stressful family situations (Belsky, 2012).

> **How has the onset of puberty changed over the last century?**

The increasingly early onset of puberty has important psychological consequences. Just two centuries ago, the gap between childhood and adulthood was relatively brief because people became physically mature at roughly the same time that they were ready to accept adult roles in society, and these roles did not normally require them to have extensive schooling. But in modern societies, people typically spend 3 to 10 years in school after they reach puberty. Thus, while the age at which people become physically adult has decreased, the age at which they are prepared or allowed to take on adult responsibilities has increased, and so the period between childhood

About 60% of preindustrial societies don't even have a word for adolescence (Schlegel & Barry, 1991). When a Krobo female menstruates for the first time, older women take her into seclusion for 2 weeks and teach her about sex, birth control, and marriage. Afterward, a public ceremony called the durbar is held, and the young female who that morning was regarded as a child is thereafter regarded as an adult.

and adulthood has become *protracted*. What are the consequences of a protracted adolescence?

Adolescence is often characterized as a time of internal turmoil and external recklessness, and some psychologists have speculated that the protraction of adolescence is in part to blame for its sorry reputation (Moffitt, 1993). According to these theorists, adolescents are adults who have temporarily been denied a place in adult society. American teenagers are subjected to 10 times as many restrictions as older adults, and twice as many restrictions as active-duty U.S. Marines or incarcerated felons (Epstein, 2007a). As such, they feel especially compelled to do things to protest these restrictions and demonstrate their adulthood, such as smoking, drinking, using drugs, having sex, and committing crimes. In a sense, adolescents are people who are forced to live in a strange gap between two worlds, and the pathologies of adolescence are partly a result of this predicament. As one researcher noted, "Trapped in the frivolous world of peer culture, they learn virtually everything they know from one another rather than from the people they are about to become. Isolated from adults and wrongly treated like children, it is no wonder that some teens behave, by adult standards, recklessly or irresponsibly" (Epstein, 2007b).

But the storm and stress of adolescence is neither as prevalent nor as inevitable as HBO would have us believe (Steinberg & Morris, 2001). Research suggests that the "moody adolescent" who is a victim of "raging hormones" is largely a myth. Adolescents are no moodier than children (Buchanan, Eccles, & Becker, 1992), and fluctuations in their hormone levels

Are adolescent problems inevitable?

have only a tiny impact on their moods (Brooks-Gunn, Graber, & Paikoff, 1994). Although they can be more impulsive and susceptible to peer influence than adults (see **FIGURE 11.12**), they are just as capable of making wise decisions based on good information (Steinberg, 2007). It is true that the majority of adolescents dabble in misbehavior, but don't actually major in it. For example, most adolescents in the United States get drunk at least once before they graduate from high school, but few develop drinking problems or allow alcohol to impair their academic success or personal relationships (Hughs, Power, & Francis, 1992; Johnston, Bachman, & O'Malley,

▶ Figure **11.12 How Do Peers Affect Decision Making?** Adolescents make better decisions when no one is around! Participants in one study played a video driving game with or without their peers in the room. The presence of peers greatly increased the number of risks taken and crashes experienced by adolescents, but had little or no effect on adults (Gardner & Steinberg, 2005).

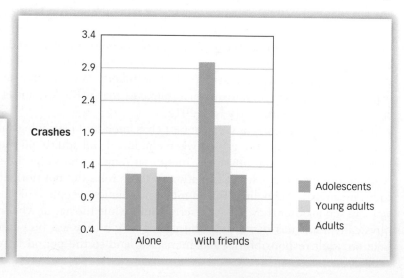

These students at the University of Missouri (*left*) may be experimenting with reckless behavior, but they are unlikely to become reckless adults. Of course, the Vermont State Trooper (*right*) who is inspecting the car in which four teens died after a night of drinking would probably like to remind them that this rule only applies to those who live.

1997). Most adolescent experiments have no long-term consequences, and the vast majority of adolescents who try drugs or break the law end up becoming sober, law-abiding adults (Steinberg, 1999). In short, the hijinks of adolescence are typically minor and temporary, and in some cultures they barely occur at all (Epstein, 2007b). Adolescence is not a terribly troubled time for most people, and most adolescents "age out" of any troubles they get themselves into (Sampson & Laub, 1995).

Sexuality

Puberty can be a difficult time, but it is especially difficult for girls who reach it earlier than their peers. These girls are more likely to experience a range of negative consequences, from distress and depression to delinquency and disease (Mendle, Turkheimer, & Emery, 2007; see **FIGURE 11.13**). This happens for several reasons (Ge & Natsuaki, 2009). First, early bloomers don't have as much time as their peers do to

> **What makes adolescence especially difficult?**

develop the skills necessary to cope with adolescence (Petersen & Grockett, 1985), but because they look so mature, people expect them to act like adults. In other words, early puberty creates unrealistic expectations and demands that the adolescent may have trouble fulfilling. Second, early blooming girls draw the attention of older men, who may lead them into a variety of unhealthy activities (Ge, Conger, & Elder, 1996). Some research suggests that for girls, the *timing* of puberty has a greater influence on emotional and behavioral problems than does the occurrence of puberty itself (Buchanan et al., 1992). The timing of puberty does not have such consistent effects on boys: some studies suggest that early maturing boys do better than their peers, some show they do worse, and some show that there is no difference at all (Ge, Conger, & Elder, 2001). Interestingly, recent research suggests that for boys, *tempo*, the speed with which they transition from the first to the last stages of puberty, may be a better predictor of negative outcomes than is timing (Mendle et al., 2010).

For some adolescents, puberty is additionally complicated by the fact that they are attracted to members of the same sex. Most gay men report having become aware of their sexual orientation between the ages of 6 and 18, and most gay women report having become

▼ Figure **11.13** **Early Puberty** Early puberty is a source of psychological distress for women (Ge, Conger, & Elder, 1996).

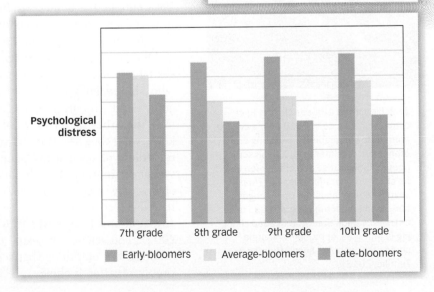

Psychological distress

| | 7th grade | 8th grade | 9th grade | 10th grade |

■ Early-bloomers ■ Average-bloomers ■ Late-bloomers

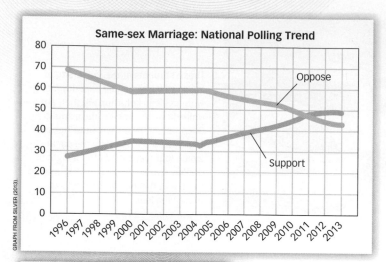

Same-sex Marriage: National Polling Trend

GRAPH FROM SILVER (2013).

▲ Figure **11.14** **Polling Trends** Americans' attitudes about homosexuality have changed dramatically in the last few years, as witnessed by their rapidly changing views on same-sex marriage.

Jane Clementi's 18-year-old son Tyler committed suicide in 2010 after a college roommate videotaped him kissing another man. She later said, "I think some people think that sexual orientation can be changed or prayed over. But I know sexual orientation is not up for negotiation. I don't think my children need to be changed. I think that what needed changing is attitudes, or myself, or maybe some other people I know" (quoted in Zernike, 2012).

REUTERS/LEE CELANO/LANDOV

aware between the ages of 11 and 26 (Calzo et al., 2011). Not only does their sexual orientation make gay adolescents different from the vast majority of their peers (a mere 3.5% of American adults identify themselves as lesbian, gay, or bisexual; Gates, 2011), but it can also subject them to disapproval from family, friends, and community. Americans are rapidly becoming more accepting of homosexuality (see **FIGURE 11.14**), but there are still plenty who disapprove. And in some nations, people do more than disapprove: They send gay citizens to prison or sentence them to death.

What determines whether a person's sexuality is primarily oriented toward the same or the opposite sex? For a long time, psychologists believed that a person's sexual orientation depended primarily on his or her upbringing. For example, psychoanalytic theorists claimed that boys who grow up with a domineering mother and a submissive father are less likely to identify with their father and are therefore more likely to become homosexual. Okay. Nice theory. But the *fact* is that scientific research has failed to identify *any* aspect of parenting that has a significant impact on a child's ultimate sexual orientation (Bell, Weinberg, & Hammersmith, 1981). Perhaps the most telling fact is that children raised by homosexual couples and children raised by heterosexual couples are equally likely to become heterosexual adults (Patterson, 1995). There is also little support for the idea that a person's early sexual encounters have a lasting impact on his or her sexual orientation (Bohan, 1996).

> **Is sexual orientation a matter of nature or nurture?**

So what *does* determine a person's sexual orientation? There is now considerable evidence to suggest that biology plays the major role. Not only do gay people have a larger proportion of gay siblings than do heterosexuals (Bailey et al., 1999), but the identical twin of a gay man (with whom he shares 100% of his genes) has a 50% chance of being gay, whereas the fraternal twin or nontwin brother of a gay man (with whom he shares 50% of his genes) has only a 15% chance (Bailey & Pillard, 1991; Gladue, 1994). A similar pattern has emerged in studies of women (Bailey et al., 1993). Some evidence suggests that the fetal environment may play a role in determining sexual orientation and that high levels of androgens in the womb may predispose a person—whether male or female—later to develop a sexual preference for women (Ellis & Ames, 1987; Meyer-Bahlberg et al., 1995). Perhaps this is why the brains of gay people tend to look like the brains of opposite-gendered straight people (Savic & Lindstrom, 2008). For example, the brain's two hemispheres tend to be unequally sized among straight men and gay women (both of whom are attracted to women), but equally sized among straight women and gay men (both of whom are attracted to men).

Of course, genes and prenatal biology cannot be the sole determinant of a person's sexual orientation because many homosexual men and women have identical twins who shared both their fetal environment and their genes, and who are nonetheless heterosexual. There must be other factors and, at present, we just don't know what they are. But one thing we do know is that regardless of what leads people to have a particular sexual orientation, there is no evidence that it can be changed by so-called conversion therapy (American Psychological Association, 2009). It is also worth noting that about 1% of people claim to have no sexual orientation of any kind and have never experienced sexual attraction to either gender (Bogaert, 2004). The science of sexual orientation is still young and fraught with conflicting findings, but one thing that seems abundantly clear is that sexual orientation is *not* simply a matter of choice.

> **Why do many adolescents make unwise choices about sex?**

But sexual behavior *is* a matter of choice, and many American teenagers choose it. Although the percentage of American teenagers who have had sex has been steadily declining (see **FIGURE 11.15**), it is still more than a third. The problem with this is that teenagers' interest in sex typically surpasses their knowledge about it. Most American parents never talk in great depth with their children about sex (Ansuini, Fiddler-Woite, & Woite, 1996), and those who do tend to start late because they overestimate the age at which their children become sexually active (Jaccard, Dittus, & Gordon, 1998; see **FIGURE 11.16**). Ignorance has consequences. A quarter of American teenagers have had four or more sexual partners by their senior year in high school, but only about half report using a condom during their last intercourse (Centers for Disease Control, 2002). Although teen birth rates have been falling in the United States for about 20 years, they are still the highest in in the developed world, and consequently, so is the rate of abortion.

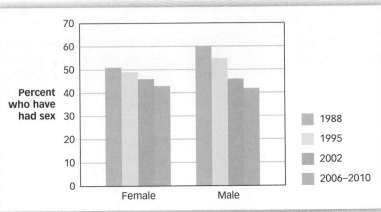

▲ Figure **11.15** **Teenage Sex** The percentage of American teenagers who have had sex has been declining in recent years (Martinez et al., 2011).

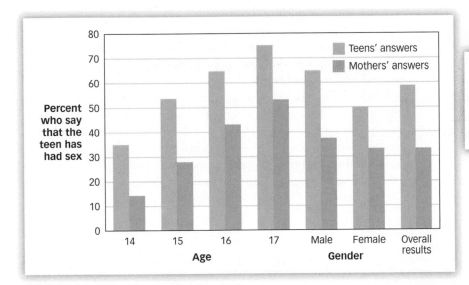

◀ Figure **11.16** **What Parents Think about Teenage Sex** When American parents talk to teens about sex, it is often too little and too late. Research shows that American teens have sex earlier than their parents think they do (Jaccard et al., 1998).

The human papilloma virus is a sexually transmitted disease that can lead to cervical cancer. Luckily, there is a vaccine that can prevent it. Some parents worry that being vaccinated will encourage their daughters to have sex early, but studies show that young women who have been vaccinated do not have sex earlier than those who have not been vaccinated (Bednarczyk et al., 2012).

What can be done? Despite what some people say, the best scientific evidence suggests that sex education does not increase the likelihood that teenagers will have sex. Instead, sex education leads teens to delay having sex for the first time, increases the likelihood they will use birth control when they do have sex, and lowers the likelihood that they will get pregnant or catch a sexually transmitted disease (Mueller, Gavin, & Kulkarni, 2008; Satcher, 2001). Despite these documented benefits, sex education in American schools is often absent, sketchy, or based on the goal of abstinence rather than harm prevention. Alas, there is little evidence to suggest that abstinence-only programs are effective (Kohler, Manhart, & Lafferty, 2008), and some studies suggest that teens who take abstinence pledges are just as likely to have sex as those who don't, but are less likely to use birth control (Rosenbaum, 2009). That's too bad, because teenage mothers fare more poorly than teenage women without children on almost every measure of academic and economic achievement, and their children fare more poorly on most measures of educational success and emotional well-being than do the children of older mothers (Olausson et al., 2001).

Parents and Peers

"Who am I?" is a question asked by amnesiacs and adolescents, who tend to ask it for different reasons. Children's views of themselves and their world are tightly tied to the views of their parents, but puberty creates a new set of needs that begins to snip away at those bonds by orienting adolescents toward peers rather than parents. Psychologist Erik Erikson (1959) characterized each stage of life by the major task confronting the individual at that stage. His *stages of psychosocial development* (shown in **TABLE 11.2**) suggest that the major task of adolescence is the development of an adult identity. Whereas children define themselves almost entirely in terms of their relationships with parents and siblings, adolescence marks a shift in emphasis from family relations to peer relations.

Two things can make this shift difficult. First, children cannot choose their parents, but adolescents can choose their peers. As such, adolescents have the power to shape themselves by joining groups that will lead them to develop new values, attitudes, beliefs, and perspectives. In a sense, the adolescent has the opportunity to invent the adult he or she will soon become, and the responsibility this opportunity entails can be overwhelming. Second, as adolescents strive for greater autonomy, their parents naturally rebel. For instance, parents and adolescents tend to disagree about the age at which certain adult behaviors—such as staying out late or having sex—are permissible, and you don't need a scientist to tell you which position each party in this conflict tends to hold (Holmbeck & O'Donnell, 1991). Because adolescents and parents often have different ideas about who should control the adolescent's behavior, their relationships become more conflictive and less close, and their interactions become briefer and less frequent (Larson & Richards, 1991). Even so, adolescents and their parents have

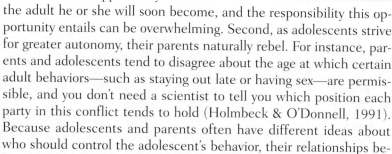

How do family and peer relationships change during adolescence?

"You're free-range when I say you're free-range."

©CHARLES BARSOTTI/THE NEW YORKER COLLECTION/CARTOONBANK.COM

Table 11.2

Erikson's Stages of Psychosocial Development

According to Erikson, at each "stage" of development a "key event" creates a challenge or "crisis" that a person can resolve positively or negatively.

Ages	Stage	Key Event	Crisis	Positive Resolution
1. Birth to 12–18 months	Oral–sensory	Feeding	Trust vs. mistrust	Child develops a belief that the environment can be counted on to meet his or her basic physiological and social needs.
2. 18 months to 3 years	Muscular–anal	Toilet training	Autonomy vs. shame/doubt	Child learns what he or she can control and develops a sense of free will and corresponding sense of regret and sorrow for inappropriate use of self-control.
3. 3–6 years	Locomotor	Independence	Initiative vs. guilt	Child learns to begin action, to explore, to imagine, and to feel remorse for actions.
4. 6–12 years	Latency	School	Industry vs. inferiority	Child learns to do things well or correctly in comparison to a standard or to others.
5. 12–18 years	Adolescence	Peer relationships	Identity vs. role confusion	Adolescent develops a sense of self in relationship to others and to own internal thoughts and desires.
6. 19–40 years	Young adulthood	Love relationships	Intimacy vs. isolation	Person develops the ability to give and receive love; begins to make long-term commitment to relationships.
7. 40–65 years	Middle adulthood	Parenting	Generativity vs. stagnation	Person develops interest in guiding the development of the next generation.
8. 65 to death	Maturity	Reflection on and acceptance of one's life	Ego integrity vs. despair	Person develops a sense of acceptance of life as it was lived and the importance of the people and relationships that the individual developed over the life span.

surprisingly few conflicts (Chung, Flook, & Fuligni, 2009), and when they do argue it tends to be over minor issues, such as dress and language (which may explain why teenagers argue more with their mothers, who are typically in charge of such issues, than with their fathers; Caspi et al., 1993).

Adolescents pull away from their parents, but more importantly, they move toward their peers. Studies show that across a wide variety of cultures, historical epochs, and even species, peer relations evolve in a similar way (Dunphy, 1963; Weisfeld, 1999). Young adolescents initially form groups or "cliques" with same-sexed peers, many of whom were friends during childhood (Brown, Mory, & Kinney, 1994). Next, male cliques and female cliques begin to meet in public places, such as town squares or shopping malls, and they begin to interact—but only in groups and only in public. After a few years, the older members of these same-sex cliques peel off and form smaller, mixed-sex cliques, which may assemble in private as well as in public, but usually assemble as a group. Finally, couples (typically a male and a female) peel off from the small, mixed-sex clique and begin romantic relationships.

Adolescents form same-sex cliques that meet opposite-sex cliques in public places. Eventually, these people will form mixed-sex cliques, pair off into romantic relationships, get married, have children, and then worry about them when they do all the same things.

Studies show that throughout adolescence, people spend increasing amounts of time with opposite-sex peers while maintaining the amount of time they spend with same-sex peers (Richards et al., 1998), and they accomplish this by spending less time with their parents (Larson & Richards, 1991). Although peers exert considerable influence on the adolescent's beliefs and behaviors, this influence generally occurs because adolescents respect, admire, and like their peers and not because their peers pressure them (Susman et al., 1994). In fact, as they age, adolescents show an increasing tendency to resist peer pressure (Steinberg & Monahan, 2007). Acceptance by peers is of tremendous importance to adolescents, and those who are rejected by their peers tend to be withdrawn, lonely, and depressed (Pope & Bierman, 1999). Fortunately for those of us who were seventh-grade nerds, individuals who are unpopular in early adolescence can become popular in later adolescence as their peers become less rigid and more tolerant (Kinney, 1993).

IN SUMMARY

▶ Adolescence is a stage of development that is distinct from those stages that come before and after it. It begins with a growth spurt and with puberty, the onset of sexual maturity of the human body. Puberty is occurring earlier than ever before, and the entrance of young people into adult society is occurring later.

▶ During this "in-between stage," adolescents are somewhat more prone to do things that are risky or illegal, but they rarely inflict serious or enduring harm on themselves or others.

▶ During adolescence, sexual interest intensifies, and in some cultures, sexual activity begins. Sexual activity typically follows a script, many aspects of which are standard across cultures. Although most people are attracted to members of the opposite sex, some are not, and research suggests that biology plays a key role in determining a person's sexual orientation.

▶ As adolescents seek to develop their adult identities, they seek increasing autonomy from their parents and become more peer-oriented, forming single-sex cliques, followed by mixed-sex cliques, and finally pairing off as couples.

adulthood
The stage of development that begins around 18 to 21 years and ends at death.

Adulthood: Change We Can't Believe In

It takes fewer than 7,000 days for a single-celled zygote to become a registered voter. **Adulthood** is *the stage of development that begins around 18 to 21 years and ends at death*. Because physical change slows from a gallop to a crawl, many of us think of adulthood as the destination to which the process of development finally delivers us, and that once we've arrived, our journey is pretty much complete. Nothing could be further from the truth because a whole host of physical, cognitive, and emotional changes take place between our first legal beer and our last legal breath.

Changing Abilities

The early 20s are the peak years for health, stamina, vigor, and prowess, and because our psychology is so closely tied to our biology, these are also the years during which most of our cognitive abilities are at their sharpest. At this very moment you probably see farther, hear better, remember more, and weigh less than you ever will again. Enjoy it while you can. This glorious moment at your physical peak will last for just a few dozen months more—and then, somewhere between the ages of 26 and 30, you will begin the slow and steady decline that will not end until you do. Just 10 or 15 years after puberty, your body will begin to break down in almost every way. Your muscles will be replaced by fat, your skin will become less elastic, your hair will thin

HOT SCIENCE

The End of History Illusion

"I've finally arrived." That's the feeling that many young adults have when they look back at the fast-paced changes of childhood and adolescence, and look forward to the relatively smooth sailing of adulthood. But recent research suggests that this feeling of having arrived is actually an illusion—and one that people succumb to throughout their entire lives.

In a recent study (Quoidbach, Gilbert, & Wilson, 2013), researchers asked thousands of people to recall how much their personalities had changed in the last 10 years, or to predict how much their personalities would change in the next 10 years.

They then compared the "looking back" memories of people who were a particular age with the "looking forward" predictions of people who were 10 years younger. So, for example, they compared how much 18-year-olds thought their personalities *would change* with how much 28-year-olds remembered their personalities *had changed,* and they did this for people from 18 to 68 years old.

As the graph shows, people who were looking back at a particular decade of life saw much more change than people who were looking forward to it—and this was true of every decade between 18 and 68! The researchers found precisely the same

pattern when they asked people to remember and predict changes in their basic values and preferences. They called this phenomenon the *end of history illusion*.

Adulthood, it seems, is a period of life that is characterized by unanticipated change, or "change we can't believe in." Although both teenagers and their grandparents seem to think that the pace of personal change has slowed to a crawl and that they have finally become the people they will forever be, the data suggest that it simply isn't so. Change slows but never stops, and its pace is faster than we expect.

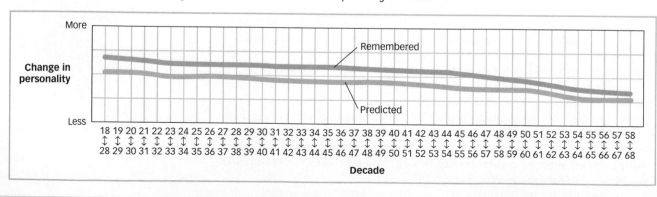

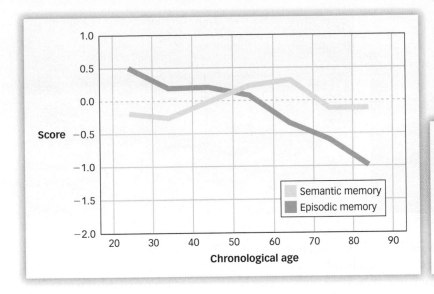

After the age of 20, people show dramatic declines on some measures of cognitive performance but not others (Salthouse, 2006). For example, the ability to recall past events (episodic memory) declines as we age, but the ability to recall the meanings of words (semantic memory) does not.

and your bones will weaken, your sensory abilities will become less acute, and your brain cells will die at an accelerated rate. Eventually, if you are a woman, your ovaries will stop producing eggs and you will become infertile. Eventually, if you are a man, your erections will be softer and fewer and farther between. Indeed, other than being more resistant to colds and less sensitive to pain, your elderly body just won't work as well as your youthful body does.

But don't worry, it gets worse. Because as these physical changes accumulate, they will begin to have measurable psychological consequences (Salthouse, 2006); see **FIGURE 11.17**). For instance, as your brain ages, your prefrontal cortex and its associated subcortical connections will deteriorate more quickly than the other areas of your brain (Raz, 2000), and you will experience a noticeable decline on cognitive tasks that require effort, initiative, or strategy. Your memory will worsen, though not all kinds will worsen at the same rate. You will experience a greater decline in working memory (the ability to hold information "in mind") than in long-term memory (the ability to retrieve information), a greater decline in episodic memory (the ability to remember particular past events) than in semantic memory (the ability to remember general information such as the meanings of words), a greater decline in retrieval accuracy than recognition accuracy, a greater decline in . . . um . . . something else that we can't remember just now.

> **What physical and psychological changes are associated with adulthood?**

Is the news all bad? Not really. Because even though your cognitive machinery will get rustier, research suggests that you will partially compensate by using it much more skillfully (Bäckman & Dixon, 1992; Salthouse, 1987). Older chess players *remember* chess positions much more poorly than younger players do, but they *play* just as well because they learn to search the board more efficiently (Charness, 1981). Older typists *react* more slowly than younger typists do, but they *type* just as quickly and accurately as because they are better at anticipating the next word in spoken or written text (Salthouse, 1984). Older airline pilots are considerably worse than younger pilots when it comes to keeping a list of words in short-term memory, but this age difference disappears when those words are the heading commands that pilots receive from the control tower every day (Morrow et al., 1994). All of this suggests that older adults are compensating for the age-related declines they experience in memory and attention (Park & McDonough, 2013).

> **Why how do adults compensate for their declining abilities?**

One week before his 58th birthday, US Airways pilot Chesley Sullenberger made a perfect emergency landing in the Hudson River and saved the lives of everyone on board. None of the passengers wish they'd had a younger pilot.

How do they do that? As you know from the Neuroscience and Behavior chapter, young brains are highly differentiated, that is, they have different parts that do different things. We now know that as the brain ages it becomes *de-differentiated* (Lindenberger & Baltes, 1994). For example, regions of the visual cortex that specialize in face and scene perception in younger people are much less specialized in older people (Grady et al., 1992; Park et al., 2004). It appears that the brain is like a group of specialists that work independently when they are young and able, but that pull together as a team when each of the specialists get older and slower (Park & McDonough, 2013). For example, when young adults try to keep verbal information in working memory, the left prefrontal cortex is more strongly activated than the right, and when young adults try to keep spatial information in working memory, the right prefrontal cortex is more strongly activated than the left (Smith & Jonides, 1997). But this *bilateral asymmetry* pretty much disappears in older adults, which suggests that the older brain is compensating for the declining abilities of each individual neural structure by calling on its other neural structures to help out (Cabeza, 2002; see **FIGURE 11.18**). The physical machinery breaks down as time passes, and one of the ways in which the brain rises to that challenge is by changing its division of labor.

► Figure **11.18** **Bilaterality in Older and Younger Brains** Across a variety of tasks, older adult brains show bilateral activation and young adult brains show unilateral activation. One explanation for this is that older brains compensate for the declining abilities of one neural structure by calling on other neural structures for help (Cabeza, 2002).

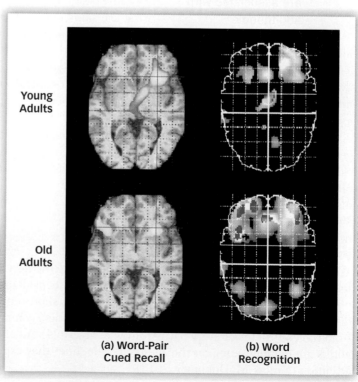

Young Adults

Old Adults

(a) Word-Pair Cued Recall

(b) Word Recognition

ROBERTO CABEZA, CENTER FOR COGNITIVE NEUROSCIENCE, DUKE UNIVERSITY. (A) CABEZA ET AL. (1997); (B) BACKMAN ET AL. (1997).

Changing Goals

One reason why Grandpa can't find his car keys is that his prefrontal cortex doesn't work as well as it used to. But another reason is that the location of car keys just isn't the sort of thing that grandpas want to spend their precious time memorizing (Haase, Heckhausen, & Wrosch, 2013). According to *socioemotional selectivity theory* (Carstensen & Turk-Charles, 1994), younger adults are largely oriented toward the acquisition of information that will be useful to them in the future (e.g., reading reviews), whereas older adults are generally oriented toward information that brings emotional satisfaction in the present (e.g., reading novels). Because young people have such long futures, they invest their time attending to, thinking about, and remembering potentially useful information that can serve them well tomorrow. Because older people have much shorter futures, they spend their time attending to, thinking about, and remembering positive information that serves them well today (see **FIGURE 11.19**).

> **How do informational goals change in adulthood?**

For example, older people perform *much* more poorly than younger people when they are asked to remember a series of unpleasant faces, but only *slightly* more poorly when they are asked to remember a series of pleasant faces (Mather & Carstensen, 2003). Whereas younger adults show equal amounts of amygdala activation when they see very pleasant or very unpleasant pictures, older adults show much more activation when they see very pleasant than very unpleasant pictures, suggesting that older adults just aren't attending to information that doesn't make them happy (Mather et al., 2004). Indeed, compared to younger adults, older adults are generally better at sustaining positive emotions and curtailing negative ones (Isaacowitz, 2012; Isaacowitz & Blanchard-Fields, 2012; Lawton et al., 1992; Mather & Carstensen, 2005). They also experience fewer negative emotions (Carstensen et al., 2000; Charles, Reynolds, & Gatz, 2001; Mroczek & Spiro, 2005; Schilling, Wahl, & Wiegering, 2013), and are more accepting of them when they do (Shallcross et al., 2013). Given all this, you shouldn't be surprised to learn that late adulthood is consistently reported to be one of the happiest and most satisfying periods of life (see **FIGURE 11.20**). You *shouldn't* be surprised, but you probably are because young adults vastly overestimate the problems of aging (Pew Research Center for People & the Press, 2009; see **FIGURE 11.21**).

> **Is late adulthood a happy or unhappy time for most people?**

Because having a short future orients people toward emotionally satisfying rather than intellectually profitable experiences, older adults become more selective about their interaction partners, choosing to spend time

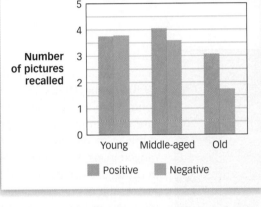

Number of pictures recalled

Young   Middle-aged   Old

■ Positive   ■ Negative

◄ Figure **11.19** **Memory for Pictures** Memory generally declines with age, but the ability to remember negative information—such as unpleasant pictures—declines much more quickly than the ability to remember positive information (Carstensen et al., 2000).

COURTESY OF DANIEL GILBERT

As people age, they prefer to spend time with family and a few close friends rather than large circles of acquaintances.

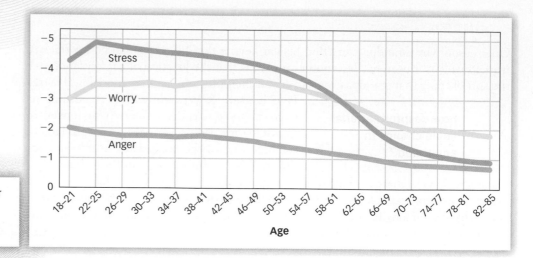

▶ Figure **11.20** **Emotions and Age** Older adults experience much lower levels of stress, worry, and anger than younger adults do (Stone et al., 2010).

Getting old isn't as bad as people think, and even holds a few nice surprises. For example, one study of women aged 40 to 100 showed that the oldest women were nearly twice as likely as the youngest ones to report being "very satisfied" with their sex lives (Trompeter, Bettencourt, & Barrett-Connor, 2012).

with family and a few close friends rather than with a large circle of acquaintances. One study monitored a group of people from the 1930s to the 1990s and found that their rate of interaction with acquaintances declined from early to middle adulthood, but their rate of interaction with spouses, parents, and siblings remained stable or increased (Carstensen, 1992). A study of older adults who ranged in age from 69 to 104 found that the oldest adults had fewer peripheral social partners than the younger adults did, but they had just as many emotionally close partners whom they identified as members of their "inner circle" (Lang & Carstensen, 1994). "Let's go meet some new people" isn't something that most 60-year-olds tend to say, but "Let's go hang out with some old friends" is. It is sad but instructive to note that many of these same cognitive and emotional changes can be observed among younger people who have discovered that their futures will be short because of a terminal illness (Carstensen & Fredrickson, 1998).

▶ Figure **11.21** **It's Better Than You Think** Research shows that young adults overestimate the problems of old age (Pew Research Center for People & the Press, 2009).

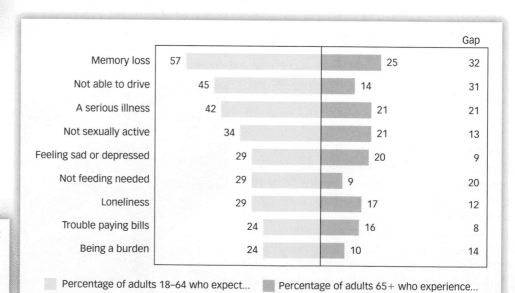

Changing Roles

The psychological separation from parents that begins in adolescence usually becomes a physical separation in adulthood. In virtually all human societies, young adults leave home, get married, and have children of their own. Marriage and parenthood are two of the most significant aspects of adult life. Census statistics suggest that if you are right now a college-age American, then you are likely to get married at around the age of 27, have approximately 1.8 children, and consider both your partner and your children to be your greatest sources of joy. Indeed, a whopping 93% of American mothers say that their children are a source of happiness all or most of the time (Pew Research Center, 1997).

But do marriage and children really make us happy? Research shows that married people live longer (see **FIGURE 11.22**), have more frequent sex (and enjoy that sex more), and earn several times as much money as unmarried people do (Waite, 1995). Given these differences, it is no surprise that married people report being happier than unmarried people—whether those unmarried people are single, widowed, divorced, or cohabiting (Johnson & Wu, 2002). That's why many researchers consider marriage one of the best investments individuals can make in their own happiness. But other researchers suggest that married people may be happier because happy people may be more likely to get married, and that marriage may be the consequence—and not the cause—of happiness (Lucas et al., 2003). The general consensus among scientists seems to be that both of these positions have merit: Even before marriage, people who end up married tend to be happier than those who never marry, but marriage does seem to confer further benefits.

> **What does research say about marriage, children, and happiness?**

Children are another story. In general, research suggests that children do not increase their parents' happiness, and may even decrease it (DiTella, MacCulloch, & Oswald, 2003; Simon, 2008; Senior, 2014). For example, parents typically report lower marital satisfaction than do nonparents—and the more children they have, the less satisfaction they report (Twenge, Campbell, & Foster, 2003). Studies of marital satisfaction at different points in the life span reveal an interesting pattern of peaks

Does marriage make people happy or do happy people tend to get married?

▼ Figure **11.22 Til Death Do Us Part**
Married people live longer than unmarried people, and this is true of both men and women. But while widowed men die as young as never-married and divorced men do (a), widowed women live longer than never-married or divorced women do (b). In other words, the loss of a wife is always bad, but the loss of a husband is only bad if you let him live! (Lillard & Waite, 1995)

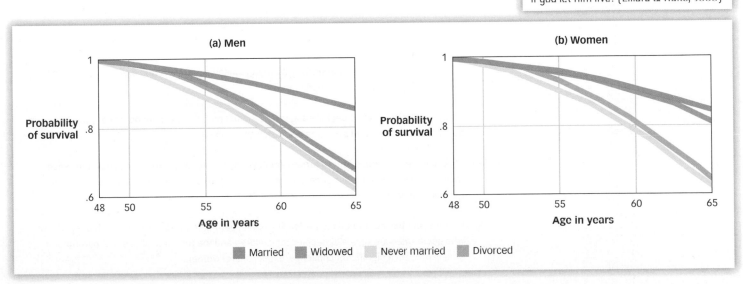

(a) Men

(b) Women

Probability of survival

Age in years

■ Married ■ Widowed ■ Never married ■ Divorced

and valleys: Marital satisfaction starts out high, plummets at about the time that the children are in diapers, begins to recover, plummets again when the children are in adolescence, and returns to its premarital levels only when children leave home (see **FIGURE 11.23**). Given that mothers typically do much more child care than fathers, it is not surprising that the negative impact of parenthood is stronger for women than for men. Women with young children are especially likely to experience role conflicts ("How am I supposed to manage being a full-time lawyer and a full-time mother?") and restrictions of freedom ("I never get to play tennis anymore"). A study that measured the moment-to-moment happiness of American women as they went about their daily activities found that women were less happy when taking care of their children than when eating, exercising, shopping, napping, or watching television—and only slightly happier than when they were doing housework (Kahneman et al., 2004).

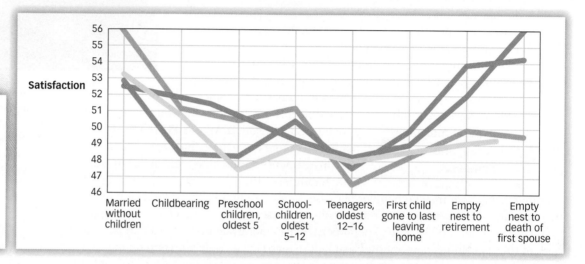

► Figure **11.23 Marital Satisfaction over the Life Span** This graph shows the results of four independent studies of marital satisfaction among men and women. All four studies suggest that marital satisfaction is highest before children are born and after they leave home (Walker, 1977).

Does all of this mean that people would be happier if they didn't have children? Not necessarily. Because researchers cannot randomly assign people to be parents or nonparents, studies of the effects of parenthood are necessarily correlational. People who want children and have children may be somewhat less happy than people who neither want them nor have them, but it is possible that people who want children would be even less happy if they didn't have them. What does seem clear is that raising children is a challenging job that most people find especially rewarding when they're not in the middle of doing it.

IN SUMMARY

► Older adults show declines in working memory, episodic memory, and retrieval tasks, but they often develop strategies to compensate.

► Gradual physical decline begins early in adulthood and has clear psychological consequences, some of which are offset by increases in skill and expertise.

► Older people are more oriented toward emotionally satisfying information, which influences their basic cognitive performance, the size and structure of their social networks, and their general happiness.

► For most people, adulthood means leaving home, getting married, and having children. People who get married are typically happier, but children and the responsibilities that parenthood entails present a significant challenge, especially for women.

OTHER VOICES

You Are Going to Die

Tim Kreider is an essayist and cartoonist whose newest book is *We Learn Nothing.*

PHOTO: TIM KREIDER/EINSTEIN THOMPSON AGENCY, NY, NY

Human development begins at conception and ends at death. Most of us would rather think about the conception part. Getting old seems scary and depressing, and one of the reasons why we send elderly people to retirement homes is so we don't have to watch as they wrinkle and wither and die. The essayist Tim Kreider (2013) thinks this is a terrible loss—not for older people, but for younger ones.

My sister and I recently toured the retirement community where my mother has announced she'll be moving. I have been in some bleak clinical facilities for the elderly where not one person was compos mentis and I had to politely suppress the urge to flee, but this was nothing like that. It was a very cushy modern complex housed in what used to be a seminary, with individual condominiums with big kitchens and sun rooms, equipped with fancy restaurants, grills and snack bars, a fitness center, a concert hall, a library, an art room, a couple of beauty salons, a bank and an ornate chapel of Italian marble. You could walk from any building in the complex to another without ever going outside, through underground corridors and glass-enclosed walkways through the woods. Mom described it as "like a college dorm, except the boys aren't as good-looking." Nonetheless I spent much of my day trying not to cry.

At all times of major life crisis, friends and family will crowd around and press upon you the false emotions appropriate to the occasion. "That's so great!" everyone said of my mother's decision to move to an assisted-living facility. "It's really impressive that she decided to do that herself." They cited their own stories of 90-year-old parents grimly clinging to drafty dilapidated houses, refusing to move until forced out by strokes or broken hips. "You should be really relieved and grateful." "She'll be much happier there." The overbearing unanimity of this chorus suggests to me that its real purpose is less to reassure than to suppress, to deny the most obvious and natural emotion that attends this occasion, which is sadness.

My sadness is purely selfish, I know. My friends are right; this was all Mom's idea, she's looking forward to it, and she really will be happier there. But it also means losing the farm my father bought in 1976, where my sister and I grew up, where Dad died in 1991. We're losing *our old phone number,* the one we've had since the Ford administration, a number I know as well as my own middle name. However infrequently I go there, it is the place on earth that feels like home to me, the place I'll always have to go back to in case adulthood falls through. I hadn't realized, until I was forcibly divested of it, that I'd been harboring the idea that someday, when this whole crazy adventure was over, I would at some point be nine again, sitting around the dinner table with Mom and Dad and my sister. And beneath it all, even at age 45, there is the irrational, little-kid fear: Who's going to take care of me? I remember my mother telling me that when her own mother died, when Mom was in her 40s, her first thought was: *I'm an orphan.*

Plenty of people before me have lamented the way that we in industrialized countries regard our elderly as unproductive workers or obsolete products, and lock them away in institutions instead of taking them into our own homes out of devotion and duty. Most of these critiques are directed at the indifference and cruelty thus displayed to the elderly; what I wonder about is what it's doing to the rest of us.

Segregating the old and the sick enables a fantasy, as baseless as the fantasy of capitalism's endless expansion, of youth and health as eternal, in which old age can seem to be an inexplicably bad lifestyle choice, like eating junk food or buying a minivan, that you can avoid if you're well-educated or hip enough. So that when through absolutely no fault of your own your eyesight begins to blur and you can no longer eat whatever you want without consequence and the hangovers start lasting for days, you feel somehow ripped off, lied to. Aging feels grotesquely unfair. As if there ought to be someone to sue.

We don't see old or infirm people much in movies or on TV. We love explosive gory death onscreen, but we're not so enamored of the creeping, gray, incontinent kind. Aging and death are embarrassing medical conditions, like hemorrhoids or eczema, best kept out of sight. Survivors of serious illness or injuries have written that, once they were sick or disabled, they found themselves confined to a different world, a world of sick people, invisible to the rest of us. Denis Johnson writes in his novel *Jesus' Son:* "You and I don't know about these diseases until we get them, in which case we also will be put out of sight."

My own father died at home, in what was once my childhood bedroom. He was, in this respect at least, a lucky man. Almost everyone dies in a hospital now, even though absolutely nobody wants to, because by the time we're dying all the decisions have been taken out of our hands by the well, and the well are without mercy. Of course we hospitalize the sick and the old for some good reasons (better care, pain relief), but I think we also segregate the elderly from the rest of society because we're afraid of them, as if age might be contagious. Which, it turns out, it is.

. . . You are older at this moment than you've ever been before, and it's the youngest you're ever going to get. The mortality rate is holding at a scandalous 100 percent. Pretending death can be indefinitely evaded with hot yoga or a gluten-free diet or antioxidants or just by refusing to look is craven denial. "Facing it, always facing it, that's the way to get through," Conrad wrote in *Typhoon.* "Face it." He was talking about more than storms. The sheltered prince Siddartha Gautama was supposedly set on the path to becoming the Buddha when he was out riding and happened to see an old man, a sick man and a dead man. Today he'd be spared the discomfiture, and the enlightenment, unless he were riding mass transit.

Just yesterday my mother sent me a poem she first read in college—Langston Hughes's "Mother to Son." She said she could still remember where she was, in her dorm room at Goshen College, when she came across it in her American Lit book. The title notwithstanding, it does not make for Hallmark-card copy. *Life for me ain't been no crystal stair.* It tells us that this life is not a story or an adventure or a journey of spiritual self-discovery; it's a slog. And it orders us to keep going, don't you dare give up, no matter what. Because I'm your mother, that's why.

Do you agree with Kreider: Do we do a disservice to the young when we segregate the old?

Chapter Review

KEY CONCEPT QUIZ

1. The sequence of prenatal development is
   a. fetus, embryo, zygote.
   b. zygote, embryo, fetus.
   c. embryo, zygote, fetus.
   d. zygote, fetus, embryo.

2. Learning begins
   a. in the womb.
   b. at birth.
   c. in the newborn stage.
   d. in infancy.

3. The proximodistal rule states that
   a. motor skills emerge in sequence from the center to the periphery.
   b. motor skills emerge in sequence from the top to the bottom.
   c. motor skills such as rooting are hardwired by nature.
   d. simple motor skills disappear as more sophisticated motor skills emerge.

4. Motor skills, such as reaching, are
   a. acquired in an orderly sequence and on a strict timetable.
   b. acquired on a strict timetable, but not in an orderly sequence.
   c. influenced by the infant's incentive.
   d. acquired by the same method by all infants.

5. Piaget believed that infants construct _____, which are theories about the way the world works.
   a. assimilations
   b. accommodations
   c. schemas
   d. habituations

6. Once children understand that human behavior is guided by mental representations, they are said to have acquired
   a. joint attention.
   b. a theory of mind.
   c. formal operational ability.
   d. egocentrism.

7. When infants in a new situation examine their mother's face for cues about what to do, they are demonstrating an ability known as
   a. joint attention.
   b. social referencing.
   c. imitation.
   d. all of the above.

8. The capacity for attachment may be innate, but the quality of attachment is influenced by
   a. the child's temperament.
   b. the primary caregiver's ability to read their child's emotional state.
   c. the interaction between the child and the primary caregiver.
   d. all of the above.

9. A child's attachment style is
   a. assessed by a behavioral test known as the Strange Situation.
   b. most commonly a secure attachment style, except across cultures.
   c. generally different in the home than it appears in the laboratory.
   d. unchangeable over time.

10. According to Kohlberg, each stage in the development of moral reasoning is characterized by a specific focus. What is the correct sequence of these stages?
    a. focus on consequences, focus on ethical principles, focus on social rules
    b. focus on ethical principles, focus on social rules, focus on consequences
    c. focus on consequences, focus on social rules, focus on ethical principles
    d. focus on social rules, focus on consequences, focus on ethical principles

11. Evidence indicates that American adolescents are
    a. moodier than children.
    b. victims of raging hormones.
    c. likely to develop drinking problems.
    d. living in a protracted gap between childhood and adulthood.

12. Scientific evidence suggests that _____ play(s) a key role in determining a person's sexual orientation.
    a. personal choices
    b. parenting styles
    c. sibling relationships
    d. biology

13. Adolescents place the greatest emphasis on relationships with
    a. peers.
    b. parents.
    c. siblings.
    d. nonparental authority figures.

14. The peak years for health, stamina, vigor, and prowess are
    a. childhood.
    b. the early teens.
    c. the early 20s.
    d. the early 30s.

15. Data suggest that, for most people, the last decades of life are
    a. characterized by an increase in negative emotions.
    b. spent attending to the most useful information.
    c. extremely satisfying.
    d. a time during which they begin to interact with a much wider circle of people.

KEY TERMS

developmental psychology (p. 426)

zygote (p. 427)

germinal stage (p. 427)

embryonic stage (p. 427)

fetal stage (p. 428)

myelination (p. 428)

teratogens (p. 428)

fetal alcohol syndrome (FAS) (p. 429)

infancy (p. 431)

motor development (p. 431)

reflexes (p. 431)

cephalocaudal rule (p. 432)

proximodistal rule (p. 432)

cognitive development (p. 433)

sensorimotor stage (p. 433)

schemas (p. 433)

assimilation (p. 433)

accommodation (p. 434)

object permanence (p. 434)

childhood (p. 435)

preoperational stage (p. 435)

concrete operational stage (p. 436)

conservation (p. 436)

formal operational stage (p. 437)

egocentrism (p. 437)

theory of mind (p. 438)

attachment (p. 444)

Strange Situation (p. 444)

temperaments (p. 445)

internal working model of relationships (p. 445)

preconventional stage (p. 448)

conventional stage (p. 448)

postconventional stage (p. 448)

adolescence (p. 451)

puberty (p. 452)

primary sex characteristics (p. 452)

secondary sex characteristics (p. 452)

adulthood (p. 460)

CHANGING MINDS

1. One of your friends recently got married and she and her husband are planning to have children. You mention to your friend that once this happens she'll have to stop drinking. She scoffs. "They make it sound as though a pregnant woman who drinks alcohol is murdering her baby. Look, my mom drank wine every weekend when she was pregnant with me and I'm just fine." What is your friend failing to understand about the effects of alcohol on prenatal development? What other teratogens might you tell her about?

2. You are at the grocery store when you spot a crying child in a stroller. The mother picks up the child and cuddles it until it stops crying. A grocery clerk is standing next to you, stocking the shelves. He leans over and says, "Now, that's bad parenting. If you pick up and cuddle a child every time it cries, you're reinforcing the behavior, and the result will be a very spoiled child." Do you agree? What do

studies of attachment tell us about the effects of picking up and holding children when they cry?

3. You and your roommate are watching a movie in which a young man tells his parents that he's gay. The parents react badly and decide that they should send him to a "camp" where he can learn to change his sexual orientation. Your roommate turns to you: "Do you know anything about this? Can people really be changed from gay to straight?" Based on what you've read in this text, what would you tell your friend about the factors determining sexual orientation?

4. One of your cousins has just turned 30 and, to his horror, has discovered a gray hair. "This is the end," he says. "Soon I'll start losing my eyesight, growing new chins, and forgetting how to use a cell phone. Aging is just one long, slow, agonizing decline." What could you tell your cousin to cheer him up? Does everything in life get worse with aging?

ANSWERS TO KEY CONCEPT QUIZ

1. b; 2. a; 3. c; 4. c; 5. c; 6. b; 7. b; 8. d; 9. a; 10. c; 11. d; 12. d; 13. a; 14. c; 15. c.

Need more help? Additional resources are located in LaunchPad at: http://www.worthpublishers.com/launchpad/schacter3e

Personality

Growing up, Stefani Joanne Angelina Germanotta seemed to have personality. As a child, she was said to have shown up at the occasional family gathering naked. As the pop star now known as Lady Gaga, she continues the tradition of being different. Her first albums, *The Fame* and *The Fame Monster,* and the fact that she calls her fans "Little Monsters" and herself the "Mother Monster," hinted she might have issues. But she, like most of us, is not one-dimensional. Yes, her style is eccentric and seems silly to many (we're looking at you, raw meat dress), but she also is a serious supporter of humanitarian and personal causes, including equality for people who are gay, bisexual, lesbian, or transgendered (as in her song "Born This Way"). Lady Gaga is one of a kind. She has personality in an important sense— she has qualities that make her psychologically different from other people.

Singer Lady Gaga in her meat dress at the MTV Video Music Awards, September 2010.

PRESS ASSOCIATION VIA AP IMAGES

471

Howard Stern

Hillary Clinton

Rihanna

How would you describe each of these personalities?

Cristiano Ronaldo

THE FORCES THAT CREATE ANY ONE PERSONALITY ARE ALWAYS something of a mystery. Your personality is different from anyone else's and expresses itself pretty consistently across settings—at home, in the classroom, and elsewhere. But how and why do people differ psychologically? By studying many unique individuals, psychologists seek to gather enough information to answer these central questions of personality psychology scientifically.

Personality is *an individual's characteristic style of behaving, thinking, and feeling.* Whether Lady Gaga's quirks are real or merely for publicity, they are certainly hers and they show her distinct personality. In this chapter, we will explore personality, first by looking at what it is and how it is measured, and then by focusing on each of four main approaches to understanding personality: trait—biological, psychodynamic, humanistic—existential, and social cognitive. Psychologists have personalities, too (well, *most* of them), so their different approaches, even to the topic of personality, shouldn't be that surprising. At the end of the chapter, we discuss the psychology of self to see how our views of what we are like can shape and define our personality.

Personality: What It Is and How It Is Measured

If someone said, "You have no personality," how would you feel? Like a cookie-cutter person, a boring, grayish lump who should go out and get a personality as soon as possible? As a rule, people don't usually strive for a personality—one seems to develop naturally as we travel through life. As psychologists have tried to understand the process of personality development, they have pondered questions of description (*how* do people differ?), explanation (*why* do people differ?), and the more quantitative question of measurement (how can personality be *assessed*?).

Describing and Explaining Personality

As the first biologists earnestly attempted to classify all plants and animals (whether lichens or ants or fossilized lions), personality psychologists began by labeling and describing different personalities. And just as biology came of age with Darwin's theory of evolution, which *explained* how differences among species arose, the maturing study of personality also has developed explanations of the basis for psychological differences among people.

Most personality psychologists focus on specific, psychologically meaningful individual differences, characteristics such as honesty, anxiousness, or moodiness. Still, personality is often in the eye of the beholder. When one person describes another as "a conceited jerk," for example, you may wonder whether you have just learned more about the describer or the person being described. Interestingly, studies that ask acquaintances to describe each other find a high degree of similarity among any one individual's descriptions of many different people ("Jason thinks that Carlos is considerate, Renata is kind, and Jean Paul is nice to others"). In contrast, resemblance is quite low when many people describe one person ("Carlos thinks Jason is smart, Renata thinks he is competitive, and Jean Paul thinks he has a good sense of humor"; Dornbusch et al., 1965).

> **What does it mean to say that personality is in the eye of the beholder?**

What leads Lady Gaga to all of her entertaining extremes? In general, explanations of personality differences are concerned with (1) *prior events* that can shape an individual's personality or (2) *anticipated events* that might motivate the person to reveal particular personality characteristics. In a biological prior event, Stefani Germanotta received genes from her parents that may have led her to develop into the sort of person who loves putting on a display (not to mention putting on raw meat) and stirring up controversy. Researchers interested in events that happen prior to our behavior study our genes, brains, and other aspects of our biological makeup, and also delve into our subconscious and into our circumstances and interpersonal surroundings. The consideration of *anticipated events* emphasizes the person's own, subjective perspective and often seems intimate and personal in its reflection of the person's inner life (hopes, fears, and aspirations).

Of course, our understanding of how the baby named Stefani Germanotta grew into the adult Lady Gaga (or the life of any woman or man) also depends on insights into the interaction between the prior and anticipated events: We need to know how her history may have shaped her motivations.

Measuring Personality

Of all the things psychologists have set out to measure, personality may be one of the toughest. How do you capture the uniqueness of a person? What aspects of people's personalities are important to know about, and how should we quantify them? The general personality measures can be classified broadly into personality inventories and projective techniques.

Personality Inventories

To learn about an individual's personality, you could follow the person around and, clipboard in hand, record every single thing the person does, says, thinks, and feels (including how long this goes on before the person calls the police). Some observations might involve your own impressions (Day 5: seems to be getting irritable); others would involve objectively observable events that anyone could verify (Day 7: grabbed my pencil and broke it in half, then bit my hand).

Psychologists have figured out ways to obtain objective data on personality without driving their subjects to violence. The most popular technique is **self-report,** *a method in which people provide subjective information about their own thoughts, feelings, or behaviors, typically via questionnaire or interview.* In most self-report measures, the respondent is asked to circle a number on a scale indicating the degree to which they endorse that item as being self-descriptive (e.g., reporting on a scale of 0–5 to what extent they believe they are a "worrier") or to indicate whether an item is true or false in describing them. The researcher then combines the answers to get a general sense of the individual's personality with respect to a particular domain. **TABLE 12.1** shows the 10 items from a self-report test of different personality traits (Gosling, Rentfrow & Swann, 2003). In this case, the respondent is asked to indicate whether each personality trait applies to him or her. To score the measure you simply add up the two items for each of the five traits listed at the bottom of the table.

How is a self-report scale created? The usual strategy is to collect sets of self-descriptive statements that indicate different degrees of a personality characteristic. To measure friendliness, for example, you could ask people to rate their agreement with statements ranging from "I am somewhat friendly" to "I am very outgoing," and even to "I love being around people every minute of the day." Adding up the number of statements the person endorses that indicate friendliness (and subtracting endorsements of those that indicate unfriendliness) yields a measure of the person's self-reported friendliness. Scales based on the content of self-reports have been devised to assess a whole range of personality characteristics, all the way from general tendencies such as overall happiness (Lyubomirsky, 2008; Lyubomirsky & Lepper, 1999)

personality
An individual's characteristic style of behaving, thinking, and feeling.

self-report
A method in which a person provides subjective information about their own thoughts, feelings, or behaviors, typically via questionnaire or interview.

Table 12.1

Ten-Item Personality Inventory (TIPI)

Here are a number of personality traits that may or may not apply to you. Please write a number next to each statement to indicate the extent to which *you agree or disagree with that statement*. You should rate the extent to which the pair of traits applies to you, even if one characteristic applies more strongly than the other.

1 = Disagree strongly
2 = Disagree moderately
3 = Disagree a little
4 = Neither agree nor disagree
5 = Agree a little
6 = Agree moderately
7 = Agree strongly

I see myself as:

1. ____ Extraverted, enthusiastic
2. ____ Critical, quarrelsome
3. ____ Dependable, self-disciplined
4. ____ Anxious, easily upset
5. ____ Open to new experiences, complex
6. ____ Reserved, quiet
7. ____ Sympathetic, warm
8. ____ Disorganized, careless
9. ____ Calm, emotionally stable
10. ____ Conventional, uncreative

TIPI scale scoring (R = reverse-scored items): Extraversion (1, 6R); Agreeableness (2R, 7); Conscientiousness (3, 8R); Emotional Stability (4R, 9); Openness to Experience (5, 10R).

Source: Gosling, Rentfrow, & Swann, 2003.

to specific ones such as responding rapidly to insults (Swann & Rentfrow, 2001) or complaining about poor service (Lerman, 2006).

One of the most commonly used personality tests is the **Minnesota Multiphasic Personality Inventory (MMPI),** *a well-researched, clinical questionnaire used to assess personality and psychological problems.* The MMPI was developed in 1939 and has been revised several times over the years, leading up to the current version, the MMPI–2–RF (restructured form; Ben-Porath & Tellegen, 2008). The MMPI–2–RF consists of 338 self-descriptive statements to which the respondent answers "true," "false," or "cannot say." The MMPI–2–RF measures a wide range of psychological constructs: clinical problems (e.g., antisocial behavior, thought dysfunction), somatic problems (e.g., head pain, cognitive complaints), internalizing problems (e.g., anxiety, self-doubt), externalizing problems (e.g., aggression, substance abuse), and interpersonal problems (e.g., family problems, avoidance). The MMPI–2–RF also includes *validity scales* that assess a person's attitudes toward test taking and any tendency to try to distort the results by faking answers.

> Personality inventories ask people to report what traits they possess; however, many psychologists believe that people do not always know what's in their mind. Can we rely on people to accurately report on their personality?

JEFF GREENBERG/GETTY IMAGES

Personality inventories such as the MMPI–2–RF are easy to administer: All that is needed is the test and a pencil (or a computer-based version). The respondent's scores are then calculated and compared with the average ratings of thousands of other test takers. Because no human interpretation of the responses is needed (i.e., "true" means true, "false" means false, etc.), any potential biases of the person giving the test are minimized. Of course, an accurate measurement of personality will only occur if people provide accurate responses. Although self-report test results are easy to obtain, critics of this approach highlight several limitations. One problem is that many people have a tendency to respond in a socially desirable way, such that they underreport things that are unflattering or embarrassing. Perhaps even more problematic is that there are many things we don't know about ourselves and so are unable to report! Studies show that people often are inaccurate in their self-report about what they have experienced in the past, what factors are motivating their behaviors in the present, or how they will feel or behave in the future (Wilson, 2009).

> **What are some limitations of personality inventories?**

Projective Techniques

A second, somewhat controversial, class of tools for evaluating personality designed to circumvent the limitations of self-report mentioned above, is **projective tests,** which are *tests designed to reveal inner aspects of individuals' personalities by analysis of their responses to a standard series of ambiguous stimuli.* The developers of projective tests assume that people will project personality factors that are below awareness—wishes, concerns, impulses, and ways of seeing the world—onto the ambiguous stimuli and will not censor these responses. Probably best-known is the **Rorschach Inkblot Test,** *a projective technique in which respondents' inner thoughts and feelings are believed to be revealed by analysis of their responses to a set of unstructured inkblots.* An example inkblot is shown in **FIGURE 12.1.** Responses are scored according to complicated systems (derived in part from research with people with psychological disorders) that classify what people see (Exner, 1993; Rapaport, 1946). For example, most people who look at Figure 12.1 report seeing birds or people. Someone who reports seeing something very unusual (e.g., "I see two purple tigers eating a velvet cheeseburger") may be experiencing thoughts and feelings that are very different from most other people.

▼ Figure **12.1 Sample Rorschach Inkblot**
Test takers are shown a card such as this sample and asked, "What might this be?" What they perceive, where they see it, and why it looks that way are assumed to reflect unconscious aspects of their personality.

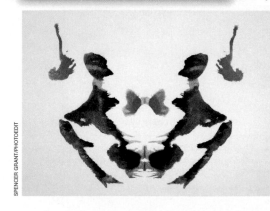

SPENCER GRANT/PHOTOEDIT

The **Thematic Apperception Test (TAT)** is *a projective technique in which respondents' underlying motives, concerns, and the way they see the social world are believed to be revealed through analysis of the stories they make up about ambiguous pictures of people.* To get a sense of the test, look at **FIGURE 12.2**. The test administrator shows the respondent the card and asks him or her to tell a story about the picture, asking questions such as: Who are those people? What is happening? What led them to this moment? What will happen next? Different people tell very different stories about the image. In creating the stories, the respondent is thought to identify with the main characters and to project his or her view of others and the world onto the other details in the drawing. Thus, any details that are not obviously drawn from the picture are believed to be projected onto the story from the respondent's own desires and internal conflicts.

Many of the TAT drawings tend to elicit a consistent set of themes, such as successes and failures, competition and jealousy, conflict with parents and siblings, feelings about intimate relationships, aggression, and sexuality. For instance, one card that shows an older man standing over a child lying in bed tends to elicit themes regarding relationships that respondents have with an older man in their life, such as a relationship with a father, teacher, boss, or therapist. The interviewer might be interested in learning whether respondents see the person lying down as a male or female, and whether they report that the man standing is trying to help or harm the person lying down. Consider a story proposed by a young man in response to this card: "The boy lying down had a hard day at school. He worked so hard studying for his exam that when he came home after taking the test he fell asleep with his clothes on. No matter how hard the boy tries, he can never make his father happy. The father is sick and tired of the son not doing well in school and so he is going to kill him. He suffocates the boy and the boy dies." The test administrator might interpret this response as indicating that the respondent perceives that his father has high expectations that are not being met, and perhaps that the father is disappointed and angry with the young man.

The value of projective tests is debated by psychologists. Although they continue to be widely used by practicing clinicians, critics argue that tests such as the Rorschach and the TAT are open to the biases of the examiner. A TAT story like the one above may *seem* revealing; however, the examiner must always add an interpretation (Was this about the respondent's actual father, about his own concerns about his academic failures, or about trying to be funny or provocative?), and that interpretation could well be the scorer's *own* projection into the mind of the test taker. Thus, despite the rich picture of a personality and the insights into an individual's motives that these tests offer, projective tests should be understood primarily as a way in which a psychologist can get to know someone personally and intuitively (McClelland et al., 1953). When measured by rigorous scientific criteria, projective tests such as the TAT and the Rorschach have not been found to be reliable or valid in predicting behavior (Lilienfeld, Lynn, & Lohr, 2003).

Newer personality measurement methods are moving beyond both self-report inventories and projective tests (Robins, Fraley, & Krueger, 2007). High-tech methods such as wireless communication, real-time computer analysis, and automated behavior

> **What might limit the validity of the information obtained from projective tests?**

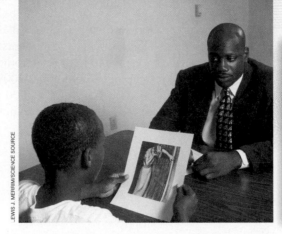

◀ Figure **12.2** **Sample TAT Card**
Test takers are shown cards with ambiguous scenes such as this sample and are asked to tell a story about what is happening in the picture. The main themes of the story, the thoughts and feelings of the characters, and how the story develops and resolves are considered useful indices of unconscious aspects of an individual's personality [Murray, 1943].

LEWIS J. MERRIM/SCIENCE SOURCE

Minnesota Multiphasic Personality Inventory (MMPI)
A well-researched, clinical questionnaire used to assess personality and psychological problems.

projective tests
Tests designed to reveal inner aspects of individuals' personalities by analysis of their responses to a standard series of ambiguous stimuli.

Rorschach Inkblot Test
A projective technique in which respondents' inner thoughts and feelings are believed to be revealed by analysis of their responses to a set of unstructured inkblots.

Thematic Apperception Test (TAT)
A projective technique in which respondents' underlying motives, concerns, and the way they see the social world are believed to be revealed through analysis of the stories they make up about ambiguous pictures of people.

The EAR (electronically activated recorder) sampled conversations of hundreds of participants and found that women and men are equally talkative (Mehl et al., 2009).

identification open the door to personality measurements that are leaps beyond following the person around with a clipboard—and can lead to surprising findings. The stereotype that women are more talkative than men, for example, was challenged by findings when 396 college students in the United States and Mexico each spent several days wearing an EAR (electronically activated recorder) that captured random snippets of their talk (Mehl et al., 2009). The result? Women and men were *equally* talkative, each averaging about 16,000 words per day. The advanced measurement of how people differ (and how they do not) is a key step in understanding personality.

IN SUMMARY

▶ In psychology, personality refers to a person's characteristic style of behaving, thinking, and feeling.

▶ Personality psychologists attempt to find the best ways to describe personality, to explain how personalities come about, and to measure personality.

▶ Two general classes of personality tests are personality inventories, such as the MMPI–2–RF, and projective techniques, such as the Rorschach Inkblot Test and the TAT. Newer high-tech methods are proving to be even more effective.

The Trait Approach: Identifying Patterns of Behavior

Imagine writing a story about the people you know. To capture their special qualities, you might describe their traits: Keesha is *friendly, aggressive,* and *domineering;* Seth is *flaky, humorous,* and *superficial*. With a dictionary and a free afternoon, you might even be able to describe William as *perspicacious, flagitious,* and *callipygian*. The trait approach to personality uses such trait terms to characterize differences among individuals. In attempting to create manageable and meaningful sets of descriptors, trait theorists face two significant challenges: narrowing down the almost infinite set of adjectives and answering the more basic question of why people have particular traits and whether they arise from biological or hereditary foundations.

Traits as Behavioral Dispositions and Motives

One way to think about personality is as a combination of traits. This was the approach of Gordon Allport (1937), one of the first trait theorists, who believed people could be described in terms of traits just as an object could be described in terms of its properties. He saw a **trait** as *a relatively stable disposition to behave in a particular and consistent way*. For example, a person who keeps his books organized alphabetically in bookshelves, hangs his clothing neatly in the closet, knows the schedule for the local bus, keeps a clear agenda in a daily planner, and lists birthdays of friends and family in his calendar can be said to have the trait of *orderliness*. This trait consistently manifests itself in a variety of settings.

The orderliness trait *describes* a person but doesn't *explain* his or her behavior. Why does the person behave in this way? There are two basic ways in which a trait might serve as an explanation: The trait may be a preexisting disposition of the person that causes the person's behavior, or it may be a motivation that guides the person's behavior. Allport saw traits as preexisting dispositions, causes of behavior that reliably trigger the behavior. The person's orderliness, for

How might traits explain behavior?

trait
A relatively stable disposition to behave in a particular and consistent way.

example, is an inner property of the person that will cause the person to straighten things up and be tidy in a wide array of situations. Other personality theorists, such as Henry Murray (the creator of the TAT), suggested instead that traits reflect motives. Just as a hunger motive might explain someone's many trips to the snack bar, a need for orderliness might explain the neat closet, organized calendar, and familiarity with the bus schedule (Murray & Kluckhohn, 1953). Researchers examining traits as causes have used personality inventories to measure them, whereas those examining traits as motives have more often used projective tests.

Researchers have described and measured hundreds of different personality traits over the past several decades. Back in the 1940s, in the wake of World War II, psychologists were very interested in right-wing *authoritarianism,* or the tendency toward political conservatism, obedience to authority, and conformity. At that time, researchers were trying to understand what had made people support the rise of Nazi Germany and Fascism (Adorno et al., 1950). Although research on the personality traits that lead to authoritarianism continues (Perry & Sibley, 2012), the topic became less focal for researchers once World War II receded into history. Examples of other traits that have come into vogue over the years include cognitive complexity, defensiveness, sensation seeking, and optimism. As with television shows and hairstyles, fashions in trait dimensions come and go over time.

By many accounts, Bashar al-Assad is a despotic ruler who imprisons, tortures, and kills those who oppose him. Why would anyone want to follow such a dictator? The study of the authoritarian personality was inspired by the idea that some people might follow most anyone because their personalities make them adhere to hierarchies of authority, submitting to those above them and dominating those below them.

The Search for Core Traits

Picking a fashionable trait and studying it in depth doesn't get us very far in the search for the core of human character: the basic set of traits that defines how humans differ from one another. People may differ strongly in their choice of Coke versus Pepsi, or dogs versus cats, but are these differences important? How have researchers tried to discover the core personality traits?

Classification Using Language

The study of core traits began with an exploration of how personality is represented in the store of wisdom we call *language.* Generation after generation, people have described people with words, so early psychologists proposed that core traits could be discerned by finding the main themes in all the adjectives used to describe personality. In one such analysis, a painstaking count of relevant words in a dictionary of English resulted in a list of over 18,000 potential traits (Allport & Odbert, 1936)! Attempts to narrow down the list to a more manageable set depend on the idea that traits might be related in a hierarchical pattern (see **FIGURE 12.3**), with more general or abstract traits at higher levels than more specific or concrete traits. Perhaps the more abstract traits represent the core of personality.

To identify this core, researchers have used the computational procedure called *factor analysis,* described in the Intelligence chapter, which sorts trait terms or self-descriptions into a small number of underlying dimensions, or *factors,* based on how people use the traits to rate themselves. In a typical study using factor analysis, hundreds of people rate themselves on hundreds of adjectives, indicating how accurately

How do psychologists identify the core personality traits?

each one describes their personality. The researcher then conducts calculations to determine similarities in the raters' usage, for example, whether people who describe themselves as *ambitious* also describe themselves as *active* but not *laid-back* or *contented.* Factor analysis also can reveal which adjectives are unrelated. For example, if people who describe themselves as *ambitious* are neither more nor less likely to describe themselves as *creative* or *innovative,* the factor analysis would reveal that *ambitiousness* and *creativity/innovativeness* represent different factors. Each factor is

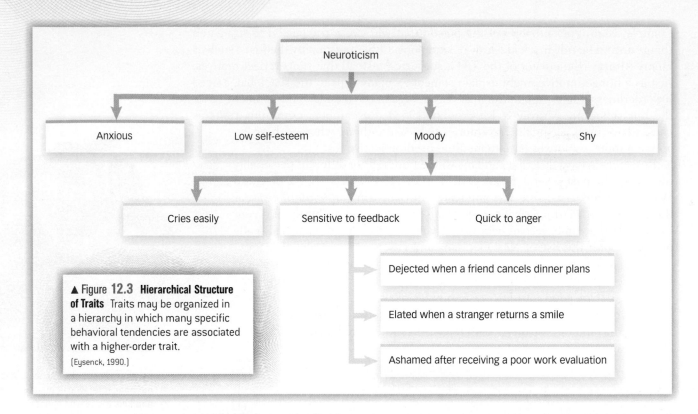

▲ Figure **12.3 Hierarchical Structure of Traits** Traits may be organized in a hierarchy in which many specific behavioral tendencies are associated with a higher-order trait. [Eysenck, 1990.]

typically presented as a continuum, ranging from one extreme trait (such as *ambitious*) to its opposite (in this case, *laid-back*).

Different factor analysis techniques have yielded different views of personality structure. Cattell (1950) proposed a 16-factor theory of personality (way down from 18,000, but still a lot), whereas others proposed theories with far fewer basic dimensions (John, Naumann, & Soto, 2008). Hans Eysenck (1967) simplified things nicely with a model of personality with only two major traits (although he later expanded it to three). Eysenck's two-factor analysis identified one dimension that distinguished people who are sociable and active (extraverts) from those who are more introspective and quiet (introverts). His analysis also identified a second dimension ranging from the tendency to be very neurotic or emotionally unstable to the tendency to be more emotionally stable. He believed that many behavioral tendencies could be understood in terms of their relation to the core traits of Extraversion and Neuroticism. The third factor he proposed was Psychoticism, which refers to the extent to which a person is impulsive or hostile. (Notably, the term "psychotic" nowadays refers to an abnormal mental state marked by detachment from reality. This is discussed further in the Disorders chapter.)

The Big Five Dimensions of Personality

Today most researchers agree that personality is best captured by 5 factors rather than 2, 3, 16, or 18,000 (John & Srivastava, 1999; McCrae & Costa, 1999). The **Big Five,** as they are affectionately called, are *the traits of the five-factor personality model: openness to experience, conscientiousness, extraversion, agreeableness, and neuroticism* (see **TABLE 12.2;** remember them by the initials O.C.E.A.N.) The five-factor model, which overlaps with the pioneering work of Cattell and Eysenck, is now widely preferred for several reasons. First, modern factor analysis techniques confirm that this set of five factors

Table 12.2

The Big Five Factor Model

	High on trait	Low on trait
Openness to experience	imaginative . . . . down-to-earth variety . . . . routine independent . . . . conforming	
Conscientiousness	organized . . . . disorganized careful . . . . careless self-disciplined . . . . weak-willed	
Extraversion	social . . . . retiring fun loving . . . . sober affectionate . . . . reserved	
Agreeableness	softhearted . . . . ruthless trusting . . . . suspicious helpful . . . . uncooperative	
Neuroticism	worried . . . . .calm insecure . . . . secure self-pitying . . . . self-satisfied	

Source: McCrae & Costa, 1990, 1999.

strikes the right balance between accounting for as much variation in personality as possible while avoiding overlapping traits. Second, in a large number of studies using different kinds of data (people's descriptions of their own personalities, other people's descriptions of their personalities, interviewer checklists, and behavioral observation) the same five factors have emerged. Third, and perhaps most important, the basic five-factor structure seems to show up across a wide range of participants, including children, adults in other cultures, and even among those who use other languages, suggesting that the Big Five may be universal (John & Srivastava, 1999).

> **What are the strengths of the five-factor model?**

Big Five
The traits of the five-factor model: openness to experience, conscientiousness, extraversion, agreeableness, and neuroticism.

In fact, the Big Five dimensions are so universal that they show up even when people are asked to evaluate the traits of complete strangers (Passini & Norman, 1966). This finding suggests that these dimensions of personality might reside in the eye of the beholder: categories that people use to evaluate others regardless of how well they know them. However, it's not all perception. The reality of these traits has been clearly established in research showing that self-reports on the Big Five are associated with predictable patterns of behavior and social outcomes. People identified as high in extraversion, for example, tend to spend time with lots of other people and are more likely than introverts to look people in the eye. People high in conscientiousness generally perform well at work and tend to live longer. People low on conscientiousness and low in agreeableness are more likely than average to be juvenile delinquents (John & Srivastava, 1999). It turns out that the Big Five personality traits also predict people's online behavior on social networking sites like Facebook (see the Hot Science box).

HOT SCIENCE

Personality on the Surface

When you judge someone as friend or foe, interesting or boring, worth hiring or firing, how do you do it? It's nice to think that your impressions of personality are based on solid foundations—something deep. You wouldn't judge personality based on something as shallow as someone's looks, would you? You wouldn't form an impression of them from looking at what pops up on Google images, or on their Facebook page, would you? These things may seem to be flimsy bases for understanding personality, but it turns out that some valid personality judgments can be made from exactly such superficial cues. And in certain cases, such judgments are remarkably accurate.

It turns out that you can get some accurate information about a book by judging its cover. Recent studies have shown that extraverts smile more than others and appear more stylish and healthy (Naumann et al., 2009), and people high in openness to experience are more likely to have tattoos and other body modifications (Nathanson, Paulhus, & Williams, 2006). Findings like these suggest that people can manipulate their surface identities to try to make desired impressions on others, and that surface signs of personality might therefore be false or misleading. However, one recent study of people's Facebook pages, which are clearly surface expressions of personality intended for others to see, found that the personalities people project online are more highly related to their real personalities than to the personalities they describe as their ideals (Back et al., 2010). The signs of personality that appear on the surface may be more than skin deep.

Going one step further, it turns out that people's Facebook activity is significantly associated with their self-reported personality traits. For instance, people high on extraversion report having more Facebook friends as well as making more status updates and comments. Posting updates and comments also is higher in Facebook users with elevated self-esteem. People high on agreeableness make more comments on their friends' posts, whereas those high on sensation seeking and openness to experience report playing a lot of games. And as you might have guessed, people high on narcissism post lots of comments, especially about their ideal self, as well as lots of pictures of themselves (Seidman, 2013; Wang et al., 2012).

▲ They say you can't judge a book by its cover, but some new research suggests you can judge a person by their facebook.

AP PHOTO/PABLO MARTINEZ MONSIVAIS

Interestingly, research on the Big Five has shown that people's personalities tend to remain fairly stable through their lifetime: Scores at one time in life correlate strongly with scores at later dates, even decades later (Caspi, Roberts, & Shiner, 2005). William James offered the opinion that "in most of us, by the age of thirty, the character has set like plaster, and will never soften again" (James, 1890, p. 121), but this turns out to be too strong a view. Some variability is typical in childhood, and though there is less in adolescence, some personality change can even occur in adulthood for some people (Srivistava et al., 2003).

Traits as Biological Building Blocks

Can we explain *why* a person has a stable set of personality traits? Many trait theorists have argued that unchangeable brain and biological processes produce the remarkable stability of traits over the life span. Allport viewed traits as characteristics of the brain that influence the way people respond to their environment. And, as you will see, Eysenck searched for a connection between his trait dimensions and specific individual differences in the workings of the brain.

Brain damage certainly can produce personality change, as the classic case of Phineas Gage so vividly demonstrates (see the Neuroscience and Behavior chapter). You may recall that after the blasting accident that blew a steel rod through his frontal lobes, Gage showed a dramatic loss of social appropriateness and conscientiousness (Damasio, 1994). In fact, when someone experiences a profound change in personality, testing often reveals the presence of such brain pathologies as Alzheimer's disease, stroke, or brain tumor (Feinberg, 2001). The administration of antidepressant medication and other pharmaceutical treatments that change brain chemistry also can trigger personality changes, making people, for example, somewhat more extraverted and less neurotic (Bagby et al., 1999; Knutson et al., 1998).

Genes, Traits, and Personality

Some of the most compelling evidence for the importance of biological factors in personality comes from the domain of behavioral genetics. Like researchers studying genetic influences on intelligence (see the Intelligence chapter), personality psychologists have looked at correlations between the traits in monozygotic, or identical, twins, who share the same genes, and dizygotic, or fraternal, twins, who on average share only half of their genes. The evidence has been generally consistent: In one review of studies involving over 24,000 twin pairs, for example, identical twins proved markedly more similar to each other in personality than did fraternal twins (Loehlin, 1992).

Simply put, the more genes you have in common with someone, the more similar your personalities are likely to be. Genes seem to influence most personality traits, and current estimates place the average genetic component of personality in the range of .40 to .60. These heritability coefficients, as you learned in the Intelligence chapter, indicate that roughly half the variability among individuals results from genetic factors (Bouchard & Loehlin, 2001). Of course, genetic factors do not account for everything and the remaining half of the variability in personality remains to be explained by differences in life experiences and other factors (see also the Real World box). Studies of twins suggest that the extent to which the Big Five traits derive from genetic differences ranges from .35 to .49 (see **TABLE 12.3**).

> **What do studies of twins tell us about personality?**

As in the study of intelligence, potential confounding factors must be ruled out to ensure that effects are truly due to genetics and not to environmental experiences. Are identical twins treated more similarly, and do they have a greater *shared environment* than fraternal twins? As children, were they dressed in the same snappy outfits

Table 12.3	
Heritability Estimates for the Big Five Personality Traits	
Trait Dimension	Heritability
Openness	.45
Conscientiousness	.38
Extraversion	.49
Agreeableness	.35
Neuroticism	.41

Source: Loehlin, 1992.

THE REAL WORLD

Are There "Male" and "Female" Personalities?

Do you think there is a typical female personality or a typical male personality? Researchers have found some reliable differences between men and women with respect to their self-reported traits, attitudes, and behaviors. Some of these findings conform to North American stereotypes of masculine and feminine. For example, researchers have found women to be more verbally expressive, more sensitive to nonverbal cues, and more nurturing than are men. Males are more physically aggressive than females, but females engage in more relational aggression (e.g., using relationships to harm someone, such as intentionally excluding them from a social group) than do males, even from a very young age (Crick & Grotpeter, 1995). Other gender differences include males having more assertiveness, slightly higher self-esteem, a more casual approach to sex, and greater sensation seeking than females. On the Big Five, studies across dozens of cultures around the world show that women are higher on neuroticism, extraversion, agreeableness, and conscientiousness; in terms of openness, women report greater openness to feelings and men greater openness to ideas (Costa, Terracciano, & McCrae, 2001; Schmitt et al., 2008). On a variety of other personality characteristics, including helpfulness, men and women on average show no reliable differences. Overall, men and women seem to be far more similar in personality than they are different (Hyde, 2005).

Although the gender differences in personality are quite small, they tend to get a lot of attention. There is debate about the origins of gender differences in personality, which often involves contrasting an evolutionary biological perspective with a social-cognitive perspective known as *social role theory*. The evolutionary perspective holds that men and women have evolved different personality characteristics, in part because their reproductive success depends on different behaviors. For instance, aggressiveness in men may have an adaptive value in intimidating sexual rivals; women who are agreeable and nurturing may have evolved to protect and ensure the survival of their offspring (Campbell, 1999) as well as to secure a reliable mate and provider (Buss, 1989).

GIFT OF JEAN AND FRANCIS MARSHALL/BERKELEY ART MUSEUM/PACIFIC FILM ARCHIVE

◀ Cultures differ in their appreciation of male and female characteristics, but the Hindu deity Ardhanarishwara represents the value of combining both parts of human nature. Male on one side and female on the other, this god is symbolic of the dual nature of the sacred. The only real problem with such side-by-side androgyny comes in finding clothes that fit.

According to social role theory, personality characteristics and behavioral differences between men and women result from cultural standards and expectations that assign them: socially permissible jobs, activities, and family positions (Eagly & Wood, 1999). Because of their physical size and their freedom from childbearing, men historically took roles of greater power—roles that in postindustrial society don't necessarily require physical strength. These differences then snowball, with men generally taking roles that require assertiveness and aggression (e.g., executive, school principal, surgeon) and women pursuing roles that emphasize greater supportiveness and nurturance (e.g., nurse, day care worker, teacher).

Regardless of the source of gender differences in personality, the degree to which people identify personally with masculine and feminine stereotypes may tell us about important personality differences between individuals. Sandra Bem (1974) designed a scale (the Bem Sex Role Inventory) that assesses the degree of identification with stereotypically masculine and feminine traits. Bem suggested that psychologically *androgynous* people (those who adopt the best of both worlds and identify with positive feminine traits such as kindness and positive masculine traits such as assertiveness) might be better adjusted than people who identify strongly with only one sex role.

An interesting wrinkle to this whole story is that although personality traits are fairly stable, they do shift a bit over time. In general, people become more conscientious in their 20s (got to keep that job!), and more agreeable in their 30s (got to keep those friends!). Neuroticism decreases with age, but only among women (Srivastava et al., 2003). So enjoy the personality you have now, because it may be changing soon.

Bem Sex Role Inventory Sample Items

Respondents taking the Bem Sex Role Inventory rate themselves on each of the items without seeing the gender categorization. Then the scale is scored for masculinity (use of stereotypically masculine items), femininity (use of stereotypically feminine items), and androgyny (the tendency to use both the stereotypically masculine and feminine adjectives to describe oneself) (Bem, 1974).

Masculine items	Feminine items
Self-reliant	Yielding
Defends own beliefs	Affectionate
Independent	Flatterable
Assertive	Sympathetic
Forceful	Sensitive to the needs of others

and placed on the same Little League teams, and could this somehow have produced similarities in their personalities? Studies of identical twins reared far apart in adoptive families—an experience that pretty much eliminates the potential effect of shared environmental factors—suggest that shared environments have little impact: Reared-apart identical twins end up just as similar in personality as those who grow up together (McGue & Bouchard, 1998; Tellegen et al., 1988).

Indeed, one provocative, related finding is that such shared environmental factors as parental divorce or parenting style may have little direct impact on personality (Plomin & Caspi, 1999). According to these researchers, simply growing up in the same family does not make people very similar. In fact, when two siblings are similar, this is thought to be primarily due to genetic similarities.

Researchers also have assessed specific behavioral and attitude similarities in twins, and the evidence for heritability in these studies is often striking. One study that examined 3,000 pairs of identical and fraternal twins found evidence for the genetic transmission of conservative views regarding topics such as socialism, church authority, the death penalty, and mixed-race marriage (Martin et al., 1986). It is very unlikely that a specific gene is directly responsible for a complex psychological outcome like beliefs about social or political issues. Rather, a set of genes (or, more likely, many sets of genes interacting) may produce specific characteristics or tendencies to think in a conservative versus liberal manner. One recent study examined the DNA of 13,000 people and measured the extent to which they reported conservative versus liberal attitudes and found associations between conservatism–liberalism and chromosomal regions linked to mental flexibility, or the extent to which a person changes their thinking in response to shifts in their environment, which could be one of the factors influencing our views on social and political issues (Hatemi et al., 2011). Current research by psychological scientists is aimed at better understanding how variations in our genetic code may contribute to the development of personality.

Our genes influence our personality in various ways. For instance, genetic factors can impact how rigidly versus flexibly we think about things like religion and politics. This Tea Party advocate probably shares the same religious and political leanings as other members of his family.

Do Animals Have Personalities?

Another source of evidence for the biological basis of human personality comes from the study of nonhuman animals. Any dog owner, zookeeper, or cattle farmer can tell you that individual animals have characteristic patterns of behavior. One Missouri woman who reportedly enjoyed raising chickens in her suburban home said that "the best part" was "knowing them as individuals" (Tucker, 2003). As far as we know, this pet owner did not give her feathered companions a personality test, though researcher Sam Gosling (1998) used this approach in a study of a group of spotted hyenas. Well, not exactly. He recruited four human observers to use personality scales to rate the different hyenas in the group. When he examined ratings on the scales, he found five dimensions; three closely resembled the Big Five traits of neuroticism (i.e., fearfulness, emotional reactivity), openness to experience (i.e., curiosity), and agreeableness (i.e., absence of aggression).

In similar studies of guppies and octopi, individual differences in traits resembling extraversion and neuroticism were reliably observed (Gosling & John, 1999). In each study, researchers identified particular behaviors that they felt reflected each trait based on their observation of the animals' normal repertoire of activities. Octopi, for example, seldom get invited to parties, so they cannot be assessed for their socializing tendencies ("He was all hands!"), but they do vary in terms of whether they prefer to eat in the safety of their den or are willing to venture out at feeding time, and so a behavior that corresponds to extraversion can reasonably be assessed (Gosling & John, 1999). Because different observers seem to agree on where an animal falls on a given dimension, the findings do not simply reflect a particular observer's imagination or tendency to *anthropomorphize* (i.e., to attribute human characteristics to nonhuman animals). Such findings of cross-species commonality in behavioral styles help support the idea that there are biological mechanisms that underlie personality traits shared by many species.

DOUG CHEESEMAN/GETTY IMAGES

Why study animal behavioral styles?

From an evolutionary perspective, differences in personality reflect alternative adaptations that species—human and nonhuman—have evolved to deal with the challenges of survival and reproduction. For example, if you were to hang around a bar for an evening or two, you would soon see that humans have evolved more than one way to attract and keep a mate. People who are extraverted would probably show off to attract attention, whereas you'd be likely to see people high in agreeableness displaying affection and nurturance (Buss, 1996). Both approaches might work well to attract mates and reproduce successfully—depending on the environment. Through this process of natural selection, those characteristics that have proved successful in our evolutionary struggle for survival have been passed on to future generations.

How would you rate this honey badger? Is it antagonistic or agreeable? Neurotic or emotionally stable? Researchers have found that even animals appear to have personalities. Or should they be called "animalities"?

Traits in the Brain

What neurophysiological mechanisms might influence the development of personality traits? Much of the thinking on this topic has focused on the extraversion–introversion dimension. In his personality model, Eysenck (1967) speculated that extraversion and introversion might arise from individual differences in cortical arousal. Eysenck suggested that extraverts pursue stimulation because their *reticular formation* (the part of the brain that regulates arousal or alertness, as described in the Neuroscience and Behavior chapter) is not easily stimulated. To achieve greater cortical arousal and feel fully alert, Eysenck argued, extraverts seek out social interaction, parties, and other activities to achieve mental stimulation. In contrast, introverts may prefer reading or quiet activities because their cortex is very easily stimulated to a point higher than optimal alertness.

What neurological differences explain why extraverts pursue more stimulation than introverts?

Behavioral and physiological research generally supports Eysenck's view. When introverts and extraverts are presented with a range of intense stimuli, introverts respond more strongly, including salivating more when a drop of lemon juice is placed on their tongues and reacting more negatively to electric shocks or loud noises (Bartol & Costello, 1976; Stelmack, 1990). This reactivity has an impact on the ability to concentrate: Extraverts tend to perform well at tasks that are done in a noisy, arousing context (such as bartending or teaching), whereas introverts are better at tasks that require concentration in tranquil contexts (such as the work of a librarian or nighttime security guard; Geen, 1984; Lieberman & Rosenthal, 2001; Matthews & Gilliland, 1999).

In a refined version of Eysenck's ideas about arousability, Jeffrey Gray (1970) proposed that the dimensions of extraversion–introversion and neuroticism reflect two basic brain systems. The *behavioral activation system (BAS)*, essentially a "go" system, activates approach behavior in response to the anticipation of reward. The extravert has a highly reactive BAS and will actively engage the environment, seeking social reinforcement and be on the go. The *behavioral inhibition system (BIS)*, a "stop" system, inhibits behavior in response to stimuli signaling punishment. The anxious person, in turn, has a highly reactive BIS and will focus on negative outcomes and be on the lookout for stop signs. Because these two systems operate independently, it is possible for someone to be both a go and a stop person (simultaneously activated and inhibited), caught in a constant conflict between these two traits. Studies of brain electrical activity (EEG) and functional brain imaging (fMRI) suggest that individual differences in activation and inhibition arise through the operation of distinct brain systems underlying these

DIPASUPIL/ FILMMAGIC/GETTY IMAGES

Extraverts pursue stimulation in the form of people, loud noise, and bright colors. Introverts tend to prefer softer, quieter settings. Pop quiz: Nikki Minaj: introvert or extrovert?

tendencies (DeYoung & Gray, 2009). Even more recently, studies have suggested that the core personality traits described above may arise from individual differences in the volume of the different brain regions associated with each trait. For instance, self-reported neuroticism is correlated with the volume of brain regions involved in sensitivity to threat; agreeableness with areas associated with processing information about the mental states of other people; conscientiousness with regions involved in self-regulation; and extraversion with areas associated with processing information about reward (DeYoung et al., 2010). Research aimed at understanding how the structure and activity of our brains can contribute to the formation of our personality traits is still in its early stages, but represents a growing area of the field that many believe holds great promise for helping us better understand how we each develop into the unique people that we are.

IN SUMMARY

▶ The trait approach tries to identify personality dimensions that can be used to characterize an individual's behavior. Researchers have attempted to boil down the potentially huge array of things people do, think, and feel into some core personality dimensions.

▶ Many personality psychologists currently focus on the Big Five personality factors: openness to experience, conscientiousness, extraversion, agreeableness, and neuroticism.

▶ To address the question of why traits arise, trait theorists often adopt a biological perspective, seeing personality largely as the result of genetic influences on brain functioning.

The Psychodynamic Approach: Forces That Lie beneath Awareness

Rather than trying to understand personality in terms of broad theories for describing individual differences, Freud looked for personality in the details: the meanings and insights revealed by careful analysis of the tiniest blemishes in a person's thought and behavior. Working with patients who came to him with disorders that did not seem to have any physical basis, he began by interpreting the origins of their everyday mistakes and memory lapses, errors that have come to be called *Freudian slips*.

Freud used the term *psychoanalysis* to refer to both his theory of personality and his method of treating patients. Freud's ideas were the first of many theories building on his basic idea that personality is a mystery to the person who "owns" it because we can't know our own deepest motives. The theories of Freud and his followers (discussed in the Treatment chapter) are referred to as the **psychodynamic approach,** *an approach that regards personality as formed by needs, strivings, and desires largely operating outside of awareness—motives that can produce emotional disorders.* The real engines of personality, in this view, are forces of which we are largely unaware.

Sigmund Freud was the first psychology theorist to be honored with his own bobble-head doll. Let's hope he's not the last.

THE PHOTO WORKS

Psychologists call this construct the **dynamic unconscious,** *an active system encompassing a lifetime of hidden memories, the person's deepest instincts and desires, and the person's inner struggle to control those forces.* The power of the unconscious is believed to come from its early origins—experiences that shaped the mind before a person could even put thoughts and feelings into words—and from its contents, which are embarrassing, unspeakable, and even frightening because they operate without any control by consciousness. Imagine having violent competitive feelings toward your father ("I wish I could beat the old man at something, or just beat him up") or a death wish toward a sibling ("It would be so great if my punk sister fell down the stairs"). Whew! Impulses like that are assumed to remain in the unconscious because such powerful forces would be too much for consciousness to bear. This battle, psychodynamic psychologists believe, goes on beneath the surface in an ongoing struggle among parts of the mind.

The Structure of the Mind: Id, Ego, and Superego

To explain the emotional difficulties that beset his patients, Freud proposed that the mind consists of three independent, interacting, and often conflicting systems: the id, the superego, and the ego.

The most basic system, the **id,** is *the part of the mind containing the drives present at birth; it is the source of our bodily needs, wants, desires, and impulses, particularly our sexual and aggressive drives.* The id operates according to the *pleasure principle,* the psychic force that motivates the tendency to seek immediate gratification of any impulse. If governed by the id alone, you would never be able to tolerate the buildup of hunger while waiting to be served at a restaurant but would simply grab food from tables nearby.

Opposite the id is the **superego,** *the mental system that reflects the internalization of cultural rules, mainly learned as parents exercise their authority.* The superego consists of a set of guidelines, internal standards, and other codes of conduct that regulate and control our behaviors, thoughts, and fantasies. It acts as a kind of conscience, punishing us when it finds we are doing or thinking something wrong (by producing guilt or other painful feelings) and rewarding us (with feelings of pride or self-congratulation) for living up to ideal standards.

The final system of the mind, according to psychoanalytic theory, is the **ego,** *the component of personality, developed through contact with the external world, that enables us to deal with life's practical demands.* The ego operates according to the *reality principle,* the regulating mechanism that enables the individual to delay gratifying immediate needs and function effectively in the real world. It is the mediator between the id and the superego. The ego helps you resist the impulse to snatch others' food and also finds the restaurant and pays the check.

Freud believed that the relative strength of the interactions among the three systems of mind (i.e., which system is usually dominant) determines an individual's basic personality structure. Together the id force of personal needs, the superego force of pressures to quell those needs, and the ego force of reality's demands create constant internal conflict. He believed that the dynamics among the id, superego, and ego are largely governed by

> **According to Freud, how is personality shaped by the interaction of the id, superego, and ego?**

anxiety, an unpleasant feeling that arises when unwanted thoughts or feelings occur, such as when the id seeks a gratification that the ego thinks will lead to real-world dangers or that the superego sees as leading to punishment. When the ego receives an "alert signal" in the form of anxiety, it launches into a defensive position in an attempt to ward off the anxiety. According to Freud, it does so using one of several

psychodynamic approach
An approach that regards personality as formed by needs, strivings, and desires largely operating outside of awareness—motives that also can produce emotional disorders.

dynamic unconscious
An active system encompassing a lifetime of hidden memories, the person's deepest instincts and desires, and the person's inner struggle to control those forces.

id
The part of the mind containing the drives present at birth; it is the source of our bodily needs, wants, desires, and impulses, particularly our sexual and aggressive drives.

superego
The mental system that reflects the internalization of cultural rules, mainly learned as parents exercise their authority.

ego
The component of personality, developed through contact with the external world, that enables us to deal with life's practical demands.

"I'm sorry, I'm not speaking to anyone tonight. My defense mechanisms seem to be out of order."

different **defense mechanisms,** *unconscious coping mechanisms that reduce anxiety generated by threats from unacceptable impulses* (see **TABLE 12.4**). Psychodynamically oriented psychologists believe that defense mechanisms help us overcome anxiety and engage effectively with the outside world and that our characteristic style of defense becomes our signature in dealing with the world—and an essential aspect of our personality.

▶ **Table 12.4**

Defense Mechanisms

Repression is the first defense the ego tries, but if it is inadequate, then other defense mechanisms may come into play.

Defense Mechanism	Description	Example
Repression	Removing painful experiences and unacceptable impulses from the conscious mind: "motivated forgetting."	Not lashing out physically in anger; putting a bad experience out of your mind.
Rationalization	Supplying a reasonable sounding explanation for unacceptable feelings and behavior to conceal (mostly from oneself) one's underlying motives or feelings.	Dropping calculus "allegedly" because of poor ventilation in the classroom.
Reaction formation	Unconsciously replacing threatening inner wishes and fantasies with an exaggerated version of their opposite.	Being rude to someone you're attracted to.
Projection	Attributing one's own threatening feelings, motives, or impulses to another person or group.	Judging others as being dishonest because you believe that you are dishonest.
Regression	Reverting to an immature behavior or earlier stage of development, a time when things felt more secure, to deal with internal conflict and perceived threat.	Using baby talk, even though able to use appropriate speech, in response to distress.
Displacement	Shifting unacceptable wishes or drives to a neutral or less threatening alternative.	Slamming a door; yelling at someone other than the person you're mad at.
Identification	Dealing with feelings of threat and anxiety by unconsciously taking on the characteristics of another person who seems more powerful or better able to cope.	A bullied child becoming a bully.
Sublimation	Channeling unacceptable sexual or aggressive drives into socially acceptable and culturally enhancing activities.	Diverting anger to the football or rugby field, or other contact sport.

Psychosexual Stages and the Development of Personality

Freud also proposed that a person's basic personality is formed before 6 years of age during a series of sensitive periods, or life stages, when experiences influence all that will follow. Freud called these periods **psychosexual stages,** *distinct early life stages through which personality is formed as children experience sexual pleasures from specific body areas and caregivers redirect or interfere with those pleasures.* He argued that as a result of adult interference with pleasure-seeking energies, the child experiences conflict. At each stage, a different bodily region, or *erotogenic* zone, dominates the child's subjective experience (e.g., during the oral stage, pleasure centers on the mouth). Each region represents a battleground between the child's id impulses and the adult external world.

Problems and conflicts encountered at any psychosexual stage, Freud believed, will influence personality in adulthood. Conflict resulting from a person's being deprived or, paradoxically, overindulged at a given stage could result in **fixation,** *a phenomenon in which a person's pleasure-seeking drives become psychologically stuck, or arrested, at a particular psychosexual stage.* Freud described particular personality traits as being derived from fixations at the different psychosexual stages. Here's how he explained each stage and the effects of fixation at each stage.

> In the 1st year and a half of life, the infant is in the **oral stage,** *the first psychosexual stage, in which experience centers on the pleasures and frustrations associated with the mouth, sucking, and being fed.* Infants who are deprived of pleasurable feeding or indulgently overfed are believed to have a personality style in which they are focused on issues related to fullness and emptiness and what they can "take in" from others.

> Between 2 and 3 years of age, the child moves on to the **anal stage,** *the second psychosexual stage, in which experience is dominated by the pleasures and frustrations associated with the anus, retention and expulsion of feces and urine, and toilet training.* Individuals who have had difficulty negotiating this conflict are believed to develop a rigid personality and remain preoccupied with issues of control.

> Between the ages of 3 and 5 years, the child is in the **phallic stage,** *the third psychosexual stage, in which experience is dominated by the pleasure, conflict, and frustration associated with the phallic–genital region as well as coping with powerful incestuous feelings of love, hate, jealousy, and conflict.* According to Freud, children in the phallic stage experience the **Oedipus conflict,** *a developmental experience in which a child's conflicting feelings toward the opposite-sex parent are (usually) resolved by identifying with the same-sex parent.*

> A more relaxed period in which children are no longer struggling with the power of their sexual and aggressive drives occurs between the ages of 5 and 13, as children experience the **latency stage,** *the fourth psychosexual stage, in which the primary focus is on the further development of intellectual, creative, interpersonal, and athletic skills.* Because Freud believed that the most significant aspects of personality development

MARTHA HOLMES/TIME LIFE PICTURES/GETTY IMAGES

One of the id's desires is to make a fine mess (a desire that is often frustrated early in life, perhaps during the anal stage). Famous painter Jackson Pollock found a way to make extraordinarily fine messes—behavior that at some level all of us envy.

defense mechanisms
Unconscious coping mechanisms that reduce anxiety generated by threats from unacceptable impulses.

psychosexual stages
Distinct early life stages through which personality is formed as children experience sexual pleasures from specific body areas and caregivers redirect or interfere with those pleasures.

fixation
A phenomenon in which a person's pleasure-seeking drives become psychologically stuck, or arrested, at a particular psychosexual stage.

oral stage
The first psychosexual stage, in which experience centers on the pleasures and frustrations associated with the mouth, sucking, and being fed.

anal stage
The second psychosexual stage, in which experience is dominated by the pleasures and frustrations associated with the anus, retention and expulsion of feces and urine, and toilet training.

phallic stage
The third psychosexual stage, in which experience is dominated by the pleasure, conflict, and frustration associated with the phallic-genital region as well as coping with powerful incestuous feelings of love, hate, jealousy, and conflict.

Oedipus conflict
A developmental experience in which a child's conflicting feelings toward the opposite-sex parent are (usually) resolved by identifying with the same-sex parent.

latency stage
The fourth psychosexual stage, in which the primary focus is on the further development of intellectual, creative, interpersonal, and athletic skills.

genital stage
The fifth and final psychosexual stage, the time for the coming together of the mature adult personality with a capacity to love, work, and relate to others in a mutually satisfying and reciprocal manner.

self-actualizing tendency
The human motive toward realizing our inner potential.

existential approach
A school of thought that regards personality as governed by an individual's ongoing choices and decisions in the context of the realities of life and death.

occur before the age of 6 years, psychodynamic psychologists do not speak of fixation at the latency period. Simply making it to the latency period relatively undisturbed by conflicts of the earlier stages is a sign of healthy personality development.

> At puberty and thereafter, the fifth and final stage of personality development occurs. The **genital stage** is *the time for the coming together of the mature adult personality with a capacity to love, work, and relate to others in a mutually satisfying and reciprocal manner.* Freud believed that people who are fixated in a prior stage fail to develop healthy adult sexuality and a well-adjusted adult personality.

What should we make of all this? On the one hand, the psychoanalytic theory of psychosexual stages offers an intriguing picture of early family relationships and the extent to which they allow the child to satisfy basic needs and wishes. On the other hand, critics argue that psychodynamic explanations lack any real evidence and tend to focus on provocative after-the-fact interpretation rather than testable prediction. The psychosexual stage theory offers a compelling set of story plots for interpreting lives once they have unfolded, but has not generated clear-cut predictions supported by research.

? Why do critics say Freud's psychosexual stages are more interpretation than explanation?

IN SUMMARY

▶ Freud believed that the personality results from forces that are largely unconscious, shaped by the interplay among id, superego, and ego.

▶ Defense mechanisms are methods the mind may use to reduce anxiety generated from unacceptable impulses.

▶ Freud also believed that the developing person passes through a series of psychosexual stages and that failing to progress beyond one of the stages results in fixation, which is associated with corresponding personality traits.

Decades of research have shown that growing up in a distressed neighborhood is associated with worse educational, occupational, and health outcomes. Humanistic psychologists would suggest that people in such settings must struggle to meet their basic daily needs and so do not have opportunities for self-actualization.

IMAGE SOURCE/GETTY IMAGES

The Humanistic–Existential Approach: Personality as Choice

In the 1950s and 1960s, psychologists began to try to understand personality from a viewpoint quite different from trait theory's biological determinism and Freud's focus on unconscious drives from unresolved childhood experiences. These new humanistic and existential theorists turned attention to how humans make *healthy choices* that create their personalities. *Humanistic psychologists* emphasized a positive, optimistic view of human nature that highlights people's inherent goodness and their potential for personal growth. *Existentialist psychologists* focused on the individual as a responsible agent who is free to create and live his or her life while negotiating the issue of meaning and the reality of death. The *humanistic–existential approach* integrates these insights with a focus on how a personality can become optimal.

Human Needs and Self-Actualization

Humanists see the **self-actualizing tendency,** *the human motive toward realizing our inner potential,* as a major factor in personality. The pursuit of knowledge, the expression of one's creativity, the quest for spiritual enlightenment, and the desire to give to society all are examples of self-actualization. As you saw in the Emotion and Motivation chapter, the noted humanistic theorist Abraham Maslow (1943) proposed a *hierarchy of needs*, a model of essential human needs arranged according to their priority, in which basic physiological and safety needs must be satisfied before a person can afford to focus on higher-level psychological needs. Only when these basic needs are satisfied can one pursue higher needs, culminating in *self-actualization*: the need to be good, to be fully alive, and to find meaning in life.

What is it to be self-actualized?

Humanist psychologists explain individual personality differences as arising from the various ways that the environment facilitates—or blocks—attempts to satisfy psychological needs. For example, someone with the inherent potential to be a great scientist, artist, parent, or teacher might never realize these talents if his or her energies and resources are instead directed toward meeting basic needs of security, belongingness, and the like. Research indicates that when people shape their lives around goals that do not match their true nature and capabilities, they are less likely to be happy than those whose lives and goals do match (Ryan & Deci, 2000).

It feels great to be doing exactly what you are capable of doing. Mihaly Csikszentmihalyi (1990) found that engagement in tasks that exactly match one's abilities creates a mental state of energized focus that he called *flow* (see **FIGURE 12.4**). Tasks that are below our abilities cause boredom, those that are too challenging cause anxiety, and those that are "just right" lead to the experience of flow. If you know how to play the piano, for example, and are playing a Chopin prelude that you know well enough that it just matches your abilities, you are likely to experience this optimal state. People report being happier at these times than at any other times. Humanists believe that such peak experiences, or states of flow, reflect the realization of one's human potential and represent the height of personality development.

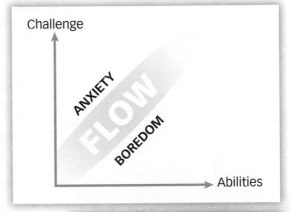

▲ Figure **12.4 Flow Experience** It feels good to do things that challenge your abilities but that don't challenge them too much. Csikszentmihalyi (1990) described this feeling between boredom and anxiety as the "flow experience."

Personality as Existence

Existentialists agree with humanists about many of the features of personality but focus on challenges to the human condition that are more profound than the lack of a nurturing environment. Rollo May (1983) and Victor Frankl (2000), for example, argued that specific aspects of the human condition, such as awareness of our own existence and the ability to make choices about how to behave, have a double-edged quality: They bring an extraordinary richness and dignity to human life, but they also force us to confront realities that are difficult to face, such as the prospect of our own death. The **existential approach** is *a school of thought that regards personality as governed by an individual's ongoing choices and decisions in the context of the realities of life and death*.

According to the existential perspective, the difficulties we face in finding meaning in life and in accepting the responsibility of making free choices provoke a type of anxiety existentialists call *angst* (the anxiety of fully being). The human ability to consider limitless numbers of goals and actions is exhilarating, but it can also open the door to profound questions such as: Why am I here? What is the meaning of my life?

What is angst, and how is it created?

Thinking about the meaning of existence also can evoke an awareness of the inevitability of death. What, then, should we do with each moment? What is the purpose of living if life as we know it will end one day, perhaps even today? Alternatively, does life have more meaning given that it is so temporary? Existential theorists do not suggest that people consider these profound existential issues on a day-to-day and moment-to-moment basis. Rather than ruminate about death and meaning, people typically pursue superficial answers that help them deal with the angst and dread they experience, and the defenses they construct form the basis of their personalities (Binswanger, 1958; May, 1983). Some people organize their lives around obtaining material possessions; others may immerse themselves in drugs or addictive behaviors such as compulsive web browsing, video gaming, or television watching in order to numb the mind to existential realities.

For existentialists, a healthier solution is to face the issues head-on and learn to accept and tolerate the pain of existence. Indeed, being fully human means confronting existential realities rather than denying them or embracing comforting illusions. This requires the courage to accept the inherent anxiety and the dread of nonbeing that is part of being alive. Such courage may be bolstered by developing supportive relationships with others who can supply unconditional positive regard. There's something about being loved that helps take away the angst.

IN SUMMARY

▶ The humanistic–existential approach to personality grew out of philosophical traditions that are at odds with most of the assumptions of the trait and psychoanalytic approaches.

▶ Humanists see personality as directed by an inherent striving toward self-actualization and development of our unique human potentials.

▶ Existentialists focus on angst and the defensive response people often have to questions about the meaning of life and the inevitability of death.

The Social-Cognitive Approach: Personalities in Situations

What is it like to be a person? The **social-cognitive approach** *views personality in terms of how the person thinks about the situations encountered in daily life and behaves in response to them.* Bringing together insights from social psychology, cognitive psychology, and learning theory, this approach emphasizes how the person experiences and interprets situations (Bandura, 1986; Mischel & Shoda, 1999; Ross & Nisbett, 1991; Wegner & Gilbert, 2000).

Researchers in social cognition believe that both the current situation and learning history are key determinants of behavior, and focus on how people *perceive* their environments. People think about their goals, the consequences of their behavior, and how they might achieve certain things in different situations (Lewin, 1951). The social-cognitive approach looks at how personality and situation interact to cause behavior, how personality contributes to the way people construct situations in their own minds, and how people's goals and expectancies influence their responses to situations.

> **Do researchers in social cognition think that personality arises from past experiences or from the current environment?**

"He's not very exciting in social situations, but on the net he's a wildman!"

Consistency of Personality across Situations

Although social-cognitive psychologists attribute behavior both to the individual's personality and to his or her situation, situation can often trump personality. For example, a person would have to be pretty strange to act exactly the same way at a memorial service and at a keg party. In their belief that the strong push and pull of situations can influence almost everyone, social-cognitive psychologists are somewhat at odds with the basic assumptions of classic personality psychology; that is, that personality characteristics (such as traits, needs, unconscious drives) cause people to behave in the same way across situations and over time. At the core of the social-cognitive approach is a natural puzzle, the **person–situation controversy,** which focuses on *the question of whether behavior is caused more by personality or by situational factors.*

This controversy began in earnest when Walter Mischel (1968) argued that measured personality traits often do a poor job of predicting individuals' behavior. Mischel reviewed decades of research that compared scores on standard personality tests with actual behavior, looking at evidence from studies asking questions such as "Does a person with a high score on a test of introversion actually spend more time alone than someone with a low score?" Mischel's disturbing conclusion: The average correlation between trait and behavior is only about .30. This is certainly better than zero (i.e., no relation at all) but not very good when you remember that a perfect prediction is represented by a correlation of 1.0.

Mischel also noted that knowing how a person will behave in one situation is not particularly helpful in predicting the person's behavior in another situation. For example, in classic studies, Hugh Hartshorne and M.A. May (1928) assessed children's honesty by examining their willingness to cheat on a test and found that such dishonesty was not consistent from one situation to another. The assessment of a child's trait of honesty in a cheating situation was of almost no use in predicting whether the child would act honestly in a different situation, such as when given the opportunity to steal money. Mischel proposed that measured traits do not predict behaviors very well because behaviors are determined more by situational factors than personality theorists were willing to acknowledge.

Is there no personality, then? Do we all just do what situations require? The person–situation controversy has inspired many studies in the years since Mischel's critique, and it turns out that information about both personality and situation are necessary to predict behavior accurately (Fleeson, 2004; Mischel, 2004). Some situations are particularly powerful, leading most everyone to behave similarly regardless of personality (Cooper & Withey, 2009). At a funeral, almost everyone looks somber, and during an earthquake, almost everyone shakes. But in more moderate situations, personality can come forward to influence behavior (Funder, 2001). Among the children in Hartshorne and May's (1928) studies, cheating versus not cheating on a test was actually a fairly good predictor of cheating on a test later—as long as the situation was similar. Personality consistency, then, appears to be a matter of when and where a certain kind of behavior tends to be shown (see the Culture & Community box). Social-cognitive theorists believe these patterns of personality consistency arise from the way different people interpret situations and from the ways different people pursue goals within situations.

> **?** Does personality or the current situation predict a person's behavior?

Personal Constructs

How can we understand differences in the way situations are interpreted? Recall our notion of personality often existing in the eye of the beholder. Situations may exist in the eye of the beholder as well. One person's gold mine may be another person's useless

Is a student who cheats on a test more likely than others to steal candy or lie to his grandmother? Social-cognitive research indicates that behavior in one situation does not necessarily predict behavior in a different situation.

social-cognitive approach
An approach that views personality in terms of how the person thinks about the situations encountered in daily life and behaves in response to them.

person–situation controversy
The question of whether behavior is caused more by personality or by situational factors.

personal constructs
Dimensions people use in making sense of their experiences.

outcome expectancies
A person's assumptions about the likely consequences of a future behavior.

locus of control
A person's tendency to perceive the control of rewards as internal to the self or external in the environment.

CULTURE & COMMUNITY

Does your personality change according to which language you're speaking? The personalities of people from different cultures often can diverge. For instance, one study revealed that personality tests taken by Americans and Mexicans differ reliably: Americans report being more extraverted, more agreeable, and more conscientious than Mexicans (Ramirez-Esparza et al., 2004). Why is this? The authors suggested that this may be due to differences in how individualistic versus collectivistic people are in each culture. Individualistic cultures (like America) emphasize personal achievement, whereas collectivistic cultures (like Mexico) focus on the importance of family and community outcomes. The authors noted that some facets of the Big Five map onto this distinction. For instance, achievement is measured as part of conscientiousness, assertiveness as part of extraversion, and superficial friendliness as part of agreeableness.

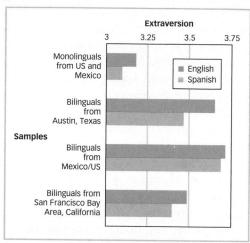

Interestingly, however, when the researchers tested Spanish–English bilinguals in Texas, California, and Mexico in both languages, scores of the bilingual participants were more extraverted, agreeable, and conscientious when they took the test in English than when they took it in Spanish! The authors proposed that this difference is the result of cultural frame switching, which refers to the tendency of bi- or multicultural people to adjust their style of thinking, feeling, and behaving to more closely match the group with which they are currently interacting. Importantly, the changes are pretty subtle (more toning it up or down rather than total personality transplant), but highlight the importance of considering culture and context when thinking about personality.

Are two of these people taller and one shorter? Are two bareheaded while one wears a hood? Or are two the daughters and one the mom? George Kelly held that the personal constructs we use to distinguish among people in our lives are basic elements of our own personalities.

hole in the ground. George Kelly (1955) long ago realized that these differences in perspective could be used to understand the *perceiver's* personality. He suggested that people view the social world from differing perspectives and that these different views arise through the application of **personal constructs,** *dimensions people use in making sense of their experiences.* Consider, for example, different individuals' personal constructs of a clown: One person may see him as a source of fun, another as a tragic figure, and yet another as so frightening that McDonald's must be avoided at all costs.

Why doesn't everyone love clowns?

Kelly assessed personal constructs about social relationships by asking people to (1) list the people in their life, (2) consider three of the people and state a way in which two of them are similar to each other and different from the third, and (3) repeat this for other triads of people to produce a list of the dimensions used to classify friends and family. One respondent might focus on the degree to which people (self included) are lazy or hardworking, for example; someone else might attend to the degree to which people are sociable or unfriendly.

Kelly proposed that different personal constructs (*construals*) are the key to personality differences; that is, different construals lead people to engage in different behaviors. Taking a long break from work for a leisurely lunch might seem lazy to you. To your friend, the break might seem an ideal opportunity for catching up with friends and wonder why you always choose to eat at your desk. Social-cognitive theory explains different responses to situations with the idea that people experience and interpret the world in different ways.

Personal Goals and Expectancies

Social-cognitive theories also recognize that a person's unique perspective on situations is reflected in his or her personal goals, which are often conscious. In fact, people can usually tell you their goals, whether they are to find a date for this weekend, get a good grade in psych, establish a fulfilling career, or just get this darn bag of chips open. These goals often reflect the tasks that are appropriate to the person's situation and, in a larger sense, fit the person's role and stage of life (Cantor, 1990; Klinger, 1977; Little, 1983; Vallacher & Wegner, 1985). For instance, common goals for adolescents include being popular, achieving greater independence from parents and family, and getting into a good college. Common goals for adults include developing a meaningful career, finding a mate, securing financial stability, and starting a family.

People translate goals into behavior in part through **outcome expectancies,** *a person's assumptions about the likely consequences of a future behavior.* Just as a laboratory rat learns that pressing a bar releases a food pellet, we learn that "if I am friendly toward people, they will be friendly in return," and "if I ask people to pull my finger, they will withdraw from me." So we learn to perform behaviors that we expect will have the outcome of moving us closer to our goals. Outcome expectancies are learned through direct experience, both bitter and sweet, and through merely observing other people's actions and their consequences.

Outcome expectancies combine with a person's goals to produce the person's characteristic style of behavior. An individual with the goal of making friends and the expectancy that being kind will produce warmth in return is likely to behave very differently from an individual whose goal is to achieve fame at any cost and who believes that shameless self-promotion is the route to fame. We do not all want the same things from life, clearly, and our personalities largely reflect the goals we pursue and the expectancies we have about the best ways to pursue them.

People differ in their generalized expectancy for achieving goals. Some people seem to feel that they are fully in control of what happens to them in life, whereas others feel that the world doles out rewards and punishments to them irrespective of their actions. Julian Rotter (1966) developed a questionnaire (see **TABLE 12.5**) to measure *a person's tendency to perceive the control of rewards as internal to the self or external in the environment,* a disposition he called **locus of control.** People whose answers suggest that they believe they control their own destiny are said to have an *internal* locus of control, whereas those who believe that outcomes are random, determined by luck, or controlled by other people are described as having an *external* locus of control. These beliefs translate into individual differences in emotion and behavior. For example, people with an internal locus of control tend to be less anxious, achieve more, and cope better with stress than do people with an external orientation (Lefcourt, 1982). To get a sense of your standing on this trait dimension, choose one of the options for each of the sample items from the locus-of-control scale in Table 12.5.

> **What is the advantage of an internal locus of control?**

Some days you feel like a puppet on a string. If you have an external locus of control, you may feel that way most days.

ASIA IMAGES/SUPERSTOCK

Table 12.5
Rotter's Locus-of-Control Scale
For each pair of items, choose the option that most closely reflects your personal belief. Then check the answer key below to see if you have more of an internal or external locus of control.
1. a. Many of the unhappy things in people's lives are partly due to bad luck. b. People's misfortunes result from the mistakes they make.
2. a. I have often found that what is going to happen will happen. b. Trusting to fate has never turned out as well for me as making a decision to take a definite course of action.
3. a. Becoming a success is a matter of hard work; luck has little or nothing to do with it. b. Getting a good job depends mainly on being in the right place at the right time.
4. a. When I make plans, I am almost certain that I can make them work. b. It is not always wise to plan too far ahead because many things turn out to be a matter of good or bad fortune anyhow.

Source: Rotter, 1966.

Answers: A more internal locus of control would be reflected in choosing options 1b, 2b, 3a, and 4a.

> ## IN SUMMARY
>
> ▶ The social-cognitive approach focuses on personality as arising from individuals' behavior in situations. Situations mean different things to different people, as suggested by Kelly's personal construct theory.
>
> ▶ According to social-cognitive personality theorists, the same person may behave differently in different situations but should behave consistently in similar situations.
>
> ▶ People translate their goals into behavior through outcome expectancies, their assumptions about the likely consequences of future behaviors.

The Self: Personality in the Mirror

Imagine that you wake up tomorrow morning, drag yourself into the bathroom, look into the mirror, and don't recognize the face looking back at you. This was the plight of a patient studied by neurologist Todd Feinberg (2001). The woman, married for 30 years and the mother of two grown children, one day began to respond to her mirror image as if it were a different person. She talked to and challenged the person in the mirror. When there was no response, she tried to attack it as if it were an intruder. Her husband, shaken by this bizarre behavior, brought her to the neurologist, who was gradually able to convince her that the image in the mirror was in fact herself.

Most of us are pretty familiar with the face that looks back at us from every mirror. We develop the ability to recognize ourselves in mirrors by 18 months of age (as

What do these self-portraits of Frida Kahlo, Vincent van Gogh, Pablo Picasso, Salvador Dalí, Wanda Wulz, and Jean-Michel Basquiat reveal about each artist's self-concept?

KAHLO • © ALBRIGHT-KNOX ART GALLERY/CORBIS

VAN GOGH • ©DEAGOSTINI/SUPERSTOCK

PICASSO • PAINTING/ALAMY

DALÍ • BY PERMISSION OF THE SALVADOR DALÍ ESTATE. © PHILIPPE HALSMAN/MAGNUM

WULZ • ALINARI/ART RESOURCE, NY

BASQUIAT • BANQUE D'IMAGES, ADAGP/ART RESOURCE, NY

discussed in the Consciousness chapter), and we share this skill with chimpanzees and other apes that have been raised in the presence of mirrors. Self-recognition in mirrors signals our amazing capacity for reflexive thinking, for directing attention to our own thoughts, feelings, and actions—an ability that enables us to construct ideas about our own personality. Unlike a cow, which will never know that it has a poor sense of humor, or a cat, which will never know that it is awfully friendly, humans have rich and detailed self-knowledge.

Admittedly, none of us know all there is to know about our own personality. In fact, sometimes others may know us better than we know ourselves (Vazire & Mehl, 2008). But we do have enough self-knowledge to respond reliably to personality inventories and report on our traits and behaviors. These observations draw on what we think about ourselves (our *self-concept*) and on how we feel about ourselves (our *self-esteem*). Self-concept and self-esteem are critically important facets of personality, not just because they reveal how people see their own personalities, but because they also guide how people think others will see them.

self-concept
A person's explicit knowledge of his or her own behaviors, traits, and other personal characteristics.

Self-Concept

In his renowned psychology textbook, William James (1890) included a theory of self in which he pointed to the self's two facets, the *I* and the *Me*. The *I* is the self that thinks, experiences, and acts in the world; it is the self as a *knower*. The *Me* is the self that is an object in the world; it is the self that is *known*. The *I* is much like consciousness, then, a perspective on all of experience (see the Consciousness chapter), but the *Me* is less mysterious: It is just a concept of a person.

> **Explain the difference between *I* and *Me*.**

If asked to describe your *Me*, you might mention your physical characteristics (male or female, tall or short, dark-skinned or light), your activities (listening to hip-hop, alternative rock, jazz, or classical music), your personality traits (extraverted or introverted, agreeable or independent), or your social roles (student, son or daughter, member of a hiking club, krumper). These features make up the **self-concept,** *a person's explicit knowledge of his or her own behaviors, traits, and other personal characteristics.* A person's self-concept is an organized body of knowledge that develops from social experiences and has a profound effect on a person's behavior throughout life.

Self-Concept Organization

Almost everyone has a place for memorabilia, a drawer or box somewhere that holds all those sentimental keepsakes—photos, yearbooks, cards and letters, maybe that scrap of the old security blanket—all memories of "life as *Me*." Perhaps you've wanted to organize these things sometime but have never gotten around to it. Fortunately, the knowledge of ourselves that we store in our *autobiographical memory* seems to be organized naturally in two ways: as narratives about episodes in our lives and in terms of traits (as would be suggested by the distinction between episodic and semantic memory discussed in the Memory chapter).

The aspect of the self-concept that is a *self-narrative* (a story that we tell about ourselves) can be brief or very lengthy. Your life story could start with your birth and upbringing, describe a series of defining moments, and end where you are today. You could select specific events and experiences, goals and life tasks, and memories of places and people that have influenced you. Self-narrative organizes the highlights (and low blows) of your life into a story in which you are the leading character and binds them together into your self-concept (McAdams, 1993; McLean,

> **What is your life story as you see it— your self-narrative?**

A key aspect of our personality involves our self-narrative, or the story we tell about ourselves. In the award winning movie *Forrest Gump*, the title character shared his self-narrative with others. What would you include in the self-narrative of your life?

Think about your own self-narrative (what you have done) and self-concept (how you view yourself). Are there areas that don't match up? Are there things that you've done, good or bad, that are not part of your self-concept? How might you explain that?

2008). Psychodynamic and humanistic–existential psychologists suggest that people's self-narratives reflect their fantasies and thoughts about core motives and approaches to existence.

Self-concept is also organized in a more abstract way, in terms of personality traits. Just as you can judge an object on its attributes (Is this apple green?), you are able to judge yourself on any number of traits—whether you are considerate or smart or lazy or active or, for that matter, green—and do so quite reliably, making the same rating on multiple occasions. Hazel Markus (1977) observed that each person finds certain unique personality traits particularly important for conceptualizing the self. One person might define herself as independent, for example, whereas another might not care much about her level of independence but instead emphasize her sense of style. Markus called the traits people use to define themselves *self-schemas,* emphasizing that they draw information about the self into a coherent scheme. Markus asked people to indicate whether they had a trait by pressing response buttons labeled *me* or *not me.* She found that participants' judgment reaction times were faster for self-schemas than for other traits. It's as though some facets of the self-concept have almost a knee-jerk quality—letting us tell quickly who we are and who we are not.

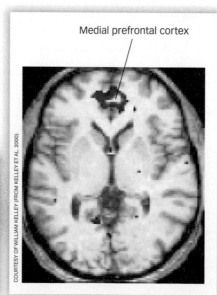

Medial prefrontal cortex

▶ Figure 12.5 **Self-Concept in the Brain** fMRI scans reveal that the medial prefrontal cortex (MPFC) is activated (shown here in red and yellow) when people make judgments of whether they possess certain personality traits compared to judging whether the traits apply to someone else. (From Kelley et al., 2002.)

Research also shows that the traits people use to judge the self tend to stick in memory. When people make judgments of themselves on traits, they later recall the traits better than when they judge other people on the same traits (Rogers, Kuiper, & Kirker, 1977). For example, answering a question such as "Are you generous?"—no matter what your answer—is likely to enhance your memory for the trait generous. In studies of this effect of *self-relevance* on memory, researchers using brain imaging technologies have found that the simple activity of making judgments about the trait self-concept is accompanied by activation of the medial prefrontal cortex (MPFC), a brain area involved in understanding people (Mitchell, Heatherton, & Macrae, 2002). This activation is stronger, however, when people are judging their own standing on traits (see **FIGURE 12.5**) than when they are judging the standing of someone else (Kelley et al., 2002). Such stronger activation, then, is linked with better memory for the traits being judged (Macrae et al., 2004). Studies have not been entirely conclusive about which brain areas are most involved in the processing of self-information (Morin, 2002), but they do show that memory for traits is strengthened when the MPFC is activated during self-judgments.

How do our behavior self-narratives and trait self-concepts compare? These two methods of self-conceptualization don't always match up. You may think of yourself as an honest person, for example, but also recall that time you nabbed a handful of change from your parents' dresser and conveniently forgot to replace it. The traits we use to describe ourselves are generalizations, and not every episode in our life stories may fit. In fact, research suggests that the stores of knowledge about our behaviors and traits are not very well integrated (Kihlstrom, Beer, & Klein, 2002). In people who develop amnesia, for example, memory for behaviors can be lost even though the trait self-concept remains stable (Klein, 2004). People can have a pretty strong sense of who they are even though they may not remember a single example of when they acted that way.

> **Why don't traits always reflect knowledge of behavior?**

Causes and Effects of Self-Concept

How do self-concepts arise, and how do they affect us? In some sense, you learn something about yourself every day. Although we can gain self-knowledge in private moments of insight, we more often arrive at our self-concepts through interacting with others. Young children in particular receive plenty of feedback from their parents, teachers, siblings, and friends about their characteristics, and this helps them to form an idea of who they are. Even adults would find it difficult to hold a view of the self as "kind" or "smart" if no one else ever shared this impression. The sense of self, then, is largely developed and maintained in relationships with others.

Over the course of a lifetime, however, we become less and less impressed with what others have to say about us. Social theorist George Herbert Mead (1934) observed that all the things people have said about us accumulate after a while into what we see as a kind of consensus held by the "generalized other." We typically adopt this general view of ourselves and hold on to it stubbornly. As a result, the person who says you're a jerk may upset you momentarily, but you bounce back, secure in the knowledge that you actually are not a jerk. And just as we might argue vehemently with someone who tried to tell us a refrigerator is a pair of underpants, we are likely to defend our self-concept against anyone whose view of us departs from our own.

"I don't want to be defined by who I am."

Because it is so stable, a major effect of the self-concept is to promote consistency in behavior across situations (Lecky, 1945). As existential theorists emphasize, people derive a comforting sense of familiarity and stability from knowing who they are. We tend to engage in what William Swann (1983, 2012) called **self-verification,** *the tendency to seek evidence to confirm the self-concept,* and we find it disconcerting if someone sees us quite differently from the way we see ourselves. In one study, Swann (1983) gave people who considered themselves submissive feedback that they seemed very dominant and forceful. Rather than accepting this discrepant information, they went out of their way to act in an extremely submissive manner. Our tendency to project into the world our concept of the self contributes to personality coherence. This talent for self-reflection enables the personality to become self-sustaining.

> **How does self-concept influence behavior?**

self-verification
The tendency to seek evidence to confirm the self-concept.

self-esteem
The extent to which an individual likes, values, and accepts the self.

Self-Esteem

When you think about yourself, do you feel good and worthy? Do you like yourself, or do you feel bad and have negative, self-critical thoughts? **Self-esteem** is *the extent to which an individual likes, values, and accepts the self.* Thousands of studies have examined differences between people with high self-esteem (who generally like themselves) and those with relatively low self-esteem (who are less keen on, and may actively dislike, themselves). Researchers who study self-esteem typically ask participants to fill out a self-esteem questionnaire, such as one shown in **TABLE 12.6** (Rosenberg, 1965). This widely used measure of self-esteem asks people to evaluate themselves in terms of each statement. People who strongly agree with the positive statements about themselves and strongly disagree with the negative statements are considered to have high self-esteem.

Although some personality psychologists have argued that self-esteem determines virtually everything about a person's life (from the tendency to engage in criminal activity and violence to professional success), evidence has accumulated that the benefits of high self-esteem are less striking and all-encompassing but still significant. In general, compared with people with low self-esteem, those with high self-esteem tend to live happier and healthier lives, cope better with stress, and be more likely to persist at difficult tasks. In contrast, individuals with low self-esteem are more likely, for example, to perceive rejection in ambiguous feedback from others and develop eating disorders than those with high self-esteem (Baumeister et al., 2003). How does this aspect of personality develop, and why does everyone—whether high or low in self-esteem—seem to *want* high self-esteem?

Sources of Self-Esteem

Some psychologists contend that high self-esteem arises primarily from being accepted and valued by significant others (Brown, 1993). Other psychologists focus on the influence of specific self-evaluations: judgments about one's value or competence in specific domains such as appearance, athletics, or scholastics.

Table 12.6

Rosenberg Self-Esteem Scale

Consider each statement and circle SA for strongly agree, A for agree, D for disagree, and SD for strongly disagree.

1. On the whole, I am satisfied with myself.	SA	A	D	SD
2. At times, I think I am no good at all.	SA	A	D	SD
3. I feel that I have a number of good qualities.	SA	A	D	SD
4. I am able to do things as well as most other people.	SA	A	D	SD
5. I feel I do not have much to be proud of.	SA	A	D	SD
6. I certainly feel useless at times.	SA	A	D	SD
7. I feel that I'm a person of worth, at least on an equal plane with others.	SA	A	D	SD
8. I wish I could have more respect for myself.	SA	A	D	SD
9. All in all, I am inclined to feel that I am a failure.	SA	A	D	SD
10. I take a positive attitude toward myself.	SA	A	D	SD

Source: Rosenberg, 1965.

Scoring: For items 1, 3, 4, 7, and 10, SA = 3, A = 2, D = 1, SD = 0; for items 2, 5, 6, 8, and 9, the scoring is reversed, with SA = 0, A = 1, D = 2, SD = 3. The higher the total score, the higher one's self-esteem.

An important factor is whom people choose for comparison. For example, James (1890) noted that an accomplished athlete who is the second best in the world should feel pretty proud, but this athlete might not if the standard of comparison involves being best in the world. In fact, athletes in the 1992 Olympics who had won silver medals looked less happy during the medal ceremony than those who had won bronze medals (Medvec, Madey, & Gilovich, 1995). If the actual self is seen as falling short of the ideal self (the person that they would like to be) people tend to feel sad or dejected; when they become aware that the actual self is inconsistent with the self they have a duty to be, they are likely to feel anxious or agitated (Higgins, 1987).

How do comparisons with others affect self-esteem?

Unconscious perspectives we take on feedback also can affect our sense of self-worth. In one study, researchers looked at the effect of an authority figure's disapproval on self-esteem. They examined the self-esteem of young, Catholic, female undergraduates who had read an article from *Cosmopolitan*, which described a woman's sexual dream (in PG-13 language), and who had either seen a photo of a disapproving-looking pope or a photo of an unfamiliar disapproving person. The photos were shown subliminally, that is, in such brief flashes that the women could not consciously recognize whom they had seen. In self-ratings made afterward, the women in the disapproving-pope group showed a marked reduction in self-esteem compared with the other women: They rated themselves as less competent, more anxious, and less moral. In the words of the researchers, self-esteem can be influenced when an important authority figure is "watching you from the back of your mind" (Baldwin, Carrell, & Lopez, 1989, p. 435).

Self-esteem is also affected by what kinds of domains we consider most important in our self-concept. One person's self-worth might be entirely contingent on, for example, how well she does in school, whereas another's self-worth might be based on her physical attractiveness (Crocker & Wolfe, 2001; Pelham, 1985). The first person's self-esteem might receive a big boost when she gets an A on an exam, but much less of a boost when she's complimented on her new hairstyle, and this effect might be exactly reversed in the second person.

This is silver medalist Bo Qui of China, gold medalist David Boudia of the US, and bronze medalist Tom Daley of the UK following the 10m platform diving competition at the 2012 London Olympics. Notice the expression on Bo Qui's face compared to those of the gold and bronze medal winders.

The Desire for Self-Esteem

What's so great about self-esteem? Why do people want to see themselves in a positive light and avoid seeing themselves negatively? The key theories on the benefits of self-esteem focus on status, belonging, and security.

Does self-esteem feel good because it reflects our degree of social dominance or status? People with high self-esteem seem to carry themselves in a way that is similar to high-status animals of other social species. Dominant male gorillas, for example, appear confident and comfortable and not anxious or withdrawn. Perhaps high self-esteem in humans reflects high social status or suggests that the person is worthy of respect, and this perception triggers natural affective responses (Barkow, 1980; Maslow, 1937).

How might self-esteem have played a role in evolution?

Could the desire for self-esteem come from a basic need to belong or be related to others? Evolutionary theory holds that early humans who managed to survive to pass on their genes were those able to maintain good relations with others rather than being cast out to fend for themselves. Clearly, belonging to groups is adaptive, as is knowing whether you are

Survivor, The Bachelor, Big Brother. Why are shows in which everyone is fighting to remain a part of the group so popular today? Is it because they play on evolutionary desire to belong? (Or do people just like to see other people get kicked out of the club?)

accepted. Thus, self-esteem could be a kind of "sociometer," an inner gauge of how much a person feels included by others at any given moment (Leary & Baumeister, 2000). According to evolutionary theory, then, we seek higher self-esteem because we have evolved to seek out belongingness in our families, work groups, and culture, and higher self-esteem indicates that we are being accepted.

The idea that self-esteem is a matter of security is consistent with the existential and psychodynamic approaches to personality. The studies of mortality salience discussed in the Emotion and Motivation chapter suggest that the source of distress underlying negative self-esteem is ultimately the fear of death (Solomon, Greenberg, & Pyszczynski, 1991). In this view, humans find it anxiety provoking, in fact terrifying, to contemplate their own mortality, and so they try to defend against this awareness by immersing themselves in activities (such as earning money or dressing up to appear attractive) that their culture defines as meaningful and valuable. The desire for self-esteem may stem from a need to find value in ourselves as a way of escaping the anxiety associated with recognizing our mortality. The higher our self-esteem, the less anxious we feel with the knowledge that someday we will no longer exist.

Whatever the reason that low self-esteem feels so bad and high self-esteem feels so good, people are generally motivated to see themselves positively. In fact, we often process information in a biased manner in order to feel good about the self. Research on the **self-serving bias** shows that *people tend to take credit for their successes but downplay responsibility for their failures.* You may have noticed this tendency in yourself, particularly in terms of the attributions you make about exams when you get a good grade (I studied really intensely, and I'm good at that subject) or a bad grade (The test was ridiculously tricky and the professor is unfair).

On the whole, most people satisfy the desire for high self-esteem and maintain a reasonably positive view of self by engaging in the self-serving bias (Miller & Ross, 1975; Shepperd, Malone, & Sweeny, 2008). In fact, if people are asked to rate themselves across a range of characteristics, they tend to see themselves as better than the average person in most domains (Alicke et al., 1995). For example, 90% of drivers describe their driving skills as better than average, and 86% of workers rate their performance on the job as above average. Even among university professors, 94% feel they are above average in teaching ability

"I suffer from accurate self-esteem."

compared with other professors (Cross, 1977). These kinds of judgments simply cannot be accurate, statistically speaking, because the average of a group of people has to be the average, not better than average! This particular error may be adaptive, however. People who do not engage in this self-serving bias to boost their self-esteem tend to be more at risk for depression, anxiety, and related health problems (Taylor & Brown, 1988).

> **What is the relationship between self-serving bias and depression?**

On the other hand, a few people take positive self-esteem to the extreme. Unfortunately, seeing yourself as way, way better than average (a trait called **narcissism,** *a grandiose view of the self combined with a tendency to seek admiration from and exploit others*) brings some costs. In fact, at its extreme, narcissism is considered a personality disorder (see the Psychological Disorders chapter). Research has documented disadvantages of an overinflated view of self, most of which arise from the need to defend that grandiose view at all costs. For example, when highly narcissistic adolescents were given reason to be ashamed of their performance on a task, their aggressiveness increased in the form of willingness to deliver loud blasts of noise to punish their opponent in a laboratory game (Thomaes et al., 2008).

Implicit Egotism

What's your favorite letter of the alphabet? About 30% of people answer by picking what just happens to be the first letter of their first name. Could this choice indicate that some people think so highly of themselves that they base judgments of seemingly unrelated topics on how much it reminds them of themselves?

This *name-letter effect* was discovered some years ago (Nuttin, 1985), but more recently researchers have gone on to discover how broad the egotistic bias in preferences can be. Brett Pelham and his colleagues have found subtle yet systematic biases toward this effect when people choose their home cities, streets, and even occupations (Pelham, Mirenberg, & Jones, 2002). When the researchers examined the rolls of people moving into several southern states, for example, they found people named George were more likely than those with other names to move to Georgia. The same was true for Florences (Florida),

> **Do people choose homes and occupations based in part on their own names?**

Kenneths (Kentucky), and Louises (Louisiana). You can guess where the Virginias tended to relocate. People whose last name is Street seem biased toward addresses ending in *street,* whereas Lanes like lanes. The name effect seems to work for occupations as well: Slightly more people named Dennis and Denise chose dentistry and Lauras and Lawrences chose law compared with other occupations. Although the biases are small, they are consistent across many tests of the hypothesis.

These biases have been called expressions of *implicit egotism* because people are not typically aware that they are influenced by the wonderful sound of their own names (Pelham, Carvallo, & Jones, 2005). When Buffy moves to Buffalo, she is not likely to volunteer that she did so because it matched her name. Yet people who show this egotistic bias in one way also tend to show it in others: People who strongly prefer their own name letter also are likely to pick their birth date as their favorite number (Koole, Dijksterhuis, & van Knippenberg, 2001). And people who like their name letter were also found to evaluate themselves positively on self-ratings of personality traits. This was especially true when the self-ratings were made in response to instructions to work *quickly.* The people who preferred their name letter made snap judgments of themselves that leaned in a positive direction, suggesting that their special self-appreciation was an automatic response.

self-serving bias
People's tendency to take credit for their successes but downplay responsibility for their failures.

narcissism
A trait that reflects a grandiose view of the self combined with a tendency to seek admiration from and exploit others.

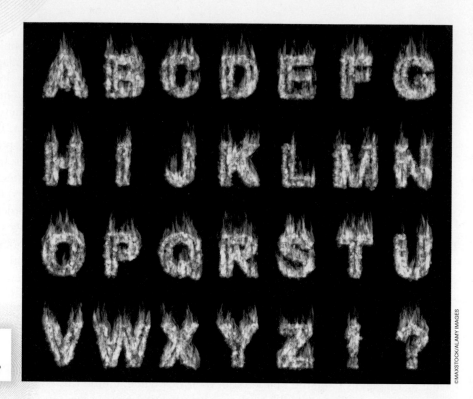

If you were trying to light up a room with a letter, would your first choice also be your initial?

©MAXSTOCK/ALAMY IMAGES

At some level, of course, a bit of egotism is probably good for us. It's sad to meet someone who hates her own name or whose snap judgment of self is "I'm worthless." Yet in another sense, implicit egotism is a curiously subtle error: a tendency to make biased judgments of what we will do and where we will go in life just because we happen to have a certain name. Yes, the bias is only a small one. But your authors wonder: Could we have found better people to work with had we not fallen prey to this bias in our choice of colleagues? The first three authors (Dan, Dan, and Dan) thought they were breaking this cycle by adding a non-Dan author, only to realize that Matt was being added shortly after he decided to move his family (including children Matthew and Maya) to Massachusetts.

The self is the part of personality that the person knows and can report about. Some of the personality measures we have seen in this chapter (such as personality inventories based on self-reports) are really no different from measures of self-concept. Both depend on the person's perceptions and memories of the self's behavior and traits. But personality runs deeper than this as well. The unconscious forces identified in psychodynamic approaches provide themes for behavior and sources of mental disorder that are not accessible for self-report. The humanistic and existential approaches remind us of the profound concerns we humans face and the difficulties we may have in understanding all the forces that shape our self-views. Finally, in emphasizing how personality shapes our perceptions of social life, the social-cognitive approach brings the self back to center stage. The self, after all, is the hub of each person's social world.

IN SUMMARY

▶ The self-concept is a person's knowledge of self, including both specific self-narratives and more abstract personality traits or self-schemas.

▶ People's self-concept develops through social feedback, and people often act to try to confirm these views through a process of self-verification.

▶ Self-esteem is a person's evaluation of self; it is derived from being accepted by others, as well as by how we evaluate ourselves by comparison to others. Theories proposed to explain why we seek positive self-esteem suggest that we do so to achieve perceptions of status, or belonging, or of being symbolically protected against mortality.

▶ People strive for positive self-views through self-serving biases and implicit egotism.

OTHER VOICES

Does the Study of Personality Lack . . . Personality?

David Brooks is a columnist for the *New York Times*, a commentator on *CNN*, and the author of several popular books on behavioral science.

PHOTO: ©JOSH HANER/COURTESY OF THE NEW YORK TIMES

As described in this chapter, some of the field's older ideas about personality (such as those described in the sections on psychodynamic and humanistic–existential approaches) are very intriguing but lacking in evidence, and so are not widely studied these days. Instead, personality researchers today are aiming to understand what aspects of our personalities are passed through which genes, and how the Big Five might map onto brain structure and functioning. The old approaches lacked evidence, but is something lacking in the newer approaches to studying personality? David Brooks seems to think so.

. . . . In the 20th century, psychoanalysts were a big deal. There were a number of best-selling authors spinning theories about the psyche, which had a large impact on how people saw the world and themselves. This includes not only Freud and Jung, but also people like Erick Erikson, Erich Fromm, Carl Rogers, Viktor Frankl and Philip Rieff. Today we're more into cognition and the brain. Over the years, attention has shifted from the soul to the personality to decision-making. Preoccupations have migrated from salvation to psychic security to success.

When it comes to treating mental illness, I guess I'm glad we've made this shift. I put more faith in medications and cognitive therapies than in Freudian or Jungian analysis. But something has been lost as well as gained. We're less adept at talking about personalities and neuroses than we were when psychoanalysts held center stage.

For example, in the middle of the 20th century, a woman named Karen Horney (pronounced HOR-nigh) crafted a series of influential theories about personality. Like many authors of these intellectually ambitious theories, she was raised in Europe and migrated to the United States before World War II. More than most of her male counterparts, Horney felt that people were driven by anxiety and the desire for security. People who have been seriously damaged, she argued, tend to react in one of three ways.

Some people respond to their wounds by moving against others. These domineering types seek to establish security by conquering and outperforming other people. They deny their own weaknesses. They are rarely plagued by self-doubt. They fear dependence and helplessness. They use their children and spouses as tools to win prestige for themselves. . . .

Other people respond to anxiety by moving toward others. These dependent types try to win people's affections by being compliant.

They avoid conflict. They become absorbed by their relationships, surrendering their individual opinions. They regard everyone else as essentially good, even people who have been cruel. . . .

Other people move away from others. These detached types try to isolate themselves and adopt an onlooker's attitude toward life. As Terry D. Cooper summarizes the category in his book, *Sin, Pride and Self-Acceptance,* "To guarantee peace, it is necessary to leave the battleground of interpersonal relationships, where there is constant threat of being captured." . . .

The domineering person believes that, if he wins life's battles, nothing can hurt him. The dependent person believes that, if he shuns private gain and conforms to the wishes of others, then the world will treat him nicely. The detached person believes that, if he asks nothing of the world, the world will ask nothing of him. These are ideal types, obviously, conceptual categories. They join a profusion of personality types that were churned out by various writers in the mid-20th century: the inner directed, the outer directed, the Organization Man, the anal retentive, the narcissist, the outsider.

The books that explained these theories were good bad books. The good bad book (I'm deriving the category from a phrase from Orwell) makes sweeping claims, and lumps people into big groups. Sometimes these claims are not really defensible intellectually. But they are thought-provoking and useful. They provide categories and handles the rest of us can use to understand the people around us, seeing where the category fits and thinking more precisely about where it doesn't.

We're probably poorer now that people like Horney have sunk to near oblivion—less adept at analyzing personality. We probably have less practice analyzing personalities. . . .

Is David Brooks right? As the study of personality has moved away from big picture explanations like those of Freud, Maslow, and Frankl, which attempt to explain why we behave the way we do with one overarching theory, and toward efforts to break down personality into smaller constructs and understand how nature and nurture produce these core traits, have we actually gotten worse at understanding personality? On balance, should interesting theories that make intriguing assumptions about people's personalities, but have no data to support their accuracy, be retained simply because they tell a more interesting story? If you are reading this book, you represent the future of psychology. How can we better understand and measure human personality? What are the most important future steps?

Chapter Review

KEY CONCEPT QUIZ

1. From a psychological perspective, personality refers to
   a. a person's characteristic style of behaving, thinking, and feeling.
   b. physiological predispositions that manifest themselves psychologically.
   c. past events that have shaped a person's current behavior.
   d. choices people make in response to cultural norms.

2. Projective techniques to assess personality involve
   a. personal inventories.
   b. self-reporting.
   c. responses to ambiguous stimuli.
   d. actuarial methodology.

3. A relatively stable disposition to behave in a particular and consistent way is a
   a. motive.
   b. goal.
   c. trait.
   d. reflex.

4. Which of the following is NOT one of the Big Five personality factors?
   a. conscientiousness
   b. agreeableness
   c. neuroticism
   d. orderliness

5. Compelling evidence for the importance of biological factors in personality is best seen in studies of
   a. parenting styles.
   b. identical twins reared apart.
   c. brain damage.
   d. factor analysis.

6. Which of Freud's systems of the mind would impel you to, if hungry, start grabbing food off people's plates upon entering a restaurant?
   a. the id
   b. the reality principle
   c. the ego
   d. the pleasure principle

7. After performing poorly on an exam, you drop a class, saying that you and the professor are just a poor match. According to Freud, what defense mechanism are you employing?
   a. regression
   b. rationalization
   c. projection
   d. reaction formation

8. According to Freud, a person who is preoccupied with his or her possessions, money, issues of submission and rebellion, and concerns about cleanliness versus messiness is fixated at which psychosexual stage?
   a. the oral stage
   b. the anal stage

   c. the latency stage
   d. the genital stage

9. Humanists see personality as directed toward the goal of
   a. existentialism.
   b. self-actualization.
   c. healthy adult sexuality.
   d. sublimation.

10. According to the existential perspective, the difficulties we face in finding meaning in life and in accepting the responsibility for making free choices provoke a type of anxiety called
    a. angst.
    b. flow.
    c. the self-actualizing tendency.
    d. mortality salience.

11. Which of the following is NOT an emphasis of the social-cognitive approach?
    a. how personality and situation interact to cause behavior
    b. how personality contributes to the way people construct situations in their own minds
    c. how people's goals and expectancies influence their responses to situations
    d. how people confront realities rather than embrace comforting illusions

12. According to social-cognitive theorists, _____ are the dimensions people use in making sense of their experiences.
    a. personal constructs
    b. outcome expectancies
    c. loci of control
    d. personal goals

13. What we think about ourselves is referred to as our _____ and how we feel about ourselves is referred to as our _____ .
    a. self-narrative; self-verification
    b. self-concept; self-esteem
    c. self-concept; self-verification
    d. self-esteem; self-concept

14. On what do the key theories on the benefits of self-esteem focus?
    a. status
    b. belonging
    c. security
    d. all of the above

15. When people take credit for their successes but downplay responsibility for their failures, they are exhibiting
    a. narcissism.
    b. implicit egotism.
    c. the self-serving bias.
    d. the name-letter effect.

KEY TERMS

personality (p. 472)

self-report (p. 473)

Minnesota Multiphasic Personality
Inventory (MMPI) (p. 474)

projective tests (p. 474)

Rorschach Inkblot Test (p. 474)

Thematic Apperception Test (TAT)
(p. 475)

trait (p. 476)

Big Five (p. 478)

psychodynamic approach (p. 484)

dynamic unconscious (p. 485)

id (p. 485)

superego (p. 485)

ego (p. 485)

defense mechanisms (p. 486)

psychosexual stages (p. 487)

fixation (p. 487)

oral stage (p. 487)

anal stage (p. 487)

phallic stage (p. 487)

Oedipus conflict (p. 487)

latency stage (p. 487)

genital stage (p. 488)

self-actualizing tendency (p. 488)

existential approach (p. 489)

social-cognitive approach (p. 490)

person–situation controversy
(p. 491)

personal constructs (p. 492)

outcome expectancies (p. 493)

locus of control (p. 493)

self-concept (p. 495)

self-verification (p. 497)

self-esteem (p. 498)

self-serving bias (p. 500)

narcissism (p. 501)

CHANGING MINDS

1. A presidential candidate makes a Freudian slip on live TV, calling his mother "petty"; he corrects himself quickly and says he meant to say "pretty." The next day the video has gone viral, and the morning talk shows discuss the possibility that the candidate has an unresolved Oedipal conflict; if so, he's stuck in the phallic stage and is likely a relatively unstable person preoccupied with issues of seduction, power, and authority (which may be why he wants to be president). Your roommate knows you're taking a psychology class and asks for your opinion: "Can we really tell that a person is sexually repressed, and maybe in love with his own mother, just because he stumbled over a single word?" How would you reply? How widely are Freud's ideas about personality accepted by modern psychologists?

2. While reading a magazine, you come across an article on the nature–nurture controversy in personality. The magazine describes several adoption studies in which adopted children (who share no genes with each other, but grow up in the same household) are no more like each other than complete strangers. This suggests that family environment—and the influence of parental behavior—on personality is very weak. You show the article to a friend, who has trouble believing the results: "I always thought parents who don't show affection produce kids who have trouble forming lasting relationships."

How would you explain to your friend the relationship between nature, nurture, and personality?

3. One of your friends has found an online site that offers personality testing. He takes the test and reports that the results prove he's an "intuitive" rather than a "sensing" personality, who likes to look at the big picture rather than focusing on tangible here-and-now experiences. "This explains a lot," he says, "like why I have trouble remembering details like other people's birthdays, and why it's hard for me to finish projects before the deadline." Aside from warning your friend about the dangers of self-diagnosis via Internet quizzes, what would you tell him about the relationship between personality types and behavior? How well do scores on personality tests predict a person's actual behavior?

4. One of your friends tells you that her boyfriend cheated on her, so she will never date him or anyone who has ever been unfaithful because "once a cheat, always a cheat." She goes on to explain that personality and character are stable over time, so people will always make the same decisions and repeat the same mistakes over time. What do we know about the interaction between personality and situations that might confirm or deny her statements?

ANSWERS TO KEY CONCEPT QUIZ

1. a; 2. c; 3. c; 4. d; 5. b; 6. a; 7. b; 8. b; 9. b; 10. a; 11. d; 12. a; 13. b;
14. d; 15. c.

Need more help? Additional resources are located in LaunchPad at:
*http://www.worthpublishers.com/launchpad/
schacter3e*

Social Psychology

ERRY, ROBERT, AND JOHN HAVE SOMETHING IN COMMON: They've all been tortured. Terry was an American journalist working in Lebanon when he was kidnapped by Hezbollah guerrillas; Robert was a semi-pro boxer living in Louisiana when he was arrested and sent to prison; and John was a naval aviator when he was shot down and captured by the North Vietnamese. All three men experienced a variety of tortures, and all agree about which was the worst.

> **John:** It's an awful thing. It crushes your spirit and weakens your resistance more effectively than any other form of mistreatment.

> **Robert:** It was a nightmare. I saw men so desperate that they ripped prison doors apart, starved and mutilated themselves . . . it takes every scrap of humanity to stay focused and sane.

> **Terry:** I'm afraid I'm beginning to lose my mind, to lose control completely. I wish I could die. I ask God often to finish this, to end it any way that pleases Him.

The cruel technique that these three men are describing has nothing to do with electric shock or waterboarding. It does not require wax, rope, or razor blades. It is a remarkably simple technique that has been used for thousands of years to break the body and destroy the mind. It is called solitary confinement. John McCain spent 2 years in a cell by himself, Terry Anderson spent 7, and Robert King spent 29.

When we think of torture, we usually think of techniques designed to cause pain by depriving people of something they desperately need, such as oxygen, water, food, or sleep. But the need for social interaction is every bit as vital. Studies of prisoners show that extensive periods of isolation can induce symptoms of psychosis (Grassian, 2006), and even in smaller doses, social isolation takes a toll. Ordinary people who are socially isolated are more likely to become depressed, to become ill, and to die prematurely. In fact, social isolation is as bad for your health as being obese or smoking (Cacioppo & Patrick, 2008; House, Landis, & Umberson, 1988).

Terry Anderson, Robert King, and John McCain each spent years in isolation and described it as the worst form of torture.

social psychology
The study of the causes and consequences of sociality.

aggression
Behavior with the purpose of harming another.

frustration–aggression hypothesis
A principle stating that animals aggress when their goals are thwarted.

WHAT KIND OF ANIMAL GETS SICK OR GOES CRAZY when left alone? Our kind. Human beings are the most social species on the planet and everything about us—from the structure of our brains to the structure of our societies—is influenced by that fact. **Social psychology** is *the study of the causes and consequences of sociality.* We'll start our tour of this field by examining *social behavior* (how people interact with each other) and see how social behavior solves problems that every living creature faces. Next we'll examine *social influence* (how people change each other) and see that people have three basic motivations that make them responsive to the actions of others. Finally, we'll examine *social cognition* (how people think about each other) and see how people use information to make judgments about others.

Social Behavior: Interacting with People

Centipedes aren't social. Neither are snails or brown bears. In fact, most animals are loners who prefer solitude to company. So why don't we?

All animals must survive and reproduce, and being social is one strategy for accomplishing these two important goals. When it comes to finding food or fending off enemies, herds and packs and flocks can often do what individuals can't, and that's why over millions of years many different species have found it useful to become social. But of the thousands and thousands of social species on our planet, only four have become *ultrasocial,* which means that they form societies in which large numbers of individuals divide labor and cooperate for mutual benefit. Those four species are the hymenoptera (i.e., ants, bees, and wasps), the termites, the naked mole rats, and us (Haidt, 2006). Even in this fine company we distinguish ourselves, because only we form societies of genetically *un*related individuals. Indeed, some scientists believe that the complexity of living in large social groups is the primary reason why nature endowed us with such big brains (Sallet et al., 2011; Shultz & Dunbar, 2010; Smith et al., 2010). If 10,000 years ago you had rounded up all the mammals on Earth and placed them on a gigantic bathroom scale, human beings would have accounted for about 0.01% of the total mass, but today we would account for 98%. We are the heavyweight champions of survival and reproduction because we are deeply social, and as you are about to see, much of our social behavior revolves around these two basic goals.

ERIKA GOLDRING/FILMMAGIC/GETTY IMAGES

Human beings are the only animals that build large-scale social networks of unrelated individuals. According to Facebook, Lady Gaga has about 60 million friends, virtually none of whom share her genes.

Survival: The Struggle for Resources

Animals have a problem: survival. To survive, animals must find resources such as food, water, and shelter. The problem is that these resources are necessarily scarce, because if they weren't, then the population would increase until they were. Animals often solve this problem by hurting or helping each other. *Hurting* and *helping* are antonyms and you might expect them to have little in common, but as you will see, these disparate behaviors are actually two solutions to the same problem (Hawley, 2002).

Aggression

The simplest way to solve the problem of scarce resources is to take those resources and then kick the stuffing out of anyone who tries to stop you. **Aggression** is *behavior with the purpose of harming another* (Anderson & Bushman, 2002; Bushman &

Huesmann, 2010), and it is a strategy used by just about every animal on the planet. Aggression is not something that animals do for its own sake but, rather, as a way of getting the resources they need. The **frustration–aggression hypothesis** suggests that *animals aggress when their desires are frustrated* (Dollard et al., 1939). The chimp wants the banana (*desire*) but the pelican is about to take it (*frustration*), so the chimp threatens the pelican with its fist (*aggression*). The robber wants the money (*desire*) but the teller has it all locked up (*frustration*), so the robber threatens the teller with a gun (*aggression*).

The frustration–aggression hypothesis is right as far as it goes, but many scientists think it doesn't go far enough. They argue that the *cause* of aggressive behavior is negative affect (more commonly known as *feeling bad*) and that a frustrated desire is just one of many things that might induce negative affect (Berkowitz, 1990). If animals aggress when they feel bad, then *anything* that makes them feel bad should increase aggression—and evidence suggests that it does. Laboratory rats that are given painful electric shocks will attack anything in their cage, including other animals, stuffed dolls, or even tennis balls (Kruk et al., 2004). People who are made to put their hands in ice water or to sit in a very hot room are more likely to blast others with noise weapons or make others eat hot chili in subsequent experiments (Anderson, 1989; Anderson, Bushman, & Groom, 1997). The idea that aggression is a response to negative affect may even explain why so many acts of aggression—from violent crime to athletic brawls—are more likely to occur on hot days when people are feeling irritated and uncomfortable (see **FIGURE 13.1**). It is worth noting that not every kind of negative affect gives rise to aggression; for example, when people feel disgusted they actually become less likely to aggress (Pond et al., 2012).

Of course, not everyone aggresses every time they feel bad. So who does and why? Research suggests that both biology and culture play important roles in determining if and when people will aggress.

Biology and Aggression. If you wanted to know whether someone was likely to engage in aggression and you could ask them just one question, it should be "Are you male or female?" (Wrangham & Peterson, 1997). Crimes such as assault, battery, and murder are almost exclusively perpetrated by men—and especially by young men—who are responsible for about 90% of the murders and 80% of the violent crimes in the United States (Strueber, Lueck, & Roth, 2006). Although most societies encourage males to be more aggressive than females (more on that shortly), male aggressiveness

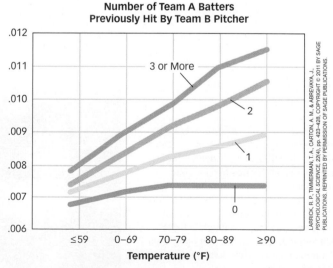

▼ Figure **13.1 Hot and Bothered**
Professional pitchers have awfully good aim, so when they hit batters with the baseball, it's safe to assume that it wasn't an accident. This graph shows data from nearly 60,000 major league baseball games. As you can see, as the temperature on the field increases, so does the likelihood that Team A batters will be hit by Team B pitchers. This effect becomes even stronger when Team B batters have previously been hit by Team A pitchers, suggesting that the Team B pitcher is seeking revenge (Larrick et al., 2011).

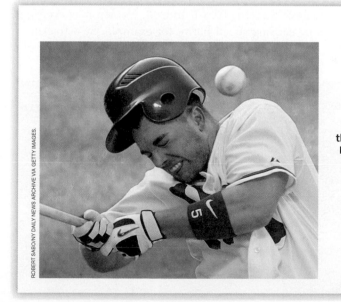

is not merely the product of socialization. Studies show that aggression is strongly correlated with the presence of a hormone called *testosterone*, which is typically higher in men than in women, in younger men than in older men, and in violent criminals than in nonviolent criminals (Dabbs et al., 1995).

Testosterone doesn't directly cause aggression, but rather, seems to make people feel powerful and confident in their ability to prevail (Eisenegger et al., 2010; Eisenegger, Haushofer, & Fehr, 2011). Male chimpanzees with high testosterone tend to stand tall and hold their chins high (Muller & Wrangham, 2004), and human beings with high testosterone walk more purposefully, focus more directly on the people they are talking to, and speak in a more forward and independent manner (Dabbs et al., 2001). Testosterone also makes people more sensitive to provocation (Ronay & Galinsky, 2011) and less sensitive to signs of retaliation. Participants in one experiment watched a face as its expression changed from neutral to threatening and were asked to respond as soon as the expression became threatening (see **FIGURE 13.2**). Participants who were given a small dose of testosterone before the experiment were slower to recognize the threatening expression (van Honk & Schutter, 2007). Failing to recognize that the person you are criticizing is getting angry is a good way to end up in a fight.

One of the most reliable ways to elicit aggression in males is to challenge their status or dominance. Indeed, three quarters of all murders can be classified as "status competitions" or "contests to save face" (Daly & Wilson, 1988). Contrary to popular wisdom, it isn't men with *low* self-esteem but men with unrealistically *high* self-esteem who are most prone to aggression, because such men are especially likely to perceive others' actions as a challenge to their inflated sense of their own status (Baumeister, Smart, & Boden, 1996). Men seem especially sensitive to these challenges when they are competing for the attention of women (Ainsworth & Maner, 2012).

Although women can be just as aggressive as men, their aggression tends to be more premeditated than impulsive and more likely to be focused on attaining or protecting a resource than on attaining or protecting their status. Women are *much* less likely than men to aggress without provocation or to aggress in ways that cause physical injury, but they are only *slightly* less likely than men to aggress when provoked or to aggress in ways that cause psychological injury (Bettencourt & Miller, 1996; Eagly & Steffen, 1986). Indeed, women may even be *more* likely than men to aggress by causing social harm, for example, by ostracizing others (Benenson et al., 2011) or by spreading malicious rumors about them (Crick & Grotpeter, 1995).

Under what circumstances do women aggress?

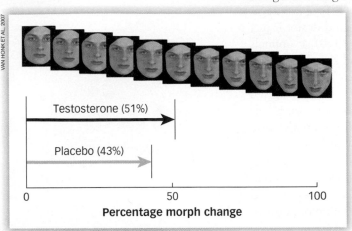

VAN HONK ET AL., 2007

Testosterone (51%)

Placebo (43%)

0   50   100
Percentage morph change

▲ Figure **13.2 I Spy Threat** Subjects who were given testosterone needed to see a more threatening expression before they were able to recognize it as such (van Honk & Schutter, 2007).

Men often aggress in response to status threats. In 2005, John Anderson (*right*) called Russell Tavares (*left*) a "nerd" on a social networking site. So Tavares got in his car, drove 1,300 miles, and burned down Anderson's trailer. "I didn't think anybody was stupid enough to try to kill anybody over an Internet fight," said Anderson. Tavares was later sentenced to 7 years in prison.

AP PHOTO/MCLENNAN COUNTY SHERIFF'S DEPARTMENT

AP PHOTO/JERRY LARSON

Culture and Aggression. William James (1911, p. 272) wrote that "our ancestors have bred pugnacity into our bone and marrow and thousands of years of peace won't breed it out of us." Was he right? Although aggression is clearly part of our evolutionary heritage, that doesn't mean it is inevitable. Indeed, the number of wars and the rate of murder have decreased by orders of magnitude in the last century alone. As psychologist Steven Pinker (2007) noted:,

> We have been getting kinder and gentler. Cruelty as entertainment, human sacrifice to indulge superstition, slavery as a labor-saving device, conquest as the mission statement of government, genocide as a means of acquiring real estate, torture and mutilation as routine punishment, the death penalty for misdemeanors and differences of opinion, assassination as the mechanism of political succession, rape as the spoils of war, pogroms as outlets for frustration, homicide as the major form of conflict resolution—all were unexceptionable features of life for most of human history. But, today, they are rare to nonexistent in the West, far less common elsewhere than they used to be, concealed when they do occur, and widely condemned when they are brought to light.

Just as aggression varies with time, so too does it vary with geography (see **FIGURE 13.3**). For example, violent crime in the United States is more prevalent in the South, where men are taught to react aggressively when they feel their status has been

What evidence suggests that culture can influence aggression?

challenged (Brown, Osterman, & Barnes, 2009; Nisbett & Cohen, 1996). In one set of experiments, researchers insulted American volunteers from Northern and Southern states and found that Southerners were more likely to experience a surge of testosterone and to feel that their status had been diminished by the insult (Cohen et al., 1996). When a large man walked directly toward them as they were leaving the experiment, insulted Southerners got "right up in his face" before giving way, whereas Northerners just stepped aside. Of course, in the control condition in which participants were *not* insulted, Southerners stepped aside *before* Northerners did, which is to say that when they aren't being insulted, Southerners are *more* polite than Northerners!

Variation over time and geography shows that culture can play an important role in determining whether our innate capacity for aggression will result in aggressive behavior (Leung & Cohen, 2011). People learn by example, which is why some researchers

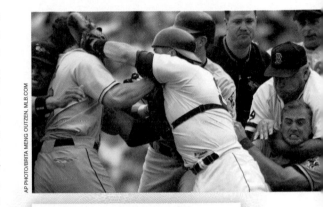

Pitchers born in Southern states are 40% more likely than those born in Northern states to hit batters with their pitches (Timmerman, 2007).

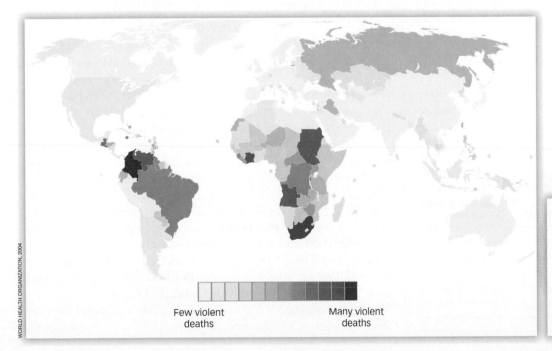

Few violent deaths

Many violent deaths

◂ Figure **13.3 The Geography of Violence** When it comes to violence, culture matters a lot. Interestingly, one factor that distinguishes between more and less violent nations is gender equality (Caprioli, 2003; Melander, 2005). The better a nation's women are treated, the lower that nation's likelihood of going to war.

WORLD HEALTH ORGANIZATION, 2004

Culture has a strong influence on violence. In Iraq, where murder is a part of everyday life, young boys stage a mock execution. In India, a teenager who is a member of the Jain religion wears a mask at all times so that she will not harm insects or microbes by inhaling them.

believe that watching violent television shows and playing violent video games can make people more aggressive (Anderson et al., 2010) and less cooperative (Sheese & Graziano, 2005; cf. Ferguson, 2010). But cultures can provide good examples as well as bad ones (Fry, 2012). In the mid-1980s, an unusual disease killed the most aggressive males in a particular troop of wild baboons in Kenya, leaving only the least aggressive males. A decade later, researchers discovered that a new "pacifist culture" had emerged among the descendants of the peaceful males. This new generation of male baboons was less aggressive, more likely to affiliate with females, and more tolerant of low-ranking males (Sapolsky & Share, 2004). If baboons can learn to get along, then surely people can too.

Cooperation

Aggression is one way to solve the problem of scarce resources, but it is not the most inventive way, because when individuals work together they can often each get more resources than either could get alone. **Cooperation** is *behavior by two or more individuals that leads to mutual benefit* (Deutsch, 1949; Pruitt, 1998), and it is one of our species' greatest achievements—right up there with language, fire, and the electric guitar (Axelrod, 1984; Axelrod & Hamilton, 1981; Nowak, 2006). Every roadway and supermarket, every iPod and cell phone, every ballet and surgery is the result of cooperation, and it is difficult to think of an important human achievement that could have occurred without it.

Risk and Trust. So if the benefits of cooperation are clear, then why don't we cooperate all the time? Cooperation is potentially beneficial, but it is also *risky,* and a simple game called *the prisoner's dilemma* illustrates why. Imagine that you and your friend have been arrested for hacking into your bank's mainframe computer and directing a few million dollars to your personal accounts. You are now being interrogated separately. The detectives tell you that if you and your friend both confess, you'll each get 10 years in prison for felony theft, and if you both refuse to confess, you'll each get 1 year in prison for, oh say, disturbing the peace. However, if one of you confesses and the other doesn't, then the one who confesses will go free and the one who doesn't confess will be put away for 30 years. What should you do? If you study **FIGURE 13.4**, you'll see that you and your friend would be wise to cooperate. If you trust your friend and refuse to confess, and if your friend trusts you and refuses to confess, then you will both get a light sentence. But look what happens if you trust your friend and then your friend double-crosses you: Your friend gets to go home and wash his car while you spend the next three decades making his license plates.

▼ Figure **13.4** **The Prisoner's Dilemma Game** The prisoner's dilemma game illustrates the benefits and costs of cooperation. Players A and B receive benefits whose size depends on whether they independently decide to cooperate. Mutual cooperation leads to a relatively moderate benefit to both players, but if only one player cooperates, then the cooperator gets no benefit and the noncooperator gets a large benefit.

	COOPERATION (B does not confess)	NONCOOPERATION (B confesses)
COOPERATION (A does not confess)	A gets 1 year B gets 1 year	A gets 30 years B gets 0 years
NONCOOPERATION (A confesses)	A gets 0 years B gets 30 years	A gets 10 years B gets 10 years

The prisoner's dilemma is more than a game. It mirrors the potential costs and benefits of cooperation in everyday life. For example, if everyone pays his or her taxes, then the tax rate stays low and everyone enjoys the benefits of sturdy bridges and first-rate museums. If no one pays taxes, then the bridges fall down and the museums shut

> **What makes cooperation risky?**

their doors. There is clearly a *moderate* benefit to everyone if everyone pays taxes, but there is a *huge* benefit to the few noncooperators who don't pay taxes while everyone else does because they get to use the bridges and enjoy the museums for free. This dilemma makes it difficult for people to decide whether to pay taxes and risk being chumps or to cheat and risk having the bridges collapse and the museums shut down. If you are like most people, you would be perfectly willing to cooperate in this sort of dilemma but you worry that others won't do the same.

Life is a strategic game, and we value those who play it honorably and despise those who don't. When people are asked what single trait they most want those around them to have, the answer is *trustworthiness* (Cottrell, Neuberg, & Li, 2007), and when those around us fail to demonstrate that quality we react bitterly. For example, the *ultimatum game* requires one player (the divider) to divide a monetary prize into two parts and offer one of the parts to a second player (the decider), who can either accept or reject the offer. If the decider rejects the offer, then both players get nothing and the game is over. Studies show that deciders typically reject offers that they consider unfair because they'd rather get nothing than get cheated (Fehr & Gaechter, 2002; Thaler, 1988). In other words, people will *pay* to punish someone who has treated them unfairly. Nonhumans also seem to dislike unfair treatment. In one study, monkeys were willing to work for a slice of cucumber until they saw the experimenter give another monkey a more delicious food for doing less work (Brosnan & DeWaal, 2003). At that point the first set of monkeys went on strike and refused to participate further.

Kevin Hart owns the Gator Motel in Fargo, Georgia, which he runs on an honor system: Guests arrive, stay as long as they like, and leave their payment on the dresser. If just a few people cheated, it would not affect the room rates, but if too many cheated, then prices would have to rise. How would you decide whether to pay or to cheat? Before answering this question, please notice the large dog.

Groups and Favoritism. Cooperation requires that we take a risk by benefiting those who have not yet benefited us and then *trusting* them to do the same. But whom can we trust?

A **group** is *a collection of people who have something in common that distinguishes them from others*. Every one of us is a member of many groups—from families and teams to religions and nations. Although these groups are quite different, they have one thing in common, which is that the people in them tend to be especially nice to each other. **Prejudice** is *a positive or negative evaluation of another person based on their group membership*, and **discrimination** is *a positive or negative behavior toward another person based on their group membership*

(Dovidio & Gaertner, 2010). One of the defining characteristics of groups is that members are positively prejudiced toward fellow members and tend to discriminate in their favor (DiDonato, Ull-

> **What is the difference between prejudice and discrimination?**

rich, & Krueger, 2011). The tendency to favor one's own group is evolutionarily ancient (Fu et al., 2012; Mahajan et al., 2011), arises early in development (Dunham, Chen, & Banaji, 2013), and is easily elicited (Efferson, Lalive, & Fehr, 2008). Even when people are randomly assigned to be members of meaningless groups such as "Group 1" or "Group 2," they still give preferential treatment to members of their own group (Hodson & Sorrentino, 2001; Locksley, Ortiz, & Hepburn, 1980). It appears that simply knowing that "I'm one of *us* and not one of *them*" is sufficient to produce prejudice and discrimination (Tajfel et al., 1971). Because group members can be relied on to favor each other, group membership makes cooperation less risky.

cooperation
Behavior by two or more individuals that leads to mutual benefit.

group
A collection of people who have something in common that distinguishes them from others.

prejudice
A positive or negative evaluation of another person based on their group membership.

discrimination
Positive or negative behavior toward another person based on their group membership.

common knowledge effect
The tendency for group discussions to focus on information that all members share.

group polarization
The tendency for groups to make decisions that are more extreme than any member would have made alone.

groupthink
The tendency for groups to reach consensus in order to facilitate interpersonal harmony.

deindividuation
A phenomenon that occurs when immersion in a group causes people to become less aware of their individual values.

diffusion of responsibility
The tendency for individuals to feel diminished responsibility for their actions when they are surrounded by others who are acting the same way.

social loafing
The tendency for people to expend less effort when in a group than when alone.

bystander intervention
The act of helping strangers in an emergency situation.

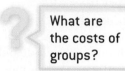

What are the costs of groups?

But if groups have benefits, they also have costs. For example, when groups try to make decisions, they rarely do better than the best member would have done alone—and they quite often do worse (Minson & Mueller, 2012). One reason is that groups don't fully capitalize on the expertise of their members (Hackman & Katz, 2010). For instance, groups (such as a school board) often give too little weight to the opinions of members who are experts (the professor) and too much weight to the opinions of members who happen to be high in status (the mayor) or especially talkative (the mayor). Groups are also susceptible to the **common knowledge effect** which is *the tendency for group discussions to focus on information that all members share* (Gigone & Hastie, 1993). The problem with this is that the information everyone shares (the size of the gymnasium) is often relatively unimportant, whereas the truly important information (how a school in a different district solved its budget crisis) is known to just a few. In addition, group discussion often acts as an "amplifier" of initial opinions. **Group polarization** is *the tendency for groups to make decisions that are more extreme than any member would have made alone* (Myers & Lamm, 1975). A group whose members come to the table with moderate opinions ("We should probably just renovate the auditorium") can end up making an extreme decision ("We're going to build a new high school!") simply because, in the course of discussion, each member was exposed to many different arguments in favor of a single position (Isenberg, 1986). Finally, members of groups care about how other members feel and are sometimes reluctant to "rock the boat" even when it needs a good rocking. **Groupthink** is *the tendency for groups to reach consensus in order to facilitate interpersonal harmony* (Janis, 1982). Harmony is important (especially if the group is a choir), but studies show that groups often sacrifice the goodness of their decisions in order to achieve it (Turner & Pratkanis, 1998). For all of these reasons, groups underperform individuals in a wide variety of tasks.

The costs of groups go beyond bad decisions because people in groups sometimes do terrible things that none of their members would do alone (Yzerbyt & Demoulin, 2010). Lynching, rioting, gang-raping—why do we sometimes behave badly when we assemble in groups?

One reason is **deindividuation**, which occurs *when immersion in a group causes people to become less concerned with their personal values*. We may want to grab the Rolex from the jeweler's window or plant a kiss on the attractive stranger in the library, but we don't do these things because they conflict with our personal values. Research shows that people are most likely to consider their personal values when their attention is focused on themselves (Wicklund, 1975), and being assembled in groups

"Hey, we're sheep. Everything seems like a good idea."

draws our attention to others and *away* from ourselves. As a result, we are less likely to consider our own personal values and instead adopt the group's values (Postmes & Spears, 1998).

A second reason why groups behave badly is **diffusion of responsibility,** which refers to *the tendency for individuals to feel diminished responsibility for their actions when they are surrounded by others who are acting the same way*. Diffusion of responsibility is the main culprit behind something you've probably observed many times—a phenomenon known as **social loafing** which refers to *the tendency for people to expend less effort when in a group than alone*. For example, individuals in large groups are less likely than individuals in small groups to clap loudly after a performance (Latané, Williams, & Harkins, 1979), exert effort in a team sport (Williams et al.,

When are people most and least likely to cheat? Researchers posted a picture above the coffee pot in an office that had an "honor system," and found that people were less likely to cheat when the picture showed eyes than when it showed flowers (Bateson, Nettle, & Roberts, 2006). Other researchers paid people to sit alone in a room and complete puzzles for cash, and found that people were less likely to cheat when the lights was bright than when the lights were low (Zhong, Bohns, & Gino, 2010).

1989), leave good tips at restaurants (Freeman et al., 1975), donate money to charity (Wiesenthal, Austrom, & Silverman, 1983), and even say hello to passersby (Jones & Foshay, 1984). But the diffusion of responsibility has much more pernicious effects. For example, studies of **bystander intervention**—which is *the act of helping strangers in an emergency situation*—reveal that people are less likely to help an innocent person in distress when there are many other bystanders present, simply because they assume that one of the other bystanders is more responsible than they are (Darley & Latané, 1968; Latané & Nida, 1981). If you saw a fellow student cheat on an exam, you'd probably feel more responsible for reporting the incident if you were taking the test in a group of 3 than in a group of 3,000 (see **FIGURE 13.5**).

If groups make bad decisions and foster bad behavior, then might we be better off without them? Probably not. One of the best predictors of a person's general well-being is the quality and extent of their group memberships (Myers & Diener, 1995). People who are excluded from groups are typically anxious, lonely, depressed, and at increased risk for illness and premature death (Cacioppo & Patrick, 2008; Cohen, 1988; Leary, 1990). Belonging is not just a source of psychological and physical well-being but also a source of identity (Ellemers, 2012; Leary, 2010; Tajfel & Turner, 1986), which is why people typically describe themselves by listing the groups of which they are members ("I'm a Canadian architect"). Groups may cause us to misjudge and misbehave, but are also the key to our happiness and well-being. Can't live with 'em, can't live without 'em.

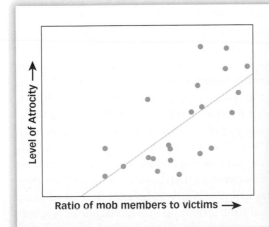

◄ Figure **13.5 Mob Size and Level of Atrocity** Groups are capable of horrible things. These two men were rescued by police just as residents of their town prepared to lynch them for stealing a car. Because larger groups provide more opportunity for deindividuation and diffusion of responsibility, their atrocities become more horrible as the ratio of mob members to victims becomes larger (Leader, Mullen, & Abrams, 2007).

HOT SCIENCE

Mouse Over

How much would you pay to save a life? The answer may depend on whether the decision is yours alone. Genetics laboratories that breed mice for experiments often end up with surplus mice. Because it is so expensive to house and feed these mice for their entire life spans, surplus mice are typically killed. Researchers at the University of Bonn decided to see how much people would pay to keep just one surplus mouse alive (Falk & Szech, 2013). They offered participants 10 Euros (about $15) to participate in their study. After participants accepted, they showed them a picture of a mouse that was destined to be killed and told them that if they would give back the 10 Euros, it would be used to support the mouse for the rest of its natural life. The majority of participants—54% to be exact—offered to give back their payment in order to save the mouse's life.

But when the researchers put the mouse's fate in the hands of *two* participants, the results changed dramatically. In a second condition of the study, the participants negotiated about what would happen to the mouse. Specifically, the participants were told that if they could agree on a way to split 20 Euros, then they would each receive the amount they agreed to and the mouse would die. If they could not agree on a way to split the money, then they would

TETRA IMAGES/ALAMY

each receive nothing and the mouse would be allowed to live out its natural life. If a participant wanted the mouse to live, then all he or she had to do was to refuse to come to an agreement about how to split the money. So what did these participants do? This time the majority of participants—72% to be exact—came to an agreement with their partner and sent the mouse to its demise.

Why did this happen? When people make joint decisions, each feels diminished responsibility for it. Participants in the first condition were faced with a moral dilemma: *Do I take the money, which I'm tempted to do, or save the mouse, which I suppose is the right thing to do?* No matter what they decided, the decision was theirs. But participants in the second condition made their decision together, and thus probably found it easier to give in to temptation because they had someone else with whom to share the blame.

Altruism

Cooperation solves the problem of scarce resources. But is that the only reason we cooperate with others? Aren't we ever just . . . well, *nice?* **Altruism** is *behavior that benefits another without benefiting oneself,* and for centuries, scientists and philosophers have argued about whether people are ever truly altruistic. That might seem like an odd argument to have. After all, people give their blood to the injured, their food to the homeless, and their arms to the elderly. We volunteer, we tithe, we donate. People do nice things all the time! Isn't that evidence of altruism?

Well, not exactly. Behaviors that appear to be altruistic often have hidden benefits for those who do them. Consider some simple examples in the realm of animal behavior. Birds and squirrels make alarm calls when they see a predator, which puts them at increased risk of being eaten but allows their fellow birds and squirrels to escape. Ants and bees spend their lives caring for the offspring of the queen rather than bearing offspring of their own. Although these behaviors appear to be altruistic, they actually aren't because the helpers are *genetically related* to the helpees. The squirrels most likely to make alarm calls are those most closely related to the other squirrels in the den (Maynard-Smith, 1965), and although honeybees do raise the queen's offspring, an odd genetic quirk causes honeybees to be more closely related to those offspring than they would be to their own. Any animal that promotes the survival of its relatives is actually promoting the survival of its own genes (Hamilton, 1964). **Kin selection** is *the process by which evolution selects for individuals who cooperate with their relatives,* and cooperating with related individuals is not really altruistic. Cooperating with unrelated individuals isn't necessarily altruistic either. Male baboons will risk injury to help an unrelated male baboon win a fight, and monkeys will spend time grooming unrelated monkeys when they could be doing something else, but as it turns out, the animals that give favors

> **Are human beings ever truly altruistic?**

altruism
Behavior that benefits another without benefiting oneself.

kin selection
The process by which evolution selects for individuals who cooperate with their relatives.

reciprocal altruism
Behavior that benefits another with the expectation that those benefits will be returned in the future.

Ground squirrels put themselves in danger when they warn others about predators, but those they warn share their genes, so the behavior is not truly altruistic. In contrast, Christine Karg-Palerio donated her kidney anonymously to someone she'd never even met. "If I had a spare, I'd do it again," she said.

tend to get favors in return. **Reciprocal altruism** is *behavior that benefits another with the expectation that those benefits will be returned in the future,* and despite the second word in this term, it isn't actually altruistic (Trivers, 1972). Indeed, reciprocal altruism is merely cooperation extended over time.

The behavior of nonhuman animals provides little if any evidence of genuine altruism (cf. Bartal, Decety, & Mason, 2011). So what about us? Are we any different? Like other animals, we tend to help our kin more than strangers (Burnstein, Crandall, & Kitayama, 1994; Komter, 2010) and we tend to expect those we help to help us in return (Burger et al., 2009). But unlike other animals, we *do* sometimes provide benefits to complete strangers who have no chance of repaying us (Batson, 2002; Warneken & Tomasello, 2009). We hold the door for people who share precisely none of our genes and tip waiters in restaurants to which we will never return. And we do more than that. As the World Trade Center burned on the morning of September 11, 2001, civilians in sailboats headed *toward* the destruction rather than away from it, initiating the largest waterborne evacuation in U.S. history. As one observer remarked, "If you're out on the water in a pleasure craft and you see those buildings on fire, in a strictly rational sense you should head to New Jersey. Instead, people went into potential danger and rescued strangers. That's social" (Dreifus, 2003). Human beings can be truly altruistic, and some studies suggest that they are actually more altruistic than they realize (Miller & Ratner, 1998).

Reproduction: The Quest for Immortality

All animals must survive and reproduce. Social behavior is useful for survival, but it is an absolute prerequisite for reproduction, which doesn't happen until people get very, very social. The first step on the road to reproduction is finding someone who wants to travel that road with us. How do we do that?

Selectivity

With the exception of a few well-known rock stars, people don't mate randomly. Rather, they *select* their sexual partners, and as anyone who has lived on earth for more than 7 full minutes knows, women tend to be more selective than men (Feingold, 1992a; Fiore et al., 2010). When researchers asked an attractive person to approach strangers on a college campus and ask, "Would you go out with me?" they found that roughly half of the men and half of the women agreed to the request for a date. On the other hand, when the attractive person

Why are women choosier than men?

said to strangers, "would you go to bed with me?" the researchers found that *none* of the women and *three quarters* of the men agreed to the request for sex (Clark & Hatfield, 1989). There are many reasons why a woman in this situation might turn down a sexual offer (Conley, 2011), but research suggests that women tend to be choosier than men in most other situations as well (Buss & Schmitt, 1993; Schmitt et al., 2012).

One reason for this is biology. Men produce billions of sperm in their lifetimes, their ability to conceive a child tomorrow is not inhibited by having conceived one today, and conception has no significant physical costs. On the other hand, women produce a small number of eggs in their lifetimes, conception eliminates their ability to conceive for at least 9 more months, and pregnancy produces physical changes that increase their nutritional requirements and put them at risk of illness and death. Therefore, if a man mates with a woman who does do not produce healthy offspring or who won't do her part to raise them, he's lost nothing but 10 minutes and a teaspoon of bodily fluid. But if a woman makes the same mistake, she has lost a precious egg, borne the costs of pregnancy, risked her life in childbirth, and missed at least 9 months of other reproductive opportunities. Clearly, our basic biology makes sex a riskier proposition for women than for men.

But if basic biology pushes women to be choosier then men, culture and experience can push every bit as hard (Petersen & Hyde, 2010; Zentner, & Mitura, 2012). For example, women may be choosier than men simply because they are approached more often (Conley et al., 2011) or because the reputational costs of promiscuity are higher (Eagly & Wood, 1999; Kasser & Sharma, 1999). Indeed, when sex becomes expensive for men (e.g., when they are choosing a long-term mate rather than a short-term date), they can be every bit as choosey as women (Kenrick et al., 1990). In fact, relatively minor changes in the courtship ritual can actually cause men to be *choosier* than women (see the Real World box). The point is that biology makes sex a riskier proposition for women than for men, but cultures can exaggerate, equalize, or even reverse those risks. The higher the risk, the more selective people of both genders tend to be.

CREATAS IMAGES/ PICTUREQUEST

DR. PAUL ZAHL/ PHOTO RESEARCHERS

If men could become pregnant, how might their behavior change? Among sea horses, it is the male that carries the young, and not coincidentally, males are more selective than are females.

Attraction

For most of us, there is a very small number of people with whom we are willing to have sex, an even smaller number of people with whom we are willing to have children, and a staggeringly large number of people with whom we are unwilling to have either. So when we meet someone new, how do we decide which of these categories they belong in? Many things go into choosing a date, a lover, or a partner for life, but perhaps none is more important than the simple feeling we call *attraction* (Berscheid & Reis, 1998). Research suggests that this feeling is caused by a range of factors that can be roughly divided into three kinds: the situational, the physical, and the psychological.

Situational Factors. One of the best predictors of any kind of interpersonal relationship is the physical proximity of the people involved (Nahemow & Lawton, 1975). In one study, students who had been randomly assigned to university housing almost a year earlier were asked to name their three closest friends, and nearly half named their next-door neighbor (Festinger, Schachter, & Back, 1950). We tend to think that we select our romantic partners on the basis of their personalities, appearances, and so on—and we do—but we only get to select from the pool of people we've met, and the likelihood of meeting a potential partner naturally increases with proximity. Before you ever start ruling out potential mates, geography has already ruled out 99.999% of the world's population for you. Proximity not only provides the opportunity for attraction,

Making the Move

When it comes to selecting romantic partners, women tend to be choosier than men, and most scientists think that has a lot to do with differences in their reproductive biology. But psychologists Eli Finkel and Paul Eastwick (2009) thought that it might also have something to do with the nature of the courtship dance itself.

When it comes to approaching a potential romantic partner, the person with the most interest should be most inclined to "make the first move." Of course, in most cultures, men are *expected* to make the first move. Could it be that making the first move *causes* men to think that they have more interest than women do and causes women to think they have less? In other words, could the rule about first moves be one of the *reasons* why women are choosier?

To find out, the researchers teamed up with a local speed dating service and created two kinds of speed dating events. In the traditional event, the women stayed in their seats and the men moved around the room, stopping to spend a few minutes chatting with each woman. In the nontraditional event, the men stayed in their seats and the women moved around the room, stopping to spend a few minutes chatting with each man. When the event was over, the researchers asked

each man and woman privately to indicate whether they wanted to exchange phone numbers with any of the potential partners they'd met.

The results were striking (see the accompanying figure). When men made the move (as they traditionally do), women were the choosier gender. That is, men wanted to get a lot more phone numbers than women wanted to give. But when women made the move, men were the choosier gender, and women asked for more numbers than men were willing to hand over. Apparently, approaching someone makes us eager and being approached makes us cautious. One reason why women are so often the choosier gender may simply be that, in most cultures, men are expected to make the first move.

it also provides the motivation: People work especially hard to like those with whom they expect to have interaction (Darley & Berscheid, 1967). When you are assigned a roommate or an office mate, you know that your day-to-day existence will be a whole lot easier if you like them than if you don't, and so you go out of your way to notice their good qualities and ignore their bad ones.

Proximity provides something else as well. Every time we encounter a person, that person becomes a bit more familiar to us, and people generally prefer familiar to novel stimuli. The **mere exposure effect** is *the tendency for liking to increase with the frequency of exposure* (Bornstein, 1989; Zajonc, 1968). For instance, in some experiments, geometric shapes, faces, or alphabetical characters were flashed on a computer screen so quickly that participants were unaware of having seen them. Participants were then shown some of the "old" stimuli that had been flashed across the screen as well as some "new" stimuli that had not. Although they could not reliably say which stimuli were old and which were new, they did tend to *like* the old stimuli better than the new ones (Monahan, Murphy, & Zajonc, 2000). The fact that mere exposure leads to liking may explain why college students who were randomly assigned to seats during a brief psychology experiment were likely to be friends with the person they sat next to a full year later (Back, Schmukle, & Egloff, 2008). There are some

Why does proximity influence attraction?

mere exposure effect
The tendency for liking to increase with the frequency of exposure.

"I'm a beast, I'm an animal, I'm that monster in the mirror." Like it or not, the mirror is the place where Usher most often sees himself. As a result, he probably prefers pictures of himself that are horizontally reversed (*above left*), whereas his fans probably prefer pictures of him that are not (*above right*). One consequence of the mere exposure effect is that people tend to like the photographic images with which they are most familiar (Mita, Dermer, & Knight, 1977).

circumstances under which "familiarity breeds contempt" (Norton, Frost, & Ariely, 2007), but for the most part familiarity seems to breed liking (Reis et al., 2011).

Attraction can be the result of geographical accidents that put people in the same place at the same time, but some places and times are clearly better than others. In one study, researchers observed men as they crossed a swaying suspension bridge. An attractive female researcher approached the men, either when they were in the middle of the bridge or after they had finished crossing it, and asked them to complete a survey. After they did so, she gave each man her telephone number and offered to explain her project in greater detail if he called. Results showed that the men were more likely to call the woman when they had met her in the middle of the swaying bridge (Dutton & Aron, 1974). Why? You may recall from the Emotion and Motivation chapter that people can misinterpret physiological arousal as a sign of attraction (Byrne et al., 1975; Schachter & Singer, 1962). The men were presumably more aroused when they were in the middle of a swaying bridge, and some of those men mistook their arousal for attraction.

Physical Factors. Once people are in the same place at the same time, they can begin to learn about each other's personal qualities, and in most cases, the first quality they learn about is the other person's appearance. You probably knew that appearance influences attraction, but this influence may be stronger than you thought. In one study, researchers arranged a dance for first-year university students and randomly assigned each student to an opposite-sex partner. Midway through the dance, the students confidentially reported how much they liked their partner, how attractive they thought their partner was, and how much they would like to see their partner again. The researchers measured many of the students' attributes—from their attitudes to their personalities—and they found that the partner's physical appearance was the *only* attribute that influenced the students' feelings of attraction (Walster et al., 1966). Field studies confirm this finding. For instance, one study found that a man's height and a woman's weight were among the best predictors of how many responses a personal ad received (Lynn & Shurgot, 1984), and another study found that physical attractiveness was the *only* factor that predicted the online dating choices of both women and men (Green, Buchanan, & Heuer, 1984). Superficiality, thy name is human!

When people are in arousing situations together, they may become attracted. Ben Bostic and Laura Zych were strangers when their US Airways flight crash-landed in the Hudson River in 2009. Now they are a couple.

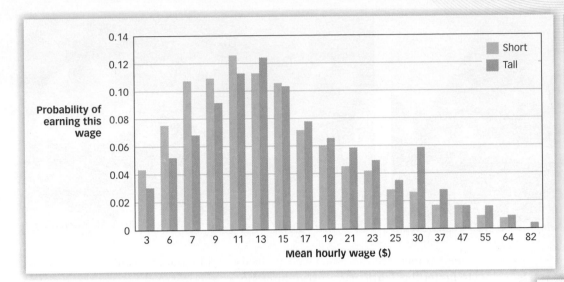

▲ Figure **13.6 Height Matters** NFL quarterback Tom Brady is 6'4" and his wife, supermodel Gisele Bunchen, is 5'10". Research shows that tall people earn $789 more per inch per year. The graph shows the average hourly wage of adult White men in the United States classified by height (Mankiw & Weinzierl, 2010).

Beauty gets us more than dates (Etcoff, 1999; Langlois et al., 2000). Beautiful people have more sex, more friends, and more fun than the rest of us do (Curran & Lippold, 1975), and they even earn about 10% more money over the course of their lives (Hamermesh & Biddle, 1994; see **FIGURE 13.6**). We tend to think that beautiful people also have superior personal qualities (Dion, Berscheid, & Walster, 1972; Eagly et al., 1991), and in some cases they do. For instance, because beautiful people have more friends and more opportunities for social interaction, they tend to have better social skills than less beautiful people (Feingold, 1992b). Appearance is so powerful that it even influences how mothers treat their own children: Mothers are more affectionate and playful when their children are attractive than unattractive (Langlois et al., 1995). Indeed, the only real disadvantage of being beautiful is that it can sometimes cause others to feel threatened (Agthe, Spörrle, & Maner, 2010). It is interesting to note that men and women are equally influenced by the appearance of their potential partners (Eastwick et al., 2011), but men are more willing to admit it (Feingold, 1990).

> **Why is physical appearance so important?**

So yes, it pays to be beautiful. But what exactly constitutes beauty? The answer to that question varies across cultures. In the United States, for example, most women want to be slender, but in Mauritania, young girls are forced to drink up to 5 gallons of high-fat milk every day so that they will someday be obese enough to attract a husband. As one Mauritanian woman noted, "Men want women to be fat, and so they are fat. Women want men to be skinny, and so they are skinny" (LaFraniere, 2007). In the United States, most men want to be tall, but in Ghana, most men are short and consider height a curse. "To be a tall person can be quite embarrassing," said one particularly altitudinous Ghanaian man. "When you are standing in a crowd, the short people start to jeer at you," said another (French, 1997).

Beauty may vary across cultures, but it is not entirely in the eye of the beholder. Different cultures have different standards of beauty, but those standards have a lot in common (Cunningham et al., 1995). For example, people in all cultures seem to have similar preferences about the ideal body, face, and age of their romantic partners.

> *Body shape.* Male bodies are considered most attractive when they approximate an inverted triangle (i.e., broad shoulders with a narrow waist and hips), and female bodies are considered most attractive when they approximate an hourglass (i.e., broad shoulders and hips with a narrow waist). In fact, the most attractive female body across many cultures seems to be the "perfect hourglass" in which the waist is precisely 70% the size of the hips (Singh, 1993). Culture may determine

Standards of beauty can vary across cultures. Mauritanian women long to be obese (*left*). Ghanian men are grateful to be short (*right*).

whether men prefer women who are heavy or thin, but in all cultures men seem to prefer this particular waist-to-hip ratio.

> *Symmetry.* People in all cultures seem to prefer faces and bodies that are *bilaterally symmetrical*—that is, faces and bodies whose left half is a mirror image of the right half (Perilloux, Webster, & Gaulin, 2010; Perrett et al., 1999).

> *Age.* Characteristics such as large eyes, high eyebrows, and a small chin make people look immature or "baby-faced" (Berry & McArthur, 1985). As a general rule, female faces are considered more attractive when they have immature features, and male faces are considered more attractive when they have mature features (Cunningham, Barbee, & Pike, 1990; Zebrowitz & Montepare, 1992). Women prefer older men and men prefer younger women in every human culture ever studied (Buss, 1989).

But why? Is there any rhyme or reason to this list of scenic attractions? Some psychologists think so. They suggest that nature has designed us to be attracted to people who (a) have good genes and (b) will be good parents (Gallup & Frederick, 2010; Neuberg, Kenrick, & Schaller, 2010). The features we all find attractive happen to be reliable indicators of these things. For example:

> *Body shape.* Testosterone causes male bodies to become "inverted triangles" just as estrogen causes female bodies to become "hourglasses." Men who are high in testosterone tend to be socially dominant and therefore have more resources to devote to their offspring, whereas women who are high in estrogen tend to be especially fertile and potentially have more offspring to make use of those resources. In other words, body shape is an indicator of male dominance and female fertility. In fact, women who have the perfect hourglass figure do tend to bear healthier children than do women with other waist-to-hip ratios (Singh, 1993).

> *What kind of information does physical appearance convey?*

> *Symmetry.* Symmetry is a sign of genetic health (Jones et al., 2001; Thornhill & Gangestad, 1993), which may explain why people are so good at detecting it. Indeed, women can distinguish between symmetrical and asymmetrical men *by smell,* and their preference for symmetrical men is especially pronounced when they are ovulating (Thornhill & Gangestad, 1999).

> *Age.* Younger women are generally more fertile than older women, whereas older men generally have more resources than younger men. Thus, a youthful appearance is a signal of a woman's ability to bear children, just as a mature appearance is a signal of a man's ability to raise them.

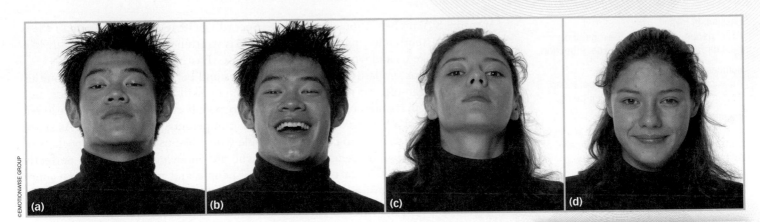

(a) (b) (c) (d)

Straight women find men sexiest when their faces are displaying pride (a) and least sexy when they are displaying happiness (b); straight men find women least sexy when their faces are displaying pride (c) and sexiest when they are displaying (d) happiness (Tracy & Beall, 2011).

If the feeling we call *attraction* is simply nature's way of telling us that we are in the presence of a person who has good genes and a propensity to be a good parent, then it isn't any wonder that people in different cultures appreciate so many of the same features in the opposite sex. Of course, appreciation is one thing and action is another, and studies show that while everyone may *desire* the most beautiful person in the room, most people tend to approach, date, and marry someone who is about as attractive as they are (Berscheid et al., 1971; Lee et al., 2008).

Psychological Factors. If attraction is all about big biceps and high cheekbones, then why don't we just skip the small talk and pick our mates from photographs? Because for human beings, attraction is about much more than that. Physical appearance is assessed easily and early (Lenton & Francesconi, 2010), and it determines who draws our attention and quickens our pulse. But once people begin interacting they quickly move beyond appearances (Cramer, Schaefer, & Reid, 1996; Regan, 1998). People's *inner* qualities—their personalities, points of view, attitudes, beliefs, values, ambitions, and abilities—play an important role in determining their sustained interest in each other, and there isn't much mystery about the kinds of inner qualities that most people find attractive. For example, intelligence, sense of humor, sensitivity, and ambition seem to be high on just about everybody's list, whereas "experienced serial killer" doesn't seem to make anyone's list (Daniel et al., 1985).

How much wit and wisdom do we want our mate to have? Research suggests that people are most attracted to those who are similar (Byrne, Ervin, & Lamberth, 1970; Byrne & Nelson, 1965; Hatfield & Rapson, 1992; Neimeyer & Mitchell, 1988). We marry people with similar levels of education, religious backgrounds, ethnicities, socioeconomic statuses, and personalities (Botwin, Buss, & Shackelford, 1997; Buss, 1985; Caspi & Herbener, 1990). We're even attracted to those who use pronouns the same way we do (Ireland et al., 2010). In fact, of all the variables psychologists have ever studied, *gender* appears to be the only one for which the majority of people have a consistent preference for dissimilarity.

Why is similarity such a powerful determinant of attraction?

Why is similarity so attractive? First, it's easy to interact with people who are similar to us because we can instantly agree on a wide range of issues, such as what to eat, where to live, how to raise children, and how to spend our money. Second, when someone shares our attitudes and beliefs, we feel more confident that those attitudes and beliefs are correct (Byrne & Clore, 1970). Indeed, research shows that when a person's attitudes or beliefs are challenged, they become even more attracted to similar others (Greenberg et al., 1990; Hirschberger, Florian, & Mikulincer, 2002). Third, if we like people who share our attitudes and beliefs, then we can reasonably expect them to like us for the same reason, and *being liked* is a powerful source of attraction

Similarity is a very strong source of attraction.

passionate love
An experience involving feelings of euphoria, intimacy, and intense sexual attraction.

companionate love
An experience involving affection, trust, and concern for a partner's well-being.

social exchange
The hypothesis that people remain in relationships only as long as they perceive a favorable ratio of costs to benefits.

comparison level
The cost–benefit ratio that people believe they deserve or could attain in another relationship.

equity
A state of affairs in which the cost–benefit ratios of two partners are roughly equal.

Humans and birds have something in common: Their offspring are utterly helpless at birth and require a lot of parental care. As a result, both people and birds have enduring relationships. And both seem to sing about it.

(Aronson & Worchel, 1966; Backman & Secord, 1959; Condon & Crano, 1988). Although we tend to like people who like us, it is worth noting that we *especially* like people who like us and who *don't* like anyone else (Eastwick et al., 2007).

Our desire for similarity goes beyond attitudes and beliefs and extends to abilities as well. For example, we may admire extraordinary skill in athletes and actors, but when it comes to friends and lovers, extraordinary people can threaten our self-esteem and make us feel a bit nervous about our own competence (Tesser, 1991). As such, we are generally attracted to competent people who—like us—have small pockets of incompetence. Why? It seems that people who are annoyingly perfect are perfectly annoying. Having a flaw or two "humanizes" people and makes them seem more accessible—and more similar to us (Aronson, Willerman, & Floyd, 1966).

Relationships

Once we have selected and attracted a mate, we are ready to reproduce. (Note: It is perfectly fine to pause for dinner.) Human reproduction ordinarily happens in the context of committed, long-term relationships (Clark & Lemay, 2010). Only a few animals have such relationships, so why are we among them?

> **Why do people form long-term romantic relationships?**

One answer is that we're born half-baked. Because human beings have large heads to house their large brains, a fully developed human infant could not pass through its mother's birth canal. So human infants are *born before they are fully developed.* That means they need a lot more care than one parent can provide. If human infants were like tadpoles—ready at birth to swim, find food, and escape predators—then their parents might not need to form and maintain relationships. But human infants are remarkably helpless creatures that require years of intense care before they can fend for themselves, and that's one reason why human adults tend to do their reproducing in the context of committed, long-term relationships. (By the way, some baby birds also require more food than one adult caretaker can provide, and the adults of those species also tend to form long-term relationships.)

Love and Marriage. In most cultures, committed, long-term relationships are signified by marriage, and ours is no exception. The probability of marrying by age 40 is about 81% for American men and 86% for American women (Goodwin, McGill, & Chandra, 2009). But when asked, people don't say that they married to solve the big-headed baby problem; they say that they married for love. Indeed, about 85% of Americans say that they would not marry without love (Kephart, 1967; Simpson, Campbell, & Berscheid, 1986); the vast majority say they would sacrifice their other life goals to attain it (Hammersla & Frease-McMahan, 1990); and most list love as one of the two most important sources of happiness in life (Freedman, 1978). The fact that people marry for love seems so obvious that you may be surprised to learn that it only became obvious in the past century or so (Brehm, 1992; Fisher, 1993; Hunt, 1959). Ancient Greeks and Romans married, but they considered love a form of madness (Heine, 2010). Twelfth-century Europeans married but thought of love as a game to be played by knights and ladies of the court (who happened to be married and not to the knights). Throughout history, marriage has traditionally served a variety of economic (and decidedly unromantic) functions—ranging from cementing agreements between clans to paying back debts—and in many cultures, that's how it is still regarded. In fact, it wasn't until the 17th century that Westerners started to think that love might be a *reason* to get married.

But what exactly is love? Psychologists distinguish between two basic kinds: **passionate love,** which is *an experience involving feelings of euphoria, intimacy, and intense sexual attraction,* and **companionate love,** which is *an experience involving affection, trust, and concern for a partner's well-being* (Acevedo & Aron, 2009; Hatfield, 1988; Rubin, 1973; Sternberg, 1986). The ideal romantic relationship gives rise to both types of love, but the speeds, trajectories, and durations of the two experiences are markedly different (see **FIGURE 13.7**). Passionate love is what brings people together: It has a rapid onset, reaches its peak quickly, and begins to diminish within just a few months (Aron et al., 2005). Companionate love is what keeps people together: It takes some time to get started, grows slowly, and need never stop growing (Gonzaga et al., 2001).

Divorce: When the Costs Outweigh the Benefits

The most recent U.S. government census statistics indicate that for every two couples who get married, one couple gets divorced.

How do people weigh the costs and benefits of their relationships?

But why? Although feelings of love, happiness, and satisfaction may lead us to marriage, the lack of those feelings doesn't seem to lead us to divorce. Marital satisfaction is only weakly correlated with marital stability (Karney & Bradbury, 1995), suggesting that relationships break up or remain intact for reasons other than the satisfaction of those involved (Drigotas & Rusbult, 1992; Rusbult & Van Lange, 2003). Relationships offer both benefits (love, sex, and financial security) and costs (responsibility, conflict, loss of freedom). **Social exchange** is *the hypothesis that people remain in relationships only as long as they perceive a favorable ratio of costs to benefits* (Homans, 1961; Thibaut & Kelley, 1959). For example, a relationship that provides an acceptable level of benefits at a reasonable cost will probably be maintained, and one that doesn't won't. Research suggests that this hypothesis is generally true, but there are three important caveats:

> The acceptableness of any cost–benefit ratio depends on the alternatives. A person's **comparison level** refers to *the cost-benefit ratio that people believe they deserve or could attain in another relationship* (Rusbult et al., 1991; Thibaut & Kelley, 1959). A cost–benefit ratio that is acceptable to two people who are stranded on a desert island might not be acceptable to the same two people if they were living in a large city where each had access to other potential partners. A cost–benefit ratio is acceptable when we feel that it is the best we can or should do.

> People may want their cost–benefit ratios to be high, but they also want them to be roughly the same as their partner's. Studies show that people care about **equity,** which is *a state of affairs in which the cost–benefit ratios of two partners are roughly equal* (Bolton & Ockenfels, 2000; Messick & Cook, 1983; Walster, Walster, & Berscheid, 1978). For example, spouses are more distressed when their respective cost–benefit ratios are *different* than when their cost–benefit ratios are *unfavorable*, and this is true even when their cost–benefit ratio is *more* favorable than their partner's (Schafer & Keith, 1980). Indeed, people who give too much are sometimes disliked just as much as those who give too little (Parks & Stone, 2010).

> Relationships can be thought of as investments into which people pour resources such as time, money, and affection, and research suggests that once people have poured resources into a relationship, they are willing to settle for less favorable cost–benefit ratios (Kelley, 1983; Rusbult, 1983). This is one of the reasons why people are much more likely to end new marriages than old ones (Bramlett & Mosher, 2002; Cherlin, 1992).

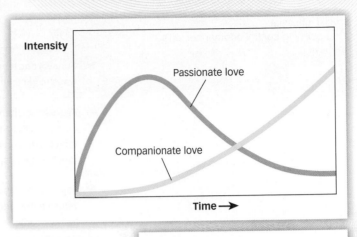

▲ Figure **13.7 Passionate and Companionate Love** Companionate and passionate love have different time courses and trajectories. Passionate love begins to cool within just a few months, but companionate love can grow slowly but steadily over years.

TOM CHENEY/THE NEW YORKER COLLECTION/CARTOONBANK.COM

"This next one goes out to all those who have ever been in love, then become engaged, gotten married, participated in the tragic deterioration of a relationship, suffered the pains and agonies of a bitter divorce, subjected themselves to the fruitless search for a new partner, and ultimately resigned themselves to remaining single in a world full of irresponsible jerks, noncommittal weirdos, and neurotic misfits."

social influence
The ability to control another person's behavior.

IN SUMMARY

▶ Survival and reproduction require scarce resources, and aggression and cooperation are two ways to get them.

▶ Aggression often results from negative affect, which can be caused by almost anything—from being insulted to being hot. The likelihood that a person will aggress when they feel negative affect is determined both by biological factors (such as testosterone level) and cultural factors (such as geography).

▶ Cooperation is beneficial but risky, and one strategy for reducing its risks is to form groups whose members are biased in favor of each other. Unfortunately, groups often decide and behave badly.

▶ Although behaviors that appear to be altruistic often have hidden benefits for the person who does them, there is little doubt that human beings can behave altruistically.

▶ Both biology and culture tend to make the costs of reproduction higher for women than for men, which is one reason why women tend to be choosier when selecting potential mates.

▶ Attraction is determined by situational factors (such as proximity), physical factors (such as symmetry), and psychological factors (such as similarity).

▶ Human reproduction usually occurs within the context of a long-term relationship. People weigh the costs and benefits of their relationships and tend to dissolve them when they think they can or should do better, when they and their partners have very different cost–benefit ratios, or when they have little invested in the relationship.

Social Influence: Controlling People

Those of us who grew up watching cartoons on Saturday mornings have usually thought a bit about which of the standard superpowers we'd most like to have. Super strength and super speed have obvious benefits, invisibility and X-ray vision could be interesting as well as lucrative, and there's a lot to be said for flying. But when it comes right down to it, the ability to control other people would probably be the most

Malala Yousafzai, a 15-year-old Pakistani girl who stood up for women's rights despite being hunted by the Taliban, was named one of the world's 100 most influential people by *Time* magazine.

useful. After all, who needs to lift a tractor or catch a bad guy if someone else can be convinced to do it? The things we want from life—gourmet food, interesting jobs, big houses, fancy cars—can be given to us by others, and the things we want most—loving families, loyal friends, admiring children, appreciative employers—cannot be had in any other way.

Social influence is *the ability to control another person's behavior* (Cialdini & Goldstein, 2004). But how does it work? If you want someone to give you their time, money, allegiance, or affection, you'd be wise to consider first what it is *they* want. People have three basic motivations that make them susceptible to social influence (Bargh, Gollwitzer, & Oettingen, 2010; Fiske, 2010). First, people are motivated to experience pleasure and to avoid experiencing pain (the *hedonic motive*). Second, people are motivated to be accepted and to avoid being rejected (the *approval motive*). Third, people are motivated to believe what is right and to avoid believing what is wrong (the *accuracy motive*). As you will see, most social influence attempts appeal to one or more of these motives.

The Hedonic Motive: Pleasure Is Better Than Pain

If there is an animal that prefers pain to pleasure it must be very good at hiding because no one has ever seen it. Pleasure seeking is the most basic of all motives, and social influence often involves creating situations in which others can achieve more pleasure by doing what we want them to do than by doing something else. Parents, teachers, governments, and businesses influence our behavior by offering rewards and threatening punishments (see **FIGURE 13.8**). There's nothing mysterious about how these influence attempts work, and they are often quite effective. When the Republic of Singapore warned its citizens that anyone caught chewing gum in public would face a year in prison and a $5,500 fine, the rest of the world was outraged; but when the outrage subsided, it was hard to ignore the fact that gum chewing in Singapore had fallen to an all-time low. A good caning gets your attention every time.

> **How effective are rewards and punishments?**

You'll recall from the Memory chapter that even a sea slug will repeat behaviors that are followed by rewards and avoid behaviors that are followed by punishments. Although the same is generally true of human beings, there are some instances in which rewards and punishments can backfire. For example, children in one study were allowed to play with colored markers and then some were given a "Good Player Award." When the children were given markers the next day, those who had received an award were less likely to play with them than were those who had not received an award (Lepper, Greene, & Nisbett, 1973). Why? Because children who had received an award the first day came to think of drawing as something one does to receive rewards, and if no one was going to give them an award, then why the heck should they do it (Deci, Koestner, & Ryan, 1999)? Similarly, rewards and punishments can backfire simply because people don't like being manipulated with them. Researchers placed signs in two restrooms on a college campus: "Please don't write on these walls" and "Do not write on these walls under any

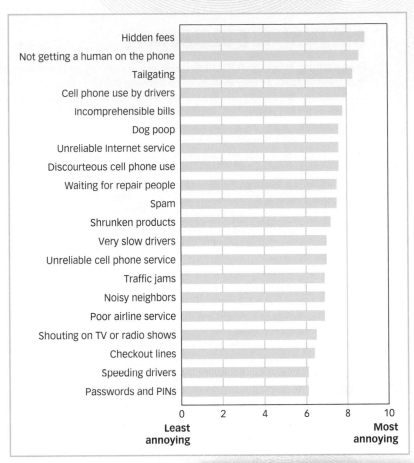

Graph categories from most annoying to least: Hidden fees, Not getting a human on the phone, Tailgating, Cell phone use by drivers, Incomprehensible bills, Dog poop, Unreliable Internet service, Discourteous cell phone use, Waiting for repair people, Spam, Shrunken products, Very slow drivers, Unreliable cell phone service, Traffic jams, Noisy neighbors, Poor airline service, Shouting on TV or radio shows, Checkout lines, Speeding drivers, Passwords and PINs

Scale: 0 2 4 6 8 10 — Least annoying to Most annoying

Other people are the source of most of our rewards—and, it appears, most of our punishments. In a 2010 survey that asked Americans to identify the things that annoyed them most, 19 of the top 20 annoyances were caused by other people. The remaining annoyance was caused by other people's dogs.

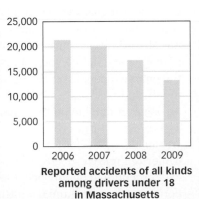

Reported accidents of all kinds among drivers under 18 in Massachusetts

(Bar graph: 2006 ≈ 21,000; 2007 ≈ 20,000; 2008 ≈ 17,000; 2009 ≈ 13,000)

◄ Figure **13.8** **The Cost of Speeding** The penalty for speeding in Massachusetts used to be a modest fine. In 2006, the legislature changed the law so that drivers under 18 who are caught speeding now lose their licenses for 90 days—and to get them back they have to pay $500, attend 8 hours of training classes, and retake the state's driving exam. Guess what? Deaths among drivers under 18 fell by 38% in just 3 years. In other words, more than 8,000 young lives were saved by appealing to the hedonic motive.

http://www.boston.com/news/local/massachusetts/articles/2010/04/18/steep_drop_in_teen_driver_fatalities/

CULTURE & COMMUNITY

Free parking. People don't like to be manipulated, and they get upset when someone threatens their freedom to do as they wish. Is this a uniquely Western reaction? To find out, psychologist Eva Jonas and her colleagues asked college students one of two favors and then measured how irritated they felt (Jonas et al., 2009). In one case, they asked students if they would give up their right to park on campus for a week ("Would you mind if I used your parking card so I can participate in a research project in this building?"). In the other case, they asked students if they would give up *everyone's* right to park on campus for a week ("Would you mind if we closed the entire parking lot for a tennis tournament?"). How did students react to these requests?

It depended on their culture. As the figure shows, European American students were more irritated by a request that limited their freedom than by a request that limited everyone's freedom ("If nobody can park, that's inconvenient. But if everybody except *me* can park, that's unfair!"). But Latino and Asian American students had precisely the opposite reactions ("The needs of the requestor outweigh the needs of one student, but they don't outweigh the needs of all students"). It appears that people do indeed value freedom—but not necessarily their own.

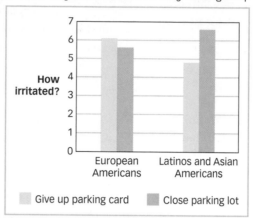

circumstances." Two weeks later, the walls in the second restroom had more graffiti on the walls, presumably because students didn't appreciate the threatening tone of the second sign and wrote on the walls just to prove that they could (Pennebaker & Sanders, 1976).

The Approval Motive: Acceptance Is Better Than Rejection

Other people stand between us and starvation, predation, loneliness, and all the other things that make getting shipwrecked such an unpopular pastime. We depend on others for safety, sustenance, and solidarity, and so we are powerfully motivated to have others like us, accept us, and approve of us (Baumeister & Leary, 1995; Leary, 2010). Like the hedonic motive, this one leaves us vulnerable to social influence.

Normative Influence

norms
Customary standards for behavior that are widely shared by members of a culture.

norm of reciprocity
The unwritten rule that people should benefit those who have benefited them.

normative influence
A phenomenon that occurs when another person's behavior provides information about what is appropriate.

door-in-the-face technique
An influence strategy that involves getting someone to deny an initial request.

conformity
The tendency to do what others do simply because others are doing it.

Consider the many things you know about elevators. When you get on an elevator you are supposed to face forward and not talk to the person next to you even if you were talking to that person before you got on the elevator unless you are the only two people on the elevator in which case it's okay to talk and face sideways but still not backward. Although no one ever taught you this rule, you probably picked it up somewhere along the way. The unwritten rules that govern social behavior are called **norms,** which are *customary standards for behavior that are widely shared by members of a culture* (Cialdini, 2013; Miller & Prentice, 1996). We learn norms with exceptional ease and we obey them with exceptional fidelity because we know that if we don't, others won't approve of us. For example, every human culture has a **norm of reciprocity,** which is *the unwritten*

> How are we influenced by other people's behavior?

rule that people should benefit those who have benefited them (Gouldner, 1960). When a friend buys you lunch, you return the favor; and if you don't, your friend gets miffed. Indeed, the norm of reciprocity is so strong that when researchers randomly pulled the names of strangers from a telephone directory and sent them all Christmas cards, they received Christmas cards back from most (Kunz & Woolcott, 1976).

Norms are a powerful weapon in the game of social influence. **Normative influence** occurs when *another person's behavior provides information about what is appropriate* (see **FIGURE 13.9**). For example, waiters and waitresses know all about the norm of reciprocity, which is why they often give customers a piece of candy along with the bill. Studies show that customers who receive a candy feel obligated to do "a little extra" for the waiter who did "a little extra" for them (Strohmetz et al., 2002). Indeed, people will sometimes refuse small gifts precisely because they don't want to feel indebted to the gift giver (Shen, Wan, & Wyer, 2011).

The norm of reciprocity involves swapping, but the thing being swapped doesn't have to be a favor. The **door-in-the-face technique** is *an influence strategy that involves getting someone to deny an initial request.* Here's how it works: You ask someone for something more valuable than you really want, you wait for that person to refuse (to "slam the door in your face"), and then you ask the person for what you really want. For example, when researchers asked college students to volunteer to supervise adolescents who were going on a field trip, only 17% of the students agreed. But when the researchers first asked students to commit to spending 2 hours per week for 2 years working at a youth detention center (to which every one of the students said no) and *then* asked them to supervise a field trip, 50% of the students agreed (Cialdini et al., 1975). Why? The norm of reciprocity! The researchers began by asking for a large favor, which the student refused. Then the researchers made a concession by asking for a smaller favor. Because the researchers made a concession, the norm of reciprocity demanded that the student make one too—and half of them did!

Conformity

People can influence us by invoking familiar norms, such as the norm of reciprocity. But if you've ever found yourself sneaking a peek at the diner next to you, hoping to

> **Why do we do what we see other people doing?**

discover whether the little fork is supposed to be used for the shrimp or the salad, then you know that other people can influence us by defining *new* norms in ambiguous, confusing, or novel situations. **Conformity** is *the tendency to do what others do simply because others are doing it,* and it results in part from normative influence.

In a classic study, psychologist Solomon Asch had participants sit in a room with seven other people who appeared to be ordinary participants, but who were actually trained actors (Asch, 1951, 1956). An experimenter explained that the participants would be shown cards with three printed lines and that his or her job was simply to say which of the three lines matched a "standard line" that was printed on another card (see **FIGURE 13.10**). The experimenter held up a card and then asked each person to answer in turn. The real participant was among the last to be called on. Everything went

On average, your risk of becoming obese increases by ...

... **57%**
if someone you consider a friend becomes obese.

... **37%**
if your spouse becomes obese.

... **171%**
if a very close friend becomes obese.

... **40%**
if one of your siblings becomes obese.

... **100%**
if you are a man and your male friend becomes obese.

... **67%**
if you are a woman and your sister becomes obese.

... **38%**
if you are a woman and your female friend becomes obese.

... **44%**
if you are a man and your brother becomes obese.

©FRANCIS DEAN/DEAN PICTURES/THE IMAGE WORKS

▲ Figure **13.9 The Perils of Connection**
Other people's behavior defines what is "normal," which is one of the reasons why obesity "spreads" through social networks (Christakis & Fowler, 2007).
Source: Analysis of 12,067 participants in the Framingham Heart Study from 1971 to 2003
James Abundis/Globe Staff

Have you ever wondered which big spender left the bill as a tip? In fact, the bills are often put there by the very people you are tipping because they know that the presence of paper money will suggest to you that others are leaving big tips and that it would be socially appropriate for you to do the same. By the way, the customary gratuity for someone who writes a textbook for you is 15%. But most students spend more.

DON PAULSON PHOTOGRAPHY/
PURESTOCK/SUPERSTOCK

The perplexed research participant (center), flanked by confederates (who are "in" on the experiment), is on the verge of conformity in one of Solomon Asch's line-judging experiments.

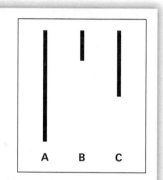

Standard

A B C

▲ Figure **13.10 Asch's Conformity Study**
If you were asked which of the lines on the right (A, B, or C) matches the standard line on the left, what would you say? Research on conformity suggests that your answer would depend, in part, on how other people in the room answered the same question.

well on the first two trials, but then on the third trial something really strange happened: the actors all began giving the same wrong answer! What did the real participants do? Seventy-five percent of them conformed and announced the wrong answer on at least one trial. Subsequent research has shown that these participants didn't actually misperceive the length of the lines, but were instead succumbing to normative influence (Asch, 1955; Nemeth & Chiles, 1988). Giving the wrong answer was apparently "the right thing to do" and so participants did it.

The behavior of others can tell us what is proper, appropriate, expected, and accepted (in other words, it can define a norm) and once a norm is defined, we feel obliged to honor it. When a Holiday Inn in Tempe, Arizona, left a variety of different "message cards" in guests' bathrooms in the hopes of convincing those guests to reuse their towels rather than laundering them every day, it discovered that the single most effective message was the one that simply read: "Seventy five percent of our guests use their towels more than once" (Cialdini, 2005). When the Sacramento Municipal Utility District randomly selected 35,000 customers and sent them electric bills showing how their energy consumption compared to that of their neighbors (see **FIGURE 13.11**), consumption fell by 2% (Kaufman, 2009). Clearly, normative influence can be a force for good.

Obedience

Other people's behavior can provide information about norms, but in most situations there are a few people whom we all recognize as having special authority both to define the norms and to enforce them. The guy who works at the movie theater may be some high school fanboy with a bad haircut and a 10:00 p.m. curfew, but in the context of the theater, he is the authority. So when he asks you to put away your cell and stop texting in the middle of the movie, you do as you are told. **Obedience** is *the tendency to do what powerful people tell us to do.*

▶ Figure **13.11 Normative Influence at Home** In 2008, the Sacramento Municipal Utility District randomly selected 35,000 of its customers and sent them electric bills like the one above. The bill didn't just show how much electricity the customer had used, it also showed how much electricity was used by neighbors who lived in similar-sized homes. When the utility crunched the numbers, they discovered that customers who had received this "compare with the neighbors" bill had reduced their electricity consumption by 2% compared to customers who had received a traditional bill (Kaufman, 2009). Clearly, normative influence can be a force for good.

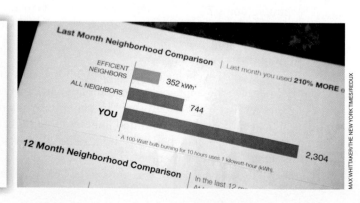

OTHER VOICES

91% of All Students Read This Box and Love It

Tina Rosenberg is an editorial writer for the *New York Times*. Her 1995 book *The Haunted Land: Facing Europe's Ghosts After Communism* won both the Pulitzer Prize and the National Book Award.

PHOTO: NOAH GREENBERG PHOTOGRAPHY

Binge drinking is a problem on college campuses across America (Wechsler & Nelson, 2001). About half of all students report doing it, and those who do are much more likely to miss classes, get behind in their school work, drive drunk, and have unprotected sex. So what to do?

Colleges have tried a number of remedies—from education to abstinence—and none of them has worked particularly well. But lately, some schools have taken a new approach called "social norming." Although this approach is surprisingly effective, it is also controversial. Tina Rosenberg's most recent book is *Join the Club: How Peer Pressure Can Transform the World*. In the following essay, she describes both the technique and the controversy.

... Like most universities, Northern Illinois University in DeKalb has a problem with heavy drinking. In the 1980s, the school was trying to cut down on student use of alcohol with the usual strategies. One campaign warned teenagers of the consequences of heavy drinking. "It was the 'don't run with a sharp stick you'll poke your eye out' theory of behavior change," said Michael Haines, who was the coordinator of the school's Health Enhancement Services. When that didn't work, Haines tried combining the scare approach with information on how to be well: "It's O.K. to drink if you don't drink too much—but if you do, bad things will happen to you."

That one failed, too. In 1989, 45 percent of students surveyed said they drank more than five drinks at parties. This percentage was slightly higher than when the campaigns began. And students thought heavy drinking was even more common; they believed that 69 percent of their peers drank that much at parties.

But by then Haines had something new to try. In 1987 he had attended a conference on alcohol in higher education sponsored by the United States Department of Education. There Wes Perkins, a professor of sociology at Hobart and William Smith Colleges, and Alan Berkowitz, a psychologist in the school's counseling center, presented a paper that they had just published on how student drinking is affected by peers. "There are decades of research on peer influence—that's nothing new," Perkins said at the meeting. What was new was their survey showing that when students were asked how much their peers drank, they grossly overestimated the amount. If the students were responding to peer pressure, the researchers said, it was coming from imaginary peers.

The "aha!" conclusion Perkins and Berkowitz drew was this: maybe students' drinking behavior could be changed by just telling them the truth.

Haines surveyed students at Northern Illinois University and found that they also had a distorted view of how much their peers drink. He decided to try a new campaign, with the theme "most students drink moderately." The centerpiece of the campaign was a series of ads in the *Northern Star*, the campus newspaper, with pictures of students and the caption "two thirds of Northern Illinois University students (72%) drink 5 or fewer drinks when they 'party'." ...

Haines's staff also made posters with campus drinking facts and told students that if they had those posters on the wall when an inspector came around, they would earn $5. (35 percent of the students did have them posted when inspected.) Later they made buttons for students in the fraternity and sorority system—these students drank more heavily—that said "Most of Us," and offered another $5 for being caught wearing one. The buttons were deliberately cryptic, to start a conversation.

After the first year of the social norming campaign, the perception of heavy drinking had fallen from 69 to 61 percent. Actual heavy drinking fell from 45 to 38 percent. The campaign went on for a decade, and at the end of it NIU students believed that 33 percent of their fellow students were episodic heavy drinkers, and only 25 percent really were—a decline in heavy drinking of 44 percent. ...

Why isn't this idea more widely used? One reason is that it can be controversial. Telling college students "most of you drink moderately" is very different than saying "don't drink." (It's so different, in fact, that the National Social Norms Institute, with headquarters at the University of Virginia, gets its money from Anheuser Busch—a decision that has undercut support for the idea of social norming.) The approach angers people who lobby for a strong, unmuddied message of disapproval—even though, of course, disapproval doesn't reduce bad behavior, and social norming does. ...

Social norming is a powerful but controversial tool for changing behavior. When we tell students about drinking on campus, should we tell them what's true (even if the truth is a bit ugly) or should we tell them what's best (even if they are unlikely to do it)?

Why do we obey powerful people? Well, yes, sometimes they have guns. But while powerful people are often capable of rewarding and punishing us, research shows that much of their influence is *normative* (Tyler, 1990). Psychologist Stanley Milgram (1963) demonstrated this in one of psychology's most infamous experiments. The participants in this experiment met a middle-aged man who was introduced as another participant, but who

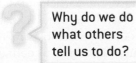

Why do we do what others tell us to do?

obedience
The tendency to do what powerful people tell us to do.

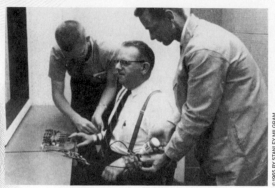

► Figure **13.12 Milgram's Obedience Studies** The learner (*left*) is being hooked up to the shock generator (*right*) that was used in Stanley Milgram's obedience studies.

was actually a trained actor. An experimenter in a lab coat explained that the participant would play the role of *teacher* and the actor would play the role of *learner*. The teacher and learner would sit in different rooms, the teacher would read words to the learner over a microphone, and the learner would then repeat the words back to the teacher. If the learner made a mistake, the teacher would press a button that delivered an electric shock to the learner (see **FIGURE 13.12**). The shock-generating machine (which was totally fake) offered 30 levels of shock, ranging from 15 volts (labeled *slight shock*) to 450 volts (labeled *Danger: severe shock*).

After the learner was strapped into his chair, the experiment began. When the learner made his first mistake, the participant dutifully delivered a 15-volt shock. As the learner made more mistakes, he received more shocks. When the participant delivered the 75-volt shock, the learner cried out in pain. At 150 volts, the learner screamed, "Get me out of here. I told you I have heart trouble . . . I refuse to go on. Let me out!" With every shock, the learner's screams became more agonized as he pleaded pitifully for his freedom. Then, after receiving the 330-volt shock, the learner stopped responding altogether. Participants were naturally upset by all this and typically asked the experimenter to stop, but the experimenter simply replied, "You have no choice; you must go on." The experimenter never threatened the participant with punishment of any kind. Rather, he just stood there with his clipboard in hand and calmly instructed the participant to continue. So what did the participants do? Eighty percent of the participants continued to shock the learner even after he screamed, complained, pleaded, and then fell silent. And 62% went all the way, delivering the highest possible voltage. Although Milgram's study was conducted nearly half a century ago, a recent replication revealed about the same rate of obedience (Burger, 2009).

In 1971, Psychologist Philip Zimbardo built a mock prison in the basement of the Stanford Psychology Department and invited two dozen students to play the roles of either a prisoner or a guard. After 6 days he was forced to halt his observational study because many of the guards had become so abusive toward the prisoners that he feared for their safety (Haney, Banks, & Zimbardo, 1973).

Were these people psychopathic sadists? Would normal people electrocute a stranger just because some guy in a lab coat told them to? The answer, it seems, is *yes*—as long as *normal* means being sensitive to social norms. The participants in this experiment knew that hurting others is *often* wrong but not *always* wrong: Doctors give painful injections, and teachers give painful exams. There are many situations in which it is permissible—and even desirable—to cause someone to suffer in the service of a higher goal. The experimenter's calm demeanor and persistent instruction suggested that he, and not the participant, knew what was appropriate in this particular situation, and so the participant did as ordered. Subsequent research confirmed that participants' obedience was due to normative pressure. When the experimenter's authority to define the norm was undermined (e.g., when a second experimenter appeared to disagree with the first or when the instructions were given by a person who wasn't wearing a lab coat), participants rarely obeyed the instructions (Milgram, 1974; Miller, 1986).

The Accuracy Motive: Right Is Better Than Wrong

When you are hungry, you open the refrigerator and grab an apple because you know that apples (a) taste good and (b) are in the refrigerator. This action, like most actions, relies on both an **attitude**, which is *an enduring positive or negative evaluation of an object or event,* and a **belief**, which is *an enduring piece of knowledge about an object or event.* In a sense, our attitudes tell us what we should do (*eat an apple*) and our beliefs tell us how to do it (*start by opening the fridge*). If our attitudes or beliefs are inaccurate—that is, if we can't tell good from bad or true from false—then our actions are likely to be fruitless. Because we rely so much on our attitudes and beliefs, it isn't surprising that we are motivated to have the right ones, and that motivation leaves us vulnerable to social influence.

Informational Influence

If everyone in the mall suddenly ran screaming for the exit, you'd probably join them—not because you were afraid that they would disapprove of you if you didn't—but because their behavior would suggest to you that there was something worth running

> How do informational and normative influences differ?

from. **Informational influence** occurs when *another person's behavior provides information about what is true.* You can observe the power of informational influence yourself just by standing in the middle of the sidewalk, tilting back your head, and staring at the top of a tall building. Research shows that within just a few minutes, other people will stop and stare too (Milgram, Bickman, & Berkowitz, 1969). Why? They will assume that if you are looking, then there must be something worth looking at.

You are the constant target of informational influence. When a salesperson tells you that "most people buy the iPad with extra memory," she is artfully suggesting that you should take other people's behavior as information about the product. Advertisements that refer to soft drinks as "popular" or books as "best sellers" are reminding you that

attitude
An enduring positive or negative evaluation of an object or event.

belief
An enduring piece of knowledge about an object or event.

informational influence
A phenomenon that occurs when another person's behavior provides information about what is true.

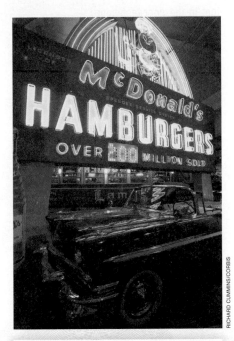

RICHARD CUMMINS/CORBIS

Is McDonald's trying to keep track of sales from the parking lot? Probably not. Rather, they want you to know that other people are buying their hamburgers, which suggests that they are worth buying.

AP PHOTO/PAELO MARTINEZ

Obama

Romney

It is now common during political debates for broadcasters to display real-time information about people's reactions to the candidates. But recent studies show that this information influences viewers' opinions about who won the debate as well as their voting decisions (Davis, Bowers, & Memon, 2011).

persuasion
A phenomenon that occurs when a person's attitudes or beliefs are influenced by a communication from another person.

systematic persuasion
The process by which attitudes or beliefs are changed by appeals to reason.

heuristic persuasion
The process by which attitudes or beliefs are changed by appeals to habit or emotion.

foot-in-the-door technique
A technique that involves making a small request and following it with a larger request.

Why do advertisers hire celebrities to endorse shoes but not cars? Cars are relatively expensive, so people are motivated to process information about them and are therefore persuaded by facts about quality and price. Shoes are relatively inexpensive, so people are not motivated to process information about them and are therefore persuaded by celebrity endorsements.

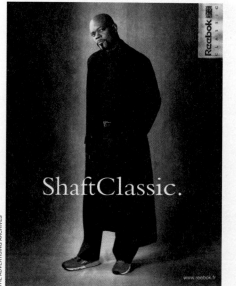

other people are buying these particular drinks and books, which suggests that they know something you don't and that you'd be wise to follow their example. Situation comedies provide laugh tracks because the producers know that when you hear other people laughing, you will mindlessly assume that something must be funny (Fein, Goethals, & Kugler, 2007; Nosanchuk & Lightstone, 1974). Bars and nightclubs make people stand in line even when there is plenty of room inside because they know that passersby will see the line and assume that the club is worth waiting for. In short, the world is full of objects and events that we know little about, and we can often cure our ignorance by paying attention to the way in which others are acting toward them. Alas, the very thing that makes us open to information leaves us open to manipulation as well.

Persuasion

When the next presidential election rolls around, two things will happen. First, the candidates will say that they intend to win your vote by making arguments that focus on the issues. Second, the candidates will then avoid arguments, ignore issues, and attempt to win your vote with a variety of cheap tricks and emotional appeals. What the candidates promise to do and what they actually do reflect two basic forms of **persuasion**, which occurs when *a person's attitudes or beliefs are influenced by a communication from another person* (Albarracín & Vargas, 2010; Petty & Wegener, 1998). The candidates will promise to persuade you by demonstrating that their positions on the issues are the most practical, intelligent, fair, and beneficial. Having made that promise, they will then devote most of their financial resources to persuading you by other means: for example, by dressing nicely and smiling a lot, by surrounding themselves with famous athletes and movie stars, by repeatedly pairing their opponent's picture with Osama bin Laden's, and so on. In other words, the candidates will promise to engage in **systematic persuasion**, which refers to *the process by which attitudes or beliefs are changed by appeals to reason,* but they will spend most of their time and money engaged in **heuristic persuasion**, which refers to *the process by which attitudes or beliefs are changed by appeals to habit or emotion* (Chaiken, 1980; Petty & Cacioppo, 1986).

> **When is it more effective to appeal to reason or to emotion?**

How do these two forms of persuasion work? *Systematic persuasion* appeals to logic and reason, and assumes that people will be more persuaded when evidence and arguments are strong rather than weak. *Heuristic persuasion* appeals to habit and emotion, and assumes that rather than weighing evidence and analyzing arguments, people will often use *heuristics* (simple shortcuts or "rules of thumb") to help them decide whether to believe a communication (see the Language and Thought chapter). Which form of persuasion will be more effective depends on whether the person is willing and able to weigh evidence and analyze arguments.

In one study, students heard a speech that contained either strong or weak arguments in favor of instituting comprehensive exams at their school (Petty, Cacioppo, & Goldman, 1981). Some students were told that the speaker was a Princeton University professor, and others were told that the speaker was a

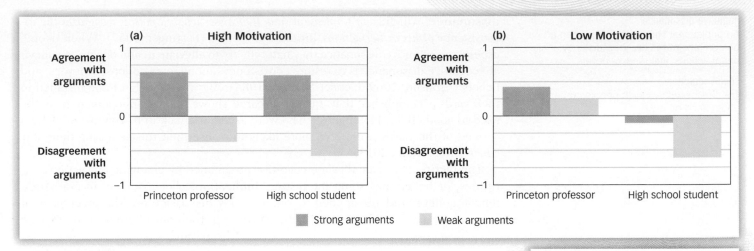

high school student—a bit of information that could be used as a shortcut to decide whether to believe the speech. Some students were told that their university was considering implementing these exams right away, whereas others were told that their university was considering implementing these exams in 10 years—a bit of information that made students feel motivated or unmotivated to analyze the evidence. As **FIGURE 13.13** shows, when students were motivated to analyze the evidence, they were systematically persuaded—that is, their attitudes and beliefs were influenced by the strength of the arguments but not by the status of the speaker. But when students were not motivated to analyze the evidence, they were heuristically persuaded—that is, their attitudes and beliefs were influenced by the status of the speaker but not by the strength of the arguments.

Consistency

If a friend told you that rabbits had just staged a coup in Antarctica and were halting all carrot exports, you probably wouldn't turn on CNN. You'd know right away that your friend was joking (or stupid) because the statement is logically inconsistent with other things that you know are true, for example, that rabbits do not foment revolution and that Antarctica does not export carrots. People

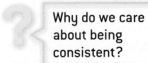

Why do we care about being consistent?

evaluate the accuracy of new beliefs by assessing their *consistency* with old beliefs, and although this is not a foolproof method for determining whether something is true, it provides a pretty good approximation. We are motivated to be accurate, and because consistency is a rough measure of accuracy, we are motivated to be consistent as well (Cialdini, Trost, & Newsom, 1995).

That motivation leaves us vulnerable to social influence. For example, the **foot-in-the-door** technique involves *making a small request and then following it with a larger request* (Burger, 1999). In one study (Freedman & Fraser, 1966), experimenters went to a neighborhood and knocked on doors to see if they could convince homeowners to agree to have a big ugly "Drive Carefully" sign installed in their front yards. One group of homeowners was simply asked to install the sign, and only 17% said yes. A second group of homeowners was first asked to sign a petition urging the state legislature to promote safe driving (which almost all agreed to do) and was *then* asked to install the ugly sign. And 55% said yes! Why would homeowners be more likely to grant two requests than one?

Just imagine how the homeowners in the second group felt. They had already signed a petition stating that they thought safe driving was important, and yet they knew they didn't want to install an ugly sign in their front yards. As they wrestled with this inconsistency, they probably began to experience a feeling called **cognitive**

▲ Figure **13.13 Systematic and Heuristic Persuasion** [*a*] *Systematic persuasion.* When students were motivated to analyze arguments because they would be personally affected by them, their attitudes were influenced by the strength of the arguments (strong arguments were more persuasive than weak arguments), but not by the status of the communicator (the Princeton professor was not more persuasive than the high school student). [*b*] *Heuristic persuasion.* When students were not motivated to analyze arguments because they would not be personally affected by them, their attitudes were influenced by the status of the communicator (the Princeton professor was more persuasive than the high school student), but not by the strength of the arguments (strong arguments were no more persuasive than weak arguments; Petty, Cacioppo, & Goldman, 1981).

cognitive dissonance
An unpleasant state that arises when a person recognizes the inconsistency of his or her actions, attitudes, or beliefs.

social cognition
The processes by which people come to understand others.

dissonance, which is *an unpleasant state that arises when a person recognizes the inconsistency of his or her actions, attitudes, or beliefs* (Festinger, 1957). When people experience cognitive dissonance they naturally try to alleviate it, and one way to alleviate cognitive dissonance is to restore consistency among one's actions, attitudes, and beliefs (Aronson, 1969; Cooper & Fazio, 1984). Allowing the sign to be installed in their yards accomplished that. Recent research shows that this phenomenon can be used to good effect: Hotel guests who were asked at check-in to commit to being a "Friend of the Earth" were 25% more likely to re-use their towels during their stay (Baca-Motes et al., 2013).

The fact that we can alleviate cognitive dissonance by changing our actions, attitudes, or beliefs has some interesting implications. For instance, in one study, female college students applied to join a weekly discussion on "the psychology of sex." Women in the control group were allowed to join the discussion, but women in the experimental group were allowed to join the discussion only after first passing an embarrassing test that involved reading pornographic fiction to a strange man. Although the carefully staged discussion was as dull as possible, women in the experimental group found it more interesting than did women in the control group (Aronson & Mills, 1958). Why? Women in the experimental group knew that they had paid a steep price to join the group ("I read all that porn out loud!"), but that belief was inconsistent with the belief that the discussion was worthless. As such, the women experienced cognitive dissonance, which they alleviated by changing their beliefs about the value of the discussion (see the top half of **FIGURE 13.14.**). We normally think that people pay for things because they value them, but as this study shows, people sometimes value things because they've paid for them—with money, time, attention, blood, sweat, or tears. It is little wonder that some fraternities use hazing to breed loyalty, that some religions require their adherents to make large personal or monetary sacrifices, that some gourmet restaurants charge outrageous amounts to keep their patrons coming back, or that some men and women play hard to get to maintain their suitors' interest.

What happens when we are inconsistent?

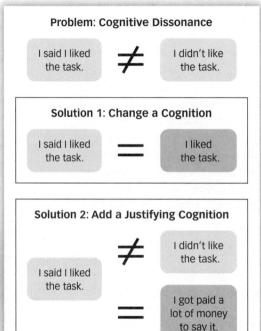

▲ Figure **13.14 Alleviating Cognitive Dissonance** Suffering for something of little value can cause cognitive dissonance. One way to alleviate that dissonance is to change your belief about the value of the thing you suffered for.

Problem: Cognitive Dissonance

I said I liked the task. ≠ I didn't like the task.

Solution 1: Change a Cognition

I said I liked the task. = I liked the task.

Solution 2: Add a Justifying Cognition

I said I liked the task. ≠ I didn't like the task.
= I got paid a lot of money to say it.

We are motivated to be consistent, but there are inevitably times when we just can't, for example, when we tell a friend that her new hairstyle is "daring" when it actually resembles a wet skunk after an unfortunate encounter with a snowblower. Why don't we experience cognitive dissonance under such circumstances and come to believe our own lies? Because while telling a friend that her hairstyle is daring is inconsistent with the belief that her hairstyle is hideous, it is perfectly consistent with the belief that one should be nice to one's friends. When small inconsistencies are *justified* by large consistencies, cognitive dissonance is reduced.

Members of Michigan Tech University's Sigma Tau Gamma fraternity brave subzero wind chill to participate in the group's annual "Grundy Run" through the campus.

AP PHOTO/DAILY MINING GAZETTE, MICHELE JOKINEN

For example, participants in one study were asked to perform a dull task that involved turning knobs one way, then the other way, and then back again. After the participants were sufficiently bored, the experimenter explained that he desperately needed a few more people to volunteer for the study, and he asked the participants to go into the hallway, find another person, and tell that person that the knob-turning task was great fun. The experimenter offered some participants $1 to tell this lie, and he offered other participants $20. All participants agreed to tell the lie, and after they did so, they were asked to report their true enjoyment of the knob-turning task. The results showed that participants liked the task *more* when they were paid $1 than $20 to lie about it (Festinger & Carlsmith, 1959). Why? Because the belief *this knob-turning task is dull* was inconsistent with the belief *I recommended the task to that person in the hallway,* but the latter belief was perfectly consistent with the belief that *$20 is a lot of money.* For some participants, the large payment justified the lie, so only those people who received the small payment experienced cognitive dissonance. As such, only the participants who received $1 felt the need to restore consistency by changing their beliefs about the enjoyableness of the task (see the bottom half of Figure 13.14).

IN SUMMARY

▶ People are motivated to experience pleasure and avoid pain (the hedonic motive), and thus can be influenced by rewards and punishments, although these can sometimes backfire.

▶ People are motivated to attain the approval of others (the approval motive), and thus can be influenced by social norms, such as the norm of reciprocity. People often look to the behavior of others to determine what's normative, and they often end up conforming or obeying, sometimes with disastrous results.

▶ People are motivated to know what is true (the accuracy motive), and thus can be influenced by other people's behaviors and communications. This motivation also causes them to seek consistency among their attitudes, beliefs, and actions.

Social Cognition: Understanding People

Frank Ocean is sexy and talented. Whether or not you agree with that sentence, it almost certainly activated your medial prefrontal cortex, which is an area of your brain that is activated when you think about the attributes of other people but not about the attributes of inanimate objects such as houses or tools (Mitchell, Heatherton, & Macrae, 2002). Although most of your brain shows diminished activity when you are at rest, this area remains active all the time (Buckner, Andrews-Hanna, & Schacter, 2008). Why does your brain have a specific area that is dedicated to processing information about just *one* of the millions of objects you might encounter, and why is this area constantly switched on?

Of the millions of objects you might encounter, other human beings are the single most important. **Social cognition** is *the processes by which people come to understand others,* and your brain is doing it all day long. Whether you know it or not, your brain is constantly making inferences about others people's thoughts and feelings, beliefs and desires, abilities and aspirations, intentions, needs, and characters. It bases these inferences on two kinds of information: the categories to which people belong, and the things they do and say.

Thinking about singer Frank Ocean activates your medial prefrontal cortex. Do you think about him still? Do ya, do ya?

KARL WALTER/GETTY IMAGES FOR COACHELLA

HOT SCIENCE

The Wedding Planner

The human brain has nearly tripled in size in just 2 million years. The *social brain hypothesis* (Shultz & Dunbar, 2010) suggests that this happened primarily so that people could manage the everyday complexities of living in large social groups. What are those complexities?

Well, just think of what you'd need to know in order to seat people at a wedding. Does Uncle Jacob like Grandma Nora, does Grandma Nora hate Cousin Caleb, and if so, does Uncle Jacob hate Cousin Caleb too? With a guest list of just 150 people there are more than 10,000 of these dyadic relationships to consider—and yet, people who can't balance a checkbook or solve a Sudoku somehow manage to do tasks like this one all the time. Are people social savants?

In a recent study (Mason et al., 2010), researchers sought to answer this question by directly comparing people's abilities to solve social and nonsocial problems. The nonsocial problem involved drawing inferences about metals. Participants were told that there were two basic groups of metals, and that metals in the same group

AMANA IMAGES INC./ALAMY

"attracted" each other, whereas metals in different groups "repelled" each other. Then, over a series of trials, participants were told about the relationships between particular metals and were asked to draw inferences about the missing relationship. For example, participants were told that *gold* and *tin* were both repelled by *platinum*, and they were then asked to infer the relationship between *gold* and *tin*. (The correct answer is "They are attracted to each other.")

The experimenters also gave participants a social version of this problem. Participants were told about two groups of people. People who were in the same group were said to be attracted to each other, whereas people who were in different groups were said to be repelled by each other. Then, over a series of trials, participants learned about the relationships between particular people—for example, they learned that *Goldie* and *Tim* were both repelled by *Patrick*—and were then asked to infer the missing relationship between *Goldie* and *Tim*. (The correct answer is "They are attracted to each other.")

Although the social and nonsocial tasks were logically identical, results showed that participants were considerably faster *and* more accurate when drawing inferences about people than about metals. When the researchers replicated the study inside an MRI machine, they discovered that both tasks activated brain areas known to play a role in deductive reasoning, but that only the social task activated brain regions known to play a role in understanding other minds.

It appears that our ability to think about people outshines our ability to think about most everything else, which is good news for the social brain hypothesis—as well as for wedding planners far and wide.

Stereotyping: Drawing Inferences from Categories

You'll recall from the Language and Thought chapter that categorization is the process by which people identify a stimulus as a member of a class of related stimuli. Once we have identified a novel stimulus as a member of a category ("That's a textbook"), we can then use our knowledge of the category to make educated guesses about the properties of the novel stimulus ("It's probably expensive") and act accordingly ("I think I'll download it illegally").

What we do with textbooks we also do with people. No, not the illegal downloading part. The educated guessing part. **Stereotyping** is *the process by which people draw inferences about others based on their knowledge of the categories to which others belong.* The moment we categorize a person as an adult, a male, a baseball player, and a Russian, we can use our knowledge of those categories to make some educated guesses about him, for example, that he shaves his face but not his legs, that he understands the infield fly rule, and that he knows more about Vladimir Putin than we do. When we offer children candy instead of cigarettes or ask gas station attendants for directions instead of financial advice, we are making inferences about people whom we have never met before based solely on their category membership. As these examples suggest, stereotyping is a very helpful process (Allport, 1954). And yet, ever since the word was coined by the journalist Walter Lippmann in 1936, it has had a distasteful connotation. Why? Because stereotyping

How are stereotypes useful?

AP PHOTO/GINO DOMENICO

Stereotypes can be inaccurate. Shlomo Koenig does not fit most people's stereotype of a police officer or a rabbi, but he is both.

is a helpful process that can often produce harmful results, and it does so because stereotypes tend to have four properties: They are inaccurate, overused, self-perpetuating, and automatic.

Stereotypes Can Be Inaccurate

The inferences we draw about individuals are only as accurate as our stereotypes about the categories to which they belong. Although there was no evidence to indicate that Jews were especially materialistic or that African Americans were especially lazy, American college students held such beliefs for most of the last century (Gilbert, 1951; Karlins, Coffman, & Walters, 1969; Katz & Braly, 1933). They weren't born holding these beliefs, so how did they acquire them? There are only two ways to acquire a belief about anything: to see for yourself or to take somebody else's word for it. In fact, most of what we know about the members of human categories is hearsay—stuff we picked up from hearing other people talk. Many of the people who believe stereotypes about Jews or African Americans have never actually met a member of either group, and their beliefs are a result of listening too closely to what others told them. In the process of inheriting the wisdom of our culture, it is inevitable that we also will inherit its ignorance too.

stereotyping
The process by which people draw inferences about others based on their knowledge of the categories to which others belong.

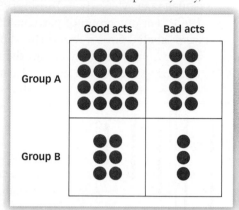

◄ Figure **13.15** **Seeing Correlations That Aren't Really There** Both Group A and Group B each perform two-thirds good acts and one-third bad acts. However, Group B and bad acts are both rare, leading people to notice and remember their co-occurrence, which leads them to perceive a correlation between group membership and behavior that isn't really there.

But even direct observation can produce inaccurate stereotypes. For example, research participants in one study were shown a long series of positive and negative behaviors and were told that each behavior had been performed by a member of one of two groups: Group A or Group B (see **FIGURE 13.15**). The behaviors were carefully arranged so that each group behaved negatively exactly one third of the time. However, there were more positive than negative behaviors in the series, and there were more members of Group A than of Group B. As such, negative behaviors were rarer than positive behaviors, and Group B members were rarer than Group A members. After seeing the behaviors, participants correctly reported that Group A had behaved negatively one third of the time. However, they incorrectly reported that Group B had behaved negatively more than *half* the time (Hamilton & Gifford, 1976).

 Why might we have inaccurate beliefs about groups even after directly observing them?

Why did this happen? Bad behavior was rare and being a member of Group B was rare. Thus, participants were especially likely to notice when the two co-occurred ("Aha! There's one of those unusual Group B people doing an unusually awful thing again"). These findings help explain why members of majority groups tend to overestimate the number of crimes (which are relatively rare events) committed by members of minority groups (who are relatively rare people, hence the word *m-i-n-o-r-i-t-y*). The point here is that even when we directly observe people, we can end up with inaccurate beliefs about the groups to which they belong.

Stereotypes Can Be Overused

Because all thumbtacks are pretty much alike, our stereotypes about thumbtacks (small, cheap, painful when chewed) are quite useful. We will rarely be mistaken if we generalize from one thumbtack to another. But human categories are so variable that our stereotypes may offer only the vaguest of clues about the individuals who populate those categories.

"Great—now I'm gonna be suspicious of every poodle I meet."

self-fulfilling prophecy
The tendency for people to behave as they are expected to behave.

stereotype threat
The fear of confirming the negative beliefs that others may hold.

perceptual confirmation
The tendency for people to see what they expect to see.

subtyping
The tendency for people who receive disconfirming evidence to modify their stereotypes rather than abandon them.

You probably believe that men have greater upper body strength than women do, and this belief is right *on average*. But the upper body strength of individuals *within* each of these categories is so varied that you cannot easily predict how much weight a particular person can lift simply by knowing that person's gender. The inherent variability of human categories makes stereotypes much less useful than they seem.

Alas, we don't always recognize this because the mere act of categorizing a stimulus tends to warp our perceptions of that category's variability. For instance, participants in some studies were shown a series of lines of different lengths (see **FIGURE 13.16**; McGarty & Turner, 1992; Tajfel & Wilkes, 1963). For one group of participants, the longest lines were labeled *Group A* and the shortest lines were labeled *Group B,* as they are on the right side of Figure 13.16. For the second group of participants, the lines

> How does categorization warp perception?

were shown without these category labels, as they are on the left side of Figure 13.16. Interestingly, those participants who saw the category labels *overestimated* the similarity of the lines that shared a label and *underestimated* the similarity of lines that did not.

You've probably experienced this phenomenon yourself. For instance, we all identify colors as members of categories such as *blue* or *green,* and this leads us to overestimate the similarity of colors that share a category label and to underestimate the similarity of colors that do not. That's why we see discrete *bands* of color when we look at rainbows, which are actually a smooth chromatic continuum (see **FIGURE 13.17**).

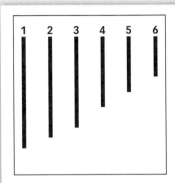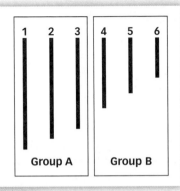

When two cities are in the same country (Memphis and Pierre) people tend to underestimate their distance, but when two cities are in different countries (Memphis and Toronto) they tend to overestimate their distance (Burris & Branscombe, 2005). Indeed, people believe that they are more likely to feel an earthquake that happens 230 miles away when the earthquake happens in their state rather than a neighboring state (Mishra & Mishra, 2010).

What's true of colors and cities is true of people as well. The mere act of categorizing people as Blacks or Whites, Jews or Gentiles, artists or accountants, can cause us to underestimate the variability within those categories ("All artists are wacky") and to overestimate the variability between them ("Artists are much wackier than accountants"). When we underestimate the variability of a human category, we overestimate how useful our stereotypes can be (Park & Hastie, 1987; Rubin, & Badea, 2012).

▲ Figure **13.16 How Categorization Warps Perception** People who see the lines on the right tend to *overestimate the similarity* of lines 1 and 3 and *underestimate the similarity* of lines 3 and 4. Simply labeling lines 1–3 *Group A* and lines 4–6 *Group B* causes the lines within a group to seem more similar to each other than they really are, and the lines in different groups to seem more different from each other than they really are.

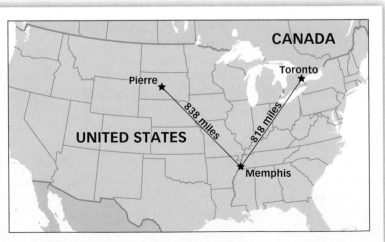

▶ Figure **13.17 Perceiving Categories** Categorization can influence how we see colors and estimate distances.

Stereotypes Can Be Self-Perpetuating

When we meet a truck driver who likes ballet more than football or a senior citizen who likes Jay-Z more than Bach, why don't we simply abandon our stereotypes of these groups? The answer is that stereotypes tend to be self-perpetuating. Like viruses and parasites, once they take up residence inside us, they resist even our most concerted efforts to eradicate them. Here's three reasons why:

> **In what way is a stereotype like a virus?**

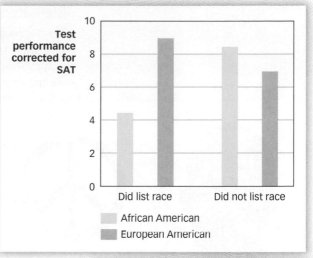

▲ Figure **13.18** **Stereotype Threat** When asked to indicate their race before taking an exam, African American students performed below their academic level (as determined by their SAT scores).

> **Self-fulfilling prophecy** is *the tendency for people to behave as they are expected to behave.* When people know that observers have a negative stereotype about them, they may experience **stereotype threat**, which is *the fear of confirming the negative beliefs that others may hold* (Aronson & Steele, 2004; Schmader, Johns, & Forbes, 2008; Walton & Spencer, 2009). Ironically, this fear may cause them to behave in ways that confirm the very stereotype that threatened them. In one study (Steele & Aronson, 1995), African American and White students took a test, and half the students in each group were asked to list their race at the top of the exam. When students were not asked to list their races they performed at their academic level, but when students were asked to list their races, African American students became anxious about confirming a negative stereotype of their group, which caused them to perform well below their academic level (see **FIGURE 13.18**). Stereotypes perpetuate themselves in part by causing the stereotyped individual to behave in ways that confirm the stereotype.

> Even when people do *not* confirm stereotypes, observers often think they have. **Perceptual confirmation** is *the tendency for people to see what they expect to see* and this tendency helps perpetuate stereotypes. In one study, participants listened to a radio broadcast of a college basketball game and were asked to evaluate the performance of one of the players. Although all participants heard the same prerecorded game, some were led to believe that the player was African American and others were led to believe that the player was White. Participants' stereotypes led them to expect different performances from athletes of different ethnic origins—and the participants perceived just what they expected. Those who believed the player was African American thought he had demonstrated greater athletic ability but less intelligence than did those who thought he was White (Stone, Perry, & Darley, 1997). Stereotypes perpetuate themselves in part by biasing our perception of individuals, leading us to believe that those individuals have confirmed our stereotypes even when they have not (Fiske, 1998).

Many of us think that nuns are traditional and proper. Does this photo of Sister Rosa Elena nailing Sister Amanda de Jesús with a snowball change your stereotype, or are you tempted to subtype them instead?

> So what happens when people clearly *dis*confirm our stereotypes? **Subtyping** is *the tendency for people who receive disconfirming evidence to modify their stereotypes rather than abandon them* (Weber & Crocker, 1983). For example, most of us think of people who work in public relations as sociable. In one study, participants learned about a PR agent who was *slightly* unsociable, and the results showed that their stereotypes about PR agents shifted a bit to accommodate this new information. So far, so good. But when participants learned about a PR agent who was *extremely* unsociable, their stereotypes did not change at all (Kunda & Oleson, 1997). Instead, they decided that extremely unsociable PR agent was "an exception to the rule" which allowed them to keep their stereotypes intact. Subtyping is a powerful method for preserving our stereotypes in the face of contradictory evidence.

Stereotyping Can Be Automatic

If we recognize that stereotypes are inaccurate and self-perpetuating (as you now do), then why don't we just make a firm resolution to stop using them? The answer is that stereotyping happens *unconsciously* (which means that we don't always know we are doing it) and *automatically* (which means that we often cannot avoid doing it even when we try; Banaji & Heiphetz, 2010; Greenwald, McGhee, & Schwartz, 1998; Greenwald & Nosek, 2001).

For example, in one study, participants played a video game in which photos of Black or White men holding either guns or cameras were flashed on the screen for less than 1 second each. Participants earned money by shooting men with guns and lost money by shooting men with cameras. The results showed that participants made two kinds of mistakes: They tended to shoot Black men holding cameras and tended not to shoot White men holding guns (Correll et al., 2002). Although the photos appeared on the screen so quickly that participants did not have enough time to consciously consider their stereotypes, those stereotypes worked unconsciously, causing them to mistake a camera for a gun when it was in the hands of a Black man and a gun for a camera when it was in the hands of a White man. Sadly, Black participants were just as likely to make this pattern of errors as were White participants. Why did this happen?

> **Can we decide not to stereotype?**

Stereotypes comprise all the information about human categories that we have absorbed over the years from friends and uncles, books and blogs, jokes and movies and late-night television. When we see Black men holding guns in rap videos, our minds associate these two things, and although we realize that we are watching art and not real life, the association is made and remembered. Later, we can't *decide* not to be influenced by that association any more than we can *decide* not to be influenced by our second-grade teacher or the smell of French fries.

In fact, some research suggests that trying not to use our stereotypes can make matters worse instead of better. Participants in one study were shown a photograph of a tough-looking male "skinhead" and were asked to write an essay describing a typical day in his life. Some of the participants were told that they should not allow their stereotypes about skinheads to influence their essays, and others were given no such instructions. Next, the experimenter brought each participant to a room with eight empty chairs. The first chair had a jacket draped over it, and the experimenter explained that it belonged to a skinhead, who had gone to use the restroom. Where did participants choose to sit? Participants who had earlier been told not to use their stereotypes sat farther away from the jacket than did participants who had been given no instructions (Macrae et al., 1994). As you know from reading the Consciousness chapter, thought suppression is ironic business that often causes us to do the very thing we were trying to avoid doing (Wegner et al., 1987).

Although stereotyping is unconscious and automatic, it is not inevitable (Blair, 2002; Kawakami et al., 2000; Milne & Grafman, 2001; Rudman, Ashmore, & Gary, 2001). For

Research using the Implicit Association Test shows that 70% of White Americans find it easier to associate White faces with positive concepts such as "peace," and Black faces with negative concepts such as "bomb," than the other way around. Surprisingly, 40% of African Americans show this same pattern.

In 2007, Reuters news photographer Namir Noor-Eldeen was shot to death in Iraq by American soldiers in a helicopter who mistook his camera for a weapon. Would they have made the same mistake if Noor-Eldeen had been blonde or female?

instance, police officers who receive special training before playing the camera or gun video game described earlier do not show the same biases that ordinary people do (Correll et al., 2007). Like ordinary people, they take a few milliseconds longer to decide not to shoot a Black man than a White man, indicating that their stereotypes are unconsciously and automatically influencing their thinking. But unlike ordinary people, they don't actually *shoot* Black men more often than White men, indicating that they have learned how to keep those stereotypes from influencing their behavior. Other studies show that even simple games and exercises can reduce the automatic influence of stereotypes (Phills et al., 2011; Todd et al., 2011).

Attribution: Drawing Inferences from Actions

In 1963, Dr. Martin Luther King Jr. gave a speech in which he described his vision for America: "I have a dream that my four children will one day live in a nation where they will not be judged by the color of their skin but by the content of their character." Research on stereotyping demonstrates that Dr. King's concerns are still well justified. We do indeed judge others by the color of their skin—as well as by their gender, nationality, religion, age, and occupation—and in so doing, we sometimes make mistakes. But are we any better at judging people by the content of their character? If we could somehow turn off our stereotypes and treat each person as an individual, would we judge these individuals accurately?

Not necessarily. Treating a person as an individual means judging them by their own words and deeds. This is more difficult than it sounds because the relationship between what a person *is* and what a person *says or does* is not always straightforward.

> **When does a person's behavior tell us something about them?**

An honest person may lie to save a friend from embarrassment, and a dishonest person may tell the truth to bolster her credibility. Happy people have some weepy moments, polite people can be rude in traffic, and people who despise us can be flattering when they need a favor. In short, people's behavior sometimes tells us about the kinds of people they are, but sometimes it simply tells us about the kinds of situations they happen to be in.

To understand people, we need to know not only *what* they did but also *why* they did it. Is the batter who hit the home run a talented slugger, or was the wind blowing in just the right direction at just the right time? Is the politician who gave the pro-life speech really opposed to abortion, or was she just trying to win the conservative vote? When we answer questions such as these, we are making **attributions**, which are *inferences about the causes of people's behaviors* (Epley & Waytz, 2010; Gilbert, 1998). We make *situational attributions* when we decide that a person's behavior was caused by some temporary aspect of the situation in which it happened ("He was lucky that the wind carried the ball into the stands"), and we make *dispositional attributions* when we decide that a person's behavior was caused by a relatively enduring tendency to think, feel, or act in a particular way ("He's got a great eye and a powerful swing").

How do we know whether to make a dispositional or a situational attribution? According to the *covariation model* (Kelley, 1967), we must consider the consistency, consensuality, and distinctiveness of the action. For example, why is the man in photo **FIGURE 13.19** wearing a cheese-shaped hat? Does he have a goofy personality (*dispositional attribution*) or is he just a regular guy who is on his way to a Wisconsin football game (*situational attribution*)? According to the covariation model, you can answer this question by asking whether his behavior is *consistent* (does he usually wear this hat?), *consensual* (are other people wearing this hat?), and *distinctive* (does he do other goofy things?). If it turns out that he wears this hat every day (*high consistency*), and if

S. GROSS

"For God's sake, think! Why is he being so nice to you?"

attribution
An inference about the cause of a person's behavior.

Low Consistency + High Consensus + High Distinctiveness = **Situational Attribution**

Consistency Does the person perform this action regularly?	**Consensus** Do most people perform this action?	**Distinctiveness** Does the person perform similar actions?

High Consistency + Low Consensus + Low Distinctiveness = **Dispositional Attribution**

AL MESSERSCHMIDT/GETTY IMAGES

► Figure **13.19** **The Covariation Model of Attribution** The covariation model tells us whether to make a dispositional or situational attribution for a person's action.

today no one else is wearing a cheese hat (*low consensus*), and if he tends to do other goofy things, such as wear clown shoes and say "honk, honk" to passersby (*low distinctiveness*), then you should probably make a dispositional attribution ("He's a certified goofball"). On the other hand, if he rarely wears this hat (*low consistency*), if today lots of other people are wearing cheese hats (*high consensus*), and if he doesn't tend to do other goofy things (*high distinctiveness*), then you should probably make a situational attribution ("He's a Packers fan on game day"). As Figure 13.19 shows, patterns of consistency, consensus, and distinctiveness provide useful information about the cause of a person's behavior.

As sensible as this seems, research suggests that people don't always use this information as they should. The **correspondence bias** is *the tendency to make a dispositional attribution when we should instead make a situational attribution* (Gilbert & Malone, 1995; Jones & Harris, 1967; Ross, 1977). This bias is so common and so basic that it is often called the *fundamental attribution error*. For example, volunteers in one experiment played a trivia game in which one participant acted as the quizmaster and made up a list of unusual questions, another participant acted as the contestant and tried to answer those questions, and a third participant acted as the observer and simply

Why do we tend to make dispositional attributions?

In 2011, presidential candidate Herman Cain said, "Don't blame Wall Street, don't blame the big banks. If you don't have a job and you are not rich, blame yourself!" Research on the correspondence bias suggests that it is easy to blame people's outcomes on their dispositions, such as stupidity and laziness, and difficult to consider the ways in which they might be victims of their situations.

©JASON MOORE/ZUMA PRESS, INC./ALAMY

watched the game. The quizmasters tended to ask tricky questions based on their own idiosyncratic knowledge, and contestants were generally unable to answer them. After watching the game, the observers were asked to decide how knowledgeable the quizmaster and the contestant were. Although the quizmasters had asked good questions and the contestants had given bad answers, it should have been clear to the observers that all this asking and answering was a product of the roles they had been assigned to play and that the contestant would have asked equally good questions and the quizmaster would have given equally bad answers had their roles been reversed. And yet observers tended to rate the quizmaster as more knowledgeable than the contestant (Ross, Amabile, & Steinmetz, 1977) and were more likely to choose the quizmaster as their own partner in an upcoming game (Quattrone, 1982). Even when we know that a successful athlete had a home field advantage or that a successful entrepreneur had family connections, we tend to attribute their success to talent and tenacity.

What causes the correspondence bias? First, the situational causes of behavior are often invisible (Ichheiser, 1949). For example, professors tend to assume that fawning students really do admire them in spite of the strong incentive for students to kiss up to those who control their grades. The problem is that professors can literally *see* students laughing at witless jokes and applauding after boring lectures, but they cannot *see* "control over grades." Situations are not as tangible or visible as behaviors, so it

The Kennedy brothers (Senator Robert, Senator Ted, and President John) and the Bush brothers (Governor Jeb and President George) were very successful men. Was their success due to the content of their characters, or to the money and fame that came with their family names?

is all too easy to ignore them (Taylor & Fiske, 1978). Second, situational attributions tend to be more complex than dispositional attributions and require more time and attention. When participants in one study were asked to make attributions while performing a mentally taxing task (namely, keeping a seven-digit number in mind), they had no difficulty making dispositional attributions, but they found it quite difficult to make situational attributions (Gilbert, Pelham, & Krull, 1988; Winter & Uleman, 1984). In short, information about situations is hard to get and hard to use, so we tend to believe that other peoples' actions are caused by their dispositions even when there is a perfectly reasonable situational explanation.

The correspondence bias is stronger in some cultures than others (Choi, Nisbett, & Norenzayan, 1999), among some people than others (D'Agostino & Fincher-Kiefer, 1992; Li et al., 2012), and under some circumstances than others. For example, we seem to be more prone to correspondence bias when judging other people's behavior than when judging our own. The **actor–observer effect** is *the tendency to make situational attributions for our own behaviors while making dispositional attributions for the identical behavior of others* (Jones & Nisbett, 1972). When college students are asked to explain why they and their friends chose their majors, they tend to explain their own choices in terms of situations ("I chose economics because my parents told me I have to support myself as soon as I'm done with college") and their friends' choices in terms of dispositions ("Leah chose economics because she's materialistic") (Nisbett et al., 1973). The actor–observer effect occurs because people typically have more information about the situations that caused their own behavior than about the situations that caused other people's behavior. We can remember getting the please-major-in-something-practical lecture from our parents, but we weren't at Leah's house to see her get the same lecture. As observers, we are naturally focused on another person's behavior, but as actors, we are quite literally focused on the situations in which our behavior occurs. Indeed, when people are shown videotapes of their conversations that allow them to see themselves from their partner's point of view, they tend to make dispositional attributions for their own behavior and situational attributions for their partner's (Storms, 1973; Taylor & Fiske, 1975).

IN SUMMARY

▶ People make inferences about others based on the categories to which they belong (stereotyping). This method can lead them to misjudge others because stereotypes can be inaccurate, overused, self-perpetuating, unconscious, and automatic.

▶ People make inferences about others based on their behaviors. This method can lead them to misjudge others because people tend to attribute actions to dispositions even when they should attribute them to situations.

correspondence bias
The tendency to make a dispositional attribution even when we should instead make a situational attribution.

actor–observer effect
The tendency to make situational attributions for our own behaviors while making dispositional attributions for the identical behavior of others.

Chapter Review

KEY CONCEPT QUIZ

1. _____ describes the use of force to acquire scarce resources.
   a. Aggression
   b. Frustration
   c. Goal setting
   d. Sociality

2. Someone who hacks into your computer, steals your personal information, and uses it to purchase goods and services in your name is acting on the principle of
   a. aggression.
   b. social cognition.
   c. negative affect.
   d. frustration–aggression.

3. Why are acts of aggression—from violent crime to athletic brawls—more likely to occur on hot days when people are feeling irritated and uncomfortable?
   a. frustration
   b. negative affect
   c. resource scarcity
   d. biology and culture interaction

4. What is the single best predictor of aggression?
   a. temperament
   b. age
   c. gender
   d. status

5. The prisoner's dilemma game illustrates
   a. the hypothesis-confirming bias.
   b. the diffusion of responsibility.
   c. group polarization.
   d. the benefits and costs of cooperation.

6. Which of the following is NOT a downside of being in a group?
   a. Groups are positively prejudiced toward other members and tend to discriminate in their favor.
   b. Groups often show prejudice and discrimination toward nonmembers.
   c. Groups sometimes make poor decisions.
   d. Groups may take extreme actions an individual member would not take alone.

7. Which of the following BEST describes reciprocal altruism?
   a. people becoming less concerned with personal values through immersion in a group
   b. anxiety, loneliness, and depression being caused by exclusion from a group
   c. cooperation extended over long periods of time
   d. the evolutionary process by which individuals cooperate with their relatives

8. Which of the following is NOT an explanation for increased selectivity by women in choosing a mate?
   a. Sex is potentially more costly for women than for men.
   b. Communal styles of child-rearing argue for increased selectivity.
   c. The reputational costs of sex are historically much higher for women than for men.
   d. Pregnancy increases women's nutritional requirements and puts them at risk of illness and death.

9. In terms of attraction, which of the following is a situational factor?
   a. proximity
   b. similarity
   c. appearance
   d. personality

10. Currently, the probability of marrying by age 40 is approximately _____ for American men and _____ for American women.
    a. 50%; 50%
    b. 90%; 10%
    c. 80%; 85%
    d. 10%; 90%

11. The hypothesis that people remain in relationships only as long as they perceive a favorable ratio of costs to benefits is referred to as
    a. companionate love.
    b. the exposure effect.
    c. social exchange.
    d. equity.

12. The _____ motive describes how people are motivated to experience pleasure and to avoid experiencing pain.
    a. emotional
    b. accuracy
    c. approval
    d. hedonic

13. The tendency to do what authorities tell us to do is known as
    a. persuasion.
    b. obedience.
    c. conformity.
    d. the self-fulfilling prophecy.

14. What is the process by which people come to understand others?
    a. dispositional attribution
    b. the accuracy motive
    c. social cognition
    d. cognitive dissonance

15. The tendency to make a dispositional attribution even when a person's behavior was caused by the situation is referred to as
    a. comparison leveling.
    b. stereotyping.
    c. covariation.
    d. correspondence bias.

KEY TERMS

social psychology (p. 508)

aggression (p. 508)

frustration–aggression hypothesis (p. 509)

cooperation (p. 512)

group (p. 513)

prejudice (p. 513)

discrimination (p. 513)

common knowledge effect (p. 514)

group polarization (p. 514)

groupthink (p. 514)

deindividuation (p. 514)

diffusion of responsibility (p. 514)

social loafing (p. 514)

bystander intervention (p. 515)

altruism (p. 516)

kin selection (p. 516)

reciprocal altruism (p. 517)

mere exposure effect (p. 519)

passionate love (p. 524)

companionate love (p. 524)

social exchange (p. 525)

comparison level (p. 525)

equity (p. 525)

social influence (p. 526)

norms (p. 528)

norm of reciprocity (p. 528)

normative influence (p. 529)

door-in-the-face technique (p. 529)

conformity (p. 529)

obedience (p. 530)

attitude (p. 533)

belief (p. 533)

informational influence (p. 533)

persuasion (p. 534)

systematic persuasion (p. 534)

heuristic persuasion (p. 534)

foot-in-the-door technique (p. 535)

cognitive dissonance (p. 536)

social cognition (p. 537)

stereotyping (p. 538)

self-fulfilling prophecy (p. 541)

stereotype threat (p. 541)

perceptual confirmation (p. 541)

subtyping (p. 541)

attribution (p. 543)

correspondence bias (p. 544)

actor–observer effect (p. 545)

CHANGING MINDS

1. One of the senators from your state is supporting a bill that would impose heavy fines on aggressive drivers who run red lights. One of your classmates thinks this is a good idea. "The textbook taught us a lot about punishment and reward. It's simple. If we punish aggressive driving, its frequency will decline." Is your classmate right? Might the new law backfire? Might another policy be more effective in promoting safe driving?

2. One of your friends is outgoing, funny, and a star athlete on the women's basketball team. She has started to date a man who is introverted and prefers playing computer games to attending parties. You tease her about the contrast in personalities, and she replies, "Well, opposites attract." Is she right?

3. In late 2011, a federal judge ruled that the New York City Fire Department had long pursued discriminatory hiring practices, resulting in systematic exclusion of minorities from the force, which at the time included almost 97% Whites although the city's population is about 25% Black. Your friend reads about the case and scoffs. "People are always so quick to claim racism. Sure, there are still a few racist people out there, but if you do surveys and ask people what they think about people of other races, they say they are fine with them." What would you tell your friend?

4. One of your friends has a very unique fashion sense and always wears clothes that are just a little bit different from what everyone else is wearing, for example, a neon orange track suit with a battered fedora.

Most of the time, you appreciate your friend for his quirky personality. One day he tells you that he chooses his clothes carefully to make a fashion statement. "Most people follow the crowd," he announces. "I don't. I'm an individual, and I make my own choices, without influence from anyone else." Could he be right? What examples might you provide for or against your friend's claim?

5. A classmate is shaken after learning about the Milgram (1963) study, in which participants were willing to obey orders to administer painful electric shocks to another human, even after he begged them to stop. Worse, the Burger (2009) study shows that it wasn't just participants "back then" who were capable of this behavior: Modern participants do the same thing. "Some people are just sheep!" she says. "I know that you and I wouldn't behave like that." Is she right? What evidence would you give her to support or oppose her claim?

6. When your family gathers for Thanksgiving, your cousin Wendy brings her fiancée, Amanda. It's the first time Amanda has met the whole family, and she seems nervous. She talks too much, laughs too loud, and rubs everyone the wrong way. Later, when you're alone with your mother, she rolls her eyes. "It's hard to imagine Wendy wanting to spend the rest of her life married to someone that annoying." You decide to be more generous, because you think your mother might have fallen prey to the correspondence bias. How could you change your mother's mind?

ANSWERS TO KEY CONCEPT QUIZ

1. a; 2. d; 3. b; 4. c; 5. d; 6. a; 7. c; 8. b; 9. a; 10. c; 11. c; 12. d; 13. b; 14. c; 15. d.

Need more help? Additional resources are located in LaunchPad at:
http://www.worthpublishers.com/launchpad/schacter3e

14

Stress and Health

"HAVE A KNIFE TO YOUR NECK. Don't make a sound. Get out of bed and come with me or I will kill you and your family." These are the words that awoke 14-year-old Elizabeth Smart in the middle of the night of June 5, 2002 while sleeping in her bedroom next to her 9-year-old sister Mary Katherine. Fearing for her life, and that of her family, she kept quiet and left with her abductor. Her little sister, terrified, hid in her bedroom for several hours before waking the girls' parents, who awoke to their daughter saying: "She's gone. Elizabeth is gone." Elizabeth was kidnapped by Brian David Mitchell, a man Elizabeth's parents had hired previously to do some roof work on their home. Mitchell broke into the family's home in Salt Lake City through an open window, abducted Elizabeth, and he and his wife Wanda Ileen Barzee held her in captivity for nine months, during which time Mitchell repeatedly raped her and threatened to kill her and her entire family. Mitchell, Barzee, and Smart were spotted walking down the street by a couple who recognized them from a recent airing of the television show *America's Most Wanted* and called the police. Mitchell and Barzee were apprehended and Elizabeth was returned to her family.

Elizabeth suffered unimaginable circumstances for a prolonged period of time in what can be thought of as one of the most stressful situations possible, especially for a 14-year-old girl. So what became of Elizabeth? Fortunately, she is now safe and sound, happily married, and working as an activist and commentator for ABC News. She endured life-threatening stressors for months, and those experiences undoubtedly affected her in ways that will last her entire lifetime. At the same time, hers is a story of resilience. Despite the very difficult hand she was dealt, she appears to have bounced back and to be leading a happy, productive, and rewarding life. Hers is a story of both stress and health.

This smiling young face is that of Elizabeth Smart, who, between the times of these two photographs, was kidnapped, raped, and tortured for nearly a year. Stressful life events often affect us in ways that cannot be seen from the outside. Fortunately, there are things that we can do in response to even the most stressful of life events that can get us smiling again.

stressors
Specific events or chronic pressures that place demands on a person or threaten the person's well-being.

stress
The physical and psychological response to internal or external stressors.

health psychology
The subfield of psychology concerned with ways psychological factors influence the causes and treatment of physical illness and the maintenance of health.

chronic stressors
Sources of stress that occur continuously or repeatedly.

FORTUNATELY, VERY FEW OF US WILL EVER HAVE TO ENDURE the type of stress that Elizabeth Smart lived through. But life can present a welter of frights, bothers, and looming disasters that can be quite difficult to manage. A reckless driver may nearly run you over; you may be discriminated against, threatened, or intimidated in some way; or a fire may leave you out on the street. Life has its **stressors**, *specific events or chronic pressures that place demands on a person or threaten the person's well-being*. Although such stressors rarely involve threats of death, they do have both immediate and cumulative effects that can influence health.

In this chapter, we'll look at what psychologists and physicians have learned about the kinds of life events that produce **stress**, *the physical and psychological response to internal or external stressors;* typical responses to such stressors; and ways to manage stress. Stress has such a profound influence on health that we consider stress and health together in this chapter. And because sickness and health are not merely features of the physical body, we then consider the more general topic of **health psychology**, *the subfield of psychology concerned with ways psychological factors influence the causes and treatment of physical illness and the maintenance of health*. You will see how perceptions of illness can affect its course and how health-promoting behaviors can improve the quality of people's lives.

Sources of Stress: What Gets to You

First of all, what are the sources of stress? A natural catastrophe, such as a hurricane, earthquake, or volcanic eruption, is an obvious source. But, for most of us, stressors are personal events that affect the comfortable pattern of our lives and little annoyances that bug us day after day. Let's look at the life events that can cause stress, chronic sources of stress, and the relationship between lack of perceived control and the impact of stressors.

Stressful Events

Weddings are positive events, but they also can be stressful due to the often overwhelming amount of planning and decision making involved (and occasionally because of the difficulties managing the interactions of friends and family).

People often seem to get sick after major life events. In pioneering work, Thomas Holmes and Richard Rahe (1967) followed up on this observation, proposing that major life changes cause stress and that increased stress causes illness. To test their idea, they asked people to rate the magnitude of readjustment required by each of many events found to be associated with the onset of illness (Rahe et al., 1964).

The resulting list of life events is remarkably predictive: Simply adding up the stress ratings of each life change experienced is a significant indicator of a person's likelihood of future illness (Miller, 1996). Someone who becomes divorced, loses a job, and has a friend die all in the same year, for example, is more likely to get sick than someone who escapes the year with only a divorce.

A version of this list adapted for the life events of college students (and sporting the snappy acronym CUSS, for College Undergraduate Stress Scale) is shown in **TABLE 14.1**. To assess your stressful events, check off any events that have happened to you in the past year and sum your point total. In a large sample of students in an introductory psychology class, the average was 1,247 points, ranging from 182 to 2,571 (Renner & Mackin, 1998).

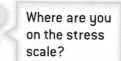

Where are you on the stress scale?

Looking at the list, you may wonder why positive events are included. Stressful life events are unpleasant, right? Why would getting married be stressful? Isn't a wedding supposed to be fun? Research has shown that compared with negative events, positive events produce less psychological

> Table 14.1

College Undergraduate Stress Scale

Event	Stress Rating	Event	Stress Rating
Being raped	100	Lack of sleep	69
Finding out that you are HIV positive	100	Change in housing situation (hassles, moves)	69
Being accused of rape	98	Competing or performing in public	69
Death of a close friend	97	Getting in a physical fight	66
Death of a close family member	96	Difficulties with a roommate	66
Contracting a sexually transmitted disease (other than AIDS)	94	Job changes (applying, new job, work hassles)	65
Concerns about being pregnant	91	Declaring a major or concerns about future plans	65
Finals week	90	A class you hate	62
Concerns about your partner being pregnant	90	Drinking or use of drugs	61
Oversleeping for an exam	89	Confrontations with professors	60
Flunking a class	89	Starting a new semester	58
Having a boyfriend or girlfriend cheat on you	85	Going on a first date	57
Ending a steady dating relationship	85	Registration	55
Serious illness in a close friend or family member	85	Maintaining a steady dating relationship	55
Financial difficulties	84	Commuting to campus or work or both	54
Writing a major term paper	83	Peer pressures	53
Being caught cheating on a test	83	Being away from home for the first time	53
Drunk driving	82	Getting sick	52
Sense of overload in school or work	82	Concerns about your appearance	52
Two exams in one day	80	Getting straight A's	51
Cheating on your boyfriend or girlfriend	77	A difficult class that you love	48
Getting married	76	Making new friends; getting along with friends	47
Negative consequences of drinking or drug use	75	Fraternity or sorority rush	47
Depression or crisis in your best friend	73	Falling asleep in class	40
Difficulties with parents	73	Attending an athletic event	20
Talking in front of class	72		

Note: To compute your personal life change score, sum the stress ratings for all events that have happened to you in the last year.
Source: Renner & Mackin (1998).

distress and fewer physical symptoms (McFarlane et al., 1980), and that happiness can sometimes even counteract the effects of negative events (Fredrickson, 2000). However, positive events often require readjustment and preparedness that many people find extremely stressful (e.g., Brown & McGill, 1989), so these events are included in computing life-change scores.

Chronic Stressors

Life would be simpler if an occasional stressful event such as a wedding or a lost job were the only pressures we faced. At least each event would be limited in scope, with a beginning, a middle, and, ideally, an end. But unfortunately, life brings with it continued exposure to **chronic stressors,** *sources of stress that occur continuously or repeatedly*. Strained relationships, discrimination, bullying, overwork, money troubles—small stressors that may be easy to ignore if they happen only occasionally—can accumulate to produce distress and illness. People who report being affected by

City life can be fun, but the higher levels of noise, crowding, and violence can also be sources of chronic stress.

daily hassles also report more psychological symptoms (LaPierre et al., 2012) and physical symptoms (Piazza et al., 2013), and these effects often have a greater and longer-lasting impact than major life events.

Many chronic stressors are linked to social relationships. For instance, as described in the Social Psychology chapter, people often form different social groups based on race, culture, interests, popularity, and so on. Being outside the in-group can be stressful. Being actively targeted by members of the in-group can be even more stressful, especially if this happens repeatedly over time (see Hot Science Box). Chronic stressors also can be linked to particular environments. For example, features of city life—noise, traffic, crowding, pollution, and even the threat of violence—provide particularly insistent sources of chronic stress (Evans, 2006). Rural areas have their own chronic stressors, of course, especially isolation and lack of access to amenities such as health care. The realization that chronic stressors are linked to environments has spawned the subfield of *environmental psychology*, the scientific study of environmental effects on behavior and health.

What are some examples of environmental factors that cause chronic stress?

In one study of the influence of noise on children, environmental psychologists looked at the impact of attending schools under the flight path to Heathrow Airport in London, England. Did the noise of more than 1,250 jets flying overhead each day have an influence beyond making kids yell to be heard? Compared with children from

HOT SCIENCE

Can Discrimination Cause Stress and Illness?

Have you ever been discriminated against because of your race, gender, sexual orientation, or some other characteristic? If so, then you know that this can be a pretty stressful experience. Discrimination that occurs repeatedly over time can be an especially powerful stressor for anyone. But what exactly does it *do* to people?

Recent research has shown that there are a number of ways that discrimination can lead to elevated stress and negative health outcomes. People from socially disadvantaged groups who experience higher levels of stress as a result of discrimination engage more frequently in maladaptive behaviors (e.g., drinking, smoking and overeating) in efforts to cope with stress. They also can experience difficulties in their interactions with healthcare professionals (e.g., clinician biases, patient suspiciousness about treatment; Major, Mendes & Dovidio, 2013). Taken together, these factors may help to explain why members of

socially disadvantaged groups have significantly higher rates of health problems than do members of socially advantaged groups (Penner et al., 2010).

New studies are revealing how discrimination can literally "get under the skin" to cause negative health outcomes. One recent study by Wendy Mendes and colleagues (Jamieson, Koslov, et al., 2013) exposed Black and White participants to social rejection by either a person of the same race or a different race to test whether there is something particularly harmful about discrimination, versus social rejection in general. To test this, they had research participants deliver a speech to two confederates in different rooms via a video chat program, after which the confederates provided negative feedback about the participant's speech. The confederates were not seen by the participant, but were represented by computer avatars that either matched the participant's race or did not. Interestingly, although the nature

of the rejection was the same in all cases, participants responded very differently if the people rejecting them were from a different race than the same race. Specifically, whereas being rejected by people from your own race was associated with greater displays of shame and physiological changes associated with an avoidance state (increased cortisol), being rejected by members of a different race was associated with displays of anger, greater vigilance for danger, physiological changes associated with an approach state (i.e., higher cardiac output and lower vascular resistance), and higher risk taking.

Studies like this one help to explain some of the health disparities that currently exist across different social groups. The results suggest that discrimination can lead to physiological, cognitive, and behavioral changes that in the short term prepare a person for action, but in the long-term could lead to negative health outcomes.

matched control schools in low-noise areas, children going to school in the flight path reported higher levels of noise annoyance and showed poorer reading comprehension (Haines et al., 2001). Next time you fly into an airport, please try to do so more quietly for the children.

Perceived Control over Stressful Events

What do catastrophes, stressful life changes, and daily hassles have in common? Right off the bat, of course, their threat to the person or the status quo is easy to see. Stressors challenge you to *do something*—to take some action to eliminate or overcome the stressor.

Paradoxically, events are most stressful when there is *nothing to do*—no way to deal with the challenge. Expecting that you will have control over what happens to you is associated with effectiveness in dealing with stress. Researchers David Glass and Jerome Singer (1972), in classic studies of *perceived control*, looked at the aftereffects of loud noise on people who could or could not control it. Participants were asked to solve puzzles and proofread in a quiet room or in a room filled with loud noise. Glass and Singer found that bursts of such noise hurt people's performance on the tasks

> **What makes events most stressful?**

after the noise was over. However, this dramatic decline in performance was prevented among participants who were told during the noise period that they could stop the noise just by pushing a button. They didn't actually take this option, but access to the "panic button" shielded them from the detrimental effects of the noise.

Subsequent studies have found that a lack of perceived control underlies other stressors too. The stressful effects of crowding, for example, appear to stem from the feeling that you can't control getting away from the crowded conditions (Evans & Stecker, 2004). Being jammed into a crowded dormitory room may be easier to handle, after all, the moment you realize you could take a walk and get away from it all.

Some stressful life events, like those associated with drunk driving, are within our power to control. We gain control when we give away the car keys to a designated driver.

IN SUMMARY

▶ Stressors are events and threats that place specific demands on a person or threaten well-being.

▶ Sources of stress include major life events (even happy ones), catastrophic events, and chronic hassles, some of which can be traced to a particular environment.

▶ Events are most stressful when we perceive that there is no way to control or deal with the challenge.

Stress Reactions: All Shook Up

It was a regular Tuesday morning in New York City. College students were sitting in their morning classes. People were arriving at work and the streets were beginning to fill with shoppers and tourists. Then, at 8:46 a.m., American Airlines Flight 11 crashed into the North Tower of the World Trade Center. People watched in horror. How could this have happened? This seemed like a terrible accident. Then at 9:03 a.m., United Airlines Flight 175 crashed into the South Tower of the World Trade Center. There were then reports of a plane crashing into the Pentagon. And another somewhere in Pennsylvania. America was under attack, and no one knew what would

The threat of death or injury, such as that experienced by many in New York City at the time of the September 11 attacks, can cause significant and lasting physical and psychological stress reactions.

happen next on this terrifying morning of September 11, 2001. The terrorist attacks on the World Trade Center were an enormous stressor that had a lasting impact on many people, physically and psychologically. People living in close proximity to the World Trade Center (within 1.5 miles) during 9/11 were found to have less gray matter in the amygdala, hippocampus, insula, anterior cingulate, and medial prefrontal cortex relative to those living more than 200 miles away during the attacks, suggesting that the stress associated with the attacks may have reduced the size of these parts of the brain that play an important role in emotion, memory, and decision making (Ganzel et al., 2008). Children who watched more television coverage of 9/11 had higher symptoms of posttraumatic stress disorder than children who watched less coverage (Otto et al., 2007). People around the country who had a stronger acute stress response to the events of 9/11 had a 53% increased incidence of heart problems over the next 3 years (Holman et al., 2008). Stress can produce changes in every system of the body and mind, stimulating both physical reactions and psychological reactions. Let's consider each in turn.

Physical Reactions

Walter Cannon (1929) coined a phrase to describe the body's response to any threatening stimulus: the **fight-or-flight response**, *an emotional and physiological reaction to an emergency that increases readiness for action.* The mind asks, "Should I stay and battle this somehow, or should I run like mad?" And the body prepares to react. If you're a cat at this time, your hair stands on end. If you're a human, your hair stands on end, too, but not as visibly. Cannon recognized this common response across species and suspected that it might be the body's first mobilization to any threat.

Research conducted since Cannon's discovery has revealed what is happening in the brain and body during this reaction. Brain activation in response to threat occurs in the hypothalamus, stimulating the nearby pituitary gland, which in turn releases a hormone known as ACTH (short for adrenocorticotropic hormone). ACTH travels through the bloodstream and stimulates the adrenal glands atop the kidneys (see **FIGURE 14.1**). In this cascading response of the HPA (hypothalamic– pituitary–adrenocortical) axis, the adrenal glands are stimulated to release hormones, including the *catecholamines* (epinephrine and norepinephrine), which increase sympathetic nervous system activation (and therefore increase heart rate, blood pressure, and respiration rate) and decrease parasympathetic activation (see the Neuroscience and Behavior chapter). The increased respiration and blood pressure make more oxygen available to the muscles to energize attack or to initiate escape. The adrenal glands also release *cortisol*, a hormone that increases the concentration of glucose in the blood to make fuel available to the muscles. Everything is prepared for a full-tilt response to the threat.

> **How does the body react to a fight-or-flight situation?**

▼ Figure **14.1** **HPA Axis** Just a few seconds after a fearful stimulus is perceived, the hypothalamus activates the pituitary gland to release adrenocorticotropic hormone (ACTH). The ACTH then travels through the bloodstream to activate the adrenal glands to release catecholamines and cortisol, which energize the fight-or-flight response.

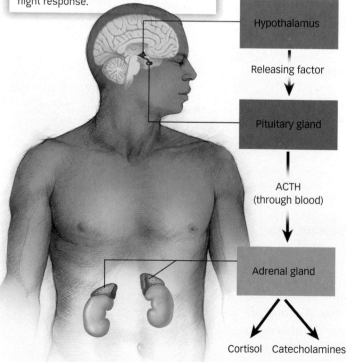

Hypothalamus

Releasing factor

Pituitary gland

ACTH (through blood)

Adrenal gland

Cortisol   Catecholamines

General Adaptation Syndrome

What might have happened if the terrorist attacks of 9/11 were spaced out over a period of days or weeks? Starting in the 1930s, Hans Selye, a Canadian physician, undertook a variety of experiments that looked at the physiological consequences of severe threats to well-being. He subjected rats to heat, cold, infection, trauma, hemorrhage, and other pro-longed stressors, making few friends among the rats or their sympathizers, but learning a lot about stress. His stressed-out rats developed physiological responses that included an enlarged adrenal cortex, shrinking of the lymph glands, and ulceration of the stomach. Noting that many different kinds of stressors caused similar patterns of physiological change, he called the reaction the **general adaptation syndrome (GAS)**, which he defined as a *three-stage physiological stress response that appears regardless of the stressor that is encountered*. The GAS is *nonspecific*; that is, the response doesn't vary, no matter what the source of the repeated stress.

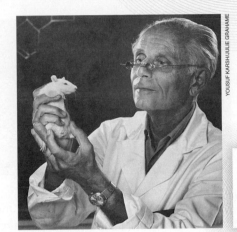

Hans Selye with rat. Given all the stress Selye put rats under, this one looks surprisingly calm.

What are the three phases of GAS?

None of this is very good news. Although Friedrich Nietzsche once said, "What does not kill me makes me stronger," Selye found that severe stress takes a toll on the body. He saw the GAS as occurring in three phases (see **FIGURE 14.2**):

> First comes the *alarm phase*, in which the body rapidly mobilizes its resources to respond to the threat. Energy is required, and the body calls on its stored fat and muscle. The alarm phase is equivalent to Cannon's fight-or-flight response.

> Next, in the *resistance phase*, the body adapts to its high state of arousal as it tries to cope with the stressor. Continuing to draw on resources of fat and muscle, it shuts down unnecessary processes: digestion, growth, and sex drive stall; menstruation stops; production of testosterone and sperm decreases. The body is being taxed to generate resistance, and all the fun stuff is put on hold.

> If the GAS continues long enough, the *exhaustion phase* sets in. The body's resistance collapses. Many of the resistance-phase defenses create gradual damage as they operate, leading to costs for the body that can include susceptibility to infection, tumor growth, aging, irreversible organ damage, or death.

▲ Figure **14.2 Selye's Three Phases of Stress Response** In Selye's theory, resistance to stress builds over time, but then can only last so long before exhaustion sets in.

Stress Effects on Health and Aging

Right now, you are (we hope!) enjoying years of healthy living. Unfortunately, as people age, the body slowly begins to break down (just ask any of the authors of this book). Interestingly, recent research has revealed that stress significantly accelerates the aging process. Elizabeth Smart's parents noted that, upon being reunited with her after 9 months of separation, they almost did not recognize her because she appeared to have aged so much (Smart, Smart, & Morton, 2003). Theirs is an extreme example; you can see examples of the effects of stress on aging around you in everyday life. People exposed to chronic stress, whether due to their relationships, job, or something else, experience actual wear and tear on their bodies and increased aging. Take a look at the pictures of the past three presidents before and after their terms as president

fight-or-flight response
An emotional and physiological reaction to an emergency that increases readiness for action.

general adaptation syndrome (GAS)
A three-stage physiological response that appears regardless of the stressor that is encountered.

Chronic stress can actually speed the aging process. Just look at how much each of our last three presidents aged while in office. College can be stressful too, but hopefully not so much so that you have white hair by graduation.

of the United States (arguably, one of the most stressful jobs in the world). As you can see, they appear to have aged much more than the 4-8 years that passed between their first and second photographs. How exactly can stressors in the environment increase the aging process?

Understanding this process requires knowing a little bit about how aging occurs. The cells in our bodies are constantly dividing, and as part of this process, our chromosomes are repeatedly copied so that our genetic information is carried into the new cells. This process is facilitated by the presence of **telomeres**, *caps at the ends of each chromosome that protect the ends of chromosomes and prevent them from sticking to each other.* They are kind of like the tape at the end of your shoelaces that keeps them from being frayed and not working as efficiently. Each time a cell divides, the telomeres become slightly shorter. If they become too short, cells can no longer divide and this can lead to the development of tumors and a range of diseases. Fortunately, our bodies fix this problem by producing a substance called **telomerase**, *an enzyme that rebuilds telomeres at the tips of chromosomes.* As cells repeatedly divide over the course of our lives, telomerase does its best to re-cap our chromosomes with telomeres. Ultimately, in the end, telomerase cannot keep up telomere production at a sufficient pace, and over time cells lose their ability to divide, causing aging and in the end, cell death. The recent discovery of the function of telomeres and telomerase and their relation to aging and disease by Elizabeth Blackburn and colleagues has been one of the most exciting advances in science in the past several decades.

What is telomerase and what does it do for us?

Interestingly, social stressors can play an important role in this process. People exposed to chronic stress have shorter telomere length and lower telomerase activity (Epel et al., 2004). Laboratory studies suggest that cortisol can reduce the activity of

Dr. Elizabeth Blackburn was awarded a Nobel Prize in 2009 for her groundbreaking discoveries on the functions of telomeres (shown here in yellow) and telomerase.

telomerase, which in turn leads to shortened telomeres, which has downstream negative effects in the form of accelerated aging and increased risk of a wide range of diseases including cancer, cardiovascular disease, diabetes, and depression (Blackburn & Epel, 2012). This sounds dire, but there are things that you can do to combat this process and potentially live a healthier and longer life! Activities like exercise and meditation seem to prevent chronic stress from shortening telomere length, providing a potential explanation of how these activities may convey health benefits such as longer life and lower risk of disease (Epel et al., 2009; Puterman et al., 2010).

Stress Effects on the Immune Response

The **immune system** is *a complex response system that protects the body from bacteria, viruses, and other foreign substances.* The system includes white blood cells, such as **lymphocytes** (including T cells and B cells), *that produce antibodies that fight infection.* The immune system is remarkably responsive to psychological influences. *Psychoneuroimmunology* is the study of how the immune system responds to psychological variables, such as the presence of stressors. Stressors can cause hormones known as *glucocorticoids* to flood the brain (described in the Neuroscience and Behavior chapter), wearing down the immune system and making it less able to fight invaders (Webster Marketon & Glaser, 2008).

> **How does stress affect the immune system?**

For example, in one study, medical student volunteers agreed to receive small wounds to the roof of the mouth. Researchers observed that these wounds healed more slowly during exam periods than during summer vacation (Marucha, Kiecolt-Glaser, & Favagehi, 1998). In another study, a set of selfless, healthy volunteers permitted researchers to swab the common cold virus in their noses (Cohen et al., 1998). You might think that a direct application of the virus would be like exposure to a massive full-facial sneeze and that all the participants would catch colds. The researchers observed, though, that some people got colds and others didn't—and stress helped account for the difference. Volunteers who had experienced chronic stressors (lasting a month or longer) were especially likely to suffer colds. In particular, participants who had lost a job or who were going through extended interpersonal problems with family or friends were most susceptible to the virus. Brief stressful life events (those lasting less than a month) had no impact. So if you're fighting with your friends or family, best to get it over with quickly, it's better for your health.

The effect of stress on immune response may help to explain why social status is related to health. Studies of British civil servants beginning in the 1960s found that mortality varied precisely with civil service grade: the higher the classification, the lower the death rate, regardless of cause (Marmot et al., 1991). One explanation is that people in lower-status jobs more often engage in unhealthy behavior such as smoking and drinking alcohol, and there is evidence of this. But there is also evidence that the stress of living life at the bottom levels of society increases risk of infections by weakening the immune system. People who perceive themselves as low in social status are more prone to suffer from respiratory infections, for example, than those who do not bear this social burden—and the same holds true for low-status male monkeys (Cohen, 1999).

Stress and Cardiovascular Health

The heart and circulatory system are also sensitive to stress. For example, for several days after Iraq's 1991 missile attack on Israel, heart attack rates went up markedly among citizens in Tel Aviv (Meisel et al., 1991). The full story of how stress affects the cardiovascular system starts earlier than the occurrence of a heart attack: Chronic stress creates changes in the body that increase later vulnerability.

---

telomeres
Caps at the end of each chromosome that protect the ends of chromosomes and prevent them from sticking to each other.

telomerase
An enzyme that rebuilds telomeres at the tips of chromosomes.

immune system
A complex response system that protects the body from bacteria, viruses, and other foreign substances.

lymphocytes
White blood cells that produce antibodies that fight infection, including T cells and B cells.

The main cause of coronary heart disease is *atherosclerosis,* a gradual narrowing of the arteries that occurs as fatty deposits, or plaque, build up on the inner walls of the arteries. Narrowed arteries result in a reduced blood supply and, eventually, when an artery is blocked by a blood clot or detached plaque, in a heart attack. Although smoking, a sedentary lifestyle, and a diet high in fat and cholesterol can cause coronary heart disease, chronic stress also is a major contributor (Krantz & McCeney, 2002). As a result of stress-activated arousal of the sympathetic nervous system, blood pressure goes up and stays up, and this gradually damages the blood vessels. The damaged vessels accumulate plaque, and the more plaque, the greater the likelihood of coronary heart disease. For example, a large study of Finnish men age 42 to 60 found that those who exhibited elevated blood pressure in response to stress and who reported that their work environment was especially stressful showed progressive atherosclerosis of a major artery in the neck during the 4-year study (Everson et al., 1997).

> **How does chronic stress increase the chance of a heart attack?**

In the 1950s, cardiologists Meyer Friedman and Ray Rosenman (1974) conducted a revolutionary study that demonstrated a link between work-related stress and coronary heart disease. They interviewed and tested 3,000 healthy middle-aged men and then tracked their subsequent cardiovascular health. Based on their research, Friedman and Rosenman developed the concept of the **Type A behavior pattern,** which is characterized by *a tendency toward easily aroused hostility, impatience, a sense of time urgency, and competitive achievement strivings.* They compared Type A individuals to those with a less driven behavior pattern (sometimes called *Type B*). The Type A men were identified not only by their answers to questions in the interview (agreeing that they walk and talk fast, work late, set goals for themselves, work hard to win, and easily get frustrated and angry at others), but also by the pushy and impatient way in which they answered the questions. They watched the clock, barked back answers, and interrupted the interviewer, at some points even slapping him with a fish. Okay, the part about the fish is wrong, but you get the idea: These people were intense. The researchers found that of the 258 men who had heart attacks in the 9 years following the interview, over two thirds had been classified as Type A and only one third had been classified as Type B.

A later study of stress and anger tracked medical students for up to 48 years to see how their behavior while they were young related to their later susceptibility to coronary problems (Chang et al., 2002). Students who responded to stress with anger and hostility were found to be 3 times more likely later to develop premature heart disease and 6 times more likely to have an early heart attack than were students who did not respond with anger. Hostility, particularly in men, predicts heart disease better than any other major causal factor, such as smoking, high caloric intake, or even high levels of LDL cholesterol (Niaura et al., 2002; see also **FIGURE 14.3**). Stress affects the cardiovascular system to some degree in everyone, but is particularly harmful in those people who respond to stressful events with hostility.

> **What causal factor most predicts heart attacks?**

Anywhere in the world, road rage starts to make sense when you believe that all the other drivers on the road are trying to kill you.

CHRIS ROUTI/ALAMY

▼ Figure **14.3** **Hostility and Coronary Heart Disease** Of 2,280 men studied over the course of 3 years, 45 suffered coronary heart disease (CHD) incidents, such as heart attack. Many more of these incidents occurred in the group who initially scored above the 80th percentile in hostility (Niaura et al., 2002).

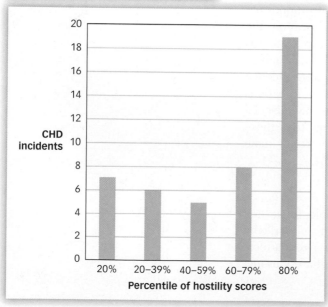

Psychological Reactions

The body's response to stress is intertwined with responses of the mind. Perhaps the first thing the mind does is try to sort things out—to interpret whether an event is threatening or not—and if it is, whether something can be done about it.

Stress Interpretation

The interpretation of a stimulus as stressful or not is called *primary appraisal* (Lazarus & Folkman, 1984). Primary appraisal allows you to realize that a small dark spot on your shirt is a stressor (spider!) or that a 70-mile-per-hour drop from a great height in a small car full of screaming people may not be (roller coaster!). In a demonstration of the importance of interpretation, researchers used a gruesome film of a subincision (a kind of genital surgery that is part of some tribal initiation rites) to severely stress volunteer participants (Speisman et al., 1964). Self-reports and participants' autonomic arousal (heart rate and skin conductance level) were the measures of stress. Before viewing the film, one group heard an introduction that downplayed the pain and emphasized the coming-of-age aspect of the initiation. This interpretation markedly reduced the film viewers' stress compared with another group whose viewing was preceded by a lecture accentuating the pain and trauma.

Changing your perception of a stressful situation from a "threat" to a "challenge" can actually modify your body's response to the situation and lead to better performance. This approach worked for Eminem's character (B. Rabbit) in the movie *8 Mile,* and it can work for you too.

UNIVERSAL PICTURES/PHOTOFEST

The next step in interpretation is *secondary appraisal*, determining whether the stressor is something you can handle or not; that is, whether you have control over the event (Lazarus & Folkman, 1984). Interestingly, the body responds differently depending on whether the stressor is perceived as a *threat* (a stressor you believe you might *not* be able to overcome) or a *challenge* (a stressor you feel fairly confident you can control; Blascovich & Tomaka, 1996). The same midterm exam is seen as a challenge if you are well prepared, but a threat if you didn't study. Fortunately, interpretations of stressors can change them from threats to challenges. One recent study (Jamieson et al., 2010) showed that instructing students to reframe their anxiety about an upcoming exam as arousal that will help them on the test actually boosted their sympathetic arousal (signaling a challenge orientation) and improved test performance. Remember this technique next time you are feeling anxious about a test: Increased arousal can improve your performance!

> **?** What is the difference between a threat and a challenge?

Although both threats and challenges raise heart rate, threats increase vascular reactivity (such as constriction of the blood vessels, which can lead to high blood pressure; see the Hot Science box, p. 552). In one study, researchers found that even interactions as innocuous as conversations can produce threat or challenge responses depending on the race of the conversation partner. Asked to talk with another, unfamiliar student, White students showed a challenge reaction when the student was White and a threat reaction when the student was African American (Mendes et al., 2002). Similar threat responses were found when White students interacted with an unexpected partner, such as an Asian student with a Southern U.S. accent (Mendes et al., 2007). It's as if social unfamiliarity creates the same kind of stress as lack of preparedness for an exam. Interestingly, having previously interacted with members of an unfamiliar group tempers the threat reaction (Blascovich et al., 2001).

Burnout

Did you ever take a class from an instructor who had lost interest in the job? The syndrome is easy to spot: The teacher looks distant and blank, almost robotic, giving predictable and humdrum lessons each day, as if it doesn't matter whether anyone is listening. Now imagine *being* this instructor. You decided to teach because you wanted to shape young minds. You worked hard, and for a while things were great. But one day, you looked up to see a room full of miserable students who were bored and didn't care about anything you had to say. They updated their Facebook pages while you talked and started shuffling papers and putting things away long before the end of class. You're happy at work only when you're not in class. When people feel this way, especially about their jobs or careers, they are suffering from **burnout**, *a state of*

Type A behavior pattern
The tendency toward easily aroused hostility, impatience, a sense of time urgency, and competitive achievement strivings.

burnout
A state of physical, emotional, and mental exhaustion created by long-term involvement in an emotionally demanding situation and accompanied by lowered performance and motivation.

©STOCK4B GMBH/ALAMY

Is there anything worse than taking a horribly boring class? How about being the teacher of that class? What techniques could be used to help people in helping professions (teachers, doctors, nurses, etc.) to prevent burnout from stress?

physical, emotional, and mental exhaustion created by long-term involvement in an emotionally demanding situation and accompanied by lowered performance and motivation.

Burnout is a particular problem in the helping professions (Maslach, Schaufeli, & Leiter, 2001). Teachers, nurses, clergy, doctors, dentists, psychologists, social workers, police officers, and others who repeatedly encounter emotional turmoil on the job may only be able to work productively for a limited time. Eventually, many succumb to symptoms of burnout: overwhelming exhaustion, a deep cynicism and detachment from the job, and a sense of ineffectiveness and lack of accomplishment (Maslach, 2003). Their unhappiness can even spread to others; people with burnout tend to become disgruntled employees who revel in their coworkers' failures and ignore their coworkers' successes (Brenninkmeijer, Vanyperen, & Buunk, 2001).

Why is burnout a problem especially in the helping professions?

What causes burnout? One theory suggests that the culprit is using your job to give meaning to your life (Pines, 1993). If you define yourself only by your career and gauge your self-worth by success at work, you risk having nothing left when work fails. For example, a teacher in danger of burnout might do well to invest time in family, hobbies, or other self-expressions. Others argue that some emotionally stressful jobs lead to burnout no matter how they are approached, and active efforts to overcome the stress before burnout occurs are important. The stress management techniques discussed in the next section may be lifesavers for people in such jobs.

IN SUMMARY

► The body responds to stress with an initial fight-or-flight reaction, which activates the hypothalamic–pituitary–adrenocortical (HPA) axis and prepares the body to face the threat or run away from it.

► The general adaptation syndrome (GAS) outlines three phases of stress response that occur regardless of the type of stressor: alarm, resistance, and exhaustion.

► Chronic stress can wear down the immune system, causing susceptibility to infection, aging, tumor growth, organ damage, and death.

► Response to stress varies if it's interpreted as something that can be overcome or not.

► The psychological response to stress can, if prolonged, lead to burnout.

Stress Management: Dealing with It

Most college students (92%) say they occasionally feel overwhelmed by the tasks they face, and over a third say they have dropped courses or received low grades in response to severe stress (Duenwald, 2002). No doubt you are among the lucky 8% who are entirely cool and report no stress. But just in case you're not, you may be interested in our exploration of stress management techniques: ways to counteract psychological and physical stress reactions directly by managing your mind and body, and ways to sidestep stress by managing your situation.

Mind Management

Stressful events are magnified in the mind. If you fear public speaking, for example, just the thought of an upcoming presentation to a group can create anxiety. And if you do break down during a presentation (going blank, for example, or blurting out something embarrassing), intrusive memories of this stressful event could echo in your mind afterward. A significant part of stress management, then, is control of the mind.

Repressive Coping

Controlling your thoughts is not easy, but some people do seem to be able to banish unpleasant thoughts from the mind. This style of dealing with stress, called **repressive coping**, is characterized by *avoiding situations or thoughts that are reminders of a stressor and maintaining an artificially positive viewpoint*. Everyone has some problems, of course, but repressors are good at deliberately ignoring them (Barnier, Levin, & Maher, 2004). So, for example, when repressors suffer a heart attack, they are less likely than other people to report intrusive thoughts of their heart problems in the days and weeks that follow (Ginzburg, Solomon, & Bleich, 2002).

Like Elizabeth Smart, who for years after her rescue focused in interviews on what was happening in her life now, rather than repeatedly discussing her past in captivity, people often rearrange their lives in order to avoid stressful situations. Many victims of rape, for example, not only avoid the place where the rape occurred, but may move away from their home or neighborhood (Ellis, 1983).

> **When is it useful to avoid stressful thoughts and when is avoidance a problem?**

Anticipating and attempting to avoid reminders of the traumatic experience, they become wary of strangers, especially men who resemble the assailant, and they check doors, locks, and windows more frequently than before. It may make sense to try to avoid stressful thoughts and situations if you're the kind of person who is good at putting unpleasant thoughts and emotions out of mind (Coifman et al., 2007). For some people, however, the avoidance of unpleasant thoughts and situations is so difficult that it can turn into a grim preoccupation (Parker & McNally, 2008; Wegner & Zanakos, 1994). For those who can't avoid negative emotions effectively, it may be better to come to grips with them. This is the basic idea of rational coping.

Rational Coping

Rational coping involves *facing the stressor and working to overcome it*. This strategy is the opposite of repressive coping and so may seem to be the most unpleasant and unnerving thing you could do when faced with stress. It

repressive coping
Avoiding situations or thoughts that are reminders of a stressor and maintaining an artificially positive viewpoint.

rational coping
Facing a stressor and working to overcome it.

Some people are good at deliberately ignoring negative events or thoughts after they occur, and their functioning may be improved as a result. However, those who are not as good at repressing this negative information may do better trying rational coping.

CPL. MARCO MANCHA/DEFENSE VIDEO & IMAGERY DISTRIBUTION SYSTEM

requires approaching, rather than avoiding, a stressor in order to lessen its longer-term negative impact (Hayes, Strosahl, & Wilson, 1999). Rational coping is a three-step process: *acceptance,* coming to realize that the stressor exists and cannot be wished away; *exposure,* attending to the stressor, thinking about it, and even seeking it out; and *understanding,* working to find the meaning of the stressor in your life.

What are the three steps in rational coping?

When the trauma is particularly intense, rational coping may be difficult to undertake. In rape trauma, for example, even accepting that the rape happened takes time and effort; the initial impulse is to deny the event and try to live as though it had never occurred. Psychological treatment may help during the exposure step by helping victims to confront and think about what happened. Using a technique called *prolonged exposure,* rape survivors relive the traumatic event in their imagination by recording a verbal account of the event and then listening to the recording daily. In one study, rape survivors were instructed to seek out objectively safe situations that caused them anxiety or that they had avoided. This sounds like bitter medicine indeed, but it is remarkably effective, producing significant reductions in anxiety and symptoms of posttraumatic stress disorder compared to no therapy and compared to other therapies that promote more gradual and subtle forms of exposure (Foa et al., 1999).

The third element of rational coping involves coming to an understanding of the meaning of the stressful events. A trauma victim may wonder again and again: Why me? How did it happen? Why? Survivors of incest frequently voice the desire to make sense of their trauma (Silver, Boon, & Stones, 1983), a process that is difficult, even impossible, during bouts of suppression and avoidance.

Extremely stressful events, such as rape, are not only acute stressors but often have lasting psychological consequences. Fortunately, there are effective techniques for learning to cope with such events that can lead to improved psychological health.

Reframing

Changing the way you think is another way to cope with stressful thoughts. **Reframing** involves *finding a new or creative way to think about a stressor that reduces its threat.* If you experience anxiety at the thought of public speaking, for example, you might reframe by shifting from thinking of an audience as evaluating you to thinking of yourself as evaluating them, and this might make speech giving easier.

Reframing can be an effective way to prepare for a moderately stressful situation, but if something like public speaking is so stressful that you can't bear to think about it until you absolutely must, the technique may be not be usable. **Stress inoculation training (SIT)** is *a reframing technique that helps people to cope with stressful situations by developing positive ways to think about the situation.* For example, in one study, people who had difficulty controlling their anger were trained to rehearse and reframe their thoughts with phrases like these: "Just roll with the punches, don't get bent out of shape," "you don't need to prove yourself," "I'm not going to let him get to me," "it's really a shame he has to act like this," and "I'll just let him make a fool of himself." Anger-prone people who practiced these thoughts were less likely to become physiologically aroused in response to laboratory-based provocations, both imaginary and real. Subsequent research on SIT has revealed that it can be useful, too, for helping people who have suffered prior traumatic events to become more comfortable living with those events (Foa & Meadows, 1997).

Writing about your deepest thoughts and feelings has been shown to have a range of beneficial health effects. Just make sure you keep your journal in a safe place.

Reframing can take place spontaneously if people are given the opportunity to spend time thinking and writing about stressful events. In an important series of studies, Jamie Pennebaker (1989) found that the physical health of college students improved after they spent a few

How has writing about stressful events been shown to be helpful?

hours writing about their deepest thoughts and feelings. Compared with students who had written about something else, members of the self-disclosure group were less likely in subsequent months to visit the student health center; they also used less aspirin and achieved better grades (Pennebaker & Chung, 2007). In fact, engaging in such expressive writing was found to improve immune function (Pennebaker, Kiecolt-Glaser, & Glaser, 1988), whereas suppressing emotional topics weakened it (Petrie, Booth, & Pennebaker, 1998). The positive effect of self-disclosing writing may reflect its usefulness in reframing trauma and reducing stress.

Body Management

Stress can express itself as tension in your neck muscles, back pain, a knot in your stomach, sweaty hands, or the harried face you glimpse in the mirror. Because stress so often manifests itself through bodily symptoms, bodily techniques such as meditation, relaxation therapy, biofeedback, and aerobic exercise are useful in its management.

Meditation

Meditation is *the practice of intentional contemplation*. Techniques of meditation are associated with a variety of religious traditions and are also practiced outside religious contexts. The techniques vary widely. Some forms of meditation call for attempts to clear the mind of thought, others involve focusing on a single thought (e.g., thinking about a candle flame), and still others involve concentration on breathing or on a *mantra* (a repetitive sound such as *om*). At a minimum, the techniques have in common a period of quiet.

Time spent meditating can be restful and revitalizing. Beyond these immediate benefits, many people also meditate in an effort to experience deeper or transformed consciousness. Whatever the reason, meditation does appear to have positive psychological effects (Hölzel et al., 2011). Many believe it does so, in part, by improving control over attention. The focus of many forms of meditation, such as mindfulness meditation, is on teaching ourselves how to remain focused on, and accepting of, our immediate experience. Interestingly, experienced meditators show deactivation in the default mode network (which is associated with mind wandering; see Figure 5.6 in the Consciousness chapter) during meditation relative to non-meditators (Brewer et al., 2011). Even short-term meditation training administered to college undergraduates has been shown to improve the connectivity between parts of the brain involved in conflict monitoring and cognitive and emotional control, and to do so via increased myelination (perhaps due to increased neuron firing) and other axonal changes (see the Neuroscience and Behavior chapter; Tang et al., 2012). Taken together, these findings suggest that meditators may be better able to regulate their thoughts and emotions, which may translate to a better ability to manage interpersonal relations, anxiety, and a range of other activities that require conscious effort (Sedlmeier et al., 2012).

> **What are some positive outcomes of meditation?**

Meditation is the practice of intentional contemplation, and it can also temporarily influence brain activity and enhance the sense of well-being.

Aung San Suu Kyi, the leader of the Myanmar opposition party who was awarded the Nobel Peace Prize in 1991, endured house arrest from 1989 until 2010. She has said that daily meditation helped her through this difficult time by improving her mood, awareness, and clarity.

relaxation therapy
A technique for reducing tension by consciously relaxing muscles of the body.

relaxation response
A condition of reduced muscle tension, cortical activity, heart rate, breathing rate, and blood pressure.

biofeedback
The use of an external monitoring device to obtain information about a bodily function and possibly gain control over that function.

Relaxation

Imagine for a moment that you are scratching your chin. Don't actually do it; just think about it and notice that your body participates by moving ever so slightly, tensing and relaxing in the sequence of the imagined action. Edmund Jacobson (1932) discovered these effects with *electromyography* (EMG), a technique used to measure the subtle activity of muscles. A person asked to imagine rowing a boat or plucking a flower from a bush would produce slight levels of tension in the muscles involved in performing the act. Jacobson also found that thoughts of relaxing the muscles sometimes reduced EMG readings when people didn't even report feeling tense. Our bodies respond to all the things we think about doing every day. These thoughts create muscle tension even when we think we're doing nothing at all.

These observations led Jacobson to develop **relaxation therapy**, *a technique for reducing tension by consciously relaxing muscles of the body.* A person in relaxation therapy may be asked to relax specific muscle groups one at a time or to imagine warmth flowing through the body or to think about a relaxing situation. This activity draws on a **relaxation response**, *a condition of reduced muscle tension, cortical activity, heart rate, breathing rate, and blood pressure* (Benson, 1990). Basically, as soon as you get in a comfortable position, quiet down, and focus on something repetitive or soothing that holds your attention, you relax.

Relaxing on a regular basis can reduce symptoms of stress (Carlson & Hoyle, 1993) and even reduce blood levels of cortisol, the biochemical marker of the stress response (McKinney et al., 1997). For example, in individuals who are suffering from tension headache, relaxation reduces the tension that causes the headache; in people with cancer, relaxation makes it easier to cope with stressful treatments; in people with stress-related cardiovascular problems, relaxation can reduce the high blood pressure that puts the heart at risk (Mandle et al., 1996).

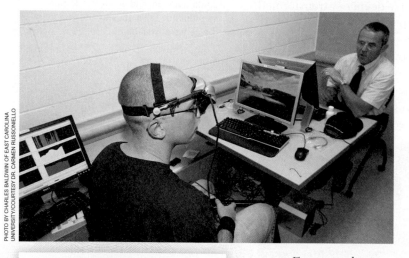

Biofeedback gives people access to visual or audio feedback showing levels of psychophysiological functions such as heart rate, breathing, brain electrical activity, or skin temperature that they would otherwise be unable to sense directly.

Biofeedback

Wouldn't it be nice if, instead of having to learn to relax, you could just flip a switch and relax as fast as possible? **Biofeedback**, *the use of an external monitoring device to obtain information about a bodily function and possibly gain control over that function,* was developed with this goal of high-tech relaxation in mind. You might not be aware right now of whether your fingers are warm or cold, for example, but with an electronic thermometer displayed before you, the ability to sense your temperature might allow you (with a bit of practice) to make your hands warmer or cooler at will (e.g., Roberts & McGrady, 1996).

Biofeedback can help people control physiological functions they are not likely to become aware of in other ways. For example, you probably have no idea right now what brain-wave patterns you are producing. In the late 1950s, Joe Kamiya (1969), a psychologist using the electroencephalograph (also called the EEG and discussed in the Neuroscience and Behavior chapter), initiated a brain-wave biofeedback revolution when he found that people could change their brain waves from alert beta patterns to relaxed alpha patterns and back again when they were permitted to monitor their own EEG readings.

How does biofeedback work?

Recent studies suggest that EEG biofeedback (or neurofeedback) is moderately successful in treating brain-wave abnormalities in disorders such as epilepsy (Yucha & Gilbert, 2004), and in teaching people to down-regulate activity in regions of the brain involved in the strong emotional responses seen in some forms of psychopathology (Hamilton et al., 2010). Often, however, the use of biofeedback to produce relaxation in the brain turns out to be a bit of technological overkill and may not be much more effective than simply having the person stretch out in a hammock and hum a happy tune. Although biofeedback is not a magic bullet that gives people control over stress-induced health troubles, it has proven to be a useful technique for things like increasing relaxation and decreasing chronic pain (Palermo et al., 2011). People who do not benefit from relaxation therapy may find that biofeedback provides a useful alternative.

Aerobic Exercise

A jogger nicely decked out in a neon running suit bounces in place at the crosswalk and then springs away when the signal changes. It is tempting to assume that this jogger is the picture of psychological health: happy, unstressed, and even downright exuberant. As it turns out, the stereotype is true: Studies indicate that *aerobic exercise* (exercise that increases heart rate and oxygen intake for a sustained period) is associated with psychological well-being (Hassmen, Koivula, & Uutela, 2000). But does exercise *cause* psychological well-being, or does psychological well-being cause people to exercise? Perhaps general happiness is what inspires the jogger's bounce. Or could some unknown third factor (neon pants?) cause both the need to exercise and the sense of well-being? As we've mentioned many times, correlation does not always imply causation.

To try to tease apart causal factors, researchers have randomly assigned people to aerobic exercise activities and no-exercise comparison groups and have found that exercise actually does promote stress relief and happiness. One recent meta-analysis (a quantitative review of existing studies) compiled data from 90 studies including

What are the benefits of exercise?

over 10,000 people with chronic illness who were randomly assigned either to exercise or a no-exercise condition, and found that people assigned to the aerobic exercise condition experienced a significant reduction in depressive symptoms (Herring et al., 2012). Other recent meta-analyses have come to similar conclusions, showing, for instance, that exercise is as effective as the most effective psychological interventions for depression (Rimer et al., 2012), and that exercise even shows positive physical and mental health benefits for individuals with schizophrenia (Gorczynski & Faulkner, 2011). Pretty good effects for a simple, timeless intervention with no side effects!

The reasons for these positive effects are unclear. Researchers have suggested that the effects result from increases in the body's production of neurotransmitters such as serotonin, which can have a positive effect on mood (as discussed in the Neuroscience and Behavior chapter) or from increases in the production of endorphins (the endogenous opioids discussed in the Neuroscience and Behavior and Consciousness chapters; Jacobs, 1994).

Beyond boosting positive mood, exercise also stands to keep you healthy into the future. Current U.S. government recommendations suggest that 30 minutes of moderately vigorous exercise per day will reduce the risk of chronic illness (Dietary Guidelines Advisory Committee, 2005). Perhaps the simplest thing you can do to improve your happiness and health, then, is to participate regularly in an aerobic activity. Pick something you find fun: Sign up for a dance class, get into a regular basketball game, or start paddling a canoe—just not all at once.

Exercise is helpful for the reduction of stress, unless, like John Stibbard, your exercise involves carrying the Olympic torch on a wobbly suspension bridge over a 70-meter gorge.

Situation Management

After you have tried to manage stress by managing your mind and managing your body, what's left to manage? Look around and you'll notice a whole world out there. Perhaps that could be managed as well. Situation management involves changing your life situation as a way of reducing the impact of stress on your mind and body. Ways to manage your situation can include seeking out social support, religious or spiritual practice, and finding a place for humor in your life.

social support
The aid gained through interacting with others.

Social Support

The wisdom of the National Safety Council's first rule—"Always swim with a buddy"—is obvious when you're in water over your head, but people often don't realize that the same principle applies whenever danger threatens. Other people can offer help in times of stress. **Social support** is *aid gained through interacting with others*. One of the more self-defeating things you can do in life is fail to connect to people in this way. Just failing to get married, for example, is bad for your health. Unmarried individuals have an elevated risk of mortality from cardiovascular disease, cancer, pneumonia and influenza, chronic obstructive pulmonary disease, and liver disease and cirrhosis (Johnson, Backlund, et al., 2000). More generally, good ongoing relationships with friends and family and participation in social activities and religious groups can be as healthy for you as exercising and avoiding smoking (Umberson et al., 2006). Social support is helpful on many levels:

> An intimate partner can help you remember to get your exercise and follow your doctor's orders, and together you'll probably follow a more healthy diet than you would all alone with your snacks.

> Talking about problems with friends and family can offer many of the benefits of professional psychotherapy, usually without the hourly fees.

> Sharing tasks and helping each other when times get tough can reduce the amount of work and worry in each other's lives.

The helpfulness of strong social bonds, though, transcends mere convenience. Lonely people are more likely than others to be stressed and depressed (Baumeister & Leary, 1995), and they can be more susceptible to illness because of lower-than-normal levels of immune functioning (Kiecolt-Glaser et al., 1984). Many first-year college students experience something of a crisis of social support. No matter how outgoing and popular they were in high school, newcomers typically find the task of developing satisfying new social relationships quite daunting. New friendships can seem shallow, connections with teachers may be perfunctory and even threatening, and social groups that are encountered can seem like islands of lost souls ("Hey, we're forming a club to investigate the lack of clubs on campus—want to join?"). Not surprisingly, research shows that students reporting the greatest feelings of isolation also show reduced immune responses to flu vaccinations (Pressman et al., 2005). Time spent getting to know people in new social situations can be an investment in your own health.

The value of social support in protecting against stress may be very different for women and men: Whereas women seek support under stress,

CULTURE & COMMUNITY

Land of the free, home of the . . . stressed? Chances are that you, your parents, grandparents, or someone further back in your family immigrated to the United States. Many families have moved to the United States in pursuit of a better life. Are things immediately better after the move to a new land, or does the process of picking up and moving to a strange land increase stress and lead to negative health consequences?

To answer these questions, Joshua Breslau and colleagues (2007) used survey data from large representative samples of English-speaking Mexicans residing in either the United States or Mexico to examine rates of anxiety and mood disorders throughout their lives. They found that the presence of an anxiety disorder while living in Mexico predicted immigration to the United States (i.e., if you are anxious in Mexico, you are more likely to move to the United States). In addition, they also learned that moving to the United States increased the likelihood of developing an anxiety or mood disorder, and of having more persistent anxiety. The authors interpreted these results as support for the "acculturation stress" hypothesis, which suggests that living in a foreign culture increases stress (due to trouble with communication, knowledge of local customs, etc.) and decreases social support, which together increase the risk of negative health outcomes. The highest risk of experiencing a mental disorder after moving to the United States was observed for children ages 0–12 years old when they moved, suggesting that this early disruption can be especially difficult. Interestingly, the increased risk of mental disorders among recent immigrants has been observed in other studies (perhaps due to stress), but those studies also consistently show that U.S. immigrants have lower levels of mental disorders than those born in the United States (which is among the highest in the world in rates of mental disorders, as described in the Psychological Disorders chapter; Borges et al., 2011; Breslau & Chang, 2006). So moving to a new country and culture can be very stressful, perhaps in part due to the stress and health levels of those in your new environment.

VISIONS OF AMERICA/UIG VIA GETTY IMAGES

men are less likely to do so. The fight-or-flight response to stress may be largely a male reaction, according to research on sex differences by Shelley Taylor (2002). Taylor suggested that the female response to stress is to *tend-and-befriend* by taking care of people and bringing them together. Like men, women respond to stressors with sympathetic nervous system arousal and the release of epinephrine and norepinephrine; but unlike

> **Why is the hormone oxytocin a health advantage for women?**

men, they also release *oxytocin,* a hormone secreted by the pituitary gland in pregnant and nursing mothers. In the presence of estrogen, oxytocin triggers social responses: a tendency to seek out social contacts, nurture others, and create and maintain cooperative groups. After a hard day at work, a man may come home frustrated and worried about his job and end up drinking a beer and fuming alone. A woman under the same type of stress may instead play with her kids or talk to friends on the phone. The tend-and-befriend response to stress may help to explain why women are healthier and have a longer life span than do men. The typical male response amplifies the unhealthy effects of stress, whereas the female response takes a lesser toll on her mind and body and provides social support for the people around her as well.

Women are more likely than men to respond to stress with a "tend-and-befriend" style in which they seek out social contact and cooperative relationships. The commonality of this response style may partly explain the success of the television show *Sex and the City,* in which four young women helped one another through many difficult times (the fabulous outfits didn't hurt either).

Religious Experiences

Many people spend a significant amount of time in quiet prayer, reflection, and contemplation. National polls indicate that over 90% of Americans believe in God, and most who do, pray at least once per day. Although many who believe in a higher power believe that their faith will be rewarded in an afterlife, it turns out that there may be some benefits here on Earth as well. An enormous body of research has examined the associations between *religiosity* (affiliation with or engagement in the practices of a particular religion) and *spirituality* (having a belief in and engagement with some higher power, not necessarily linked to any particular religion), and positive health outcomes. The helpful effects of religiosity and spirituality have been observed in a wide range of areas including lower rates of heart disease, decreases in chronic pain, and improved psychological health (Seybold & Hill, 2001).

Why do people who endorse religiosity or spirituality have better mental and physical health? Is it divine intervention? Several testable ideas have been proposed. Engagement in religious/spiritual practices, such as attendance at weekly religious services, may lead to the development of a stronger and more extensive social network,

> **Why are religiosity and spirituality associated with health benefits?**

which has well-known health benefits. Those who are religious/spiritual also may fare better psychologically and physically as a result of following the healthy recommendations offered in many religious/spiritual teachings. That is, they may be more likely to follow dietary restrictions, restrain from the use of drugs or alcohol, and endorse a more hopeful and optimistic perspective of daily life events, all of which can lead to more positive health outcomes (Seeman, Dubin, & Seeman, 2003; Seybold & Hill, 2001). On balance, many claims made by some religious groups have not been supported, such as the beneficial effects of intercessory prayer (see **FIGURE 14.4**). Psychologists are actively testing the effectiveness of various religious and spiritual practices with the goal of better understanding how they might help to explain, and improve, the human condition.

▼ Figure **14.4** **Pray for me?** To test whether praying for someone in their time of need actually helped them, researchers randomly assigned 1,802 patients about to undergo cardiac bypass surgery to one of three conditions: those told that they may be prayed for and were; those told that they may be prayed for and weren't; and those told that they definitely would be prayed for and were. Unfortunately, there were no differences in the presence of complications between those who were or were not prayed for. To make matters worse, those who knew they would be prayed for and were, experienced significantly more complications than the other two groups (Benson et al., 2006).

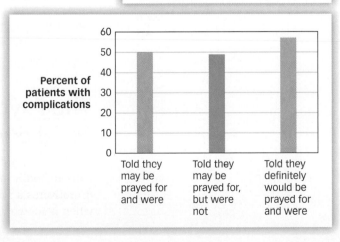

Humor

Wouldn't it be nice to laugh at your troubles and move on? Most of us recognize that humor can diffuse unpleasant situations and bad feelings, and it makes sense that bringing some fun into your life could help to reduce stress. The extreme point of view on this topic is staked out in self-help books with titles such as *Health, Healing, and the Amuse System* and *How Serious Is This? Seeing Humor in Daily Stress.* Is laughter truly the best medicine? Should we close down the hospitals and send in the clowns?

How does humor mitigate stress?

There is a kernel of truth to the theory that humor can help us cope with stress. For example, humor can reduce sensitivity to pain and distress, as researchers found when they subjected volunteers to an overinflated blood pressure cuff. Participants were more tolerant of the pain during a laughter-inducing comedy audiotape than during a neutral tape or instructed relaxation (Cogan et al., 1987).

Humor can also reduce the time needed to calm down after a stressful event. For example, men viewing a highly stressful film about three industrial accidents were asked to narrate the film aloud, either by describing the events seriously or by making their commentary as funny as possible. Although men in both groups reported feeling tense while watching the film and showed increased levels of sympathetic nervous arousal (increased heart rate and skin conductance, decreased skin temperature), those looking for humor in the experience bounced back to normal arousal levels more quickly than did those in the serious story group (Newman & Stone, 1996).

If laughter and fun can alleviate stress quickly in the short term, do the effects accumulate to improve health and longevity? Sadly, the evidence suggests not (Provine, 2000). A study titled "Do Comics Have the Last Laugh?" tracked the longevity of comedians in comparison to other entertainers and nonentertainers (Rotton, 1992). It was found that the comedians died younger—perhaps after too many nights on stage thinking, *I'm dying out here.*

When Andrew Mason, CEO of the Internet company Groupon, left his position, his resignation letter read: "After four and a half intense and wonderful years as CEO of Groupon, I've decided that I'd like to spend more time with my family. Just kidding—I was fired today." He went on to add, "I am so lucky to have had the opportunity to take the company this far with all of you. I'll now take some time to decompress (FYI I'm looking for a good fat camp to lose my Groupon 40, if anyone has a suggestion), and then maybe I'll figure out how to channel this experience into something productive." This seems like a textbook case of using humor to mitigate stress, which is why we put it, um, you know where.

IN SUMMARY

▶ The management of stress involves strategies for influencing the mind, the body, and the situation.

▶ People try to manage their minds by trying to suppress stressful thoughts or avoid the situations that produce them, by rationally coping with the stressor, and by reframing.

▶ Body management strategies involve attempting to reduce stress symptoms through meditation, relaxation, biofeedback, and aerobic exercise.

▶ Overcoming stress by managing your situation can involve seeking out social support, engaging in religious experiences, or attempting to find humor in stressful events.

The Psychology of Illness: Mind over Matter

One of the mind's main influences on the body's health and illness is the mind's sensitivity to bodily symptoms. Noticing what is wrong with the body can be helpful when it motivates a search for treatment, but sensitivity can also lead to further problems when it snowballs into a preoccupation with illness that itself can cause harm.

Psychological Effects of Illness

Why does it feel so bad to be sick? You notice scratchiness in your throat or the start of sniffles, and you think you might be coming down with something. And in just a few short hours, you're achy all over, energy gone, no appetite, feverish, feeling dull and listless. You're sick. The question is, why does it have to be like this? Why couldn't it feel good? As long as you're going to have to stay at home and miss out on things anyway, couldn't sickness be less of a pain?

Sickness makes you miserable for good reason. Misery is part of the *sickness response*, a coordinated, adaptive set of reactions to illness organized by the brain (Hart, 1988; Watkins & Maier, 2005). Feeling sick keeps you home, where you'll spread germs to fewer people. More importantly, the sickness response makes you withdraw from activity and lie still, conserving the energy for fighting illness that you'd normally expend on other behavior. Appetite loss is similarly helpful: The energy spent on digestion is conserved. Thus, the behavioral changes that accompany illness are not random side effects; they help the body fight disease. These responses become prolonged and exaggerated with aging—subtle signs that we are losing the fight (Barrientos et al., 2009).

> **What is the benefit of the sickness response?**

How does the brain know it should do this? The immune response to an infection begins with one of the components of the immune response, the activation of white blood cells that "eat" microbes and also release *cytokines,* proteins that circulate through the body and communicate among the other white blood cells, and also communicate the sickness response to the brain (Maier & Watkins, 1998). Administration of cytokines to an animal can artificially create the sickness response, and administration of drugs that oppose the action of cytokines can block the sickness response even during an ongoing infection. Cytokines do not enter the brain, but they activate the vagus nerve that runs from the intestines, stomach, and chest to the brain and induce the "I am infected" message (Goehler et al., 2000). Perhaps this is why we often feel sickness in the "gut," a gnawing discomfort in the very center of the body.

Interestingly, the sickness response can be prompted without any infection at all, merely by the introduction of stress. The stressful presence of a predator's odor, for instance, can produce the sickness response of lethargy in an animal, along with symptoms of infection such as fever and increased white blood cell count (Maier & Watkins, 2000). In humans, the connection between sickness response, immune reaction, and stress is illustrated in depression, a condition in which all the sickness machinery runs at full speed. So, in addition to fatigue and malaise, depressed people show signs characteristic of infection, including high levels of cytokines circulating in the blood (Maes, 1995). Just as illness can make you feel a bit depressed, severe depression seems to recruit the brain's sickness response and make you feel ill (Watkins & Maier, 2005).

Recognizing Illness and Seeking Treatment

You probably weren't thinking about your breathing a minute ago, but now that you're reading this sentence, you notice it. Sometimes we are very attentive to our bodies. At other times, the body seems to be on "automatic," running along unnoticed until specific symptoms announce themselves or are pointed out by an annoying textbook writer.

Directing attention toward the body or away from it can influence the symptoms we perceive. When people are bored, for example, they have more attention available to direct toward their bodies, so they focus more on their physical symptoms.

BETSIE VAN DER MEER/GETTY IMAGES

If you have been reading this very exciting textbook, there is no chance you have been yawning. However, seeing this guy yawning may cause your brain to initiate a yawn response as well.

Pennebaker (1980) audiotaped classrooms and found that people are more likely to cough when someone else has just coughed, but that such psychological contagion is much more likely at boring points in a lecture. Interestingly, coughing is not something people do on purpose (as Pennebaker found when he recorded clusters of coughs among sleeping firefighters). Thus, awareness and occurrence of physical symptoms can be influenced by psychological factors beyond our control.

People differ substantially in the degree to which they attend to and report bodily symptoms. People who report many physical symptoms tend to be negative in other ways as well, describing themselves as anxious, depressed, and under stress (Watson & Pennebaker, 1989). Do people with many symptom complaints truly have a lot of problems or are they just high-volume complainers?

> **What is the relationship between pain and activity in the brain?**

To answer this question, researchers used fMRI brain scans to compare the severity of reported sensation of pain with the degree of activation in brain areas usually associated with pain experience. Volunteers underwent several applications of a thermal stimulus (110–120° F) to the leg, and, as you might expect, some of the participants found it more painful than did others. Scans during the painful events revealed that the anterior cingulate cortex, somatosensory cortex, and prefrontal cortex (areas known to respond to painful body stimulation) were particularly active in those participants who reported higher levels of pain experience (see **FIGURE 14.5**), suggesting that people can report accurately on the extent to which they experience pain (Coghill, McHaffie, & Yen, 2003; see the Real World box).

In contrast to complainers are those who underreport symptoms and pain or ignore or deny the possibility that they are sick. Insensitivity to symptoms comes with costs: It can delay the search for treatment, sometimes with serious repercussions. Of 2,404 patients in one study who had been treated for a heart attack, 40% had delayed going to the hospital for over 6 hours from the time they first noticed suspicious symptoms (Gurwitz et al., 1997). Severe chest pain or a history of prior heart surgery did send people to the hospital in a hurry. Those with more subtle symptoms often waited around for hours, however, not calling an ambulance or their doctor, just hoping the

| 0 | 1 | 2 | 3 | 4 | 5 |
| No Hurt | Hurts Little Bit | Hurts Little More | Hurts Even More | Hurts Whole Lot | Hurts Worst |

FACES FROM HOCKENBERRY MJ, WILSON D: WONG'S ESSENTIALS OF PEDIATRIC NURSING, ED. 8, ST. LOUIS, 2009, MOSBY. USED WITH PERMISSION. COPYRIGHT MOSBY.

How much does it hurt? Pain is a psychological state that can be difficult to measure. One way to put a number on a pain is to have people judge with reference to the external expression of the internal state.

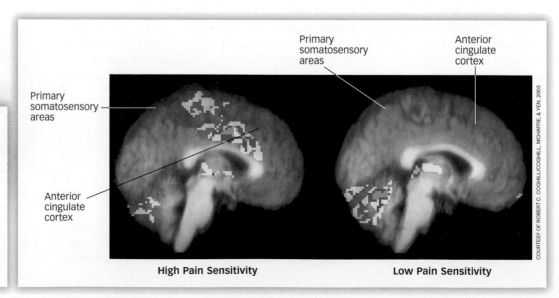

▶ Figure **14.5 The Brain in Pain**
fMRI scans of brain activation in high- (*left*) and low-pain-sensitive (*right*) individuals during painful stimulation. The anterior cingulate cortex and primary somatosensory areas show greater activation in high-pain-sensitive individuals. Levels of activation are highest in yellow and red, then light blue and dark blue (Coghill, McHaffie, & Yen, 2003).

Primary somatosensory areas

Anterior cingulate cortex

Primary somatosensory areas

Anterior cingulate cortex

High Pain Sensitivity

Low Pain Sensitivity

COURTESY OF ROBERT C. COGHILL/COGHILL, MCHAFFIE, & YEN, 2003

problem would go away, which is not a good idea because many of the treatments that can reduce the damage of a heart attack are most useful when provided early. When it comes to your own health, protecting your mind from distress through the denial of illness can result in exposing your body to great danger.

THE REAL WORLD

This Is Your Brain on Placebos

There is something miraculous about Band-Aids. Your standard household toddler typically *requires* one for any injury at all, expecting and often achieving immediate relief. It is not unusual to find a child who reports that aches or pains are "cured" if a Band-Aid has been applied by a helpful adult. Of course, the Band-Aid is not *really* helping the pain—or is it?

Physicians and psychologists have long puzzled over the *placebo effect*, a clinically significant psychological or physiological response to a therapeutically inert substance or procedure. The classic placebo is the sugar pill, but Band-Aids, injections, heating pads, neck rubs, homeopathic remedies, and kind words can have placebo effects (Diederich & Goetz, 2008). Even sham brain surgery can be more effective than no treatment at all (McRae et al., 2004). The effect is most marked, however, when the patient knows that a treatment is taking place (Stewart-Williams, 2004). This is also true of active treatments: A morphine injection works much better if you know you're getting it (Benedetti, Maggi, & Lopiano, 2003). Knowledge effects can be remarkably specific, mirroring in detail what patients believe about the nature of medicine, for example, that two pills work better than one and an injection works better than just a pill (de Craen et al., 1999).

How do placebos operate? Do people being treated for pain really feel the pain but distort their report of the experience to make it fit their beliefs about treatment? Or does the placebo actually reduce the pain a patient experiences? Howard Fields and Jon Levine (1984) discovered that placebos trigger the release of endorphins (or *endogenous opioids*), painkilling chemicals similar to morphine that are produced by the brain (see the Consciousness chapter). In their experiments, they found that an injection of naloxone, an opioid-blocking drug, typically reduces the benefit both of an opioid such as morphine and a placebo injection, suggesting that the placebo has its painkilling effects because it triggers the release of endorphins.

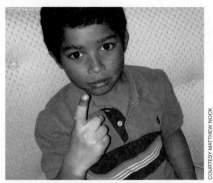

▲ Can a Band-Aid cure all of your aches and pains? Many children, like this little guy, report immediate pain relief following application of a Band-Aid to whatever spot is hurting them. Although most adults know that Band-Aids don't treat pain, the placebo effect remains powerful throughout the life span.

In another advance in the study of these effects, placebos were found to lower the activation of specific brain areas associated with pain. One set of fMRI studies examined brain activation as volunteers were exposed to electric shock or heat (Wager et al., 2004). In preparation for some exposures to these painful stimuli, a placebo cream was applied to the skin, and the participant was told it was an analgesic that would reduce the pain. Other participants merely experienced the pain. As you can see in the accompanying figure, the fMRI scans showed decreased activation during placebo analgesia in the *thalamus, anterior cingulate cortex,* and *insula,* pain-sensitive brain regions that were activated during untreated pain. These findings suggest that placebos are not leading people to misreport their pain experience, but rather are reducing brain activity in areas that normally are active during pain experience.

Such findings don't mean that next time your stomach aches, you can break out a Band-Aid and heal yourself. Part of the placebo effect is dependent on the conscious expectation that the placebo will work, and it could be a challenge to make yourself believe you will feel better when you don't. Part of the placebo effect is unconscious, though, a tendency to feel better that is learned through classical conditioning. When you've been healed in the past by a particular doctor or form of treatment, or in a certain setting, unconscious learning mechanisms may lead to improvement if you simply encounter a similar doctor, treatment, or setting again, even if you don't consciously expect to improve (Benedetti, Pollo, et al., 2003). There's something comforting about returning to things that have given you comfort in the past.

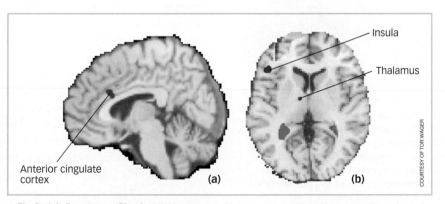

▲ **The Brain's Response to Placebo** fMRI scans reveal that some brain regions normally activated when individuals report pain in response to shocks are deactivated when those individuals are given a placebo analgesic during the shock. These regions include the anterior cingulate cortex (shown in the top image, a right medial view of the brain) and the insula and thalamus (both shown in the bottom image, a ventral view of the brain; Wager et al., 2004).

psychosomatic illness
An interaction between mind and body that can produce illness.

somatic symptom disorders
The set of psychological disorders in which a person with at least one bodily symptom displays significant health-related anxiety, expresses disproportionate concerns about their symptoms, and devotes excessive time and energy to their symptoms or health concerns.

sick role
A socially recognized set of rights and obligations linked with illness.

Somatic Symptom Disorders

The flip side of denial is excessive sensitivity to illness, and it turns out that sensitivity also has its perils. Indeed, hypersensitivity to symptoms or to the possibility of illness underlies a variety of psychological problems and can also undermine physical health. Psychologists studying **psychosomatic illness**, *an interaction between mind and body that can produce illness*, explore ways in which mind (*psyche*) can influence body (*soma*) and vice versa. The study of mind–body interactions focuses on psychological disorders called **somatic symptom disorders**, in which *a person with at least one bodily symptom displays significant health-related anxiety, expresses disproportionate concerns about their symptoms, and devotes excessive time and energy to their symptoms or health concerns*. These are disorders like those that will be discussed in the Psychological Disorders chapter, but their association with symptoms in the body makes them relevant to this chapter's concern with stress and health. Disorders focused on concerns about physical illness used to be called *somatoform*

> **How can hypersensitivity to symptoms undermine health?**

disorders and included categories like hypochondriasis. Somatoform disorders were those in which people experienced unexplained medical symptoms believed to be generated by a person's mind. However, the focus on psychosomatic illness has shifted from concerns about mentally generated physical symptoms, to excessive psychological concerns about explainable medical symptoms, with the idea that the latter are serious and could benefit from psychological intervention. Some believe this shift in focus is problematic and will lead psychologists and psychiatrists to label normal concern about one's health as a psychological disorder. The interesting and somewhat complicated question of what should be considered a psychological disorder and what should not is something we tackle more directly in the next chapter.

On Being a Patient

Getting sick is more than a change in physical state: It can involve a transformation of identity. This change can be particularly profound with a serious illness: A kind of cloud settles over you, a feeling that you are now different, and this transformation can influence everything you feel and do in this new world of illness. You even take on a new role in life, a **sick role**: *a socially recognized set of rights and obligations linked with illness* (Parsons, 1975). The sick person is absolved of responsibility for many everyday obligations and enjoys exemption from normal activities. For example, in addition to skipping school and homework and staying on the couch all day, a sick child can watch TV and avoid eating anything unpleasant at dinner. At the extreme, the sick person can get away with being rude, lazy, demanding, and picky. In return for these exemptions, the sick role also incurs obligations. The properly "sick" individual cannot appear to enjoy the illness or reveal signs of wanting to be sick and must also take care to pursue treatment to end this "undesirable" condition. Parsons observed that illness has psychological, social, and even moral components. You may recall times when you have felt the conflict between sickness and health as though it were a moral decision: Should you drag yourself out of bed and try to make it to the chemistry exam or just slump back under the covers and wallow in your "pain"?

Some people feign medical or psychological symptoms to achieve something they want, a type of behavior called *malingering*. Because many symptoms of illness cannot be faked (even facial expressions of pain are difficult to simulate; Williams, 2002), malingering is possible only with a restricted number of illnesses. Faking illness is suspected when the secondary gains of illness, such as the ability to rest, to be freed from performing unpleasant

> **What benefits might come from being ill?**

Have you ever ridden on public transportation sitting next to a person with a hacking cough? We are bombarded by advertisements for medicines designed to suppress symptoms of illness so we can keep going. Is staying home with a cold socially acceptable or considered malingering? How does this jibe with the concept of the *sick role*?

IMAGE SOURCE/GETTY SOURCE

tasks, or to be helped by others, outweigh the costs. Such gains can be very subtle, as when a child stays in bed because of the comfort provided by an otherwise distant parent, or they can be obvious, as when insurance benefits turn out to be a cash award for Best Actor. Some behaviors that may lead to illness may not be under the patient's control; for example, self-starvation may be part of an uncontrollable eating disorder (see the Emotion and Motivation chapter). For this reason, malingering can be difficult to diagnose and treat (Feldman, 2004).

Patient–Practitioner Interaction

Medical care usually occurs through a strange interaction. On one side is a patient, often miserable, who expects to be questioned and examined and possibly prodded, pained, or given bad news. On the other side is a health care provider, who comes in knowing nothing about what brings the patient in to see them, but hopes to quickly obtain information from the patient by asking lots of extremely personal questions (and examining extremely personal parts of the body); identify the problem and potential solution; help in some way; and achieve all of this as efficiently as possible because more patients are waiting. It seems less like a time for healing than an occasion for major awkwardness. One of the keys to an effective medical care interaction is physician empathy (Spiro et al., 1994). To offer successful treatment, the clinician must simultaneously understand the patient's

> **Why is it important that a physician express empathy?**

physical state *and* psychological state. Physicians often err on the side of failing to acknowledge patients' emotions, focusing instead on technical issues of the case (Suchman et al., 1997). This is particularly unfortunate because a substantial percentage of patients who seek medical care do so for treatment of psychological and emotional problems (Taylor, 1986). As the Greek physician Hippocrates wrote in the 4th century BCE: "Some patients, though conscious that their condition is perilous, recover their health simply through their contentment with the goodness of the physician." The best physician treats the patient's mind as well as the patient's body.

Another important part of the medical care interaction is motivating the patient to follow the prescribed regimen of care (Miller & Rollnick, 2012). When researchers check compliance by counting the pills remaining in a patient's bottle after a prescription has been underway, they find that patients often do an astonishingly poor job of following doctors' orders (see **FIGURE 14.6**). Compliance deteriorates when the treatment must be *frequent,* as when eyedrops for glaucoma are required every few hours, or *inconvenient* or *painful,* such as drawing blood or performing injections in managing diabetes. Finally, compliance decreases *as the number of treatments increases.* This is a worrisome problem, especially for older patients, who may have difficulty remembering when to take which pill. Failures in medical care may stem from the failure of health care providers to recognize the psychological challenges that are involved in self-care. Helping people to follow doctors' orders involves psychology, not medicine, and is an essential part of promoting health.

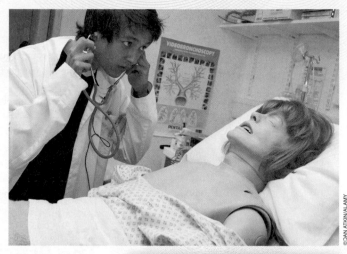

Doctor and patient have two modes of interaction, the technical and the interpersonal. Medical training with robot patients may help doctors learn the technical side of health care, but it is likely to do little to improve the interpersonal side.

▼ Figure **14.6** **Antacid Intake** A scatterplot of antacid intake measured by bottle count plotted against patient's stated intake for 116 patients. When the actual and stated intakes are the same, the point lies on the diagonal line; when stated intake is greater than actual, the point lies above the line. Most patients exaggerated their intake (Roth & Caron, 1978).

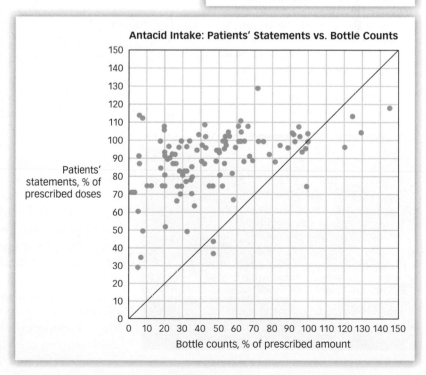

Antacid Intake: Patients' Statements vs. Bottle Counts

Patients' statements, % of prescribed doses (y-axis, 0–150)

Bottle counts, % of prescribed amount (x-axis, 0–150)

"Whoa — way too much information."

IN SUMMARY

▶ The psychology of illness concerns how sensitivity to the body leads people to recognize illness and seek treatment.

▶ Somatic symptom disorders can stem from excessive sensitivity to physical problems.

▶ The sick role is a set of rights and obligations linked with illness; some people fake illness in order to accrue those rights.

▶ Successful health care providers interact with their patients to understand both the physical state and the psychological state.

The Psychology of Health: Feeling Good

Two kinds of psychological factors influence personal health: health-relevant personality traits and health behavior. Personality can influence health through relatively enduring traits that make some people particularly susceptible to health problems or stress while sparing or protecting others. The Type A behavior pattern is an example. Because personality is not typically something we choose ("I'd like a bit of that sense of humor and extraversion over there, please, but hold the whininess"), this source of health can be outside personal control. In contrast, engaging in positive health behaviors is something anyone can do, at least in principle.

Personality and Health

Different health problems seem to plague different social groups. For example, men are more susceptible to heart disease than are women, and African Americans are more susceptible to asthma than are Asian or European Americans. Beyond these general social categories, personality turns out to be a factor in wellness, with individual differences in optimism and hardiness important influences.

Optimism

Pollyanna is one of literature's most famous optimists. Eleanor H. Porter's 1913 novel portrayed Pollyanna as a girl who greeted life with boundless good cheer, even when she was orphaned and sent to live with her cruel aunt. Her response to a sunny day was to remark on the good weather, of course, but her response to a gloomy day was to point out how lucky it is that not every day is gloomy! Her crotchety Aunt Polly had exactly the opposite attitude, somehow managing to turn every happy moment into an opportunity for strict correction. A person's level of optimism or pessimism tends to be fairly stable over time, and research comparing the personalities of twins reared together versus those reared apart suggests that this stability arises because these traits are moderately heritable (Plomin et al., 1992). Perhaps Pollyanna and Aunt Polly were each "born that way."

An optimist who believes that "in uncertain times, I usually expect the best" is likely to be healthier than a pessimist who believes that "if something can go wrong for me, it will." One recent review of dozens of studies including tens of thousands of participants concluded that of all of the measures of psychological well-being examined, optimism is the one that most strongly predicted a positive outcome for cardiovascular health (Boehm & Kubzansky, 2012). Importantly, the association between optimism and cardiovascular health remains even after statistically controlling for traditional risk factors

Adrianne Haslet was approximately four feet away from one of the bombs that exploded at the Boston Marathon in 2013. Although the explosion caused her to lose her left foot, Adrianne vowed that she will continue her career as a dancer—and will run the Boston Marathon in 2014. She is an optimist, and optimism can lead to positive health outcomes.

for heart disease including depression and anxiety, suggesting that it is not just the absence of psychopathology, but the presence of positive expectancies for the future, that predict positive health outcomes. Does just having positive thoughts about the future make it so? Unfortunately not.

Rather than improving physical health directly, optimism seems to aid in the maintenance of *psychological* health in the face of physical health problems. When sick, optimists are more likely than pessimists to maintain positive emotions, avoid negative emotions such as anxiety and depression, stick to medical regimens their caregivers have prescribed, and keep up their relationships with others. Among women who have surgery for breast cancer, for example, optimists are less likely to experience distress and fatigue after treatment than are pessimists, largely because they keep up social contacts and recreational activities during their treatment (Carver, Lehman, & Antoni, 2003). Optimism also seems to aid in the maintenance of physical health. For instance, optimism appears to be associated with cardiovascular health because optimistic people tend to engage in healthier behaviors like eating a balanced diet and exercising, which in turn leads to a healthier lipid profile (i.e., higher levels of high-density lipoprotein cholesterol that help to prevent buildup in your arteries, and lower triglycerides, which are the chemical form of fat storage in the body), which decreases the risk of heart disease (Boehm et al., 2013). So being optimistic is a positive asset, but it takes more than just hope to obtain positive health benefits.

> **Who's healthier, the optimist or the pessimist? Why?**

The benefits of optimism raise an important question: If the traits of optimism and pessimism are stable over time—even resistant to change—can pessimists ever hope to gain any of the advantages of optimism (Heatherton & Weinberger, 1994)? Research has shown that even die-hard pessimists can be trained to become significantly more optimistic and that this training can improve their psychosocial health outcomes. For example, pessimistic breast cancer patients who received 10 weeks of training in stress management techniques became more optimistic and were less likely than those who received only relaxation exercises to suffer distress and fatigue during their cancer treatments (Antoni et al., 2001).

Hardiness

Some people seem to be thick-skinned, somehow able to take stress or abuse that could be devastating to others. Are there personality traits that contribute to such resilience and offer protection from stress-induced illness? To identify such traits, Suzanne Kobasa (1979) studied a group of stress-resistant business executives. These individuals reported high levels of stressful life events but had histories of relatively few illnesses compared with a similar group who succumbed to stress by getting sick. The stress-resistant group (Kobasa labeled them *hardy*) shared several traits, all conveniently beginning with the letter *C*. They showed a sense of *commitment*, an ability to become involved in life's tasks and encounters rather than just dabbling. They exhibited a belief in *control*, the expectation that their actions and words have a causal influence over their lives and environment. And they were willing to accept *challenge*, undertaking change and accepting opportunities for growth.

Can just anyone develop hardiness? Researchers have attempted to teach hardiness with some success. In one such attempt, participants attended 10 weekly hardiness-training sessions, in which they were encouraged to examine their stresses, develop action plans for dealing with them, explore their bodily reactions to stress, and find ways to compensate for unchangeable situations without falling into

Sometimes hardiness tips over the edge into foolhardiness. Members of the Coney Island Polar Bear Club take that plunge every Sunday of winter.

AP PHOTO/KATHY WILLENS

self-pity. Compared with control groups (who engaged in relaxation and meditation training or in group discussions about stress), the hardiness-training group reported greater reductions in their perceived personal stress as well as fewer symptoms of illness (Maddi, Kahn, & Maddi, 1998). Hardiness training can have similar positive effects in college students, for some even boosting their GPA (Maddi et al., 2009).

Health-Promoting Behaviors and Self-Regulation

Even without changing our personalities at all, we can do certain things to be healthy. The importance of healthy eating, safe sex, and giving up smoking are common knowledge. But we don't seem to be acting on the basis of this knowledge. At the turn of the 21st century, 69% of Americans over 20 are overweight or obese (National Center for Health Statistics, 2012). The prevalence of unsafe sex is difficult to estimate, but 65 million Americans currently suffer from an incurable sexually transmitted disease (STD), and 20 million contract one or more new STDs each year (Satterwhite et al., 2013). Another million people live with human immunodeficiency virus/acquired immune deficiency syndrome (HIV/AIDS), 18.1% of whom are unaware of their infection, which is usually contracted through unprotected sex with an infected partner (Centers for Disease Control, 2012). And despite endless warnings, 21% of Americans still smoke cigarettes (Pleis et al., 2009). What's going on?

Self-Regulation

Doing what is good for you is not necessarily easy. Mark Twain once remarked, "The only way to keep your health is to eat what you don't want, drink what you don't like, and do what you'd rather not." Engaging in health-promoting behaviors involves **self-regulation**, *the exercise of voluntary control over the self to bring the self into line with preferred standards.* When you decide on a salad rather than a cheeseburger, for

> **Why is it difficult to achieve and maintain self-control?**

instance, you control your impulse and behave in a way that will help to make you the kind of person you would prefer to be—a healthy one. Self-regulation often involves putting off immediate gratification for longer-term gains.

Self-regulation requires a kind of inner strength or willpower. One theory suggests that self-control is a kind of strength that can be fatigued (Baumeister, Heatherton, & Tice, 1995; Baumeister, Vohs, & Tice, 2007). In other words, trying to exercise control in one area may exhaust self-control, leaving behavior in other areas unregulated. To test this theory, researchers seated hungry volunteers near a batch of fresh, hot, chocolate chip cookies. They asked some participants to leave the cookies alone but help themselves to a healthy snack of radishes, whereas others were allowed to indulge. When later challenged with an impossibly difficult figure-tracing task, the self-control group was more likely than the self-indulgent group to abandon the difficult task—behavior interpreted as evidence that they had depleted their pool of self-control (Baumeister et al., 1998). The take-home message from this experiment is that to control behavior successfully, we need to choose our battles, exercising self-control mainly on the personal weaknesses that are most harmful to health.

Sometimes, though, self-regulation is less a matter of brute force than of strategy. Martial artists claim that anyone can easily overcome a large attacker with the use of the right moves, and overcoming our own unhealthy impulses may also be a matter of finesse. Let's look carefully at healthy approaches to some key challenges for self-regulation—eating, safe sex, and smoking—to learn what "smart moves" can aid us in our struggles.

JEAN SANDER/FEATUREPICS

Nobody ever said self-control was easy. Probably the only reason you're able to keep yourself from eating this cookie is that it's just a picture of a cookie. Really. Don't eat it.

self-regulation
The exercise of voluntary control over the self to bring the self into line with preferred standards.

Eating Wisely

In many Western cultures, the weight of the average citizen is increasing alarmingly. One explanation is based on our evolutionary history: In order to ensure their survival, our ancestors found it useful to eat well in times of plenty to store calories for leaner times. In postindustrial societies in the 21st century, however, there are no leaner times, and people can't burn all of the calories they consume (Pinel, Assanand, & Lehman, 2000). But why, then, isn't obesity endemic throughout the Western world? Why are people in France leaner on average than Americans, even though their foods are high in fat? One reason has to do with the fact that activity level in France is greater. Research by Paul Rozin and his colleagues also finds that portion sizes in France are significantly smaller than in the United States, but at the same time, people in France take longer to finish their smaller meals. At a McDonald's in France, diners take an average of 22 minutes to consume a meal, whereas in the United States, they take under 15 minutes (Rozin, Kabnick, et al., 2003). Right now, Americans seem to be involved in some kind of national eating contest, whereas in France people are eating less food more slowly, perhaps leading them to be more conscious of what they are eating. This, ironically, probably leads to lower French fry consumption.

One of the reasons that people in France are leaner than people in the United States is because the average French diner spends 22 minutes to consume a fast-food meal, whereas the average American diner spends only 15 minutes. How could the length of the average meal influence an individual's body weight?

Short of moving to France, what can you do? Studies indicate that dieting doesn't always work because the process of conscious self-regulation can be easily undermined by stress, leading people who are trying to control themselves to lose control by overindulging in the very behavior they had been trying to overcome. This may remind you of a general principle discussed in the Consciousness chapter: Trying hard not to do something can often directly produce the unwanted behavior (Wegner, 1994a, 1994b).

The restraint problem may be inherent in the very act of self-control (Polivy & Herman, 1992). Rather than dieting, then, heading toward normal weight should involve a new emphasis on exercise and nutrition (Prochaska & Sallis, 2004). In emphasizing what is good to eat, the person can freely think about food rather than trying to suppress thoughts about it. A focus on increasing activity rather than reducing food intake, in turn, gives people another positive and active goal to pursue. Self-regulation is more effective when it focuses on what to do rather than on what *not* to do (Molden, Lee, & Higgins, 2009; Wegner & Wenzlaff, 1996).

> **Why is exercise a more effective weight-loss choice than dieting?**

Avoiding Sexual Risks

People put themselves at risk when they have unprotected vaginal, oral, or anal intercourse. Sexually active adolescents and adults are usually aware of such risks, not to mention the risk of unwanted pregnancy, and yet many behave in risky ways nonetheless. Why doesn't awareness translate into avoidance? Risk takers harbor an *illusion of unique invulnerability*, a systematic bias toward believing that they are less likely to fall victim to the problem than are others (Perloff & Fetzer, 1986). For example, a study of sexually active female college students found that respondents judged their own likelihood of getting pregnant in the next year as less than 10%, but estimated the average for other women at the university to be 27% (Burger & Burns, 1988). Paradoxically, this illusion was even stronger among women in the sample who reported using inadequate or no contraceptive techniques. The tendency to think "It won't happen to me" may be most pronounced when it probably will.

Unprotected sex often is the impulsive result of last-minute emotions. When thought is further blurred by alcohol or recreational drugs, people often fail to use the latex condoms that can reduce their exposure to the risks of pregnancy, HIV, and many other STDs. Like other forms of self-regulation, the avoidance of sexual risk requires the kind of planning that can be easily undone by circumstances that hamper the ability to think ahead. One approach to reducing sexual risk taking, then, is simply finding ways to help people plan ahead. Sex education programs offer adolescents just such a chance by encouraging them, at a time when they have not had much sexual experience, to think about what they might do when they need to make decisions. Although sex education is sometimes criticized as increasing adolescents' awareness of and interest in sex, the research evidence is clear: Sex education reduces the likelihood that adolescents will engage in unprotected sexual activity and benefits their health (American Psychological Association, 2005). The same holds true for adults.

> **Why does planning ahead reduce sexual risk taking?**

Not Smoking

One in two smokers dies prematurely from smoking-related diseases such as lung cancer, heart disease, emphysema, and cancer of the mouth and throat. Lung cancer alone kills more people than any other form of cancer, and smoking causes 80% of lung cancers. Although the overall rate of smoking in the United States is declining, new smokers abound, and many can't seem to stop. College students are puffing away along with everyone else, with 20% of college students currently smoking (Thompson et al., 2007). In the face of all the devastating health consequences, why don't people quit?

Nicotine, the active ingredient in cigarettes, is addictive, so smoking is difficult to stop once the habit is established (discussed in the Consciousness chapter). As in other forms of self-regulation, the resolve to quit smoking is fragile and seems to break down under stress. In the months following 9/11, for example, cigarette sales jumped 13% in Massachusetts (Phillips, 2002). And for some time after quitting, ex-smokers remain sensitive to cues in the environment: Eating or drinking, a bad mood, anxiety, or just seeing someone else smoking is enough to make them want a cigarette (Shiffman et al., 1996). The good news is that the urge decreases and people become less likely to relapse the longer they've been away from nicotine.

"Boy, I'm going to pay for this tomorrow at yoga class."

Psychological programs and techniques to help people kick the habit include nicotine replacement systems such as gum and skin patches, counseling programs, and hypnosis, but these programs are not always successful. Trying again and again in different ways is apparently the best approach (Schachter, 1982). After all, to quit smoking forever, you only need to quit one more time than you start up. But like the self-regulation of eating and sexuality, the self-regulation of smoking can require effort and thought. The ancient Greeks blamed self-control problems on *akrasia* (weakness of will). Modern psychology focuses less on blaming a person's character for poor self-regulation and points instead toward the difficulty of the task. Keeping healthy by behaving in healthy ways is one of the great challenges of life (see Other Voices box).

> **To quit smoking forever, how many times do you need to quit?**

IN SUMMARY

► The connection between mind and body can be revealed through the influences of personality and self-regulation of behavior on health.

► The personality traits of optimism and hardiness are associated with reduced risk for illnesses, perhaps because people with these traits can fend off stress.

► The self-regulation of behaviors such as eating, sexuality, and smoking is difficult for many people because self-regulation is easily disrupted by stress; strategies for maintaining self-control can pay off with significant improvements in health and quality of life.

OTHER VOICES

Freedom to Be Unhealthy?

Robert H. Frank is an economics professor at the Johnson Graduate School of Management at Cornell University.

PHOTO: BLOOMBERG VIA GETTY IMAGES

In the chapter on Emotion and Motivation you learned about the health benefits and risks associated with what you eat. In this chapter, you learned that what you do (Do you exercise?) and what you think (Are you an optimist?) also can influence your experience of stress and health. The research is clear that people who eat right and exercise regularly have better mental and physical health outcomes. Is it our business, then, to try to get people to eat better and exercise more?

The mayor of New York City, Michael Bloomberg, recently advocated for a tax on large, sugary drinks, which has been nicknamed the "soda tax." Some have praised this idea, believing that it is our responsibility to structure society in a way that improves the health of our citizens, and especially our children. Others have criticized this initiative, arguing that we live in a free country and people should be free to drink all of the soda and avoid all of the exercise they want. Economist Robert Frank recently weighed in on this issue, considering the pros and cons of a soda tax.

On narrow technical grounds, a New York State court recently rejected Mayor Michael R. Bloomberg's proposed curbs on large sodas and other sugary drinks. The ruling is being appealed, but many people who viewed the proposal as a step down a slippery slope to a nanny state were quick to celebrate the court's move. Beyond questioning the mayor's legal authority to impose a 16-ounce limit on the size of sugary beverages sold in certain places, critics objected on philosophical grounds, arguing that people should be free to make such choices for themselves.

But while almost everyone celebrates freedom in the abstract, defending one cherished freedom often requires sacrificing another. Whatever the flaws in Mr. Bloomberg's proposal, it sprang from an entirely commendable concern: a desire to protect parents' freedom to raise healthy children.

Being free to do something doesn't just mean being legally permitted to do it. It also means having a reasonable prospect of being able to do it. Parents don't want their children to become obese, or to suffer the grave consequences of diet-induced diabetes. Yet our current social environment encourages heavy consumption of sugary soft drinks, making such outcomes much more likely. So that environment clearly limits parents' freedom to achieve an eminently laudable goal.

The mayor's critics want to protect their own freedom to consume soft drinks in 32-ounce containers. But pro-freedom slogans provide no guidance about what to do when specific freedoms are in conflict, as they are here. Nor do they alert us to the possibility that taxes or other alternative policies often render such tough choices unnecessary. Sensible policy decisions spring less reliably from slogans than from careful assessment of the pros and cons of the relevant alternatives.

Does frequent exposure to supersize sodas really limit parents' freedom to raise healthy children? There's room for skepticism, because people often believe that they're not much influenced by others' opinions and behavior. But believing doesn't make it so.

As an Illinois state legislator in 1842, Abraham Lincoln deftly illustrated the absurdity of this particular conceit: "Let me ask the man who could maintain this position most stiffly, what compensation he will accept to go to church some Sunday and sit during the sermon with his wife's bonnet upon his head?" Most men, Lincoln conjectured, would demand a considerable sum—not because wearing a woman's bonnet would be illegal or immoral, obviously, but just because it would be so unseemly.

Even those who concede the obvious power of the social environment have little reason to worry about how their own choices might alter it. Collectively, however, our choices can profoundly transform the environment, often in ways that cause serious problems. And that makes the social environment an object of legitimate public concern.

Imagine a society like the United States before 1964, where unregulated individual choices produced high percentages of smokers in the population—more than 50 percent among adult men. Not even the staunchest libertarians should deny that their children would be more likely to become smokers in such an environment.

Smokers harm not only themselves and those who inhale secondhand smoke but also those who simply want their children to grow

(continued on next page)

up to be nonsmokers. People can urge their children to ignore peer influences, of course, but that's often a losing battle.

No rational deliberation about smoking policies can ignore the fact that smoking harms others in this way. Such considerations helped give rise to a variety of policies that discourage smoking. In New York City, for example, smoking is no longer permitted in many public places, and state and city taxes on a pack of cigarettes are now near $6.

Such policies have reduced the national smoking rate by more than half since 1965, making it much easier for parents to raise their children to be nonsmokers. That's an enormous benefit. Opponents of smoking restrictions must be prepared to show that those adversely affected by them suffer harm that outweighs that benefit. Given that the overwhelming majority of smokers themselves regret having taken up the habit, that's a tall order.

Parallel arguments apply to sugary drinks. Unless we're prepared to deny, against all evidence, that the environment powerfully influences children's choices, we're forced to conclude that rejecting Mr. Bloomberg's proposal significantly curtails parents' freedom to achieve the perfectly reasonable goal of raising healthy children. Why should opponents of the mayor's proposal be permitted to limit parents' freedom in this way, merely to spare themselves the trivial inconvenience of having to order a second 16-ounce soda?

Fortunately, society's legitimate interest in the social environment needn't be expressed by means of invasive prohibitions. The public policy goal that prompted the mayor's proposal could also be served in more direct and less intrusive ways.

For example, we could tax sugary soft drinks. In 2010, the mayor himself praised a proposal for a penny-per-ounce tax on soda in New York State; the idea was dropped after heavy opposition from the beverage industry.

The case for reintroducing such a proposal is strong. We have to tax something, after all, and taxing soft drinks would let us reduce taxes now imposed on manifestly useful activities. At the federal level, for example, a tax on soda would permit a reduction in the payroll tax, which would encourage businesses to hire more workers.

Just as few smokers are glad that they smoke, few people go to their graves wishing that they and their loved ones had drunk more sugary soft drinks. Evidence suggests that the current high volume of soft-drink consumption has generated enormous social costs. So to those who have lobbied successfully against a soda tax, I pose a simple question: How do the benefits of your right to drink tax-free sodas outweigh the substantial costs of defending it?

Where do you stand? The research described in this textbook makes clear that healthier eating and behavior lead to better health outcomes—benefiting both the individual and society more generally in the form of greater productivity and lower health costs due to later illness. But does the government really have the right to penalize people for choosing to drink soda and other sugary drinks? On the other hand, does it really impinge upon people's freedom to be charged a few more cents for drinks that are bad for them (and costlier to society in the form of health expenses)? How should the science of human health and behavior be used to influence actual human health and behavior?

Chapter Review

KEY CONCEPT QUIZ

1. What kinds of stressors are you likely to be exposed to if you live in a dense urban area with considerable traffic, noise, and pollution?
   a. cultural stressors
   b. intermittent stressors
   c. chronic stressors
   d. positive stressors

2. In an experiment, two groups are subject to distractions while attempting to complete a task. Group A is told they can quiet the distractions by pushing a button. This information is withheld from Group B. Why will Group A's performance at the task likely be better than Group B's?
   a. Group B is working in a different environment.
   b. Group A has perceived control over a source of performance-impeding stress.
   c. Group B is less distracted than Group A.
   d. The distractions affecting Group B are now chronic.

3. The brain activation that occurs in response to a threat begins in the
   a. pituitary gland.
   b. hypothalamus.
   c. adrenal gland.
   d. corpus callosum.

4. According to the general adaptation syndrome, during the ___ phase, the body adapts to its high state of arousal as it tries to cope with a stressor.
   a. exhaustion
   b. alarm
   c. resistance
   d. energy

5. Which of the following statements is most accurate regarding the physiological response to stress?
   a. Type A behavior patterns have psychological but not physiological ramifications.
   b. The link between work-related stress and coronary heart disease is unfounded.
   c. Stressors can cause hormones to flood the brain, strengthening the immune system.
   d. The immune system is remarkably responsive to psychological influences.

6. Meditation is an altered state of consciousness that occurs
   a. with the aid of drugs.
   b. through hypnosis.
   c. naturally or through special practices.
   d. as a result of dreamlike brain activity.

7. Engaging in aerobic exercise is a way of managing stress by managing the
   a. environment
   b. body.
   c. situation.
   d. intake of air.

8. Finding a new or creative way to think about a stressor that reduces its threat is called
   a. stress inoculation.
   b. repressive coping.
   c. reframing.
   d. rational coping.

9. The positive health outcomes associated with religiosity and spirituality are believed to be the result of all of the following except
   a enhanced social support.
   b engagement in healthier behavior.
   c endorsement of hope and optimism.
   d intercessory prayer.

10. Faking an illness is a violation of
    a. malingering.
    b. somatoform disorder.
    c. the sick role.
    d. the Type B pattern of behavior.

11. Which of the following describes a successful health care provider?
    a. displays empathy
    b. pays attention to both the physical and psychological state of the patient
    c. uses psychology to promote patient compliance
    d. all of the above

12. When sick, optimists are more likely than pessimists to
    a. maintain positive emotions.
    b. become depressed.
    c. ignore their caregiver's advice.
    d. avoid contact with others.

13. Which of the following is NOT a trait associated with hardiness?
    a. a sense of commitment
    b. an aversion to criticism
    c. a belief in control
    d. a willingness to accept challenge

14. Stress ___ the self-regulation of behaviors such as eating and smoking.
    a. strengthens
    b. has no effect on
    c. disrupts
    d. normalizes

KEY TERMS

stressors (p. 550)
stress (p. 550)
health psychology (p. 550)
chronic stressor (p. 551)
fight-or-flight response (p. 554)
general adaptation syndrome (GAS) (p. 555)

telomeres (p. 556)
telomerase (p. 556)
immune system (p. 557)
lymphocytes (p. 557)
Type A behavior pattern (p. 558)
burnout (p. 559)
repressive coping (p. 561)

rational coping (p. 561)
reframing (p. 562)
stress inoculation training (SIT) (p. 562)
meditation (p. 563)
relaxation therapy (p. 564)
relaxation response (p. 564)

biofeedback (p. 564)
social support (p. 566)
psychosomatic illness (p. 572)
somatic symptom disorders (p. 572)
sick role (p. 572)
self-regulation (p. 576)

CHANGING MINDS

1. In 2002, researchers compared severe acne in college students during a relatively stress-free period and during a highly stressful exam period. After adjusting for other variables such as changes in sleep or diet, the researchers concluded that increased acne severity was strongly correlated with increased levels of stress. Learning about the study, your roommate is surprised. "Acne is a skin disease," your roommate says. "I don't see how it could have anything to do with your mental state." How would you weigh in on the role of stress in medical diseases? What other examples could you give of ways in which stress can affect health?

2. A friend of yours, who is taking a heavy course load, confides that he's feeling overwhelmed. "I can't take the stress," he says. "Sometimes I daydream of living on an island somewhere, where I can just lie in the

sun and have no stress at all." What would you tell your friend about stress? Is all stress bad? What would a life with no stress really be like?

3. One of your classmates spent the summer interning in a neurologist's office. "One of the most fascinating things," she says, "was the patients with psychosomatic illness. Some had seizures or partial paralysis of an arm, and there were no neurological causes—so it was all psychosomatic. The neurologist tried to refer these patients to psychiatrists, but a lot of the patients thought he was accusing them of faking their symptoms, and were very insulted." What would you tell your friend about psychosomatic illness? Could a disease that's "all in the head" really produce symptoms such as seizures or partial paralysis, or are these patients definitely faking their symptoms?

ANSWERS TO KEY CONCEPT QUIZ

1. c; 2. b; 3. b; 4. c; 5. d; 6. c; 7. b; 8. c; 9. d; 10. c; 11. d; 12. a; 13. b, 14. c.

Need more help? Additional resources are located in LaunchPad at:
http://www.worthpublishers.com/launchpad/ schacter3e

15

Psychological Disorders

VIRGINIA WOOLF LEFT HER WALKING STICK on the bank of the river, put a large stone in the pocket of her coat, and made her way into the water. Her body was found 3 weeks later. She had written to her husband: "Dearest, I feel certain I am going mad again. . . . And I shan't recover this time. I begin to hear voices, and I can't concentrate. So I am doing what seems the best thing to do" (Dally, 1999, p. 182). Thus, near Rodmell, Sussex, England, on March 28, 1941, life ended for the prolific novelist and essayist, central figure of the avant-garde literary salon known as the Bloomsbury Group, influential feminist—and unfortunate victim of lifelong "breakdowns," with swings in mood between severe depression and unbridled mania.

The condition afflicting Woolf is now known as bipolar disorder. At one extreme were her episodes of depression: She was sullen and despondent; her creativity came to a halt; and sometimes she was bedridden for months by her illness. These periods alternated with mania, when, as her husband, Leonard, recounted, "She talked almost without stopping for 2 or 3 days, paying no attention to anyone in the room or anything said to her." Her language "became completely incoherent, a mere jumble of dissociated words." At the height of her spells, birds spoke to her in Greek, her dead mother reappeared and scolded her, and voices commanded her to "do wild things." She refused to eat, wrote pages of nonsense, and launched tirades of abuse at her husband and her companions (Dally, 1999, p. 240).

Between these phases, Woolf somehow managed a brilliant literary life. Her Victorian family had seen no reason for a woman to attend university, but the absence of schooling did not prevent her from becoming the extraordinary intellectual figure celebrated in the title of Edward Albee's (1962) play, *Who's Afraid of Virginia Woolf?* All told, she wrote nine novels, a play, five volumes of essays, and more than 14 volumes of diaries and letters. Her novels broke away from traditions of strict plot and setting to explore the inner lives and musings of her characters, and

English novelist and critic, Virginia Woolf (1882–1941), in 1937. Her lifelong affliction with bipolar disorder ended in suicide, but the manic phases of her illness helped to fuel her prolific writing.

©THE PRINT COLLECTOR/ALAMY

her observations revealed a keen appreciation of her own experience of psychological disorder. In a letter to a friend, she remarked, "As an experience, madness is terrific . . . and not to be sniffed at, and in its lava I still find most of the things I write about" (Dally, 1999, p. 240). The price that Woolf paid for her genius, of course, was a dear one, and her husband and companions shared the burden of dealing with her disorder and her death. Disorders of the mind can create immense pain.

IN THIS CHAPTER, WE FIRST CONSIDER THE QUESTION: What is abnormal? Virginia Woolf's bouts of depression and mania and her eventual suicide certainly are abnormal in the sense that most people do not have these experiences, but at times she led a perfectly normal life. The enormously complicated human mind can produce behaviors, thoughts, and emotions that change radically from moment to moment. How do psychologists decide when a person's thoughts, emotions, and behaviors are "disordered?" We will first examine the key factors that must be weighed in making such a decision. We'll then focus on several major forms of *mental disorder*: depressive and bipolar disorders; anxiety, obsessive-compulsive, and trauma-related disorders; schizophrenia; disorders that begin in childhood and adolescence; and self-harm behaviors. As we view each type of disorder, we will examine how they manifest and what is known about their prevalence and causes.

The disorders examined in this chapter represent a tragic loss of human potential. The contentment, peace, and love that people could be enjoying are crowded out by pain and suffering when the mind goes awry to create disorders. A scientific approach to mental disorders that views them through a model that considers the biological, psychological, and social factors that combine to cause disorders (appropriately called the *biopsychosocial model*) is beginning to sort out their symptoms and causes. As we see in the next chapter, this approach already offers treatments for some disorders that are remarkably effective, and for other disorders, it offers hope that pain and suffering can be alleviated in the future.

Defining Mental Disorders: What Is Abnormal?

The concept of a mental disorder is one of those things that seems simple at first glance, but turns out to be very complex and quite tricky (similar to clearly defining "consciousness," "stress," or "personality"). Any extreme variation in your thoughts, feelings, or behaviors is not a mental disorder. For instance, severe anxiety before a test, sadness after the loss of a loved one, or a night of excessive alcohol consumption—although unpleasant—is not necessarily pathological. Similarly, a persistent pattern of deviating from the norm does not qualify a person for a mental disorder. If it did, we would diagnose mental disorders in the most creative and visionary people—anyone whose ideas deviate from those around them.

So what *is* a mental disorder? Perhaps surprisingly, there is not universal agreement on a precise definition of the term "mental disorder." However, there is general agreement that a **mental disorder** can be defined as *a persistent disturbance or dysfunction in behavior, thoughts, or emotions that causes significant distress or impairment* (Stein et al., 2010; Wakefield, 2007). One way to think about mental disorders is as dysfunctions or deficits in the normal human psychological processes you have learned about throughout this book. People with mental disorders have problems with their perception, memory, learning, emotion, motivation, thinking, and social processes. You might ask: But this is still a broad definition, what kinds of disturbances "count" as mental disorders? How long must they last to be considered "persistent?" And how

mental disorder
A persistent disturbance or dysfunction in behavior, thoughts, or emotions that causes significant distress or impairment.

medical model
Abnormal psychological experiences are conceptualized as illnesses that, like physical illnesses, have biological and environmental causes, defined symptoms, and possible cures.

Although mental disorders represent deviations from normal behavior, all deviations from the norm are not disordered. Indeed, people thinking differently about the world, and behaving in ways that deviated from the norm, have brought remarkable advances, such as Mickey Mouse, iPhones, and racial equality.

much distress or impairment is required? These are all hotly debated questions in the field. They have been for many years, and likely will be for years to come (as discussed in more detail later).

Conceptualizing Mental Disorders

Historically speaking, there are reports of people acting strangely or reporting bizarre thoughts or emotions since ancient times. Until fairly recently, such difficulties were conceptualized as the result of religious or supernatural forces. In some cultures, psychopathology is still interpreted as possession by spirits or demons, as enchantment by a witch or shaman, or as God's punishment for wrongdoing. In many societies, including our own, people with psychological disorders have been feared and ridiculed, and often treated as criminals: punished, imprisoned, or put to death for their "crime" of deviating from the normal.

According to the theory of physiognomy, mental disorders could be diagnosed from facial features. This fanciful theory is now considered superstition but was popular from antiquity until the early 20th century.

Over the past 200 years, these ways of looking at psychological abnormalities have largely been replaced in most parts of the world by a **medical model**, in which *abnormal psychological experiences are conceptualized as illnesses that, like physical illnesses, have biological and environmental causes, defined symptoms, and possible cures.* Conceptualizing abnormal thoughts and behaviors as illness suggests that a first step is to determine the nature of the problem through *diagnosis.*

What's the first step in helping someone with a psychological disorder?

In diagnosis, clinicians seek to determine the nature of a person's mental disorder by assessing *signs* (objectively observed indicators of a disorder) and *symptoms* (subjectively reported behaviors, thoughts, and emotions) that suggest an underlying illness. So, for example, just as self-reported sniffles, and cough are symptoms of a cold, Virginia Woolf's extreme moods, alternating between despondency and wild euphoria, can be seen as symptoms of her

Extreme shyness or social anxiety disorder? What are some of the criticisms of the medical model?

SIMONE BECCHETTI/GETTY IMAGES

bipolar disorder. It is important to note the differences among three related general medical and classification terms:

> A *disorder* refers to a common set of signs and symptoms;

> A *disease* is a known pathological process affecting the body; and

> A *diagnosis* is a determination as to whether a disorder or disease is present (Kraemer, Shrout, & Rubio-Stipec, 2007).

Importantly, knowing that a disorder is present (i.e., diagnosed) does not necessarily mean that we know the underlying disease process in the body that gives rise to the signs and symptoms of the disorder.

Viewing mental disorders as medical problems reminds us that people who are suffering deserve care and treatment, not condemnation. Nevertheless, there are some criticisms of the medical model. Some psychologists argue that it is inappropriate to use clients' subjective self-report, rather than physical tests of pathology (as in other areas of medical diagnostics), to determine underlying illness. Others argue that the model often "medicalizes" or "pathologizes" normal human behavior. For instance, extreme sadness can be considered to be an illness called *major depressive disorder*; extreme shyness can be diagnosed as an illness called *social anxiety disorder*; and trouble concentrating in school is called *attention-deficit/hyperactivity disorder*. Although there are some valid concerns about the current method of defining and classifying mental disorders, it inarguably is a huge advance over older alternatives, such as viewing mental disorders as the work of witchcraft or as punishment for sin. Moreover, psychologists keep these concerns in mind as they work to improve the diagnostic procedures.

Classifying Disorders: The *DSM*

So how is the medical model used to classify the wide range of abnormal behaviors that occur among humans? Psychologists, psychiatrists (physicians concerned with the study and treatment of mental disorders) and most other people working in the area of mental disorders use a standardized system for classifying mental disorders. In 1952, in recognition of the need to have a consensual diagnostic system for clinicians and researchers, the American Psychiatric Association published the first version of the **Diagnostic and Statistical Manual of Mental Disorders (DSM)**. The *DSM*

Diagnostic and Statistical Manual of Mental Disorders (DSM)
A classification system that describes the features used to diagnose each recognized mental disorder and indicates how the disorder can be distinguished from other, similar problems.

comorbidity
The co-occurrence of two or more disorders in a single individual.

biopsychosocial perspective
Explains mental disorders as the result of interactions among biological, psychological, and social factors.

is *a classification system that describes the features used to diagnose each recognized mental disorder and indicates how the disorder can be distinguished from other, similar problems.* Each disorder is named and classified as a distinct illness. The initial version of the *DSM*, and its revision, *DSM–II*, published in 1968, provided a common language for talking about disorders. This was a major advance in the study of mental disorders; however, the diagnostic criteria listed in these early volumes were quite vague and based on thin theoretical assumptions. For instance, people who were extremely depressed or anxious for long periods of time might be given the general diagnosis of "neurosis reaction."

The next two editions of the *DSM* (*DSM–III*, published in 1980 and *DSM–IV*, published in 1994) moved from vague descriptions of disorders to very detailed lists of symptoms (or *diagnostic criteria*) that had to be present in order for a disorder to be di-

How has the *DSM* changed over time?

agnosed. For instance, in addition to being extremely sad or depressed (for at least 2 weeks), a person must have at least five of nine agreed upon symptoms of depression (e.g., diminished interest in normally enjoyable activities, significant weight loss or gain, significantly increased or decreased sleep, loss of energy, feelings of worthlessness or guilt, trouble concentrating). The use of these detailed lists of symptoms for each of more than 200 disorders listed led to a dramatic increase in the reliability, or consistency, in diagnosing mental disorders. Two clinicians interviewing the same individual were now much more likely to agree on what mental disorders were present, greatly increasing the credibility of the diagnostic process (and the fields of psychiatry and clinical psychology).

In May 2013, the American Psychiatric Association released an updated manual: *DSM–5*. The *DSM–5* describes 22 major categories containing more than 200 different mental disorders (see **TABLE 15.1**). Along with the disorders listed in these 22 categories, the *DSM–5* describes conditions that may be included as formal disorders, but that, for now, require additional research. In addition, there is a section devoted to cultural considerations in diagnosing mental disorders. Why the switch from Roman to Arabic numerals? The hope is that with more rapid advances in our understanding of mental disorders, rather than wait another 20 years to update the *DSM*, we can make revisions as we learn more (*DSM–5.1, 5.2, 5.3,* and so on).

Each of the 22 chapters in the main body of the *DSM–5* lists the specific criteria that must be met in order for a person to be diagnosed with each disorder. Studies of large, representative samples of the U.S. population reveals that approximately half of Americans report experiencing at least one mental disorder during the course of their lives (Kessler, Berglund, et al., 2005). And, most of those with a mental disorder (greater than 80%) report **comorbidity**, which refers to *the co-occurrence of two or more disorders in a single individual* (Gadermann et al., 2012).

Causation of Disorders

The medical model of mental disorder suggests that knowing a person's diagnosis is useful because any given category of mental illness is likely to have a distinctive cause. In other words, just as different viruses, bacteria, or genetic abnormalities cause different physical illnesses, so a specifiable pattern of causes (or *etiology*) may exist for different psychological disorders. The medical model also suggests that each category of mental disorder is likely to have a common *prognosis*, a typical course over time and susceptibility to treatment and cure. Unfortunately, this basic medical model is usually an oversimplification; it is rarely useful to focus on a *single cause* that is *internal* to the person and that suggests a *single cure*.

To understand what factors might cause mental disorders, most psychologists take an integrated **biopsychosocial perspective** that *explains mental disorders as the result of interactions among biological, psychological, and social factors.* On the biological

Table 15.1

Main *DSM–5* Categories of Mental Disorders

1. **Neurodevelopmental Disorders:** These are conditions that begin early in development and cause significant impairments in functioning, such as intellectual disability (formerly called "mental retardation"), autism spectrum disorder, and attention-deficit/hyperactivity disorder.

2. **Schizophrenia Spectrum and Other Psychotic Disorders:** This is a group of disorders characterized by major disturbances in perception, thought, language, emotion, and behavior.

3. **Bipolar and Related Disorders:** These disorders include major fluctuations in mood—from mania to depression—and also can include psychotic experiences, which is why they are placed between the psychotic and depressive disorders in *DSM–5*.

4. **Depressive Disorders:** These are conditions characterized by extreme and persistent periods of depressed mood.

5. **Anxiety Disorders:** These are disorders characterized by excessive fear and anxiety that are extreme enough to impair a person's functioning, such as panic disorder, generalized anxiety disorder, and specific phobia.

6. **Obsessive-Compulsive and Related Disorders:** These are conditions characterized by the presence of obsessive thinking followed by compulsive behavior in response to that thinking.

7. **Trauma- and Stressor-Related Disorders:** These are disorders that develop in response to a traumatic event, such as posttraumatic stress disorder.

8. **Dissociative Disorders:** These are conditions characterized by disruptions or discontinuity in consciousness, memory, or identity, such as dissociative identity disorder (formerly called "multiple personality disorder").

9. **Somatic Symptom and Related Disorders:** These are conditions in which a person experiences bodily symptoms (e.g., pain, fatigue) associated with significant distress or impairment.

10. **Feeding and Eating Disorders:** These are problems with eating that impair health or functioning, such as anorexia nervosa and bulimia nervosa.

11. **Elimination Disorders:** These involve inappropriate elimination of urine or feces (e.g., bed-wetting).

12. **Sleep–Wake Disorders:** These are problems with the sleep–wake cycle, such as insomnia, narcolepsy, and sleep apnea.

13. **Sexual Dysfunctions:** These are problems related to unsatisfactory sexual activity, such as erectile disorder and premature ejaculation.

14. **Gender Dysphoria:** This is a single disorder characterized by incongruence between a person's experienced/expressed gender and assigned gender.

15. **Disruptive, Impulse-Control, and Conduct Disorders:** These are conditions involving problems controlling emotions and behaviors, such as conduct disorder, intermittent explosive disorder, and kleptomania.

16. **Substance-Related and Addictive Disorders:** This collection of disorders involves persistent use of substances or some other behavior (e.g., gambling) despite the fact that it leads to significant problems.

17. **Neurocognitive Disorders:** These are disorders of thinking caused by conditions such as Alzheimer's disease or traumatic brain injury.

18. **Personality Disorders:** These are enduring patterns of thinking, feeling, and behaving that lead to significant life problems.

19. **Paraphilic Disorders:** These are conditions characterized by inappropriate sexual activity, such as pedophilic disorder.

20. **Other Mental Disorders:** This is a residual category for conditions that do not fit into one of the above categories but are associated with significant distress or impairment, such as an unspecified mental disorder due to a medical condition.

21. **Medication-Induced Movement Disorders and Other Adverse Effects of Medication:** These are problems with physical movement (e.g., tremors, rigidity) that are caused by medication.

22. **Other Conditions that May be the Focus of Clinical Attention:** These include problems related to abuse, neglect, relationship, and other problems.

Source: From *DSM–5* (American Psychiatric Association, 2013).

CULTURE & COMMUNITY

What do mental disorders look like in different parts of the world? Are the mental disorders that we see in the United States also experienced by people in other parts of the world? In an effort to better understand the *epidemiology* (the study of the distribution and causes of health and disease) of mental disorders, Ronald Kessler and colleagues launched the World Health Organization World Mental Health Surveys, a large-scale study in which people from nearly two dozen countries around the world were assessed for the presence of mental disorders (Kessler & Üstün, 2008). The results of this study reveal that the major mental disorders seen in the United States appear similarly in countries and cultures all around the world. For instance, depression, anxiety, attention-deficit/hyperactivity disorder, and substance use are seen all over the globe.

They are reported at different rates in different countries (people in the United States reported the highest rates of mental disorders), but depression and anxiety are always the most common, followed by impulse-control and substance use disorders (Kessler et al., 2007).

Although all countries appear to have the common mental disorders described above, it is clear that cultural context can influence how mental disorders are experienced, described, assessed, and treated. To address this issue, the *DSM–5* includes a cultural formulation section that contains a Cultural Formulation Interview (CFI). The CFI includes 16 questions that the clinician asks a client during a mental health assessment in order to help the clinician understand how the client's culture might influence the experience, expression, and explanation of their mental disorder.

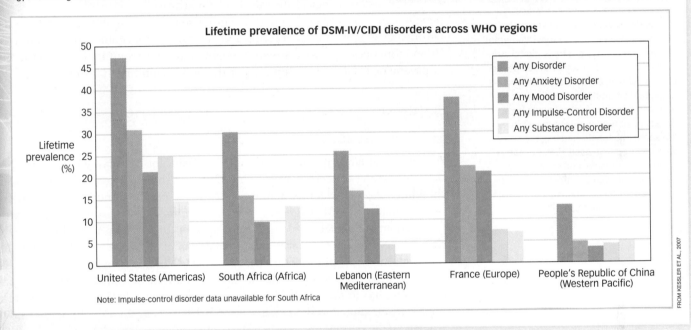

Lifetime prevalence of DSM-IV/CIDI disorders across WHO regions

Note: Impulse-control disorder data unavailable for South Africa

FROM KESSLER ET AL. 2007

---

side, the focus is on genetic and epigenetic (see Figure 3.23) influences, biochemical imbalances, and abnormalities in brain structure and function. The psychological perspective focuses on maladaptive learning and coping, cognitive biases, dysfunctional attitudes, and interpersonal problems. Social factors include poor socialization, stressful life experiences, and cultural and social inequities. The complexity of causation suggests that different individuals can experience a similar psychological disorder (e.g., depression) for different reasons. A person might fall into depression as a result of biological causes (e.g., genetics, hormones), psychological causes (e.g., faulty beliefs, hopelessness, poor strategies for coping with loss), environmental causes (e.g., stress or loneliness), or more likely as a result of some combination of these factors. And, of course, multiple causes mean there may not be a single cure.

> **Why does assessment require looking at a number of factors?**

The observation that most disorders have both internal (biological and psychological) *and* external (environmental) causes has given rise to a theory known as the **diathesis–stress model,** which suggests that *a person may be predisposed for a psychological disorder that remains unexpressed until triggered by stress.* The diathesis is the

diathesis–stress model
Suggests that a person may be predisposed for a psychological disorder that remains unexpressed until triggered by stress.

Mental disorders can be caused by biological, psychological, and environmental factors. The diathesis–stress model suggests that a person may be predisposed for a psychological disorder that remains unexpressed until triggered by stress. Suppose that two identical twins (with the same genetic profile) grow up in the same household (sharing the same parents, the same basic diet, the same access to television, and so on). As a teenager, one twin but not the other develops a mental disorder such as schizophrenia. How could this be?

internal predisposition and the stress is the external trigger. For example, most people were able to cope with their strong emotional reactions to the terrorist attack of September 11, 2001. However, for some who had a predisposition to negative emotions, the horror of the events may have overwhelmed their ability to cope, thereby precipitating a psychological disorder. Although diatheses can be inherited, it's important to remember that heritability is not destiny. A person who inherits a diathesis may never encounter the precipitating stress, whereas someone with little genetic propensity to a disorder may come to suffer from it given the right pattern of stress. The tendency to oversimplify mental disorders by attributing them to single, internal causes is nowhere more evident than in the interpretation of the role of the brain in psychological disorders. Brain scans of

> **What are the limitations of using brain scans for diagnosing?**

people with and without disorders can give rise to an unusually strong impression that psychological problems are internal and permanent, inevitable, and even untreatable. Brain influences and processes are fundamentally important for knowing the full story of psychological disorders, but are not the only chapter in that story.

A New Approach to Understanding Mental Disorders: RDoC

Although the *DSM* provides a useful framework for classifying disorders, there has been a growing concern over the fact that the findings from scientific research on the biopsychosocial factors that appear to cause psychopathology do not map neatly onto individual *DSM* diagnoses. Succinctly characterizing the current state of affairs, Thomas R. Insel, Director of the National Institute of Mental Health (NIMH; the primary funder of research on mental disorders in the United States), noted that although many people describe the *DSM* as a bible, it is more accurate to think of it like a dictionary that provides labels and current definitions: "People think that everything has to match *DSM* criteria, but you know what? Biology never read that book" (Insel, quoted in Belluck & Carey, 2013, p. A13). In order to better understand what actually causes mental disorders, researchers at the NIMH have proposed a new framework for thinking about mental disorders focused not on the currently defined *DSM* categories of disorders, but on the more basic biological, cognitive, and behavioral constructs that are believed to be the building blocks of mental disorders. This new system is called the **Research Domain Criteria Project (RDoC),** *a new initiative that aims to guide the classification and understanding of mental disorders by revealing the basic processes that give rise to them.* The RDoC is not intended to immediately replace the *DSM*, but to inform future revisions to it in the coming years (see the Real World box).

Using the RDoC, researchers study the causes of abnormal functioning by focusing on biological factors from genes to cells to brain circuits; psychological domains, such as learning, attention, memory; and various social processes and behavior (see **TABLE 15.2** for a list of domains). Through the RDoC approach, the NIMH would like to shift researchers away from studying currently defined *DSM* categories, and toward the study of the dimensional biopsychosocial processes believed, at the extreme end of the continuum, to lead to mental disorders. The long-term goal is to better understand what abnormalities cause different disorders, and to classify disorders based on those underlying causes, rather than on observed symptoms. This approach would bring the study of mental disorders in line with the study of other medical disorders. For example, if you are experiencing chest pain, severe headaches, fatigue,

Research Domain Criteria Project (RDoC) A new initiative that aims to guide the classification and understanding of mental disorders by revealing the basic processes that give rise to them.

► Table 15.2

Draft Research Domain Criteria (RDoC) Matrix

Domain / Construct	Units of Analysis							
	Genes	Molecules	Cells	Circuits	Physiology	Behavior	Self-reports	Paradigms
Negative Valence Systems								
Acute threat ("fear")								
Potential threat ("anxiety")								
Sustained threat								
Loss								
Frustrative nonreward								
Positive Valence Systems								
Approach motivation								
Initial responsiveness to reward								
Sustained responsiveness to reward								
Reward learning								
Habit								
Cognitive Systems								
Attention								
Perception								
Working memory								
Declarative memory								
Language behavior								
Cognitive (effortful) control								
Systems for Social Processes								
Affiliation and attachment								
Social communication								
Perception and understanding of self								
Perception and understanding of others								
Arousal and Regulatory Systems								
Arousal								
Circadian rhythms								
Sleep and wakefulness								

and difficulty breathing, it is unlikely that you are experiencing four separate disorders (*chest pain disorder, headache disorder*, etc.). Instead, we now know that these are all symptoms of an underlying disease process called hypertension. The RDoC approach similarly aims to shift the focus away from classifying based on surface symptoms and toward an understanding of the processes that give rise to disordered behavior. For instance, rather than studying cocaine addiction as a distinct disorder, from an RDoC perspective researchers might try to understand what causes abnormalities in "responsiveness to reward," a factor seen in those with excessive cocaine use as well as those with other addictive behaviors. Indeed, recent research has shown that variations in a gene (*DRD2*) that codes for dopamine receptors are associated with abnormalities in connectivity between parts of the frontal lobe and the striatum (described in the Neuroscience and Behavior chapter). This lack of connectivity is, in turn, related to the impulsiveness and responsiveness to rewards associated with a range of addictive behavior disorders (Buckholtz & Meyer-Lindenberg, 2012). This may help explain why some people seem to have addictive personalities in which they have trouble

How Are Mental Disorders Defined and Diagnosed?

Who decides what goes in the *DSM*? How are these decisions made? In psychology and psychiatry, as in the early days of most areas of the study of human health and behavior, these decisions currently are made by consensus among leaders in the research field. These leaders meet repeatedly over several years to make decisions about which disorders should be included in the new revision of the *DSM*, and how they should be defined. Over the years, these decisions have been based on descriptive research reporting on which clinical symptoms tend to cluster together. Everyone agrees that we need a system for classifying and defining mental disorders; however, as the currently available body of knowledge about mental disorders grows,

the field is moving beyond simple descriptive diagnostic categories toward ones based on underlying biopsychosocial processes (i.e., the Research Domain Criteria Project). Future decisions about how mental disorders are defined will likely continue to be reached by consensus among leaders in the field, but will be driven more directly by research on the underlying causes of these disorders.

Who decides whether someone has a diagnosis? And how are these decisions made? Over the years, researchers have developed structured clinical interviews that convert the lists of symptoms included in the *DSM* into sets of interview questions through which the clinician (psychologist, psychiatrist, social worker) makes a determination about whether or not a given per-

son meets criteria for each disorder (Nock et al., 2007). For instance, according to *DSM–5*, a person must have at least five of the nine symptoms of major depressive disorder in order to meet criteria for this disorder. Structured clinical interviews typically include nine questions about depression (one per symptom), and if the person reports that they have at least five of these symptoms, the clinician may conclude that this person is suffering from major depression. Right now diagnoses are determined primarily by client self-report of symptoms. With increasing attention to the underlying causes of mental disorders, many hope that in the future we will have biological and behavioral tests to help us make decisions about who has a mental illness and who does not.

The new Research Domain Criteria are trying to help us better understand why people seem to have "addictive personalities" in which they have trouble limiting their engagement in pleasurable experiences.

inhibiting their reward-seeking behavior. Importantly, understanding what processes cause problems like addiction will help us to develop more effective treatments, a topic we address in more detail in the next chapter.

You might have noticed that the list of domains in Table 15.2 looks like a slightly more detailed version of the table of contents for this book! The RDoC approach has an overall emphasis on neuroscience (Chapter 3), and specific focuses on abnormalities in emotional and motivational systems (Chapters 8), cognitive systems such as memory (Chapter 6), learning (Chapter 7), language and cognition (Chapter 9), social processes (Chapter 13), and stress and arousal (Chapter 14). From the RDoC perspective, mental disorders can be thought of as the result of abnormalities or dysfunctions in normal psychological processes. By learning about many of these processes in this book, you will likely have a good understanding of new definitions of mental disorders as they are developed in the years ahead.

Dangers of Labeling

An important complication in the diagnosis and classification of psychological disorders is the effect of labeling. Psychiatric labels can have negative consequences because many carry the baggage of negative stereotypes and stigma, such as the idea that mental disorder is a sign of personal weakness or the idea that psychiatric patients are dangerous. The stigma associated with mental disorders may explain why most people with diagnosable psychological disorders (approximately 60%) do not seek treatment (Kessler, Demler, et al., 2005; Wang, Berglund, et al., 2005).

Unfortunately, educating people about mental disorders does not dispel the stigma borne by those with these conditions (Phelan et al., 1997). In fact, expectations created by psychiatric labels can sometimes even compromise the judgment of mental health professionals (Garb, 1998; Langer & Abelson, 1974; Temerlin & Trousdale, 1969). In a classic demonstration of this phenomenon, psychologist David Rosenhan and six associates reported to different mental hospitals complaining of "hearing voices," a symptom sometimes

Why might someone avoid seeking help?

found in people with schizophrenia. Each was admitted to a hospital, and each promptly reported that the symptom had ceased. Even so, hospital staff were reluctant to identify these people as normal: It took an average of 19 days for these "patients" to secure their release, and even then they were released with the diagnosis of "schizophrenia in remission" (Rosenhan, 1973). Apparently, once hospital staff had labeled these patients as having a psychological disease, the label stuck.

These effects of labeling are particularly disturbing in light of evidence that the hospitalization of people with mental disorders is seldom necessary. One set of studies in Vermont followed the lives of patients who were thought to be too dangerous to release and therefore had been kept in the back wards of institutions for years. Their release resulted in no harm to the community (Harding et al., 1987), and further studies have shown that those with a mental disorder are no more likely to be violent than those without a disorder (Elbogen & Johnson, 2009; Monahan, 1992).

Labeling may even affect how labeled individuals view themselves; persons given such a label may come to view themselves not just as mentally disordered, but as hopeless or worthless. Such a view may cause them to develop an attitude of defeat and, as a result, to fail to work toward their own recovery. As one small step toward counteracting such consequences, clinicians have adopted the important practice of applying labels to the disorder and not to the person with the disorder. For example, an individual might be described as "a person with schizophrenia," not as "a schizophrenic." You'll notice that we follow this convention in the text.

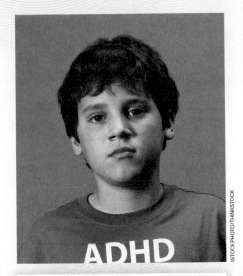

Although we label mental disorders, we should not apply those labels to people. For instance, rather than saying someone "is ADHD," we would say that the person currently meets diagnostic criteria for ADHD.

IN SUMMARY

▶ The *DSM–5* is a classification system that defines a mental disorder as occurring when the person experiences disturbances of thought, emotion, or behavior that produce distress or impairment and that arise from internal sources.

▶ According to the biopsychosocial model, mental disorders arise from an interaction of biological, psychological, and social factors, often thought of as a combination of a diathesis (internal predisposition) and stress (environmental life event).

▶ The RDoC is a new classification system that focuses on biological, cognitive, and behavioral aspects of mental disorders.

Anxiety Disorders: When Fears Take Over

"Okay, time for a pop quiz that will be half your grade for this class." If your instructor had actually said that, you would probably have experienced a wave of anxiety and dread. Your reaction would be appropriate and—no matter how intense the feeling— would not be a sign that you have a mental disorder. In fact, situation-related anxiety is normal and adaptive: in this case, perhaps by reminding you to keep up with your textbook assignments so you are prepared for pop quizzes. When anxiety arises that is out of proportion to real threats and challenges, however, it is maladaptive: It can take hold of people's lives, stealing their peace of mind and undermining their ability to function normally. Pathological anxicty is expressed as an **anxiety disorder,** *the class of mental disorder in which anxiety is the predominant feature.* People commonly experience more than one type of anxiety disorder at a given time, and there is significant *comorbidity* between anxiety and depression (Beesdo et al., 2010; Brown & Barlow, 2002). Among the anxiety disorders recognized in the *DSM–5* are phobic disorders, panic disorder, and generalized anxiety disorder.

> **When is anxiety harmful, and when is it helpful?**

anxiety disorder
The class of mental disorder in which anxiety is the predominant feature.

phobic disorders
Disorders characterized by marked, persistent, and excessive fear and avoidance of specific objects, activities, or situations.

specific phobia
A disorder that involves an irrational fear of a particular object or situation that markedly interferes with an individual's ability to function.

social phobia
A disorder that involves an irrational fear of being publicly humiliated or embarrassed.

preparedness theory
The idea that people are instinctively predisposed toward certain fears.

The preparedness theory explains why most merry-go-rounds carry children on beautiful horses. This mom might have some trouble getting her daughter to ride on a big spider or snake.

COURTESY OF DANIEL WEGNER

Phobic Disorders

Consider Mary, a 47-year-old mother of three, who sought treatment for *claustrophobia*—an intense fear of enclosed spaces. She traced her fear to childhood, when her older siblings would scare her by locking her in closets and confining her under blankets. Her own children grown, she wanted to find a job but could not because of a terror of elevators and other confined places that, she felt, shackled her to her home (Carson, Butcher, & Mineka, 2000). Many people feel a little anxious in enclosed spaces, but Mary's fears were abnormal and dysfunctional because they were disproportionate to any actual risk and impaired her ability to carry out a normal life. The *DSM–5* describes **phobic disorders** as characterized by *marked, persistent, and excessive fear and avoidance of specific objects, activities, or situations.* An individual with a phobic disorder recognizes that the fear is irrational but cannot prevent it from interfering with everyday functioning.

A **specific phobia** is *an irrational fear of a particular object or situation that markedly interferes with an individual's ability to function.* Specific phobias fall into five categories: (1) animals (e.g., dogs, cats, rats, snakes, spiders); (2) natural environments (e.g., heights, darkness, water, storms); (3) situations (e.g., bridges, elevators, tunnels, enclosed places); (4) blood, injections, and injury; and (5) other phobias, including choking or vomiting; and in children, loud noises or costumed characters. Approximately 12% of people in the United States will develop a specific phobia during their lives (Kessler, Berglund, et al., 2005), with rates slightly higher among women than men (Kessler et al., 2012).

Social phobia involves *an irrational fear of being publicly humiliated or embarrassed.* Social phobia can be restricted to situations such as public speaking, eating in public, or urinating in a public bathroom or generalized to a variety of social situations that involve being observed or interacting with unfamiliar people. Individuals with social phobia try to avoid situations where unfamiliar people might evaluate them, and they experience intense anxiety and distress when public exposure is unavoidable. Social phobia can develop in childhood, but it typically emerges between early adolescence and early adulthood (Kessler, Berglund, et al., 2005). Many people experience social phobia, with about 12% of men and 14% of women qualify for a diagnosis at some time in their lives (Kessler et al., 2012).

Why are phobias so common? The high rates of both specific and social phobias suggest a predisposition to be fearful of certain objects and situations. Indeed, most of the situations and objects of people's phobias could pose a real threat, for example, falling from a high place or being attacked by a vicious dog or poisonous snake or spider. Social situations have their own dangers. A roomful of strangers may not attack or bite, but they could form impressions that affect your prospects for friends, jobs, or marriage. And of course, in some very rare cases, they could attack or bite.

Observations such as these are the basis for the **preparedness theory** of phobias, which maintains that *people are instinctively predisposed toward certain fears.* The preparedness theory, proposed by Martin E. P. Seligman (1971), is supported by research showing that both humans and monkeys can quickly be conditioned to have a fear response for stimuli such as snakes and spiders, but not for neutral stimuli such as flowers or toy rabbits (Cook & Mineka, 1989; Öhman, Dimberg, & Öst, 1985). Similarly, research on facial expressions has shown that people are more easily conditioned to fear angry facial expressions than other types of expressions (Öhman, 1996; Woody & Nosen, 2008). Phobias are particularly likely to form for objects that evolution has predisposed us to avoid. This idea is also supported by studies of the heritability of phobias. Family studies of specific phobias indicate greater concordance rates for identical than for fraternal twins (Kendler, Myers, & Prescott, 2002; O'Laughlin & Malle, 2002). Other studies have found that over 30% of first-degree relatives (parents, siblings, or children) of individuals with specific phobias also have a phobia (Fryer et al., 1990).

> **Why might we be predisposed to certain phobias?**

Temperament may also play a role in vulnerability to phobias. Researchers have found that infants who display excessive shyness and inhibition are at an increased risk for developing a phobic behavior later in life (Morris, 2001; Stein, Chavira, & Jang, 2001). Neurobiological factors may also play a role. Abnormalities in the neurotransmitters serotonin and dopamine are more common in individuals who report phobias than they are among people who don't (Stein, 1998). In addition, individuals with phobias sometimes show abnormally high levels of activity in the amygdala, an area of the brain linked with the development of emotional associations (discussed in the chapter on Emotion and Motivation and in Stein et al., 2001). Interestingly, although people with social phobia report feeling much more distressed than those without social phobia during tasks involving social evaluation (such as giving a speech), they are actually no more physiologically aroused than others (Jamieson, Nock, & Mendes, 2013). This suggests that social phobia may be due to a person's subjective experience of the situation, rather than an abnormal physiological stress response to such situations.

This evidence does not rule out the influence of environments and upbringing on the development of phobic overreactions. As learning theorist John Watson (1924) demonstrated many years ago, phobias can be classically conditioned (see the discussion of Little Albert and the white rat in the Learning chapter). Similarly, the discomfort of a dog bite could create a conditioned association between dogs and pain, resulting in an irrational fear of all dogs. The idea that phobias are learned from emotional experiences with feared objects, however, is not a complete explanation for the occurrence of phobias. Most studies find that people with phobias are no more likely than people without phobias to recall personal experiences with the feared object that could have provided the basis for classical conditioning (Craske, 1999; McNally & Steketee, 1985). Moreover, many people are bitten by dogs, but few develop phobias. Despite its shortcomings, however, the idea that this is a matter of learning provides a useful model for therapy (see the Treatment chapter).

Panic Disorder

If you suddenly found yourself in danger of death (That lion is headed straight for us!), a wave of panic might wash over you. People who suffer panic attacks are frequently overwhelmed by such intense fears and by powerful physical symptoms of anxiety, but in the complete absence of actual danger. Wesley, a 20-year-old college student began having panic attacks with increasing frequency, often two or three times a day, when he finally sought help at a clinic. The attacks began with a sudden wave of "intense, terrifying fear" that seemed to come out of nowhere, often accompanied by dizziness, a tightening of the chest, and the thought that he was going to pass out or possibly die. Wesley's attacks had started a few years earlier and occurred intermittently ever since. Wesley decided to come in for treatment because he had begun to avoid buses, trains, and public places for fear that he would have an attack like this and not be able to escape.

THINKSTOCK

Phobias are anxiety disorders that involve excessive and persistent fear of a specific object, activity, or situation. Some phobias may be learned through classical conditioning, in which a conditioned stimulus (CS) that is paired with an anxiety-evoking unconditioned stimulus (US) itself comes to elicit a conditioned fear response (CR). Suppose your friend has a phobia of dogs that is so intense that he is afraid to go outside in case one of his neighbors' dogs barks at him. Using the principles of classical conditioning you learned in the Learning chapter, how might you help him overcome his fear?

panic disorder
A disorder characterized by the sudden occurrence of multiple psychological and physiological symptoms that contribute to a feeling of stark terror.

agoraphobia
A specific phobia involving a fear of public places.

generalized anxiety disorder (GAD)
A disorder characterized by chronic excessive worry accompanied by three or more of the following symptoms: restlessness, fatigue, concentration problems, irritability, muscle tension, and sleep disturbance.

In panic disorder with agoraphobia, the fear of having a panic attack in public may prevent the person from going outside.

Wesley's condition, called **panic disorder,** is characterized by *the sudden occurrence of multiple psychological and physiological symptoms that contribute to a feeling of stark terror.* The acute symptoms of a panic attack typically last only a few minutes and include shortness of breath, heart palpitations, sweating, dizziness, depersonalization (a feeling of being detached from one's body) or derealization (a feeling that the external world is strange or unreal), and a fear that one is going crazy or about to die. Not surprisingly, panic attacks often send people rushing to emergency rooms or their physicians' offices for what they believe are heart attacks. Unfortunately, because many of the symptoms mimic various medical disorders, a correct diagnosis may take years in spite of costly medical tests that produce normal results (Katon, 1994). According to the *DSM–5* diagnostic criteria, a person has panic disorder only if they experience recurrent unexpected attacks and report significant anxiety about having another attack.

A common complication of panic disorder is **agoraphobia,** *a specific phobia involving a fear of public places.* Many people with agoraphobia, including Wesley, are not frightened of public places in themselves; instead, they are afraid of having a panic attack in a public place or around strangers who might view them with disdain or fail to help them. In severe cases, people who have panic disorder with agoraphobia are unable to leave home, sometimes for years.

> **What is it about public places that many people with agoraphobia fear?**

Approximately 22% of the U.S. population reports having had at least one panic attack (Kessler, Chiu, et al., 2006), typically during a period of intense stress (Telch, Lucas, & Nelson, 1989). An occasional episode is not sufficient for a diagnosis of panic disorder: The individual also has to experience significant dread and anxiety about having another attack. When this criterion is applied, approximately 5% of people will have diagnosable panic disorder sometime in their lives (Kessler, Berglund, et al., 2005). Panic disorder is more prevalent among women (7%) than men (3%; Kessler et al., 2012). Family studies suggest some hereditary component to panic disorder, with 30 to 40% of the variance in liability for developing panic disorder attributed to genetic influence (Hettema, Neale, & Kendler, 2001).

In an effort to understand the role that physiological arousal plays in panic attacks, researchers have compared the responses of experimental participants with and without panic disorder to *sodium lactate,* a chemical that produces rapid, shallow breathing and heart palpitations. Those with panic disorder were found to be acutely sensitive to the drug; within a few minutes after administration, 60 to 90% experienced a panic attack. Participants without the disorder rarely responded to the drug with a panic attack (Liebowitz et al., 1985).

The difference in responses to the chemical may be due to differing interpretations of physiological signs of anxiety; that is, people who experience panic attacks may be hypersensitive to physiological signs of anxiety, which they interpret as having disastrous consequences for their well-being. Supporting this cognitive explanation is research showing that people who are high in anxiety sensitivity (i.e., they believe that bodily arousal and other symptoms of anxiety can have dire consequences) have an elevated risk for experiencing panic attacks (Olatunji & Wolitzky-Taylor, 2009). Thus, panic attacks may be conceptualized as a "fear of fear" itself.

Generalized Anxiety Disorder

Gina, a 24-year-old woman, began to experience debilitating anxiety during her first year of graduate school for clinical psychology. At first she worried about whether she was sufficiently completing all of her assignments, then she worried about whether her clients were improving or if she was actually making them worse. Soon her concerns spread to focus on her health (did she have an undiagnosed medical problem?) as well as that of her boyfriend (he smokes cigarettes . . . perhaps he is currently giving himself cancer?). She worried incessantly for a year and ultimately took time off from school to get treatment for her worries, extreme agitation, fatigue, and feelings of sadness and depression.

Gina's symptoms are typical of **generalized anxiety disorder (GAD)**—called *generalized* because the unrelenting worries are not focused on any particular threat; they are, in fact, often exaggerated and irrational. GAD is *chronic excessive worry accompanied by three or more of the following symptoms: restlessness, fatigue, concentration problems, irritability, muscle tension, and sleep disturbance.* In people suffering from GAD, the uncontrollable worrying produces a sense of loss of control that can so erode self-confidence that simple decisions seem fraught with dire consequences. For example, Gina struggled to make everyday decisions as basic as which vegetables to buy at the market and how to prepare her dinner.

What factors contribute to GAD?

Approximately 6% of people in the United States suffer from GAD at some time in their lives (Kessler, Berglund, et al., 2005), with women experiencing GAD at higher rates (8%) than men (5%; Kessler et al., 2012). Research suggests that both biological and psychological factors contribute to the risk of GAD. Family studies indicate a mild to modest level of heritability (Norrholm & Ressler, 2009). Although identical twin studies of GAD are rare, some evidence suggests that compared with fraternal twins, identical twins have modestly higher *concordance rates* (the percentage of pairs that share the characteristic; Hettema et al., 2001). Moreover, teasing out environmental versus personality influences on concordance rates is quite difficult.

Biological explanations of GAD suggest that neurotransmitter imbalances may play a role in the disorder. The precise nature of this imbalance is not clear. *Benzodiazepines* (a class of sedative drugs discussed in the Treatment chapter; e.g., Valium, Librium) that appear to stimulate the neurotransmitter *gamma-aminobutyric acid (GABA)* can sometimes reduce the symptoms of GAD, suggesting a potential role for this neurotransmitter in the occurrence of GAD. However, other drugs that do not directly affect GABA levels (e.g., buspirone and antidepressants such as Prozac) can also be helpful in the treatment of GAD (Gobert et al., 1999; Michelson et al., 1999; Roy-Byrne & Cowley, 1998). To complicate matters, these different prescription drugs do not help all individuals and, in some cases, can produce serious side effects and dependency.

Psychological explanations focus on anxiety-provoking situations in explaining high levels of GAD. The condition is especially prevalent among people who have low incomes, are living in large cities, and/or are in environments rendered unpredictable by political and economic strife. The relatively high rates of GAD among women may also be related to stress because women are more likely than men to live in poverty, experience discrimination, or be subjected to sexual or physical abuse (Koss, 1990; Strickland, 1991). Research shows that unpredictable traumatic experiences in childhood increase the risk of developing GAD, and this evidence also supports the idea that stressful experiences play a role (Torgensen, 1986). Risk of GAD also increases following the experience of a loss or situation associated with future perceived danger (Kendler et al., 2003), such as loss of a home due to foreclosure (McLaughlin et al., 2012). Still, many people who might be expected to develop GAD don't, supporting the diathesis–stress notion that personal vulnerability must also be a key factor in this disorder.

The experience of major stressful life events, such as losing a job or home, can lead to generalized anxiety disorder, a condition characterized by chronic, excessive worry.

STURTI/GETTY IMAGES

> ### IN SUMMARY
>
> ▶ People with anxiety disorders have irrational worries and fears that undermine their ability to function normally.
>
> ▶ Phobic disorders are characterized by excessive fear and avoidance of specific objects, activities, or situations.
>
> ▶ People who suffer from panic disorder experience a sudden and intense attack of anxiety that is terrifying and can lead them to become agoraphobic and housebound for fear of public humiliation.
>
> ▶ Generalized anxiety disorder (GAD) involves a chronic state of anxiety, whereas phobic disorders involve anxiety tied to a specific object or situation.

Obsessive-Compulsive Disorder: Trapped in a Loop

You may have had the experience of having an irresistible urge to go back to check whether you actually locked the door or turned off the oven, even when you're pretty sure that you did. Or you may have been unable to resist engaging in some superstitious behavior, such as wearing your lucky shirt on a date or to a sporting event. In some people, such thoughts and actions spiral out of control and become a serious problem.

Karen, a 34-year-old with four children, sought treatment after several months of experiencing intrusive, repetitive thoughts in which she imagined that one or more of her children was having a serious accident. In addition, an extensive series of protective counting rituals hampered her daily routine. For example, when grocery shopping, Karen had the feeling that if she selected the first item (say, a box of cereal) on a shelf, something terrible would happen to her oldest child. If she selected the second item, some unknown disaster would befall her second child, and so on for the four children. The children's ages were also important. The sixth item in a row, for example, was associated with her youngest child, who was 6 years old.

Karen's preoccupation with numbers extended to other activities, most notably, the pattern in which she smoked cigarettes and drank coffee. If she had one cigarette, she felt that she had to smoke at least four in a row or one of her children would be harmed in some way. If she drank one cup of coffee, she felt compelled to drink four more to protect her children from harm. She acknowledged that her counting rituals were irrational, but she became extremely anxious when she tried to stop (Oltmanns, Neale, & Davison, 1991).

Karen's symptoms are typical of **obsessive-compulsive disorder (OCD),** in which *repetitive, intrusive thoughts (obsessions) and ritualistic behaviors (compulsions)*

obsessive-compulsive disorder (OCD)
A disorder in which repetitive, intrusive thoughts (obsessions) and ritualistic behaviors (compulsions) designed to fend off those thoughts interfere significantly with an individual's functioning.

posttraumatic stress disorder (PTSD)
A disorder characterized by chronic physiological arousal, recurrent unwanted thoughts or images of the trauma, and avoidance of things that call the traumatic event to mind.

? How effective is willful effort at curing OCD?

designed to fend off those thoughts interfere significantly with an individual's functioning. Anxiety plays a role in this disorder because the obsessive thoughts typically produce anxiety, and the compulsive behaviors are performed to reduce it. In OCD, these obsessions and compulsions are intense, frequent, and experienced as irrational and excessive. Attempts to cope with the obsessive thoughts by trying to suppress or ignore them are of little or no benefit. In fact (as discussed in the Consciousness chapter), thought suppression can backfire, increasing the frequency and intensity of the obsessive thoughts (Wegner, 1989; Wenzlaff & Wegner, 2000). Despite anxiety's role, in *DSM–5* OCD is classified separately from anxiety disorders because the disorder is believed to have a distinct cause and to be maintained via different neural circuitry in the brain than the anxiety disorders.

Although 28% of adults in the United States report experiencing obsessions or compulsions at some point in their lives (Ruscio et al., 2010), only 2% will develop actual OCD (Kessler, Berglund, et al., 2005). Similar to anxiety disorders, rates of OCD are higher among women than men (Kessler et al., 2012). Among those with OCD, the most common obsessions and compulsions involve checking (79% of those with OCD), ordering (57%), moral concerns (43%), and contamination (26%; Ruscio et al., 2010). Although compulsive behavior is always excessive, it can vary considerably in intensity and frequency. For example, fear of contamination may lead to 15 minutes of hand washing in some individuals, whereas others may need to spend hours with disinfectants and extremely hot water, scrubbing their hands until they bleed.

The obsessions that plague individuals with OCD typically derive from concerns that could pose a real threat (such as contamination or disease), which supports preparedness theory. Thinking repeatedly about whether we've left a stove burner on when we leave the house makes sense, after all, if we want to return to a house that is not "well done." The concept of preparedness places OCD in the same evolutionary context as phobias (Szechtman & Woody, 2006). However, as with phobias, we need to consider other factors to explain why fears that may have served an evolutionary purpose can become so distorted and maladaptive.

Family studies indicate a moderate genetic heritability for OCD: Identical twins show a higher concordance than do fraternal twins. Relatives of individuals with OCD may not have the disorder themselves, but they are at greater risk for other types of anxiety disorders than are members of the general public (Billet, Richter, & Kennedy, 1998). Researchers have not determined the biological mechanisms that may contribute to OCD (Friedlander & Desrocher, 2006), but one hypothesis implicates heightened neural activity in the caudate nucleus of the brain, a portion of the basal ganglia (discussed in the Neuroscience and Behavior chapter) known to be involved in the initiation of intentional actions (Rappoport, 1990). Drugs that increase the activity of the neurotransmitter serotonin in the brain can inhibit the activity of the caudate nucleus and relieve some of the symptoms of obsessive-compulsive disorder (Hansen et al., 2002). However, this finding does not indicate that overactivity of the caudate nucleus is the cause of OCD. It could also be an effect of the disorder: People with OCD often respond favorably to psychotherapy and show a corresponding reduction in activity in the caudate nucleus (Baxter et al., 1992).

Howie Mandel is a successful comedian, but his struggle with OCD is no laughing matter. Like approximately 2% of people in the United States, Mandel struggles with extreme fears of being contaminated by germs and engages in repeated checking and cleaning behaviors that often interfere with his daily life. He has spoken publicly about his struggles with OCD and about the importance of seeking effective treatment for this condition.

IN SUMMARY

▶ People with obsessive-compulsive disorder experience recurring, anxiety-provoking thoughts that compel them to engage in ritualistic, irrational behavior.

Posttraumatic Stress Disorder: Troubles after a Trauma

Psychological reactions to stress can lead to stress disorders. For example, a person who lives through a terrifying and uncontrollable experience may develop **posttraumatic stress disorder (PTSD)**, a disorder characterized by *chronic physiological arousal, recurrent unwanted thoughts or images of the trauma, and avoidance of things that call the traumatic event to mind.*

Psychological scars left by traumatic events are nowhere more apparent than in war. Many soldiers returning from combat experience symptoms of PTSD, including flashbacks of battle, exaggerated anxiety and startle reactions, and even medical conditions

JIM BARBER/SHUTTERSTOCK

The traumatic events of war leave many debilitated by PTSD. But because PTSD is an invisible wound that is difficult to diagnose with certainty, the Pentagon has decided that psychological casualties of war are not eligible for the Purple Heart—the hallowed medal given to those wounded or killed by enemy action (Alvarez & Eckholm, 2009).

that do not arise from physical damage (e.g., paralysis or chronic fatigue). Most of these symptoms are normal, appropriate responses to horrifying events, and for most people, the symptoms subside with time. In PTSD, the symptoms can last much longer. For example, approximately 12% of U.S. veterans of recent operations in Iraq met criteria for PTSD after their deployment; and the observed rates of PTSD are even higher in non-Western and developing countries (Keane, Marshall, & Taft, 2006). The effects of PTSD are now recognized not only among the victims, witnesses, and perpetrators of war, but also among ordinary people who are traumatized by terrible events in civilian life. At some time over the course of their lives, about 7% of Americans are estimated to suffer from PTSD (Kessler, Berglund, et al., 2005).

What structure in the brain might be an indicator for susceptibility to PTSD?

Not everyone who is exposed to a traumatic event develops PTSD, suggesting that people differ in their degree of sensitivity to trauma. Research using brain imaging techniques to examine brain structure and function has identified important neural correlates of PTSD. Specifically, those with PTSD show heightened activity in the amygdala (a region associated with the evaluation of threatening information and fear conditioning), decreased activity in the medial prefrontal cortex (a region important in the extinction of fear conditioning), and a smaller sized hippocampus (the part of the brain most linked with memory, as described in the Neuroscience and Behavior and Memory chapters; Shin, Rauch, & Pitman, 2006). Of course, an important question is whether people whose brains have these characteristics are at greater risk for PTSD if traumatized, or if these are the consequences of trauma in some people. For instance, does reduced hippocampal volume reflect a preexisting condition that makes the brain sensitive to stress, or does the traumatic stress itself somehow kill nerve cells? One important study suggests that although a group of combat veterans with PTSD showed reduced hippocampal volume, so did the identical (monozygotic) twins of those men (see **FIGURE 15.1**), even though the twins had never had any combat exposure or developed PTSD (Gilbertson et al., 2002). This suggests that the veterans' reduced hippocampal volumes weren't caused by the combat exposure; instead, both these veterans and their twin brothers might have had a smaller hippocampus to begin with, a preexisting condition that made them susceptible to developing PTSD when they were later exposed to trauma.

► Figure **15.1** **Hippocampal Volumes of Vietnam Veterans and Their Identical Twins** Average hippocampal volumes for four groups of participants: (1) combat-exposed veterans who developed PTSD; (2) their combat-unexposed twins with no PTSD themselves; (3) combat-exposed veterans who never developed PTSD; and (4) their unexposed twins, also with no PTSD. Smaller hippocampal volumes were found both for the combat-exposed veterans with PTSD (Group 1) and their twins who had not been exposed to combat (Group 2) in comparison to veterans without PTSD (Group 3) and their twins (Group 4). This pattern of findings suggests that an inherited smaller hippocampus may make some people sensitive to conditions that cause PTSD (Gilbertson et al., 2002).

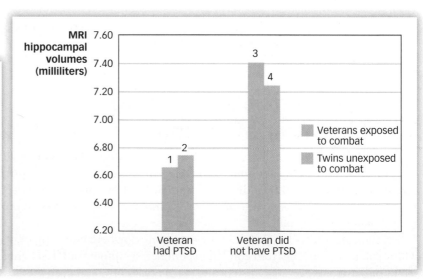

IN SUMMARY

► Terrifying, life-threatening events, such as combat experience or rape, can lead to the development of posttraumatic stress disorder (PTSD) in which a person experiences chronic physiological arousal, unwanted thoughts or images of the event, and avoidance of things that remind the person of the event.

Depressive and Bipolar Disorders: At the Mercy of Emotions

You're probably in a mood right now. Maybe you're happy that it's almost time to get a snack or saddened by something you heard from a friend—or you may feel good or bad without having a clue why. As you learned in the Emotion and Motivation chapter, moods are relatively long-lasting, nonspecific emotional states—and *nonspecific* means we often may have no idea what has caused a mood. Changing moods lend variety to our experiences, like different-colored lights shining on the stage as we play out our lives. However, for people like Virginia Woolf and others with mood disorders, moods can become so intense that they are pulled or pushed into life-threatening actions. **Mood disorders** are *mental disorders that have mood disturbance as their predominant feature* and take two main forms: *depression* (also called *unipolar depression*) and *bipolar disorder* (so named because people go from one end of the emotional pole [extreme depression] to the other [extreme mania]).

Depressive Disorders

Everyone feels sad, pessimistic, and unmotivated from time to time. But for most people these periods are relatively short-lived and mild. Depression is much more than typical sadness. The experience of Mark, a 34-year-old man who visited his primary care physician complaining of chronic fatigue, is fairly typical. During the visit, he mentioned difficulties falling asleep and staying asleep that left him chronically tired, so much so that he feared maybe he had some kind of medical problem. He complained that over the past 6 months, he no longer had the energy to exercise and had gained 10 pounds. He also lost all interest in going out with his friends or even talking to other people. Nothing he normally enjoyed, even sexual activity, gave him pleasure anymore; he had trouble concentrating and was forgetful, irritable, impatient, and frustrated. Mark's change in mood and behavior, and the sense of hopelessness and weariness he felt goes far beyond normal sadness. Instead, depressive disorders are dysfunctional, chronic, and fall outside the range of socially or culturally expected responses.

? **What is the difference between depression and sadness?**

Major depressive disorder (or **unipolar depression**), which we refer to here simply as "depression," is characterized by *a severely depressed mood and/or inability to experience pleasure that lasts 2 or more weeks and is accompanied by feelings of worthlessness, lethargy, and sleep and appetite disturbance.* In a related condition called **dysthymia**, *the same cognitive and bodily problems as in depression are present, but they are less severe and last longer, persisting for at*

mood disorders
Mental disorders that have mood disturbance as their predominant feature.

major depressive disorder (or unipolar depression)
A disorder characterized by a severely depressed mood and/or inability to experience pleasure that lasts 2 or more weeks and is accompanied by feelings of worthlessness, lethargy, and sleep and appetite disturbance.

dysthymia
The same cognitive and bodily problems as in depression are present, but they are less severe and last longer, persisting for at least 2 years.

The Blue Devils. George Cruikshank (1792–1878) portrayed a depressed man tormented by demons offering him methods of suicide, appearing as bill collectors, and making a funeral procession.

BRIDGEMAN ART LIBRARY

Seasonal affective disorder is not merely having the blues because of the weather. It appears to be due to reduced exposure to light in the winter months.

Postpartum depression can strike women out of the blue, often causing new mothers to feel extreme sadness, guilt, and disconnection, and even to experience serious thoughts of suicide. Actress Brooke Shields wrote about her experience with postpartum depression in a popular book on this condition.

least 2 years. When both types co-occur, the resulting condition is called **double depression,** defined as *a moderately depressed mood that persists for at least 2 years and is punctuated by periods of major depression.*

Some people experience *recurrent depressive episodes in a seasonal pattern,* commonly known as **seasonal affective disorder (SAD)**. In most cases, the episodes begin in fall or winter and remit in spring, and this pattern is due to reduced levels of light over the colder seasons (Westrin & Lam, 2007). Nevertheless, recurrent summer depressive episodes have been reported. A winter-related pattern of depression appears to be more prevalent in higher latitudes.

Approximately 18% of people in the United States meet criteria for depression at some point in their lives (Kessler et al., 2012). On average, major depression lasts about 12 weeks (Eaton et al., 2008). However, without treatment, approximately 80% of individuals will experience at least one recurrence of the disorder (Judd, 1997; Mueller et al., 1999). Compared with people who have a single episode, individuals with recurrent depression have more severe symptoms, higher rates of depression in their families, more suicide attempts, and higher rates of divorce (Merikangas, Wicki, & Angst, 1994).

Similar to anxiety disorders, the rate of depression is much higher in women (22%) than in men (14%; Kessler et al., 2012). Socioeconomic standing has been invoked as an explanation for women's heightened risk: Their incomes are lower than those of men, and poverty could cause depression. Sex differences in hormones are another possibility: Estrogen, androgen, and progesterone influence depression; some

> **Why do more women than men experience depression?**

women experience *postpartum depression* (depression following childbirth) due to changing hormone balances. It is also possible that the higher rate of depression in women reflects greater willingness by women to face their depression and seek out help, leading to higher rates of diagnosis (Nolen-Hoeksema, 2008). Women have a tendency to accept, disclose, and ruminate on their negative emotions, whereas men are more likely to deny negative emotions and engage in self-distraction such as work and drinking alcohol.

Biological Factors

Heritability estimates for major depression typically range from 33 to 45% (Plomin et al., 1997; Wallace, Schnieder, & McGuffin, 2002). However, like most types of mental disorders, heritability rates vary as a function of severity. For example, a relatively large study of twins found that the concordance rates for severe major depression (defined as three or more episodes) were quite high, with a rate of 59% for identical twins and 30% for fraternal twins (Bertelsen, Harvald, & Hauge, 1977). In contrast, concordance rates for less severe major depression (defined as fewer than three episodes) fell to 33% for identical twins and 14% for fraternal twins. Heritability rates for dysthymia are low and inconsistent (Plomin et al., 1997). This makes depression about as heritable as complex medical conditions, like type 2 diabetes and asthma.

Beginning in the 1950s, researchers noticed that drugs that increased levels of the neurotransmitters norepinephrine and serotonin could sometimes reduce depression. This observation suggested that depression might be caused by an absolute or relative depletion of these neurotransmitters and sparked a revolution in the pharmacological treatment of depression (Schildkraut, 1965), leading to the development and widespread use of such popular prescription drugs as Prozac and Zoloft, which increase the availability of serotonin in the brain. Further research has shown, however, that reduced levels of these neurotransmitters cannot be the whole story regarding the causes of depression. For example, some studies have found *increases* in norepinephrine activity among depressed individuals (Thase & Howland, 1995). Moreover, even though the antidepressant medications change neurochemical transmission in less than a day, they typically take at least 2 weeks to relieve depressive symptoms and are not effective in decreasing depressive symptoms in many cases. A biochemical model of depression has yet to be developed that accounts for all the evidence.

Newer biological models of depression have tried to understand depression using a diathesis–stress framework. For instance, Avshalom Caspi and his colleagues (2003) found that stressful life events are much more likely to lead to depression among those with a certain genetic trait (vulnerability) related to the activity of the neurotransmitter serotonin: a finding showing that nature and nurture interact to influence brain structure, function, and chemistry in depression (see **FIGURE 15.2**).

Recent research also has begun to tell us what parts of the brain show abnormalities in depression. For instance, some important findings came out of a recent meta-analysis (which is a quantitative synthesis of the results of many individual studies) of 24 brain imaging studies. Results showed that when viewing negative stimuli (words or images), people suffering from depression showed both increased activity in regions of the brain associated with processing emotional information and decreased activity in areas associated with cognitive control (see **FIGURE 15.3**; Hamilton et al., 2012). Of course, this is not the whole picture and these findings don't explain all of the symptoms seen in depression, why and when depression comes and goes, or how treatment works. Given that depression does not arise due to a single gene or brain region, but likely from the interactions of different biological systems that each give rise to the different psychological traits seen in depression, it will likely be many years before we fully understand the biological causes of this disorder (Krishnan & Nestler, 2008).

double depression
A moderately depressed mood that persists for at least 2 years and is punctuated by periods of major depression.

seasonal affective disorder (SAD)
Recurrent depressive episodes in a seasonal pattern.

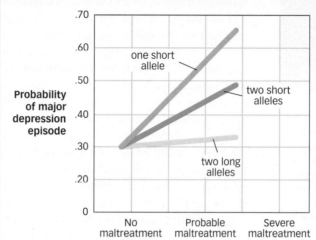

◄ Figure **15.2 Gene × Environment Interactions in Depression** Stressful life experiences are much more likely to lead to later depression among those with one short, and especially two short, alleles of the serotonin transporter gene. Those with two long alleles (long alleles are associated with more efficient serotonergic functioning) showed no increased risk of depression, even those who experienced severe maltreatment.

COURTESY PAUL HAMILTON

	Structure	Activity in depression
A	Amygdala	Increased
B	Dorsal ACC	Increased
C	Insula and superior temporal gyrus	Increased
D	DLPFC	Decreased
E	Caudate body	Decreased

◄ Figure **15.3 Brain and Depression** When presented with negative information, people with depression show increased activation in regions of the brain associated with emotional processing such as the amygdala, insula, and dorsal anterior cingulate cortex (ACC); and decreased activity in regions associated with cognitive control such as the dorsal striatum and dorsolateral prefrontal cortex (DLPFC; Hamilton et al., 2012).

The cognitive model of depression is based on approaches to thinking used by the Greek Stoic philosophers nearly 2,000 years ago. Epictetus's famous quote: "Men are disturbed not by things, but by the principles and notions which they form concerning things" is commonly cited by cognitive theorists as a guiding principle of the cognitive model of depression.

Psychological Factors

If optimists see the world through rose-colored glasses, people who suffer with depression tend to view the world through dark gray lenses. Their negative cognitive style is remarkably consistent and, some argue, begins in childhood with experiences that create a pattern of negative self thoughts (Blatt & Homann, 1992; Gibb, Alloy, & Tierney, 2001). One of the first theorists to emphasize the role of thought in depression, Aaron T. Beck (1967), noted that his depressed patients distorted perceptions of their experiences and embraced dysfunctional attitudes that promoted and maintained negative mood states. His observations led him to develop a *cognitive model of depression*, which states that biases in how information is attended to, processed, and remembered lead to and maintain depression.

Elaborating on this initial idea, researchers proposed a theory of depression that emphasizes the role of people's negative inferences about the causes of their experiences (Abramson, Seligman, & Teasdale, 1978). **Helplessness theory**, which is a part of the cognitive model of depression, maintains that *individuals who are prone to depression automatically attribute negative experiences to causes that are internal (i.e., their own fault), stable (i.e., unlikely to change), and global (i.e., widespread)*. For example, a student at risk for depression might view a bad grade on a math test as a sign of low intelligence (internal) that will never change (stable) and that will lead to failure in all his or her future endeavors (global). In contrast, a student without this tendency might have the opposite response, attributing the grade to something external (poor teaching), unstable (a missed study session), and/or specific (boring subject).

> **What is helplessness theory?**

The relationship between one's perceptions and depression has been further developed and supported over the past several decades. The update to Beck's cognitive model suggests that due to a combination of a genetic vulnerability and negative early life events, people with depression have developed a negative *schema* (described in the Development chapter). This negative schema is characterized by biases in

> - interpretations of information (a tendency to interpret neutral information negatively—seeing the world through grey glass);
> - attention (trouble disengaging from negative information);
> - memory (better recall of negative information; Gotlib & Joormann, 2010).

For example, a student at risk for depression who got a bad grade on a test might interpret a well-intentioned comment from the teacher ("Good job on the test") negatively ("She's being sarcastic!"); have trouble forgetting about both the test score and the perceived negative comment; and have better memory about this test in the future ("Sure, I did well on my English exam, but don't forget about that bad math test last month"). The presence of these biases may help to explain the internal, stable, and global attributions seen in depression. In addition, recent research suggests that some of the differences in brain structure and function seen in those with depression can help to explain some of these cognitive biases. For instance, people with depression show abnormalities in parts of the brain involved in attention and memory, especially when presented with negative information (Disner et al., 2011). Although we don't fully understand the causes of depression, pieces of the puzzle are being discovered and put together as you read this.

Bipolar Disorder

If depression is distressing and painful, would the opposite extreme be better? Not for Virginia Woolf or for Julie, a 20-year-old college sophomore. When first seen by a clinician, Julie had gone 5 days without sleep and, like Woolf, was extremely active and

helplessness theory
The idea that individuals who are prone to depression automatically attribute negative experiences to causes that are internal (i.e., their own fault), stable (i.e., unlikely to change), and global (i.e., widespread).

bipolar disorder
A condition characterized by cycles of abnormal, persistent high mood (mania) and low mood (depression).

expressing bizarre thoughts and ideas. She proclaimed to friends that she did not menstruate because she was "of a third sex, a gender above the two human sexes." She claimed to be a "superwoman," capable of avoiding human sexuality and yet still able to give birth. Preoccupied with the politics of global disarmament, she felt that she had switched souls with the senior senator from her state, had tapped into his thoughts and memories, and could save the world from nuclear destruction. She began to campaign for an elected position in the U.S. government (even though no elections were scheduled at that time). Worried that she would forget some of her thoughts, she had been leaving hundreds of notes about her ideas and activities everywhere, including on the walls and furniture of her dormitory room (Vitkus, 1999).

In addition to her manic episodes, Julie (like Woolf) had a history of depression. The diagnostic label for this constellation of symptoms is **bipolar disorder,** *a condition characterized by cycles of abnormal, persistent high mood (mania) and low mood (depression).* In about two thirds of people with bipolar disorder, manic episodes immediately precede or immediately follow depressive episodes (Whybrow, 1997). The depressive phase of bipolar disorder is often clinically indistinguishable from major depression (Johnson, Cuellar, & Miller, 2009). In the manic phase, which must last at least 1 week to meet *DSM* requirements, mood can be

TROELS GRAUGAARD/GETTY IMAGES

Mania is not simply being very happy. People experiencing a manic episode may fail to sleep for several days, purchase four cars in one day, and have thoughts racing through their mind so fast that they are literally unable to form a coherent sentence.

> **?** Why is bipolar disorder sometimes misdiagnosed as schizophrenia?

elevated, expansive, or irritable. Other prominent symptoms include grandiosity, decreased need for sleep, talkativeness, racing thoughts, distractibility, and reckless behavior (such as compulsive gambling, sexual indiscretions, and unrestrained spending sprees). Psychotic features such as hallucinations (erroneous perceptions) and delusions (erroneous beliefs) may be present, so the disorder can be misdiagnosed as schizophrenia (described in a later section).

Here's how Kay Redfield Jamison (1995, p. 67) described her own experience with bipolar disorder in *An Unquiet Mind: A Memoir of Moods and Madness.*

> There is a particular kind of pain, elation, loneliness, and terror involved in this kind of madness. When you're high it's tremendous. The ideas and feelings are fast and frequent like shooting stars, and you follow them until you find better and brighter ones . . . . But, somewhere, this changes. The fast ideas are far too fast, and there are far too many; overwhelming confusion replaces clarity. Memory goes. Humor and absorption on friends' faces are replaced by fear and concern. Everything previously moving with the grain is now against—you are irritable, angry, frightened, uncontrollable, and enmeshed totally in the blackest caves of the mind. You never knew those caves were there. It will never end, for madness carves its own reality.

BASSO CANNARSA/LUZPHOTO/REDUX

Psychologist Kay Redfield Jamison has written several best-selling books about her own struggles with bipolar disorder.

The lifetime risk for bipolar disorder is about 2.5% and does not differ between men and women (Kessler et al., 2012). Bipolar disorder is typically a recurrent condition, with approximately 90% of afflicted people suffering from several episodes over a lifetime (Coryell et al., 1995). About 10% of people with bipolar disorder have *rapid cycling bipolar disorder,* characterized by at least four mood episodes (either manic or depressive) every year, and this form of the disorder is particularly difficult to treat (Post et al., 2008). Rapid cycling is more common in women than in men and is sometimes precipitated by taking certain kinds of antidepressant drugs (Liebenluft, 1996; Whybrow, 1997). Unfortunately, bipolar disorder tends to be persistent. In one study, 24% of the participants had relapsed within 6 months of recovery from an episode, and 77% had at least one new episode within 4 years of recovery (Coryell et al., 1995).

Some have suggested that people with psychotic and mood (especially bipolar) disorders have higher creativity and intellectual ability (Andreasen, 2011). In bipolar disorder, the suggestion goes, before the mania becomes too pronounced, the energy, grandiosity, and ambition that it supplies may help people achieve great things. In addition to Virginia Woolf, notable individuals thought to have had the disorder include Isaac Newton, Vincent Van Gogh, Abraham Lincoln, Ernest Hemingway, Winston Churchill, and Theodore Roosevelt.

Biological Factors

Among the various mental disorders, bipolar disorder has one of the highest rates of heritability, with concordance from 40 to 70% for identical twins and 10% for fraternal twins (Craddock & Jones, 1999). Like most other disorders, it is likely that bipolar disorder is *polygenic,* arising from the interaction of multiple genes that combine to create the symptoms observed in those with this disorder; however, these have been difficult to identify. Adding to the complexity, there also is evidence of *pleiotropic effects*, in which one gene influences one's susceptibility to multiple disorders. For instance, one recent study revealed a shared genetic vulnerability for bipolar disorder and schizophrenia. The genes linked to both disorders are associated with compromised abilities both in filtering unnecessary information and recognition memory, as well as problems with dopamine and serotonin transmission—factors present in both types of disorders (Huang et al., 2010). A follow-up study examining more than 60,000 people revealed that common genetic risk factors are associated with bipolar disorder and schizophrenia, as well as major depression, autism spectrum disorder, and attention-deficit/hyperactivity disorder. These disorders share overlapping symptoms such as problems with mood regulation, cognitive impairments, and social withdrawal (Cross-Disorder Group of the Psychiatric Genomics Consortium, 2013). Findings like these are exciting because they help us begin to understand why we see similar symptoms in people with what we previously thought were unrelated disorders. Although some genetic links have been made, we currently lack an understanding of how different biological factors work together to create the symptoms observed in bipolar and other disorders.

> **What findings offer exciting new evidence of why symptoms of different disorders seem to overlap?**

There is growing evidence that the epigenetic changes you learned about in the Neuroscience and Behavior chapter can help to explain how it is that genetic risk factors influence the development of bipolar and related disorders. Remember how rat pups whose moms spent less time licking and grooming them experienced epigenetic changes (decreased DNA methylation) that led to a poorer stress response? As you might expect, these same kinds of epigenetic effects seem to help explain who develops symptoms of mental disorders and who doesn't. For instance, studies examining monozygotic twin pairs (identical twins who share 100% of their DNA) in which one develops bipolar disorder or schizophrenia and one doesn't, reveal significant epigenetic differences between the two, with decreased methylation at genetic locations known to be important in brain development and the occurrence of bipolar disorders and schizophrenia (Dempster et al., 2011; Labrie, Pai, & Petronis, 2012).

Psychological Factors

Stressful life experiences often precede manic and depressive episodes (Johnson, Cuellar, et al., 2008). One study found that severely stressed individuals took an average of 3 times longer to recover from an episode than did individuals not affected by stress (Johnson & Miller, 1997). The stress–disorder relationship is not simple, however: High levels of stress have less impact on people with extraverted personalities than on those with more introverted personalities (Swednsen et al., 1995). Personality characteristics such as neuroticism and conscientiousness have also been

> **How does stress relate to manic-depressive episodes?**

found to predict increases in bipolar symptoms over time (Lozano & Johnson, 2001). Finally, people living with family members high on **expressed emotion,** which in this context is *a measure of how much hostility, criticism, and emotional overinvolvement are used when speaking about a family member with a mental disorder*, are more likely to relapse than people with supportive families (Miklowitz & Johnson, 2006). This is true not just of those with bipolar disorder: Expressed emotion is associated with higher rates of relapse across a wide range of mental disorders (Hooley, 2007).

IN SUMMARY

▶ Mood disorders are mental disorders in which a disturbance in mood is the predominant feature.

▶ Major depression (or unipolar depression) is characterized by a severely depressed mood and/or inability to experience pleasure lasting at least 2 weeks; symptoms include excessive self-criticism, guilt, difficulty concentrating, suicidal thoughts, sleep and appetite disturbances, and lethargy. Dysthymia, a related disorder, involves less severe symptoms that persist for at least 2 years.

▶ Bipolar disorder is an unstable emotional condition involving extreme mood swings of depression and mania. The manic phase is characterized by periods of abnormally and persistently elevated, expansive, or irritable mood, lasting at least 1 week.

Schizophrenia and Other Psychotic Disorders: Losing the Grasp on Reality

Margaret, a 39-year-old mother, believed that God was punishing her for marrying a man she did not love and bringing two children into the world. As her punishment, God had made her and her children immortal so that they would have to suffer in their unhappy home life forever—a realization that came to her one evening when she was washing dishes and saw a fork lying across a knife in the shape of a cross. Margaret found further support for her belief in two pieces of evidence: First, a local television station was rerunning old episodes of *The Honeymooners,* a 1950s situation comedy in which the main characters often argue and shout at each other. She saw this as a sign from God that her own marital conflict would go on forever. Second, she believed (falsely) that the pupils of her children's eyes were fixed in size and would neither dilate nor constrict—a sign of their immortality. At home, she would lock herself in her room for hours and sometimes days. The week before her diagnosis, she kept her 7-year-old son home from school so that he could join her and his 4-year-old sister in reading aloud from the Bible (Oltmanns et al., 1991). Margaret was suffering from the most well-known and widely studied psychotic disorder: schizophrenia. Schizophrenia is one of the most mystifying and devastating of all the mental disorders.

Symptoms and Types of Schizophrenia

Schizophrenia is a psychotic disorder (*psychosis* is a break from reality) characterized by *the profound disruption of basic psychological processes; a distorted perception of reality; altered or blunted emotion; and disturbances in thought, motivation, and behavior.* Traditionally, schizophrenia was regarded primarily as a disturbance of thought and perception, in which the sense of reality becomes severely distorted and confused. However, this condition is now understood to take different

What is schizophrenia?

expressed emotion
A measure of how much hostility, criticism, and emotional overinvolvement are used when speaking about a family member with a mental disorder.

schizophrenia
A disorder characterized by the profound disruption of basic psychological processes; a distorted perception of reality; altered or blunted emotion; and disturbances in thought, motivation, and behavior.

Those suffering from schizophrenia often experience hallucinations and delusions, unable to determine what is real and what has been created by their own mind. The experience of John Nash, a Nobel Prize–winning economist, with schizophrenia was depicted in the book and movie *A Beautiful Mind*.

positive symptoms
Thoughts and behaviors present in schizophrenia but not seen in those without the disorder, such as delusions and hallucinations.

hallucination
A false perceptual experience that has a compelling sense of being real despite the absence of external stimulation.

delusion
A patently false belief system, often bizarre and grandiose, that is maintained in spite of its irrationality.

disorganized speech
A severe disruption of verbal communication in which ideas shift rapidly and incoherently among unrelated topics.

grossly disorganized behavior
Behavior that is inappropriate for the situation or ineffective in attaining goals, often with specific motor disturbances.

forms affecting a wide range of functions. According to the *DSM–5*, schizophrenia is diagnosed when two or more symptoms emerge during a continuous period of at least 1 month with signs of the disorder persisting for at least 6 months. The symptoms of schizophrenia often are separated into *positive, negative,* and *cognitive symptoms*.

Positive symptoms of schizophrenia include *thoughts and behaviors not seen in those without the disorder,* such as

> **Hallucinations** are *false perceptual experiences that have a compelling sense of being real despite the absence of external stimulation.* The perceptual disturbances associated with schizophrenia can include hearing, seeing, smelling, or having a tactile sensation of things that are not there. Schizophrenic hallucinations are often auditory (e.g., hearing voices that no one else can hear). Among people with schizophrenia, some 65% report hearing voices repeatedly (Frith & Fletcher, 1995). British psychiatrist Henry Maudsley (1886) long ago proposed that these voices are in fact produced in the mind of the person with schizophrenia, and recent research substantiates his idea. In one PET imaging study, auditory hallucinations were accompanied by activation in Broca's area (as discussed in the Neuroscience and Behavior chapter), the part of the brain associated with the production of language (McGuire, Shah, & Murray, 1993). Unfortunately, the voices heard in schizophrenia seldom sound like the self or like a kindly uncle offering advice. They command, scold, suggest bizarre actions, or offer snide comments. One individual reported a voice saying, "He's getting up now. He's going to wash. It's about time" (Frith & Fletcher, 1995).

> **Delusions** are *patently false beliefs, often bizarre and grandiose, that are maintained in spite of their irrationality.* For example, an individual with schizophrenia may believe that he or she is Jesus Christ, Napoleon, Joan of Arc, or some other well-known person. Such delusions of identity have helped foster the misconception that schizophrenia involves multiple personalities. However, adopted identities in schizophrenia do not alternate, exhibit amnesia for one another, or otherwise "split." Delusions of persecution are also common. Some individuals believe that the CIA, demons, extraterrestrials, or other malevolent forces are conspiring to harm them or control their minds, which may represent an attempt to make sense of the tormenting delusions (Roberts, 1991). People with schizophrenia have little or no insight into their disordered perceptual and thought processes (Karow et al., 2007). Without understanding that they have lost control of their own minds, they may develop unusual beliefs and theories that attribute control to external agents.

> **Disorganized speech** is *a severe disruption of verbal communication in which ideas shift rapidly and incoherently among unrelated topics.* The abnormal speech patterns in schizophrenia reflect difficulties in organizing thoughts and focusing attention. Responses to questions are often irrelevant, ideas are loosely associated, and words are used in peculiar ways. For example, asked by her doctor, "Can you tell me the name of this place?" one patient with schizophrenia responded, "I have not been a drinker for 16 years. I am taking a mental rest after a 'carter' assignment of 'quill.' You know, a 'penwrap.' I had contracts with Warner Brothers Studios and Eugene broke phonograph records but Mike protested. I have been with the police department for 35 years. I am made of flesh and blood—see, Doctor" [pulling up her dress] (Carson et al., 2000, p. 474).

> **Grossly disorganized behavior** is *behavior that is inappropriate for the situation or ineffective in attaining goals, often with specific motor disturbances.* An individual might exhibit constant childlike silliness, improper sexual behavior (such as masturbating in public), disheveled appearance, or loud shouting or swearing. Specific motor disturbances might include strange movements, rigid posturing,

odd mannerisms, bizarre grimacing, or hyperactivity. **Catatonic behavior** is *a marked decrease in all movement or an increase in muscular rigidity and overactivity.* Individuals with *catatonia* may actively resist movement (when someone is trying to move them) or become completely unresponsive and unaware of their surroundings in a *catatonic stupor.* In addition, individuals receiving drug therapy may exhibit motor symptoms (such as rigidity or spasm) as a side effect of the medication. Indeed, the *DSM–5* includes a diagnostic category labeled *medication-induced movement disorders* that identifies motor disturbances arising from the use of medications of the sort commonly used to treat schizophrenia.

Negative symptoms are *deficits or disruptions to normal emotions and behaviors.* They include emotional and social withdrawal; apathy; poverty of speech; and other indications of the absence or insufficiency of normal behavior, motivation, and emotion. These symptoms refer to things missing in people with schizophrenia. Negative symptoms may rob people of emotion, for example, leaving them with flat, deadpan responses; their interest in people or events may be undermined, or their capacity to focus attention may be impaired.

Cognitive symptoms are *deficits in cognitive abilities, specifically in executive functioning, attention, and working memory.* These are the most difficult symptoms to notice because they are much less bizarre and public than the positive and negative symptoms. However, these cognitive deficits often play a large role in terms of preventing people with schizophrenia from achieving a high level of functioning, such as maintaining friendships and holding down a job (Green et al., 2000).

Schizophrenia occurs in about 1% of the population (Jablensky, 1997) and is slightly more common in men than in women (McGrath et al., 2008). Early versions of the *DSM* suggested that schizophrenia might have a very early onset—in the form of infantile autism—but more recent studies suggest that these disorders are distinct and that schizophrenia rarely develops before early adolescence (Rapoport et al., 2009). The first episode typically occurs in late adolescence or early adulthood (Gottesman, 1991). Despite its relatively low frequency, schizophrenia is the primary diagnosis for nearly 40% of all admissions to state and county mental hospitals; it is the second most frequent diagnosis for inpatient psychiatric admission at other institutions (Rosenstein, Milazzo-Sayre, & Manderscheid, 1990). The disproportionate rate of hospitalization for schizophrenia is a testament to the devastation it causes in people's lives.

A person suffering from catatonic schizophrenia may assume an unusual posture and fail to move for hours.

Biological Factors

In 1899, when German psychiatrist Emil Kraepelin first described the syndrome we now know as schizophrenia, he remarked that the disorder was so severe that it suggested "organic," or biological, origins. Over the years, accumulating evidence for the role of biology in schizophrenia has come from studies of genetic factors, biochemical factors, and neuroanatomy.

Genetic Factors

Family studies indicate that the closer a person's genetic relatedness to a person with schizophrenia, the greater the likelihood of developing the disorder (Gottesman, 1991). As shown in **FIGURE 15.4**, concordance rates increase dramatically with biological relatedness. The rates are estimates and vary considerably from study to study, but almost every study finds the average concordance rates higher for identical twins (48%) than for fraternal twins (17%), which suggests a genetic component for the disorder (Torrey et al., 1994).

What is the role of genetics in schizophrenia?

catatonic behavior
A marked decrease in all movement or an increase in muscular rigidity and overactivity.

negative symptoms
Deficits or disruptions to normal emotions and behaviors (e.g., emotional and social withdrawal; apathy; poverty of speech; and other indications of the absence or insufficiency of normal behavior, motivation, and emotion).

cognitive symptoms
Deficits in cognitive abilities, specifically executive functioning, attention, and working memory.

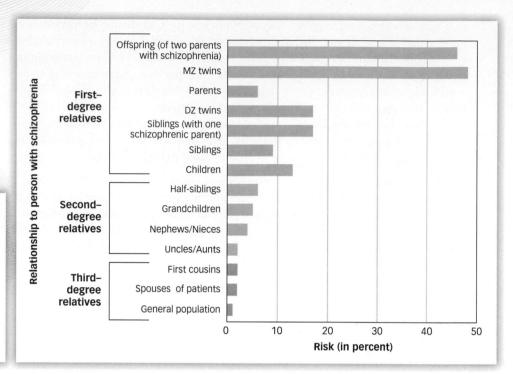

► Figure **15.4** **Average Risk of Developing Schizophrenia** The risk of schizophrenia among biological relatives is greater for those with greater degrees of relatedness. An identical (MZ) twin of a twin with schizophrenia has a 48% risk of developing schizophrenia, for example, and offspring of two parents with schizophrenia have a 46% risk of developing the disorder.

Adapted from Gottesman, 1991.

Although genetics clearly have a strong predisposing role in schizophrenia, considerable evidence suggests that environmental factors, such as the prenatal and perinatal environments, also affect concordance rates (Jurewicz, Owen, & O'Donovan, 2001; Thaker, 2002; Torrey et al., 1994). For example, because approximately 70% of identical twins share the same prenatal blood supply, toxins in the mother's blood could contribute to the high concordance rate. More recent studies (discussed in the earlier section on bipolar disorder) are contributing to a better understanding of how environmental stressors can trigger epigenetic changes that increase susceptibility to this disorder.

Biochemical Factors

During the 1950s, major tranquilizers were discovered that could reduce the symptoms of schizophrenia by lowering levels of the neurotransmitter dopamine. The effectiveness of many drugs in alleviating schizophrenic symptoms is related to the drugs' capacity to reduce dopamine's role in neurotransmission in certain brain tracts. This finding suggested the **dopamine hypothesis,** *the idea that schizophrenia involves an excess of dopamine activity.* The hypothesis has been invoked to explain why amphetamines, which increase dopamine levels, often exacerbate symptoms of schizophrenia (Iverson, 2006).

If only things were so simple. Considerable evidence suggests that this hypothesis is inadequate (Moncrieff, 2009). For example, many individuals with schizophrenia do not respond favorably to dopamine-blocking drugs (e.g., major tranquilizers), and those who do seldom show a complete remission of symptoms. Moreover, the drugs block dopamine receptors very rapidly, yet individuals with schizophrenia typically do not show a beneficial response for weeks. Finally, research has implicated other neurotransmitters in schizophrenia, suggesting that the disorder may involve a complex interaction among a host of different biochemicals (Risman et al., 2008; Sawa & Snyder, 2002). In sum, the precise role of neurotransmitters in schizophrenia has yet to be determined.

dopamine hypothesis
The idea that schizophrenia involves an excess of dopamine activity.

Neuroanatomy

When neuroimaging techniques became available, researchers immediately started looking for distinctive anatomical features of the brain in individuals with schizophrenia. The earliest observations revealed enlargement of the *ventricles,* hollow areas filled with cerebrospinal fluid, lying deep within the core of the brain (see **FIGURE 15.5**; Johnstone et al., 1976). In some individuals (primarily those with chronic, negative symptoms), the ventricles were abnormally enlarged, suggesting a loss of brain tissue mass that could arise from an anomaly in prenatal development (Arnold et al., 1998; Heaton et al., 1994).

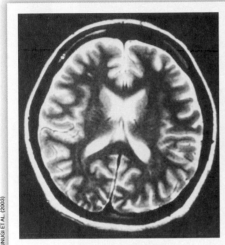

(a) Twin with schizophrenia   **(b)** Twin without schizophrenia

◄ Figure **15.5 Enlarged Ventricles in Schizophrenia** These MRI scans of monozygotic twins reveal that (*a*) the twin affected by schizophrenia shows enlarged ventricles (all the central white space) as compared to (*b*) the unaffected twin (Kunugi et al., 2003).

Understanding the significance of this brain abnormality for schizophrenia is complicated by several factors, however. First, such enlarged ventricles are found in only a minority of cases of schizophrenia. Second, some individuals who do not have schizophrenia also show evidence of enlarged ventricles. Finally, this type of brain abnormality can be caused by the long-term use of some types of antipsychotic medications commonly prescribed in schizophrenia (Breggin, 1990; Gur et al., 1998).

How are the brains of people with schizophrenia different from those without this disorder?

Neuroimaging studies provide evidence of a variety of brain abnormalities in schizophrenia. Paul Thompson and his colleagues (2001) examined changes in the brains of adolescents whose MRI scans could be traced sequentially from the onset of schizophrenia. By morphing the images onto a standardized brain, the researchers were able to detect progressive tissue loss beginning in the parietal lobe and eventually encompassing much of the brain (see **FIGURE 15.6**). All adolescents lose some gray matter over time in a kind of normal "pruning" of the brain, but in the case of those developing schizophrenia, the loss was dramatic enough to seem pathological. A variety of specific brain changes found in other studies suggests a clear relationship between biological changes in the brain and the progression of schizophrenia (Shenton et al., 2001).

Psychological Factors

With all these potential biological contributors to schizophrenia, you might think there would be few psychological or social causes of the disorder. However, several studies do suggest that the family environment plays a role in the development of and recovery

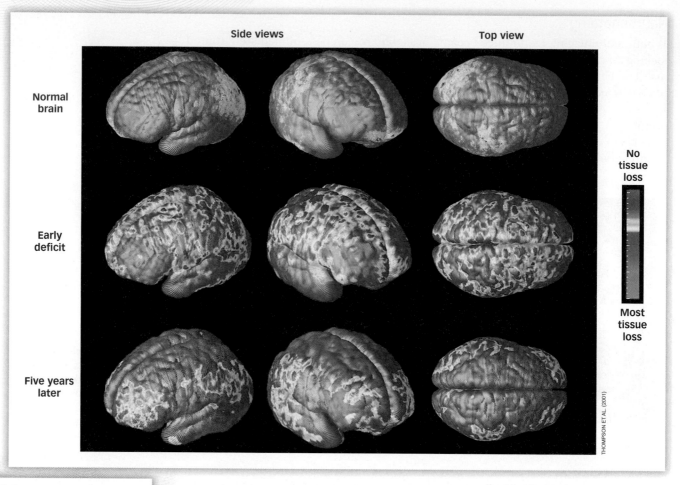

Side views   Top view

Normal brain

Early deficit

Five years later

No tissue loss

Most tissue loss

THOMPSON ET AL. (2001)

▲ Figure **15.6 Brain Tissue Loss in Adolescent Schizophrenia** MRI scan composites reveal brain tissue loss in adolescents diagnosed with schizophrenia. Normal brains show minimal loss due to "pruning" (*top*). Early-deficit scans reveal loss in the parietal areas (*middle*); individuals at this stage may experience symptoms such as hallucinations or bizarre thoughts. Scans 5 years later reveal extensive tissue loss over much of the cortex (*bottom*); individuals at this stage are likely to suffer from delusions, disorganized speech and behavior, and negative symptoms such as social withdrawal (Thompson et al., 2001).

from the condition. One large-scale study compared the risk of schizophrenia in children adopted into healthy families and those adopted into severely disturbed families (Tienari et al., 2004). (Disturbed families were defined as those with extreme conflict, lack of communication, or chaotic relationships.) Among children whose biological mothers had schizophrenia, the disturbed environment increased the likelihood of developing schizophrenia—an outcome that was not found among children who were also reared in disturbed families but whose biological mothers did *not* have schizophrenia. This finding provides support for the diathesis–stress model described earlier.

IN SUMMARY

▶ Schizophrenia is a severe psychological disorder involving hallucinations, disorganized thoughts and behavior, and emotional and social withdrawal.

▶ Schizophrenia affects only 1% of the population, but it accounts for a disproportionate share of psychiatric hospitalizations.

▶ The first drugs that reduced the availability of dopamine sometimes reduced the symptoms of schizophrenia, suggesting that the disorder involved an excess of dopamine activity, but recent research suggests that schizophrenia may involve a complex interaction among a variety of neurotransmitters.

▶ Risks for developing schizophrenia include genetic factors, biochemical factors (perhaps a complex interaction among many neurotransmitters), brain abnormalities, and a stressful home environment.

OTHER VOICES

Successful and Schizophrenic

Elyn R. Saks is a law professor at the University of Southern California and the author of the memoir *The Center Cannot Hold: My Journey Through Madness.*

PHOTO BY MIKEL HEALEY, COURTESY ELYN R. SAKS

This chapter describes what we know about the characteristics and causes of mental disorders, and the next chapter describes how these disorders are commonly treated. For some of the more severe disorders, such as schizophrenia, the picture does not look good. People diagnosed with schizophrenia often are informed that it is a lifelong condition, and although current treatments show some effectiveness in decreasing the delusional thinking and hallucinations often present in those with schizophrenia, people with this disorder often are unable to hold down a full-time job, maintain healthy relationships, and achieve a high quality of life.

Elyn Saks is one such person who received a diagnosis of schizophrenia and was informed of this prognosis. She described what happened next in a longer version of the following article that appeared in the *New York Times* (2013).

Thirty years ago, I was given a diagnosis of schizophrenia. My prognosis was "grave": I would never live independently, hold a job, find a loving partner, get married. My home would be a board-and-care facility, my days spent watching TV in a day room with other people debilitated by mental illness. . . .

Then I made a decision. I would write the narrative of my life. Today I am a chaired professor at the University of Southern California Gould School of Law. I have an adjunct appointment in the department of psychiatry at the medical school of the University of California, San Diego. The MacArthur Foundation gave me a genius grant.

Although I fought my diagnosis for many years, I came to accept that I have schizophrenia and will be in treatment the rest of my life. . . . What I refused to accept was my prognosis.

Conventional psychiatric thinking and its diagnostic categories say that people like me don't exist. Either I don't have schizophrenia (please tell that to the delusions crowding my mind), or I couldn't have accomplished what I have (please tell that to U.S.C.'s committee on faculty affairs). But I do, and I have. And I have undertaken research with colleagues at U.S.C. and U.C.L.A. to show that I am not alone. There are others with schizophrenia and such active symptoms as delusions and hallucinations who have significant academic and professional achievements.

Over the last few years, my colleagues . . . and I have gathered 20 research subjects with high-functioning schizophrenia in Los Angeles. They suffered from symptoms like mild delusions or hallucinatory behavior. Their average age was 40. Half were male, half female, and more than half were minorities. All had high school diplomas, and a majority either had or were working toward college or graduate degrees. They were graduate students, managers, technicians and professionals, including a doctor, lawyer, psychologist and chief executive of a nonprofit group. At the same time, most were unmarried and childless, which is consistent with their diagnoses. . . . More than three-quarters had been hospitalized between two and five times because of their illness, while three had never been admitted.

How had these people with schizophrenia managed to succeed in their studies and at such high-level jobs? We learned that, in addition to medication and therapy, all the participants had developed techniques to keep their schizophrenia at bay. For some, these techniques were cognitive. An educator with a master's degree said he had learned to face his hallucinations and ask, "What's the evidence for that? Or is it just a perception problem?" Another participant said, "I hear derogatory voices all the time. . . . You just gotta blow them off." . . .

Other techniques that our participants cited included controlling sensory inputs. For some, this meant keeping their living space simple (bare walls, no TV, only quiet music), while for others, it meant distracting music. "I'll listen to loud music if I don't want to hear things," said a participant who is a certified nurse's assistant. Still others mentioned exercise, a healthy diet, avoiding alcohol and getting enough sleep. . . .

One of the most frequently mentioned techniques that helped our research participants manage their symptoms was work. "Work has been an important part of who I am," said an educator in our group. "When you become useful to an organization and feel respected in that organization, there's a certain value in belonging there." This person works on the weekends too because of "the distraction factor." In other words, by engaging in work, the crazy stuff often recedes to the sidelines. . . .

THAT is why it is so distressing when doctors tell their patients not to expect or pursue fulfilling careers. Far too often, the conventional psychiatric approach to mental illness is to see clusters of symptoms that characterize people. Accordingly, many psychiatrists hold the view that treating symptoms with medication is treating mental illness. But this fails to take into account individuals' strengths and capabilities, leading mental health professionals to underestimate what their patients can hope to achieve in the world. . . . A recent *New York Times Magazine* article described a new company that hires high-functioning adults with autism, taking advantage of their unusual memory skills and attention to detail. . . .

An approach that looks for individual strengths, in addition to considering symptoms, could help dispel the pessimism surrounding mental illness. Finding "the wellness within the illness," as one person with schizophrenia said, should be a therapeutic goal. Doctors should urge their patients to develop relationships and engage in meaningful work. They should encourage patients to find their own repertory of techniques to manage their symptoms and aim for a quality of life as they define it. And they should provide patients with the resources—therapy, medication and support—to make these things happen. . . .

Elyn Saks's story is amazing and inspiring. It also is quite unusual. How should we incorporate stories like hers and the people in the research study she described? Are these people outliers—simply a carefully selected collection of people who had unusually favorable outcomes (given the large size of Los Angeles, it is reasonable to think one could amass a small sample of such cases)? Or has Professor Saks touched on an important limitation to the way in which the field currently conceptualizes, classifies, and treats mental disorders? Do we focus too much on what is wrong and on how professionalized healthcare can treat the pathology and not enough on what inherent strengths people have that can help them overcome their challenges, function at a high level, and achieve a high quality of life? These are all questions that are testable with the methods of psychological science, and the answers may help to improve the lives of many people.

Disorders of Childhood and Adolescence

All of the disorders described above can have their onset during childhood, adolescence, or adulthood. Some often begin early in life (lots of adolescents develop anxiety disorders or depression), and in fact half of all disorders begin by age 14, and three-quarters by age 24 (Kessler, Berglund, et al., 2005), which means if you are 24 years or older, you're almost out of the woods. However, other disorders tend not to begin until early adulthood, such as bipolar disorder and schizophrenia (we did say "almost"). Some disorders *always*, by definition, begin in childhood or adolescence, and if they don't, you are never going to have them. These include autism spectrum disorder, attention-deficit/hyperactivity disorder, conduct disorder, intellectual disability (formerly called *mental retardation*), learning disorders, communication disorders, and motor skill disorders, in addition to many others. The first three are among the most common and well known, so we will review them briefly here.

Autism Spectrum Disorder

Marco is a 4-year-old only child. His parents have become worried because, although his mother stays home with him all day and tries to play with him and talk with him, he still has not spoken a single word and he shows little interest in trying. He spends much of his time playing with his toy trains, which seem to be the thing he enjoys most in life. He often sits for hours staring at spinning train wheels or pushing a single train back and forth, seeming completely in his own world, uninterested in playing with anyone else. Marco's parents have become concerned about Marco's apparent inability to speak, disinterest in others, and development of some peculiar mannerisms, such as flapping his arms repeatedly for no apparent reason.

Autism Spectrum Disorder (ASD) is *a condition beginning in early childhood in which a person shows persistent communication deficits as well as restricted and repetitive patterns of behaviors, interests or activities.* In *DSM–5*, ASD now subsumes multiple disorders that were considered separate in *DSM–IV*: autistic disorder, Asperger's disorder, childhood disintegrative disorder, and pervasive developmental disorder not otherwise specified (i.e., these disorders are no longer recognized in the *DSM*).

The true rate of ASD is difficult to pinpoint, especially given the recent change in diagnostic definition. Estimates from the 1960s indicated that autism was a rare diagnosis, occurring in 4 per 10,000 children. Estimates have been creeping up over time and now stand at approximately 10 to 20 per 10,000 children. If one considers the full range of disorders that now fall under the ASD umbrella in the *DSM–5*, the rate is 60 per 10,000 children (Newschaffer et al., 2007). It is unclear whether this increased rate is due to increased awareness and recognition of ASD, better screening and diagnostic tools, or to some other factor. Boys have higher rates of ASD than girls by a ratio of about 4:1.

Early theories of autism described it as "childhood schizophrenia," but it is now understood to be separate from schizophrenia, which is rarely diagnosed in children, emerging mainly in adolescence or young adulthood (Kessler & Wang, 2008). ASD is currently viewed as a heterogeneous set of traits that cluster together in some families (heritability estimates for ASD are as high as 90%), leaving some children with just a few mild ASD traits and others with a more severe form of the disorder (Geschwind, 2009). Interestingly, some people with ASD have unique strengths. For instance, some people with ASD have remarkable abilities to perceive or remember details, or to master symbol systems such as mathematics or music (Happé & Vital, 2009).

One current model suggested that ASD can be understood as an impaired capacity for *empathizing,* knowing the mental states of others, combined with a superior ability for *systematizing,* understanding the rules that organize the structure and function of

> **What is the relationship between ASD and empathy?**

autism spectrum disorder (ASD)
A condition beginning in early childhood in which a person shows persistent communication deficits as well as restricted and repetitive patterns of behaviors, interests, or activities.

objects (Baron-Cohen & Belmonte, 2005). Consistent with this model, brain imaging studies show that people with autism have comparatively decreased activity in regions associated with understanding the minds of others and greater activation in regions related to basic object perception (Sigman, Spence & Wang, 2006).

Although many people with ASD experience impairments throughout their lives that prevent them from having relationships and holding down a job, many go on to very successful careers. The renowned behavioral scientist and author Temple Grandin (2006) has written of her personal experience with autism. She was diagnosed with autism at age 3, started learning to talk late, and then suffered teasing for odd habits and "nerdy" behavior. Fortunately, she developed ways to cope and found a niche through her special talent—the ability to understand animal behavior (Sacks, 1996). She is now a Professor of Animal Sciences at Colorado State University; celebrated author of books such as *Animals in Translation*; designer of animal handling systems used widely in ranching, farming, and zoos; and the central character in an HBO movie based on her life. Temple Grandin's story lets us know that there are happy endings. Overall, those diagnosed with ASD as children have highly variable trajectories, with some achieving normal or better-than-normal functioning and others struggling with profound disorder. Autism is a childhood disorder that in adulthood can turn out many ways (see the Hot Science box).

Temple Grandin, Professor of Animal Sciences at Colorado State University, is living proof that people with Autism Spectrum Disorder are able to have very successful professional careers.

HOT SCIENCE

Optimal Outcome in Autism Spectrum Disorder

What comes to mind when you think of the word *autism*? What kind of person do you imagine? If an adult, what do you imagine that they do for a living? Can they hold a job? Can they care for themselves? Autism spectrum disorder (ASD) is considered by many to be a lifelong condition in which those affected will forever experience significant difficulties and disability in their interpersonal, education, and occupational functioning. Several recent studies are helping to change this outlook.

Deborah Fein and colleagues (2013) recently described a sample of people who were diagnosed with autism as children, but who no longer met criteria for ASD. How could this be? For years, researchers have noticed that some portion of children diagnosed with autism later fail to meet diagnostic criteria. One recent review suggested that 3 to 25% of children ultimately lose their ASD diagnosis over time (Helt et al., 2008). There are several potential explanations for this. The most obvious is that some portion of children diagnosed with ASD are misdiagnosed and don't really have this disorder. Perhaps they are overly shy, or quiet, or develop speech later than other children, and this is misinterpreted as ASD. Another possibility is that children who lose their ASD diagnosis had a milder form of the disorder and/or were identified and treated earlier. There is some support for this idea,

▲ Autism was once viewed as a condition with lifelong impairments. New research suggests that early intervention can help many of those in whom ASD is diagnosed to achieve normal levels of functioning.

as predictors of recovery from ASD include high IQ, stronger language abilities, and earlier age of identification and treatment (Helt et al., 2008).

The possibility of effectively treating ASD initially was raised in an important study by Ivar Lovaas in 1987. Lovaas assigned 19 children with autism to an intensive behavioral intervention in which they received over 40 hours per week of one-on-one behavior therapy for 2 years, and 40 children to control conditions in which they received fewer than 10 hours per week of treatment. Amazingly, follow-up of the treated children revealed that 47% of those in the intensive behavior therapy condition obtained a normal level of intellectual and educational

functioning—passing through a normal first grade class—compared to only 2% of those in the control conditions.

Extending this earlier work, Geraldine Dawson and colleagues (2010) are testing a program called the Early Start Denver Model (ESDM), an intensive behavioral intervention (20 hours per week for 2 years) similarly designed to improve outcomes among those with ASD. Using randomized, controlled trials, Dawson and colleagues found that toddlers with ASD who received ESDM, compared to those receiving standard community treatment, showed significant improvements in IQ (a 17-point raise!), language, adaptive and social functioning, and ASD diagnosis. Interestingly, children in the ESDM showed normalized brain activity after treatment (i.e., greater brain activation when viewing faces), which was in turn associated with improved social behavior; those in the control condition showed the opposite pattern (Dawson et al., 2012).

How effective are intensive behavioral interventions like those described here? Fein and colleagues' (2013) data suggest that some people diagnosed with ASD can achieve optimal outcomes, meaning they do not differ from typically developing people in IQ, language, communication, or socialization—the key deficit areas that characterize ASD. This is currently a very hot area of research, and one that could have implications for those in whom ASD is diagnosed.

attention deficit/hyperactivity disorder (ADHD)
A persistent pattern of severe problems with inattention and/or hyperactivity or impulsiveness that cause significant impairments in functioning.

conduct disorder
A persistent pattern of deviant behavior involving aggression to people or animals, destruction of property, deceitfulness or theft, or serious rule violations.

Attention-Deficit/Hyperactivity Disorder

Chances are you have had the experience of being distracted during a lecture or while reading one of your *other* textbooks. We all have trouble focusing from time to time. Far beyond normal distraction, **attention deficit/hyperactivity disorder (ADHD),** is *a persistent pattern of severe problems with inattention and/or hyperactivity or impulsiveness that cause significant impairments in functioning.* This is quite different than occasional mind wandering or bursts of activity. Meeting criteria for ADHD requires having multiple symptoms of inattention (e.g., persistent problems with sustained attention, organization, memory, following instructions), hyperactivity–impulsiveness (e.g., persistent difficulties with remaining still, waiting for a turn, interrupting others), or both. Most children experience some of these behaviors at some point, but to meet criteria for ADHD, a child has to have many of these behaviors for at least 6 months in at least two settings (e.g., home and school) to the point where they impair the child's ability to perform at school or get along at home.

> **What are the criteria for an ADHD diagnosis?**

Approximately 10% of boys and 4% of girls meet criteria for ADHD (Polanczyk et al., 2007). The *DSM–5* requires that symptoms of ADHD be present before the age of 12 in order to meet criteria for this disorder. As you can imagine, children and adolescents with ADHD often struggle in the classroom. One recent study of 500 people with ADHD found that about half had a C average or lower, and about one-third were in special classes (Biederman et al., 2006). For a long time ADHD was thought of as a disorder that affects only children and adolescents and that people "age out" of the disorder. However, we now know that in many instances this disorder persists into adulthood. The same symptoms are used to diagnose both children and adults (e.g., children with ADHD may struggle with attention and concentration in the classroom, whereas adults may experience the same problems in meetings). Approximately 4% of adults meet criteria for ADHD, and adults with this disorder are more likely to be male, divorced, and unemployed—and most did not receive any treatment for their ADHD (Kessler, Adler, et al., 2006). Unfortunately, most people still think of this as a disorder of childhood and don't realize that adults can suffer from ADHD as well, which could be why so few adults with ADHD receive treatment, and why the disorder often wreaks havoc on job performance and relationships.

Because ADHD, like most disorders, is defined by the presence of a wide range of symptoms, it is unlikely that it emerges from one single cause or dysfunction. The exact cause of ADHD is not known, but there are some promising leads. Genetic studies suggest that there is a strong biological influence and estimate that the heritability of ADHD is 76% (Faraone et al., 2005). Brain imaging studies suggest that those with ADHD have smaller brain volumes (Castellanos et al., 2002) as well as structural and functional abnormalities in frontosubcortical networks associated with attention and behavioral inhibition (Makris et al., 2009). The good news is that current drug treatments for ADHD are effective and appear to decrease the risk of later psychological and academic problems (Biederman et al., 2009).

Conduct Disorder

Michael is an 8-year-old boy whose mother brought him into a local clinic because his behavior had been getting progressively out of control and his parents and teachers were no longer able to control him. Although Michael's two older brothers and little sisters got along perfectly fine at home and at school, Michael had always gotten into trouble. At home he routinely bullied his siblings, threw glasses and dishes at family members, and on numerous occasions punched and kicked his parents. Outside of the house, Michael had been getting into trouble for stealing from the local store, yelling at his teacher, and spitting at the principal of his school. The last straw came when Michael's parents found him trying to set fire to his bedspread one night. They tried punishing him by taking away his toys, restricting his privileges, and trying to encourage him with a sticker chart, but nothing seemed to change his behavior.

Conduct disorder is a condition in which a child or adolescent engages in a *persistent pattern of deviant behavior involving aggression to people or animals, destruction of property, deceitfulness or theft, or serious rule violations*. Approximately 9% of people in the United States report a lifetime history of conduct disorder (12% of boys and 7% of girls; Nock et al., 2006). This number may seem a bit high, but approximately 40% of those with conduct disorder have, on average, only 3 symptoms that cluster into one of three areas: rule breaking, theft/deceit, or aggression toward others. The other 60% have more symptoms, on average 6 to 8 of the 15 defined symptoms, with problems in many more areas and a much higher risk of having other mental disorders later in life (Nock et al., 2006).

> Why is it difficult to pin down the causes of conduct disorder?

Meeting criteria for conduct disorder requires having any 3 of the 15 symptoms of conduct disorder. This means there are approximately 32,000 different combinations of symptoms that could lead to a diagnosis, which makes those with conduct disorder a pretty diverse group. This diversity makes it difficult to pin down the causes of conduct disorder. One thing that seems clear is that a wide range of genetic, biological, and environmental factors interact to produce this disorder. Indeed, risk factors for conduct disorder include maternal smoking during pregnancy, exposure to abuse and family violence during childhood, affiliation with deviant peer groups, and the presence of deficits in executive functioning (e.g., decision making, impulsiveness; Boden et al., 2010; Burke et al., 2002). Researchers currently are attempting to better understand the pathways through which inherited genetic factors interact with environmental stressors (e.g., childhood adversities) to create characteristics in brain structure and function (e.g., reduced activity in brain regions associated with planning and decision making) that interact with environmental factors (e.g., affiliation with deviant peers) to lead to the behaviors that are characteristic of conduct disorder. Not surprisingly, conduct disorder tends to be comorbid with other disorders characterized by problems with decision making and impulsiveness, such as ADHD, substance use disorders, and antisocial personality disorder, which is described in more detail in the next section.

Psychologists are attempting to identify the causes of conduct disorder with the hopes of being able to decrease the harmful behaviors, like bullying, that often accompany it.

IN SUMMARY

▶ Some mental disorders always begin during childhood or adolescence, and in some cases (ASD, ADHD) persist into adulthood.

▶ ASD emerges in early childhood and is a condition in which a person has persistent communication deficits as well as restricted and repetitive patterns of behavior, interests, or activities.

▶ ADHD begins by age 12 and involves a persistent pattern of severe problems with inattention and/or hyperactivity or impulsiveness that cause significant impairments in functioning.

▶ Conduct disorder begins in childhood or adolescence and involves a persistent pattern of deviant behavior involving aggression to people or animals, destruction of property, deceitfulness or theft, or serious rule violations.

personality disorders
Enduring patterns of thinking, feeling, or relating to others or controlling impulses that deviate from cultural expectations and cause distress or impaired functioning.

Personality Disorders: Going to Extremes

Think for a minute about high school acquaintances whose personalities made them stand out—not necessarily in a good way. Was there an odd person who didn't seem to make sense, wore strange outfits, sometimes wouldn't respond in conversation—or would respond by bringing up weird things like astrology or mind reading? Or perhaps a drama queen, someone whose theatrics and exaggerated emotions turned everything into a big deal? And don't forget the neat freak, the perfectionist obsessed with control, who had the perfectly organized locker, precisely arranged hair, and sweater with zero lint balls. One way to describe such people is to say they simply have *personalities*, the unique patterns of traits we explored in the Personality chapter. But sometimes personality traits can become so rigid and confining that they blend into mental disorders. **Personality disorders** are *enduring patterns of thinking, feeling, or relating to others or controlling impulses that deviate from cultural expectations and cause distress or impaired functioning*. Personality disorders begin in adolescence or early adulthood and are relatively stable over time. Let's look at the types of personality disorders and then take a closer look at one that sometimes lands people in jail: antisocial personality disorder.

Types of Personality Disorders

The *DSM–5* lists 10 specific personality disorders (see **TABLE 15.3**). They fall into three clusters: (a) *odd/eccentric*, (b) *dramatic/erratic*, and (c) *anxious/inhibited*. The strange high school student, for example, could have *schizotypal personality disorder* (odd/eccentric cluster); the drama queen could have *histrionic personality disorder* (dramatic/erratic cluster); the neat freak could have *obsessive-compulsive personality disorder*

(anxious/inhibited cluster). In fact, browsing through the list may awaken other high school memories. Don't rush to judgment, however. Most of those kids are probably quite healthy and fall far short of qualifying for a diagnosis; after all, high school can be a rocky time for everyone, which is why personality disorders are not diagnosed in children or adolescents. The *DSM–5* even notes that early personality problems often do not persist into adulthood. Still, the array of personality disorders suggests that there are multiple ways an individual's gift of a unique personality could become a problem.

Personality disorders have been a bit controversial for several reasons. First, critics question whether having a problematic personality is really a disorder. Given that approximately 15% of the U.S. population has a personality disorder according to the *DSM–5*, perhaps it might be better just to admit that a lot of people are difficult and leave it at that. Another question is whether personality problems correspond to "disorders" in that there are distinct *types* or whether such problems might be better understood as extreme values on trait *dimensions* such as the Big Five traits discussed in the Personality chapter (Trull & Durrett, 2005). In *DSM–IV*, personality disorders appeared as a separate type of disorder from all of

Ever browse a copy of *Architectural Digest* and wonder who would live in one of those perfect homes? A person with obsessive-compulsive personality disorder might fit right in. This personality disorder (characterized by excessive perfectionism) should not be mistaken, by the way, for obsessive-compulsive disorder—the anxiety disorder in which the person suffers from repeated unwanted thoughts or actions.

GETTY IMAGES/IMAGE SOURCE

> **Table 15.3**

Clusters of Personality Disorders

Cluster	Personality Disorder	Characteristics
A. Odd/Eccentric	Paranoid	Distrust in others, suspicion that people have sinister motives. Apt to challenge the loyalties of friends and read hostile intentions into others' actions. Prone to anger and aggressive outbursts but otherwise emotionally cold. Often jealous, guarded, secretive, overly serious.
	Schizoid	Extreme introversion and withdrawal from relationships. Prefers to be alone, little interest in others. Humorless, distant, often absorbed with own thoughts and feelings, a daydreamer. Fearful of closeness, with poor social skills, often seen as a "loner."
	Schizotypal	Peculiar or eccentric manners of speaking or dressing. Strange beliefs. "Magical thinking" such as belief in ESP or telepathy. Difficulty forming relationships. May react oddly in conversation, not respond, or talk to self. Speech elaborate or difficult to follow. (Possibly a mild form of schizophrenia.)
B. Dramatic/Erratic	Antisocial	Impoverished moral sense or "conscience." History of deception, crime, legal problems, impulsive and aggressive or violent behavior. Little emotional empathy or remorse for hurting others. Manipulative, careless, callous. At high risk for substance abuse and alcoholism.
	Borderline	Unstable moods and intense, stormy personal relationships. Frequent mood changes and anger, unpredictable impulses. Self-mutilation or suicidal threats or gestures to get attention or manipulate others. Self-image fluctuation and a tendency to see others as "all good" or "all bad."
	Histrionic	Constant attention seeking. Grandiose language, provocative dress, exaggerated illnesses, all to gain attention. Believes that everyone loves them. Emotional, lively, overly dramatic, enthusiastic, and excessively flirtatious. Shallow and labile emotions. "Onstage."
	Narcissistic	Inflated sense of self-importance, absorbed by fantasies of self and success. Exaggerates own achievement, assumes others will recognize they are superior. Good first impressions but poor longer-term relationships. Exploitative of others.
C. Anxious/Inhibited	Avoidant	Socially anxious and uncomfortable unless they are confident of being liked. In contrast with schizoid person, yearns for social contact. Fears criticism and worries about being embarrassed in front of others. Avoids social situations due to fear of rejection.
	Dependent	Submissive, dependent, requiring excessive approval, reassurance, and advice. Clings to people and fears losing them. Lacking self-confidence. Uncomfortable when alone. May be devastated by end of close relationship or suicidal if breakup is threatened.
	Obsessive-compulsive	Conscientious, orderly, perfectionist. Excessive need to do everything "right." Inflexibly high standards and caution can interfere with their productivity. Fear of errors can make them strict and controlling. Poor expression of emotions. (*Not* the same as obsessive-compulsive disorder.)

Source: From *DSM–5* (American Psychiatric Association, 2013).

the other disorders described above (specifically, those major disorders were all in a category called *Axis I* and personality disorders were in *Axis II*). However, in *DSM–5* personality disorders have earned equal footing as full-fledged disorders. One of the most well studied of all the personality disorders is antisocial personality disorder.

Antisocial Personality Disorder

Henri Desiré Landru began using personal ads to attract a woman "interested in matrimony" in Paris in 1914, and he succeeded in seducing 10 of them. He bilked them of their savings, poisoned them, and cremated them in his stove, also disposing of a boy and two dogs along the way. He recorded his murders in a notebook and maintained a marriage and a mistress all the while. The gruesome actions of serial killers such as Landru leave us frightened and wondering; however, bullies, compulsive liars, and

Henri Desiré Landru (1869–1922) was a serial killer who met widows through ads he placed in newspapers' lonely hearts columns. After obtaining enough information to embezzle money from them, he murdered 10 women and the son of one of the women. He was executed for serial murder in 1922.

even drivers who regularly speed through a school zone share the same shocking blindness to human pain. The *DSM–5* includes the category of **antisocial personality disorder (APD)** and defines it as *a pervasive pattern of disregard for and violation of the rights of others that begins in childhood or early adolescence and continues into adulthood.*

Adults with an APD diagnosis typically have a history of *conduct disorder* before the age of 15. In adulthood, a diagnosis of APD is given to individuals who show three or more of a set of seven diagnostic signs: illegal behavior, deception, impulsivity, physical aggression, recklessness, irresponsibility, and a lack of remorse for wrongdoing. About 3.6% of the general population has APD, and the rate of occurrence in men is 3 times the rate in women (Grant et al., 2004).

The terms *sociopath* and *psychopath* describe people with APD who are especially coldhearted, manipulative, and ruthless—yet may be glib and charming (Cleckley, 1976; Hare, 1998). Although psychologists usually try to explain the development of abnormal behavior as a product of childhood experiences or difficult life circumstances, those who work with APD seem less forgiving, often noting the sheer dangerousness of people with this disorder. Many people with APD do commit crimes, and many are caught because of the frequency and flagrancy of their infractions. Among 22,790 prisoners in one study, 47% of the men and 21% of the women were diagnosed with APD (Fazel & Danesh, 2002). Statistics such as these support the notion of a "criminal personality."

Both the early onset of conduct problems and the lack of success in treatment suggest that career criminality often has an internal cause (Lykken, 1995). Evidence of brain abnormalities in people with APD is also accumulating (Blair, Peschardt, & Mitchell, 2005). One line of investigation has looked at sensitivity to fear in psychopaths and individuals who show no such psychopathology. For example, criminal psychopaths who are shown negative emotional words such as *hate* or *corpse* exhibit less activity in the amygdala and hippocampus than do noncriminals (Kiehl et al., 2001). The two brain areas

> **What are some of the factors that contribute to APD?**

are involved in the process of fear conditioning (Patrick, Cuthbert, & Lang, 1994), so their relative inactivity in such studies suggests that psychopaths are less sensitive to fear than are other people. Violent psychopaths can target their aggression toward the self as well as others, often behaving in reckless ways that lead to violent ends. It might seem peaceful to go through life "without fear," but perhaps fear is useful in keeping people from the extremes of antisocial behavior.

antisocial personality disorder (APD)
A pervasive pattern of disregard for and violation of the rights of others that begins in childhood or early adolescence and continues into adulthood.

suicide
Intentional self-inflicted death.

suicide attempt
When a person engages in potentially harmful behavior with some intention of dying.

IN SUMMARY

► Personality disorders are enduring patterns of thinking, feeling, relating to others, or controlling impulses that cause distress or impaired functioning.

► They include three clusters: odd/eccentric, dramatic/erratic, and anxious/inhibited.

► Antisocial personality disorder is associated with a lack of moral emotions and behavior; people with antisocial personality disorder can be manipulative, dangerous, and reckless, often hurting others and sometimes hurting themselves.

Self-Harm Behaviors: When the Mind Turns against Itself

We all have an innate drive to keep ourselves alive. We eat when we are hungry, get out of the way of fast-moving vehicles, and go to school so we can earn a living to keep ourselves, and our families, alive (see the discussion of evolutionary psychology in the Psychology: Evolution of a Science chapter). One of the most extreme manifestations of abnormal human behavior is when a person acts in direct opposition to this drive for self-preservation and engages in intentionally self-destructive behavior. Accounts of people intentionally harming themselves date back to the beginning of recorded history. However, it is only over the past several decades that we have begun to gain an understanding of why people purposely do things to hurt themselves. *DSM–5* includes two self-destructive behaviors in its Section III (disorders in need of further study): suicide behavior disorder and nonsuicidal self-injury disorder.

Suicidal Behavior

Tim, a 35-year-old accountant, had by all appearances been living a pretty happy, successful life. He was married to his high school sweetheart and had two young children. Over the past several years, though, his workload had increased and he started to experience severe job-related stress. At around the same time, he and his wife began to experience some financial problems, and his alcohol consumption increased, all of which put significant strain on the family and began to affect his work. Tim's co-workers noted that he had become pretty angry and agitated lately—even yelling at co-workers on a few occasions. One evening Tim and his wife got into a heated argument about the family's finances and Tim's excessive alcohol use; Tim went into the bathroom and swallowed a bottle full of prescription medicine in an effort to end his life. He was taken to the hospital and kept there to be treated for suicidal behavior.

Suicide, which refers to *intentional self-inflicted death*, is the 10th leading cause of death in the United States and the 2nd leading cause of death among people 15 to 24 years old. It takes the lives of more than 5 times as many people as HIV-AIDS each year in the United States, and more than twice as many people as homicide (Hoyert & Xu, 2012). There are large demographic differences in the suicide rate. For instance, approximately 80% of suicides in the United States and around the world occur among men, and in the United States, White people are much more likely to kill themselves than members of other racial and ethnic groups, accounting for 90% of all suicides (Centers for Disease Control and Prevention, 2013). Unfortunately, we currently do not have a good understanding of why these enormous sociodemographic differences exist.

Nonfatal **suicide attempt,** in which a person engages in *potentially harmful behavior with some intention of dying*, occurs much more frequently than suicide deaths. In the United States, approximately 15% of adults report that they have seriously considered suicide at some point in their lives, 5% have made a plan to kill themselves, and 5% have actually made a suicide attempt. The rates of these behaviors in the United States are slightly above the percentages seen across a wide range of countries, which are 9% (considered suicide), 3% (planned suicide), and 3% (made an attempt), respectively (Nock et al., 2008). As these numbers suggest, only one third of those who think about suicide actually go on to make a suicide attempt. Although many more men than women die by suicide, women experience suicidal thoughts and (nonfatal) suicide attempts at significantly higher rates than do men (Nock et al., 2008). Moreover, the rates of suicidal thoughts and attempts increase dramatically during adolescence and young adulthood. A recent study of a representative sample of approximately 10,000 U.S. adolescents revealed that suicidal

We all have an innate desire to keep ourselves alive. So why do some people purposely do things to harm themselves?

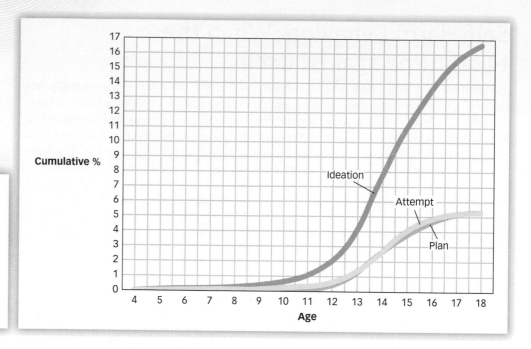

► Figure **15.7 Age of Onset of Suicidal Behavior During Adolescence** A recent survey of a nationally representative sample of U.S. adolescents shows that although suicidal thoughts and behaviors are quite rare among children (the rate was 0.0 for ages 1–4), they increase dramatically starting at age 12 and continuing to climb throughout adolescence.

Adapted from Nock et al., 2013

thoughts and behaviors are virtually nonexistent before age 10, but then increase dramatically from age 12 to 18 years (see **FIGURE 15.7**) before leveling off during early adulthood (Nock et al., 2013).

So the numbers are staggering, but *why* do people try to kill themselves? The short answer is: We do not yet know, and it's complicated. When interviewed in the hospital following their suicide attempt, most people who have tried to kill themselves report that they did so in order to escape from an intolerable state of mind or impossible situation (Boergers, Spirito, & Donaldson, 1998). Consistent with this explanation, research has documented that the risk of suicidal behavior is significantly increased if a person experiences factors that can create severely distressing states such as the presence of multiple mental disorders (more than 90% of people who die by suicide have at least one mental disorder); the experience of significant negative life events during childhood and adulthood (e.g., physical and sexual assault); and the presence of severe medical problems (Nock, Borges, & Ono, 2012). The search is ongoing for a more comprehensive understanding of how and why some people respond to negative life events with suicidal thoughts and behaviors, as well as on methods of better predicting and preventing these devastating outcomes.

What are some of the factors that contribute to suicidal behavior?

Nonsuicidal Self-Injury

Louisa, an 18-year-old college student, secretly cuts her lower waist and upper thighs about once per week, typically when she is in the midst of feeling intense anger and hatred, either toward herself or someone else. She has always had a bit of a "hot streak" as she calls it, but it wasn't until she turned 14 that she started to use self-injury as a way to calm herself down. Louisa says that she actually feels a little ashamed after each episode of cutting, but she doesn't know how else to calm down when she gets really upset and so she has no plans of stopping this behavior.

Louisa is engaging in a behavior called **nonsuicidal self-injury (NSSI),** the *direct, deliberate destruction of body tissue in the absence of any intent to die.* NSSI has been reported since the beginning of recorded history; however, it is a behavior that appears to be on the rise over the past few decades. Recent studies suggest that as many as 15 to 20% of adolescents and 3 to 6% of adults report engaging in NSSI at some point in their lifetime (Klonsky, 2011; Muehlenkamp et al., 2012). The rates appear to be even between males and females, and for people of different races and ethnicities. Like suicidal behavior, NSSI is virtually absent during childhood, increases dramatically during adolescence, and then appears to decrease across adulthood.

> **What is known so far about why people engage in self-injury?**

nonsuicidal self-injury (NSSI) Direct, deliberate destruction of body tissue in the absence of any intent to die.

In some parts of the world, cutting or scarification of the skin is socially accepted, and in some cases encouraged as a rite of passage (Favazza, 2011). In parts of the world where self-cutting is not socially encouraged, why would a person purposely hurt him- or herself if not to die? Recent studies suggest that people who engage in self-injury have very strong emotional and physiological responses to negative events, that they perceive this response as intolerable, and that NSSI serves to diminish the intensity of this response (Nock, 2009). There also is some evidence that in many instances, people engage in self-injury as a means to communicate distress or elicit help from others (Nock, 2010). Although we are beginning to get an understanding of why some people engage in NSSI, there are many aspects of this behavior that we do not yet understand, and the study of NSSI is an increasingly active area of research.

Unfortunately, like suicidal behavior, our understanding of the genetic and neurobiological influences on NSSI is limited, and there currently are no effective medications for these problems. There also is very limited evidence for behavioral interventions or prevention programs (Mann et al., 2005). So, whereas suicidal behavior and NSSI are some of the most disturbing and dangerous mental disorders, they also, unfortunately, are among the most perplexing. The field has made significant strides in our understanding of these behavior problems in recent years, but there is a long way to go before we are able to predict and prevent them accurately and effectively.

Although in the United States self-injury is considered to be pathological, in some parts of the world scarification of the skin is viewed as a rite of passage into adulthood and a symbol of one's tribe, as in the case of this young man from the Republic of Benin in West Africa.

IN SUMMARY

▶ Suicide is among the leading causes of death in the United States and the world. Most people who die by suicide have a mental disorder, and suicide attempts most often are motivated by an attempt to escape intolerable mental states or situations.

▶ NSSI, like suicidal behavior, increases dramatically during adolescence, but for many is a persistent problem throughout adulthood. Although NSSI is performed without suicidal intent, like suicidal behavior, it is most often motivated by an attempt to escape from painful mental states.

Chapter Review

KEY CONCEPT QUIZ

1. The conception of psychological disorders as diseases that have symptoms and possible cures is referred to as
   a. the medical model.
   b. physiognomy.
   c. the root syndrome framework.
   d. a diagnostic system.

2. The *DSM–5* is best described as a
   a. medical model.
   b. classification system.
   c. set of theoretical assumptions.
   d. collection of physiological definitions.

3. Comorbidity of disorders refers to
   a. symptoms stemming from internal dysfunction.
   b. the relative risk of death arising from a disorder.
   c. the co-occurrence of two or more disorders in a single individual.
   d. the existence of disorders on a continuum from normal to abnormal.

4. Irrational worries and fears that undermine one's ability to function normally are an indication of
   a. a genetic abnormality.
   b. dysthymia.
   c. diathesis.
   d. an anxiety disorder.

5. A(n) __ disorder involves anxiety tied to a specific object or situation.
   a. generalized anxiety
   b. environmental
   c. panic
   d. phobic

6. Agoraphobia often develops as a result of
   a. preparedness theory.
   b. obsessive-compulsive disorder.
   c. panic disorder.
   d. social phobia.

7. Kelly's fear of germs leads her to wash her hands repeatedly throughout the day, often for a half hour or more, under extremely hot water. From which disorder does Kelly suffer?
   a. panic attacks
   b. obsessive-compulsive disorder
   c. phobia
   d. generalized anxiety disorder

8. Major depression is characterized by a severely depressed mood that lasts at least
   a. 2 weeks.
   b. 1 week.
   c. 1 month.
   d. 6 months.

9. Extreme moods swings between __ characterize bipolar disorder.
   a. depression and mania
   b. stress and lethargy
   c. anxiety and arousal
   d. obsessions and compulsions

10. Schizophrenia is characterized by which of the following?
    a. hallucinations
    b. disorganized thoughts and behavior
    c. emotional and social withdrawal
    d. all of the above

11. Schizophrenia affects approximately __ % of the population and accounts for approximately __ % of admissions to state and county mental hospitals.
    a. 5; 20
    b. 5; 5
    c. 1; 1
    d. 1; 40

12. Autism spectrum disorder is characterized by which of the following?
    a. communication deficits and restricted, repetitive behavior
    b. hallucinations and delusions
    c. suicidal thoughts
    d. all of the above

13. Attention-deficit/hyperactivity disorder
    a. must begin before the age of 7.
    b. never persists into adulthood.
    c. sometimes persists into adulthood.
    d. affects only boys.

14. In the United States, those at highest risk for suicide are
    a. men.
    b. White people.
    c. those with a mental disorder.
    d. all of the above

15. Nonsuicidal self-injury occurs among _% of adolescents.
    a. 1–2
    b. 3–5
    c. 15–20
    d. 50

KEY TERMS

mental disorder (p. 584)

medical model (p. 585)

Diagnostic and Statistical Manual of Mental Disorders (DSM) (p. 586)

comorbidity (p. 587)

biopsychosocial perspective (p. 587)

diathesis–stress model (p. 589)

Research Domain Criteria Project (RDoC) (p. 590)

anxiety disorder (p. 593)

phobic disorders (p. 594)

specific phobia (p. 594)

social phobia (p. 594)

preparedness theory (p. 594)

panic disorder (p. 596)

agoraphobia (p. 596)

generalized anxiety disorder (GAD) (p. 597)

obsessive-compulsive disorder (OCD) (p. 598)

posttraumatic stress disorder (PTSD) (p. 599)

mood disorders (p. 601)

major depressive disorder (or unipolar depression) (p. 601)

dysthymia (p. 601)

double depression (p. 602)

seasonal affective disorder (SAD) (p. 602)

helplessness theory (p. 604)

bipolar disorder (p. 605)

expressed emotion (p. 607)

schizophrenia (p. 607)

positive symptoms (p. 608)

hallucination (p. 608)

delusion (p. 608)

disorganized speech (p. 608)

grossly disorganized behavior (p. 608)

catatonic behavior (p. 609)

negative symptoms (p. 609)

cognitive symptoms (p. 609)

dopamine hypothesis (p. 610)

autism spectrum disorder (ASD) (p. 614)

attention-deficit/hyperactivity disorder (ADHD) (p. 614)

conduct disorder (p. 616)

personality disorders (p. 618)

antisocial personality disorder (APD) (p. 620)

suicide (p. 621)

suicide attempt (p. 621)

nonsuicidal self-injury (NSSI) (p. 622)

CHANGING MINDS

1. You catch a TV interview with a celebrity who describes his difficult childhood, living with a mother who suffered from major depression. "Sometimes my mother stayed in her bed for days, not even getting up to eat," he says. "At the time, the family hushed it up. My parents were immigrants, and they came from a culture where it was considered shameful to have mental problems. You are supposed to have enough strength of will to overcome your problems, without help from anyone else. So my mother never got treatment." How might the idea of a medical model of psychiatric disorders have helped the woman and her family in the decision whether to seek treatment?

2. You're studying for your upcoming psychology exam when your roommate breezes in, saying: "I was just at the gym and I ran into Sue. She's totally schizophrenic: nice one minute, mean the next." You can't resist the opportunity to set the record straight. What psychiatric disorder is your roommate (incorrectly) attributing to Sue? How is this different from schizophrenia?

3. A friend of yours has a family member who is experiencing severe mental problems, including delusions and loss of motivation. "We went to one psychiatrist," she says, "and got a diagnosis of schizophrenia. We went for a second opinion, and the other doctor said it was probably bipolar disorder. They're both good doctors, and they're both using the same *DSM*—how can they come up with different diagnoses?"

4. After reading the chapter, one of your classmates turns to you with a sigh of relief. "I finally figured it out. I have a deadbeat brother, who always gets himself into trouble and then blames other people for his problems. Even when he gets a ticket for speeding, he never thinks it's his fault—the police were picking on him, or his passengers were urging him to go too fast. I always thought he was just a loser, but now I realize he has a personality disorder!" Do you agree with your classmate's diagnosis of his brother? How would you caution your classmate about the dangers of self-diagnosis, or diagnosis of friends and family?

ANSWERS TO KEY CONCEPT QUIZ

1. a; 2. b; 3. c; 4. d; 5. d; 6. c; 7. b; 8. a; 9. a; 10. d; 11. d; 12. a; 13. c; 14. d; 15. c.

16

Treatment of Psychological Disorders

"TODAY WE'RE GOING TO BE TOUCHING A DEAD MOUSE I saw in the alley outside my office building," Dr. Jenkins said. "OK, let's do it, I'm ready," Christine responded. The pair walked down to the alley and spent the next 50 minutes touching, then stroking, the dead mouse. They then went back upstairs to plan out what other disgusting things Christine was going to touch over the next 7 days before coming back for her next therapy session. Yes, this is all part of the psychological treatment of Christine's obsessive-compulsive disorder (OCD). It is an approach called *exposure and response prevention* (ERP), in which people are gradually exposed to the content of their obsessions and prevented from engaging in their compulsions. Christine's obsession is that she is going to be contaminated by germs and die of cancer; her compulsive behavior involves several hours per day of washing her body and scrubbing everything around her with alcohol wipes. After dozens and dozens of exposures, without performing the behaviors that they believe have been keeping them safe, people eventually learn that their obsessive thoughts are not accurate and that they don't have to act out their compulsions. ERP can be a very scary treatment, but it has proven amazingly effective at decreasing obsessions and compulsions and helping people with OCD return to a high level of daily functioning. OCD was widely considered untreatable until the development of ERP, which is now considered to be the most effective way to treat OCD (Foa, 2010). ERP is just one of many approaches currently being used to help people to overcome the mental disorders you learned about in the last chapter.

Exposure-based treatments, in which a person learns to face the source of their fear and anxiety, have proven to be an effective way to treat anxiety disorders.

KEITH BINNS/GETTY IMAGES

THERE ARE MANY DIFFERENT WAYS TO TREAT PSYCHOLOGICAL DISORDERS and to change the thoughts, behaviors, and emotions associated with them. In this chapter, we will explore the most common approaches to psychological treatment. We will examine why people need to seek psychological help in the first place, and then explore how psychotherapy for individuals is built on the major theories of the causes and cures of disorders, including psychoanalytic, humanistic, existential, behavioral, and cognitive theories. We also will look into biological approaches to treatment that focus on directly modifying brain structure and function. We'll discuss whether treatment works, as well as how we know that treatment works. We'll also look to the future by exploring some exciting new directions in the assessment and treatment of disorders using innovative technologies.

Treatment: Getting Help to Those Who Need It

Estimates suggest that 46.4% of people in the United States suffer from some type of mental disorder at some point in their lifetime (Kessler, Berglund, et al., 2005), and 26.2% suffer from at least one disorder during a given year (Kessler, Chiu, et al., 2005). The personal costs of these disorders involve anguish to the sufferers as well as interference in their ability to carry on the activities of daily life. Think about

What are some of the personal, social, and financial costs of mental illness?

Christine from the example above. If she did not (or could not) seek treatment, she would continue to be crippled by her OCD, which was causing major problems in her life. She had to quit her job at the local coffee shop because she was no longer able to touch money or anything else that had been touched by other people without washing it first. Her relationship with her boyfriend was in trouble because he was growing tired of her constant reassurance seeking regarding cleanliness (hers and his). All of these problems were in turn increasing her anxiety and depression, making her obsessions even stronger. She desperately wanted and needed some way to break out of this vicious cycle. She needed an effective treatment.

The personal and social burdens associated with mental disorders are also enormous. Mental disorders typically have earlier ages of onset than physical disorders and are associated with significant impairments in the form of an inability to carry out daily activities, such as days out of school or work or problems in family and personal relationships. Impairments associated with mental disorders are as severe, and in many cases more severe, than those associated with physical disorders such as cancer, chronic pain, and heart disease (Ormel et al., 2008). For instance, a person with severe depression may be unable to hold down a job or even get organized enough to collect a disability check, and people with many disorders stop getting along with family, caring for their children, or trying to help.

There are financial costs too. Depression is the fourth leading cause of disability worldwide, and it is expected to rise to the second leading cause of disability by 2020 (Murray & Lopez, 1996a, 1996b). People with severe depression often are unable to make it into work due to their disorder, and even when they make it into work they often suffer from poor work performance. Recent estimates suggest that depression-related lost work productivity costs somewhere from $30 to $50 billion per year (Kessler, 2012). If we add in similar figures for anxiety disorders, psychotic disorders, substance disorders, and all the other psychological problems, the overall costs are astronomical. In addition to the personal benefits of treatment, then, society also stands to benefit from the effective treatment of psychological disorders.

Do all people with a mental disorder receive treatment? Not by a long shot. Only about 18% of people in the United States with a mental disorder in the past 12 months received treatment during the same time frame. Treatment rates are even lower elsewhere around the world, especially in low-income or developing countries (Wang et al., 2007). Treatment rates are higher for those with more severe mental disorders. Approximately 40% of those in the United States with a serious mental disorder (one that substantially interferes with major life activities) have received treatment in the past year (Wang, Demler, & Kessler, 2002). However, it is clear from these numbers that most people with a mental disorder do not receive treatment, and among those who do, the average delay from onset until treatment is first received is over a decade (Wang et al., 2004)!

Why Many People Fail to Seek Treatment

A physical symptom such as a toothache would send most people to the dentist—a trip that usually results in a successful treatment. The clear source of pain and the obvious solution make for a quick and effective response. In contrast, the path from a mental disorder to a successful treatment is often far less clear and many people are less familiar with when they should seek treatment for a mental disorder

> **What are the obstacles to treatment for the mentally ill?**

or where they should go. In the case of mental disorders, people may fail to get treatment for a number of reasons. Here are three of the most often reported:

1. *People may not realize that they have a mental disorder that could be effectively treated.* Approximately 45% of those with a mental disorder who do not seek treatment report that they did not do so because they didn't think that they needed to be treated (Mojtabai et al., 2011). Mental disorders often are not taken nearly as seriously as physical illness, perhaps because the origin of mental illness is "hidden" and usually cannot be diagnosed by a blood test or X-ray. Moreover, although most people know what a toothache is and that it can be successfully treated, far fewer people know when they have a mental disorder and what treatments might be available.

2. *There may be barriers to treatment, such as beliefs and circumstances that keep people from getting help.* Individuals may believe that they should be able to handle things themselves. In fact, this is the primary reason that people with a mental disorder give for not seeking treatment (72.6%) and for dropping out of treatment prematurely (42.2%; Mojtabai et al., 2011). Other attitudinal barriers for not seeking treatment include believing that the problem was not that severe (16.9% of nontreatment seekers), the belief that treatment would be ineffective (16.4%), and perceived stigma from others (9.1%).

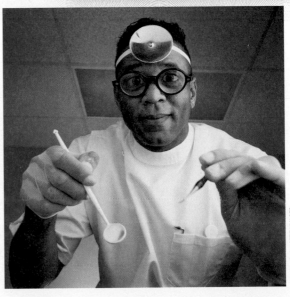

> When your tooth hurts, you go to a dentist. But how do you know when to see a psychologist?

ALLISON LEACH/GETTY IMAGES

3. *Structural barriers prevent people from physically getting to treatment.* Like finding a good lawyer or plumber, finding the right psychologist can be more difficult than simply flipping through the yellow pages or searching online. This confusion is understandable given the plethora of different types of treatments available (see the Real World box, Types of Psychotherapists). Once you find the therapist for you, you may encounter structural barriers related to not being able to afford treatment (15.3% of nontreatment seekers), lack of clinician availability (12.8%), inconvenience of attending treatment (9.8%), and trouble finding transportation to the clinic (5.7%; Mojtabai et al., 2011).

Even when people seek and find help, they sometimes do not receive the most effective treatments, which further complicates things. For starters, most of the treatment of mental disorders is not provided by mental

THE REAL WORLD

Types of Psychotherapists

What do you do if you're ready to seek the help of a mental health professional? To whom do you turn? Therapists have widely varying backgrounds and training, and this affects the kinds of services they offer. Before you choose a therapist, it is useful to have an understanding of a therapist's background, training, and areas of expertise. There are several major "flavors."

• **Psychologist** A psychologist who practices psychotherapy holds a doctorate with specialization in clinical psychology (a PhD or PsyD). This degree takes about 5 years to complete and includes extensive training in therapy, the assessment of psychological disorders, and research. The psychologist will sometimes have a specialty, such as working with ado-

lescents or helping people overcome sleep disorders, and will usually conduct therapy that involves talking. Psychologists must be licensed by the state, and most states require candidates to complete about 2 years of supervised practical training and a competency exam. If you look for a *psychologist* in the Yellow Pages or through a clinic, you will usually find someone with this background.

• **Psychiatrist** A psychiatrist is a medical doctor who has completed an M.D. with specialized training in assessing and treating mental disorders. Psychiatrists can prescribe medications, and some also practice psychotherapy. General practice physicians can also prescribe medications for mental disorders and often are the first to see people with such

ZIGY KALUZNY/GETTY IMAGES

WAVEBREAKMEDIA LTD./GETTY IMAGES

disorders because people consult them for a wide range of health problems. However, general practice physicians do not typically receive much training in the diagnosis or treatment of mental disorders, and they do not practice psychotherapy.

• **Social worker** Social workers have a master's degree in social work and have training in working with people in dire life situations such as poverty, homelessness, or family conflict. Clinical or psychiatric social workers also receive special training to help people in these situations who have mental disorders. Social workers often work in government

health specialists, but by general medical practitioners (Wang et al., 2007). And even when people make it to a mental health specialist, they do not always receive the most effective treatment possible. In fact, only a small percentage of those with a mental disorder (< 40%) receive what would be considered minimally adequate treatment, and only 15.3% of those with serious mental illness receive treatment that is considered minimally adequate. Inadequate treatment is especially a problem among those who are younger, African American, living in the Southern United States, diagnosed with a psychotic disorder, and treated in a general medical setting (Wang et al., 2002). Clearly, before choosing or prescribing a therapy, we need to know what kinds of treatments are available and understand which treatments are best for particular disorders.

or private social service agencies and may also work in hospitals or have a private practice.

- **Counselor** Counselors have a wide range of training. To be a counseling psychologist, for example, requires a doctorate and practical training—the title uses that key term *psychologist* and is regulated by state laws. But states vary in how they define *counselor*. In some cases, a counselor must have a master's degree and extensive training in therapy, whereas in others, a counselor may have minimal training or relevant education. Counselors who work in schools usually have a master's degree and specific training in counseling in educational settings.

Some people offer therapy under made-up terms that sound professional—"mind/body healing therapist," for example, or "marital adjustment adviser." Often these terms are simply invented to mislead clients and avoid licensing boards, and the "therapist" may have no training or expertise at all. And, of course, there are a few people who claim to be licensed practitioners who are not: Louise Wightman, who had once worked as stripper "Princess Cheyenne," was convicted of fraud in 2007 after conducting psychotherapy as a psychologist with dozens of clients. She claimed she didn't know the PhD degree she had purchased over the Internet was bogus (Associated Press, 2007). People who offer therapy may be well-meaning and even helpful, but they could do harm too. To be safe, it is important to shop wisely for a therapist whose

BSIP/JIG/GETTY IMAGES

training and credentials reflect expertise and inspire confidence.

How should you shop? One way is to start with people you know: your general practice physician, a school counselor, or a trusted friend or family member who might know of a good therapist. Or you can visit your college clinic or hospital or contact an Internet site of an organization such as the American Psychological Association that offers referrals to licensed mental health care providers. When you do contact someone, he or she will often be able to provide you with further advice about who would be just the right kind of therapist to consult.

Before you agree to see a therapist for treatment, you should ask questions such as those below to evaluate whether the therapist's style or background is a good match for your problem:

- What type of therapy do you practice?
- What types of problems do you usually treat?
- For how long do you usually see people in therapy?
- Will our work involve "talking" therapy, medications, or both?
- How effective is this type of therapy for the type of problem I'm having?
- What are your fees for therapy, and will health insurance cover them?

Not only will the therapist's answers to these questions tell you about his or her background and experience, but they will also tell you about his or her approach to treating clients. You can then make an informed decision about the type of service you need.

Although you should consider what type of therapist would best fit your needs, the therapist's personality and approach can sometimes be as important as his or her background or training. You should seek out someone who is willing and open to answer questions, who has a clear understanding about the type of problem leading you to seek therapy, and who shows general respect and empathy for you. A therapist is someone you are entrusting with your mental health, and you should only enter into such a relationship when you and the therapist have good rapport.

Approaches to Treatment

Treatments can be divided broadly into two kinds: (a) psychological treatment, in which people interact with a clinician in order to use the environment to change their brain and behavior; and (b) biological treatment, in which the brain is treated directly with drugs, surgery or some other direct intervention. In some cases, both psychological *and* biological treatments are used. Christine's OCD, for example, might be treated not only with the ERP but also with medication that decreases her obsessive thoughts and compulsive urges. For many years, psychological treatment was the main form of intervention for psychological disorders because few biological options were available. There have always been folk remedies that propose to have

Early mental health workers used water dowsing, or "hydrotherapy," for psychological disorders. Here a patient at the Pennsylvania Hospital for the Insane gets a cold "douche bath" (Haskell, 1869). Such treatments were given in the forlorn hope that something might work, but often they were simply torture.

COURTESY UNIVERSITY OF MICHIGAN'S MAKING OF AMERICA/HTTP://MOA.UMDL.UMICH.EDU

a biological basis—such as hydrotherapy (pouring cold water on those with mental disorders), trephination (drilling holes in the skull to let the evil spirits escape), and bloodletting (the removal of blood from the body)—used to try to cure psychological disorders (Note: Do not try these at home. Turns out they don't work). As we learn more about the biology and chemistry of the brain, approaches to mental health that begin with the brain are becoming increasingly widespread. As you'll see later in the chapter, many effective treatments combine both psychological and biological interventions.

CULTURE & COMMUNITY

Treatment of Psychological Disorders around the World Barriers that keep people from receiving treatment for mental disorders exist all around the world. However, they are greater in some places than in others. One recent study examined what percentage of people with a mental disorder in 17 different countries around the world received treatment for their disorder in the past year (Wang et al., 2007). Several different findings are interesting to note. First, people with a severe mental disorder are much more likely to be treated. This makes sense. For instance, if your disorder is so severe that it prevents you from going to school or work you will probably seek treatment, but if it doesn't really interfere with your daily life you may not go for help. Second, people living in high-income countries (as defined by the World Bank) are much more likely to get treatment than those in middle- or low-income countries. This makes sense too. The more resources a country has, the more able it is to make psychological treatments available to its people. Third, most people with a mental disorder do not receive any treatment. This is true even in the countries with the highest income. This means that although we have a better understanding of mental disorders than we ever had before (as described in the last chapter), and we have better treatments than ever before (as described in this chapter), we still have to do a much better job removing the barriers that prevent those with mental disorders from getting help.

Percent of people with a mental disorder who receive treatment

Percent in treatment

Legend: Serious, Moderate, Mild

Countries: Nigeria, China, Colombia, S. Africa, Ukraine, Lebanon, Mexico, Belgium, France, Israel, Germany, Italy, Japan, Netherlands, New Zealand, Spain, USA

Low Income / Low Middle Income / High Middle Income / High Income

IN SUMMARY

▶ Mental illness is often misunderstood, and because of this, it too often goes untreated.

▶ Untreated mental illness can be extremely costly, affecting an individual's ability to function and also causing social and financial burdens.

▶ Many people who suffer from mental illness do not get the help they need; they may be unaware that they have a problem, they may be uninterested in getting help for their problem, or they may face structural barriers to getting treatment.

▶ Treatments include psychotherapy, which focuses on the mind, and medical and biological methods, which focus on the brain and body.

psychotherapy
An interaction between a socially sanctioned clinician and someone suffering from a psychological problem, with the goal of providing support or relief from the problem.

eclectic psychotherapy
A form of psychotherapy that involves drawing on techniques from different forms of therapy, depending on the client and the problem.

psychodynamic psychotherapies
Therapies that explore childhood events and encourage individuals to use this understanding to develop insight into their psychological problems.

Psychological Treatments: Healing the Mind through Interaction

Psychological therapy, or **psychotherapy**, *is an interaction between a socially sanctioned clinician and someone suffering from a psychological problem, with the goal of providing support or relief from the problem.* Currently over 500 different forms of psychotherapy exist. Although there are similarities among all the psychotherapies, each approach is unique in its goals, aims, and methods. A survey of 1,000 psychotherapists asked them to describe their main theoretical orientation (Norcross, Hedges, & Castle, 2002; see **FIGURE 16.1**). Over a third reported using **eclectic psychotherapy**, *a form of psychotherapy that involves drawing on techniques from different forms of therapy, depending on the client and the problem.* This allows therapists to apply an appropriate theoretical perspective suited to the problem at hand, rather than adhering to a single theoretical perspective for all clients and all types of problems. Nevertheless, as Figure 16.1 shows, the majority of psychotherapists use a single approach, such as psychodynamic therapy, humanistic and existential therapies, behavioral and cognitive therapies, or group therapy. We'll examine each of those four major branches of psychotherapy in turn.

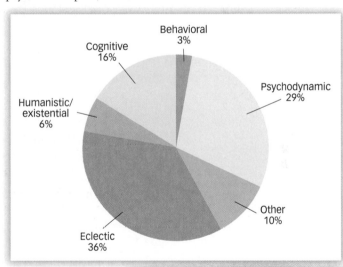

▲ Figure **16.1** **Approaches to Psychotherapy in the 21st Century** This chart shows the percentage of psychologists (from among 1,000 members of the American Psychological Association's Division of Psychotherapy) who have various primary psychotherapy orientations (adapted from Norcross et al., 2002).

Psychodynamic Therapy

Psychodynamic psychotherapy has its roots in Freud's psychoanalytically oriented theory of personality. **Psychodynamic psychotherapies** *explore childhood events and encourage individuals to use this understanding to develop insight into their psychological problems.* Psychoanalysis was the first psychodynamic therapy to develop, but it has largely been replaced by modern psychodynamic therapies, such as interpersonal psychotherapy.

Psychoanalysis

As you saw in the Personality chapter, *psychoanalysis* assumes that people are born with aggressive and sexual urges that are repressed during childhood development through the use of defense mechanisms. Psychoanalysts encourage their clients to bring these repressed conflicts into consciousness so that the clients can understand them and reduce their unwanted influences. Psychoanalysts focus a great deal on early childhood events because they believe that urges and conflicts were likely to be repressed during this time.

Traditional psychoanalysis involves four or five sessions per week over an average of 3 to 6 years (Ursano & Silberman, 2003). During a session, the client reclines on a couch, facing away from the analyst, and is asked to express whatever thoughts and feelings come to mind. Occasionally, the therapist may comment on some of the information presented by the client, but does not express his or her values and judgments. The stereotypic image you might have of psychological therapy—a person lying on a couch talking to a person sitting in a chair—springs from this approach.

In traditional psychoanalysis, the client lies on a couch, with the therapist sitting behind, out of the client's view.

What Happens in Psychoanalysis

The goal of psychoanalysis is for the client to understand the unconscious in a process Freud called *developing insight*. A psychoanalyst can use several key techniques to help the client develop insight, including the following.

Free Association. In free association, the client reports every thought that enters the mind, without censorship or filtering. This strategy allows the stream of consciousness to flow unimpeded. If the client stops, the therapist prompts further associations ("And what does that make you think of?"). The therapist may then look for themes that recur during therapy sessions.

Dream Analysis. Psychoanalysis may treat dreams as metaphors that symbolize unconscious conflicts or wishes and that contain disguised clues that the therapist can help the client understand. A psychoanalytic therapy session might begin with an invitation for the client to recount a dream, after which the client might be asked to participate in the interpretation by freely associating to the dream.

Interpretation. This is the process by which the therapist deciphers the meaning (e.g., unconscious impulses or fantasies) underlying what the client says and does. Interpretation is used throughout therapy, during free association and dream analysis, as well as in other aspects of the treatment. During the process of interpretation, the therapist suggests possible meanings to the client, looking for signs that the correct meaning has been discovered.

Analysis of Resistance. In the process of "trying on" different interpretations of the client's thoughts and actions, the therapist may suggest an interpretation that the client finds particularly unacceptable. **Resistance** *is a reluctance to cooperate with treatment for fear of confronting unpleasant unconscious material.* For example, the therapist might suggest that the client's problem with obsessive health worries could be traced to a childhood rivalry with her mother for her father's love and attention. The client could find the suggestion insulting and resist the interpretation. The therapist might interpret this resistance as a signal not that the interpretation is wrong but instead that the interpretation is on the right track. If a client always shifts the topic of discussion away from a particular idea, it might signal to the therapist that this is indeed an issue the client could be directed to confront in order to develop insight.

Through the course of meeting so frequently over such a long period of time, the client and psychoanalyst often develop a close relationship. Freud noticed this relationship developing in his analyses and was at first troubled by it: Clients would develop an unusually strong

> **What might a client's resistance signal to a psychoanalyst?**

"Before we begin, I'd like to say a few words about the concept of 'defence mechanisms'."

attachment to him, almost as though they were viewing him as a parent or a lover, and he worried that this could interfere with achieving the goal of insight. Over time, however, he came to believe that the development and resolution of this relationship was a key process of psychoanalysis. **Transference** occurs *when the analyst begins to assume a major significance in the client's life and the client reacts to the analyst based on unconscious childhood fantasies.* Successful psychoanalysis involves analyzing the transference so that the client understands this reaction and why it occurs.

Beyond Psychoanalysis

Although Freud's insights and techniques are fundamental, modern psychodynamic treatments differ from classic psychoanalysis in both their content and procedures. One of the most widely used psychodynamic treatments is **interpersonal psychotherapy (IPT)**, *a form of psychotherapy that focuses on helping clients improve current relationships* (Weissman, Markowitz, & Klerman, 2000). In terms of content, rather than using free association, therapists using IPT talk to clients about their interpersonal behaviors and feelings. They pay particular attention to the client's grief (an exaggerated

> **In what common ways do other psychodynamic theories differ from Freudian analysis?**

reaction to the loss of a loved one), role disputes (conflicts with a significant other), role transitions (changes in life status, such as starting a new job, getting married, or retiring), or interpersonal deficits (lack of the necessary skills to start or maintain a relationship). The treatment focuses on interpersonal functioning with the assumption that, as interpersonal relations improve, symptoms will subside.

Modern psychodynamic psychotherapies such as IPT also differ from classical psychoanalysis in the procedures used. For starters, in modern psychodynamic therapy the therapist and client typically sit face-to-face. In addition, therapy is less intensive, with meetings often occurring only once a week and therapy lasting months rather than years. In contrast to classical psychoanalysis, modern psychodynamic therapists are more likely to see relief from symptoms as a reasonable goal for therapy (in addition to the goal of facilitating insight), and they are more likely to offer support or advice in addition to interpretation (Barber et al., 2013). Therapists are also now less likely to interpret a client's statements as a sign of unconscious sexual or aggressive impulses. However, other concepts, such as transference and fostering insight into unconscious processes, remain features of most psychodynamic therapies. Freud's couch cast a long shadow.

Although psychodynamic therapy has been around for a long time and continues to be widely practiced, there is relatively little evidence for its effectiveness. Comparisons to other forms of treatment such as cognitive behavior therapy (described later) suggest that psychodynamic therapy is somewhat less effective (Watzke et al., 2012). Moreover, there is some evidence that some of the aspects of psychodynamic therapy long believed to be effective may actually be harmful. For instance, research suggests that the more a therapist makes interpretations about perceived transference in the client, the worse the therapeutic alliance and the worse the clinical outcome (Henry et al., 1994). Despite findings like these, there is some evidence that long-term psychodynamic psychotherapy (lasting at least a year) is more effective than short-term psychotherapy (Leichsenring & Rabung, 2008). Psychodynamic therapy is not as widely used as it once was, but many psychologists still use it in practice, and many people say that they find it helpful.

resistance
A reluctance to cooperate with treatment for fear of confronting unpleasant unconscious material.

transference
An event that occurs in psychoanalysis when the analyst begins to assume a major significance in the client's life and the client reacts to the analyst based on unconscious childhood fantasies.

interpersonal psychotherapy (IPT)
A form of psychotherapy that focuses on helping clients improve current relationships.

MIRAMAX/THE KOBAL COLLECTION

In the movie *Good Will Hunting,* the lead character, played by actor Matt Damon, forms a strong bond with his therapist, played by Robin Williams. As in psychodynamic therapy, the therapist uses their relationship to help break down the patient's defense mechanisms and resolve an inner conflict. The amazing bond that was formed between therapist and patient, and the life-changing treatment delivered is the stuff of therapists' dreams (and Hollywood scripts).

Humanistic and Existential Therapies

Humanistic and existential therapies emerged in the middle of the 20th century, in part as a reaction to the negative views that psychoanalysis holds about human nature. Humanistic and existential therapies assume that human nature is generally positive, and they emphasize the natural tendency of each individual to strive for personal improvement. Humanistic and existential therapies share the assumption that psychological problems stem from feelings of alienation and loneliness, and that those feelings can be traced to failures to reach one's potential (in the humanistic approach) or from failures to find meaning in life (in the existential approach). Although interest in these approaches peaked in the 1960s and 1970s, some therapists continue to use these approaches today. Two well-known types are person-centered therapy (a humanistic approach) and gestalt therapy (an existential approach).

> **How does a humanistic view of human nature differ from a psychodynamic view?**

Person-Centered Therapy

Person-centered therapy (or **client-centered therapy**) *assumes that all individuals have a tendency toward growth and that this growth can be facilitated by acceptance and genuine reactions from the therapist.* Psychologist Carl Rogers (1902–1987) developed person-centered therapy in the 1940s and 1950s (Rogers, 1951). Person-centered therapy assumes that each person is qualified to determine his or her own goals for therapy, such as feeling more confident or making a career decision, and even the frequency and length of therapy. In this type of nondirective treatment, the therapist tends not to provide advice or suggestions about what the client should be doing, but instead paraphrases the client's words, mirroring the client's thoughts and sentiments (e.g., "I think I hear you saying . . ."). Person-centered therapists believe that with adequate support, the client will recognize the right things to do.

Rogers encouraged person-centered therapists to demonstrate three basic qualities: congruence, empathy, and unconditional positive regard. Congruence refers to openness and honesty in the therapeutic relationship and ensuring that the therapist communicates the same message at all levels. For example, the same message must be communicated in the therapist's words, the therapist's facial expression, and the therapist's body language. Saying "I think your concerns are valid" while smirking would simply not do. Empathy refers to the continuous process of trying to understand the client by getting inside his or her way of thinking, feeling, and understanding the world. Interestingly, research has shown that the more empathic a client says their clinician is being, the more similarity there is between the client's and therapist's level of physiological arousal in that moment (Marci et al., 2007). This suggests that therapists who are being empathic may really be feeling some of what their clients are feeling. Seeing the world from the client's perspective enables the therapist to better appreciate the client's apprehensions, worries, or fears. Finally, the therapist must treat the client with unconditional positive regard by providing a nonjudgmental, warm, and accepting environment in which the client can feel safe expressing his or her thoughts and feelings.

The goal is not to uncover repressed conflicts, as in psychodynamic therapy, but instead to try to understand the client's experience and reflect that experience back to the client in a supportive way, encouraging the client's natural tendency toward growth. This style of therapy is reminiscent of psychoanalysis in its way of encouraging the client toward the free expression of thoughts and feelings.

Gestalt Therapy

Gestalt therapy was founded by Frederick "Fritz" Perls (1893–1970) and colleagues in the 1940s and 1950s (Perls, Hefferkine, & Goodman, 1951). **Gestalt therapy** *has the goal of helping the client become aware of his or her thoughts, behaviors, experiences,*

---

person-centered therapy (or client-centered therapy) Assumes that all individuals have a tendency toward growth and that this growth can be facilitated by acceptance and genuine reactions from the therapist.

gestalt therapy Has the goal of helping the client become aware of his or her thoughts, behaviors, experiences, and feelings and to "own" or take responsibility for them.

behavior therapy A type of therapy that assumes that disordered behavior is learned and that symptom relief is achieved through changing overt maladaptive behaviors into more constructive behaviors.

and feelings and to "own" or take responsibility for them. Gestalt therapists are encouraged to be enthusiastic and warm toward their clients, an approach they share with person-centered therapists. To help facilitate the client's awareness, gestalt therapists also reflect back to the client their impressions of the client.

Gestalt therapy emphasizes the experiences and behaviors that are occurring at that particular moment in the therapy session. For example, if a client is talking about something stressful that occurred during the previous week, the therapist might shift the attention to the client's current experience by asking, "How do you feel as you describe what happened to you?" This technique is known as focusing. Clients are also encouraged to put their feelings into action. One way to do this is the empty chair technique, in which the client imagines that another person (e.g., a spouse, a parent, a coworker) is in an empty chair, sitting directly across from the client. The client then moves from chair to chair, alternating from role-playing what he or she would say to the other person and how he or she imagines the other person would respond. Gestalt techniques originated as a form of psychotherapy but are now often used in counseling or "life coaching" to help people prepare for new job or family situations (Grant, 2008).

As part of gestalt therapy, clients may be encouraged to imagine that another person is sitting across from them in a chair. The client then moves from chair to chair, role-playing what he or she would say to the imagined person and what that person would answer.

Behavioral and Cognitive Therapies

Unlike the talk therapies described before, behavioral and cognitive treatments emphasize actively changing a person's current thoughts and behaviors as a way to decrease or eliminate their psychopathology. In the evolution of psychological treatments, clients started out lying down in psychoanalysis, then sitting in psychodynamic and related approaches, but are often standing and engaging in behavior-change homework assignments in their everyday life in behavioral and cognitive therapies.

Behavior Therapy

Whereas Freud developed psychoanalysis as an offshoot of hypnosis and other techniques used by other clinicians before him, behavior therapy was developed based on laboratory findings from earlier behavioral psychologists. As you read in the Psychology: Evolution of a Science chapter, behaviorists rejected theories that were based on "invisible" mental properties that were difficult to test and impossible to observe directly. Behaviorists found psychoanalytic ideas particularly hard to test: How do you know whether a person has an unconscious conflict or whether insight has occurred? Behavioral principles, in contrast, focused solely on behaviors that could be observed (e.g., avoidance of a feared object, such as refusing to get on an airplane). **Behavior therapy** assumes that *disordered behavior is learned and that symptom relief is achieved through changing overt maladaptive behaviors into more constructive behaviors.* A variety of behavior therapy techniques have been developed for many disorders, based on the learning principles you encountered in the Learning chapter, including operant conditioning procedures (which focus on reinforcement and punishment) and classical conditioning procedures (which focus on extinction). Here are three examples of behavior therapy techniques in action:

> **?** **What primary problem did behaviorists have with psychoanalytic ideas?**

A behavioral psychologist might treat a temper tantrum using time-out from reinforcement, which is based on the behavioral principle of operant conditioning and ensures that a child will not be rewarded for her undesired behavior.

MATTHEW NOCK

token economy
A form of behavior therapy in which clients are given "tokens" for desired behaviors, which they can later trade for rewards.

exposure therapy
An approach to treatment that involves confronting an emotion-arousing stimulus directly and repeatedly, ultimately leading to a decrease in the emotional response.

cognitive therapy
Focuses on helping a client identify and correct any distorted thinking about self, others, or the world.

cognitive restructuring
A therapeutic approach that teaches clients to question the automatic beliefs, assumptions, and predictions that often lead to negative emotions and to replace negative thinking with more realistic and positive beliefs.

Eliminating Unwanted Behaviors. How would you change a 3-year-old boy's habit of throwing tantrums at the grocery store? A behavior therapist might investigate what happens immediately before and after the tantrum: Did the child get candy to "shut him up?" The study of operant conditioning shows that behavior can be influenced by its *consequences* (the reinforcing or punishing events that follow). Adjusting these might help change the behavior. Making the consequences less reinforcing (no candy!) and more punishing (a period of time-out facing the wall in the grocery store while the parent watches from nearby rather than providing a rush of attention) could eliminate the problem behavior.

Promoting Desired Behaviors. Candy and time-out can have a strong influence on child behavior, but they work less well with adults. How might you get an individual with schizophrenia to engage in activities of daily living? How would you get a cocaine addict to stop using drugs? A behavior therapy technique that has proven to be quite effective in such cases is the **token economy**, which involves *giving clients "tokens" for desired behaviors, which they can later trade for rewards.* For instance, in the case of cocaine dependence, the desired behavior is not using cocaine. Programs that reward non-use (verified by urine samples) with vouchers that can be exchanged for rewards such as money, bus passes, clothes, and so on, have shown an ability to significantly reduce cocaine use and associated psychological problems (Petry, Alessi, & Rash, 2013). Similar systems are used to promote desired behaviors in classrooms, the workplace, and commercial advertising (e.g., airline and credit card rewards programs).

Reducing Unwanted Emotional Responses. One of the most powerful ways to reduce fear is by gradual exposure to the feared object or situation. **Exposure therapy** involves *confronting an emotion-arousing stimulus directly and repeatedly, ultimately leading to a decrease in the emotional response.* This technique depends on the processes of habituation and response extinction. For example, in Christine's case her clinician gradually exposed her to the content of her obsessions (dirt and germs), which became less and less distressing with repeated exposure. Similarly, for clients who are afraid of social interaction and unable to function at school or work, a behavioral treatment might involve exposure first to imagined situations in which they talk briefly with one person, then a bit longer talk to a medium-sized group, and finally, giving a speech to a large group. It's now known that *in vivo* (live) exposure is more effective than imaginary exposure (Choy, Fyer, & Lipsitz, 2007). In other words, if a person fears social situations, it is better for that person to practice social interaction than merely to imagine it. Behavioral therapists use an exposure hierarchy to expose the client gradually to the feared object or situation. Easier situations are practiced first, and as fear decreases, the client progresses to more difficult or frightening situations (see **TABLE 16.1**).

> How might exposure therapy help treat a phobia or fear of a specific object?

Table 16.1

Exposure Hierarchy for Social Phobia

Item	Fear (0–100)
1. Have a party and invite everyone from work	99
2. Go to a holiday party for 1 hour without drinking	90
3. Invite Cindy to have dinner and see a movie	85
4. Go for a job interview	80
5. Ask boss for a day off work	65
6. Ask questions in a meeting at work	65
7. Eat lunch with co-workers	60
8. Talk to a stranger on the bus	50
9. Talk to cousin on the telephone for 10 minutes	40
10. Ask for directions at the gas station	35

Source: Ellis (1991).

Exposure therapy can also help people overcome unwanted emotional and behavioral responses through *exposure and response prevention*. Persons with OCD, for example, might have recurrent thoughts that their hands are dirty and need washing. Washing stops the uncomfortable feelings of contamination only briefly, though, and they wash again and again in search of relief. In exposure with response prevention, they might be asked in therapy to get their hands dirty on purpose (first by touching a coin picked up from the ground, then by touching a public toilet, and later by touching a dead mouse) and leave them dirty for hours. They may need to do this only a few times to break the cycle and be freed from the obsessive ritual (Foa et al., 2007).

Cognitive Therapy

Whereas behavior therapy focuses primarily on changing a person's behavior, **cognitive therapy**, as the name suggests, focuses on *helping a client identify and correct any distorted thinking about self, others, or the world* (Beck, 2005). For example, behaviorists might explain a phobia as the outcome of a

> **?** How might a client restructure a negative self-image into a positive one?

classical conditioning experience such as being bitten by a dog, where the dog bite leads to the development of a dog phobia through the association of the dog with the experience of pain. Cognitive theorists might instead emphasize the *interpretation* of the event. It might not be the event itself that caused the fear, but rather the individual's beliefs and assumptions about the event and the feared stimulus. In the case of a dog bite, cognitive theorists might focus on a person's new or strengthened belief that dogs are dangerous to explain the fear.

Cognitive therapies use a principal technique called **cognitive restructuring**, which *involves teaching clients to question the automatic beliefs, assumptions, and predictions that often lead to negative emotions and to replace negative thinking with more realistic and positive beliefs.* Specifically, clients are taught to examine the evidence for and against a particular belief or to be more accepting of outcomes that may be undesirable yet still manageable. For example, a depressed client may believe that she is stupid and will never pass her college courses—all on the basis of one poor grade. In this situation, the therapist would work with the client to examine the validity of this belief. The therapist would consider relevant evidence such as grades on previous exams, performance on other coursework, and examples of intelligence outside school. It may be that the client has never failed a course before and has achieved good grades in this particular course in the past. In this case, the therapist would encourage the client to consider all this information in determining whether she is truly "stupid." **TABLE 16.2** shows a variety of potentially irrational ideas that serve to unleash unwanted emotions such as anger, depression, or anxiety. Any of these irrational beliefs might bedevil a person with serious emotional problems if left unchallenged and are potential targets for cognitive restructuring. In therapy sessions, the cognitive therapist will help the client to identify evidence that supports, and fails to support, each negative thought in order to help the

An exposure therapy client with obsessive-compulsive disorder who fears contamination in public restrooms might be given "homework" to visit three such restrooms in a week, touch the toilets, and then *not* wash up.

Table 16.2

Common Irrational Beliefs and the Emotional Responses They Can Cause

Belief	Emotional Response
I have to get this done immediately.	Anxiety, stress
I must be perfect.	
Something terrible will happen.	
Everyone is watching me.	Embarrassment, social anxiety
I won't be able to make friends.	
People know something is wrong with me.	
I'm a loser and will always be a loser.	Sadness, depression
Nobody will ever love me.	
She did that to me on purpose.	Anger, irritability
He is evil and should be punished.	
Things ought to be different.	

Source: Ellis (1991).

Cognitive therapist Aaron Beck's approach to psychotherapy helps people change maladaptive thinking patterns using a direct and rational approach.

client generate more balanced thoughts that accurately reflect the true state of affairs. In other words, the clinician tries to remove the dark lens through which the client views the world, not with the goal of replacing it with rose-colored glasses, but instead with clear glass. Here is a brief sample transcript of what part of a cognitive therapy session might sound like.

Clinician Last week I asked you to keep a thought record of situations that made you feel very depressed, at least one per day, and the automatic thoughts that popped into your mind. Were you able to do that?

Client Yes.

Clinician Great. Did you bring it in with you today?

Client Yes, here it is.

Clinician Wonderful, I'm glad you were able to complete this assignment. Let's take a look at this together. What's the first situation that you recorded?

Client Well . . . I went out on Friday night with my friends, which I thought would be fun and help me to feel better. But I was feeling kind of down about things and I ended up not really talking to anyone, which led me to just sit in the corner and drink all night, which caused me to get so drunk that I passed out at the party. I woke up the next day feeling embarrassed and more depressed than ever.

Clinician OK, sounds like a tough situation. So the situation is you had too much to drink and passed out. The resulting emotion you had was depression. How intense was your feeling of depression on a scale of 0 to 100?

Client 90.

Clinician OK, and what thoughts automatically popped into your head?

Client I can't control myself. I'll never be able to control myself. My friends think I'm a loser and will never want to hang out with me again.

Clinician OK, and which of these thoughts led you to feel most depressed?

Client That my friends think I'm a loser and won't want to hang out with me anymore.

Clinician Alright, so let's focus on that one for a minute. What evidence can you think of that supports this thought?

Client Well . . . um . . . I got really drunk and so they *have* to think I'm a loser. I mean, who does that?

Clinician OK, write that down on your thought record in this column here. Anything else? Is there any other evidence you can think of that supports those thoughts?

Client No.

Clinician All right. Now let's take a moment to think about whether there is any evidence that doesn't support those thoughts. Did anything happen that suggests that your friends don't think you are a loser or that they do want to keep hanging out with you?

Client Well . . . apparently some kids were making fun of me when I was passed out and my friends stopped them. And they also brought me home safely and then called the next day and joked about what happened and my one friend Tommy said something like "we've all been there" and that he wants to hang out again this weekend.

Clinician OK, great, write that down in this next column. This is very interesting. So on one hand, you feel depressed and have thoughts that you are a loser and your friends don't like you. But on the other hand, you have some pretty real-world evidence that even though you drank too much, they were still there for you and they do in fact want to hang out with you again, yes?

Client: Yeah, I guess you're right if you put it that way. I didn't think about it like that.

Clinician So now if we were going to replace your first thoughts, which don't seem to have a lot of real-world evidence, with a more balanced thought based on the evidence, what would that new thought be?

Client Probably something like, my friends probably weren't happy about the fact that I got so drunk because then they had to take care of me, but they are my friends and were there for me and want to keep hanging out with me.

Clinician Excellent job. I think that sounds just right based on the evidence, write that down in the next column. And how much do you believe in this new thought on a scale of 0 to 100?

Client I think it's actually pretty accurate, so I would say 95.

Clinician: And thinking about this new more balanced thought rather than your first one, how would you rate your depression?

Client: Much lower than before. Probably a 40. I'm still not happy that I got so drunk, but less depressed about my friends.

In addition to cognitive restructuring techniques, which try to change a person's thoughts to be more balanced or accurate, some forms of cognitive therapy also include techniques for coping with unwanted thoughts and feelings, techniques that resemble meditation (see the Consciousness chapter). Clients may be encouraged to attend to their troubling thoughts or emotions or be given meditative techniques that allow them to gain a new focus (Hofmann & Asmundson, 2008). One such technique, called **mindfulness meditation**, *teaches an individual to be fully present in each moment; to be aware of his or her thoughts, feelings, and sensations; and to detect symptoms before they become a problem.* Researchers have found mindfulness meditation to be helpful for preventing relapse in depression. In one study, people recovering from depression were about half as likely to relapse during a 60-week assessment period if they received mindfulness meditation-based cognitive therapy than if they received treatment as usual (Teasdale, Segal, & Williams, 2000).

Cognitive Behavioral Therapy

Historically, cognitive and behavioral therapies were considered distinct systems of therapy, and some people continue to follow this distinction, using solely behavioral *or* cognitive techniques. Today, the extent to which therapists use cognitive versus behavioral techniques depends on the individual therapist as well as the type of problem being treated. Most therapists working with anxiety and depression use *a blend of cognitive and behavioral therapeutic strategies*, often referred to as **cognitive behavioral therapy** (**CBT**). In a way, this technique acknowledges that there may be behaviors that people cannot control through rational thought, but also that there are ways of helping people think more rationally when thought does play a role. In contrast to traditional behavior therapy and cognitive therapy, CBT is *problem focused*, meaning that it is undertaken for specific problems (e.g., reducing the frequency of panic attacks or returning to work after a bout of depression), and *action oriented*, meaning that the therapist tries to assist the client in selecting specific strategies to help address those problems. The client is expected to *do* things, such as engage in exposure exercises, practice behavior change skills or use a diary to monitor relevant symptoms (e.g., the severity of depressed mood, panic attack symptoms). This is in contrast to psychodynamic or other therapies where goals may not be explicitly discussed or agreed on and the client's only necessary action is to attend the therapy session.

> Why do most therapists use a blend of cognitive and behavioral strategies?

mindfulness meditation
Teaches an individual to be fully present in each moment; to be aware of his or her thoughts, feelings, and sensations; and to detect symptoms before they become a problem.

cognitive behavioral therapy (CBT)
A blend of cognitive and behavioral therapeutic strategies.

How might the use of behavior change homework improve the effectiveness of behavior therapy?

©EONNIE KAMIN/PHOTOEDIT

CBT also contrasts with psychodynamic approaches in its assumptions about what the client can know. CBT is *transparent* in that nothing is withheld from the client. By the end of the course of therapy, most clients have a very good understanding of the treatment they have received as well as the specific techniques that are used to make the desired changes. For example, clients with OCD who fear contamination would feel confident in knowing how to confront feared situations such as public washrooms and why confronting this situation is helpful.

Cognitive behavioral therapies have been found to be effective for a number of disorders (Butler et al., 2006; see the Hot Science box). Substantial effects of CBT have been found for unipolar depression, generalized anxiety disorder, panic disorder, social phobia, posttraumatic stress disorder, and childhood depressive and anxiety disorders. CBT has moderate but less substantial effects for marital distress, anger, somatic disorders, and chronic pain.

HOT SCIENCE

"Rebooting" Psychological Treatment

Modern psychotherapy has advanced far beyond the days of Freud and his free-associating patients. We now have more sophisticated treatments that have been developed based on recent advances in psychological science and supported in experimental studies showing that they actually do decrease peoples' psychological suffering. However, psychological treatment is still pretty primitive in many ways. It usually involves a patient meeting once per week with a clinician who attempts to talk them out of their psychological disorder – just as it did in the earliest days of psychological treatment. In a recent paper, Alan Kazdin (and his student Stacey Blase) called for a "rebooting" of psychotherapy research and practice (Kazdin & Blase, 2011).What is needed, they argue, is a portfolio of treatment delivery approaches that take advantage of recent advances in technology.

Although most psychologists providing treatment to those with psychological disorders still use traditional psychotherapy, researchers are developing and testing new methods of assessing and treating disorders that make creative use of new technologies. One of the most exciting recent advances in psychological treatment involves computerized training programs. For example, research suggests that biases in the ways that people process information cause psychological disorders. Cognitive bias modification (CBM) is a computerized intervention that focuses on eliminating these biases (MacLeod & Mathews, 2012). Specifically, people with social anxiety

show selective attention for threatening information (e.g., when shown several faces they have an automatic tendency to look at the angrier one). In one form of CBM for social anxiety, the patient completes a computerized training program in which he or she is repeatedly shown pairs of faces, one angry and one neutral, that flash on the screen very quickly (for 500 milliseconds) after which the letter "E" or "F" appears behind one of them and the patient's task is to indicate whether the letter is an "E" or "F." In CBM, the "E" or "F" always, or nearly always, appears behind the neutral face, which over time teaches the person to ignore the angry face and attend to the neutral face, thus reducing their tendency to attend to threatening faces. The training is intended to generalize beyond faces to reduce attention to threatening stimuli in general. In a recent placebo-controlled trial, Eldar and colleagues (2012) recently found that four sessions of CBM led to significant

COURTESY PHILIP M. ENOCK

reductions in symptoms of various anxiety disorders in a sample of anxious children. CBM has been tested for the treatment of a range of different psychological disorders (Beard, Sawyer & Hofmann, 2012) and represents an exciting new direction in treatment development. However, it is important to note that in CBM, as with many novel treatments, several non-replications followed the initial successful trials (e.g., Enock & McNally, 2013), suggesting that the jury is still out regarding the effectiveness of this new type of treatment.

In addition to new forms of treatment that can be administered in clinics, advances in technology are allowing psychologists to bring the clinic into people's everyday life. Psychologists are now using computers, cellular phones, and wearable bio-sensors to measure patients' experiences in the real world in real-time, and also to administer interventions well beyond the clinic walls (e.g., using text messages to remind patients not to smoke or to practice the skills they learned during their last therapy session). The development of 'mobile health' or 'mHealth' interventions has been extremely exciting; however, one recent review found that more than half of interventions that used mobile technologies fail to show any benefit (Kaplan & Stone, 2013). So although the development of portable technological devices has opened up lots of new opportunities for intervention, it is important that psychologists carefully evaluate which can help improve health outcomes, and which are simply fancier ways of providing ineffective treatment.

Group Treatments: Healing Multiple Minds at the Same Time

group therapy
A technique in which multiple participants (who often do not know one another at the outset) work on their individual problems in a group atmosphere.

It is natural to think of psychopathology as an illness that affects only the individual. A particular person "is depressed," for example, or "has anxiety." Yet each person lives in a world of other people, and interactions with others may intensify and even create disorders. A depressed person may be lonely after moving away from friends and loved ones, or an anxious person could be worried about pressures from parents. These ideas suggest that people might be able to recover from disorders in the same way they got into them—not just as an individual effort, but through social processes.

When is group therapy the best option?

Couples and Family Therapy

When a couple is "having problems," neither individual may be suffering from any psychopathology. Rather, it may be the relationship itself that is disordered. *Couples therapy* is when a married, cohabitating, or dating couple is seen together in therapy to work on problems usually arising within the relationship. A traditional use of couples therapy might involve a couple seeking help because they are unhappy with their relationship. In this scenario, both members of the couple are expected to attend therapy sessions and the problem is seen as arising from their interaction rather than from the problems of one half of the couple. Treatment strategies would target changes in *both* parties, focusing on ways to break their repetitive dysfunctional pattern.

What do you do when your relationship is in trouble? One option is couples therapy. In the romantic comedy, *Couples Retreat,* four couples take a weeklong resort vacation that includes daily couples therapy. Hilarity ensues.

There are cases when therapy with even larger groups is warranted. An individual may be having a problem—say, an adolescent is abusing alcohol—but the source of the problem is the individual's relationships with family members; perhaps the mother is herself an alcoholic who subtly encourages the adolescent to drink and the father travels and neglects the family. In this case, it could be useful for the therapist to work with the whole group at once in *family therapy*—psychotherapy involving members of a family. Family therapy can be particularly effective when adolescent children are having problems (Masten, 2004).

In family therapy, the "client" is the entire family. Family therapists believe that problem behaviors exhibited by a particular family member are the result of a dysfunctional family. For example, an adolescent girl suffering from bulimia might be treated in therapy with her mother, father, and older brother. The therapist would work to understand how the family members relate to one another, how the family is organized, and how it changes over time. In discussions with the family, the therapist might discover that the parents' excessive enthusiasm about her brother's athletic career led the girl to try to gain their approval by controlling her weight to become "beautiful." Both couples and family therapy involve more than one person attending therapy together, and the problems and solutions are seen as arising from the *interaction* of these individuals rather than simply from any one individual.

Families enter therapy for many reasons, sometimes to help particular members and other times because there are problems in one or more of the relationships in the family.

Group Therapy

Taking these ideas one step further, if individuals (or families) can benefit from talking with a psychotherapist, perhaps they can also benefit from talking with other clients who are talking with the therapist. This is **group therapy**, *a technique in which multiple participants (who often do not know one another at the outset) work on their individual* *problems in a group atmosphere.* The therapist in group therapy serves more as a discussion leader than as a personal therapist, conducting the sessions both by talking with individuals and by encouraging them to talk with one another. Group therapy is often used for people who have a common problem, such as substance abuse, but it can also be used for those with differing problems.

> **What are the pros and cons of a group therapy approach?**

Why do people choose group therapy? One advantage is that attending a group with others who have similar problems shows clients that they are not alone in their suffering. In addition, group members model appropriate behaviors for one another and share their insights about how to deal with their problems. Group therapy is often just as effective as individual therapy (e.g., Jonsson & Hougaard, 2008). So, from a societal perspective, group therapy is much more efficient.

Group therapy also has disadvantages. It may be difficult to assemble a group of individuals who have similar needs. This is particularly an issue with CBT, which tends to focus on specific problems such as depression or panic disorder. Group therapy may become a problem if one or more members undermine the treatment of other group members. This can occur if some group members dominate the discussions, threaten other group members, or make others in the group uncomfortable (e.g., attempting to date other members). Finally, clients in group therapy get less attention than they might in individual psychotherapy.

Self-Help and Support Groups

An important offshoot of group therapy is the concept of *self-help groups* and *support groups,* which are discussion groups that focus on a particular disorder or difficult life experience and are often run by peers who have themselves struggled with the same issues. The most famous self-help and support groups are Alcoholics Anonymous (AA), Gamblers Anonymous, and Al-Anon (a program for the family and friends of those with alcohol problems). Other self-help groups offer support to cancer survivors or to parents of children with autism or to people with mood disorders, eating disorders, and substance abuse problems. In fact, self-help and support groups exist for just about every psychological disorder. In addition to being cost-effective, self-help and support groups allow people to realize that they are not the only ones with a particular

> **What are the pros and cons of self-help support groups?**

Self-help groups are a cost-effective, time-effective, and treatment-effective solution for dealing with some types of psychological problems. Many people like self-help groups, but are they effective? How could you test this?"

©RICHARD T. NOWITZ/CORBIS

problem and give them the opportunity to offer guidance and support to each other based on personal experiences of success.

In some cases, though, self-help and support groups can do more harm than good. Some members may be disruptive or aggressive or encourage one another to engage in behaviors that are countertherapeutic (e.g., avoiding feared situations or using alcohol to cope). People with moderate problems may be exposed to others with severe problems and may become oversensitized to symptoms they might not otherwise have found disturbing. Because self-help and support groups are usually not led by trained therapists, mechanisms to evaluate these groups or to ensure their quality are rarely in place.

AA has more than 2 million members in the United States, with 185,000 group meetings that occur around the world (Mack, Franklin, & Frances, 2003). Members are encouraged to follow "12 steps" to reach the goal of lifelong abstinence from all drinking, and the steps include believing in a higher power, practicing prayer and meditation, and making amends for harm to others. Most members attend group meetings several times per week, and between meetings they receive additional support from their "sponsor." A few studies examining the effectiveness of AA have been conducted, and it appears that individuals who participate tend to overcome problem drinking with greater success than those who do not participate in AA (Fiorentine, 1999; Morgenstern et al., 1997). However, several tenets of the AA philosophy are not supported by the research. We know that the general AA program is useful, but questions about which parts of this program are most helpful have yet to be studied.

Considered together, the many social approaches to psychotherapy reveal how important interpersonal relationships are for each of us. It may not always be clear how psychotherapy works, whether one approach is better than another, or what particular theory should be used to understand how problems have developed. What is clear, however, is that social interactions between people—both in individual therapy and in all the different forms of therapy in groups—can be useful in treating psychological disorders.

IN SUMMARY

▶ Psychodynamic therapies, including psychoanalysis, emphasize helping clients gain insight into their unconscious conflicts. Traditional psychoanalysis involves 4 to 5 sessions per week of treatment with a client lying on a couch free-associating, whereas modern psychodynamic therapies involve one session per week with face-to-face interactions in which therapists help clients solve interpersonal problems.

▶ Humanistic approaches (e.g., person-centered therapy) and existential approaches (e.g., gestalt therapy) focus on helping people to develop a sense of personal worth.

▶ Behavior therapy applies learning principles to specific behavior problems.

▶ Cognitive therapy is focused on helping people to change the way they think about events in their lives, and teaching them to challenge irrational thoughts.

▶ Cognitive behavior therapy (CBT), which merges cognitive and behavioral approaches, has been shown to be effective for treating a wide range of psychological disorders.

▶ Group therapies target couples, families, or groups of clients brought together for the purpose of working together to solve their problems.

▶ Self-help and support groups, such as AA, are common in the United States and around the world but are not well studied.

This is a trephined skull from a Stone Age burial site (about 5900–6200 BCE) in the Alsace region of France. Two holes were drilled in the skull and the individual survived, as shown by the regrowth of bone covering the holes (from Alt et al., 1997). Don't try this at home.

SSPL/GETTY IMAGES

Medical and Biological Treatments: Healing the Mind by Physically Altering the Brain

Ever since someone discovered that a whack to the head can affect the mind, people have suspected that direct brain interventions might hold the keys to a cure for psychological disorders. Archaeological evidence, for example, indicates that the occasional human thousands of years ago was "treated" for some malady by the practice of *trephining* (drilling a hole in the skull), perhaps in the belief that this would release evil spirits that were affecting the mind (Alt et al., 1997). Surgery for psychological disorders is a last resort nowadays, and treatments that focus on the brain usually involve interventions that are less dramatic. The use of drugs to influence the brain was also discovered in prehistory (alcohol, for example, has been around for a long time). Since then, drug treatments have grown in variety, effectiveness, and popularity and they are now the most common medical approach in treating psychological disorders (see **FIGURE 16.2**).

► Figure **16.2 Antidepressant Use** The popularity of psychiatric medications has skyrocketed in recent years. A recent government report showed that the use of antidepressant medications increased 400% over the period of 1988 to 2008 (National Center for Health Statistics, 2012). This rise may be due to a number of factors, including the publication of data on the effectiveness of these medications, increasing efforts to disseminate them to prescribers, and enhanced efforts to market these drugs directly to consumers. The higher rates of use shown here for females may be due in part to the fact that women have higher rates of both depression and treatment use in general, compared to men.

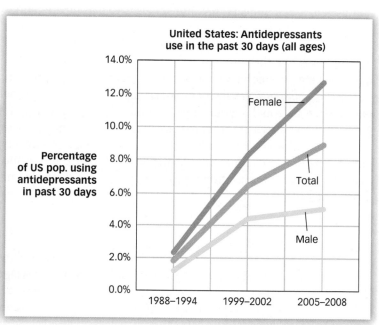

Antipsychotic Medications

The story of drug treatments for severe psychological disorders starts in the 1950s, with chlorpromazine (brand name Thorazine), which was originally developed as a sedative, but when administered to people with schizophrenia, often left them euphoric and docile, although they had formerly been agitated and incorrigible (Barondes, 2003). Chlorpromazine was the first in a series of **antipsychotic drugs**, which *treat schizophrenia and related psychotic disorders,* and completely changed the way schizophrenia was managed. Other related medications, such as thioridazine (Mellaril) and haloperidol (Haldol), followed. Before the introduction of antipsychotic drugs, people with schizophrenia often exhibited bizarre symptoms and were sometimes so disruptive and difficult to manage that the only way to protect them (and other people) was to keep them in hospitals for people with mental disorders, which were initially called *asylums* but now are referred to as *psychiatric hospitals* (see the Real World box, Treating Severe Mental Disorders). In the period following the introduction of these drugs, the number of people in psychiatric hospitals decreased by more than

antipsychotic drugs
Medications that are used to treat schizophrenia and related psychotic disorders.

THE REAL WORLD

Treating Severe Mental Disorders

Society has never quite known what to do with people who have severe mental disorders. For much of recorded history, mentally ill people have been victims of maltreatment, languishing as paupers in the streets or, worse, suffering inhumane conditions in prisons. It was something of a reform, then, when in the 18th century, the few private "madhouses" for the rich became models for the establishment of public asylums in England and France.

In North America, the asylum movement for humane treatment of the mentally ill was fostered initially by Dr. Benjamin Rush (a signer of the Constitution) and later by mental health crusader Dorothea Dix. Dix visited jails and almshouses in Massachusetts and in 1843 reported to the legislature widespread cruelty toward the insane. She developed a remarkably effective personal campaign across North America and Europe that eventually resulted in the building of hundreds of asylums for the mentally ill.

The creation of asylums encouraged humane treatment but did not guarantee it. London's St. Mary's of Bethlehem Hospital, known for inspiring the term **bedlam**, was typical—even charging visitors to view the inmates as a way of financing the institution. One visitor to this human zoo in 1753 remarked, "To my great surprise, I found at least a hundred people, who, having paid their two pence apiece, were suffered, unattended, to run rioting up and down the wards, making sport and diversion of the miserable inhabitants" (Hitchcock, 2005). To some degree, the abuse of insane inmates by jailers simply was transformed into the abuse of mental patients by asylum workers. For severe disorders, there often was no "treatment" at all, and the focus of the asylum instead was merely on custody (Jones, 1972).

These weaknesses of the asylum movement eventually led to another revolution in mental health treatment—the deinstitutionalization movement of the 1960s. Drugs were being discovered that helped people to manage their disorders and live outside hospitals. With the funding of a "community mental health" initiative by the Kennedy administration, dozens of mental hospitals across the United States were closed, and thousands of patients were trained to shop, cook, take public transportation, and otherwise deal with living outside the hospital. Former asylum patients were returned to their families or placed in foster homes or group apartments, but in too many cases they were simply released with nowhere to go and ultimately became homeless. Treatment of all but the most untreatable patients was managed through community mental health centers: support units to provide emergency inpatient care as needed but mainly supplying outpatient treatment and assistance in community living (Levine, 1981).

Has this experiment worked? On one hand, treatment for some severe disorders has improved since deinstitutionalization began. The basic drugs that helped people to manage their lives outside mental hospitals have been refined and improved. In addition, the conditions and treatments available in psychiatric hospitals have improved immensely. Contrary to what you may see in the movies, psychiatric units and hospitals look just like other medical floors in general hospitals.

However, outside the hospital walls, federal funding of the network of community mental health centers was abandoned by the Reagan administration in the 1980s, and state-funded programs and private managed care providers have not made up the difference (Cutler, Bevilacqua, & McFarland, 2003). So, although deinstitutionalization has allowed people with severe mental illnesses greater freedom from asylums, many of these people have ended up on the streets, where they remain homeless, poor, and vulnerable to danger. Treatment for those with serious mental illness has improved over the past 100+ years, but we still clearly have a long way to go.

▲ What does a modern psychiatric hospital look like? In Hollywood movies, they typically are dirty, scary, painted in a drab gray or green color, and it is always night time. In the real world, they look just like other hospital units in terms of cleanliness, scariness, paint scheme, and the experience of both day and night.

psychopharmacology
The study of drug effects on psychological states and symptoms.

antianxiety medications
Drugs that help reduce a person's experience of fear or anxiety.

antidepressants
A class of drugs that help lift people's moods.

two thirds. Antipsychotic drugs made possible the deinstitutionalization of hundreds of thousands of people and gave a major boost to the field of **psychopharmacology**, *the study of drug effects on psychological states and symptoms.*

Antipsychotic medications are believed to block dopamine receptors in parts of the brain such as the mesolimbic area, an area between the tegmentum (in the midbrain) and various subcortical structures (see the Neuroscience and Behavior chapter). The medication reduces dopamine activity in these areas. The effectiveness of schizophrenia medications led to the dopamine hypothesis (described in the Psychological Disorders chapter), suggesting that schizophrenia may be caused by excess dopamine in the synapse. Research has indeed found that dopamine overactivity in the mesolimbic area of the brain is related to the more bizarre positive symptoms of schizophrenia, such as hallucinations and delusions (Marangell et al., 2003).

> **What do antipsychotic drugs do?**

Although antipsychotic drugs work well for positive symptoms, it turns out that negative symptoms of schizophrenia, such as emotional numbing and social withdrawal, may be related to dopamine *under*activity in the mesocortical areas of the brain (connections between parts of the tegmentum and the cortex). This may help explain why antipsychotic medications do not relieve negative symptoms well. Instead of a medication that blocks dopamine receptors, negative symptoms require a medication that *increases* the amount of dopamine available at the synapse. This is a good example of how medical treatments can have broad psychological effects but not target specific psychological symptoms.

After the introduction of antipsychotic medications, there was little change in the available treatments for schizophrenia for more than a quarter of a century. However, in the 1990s, a new class of antipsychotic drugs was introduced. These newer drugs, which include clozapine (Clozaril), risperidone (Risperidal), and olanzepine (Zyprexa), have become known as *atypical* antipsychotics (the older drugs are now often referred to as *conventional* or *typical* antipsychotics). Unlike the older antipsychotic medications, these newer drugs appear to affect both the dopamine and serotonin systems, blocking both types of receptors. The ability to block serotonin receptors appears to be a useful addition because enhanced serotonin activity in the brain has been implicated in some of the core difficulties in schizophrenia, such as cognitive and perceptual disruptions, as well as mood disturbances. This may explain why atypical antipsychotics work at least as well as older drugs for the positive symptoms of schizophrenia and also work fairly well for the negative symptoms (Bradford, Stroup, & Lieberman, 2002).

> **What are the advantages of the newer, atypical antipsychotic medications?**

Like most medications, antipsychotic drugs have side effects. The side effects can be sufficiently unpleasant that some people "go off their meds," preferring their symptoms to the drug. One side effect that often occurs with long-term use is *tardive dyskinesia*, a condition of involuntary movements of the face, mouth, and extremities. In fact, people often need to take another medication to treat the unwanted side effects of the conventional antipsychotic drugs. Side effects of the newer medications tend to be different and sometimes milder than those of the older antipsychotics. For that reason, the atypical antipsychotics are now usually the front-line treatments for schizophrenia (Meltzer, 2013).

"The drug has, however, proved more effective than traditional psychoanalysis."

PAUL NOTH/THE NEW YORKER COLLECTION/CARTOONBANK.COM

Antianxiety Medications

Antianxiety medications are *drugs that help reduce a person's experience of fear or anxiety.* The most commonly used antianxiety medications are the benzodiazepines, a type of tranquilizer that works by facilitating the action of the neurotransmitter gamma-aminobutyric acid (GABA). As you read in the Neuroscience and Behavior chapter, GABA inhibits certain neurons in the brain. This inhibitory action can produce a calming effect for the person. Commonly prescribed benzodiazepines include diazepam (Valium), lorazepam (Ativan), and alprazolam (Xanax). The benzodiazepines typically take effect in a matter of minutes and are effective for reducing symptoms of anxiety disorders (Roy-Byrne & Cowley, 2002).

> **What are some reasons for caution when prescribing antianxiety medications?**

Nonetheless, these days doctors are relatively cautious when prescribing benzodiazepines. One concern is that these drugs have the potential for abuse. They are often associated with the development of *drug tolerance,* which is the need for higher dosages over time to achieve the same effects following long-term use (see the Consciousness chapter). Furthermore, after people become tolerant of the drug, they risk significant withdrawal symptoms when it's discontinued. Some withdrawal symptoms include increased heart rate, shakiness, insomnia, agitation, and anxiety—the very symptoms the drug was taken to eliminate! Therefore, people who take benzodiazepines for extended periods may have difficulty coming off these drugs and should discontinue their medications gradually to minimize withdrawal symptoms (Schatzberg, Cole, & DeBattista, 2003). Another consideration when prescribing benzodiazepines is their side effects. The most common side effect is drowsiness, although benzodiazepines can also have negative effects on coordination and memory. And, benzodiazapines combined with alcohol can depress respiration, potentially causing accidental death.

When anxiety leads to insomnia, drugs known as hypnotics may be useful as sleep aids. One such drug, zolpidem (Ambien), is in wide use and is often effective, but with some reports of sleepwalking, sleep-eating, and even sleep-driving (Hughes, 2007). Another alternative for anxiety is buspirone (Buspar), which has been shown to reduce anxiety among individuals who suffer from generalized anxiety disorder (Roy-Byrne & Cowley, 2002).

Antidepressants and Mood Stabilizers

Antidepressants are *a class of drugs that help lift people's moods.* They were first introduced in the 1950s, when iproniazid, a drug that was used to treat tuberculosis, was found to elevate mood (Selikoff, Robitzek, & Ornstein, 1952). Iproniazid is a *monoamine oxidase inhibitor (MAOI),* a medication that prevents the enzyme monoamine oxidase from breaking down neurotransmitters such as norepinephrine, serotonin, and dopamine. However, despite their effectiveness, MAOIs are rarely prescribed anymore. MAOI side effects such as dizziness and loss of sexual interest are often difficult to tolerate, and these drugs interact with many different medications, including over-the-counter cold medicines. They also can cause dangerous increases in blood pressure when taken with foods that contain tyramine, a natural substance formed from the breakdown of protein in certain cheeses, beans, aged meats, soy products, and draft beer.

A second category of antidepressants is the tricyclic antidepressants, which were also introduced in the 1950s. These include drugs such as imipramine (Tofranil) and amitriptyline (Elavil). These medications block the reuptake of norepinephrine and

If you watch television you have seen advertisements for specific drugs. Does this direct-to-consumer advertising really work? Sure does! One recent study sent people acting as patients to physicians' offices asking for specific drugs and found that patient requests had a huge impact on doctors' behavior: Those asking about specific drugs were much more likely to receive a prescription than those who did not make a request (Kravitz et al., 2005).

THINKSTOCK

serotonin, thereby increasing the amount of neurotransmitter in the synaptic space between neurons. The most common side effects of tricyclic antidepressants include dry mouth, constipation, difficulty urinating, blurred vision, and racing heart (Marangell et al., 2003). Although these drugs are still prescribed, they are used much less frequently than they were in the past because of these side effects.

Among the most commonly used antidepressants today are the *selective serotonin reuptake inhibitors,* or SSRIs, which include drugs such as fluoxetine (Prozac), citalopram (Celexa), and paroxetine (Paxil). The SSRIs work by blocking the reuptake of serotonin in the brain, which makes more serotonin available in the synaptic space between neurons. The greater availability of serotonin in the synapse gives the neuron a better chance of "recognizing" and using this neurotransmitter in sending the desired signal. The SSRIs were developed based on hypotheses that low levels of serotonin are a causal factor in depression. Supporting this hypothesis, SSRIs are effective for depression, as well as for a wide range of other problems. SSRIs are called *selective* because, unlike the tricyclic antidepressants, which work on the serotonin and norepinephrine systems, SSRIs work more specifically on the serotonin system (see **FIGURE 16.3**).

> **What are the most common antidepressants used today? How do they work?**

Finally, antidepressants such as Effexor (venlafaxine) and Wellbutrin (ibupropion) offer other alternatives. Effexor is an example of a serotonin and norepinephrine reuptake inhibitor (SNRI); whereas SSRIs act only upon serotonin, SNRIs act on both serotonin and norepinephrine. Wellbutrin, in contrast, is a norepinephrine and dopamine reuptake inhibitor. These and other newly developed antidepressants appear to have fewer (or at least different) side effects than the tricyclic antidepressants and MAOIs.

Most antidepressants can take up to a month before they start to have an effect on mood. Besides relieving symptoms of depression, almost all of the antidepressants effectively treat anxiety disorders, and many of them can resolve other problems, such

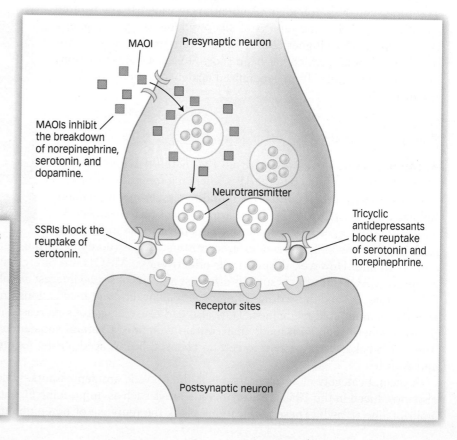

▶ Figure **16.3 Antidepressant Drug Actions** Antidepressant drugs, such as MAOIs, SSRIs, and tricyclic antidepressants, act on neurotransmitters such as serotonin, dopamine, and norepinephrine by inhibiting their breakdown and blocking reuptake. These actions make more of the neurotransmitter available for release and leave more of the neurotransmitter in the synaptic gap to activate the receptor sites on the postsynaptic neuron. These drugs relieve depression and often alleviate anxiety and other disorders.

as eating disorders. In fact, several companies that manufacture SSRIs have marketed their drugs as treatments for anxiety disorders rather than for their antidepressant effects. Although antidepressants can be effective in treating major depression, they are not recommended for treating bipolar disorder, which is characterized by manic or hypomanic episodes (see the Psychological Disorders chapter). Antidepressants are not prescribed because, in the process of lifting one's mood, they might actually trigger a manic episode in a person with bipolar disorder. Instead, bipolar disorder is treated with *mood stabilizers,* which are medications used to suppress swings between mania and depression. Commonly used mood stabilizers include lithium and valproate. Even in unipolar depression, lithium is sometimes effective when combined with traditional antidepressants in people who do not respond to antidepressants alone.

> **Why aren't antidepressants prescribed for bipolar disorder?**

Lithium has been associated with possible long-term kidney and thyroid problems, so people taking lithium must monitor their blood levels of lithium on a regular basis. Furthermore, lithium has a precise range in which it is useful for each person, another reason it should be closely monitored with blood tests. Valproate, in contrast, does not require such careful blood monitoring. Although valproate may have side effects, it is currently the most commonly prescribed drug in the United States for bipolar disorder (Schatzberg et al., 2003). In sum, although the antidepressants are effective for a wide variety of problems, mood stabilizers may be required when a person's symptoms include extreme swings between highs and lows, such as experienced with bipolar disorder.

Herbal and Natural Products

In a survey of more than 2,000 Americans, 7% of those suffering from anxiety disorders and 9% of those suffering from severe depression reported using alternative "medications" such as herbal medicines, megavitamins, homeopathic remedies, or naturopathic remedies to treat these problems (Kessler et al., 2001). Major reasons people use these products are that they are easily available over the counter, are less expensive, and are perceived as "natural" alternatives to synthetic or manmade "drugs." Are herbal and natural products effective in treating mental health problems, or are they just "snake oil?"

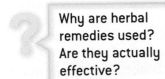

> **Why are herbal remedies used? Are they actually effective?**

The answer to this question isn't simple. Herbal products are not considered medications by regulatory agencies like the U.S. Food and Drug Administration, so they are exempt from rigorous research to establish their safety and effectiveness. Instead, herbal products are classified as nutritional supplements and regulated in the same way as food. There is little scientific information about herbal products, including possible interactions with other medications, possible tolerance and withdrawal symptoms, side effects, appropriate dosages, how they work, or even *whether* they work—and the purity of these products often varies from brand to brand (Jordan, Cunningham, & Marles, 2010).

There is research support for the effectiveness of some herbal and natural products, but the evidence is not overwhelming (Lake, 2009). Products such as inositol (a bran derivative), kava (an herb related to black pepper), omega-3 fatty acid (a fish oil), and SAM-e (an amino acid derivative) are sold as health foods and are described as having positive psychological effects of various kinds, but the evidence is mixed. For example, in the case of St. John's wort (a wort, it turns out, is an herb), some studies have shown it has an advantage over a placebo condition (e.g., Lecrubier et al., 2002) for the treatment of depression, whereas others show no advantage (e.g., Hypericum Depression Trial Study Group, 2002). Omega-3 fatty acids have been

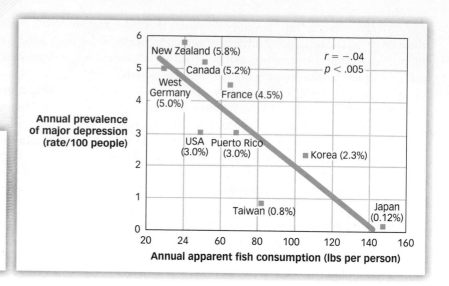

▶ Figure **16.4** **Omega-3 Fatty Acids and Depression** Recent studies have shown that consumption of omega-3 fatty acids is associated with a wide range of positive mental health outcomes. For instance, Joe Hibbeln (1998) showed that countries that consume more fish (a main dietary source of omega-3s) have significantly lower rates of depression.

linked with lower rates of depression and suicide, and several treatment studies have repeatedly shown that omega-3s are superior to placebo at decreasing depression (see **FIGURE 16.4**; Lewis et al., 2011; Parker, Gibson, et al., 2006). Overall, although herbal medications and treatments are worthy of continued research, these products should be closely monitored and used judiciously until more is known about their safety and effectiveness.

Combining Medication and Psychotherapy

Given that psychological treatments and medications both have shown an ability to treat mental disorders effectively, some natural next questions are: Which is more effective? Is the combination of psychological and medicinal treatments better than either by itself? Many studies have compared psychological treatments, medication, and combinations of these approaches for addressing psychological disorders. The results of these studies often depend on the particular problem being considered. For example, in the cases of schizophrenia and bipolar disorder, researchers have found that medication is more effective than psychological treatment and so is considered a necessary part of treatment; recent studies have tended to examine whether adding psychotherapeutic treatments such as social skills training or cognitive behavioral treatment can be helpful (they can). In the case of mood and anxiety disorders, medication and psychological treatments are equally effective. One study compared cognitive behavior therapy, imipramine (the antidepressant also known as Tofranil), and the combination of these treatments (CBT plus imipramine) with a placebo (administration of an inert medication) for the treatment of panic disorder (Barlow et al., 2000). After 12 weeks of treatment, either CBT alone or imipramine alone was found to be superior to a placebo. For the CBT plus imipramine condition, the response rate also exceeded the rate for the placebo, but was not significantly better than that for either CBT or imipramine alone. In other words, either treatment was better than nothing, but the combination of treatments was not significantly more effective than one or the other (see **FIGURE 16.5**). More is not always better.

▼ Figure **16.5** **The Effectiveness of Medication and Psychotherapy for Panic Disorder** One study of CBT and medication (imipramine) for panic disorder found that the effects of CBT, medication, and treatment that combined CBT and medication were not significantly different over the short term, though all three were superior to the placebo condition (Barlow et al., 2000).

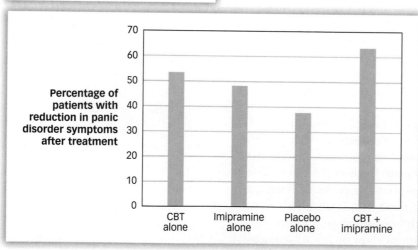

OTHER VOICES

Diagnosis: Human

Ted Gup is an author and fellow of the Edmond J. Safra Center for Ethics at Harvard University.

PHOTO: SUSAN SYMONES/ INFINITY PORTRAIT DESIGN

Should more people receive psychological treatment or medications? Or should fewer? On one hand, data indicate that most people with a mental disorder do not receive treatment and that untreated mental disorders are an enormous source of pain and suffering. On the other hand, some argue that we have become too quick to label normal human behavior as "disordered" and too willing to medicate any behavior, thought, or feeling that makes us uncomfortable. Ted Gup is one of these people. The following is a version of his op-ed piece that appeared in *The New York Times* on April 3, 2013 under the headline "Diagnosis: Human."

The news that 11 percent of school-age children now receive a diagnosis of attention deficit hyperactivity disorder—some 6.4 million— gave me a chill. My son David was one of those who received that diagnosis.

In his case, he was in the first grade. Indeed, there were psychiatrists who prescribed medication for him even before they met him. One psychiatrist said he would not even see him until he was medicated. For a year I refused to fill the prescription at the pharmacy. Finally, I relented. And so David went on Ritalin, then Adderall, and other drugs that were said to be helpful in combating the condition.

In another age, David might have been called "rambunctious." His battery was a little too large for his body. And so he would leap over the couch, spring to reach the ceiling and show an exuberance for life that came in brilliant microbursts.

As a 21-year-old college senior, he was found on the floor of his room, dead from a fatal mix of alcohol and drugs. The date was Oct. 18, 2011. No one made him take the heroin and alcohol, and yet I cannot help but hold myself and others to account. I had unknowingly colluded with a system that devalues talking therapy and rushes to medicate, inadvertently sending a message that self-medication, too, is perfectly acceptable.

My son was no angel (though he was to us) and he was known to trade in Adderall, to create a submarket in the drug among his classmates who were themselves all too eager to get their hands on it. What he did cannot be excused, but it should be understood. What he did was to create a market that perfectly mirrored the society in which he grew up, a culture where Big Pharma itself prospers from the off-label uses of drugs, often not tested in children and not approved for the many uses to which they are put.

And so a generation of students, raised in an environment that encourages medication, are emulating the professionals by using drugs in the classroom as performance enhancers. And we wonder why it is that they use drugs with such abandon. As all parents learn—at times to their chagrin—our children go to school not only in the classroom but also at home, and the culture they construct for themselves as teenagers and young adults is but a tiny village imitating that to which they were introduced as children.

The issue of permissive drug use and over-diagnosis goes well beyond hyperactivity. In May, the American Psychiatric Association will publish its *DSM–5*, the *Diagnostic and Statistical Manual of Mental Disorders*. It is called the bible of the profession. Its latest iteration, like those before, is not merely a window on the profession but on the culture it serves, both reflecting and shaping societal norms. (For instance, until the 1970s, it categorized homosexuality as a mental illness.)

One of the new, more controversial provisions expands depression to include some forms of grief. On its face it makes sense. The grieving often display all the common indicators of depression—loss of interest in life, loss of appetite, irregular sleep patterns, low functionality, etc. But as others have observed, those same symptoms are the very hallmarks of grief itself.

Ours is an age in which the airwaves and media are one large drug emporium that claims to fix everything from sleep to sex. I fear that being human is itself fast becoming a condition. It's as if we are trying to contain grief, and the absolute pain of a loss like mine. We have become increasingly disassociated and estranged from the patterns of life and death, uncomfortable with the messiness of our own humanity, aging and, ultimately, mortality.

Challenge and hardship have become pathologized and monetized. Instead of enhancing our coping skills, we undermine them and seek shortcuts where there are none, eroding the resilience upon which each of us, at some point in our lives, must rely. Diagnosing grief as a part of depression runs the very real risk of delegitimizing that which is most human—the bonds of our love and attachment to one another. The new entry in the *DSM* cannot tame grief by giving it a name or a subsection, nor render it less frightening or more manageable.

The *DSM* would do well to recognize that a broken heart is not a medical condition, and that medication is ill-suited to repair some tears. Time does not heal all wounds, closure is a fiction, and so too is the notion that God never asks of us more than we can bear. Enduring the unbearable is sometimes exactly what life asks of us.

But there is a sweetness even to the intensity of this pain I feel. It is the thing that holds me still to my son. And yes, there is a balm even in the pain. I shall let it go when it is time, without reference to the *DSM*, and without the aid of a pill.

Have we gone too far in labeling and treatment of mental disorders? Or have we not gone far enough? How can we make sure that we are not medicating normal behavior, while at the same time ensuring that we provide help to those who are suffering with a true mental disorder?

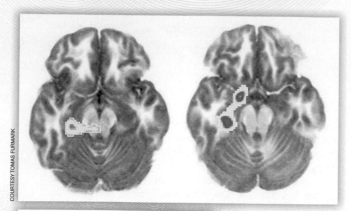

▲ Figure **16.6** **The Effects of Medication and Therapy in the Brain** PET scans of individuals with social phobia showed similar reductions in activations of the amygdala–hippocampus region after they received treatment with CBT (*left*) and with citalopram (*right*), an SSRI (from Furmark et al., 2002).

Given that both therapy and medications are effective, one question is whether they work through similar mechanisms. A study of people with social phobia examined patterns of cerebral blood flow following treatment using either citalopram (an SSRI) or CBT (Furmark et al., 2002). Participants in both groups were alerted to the possibility that they would soon have to speak in public. In both groups, those who responded to treatment showed similar reductions in activation in the amygdala, hippocampus, and neighboring cortical areas during this challenge (see **FIGURE 16.6**). The amygdala, located next to the hippocampus (see Figure 6.18) plays a significant role in memory for emotional information. These findings suggest that both therapy and medication affect the brain in regions associated with a reaction to threat. Although it might seem that events that influence the brain should be physical—after all, the brain is a physical object—it is important to keep in mind that environmental learning experiences, such as psychological treatment, produce similar influences on the brain.

? Do therapy and medications work through similar mechanisms?

One complication in combining medication and psychotherapy is that these treatments are often provided by different people. Psychiatrists are trained in the administration of medication in medical school (and they may also provide psychological treatment), whereas psychologists provide psychological treatment but not medication. This means that the coordination of treatment often requires cooperation between psychologists and psychiatrists.

The question of whether psychologists should be licensed to prescribe medications has been a source of debate among psychologists and physicians (Fox et al., 2009). Only Louisiana and New Mexico currently allow licensed and specially trained psychologists prescription privileges, but nine more states are currently considering it (Munsey, 2008). Opponents argue that psychologists do not have the medical training to understand how medications interact with other drugs. Proponents of prescription privileges argue that patient safety would not be compromised as long as rigorous training procedures were established. This issue remains a focus of debate, and at present, the coordination of medication and psychological treatment usually involves a team effort of psychiatry and psychology.

Biological Treatments beyond Medication

Medication can be an effective biological treatment, but for some people medications do not work or side effects are intolerable. If this group of people doesn't respond to psychotherapy either, what other options do they have to achieve symptom relief? Some additional avenues of help are available, but some are risky or poorly understood.

One commonly used biological treatment for severe mental disorders is **electroconvulsive therapy (ECT)**, sometimes referred to as *shock therapy*, which is *a treatment that involves inducing a brief seizure by delivering an electrical shock to the brain*. The shock is applied to the person's scalp for less than a second. ECT is primarily used to treat severe depression that has not responded to antidepressant medications, although it may

? Where do people turn if psychological treatment and medication are unsuccessful?

also be useful for treating bipolar disorder (Khalid et al., 2008; Poon et al., 2012). Patients are pretreated with muscle relaxants and are under general anesthetic, so they are not conscious of the procedure. The main side effect of ECT is impaired short-term memory, which usually improves over the

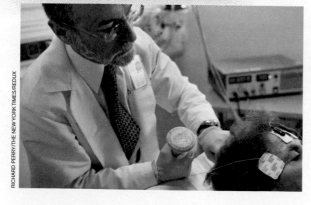

Electroconvulsive therapy (ECT) can be an effective treatment for severe depression. To reduce the side effects, it is administered under general anesthesia.

first month or two after the end of treatment. In addition, patients undergoing this procedure sometimes report headaches and muscle aches afterward (Marangell et al., 2003). Despite these side effects, the treatment can be effective: ECT is more effective than simulated ECT, than placebo, and than antidepressant drugs such as tricyclics and MAOIs (Pagnin et al., 2008).

Another biological approach that does not involve medication is **transcranial magnetic stimulation (TMS)**, *a treatment that involves placing a powerful pulsed magnet over a person's scalp, which alters neuronal activity in the brain.* As a treatment for depression, the magnet is placed just above the right or left eyebrow in an effort to stimulate the right or left prefrontal cortex (areas of the brain implicated in depression). TMS is an exciting development because it is noninvasive and has fewer side effects than ECT (see the Neuroscience and Behavior chapter). Side effects are minimal; they include mild headache and a small risk of seizure, but TMS has no impact on memory or concentration. TMS may be particularly useful in treating depression that is unresponsive to medication (Avery et al., 2009). In fact, a study comparing TMS to ECT found that both procedures were effective, with no significant differences between them (Janicak et al., 2002). Other studies have found that TMS can also be used to treat auditory hallucinations in schizophrenia (Aleman, Sommer, & Kahn, 2007).

Phototherapy, *a therapy that involves repeated exposure to bright light,* may be helpful to people who have a seasonal pattern to their depression. This could include people suffering with seasonal affective disorder (SAD; see the Psychological Disorders chapter), or those who experience depression only in the winter months due to the lack of sunlight. Typically, people are exposed to bright light in the morning, using a lamp designed for this purpose. Phototherapy has not been as well researched as psychological treatment or medication, but the handful of studies available suggest it is approximately as effective as antidepressant medication in the treatment of SAD (Thaler et al., 2011).

In very rare cases, **psychosurgery**, *the surgical destruction of specific brain areas,* may be used to treat psychological disorders. Psychosurgery has a controversial history, beginning in the 1930s with the invention of the lobotomy by Portuguese physician Egas Moniz (1874–1955). After discovering that certain surgical procedures on animal brains calmed behavior, Moniz began to use similar techniques on violent or agitated human patients. Lobotomies involved inserting an instrument into the brain through the patient's eye socket or through holes drilled in the side of the head. The objective was to sever connections between the frontal lobes and inner brain structures such as the thalamus, known to be involved in emotion. Although some lobotomies produced highly successful results and Moniz received the 1949 Nobel Prize for his work, significant side effects such as extreme lethargy or childlike impulsiveness detracted from these benefits. Lobotomy was used widely for years, leaving many people devastated by these permanent side effects, and because of this there is an ongoing movement challenging the awarding of the Nobel Prize to Moniz. The development of antipsychotic drugs in the 1950s provided a safer way to treat violent individuals and brought the practice of lobotomy to an end (Swayze, 1995).

Psychosurgery is rarely used these days and is reserved only for extremely severe cases for which no other interventions have been effective and the symptoms of the disorder are intolerable to the patient. For instance, psychosurgery is sometimes used in severe cases of OCD in which the person is completely unable to function in their daily life and psychological treatment and medication are not effective. In contrast to the earlier days of lobotomy in which broad regions of brain tissue were destroyed, modern psychosurgery involves a very precise destruction of brain tissue in order to disrupt the brain circuits known to be involved in the generation of obsessions and compulsions. This increased precision has produced better results. For example, people suffering from OCD who fail to respond to treatment (including several trials of medications and

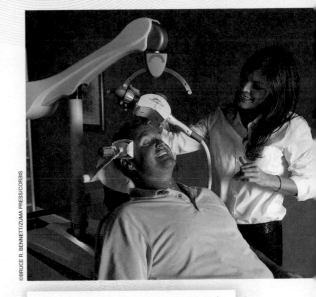

Transcranial magnetic stimulation (TMS) is an exciting new technique that allows researchers and clinicians to change brain activity using a magnetic wand—no surgery is required.

electroconvulsive therapy (ECT)
A treatment that involves inducing a brief seizure by delivering an electrical shock to the brain.

transcranial magnetic stimulation (TMS)
A treatment that involves placing a powerful pulsed magnet over a person's scalp, which alters neuronal activity in the brain.

phototherapy
A therapy that involves repeated exposure to bright light.

psychosurgery
Surgical destruction of specific brain areas.

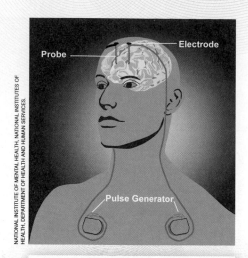

Deep brain stimulation involves the insertion of battery-powered electrodes that deliver electrical pulses to specific areas of the brain believed to be causing a person's mental disorder.

cognitive behavioral treatment) may benefit from specific surgical procedures called *cingulotomy* and *anterior capsulotomy*. Cingulotomy involves destroying part of the corpus callosum (see Figure 3.18) and cingulate gyrus (the ridge just above the corpus collosum). Anterior capsulotomy involves creating small lesions to disrupt the pathway between the caudate nucleus and putamen. Because of the relatively small number of cases of psychosurgery, there are not as many studies of these techniques as there are for other treatments; however, available studies have shown that psychosurgery typically leads to substantial improvements in both the short and long term for people with severe OCD (Csigó et al., 2010; van Vliet et al., 2013).

A final approach, called *deep brain stimulation* (DBS), combines the use of psychosurgery with the use of electrical currents (as in ECT and TMS). In DBS, a treatment pioneered only recently, a small, battery-powered device is implanted in the body to deliver electrical stimulation to specific areas of the brain known to be involved in the disorder being targeted. This technique has been successful for OCD treatment (Abelson et al., 2009) and can provide benefits for people with a variety of neurologic conditions. The tremor that accompanies Parkinson's disease has proven to be treatable in this way (Perlmutter & Mink, 2006), as have some cases of severe depression that are otherwise untreatable (Mayberg et al., 2005). The early view of psychosurgery as a treatment of last resort is being replaced by a cautious hope that newer, focused treatments that target brain circuits known to be functioning abnormally in those with certain mental disorders can have beneficial effects (Ressler & Mayberg, 2007).

IN SUMMARY

► Medications have been developed to treat many psychological disorders, including antipsychotic medications (used to treat schizophrenia and psychotic disorders), antianxiety medications (used to treat anxiety disorders), and antidepressants (used to treat depression and related disorders).

► Medications are often combined with psychotherapy.

► Other biomedical treatments include electroconvulsive therapy (ECT), transcranial magnetic stimulation (TMS), and psychosurgery—this last used in extreme cases, when other methods of treatment have been exhausted.

Treatment Effectiveness: For Better or for Worse

Think back to Christine and the dead mouse at the beginning of the chapter. What if, instead of exposure and response prevention, Christine had been assigned psychoanalysis or psychosurgery? Could these alternatives have been just as effective (and justified) for treating her OCD? Through this chapter, we have explored various psychological and biological treatments that may help people with psychological disorders. But do these treatments actually work, and which ones work better than the others?

As you learned in the Methods in Psychology chapter, pinning down a specific cause for an effect can be a difficult detective exercise. The detection is made even more difficult because people may approach treatment evaluation very unscientifically, often by simply noticing an improvement (or no improvement, or even a worsening of symptoms) and reaching a conclusion based on that sole observation. Determination of a treatment's effectiveness can be misdirected by illusions that can only be overcome by careful, scientific evaluation.

Treatment Illusions

Imagine you're sick and the doctor says, "Take a pill." You follow the doctor's orders, and you get better. To what do you attribute your improvement? If you're like most people, you reach the conclusion that the pill cured you. That's one possible explanation, but there are at least three others: Maybe you would have gotten better anyway; maybe the pill wasn't the active ingredient in your cure; or maybe after you're better, you mistakenly remember having been more ill than you really were. These possibilities point to three potential illusions of treatment: illusions produced by natural improvement, by placebo effects, and by reconstructive memory.

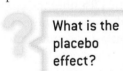

What are three kinds of treatment illusions?

placebo
An inert substance or procedure that has been applied with the expectation that a healing response will be produced.

Natural Improvement

Natural improvement is the tendency of symptoms to return to their mean or average level. The illusion in this case happens when you conclude mistakenly that a treatment has made you better when you would have gotten better anyway. People typically turn to therapy or medication when their symptoms are at their worst. When this is the case, the client's symptoms will often improve regardless of whether there was any treatment at all; when you're at rock bottom, there's nowhere to move but up. In most cases, for example, depression that becomes severe enough to make individuals candidates for treatment will tend to lift in several months *no matter what they do*. A person who enters therapy for depression may develop an illusion that the therapy works because the therapy coincides with the typical course of the illness and the person's natural return to health. How can we know if change was caused by the treatment or by natural improvement? As discussed in the Methods in Psychology chapter, we could do an experiment in which we assign half of the people who are depressed to receive treatment and the other half to receive no treatment, and then monitor them over time to see if the ones who got treatment actually show greater improvement. This is precisely how researchers test out different interventions, as described in more detail below.

Placebo Effects

Recovery could be produced by *nonspecific treatment effects* that are not related to the specific mechanisms by which treatment is supposed to be working. For example, the

What is the placebo effect?

doctor prescribing the medication might simply be a pleasant and hopeful individual who gives the client a sense of hope or optimism that things will improve. Client and doctor alike might attribute the client's improvement to the effects of medication on the brain, whereas the true active ingredient was the warm relationship with the doctor or improved outlook on life.

Simply knowing that you are getting a treatment can be a nonspecific treatment effect. These instances include the positive influences that can be produced by a **placebo**, *an inert substance or procedure that has been applied with the expectation that a healing response will be produced*. For example, if you take a sugar pill that does not contain any painkiller for a headache thinking it is Tylenol or aspirin, this pill is a placebo. Placebos can have profound effects in the case of psychological treatments. Research shows that a large percentage of individuals with anxiety, depression, and other emotional and medical problems experience significant improvement after a placebo treatment (see The Real World: This is Your Brain on Placebos, p. 571).

One recent study compared the decrease in symptoms of depression seen in 718 patients randomly assigned to receive either antidepressant medication or pill placebo (Fournier et al., 2010). Participants receiving medication showed a dramatic decrease in symptoms over the course of treatment. However, so did those taking placebo. Closer examination of the data revealed that for those with mild or moderate

"If this doesn't help you don't worry, it's a placebo."

PETER C. VEY/THE NEW YORKER COLLECTION/CARTOONBANK.COM

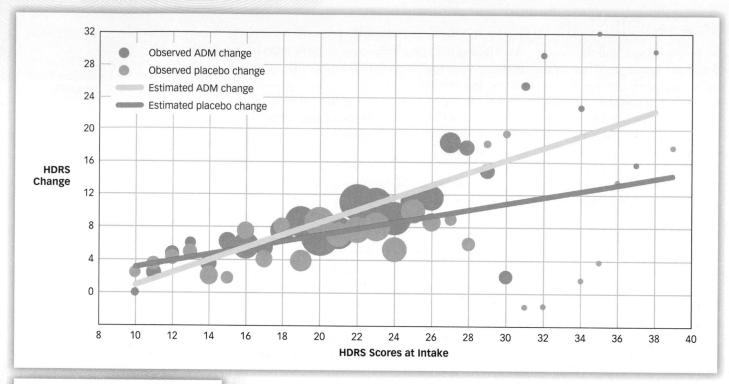

▲ Figure **16.7 Antidepressants versus Placebos for Depression** A total of 713 depressed individuals from six different studies were given pills to treat their depression. Half were randomly assigned to receive an antidepressant medication (ADM) and half to receive a pill placebo. Importantly, the participants did not know if they were taking an antidepressant or simply a placebo. For those with mild or moderate depression, as measured by the Hamilton Depression Rating Scale (HDRS), antidepressants did not work any better than placebo. However, those with severe depression showed much greater improvement on antidepressants than on placebo. The circle size represents the number of people with data at each point (from Fournier et al., 2010).

depression, placebo is just as effective as antidepressant medication at decreasing a person's symptoms, and it is only in instances of severe depression that antidepressants seem to work better than placebo (see **FIGURE 16.7**).

Reconstructive Memory

A third treatment illusion can come about when the client's motivation to get well causes errors in *reconstructive memory* for the original symptoms. You might think that you've improved because of a treatment when in fact you're simply misremembering: mistakenly believing that your symptoms before treatment were worse than they actually were. This tendency was first observed in research examining the effectiveness of a study skills class (Conway & Ross, 1984). Some students who wanted to take the class were enrolled, but others were randomly assigned to a waiting list until the class could be offered again. When their study abilities were measured afterward, those students who took the class were no better at studying than their wait-listed counterparts. However, those who took the class *said* that they had improved. How could this be? Those participants recalled their study skills before the class as being worse than they actually had been. This motivated reconstruction of the past was dubbed by Conway and Ross (1984), "Getting What You Want by Revising What You Had." A client who forms a strong expectation of success in therapy might conclude later that even a useless treatment had worked wonders by recalling past symptoms and troubles as worse than they were and thereby making the treatment seem effective.

Treatment Studies

How can we make sure that we are using treatments that actually work and not wasting time with procedures that may be useless or even harmful? Research psychologists use the approaches covered in the Methods in Psychology chapter to create experiments that test whether treatments are effective for the different mental disorders described in the previous chapter.

Treatment outcome studies are designed to evaluate whether a particular treatment works, often in relation to some other treatment or a control condition. For example, to study the outcome of treatment for depression, researchers might compare the self-reported symptoms of two groups of people who were initially depressed: those who received treatment for 6 weeks and a control group that had also been selected for the study but were assigned to a waiting list for later treatment and were simply tested 6 weeks after their selection. The outcome study could determine whether this treatment had any benefit.

Researchers use a range of methods to ensure that any observed effects are not due to the treatment illusions described earlier. For example, the treatment illusions caused by natural improvement and reconstructive memory happen when people compare their symptoms before treatment to their symptoms after treatment. To avoid this, a treatment (or experimental) group and a control group need to be randomly assigned to each condition and then compared at the end of treatment. That way, natural improvement or motivated reconstructive memory can't cause illusions of effective treatment.

Why is a double-blind experiment so important in assessing treatment effectiveness?

But what should happen to the control group during the treatment? If they simply stay home waiting until they can get treatment later (a wait-list control group), they won't receive the placebo effects. So, ideally, a treatment should be assessed in a *double-blind experiment*, a study in which both the participant and the researcher/therapist are uninformed about which treatment the participant is receiving. In the case of drug studies, this isn't hard to arrange because active drugs and placebos can be made to look alike to both the participants and the researchers during the study. Keeping both participants and researchers "in the dark" is much harder in the study of psychological treatments; in fact, in most cases it is not possible. Both the participant and the therapist can easily notice the differences in treatments such as psychoanalysis and behavior therapy, for example, so there's no way to keep the beliefs and expectations of both participant and therapist completely out of the picture in evaluating psychotherapy effectiveness. Nevertheless, by comparing treatments either to no treatment or to other active interventions (such as other psychological treatments or medications), researchers can determine which treatments work, and which are most effective for different disorders.

Which Treatments Work?

The distinguished psychologist Hans Eysenck (1916–1997) reviewed the relatively few studies of psychotherapy effectiveness available in 1957 and raised a furor among therapists by concluding that psychotherapy—particularly psychoanalysis—not only was ineffective but seemed to *impede* recovery (Eysenck, 1957). Much larger numbers of studies have been examined statistically since then, and they support a more optimistic conclusion: The typical psychotherapy client is better off than three quarters of untreated individuals

How do psychologists know which treatments work and which might be harmful?

(Seligman, 1995; Smith, Glass, & Miller, 1980). Although critiques of psychotherapy continue to point out weaknesses in how clients are tested, diagnosed, and treated (Baker, McFall, & Shoham, 2009; Dawes, 1994), strong evidence generally supports the effectiveness of many treatments (Nathan & Gorman, 2007), including psychodynamic therapy (Shedler, 2010). The key question then becomes: Which treatments are effective for which problems (Hunsley & Di Giulio, 2002)?

One of the most enduring debates in clinical psychology concerns how the various psychotherapies compare to one another. Some psychologists have argued for years that evidence supports the conclusion that most psychotherapies work about equally well. In this view, common factors shared by all forms of psychotherapy, such as

Table 16.3

Selected List of Specific Psychological Treatments Compared to Medication or Other Treatments

Disorder	Treatment	Results
Depression	CBT	PT = meds; PT+meds > either alone
Panic disorder	CBT	PT > meds at follow-up; PT=meds at end of treatment; both > placebo
Posttraumatic stress disorder	CBT	PT > present-centered therapy
Tourette's disorder	Habit reversal training	PT > supportive therapy
Insomnia	CBT	PT > medication or placebo
Depression and physical health in Alzheimer's patients	Exercise and behavioral management	PT > routine medical care
Gulf War Veterans' illnesses	CBT and exercise	PT > Usual care or alternative treatments

Note: CBT = cognitive behavior therapy; PT = psychological treatment; Meds = medication.
Source: Barlow et al. (2013).

Treatments that are shown to be effective in research studies (which often include only a small percentage of ethnic minority patients) have been found to work equally well with people of different ethnicities (Miranda et al., 2005).

iatrogenic illness
A disorder or symptom that occurs as a result of a medical or psychotherapeutic treatment itself.

contact with and empathy from a professional, contribute to change (Luborsky et al., 2002; Luborsky & Singer, 1975). In contrast, others have argued that there are important differences among therapies and that certain treatments are more effective than others, especially for treating particular types of problems (Beutler, 2002; Hunsley & Di Giulio, 2002). How can we make sense of these differing perspectives?

In 1995, the American Psychological Association (APA) published one of the first attempts to define criteria for determining whether a particular type of psychotherapy is effective for a particular problem (Task Force on Promotion and Dissemination of Psychological Procedures, 1995). The official criteria for empirically validated treatments defined two levels of empirical support: *well-established treatments,* those with a high level of support (e.g., evidence from several randomized controlled trials), and *probably efficacious treatments,* those with preliminary support. After these criteria were established, a list of empirically supported treatments was published by the APA (Chambless et al., 1998; Woody & Sanderson, 1998). A recent review of such treatments highlighted several specific psychological treatments that have been shown to work as well as, or even better than, other available treatments, including medication (Barlow et al., 2013). **TABLE 16.3** lists several of these treatments.

Some have questioned whether treatments shown to work in well-controlled studies conducted at university clinics will work in the real world. For instance, some have noted that most treatment studies reported in the literature do not have large numbers of participants who are of ethnic minority status, and so it is unclear if these treatments will work with ethnically and culturally diverse groups. One recent, comprehensive review of all available data suggests that although there are gaps in the literature, where there are data available, results suggest that current evidence-based psychological treatments work as well with ethnic minority clients as with White clients (Miranda et al., 2005).

Even trickier than the question of establishing whether a treatment works is whether a psychotherapy or medication might actually do harm. The dangers of drug treatment should be clear to anyone who has read a magazine ad for a drug and studied the fine print with its list of side effects, potential drug interactions, and complications. Many drugs used for psychological treatment may be addictive, creating long-term dependency with serious withdrawal symptoms. The strongest critics of drug treatment claim that drugs do no more than trade one unwanted symptom for another: depression for sexual disinterest, anxiety for intoxication, or agitation for lethargy and dulled emotion (e.g., see Breggin, 2000).

How might psychotherapy cause harm?

The dangers of psychotherapy are more subtle, but one is clear enough in some cases that there is actually a name for it. **Iatrogenic illness** is *a disorder or symptom that occurs as a result of a medical or psychotherapeutic treatment itself* (e.g., Boisvert & Faust, 2002). Such an illness might arise, for example, when a psychotherapist becomes convinced that a client has a disorder that in fact the client does not have. As a result, the therapist works to help the client accept that diagnosis and participate in psychotherapy to treat that disorder. Being treated for a disorder can, under certain

MARY KATE DENNY/PHOTOEDIT

conditions, make a person show signs of that very disorder—and so an iatrogenic illness is born.

There are cases of clients who have been influenced through hypnosis and repeated suggestions in therapy to believe that they have dissociative identity disorder (even coming to express multiple personalities) or to believe that they were subjected to traumatic events as a child and "recover" memories of such events when investigation reveals no evidence for these problems prior to therapy (Acocella, 1999; McNally, 2003; Ofshe & Watters, 1994). There are people who have entered therapy with a vague sense that something odd has happened to them and who emerge after hypnosis or other imagination-enhancing techniques with the conviction that their therapist's theory was right: They were abducted by space aliens (Clancy, 2005). Needless to say, a therapy that leads clients to develop such bizarre beliefs is doing more harm than good.

Just as psychologists have created lists of treatments that work, they also have begun to establish lists of treatments that *harm*. The purpose of doing so is to inform other researchers, clinicians, and the public which treatments they should avoid. Many are under the impression that although every psychological treatment may not be effective, some treatment is better than no treatment. However, it turns out that a number of interventions intended to help alleviate people's symptoms actually make them worse! Did your high school have a D.A.R.E. (Drug Abuse and Resistance Education) program? Have you heard of critical-incident stress debriefing (CISD), scared straight, and boot-camp programs? They all sound like they might work, but careful scientific experiments have determined that people who participate in these interventions are actually worse off after doing so (see **TABLE 16.4**; Lilienfeld, 2007)!

To regulate the potentially powerful influence of therapies, psychologists hold themselves to a set of ethical standards for the treatment of people with mental disorders (American Psychological Association, 2002). Adherence to these standards is required for membership in the American Psychological Association, and state licensing boards also monitor adherence to ethical principles in therapy. These ethical standards include (a) striving to benefit clients and taking care to do no harm; (b) establishing relationships of trust with clients; (c) promoting accuracy, honesty, and truthfulness; (d) seeking fairness in treatment and taking precautions to avoid biases; and (e) respecting the dignity and worth of all people. When people suffering from mental disorders come to psychologists for help, adhering to these guidelines is the least that psychologists can do. Ideally, in the hope of relieving this suffering, they can do much more.

Table 16.4		
Some Psychological Treatments that Cause Harm		
Type of Treatment	Potential Harm	Source of Evidence
CISD	Increased risk of PTSD	RCTs
Scared straight	Worsening of conduct problems	RCTs
Boot-camp interventions for conduct problems	Worsening of conduct problems	Meta-analysis (review of studies)
DARE programs	Increased use of alcohol and drugs	RCTs

Note. CISD = critical-incident stress debriefing; PTSD = posttraumatic stress disorder; RCTs = randomized controlled trials
Source: Lilienfeld (2007).

IN SUMMARY

▶ Observing improvement during treatment does not necessarily mean that the treatment was effective; it might instead reflect natural improvement, nonspecific treatment effects (e.g., the placebo effect), and reconstructive memory processes.

▶ Treatment studies focus on both treatment outcomes and processes, using scientific research methods such as double-blind techniques and placebo controls.

▶ Treatments for psychological disorders are generally more effective than no treatment at all, but some are more effective than others for certain disorders, and both medication and psychotherapy have dangers that ethical practitioners must consider carefully.

Chapter Review

KEY CONCEPT QUIZ

1. Which of the following is NOT a reason why people fail to get treatment for mental illness?
   a. People may not realize that their disorder needs to be treated.
   b. Levels of impairment for people with mental illness are comparable to or higher than those of people with chronic medical illnesses.
   c. There may be barriers to treatment, such as beliefs and circumstances that keep people from getting help.
   d. Even people who acknowledge they have a problem may not know where to look for services.

2. Eclectic psychotherapy
   a. concentrates on the interpretation of dreams.
   b. introduces clients to strange situations.
   c. draws on techniques from different forms of therapy.
   d. focuses on the analysis of resistance.

3. The different psychodynamic therapies all share an emphasis on
   a. the influence of the collective unconscious.
   b. the importance of taking responsibility for psychological problems.
   c. combining behavioral and cognitive approaches.
   d. developing insight into the unconscious sources of psychological disorders.

4. Which psychoanalytic technique involves the client reporting every thought that enters his or her mind, without censorship or filtering?
   a. transference
   b. free association
   c. interpretation
   d. resistance analysis

5. Which type of therapy would likely work best for someone with an irrational fear of heights?
   a. psychodynamic
   b. gestalt
   c. behavioral
   d. humanistic

6. Mindfulness meditation is part of which kind of therapy?
   a. interpersonal
   b. humanistic
   c. psychodynamic
   d. cognitive

7. Which type of therapy emphasizes action on the part of the client, as well as complete transparency as to the specifics of the treatment?
   a. cognitive behavioral
   b. humanistic
   c. existential
   d. group

8. Examining the failure to reach one's potential reflects the _____ approach, whereas examining one's failure to find meaning in life reflects the _____ approach.
   a. cognitive; behavioral
   b. humanistic; existential
   c. psychodynamic; cognitive behavioral
   d. existential; humanistic

9. Self-help groups are an important offshoot of
   a. cognitive behavioral therapy.
   b. support groups.
   c. person-centered therapy.
   d. group therapy.

10. Antipsychotic drugs were developed to treat
    a. depression.
    b. schizophrenia.
    c. anxiety.
    d. mood disorders.

11. Atypical antipsychotic drugs
    a. act on different neurotransmitters depending on the individual.
    b. affect only the dopamine system.
    c. affect only the serotonin system.
    d. act on both the dopamine and serotonin systems.

12. Which of the following statements is NOT accurate regarding antidepressants?
    a. Current antidepressants act on combinations of different neurotransmitter systems.
    b. Antidepressants have had significantly positive results in the treatment of bipolar disorder.
    c. Antidepressants are also prescribed to treat anxiety.
    d. Most antidepressants can take up to a month before they start to have an effect on mood.

13. What do electroconvulsive therapy, transcranial magnetic stimulation, and phototherapy all have in common?
    a. They incorporate herbal remedies in their treatment regimens.
    b. They may result in the surgical destruction of certain brain areas.
    c. They are considered biological treatments beyond medication.
    d. They are typically used in conjunction with psychotherapy.

14. Antidepressant medications have the strongest effects for people with _____ depression.
    a. no
    b. mild
    c. moderate
    d. severe

15. Current studies indicate that the typical psychotherapy client is better off than _____ of untreated individuals.
    a. one half
    b. the same number
    c. one fourth
    d. three fourths

KEY TERMS

psychotherapy (p. 633)

eclectic psychotherapy (p. 633)

psychodynamic psychotherapies (p. 633)

resistance (p. 634)

transference (p. 635)

interpersonal psychotherapy (IPT) (p. 635)

person-centered therapy (or client-centered therapy) (p. 636)

gestalt therapy (p. 636)

behavior therapy (p. 637)

token economy (p. 638)

exposure therapy (p. 638)

cognitive therapy (p. 639)

cognitive restructuring (p. 639)

mindfulness meditation (p. 641)

cognitive behavioral therapy (CBT) (p. 641)

group therapy (p. 643)

antipsychotic drugs (p. 646)

psychopharmacology (p. 648)

antianxiety medications (p. 649)

antidepressants (p. 649)

electroconvulsive therapy (ECT) (p. 654)

transcranial magnetic stimulation (TMS) (p. 655)

phototherapy (p. 655)

psychosurgery (p. 655)

placebo (p. 657)

iatrogenic illness (p. 658)

CHANGING MINDS

1. One of your friends recently lost a close family member in a tragic car accident, and he's devastated. He's not been attending classes, and when you check up on him, you learn that he's not sleeping well or eating regularly. You want to help him but feel a little out of your depth, so you suggest he visit the campus counseling center and talk to a therapist. "Only crazy people go to therapy," he says. What could you tell your friend to dispel his assumption?

2. While you're talking to your bereaved friend, his roommate comes in. The roommate agrees with your suggestion about therapy but takes it further. "I'll give you the name of my therapist. He helped me quit smoking—he'll be able to cure your depression in no time." Why is it dangerous to assume that a good therapist can cure anyone and anything?

3. In the Methods in Psychology chapter you read about Louise Hay, whose bestselling book, *You Can Heal Your Life,* promotes a kind of psychotherapy: teaching readers how to change their thoughts and thereby improve not only their inner lives but also their physical health. The chapter quotes Hay as saying that scientific evidence

is unnecessary to validate her claims. Is there a scientific basis for the major types of psychotherapy described in this chapter? How is scientific experimentation used to assess their effectiveness?

4. In June 2009, pop icon Michael Jackson died after receiving a fatal dose of the anesthetic propofol, which is sometimes used off-label as an antianxiety drug; autopsy confirmed that his body contained a cocktail of prescription drugs, including the benzodiazepines lorazepam and diazepam. (Jackson's cardiologist, Dr. Conrad Murray, was later convicted of involuntary manslaughter for administering the fatal dose.) Other celebrities whose deaths have been attributed to medications commonly prescribed for anxiety and depression include Heath Ledger in 2008 and Anna Nicole Smith in 2007. "These drugs are dangerous," your roommate notes. "People who have psychological problems should seek out talk therapy for their problems and stay away from the medications, even if they're prescribed by a responsible doctor." You agree that medications can be dangerous if misused, but how would you justify the use of drug treatment for serious mental disorders?

ANSWERS TO KEY CONCEPT QUIZ

1. b; 2. c; 3. d; 4. b; 5. c; 6. d; 7. a; 8. b; 9. d; 10. b; 11. d; 12. b; 13. c; 14. d; 15. d

Need more help? Additional resources are located in LaunchPad at:
http://www.worthpublishers.com/launchpad/ schacter3e

Glossary

absentmindedness A lapse in attention that results in memory failure. (p. 250)

absolute threshold The minimal intensity needed to just barely detect a stimulus in 50% of the trials. (p. 132)

accommodation The process by which infants revise their schemas in light of new information. (p. 434)

accommodation The process by which the eye maintains a clear image on the retina. (p. 138)

acetylcholine (ACh) A neurotransmitter involved in a number of functions, including voluntary motor control. (p. 88)

acquisition The phase of classical conditioning when the CS and the US are presented together. (p. 269)

action potential An electric signal that is conducted along a neuron's axon to a synapse. (p. 86)

activation–synthesis model The theory that dreams are produced when the brain attempts to make sense of random neural activity that occurs during sleep. (p. 201)

actor–observer effect The tendency to make situational attributions for our own behaviors while making dispositional attributions for the identical behavior of others. (p. 545)

adolescence The period of development that begins with the onset of sexual maturity (about 11 to 14 years of age) and lasts until the beginning of adulthood (about 18 to 21 years of age). (p. 451)

adulthood The stage of development that begins around 18 to 21 years and ends at death. (p. 460)

aggression Behavior with the purpose of harming another. (p. 508)

agonists Drugs that increase the action of a neurotransmitter. (p. 89)

agoraphobia A specific phobia involving a fear of public places. (p. 596)

alcohol myopia A condition that results when alcohol hampers attention, leading people to respond in simple ways to complex situations. (p. 208)

algorithm A well-defined sequence of procedures or rules that guarantees a solution to a problem. (p. 375)

altered state of consciousness A form of experience that departs significantly from the normal subjective experience of the world and the mind. (p. 193)

altruism Behavior that benefits another without benefiting oneself. (p. 516)

amygdala A part of the limbic system that plays a central role in many emotional processes, particularly the formation of emotional memories. (p. 99)

anal stage The second psychosexual stage, in which experience is dominated by the pleasures and frustrations associated with the anus, retention and expulsion of feces and urine, and toilet training. (p. 487)

analogical problem solving Solving a problem by finding a similar problem with a known solution and applying that solution to the current problem. (p. 383)

anorexia nervosa An eating disorder characterized by an intense fear of being fat and severe restriction of food intake. (p. 334)

antagonists Drugs that block the function of a neurotransmitter. (p. 89)

anterograde amnesia The inability to transfer new information from the short-term store into the long-term store. (p. 232)

antianxiety medications Drugs that help reduce a person's experience of fear or anxiety. (p. 649)

antidepressants A class of drugs that help lift people's moods. (p. 649)

antipsychotic drugs Medications that are used to treat schizophrenia and related psychotic disorders. (p. 646)

antisocial personality disorder (APD) A pervasive pattern of disregard for and violation of the rights of others that begins in childhood or early adolescence and continues into adulthood. (p. 620)

anxiety disorder The class of mental disorder in which anxiety is the predominant feature. (p. 593)

aphasia Difficulty in producing or comprehending language. (p. 362)

apparent motion The perception of movement as a result of alternating signals appearing in rapid succession in different locations. (p. 154)

appraisal An evaluation of the emotion-relevant aspects of a stimulus. (p. 319)

approach motivation A motivation to experience a positive outcome. (p. 345)

area A1 A portion of the temporal lobe that contains the primary auditory cortex. (p. 160)

area V1 The part of the occipital lobe that contains the primary visual cortex. (p. 143)

assimilation The process by which infants apply their schemas in novel situations. (p. 433)

association areas Areas of the cerebral cortex that are composed of neurons that help provide sense and meaning to information registered in the cortex. (p. 102)

attachment The emotional bond that forms between newborns and their primary caregivers. (p. 444)

attention deficit/hyperactivity disorder (ADHD) A persistent pattern of severe problems with inattention and/or hyperactivity or impulsiveness that cause significant impairments in functioning. (p. 616)

attitude An enduring positive or negative evaluation of an object or event. (p. 533)

attribution An inference about the cause of a person's behavior. (p. 543)

autism spectrum disorder (ASD) A condition beginning in early childhood in which a person shows persistent communication deficits as well as restricted and repetitive patterns of behaviors, interests, or activities. (p. 614)

autonomic nervous system (ANS) A set of nerves that carries involuntary and automatic commands that control blood vessels, body organs, and glands. (p. 93)

availability bias Items that are more readily available in memory are judged as having occurred more frequently. (p. 375)

avoidance motivation A motivation not to experience a negative outcome. (p. 345)

axon The part of a neuron that carries information to other neurons, muscles, or glands. (p. 81)

balanced placebo design A study design in which behavior is observed following the presence or absence of an actual stimulus and also following the presence or absence of a placebo stimulus. (p. 208)

basal ganglia A set of subcortical structures that directs intentional movements. (p. 100)

basilar membrane A structure in the inner ear that undulates when vibrations from the ossicles reach the cochlear fluid. (p. 159)

behavior Observable actions of human beings and nonhuman animals. (p. 3)

behavior therapy A type of therapy that assumes that disordered behavior is learned and that symptom relief is achieved through changing overt maladaptive behaviors into more constructive behaviors. (p. 637)

behavioral neuroscience An approach to psychology that links psychological processes to activities in the nervous system and other bodily processes. (p. 24)

behaviorism An approach that advocates that psychologists restrict themselves to the scientific study of objectively observable behavior. (p. 16)

belief An enduring piece of knowledge about an object or event. (p. 533)

belief bias People's judgments about whether to accept conclusions depend more on how believable the conclusions are than on whether the arguments are logically valid. (p. 390)

bias The distorting influences of present knowledge, beliefs, and feelings on recollection of previous experiences. (p. 256)

Big Five The traits of the five-factor model: openness to experience, conscientiousness, extraversion, agreeableness, and neuroticism. (p. 478)

binding problem How features are linked together so that we see unified objects in our visual world rather than free-floating or mis-combined features. (p. 146)

binocular disparity The difference in the retinal images of the two eyes that provides information about depth. (p. 152)

biofeedback The use of an external monitoring device to obtain information about a bodily function and possibly gain control over that function. (p. 564)

biological preparedness A propensity for learning particular kinds of associations over others. (p. 276)

biopsychosocial perspective Explains mental disorders as the result of interactions among biological, psychological, and social factors. (p. 587)

bipolar disorder A condition characterized by cycles of abnormal, persistent high mood (mania) and low mood (depression). (p. 605)

blind spot A location in the visual field that produces no sensation on the retina. (p. 140)

blocking A failure to retrieve information that is available in memory even though you are trying to produce it. (p. 252)

bulimia nervosa An eating disorder characterized by binge eating followed by purging. (p. 334)

burnout A state of physical, emotional, and mental exhaustion created by long-term involvement in an emotionally demanding situation and accompanied by lowered performance and motivation. (p. 559)

bystander intervention The act of helping strangers in an emergency situation. (p. 515)

Cannon–Bard theory The theory that a stimulus simultaneously triggers activity in the body and emotional experience in the brain. (p. 316)

case method A procedure for gathering scientific information by studying a single individual. (p. 64)

catatonic behavior A marked decrease in all movement or an increase in muscular rigidity and overactivity. (p. 609)

category-specific deficit A neurological syndrome that is characterized by an inability to recognize objects that belong to a particular category, although the ability to recognize objects outside the category is undisturbed. (p. 372)

cell body (or soma) The part of a neuron that coordinates information-processing tasks and keeps the cell alive. (p. 81)

central nervous system (CNS) The part of the nervous system that is composed of the brain and spinal cord. (p. 92)

cephalocaudal rule The "top-to-bottom" rule that describes the tendency for motor skills to emerge in sequence from the head to the feet. (p. 432)

cerebellum A large structure of the hindbrain that controls fine motor skills. (p. 96)

cerebral cortex The outermost layer of the brain, visible to the naked eye and divided into two hemispheres. (p. 97)

change blindness When people fail to detect changes to the visual details of a scene. (p. 154)

childhood The stage of development that begins at about 18 to 24 months and lasts until adolescence, which begins between 11 and 14 years. (p. 435)

chromosomes Strands of DNA wound around each other in a double-helix configuration. (p. 108)

chronic stressors Sources of stress that occur continuously or repeatedly. (p. 551)

chunking Combining small pieces of information into larger clusters or chunks that are more easily held in short-term memory. (p. 229)

circadian rhythm A naturally occurring 24-hour cycle. (p. 193)

classical conditioning A type of learning that occurs when a neutral stimulus produces a response after being paired with a stimulus that naturally produces a response. (p. 267)

cochlea A fluid-filled tube that is the organ of auditory transduction. (p. 159)

cocktail-party phenomenon A phenomenon in which people tune in one message even while they filter out others nearby. (p. 182)

cognitive behavioral therapy (CBT) A blend of cognitive and behavioral therapeutic strategies. (p. 641)

cognitive development The emergence of the ability to think and understand. (p. 433)

cognitive dissonance An unpleasant state that arises when a person recognizes the inconsistency of his or her actions, attitudes, or beliefs. (p. 536)

cognitive map A mental representation of the physical features of the environment. (p. 289)

cognitive neuroscience The field of study that attempts to understand the links between cognitive processes and brain activity. (p. 25)

cognitive psychology The scientific study of mental processes, including perception, thought, memory, and reasoning. (p. 22)

cognitive restructuring A therapeutic approach that teaches clients to question the automatic beliefs, assumptions, and predictions that often lead to negative emotions and to replace negative thinking with more realistic and positive beliefs. (p. 639)

cognitive symptoms Deficits in cognitive abilities, specifically executive functioning, attention, and working memory. (p. 609)

cognitive therapy Focuses on helping a client identify and correct any distorted thinking about self, others, or the world. (p. 639)

cognitive unconscious All the mental processes that give rise to a person's thoughts, choices, emotions, and behavior even though they are not experienced by the person. (p. 191)

color-opponent system Pairs of visual neurons that work in opposition. (p. 142)

common knowledge effect The tendency for group discussions to focus on information that all members share. (p. 514)

comorbidity The co-occurrence of two or more disorders in a single individual. (p. 587)

companionate love An experience involving affection, trust, and concern for a partner's well-being. (p. 524)

comparison level The cost–benefit ratio that people believe they deserve or could attain in another relationship. (p. 525)

concept A mental representation that groups or categorizes shared features of related objects, events, or other stimuli. (p. 369)

concrete operational stage The stage of cognitive development that begins at about 6 years and ends at about 11 years, during which children learn how various actions or "operations" can affect or transform "concrete" objects. (p. 436)

conditioned response (CR) A reaction that resembles an unconditioned response but is produced by a conditioned stimulus. (p. 268)

conditioned stimulus (CS) A previously neutral stimulus that produces a reliable response in an organism after being paired with a US. (p. 268)

conduct disorder A persistent pattern of deviant behavior involving aggression to people or animals, destruction of property, deceitfulness or theft, or serious rule violations. (p. 617)

cones Photoreceptors that detect color, operate under normal daylight conditions, and allow us to focus on fine detail. (p. 138)

conformity The tendency to do what others do simply because others are doing it. (p. 529)

conjunction fallacy When people think that two events are more likely to occur together than either individual event. (p. 376)

conscious motivations Motivations of which people are aware. (p. 344)

consciousness A person's subjective experience of the world and the mind. (pp. 8, 178)

conservation The notion that the quantitative properties of an object are invariant despite changes in the object's appearance. (p. 436)

consolidation The process by which memories become stable in the brain. (p. 232)

control group The group of people who are not exposed to the particular manipulation, as compared to the experimental group, in an experiment. (p. 59)

conventional stage A stage of moral development in which the morality of an action is primarily determined by the extent to which it conforms to social rules. (p. 448)

cooperation Behavior by two or more individuals that leads to mutual benefit. (p. 512)

corpus callosum A thick band of nerve fibers that connects large areas of the cerebral cortex on each side of the brain and supports communication of information across the hemispheres. (p. 101)

correlation coefficient A mathematical measure of both the direction and strength of a correlation, which is symbolized by the letter r. (p. 53)

correlation Two variables are said to "be correlated" when variations in the value of one variable are synchronized with variations in the value of the other. (p. 52)

correspondence bias The tendency to make a dispositional attribution even when we should instead make a situational attribution. (p. 544)

crystallized intelligence The ability to retain and use knowledge that was acquired through experience. (p. 405)

cultural psychology The study of how cultures reflect and shape the psychological processes of their members. (p. 28)

debriefing A verbal description of the true nature and purpose of a study. (p. 72)

deep structure The meaning of a sentence. (p. 354)

defense mechanisms Unconscious coping mechanisms that reduce anxiety generated by threats from unacceptable impulses. (p. 486)

deindividuation A phenomenon that occurs when immersion in a group causes people to become less aware of their individual values. (p. 514)

delusion A patently false belief system, often bizarre and grandiose, that is maintained in spite of its irrationality. (p. 608)

demand characteristics Those aspects of an observational setting that cause people to behave as they think someone else wants or expects. (p. 45)

dendrite The part of a neuron that receives information from other neurons and relays it to the cell body. (p. 81)

dependent variable The variable that is measured in a study. (p. 59)

depressants Substances that reduce the activity of the central nervous system. (p. 207)

developmental psychology The study of continuity and change across the life span. (p. 426)

deviation IQ A statistic obtained by dividing a person's test score by the average test score of people in the same age group and then multiplying the quotient by 100 (see ratio IQ). (p. 398)

Diagnostic and Statistical Manual of Mental Disorders (DSM) A classification system that describes the features used to diagnose each recognized mental disorder and indicates how the disorder can be distinguished from other, similar problems. (p. 586)

diathesis–stress model Suggests that a person may be predisposed for a psychological disorder that remains unexpressed until triggered by stress. (p. 589)

dichotic listening A task in which people wearing headphones hear different messages presented to each ear. (p. 182)

diffusion chain A process in which individuals initially learn a behavior by observing another individual perform that behavior, and then serve as a model from which other individuals learn the behavior. (p. 296)

diffusion of responsibility The tendency for individuals to feel diminished responsibility for their actions when they are surrounded by others who are acting the same way. (p. 514)

discrimination Positive or negative behavior toward another person based on their group membership. (p. 513)

discrimination The capacity to distinguish between similar but distinct stimuli. (p. 271)

disorganized speech A severe disruption of verbal communication in which ideas shift rapidly and incoherently among unrelated topics. (p. 608)

display rule A norm for the appropriate expression of emotion. (p. 326)

DNA methylation Adding a methyl group to DNA. (p. 110)

door-in-the-face technique An influence strategy that involves getting someone to deny an initial request (p. 529)

dopamine A neurotransmitter that regulates motor behavior, motivation, pleasure, and emotional arousal. (p. 88)

dopamine hypothesis The idea that schizophrenia involves an excess of dopamine activity. (p. 610)

double depression A moderately depressed mood that persists for at least 2 years and is punctuated by periods of major depression. (p. 602)

double-blind An observation whose true purpose is hidden from both the observer and the person being observed. (p. 47)

drive An internal state caused by physiological needs. (p. 333)

drug tolerance The tendency for larger doses of a drug to be required over time to achieve the same effect. (p. 205)

dynamic unconscious An active system encompassing a lifetime of hidden memories, the person's deepest instincts and desires, and the person's inner struggle to control these forces. (pp. 190, 485)

dysthymia The same cognitive and bodily problems as in depression are present, but they are less severe and last longer, persisting for at least 2 years. (p. 601)

echoic memory A fast-decaying store of auditory information. (p. 228)

eclectic psychotherapy A form of psychotherapy that involves drawing on techniques from different forms of therapy, depending on the client and the problem. (p. 633)

ego The component of personality, developed through contact with the external world, that enables us to deal with life's practical demands. (p. 485)

egocentrism The failure to understand that the world appears differently to different people. (p. 437)

electroconvulsive therapy (ECT) A treatment that involves inducing a brief seizure by delivering an electrical shock to the brain. (p. 654)

electroencephalograph (EEG) A device used to record electrical activity in the brain. (p. 118)

electrooculograph (EOG) An instrument that measures eye movements. (p. 194)

embryonic stage The period of prenatal development that lasts from the 2nd week until about the 8th week. (p. 427)

emotion A positive or negative experience that is associated with a particular pattern of physiological activity. (p. 316)

emotion regulation The strategies people use to influence their own emotional experience. (p. 320)

emotional expression An observable sign of an emotional state. (p. 322)

emotional intelligence The ability to reason about emotions and to use emotions to enhance reasoning. (p. 406)

empirical method A set of rules and techniques for observation. (p. 42)

empiricism The belief that accurate knowledge can be acquired through observation. (p. 40)

encoding specificity principle The idea that a retrieval cue can serve as an effective reminder when it helps re-create the specific way in which information was initially encoded. (p. 236)

encoding The process of transforming what we perceive, think, or feel into an enduring memory. (p. 222)

endorphins Chemicals that act within the pain pathways and emotion centers of the brain. (p. 89)

epigenetic marks Chemical modifications to DNA that can turn genes on or off. (p. 110)

epigenetics Environmental influences that determine whether or not genes are expressed, or the degree to which they are expressed, without altering the basic DNA sequences that constitute the genes themselves. (p. 110)

episodic memory The collection of past personal experiences that occurred at a particular time and place. (p. 244)

equity A state of affairs in which the cost–benefit ratios of two partners are roughly equal. (p. 525)

evolutionary psychology A psychological approach that explains mind and behavior in terms of the adaptive value of abilities that are preserved over time by natural selection. (p. 25)

exemplar theory A theory of categorization that argues that we make category judgments by comparing a new instance with stored memories for other instances of the category. (p. 371)

existential approach A school of thought that regards personality as governed by an individual's ongoing choices and decisions in the context of the realities of life and death. (p. 489)

expectancy theory The idea that alcohol effects can be produced by people's expectations of how alcohol will influence them in particular situations. (p. 208)

experiment A technique for establishing the causal relationship between variables. (p. 57)

experimental group The group of people who are exposed to a particular manipulation, as compared to the control group, in an experiment. (p. 59)

explicit memory The act of consciously or intentionally retrieving past experiences. (p. 242)

exposure therapy An approach to treatment that involves confronting an emotion-arousing stimulus directly and repeatedly, ultimately leading to a decrease in the emotional response. (p. 638)

expressed emotion A measure of how much hostility, criticism, and emotional overinvolvement are used when speaking about a family member with a mental disorder. (p. 607)

external validity An attribute of an experiment in which variables have been defined in a normal, typical, or realistic way. (p. 62)

extinction The gradual elimination of a learned response that occurs when the CS is repeatedly presented without the US. (p. 271)

extrinsic motivation A motivation to take actions that lead to reward. (p. 343)

facial feedback hypothesis Emotional expressions can cause the emotional experiences they signify. (p. 324)

factor analysis A statistical technique that explains a large number of correlations in terms of a small number of underlying factors. (p. 401)

false recognition A feeling of familiarity about something that hasn't been encountered before. (p. 254)

family resemblance theory Members of a category have features that appear to be characteristic of category members but may not be possessed by every member. (p. 370)

fast mapping The fact that children can map a word onto an underlying concept after only a single exposure. (p. 356)

feature-integration theory The idea that focused attention is not required to detect the individual features that comprise a stimulus, but is required to bind those individual features together. (p. 146)

fetal alcohol syndrome (FAS) A developmental disorder that stems from heavy alcohol use by the mother during pregnancy. (p. 429)

fetal stage The period of prenatal development that lasts from the 9th week until birth. (p. 428)

fight-or-flight response An emotional and physiological reaction to an emergency that increases readiness for action. (p. 554)

fixation A phenomenon in which a person's pleasure-seeking drives become psychologically stuck, or arrested, at a particular psychosexual stage. (p. 487)

fixed-interval schedule (FI) An operant conditioning principle in which reinforcers are presented at fixed-time periods, provided that the appropriate response is made. (p. 284)

fixed-ratio schedule (FR) An operant conditioning principle in which reinforcement is delivered after a specific number of responses have been made. (p. 285)

flashbulb memories Detailed recollections of when and where we heard about shocking events. (p. 258)

fluid intelligence The ability to see abstract relationships and draw logical inferences. (p. 405)

foot-in-the-door technique A technique that involves making a small request and following it with a larger request. (p. 535)

formal operational stage The final stage of cognitive development that begins around the age of 11, during which children learn to reason about abstract concepts. (p. 437)

fovea An area of the retina where vision is the clearest and there are no rods at all. (p. 140)

framing effects When people give different answers to the same problem depending on how the problem is phrased (or framed). (p. 377)

fraternal twins (or dizygotic twins) Twins who develop from two different eggs that were fertilized by two different sperm (see identical twins). (p. 408)

frequency distribution A graphical representation of measurements arranged by the number of times each measurement was made. (p. 48)

frequency format hypothesis The proposal that our minds evolved to notice how frequently things occur, not how likely they are to occur. (p. 379)

frontal lobe A region of the cerebral cortex that has specialized areas for movement, abstract thinking, planning, memory, and judgment. (p. 102)

frustration–aggression hypothesis A principle stating that animals aggress when their goals are thwarted. (p. 509)

full consciousness Consciousness in which you know and are able to report your mental state. (p. 184)

functional fixedness The tendency to perceive the functions of objects as fixed. (p. 385)

functionalism The study of the purpose mental processes serve in enabling people to adapt to their environment. (p. 11)

GABA (gamma-aminobutyric acid) The primary inhibitory neurotransmitter in the brain. (p. 88)

gate-control theory of pain A theory of pain perception based on the idea that signals arriving from pain receptors in the body can be stopped, or gated, by interneurons in the spinal cord via feedback from two directions. (p. 165)

gateway drug A drug whose use increases the risk of the subsequent use of more harmful drugs. (p. 212)

gene The major unit of hereditary transmission. (p. 108)

general adaptation syndrome (GAS) A three-stage physiological response that appears regardless of the stressor that is encountered. (p. 555)

generalization The CR is observed even though the CS is slightly different from the CS used during acquisition. (p. 271)

generalized anxiety disorder (GAD) A disorder characterized by chronic excessive worry accompanied by three or more of the following symptoms: restlessness, fatigue, concentration problems, irritability, muscle tension, and sleep disturbance. (p. 597)

genetic dysphasia A syndrome characterized by an inability to learn the grammatical structure of language despite having otherwise normal intelligence. (p. 360)

genital stage The fifth and final psychosexual stage, the time for the coming together of the mature adult personality with a capacity to love, work, and relate to others in a mutually satisfying and reciprocal manner. (p. 488)

germinal stage The 2-week period of prenatal development that begins at conception. (p. 427)

Gestalt psychology A psychological approach that emphasizes that we often perceive the whole rather than the sum of the parts. (p. 21)

gestalt therapy Has the goal of helping the client become aware of his or her thoughts, behaviors, experiences, and feelings and to "own" or take responsibility for them. (p. 636)

glial cells Support cells found in the nervous system. (p. 82)

glutamate The major excitatory neurotransmitter in the brain. (p. 88)

grammar A set of rules that specify how the units of language can be combined to produce meaningful messages. (p. 352)

grossly disorganized behavior Behavior that is inappropriate for the situation or ineffective in attaining goals, often with specific motor disturbances. (p. 608)

group A collection of people who have something in common that distinguishes them from others. (p. 513)

group polarization The tendency for groups to make decisions that are more extreme than any member would have made alone. (p. 514)

group therapy A technique in which multiple participants (who often do not know one another at the outset) work on their individual problems in a group atmosphere. (p. 643)

groupthink The tendency for groups to reach consensus in order to facilitate interpersonal harmony. (p. 514)

habituation A general process in which repeated or prolonged exposure to a stimulus results in a gradual reduction in responding. (p. 266)

hair cells Specialized auditory receptor neurons embedded in the basilar membrane. (p. 159)

hallucination A false perceptual experience that has a compelling sense of being real despite the absence of external stimulation. (p. 608)

hallucinogens Drugs that alter sensation and perception and often cause visual and auditory hallucinations. (p. 211)

haptic perception The active exploration of the environment by touching and grasping objects with our hands. (p. 163)

harm reduction approach A response to high-risk behaviors that focuses on reducing the harm such behaviors have on people's lives. (p. 213)

health psychology The subfield of psychology concerned with ways psychological factors influence the causes and treatment of physical illness and the maintenance of health. (p. 550)

hedonic principle The claim that people are motivated to experience pleasure and avoid pain. (p. 331)

helplessness theory The idea that individuals who are prone to depression automatically attribute negative experiences to causes that are internal (i.e., their own fault), stable (i.e., unlikely to change), and global (i.e., widespread). (p. 604)

heritability A measure of the variability of behavioral traits among individuals that can be accounted for by genetic factors. (p. 111)

heritability coefficient A statistic (commonly denoted as h^2) that describes the proportion of the difference between people's scores that can be explained by differences in their genes. (p. 409)

heuristic A fast and efficient strategy that may facilitate decision making but does not guarantee that a solution will be reached. (p. 375)

heuristic persuasion The process by which attitudes or beliefs are changed by appeals to habit or emotion. (p. 534)

hindbrain An area of the brain that coordinates information coming into and out of the spinal cord. (p. 96)

hippocampus A structure critical for creating new memories and integrating them into a network of knowledge so that they can be stored indefinitely in other parts of the cerebral cortex. (p. 99)

histone modification Adding chemical modifications to proteins called histones that are involved in packaging DNA. (p. 110)

homeostasis The tendency for a system to take action to keep itself in a particular state. (p. 332)

human sexual response cycle The stages of physiological arousal during sexual activity. (p. 340)

humanistic psychology An approach to understanding human nature that emphasizes the positive potential of human beings. (p. 14)

hypnosis A social interaction in which one person (the hypnotist) makes suggestions that lead to a change in another person's (the subject's) subjective experience of the world. (p. 214)

hypnotic analgesia The reduction of pain through hypnosis in people who are susceptible to hypnosis. (p. 215)

hypothalamus A subcortical structure that regulates body temperature, hunger, thirst, and sexual behavior. (p. 98)

hypothesis A falsifiable prediction made by a theory. (p. 41)

hysteria A temporary loss of cognitive or motor functions, usually as a result of emotionally upsetting experiences. (p. 13)

iatrogenic illness A disorder or symptom that occurs as a result of a medical or psychotherapeutic treatment itself. (p. 660)

iconic memory A fast-decaying store of visual information. (p. 228)

id The part of the mind containing the drives present at birth; it is the source of our bodily needs, wants, desires, and impulses, particularly our sexual and aggressive drives. (p. 485)

identical twins (or monozygotic twins) Twins who develop from the splitting of a single egg that was fertilized by a single sperm (see fraternal twins). (p. 408)

illusions Errors of perception, memory, or judgment in which subjective experience differs from objective reality. (p. 20)

illusory conjunction A perceptual mistake where features from multiple objects are incorrectly combined. (p. 146)

immune system A complex response system that protects the body from bacteria, viruses, and other foreign substances. (p. 557)

implicit learning Learning that takes place largely independent of awareness of both the process and the products of information acquisition. (p. 300)

implicit memory The influence of past experiences on later behavior and performance, even without an effort to remember them or an awareness of the recollection. (p. 242)

inattentional blindness A failure to perceive objects that are not the focus of attention. (p. 155)

independent variable The variable that is manipulated in an experiment. (p. 59)

infancy The stage of development that begins at birth and lasts between 18 and 24 months. (p. 431)

informational influence A phenomenon that occurs when another person's behavior provides information about what is true. (p. 533)

informed consent A written agreement to participate in a study made by an adult who has been informed of all the risks that participation may entail. (p. 71)

insomnia Difficulty in falling asleep or staying asleep. (p. 197)

instrument Anything that can detect the condition to which an operational definition refers. (p. 44)

intelligence The ability to direct one's thinking, adapt to one's circumstances, and learn from one's experiences. (p. 396)

intermittent reinforcement An operant conditioning principle in which only some of the responses made are followed by reinforcement. (p. 285)

intermittent reinforcement effect The fact that operant behaviors that are maintained under intermittent reinforcement schedules resist extinction better than those maintained under continuous reinforcement. (p. 286)

internal validity An attribute of an experiment that allows it to establish causal relationships. (p. 62)

internal working model of relationships A set of beliefs about the self, the primary caregiver, and the relationship between them. (p. 445)

interneurons Neurons that connect sensory neurons, motor neurons, or other interneurons. (p. 83)

interpersonal psychotherapy (IPT) A form of psychotherapy that focuses on helping clients improve current relationships. (p. 635)

intrinsic motivation A motivation to take actions that are themselves rewarding. (p. 342)

introspection The subjective observation of one's own experience. (p. 9)

ironic processes of mental control Mental processes that can produce ironic errors because monitoring for errors can itself produce them. (p. 189)

James–Lange theory The theory that a stimulus triggers activity in the body, which in turn produces an emotional experience in the brain. (p. 316)

just noticeable difference (JND) The minimal change in a stimulus that can just barely be detected. (p. 132)

kin selection The process by which evolution selects for individuals who cooperate with their relatives. (p. 516)

language A system for communicating with others using signals that are combined according to rules of grammar and convey meaning. (p. 352)

language acquisition device (lad) A collection of processes that facilitate language learning. (p. 360)

latency stage The fourth psychosexual stage, in which the primary focus is on the further development of intellectual, creative, interpersonal, and athletic skills. (p. 487)

latent content A dream's true underlying meaning. (p. 200)

latent learning Something is learned, but it is not manifested as a behavioral change until sometime in the future. (p. 288)

law of effect Behaviors that are followed by a "satisfying state of affairs" tend to be repeated and those that produce an "unpleasant state of affairs" are less likely to be repeated. (p. 278)

learning The acquisition of new knowledge, skills, or responses from experience that results in a relatively permanent change in the state of the learner. (p. 266)

limbic system A group of forebrain structures including the hypothalamus, the hippocampus, and the amygdala, which are involved in motivation, emotion, learning, and memory. (p. 99)

linguistic relativity hypothesis The proposal that language shapes the nature of thought. (p. 367)

locus of control A person's tendency to perceive the control of rewards as internal to the self or external in the environment. (p. 493)

long-term memory A type of storage that holds information for hours, days, weeks, or years. (p. 231)

long-term potentiation (LTP) A process whereby communication across the synapse between neurons strengthens the connection, making further communication easier. (p. 235)

loudness A sound's intensity. (p. 157)

lymphocytes White blood cells that produce antibodies that fight infection, including T cells and B cells. (p. 557)

major depressive disorder (or unipolar depression) A disorder characterized by a severely depressed mood and/or inability to experience pleasure that lasts 2 or more weeks and is accompanied by feelings of worthlessness, lethargy, and sleep and appetite disturbance. (p. 601)

manifest content A dream's apparent topic or superficial meaning. (p. 200)

manipulation Changing a variable in order to determine its causal power. (p. 58)

marijuana The leaves and buds of the hemp plant, which contain a psychoactive drug called tetrahydrocannabinol (THC). (p. 211)

matched pairs A technique whereby each participant is identical to one other participant in terms of a third variable. (p. 56)

matched samples A technique whereby the participants in two groups are identical in terms of a third variable. (p. 55)

mean The average value of all the measurements. (p. 49)

means–ends analysis A process of searching for the means or steps to reduce differences between the current situation and the desired goal. (p. 382)

median The value that is in the middle; that is, greater than or equal to half the measurements and less than or equal to half the measurements. (p. 49)

medical model Abnormal psychological experiences are conceptualized as illnesses that, like physical illnesses, have biological and environmental causes, defined symptoms, and possible cures. (p. 585)

meditation The practice of intentional contemplation. (p. 563)

medulla An extension of the spinal cord into the skull that coordinates heart rate, circulation, and respiration. (p. 96)

memory misattribution Assigning a recollection or an idea to the wrong source. (p. 253)

memory The ability to store and retrieve information over time. (p. 222)

mental control The attempt to change conscious states of mind. (p. 188)

mental disorder A persistent disturbance or dysfunction in behavior, thoughts, or emotions that causes significant distress or impairment. (p. 584)

mere exposure effect The tendency for liking to increase with the frequency of exposure. (p. 519)

metabolism The rate at which energy is used by the body. (p. 338)

mind The private inner experience of perceptions, thoughts, memories, and feelings. (p. 2)

mind–body problem The issue of how the mind is related to the brain and the body. (p. 180)

mindfulness meditation Teaches an individual to be fully present in each moment; to be aware of his or her thoughts, feelings, and sensations; and to detect symptoms before they become a problem. (p. 641)

minimal consciousness A low-level kind of sensory awareness and responsiveness that occurs when the mind inputs sensations and may output behavior. (p. 184)

Minnesota Multiphasic Personality Inventory (MMPI) A well-researched, clinical questionnaire used to assess personality and psychological problems. (p. 474)

mirror neurons Neurons that are active when an animal performs a behavior, such as reaching for or manipulating an object, and are also activated when another animal observes that animal performing the same behavior. (p. 103)

mode The value of the most frequently observed measurement. (p. 49)

monocular depth cues Aspects of a scene that yield information about depth when viewed with only one eye. (p. 150)

mood disorders Mental disorders that have mood disturbance as their predominant feature. (p. 601)

morphemes The smallest meaningful units of language. (p. 353)

morphological rules A set of rules that indicate how morphemes can be combined to form words. (p. 353)

motivation The purpose for or psychological cause of an action. (p. 330)

motor development The emergence of the ability to execute physical action. (p. 431)

motor neurons Neurons that carry signals from the spinal cord to the muscles to produce movement. (p. 82)

myelin sheath An insulating layer of fatty material. (p. 82)

myelination The formation of a fatty sheath around the axons of a neuron. (p. 428)

narcissism A trait that reflects a grandiose view of the self combined with a tendency to seek admiration from and exploit others. (p. 501)

narcolepsy A disorder in which sudden sleep attacks occur in the middle of waking activities. (p. 198)

narcotics (or opiates) Highly addictive drugs derived from opium that relieve pain. (p. 210)

nativism The philosophical view that certain kinds of knowledge are innate or inborn. (p. 6)

nativist theory The view that language development is best explained as an innate, biological capacity. (p. 360)

natural correlation A correlation observed in the world around us. (p. 54)

natural selection Charles Darwin's theory that the features of an organism that help it survive and reproduce are more likely than other features to be passed on to subsequent generations. (p. 11)

naturalistic observation A technique for gathering scientific information by unobtrusively observing people in their natural environments. (p. 45)

need for achievement The motivation to solve worthwhile problems. (p. 344)

negative symptoms Deficits or disruptions to normal emotions and behaviors (e.g., emotional and social withdrawal; apathy; poverty of speech; and other indications of the absence or insufficiency of normal behavior, motivation, and emotion). (p. 609)

nervous system An interacting network of neurons that conveys electrochemical information throughout the body. (p. 92)

neurons Cells in the nervous system that communicate with one another to perform information-processing tasks. (p. 80)

neurotransmitters Chemicals that transmit information across the synapse to a receiving neuron's dendrites. (p. 87)

night terrors (or sleep terrors) Abrupt awakenings with panic and intense emotional arousal. (p. 199)

nonshared environment Those environmental factors that are not experienced by all relevant members of a household (see shared environment). (p. 410)

nonsuicidal self-injury (NSSI) Direct, deliberate destruction of body tissue in the absence of any intent to die. (p. 622)

norepinephrine A neurotransmitter that is particularly involved in states of vigilance, or heightened awareness of dangers in the environment. (p. 88)

norm of reciprocity The unwritten rule that people should benefit those who have benefited them. (p. 528)

normal distribution A mathematically defined distribution in which the frequency of measurements is highest in the middle and decreases symmetrically in both directions. (p. 48)

normative influence A phenomenon that occurs when another person's behavior provides information about what is appropriate. (p. 529)

norms Customary standards for behavior that are widely shared by members of a culture. (p. 528)

obedience The tendency to do what powerful people tell us to do. (p. 531)

object permanence The belief that objects continue to exist even when they are not visible. (p. 434)

observational learning A condition in which learning takes place by watching the actions of others. (p. 295)

obsessive-compulsive disorder (OCD) A disorder in which repetitive, intrusive thoughts (obsessions) and ritualistic behaviors (compulsions) designed to fend off those thoughts interfere significantly with an individual's functioning. (p. 598)

occipital lobe A region of the cerebral cortex that processes visual information. (p. 101)

Oedipus conflict A developmental experience in which a child's conflicting feelings toward the opposite-sex parent are (usually) resolved by identifying with the same-sex parent. (p. 487)

olfactory bulb A brain structure located above the nasal cavity beneath the frontal lobes. (p. 168)

olfactory receptor neurons (ORNs) Receptor cells that initiate the sense of smell. (p. 167)

operant behavior Behavior that an organism produces that has some impact on the environment. (p. 278)

operant conditioning A type of learning in which the consequences of an organism's behavior determine whether it will be repeated in the future. (p. 277)

operational definition A description of a property in concrete, measurable terms. (p. 44)

oral stage The first psychosexual stage, in which experience centers on the pleasures and frustrations associated with the mouth, sucking, and being fed. (p. 487)

organizational encoding The process of categorizing information according to the relationships among a series of items. (p. 225)

outcome expectancies A person's assumptions about the likely consequences of a future behavior. (p. 493)

panic disorder A disorder characterized by the sudden occurrence of multiple psychological and physiological symptoms that contribute to a feeling of stark terror. (p. 596)

parasympathetic nervous system A set of nerves that helps the body return to a normal resting state. (p. 94)

parietal lobe A region of the cerebral cortex whose functions include processing information about touch. (p. 101)

passionate love An experience involving feelings of euphoria, intimacy, and intense sexual attraction. (p. 524)

perception The organization, identification, and interpretation of a sensation in order to form a mental representation. (p. 130)

perceptual confirmation The tendency for people to see what they expect to see. (p. 541)

perceptual constancy A perceptual principle stating that even as aspects of sensory signals change, perception remains consistent. (p. 148)

peripheral nervous system (PNS) The part of the nervous system that connects the central nervous system to the body's organs and muscles. (p. 92)

persistence The intrusive recollection of events that we wish we could forget. (p. 258)

person-centered therapy (or client-centered therapy) Assumes that all individuals have a tendency toward growth and that this growth can be facilitated by acceptance and genuine reactions from the therapist. (p. 636)

person–situation controversy The question of whether behavior is caused more by personality or by situational factors. (p. 491)

personal constructs Dimensions people use in making sense of their experiences. (p. 492)

personality An individual's characteristic style of behaving, thinking, and feeling. (p. 472)

personality disorders Enduring patterns of thinking, feeling, or relating to others or controlling impulses that deviate from cultural expectations and cause distress or impaired functioning. (p. 618)

persuasion A phenomenon that occurs when a person's attitudes or beliefs are influenced by a communication from another person. (p. 534)

phallic stage The third psychosexual stage, in which experience is dominated by the pleasure, conflict, and frustration associated with the phallic-genital region as well as coping with powerful incestuous feelings of love, hate, jealousy, and conflict. (p. 487)

phenomenology How things seem to the conscious person. (p. 179)

pheromones Biochemical odorants emitted by other members of its species that can affect an animal's behavior or physiology. (p. 170)

philosophical empiricism The view that all knowledge is acquired through experience. (p. 6)

phobic disorders Disorders characterized by marked, persistent, and excessive fear and avoidance of specific objects, activities, or situations. (p. 594)

phoneme The smallest unit of sound that is recognizable as speech rather than as random noise. (p. 353)

phonological rules A set of rules that indicate how phonemes can be combined to produce speech sounds. (p. 353)

phototherapy A therapy that involves repeated exposure to bright light. (p. 655)

phrenology A now defunct theory that specific mental abilities and characteristics, ranging from memory to the capacity for happiness, are localized in specific regions of the brain. (p. 6)

physiology The study of biological processes, especially in the human body. (p. 7)

pitch How high or low a sound is. (p. 157)

pituitary gland The "master gland" of the body's hormone-producing system, which releases hormones that direct the functions of many other glands in the body. (p. 99)

place code The process by which different frequencies stimulate neural signals at specific places along the basilar membrane, from which the brain determines pitch. (p. 160)

placebo An inert substance or procedure that has been applied with the expectation that a healing response will be produced. (p. 657)

pons A brain structure that relays information from the cerebellum to the rest of the brain. (p. 96)

population A complete collection of participants who might possibly be measured. (p. 63)

positive symptoms Thoughts and behaviors present in schizophrenia but not seen in those without the disorder, such as delusions and hallucinations. (p. 608)

postconventional stage A stage of moral development in which the morality of an action is determined by a set of general principles that reflect core values. (p. 448)

posthypnotic amnesia The failure to retrieve memories following hypnotic suggestions to forget. (p. 214)

posttraumatic stress disorder (PTSD) A disorder characterized by chronic physiological arousal, recurrent unwanted thoughts or images of the trauma, and avoidance of things that call the traumatic event to mind. (p. 599)

power An instrument's ability to detect small magnitudes of the property. (p. 44)

practical reasoning Figuring out what to do, or reasoning directed toward action. (p. 388)

preconventional stage A stage of moral development in which the morality of an action is primarily determined by its consequences for the actor. (p. 448)

prejudice A positive or negative evaluation of another person based on their group membership. (p. 513)

preoperational stage The stage of cognitive development that begins at about 2 years and ends at about 6 years, during which children develop a preliminary understanding of the physical world. (p. 434)

preparedness theory The idea that people are instinctively predisposed toward certain fears. (p. 594)

primary sex characteristics Bodily structures that are directly involved in reproduction. (p. 452)

priming An enhanced ability to think of a stimulus, such as a word or object, as a result of a recent exposure to the stimulus. (p. 243)

proactive interference Situations in which information learned earlier impairs memory for information acquired later. (p. 250)

problem of other minds The fundamental difficulty we have in perceiving the consciousness of others. (p. 179)

procedural memory The gradual acquisition of skills as a result of practice, or "knowing how" to do things. (p. 242)

projective tests Tests designed to reveal inner aspects of individuals' personalities by analysis of their responses to a standard series of ambiguous stimuli. (p. 474)

prospect theory People choose to take on risk when evaluating potential losses and avoid risks when evaluating potential gains. (p. 378)

prospective memory Remembering to do things in the future. (p. 251)

prototype The "best" or "most typical" member of a category. (p. 370)

proximodistal rule The "inside-to-outside" rule that describes the tendency for motor skills to emerge in sequence from the center to the periphery. (p. 432)

psychoactive drugs Chemicals that influence consciousness or behavior by altering the brain's chemical message system. (p. 204)

psychoanalysis A therapeutic approach that focuses on bringing unconscious material into conscious awareness to better understand psychological disorders. (p. 14)

psychoanalytic theory An approach that emphasizes the importance of unconscious mental processes in shaping feelings, thoughts, and behavior. (p. 13)

psychodynamic approach An approach that regards personality as formed by needs, strivings, and desires largely operating outside of awareness—motives that also can produce emotional disorders. (p. 484)

psychodynamic psychotherapies Therapies that explore childhood events and encourage individuals to use this understanding to develop insight into their psychological problems. (p. 633)

psychology The scientific study of mind and behavior. (p. 2)

psychopharmacology The study of drug effects on psychological states and symptoms. (p. 648)

psychophysics Methods that measure the strength of a stimulus and the observer's sensitivity to that stimulus. (p. 132)

psychosexual stages Distinct early life stages through which personality is formed as children experience sexual pleasures from specific body areas and caregivers redirect or interfere with those pleasures. (p. 487)

psychosomatic illness An interaction between mind and body that can produce illness. (p. 572)

psychosurgery Surgical destruction of specific brain areas. (p. 655)

psychotherapy An interaction between a socially sanctioned clinician and someone suffering from a psychological problem, with the goal of providing support or relief from the problem. (p. 633)

puberty The bodily changes associated with sexual maturity. (p. 452)

punisher Any stimulus or event that functions to decrease the likelihood of the behavior that led to it. (p. 279)

random assignment A procedure that lets chance assign people to the experimental or control group. (p. 60)

random sampling A technique for choosing participants that ensures that every member of a population has an equal chance of being included in the sample. (p. 64)

range The value of the largest measurement in a frequency distribution minus the value of the smallest measurement. (p. 50)

ratio IQ A statistic obtained by dividing a person's mental age by the person's physical age and then multiplying the quotient by 100 (see deviation IQ). (p. 398)

rational choice theory The classical view that we make decisions by determining how likely something is to happen, judging the value of the outcome, and then multiplying the two. (p. 374)

rational coping Facing a stressor and working to overcome it. (p. 561)

reaction time The amount of time taken to respond to a specific stimulus. (p. 8)

reappraisal Changing one's emotional experience by changing the way one thinks about the emotion-eliciting stimulus. (p. 321)

reasoning A mental activity that consists of organizing information or beliefs into a series of steps in order to reach conclusions. (p. 388)

rebound effect of thought suppression The tendency of a thought to return to consciousness with greater frequency following suppression. (p. 189)

receptors Parts of the cell membrane that receive the neurotransmitter and initiate or prevent a new electric signal. (p. 87)

reciprocal altruism Behavior that benefits another with the expectation that those benefits will be returned in the future. (p. 517)

reconsolidation Memories can become vulnerable to disruption when they are recalled, requiring them to become consolidated again. (p. 234)

referred pain Feeling of pain when sensory information from internal and external areas converges on the same nerve cells in the spinal cord. (p. 164)

reflexes Specific patterns of motor response that are triggered by specific patterns of sensory stimulation. (p. 431)

refractory period The time following an action potential during which a new action potential cannot be initiated. (p. 86)

reframing Finding a new or creative way to think about a stressor that reduces its threat. (p. 562)

rehearsal The process of keeping information in short-term memory by mentally repeating it. (p. 229)

reinforcement The consequences of a behavior determine whether it will be more or less likely to occur again. (p. 18)

reinforcer Any stimulus or event that functions to increase the likelihood of the behavior that led to it. (p. 279)

relaxation response A condition of reduced muscle tension, cortical activity, heart rate, breathing rate, and blood pressure. (p. 564)

relaxation therapy A technique for reducing tension by consciously relaxing muscles of the body. (p. 564)

reliability The tendency for an instrument to produce the same measurement whenever it is used to measure the same thing. (p. 44)

REM sleep A stage of sleep characterized by rapid eye movements and a high level of brain activity. (p. 194)

representativeness heuristic A mental shortcut that involves making a probability judgment by comparing an object or event to a prototype of the object or event. (p. 377)

repression A mental process that removes unacceptable thoughts and memories from consciousness and keeps them in the unconscious. (p. 190)

repressive coping Avoiding situations or thoughts that are reminders of a stressor and maintaining an artificially positive viewpoint. (p. 561)

Research Domain Criteria Project (RDoC) A new initiative that aims to guide the classification and understanding of mental disorders by revealing the basic processes that give rise to them. (p. 590)

resistance A reluctance to cooperate with treatment for fear of confronting unpleasant unconscious material. (p. 634)

response An action or physiological change elicited by a stimulus. (p. 18)

resting potential The difference in electric charge between the inside and outside of a neuron's cell membrane. (p. 84)

reticular formation A brain structure that regulates sleep, wakefulness, and levels of arousal. (p. 96)

retina Light-sensitive tissue lining the back of the eyeball. (p. 138)

retrieval cue External information that is associated with stored information and helps bring it to mind. (p. 236)

retrieval The process of bringing to mind information that has been previously encoded and stored. (p. 222)

retrieval-induced forgetting A process by which retrieving an item from long-term memory impairs subsequent recall of related items. (p. 238)

retroactive interference Situations in which information learned later impairs memory for information acquired earlier. (p. 250)

retrograde amnesia The inability to retrieve information that was acquired before a particular date, usually the date of an injury or surgery. (p. 232)

rods Photoreceptors that become active under low-light conditions for night vision. (p. 138)

Rorschach Inkblot Test A projective technique in which respondents' inner thoughts and feelings are believed to be revealed by analysis of their responses to a set of unstructured inkblots. (p. 474)

sample A partial collection of people drawn from a population. (p. 64)

schemas Theories about the way the world works. (p. 433)

schizophrenia A disorder characterized by the profound disruption of basic psychological processes; a distorted perception of reality; altered or blunted emotion; and disturbances in thought, motivation, and behavior. (p. 607)

scientific method A procedure for finding truth by using empirical evidence. (p. 40)

seasonal affective disorder (SAD) Recurrent depressive episodes in a seasonal pattern. (p. 602)

second-order conditioning Conditioning where a CS is paired with a stimulus that became associated with the US in an earlier procedure. (p. 269)

secondary sex characteristics Bodily structures that change dramatically with sexual maturity but that are not directly involved in reproduction. (p. 452)

self-actualizing tendency The human motive toward realizing our inner potential. (p. 488)

self-concept A person's explicit knowledge of his or her own behaviors, traits, and other personal characteristics. (p. 495)

self-consciousness A distinct level of consciousness in which the person's attention is drawn to the self as an object. (p. 184)

self-esteem The extent to which an individual likes, values, and accepts the self. (p. 498)

self-fulfilling prophecy The tendency for people to behave as they are expected to behave. (p. 541)

self-regulation The exercise of voluntary control over the self to bring the self into line with preferred standards. (p. 576)

self-report A method in which a person provides subjective information about their own thoughts, feelings, or behaviors, typically via questionnaire or interview. (p. 473)

self-selection A problem that occurs when anything about a person determines whether he or she will be included in the experimental or control group. (p. 59)

self-serving bias People's tendency to take credit for their successes but downplay responsibility for their failures. (p. 500)

self-verification The tendency to seek evidence to confirm the self-concept. (p. 497)

semantic encoding The process of relating new information in a meaningful way to knowledge that is already in memory. (p. 224)

semantic memory A network of associated facts and concepts that make up our general knowledge of the world. (p. 244)

sensation Simple stimulation of a sense organ. (p. 130)

sensitization A simple form of learning that occurs when presentation of a stimulus leads to an increased response to a later stimulus. (p. 266)

sensorimotor stage A stage of development that begins at birth and lasts through infancy in which infants acquire information about the world by sensing it and moving around within it. (p. 433)

sensory adaptation Sensitivity to prolonged stimulation tends to decline over time as an organism adapts to current conditions. (p. 135)

sensory memory A type of storage that holds sensory information for a few seconds or less. (p. 228)

sensory neurons Neurons that receive information from the external world and convey this information to the brain via the spinal cord. (p. 82)

serotonin A neurotransmitter that is involved in the regulation of sleep and wakefulness, eating, and aggressive behavior. (p. 88)

shaping Learning that results from the reinforcement of successive steps to a final desired behavior. (p. 286)

shared environment Those environmental factors that are experienced by all relevant members of a household (see nonshared environment). (p. 410)

short-term memory A type of storage that holds nonsensory information for more than a few seconds but less than a minute. (p. 229)

sick role A socially recognized set of rights and obligations linked with illness. (p. 572)

signal detection theory The response to a stimulus depends both on a person's sensitivity to the stimulus in the presence of noise and on a person's response criterion. (p. 134)

sleep apnea A disorder in which the person stops breathing for brief periods while asleep. (p. 198)

sleep paralysis The experience of waking up unable to move. (p. 198)

social cognition The processes by which people come to understand others. (p. 537)

social-cognitive approach An approach that views personality in terms of how the person thinks about the situations encountered in daily life and behaves in response to them. (p. 490)

social exchange The hypothesis that people remain in relationships only as long as they perceive a favorable ratio of costs to benefits. (p. 525)

social influence The ability to control another person's behavior (p. 526)

social loafing The tendency for people to expend less effort when in a group than when alone. (p. 514)

social phobia A disorder that involves an irrational fear of being publicly humiliated or embarrassed. (p. 594)

social psychology The study of the causes and consequences of sociality. (pp. 27, 508)

social support The aid gained through interacting with others. (p. 566)

somatic nervous system A set of nerves that conveys information between voluntary muscles and the central nervous system. (p. 92)

somatic symptom disorders The set of psychological disorders in which a person with at least one bodily symptom displays significant health-related anxiety, expresses disproportionate concerns about their symptoms, and devotes excessive time and energy to their symptoms or health concerns. (p. 572)

somnambulism (or sleepwalking) Occurs when a person arises and walks around while asleep. (p. 198)

source memory Recall of when, where, and how information was acquired. (p. 253)

specific phobia A disorder that involves an irrational fear of a particular object or situation that markedly interferes with an individual's ability to function. (p. 594)

spinal reflexes Simple pathways in the nervous system that rapidly generate muscle contractions. (p. 94)

spontaneous recovery The tendency of a learned behavior to recover from extinction after a rest period. (p. 271)

standard deviation A statistic that describes the average difference between the measurements in a frequency distribution and the mean of that distribution. (p. 50)

state-dependent retrieval The tendency for information to be better recalled when the person is in the same state during encoding and retrieval. (p. 237)

stereotype threat The fear of confirming the negative beliefs that others may hold. (p. 541)

stereotyping The process by which people draw inferences about others based on their knowledge of the categories to which others belong. (p. 538)

stimulants Substances that excite the central nervous system, heightening arousal and activity levels. (p. 209)

stimulus Sensory input from the environment. (p. 8)

storage The process of maintaining information in memory over time. (p. 222)

Strange Situation A behavioral test developed by Mary Ainsworth that is used to determine a child's attachment style. (p. 444)

stress inoculation training (SIT) A reframing technique that helps people to cope with stressful situations by developing positive ways to think about the situation. (p. 562)

stress The physical and psychological response to internal or external stressors. (p. 550)

stressors Specific events or chronic pressures that place demands on a person or threaten the person's well-being. (p. 550)

structuralism The analysis of the basic elements that constitute the mind. (p. 8)

subcortical structures Areas of the forebrain housed under the cerebral cortex near the very center of the brain. (p. 97)

subliminal perception Thought or behavior that is influenced by stimuli that a person cannot consciously report perceiving. (p. 191)

subtyping The tendency for people who receive disconfirming evidence to modify their stereotypes rather than abandon them. (p. 541)

suggestibility The tendency to incorporate misleading information from external sources into personal recollections. (p. 255)

suicide attempt When a person engages in potentially harmful behavior with some intention of dying. (p. 621)

suicide Intentional self-inflicted death. (p. 621)

sunk-cost fallacy A framing effect in which people make decisions about a current situation based on what they have previously invested in the situation. (p. 377)

superego The mental system that reflects the internalization of cultural rules, mainly learned as parents exercise their authority. (p. 485)

surface structure How a sentence is worded. (p. 354)

syllogistic reasoning Determining whether a conclusion follows from two statements that are assumed to be true. (p. 390)

sympathetic nervous system A set of nerves that prepares the body for action in challenging or threatening situations. (p. 93)

synapse The junction or region between the axon of one neuron and the dendrites or cell body of another. (p. 82)

syntactical rules A set of rules that indicate how words can be combined to form phrases and sentences. (p. 354)

systematic persuasion The process by which attitudes or beliefs are changed by appeals to reason. (p. 534)

taste buds The organ of taste transduction. (p. 171)

tectum A part of the midbrain that orients an organism in the environment. (p. 96)

tegmentum A part of the midbrain that is involved in movement and arousal. (p. 96)

telegraphic speech Speech that is devoid of function morphemes and consists mostly of content words. (p. 357)

telomerase An enzyme that rebuilds telomeres at the tips of chromosomes. (p. 556)

telomeres Caps at the end of each chromosome that protect the ends of chromosomes and prevent them from sticking to each other. (p. 556)

temperaments Characteristic patterns of emotional reactivity. (p. 445)

template A mental representation that can be directly compared to a viewed shape in the retinal image. (p. 150)

temporal code The cochlea registers low frequencies via the firing rate of action potentials entering the auditory nerve. (p. 160)

temporal lobe A region of the cerebral cortex responsible for hearing and language. (p. 102)

teratogens Agents that damage the process of development, such as drugs and viruses. (p. 428)

terminal buttons Knoblike structures that branch out from an axon. (p. 87)

terror management theory The theory that people cope with their existential terror by developing a "cultural worldview." (p. 347)

thalamus A subcortical structure that relays and filters information from the senses and transmits the information to the cerebral cortex. (p. 98)

Thematic Apperception Test (TAT) A projective technique in which respondents' underlying motives, concerns, and the way they see the social world are believed to be revealed through analysis of the stories they make up about ambiguous pictures of people. (p. 475)

theoretical reasoning (or **discursive reasoning**) Reasoning directed toward arriving at a belief. (p. 388)

theory A hypothetical explanation of a natural phenomenon. (p. 40)

theory of mind The understanding that human behavior is guided by mental representations. (p. 438)

third-variable correlation Two variables are correlated only because each is causally related to a third variable. (p. 55)

third-variable problem The fact that a causal relationship between two variables cannot be inferred from the naturally occurring correlation between them because of the ever-present possibility of third-variable correlation. (p. 57)

thought suppression The conscious avoidance of a thought. (p. 188)

timbre A listener's experience of sound quality or resonance. (p. 158)

token economy A form of behavior therapy in which clients are given "tokens" for desired behaviors, which they can later trade for rewards. (p. 638)

trait A relatively stable disposition to behave in a particular and consistent way. (p. 476)

transcranial magnetic stimulation (TMS) A treatment that involves placing a powerful pulsed magnet over a person's scalp, which alters neuronal activity in the brain. (p. 655)

transduction What takes place when many sensors in the body convert physical signals from the environment into encoded neural signals sent to the central nervous system. (p. 130)

transfer-appropriate processing The idea that memory is likely to transfer from one situation to another when the encoding and retrieval contexts of the situations match. (p. 237)

transference An event that occurs in psychoanalysis when the analyst begins to assume a major significance in the client's life and the client reacts to the analyst based on unconscious childhood fantasies. (p. 635)

transience Forgetting what occurs with the passage of time. (p. 249)

two-factor theory of intelligence Spearman's theory suggesting that every task requires a combination of a general ability (which he called g) and skills that are specific to the task (which he called s). (p. 402)

two-factor theory The theory that emotions are based on inferences about the causes of physiological arousal. (p. 317)

Type A behavior pattern The tendency toward easily aroused hostility, impatience, a sense of time urgency, and competitive achievement strivings. (p. 558)

unconditioned response (UR) A reflexive reaction that is reliably produced by an unconditioned stimulus. (p. 267)

unconditioned stimulus (US) Something that reliably produces a naturally occurring reaction in an organism. (p. 267)

unconscious motivations Motivations of which people are not aware. (p. 344)

unconscious The part of the mind that operates outside of conscious awareness but influences conscious thoughts, feelings, and actions. (p. 13)

universality hypothesis Emotional expressions have the same meaning for everyone. (p. 323)

validity The goodness with which a concrete event defines a property. (p. 44)

variable A property whose value can vary across individuals or over time. (p. 52)

variable-interval schedule (VI) An operant conditioning principle in which behavior is reinforced based on an average time that has expired since the last reinforcement. (p. 284)

variable-ratio schedule (VR) An operant conditioning principle in which the delivery of reinforcement is based on a particular average number of responses. (p. 285)

vestibular system The three fluid-filled semicircular canals and adjacent organs located next to the cochlea in each inner ear. (p. 166)

visual acuity The ability to see fine detail. (p. 136)

visual form agnosia The inability to recognize objects by sight. (p. 144)

visual imagery encoding The process of storing new information by converting it into mental pictures. (p. 224)

Weber's law The just noticeable difference of a stimulus is a constant proportion despite variations in intensity. (p. 133)

working memory Active maintenance of information in short-term storage. (p. 229)

zygote A fertilized egg that contains chromosomes from both a sperm and an egg. (p. 427)

References

Aarts, H., Custers, R., & Marien, H. (2008). Preparing and motivating behavior outside of awareness. *Science, 319,* 1639.

Abbott, J. M., Klein, B., & Ciechomski, L. (2008). Best practices in online therapy. *Journal of Technology in Human Services, 26,* 360–375.

Abel, T., Alberini, C., Ghirardi, M., Huang, Y.-Y., Nguyen, P., & Kandel, E. R. (1995). Steps toward a molecular definition of memory consolidation. In D. L. Schacter (Ed.), *Memory distortion: How minds, brains and societies reconstruct the past* (pp. 298–328). Cambridge, MA: Harvard University Press.

Abelson, J., Curtis, G., Sagher, O., Albucher, R., Harrigan, M., Taylor, S., . . . Giordani, B. (2009). Deep brain stimulation for refractory obsessive-compulsive disorder. *Biological Psychiatry, 57,* 510–516.

Abrams, M., & Reber, A. S. (1988). Implicit learning: Robustness in the face of psychiatric disorders. *Journal of Psycholinguistic Research, 17,* 425–439.

Abramson, L. Y., Seligman, M. E. P., & Teasdale, J. D. (1978). Learned helplessness in humans: Critique and reformulation. *Journal of Abnormal Psychology, 87,* 49–74.

Acevedo, B. P., & Aron, A. (2009). Does a long-term relationship kill romantic love? *Review of General Psychology, 13,* 59–65.

Acevedo-Garcia, D., McArdle, N., Osypuk, T. L., Lefkowitz, B., & Krimgold, B. K. (2007). *Children left behind: How metropolitan areas are failing America's children.* Boston: Harvard School of Public Health.

Achter, J. A., Lubinski, D., & Benbow, C. P. (1996). Multipotentiality among the intellectually gifted: "It was never there and already it's vanishing." *Journal of Counseling Psychology, 43,* 65–76.

Acocella, J. (1999). *Creating hysteria: Women and multiple personality disorder.* San Francisco: Jossey-Bass.

Addis, D. R., Wong, A. T., & Schacter, D. L. (2007). Remembering the past and imagining the future: Common and distinct neural substrates during event construction and elaboration. *Neuropsychologia, 45,* 1363–1377.

Addis, D. R., Wong, A. T., & Schacter, D. L. (2008). Age-related changes in the episodic simulation of future events. *Psychological Science, 19,* 33–41.

Adelmann, P. K., & Zajonc, R. B. (1989). Facial efference and the experience of emotion. *Annual Review of Psychology, 40,* 249–280.

Adolph, K. E., & Avoilio, A. M. (2000). Walking infants adapt locomotion to changing body dimensions. *Journal of Experimental Psychology: Human Perception and Performance, 26,* 1148–1166.

Adolph, K. E., Cole, W. G., Komati, M., Garciaguirre, J. S., Badaly, D., Lingeman, J. M., . . . Sotsky, R. B. (2012). How do you learn to walk? Thousands of steps and dozens of falls per day. *Psychological Science, 23*(11), 1387–1394. doi:10.1177/0956797612446346

Adolphs, R., Russell, J. A., & Tranel, D. (1999). A role for the human amygdala in recognizing emotional arousal from unpleasant stimuli. *Psychological Science, 10,* 167–171.

Adolphs, R., Tranel, D., Damasio, H., & Damasio, A. R. (1995). Fear and the human amygdala. *The Journal of Neuroscience, 15,* 5879–5891.

Adorno, T. W., Frenkel-Brunswik, E., Levinson, D. J., & Sanford, R. N. (1950). *The authoritarian personality.* New York: Harper & Row.

Aggleton, J. (Ed.). (1992). *The amygdala: Neurobiological aspects of emotion, memory and mental dysfunction.* New York: Wiley-Liss.

Agin, D. (2007). *Junk science: An overdue indictment of government, industry, and faith groups that twist science for their own gain.* New York: Macmillan.

Agren, T., Engman, J., Frick, A., Björkstrand, J., Larsson, E. M., Furmark, T., & Fredrikson, M. (2012). Disruption of reconsolidation erases a fear memory trace in the human amygdala. *Science, 337,* 1550–1552.

Agthe, M., Spörrle, M., & Maner, J. K. (2010). Don't hate me because I'm beautiful: Anti-attractiveness bias in organizational evaluation and decision making. *Journal of Experimental Psychology, 46*(6), 1151–1154. doi:10.1016/j.jesp.2010.05.007

Aharon, I., Etcoff, N., Ariely, D., Chabris, C. F., O'Conner, E., & Breiter, H. C. (2001). Beautiful faces have variable reward value: fMRI and behavioral evidence. *Neuron, 32,* 537–551.

Ahlskog, J. E. (2011). Pathological behaviors provoked by dopamine agonist therapy of Parkinson's disease. *Physiology & Behavior, 104,* 168–172.

Ainslie, G. (2001). *Breakdown of will.* New York: Cambridge University Press.

Ainsworth, M. D. S., Blehar, M. C., Waters, E., & Wall, S. (1978). *Patterns of attachment: A psychological study of the strange situation.* Hillsdale, NJ: Erlbaum.

Ainsworth, S. E., & Maner, J. K. (2012). Sex begets violence: Mating motives, social dominance, and physical aggression in men. *Journal of Personality and Social Psychology, 103*(5), 819–829. doi: 10.1037/a0029428

Aksglaede, L., Sorensen, K., Petersen, J. H., Skakkebaek, N. E., & Juul, A. (2009). Recent decline in age at breast development: The Copenhagen puberty study. *Pediatrics, 123*(5), e932–e939.

Alasaari, J. S., Lagus, M., Ollila, H. M., Toivola, A., Kivimaki, M., Vahterra, J., . . . Paunio, T. (2012). Environmental stress affects DNA methylation of a CpG rich promoter region of serotonin transporter gene in a nurse cohort. *PLoS One, 7,* e45813. doi:10.1371/journal.pone.0045813

Albarracín, D., & Vargas, P. (2010). Attitudes and persuasion: From biology to social responses to persuasive intent. In S. T. Fiske, D. T. Gilbert, & G. Lindzey (Eds.), *The handbook of social psychology* (5th ed., Vol. 1, pp. 389–422). New York: Wiley.

Albee, E. (1962). *Who's afraid of Virginia Woolf?* New York: Atheneum.

Aleman, A., Sommer, I. E., & Kahn, R. S. (2007). Efficacy of slow repetitive transcranial magnetic stimulation in the treatment of resistant auditory hallucinations in schizophrenia: A meta-analysis. *Journal of Clinical Psychiatry, 68,* 416–421.

Allen, P., Larøi, F., McGuire, P.K., & Aleman, A. (2008). The hallucinating brain: A review of structural and functional neuroimaging studies of hallucinations. *Neuroscience and Biobehavioral Reviews, 32,* 175–191.

Alicke, M. D., Klotz, M. L., Breitenbecher, D. L., Yurak, T. J., & Vredenburg, D. S. (1995). Personal contact, individuation, and the better-than-average effect. *Journal of Personality and Social Psychology, 68,* 804–824.

Allison, D. B., Fontaine, K. R., Manson, J. E., Stevens, J., & VanItallie, T. B. (1999). Annual deaths attributable to obesity in the United States. *Journal of the American Medical Association, 282,* 1530–1538.

Allison, D. B., Kaprio, J., Korkeila, M., Koskenvuo, M., Neale, M. C., & Hayakawa, K. (1996). The heritability of body mass index among an international sample of monozygotic twins reared apart. *International Journal of Obesity, 20*(6), 501–506.

Alloway, T. P., Gathercole, S. E., Kirkwood, H., & Elliott, J. (2009). The cognitive and behavioral characteristics of children with low working memory. *Child Development, 80,* 606–621.

Allport, G. W. (1937). *Personality: A psychological interpretation.* New York: Holt.

Allport, G. W. (1954). *The nature of prejudice.* Cambridge, MA: Addison-Wesley.

Allport, G. W., & Odbert, H. S. (1936). Trait-names: A psycholexical study. *Psychological Monographs, 47,* 592.

Alt, K. W., Jeunesse, C., Buitrago-Téllez, C. H., Wächter, R., Boës, E., & Pichler, S. L. (1997). Evidence for stone age cranial surgery. *Nature, 387,* 360.

Alvarez, L. W. (1965). A pseudo experience in parapsychology. *Science, 148,* 1541.

American Academy of Pediatrics. (2000, July 26). *The impact of entertainment violence on children.* Joint statement issued at a meeting of the Congressional Public Health Summit. Retrieved from http://www.aap.org/advocacy/releases/jstmtevc.htm

American Psychiatric Association. (2000). *Diagnostic and statistical manual of mental disorders* (4th ed., text rev.). Washington, DC: Author.

American Psychiatric Association. (2013). *Diagnostic and statistical manual of mental disorders* (5th ed.). Washington, DC: Author.

American Psychological Association. (2002). *Ethical principles of psychologists and code of conduct.* Washington, DC: Author. Retrieved from apa.org/code/ethics/index.aspx [includes 2010 amendments].

American Psychological Association. (2005). *Resolution in favor of empirically supported sex education and HIV prevention programs for adolescents.* Washington, DC: Author.

American Psychological Association. (2009). *Report of the American Psychological Association task force on appropriate therapeutic responses to sexual orientation.* Washington, DC: Author.

Anand, S., & Hotson, J. (2002). Transcranial magnetic stimulation: Neurophysiological applications and safety. *Brain and Cognition, 50,* 366–386.

Anderson, C. A. (1989). Temperature and aggression: Ubiquitous effects of heat on occurrence of human violence. *Psychological Bulletin, 106,* 74–96.

Anderson, C. A., Berkowitz, L., Donnerstein, E., Huesmann, L. R., Johnson, J. D., Linz, D., . . . Wartella, E. (2003). The influence of media violence on youth. *Psychological Science in the Public Interest, 4,* 81–110.

Anderson, C. A., & Bushman, B. J. (2001). Effects of violent video games on aggressive behavior, aggressive cognition, aggressive affect, physiological arousal, and prosocial behavior: A metaanalytic review of the scientific literature. *Psychological Science, 12*(5), 353–359.

Anderson, C. A., & Bushman, B. J. (2002). Human aggression. *Annual Review of Psychology, 53,* 27–51.

Anderson, C. A., Bushman, B. J., & Groom, R. W. (1997). Hot years and serious and deadly assault: Empirical tests of the heat hypothesis. *Journal of Personality and Social Psychology, 73,* 1213–1223.

Anderson, C. A., Shibuya, A., Ihori, N., Swing, E. L., Bushman, B. J., Sakamoto, A., . . . Saleem, M. (2010). Violent video game effects on aggression, empathy, and prosocial behavior in Eastern and Western countries: A meta-analytic review. *Psychological Bulletin, 136*(2), 151–173. doi: 10.1037/a0018251

Anderson, J. R., & Schooler, L. J. (1991). Reflections of the environment in memory. *Psychological Science, 2,* 396–408.

Anderson, J. R., & Schooler, L. J. (2000). The adaptive nature of memory. In E. Tulving & F. I. M. Craik (Eds.), *Handbook of memory* (pp. 557–570). New York: Oxford University Press.

Anderson, M. C. (2003). Rethinking interference theory: Executive control and the mechanisms of forgetting. *Journal of Memory and Language, 49,* 415–445.

Anderson, M. C., Bjork, R. A., & Bjork, E. L. (1994). Remembering can cause forgetting: Retrieval dynamics in long-term memory. *Journal of Experimental Psychology: Learning, Memory, and Cognition, 20,* 1063–1087.

Anderson, M. C., Ochsner, K. N., Kuhl, B., Cooper, J., Robertson, E., Gabrieli, S. W., . . . Gabrieli, J. D. E. (2004). Neural systems underlying the suppression of unwanted memories. *Science, 303,* 232–235.

Anderson, R. C., Pichert, J. W., Goetz, E. T., Schallert, D. L., Stevens, K. V., & Trollip, S. R. (1976). Instantiation of general terms. *Journal of Verbal Learning and Verbal Behavior, 15,* 667–679.

Andreasen, N. C. (2011). A journey into chaos: Creativity and the unconscious. *Mens Sana Monographs, 9,* 42–53.

Andrewes, D. (2001). *Neuropsychology: From theory to practice.* Hove, England: Psychology Press.

Andrews, I. (1982). Bilinguals out of focus: A critical discussion. *International Review of Applied Linguistics in Language Teaching, 20,* 297–305.

Andrews-Hanna, J. R. (2012). The brain's default network and its adaptive role in internal mentation. *Neuroscientist, 18,* 251–270.

Annis, L. F., & Annis, D. B. (1982). A normative study of students' reported preferred study techniques. *Literacy Research and Instruction, 21,* 201–207.

Ansfield, M., Wegner, D. M., & Bowser, R. (1996). Ironic effects of sleep urgency. *Behavior Research and Therapy, 34,* 523–531.

Ansuini, C. G., Fiddler-Woite, J., & Woite, R. S. (1996). The source, accuracy, and impact of initial sexuality information on lifetime wellness. *Adolescence, 31,* 283–289.

Antoni, M. H., Lehman, J. M., Kilbourn, K. M., Boyers, A. E., Culver, J. L., Alferi, S. M., . . . Carver, C. S. (2001). Cognitive-behavioral stress management intervention decreases the prevalence of depression and enhances benefit finding among women under treatment for early-stage breast cancer. *Health Psychology, 20,* 20–32.

Apicella, C. L., Feinberg, D. R., & Marlowe, F. W. (2007). Voice pitch predicts reproductive success in male hunter-gatherers. *Biology Letters, 3*(6), 682–684. doi:10.1098/rsbl.2007.0410

Apperly, I. A., & Butterfill, S. A. (2009). Do humans have two systems to track beliefs and belief-like states? *Psychological Review, 116,* 953–970.

Arellano, D., Varona, J., & Perales, F. (2008). Generation and visualization of emotional states in virtual characters. *Computer Animation and Virtual Worlds, 19*(3–4), 259–270.

Aristotle. (1998). *The Nichomachean ethics* (D. W. Ross, Trans.). Oxford, England: Oxford University Press. (Original work circa 350 BCE)

Ariyasu, H., Takaya, K., Tagami, T., Ogawa, Y., Hosoda, K., Akamizu, T., . . . Hosoda, H. (2001). Stomach is a major source of circulating ghrelin, and feeding state determines plasma ghrelin-like immunoreactivity levels in humans. *Journal of Clinical Endocrinology and Metabolism, 86,* 4753–4758.

Armstrong, D. M. (1980). *The nature of mind.* Ithaca, NY: Cornell University Press.

Arnold, M. B. (Ed.). (1960). *Emotion and personality: Psychological aspects* (Vol. 1). New York: Columbia University Press.

Arnold, S. E., Trojanowski, J. Q., Gur, R. E., Blackwell, P., Han, L., & Choi, C. (1998). Absence of neurodegeneration and neural injury in the cerebral cortex in a sample of elderly patients with schizophrenia. *Archives of General Psychiatry, 55,* 225–232.

Aron, A., Fisher, H., Mashek, D., Strong, G., Li, H., & Brown, L. (2005). Reward, motivation, and emotion systems associated with early-stage intense romantic love. *Journal of Neurophysiology, 93,* 327–337.

Aronson, E. (1963). Effect of the severity of threat on the devaluation of forbidden behavior. *Journal of Abnormal and Social Psychology, 66,* 584–588.

Aronson, E. (1969). The theory of cognitive dissonance: A current perspective. In L. Berkowitz (Ed.), *Advances in experimental social psychology* (Vol. 4, pp. 1–34): Academic Press.

Aronson, E., & Mills, J. (1958). The effect of severity of initiation on liking for a group. *Journal of Abnormal and Social Psychology, 59,* 177–181.

Aronson, E., Willerman, B., & Floyd, J. (1966). The effect of a pratfall on increasing interpersonal attractiveness. *Psychonomic Science, 4,* 227–228.

Aronson, E., & Worchel, P. (1966). Similarity versus liking as determinants of interpersonal attractiveness. *Psychonomic Science, 5,* 157–158.

Aronson, J., & Steele, C. M. (2004). Stereotypes and the fragility of academic competence, motivation, and self-concept. In A. J. Elliot & C. S. Dweck (Eds.), *Handbook of competence and motivation* (pp. 436–456). New York: Guilford Press.

Asch, S. E. (1946). Forming impressions of personality. *Journal of Abnormal and Social Psychology, 41,* 258–290.

Asch, S. E. (1951). Effects of group pressure on the modification and distortion of judgments. In H. Guetzkow (Ed.), *Groups, leadership, and men* (pp. 177–190). Pittsburgh, PA: Carnegie Press.

Asch, S. E. (1955). Opinions and social pressure. *Scientific American, 193,* 31–35.

Asch, S. E. (1956). Studies of independence and conformity: 1. A minority of one against a unanimous majority. *Psychological Monographs: General and Applied, 70,* 1–70.

Aschoff, J. (1965). Circadian rhythms in man. *Science, 148,* 1427–1432.

Aserinsky, E., & Kleitman, N. (1953). Regularly occurring periods of eye motility, and concomitant phenomena, during sleep. *Science, 118,* 273–274.

Ashby, F. G., & Ell, S. W. (2001). The neurobiology of human category learning. *Trends in Cognitive Sciences, 5,* 204–210.

Ashby, F. G., & O'Brien, J. B. (2005). Category learning and multiple memory systems. *Trends in Cognitive Sciences, 9,* 83–89.

Ashcraft, M. H. (1998). *Fundamentals of cognition.* New York: Longman.

Associated Press. (2007). Former stripper guilty of posing as psychologist. *Boston Herald.* Retrieved from http://www.bostonherald.com.

Astington, J. W., & Baird, J. (2005). *Why language matters for theory of mind.* Oxford, England: Oxford University Press.

Atance, C. M., Bélanger, M., & Meltzoff, A. N. (2010). Preschoolers' understanding of others' desires: Fulfilling mine enhances my understanding of yours. *Developmental Psychology, 46*(6), 1505–1513. doi:10.1037/a0020374

Avery, D., Holtzheimer, P., III, Fawaz, W., Russo, J., Naumeier, J., Dunner, D., . . . Roy-Byrne, P. (2009). A controlled study of repetitive transcranial magnetic stimulation in medication-resistant major depression. *Biological Psychiatry, 59,* 187–194.

Aviezer, H., Hassin, R. R., Ryan, J., Grady, C., Susskind, J., Anderson, A., . . . Bentin, S. (2008). Angry, disgusted, or afraid? Studies on the malleability of emotion perception. *Psychological Science, 19,* 724–732.

Aviezer, H., Trope, Y., & Todorov, A. (2012). Body cues, not facial expressions, discriminate between intense positive and negative emotions. *Science, 338,* 1225–1229.

Avolio, B. J., & Waldman, D. A. (1994). Variations in cognitive, perceptual, and psychomotor abilities across the working life span: Examining the effects of race, sex, experience, education, and occupational type. *Psychology and Aging, 9,* 430–442.

Axelrod, R. (1984). *The evolution of cooperation.* New York: Basic Books.

Axelrod, R., & Hamilton, W. D. (1981). The evolution of cooperation. *Science, 211,* 1390–1396.

Ayduk, O., Shoda, Y., Cervone, D., & Downey, G. (2007). Delay of gratification in children: Contributions to social–personality psychology. In G. Downey, Y. Shoda, & C. Cervone (Eds.), *Persons in context: Building a science of the individual* (pp. 97–109). New York: Guilford Press.

Ayres, C. E. (1921). Instinct and capacity. 1. The instinct of belief-in-instincts. *Journal of Philosophy, 18,* 561–565.

Azuma, H., & Kashiwagi, K. (1987). Descriptors for an intelligent person: A Japanese study. *Japanese Psychological Research, 29,* 17–26.

Baars, B. J. (1986). *The cognitive revolution in psychology.* New York: Guilford Press.

Baca-Motes, K., Brown, A., Gneezy, A., Keenan, E. A., & Nelson, L. D. (2013). Commitment and behavior change: Evidence from the field. *Journal of Consumer Research, 39*(5), 1070–1084. doi:10.1086/667226

Back, M. D., Schmukle, S. C., & Egloff, B. (2008). Becoming friends by chance. *Psychological Science, 19,* 439–440.

Back, M. D., Stopfer, J. M., Vazire, S., Gaddis, S., Schmukle, S. C., Egloff, B., & Gosling, S. (2010). Facebook profiles reflect actual personality not self-idealization. *Psychological Science, 21,* 372–374.

Backman, C. W., & Secord, P. F. (1959). The effect of perceived liking on interpersonal attraction. *Human Relations, 12,* 379–384.

Bäckman, L., Almkvist, O., Andersson, J., Nordberg, A., Winblad, B., Reineck, R., & Långström, B. (1997). Brain activation in young and older adults during implicit and explicit retrieval. *Journal of Cognitive Neuroscience, 9,* 378–391.

Bäckman, L., & Dixon, R. A. (1992). Psychological compensation: A theoretical framework. *Psychological Bulletin, 112,* 259–283.

Baddeley, A. D. (2001). Is working memory still working? *American Psychologist, 56,* 851–864.

Baddeley, A. D., & Hitch, G. J. (1974). Working memory. In S. Dornic (Ed.), *Attention and performance* (Vol. 6, pp. 647–667). Hillsdale, NJ: Erlbaum.

Bagby, R. M., Levitan, R. D., Kennedy, S. H., Levitt, A. J., & Joffe, R. T. (1999). Selective alteration of personality in response to noradrenergic and serotonergic antidepressant medication in depressed sample: Evidence of non-specificity. *Psychiatry Research, 86,* 211–216.

Bahrick, H. P. (1984). Semantic memory content in permastore: 50 years of memory for Spanish learned in school. *Journal of Experimental Psychology: General, 113,* 1–29.

Bahrick, H. P. (2000). Long-term maintenance of knowledge. In E. Tulving & F. I. M. Craik (Eds.), *The Oxford handbook of memory* (pp. 347–362). New York: Oxford University Press.

Bahrick, H. P., Hall, L. K., & Berger, S. A. (1996). Accuracy and distortion in memory for high school grades. *Psychological Science, 7,* 265–271.

Bahrick, H. P., Hall, L. K., & DaCosta, L. A. (2008). Fifty years of college grades: Accuracy and distortions. *Emotion, 8,* 13–22.

Bailey, J. M., & Pillard, R. C. (1991). A genetic study of male sexual orientation. *Archives of General Psychiatry, 48,* 1089–1096.

Bailey, J. M., Pillard, R. C., Dawood, K., Miller, M. B., Farrer, L. A., Trivedi, S., . . . Murphy, R. L. (1999). A family history study of male sexual orientation using three independent samples. *Behavior Genetics, 29,* 79–86.

Bailey, J. M., Pillard, R. C., Neale, M. C., & Agyes, Y. (1993). Heritable factors influence sexual orientation in women. *Archives of General Psychiatry, 50,* 217–223.

Baillargeon, R., Scott, R. M., & He, Z. (2010). False-belief understanding in infants. *Trends in Cognitive Sciences, 14*(3), 110–118.

Baillargeon, R., Spelke, E. S., & Wasserman, S. (1985). Object permanence in 5-month-old infants. *Cognition, 20,* 191–208.

Baird, B., Smallwood, J., Mrazek, M. D., Kam, J. W. Y., Franklin, M. S., & Schooler, J. W. (2012). Inspired by distraction: Mind wandering facilitates creative incubation. *Psychological Science, 23,* 1117–1122.

Baker, E., Shelton, K. H., Baibazarova, E., Hay, D. F., & van Goozen, S. H. M. (2013). Low skin conductance activity in infancy predicts aggression in toddlers 2 years later. *Psychological Science,* 24(6), 1051–1056. doi:10.1177/0956797612465198

Baker, T. B., Brandon, T. H., & Chassin, L. (2004). Motivational influences on cigarette smoking. *Annual Review of Psychology, 55,* 463–491.

Baker, T. B., McFall, R. M., & Shoham, V. (2009). Current status and future prospects of clinical psychology: Toward a scientifically principled approach to mental and behavioral health care. *Psychological Science in the Public Interest, 9,* 67–103.

Baldwin, M. W., Carrell, S. E., & Lopez, D. F. (1989). Priming relationship schemas: My advisor and the pope are watching me from the back of my mind. *Journal of Experimental Social Psychology, 26,* 435–454.

Baler, R. D., & Volkow, N. D. (2006). Drug addiction: The neurobiology of disrupted self-control. *Trends in Molecular Medicine, 12,* 559–566.

Baltes, P. B., & Reinert, G. (1969). Cohort effects in cognitive development of children as revealed by cross-sectional sequences. *Developmental Psychology, 1,* 169–177.

Banaji, M. R., & Heiphetz, L. (2010). Attitudes. In S. T. Fiske, D. T. Gilbert, & G. Lindzey (Eds.), *The handbook of social psychology* (5th ed., Vol. 1, pp. 348–388). New York: Wiley.

Bandura, A. (1965). Influence of models' reinforcement contingencies on the acquisition of imitative responses. *Journal of Social and Personality Psychology, 1,* 589–595.

Bandura, A. (1977). *Social learning theory.* Englewood Cliffs, NJ: Prentice Hall.

Bandura, A. (1986). *Social foundations of thought and action: A social cognitive theory.* Englewood Cliffs, NJ: Prentice Hall.

Bandura, A. (1994). Social cognitive theory of mass communication. In J. Bryant & D. Zillmann (Eds.), *Media effects: Advances in theory and research* (pp. 61–90). Hillsdale, NJ: Erlbaum.

Bandura, A., Ross, D., & Ross, S. (1961). Transmission of aggression through imitation of adult models. *Journal of Abnormal and Social Psychology, 63,* 575–582.

Bandura, A., Ross, D., & Ross, S. (1963). Vicarious reinforcement and imitative learning. *Journal of Abnormal and Social Psychology, 67,* 601–607.

Banks, M. S., & Salapatek, P. (1983). Infant visual perception. In M. Haith & J. Campos (Eds.), *Handbook of child psychology: Biology and infancy* (pp. 435–572). New York: Wiley.

Banse, R., & Scherer, K. R. (1996). Acoustic profiles in vocal emotion expression. *Journal of Personality and Social Psychology, 70,* 614–636.

Barber, J. P., Muran, J. C., McCarthy, K. S., & Keefe, J. R. (2013). Research on dynamic therapies. In M. Lambert (Ed.), *Bergin and Garfield's handbook of psychotherapy and behavior change* (6th ed., pp. 443–494). Hoboken, NJ: Wiley.

Barber, S. J., Rajaram, S., & Fox, E. B. (2012). Learning and remembering with others: The key role of retrieval in shaping group recall and collective memory. *Social Cognition, 30,* 121–132.

Bard, P. (1934). On emotional experience after decortication with some remarks on theoretical views. *Psychological Review, 41,* 309–329.

Bargh, J. A., & Chartrand, T. L. (1999). The unbearable automaticity of being. *American Psychologist, 54,* 462–479.

Bargh, J. A., Chen, M., & Burrows, L. (1996). The automaticity of social behavior: Direct effects of trait concept and stereotype activation on action. *Journal of Personality and Social Psychology, 71,* 230–244.

Bargh, J. A., Gollwitzer, P. M., Lee-Chai, A., Barndollar, K., & Trötschel, R. (2001). The automated will: Nonconscious activation and pursuit of behavioral goals. *Journal of Personality and Social Psychology, 81,* 1014–1027.

Bargh, J. A., Gollwitzer, P. M., & Oettingen, G. (2010). Motivation. In S. T. Fiske, D. T. Gilbert, & G. Lindzey (Eds.), *The handbook of social psychology* (5th ed., Vol. 1, pp. 263–311). New York: Wiley.

Bargh, J. A., & Morsella, E. (2008). The unconscious mind. *Perspectives on Psychological Science, 3,* 73–89.

Barker, A. T., Jalinous, R., & Freeston, I. L. (1985). Noninvasive magnetic stimulation of the human motor cortex. *Lancet, 2,* 1106–1107.

Barkow, J. (1980). Prestige and self-esteem: A biosocial interpretation. In D. R. Omark, F. F. Stayer, & D. G. Freedman (Eds.), *Dominance relations* (pp. 319–322). New York: Garland.

Barlow, D. H., Bullis, J. R., Comer, J. S., & Ametaj, A. A. (2013). Evidence-based psychological treatments: An update and a way forward. *Annual Review of Clinical Psychology, 9,* 1–27.

Barlow, D. H., Gorman, J. M., Shear, M. K., & Woods, S. W. (2000). Cognitive-behavioral therapy, imipramine, or their combination for panic disorder: A randomized controlled trial. *Journal of the American Medical Association, 283*(19), 2529–2536.

Barnier, A. J., Levin, K., & Maher, A. (2004). Suppressing thoughts of past events: Are repressive copers good suppressors? *Cognition and Emotion, 18,* 457–477.

Baron-Cohen, S. (1991). Do people with autism understand what causes emotion? *Child Development, 62,* 385–395.

Baron-Cohen, S., & Belmonte, M. K. (2005). Autism: A window onto the development of the social and analytic brain. *Annual Review of Neuroscience, 28,* 109–126.

Baron-Cohen, S., Leslie, A., & Frith, U. (1985). Does the autistic child have a "theory of mind"? *Cognition, 21,* 37–46.

Barondes, S. (2003). *Better than Prozac.* New York: Oxford University Press.

Barrett, L. F., Mesquita, B., & Gendron, M. (2011). Context in emotion perception. *Current Directions in Psychological Science, 20*(5), 286–290. doi:10.1177/0963721411422522

Barrientos, R. M., Watkins, L. R., Rudy, J. W., & Maier, S. F. (2009). Characterization of the sickness response in young and aging rats following *E. coli* infection. *Brain, Behavior, and Immunity, 23,* 450–454.

Bartal, I. B.-A., Decety, J., & Mason, P. (2011). Empathy and prosocial behavior in rats. *Science, 334*(6061), 1427–1430.

Bartlett, F. C. (1932). *Remembering: A study in experimental and social psychology.* Cambridge, England: Cambridge University Press.

Bartol, C. R., & Costello, N. (1976). Extraversion as a function of temporal duration of electric shock: An exploratory study. *Perceptual and Motor Skills, 42,* 1174.

Bartoshuk, L. M. (2000). Comparing sensory experiences across individuals: Recent psychophysical advances illuminate genetic variation in taste perception. *Chemical Senses, 25,* 447–460.

Bartoshuk, L. M., & Beauchamp, G. K. (1994). Chemical senses. *Annual Review of Psychology, 45,* 419–445.

Basden, B. H., Basden, D. R., Bryner, S., & Thomas, R. L. (1997). A comparison of group and individual remembering: Does collaboration disrupt retrieval strategies? *Journal of Experimental Psychology: Learning, Memory, and Cognition, 23,* 1176–1191.

Bates, E., & Goodman, J. C. (1997). On the inseparability of grammar and the lexicon: Evidence from acquisition, aphasia, and real-time processing. *Language and Cognitive Processes, 12,* 507–584.

Bateson, M., Nettle, D., & Roberts, G. (2006). Cues of being watched enhance cooperation in a real-world setting. *Biology Letters, 2*(3), 412–414.

Batson, C. D. (2002). Addressing the altruism question experimentally. In S. G. Post & L. G. Underwood (Eds.), *Altruism & altruistic love: Science, philosophy, & religion in dialogue* (pp. 89–105). London: Oxford University Press.

Batty, G. D., Deary, I. J., Schoon, I., & Gale, C. R. (2007). Mental ability across childhood in relation to risk factors for premature mortality in adult life: The 1970 British Cohort Study. *Journal of Epidemiology & Community Health, 61*(11), 997–1003. doi:10.1136/jech.2006.054494

Baumeister, R. F., Bratslavsky, E., Muraven, M., & Tice, D. M. (1998). Ego depletion: Is the active self a limited resource? *Journal of Personality and Social Psychology, 74,* 1252–1265.

Baumeister, R. F., Campbell, J. D., Krueger, J. I., & Vohs, K. D. (2003). Does high self-esteem cause better performance, interpersonal success, happiness, or healthier lifestyles? *Psychological Science in the Public Interest, 4,* 1–44.

Baumeister, R. F., Cantanese, K. R., & Vohs, K. D. (2001). Is there a gender difference in strength of sex drive? Theoretical views, conceptual distinctions, and a review of relevant evidence. *Personality and Social Psychology Review, 5,* 242–273.

Baumeister, R. F., Heatherton, T. F., & Tice, D. M. (1995). *Losing control.* San Diego, CA: Academic Press.

Baumeister, R. F., & Leary, M. R. (1995). The need to belong: Desire for interpersonal attachments as a fundamental human motivation. *Psychological Bulletin, 117,* 497–529.

Baumeister, R. F., Smart, L., & Boden, J. M. (1996). Relation of threatened egotism to violence and aggression: The dark side of high self-esteem. *Psychological Review, 103,* 5–33.

Baumeister, R. F., Vohs, K. D., & Tice, D. M. (2007). The strength model of self-control. *Current Directions in Psychological Science, 16,* 351–355.

Baxter, L. R., Schwartz, J. M., Bergman, K. S., Szuba, M. P., Guze, B. H., Mazziotta, J. C., Alazraki, A., . . . Munford, P. (1992). Caudate glucose metabolic rate changes with both drug behavior therapy for obsessive-compulsive disorder. *Archives of General Psychiatry, 49,* 681–689.

Bayley, P. J., Frascino, J. C., & Squire, L. R. (2005). Robust habit learning in the absence of awareness and independent of the medial temporal lobe. *Nature, 436,* 550–553.

Bayley, P. J., Gold, J. J., Hopkins, R. O., & Squire, L. R. (2005). The neuroanatomy of remote memory. *Neuron, 46,* 799–810.

Beard, C., Sawyer, A. T., & Hoffmann, S. G. (2012). Efficacy of attention bias modification using threat and appetitive stimuli: A meta-analytic review. *Behavior Therapy, 43,* 724–740.

Bechara, A., Damasio, A. R., Damasio, H., & Anderson, S. W. (1994). Insensitivity to future consequences following damage to human prefrontal cortex. *Cognition, 50,* 7–15.

Bechara, A., Damasio, H., Tranel, D., & Damasio, A. R. (1997). Deciding advantageously before knowing the advantageous strategy. *Science, 275,* 1293–1295.

Bechara, A., Dolan, S., Denburg, N., Hindes, A., & Anderson, S. W. (2001). Decision-making deficits, linked to a dysfunctional ventromedial prefrontal cortex, revealed in alcohol and stimulant abusers. *Neuropsychologia, 39,* 376–389.

Bechara, A., Tranel, D., & Damasio, H. (2000). Characterization of the decision-making deficit of patients with ventromedial prefrontal cortex lesions. *Brain, 123,* 2189–2202.

Beck, A. T. (1967). *Depression: Causes and treatment.* Philadelphia: University of Pennsylvania Press.

Beck, A. T. (2005). The current state of cognitive therapy: A 40-year retrospective. *Archives of General Psychiatry, 62,* 953–959.

Beckers, G., & Zeki, S. (1995). The consequences of inactivating areas V1 and V5 on visual motion perception. *Brain, 118,* 49–60.

Bednarczyk, R. A., Davis, R., Ault, K., Orenstein, W., & Omer, S. B. (2012). Sexual activity-related outcomes after human papillomavirus vaccination of 11- to 12-year-olds. *Pediatrics, 130*(5), 798–805. Doi:10.1542/peds.2912-1516

Bedny, M., & Saxe, R. (2012). Insights into the origins of knowledge from the cognitive neuroscience of blindness. *Cognitive Neuropsychology, 29,* 56–84.

Beek, M. R., Levin, D. T., & Angelone, B. (2007). Change blindness blindness: Beliefs about the roles of intention and scene complexity in change detection. *Consciousness and Cognition, 16,* 31–51.

Beesdo, K., Pine, D. S., Lieb, R., & Wittchen, H. U. (2010). Incidence and risk patterns of anxiety and depressive disorders and categorization of generalized anxiety disorder. *Archives of General Psychiatry, 67,* 47–57.

Békésy, G. von. (1960). *Experiments in hearing.* New York: McGraw-Hill.

Bekinschtein, T. A., Peeters, M., Shalom, D., & Sigman, M. (2011). Sea slugs, subliminal pictures, and vegetative state patients: Boundaries of consciousness in classical conditioning. *Frontiers in Psychology, 2,* article 337. doi:10.3389/fpsyg.2011.00337

Bell, A. P., Weinberg, M. S., & Hammersmith, S. K. (1981). *Sexual preference: Its development in men and women.* Bloomington: Indiana University Press.

Belluck, P., & Carey, B. (2013, May 7). Psychiatry's guide is out of touch with science, experts say. *New York Times,* p. A13. Retreived from http://www.nytimes.com/2013/05/07/psychiatrys-new-guide-falls-short-experts-say.html

Belsky, J. (2012). The development of human reproductive strategies: Progress and prospects. *Current Directions in Psychological Science, 21*(5), 310–316. doi:10.1177/0963721412453588

Belsky, J., Spritz, B., & Crnic, K. (1996). Infant attachment security and affective-cognitive information processing at age 3. *Psychological Science, 7,* 111–114.

Bem, S. L. (1974). The measure of psychological androgyny. *Journal of Consulting and Clinical Psychology, 42,* 155–162.

Benedetti, F., Maggi, G., & Lopiano, L. (2003). Open versus hidden medical treatment: The patient's knowledge about a therapy affects the therapy outcome. *Prevention & Treatment, 6,* Article 1. Retrieved June 23, 2003, from http://content.apa.org/psycarticles/ 2003-07872-001

Benedetti, F., Pollo, A., Lopiano, L., Lanotte, M., Vighetti, S., & Rainero, I. (2003). Conscious expectation and unconscious conditioning in analgesic, motor, and hormonal placebo/nocebo responses. *The Journal of Neuroscience, 23,* 4315–4323.

Benenson, J. F., Markovits, H., Thompson, M. E., & Wrangham, R. W. (2011). Under threat of social exclusion, females exclude more than males. *Psychological Science, 22*(4), 538–544. doi: 10.1177/0956797611402511

Bennett, I. J., Romano, J. C., Howard, J. H., & Howard, D. V. (2008). Two forms of implicit learning in young adults with dyslexia. *Annals of the New York Academy of Sciences, 1145,* 184–198.

Benoit, R. G., & Anderson, M. C. (2012). Opposing mechanisms support the voluntary forgetting of unwanted memories. *Neuron, 76,* 450–460.

Benoit, S. C., Kemp, C. J., Elias, C. F., Abplanalp, W., Herman, J. P., Migrenne, S., . . . Clegg, D. J. (2009). Palmitic acid mediates hypothalamic insulin resistance by altering pkc-theta subcellular localization in rodents. *The Journal of Clinical Investigation, 119*(9), 2577–2589.

Ben-Porath, Y. S., & Tellegen, A. (2008). *Minnesota Multiphasic Personality Inventory–2–Restructured Form: Manual for administration, scoring, and interpretation.* Minneapolis: University of Minnesota Press.

Benson, H. (Ed.). (1990). *The relaxation response.* New York: Harper Torch.

Benson, H., Dusek, J. A., Sherwood, J. B., Lam, P., Bethea, C. F., Carpenter, W., . . . Hibberd, P. L. (2006). Study of the therapeutic effects of intercessory prayer (STEP) in cardiac bypass patients: A multicenter randomized trial of uncertainty and certainty of receiving intercessory prayer. *American Heart Journal, 151,* 934–942.

Berger, H. (1929). Über das Elektrenkephalogramm des Menschen [Electroencephalogram of man]. *Archiv für Psychiatrie und Nervenkrankheiten, 87,* 527–570.

Berglund, H., Lindstrom, P., & Savic, I. (2006). Brain response to putative pheromones in lesbian women. *Proceedings of the National Academy of Sciences, USA, 103,* 8269–8274.

Bering, J. (2004). A critical review of the "enculturation hypothesis": The effects of human rearing on great ape social cognition. *Animal Cognition, 7,* 201–212.

Berkowitz, L. (1990). On the formation and regulation of anger and aggression: A cognitive-neoassociationistic analysis. *American Psychologist, 45,* 494–503.

Bernard, L. L. (1924). *Instinct: A study in social psychology.* New York: Holt.

Bernat, J. L. (2009). Ethical issues in the treatment of severe brain injury: The impact of new technologies. *Annals of the New York Academy of Sciences, 1157,* 117–130.

Berridge, K. C. (2007). The debate over dopamine's role in reward: The case for incentive salience. *Psychopharmacology, 191,* 391–431.

Berry, D. S., & McArthur, L. Z. (1985). Some components and consequences of a babyface. *Journal of Personality and Social Psychology, 48,* 312–323.

Berry, J. W., Poortinga, Y. H., Segall, M. H., & Dasen, P. R. (1992). *Cross-cultural psychology: Research and applications.* New York: Cambridge University Press.

Berscheid, E., Dion, K., Walster, E., & Walster, G. W. (1971). Physical attractiveness and dating choice: A test of the matching hypothesis. *Journal of Experimental Social Psychology, 7*(2), 173–189.

Berscheid, E., & Reis, H. T. (1998). Interpersonal attraction and close relationships. In D. T. Gilbert, S. T. Fiske, & G. Lindzey (Eds.), *The handbook of social psychology* (4th ed., Vol. 2, pp. 193–281). New York: McGraw-Hill.

Bertelsen, B., Harvald, B., & Hauge, M. (1977). A Danish twin study of manic-depressive disorders. *British Journal of Psychiatry, 130,* 330–351.

Bertenthal, B. I., Rose, J. L., & Bai, D. L. (1997). Perception–action coupling in the development of visual control of posture. *Journal of Experimental Psychology: Human Perception & Performance, 23,* 1631–1643.

Berthoud, H.-R., & Morrison, C. (2008). The brain, appetite, and obesity. *Annual Review of Psychology, 59,* 55–92.

Best, J. B. (1992). *Cognitive psychology* (3rd ed.). New York: West Publishing.

Bettencourt, B., A., & Miller, N. (1996). Gender differences in aggression as a function of provocation: A meta-analysis. *Psychological Bulletin, 119,* 422–447.

Beutler, L. E. (2002). The dodo bird is extinct. *Clinical Psychology: Science and Practice, 9,* 30–34.

Bhargava, S. (2011). Diagnosis and management of common sleep problems in children. *Pediatrics in Review, 32,* 91.

Bialystok, E. (1999). Cognitive complexity and attentional control in the bilingual mind. *Child Development, 70,* 636–644.

Bialystok, E. (2009). Bilingualism: The good, the bad, and the indifference. *Bilingualism: Language and Cognitive Processes, 12,* 3–11.

Bialystok, E., Craik, F. I. M., & Luk, G. (2012). Bilingualism: Consequences for mind and brain. *Trends in Cognitive Sciences, 16,* 240–250.

Bickerton, D. (1990). *Language and species.* Chicago: University of Chicago Press.

Biederman, I. (1987). Recognition-by-components: A theory of human image understanding. *Psychological Review, 94,* 115–147.

Biederman, J., Faraone, S. V., Spencer, T. J., Mick, E., Monuteaux, M. C., & Aleardi, M. (2006). Functional impairments in adults with self-reports of diagnosed ADHD: A controlled study of 1001 adults in the community. *Journal of Clinical Psychiatry, 67,* 524–540.

Biederman, J., Monuteaux, M. C., Spencer, T., Wilens, T. E., & Faraone, S. V. (2009). Do stimulants protect against psychiatric disorders in youth with ADHD? A 10-year follow-up study. *Pediatrics, 124,* 71–78.

Billet, E., Richter, J., & Kennedy, J. (1998). Genetics of obsessive-compulsive disorder. In R. Swinson, M. Anthony, S. Rachman, & M. Richter (Eds.), *Obsessive-compulsive disorder: Theory, research, and treatment* (pp. 181–206). New York: Guilford Press.

Binet, A. (1909). *Les idées modernes sur les enfants* [Modern ideas about children]. Paris: Flammarion.

Binswanger, L. (1958). The existential analysis school of thought. In R. May (Ed.), *Existence: A new dimension in psychiatry and psychology* (pp. 191–213). New York: Basic Books.

Bjork, D. W. (1983). *The compromised scientist: William James in the development of American psychology.* New York: Columbia University Press.

Bjork, D. W. (1993). *B. F. Skinner: A life.* New York: Basic Books.

Bjork, E. L., & Bjork, R. A. (2011). Making things hard on yourself, but in a good way: Creating desirable difficulties to enhance learning. In M. A. Gernsbacher, R. W. Pewe, L. M. Hough, & J. R. Pomerantz (Eds.), *Psychology and the real world: Essays illustrating fundamental contributions to society* (pp. 56–64). New York: Worth Publishers.

Bjork, R. A. (2011). On the symbiosis of remembering, forgetting, and learning. In A. S. Benjamin (Ed.), *Successful remembering and successful forgetting: A festschrift in honor of Robert A. Bjork* (pp. 1–22). London: Psychology Press.

Bjork, R. A., & Bjork, E. L. (1988). On the adaptive aspects of retrieval failure in autobiographical memory. In M. M. Gruneberg, P. E. Morris, & R. N. Sykes (Eds.), *Practical aspects of memory: Current research and issues* (pp. 283–288). Chichester, England: Wiley.

Bjork, R. A., Dunlosky, J., & Kornell, N. (2013). Self-regulated learning: Beliefs, techniques, and illusions. *Annual Review of Psychology, 64,* 417–444.

Blackburn, E. H., & Epel, E. S. (2012). Too toxic to ignore. *Nature, 490,* 169–171.

Blair, C. (2006). How similar are fluid cognition and general intelligence? A developmental neuroscience perspective on fluid cognition as an aspect of human cognitive ability. *Behavioral and Brain Sciences, 29*(2), 109–125 (article),125–160 (discussion). doi:10.1017/S0140525X06009034

Blair, I. V. (2002). The malleability of automatic stereotypes and prejudice. *Personality and Social Psychology Review, 6,* 242–261.

Blair, J., Peschardt, K., & Mitchell, D. R. (2005). *Psychopath: Emotion and the brain.* Oxford, England: Blackwell.

Blascovich, J., Mendes, W. B., Hunter, S. B., Lickel, B., & Kowai-Bell, N. (2001). Perceiver threat in social interactions with stigmatized others. *Journal of Personality and Social Psychology, 80,* 253–267.

Blascovich, J., & Tomaka, J. (1996). The biopsychosocial model of arousal regulation. In M. P. Zanna (Ed.), *Advances in experimental social psychology* (Vol. 28, pp. 1–51). San Diego, CA: Academic Press.

Blasi, A. (1980). Bridging moral cognition and moral action: A critical review of the literature. *Psychological Bulletin, 88,* 1–45.

Blatt, S. J., & Homann, E. (1992). Parent–child interaction in the etiology of dependent and self-critical depression. *Clinical Psychology Review, 12,* 47–91.

Blesch, A., & Tuszynski, M. H. (2009). Spinal cord injury: Plasticity, regeneration and the challenge of translational drug development. *Trends in Neurosciences, 32,* 41–47.

Bliss, T. V. P. (1999). Young receptors make smart mice. *Nature, 401,* 25–27.

Bliss, T. V. P., & Lømo, W. T. (1973). Long-lasting potentiation of synaptic transmission in the dentate area of the anesthetized rabbit following stimulation of the perforant path. *Journal of Physiology, 232,* 331–356.

Bloch, C., Kaiser, A., Kuenzli, E., Zappatore, D., Haller, S., Franceschini, R., . . . Nitsch, C. (2009). The age of second language acquisition determines the variability in activation elicited by narration in three languages in Broca's and Wernicke's area. *Neuropsychologia, 47,* 625–633.

Bloom, C. M., Venard, J., Harden, M., & Seetharaman, S. (2007). Non-contingent positive and negative reinforcement schedules of superstitious behaviors. *Behavioural Process, 75,* 8–13.

Blumen, H . M., & Rajaram, S. (2008). Influence of re-exposure and retrieval disruption during group collaboration on later individual recall. *Memory, 16,* 231–244.

Boden, J. M., Fergusson, D. M., & Horwood, L. J. (2010). Risk factors for conduct disorder and oppositional/defiant disorder: Evidence from a New Zealand birth cohort. *Journal of the American Academy of Child and Adolescent Psychiatry, 49,* 1125–1133.

Boecker, H., Sprenger, T., Spilker, M. E., Henriksen, G., Koppenhoefer, M., Wagner, K. J., . . .Tolle, T. R. (2008). The runner's high: Opioidergic mechanisms in the human brain. *Cerebral Cortex, 18,* 2523–2531.

Boehm, J. K., & Kubzansky, L. D. (2012). The heart's content: The association between positive psychological well-being and cardiovascular health. *Psychological Bulletin, 138,* 655–691.

Boehm, J. K., Williams, D. R., Rimm, E. B., Ryff, C., & Kubzansky, L. D. (2013). Relation between optimism and lipids in midlife. *American Journal of Cardiology, 111,* 1425–1431.

Boergers, J., Spirito, A., & Donaldson, D. (1998). Reasons for adolescent suicide attempts: Associations with psychological functioning. *Journal of the American Academy of Child and Adolescent Psychiatry, 37,* 1287–1293.

Bogaert, A. F. (2004). Asexuality: Its prevalence and associated factors in a national probability sample. *The Journal of Sex Research, 41,* 279–287.

Bohan, J. S. (1996). *Psychology and sexual orientation: Coming to terms.* New York: Routledge.

Boinski, S., Quatrone, R. P., & Swartz, H. (2000). Substrate and tool use by brown capuchins in Suriname: Ecological contexts and cognitive bases. *American Anthropologist, 102,* 741–761.

Boisvert, C. M., & Faust, D. (2002). Iatrogenic symptoms in psychotherapy: A theoretical exploration of the potential impact of labels, language, and belief systems. *American Journal of Psychotherapy, 56,* 244–259.

Bolger, N., Davis, A., & Rafaeli, E. (2003). Diary methods: Capturing life as it is lived. *Annual Review of Psychology, 54,* 579–616.

Bolton, G. E., & Ockenfels, A. (2000). Erc: A theory of equity, reciprocity, and competition. *American Economic Review, 90,* 166–193.

Boomsma, D., Busjahn, A., & Peltonen, L. (2002). Classical twin studies and beyond. *Nature Reviews Genetics, 3,* 872–882.

Bootzin, R. R., & Epstein, D. R. (2011). Understanding and treating insomnia. *Annual Review of Clinical Psychology, 7,* 435–458.

Borges, G., Breslau, J., Orozco, R., Tancredi, D. J., Anderson, H., Aguilar-Gaxiola, S., & Medina-Mora, M.-E. (2011). A cross-national study on Mexico–US migration, substance use and substance use disorders. *Drug and Alcohol Dependence, 117,* 16–23.

Borghol, N., Suderman, M., McArdle, W., Racine, A., Hallett, M., Pembrey, M., . . . Szyf, M. (2012). Associations with early-life socioeconomic position in adult DNA methylation. *International Journal of Epidemiology, 41,* 62–74.

Borkenau, P., & Liebler, A. (1995). Observable attributes as manifestations and cues of personality and intelligence. *Journal of Personality, 63,* 1–25.

Borkevec, T. D. (1982). Insomnia. *Journal of Consulting and Clinical Psychology, 50,* 880–895.

Born, R. T., & Bradley, D. C. (2005). Structure and function of visual area MT. *Annual Review of Neuroscience, 28,* 157–189.

Börner, K., Klavans, R., Patek, M., Zoss, A. M., Biberstine, J. R., Light, R. P., Larivière, V., & Boyack, K. W. (2012). Design and update of a classification system: The UCSD map of science. *PLoS ONE, 7,* e39464.

Bornstein, R. F. (1989). Exposure and affect: Overview and metaanalysis of research, 1968–1987. *Psychological Bulletin, 106,* 265–289.

Boroditsky, L. (2001). Does language shape thought? Mandarin and English speakers' conceptions of time. *Cognitive Psychology, 43,* 1–22.

Botwin, M. D., Buss, D. M., & Shackelford, T. K. (1997). Personality and mate preferences: Five factors in mate selection and marital satisfaction. *Journal of Personality, 65,* 107–136.

Bouchard, T. J., & Loehlin, J. C. (2001). Genes, evolution, and personality. *Behavioral Genetics, 31,* 243–273.

Bouchard, S. M., Brown, T. G., & Nadeau, L. (2012). Decision making capacities and affective reward anticipation in DWI recidivists compared to non-offenders: A preliminary study. *Accident Analysis and Prevention, 45,* 580–587.

Bouchard, T. J., & McGue, M. (2003). Genetic and environmental influences on human psychological differences. *Journal of Neurobiology, 54,* 4–45.

Bouton, M. E. (1988). Context and ambiguity in the extinction of emotional learning: Implications for exposure therapy. *Behaviour Research and Therapy, 26,* 137–149.

Bower, B. (1999, October 30). The mental butler did it—research suggests that subconscious affects behavior more than thought. *Science News, 156,* 208–282.

Bower, G. H. (1981). Mood and memory. *American Psychologist, 36,* 129–148.

Bower, G. H., Clark, M. C., Lesgold, A. M., & Winzenz, D. (1969). Hierarchical retrieval schemes in recall of categorical word lists. *Journal of Verbal Learning and Verbal Behavior, 8,* 323–343.

Bowers, K. S., Regehr, G., Balthazard, C., & Parker, D. (1990). Intuition in the context of discovery. *Cognitive Psychology, 22,* 72–110.

Bowlby, J. (1969). *Attachment and loss: Vol. 1. Attachment.* New York: Basic Books.

Bowlby, J. (1973). *Attachment and loss: Vol. 2. Separation.* New York: Basic Books.

Bowlby, J. (1980). *Attachment and loss: Vol. 3. Loss: Sadness and depression.* New York: Basic Books.

Boyack, K. W., Klavans, R., & Börner, K. (2005). Mapping the backbone of science. *Scientometrics, 64,* 351–374.

Boyd, R. (2008, February 7). Do people use only 10 percent of their brains? *Scientific American.* Retrieved from http://www.scientificamerican.com/article.cfm?id=people-only-use-10-percent-of-brain&page=2

Bozarth, M. A. (Ed.). (1987). *Methods of assessing the reinforcing properties of abused drugs.* New York: Springer-Verlag.

Bozarth, M. A., & Wise, R. A. (1985). Toxicity associated with long-term intravenous heroin and cocaine self-administration in the rat. *Journal of the American Medical Association, 254,* 81–83.

Brackett, M. A., & Mayer, J. D. (2003). Convergent, discriminant, and incremental validity of competing measures of emotional intelligence. *Personality and Social Psychology Bulletin, 29,* 1147.

Brackett, M. A., Rivers, S. E., Shiffman, S., Lerner, N., & Salovey, P. (2006). Relating emotional abilities to social functioning: A comparison of self-report and performance measures of emotional intelligence. *Journal of Personality and Social Psychology, 91,* 780.

Brackett, M. A., Warner, R. M., & Bosco, J. (2005). Emotional intelligence and relationship quality among couples. *Personal Relationships, 12*(2), 197–212.

Bradford, D., Stroup, S., & Lieberman, J. (2002). Pharmacological treatments for schizophrenia. In P. E. Nathan & J. M. Gorman (Eds.), *A guide to treatments that work* (2nd ed., pp. 169–199). New York: Oxford University Press.

Bradmetz, J., & Schneider, R. (2004). The role of the counterfactually satisfied desire in the lag between false-belief and false-emotion attributions in children aged 4–7. *British Journal of Developmental Psychology, 22,* 185–196.

Braet, W., & Humphreys, G. W. (2009). The role of reentrant processes in feature binding: Evidence from neuropsychology and TMS on late onset illusory conjunctions. *Visual Cognition, 17,* 25–47.

Bramlett, M. D., & Mosher, W. D. (2002). *Cohabitation, marriage, divorce, and remarriage in the United States* (Vital and Health Statistics Series 23, No. 22). Hyattsville, MD: National Center for Health Statistics.

Brandt, K. R., Gardiner, J. M., Vargha-Khadem, F., Baddeley, A. D., & Mishkin, M. (2009). Impairment of recollection but not familiarity in a case of developmental amnesia. *Neurocase, 15,* 60–65.

Braun, A. R., Balkin, T. J., Wesensten, N. J., Gwadry, F., Carson, R. E., Varga, M., . . . Herskovitch, P. (1998). Dissociated pattern of activity in visual cortices and their projections during rapid eye movement sleep. *Science, 279,* 91–95.

Breckler, S. J. (1994). Memory for the experiment of donating blood: Just how bad was it? *Basic and Applied Social Psychology, 15,* 467–488.

Brédart, S., & Valentine, T. (1998). Descriptiveness and proper name retrieval. *Memory, 6,* 199–206.

Bredy, T. W., Wu, H., Crego, C., Zellhoefer, J., Sun, Y. E., & Barad, M. (2007). Histone modifications around individual BDNF gene promoters in prefrontal cortex are associated with extinction of conditioned fear. *Learning and Memory, 14,* 268–276.

Breggin, P. R. (1990). Brain damage, dementia, and persistent cognitive dysfunction associated with neuroleptic drugs: Evidence, etiology, implications. *Journal of Mind and Behavior, 11,* 425–463.

Breggin, P. R. (2000). *Reclaiming our children.* Cambridge, MA: Perseus Books.

Brehm, S. S. (1992). *Intimate relationships* (2nd ed.). New York: McGraw-Hill.

Breland, K., & Breland, M. (1961). The misbehavior of organisms. *American Psychologist, 16,* 681–684.

Brennan, P. A., & Zufall, F. (2006). Pheromonal communication in vertebrates. *Nature, 444,* 308–315.

Brenninkmeijer, V., Vanyperen, N. W., & Buunk, B. P. (2001). I am not a better teacher, but others are doing worse: Burnout and perceptions of superiority among teachers. *Social Psychology of Education, 4*(3–4), 259–274.

Breslau, J., Aguilar-Gaxiola, S., Borges, G., Castilla-Puentes, R. C., Kendler, K. S., Medina-Mora, M.-E., . . . Kessler, R. C. (2007). Mental disorders among English-speaking Mexican immigrants to the US compared to a national sample of Mexicans. *Psychiatry Research, 151,* 115–122.

Breslau, J., & Chang, D. F. (2006). Psychiatric disorders among foreign-born and US-born Asian-Americans in a US national survey. *Social Psychiatry & Psychiatric Epidemiology, 41,* 943–950.

Bretherton, I., & Munholland, K. A. (1999). Internal working models in attachment relationships: A construct revisited. In J. Cassidy & P. R. Shaver (Eds.), *Handbook of attachment: Theory, research and clinical applications* (pp. 89–114). New York: Guilford Press.

Brewer, J. A., Worhunsky, P. D., Gray, J. R., Tang, Y.-Y., Weber, J., & Kober, H. (2011). Meditation experience is associated with differences in default mode network activity and connectivity. *Proceedings of the National Academy of Sciences, 108,* 20254–20259.

Brewer, W. F. (1996). What is recollective memory? In D. C. Rubin (Ed.), *Remembering our past: Studies in autobiographical memory* (pp. 19–66). New York: Cambridge University Press.

Broadbent, D. E. (1958). *Perception and communication.* London: Pergamon Press.

Broberg, D. J., & Bernstein, I. L. (1987). Candy as a scapegoat in the prevention of food aversions in children receiving chemotherapy. *Cancer, 60,* 2344–2347.

Broca, P. (1861). Remarques sur le siège de la faculté du langage articulé; suivies d'une observation d'aphémie (perte de la parole) [Remarks on the seat of the faculty of articulated language, following an observation of aphemia (loss of speech)]. *Bulletin de la Société Anatomique de Paris, 36,* 330–357.

Broca, P. (1863). Localisation des fonction cérébrales: Siège du langage articulé [Localization of brain functions: Seat of the faculty of articulated language]. *Bulletin de la Société d'Anthropologie de Paris, 4,* 200–202.

Brock, A. (1993). Something old, something new: The "reappraisal" of Wilhelm Wundt in textbooks. *Theory & Psychology, 3*(2), 235–242.

Brody, N. (2003). Construct validation of the Sternberg Triarchic Abilities Test: Comment and reanalysis. *Intelligence, 31*(4), 319–329.

Brooks, D. (2011, July 7). The unexamined society. *New York Times.* Retrieved from http://www.nytimes.com/2011/07/08/opinion/08brooks.html

Brooks, D. (2012a, May 3). The campus tsunami. *New York Times.* Retreived from http://www.nytimes.com/2012/05/04/opinion/brooks the campus-tsunami.html

Brooks, D. (2012b, October 12). The personality problem. *New York Times.* Retrieved from http://www.nytimes.com/2012/10/12/opinion/brooks-the-personality-problem.html

Brooks, R., & Meltzoff, A. N. (2002). The importance of eyes: How infants interpret adult looking behavior. *Developmental Psychology, 38,* 958–966.

Brooks-Gunn, J., Graber, J. A., & Paikoff, R. L. (1994). Studying links between hormones and negative affect: Models and measures. *Journal of Research on Adolescence, 4,* 469–486.

Brosnan, S. F., & DeWaal, F. B. M. (2003). Monkeys reject unequal pay. *Nature, 425,* 297–299.

Brown, A. S. (2004). *The déjà vu experience.* New York: Psychology Press.

Brown, B. B., Mory, M., & Kinney, D. (1994). Casting crowds in a relational perspective: Caricature, channel, and context. In G. A. R. Montemayor & T. Gullotta (Eds.), *Advances in adolescent development: Personal relationships during adolescence* (Vol. 5, pp. 123–167). Newbury Park, CA: Sage.

Brown, J. D. (1993). Self-esteem and self-evaluation: Feeling is believing. In J. M. Suls (Ed.), *The self in social perspective: Psychological perspectives on the self* (Vol. 4, pp. 27–58). Hillsdale, NJ: Erlbaum.

Brown, J. D., & McGill, K. L. (1989). The cost of good fortune: When positive life events produce negative health consequences. *Journal of Personality and Social Psychology, 57,* 1103–1110.

Brown, L. E., Wilson, E. T., & Gribble, P. L. (2009). Repetitive transcranial magnetic stimulation to the primary cortex interferes with motor learning by observing. *Journal of Cognitive Neuroscience, 21,* 1013–1022.

Brown, R. (1958). *Words and things.* New York: Free Press.

Brown, R., & Hanlon, C. (1970). Derivational complexity and order of acquisition in child speech. In J. R. Hayes (Ed.), *Cognition and the development of language* (pp. 11–53). New York: Wiley.

Brown, R., & Kulik, J. (1977). Flashbulb memories. *Cognition, 5,* 73–99.

Brown, R., & McNeill, D. (1966). The "tip-of-the-tongue" phenomenon. *Journal of Verbal Learning and Verbal Behavior, 5,* 325–337.

Brown, R. P., Osterman, L. L., & Barnes, C. D. (2009). School violence and the culture of honor. *Psychological Science, 20*(11), 1400–1405.

Brown, S. C., & Craik, F. I. M. (2000). Encoding and retrieval of information. In E. Tulving & F. I. M. Craik (Eds.), *The Oxford handbook of memory* (pp. 93–107). New York: Oxford University Press.

Brown, T. A., & Barlow, D. H. (2002). Classification of anxiety and mood disorders. In D. H. Barlow (Ed.), *Anxiety and its disorders: The nature and treatment of anxiety and panic* (2nd ed.). New York: Guilford Press.

Brownell, K. D., Greenwood, M. R. C., Stellar, E., & Shrager, E. E. (1986). The effects of repeated cycles of weight loss and regain in rats. *Physiology and Behavior, 38,* 459–464.

Bruner, J. S. (1983). Education as social invention. *Journal of Social Issues, 39,* 129–141.

Brunet, A., Orr, S. P., Tremblay, J., Robertson, K., Nader, K., & Pitman, R. K. (2008). Effects of post-retrieval propranolol on psychophysiologic responding during subsequent script-driven traumatic imagery in posttraumatic stress disorder. *Journal of Psychiatric Research, 42,* 503–506.

Brunet, A., Poundjia, J., Tremblay, J., Bui, E., Thomas, E., Orr, S. P., . . . Pitman, R. K. (2011). Trauma reactivation under the influence of propranolol decreases posttraumatic stress symptoms and disorder. *Journal of Clinical Psychopharmacology, 31,* 547–550.

Brunner, D. P., Dijk, D. J., Tobler, I., & Borbely, A. A. (1990). Effect of partial sleep deprivation on sleep stages and EEG power spectra. *Electroencephalography and Clinical Neurophysiology, 75,* 492–499.

Bryck, R. L., & Fisher, P. A. (2012). Training the brain: Practical applications of neural plasticity from the intersection of cognitive neuroscience, developmental psychology, and prevention science. *American Psychologist, 67,* 87–100.

Buchanan, C. M., Eccles, J. S., & Becker, J. B. (1992). Are adolescents the victims of raging hormones? Evidence for activational effects of hormones on moods and behavior at adolescence. *Psychological Bulletin, 111,* 62–107.

Buchanan, T. W. (2007). Retrieval of emotional memories. *Psychological Bulletin, 133,* 761–779.

Buckholtz, J. W., & Meyer-Lindenberg, A. (2012). Psychopathology and the human connectome: Toward a transdiagnostic model of risk for mental illness. *Neuron, 74,* 990–1003.

Buck Louis, G. M., Gray, L. E., Marcus, M., Ojeda, S. R., Pescovitz, O. H., Witchel, S. F., . . . Euling, S. Y. (2008). Environmental factors and puberty timing: Expert panel research. *Pediatrics, 121*(Suppl. 3), S192–S207. doi:10.1542/peds1813E

Buckner, R. L., Andrews-Hanna, J. R., & Schacter, D. L. (2008). The brain's default network: Anatomy, function, and relevance to disease. *Annals of the New York Academy of Sciences, 1124,* 1–38.

Buckner, R. L., Petersen, S. E., Ojemann, J. G., Miezin, F. M., Squire, L. R., & Raichle, M. E. (1995). Functional anatomical studies of explicit and implicit memory retrieval tasks. *The Journal of Neuroscience, 15,* 12–29.

Bunce, D. M., Flens, E. A., & Neiles, K. Y. (2011). How long can students pay attention in class? A study of student attention decline using clickers. *Journal of Chemical Education, 87,* 1438–1443.

Bureau of Justice Statistics. (2008). *Prisoners in 2007* (No. NCJ224280 by H. C. West & W. J. Sabol). Washington, DC: U.S. Department of Justice.

Burger, J. M. (1999). The foot-in-the-door compliance procedure: A multiple-process analysis and review. *Personality and Social Psychology Review, 3,* 303–325.

Burger, J. M. (2009). Replicating Milgram: Would people still obey today? *American Psychologist, 64,* 1–11.

Burger, J. M., & Burns, L. (1988). The illusion of unique invulnerability and the use of effective contraception. *Personality and Social Psychology Bulletin, 14,* 264–270.

Burger, J. M., Sanchez, J., Imberi, J. E., & Grande, L. R. (2009). The norm of reciprocity as an internalized social norm: Returning favors even when no one finds out. *Social Influence, 4*(1), 11–17.

Burke, D., MacKay, D. G., Worthley, J. S., & Wade, E. (1991). On the tip of the tongue: What causes word failure in young and older adults? *Journal of Memory and Language, 30,* 237–246.

Burke, J. D., Loeber, R., & Birmaher, B. (2002). Oppositional defiant disorder and conduct disorder: Part II. A review of the past 10 years. *Journal of the American Academy of Child and Adolescent Psychiatry, 41,* 1275–1293.

Burkham, D. T., Ready, D. D., Lee, V. E., & LoGerfo, L. F. (2004). Social-class differences in summer learning between kindergarten and first grade: Model specification and estimation. *Sociology of Education, 77,* 1–31.

Burks, S. V., Carpenter, J. P., Goette, L., & Rustichini, A. (2009). Cognitive skills affect economic preferences, strategic behavior, and job attachment. *Proceedings of the National Academy of Sciences, 106*(19), 7745–7750. doi:10.1073/pnas.0812360106

Burns, D. J., Hwang, A. J., & Burns, S. A. (2011). Adaptive memory: Determining the proximate mechanisms responsible for the memorial advantages of survival processing. *Journal of Experimental Psychology: Learning, Memory, and Cognition, 37,* 206–218.

Burnstein, E., Crandall, C., & Kitayama, S. (1994). Some neo-Darwinian decision rules for altruism: Weighing cues for inclusive fitness as a function of the biological importance of the decision. *Journal of Personality and Social Psychology, 67,* 773–789.

Burris, C. T., & Branscombe, N. R. (2005). Distorted distance estimation induced by a self-relevant national boundary. *Journal of Experimental Social Psychology, 41,* 305–312.

Bushman, B. J., & Huesmann, L. R. (2010). Aggression. In S. T. Fiske, D. T. Gilbert, & G. Lindzey (Eds.), *The handbook of social psychology* (5th ed., Vol. 2, pp. 833–863). New York: Wiley.

Buss, D. M. (1985). Human mate selection. *American Scientist, 73,* 47–51.

Buss, D. M. (1989). Sex differences in human mate preferences: Evolutionary hypotheses tested in 37 cultures. *Behavioral and Brain Sciences, 12,* 1–49.

Buss, D. M. (1996). Social adaptation and five major factors of personality. In J. S. Wiggins (Ed.), *The five-factor model of personality: Theoretical perspectives* (pp. 180–208). New York: Guilford Press.

Buss, D. M. (1999). *Evolutionary psychology: The new science of the mind.* Boston: Allyn & Bacon.

Buss, D. M. (2000). *The dangerous passion: Why jealousy is as necessary as love and sex.* New York: Free Press.

Buss, D. M. (2007). The evolution of human mating. *Acta Psychologica Sinica, 39,* 502–512.

Buss, D. M., & Haselton, M. G. (2005). The evolution of jealousy. *Trends in Cognitive Sciences, 9,* 506–507.

Buss, D. M., Haselton, M. G., Shackelford, T. K., Bleske, A. L., & Wakefield, J. C. (1998). Adaptations, exaptations, and spandrels. *American Psychologist, 53,* 533–548.

Buss, D. M., & Schmitt, D. P. (1993). Sexual strategies theory: An evolutionary perspective on human mating. *Psychological Review, 100,* 204–232.

Butler, A. C., Chapman, J. E., Forman, E. M., & Beck, A. T. (2006). The empirical status of cognitive-behavioral therapy: A review of meta-analyses. *Clinical Psychology Review, 26,* 17–31.

Butler, M. A., Corboy, J. R., & Filley, C. M. (2009). How the conflict between American psychiatry and neurology delayed the appreciation of cognitive dysfunction in multiple sclerosis. *Neuropsychology Review, 19,* 399–410.

Byers-Heinlein, K., Burns, T. C., & Werker, J. F. (2010). The roots of bilingualism in newborns. *Psychological Science, 21*(3), 343–348. doi:10.1177/0956797609360758

Byrne, D., Allgeier, A. R., Winslow, L., & Buckman, J. (1975). The situational facilitation of interpersonal attraction: A three-factor hypothesis. *Journal of Applied Social Psychology, 5,* 1–15.

Byrne, D., & Clore, G. L. (1970). A reinforcement model of evaluative responses. *Personality: An International Journal, 1,* 103–128.

Byrne, D., Ervin, C. R., & Lamberth, J. (1970). Continuity between the experimental study of attraction and real-life computer dating. *Journal of Personality and Social Psychology, 16,* 157–165.

Byrne, D., & Nelson, D. (1965). Attraction as a linear function of proportion of positive reinforcements. *Journal of Personality and Social Psychology, 1,* 659–663.

Cabeza, R. (2002). Hemispheric asymmetry reduction in older adults: The HAROLD model. *Psychology and Aging, 17,* 85–100.

Cabeza, R., Grady, C. L., Nyberg, L., McIntosh, A. R., Tulving, E., Kapur, S., . . . Craik, F. I. M. (1997). Age-related differences in neural activity during memory encoding and retrieval: A positron emission tomography study. *The Journal of Neuroscience, 17,* 391–400.

Cabeza, R., Rao, S., Wagner, A. D., Mayer, A., & Schacter, D. L. (2001). Can medial temporal lobe regions distinguish true from false? An event-related fMRI study of veridical and illusory recognition memory. *Proceedings of the National Academy of Sciences, USA, 98,* 4805–4810.

Cacioppo, J. T., & Patrick, B. (2008). *Loneliness: Human nature and the need for social connection.* New York: Norton.

Cahill, L., Haier, R. J., Fallon, J., Alkire, M. T., Tang, C., Keator, D., . . . McGaugh, J. L. (1996). Amygdala activity at encoding correlated with longterm, free recall of emotional information. *Proceedings of the National Academy of Sciences, USA, 93,* 8016–8021.

Cahill, L., & McGaugh, J. L. (1998). Mechanisms of emotional arousal and lasting declarative memory. *Trends in Neurosciences, 21,* 294–299.

Calder, A. J., Young, A. W., Rowland, D., Perrett, D. I., Hodges, J. R., & Etcoff, N. L. (1996). Facial emotion recognition after bilateral amygdala damage: Differentially severe impairment of fear. *Cognitive Neuropsychology, 13,* 699–745.

Calkins, M. W. (Ed.). (1930). *Mary Whiton Calkins* (Vol. 1). Worcester, MA: Clark University Press.

Callaghan, T., Rochat, P., Lillard, A., Claux, M. L., Odden, H., Itakura, S., . . . Singh, S. (2005). Synchrony in the onset of mental-state reasoning: Evidence from five cultures. *Psychological Science, 16,* 378–384.

Calvin, C. M., Deary, I. J., Fenton, C., Roberts, B. A., Der, G., Leckenby, N., & Batty, G. D. (2010). Intelligence in youth and all-cause-mortality: Systematic review with meta-analysis. *International Journal of Epidemiology, 40*(3), 626–644. doi:10.1093/ije/dyq190

Calzo, J. P., Antonucci, T. C., Mays, V. M., & Cochran, S. D. (2011). Retrospective recall of sexual orientation identity development among gay, lesbian, and bisexual adults. *Developmental Psychology, 47*(6), 1658–1673. doi:10.1037/a0025508

Cameron, C. D., & Payne, B. K. (2011). Escaping affect: How motivated emotion regulation creates insensitivity to mass suffering. *Journal of Personality and Social Psychology, 100*(1), 1–15.

Campbell, A. (1999). Staying alive: Evolution, culture, and women's intra-sexual aggression. *Behavioral & Brain Sciences, 22,* 203–252.

Campbell, C. M., & Edwards, R. R. (2012). Ethnic differences in pain and pain management. *Pain Management, 2,* 219–230.

Campbell, C. M., Edwards, R. R., & Fillingim, R. B. (2005). Ethnic differences in responses to multiple experimental pain stimuli. *Pain, 113,* 20–26.

Cannon, W. B. (1929). *Bodily changes in pain, hunger, fear, and rage: An account of recent research into the function of emotional excitement* (2nd ed.). New York: Appleton-Century-Crofts.

Cantor, N. (1990). From thought to behavior: "Having" and "doing" in the study of personality and cognition. *American Psychologist, 45,* 735–750.

Caparelli, E. C. (2007). TMS & fMRI: A new neuroimaging combinational tool to study brain function. *Current Medical Imaging Review, 3,* 109–115.

Caprioli, M. (2003). Gender equality and state aggression: The impact of domestic gender equality on state first use of force. *International Interactions, 29*(3), 195–214. doi:10.1080/03050620304595

Carey, N. (2012). *The epigenetics revolution: How modern biology is rewriting our understanding of genetics, disease, and inheritance.* New York: Columbia University Press.

Carlson, C., & Hoyle, R. (1993). Efficacy of abbreviated progressive muscle relaxation training: A quantitative review of behavioral medicine research. *Journal of Consulting and Clinical Psychology, 61,* 1059–1067.

Carmichael Olson, H., Streissguth, A. P., Sampson, P. D., Barr, H. M., Bookstein, F. L., & Thiede, K. (1997). Association of prenatal alcohol exposure with behavioral and learning problems in early adolescence. *Journal of the American Academy of Child & Adolescent Psychiatry, 36*(9), 1187–1194.

Carolson, E. A. (1998). A prospective longitudinal study of attachment disorganization/disorientation. *Child Development, 69,* 1107–1128.

Carpenter, S. K. (2012). Testing enhances the transfer of learning. *Current Directions in Psychological Science, 21,* 279–283.

Carr, L., Iacoboni, M., Dubeau, M., Mazziotta, J. C., & Lenzi, G. L. (2003). Neural mechanisms of empathy in humans: A relay from neural systems for imitation to limbic areas. *Proceedings of the National Academy of Sciences, USA, 100,* 5497–5502.

Carroll, J. B. (1993). *Human cognitive abilities.* Cambridge, England: Cambridge University Press.

Carson, R. C., Butcher, J. N., & Mineka, S. (2000). *Abnormal psychology and modern life* (11th ed.). Boston: Allyn & Bacon.

Carstensen, L. L. (1992). Social and emotional patterns in adulthood: Support for socioemotional selectivity theory. *Psychology and Aging, 7,* 331–338.

Carstensen, L. L., & Fredrickson, B. L. (1998). Influence of HIV status and age on cognitive representations of others. *Health Psychology, 17,* 1–10.

Carstensen, L. L., Pasupathi, M., Mayr, U., & Nesselroade, J. R. (2000). Emotional experience in everyday life across the adult life span. *Journal of Personality and Social Psychology, 79,* 644–655.

Carstensen, L. L., & Turk-Charles, S. (1994). The salience of emotion across the adult life span. *Psychology and Aging, 9,* 259–264.

Carver, C. S. (2006). Approach, avoidance, and the self-regulation of affect and action. *Motivation and Emotion, 30,* 105–110.

Carver, C. S., Lehman, J. M., & Antoni, M. H. (2003). Dispositional pessimism predicts illness-related disruption of social and recreational activities among breast cancer patients. *Journal of Personality and Social Psychology, 84,* 813–821.

Carver, C. S., & White, T. L. (1994). Behavioral inhibition, behavioral activation, and affective responses to impending reward and punishment: The bis/bas scales. *Journal of Personality and Social Psychology, 67*(2), 319–333.

Casasanto, D., & Boroditsky, L. (2008). Time in the mind: Using space to think about time. *Cognition, 106,* 579–593.

Casazza, K., Fontaine, K. R., Astrup, A., Birch, L. L., Brown, A. W., Bohan Brown, M. M., . . . Allison, D. B. (2013). Myths, presumptions, and facts about obesity. *New England Journal of Medicine, 368*(5), 446–454.

Caspi, A., & Herbener, E. S. (1990). Continuity and change: Assortative marriage and the consistency of personality in adulthood. *Journal of Personality and Social Psychology, 58,* 250–258.

Caspi, A., Lynam, D., Moffitt, T. E., & Silva, P. A. (1993). Unraveling girls' delinquency: Biological, dispositional, and contextual contributions to adolescent misbehavior. *Developmental Psychology, 29,* 19–30.

Caspi, A., Roberts, B. W., & Shiner, R. L. (2005). Personality development: Stability and change. *Annual Review of Psychology, 56,* 453–484.

Caspi, A., Sugden, K., Moffitt, T. E., Taylor, A., Craig, I. W., Harrington, H., . . . Poulton, R. (2003). Influence of life stress on depression: Moderation by a polymorphism in the 5-HTT gene. *Science, 301,* 386–389.

Castel, A. D., McCabe, D. P., & Roediger, H. L. III. (2007). Illusions of competence and overestimation of associate memory for identical items: Evidence from judgments of learning. *Psychonomic Bulletin & Review, 14,* 197–111.

Castellanos, F. X., Patti, P. L., Sharp, W., Jeffries, N. O., Greenstein, D. K., Clasen, L. S., . . . Rapoport, J. L. (2002). Developmental trajectories of brain volume abnormalities in children and adolescents with attention-deficit/hyperactivity disorder. *Journal of the American Medical Association, 288,* 1740–1748. doi: 10.1001/jama.288.14.1740

Catrambone, R. (2002). The effects of surface and structural feature matches on the access of story analogs. *Journal of Experimental Psychology: Learning, Memory, & Cognition, 28,* 318–334.

Cattell, R. B. (1950). *Personality: A systematic, theoretical, and factual study.* New York: McGraw-Hill.

Ceci, S. J. (1991). How much does schooling influence general intelligence and its cognitive components? A reassessment of the evidence. *Developmental Psychology, 27,* 703–722.

Ceci, S. J., DeSimone, M., & Johnson, S. (1992). Memory in context: A case study of "Bubbles P.," a gifted but uneven memorizer. In D. J. Herrmann, H. Weingartner, A. Searleman, & C. McEvoy (Eds.), *Memory improvement: Implications for memory theory* (pp. 169–186). New York: Springer-Verlag.

Ceci, S. J., & Williams, W. M. (1997). Schooling, intelligence, and income. *American Psychologist, 52,* 1051–1058.

Ceci, S. J., Williams, W. M., & Barnett, S. M. (2009). Women's underrepresentation in science: Sociocultural and biological considerations. *Psychological Bulletin, 135*(2), 218–261. doi:10.1037/a0014412

Centers for Disease Control and Prevention (CDC). (2002, June 28). Youth risk behavior surveillance. *Surveillance Summary, 51*(SS-4), 1–64. Washington, DC: Author.

Centers for Disease Control and Prevention. (2012). Monitoring selected national HIV prevention and care objectives by using HIV surveillance data—United States and 6 U.S. dependent areas—2010. *HIV Surveillance Supplemental Report, 17*(No. 3, part A).

Centers for Disease Control and Prevention. (2013). *Injury prevention and control: Data and statistics (WISQARS).* Retrieved from http://www.cdc.gov/injury/wisqars/index.html

Cepeda, N. J., Pashler, H., Vul, E., Wixted, J. T., & Rohrer, D. (2006). Distributed practice in verbal recall tests: A review and quantitative synthesis. *Psychological Bulletin, 132,* 354–380.

Chabris, C. F., Hebert, B. M., Benjamin, D. J., Beauchamp, J., Cesarini, D., van der Loos, M., & Laibson, D. (2012). Most reported genetic associations with general intelligence are probably false positives. *Psychological Science, 23*(11), 1314–1323. doi:10.1177/0956797611435528

Chabris, C., & Simons, D. (2012, November 16). Using just 10% of your brains? Think again. *Wall Street Journal Online.* Retrieved from http://online.wsj.com/article/SB100014241278873245563045781193 5187421218.html

Chaiken, S. (1980). Heuristic versus systematic information processing and the use of source versus message cues in persuasion. *Journal of Personality and Social Psychology, 39,* 752–766.

Chalmers, D. (1996). *The conscious mind: In search of a fundamental theory.* New York: Oxford University Press.

Chambless, D. L., Baker, M. J., Baucom, D. H., Beutler, L. E., Calhoun, K. S., Crits-Christoph, P., . . . Woody, S. R. (1998).

Update on empirically validated therapies, II. *Clinical Psychologist,* 51(1), 3–14.

Chandler, J., & Schwarz, N. (2009). How extending your middle finger affects your perception of others: Learned movements influence concept accessibility. *Journal of Experimental Social Psychology, 45,* 123–128.

Chandrashekar, J., Hoon, M. A., Ryba, N. J., & Zuker, C. S. (2006). The receptors and cells for human tastes. *Nature, 444,* 288–294.

Chang, P. P., Ford, D. E., Meoni, L. A., Wang, N., & Klag, M. J. (2002). Anger in young men and subsequent premature cardiovascular disease. *Archives of Internal Medicine, 162,* 901–906.

Charles, S. T., Reynolds, C. A., & Gatz, M. (2001). Age-related differences and change in positive and negative affect over 23 years. *Journal of Personality and Social Psychology, 80,* 136–151.

Charness, N. (1981). Aging and skilled problem solving. *Journal of Experimental Psychology: General, 110,* 21–38.

Charpak, G., & Broch, H. (2004). *Debunked!: ESP, telekinesis, and other pseudoscience* (B. K. Holland, Trans.). Baltimore, MD: Johns Hopkins University Press.

Chartrand, T. L., & Bargh, J. A. (1999). The chameleon effect: The perception-behavior link and social interaction. *Journal of Personality and Social Psychology, 76,* 893–910.

Chartrand, T. L., & Kay, A. (2006). *Mystery moods and perplexing performance: Consequences of succeeding and failing at a nonconscious goal.* Unpublished manuscript.

Chen, E., Cohen, S., & Miller, G. E. (2010). How low socioeconomic status affects 2-year hormonal trajectories in children. *Psychological Science, 21(1),* 31–37.

Cheney, D. L., & Seyfarth, R. M. (1990). *How monkeys see the world.* Chicago: University of Chicago Press.

Cheng, D. T., Disterhoft, J. F., Power, J. M., Ellis, D. A., & Desmond, J. E. (2008). Neural substrates underlying human delay and trace eyeblink conditioning. *Proceedings of the National Academy of Sciences, USA, 105,* 8108–8113.

Cherlin, A. J. (Ed.). (1992). *Marriage, divorce, remarriage* (2nd ed.). Cambridge, MA: Harvard University Press.

Cherry, C. (1953). Some experiments on the recognition of speech with one and two ears. *Journal of the Acoustical Society of America, 25,* 275–279.

Choi, I., Nisbett, R. E., & Norenzayan, A. (1999). Causal attribution across cultures: Variation and universality. *Psychological Bulletin, 125,* 47–63.

Chomsky, N. (1957). *Syntactic structures.* The Hague: Mouton.

Chomsky, N. (1959). A review of *Verbal Behavior* by B. F. Skinner. *Language, 35,* 26–58.

Chomsky, N. (1986). *Knowledge of language: Its nature, origin, and use.* New York: Praeger.

Chorover, S. L. (1980). *From Genesis to genocide : The meaning of human nature and the power of behavior control.* Cambridge, MA: MIT Press.

Choy, Y., Fyer, A. J., & Lipsitz, J. D. (2007). Treatment of specific phobia in adults. *Clinical Psychology Review, 27,* 266–286.

Christakis, N. A., & Fowler, J. H. (2007). The spread of obesity in a large social network over 32 years. *New England Journal of Medicine, 357(4),* 370–379.

Christianson, S.-Å., & Loftus, E. F. (1987). Memory for traumatic events. *Applied Cognitive Psychology, 1,* 225–239.

Chung, G. H., Flook, L., & Fuligni, A. J. (2009). Daily family conflict and emotional distress among adolescents from Latin American, Asian, and European backgrounds. *Developmental Psychology, 45,* 1406–1415.

Cialdini, R. B. (2005). Don't throw in the towel: Use social influence research. *American Psychological Society, 18,* 33–34.

Cialdini, R. B. (2013). The focus theory of normative conduct. In P. A. M. van Lange, A. W. Kruglanski, & E. T. Higgins (Eds.), *Handbook of theories of social psychology* (Vol. 3, pp. 295–312). New York: Sage.

Cialdini, R. B., & Goldstein, N. J. (2004). Social influence: Compliance and conformity. *Annual Review of Psychology, 55(1),* 591–621. doi: 10.1146/annurev.psych.55.090902.142015

Cialdini, R. B., Trost, M. R., & Newsom, J. T. (1995). Preference for consistency: The development of a valid measure and the discovery of surprising behavioral implications. *Journal of Personality and Social Psychology, 69,* 318–328.

Cialdini, R. B., Vincent, J. E., Lewis, S. K., Catalan, J., Wheeler, D., & Darby, B. L. (1975). Reciprocal concessions procedure for inducing compliance: The door-in-the-face technique. *Journal of Personality and Social Psychology, 31,* 206–215.

Ciarrochi, J. V., Chan, A. Y., & Caputi, P. (2000). A critical evaluation of the emotional intelligence concept. *Personality & Individual Differences, 28,* 539.

Cicchetti, D., & Toth, S. L. (1998). Perspectives on research and practice in developmental psychopathology. In I. E. Sigel & K. A. Renninger (Eds.), *Handbook of child psychology: Vol. 4. Child psychology in practice* (5th ed., pp. 479–583). New York: Wiley.

Clancy, S. A. (2005). *Abducted: How people come to believe they were kidnapped by aliens.* Cambridge, MA: Harvard University Press.

Clark, M. S., & Lemay, E. P. (2010). Close relationships. In S. T. Fiske, D. T. Gilbert, & G. Lindzey (Eds.), *The handbook of social psychology* (5th ed., Vol. 2). New York: Wiley.

Clark, R. D., & Hatfield, E. (1989). Gender differences in receptivity to sexual offers. *Journal of Psychology and Human Sexuality, 2,* 39–55.

Clark, R. E., Manns, J. R., & Squire, L. R. (2002). Classical conditioning, awareness and brain systems. *Trends in Cognitive Sciences, 6,* 524–531.

Clark, R. E., & Squire, L. R. (1998). Classical conditioning and brain systems: The role of awareness. *Science, 280,* 77–81.

Cleckley, H. M. (1976). *The mask of sanity* (5th ed.). St. Louis: Mosby.

Coe, C. L., & Lubach, G. R. (2008). Fetal programming prenatal origins of health and illness. *Current Directions in Psychological Science, 17,* 36–41.

Cogan, R., Cogan, D., Waltz, W., & McCue, M. (1987). Effects of laughter and relaxation on discomfort thresholds. *Journal of Behavioral Medicine, 10,* 139–144.

Coghill, R. C., McHaffie, J. G., & Yen, Y. (2003). Neural correlates of individual differences in the subjective experience of pain. *Proceedings of the National Academy of Sciences, USA, 100,* 8538–8542.

Cohen, D., Nisbett, R. E., Bowdle, B. F., & Schwarz, N. (1996). Insult, aggression, and the southern culture of honor: An "experimental ethnography." *Journal of Personality and Social Psychology, 70,* 945–960.

Cohen, G. (1990). Why is it difficult to put names to faces? *British Journal of Psychology, 81,* 287–297.

Cohen, S. (1988). Psychosocial models of the role of social support in the etiology of physical disease. *Health Psychology, 7,* 269–297.

Cohen, S. (1999). Social status and susceptibility to respiratory infections. *New York Academy of Sciences, 896,* 246–253.

Cohen, S., Frank, E., Doyle, W. J., Skoner, D. P., Rabin, B. S., & Gwaltney, J. M., Jr. (1998). Types of stressors that increase susceptibility to the common cold in healthy adults. *Health Psychology, 17,* 214–223.

Coifman, K. G., Bonanno, G. A., Ray, R. D., & Gross, J. J. (2007). Does repressive coping promote resilience? Affective-autonomic response discrepancy during bereavement. *Journal of Personality and Social Psychology, 92,* 745–758.

Colcombe, S. J., Erickson, K. I., Scalf, P. E., Kim, J. S., Prakesh, R., McAuley, E., . . . Kramer, A. F. (2006). Aerobic exercise training increases brain volume in aging humans. *Journals of Gerontology Series A: Biological Sciences and Medical Sciences, 61,* 1166–1170.

Colcombe, S. J., Kramer, A. F., Erickson, K. I., Scalf, P., McAuley, E., Cohen, N. J., . . . Elavsky, S. (2004). Cardiovascular fitness, cortical plasticity, and aging. *Proceedings of the National Academy of Sciences, USA, 101,* 3316–3321.

Cole, M. (1996). *Cultural psychology: A once and future discipline.* Cambridge, MA: Belknap Press of Harvard University Press.

Coman, A., Manier, D., & Hirst, W. (2009). Forgetting the unforgettable through conversation: Social shared retrieval-induced forgetting of September 11 memories. *Psychological Science, 20,* 627–633.

Condon, J. W., & Crano, W. D. (1988). Inferred evaluation and the relation between attitude similarity and interpersonal attraction. *Journal of Personality and Social Psychology, 54,* 789–797.

Conley, T. D. (2011). Perceived proposer personality characteristics and gender differences in acceptance of casual sex offers. *Journal of Personality and Social Psychology, 100*(2), 309–329. doi: 10.1037/a0022152

Conley, T. D., Moors, A. C., Matsick, J. L., Ziegler, A., & Valentine, B. A. (2011). Women, men, and the bedroom: Methodological and conceptual insights that narrow, reframe, and eliminate gender differences in sexuality. *Current Directions in Psychological Science, 20*(5), 296–300. doi: 10.1177/0963721411418467

Conway, M., & Ross, M. (1984). Getting what you want by revising what you had. *Journal of Personality and Social Psychology, 47,* 738–748.

Cook, M., & Mineka, S. (1989). Observational conditioning of fear to fear-relevant versus fear-irrelevant stimuli in rhesus monkeys. *Journal of Abnormal Psychology, 98*(4), 448–459.

Cook, M., & Mineka, S. (1990). Selective associations in the observational conditioning of fear in rhesus monkeys. *Journal of Experimental Psychology: Animal Behavior Process, 16,* 372–389.

Coontz, P. (2008). The responsible conduct of social research. In K. Yang & G. J. Miller (Eds.), *Handbook of research methods in public administration* (pp. 129–139). Boca Raton, FL: Taylor & Francis.

Cooper, H., Nye, B., Charlton, K., Lindsay, J., & Greathouse, S. (1996). The effects of summer vacation on achievement test scores: A narrative and meta-analytic review. *Review of Educational Research, 66*(3), 227–268.

Cooper, J., & Fazio, R. H. (1984). A new look at dissonance theory. In L. Berkowitz (Ed.), *Advances in experimental social psychology* (Vol. 17, pp. 229–266). New York: Academic Press.

Cooper, J. C., Hollon, N. G., Wimmer, G. E., & Knutson, B. (2009). Available alternative incentives modulate anticipatory nucleus accumbens activation. *Social Cognitive and Affective Neuroscience, 4,* 409–416.

Cooper, J. M., & Strayer, D. L. (2008). Effects of simulator practice and real-world experience on cell-phone related driver distraction. *Human Factors, 50,* 893–902.

Cooper, J. R., Bloom, F. E., & Roth, R. H. (2003). *Biochemical basis of neuropharmacology.* New York: Oxford University Press.

Cooper, M. L. (2006). Does drinking promote risky sexual behavior? A complex answer to a simple question. *Current Directions in Psychological Science, 15,* 19–23.

Cooper, W. H., & Withey, W. J. (2009). The strong situation hypothesis. *Personality and Social Psychology Review, 13,* 62–72.

Corbetta, M., Shulman, G. L., Miezin, F. M., & Petersen, S. E. (1995). Superior parietal cortex activation during spatial attention shifts and visual feature conjunction. *Science, 270,* 802–805.

Coren, S. (1997). *Sleep thieves.* New York: Free Press.

Corkin, S. (2002). What's new with the amnesic patient HM? *Nature Reviews Neuroscience, 3,* 153–160.

Corkin, S. (2013). *Permanent present tense: The unforgettable life of the amnesic patient, H.M.* New York: Basic Books.

Correll, J., Park, B., Judd, C. M., & Wittenbrink, B. (2002). The police officer's dilemma: Using ethnicity to disambiguate potentially threatening individuals. *Journal of Personality and Social Psychology, 83,* 1314–1329.

Correll, J., Park, B., Judd, C. M., Wittenbrink, B., Sadler, M. S., & Keesee, T. (2007). Across the thin blue line: Police officers and racial bias in the decision to shoot. *Journal of Personality and Social Psychology, 92,* 1006–1023.

Corsi, P. (1991). *The enchanted loom: Chapters in the history of neuroscience.* New York: Oxford University Press.

Corti, E. (1931). *A history of smoking* (P. England, Trans.). London: Harrap.

Coryell, W., Endicott, J., Maser, J. D., Mueller, T., Lavori, P., & Keller, M. (1995). The likelihood of recurrence in bipolar affective disorder: The importance of episode recency. *Journal of Affective Disorders, 33,* 201–206.

Costa, P. T., Terracciano, A., & McCrae, R. R. (2001). Gender differences in personality traits across cultures: Robust and surprising findings. *Journal of Personality and Social Psychology, 81,* 322–331.

Costanza, A., Weber, K., Gandy, S., Bouras, C., Hof, P. R., Giannakopoulos, G., & Canuto, A. (2011). Contact sport-related chronic traumatic encephalopathy in the elderly: Clinical expression and structural substrates. *Neuropathology and Applied Neurobiology, 37,* 570–584.

Cottrell, C. A., Neuberg, S. L., & Li, N. P. (2007). What do people desire in others? A sociofunctional perspective on the importance of different valued characteristics. *Journal of Personality and Social Psychology, 92,* 208–231.

Cox, D., & Cowling, P. (1989). *Are you normal?* London: Tower Press.

Coyne, J. A. (2000, April 3). Of vice and men: Review of R. Tornhill and C. Palmer, *A natural history of rape. The New Republic,* pp. 27–34.

Craddock, N., & Jones, I. (1999). Genetics of bipolar disorder. *Journal of Medical Genetics, 36,* 585–594.

Craik, F. I. M., Govoni, R., Naveh-Benjamin, M., & Anderson, N. D. (1996). The effects of divided attention on encoding and retrieval processes in human memory. *Journal of Experimental Psychology: General, 125,* 159–180.

Craik, F. I. M., & Tulving, E. (1975). Depth of processing and the retention of words in episodic memory. *Journal of Experimental Psychology: General, 104,* 268–294.

Cramer, R. E., Schaefer, J. T., & Reid, S. (1996). Identifying the ideal mate: More evidence for male–female convergence. *Current Psychology, 15,* 157–166.

Craske, M. G. (1999). *Anxiety disorders: Psychological approaches to theory and treatment.* Boulder, CO: Westview Press.

Crick, N. R., & Grotpeter, J. K. (1995). Relational aggression, gender, and social-psychological adjustment. *Child Development, 66,* 710–722.

Crocker, J., & Wolfe, C. T. (2001). Contingencies of self-worth. *Psychological Review, 108*(3), 593–623.

Crombag, H. F. M., Wagenaar, W. A., & Van Koppen, P. J. (1996). Crashing memories and the problem of "source monitoring." *Applied Cognitive Psychology, 10,* 95–104.

Cross, E. S., Kraemer, D. J. M., Hamilton, A. F. de C., Kelley, W. M., & Grafton, S. T. (2009). Sensitivity of the action observation network to physical and observational learning. *Cerebral Cortex, 19,* 315–326.

Cross, P. (1977). Not can but will college teachers be improved? *New Directions for Higher Education, 17,* 1–15.

Cross-Disorder Group of the Psychiatric Genomics Consortium. (2013). Identification of risk loci with shared effects on five major psychiatric disorders: A genome-wide analysis. *Lancet, 381,* 1371–1379.

Cruse, D., Chennu, S., Fernández-Espejo, D., Payne, W. L., Young, G. B., & Owen, A. M. (2012). Detecting awareness in the vegetative state: Electroencephalographic evidence for attempted movements to command. *PLoS One, 7*(11), e49933. doi:10.1371/journal.pone.0049933

Csigó, K., Harsányi, A., Demeter, G., Rajkai, C., Németh, A., & Racsmány, M. (2010). Long-term follow-up of patients with obsessive-compulsive disorder treated by anterior capsulotomy: A neuropsychological study. *Journal of Affective Disorders, 126,* 198–205.

Csikszentmihalyi, M. (1990). *Flow: The psychology of optimal experience.* New York: Harper & Row.

Cuc, A., Koppel, J., & Hirst, W. (2007). Silence is not golden: A case of socially shared retrieval-induced forgetting. *Psychological Science, 18,* 727–733.

Cummins, D. D. (2012). *Good thinking: Seven powerful ideas that influence the way we think.* New York: Cambridge University Press.

Cunningham, M. R., Barbee, A. P., & Pike, C. L. (1990). What do women want? Facial metric assessment of multiple motives in the perception of male facial physical attractiveness. *Journal of Personality and Social Psychology, 59,* 61–72.

Cunningham, M. R., Roberts, A. R., Barbee, A. P., Druen, P. B., & Wu, C.-H. (1995). "Their ideas of beauty are, on the whole, the same as ours": Consistency and variability in the cross-cultural perception of female physical attractiveness. *Journal of Personality and Social Psychology, 68,* 261–279.

Cunningham, W. A., & Brosch, T. (2012). Motivational salience: Amygdala tuning from traits, needs, values, and goals. *Current Directions in Psychological Science, 21*(1), 54–59.

Curran, J. P., & Lippold, S. (1975). The effects of physical attraction and attitude similarity on attraction in dating dyads. *Journal of Personality, 43,* 528–539.

Curtiss, S. (1977). *Genie: A psycholinguistic study of a modern-day "wildchild."* New York: Academic Press.

Cutler, D. L., Bevilacqua, J., & McFarland, B. H. (2003). Four decades of community mental health: A symphony in four movements. *Community Mental Health Journal, 39,* 381–398.

Dabbs, J. M., Bernieri, F. J., Strong, R. K., Campo, R., & Milun, R. (2001). Going on stage: Testosterone in greetings and meetings. *Journal of Research in Personality, 35,* 27–40.

Dabbs, J. M., Carr, T. S., Frady, R. L., & Riad, J. K. (1995). Testosterone, crime, and misbehavior among 692 male prison inmates. *Personality and Individual Differences, 18,* 627–633.

Dael, N., Mortillaro, M., & Scherer, K. R. (2012). Emotion expression in body action and posture. *Emotion, 12,* 1085–1101.

D'Agostino, P. R., & Fincher-Kiefer, R. (1992). Need for cognition and correspondence bias. *Social Cognition, 10,* 151–163.

Dahger, A., & Robbins, T. W. (2009). Personality, addiction, dopamine: Insights from Parkinson's disease. *Neuron, 61,* 502–510.

Dahl, G., & Della Vigna, S. (2009). Does movie violence increase violent crime? *The Quarterly Journal of Economics, 124,* 677–734.

Dally, P. (1999). *The marriage of heaven and hell: Manic depression and the life of Virginia Woolf.* New York: St. Martin's Griffin.

Dalton, P. (2003). Olfaction. In H. Pashler & S. Yantis (Eds.), *Stevens' handbook of experimental psychology: Vol. 1. Sensation and perception* (3rd ed., pp. 691–746). New York: Wiley.

Daly, M., & Wilson, M. (1988). Evolutionary social psychology and family homicide. *Science, 242,* 519–524.

Damasio, A. R. (1989). Time-locked multiregional retroactivation: A systems-level proposal for the neural substrates of recall and recognition. *Cognition, 33,* 25–62.

Damasio, A. R. (1994). *Descartes' error: Emotion, reason, and the human brain.* New York: Putnam.

Damasio, A. R. (2005). *Descartes' error: Emotion, reason, and the human Brain.* New York: Penguin.

Damasio, A. R., Grabowski, T. J., Bechara, A., Damasio, H., Ponto, L. L. B., Parvisi, J., & Hichwa, R. D. (2000). Subcortical and cortical brain activity during the feeling of self-generated emotions. *Nature Neuroscience, 3,* 1049–1056.

Damasio, H., Grabowski, T., Frank, R., Galaburda, A. M., & Damasio, A. R. (1994). The return of Phineas Gage: Clues about the brain from the skull of a famous patient. *Science, 264,* 1102–1105.

Damasio, H., Grabowski, T. J., Tranel, D., Hichwa, R. D., & Damasio, A. R. (1996). A neural basis for lexical retrieval. *Nature, 380,* 499–505.

Damsma, G., Pfaus, J. G., Wenkstern, D., Phillips, A. G., & Fibiger, H. C. (1992). Sexual behavior increases dopamine transmission in the nucleus accumbens and striatum of male rats: Comparison with novelty and locomotion. *Behavioral Neurosciences, 106,* 181–191.

Daneshvar, D. H., Nowinski, C. J., McKee, A. C., & Cantu, R. C. (2011). The epidemiology of sport-related concussion. *Clinical Sports Medicine, 30,* 1–17.

Daniel, H. J., O'Brien, K. F., McCabe, R. B., & Quinter, V. E. (1985). Values in mate selection: A 1984 campus survey. *College Student Journal, 19,* 44–50.

Danner, U. N., Ouwehand, C., van Haastert, N. L., Homsveld, H., & de Ridder, D. T. (2012). Decision-making impairments in women with binge eating disorder in comparison with obese and normal weight women. *European Eating Disorders Review, 20,* e56–e62.

Darley, J. M., & Berscheid, E. (1967). Increased liking caused by the anticipation of interpersonal contact. *Human Relations, 10,* 29–40.

Darley, J. M., & Gross, P. H. (1983). A hypothesis-confirming bias in labeling effects. *Journal of Personality and Social Psychology, 44,* 20–33.

Darley, J. M., & Latané, B. (1968). Bystander intervention in emergencies: Diffusion of responsibility. *Journal of Personality and Social Psychology, 8,* 377–383.

Dar-Nimrod, I., & Heine, S. J. (2006). Exposure to scientific theories affects women's math performance. *Science, 314,* 435.

Darwin, C. (2007). *The expression of the emotions in man and animals.* New York: Bibliobazaar. (Original work published 1899)

Darwin, C. (1998). *The expression of the emotions in man and animals* (P. Ekman, Ed.). New York: Oxford University Press. (Original work published 1872)

Darwin, C. J., Turvey, M. T., & Crowder, R. G. (1972). An auditory analogue of the Sperling partial report procedure: Evidence for brief auditory storage. *Cognitive Psychology, 3,* 255–267.

Dauer, W., & Przedborski, S. (2003). Parkinson's disease: Mechanisms and models. *Neuron, 39,* 889–909.

Daum, I., Schugens, M. M., Ackermann, H., Lutzenberger, W., Dichgans, J., & Birbaumer, N. (1993). Classical conditioning after cerebellar lesions in humans. *Behavioral Neuroscience, 107,* 748–756.

Davidson, R. J., Ekman, P., Saron, C., Senulis, J., & Friesen, W. V. (1990). Emotional expression and brain physiology I: Approach/withdrawal and cerebral asymmetry. *Journal of Personality and Social Psychology, 58,* 330–341.

Davidson, R. J., Putnam, K. M., & Larson, C. L. (2000). Dysfunction in the neural circuitry of emotion regulation—a possible prelude to violence. *Science, 289,* 591–594.

Davies, G. (1988). Faces and places: Laboratory research on context and face recognition. In G. M. Davies & D. M. Thomson (Eds.), *Memory in context: Context in memory* (pp. 35–53). New York: Wiley.

Davies, G, Tenesa, A., Payton, A., Yang, J., Harris, S. E., Liewald, D., . . . Deary, I. J. (2011). Genome-wide association studies establish that human intelligence is highly heritable and polygenic. *Molecular Psychiatry, 16*(10), 996–1005. doi:10.1038/mp2011.85

Davila Ross, M., Menzler, S., & Zimmermann, E. (2008). Rapid facial mimicry in orangutan play. *Biology Letters, 4*(1), 27–30.

Davis, C. (2008, March 30). Simon Cowell admits to using Botox. *People Magazine.* Retrieved from http://www.people.com/people/article/0,,20181478,00.html

Davis, C. J., Bowers, J. S., & Memon, A. (2011). Social influence in televised election debates: A potential distortion of democracy. *PLosONE, 6*(3), e18154.

Davis, J. L., Senghas, A., Brandt, F., & Ochsner, K. N. (2010). The effects of BOTOX injections on emotional experience. *Emotion, 10*(3), 433–440. doi: 10.1037/a0018690

Dawes, R. M. (1994). *House of cards: Psychology and psychotherapy built on myth.* New York: Free Press.

Dawood, K., Kirk, K. M., Bailey, J. M., Andrews, P. W., & Martin, N. G. (2005). Genetic and environmental influences on the frequency of orgasm in women. *Twin Research, 8,* 27–33.

Dawson, G., Rogers, S., Munson, J., Smith, M., Winter, J., Greenson, J., . . . Varley, J. (2010). Randomized, controlled trial of an intervention for toddlers with autism: The Early Start Denver Model. *Pediatrics, 125,* e17–e23.

Dawson, G., Jones, E. J. H., Merkle, K., Venema, K., Lowry, R., Faja, S., . . . Webb, S. J. (2012). Early behavioral intervention is associated with normalized brain activity in young children with autism. *Journal of the American Academy of child and Adolescent Psychiatry, 51,* 1150–1159.

Dawson, M., Soulieres, I., Gernsbacher, M. A., & Mottron, L. (2007). The level and nature of autistic intelligence. *Psychological Science, 18,* 657–662.

Day, J. J., & Sweatt, J. D. (2011). Epigenetic mechanisms in cognition. *Neuron, 70,* 813–829.

Dayan, P., & Huys, Q. J. M. (2009). Serotonin in affective control. *Annual Review of Neuroscience, 32,* 95–126.

Deák, G. O. (2006). Do children really confuse appearance and reality? *Trends in Cognitive Sciences, 10*(12), 546–550.

de Araujo, I. E., Rolls, E. T., Velazco, M. I., Margot, C., & Cayeux, I. (2005). Cognitive modulation of olfactory processing. *Neuron, 46,* 671–679.

Deary, I. J. (2000). *Looking down on human intelligence: From psychometrics to the brain.* New York: Oxford University Press.

Deary, I. J. (2012). Intelligence. *Annual Review of Psychology, 63*(1), 453–482. doi:10.1146/annurev-psych-120710-100353

Deary, I. J., Batty, G. D., & Gale, C. R. (2008). Bright children become enlightened adults. *Psychological Science, 19*(1), 1–6.

Deary, I. J., Batty, G. D., Pattie, A., & Gale, C. R. (2008). More intelligent, more dependable children live longer: A 55-year longitudinal study of a representative sample of the Scottish nation. *Psychological Science, 19,* 874.

Deary, I. J., Der, G., & Ford, G. (2001). Reaction time and intelligence differences: A population based cohort study. *Intelligence, 29*(5), 389–399.

Deary, I. J., Taylor, M. D., Hart, C. L., Wilson, V., Smith, G. D., Blane, D., & Starr, J. M. (2005). Intergenerational social mobility and mid-life status attainment: Influences of childhood intelligence, childhood social factors, and education. *Intelligence, 33*(5), 455–472. doi:10.1016/j.intell.2005.06.003

Deary, I. J., Weiss, A., & Batty, G. D. (2011). Intelligence and personality as predictors of illness and death: How researchers in differential psychology and chronic disease epidemiology are collaborating to understand and address health inequalities. *Psychological Science in the Public Interest, 11*(2), 53–79. doi:10.1177/1529100610387081

Deary, I. J., Whiteman, M. C., Starr, J. M., Whalley, L. J., & Fox, H. C. (2004). The impact of childhood intelligence on later life: Following up the Scottish mental surveys of 1932 and 1947. *Journal of Personality and Social Psychology, 86,* 130–147.

Deb, S., Thomas, M., & Bright, C. (2001). Mental disorder in adults with intellectual disability: I. Prevalence of functional psychiatric illness among a community-based population aged between 16 and 64 years. *Journal of Intellectual Disability Research, 45*(Pt. 6), 495–505.

DeCasper, A. J., & Spence, M. J. (1986). Prenatal maternal speech influences newborns' perception of speech sounds. *Infant Behavior and Development, 9,* 133–150.

Deci, E. L. (1971). Effects of externally mediated rewards on intrinsic motivation. *Journal of Personality and Social Psychology, 18,* 105–115.

Deci, E. L., Koestner, R., & Ryan, R. M. (1999). A meta-analytic review of experiments examining the effects of extrinsic rewards on intrinsic motivation. *Psychological Bulletin, 125,* 627–668.

de Craen, A. J. M., Moerman, D. E., Heisterkamp, S. H., Tytgat, G. N. J., Tijssen, J. G. P., & Kleijnen, J. (1999). Placebo effect in the treatment of duodenal ulcer. *British Journal of Clinical Pharmacology, 48,* 853–860.

Deese, J. (1959). On the prediction of occurrence of particular verbal intrusions in immediate recall. *Journal of Experimental Psychology, 58,* 17–22.

DeFelipe, J., & Jones, E. G. (1988). *Cajal on the cerebral cortex: An annotated translation of the complete writings.* New York: Oxford University Press.

Degenhardt, L., Chiu, W. T., Sampson, N., Kessler, R. C., Anthony, J. C., Angermeyer, M., . . . Wells, J. E. (2008). Toward a global view of alcohol, tobacco, cannabis, and cocaine use: Findings from the WHO World Mental Health surveys. *PLoS Medicine, 5,* e141.

Degenhardt, L., Dierker, L., Chiu, W. T., Medina-Mora, M. E., Neumark, Y., Sampson, N., . . . Kessler, R. C. (2010). Evaluating the drug use "gateway" theory using cross-national data: Consistency and associations of the order of initiation of drug use among participants in the WHO World Mental Health surveys. *Drug and Alcohol Dependence, 108,* 84–97.

Dekker, M. C., & Koot, H. M. (2003). DSM–IV disorders in children with borderline to moderate intellectual disability: I. Prevalence and impact. *Journal of the American Academy of Child and Adolescent Psychiatry, 42*(8), 915–922. doi:10.1097/01.CHI.0000046892.27264.1A

Dekker, S., Lee, N. C., Howard-Jones, P., & Jolles, J. (2012). Neuromyths in education: Prevalence and predictors of misconceptions among teachers. *Frontiers in Psychology 3: 429.* doi:10.3389/fpsyg.2012.00429

Delgado, M. R., Frank, R. H., & Phelps, E. A. (2005). Perceptions of moral character modulate the neural systems of reward during the trust game. *Nature Neuroscience, 8,* 1611–1618.

Demb, J. B., Desmond, J. E., Wagner, A. D., Vaidya, C. J., Glover, G. H., & Gabrieli, J. D. E. (1995). Semantic encoding and retrieval in the left inferior prefrontal cortex: A functional MRI study of task difficulty and process specificity. *The Journal of Neuroscience, 15,* 5870–5878.

Dement, W. C. (1959, November 30). Dreams. *Newsweek*.

Dement, W. C. (1978). *Some must watch while some must sleep*. New York: Norton.

Dement, W. C. (1999). *The promise of sleep*. New York: Delacorte Press.

Dement, W. C., & Kleitman, N. (1957). The relation of eye movements during sleep to dream activity: An objective method for the study of dreaming. *Journal of Experimental Psychology, 53*, 339–346.

Dement, W. C., & Wolpert, E. (1958). Relation of eye movements, body motility, and external stimuli to dream content. *Journal of Experimental Psychology, 55*, 543–553.

Dempster, E. L., Pidsley, R., Schalkwyk, L. C., Owens, S., Georgiades, A., Kane, F., . . . Mill, J. (2011). Disease-associated epigenetic changes in monozygotic twins discordant for schizophrenia and bipolar disorder. *Human Molecular Genetics, 20*, 4786–4796.

Denison, S., Reed, C., & Xu, F. (2013). The emergence of probabilistic reasoning in very young infants: Evidence from 4.5- and 6-month-olds. *Developmental Psychology, 49*(2), 243–249. doi:10.1037/a0028278

Dennett, D. (1991). *Consciousness explained*. New York: Basic Books.

DePaulo, B. M., Charlton, K., Cooper, H., Lindsay, J. J., & Muhlenbruck, L. (1997). The accuracy–confidence correlation in the detection of deception. *Personality and Social Psychology Review, 1*, 346–357.

DePaulo, B. M., Lindsay, J. J., Malone, B. E., Muhlenbruck, L., Charlton, K., & Cooper, H. (2003). Cues to deception. *Psychological Bulletin, 129*, 74–118.

DePaulo, B. M., Stone, J. I., & Lassiter, G. D. (1985). Deceiving and detecting deceit. In B. R. Schlenker (Ed.), *The self and social life* (pp. 323–370). New York: McGraw-Hill.

Der, G., Batty, G. D., & Deary, I. J. (2009). The association between IQ in adolescence and a range of health outcomes at 40 in the 1979 U.S. national longitudinal study of youth. *Intelligence, 37*(6), 573–580.

DeRosnay, M., Pons, F., Harris, P. L., & Morrell, J. M. B. (2004). A lag between understanding false belief and emotion attribution in young children: Relationships with linguistic ability and mothers' mental-state language. *British Journal of Developmental Psychology, 24*(1), 197–218.

Des Jarlais, D. C., McKnight, C., Goldblatt, C., & Purchase, D. (2009). Doing harm reduction better: Syringe exchange in the United States. *Addiction, 104*(9), 1331–1446.

DesJardin, J. L., Eisenberg, L. S., & Hodapp, R. M. (2006). Sound beginnings: Supporting families of young deaf children with cochlear implants. *Infants and Young Children, 19*, 179–189.

Deutsch, M. (1949). A theory of cooperation and competition. *Human Relations, 2*, 129–152.

DeVilliers, P. (2005). The role of language in theory-of-mind development: What deaf children tell us. In J. W. Astington & J. A. Baird (Eds.), *Why language matters for theory of mind* (pp. 266–297). Oxford, England: Oxford University Press.

De Vries, M. H., Barth, A. C. R., Maiworm, S., Knecht, S., Zwitserlood, P., & Flöel, A. (2010). Electrical stimulation of Broca's area enhances implicit learning of an artificial grammar. *Journal of Cognitive Neuroscience, 22*, 2427–2436.

de Waal, F. B. M. (2012). The antiquity of empathy. *Science, 336*(6083), 874–876. doi:10.1126/science.1220999

Dewhurst, D. L., & Cautela, J. R. (1980). A proposed reinforcement survey schedule for special needs children. *Journal of Behavior Therapy and Experimental Psychiatry, 11*, 109–112.

De Witte, P. (1996). The role of neurotransmitters in alcohol dependency. *Alcohol & Alcoholism, 31*(Suppl. 1), 13–16.

De Wolff, M., & van IJzendoorn, M. H. (1997). Sensitivity and attachment: A meta-analysis on parental antecedents of infant attachment. *Child Development, 68*, 571–591.

DeYoung, C. G., & Gray, J. R. (2009). Personality neuroscience: Explaining individual differences in affect, behavior, and cognition. In P. J. Corr & G. Matthews (Eds.), *The Cambridge handbook of personality psychology* (pp. 323–346). New York: Cambridge University Press.

DeYoung, C. G., Hirsh, J. B., Shane, M. S., Papademetris, X., Rajeevan, N., & Gray, J. R. (2010). Testing predictions from personality neuroscience: Brain structure and the Big Five. *Psychological Science, 21*, 820–828.

Diaconis, P., & Mosteller, F. (1989). Methods for studying coincidences. *Journal of the American Statistical Association, 84*, 853–861.

Diano, S., Farr, S. A., Benoit, S. C., McNay, E. C., da Silva, I., Horvath, B., . . . Horvath, T. L. (2006). Ghrelin controls hippocampal spine synapse density and memory performance. *Nature Neuroscience, 9*(3), 381–388.

Dickens, W. T., & Flynn, J. R. (2001). Heritability estimates versus large environmental effects: The IQ paradox resolved. *Psychological Review, 108*, 346–369.

Dickinson, A., Watt, A., & Griffiths, J. H. (1992). Free-operant acquisition with delayed reinforcement. *Quarterly Journal of Experimental Psychology Section B: Comparative and Physiological Psychology, 45*, 241–258.

Didden, R., Sigafoos, J., Lang, R., O'Reilly, M., Drieschner, K., & Lancioni, G. E. (2012). Intellectual disabilities. In P. Sturmey & M. Hersen (Eds.), *Handbook of evidence-based practice in clinical psychology*. Hoboken, NJ: Wiley. Retrieved from http://doi.wiley.com/10.1002/9781118156391.ebcp001006

DiDonato, T. E., Ullrich, J., & Krueger, J. I. (2011). Social perception as induction and inference: An integrative model of intergroup differentiation, ingroup favoritism, and differential accuracy. *Journal of Personality and Social Psychology, 100*(1), 66–83. doi: 10.1037/a0021051

Diederich, N. J., & Goetz, C. G. (2008). The placebo treatments in neurosciences: New insights from clinical and neuroimaging studies. *Neurology, 71*, 677–684.

Diekelmann, S., & Born, J. (2010). The memory function of sleep. *Nature Reviews Neuroscience, 11*, 114–126.

Dietary Guidelines Advisory Committee. (2005). *Dietary guidelines for Americans 2005*. Retrieved October 15, 2007, from http://www.health.gov/dietaryguidelines

Dijksterhuis, A. (2004). Think different: The merits of unconscious thought in preference development and decision making. *Journal of Personality and Social Psychology, 87*, 586–598.

Dimberg, U. (1982). Facial reactions to facial expressions. *Psychophysiology, 19*, 643–647.

Dion, K., Berscheid, E., & Walster, E. (1972). What is beautiful is good. *Journal of Personality and Social Psychology, 24*, 285–290.

Disner, S. G., Beevers, C. G., Haigh, E. A., & Beck, A. T. (2011). Neural mechanisms of the cognitive model of depression. *Nature Reviews Neuroscience, 12*, 467–477.

DiTella, R., MacCulloch, R. J., & Oswald, A. J. (2003). The macroeconomics of happiness. *Review of Economics and Statistics, 85*, 809–827.

Dittrich, W. H., Troscianko, T., Lea, S., & Morgan, D. (1996). Perception of emotion from dynamic point-light displays represented in dance. *Perception, 25*, 727–738.

Dollard, J., Doob, L. W., Miller, N. E., Mowrer, O. H., & Sears, R. R. (1939). *Frustration and aggression*. Oxford, England: Yale University Press.

Domhoff, G. W. (2007). Realistic simulation and bizarreness in dream content: Past findings and suggestions for future research. In D. B. P. McNamara (Ed.), *The new science of dreaming: Content, recall, and personality correlates* (Vol. 22, pp. 1–27). Westport, CT: Praeger.

Domjan, M. (2005). Pavlovian conditioning: A functional perspective. *Annual Review of Psychology, 56,* 179–206.

Donner, T. H., Kettermann, A., Diesch, E., Ostendorf, F., Villiringer, A., & Brandt, S. A. (2002). Visual feature and conjunction searches of equal difficulty engage only partially overlapping frontoparietal networks. *NeuroImage, 15,* 16–25.

Dornbusch, S. M., Hastorf, A. H., Richardson, S. A., Muzzy, R. E., & Vreeland, R. S. (1965). The perceiver and perceived: Their relative influence on categories of interpersonal perception. *Journal of Personality and Social Psychology, 1,* 434–440.

Dorus, S., Vallender, E. J., Evans, P. D., Anderson, J. R., Gilbert, S. L., Mahowald, M., . . . Lahn, B. T. (2004). Accelerated evolution of nervous system genes in the origin of *Homo sapiens. Cell, 119,* 1027–1040.

Dostoevsky, F. (1988). *Winter notes on summer impressions* (D. Patterson, Trans.). Evanston, IL: Northwestern University Press. (Original work published 1863)

Dovidio, J. F., & Gaertner, S. L. (2010). Intergroup bias. In S. T. Fiske, D. T. Gilbert, & G. Lindzey (Eds.), *The handbook of social psychology* (5th ed., Vol. 2, pp. 1085–1121). New York: Wiley.

Downer, J. D. C. (1961). Changes in visual gnostic function and emotional behavior following unilateral temporal damage in the "splitbrain" monkey. *Nature, 191,* 50–51.

Downing, P. E., Chan, A. W. Y., Peelen, M. V., Dodds, C. M., & Kanwisher, N. (2006). Domain specificity in visual cortex. *Cerebral Cortex, 16,* 1453–1461.

Draguns, J. G., & Tanaka-Matsumi, J. (2003). Assessment of psychopathology across and within cultures: Issues and findings. *Behaviour Research and Therapy, 41,* 755–776.

Dreifus, C. (2003, May 20). Living one disaster after another, and then sharing the experience. *New York Times,* p. D2.

Drigotas, S. M., & Rusbult, C. E. (1992). Should I stay or should I go? A dependence model of breakups. *Journal of Personality and Social Psychology, 62,* 62–87.

Druckman, D., & Bjork, R. A. (1994). *Learning, remembering, believing: Enhancing human performance.* Washington, DC: National Academy Press.

Duckworth, A. L., & Seligman, M. E. P. (2005). Self-discipline outdoes IQ in predicting academic performance of adolescents. *Psychological Science, 16,* 939–944.

Dudai, Y. (2012). The restless engram: Consolidations never end. *Annual Review of Neuroscience, 35,* 227–247.

Dudycha, G. J., & Dudycha, M. M. (1933). Some factors and characteristics of childhood memories. *Child Development, 4,* 265–278.

Duenwald, M. (2002, September 12). Students find another staple of campus life: Stress. *New York Times.* Retrieved from http://www .nytimes.com/2002/09/17/health/students-find-another-staple-of -campus-life-stress.html?pagewanted=all&src=pm

Duncan, D. E. (2012, November 4). How science can build a better you. *The New York Times.* Retrieved from http://www.nytimes .com/2012/11/04/sunday-review/how-science-can-build-a-better-you. html_r=0

Duncan, G. J., Yeung, W. J., Brooks-Gunn, J., & Smith, J. R. (1998). How much does childhood poverty affect the life chances of children? *American Sociological Review, 63,* 406–423.

Duncker, K. (1945). On problem-solving. *Psychological Monographs, 58*(5).

Dunham, Y., Chen, E. E., & Banaji, M. R. (2013). Two signatures of implicit intergroup attitudes: Developmental invariance and early enculturation. *Psychological Science, 6,* 860–868. doi:10.1177/0956797612463081

Dunlap, K. (1919). Are there any instincts? *Journal of Abnormal Psychology, 14,* 307–311.

Dunlop, S. A. (2008). Activity-dependent plasticity: Implications for recovery after spinal cord injury. *Trends in Neurosciences, 31,* 410–418.

Dunlosky, J., & Rawson, K. A. (2012). Overconfidence produces underachievement: Inaccurate self-evaluations undermine students' learning and retention. *Learning and Instruction, 22,* 271–280.

Dunlosky, J., Rawson, K. A., Marsh, E. J., Nathan, M. J., & Willingham, D. T. (2013). Improving students' learning with effective learning techniques: Promising directions from cognitive and educational psychology. *Psychological Science in the Public Interest, 14*(1), 4–58.

Dunlosky, J., & Thiede, K. W. (2013). Four cornerstones of calibration research: Why understanding students' judgments can improve their achievement. *Learning and Instruction, 24,* 58–61.

Dunphy, D. C. (1963). The social structure of urban adolescent peer groups. *Sociometry, 26,* 230–246.

Dutton, D. G., & Aron, A. P. (1974). Some evidence for heightened sexual attraction under conditions of high anxiety. *Journal of Personality and Social Psychology, 30,* 510–517.

Duval, S., & Wicklund, R. A. (1972). *A theory of objective self awareness.* New York: Academic Press.

Dyer, D., Dalzell, F., & Olegario, F. (2004). *Rising Tide: Lessons from 165 years of brand building at Procter & Gamble.* Cambridge, MA: Harvard Business School Press.

Eacott, M. J., & Crawley, R. A. (1998). The offset of childhood amnesia: Memory for events that occurred before age 3. *Journal of Experimental Psychology: General, 127,* 22–33.

Eagly, A. H., Ashmore, R. D., Makhijani, M. G., & Longo, L. C. (1991). What is beautiful is good, but . . . : A meta-analytic review of research on the physical attractiveness stereotype. *Psychological Bulletin, 110,* 109–128.

Eagly, A. H., & Steffen, V. J. (1986). Gender and aggressive behavior: A meta-analytic review of the social psychological literature. *Psychological Bulletin, 100,* 309–330.

Eagly, A. H., & Wood, W. (1999). The origins of sex differences in human behavior: Evolved dispositions versus social roles. *American Psychologist, 54,* 408–423.

Eastwick, P. W., Eagly, A. H., Finkel, E. J., & Johnson, S.E. (2011). Implicit and explicit preferences for physical attractiveness in a romantic partner: A double dissociation in predictive validity. *Journal of Personality and Social Psychology, 101*(5), 993–1011. doi: 10.1037/ a0024061

Eastwick, P. W., Finkel, E. J., Mochon, D., & Ariely, D. (2007). Selective versus unselective romantic desire: Not all reciprocity is created equal. *Psychological Science, 18,* 317–319.

Eaton, W. W., Shao, H., Nestadt, G., Lee, B. H., Bienvenu, O. J., & Zandi, P. (2008). Population-based study of first onset and chronicity of major depressive disorder. *Archives of General Psychiatry, 65,* 513–520.

Ebbinghaus, H. (1964). *Memory: A contribution to experimental psychology.* New York: Dover. (Original work published 1885)

Eddy, D. M. (1982). Probabilistic reasoning in clinical medicine: Problems and opportunities. In D. Kahneman, P. Slovic, & A. Tversky (Eds.), *Judgments under uncertainty: Heuristics and biases* (pp. 249–267). New York: Cambridge University Press.

Edgerton, V. R., Tillakaratne, J. K. T., Bigbee, A. J., deLeon, R. D., & Roy, R. R. (2004). Plasticity of the spinal neural circuitry after injury. *Annual Review of Neuroscience, 27*, 145–167.

Edwards, W. (1955). The theory of decision making. *Psychological Bulletin, 51*, 201–214.

Efferson, C., Lalive, R., & Fehr, E. (2008). The coevolution of cultural groups and ingroup favoritism. *Science, 321*, 1844–1849.

Eich, J.E. (1980). The cue-dependent nature of state-dependent retention. *Memory & Cognition, 8*, 157–173.

Eich, J.E. (1995). Searching for mood dependent memory. *Psychological Science, 6*, 67–75.

Eichenbaum, H. (2008). *Learning & memory.* New York: Norton.

Eichenbaum, H., & Cohen, N. J. (2001). *From conditioning to conscious recollection: Memory systems of the brain.* New York: Oxford University Press.

Eickhoff, S. B., Dafotakis, M., Grefkes, C., Stoecker, T., Shah, N. J., Schnitzler, A., . . . Siebler, M. (2008). fMRI reveals cognitive and emotional processing in a long-term comatose patient. *Experimental Neurology, 214*, 240–246.

Eimas, P. D., Siqueland, E. R., Jusczyk, P., & Vigorito, J. (1971). Speech perception in infants. *Science, 171*, 303–306.

Einstein, G. O., & McDaniel, M. A. (1990). Normal aging and prospective memory. *Journal of Experimental Psychology: Learning, Memory, and Cognition, 16*, 717–726.

Einstein, G. O., & McDaniel, M. A. (2005). Prospective memory: Multiple retrieval processes. *Current Direction in Psychological Science, 14*, 286–290.

Eisenberg, N., Fabes, R. A., Guthrie, I. K., & Reiser, M. (2000). Dispositional emotionality and regulation: Their role in predicting quality of social functioning. *Journal of Personality and Social Psychology, 78*, 136.

Eisenegger, C. Haushofer, J., & Fehr, E. (2011). The role of testosterone in social interaction. *Trends in Cognitive Sciences, 15*(6), 263–271. doi:10.1016/j.tics.2011.04.008

Eisenegger, C., Naef, M., Snozzi, R., Heinrichs, M., & Fehr, E. (2010). Prejudice and truth about the effect of testosterone on human bargaining behaviour. *Nature, 463*, 356–359.

Ekman, P. (1965). Differential communication of affect by head and body cues. *Journal of Personality and Social Psychology, 2*, 726–735.

Ekman, P. (1972). Universals and cultural differences in facial expressions of emotion. In J. K. Cole (Ed.), *Nebraska Symposium on Motivation, 1971* (pp. 207–283). Lincoln: University of Nebraska Press.

Ekman, P. (1992). *Telling lies.* New York: Norton.

Ekman, P. (2003). Darwin, deception, and facial expression. *Annals of the New York Academy of Sciences, 1000*, 205–221.

Ekman, P., & Friesen, W. V. (1968). Nonverbal behavior in psychotherapy research. In J. M. Shlien (Ed.), *Research in psychotherapy* (Vol. 3, pp. 179–216). Washington, DC: American Psychological Association.

Ekman, P., & Friesen, W. V. (1971). Constants across cultures in the face and emotion. *Journal of Personality and Social Psychology, 17*, 124–129.

Ekman, P., & Friesen, W. V. (1982). Felt, false, and miserable smiles. *Journal of Nonverbal Behavior, 6*, 238–252.

Ekman, P., Levenson, R. W., & Friesen, W. V. (1983). Autonomic nervous system activity distinguishes among emotions. *Science, 221*, 1208–1210.

Elbogen, E. B., & Johnson, S. C. (2009). The intricate link between violence and mental disorder. *Archives of General Psychiatry, 66*(2), 152–161.

Eldar, S., Apter, A., Lotan, D., Edgar, K. P., Naim, R., Fox, N. A., . . . Bar-Heim, Y. (2012). Attention bias modification treatment for pediatric anxiety disorders: A randomized controlled trial. *American Journal of Psychiatry, 169*, 213–220.

Eldridge, L. L., Knowlton, B. J., Furmanski, C. S., Bookheimer, S. Y., & Engel, S. A. (2000). Remembering episodes: A selective role for the hippocampus during retrieval. *Nature Neuroscience, 3*, 1149–1152.

Eldridge, M. A., Barnard, P. J., & Bekerian, D. A. (1994). Autobiographical memory and daily schemas at work. *Memory, 2*, 51–74.

Elfenbein, H. A., & Ambady, N. (2002). On the universality and cultural specificity of emotion recognition: A meta-analysis. *Psychological Bulletin, 128*, 203–235.

Elfenbein, H. A., Der Foo, M. D., White, J., & Tan, H. H. (2007). Reading your counterpart: The benefit of emotion recognition accuracy for effectiveness in negotiation. *Journal of Nonverbal Behavior, 31*, 205–223.

Ellemers, N. (2012). The group self. *Science, 336*(6083), 848–852. doi:10.10.1126/science.1220987

Ellenbogen, J. M., Payne, J. D., & Stickgold, R. (2006). The role of sleep in declarative memory consolidation: Passive, permissive, or none? *Current Opinion in Neurobiology, 16*, 716–722.

Elliott, R., Sahakian, B. J., Matthews, K., Bannerjea, A., Rimmer, J., & Robbins, T. W. (1997). Effects of methylphenidate on spatial working memory and planning in healthy young adults. *Psychopharmacology, 131*, 196–206.

Ellis, A. (1991). *Reason and emotion in psychotherapy.* New York: Carol.

Ellis, B. J., & Garber, J. (2000). Psychosocial antecedents of variation in girls' pubertal timing: Maternal depression, stepfather presence, and marital and family stress. *Child Development, 71*, 485–501.

Ellis, E. M. (1983). A review of empirical rape research: Victim reactions and response to treatment. *Clinical Psychology Review, 3*, 473–490.

Ellis, L., & Ames, M. A. (1987). Neurohormonal functioning in sexual orientation: A theory of homosexuality–heterosexuality. *Psychological Bulletin, 101*, 233–258.

Ellman, S. J., Spielman, A. J., Luck, D., Steiner, S. S., & Halperin, R. (1991). REM deprivation: A review. In S. J. Ellman & J. S. Antrobus (Eds.), *The mind in sleep: Psychology and psychophysiology* (2nd ed., pp. 329–376). New York: Wiley.

Ellsworth, P. C., & Scherer, K. R. (2003). Appraisal processes in emotion. In R. J. Davidson, K. R. Scherer, & H. H. Goldsmith (Eds.), *The handbook of affective science* (pp. 572–595). New York: Oxford University Press.

Emerson, R. C., Bergen, J. R., & Adelson, E. H. (1992). Directionally selective complex cells and the computation of motion energy in cat visual cortex. *Vision Research, 32*, 203–218.

Epel, E. S., Blackburn, E. H., Lin, J., Dhabhar, F. S., Adler, N.E., Morrow, J. D., & Cawthorn, R. M. (2004). Accelerated telomere shortening in response to life stress. *Proceedings of the National Academy of Sciences, 101*, 17312–17315.

Enock, P. M., & McNally, R. J. (2013). How mobile apps and other web-based interventions can transform psychological treatment and the treatment development cycle. *Behavior Therapist, 36*(3), 56, 58, 60, 62–66.

Epel, E. S., Daubenmier, J., Moskowitz, J. T., Foldman, S., & Blackburn, E. H. (2009). Can meditation slow rate of cellular aging? Cognitive stress, mindfulness, and telomerase. *Annals of the New York Academy of Sciences, 1172*, 34–53.

Epley, N., Savitsky, K., & Kachelski, R. A. (1999). What every skeptic should know about subliminal persuasion. *Skeptical Inquirer, 23*, 40–45, 58.

Epley, N., & Waytz, A. (2010). Mind perception. In S. T. Fiske, D. T. Gilbert, & G. Lindzey (Eds.), *The handbook of social psychology* (5th ed., Vol. 1, pp. 498–541). New York: Wiley.

Epstein, R. (2007a). *The case against adolescence: Rediscovering the adult in every teen.* New York: Quill Driver.

Epstein, R. (2007b). The myth of the teen brain. *Scientific American Mind, 18,* 27–31.

Erber, R., Wegner, D. M., & Therriault, N. (1996). On being cool and collected: Mood regulation in anticipation of social interaction. *Journal of Personality and Social Psychology, 70,* 757–766.

Erffmeyer, E. S. (1984). Rule-violating behavior on the golf course. *Perceptual and Motor Skills, 59,* 591–596.

Ericsson, K. A., & Charness, N. (1999). Expert performance: Its structure and acquisition. In S. J. Ceci & W. M. Williams (Eds.), *The nature–nurture debate: The essential readings* (pp. 200–256). Oxford, England: Blackwell.

Ericson, E. H. (1959). *Identity and the life cycle.* New York: International Universities Press.

Espy, K. A., Fang, H., Johnson, C., Stopp, C., Wiebe, S. A., & Respass, J. (2011). Prenatal tobacco exposure: Developmental outcomes in the neonatal period. *Developmental Psychology, 47*(1), 153–169. doi:10.1037/a0020724

Etcoff, N. (1999). *Survival of the prettiest: The science of beauty.* New York: Doubleday.

Evans, G. W. (2004). The environment of childhood poverty. *American Psychologist, 59*(2), 77–92.

Evans, G. W. (2006). Child development and the physical environment. *Annual Review of Psychology, 57,* 423–451.

Evans, S. W., & Kim, P. (2012). Childhood poverty and young adults' allostatic load: The mediating role of childhood cumulative risk exposure. *Psychological Science, 23*(9), 979–983. doi:10.1177/0956797612441218

Evans, G. W., & Stecker, R. (2004). Motivational consequences of environmental stress. *Journal of Environmental Psychology, 24,* 143–165.

Evans, J. St. B., Barston, J. L., & Pollard, P. (1983), On the conflict between logic and belief in syllogistic reasoning. *Memory & Cognition, 11,* 295–306.

Evans, P. D., Gilbert, S. L., Mekel-Bobrov, N., Vallender, E. J., Anderson, J. R., Vaez-Azizi, L. M., . . . Lahn, B. T. (2005). Microcephalin, a gene regulating brain size, continues to evolve adaptively to humans. *Science, 309,* 1717–1720.

Everson, S. A., Lynch, J. W., Chesney, M. A., Kaplan, G. A., Goldberg, D.E., Shade, S. B., . . . Salonen, J. T. (1997). Interaction of workplace demands and cardiovascular reactivity in progression of carotid atherosclerosis: Population based study. *British Medical Journal, 314,* 553–558.

Exner, J.E. (1993). *The Rorschach: A comprehensive system: Vol. 1. Basic Foundations.* New York: Wiley.

Eysenck, H. J. (1957). The effects of psychotherapy: An evaluation. *Journal of Consulting Psychology, 16,* 319–324.

Eysenck, H. J. (1967). *The biological basis of personality.* Springfield, IL: Charles C Thomas.

Eysenck, H. J. (1990). Biological dimensions of personality. In L. A. Pervin (Ed.), *Handbook of personality: Theory and research* (pp. 244–276). New York: Guilford Press.

Falk, A., & Szech, N. (2013). Morals and markets. *Science, 340*(6133), 707–711. doi:10.1126/science.1231566

Falk, R., & McGregor, D. (1983). The surprisingness of coincidences. In P. Humphreys, O. Svenson, & A. Vari (Eds.), *Analysing and aiding decision processes* (pp. 489–502). New York: North Holland.

Fancher, R. E. (1979). *Pioneers in psychology.* New York: Norton.

Fantz, R. L. (1964). Visual experience in infants: Decreased attention to familiar patterns relative to novel ones. *Science, 164,* 668–670.

Farah, M. J., Illes, J., Cook-Deegan, R., Gardner, H., Kandel, E., King, P., . . . Wolpe, P. R. (2004) Neurocognitive enhancement: What can we do and what should we do? *Nature Reviews Neuroscience, 5,* 421–426.

Farah, M. J., & Rabinowitz, C. (2003). Genetic and environmental influences on the organization of semantic memory in the brain: Is "living things" an innate category? *Cognitive Neuropsychology, 20,* 401–408.

Faraone, S. V., Perlis, R. H., Doyle, A. E., Smoller, J. W., Goralnick, J. J., Holmgren, M. A., & Sklar, P. (2005). Molecular genetics of attention-deficit/hyperactivity disorder. *Biological Psychiatry, 57,* 1313–1323.

Farivar, R. (2009). Dorsal–ventral integration in object recognition. *Brain Research Reviews, 61,* 144–153.

Farooqi, I. S., Bullmore, E., Keogh, J., Gillard, J., O'Rahilly, S., & Fletcher, P. C. (2007). Leptin regulates striatal regions and human eating behavior. *Science, 317,* 1355.

Farooqi, I. S., Matarese, G., Lord, G. M., Keogh, J. M., Lawrence, E., Agwu, C., & O'Rahilly, S. (2002). Beneficial effects of leptin on obesity, T cell hyporesponsiveness, and neuroendocrine/metabolic dysfunction of human congenital leptin deficiency. *The Journal of Clinical Investigation, 110*(8), 1093–1103.

Farrar, M. J. (1990). Discourse and the acquisition of grammatical morphemes. *Journal of Child Language, 17,* 607–624.

Favazza, A. (2011). *Bodies under siege: Self-mutilation, nonsuicidal self-injury, and body modification in culture and psychiatry.* Baltimore, MD: Johns Hopkins University Press.

Fazel, S., & Danesh, J. (2002). Serious mental disorder in 23,000 prisoners: A review of 62 surveys. *Lancet, 359,* 545–550.

Fechner, G. T. (1966). *Elements of psychophysics* (H. E. Alder, Trans.). New York: Holt, Rinehart, & Winston. (Original work published 1860)

Feczer, D., & Bjorklund, P. (2009). Forever changed: Posttraumatic stress disorder in female military veterans, a case report. *Perspectives in Psychiatric Care, 45,* 278–291.

Fehr, E., & Gaechter, S. (2002). Altruistic punishment in humans. *Nature, 415,* 137–140.

Fein, D., Barton, M., Eigsti, I.-M., Kelley, E., Naigles, L., Schultz, R. T., . . . Tyson, K. (2013). Optimal outcome in individuals with a history of autism. *Journal of child Psychology and Psychiatry, 54,* 195–205.

Fein, S., Goethals, G. R., & Kugler, M. B. (2007). Social influence on political judgments: The case of presidential debates. *Political Psychology, 28,* 165–192.

Feinberg, T. E. (2001). *Altered egos: How the brain creates the self.* New York: Oxford University Press.

Feingold, A. (1990). Gender differences in effects of physical attractiveness on romantic attraction: A comparison across five research paradigms. *Journal of Personality and Social Psychology, 59,* 981–993.

Feingold, A. (1992a). Gender differences in mate selection preferences: A test of the parental investment model. *Psychological Bulletin, 112,* 125–139.

Feingold, A. (1992b). Good-looking people are not what we think. *Psychological Bulletin, 111,* 304–341.

Feinstein, J. S., Buzza, C., Hurlemann, R., Follmer, R. L., Dahdaleh, N. S., Coryell, W. H. , . . . Wemmie, J. A. (2013). Fear and panic in humans with bilateral amygdala damage. *Nature Neuroscience, 3,* 270–272.

Feldman, D. E. (2009). Synaptic mechanisms for plasticity in neocortex. *Annual Review of Neuroscience, 32,* 33–55.

Feldman, M. D. (2004). *Playing sick.* New York: Brunner-Routledge.

Ferguson, C. J. (2010). Blazing angels or resident evil? Can violent video games be a force for good? *Review of General Psychology, 14*(2), 68–81. doi:10.1037/a0018941

Fernandez-Espejo, D., Junque, C., Vendrell, P., Bernabeu, M., Roig, T., Bargallo, N., & Mercader, J. M. (2008). Cerebral response to speech in vegetative and minimally conscious states after traumatic brain injury. *Brain Injury, 22,* 882–890.

Fernbach, P. M., Rogers, T., Fox, C. R., & Sloman, S. A. (2013). Political extremism is supported by an illusion of understanding. *Psychological Science, 24*(6), 939–946.

Fernyhough, C. (2012). *Pieces of light: The new science of memory.* London: Profile Books.

Ferster, C. B., & Skinner, B. F. (1957). *Schedules of reinforcement.* New York: Appleton-Century-Crofts.

Festinger, L. (1957). *A theory of cognitive dissonance.* Stanford, CA: Stanford University Press.

Festinger, L., & Carlsmith, J. M. (1959). Cognitive consequences of forced compliance. *Journal of Abnormal and Social Psychology, 58,* 203–210.

Festinger, L., Schachter, S., & Back, K. (1950). *Social pressures in informal groups: A study of human factors in housing.* Oxford, England: Harper & Row.

Field, G. C. (1921). Faculty psychology and instinct psychology. *Mind, 30,* 257–270.

Fields, G. (2009, May 14). White House czar calls for end to "War on Drugs." *Wall Street Journal,* p. A3. Retrieved May 14, 2009, from http://online.wsj.com/article/SB124225891527617397.html

Fields, H. L., & Levine, J. D. (1984). Placebo analgesia: A role for endorphins? *Trends in Neurosciences, 7,* 271–273.

Finkel, E. J., & Eastwick, P. W. (2009). Arbitrary social norms influence sex differences in romantic selectivity. *Psychological Science, 20,* 1290–1295.

Finkelstein, E. A., Trogdon, J. G., Cohen, J. W., & Dietz, W. (2009). Annual medical spending attributable to obesity: Payer- and servicespecific estimates. *Health Affairs, 28*(5), w822–w831.

Finkelstein, K. E. (1999, October 17). Yo-Yo Ma's lost Stradivarius is found after wild search. *New York Times,* p. 34.

Finn, R. (1991). Different minds. *Discover, 12,* 54–59.

Fiore, A. T., Taylor, L. S., Zhong, X., Mendelsohn, G. A., & Cheshire, C. (2010). Who's right and who writes: People, profiles, contacts, and replies in online dating. *Proceedings of Hawaii International Conferences on Systems Science, 43,* Persistent Conversation minitrack.

Fiorentine, R. (1999). After drug treatment: Are 12-step programs effective in maintaining abstinence? *American Journal of Drug and Alcohol Abuse, 25,* 93–116.

Fiorillo, C. D., Newsome, W. T., & Schultz, W. (2008). The temporal precision of reward prediction in dopamine neurons. *Nature Neuroscience, 11,* 966–973.

Fisher, H. E. (1993). *Anatomy of love: The mysteries of mating, marriage, and why we stray.* New York: Fawcett.

Fisher, R. P., & Craik, F. I. M. (1977). The interaction between encoding and retrieval operations in cued recall. *Journal of Experimental Psychology: Human Learning and Perception, 3,* 153–171.

Fiske, S. T. (1998). Stereotyping, prejudice, and discrimination. In D. T. Gilbert, S. T. Fiske, & G. Lindzey (Eds.), *The handbook of social psychology* (4th ed., Vol. 2, pp. 357–411). New York: McGraw-Hill.

Fiske, S. T. (2010). *Social beings: A core motives approach to social psychology.* Hoboken, NJ: Wiley.

Fleeson, W. (2004). Moving personality beyond the person-situation debate: The challenge and opportunity of within-person variability. *Current Directions in Psychological Science, 13,* 83–87.

Flegal, K. M., & Troiano, R. P. (2000). Changes in the distribution of body mass index of adults and children in the U.S. population. *International Journal of Obesity, 24,* 807–818.

Fletcher, P. C., Shallice, T., & Dolan, R. J. (1998). The functional roles of prefrontal cortex in episodic memory. I. Encoding. *Brain, 121,* 1239–1248.

Flor, H., Nikolajsen, L., & Jensen, T. S. (2006). Phantom limb pain: A case of maladaptive CNS plasticity? *Nature Reviews Neuroscience, 7,* 873–881.

Flynn, E. (2008). Investigating children as cultural magnets: Do young children transmit redundant information along diffusion chains? *Philosophical Transactions of the Royal Society of London Series B, 363,* 3541–3551.

Flynn, E., & Whiten, A. (2008). Cultural transmission of tool-use in young children: A diffusion chain study. *Social Development, 17,* 699–718.

Flynn, J. R. (2012). *Are we getting smarter? Rising IQ in the twenty-first century.* New York: Cambridge University Press.

Foa, E. B. (2010). Cognitive behavioral therapy of obsessive-compulsive disorder. *Dialogues in Clinical Neuroscience, 12,* 199–207.

Foa, E. B., Dancu, C. V., Hembree, E. A., Jaycox, L. H., Meadows, E. A., & Street, G. P. (1999). A comparison of exposure therapy, stress inoculation training, and their combination for reducing posttraumatic stress disorder in female assault victims. *Journal of Consulting and Clinical Psychology, 67,* 194–200.

Foa, E. B., Liebowitz, M. R., Kozak, M. J., Davies, S., Campeas, R., Franklin, M. E., . . . Tu, X. (2007). Randomized, placebo-controlled trial of exposure and ritual prevention, clomipramine, and their combination in the treatment of obsessive-compulsive disorder. *Focus, 5,* 368–380.

Foa, E. B., & Meadows, E. A. (1997). Psychosocial treatments for posttraumatic stress disorder: A critical review. *Annual Review of Psychology, 48,* 449–480.

Fogassi, L., Ferrari, P. F., Gesierich, B., Rozzi, S., Chersi, F., & Rizzolatti, G. (2005). Parietal lobe: From action organization to intention understanding. *Science, 308,* 662–667.

Folley, B. S., & Park, S. (2005). Verbal creativity and schizotypal personality in relation to prefrontal hemispheric laterality: A behavioral and near-infrared optical imaging study. *Schizophrenia Research, 80,* 271–282.

Forkstam, C., Hagoort, P., Fernández, G., Ingvar, M., & Petersson, K. M. (2006). Neural correlates of artificial syntactic structure classification. *NeuroImage, 32,* 956–967.

Foroni, F., & Semin, G. R. (2009). Language that puts you in touch with your bodily feelings: The multimodal responsiveness of affective expressions. *Psychological Science, 20*(8), 974–980.

Fournier, J. C., DeRubeis, R., Hollon, S. D., Dimidjian, S., Amsterdam, J. D., Shelton, R. C., & Fawcett, J. (2010). Antidepressant drug effects and depression severity. *Journal of the American Medical Association, 303,* 47–53.

Fouts, R. S., & Bodamer, M. (1987). Preliminary report to the National Geographic Society on "Chimpanzee intrapersonal signing." *Friends of Washoe, 7,* 4–12.

Fox, M. J. (2009). *Always looking up.* New York: Hyperion.

Fox, P. T., Mintun, M. A., Raichle, M. E., Miezin, F. M., Allman, J. M., & Van Essen, D. C. (1986). Mapping human visual cortex with positron emission tomography. *Nature, 323,* 806–809.

Fox, R. E., DeLeon, P. H., Newman, R., Sammons, M. T., Dunivin, D. L., & Baker, D. C. (2009). Prescriptive authority and psychology: A status report. *American Psychologist, 64,* 257–268.

Fragaszy, D. M., Izar, P., Visalberghi, E., Ottoni, E. B., & de Oliveria, M. G. (2004). Wild capuchin monkeys (*Cebus libidinosus*) use anvils and stone pounding tools. *American Journal of Primatology, 64,* 359–366.

Francis, D., Diorio, J., Liu, D., & Meaney, M. J. (1999). Nongenomic transmission across generations of maternal behavior and stress responses in the rat. *Science, 286,* 1155–1158.

François, C., Chobert, J., Besson, M., & Schon, D. (2013). Music training for the development of speech segmentation. *Cerebral Cortex, 9,* 2038–2043. doi:10.1093/cercor/bhs180

Frank, M. G., Ekman, P., & Friesen, W. V. (1993). Behavioral markers and recognizability of the smile of enjoyment. *Journal of Personality and Social Psychology, 64,* 83–93.

Frank, M. G., & Stennet, J. (2001). The forced-choice paradigm and the perception of facial expressions of emotion. *Journal of Personality and Social Psychology, 80,* 75–85.

Frankl, V. (2000). *Man's search for meaning.* New York: Beacon Press.

Fredman, T., & Whiten, A. (2008). Observational learning from tool using models by human-reared and mother-reared capuchin monkeys (*Cebus apella*). *Animal Cognition, 11,* 295–309.

Fredrickson, B. L. (2000). Cultivating positive emotions to optimize health and well-being. *Prevention and Treatment, 3,* Article 0001a. doi:10.1037/1522-3736.3.1.31a. Retrieved September 21, 2013 from http://psycnet.apa.org

Freedman, J. (1978). *Happy people: What happiness is, who has it, and why.* New York: Harcourt Brace Jovanovich.

Freedman, J. L., & Fraser, S. C. (1966). Compliance without pressure: The foot-in-the-door technique. *Journal of Personality and Social Psychology, 4,* 195–202.

Freeman, S., Walker, M. R., Borden, R., & Latané, B. (1975). Diffusion of responsibility and restaurant tipping: Cheaper by the bunch. *Personality and Social Psychology Bulletin, 1,* 584–587.

French, H. W. (1997, February 26). In the land of the small it isn't easy being tall. *New York Times.* Retrieved from http://www.nytimes.com/1997/02/26/world/in-the-land-of-the-small-it-isn-t-easy-being-tall.html

Freud, S. (1938). The psychopathology of everyday life. In A. A. Brill (Ed.), *The basic writings of Sigmund Freud* (pp. 38–178). New York: Basic Books. (Original work published 1901)

Freud, S. (1953). Three essays on the theory of sexuality. In J. Strachey (Ed. & Trans.), *The standard edition of the complete psychological works of Sigmund Freud* (Vol. 7, pp. 135–243). London: Hogarth Press. (Original work published 1905)

Freud, S. (1965). *The interpretation of dreams* (J. Strachey, Trans.). New York: Avon. (Original work published 1900)

Frick, R. W. (1985). Communicating emotion: The role of prosodic features. *Psychological Bulletin, 97,* 412–429.

Fried, P. A., & Watkinson, B. (2000). Visuoperceptual functioning differs in 9- to 12-year-olds prenatally exposed to cigarettes and marijuana. *Neurotoxicology and Teratology, 22,* 11–20.

Friedlander, L., & Desrocher, M. (2006). Neuroimaging studies of obsessive-compulsive disorder in adults and children. *Clinical Psychology Review, 26,* 32–49.

Friedman, J. M. (2003). A war on obesity, not the obese. *Science, 299*(5608), 856–858.

Friedman, J. M., & Halaas, J. L. (1998). Leptin and the regulation of body weight in mammals. *Nature, 395*(6704), 763–770.

Friedman, M., & Rosenman, R. H. (1974). *Type A behavior and your heart.* New York: Knopf.

Friedman, S. L., & Boyle, D. E. (2008). Attachment in U.S. children experiencing nonmaternal care in the early 1990s. *Attachment & Human Development, 10*(3), 225–261.

Friedman-Hill, S. R., Robertson, L. C., & Treisman, A. (1995). Parietal contributions to visual feature binding: Evidence from a patient with bilateral lesions. *Science, 269,* 853–855.

Friesen, W. V. (1972). *Cultural differences in facial expressions in a social situation: An experimental test of the concept of display rules.* Unpublished doctoral dissertation, University of California, San Francisco.

Frith, C. D., & Fletcher, P. (1995). Voices from nowhere. *Critical Quarterly, 37,* 71–83.

Frith, U. (2003). *Autism: Explaining the enigma.* Oxford, England: Blackwell.

Fry, D. P. (2012). Life without war. *Science, 336*(6083), 879–884. doi:10.1126/science.1217987

Fryer, A. J., Mannuzza, S., Gallops, M. S., Martin, L. Y., Aaronson, C., Gorman, J. M., . . . Klein, D. F. (1990). Familial transmission of simple phobias and fears: A preliminary report. *Archives of General Psychiatry, 47,* 252–256.

Fu, F., Tarnita, C. E., Christakis, N. A., Wang, L., Rand, D. G., & Novak, M. A. (2012). Evolution of in-group favoritism. *Scientific Reports, 2,* Article 460. doi:10.1038/srep00460

Fukui, H., Murai, T., Fukuyama, H., Hayashi, T., & Hanakawa, T. (2005). Functional activity related to risk anticipation during performance of the Iowa gambling task. *NeuroImage, 24,* 253–259.

Funder, D. C. (2001). Personality. *Annual Review of Psychology, 52,* 197–221.

Furmark, T., Tillfors, M., Marteinsdottir, I., Fischer, H., Pissiota, A., Långström, B., & Fredrikson, M. (2002). Common changes in cerebral blood flow in patients with social phobia treated with citalopram or cognitive behavioral therapy. *Archives of General Psychiatry, 59*(5), 425–433.

Fuster, J. M. (2003). *Cortex and mind.* New York: Oxford University Press.

Gadermann, A. M., Alonso, J., Vilagut, G., Zaslavsky, A. M., & Kessler, R. C. (2012). Comorbidity and disease burden in the National Comorbidity Survey Replication (NCS-R). *Depression and Anxiety, 29,* 797–806.

Gais, S., & Born, J. (2004). Low acetylcholine during slow-wave sleep is critical for declarative memory consolidation. *Proceedings of the National Academy of Sciences, USA, 101,* 2140–2144.

Galati, D., Scherer, K. R., & Ricci-Bitt, P. E. (1997). Voluntary facial expression of emotion: Comparing congenitally blind with normally sighted encoders. *Journal of Personality and Social Psychology, 73,* 1363–1379.

Gale, C. R., Batty, G. D., McIntosh, A. M., Porteous, D. J., Deary, I. J., & Rasmussen, F. (2012). Is bipolar disorder more common in highly intelligent people? A cohort study of a million men. *Molecular Psychiatry, 18*(2), 190–194. doi:10.1038/mp.2012.26

Gale, C. R., Batty, G. D., Tynelius, P. Deary, I. J., & Rasmussen, F. (2010). Intelligence in early adulthood and subsequent hospitalization for mental disorders. *Epidemiology, 21*(1), 70–77. doi:10.1097/EDE.0b013e3181c17da8

Galef, B. (1998). Edward Thorndike: Revolutionary psychologist, ambiguous biologist. *American Psychologist, 53,* 1128–1134.

Gallistel, C. R. (2000). The replacement of general-purpose learning models with adaptively specialized learning modules. In M. S. Gazzaniga (Ed.), *The new cognitive neurosciences* (pp. 1179–1191). Cambridge, MA: MIT Press.

Gallo, D. A. (2006). *Associative illusions of memory*. New York: Psychology Press.

Gallo, D. A. (2010). False memories and fantastic beliefs: 15 years of the DRM illusion. *Memory & Cognition, 38*, 833–848.

Gallup, G. G. (1977). Self-recognition in primates: A comparative approach to the bidirectional properties of consciousness. *American Psychologist, 32*, 329–338.

Gallup, G. G. (1997). On the rise and fall of self-conception in primates. *Annals of the New York Academy of Sciences, 818*, 73–84.

Gallup, G. G., & Frederick, D. A. (2010). The science of sex appeal: An evolutionary perspective. *Review of General Psychology, 14*(3), 240–250. doi:10.1037/a0020451

Galton, F. (1869). *Hereditary genius: An inquiry into its laws and consequences*. London: Macmillan/Fontana.

Ganzel, B. L., Kim, P., Glover, G. H., & Temple, E. (2008). Resilience after 9/11: Multimodal neuroimaging evidence for stress-related change in the healthy adult brain. *NeuroImage, 40*, 788–795.

Garb, H. N. (1998). *Studying the clinician: Judgment research and psychological assessment*. Washington, DC: American Psychological Association.

Garcia, J. (1981). Tilting at the windmills of academe. *American Psychologist,36*, 149–158.

Garcia, J., & Koelling, R. A. (1966). Relation of cue to consequence in avoidance learning. *Psychonomic Science, 4*, 123–124.

Gardner, R. A., & Gardner, B. T. (1969). Teaching sign language to a chimpanzee. *Science, 165*, 664–672.

Gardner, M., & Steinberg, L. (2005). Peer influence on risk taking, risk preference, and risky decision making in adolescence and adulthood: An experimental study. *Developmental Psychology, 41*,(4), 625–635. doi:10.1037/0012-1649.41.4.625

Garland, A. F., & Zigler, E. (1999). Emotional and behavioral problems among highly intellectually gifted youth. *Roeper Review, 22*(1), 41.

Garrett, B. L. (2011). *Convicting the innocent: Where criminal prosecutions go wrong*. Cambridge, MA: Harvard University Press.

Garry, M., Manning, C., Loftus, E. F., & Sherman, S. J. (1996). Imagination inflation: Imagining a childhood event inflates confidence that it occurred. *Psychonomic Bulletin & Review, 3*, 208–214.

Gaser, C., & Schlaug, G. (2003). Brain structures differ between musicians and nonmusicians. *Journal of Neuroscience, 23*, 9240–9245.

Gates, F. J. (2011). *How many people are lesbian, gay, bisexual, and transgender?* Los Angeles: UCLA School of Law, Williams Institute. Retrieved from http://williamsinstitute.law.ucla.edu/wp-content/uploads/Gates-How-Many-People-LGBT-Apr-2011.pdf

Gathercole, S. E. (2008). Nonword repetition and word learning: The nature of the relationship. *Applied Psycholinguistics, 27*, 513–543.

Gazzaniga, M. S. (Ed.). (2000). *The new cognitive neurosciences*. Cambridge, MA: MIT Press.

Gazzaniga, M. S. (2006). Forty-five years of split brain research and still going strong. *Nature Reviews Neuroscience, 6*, 653–659.

Ge, D., Fellay, J., Thompson, A. J., Simon, J. S., Shianna, K. V., Urban, T. J., . . . Goldstein, D. B. (2009). Genetic variation in il28b predicts hepatitis C treatment-induced viral clearance. *Nature, 461*, 399–401.

Ge, X. J., Conger, R. D., & Elder, G. H. (1996). Coming of age too early: Pubertal influences on girls' vulnerability to psychological distress. *Child Development, 67*, 3386–3400.

Ge, X. J., Conger, R. D., & Elder, G. H., Jr. (2001). Pubertal transition, stressful life events, and the emergence of gender differences in adolescent depressive symptoms. *Developmental Psychology, 37*(3), 404–417. Doi:10.1037/0012-1649.37.3.404

Ge, X. J., & Natsuaki, M. N. (2009). In search of explanations for early pubertal timing effects on developmental psychopathology. *Current Directions in Psychological Science, 18*, 327–331.

Geen, R. G. (1984). Preferred stimulation levels in introverts and extraverts: Effects on arousal and performance. *Journal of Personality and Social Psychology, 46*, 1303–1312.

Gegenfurtner, K. R., & Kiper, D. C. (2003). Color vision. *Annual Review of Neuroscience, 26*, 181–206.

Geier, A., Wansink, B., & Rozin, P. (2012). Red potato chips: Segmentation cues substantially decrease food intake. *Health Psychology, 31*, 398–401.

Gendron, M., Roberson, D., van der Vyver, J. M., & Barrett, L. F. (in press). Perceptions of emotion from facial expressions are not culturally universal: Evidence from a remote culture. *Emotion*.

Gershoff, E. T. (2002). Corporal punishment by parents and associated child behaviors and experiences: A meta-analytic and theoretical review. *Psychological Bulletin, 128*, 539–579.

Geschwind, D. H. (2009). Advances in autism. *Annual Review of Medicine, 60*, 67–80.

Gibb, B. E., Alloy, L. B., & Tierney, S. (2001). History of childhood maltreatment, negative cognitive styles, and episodes of depression in adulthood. *Cognitive Therapy and Research, 25*, 425–446.

Gibbons, F. X. (1990). Self-attention and behavior: A review and theoretical update. In M. P. Zanna (Ed.), *Advances in experimental social psychology* (Vol. 23, pp. 249–303). San Diego, CA: Academic Press.

Gick, M. L., & Holyoak, K. J. (1980). Analogical problem solving. *Cognitive Psychology, 12*, 306–355.

Giedd, J. N., Blumenthal, J., Jeffries, N. O., Castellanos, F. X., Liu, H., Zijdenbos, A., . . . Rapoport, J. L. (1999). Brain development during childhood and adolescence: A longitudinal MRI study. *Nature Neuroscience, 2*, 861–863.

Gierlach, E., Blesher, B. E., & Beutler, L. E. (2010). Cross-cultural differences in risk perceptions of disasters. *Risk Analysis, 30*, 1539–1549.

Gigerenzer, G. (1996). The psychology of good judgment: Frequency formats and simple algorithms. *Journal of Medical Decision Making, 16*, 273–280.

Gigerenzer, G., & Hoffrage, U. (1995). How to improve Bayesian reasoning without instruction: Frequency formats. *Psychological Review, 102*, 684–704.

Gigone, D., & Hastie, R. (1993). The common knowledge effect: Information sharing and group judgment. *Journal of Personality and Social Psychology, 54*, 959–974.

Gilbert, D. T. (1991). How mental systems believe. *American Psychologist, 46*, 107–119.

Gilbert, D. T. (1998). Ordinary personology. In D. T. Gilbert, S. T. Fiske, & G. Lindzey (Eds.), *The handbook of social psychology* (4th ed., Vol. 2, pp. 89–150). New York: McGraw-Hill.

Gilbert, D. T. (2006). *Stumbling on happiness*. New York: Knopf.

Gilbert, D. T., Brown, R. P., Pinel, E. C., & Wilson, T. D. (2000). The illusion of external agency. *Journal of Personality and Social Psychology, 79*, 690–700.

Gilbert, D. T., Gill, M. J., & Wilson, T. D. (2002). The future is now: Temporal correction in affective forecasting. *Organizational Behavior and Human Decision Processes, 88*, 430–444.

Gilbert, D. T., & Malone, P. S. (1995). The correspondence bias. *Psychological Bulletin, 117*, 21–38.

Gilbert, D. T., Pelham, B. W., & Krull, D. S. (1988). On cognitive busyness: When persons perceive meet persons perceived. *Journal of Personality and Social Psychology, 54*, 733–740.

Gilbert, G. M. (1951). Stereotype persistence and change among college students. *Journal of Abnormal and Social Psychology, 46,* 245–254.

Gilbertson, M. W., Shenton, M. E., Ciszewski, A., Kasai, K., Lasko, N. B., Orr, S. P., & Pitman, R. K. (2002). Smaller hippocampal volume predicts pathological vulnerability to psychological trauma. *Nature Neuroscience, 5,* 1242–1247.

Gillespie, C. F., & Nemeroff, C. B. (2007). Corticotropin-releasing factor and the psychobiology of early-life stress. *Current Directions in Psychological Science, 16,* 85–89.

Gillette, J., Gleitman, H., Gleitman, L., & Lederer, A. (1999). Human simulation of vocabulary learning. *Cognition, 73,* 135–176.

Gilligan, C. (1982). *In a different voice: Psychological theory and women's development.* Cambridge, MA: Harvard University Press.

Gilovich, T. (1991). *How we know what isn't so: The fallibility of human reason in everyday life.* New York: Free Press.

Ginzburg, K., Solomon, Z., & Bleich, A. (2002). Repressive coping style, acute stress disorder, and posttraumatic stress disorder after myocardial infarction. *Psychosomatic Medicine, 64,* 748–757.

Giovanello, K. S., Schnyer, D. M., & Verfaellie, M. (2004). A critical role for the anterior hippocampus in relational memory: Evidence from an fMRI study comparing associative and item recognition. *Hippocampus, 14,* 5–8.

Gladue, B. A. (1994). The biopsychology of sexual orientation. *Current Directions in Psychological Science, 3,* 150–154.

Glass, D. C., & Singer, J. E. (1972). *Urban stress.* New York: Academic Press.

Glenwick, D. S., Jason, L. A., & Elman, D. (1978). Physical attractiveness and social contact in the singles bar. *Journal of Social Psychology, 105,* 311–312.

Glynn, L. M., & Sandman, C. A. (2011). Prenatal origins of neurological development: A critical period for fetus and mother. *Current Directions in Psychological Science, 20*(6), 384–389. doi:10.1177/0963721411422056

Gneezy, U., & Rustichini, A. (2000). A fine is a price. *Journal of Legal Studies, 29,* 1–17.

Gobert, A., Rivet, J. M., Cistarelli, L., Melon, C., & Millan, M. J. (1999). Buspirone modulates basal and fluoxetine-stimulated dialysate levels of dopamine, noradrenaline, and serotonin in the frontal cortex of freely moving rats: Activation of serotonin 1A receptors and blockade of alpha2-adrenergic receptors underlie its actions. *Neuroscience, 93,* 1251–1262.

Goddard, H. H. (1913). *The Kallikak family: A study in the heredity of feeble-mindedness.* New York: Macmillan.

Godden, D. R., & Baddeley, A. D. (1975). Context-dependent memory in two natural environments: On land and underwater. *British Journal of Psychology, 66,* 325–331.

Goehler, L. E., Gaykema, R. P. A., Hansen, M. K., Anderson, K., Maier, S. F., & Watkins, L. R. (2000). Vagal immune-to-brain communication: A visceral chemosensory pathway. *Autonomic Neuroscience: Basic and Clinical, 85,* 49–59.

Goel, V. (2007). Anatomy of deductive reasoning. *Trends in Cognitive Sciences, 11,* 435–441.

Goel, V., & Dolan, R. J. (2003). Explaining modulation of reasoning by belief. *Cognition, 87,* 11–22.

Goetzman, E. S., Hughes, T., & Klinger, E. (1994). *Current concerns of college students in a midwestern sample.* Unpublished report, University of Minnesota, Morris.

Goff, L. M., & Roediger, H. L., III. (1998). Imagination inflation for action events—repeated imaginings lead to illusory recollections. *Memory & Cognition, 26,* 20–33.

Goldman, M. S., Brown, S. A., & Christiansen, B. A. (1987). Expectancy theory: Thinking about drinking. In H. T. Blane & K. E. Leonard (Eds.), *Psychological theories of drinking and alcoholism* (pp. 181–266). New York: Guilford Press.

Goldstein, M. H., Schwade, J. A., Briesch, J., & Syal, S. (2010). Learning while babbling: Prelinguistic object-directed vocalizations signal a readiness to learn. *Infancy, 15,* 362–391

Goldstein, R., Almenberg, J., Dreber, A., Emerson, J. W., Herschkowitsch, A., & Katz, J. (2008). Do more expensive wines taste better? Evidence from a large sample of blind tastings. *Journal of Wine Economics, 3,* 1–9.

Goldstein, R., & Herschkowitsch, A. (2008). *The wine trials.* Austin, TX: Fearless Critic Media.

Gomez, C., Argandota, E. D., Solier, R. G., Angulo, J. C., & Vazquez, M. (1995). Timing and competition in networks representing ambiguous figures. *Brain and Cognition, 29,* 103–114.

Gontier, N. (2008). Genes, brains, and language: An epistemological examination of how genes can underlie human cognitive behavior. *Review of General Psychology, 12,* 170–180.

Gonzaga, G. C., Keltner, D., Londahl, E. A., & Smith, M. D. (2001). Love and the commitment problem in romantic relations and friendship. *Journal of Personality and Social Psychology, 81,* 247–262.

Goodale, M. A., & Milner, A. D. (1992). Separate visual pathways for perception and action. *Trends in Neurosciences, 15,* 20–25.

Goodale, M. A., & Milner, A. D. (2004). *Sight unseen.* Oxford, England: Oxford University Press.

Goodale, M. A., Milner, A. D., Jakobson, L. S., & Carey, D. P. (1991). A neurological dissociation between perceiving objects and grasping them. *Nature, 349,* 154–156.

Goodwin, P., McGill, B., & Chandra, A. (2009). *Who marries and when? Age at first marriage in the United States, 2002* (Data Brief 19). Hyattsville, MD: National Center for Health Statistics.

Gootman, E. (2003, March 3). Separated at birth in Mexico, united at campuses on Long Island. *New York Times,* p. A25.

Gopnik, A. (2012). Scientific thinking in young children: Theoretical advances, empirical research, and policy implications. *Science, 337*(6102), 1623–1627. doi:10.1126/science.1223416

Gopnik, A., & Astington, J. W. (1988). Children's understanding of representational change and its relation to the understanding of false belief and the appearance reality distinction. *Child Development, 59,* 26–37.

Gopnik, M. (1990a). Feature-blind grammar and dysphasia. *Nature, 344,* 715.

Gopnik, M. (1990b). Feature blindness: A case study. *Language Acquisition: A Journal of Developmental Linguistics, 1,* 139–164.

Gorczynski, P., & Faulkner, G. (2011). Exercise therapy for schizophrenia. *Cochrane Database of Systematic Reviews, 5,* CD004412.

Gordon, P. (2004). Numerical cognition without words: Evidence from Amazonia. *Science, 306,* 496–499.

Gorno-Tempini, M. L., Price, C. J., Josephs, O., Vandenberghe, R., Cappa, S. F., Kapur, N., & Frackowiak, R. S. (1998). The neural systems sustaining face and proper-name processing. *Brain, 121,* 2103–2118.

Gosling, S. D. (1998). Personality dimensions in spotted hyenas (*Crocuta crocuta*). *Journal of Comparative Psychology, 112,* 107–118.

Gosling, S. D., & John, O. P. (1999). Personality dimensions in non-human animals: A cross-species review. *Current Directions in Psychological Science, 8,* 69–75.

Gosling, S. D., Rentfrow, P. J., & Swann, W. B., Jr. (2003). A very brief measure of the Big-Five personality domains. *Journal of Research in Personality, 37,* 504–528.

Gotlib, I. H., & Joormann, J. (2010). Cognition and depression: Current status and future directions. *Annual Review of Clinical Psychology, 6,* 285–312.

Gottesman, I. I. (1991). *Schizophrenia genesis: The origins of madness.* New York: Freeman.

Gottesman, I. I., & Hanson, D. R. (2005). Human development: Biological and genetic processes. *Annual Review of Psychology, 56,* 263–286.

Gottfredson, L. S. (1997). Mainstream science on intelligence: An editorial with 52 signatories, history, and bibliography. *Intelligence, 24,* 13–23.

Gottfredson, L. S. (2003). Dissecting practical intelligence theory: Its claims and evidence. *Intelligence, 31*(4), 343–397.

Gottfredson, L. S., & Deary, I. J. (2004). Intelligence predicts health and longevity, but why? *Current Directions in Psychological Science, 13,* 1–4.

Gottfried, J. A. (2008). Perceptual and neural plasticity of odor quality coding in the human brain. *Chemosensory Perception, 1,* 127–135.

Gouldner, A. W. (1960). The norm of reciprocity. *American Sociological Review, 25,* 161–178.

Grady, C. L., Haxby, J. V., Horwitz, B., Schapiro, M. B., Rapoport, S. I., Ungerleider, L. G., . . . Herscovitch, P. (1992). Dissociation of object and spatial vision in human extrastriate cortex: Age-related changes in activation of regional cerebral blood flow measured with [^{15}O] water and positiron emission tomography. *Journal of Cognitive Neuroscience, 4*(1), 23–34. doi:10.1162/jocn.1992.4.1.23

Graf, P., & Schacter, D. L. (1985). Implicit and explicit memory for new associations in normal subjects and amnesic patients. *Journal of Experimental Psychology: Learning, Memory, and Cognition, 11,* 501–518.

Grandin, T. (2006). *Thinking in pictures: My life with autism* (expanded edition). Visalia, CA: Vintage.

Grant, A. M. (2008). Personal life coaching for coaches-in-training enhances goal attainment, insight, and learning. *Coaching, 1*(1), 54–70.

Grant, B. F., Hasin, D. S., Stinson, F. S., Dawson, D. A., Chou, S. P., & Ruan, W. J. (2004). Prevalence, correlates, and disability of personality disorders in the U.S.: Results from the National Epidemiologic Survey on Alcohol and Related Conditions. *Journal of Clinical Psychiatry, 65,* 948–958.

Gray, H. M., Gray, K., & Wegner, D. M. (2007). Dimensions of mind perception. *Science, 315,* 619.

Gray, J. A. (1970). The psychophysiological basis of introversion–extraversion. *Behavior Research and Therapy, 8,* 249–266.

Gray, J. A. (1990). Brain systems that mediate both emotion and cognition. *Cognition and Emotion, 4,* 269–288.

Greely, H., Sahakian, B., Harris, J., Kessler, R. C., Gazzaniga, M., Campbell, P., & Farah, M. J. (2008). Towards responsible use of cognitive enhancing drugs by the healthy. *Nature, 456*(7223), 702–705.

Green, C. S., & Bavelier, D. (2007). Action video-game experience alters the spatial resolution of vision. *Psychological Science, 18,* 88–94.

Green, D. A., & Swets, J. A. (1966). *Signal detection theory and psychophysics.* New York: Wiley.

Green, M. F., Kern, R. S., Braff, D. L., & Mintz, J. (2000). Neurocognitive deficits and functional outcome in schizophrenia: Are we measuring the "right stuff"? *Schizophrenia Bulletin, 26,* 119–136.

Green, S. K., Buchanan, D. R., & Heuer, S. K. (1984). Winners, losers, and choosers: A field investigation of dating initiation. *Personality and Social Psychology Bulletin, 10,* 502–511.

Greenberg, J., Pyszczynski, T., Solomon, S., Rosenblatt, A., Veeder, M., Kirkland, S., & Lyon, D. (1990). Evidence for terror management theory II: The effects of mortality salience on reactions to those who threaten or bolster the cultural worldview. *Journal of Personality and Social Psychology, 58,* 308–318.

Greenberg, J., Solomon, S., & Arndt, J. (2008). A basic but uniquely human motivation: Terror management. In J. Y. Shah & W. L. Gardner (Eds.), *Handbook of motivation science* (pp. 114–134). New York: Guilford Press.

Greene, J. (2013). *Moral tribes: Emotion, reason, and the gap between us and them.* New York: Penguin.

Greene, J. D., Sommerville, R. B., Nystrom, L. E., Darley, J. M., & Cohen, J. D. (2001). An fMRI investigation of emotional engagement in moral judgment. *Science, 293,* 2105–2108.

Greenwald, A. G. (1992). New look 3: Unconscious cognition reclaimed. *American Psychologist, 47,* 766–779.

Greenwald, A. G., McGhee, D. E., & Schwartz, J. L. K. (1998). Measuring individual differences in implicit cognition: The implicit association test. *Journal of Personality and Social Psychology, 74,* 1464–1480.

Greenwald, A. G., & Nosek, B. A. (2001). Health of the Implicit Association Test at age 3. *Zeitschrift für Experimentelle Psychologie, 48,* 85–93.

Gropp, E., Shanabrough, M., Borok, E., Xu, A. W., Janoschek, R., Buch, T., . . . Brüning, J. C. (2005). Agouti-related peptide-expressing neurons are mandatory for feeding. *Nature Neuroscience, 8,* 1289–1291.

Gross, J. J. (1998). Antecedent- and response-focused emotion regulation: Divergent consequences for experience, expression, and physiology. *Journal of Personality and Social Psychology, 74,* 224–237.

Gross, J. J. (2002). Emotion regulation: Affective, cognitive, and social consequences. *Psychophysiology, 39,* 281–291.

Gross, J. J., & Munoz, R. F. (1995). Emotion regulation and mental health. *Clinical Psychology: Science and Practice, 2,* 151–164.

Groves, B. (2004, August 2). Unwelcome awareness. *The San Diego Union-Tribune,* p. 24.

Grün, F., & Blumberg, B. (2006). Environmental obesogens: Organotins and endocrine disruption via nuclear receptor signaling. *Endocrinology, 147,* s50–s55.

Guerin, S. A., Robbins, C. A., Gilmore, A. W., & Schacter, D. L. (2012a). Interactions between visual attention and episodic retrieval: Dissociable contributions of parietal regions during gist-based false recognition. *Neuron, 75,* 1122–1134.

Guerin, S. A., Robbins, C. A., Gilmore, A. W., & Schacter, D. L. (2012b). Retrieval failure contributes to gist-based false recognition. *Journal of Memory and Language, 66,* 68–78.

Guillery, R. W., & Sherman, S. M. (2002). Thalamic relay functions and their role in corticocortical communication: Generalizations from the visual system. *Neuron, 33,* 163–175.

Gup, T. (2013, April 3). Diagnosis: Human. *New York Times,* p. A27.

Gur, R. E., Cowell, P., Turetsky, B. I., Gallacher, F., Cannon, T., Bilker, W., & Gur, R. C. (1998). A follow-up magnetic resonance imaging study of schizophrenia: Relationship of neuroanatomical changes to clinical and neurobehavioral measures. *Archives of General Psychiatry, 55,* 145–152.

Gurwitz, J. H., McLaughlin, T. J., Willison, D. J., Guadagnoli, E., Hauptman, P. J., Gao, X., & Soumerai, S. B. (1997). Delayed hospital presentation in patients who have had acute myocardial infarction. *Annals of Internal Medicine, 126,* 593–599.

Gusnard, D. A., & Raichle, M. E. (2001). Searching for a baseline: Functional imaging and the resting human brain. *Nature Reviews: Neuroscience, 2,* 685–694.

Gustafsson, J.-E. (1984). A unifying model for the structure of intellectual abilities. *Intelligence, 8,* 179–203.

Gutchess, A. H., & Schacter, D. L. (2012). The neural correlates of gist-based true and false recognition. *NeuroImage, 59,* 3418–3426.

Guthrie, R. V. (2000). Kenneth Bancroft Clark (1914–). In A. E. Kazdin (Ed.), *Encyclopedia of Psychology* (Vol. 2, p. 91). Washington, DC: American Psychological Association.

Haase, C. M., Heckhausen, J., & Wrosch, C. (2013). Developmental regulation across the life span: Toward a new synthesis. *Developmental Psychology, 49*(5), 964–972. doi:10.1037/a0029231

Hacking, I. (1975). *The emergence of probability.* New York: Cambridge University Press.

Hackman, D. A., & Farah, M. J. (2008). Socioeconomic status and the developing brain. *Trends in Cognitive Sciences, 13,* 65–73.

Hackman, J. R., & Katz, N. (2010). Group behavior and performance. In S. T. Fiske, D. T. Gilbert, & G. Lindzey (Eds.), *The handbook of social psychology* (5th ed., Vol. 2, pp. 1208–1251). New York: Wiley.

Haedt-Matt, A. A., & Keel, P. K. (2011). Revisiting the affect regulation model of binge eating: A meta-analysis of studies using ecological momentary assessment. *Psychological Bulletin, 137*(4), 660–681.

Haggard, P., & Tsakiris, M. (2009). The experience of agency: Feelings, judgments, and responsibility. *Current Directions in Psychological Science, 18,* 242–246.

Haidt, J. (2001). The emotional dog and its rational tail: A social intuitionist approach to moral judgment. *Psychological Review, 108,* 814–834.

Haidt, J. (2006). *The happiness hypothesis: Finding modern truth in ancient wisdom.* New York: Basic Books.

Haidt, J., & Keltner, D. (1999). Culture and facial expression: Openended methods find more expressions and a gradient of recognition. *Cognition and Emotion, 13,* 225–266.

Haines, M. M., Stansfeld, S. A., Job, R. F., Berglund, B., & Head, J. (2001). Chronic aircraft noise exposure, stress responses, mental health and cognitive performance in school children. *Psychological Medicine, 31,* 265–277.

Hallett, M. (2000). Transcranial magnetic stimulation and the human brain. *Nature, 406,* 147–150.

Halliday, R., Naylor, H., Brandeis, D., Callaway, E., Yano, L., & Herzig, K. (1994). The effect of D-amphetamine, clonidine, and yohimbine on human information processing. *Psychophysiology, 31,* 331–337.

Halpern, B. (2002). Taste. In H. Pashler & S. Yantis (Eds.), *Stevens' handbook of experimental psychology: Vol. 1. Sensation and perception* (3rd ed., pp. 653–690). New York: Wiley.

Halpern, D. F. (1997). Sex differences in intelligence: Implications for education. *American Psychologist, 52,* 1091–1102.

Halpern, D. F., Benbow, C. P., Geary, D. C., Gur, R. C., Hyde, J. S., & Gernsbacher, M. A. (2007). The science of sex differences in science and mathematics. *Psychological Science in the Public Interest, 8,* 1–51.

Hambrick, D. Z., Oswald, F. L., Altmann, E. M., Meinz, E. J., Gobet, F., & Campitelli, G. (2013). Deliberate practice: Is that all it takes to become an expert? *Intelligence.* Advance online publication. doi:10.1016/j.intell.2013.04.001

Hamermesh, D. S., & Biddle, J. E. (1994). Beauty and the labor market. *American Economic Review, 84,* 1174–1195.

Hamilton, A. F., & Grafton, S. T. (2006). Goal representation in human anterior intraparietal sulcus. *The Journal of Neuroscience, 26,* 1133–1137.

Hamilton, A. F., & Grafton, S. T. (2008). Action outcomes are represented in human inferior frontoparietal cortex. *Cerebral Cortex, 18,* 1160–1168.

Hamilton, D. L., & Gifford, R. K. (1976). Illusory correlation in interpersonal perception: A cognitive basis of stereotypic judgements. *Journal of Experimental Social Psychology, 12,* 392–407.

Hamilton, J. P., Etkin, A., Furman, D. J., Lemus, M. G., Johnson, R. F., & Gotlib, I. H. (2012). Functional neuroimaging of major depressive disorder: A meta-analysis and new integration of baseline activation and neural response data. *American Journal of Psychiatry, 169,* 693–703.

Hamilton, J. P., Glover, G. H., Hsu, J. J., Johnson, R. F., & Gotlib, I. H. (2010). Modulation of subgenual anterior cingulated cortex activity with real-time neurofeedback. *Human Brain Mapping, 32,* 22–31.

Hamilton, W. D. (1964). The genetical evolution of social behaviour. *Journal of Theoretical Biology, 7,* 1–16.

Hamlin, J. K., Mahajan, N., Liberman, Z., & Wynn, K. (2013). Not like me = bad: Infants prefer those who harm dissimilar others. *Psychological Science, 24*(4), 589–594. doi:10.1177/0956797612457785

Hamlin, J. K., Wynn, K., & Bloom, P. (2007). Social evaluation by preverbal infants. *Nature, 450*(7169), 557–559.

Hammersla, J. F., & Frease-McMahan, L. (1990). University students' priorities: Life goals vs. relationships. *Sex Roles, 23,* 1–14.

Hampikian, G. (2012, August 24). Men, who needs them? *The New York Times.* Retrieved from http://www.nytimes.com/2012/08/25/opinion/men-who-needs-them.html

Haney, C., Banks, W. C., & Zimbardo, P. G. (1973). Study of prisoners and guards in a simulated prison. *Naval Research Reviews, 9,* 1–17.

Hannon, E. E., & Trainor, L. J. (2007). Music acquisition: Effects of enculturation and formal training on development. *Trends in Cognitive Sciences, 11,* 466–472.

Hansen, E. S., Hasselbalch, S., Law, I., & Bolwig, T. G. (2002). The caudate nucleus in obsessive-compulsive disorder. Reduced metabolism following treatment with paroxetine: A PET study. *International Journal of Neuropsychopharmacology, 5,* 1–10.

Happé, F. G. E. (1995). The role of age and verbal ability in the theory of mind performance of subjects with autism. *Child Development, 66,* 843–855.

Happé, F. G. E., & Vital, P. (2009). What aspects of autism predispose to talent? *Philosophical Transactions of the Royal Society B: Biological Science, 364,* 1369–1375.

Harand, C., Bertran, F., La Joie, R., Landeau, B., Mézenge, F., . . . Rauchs, G. (2012). The hippocampus remains activated over the long term for the retrieval of truly episodic memories. *PLoS ONE, 7,* e43495. doi:10.1371/journal.pone.0043495

Harding, C. M., Brooks, G. W., Ashikaga, T., Strauss, J. S., & Brier, A. (1987). The Vermont longitudinal study of persons with severe mental illness, II: Long-term outcome of subjects who retrospectively met DSM-III criteria for schizophrenia. *American Journal of Psychiatry, 144,* 727–735.

Hare, R. D. (1998). *Without conscience: The disturbing world of the psychopaths among us.* New York: Guilford Press.

Harkness, S., Edwards, C. P., & Super, C. M. (1981). Social roles and moral reasoning: A case study in a rural African community. *Developmental Psychology, 17,* 595–603.

Harlow, H. F. (1958). The nature of love. *American Psychologist, 13,* 573–685.

Harlow, H. F., & Harlow, M. L. (1965). The affectional systems. In A. M. Schrier, H. F. Harlow, & F. Stollnitz (Eds.), *Behavior of nonhuman primates* (Vol. 2, pp. 287–334). New York: Academic Press.

Harlow, J. M. (1848). Passage of an iron rod through the head. *Boston Medical and Surgical Journal, 39,* 389–393.

Harris, B. (1979). Whatever happened to Little Albert? *American Psychologist, 34,* 151–160.

Harris, P. L., de Rosnay, M., & Pons, F. (2005). Language and children's understanding of mental states. *Current Directions in Psychological Science, 14,* 69–73.

Harris, P. L., Johnson, C. N., Hutton, D., Andrews, G., & Cooke, T. (1989). Young children's theory of mind and emotion. *Cognition and Emotion, 3,* 379–400.

Hart, B. L. (1988). Biological basis of the behavior of sick animals. *Neuroscience and Biobehavioral Reviews, 12,* 123–137.

Hart, B., & Risley, T. R. (1995). *Meaningful differences in the everyday experience of young American children.* Baltimore, MD: Brookes.

Hart, W., Albarracin, D., Eagly, A. H., Lindberg, M. J., Merrill, L., & Brechan, I. (2009). Feeling validated versus being correct: A meta-analysis of selective exposure to information. *Psychological Bulletin, 135,* 555–588.

Hartshorne, H., & May, M. (1928). *Studies in deceit.* New York: Macmillan.

Hasher, L., & Zacks, R. T. (1984). Automatic processing of fundamental information: The case of frequency of occurrence. *American Psychologist, 39,* 1372–1388.

Haskell, E. (1869). *The trial of Ebenezer Haskell, in lunacy, and his acquittal before Judge Brewster, in November, 1868, together with a brief sketch of the mode of treatment of lunatics in different asylums in this country and in England: with illustrations, including a copy of Hogarth's celebrated painting of a scene in old Bedlam, in London, 1635.* Philadelphia, PA: Ebenezer Haskell.

Haslam, C., Wills, A. J., Haslam, S. A., Kay, J., Baron, R., & McNab, F. (2007). Does maintenance of colour categories rely on language? Evidence to the contrary from a case of semantic dementia. *Brain and Language, 103,* 251–263.

Hassabis, D., Kumaran, D., Vann, S. D., & Maguire, E. A. (2007). Patients with hippocampal amnesia cannot imagine new experiences. *Proceedings of the National Academy of Sciences, USA, 104,* 1726–1731.

Hasselmo, M. E. (2006). The role of acetylcholine in learning and memory. *Current Opinion in Neurobiology, 16,* 710–715.

Hassin, R. R., Bargh, J. A., & Zimerman, S. (2009). Automatic and flexible: The case of non-conscious goal pursuit. *Social Cognition, 27,* 20–36.

Hassmen, P., Koivula, N., & Uutela, A. (2000). Physical exercise and psychological well-being: A population study in Finland. *Preventive Medicine, 30,* 17–25.

Hasson, U., Hendler, T., Bashat, D. B., & Malach, R. (2001). Vase or face? A neural correlate of shape-selective grouping processes in the human brain. *Journal of Cognitive Neuroscience, 13,* 744–753.

Hatemi, P. K., Gillespie, N. A., Eaves, L. J., Maher, B. S., Webb, B. T., Heath, A. C., . . . Martin, N. G. (2011). A genome-wide analysis of liberal and conservative political attitudes. *The Journal of Politics, 73,* 271–285.

Hatfield, E. (1988). Passionate and companionate love. In R. J. Sternberg & M. L. Barnes (Eds.), *The psychology of love* (pp. 191–217). New Haven, CT: Yale University Press.

Hatfield, E., & Rapson, R. L. (1992). Similarity and attraction in close relationships. *Communication Monographs, 59,* 209–212.

Hausser, M. (2000). The Hodgkin-Huxley theory of the action potential. *Nature Neuroscience, 3,* 1165.

Havas, D. A., Glenberg, A. M., Gutowski, K. A., Lucarelli, M. J., & Davidson, R. J. (2010). Cosmetic use of botulinum toxin-A affects processing of emotional language. *Psychological Science, 21*(7), 895–900. doi:10.1177/0956797610374742

Hawley, P. H. (2002). Social dominance and prosocial and coercive strategies of resource control in preschoolers. *International Journal of Behavioral Development, 26,* 167–176.

Haxby, J. V., Gobbini, M. I., Furey, M. L., Ishai, A., Schouten, J. L., & Pietrini, P. (2001). Distributed and overlapping representations of faces and objects in ventral temporal cortex. *Science, 293,* 2425–2430.

Hayes, J. E., Bartoshuk, L. M., Kidd, J. R., & Duffy, V. B. (2008). Supertasting and PROP bitterness depends on more than the TAS2R38 gene. *Chemical Senses, 23,* 255–265.

Hayes, K., & Hayes, C. (1951). The intellectual development of a home-raised chimpanzee. *Proceedings of the American Philosophical Society, 95,* 105–109.

Hayes, S. C., Strosahl, K., & Wilson, K. G. (1999). *Acceptance and commitment therapy: An experiential approach to behavior change.* New York: Guilford Press.

Hay-McCutcheon, M. J., Kirk, K. I., Henning, S. C., Gao, S. J., & Qi, R. (2008). Using early outcomes to predict later language ability in children with cochlear implants. *Audiology and Neuro-Otology, 13,* 370–378.

Heath, S. B. (1983). *Way with words: Language, life and work in communities and classrooms.* Cambridge, England: Cambridge University Press.

Heatherton, T. F., & Weinberger, J. L. (Eds.). (1994). *Can personality change?* Washington, DC: American Psychological Association.

Heaton, R., Paulsen, J. S., McAdams, L. A., Kuck, J., Zisook, S., Braff, D., . . . Jeste, D. V. (1994). Neuropsychological deficits in schizophrenia: Relationship to age, chronicity, and dementia. *Archives of General Psychiatry, 51,* 469–476.

Heavey, C. L., Hurlburt, R. T., & Lefforge, N. L. (2012). Toward a phenomenology of feelings. *Emotion, 12*(4), 763–777.

Hebb, D. O. (1949). *The organization of behavior.* New York: Wiley.

Hebl, M. R., & Heatherton, T. F. (1997). The stigma of obesity in women: The difference is Black and White. *Personality and Social Psychology Bulletin, 24,* 417–426.

Hebl, M. R., & Mannix, L. M. (2003). The weight of obesity in evaluating others: A mere proximity effect. *Personality and Social Psychology Bulletin, 29,* 28–38.

Hedges, L. V., & Nowell, A. (1995). Sex differences in mental test scores, variability, and numbers of high-scoring individuals. *Science, 269*(5220), 41–45.

Heerey, E. A., Keltner, D., & Capps, L. M. (2003). Making sense of self-conscious emotion: Linking theory of mind and emotion in children with autism. *Emotion, 3,* 394–400.

Heine, S. J. (2010). Cultural psychology. In S. T. Fiske, D. T. Gilbert, & G. Lindzey (Eds.), *The handbook of social psychology* (5th ed., Vol. 2, pp. 1423–1464). New York: Wiley.

Heine, S. J., & Lehman, D. R. (1995). Cultural variation in unrealistic optimism: Does the West feel more invulnerable than the East? *Journal of Peronality and Social Psychology, 68,* 595–607.

Helt, M., Kelley, E., Kinsbourne, M., Pandey, J., Boorstein, H., Herbert, M., & Fein, D. (2008). Can children with autism recover? If so, how? *Neuropsychology Review, 18,* 339–366.

Henderlong, J., & Lepper, M. R. (2002). The effects of praise on children's intrinsic motivation: A review and synthesis. *Psychological Bulletin, 128,* 774–795.

Henrich, J., Heine, S. J., & Norenzayan, A. (2010). Most people are not WEIRD. *Nature, 466,* 29.

Henry, W. P., Strupp, H. H., Schacht, T. E., & Gaston, L. (1994). Psychodynamic approaches. In A. E. Bergin & S. L. Garfield (Eds.), *Handbook of psychotherapy and behavior change* (pp. 467–508). New York: Wiley.

Herman, C. P., Roth, D. A., & Polivy, J. (2003). Effects of the presence of others on food intake: A normative interpretation. *Psychological Bulletin, 129,* 873–886.

Herman-Giddens, M. E., Steffes, J., Harris, D., Slora, E., Hussey, M., Dowshen, S. A., & Reiter, E. O. (2012). Secondary sexual characteristics in boys: Data from the pediatric research in office settings network. *Pediatrics, 130*(5), e1058–e1068. doi:10.1542/peds.2011-3291

Herring, M. P., Puetz, T. W., O'Connor, P. J., & Dishman, R. K. (2010). Effect of exercise training on depressive symptoms among patients with chronic illness: A systematic review and meta-analysis of randomized controlled trials. *Archives of Internal Medicine, 172,* 101–111.

Herrnstein, R. J. (1977). The evolution of behaviorism. *American Psychologist, 32,* 593–603.

Hertenstein, M. J., Holmes, R., McCullough, M., & Keltner, D. (2009). The communication of emotion via touch. *Emotion, 9,* 566–573.

Hertig, M. M., & Nagel, B. J. (2012). Aerobic fitness relates to learning on a virtual Morris water maze task and hippocampal volume in adolescents. *Behavioral Brain Research, 233,* 517–525.

Hertwig, R., & Gigerenzer, G. (1999). The "conjunction fallacy" revisited: How intelligent inferences look like reasoning errors. *Journal of Behavioral Decision Making, 12,* 275–305.

Herz, R. S., & von Clef, J. (2001). The influence of verbal labeling on the perception of odors. *Perception, 30,* 381–391.

Hettema, J. M., Neale, M. C., & Kendler, K. S. (2001). A review and meta-analysis of the genetic epidemiology of anxiety disorders. *American Journal of Psychiatry, 158,* 1568–1578.

Heyes, C. M., & Foster, C. L. (2002). Motor learning by observation: Evidence from a serial reaction time task. *Quarterly Journal of Experimental Psychology (A), 55,* 593–607.

Heyman, G. M. (2009). *Addiction: A disorder of choice.* Cambridge, MA: Harvard University Press.

Heymsfield, S. B., Greenberg, A. S., Fujioka, K., Dixon, R. M., Kushner, R., Hunt, T., . . . McCarnish, M. (1999). Recombinant leptin for weight loss in obese and lean adults: A randomized, controlled, dose-escalation trial. *Journal of the American Medical Association, 282*(16), 1568–1575.

Hibbeln, J. R. (1998). Fish consumption and major depression. *Lancet, 351,* 1213.

Hickok, G. (2009). Eight problems for the mirror neuron theory of action understanding in monkeys and humans. *Journal of Cognitive Neuroscience, 21,* 1229–1243.

Higgins, E. T. (1987). Self-discrepancy theory: A theory relating self and affect. *Psychological Review, 94,* 319–340.

Higgins, E. T. (1997). Beyond pleasure and pain. *American Psychologist, 52,* 1280–1300.

Hilgard, E. R. (1965). *Hypnotic susceptibility.* New York: Harcourt, Brace and World.

Hilgard, E. R. (1986). *Divided consciousness: Multiple controls in human thought and action.* New York: Wiley-Interscience.

Hillman, C. H., Erickson, K. I., & Kramer, A. F. (2008). Be smart, exercise your heart: Exercise effects on brain and cognition. *Nature Reviews Neuroscience, 9,* 58–65.

Hilts, P. (1995). *Memory's ghost: The strange tale of Mr. M and the nature of memory.* New York: Simon & Schuster.

Hine, T. (1995). *The total package: The evolution and secret meanings of boxes, bottles, cans, and tubes.* Boston: Little, Brown.

Hintzman, D. L., Asher, S. J., & Stern, L. D. (1978). Incidental retrieval and memory for coincidences. In M. M. Gruneberg, P. E. Morris, & R. N. Sykes (Eds.), *Practical aspects of memory* (pp. 61–68). New York: Academic Press.

Hirschberger, G., Florian, V., & Mikulincer, M. (2002). The anxiety buffering function of close relationships: Mortality salience effects on the readiness to compromise mate selection standards. *European Journal of Social Psychology, 32,* 609–625.

Hirst, W., & Echterhoff, G. (2012). Remembering in conversations: The social sharing and reshaping of memory. *Annual Review of Psychology, 63,* 55–79.

Hirst, W., Phelps, E. A., Buckner, R. L., Budson, A. E., Cuc, A., Gabrieli, J. D. E., . . . Vaidya, C. J. (2009). Long-term memory for the terrorist attack of September 11: Flashbulb memories, event memories, and the factors that influence their retention. *Journal of Experimental Psychology: General, 138,* 161–176.

Hirstein, W., & Ramachandran, V. S. (1997). Capgras syndrome: A novel probe for understanding the neural representation of the identity and familiarity of persons. *Proceedings: Biological Sciences, 264,* 437–444.

Hishakawa, Y. (1976). Sleep paralysis. In C. Guilleminault, W. C. Dement, & P. Passouant (Eds.), *Narcolepsy: Advances in sleep research* (Vol. 3, pp. 97–124). New York: Spectrum.

Hitchcock, S. T. (2005). *Mad Mary Lamb: Lunacy and murder in literary London.* New York: Norton.

Hobson, J. A. (1988). *The dreaming brain.* New York: Basic Books.

Hobson, J. A., & McCarley, R. W. (1977). The brain as a dream-state generator: An activation–synthesis hypothesis of the dream process. *American Journal of Psychiatry, 134,* 1335–1368.

Hockley, W. E. (2008). The effects of environmental context on recognition memory and claims of remembering. *Journal of Experimental Psychology: Learning, Memory, and Cognition, 34,* 1412–1429.

Hodgkin, A. L., & Huxley, A. F. (1939). Action potential recorded from inside a nerve fibre. *Nature, 144,* 710–712.

Hodson, G., & Sorrentino, R. M. (2001). Just who favors the ingroup? Personality differences in reactions to uncertainty in the minimal group paradigm. *Group Dynamics, 5,* 92–101.

Hoek, H. W., & van Hoeken, D. (2003). Review of the prevalence and incidence of eating disorders. *International Journal of Eating Disorders, 34,* 383–396.

Hoffrage, U., & Gigerenzer, G. (1996). The impact of information representation on Bayesian reasoning. In G. Cottrell (Ed.), *Proceedings of the Eighteenth Annual Conference of the Cognitive Science Society* (pp. 126–130). Mahwah, NJ: Erlbaum.

Hoffrage, U., & Gigerenzer, G. (1998). Using natural frequencies to improve diagnostic inferences. *Academic Medicine, 73,* 538–540.

Hofmann, S. G., & Asmundson, G. J. G. (2008). Acceptance and mindfulness-based therapy: New wave or old hat? *Clinical Psychology Review, 28,* 1–16.

Hofmann, W., Vohs, K. D., & Baumeister, R. F. (2012). What people desire, feel conflicted about, and try to resist in everyday life. *Psychological Science, 23,* 582–588.

Hollins, M. (2010). Somesthetic senses. *Annual Review of Psychology, 61,* 243–271.

Holloway, G. (2001). *The complete dream book: What your dreams tell about you and your life.* Naperville, IL: Sourcebooks.

Holman, E. A., Silver, R. C., Poulin, M., Andersen, J., Gil-Rivas, V., & McIntosh, D. N. (2008). Terrorism, acute stress, and cardiovascular health. *Archives of General Psychiatry, 65,* 73–80.

Holman, M. A., Carlson, M. L., Driscoll, C. L. W., Grim, K. J., Petersson, R., Sladen, D. P., & Flick, R. P. (2013). Cochlear implantation in children 12 months of age or younger. *Otology & Neurology, 34,* 251–258.

Holmbeck, G. N., & O'Donnell, K. (1991). Discrepancies between perceptions of decision making and behavioral autonomy. In R. L. Paikoff (Ed.), *New directions for child development: Shared views in the family during* adolescence (no. 51, pp. 51–69). San Francisco: Jossey-Bass.

Holmes, J., Gathercole, S. E., & Dunning, D. L. (2009). Adaptive training leads to sustained enhancement of poor working memory in children. *Developmental Science, 12,* F9-F15.

Holmes, T. H., & Rahe, R. H. (1967). The social readjustment rating scale. *Journal of Psychosomatic Research, 11,* 213–318.

Hölzel, B. K., Carmody, J., Vangel, M., Congleton, C., Yerramsetti, S. M., Gard, T., & Lazar, S. W. (2011). Mindfulness practice leads to increases in regained gray matter density. *Psychiatry Research: Neuroimaging, 191*(1), 36–43.

Homan, K. J., Houlihan, D., Ek, K., & Wanzek, J. (2012). Cultural differences in the level of rewards between adolescents from America, Tanzania, Denmark, Honduras, Korea, and Spain. *International Journal of Psychological Studies, 4,* 264–272.

Homans, G. C. (1961). *Social behavior.* New York: Harcourt, Brace and World.

Hooley, J. M. (2007). Expressed emotion and relapse of psychopathology. *Annual Review of Clinical Psychology, 3,* 329–352.

Hopper, L. M., Flynn, E. G., Wood, L. A. N., & Whiten, A. (2010). Observational learning of tool use in children: Investigating cultural spread through diffusion chains and learning mechanisms through ghost displays. *Journal of Experimental Child Psychology, 106,* 82–97.

Horn, J. L., & Cattell, R. B. (1966). Refinement and test of the theory of fluid and crystallized general intelligences. *Journal of Educational Psychology, 5,* 253–270.

Horner, V., Whiten, A., Flynn, E., & de Waal, F. B. M. (2006). Faithful replication of foraging techniques along cultural transmission chains by chimpanzees and children. *Proceedings of the National Academy of Sciences, USA, 103,* 13878–13883.

Horrey, W. J., & Wickens, C. D. (2006). Examining the impact of cell phone conversation on driving using meta-analytic techniques. *Human Factors, 48,* 196–205.

Horta, B. L., Victoria, C. G., Menezes, A. M., Halpern, R., & Barros, F. C. (1997). Low birthweight, preterm births and intrauterine growth retardation in relation to maternal smoking. *Pediatrics and Perinatal Epidemiology, 11,* 140–151.

Hosking, S. G., Young, K. L., & Regan, M. A. (2009). The effects of text messaging on young drivers. *Human Factors, 51,* 582–592.

Houlihan, D., Jesse, V. C., Levine, H. D., & Sombke, C. (1991). A survey of rewards for use with teenage children. *Child & Family Behavior Therapy, 13,* 1–12.

House, J. S., Landis, K. R., & Umberson, D. (1988). Social relationships and health. *Science, 241,* 540–545.

Howard, I. P. (2002). Depth perception. In S. Yantis & H. Pashler (Eds.), *Stevens' handbook of experimental psychology: Vol. 1. Sensation and perception* (3rd ed., pp. 77–120). New York: Wiley.

Howard, J. H., Jr., & Howard, D. V. (1997). Age differences in implicit learning of higher order dependencies in serial patterns. *Psychology and Aging, 12,* 634–656.

Howard, M. O., Brown, S. E., Garland, E. L., Perron, B. E., & Vaughn, M. G. (2011). Inhalant use and inhalant use disorders in the United States. *Addiction Science & Clinical Practice, 6,* 18–31.

Howard-Jones, P. A., Blakemore, S.-J., Samuel, E. A., Summers, I. R., & Claxton, G. (2005). Semantic divergence and creative story generation: An fMRI investigation. *Cognitive Brain Research, 25,* 240–250.

Howes, M., Siegel, M., & Brown, F. (1993). Early childhood memories—accuracy and affect. *Cognition, 47,* 95–119.

Hoyert, D. L., & Xu, J. (2012). Deaths: Preliminary data for 2011. *National Vital Statistics Reports, 61,* 1–51.

Huang, J., Perlis, R. H., Lee, P. H., Rush, A. J., Fava, M., Sachs, G. S., . . . Smoller, J. W. (2010). Cross-disorder genomewide analysis of schizophrenia, bipolar disorder, and depression. *American Journal of Psychiatry, 167,* 1254–1263.

Hubel, D. H. (1988). *Eye, brain, and vision.* New York: Freeman.

Hubel, D. H., & Wiesel, T. N. (1962). Receptive fields, binocular interaction and functional architecture in the cat's visual cortex. *Journal of Physiology, 160,* 106–154.

Hubel, D. H., & Wiesel, T. N. (1998). Early exploration of the visual cortex. *Neuron, 20,* 401–412.

Huesmann, L. R., Moise-Titus, J., Podolski, C.-L., & Eron, L. D. (2003). Longitudinal relations between children's exposure to TV violence and their aggressive and violent behavior in young adulthood: 1977–1992. *Developmental Psychology, 39,* 201–221.

Hughes, J. R. (2007). A review of sleepwalking (somnambulism): The enigma of neurophysiology and polysomnography with differential diagnosis of complex partial seizures. *Epilepsy & Behavior, 11,* 483–491.

Hughs, S., Power, T., & Francis, D. (1992). Defining patterns of drinking in adolescence: A cluster analytic approach. *Journal of Studies on Alcohol, 53,* 40–47.

Hunsley, J., & Di Giulio, G. (2002). Dodo bird, phoenix, or urban legend? The question of psychotherapy equivalence. *Scientific Review of Mental Health Practice, 1,* 13–24.

Hunt, E. B. (2011). *Human intelligence.* New York: Cambridge University Press.

Hunt, M. (1959). *The natural history of love.* New York: Knopf.

Hunter, J. E., & Hunter, R. F. (1984). Validity and utility of alternative predictors of job performance. *Psychological Bulletin, 96,* 72–98.

Hurvich, L. M., & Jameson, D. (1957). An opponent process theory of color vision. *Psychological Review, 64,* 384–404.

Hussey, E., & Safford, A. (2009). Perception of facial expression in somatosensory cortex supports simulationist models. *The Journal of Neuroscience, 29*(2), 301–302.

Huttenlocher, P. R. (1979). Synaptic density in human frontal cortex—developmental changes and effects of aging. *Brain Research, 163,* 195–205.

Huxley, A. (1932). *Brave new world.* London: Chatto and Windus.

Huxley, A. (1954). *The doors of perception.* New York: Harper & Row.

Hyde, K. L., Lerch, J., Norton, A., Forgeard, M., Winner, E., Evans, A. C., & Schlaug, G. (2009). Musical training shapes structural brain development. *Journal of Neuroscience, 29,* 3019–3025.

Hyman, I. E., Jr., Boss, S. M., Wise, B. M., McKenzie, K. E., & Caggiano, J. M. (2010). Did you see the unicycling clown? Inattentional blindness while walking and talking on a cell phone. *Applied Cognitive Psychology, 24*(5), 597–607.

Hyman, I. E., Jr., & Pentland, J. (1996). The role of mental imagery in the creation of false childhood memories. *Journal of Memory and Language, 35,* 101–117.

Hyman, S. E. (2010). The diagnosis of mental disorders: The problem of reification. *Annual Review of Clinical Psychology, 6,* 155–179.

Hypericum Depression Trial Study Group. (2002). Effect of *Hypericum perforatum* (St. John's wort) in major depressive disorder: A randomized controlled trial. *Journal of the American Medical Association, 287,* 1807–1814.

Iacoboni, M. (2009). Imitation, empathy, and mirror neurons. *Annual Review of Psychology, 60,* 653–670.

Iacoboni, M., Molnar-Szakacs, I., Gallese, V., Buccino, G., Mazziotta, J. C., & Rizzolatti, G. (2005). Grasping the intentions of others with one's own mirror neuron system. *PLoS Biology, 3,* 529–535.

Ichheiser, G. (1949). Misunderstandings in human relations: A study in false social perceptions. *American Journal of Sociology, 55* (Pt. 2):1–70.

Imbo, I., & LeFevre, J.-A. (2009). Cultural differences in complex addition: Efficient Chinese versus adaptive Belgians and Canadians. *Journal of Experimental Psychology: Learning, Memory, and Cognition, 35,* 1465–1476.

Inciardi, J. A. (2001). *The war on drugs III.* New York: Allyn & Bacon.

Ingram, R. E., Miranda, J., & Segal, Z. V. (1998). *Cognitive vulnerability to depression.* New York: Guilford Press.

Ingvar, M., Ambros-Ingerson, J., Davis, M., Granger, R., Kessler, M., Rogers, G. A., . . . Lynch, G. (1997). Enhancement by an ampakine of memory encoding in humans. *Experimental Neurology, 146,* 553–559.

Inui, A. (2001). Ghrelin: An orexigenic and somatotrophic signal from the stomach. *Nature Reviews Neuroscience, 2,* 551–560.

Ireland, M. E., Slatcher, R. B., Eastwick, P. W., Scissors, L. E., Finkel, E. J., & Pennebaker, J. W. (2010). Language style matching predicts relationship initiation and stability. *Psychological Science, 22*(1), 39–44. doi:10.1177/0956797610392928

Irvine, J. T. (1978). Wolof magical thinking: Culture and conservation revisited. *Journal of Cross-Cultural Psychology, 9,* 300–310.

Isaacowitz, D. M. (2012). Mood regulation in real time: Age differences in the role of looking. *Current Directions in Psychological Science, 21*(4), 237–242. doi:10.1177/0963721412448651

Isaacowitz, D. M., & Blanchard-Fields, F. (2012). Linking process and outcome in the study of emotion and aging. *Perspectives on Psychological Science, 7*(1), 3–17. doi:10.1177/1745691611424750

Isabelle, R. A. (1993). Origins of attachment: Maternal interactive behavior across the first year. *Child Development, 64,* 605–621.

Isen, A. M., & Patrick, R. (1983). The effect of positive feelings on risk-taking: When the chips are down. *Organizational Behavior and Human Performance, 31,* 194–202.

Isenberg, D. J. (1986). Group polarization: A critical review and meta-analysis. *Journal of Personality and Social Psychology, 50*(6), 1141–1151. Doi:10.1037/0022-3514.50.6.1141

Ishii, K., Reyes, J. A., & Kitayama, S. (2003). Spontaneous attention to word content versus emotional tone. *Psychological Science, 14*(1), 39–46.

Ittelson, W. H. (1952). *The Ames demonstrations in perception.* Princeton, NJ: Princeton University Press.

Izard, C. E. (1971). *The face of emotion.* New York: Appleton-Century-Crofts.

Jablensky, A. (1997). The 100-year epidemiology of schizophrenia. *Schizophrenia Research, 28,* 111–125.

Jaccard, J., Dittus, P. J., & Gordon, V. V. (1998). Parent–adolescent congruency in reports of adolescent sexual behavior and in communications about sexual behavior. *Child Development, 69,* 247–261.

Jacobs, B. L. (1994). Serotonin, motor activity, and depression-related disorders. *American Scientist, 82,* 456–463.

Jacobson, E. (1932). The electrophysiology of mental activities. *American Journal of Psychology, 44,* 677–694.

Jacobson, T., & Hoffman, V. (1997). Children's attachment representations: Longitudinal relations to school behavior and academic compe-

tency in middle childhood and adolescence. *Developmental Psychology, 33,* 703–710.

Jaffee, S., & Hyde, J. S. (2000). Gender differences in moral orientation: A meta-analysis. *Psychological Bulletin, 126,* 703–726.

Jahoda, G. (1993). *Crossroads between culture and mind.* Cambridge, MA: Harvard University Press.

James, T. W., Culham, J., Humphrey, G. K., Milner, A. D., & Goodale, M. A. (2003). Ventral occipital lesions impair object recognition but not object-directed grasping: An fMRI study. *Brain, 126,* 2463–2475.

James, W. (1884). What is an emotion? *Mind, 9,* 188–205.

James, W. (1890). *The principles of psychology.* Cambridge, MA: Harvard University Press.

James, W. (1911). *Memories and studies.* New York: Longman.

Jamieson, J. P., Koslov, K., Nock, M. K., & Mendes, W. B. (2013). Experiencing discrimination increases risk-taking. *Psychological Science, 24,* 131–139.

Jamieson, J. P., Mendes, W. B., Blackstock, E., & Schmader, T. (2010). Turning the knots in your stomach into bows: Reappraising arousal improves performance on the GRE. *Journal of Experimental Social Psychology, 46,* 208–212.

Jamieson, J. P., Mendes, W. B., & Nock, M. K. (2013). Improving acute stress responses: The power of reappraisal. *Current Directions in Psychological Science, 22*(1), 51–56.

Jamieson, J. P., Nock, M. K., & Mendes, W. B. (2013). Changing the conceptualization of stress in social anxiety disorder: Affective and physiological consequences. *Clinical Psychological Science.* Advance online publication. doi:10.1177/2167702613482119

Jamison, K. R. (1993). *Touched with fire: Manic-depressive illness and the artistic temperament.* New York: Free Press.

Jamison, K. R. (1995). *An unquiet mind: A memoir of moods and madness.* New York: Random House.

Janicak, P. G., Dowd, S. M., Martis, B., Alam, D., Beedle, D., Krasuski, J., . . . Viana, M. (2002). Repetitive transcranial magnetic stimulation versus electroconvulsive therapy for major depression: Preliminary results of a randomized trial. *Biological Psychiatry, 51,* 659–667.

Janis, I. L. (1982). *Groupthink: Scientific studies of policy decisions and fiascoes.* Boston: Houghton-Mifflin.

Jarosz, A. F., Colflesh, G. J. H., & Wiley, J. (2012). Uncorking the muse: Alcohol intoxication facilitates creative problem solving. *Consciousness and Cognition, 21,* 487–493.

Jarvella, R. J. (1970). Effects of syntax on running memory span for connected discourse. *Psychonomic Science, 19,* 235–236.

Jarvella, R. J. (1971). Syntactic processing of connected speech. *Journal of Verbal Learning and Verbal Behavior, 10,* 409–416.

Jausovec, N., & Jausovec, K. (2005). Differences in induced gamma and upper alpha oscillations in the human brain related to verbal performance and emotional intelligence. *International Journal of Psychophysiology, 56,* 223.

Jausovec, N., Jausovec, K., & Gerlic, I. (2001). Differences in even-trelated and induced electroencephalography patterns in the theta and alpha frequency bands related to human emotional intelligence. *Neuroscience Letters, 311,* 93.

Jaynes, J. (1976). *The origin of consciousness in the breakdown of the bicameral mind.* London: Allen Lane.

Jenkins, H. M., Barrera, F. J., Ireland, C., & Woodside, B. (1978). Signal-centered action patterns of dogs in appetitive classical conditioning. *Learning and Motivation, 9,* 272–296.

Jenkins, J. G., & Dallenbach, K. M. (1924). Oblivscence during sleep and waking. *American Journal of Psychology, 35,* 605–612.

John, O. P., Naumann, L. P., & Soto, C. J. (2008). Paradigm shift to the integrative Big-Five trait taxonomy: History, measurement, and conceptual issues. In O. P. John, R. W. Robins, & L. A. Pervin (Eds.), *Handbook of personality: Theory and research* (pp. 114–158). New York: Guilford Press.

John, O. P., & Srivastava, S. (1999). The Big Five trait taxonomy: History, measurement, and theoretical perspectives. In L. A. Pervin & O. P. John (Eds.), *Handbook of personality: Theory and research* (2nd ed., pp. 102–138). New York: Guilford Press.

Johnson, C. A., Xiao, L., Palmer, P., Sun, P., Wang, Q., Wei, Y. L., . . . Bechara, A. (2008). Affective decision-making deficits, linked to dysfunctional ventromedial prefrontal cortex, revealed in 10th grade Chinese adolescent binge drinkers. *Neuropsychologia, 46,* 714–726.

Johnson, D. H. (1980). The relationship between spike rate and synchrony in responses of auditory-nerve fibers to single tones. *Journal of the Acoustical Society of America, 68,* 1115–1122.

Johnson, D. R., & Wu, J. (2002). An empirical test of crisis, social selection, and role explanations of the relationship between marital disruption and psychological distress: A pooled time-series analysis of four-wave panel data. *Journal of Marriage and the Family, 64,* 211–224.

Johnson, J. D., Noel, N. E., & Sutter-Hernandez, J. (2000). Alcohol and male sexual aggression: A cognitive disruption analysis. *Journal of Applied Social Psychology, 30,* 1186–1200.

Johnson, J. S., & Newport, E. L. (1989). Critical period effects in second language learning: The influence of maturational state on the acquisition of English as a second language. *Cognitive Psychology, 21,* 60–99.

Johnson, K. (2002). Neural basis of haptic perception. In H. Pashler & S. Yantis (Eds.), *Stevens' handbook of experimental psychology: Vol. 1. Sensation and perception* (3rd ed., pp. 537–583). New York: Wiley.

Johnson, M. H., Dziurawiec, S., Ellis, H. D., & Morton, J. (1991). Newborns' preferential tracking of face-like stimuli and its subsequent decline. *Cognition, 40,* 1–19.

Johnson, M. K., Hashtroudi, S., & Lindsay, D. S. (1993). Source monitoring. *Psychological Bulletin, 114,* 3–28.

Johnson, N. J., Backlund, E., Sorlie, P. D., & Loveless, C. A. (2000). Marital status and mortality: The National Longitudinal Mortality Study. *Annual Review of Epidemiology, 10,* 224–238.

Johnson, S. L., Cuellar, A. K., & Miller, C. (2009). Unipolar and bipolar depression: A comparison of clinical phenomenology, biological vulnerability, and psychosocial predictors. In I. H. Gottlib & C. L. Hammen (Eds.), *Handbook of depression* (2nd ed., pp. 142–162). New York: Guilford Press.

Johnson, S. L., Cuellar, A. K., Ruggiero, C., Winnett-Perman, C., Goodnick, P., White, R., & Miller, I. (2008). Life events as predictors of mania and depression in bipolar 1 disorder. *Journal of Abnormal Psychology, 117,* 268–277.

Johnson, S. L., & Miller, I. (1997). Negative life events and time to recover from episodes of bipolar disorder. *Journal of Abnormal Psychology, 106,* 449–457.

Johnston, L., Bachman, J., & O'Malley, P. (1997). *Monitoring the future.* Ann Arbor, MI: Institute for Social Research.

Johnstone, E. C., Crow, T. J., Frith, C., Husband, J., & Kreel, L. (1976). Cerebral ventricular size and cognitive impairment in chronic schizophrenia. *Lancet, 2,* 924–926.

Joiner, T. E., Jr. (2006). *Why people die by suicide.* Cambridge, MA: Harvard University Press.

Jonas, E., Graupmann, V., Kayser, D. N., Zanna, M., Traut-Mattausch, E., & Frey, D. (2009). Culture, self, and the emergence of reactance: Is there a "universal" freedom? *Journal of Experimental Social Psychology, 45,* 1068–1080.

Jones, B. C., Little, A. C., Penton-Voak, I. S., Tiddeman, B. P., Burt, D. M., & Perrett, D. I. (2001). Facial symmetry and judgements of apparent health: Support for a "good genes" explanation of the attractiveness–symmetry relationship. *Evolution and Human Behavior, 22,* 417–429.

Jones, E. E., & Harris, V. A. (1967). The attribution of attitudes. *Journal of Experimental Social Psychology, 3,* 1–24.

Jones, E. E., & Nisbett, R. E. (1972). The actor and the observer: Divergent perceptions of the causes of behavior. In E. E. Jones, D. E. Kanouse, H. H. Kelley, R. E. Nisbett, S. Valins, & B. Weiner (Eds.), *Attribution: Perceiving the causes of behavior* (pp. 79–94). Morristown, NJ: General Learning Press.

Jones, K. (1972). *A history of mental health services.* London: Routledge and Kegan Paul.

Jones, L. M., & Foshay, N. N. (1984). Diffusion of responsibility in a nonemergency situation: Response to a greeting from a stranger. *Journal of Social Psychology, 123,* 155–158.

Jones, S. S. (2007). Imitation in infancy. *Psychological Science, 18(7),* 593–599.

Jonsson, H., & Hougaard, E. (2008). Group cognitive behavioural therapy for obsessive-compulsive disorder: A systematic review and meta-analysis. *Acta Psychiatrica Scandinavica, 117,* 1–9.

Jordan, S. A., Cunningham, D. G., & Marles, R. J. (2010). Assessment of herbal medicinal products: Challenges and opportunities to increase the knowledge base for safety assessment. *Toxicology and Applied Pharmacology, 243,* 198–216.

Judd, L. L. (1997). The clinical course of unipolar major depressive disorders. *Archives of General Psychiatry, 54,* 989–991.

Jung-Beeman, M. (2005). Bilateral brain processes for comprehending natural language. *Trends in Cognitive Sciences, 9,* 512–518.

Jung-Beeman, M., Bowden, E. M., Haberman, J., Frymiare, J. L., Arambel-Liu, S., Greenblatt, R., . . . Kounios, J. (2004). Neural activity when people solve verbal problems with insight. *PLoS Biology, 2,* 500–510.

Jurewicz, I., Owen, R. J., & O'Donovan, M. C. (2001). Searching for susceptibility genes in schizophrenia. *European Neuropsychopharmacology, 11,* 395–398.

Kaas, J. H. (1991). Plasticity of sensory and motor maps in adult mammals. *Annual Review of Neuroscience, 14,* 137–167.

Kagan, J. (1997). Temperament and the reactions to unfamiliarity. *Child Development, 68,* 139–143.

Kahneman, D., Krueger, A. B., Schkade, D. A., Schwarz, N., & Stone, A. A. (2004). A survey method for characterizing daily life experience: The day reconstruction method. *Science, 306,* 1776–1780.

Kahneman, D., & Tversky, A. (1973). On the psychology of prediction. *Psychological Review, 80,* 237–251.

Kahneman, D., & Tversky, A. (1979). Prospect theory: An analysis of decision under risk. *Econometrica, 47,* 263–291.

Kamin, L. J. (1959). The delay-of-punishment gradient. *Journal of Comparative and Physiological Psychology, 52,* 434–437.

Kamiya, J. (1969). Operant control of the EEG alpha rhythm and some of its reported effects on consciousness. In C. S. Tart (Ed.), *Altered states of consciousness* (pp. 519–529). Garden City, NY: Anchor Books.

Kan, P. F., & Kohnert, K. (2008). Fast mapping by bilingual preschool children. *Journal of Child Language, 35,* 495–514.

Kandel, E. R. (2000). Nerve cells and behavior. In E. R. Kandel, G. H. Schwartz, & T. M. Jessell (Eds.), *Principles of neural science* (pp. 19–35). New York. McGraw-Hill.

Kandel, E. R. (2006). *In search of memory: The emergence of a new science of mind.* New York: Norton.

Kang, S. H. K., McDermott, K. B., & Roediger, H. L. III. (2007). Test format and corrective feedback modify the effect of testing on long-term retention. *European Journal of Cognitive Psychology, 19,* 528–558.

Kanwisher, N. (2000). Domain specificity in face perception. *Nature Neuroscience, 3,* 759–763.

Kanwisher, N., McDermott, J., & Chun, M. M. (1997). The fusiform face area: A module in human extrastriate cortex specialized for face perception. *The Journal of Neuroscience, 17,* 4302–4311.

Kanwisher, N., & Yovel, G. (2006). The fusiform face area: A cortical region specialized for the perception of faces. *Philosophical Transactions of the Royal Society (B), 361,* 2109–2128.

Kaplan, R. M., & Stone, A. A. (2013). Bringing the laboratory and clinic to the community: Mobile technologies for health promotion and disease prevention. *Annual Review of Psychology, 64,* 471–498.

Kapur, S., Craik, F. I. M., Tulving, E., Wilson, A. A., Houle, S., & Brown, G. M. (1994). Neuroanatomical correlates of encoding in episodic memory: Levels of processing effects. *Proceedings of the National Academy of Sciences, USA, 91,* 2008–2011.

Karau, S. J., & Williams, K. D. (1993). Social loafing: A meta-analytic review and theoretical integration. *Journal of Personality and Social Psychology, 65,* 681–706.

Karlins, M., Coffman, T. L., & Walters, G. (1969). On the fading of social stereotypes: Studies in three generations of college students. *Journal of Personality and Social Psychology, 13,* 1–16.

Karney, B. R., & Bradbury, T. N. (1995). The longitudinal course of marital quality and stability: A review of theory, methods, and research. *Psychological Bulletin, 118,* 3–34.

Karow, A., Pajonk, F. G., Reimer, J., Hirdes, F., Osterwald, C., Naber, D., & Moritz, S. (2007). The dilemma of insight into illness in schizophrenia: Self- and expert-rated insight and quality of life. *European Archives of Psychiatry and Clinical Neuroscience, 258,* 152–159.

Karpicke, J. D. (2012). Retrieval-based learning: Active retrieval promotes meaningful learning. *Current Directions in Psychological Science, 21,* 157–163.

Karpicke, J. D., & Blunt, J. R. (2011). Retrieval practice produces more learning than elaborative studying with concept mapping. *Science, 331,* 772–775.

Karpicke, J. D., & Roediger, H. L., III. (2008). The critical importance of retrieval for learning. *Science, 319,* 966–968.

Kassam, K. S., Gilbert, D. T., Swencionis, J. K., & Wilson, T. D. (2009). Misconceptions of memory: The Scooter Libby effect. *Psychological Science, 20,* 551–552.

Kasser, T., & Sharma, Y. S. (1999). Reproductive freedom, educational equality, and females' preference for resource-acquisition characteristics in mates. *Psychological Science, 10,* 374–377.

Katon, W. (1994). Primary care—psychiatry panic disorder management. In B. E. Wolfe & J. D. Maser (Eds.), *Treatment of panic disorder: A consensus development conference* (pp. 41–56). Washington, DC: American Psychiatric Press.

Katz, D., & Braly, K. (1933). Racial stereotypes of one hundred college students. *Journal of Abnormal and Social Psychology, 28,* 280–290.

Kaufman, A. S. (2001). WAIS-III IQs, Horn's theory, and generational changes from young adulthood to old age. *Intelligence, 29,* 131–167.

Kaufman, L. (2009, January 30). Utilities turn their customers green, with envy. *New York Times.* Retrieved from http://www.nytimes.com/2009/01/31/science/earth/31compete.html

Kawakami, K., Dovidio, J. F., Moll, J., Hermsen, S., & Russin, A. (2000). Just say no (to stereotyping): Effects of training in the negation of stereotypic associations on stereotype activation. *Journal of Personality and Social Psychology, 78,* 871–888.

Kazdin, A. E., & Blaise, S. L. (2011). Rebooting psychotherapy research and practice to reduce the burden of mental illness. *Perspectives on Psychological Science, 6,* 21–37.

Keane, T. M., Marshall, A. D., & Taft, C. T. (2006). Posttraumatic stress disorder: Etiology, epidemiology, and treatment outcome. *Annual Review of Clinical Psychology, 2,* 161–197.

Keefe, F. J., Abernathy, A. P., & Campbell, L. C. (2005). Psychological approaches to understanding and treating disease-related pain. *Annual Review of Psychology, 56,* 601–630.

Keefe, F. J., Lumley, M., Anderson, T., Lynch, T., & Carson, K. L. (2001). Pain and emotion: New research directions. *Journal of Clinical Psychology, 57,* 587–607.

Kelley, H. H. (1967). Attribution theory in social psychology. In D. Levine (Ed.), *Nebraska Symposium on Motivation* (Vol. 15, pp. 192–238). Lincoln: University of Nebraska Press.

Kelley, H. H. (1983). Love and commitment. In H. H. Kelley, E. Berscheid, A. Christensen, & J. H. Harvey (Eds.), *Close relationships* (pp. 265–314). New York: W. H. Freeman and Company.

Kelley, W. M., Macrae, C. N., Wyland, C. L., Caglar, S., Inati, S., & Heatherton, T. F. (2002). Finding the self? An event-related fMRI study. *Journal of Cognitive Neuroscience, 14,* 785–794.

Kellman, P. J., & Spelke, E. S. (1983). Perception of partly occluded objects in infancy. *Cognitive Psychology, 15,* 483–524.

Kelly, G. (1955). *The psychology of personal constructs.* New York: Norton.

Keltner, D. (1995). Signs of appeasement: Evidence for the distinct displays of embarrassment, amusement, and shame. *Journal of Personality and Social Psychology, 68,* 441–454.

Keltner, D., & Buswell, B. N. (1996). Evidence for the distinctness of embarrassment, shame, and guilt: A study of recalled antecedents and facial expressions of emotion. *Cognition and Emotion, 10,* 155–171.

Keltner, D., & Haidt, J. (1999). Social functions of emotions at four levels of analysis. *Cognition and Emotion, 13,* 505–521.

Keltner, D., & Harker, L. A. (1998). The forms and functions of the nonverbal signal of shame. In P. Gilbert & B. Andrews (Eds.), *Shame: Interpersonal behavior, psychopathology, and culture* (pp. 78–98). New York: Oxford University Press.

Keltner, D., & Shiota, M. N. (2003). New displays and new emotions: A commentary on Rozin and Cohen (2003). *Emotion, 3,* 86–91.

Kendler, K. S., Hettema, J. M., Butera, F., Gardner, C. O., & Prescott, C. A. (2003). Life event dimensions of loss, humiliation, entrapment, and danger in the prediction of onsets of major depression and generalized anxiety. *Archives of General Psychiatry, 60,* 789–796.

Kendler, K. S., Myers, J., & Prescott, C. A. (2002). The etiology of phobias: An evaluation of the stress–diathesis model. *Archives of General Psychiatry, 59,* 242–248.

Kenrick, D. T., Neuberg, S. L., Griskevicius, V., Becker, D. V., & Schaller, M. (2010). Goal-driven cognition and functional behavior: The fundamental motives framework. *Current Directions in Psychological Science, 19*(1), 63–67.

Kenrick, D. T., Sadalla, E. K., Groth, G., & Trost, M. R. (1990). Evolution, traits, and the stages of human courtship: Qualifying the parental investment model. *Journal of Personality, 58,* 97–116.

Kensinger, E. A., Clarke, R. J., & Corkin, S. (2003). What neural correlates underlie successful encoding and retrieval? A functional magnetic resonance imaging study using a divided attention paradigm. *The Journal of Neuroscience, 23,* 2407–2415.

Kensinger, E. A., & Schacter, D. L. (2005). Emotional content and reality monitoring ability: fMRI evidence for the influence of encoding processes. *Neuropsychologia, 43,* 1429–1443.

Kensinger, E. A., & Schacter, D. L. (2006). Amygdala activity is associated with the successful encoding of item, but not source, information for positive and negative stimuli. *The Journal of Neuroscience, 26,* 2564–2570.

Kephart, W. M. (1967). Some correlates of romantic love. *Journal of Marriage and the Family, 29,* 470–474.

Kershaw, T. C., & Ohlsson, S. (2004). Multiple causes of difficulty in insight: The case of the nine-dot problem. *Journal of Experimental Psychology: Learning, Memory, and Cognition, 30,* 3–13.

Kertai, M. D., Pal, N., Palanca, B. J., Lin, N., Searleman, S. A., Zhang, L., . . . B-Unaware Study Group. (2010). Association of perioperative risk factors and cumulative duration of low bispectral index with intermediate-term mortality after cardiac surgery in the B-Unaware trial. *Anesthesiology, 112*(5), 1116–1127.

Kessler, R. C. (2012). The costs of depression. *Psychiatric Clinics of North America, 35,* 1–14.

Kessler, R. C., Adler, L., Barkley, R., Biederman, J., Connors, C. K., Demler, O., . . . Zaslavsky, A. M. (2006). The prevalence and correlates of adult ADHD in the United States: Results from the National Comorbidity Study Replication. *American Journal of Psychiatry, 163,* 716–723.

Kessler, R. C., Angermeyer, M., Anthony, J. C., deGraaf, R., Demyittenaere, K., Gasquet, I., . . . Üstün, T. B. (2007). Lifetime prevalence and age-of-onset distributions of mental disorders in the World Health Organization World Mental Health Survey Initiative. *World Psychiatry, 6,* 168–176.

Kessler, R. C., Berglund, P., Demler, M. A., Jin, R., Merikangas, K. R., & Walters, E. E. (2005). Lifetime prevalence and age-of-onset distributions of *DSM–IV* disorders in the National Comorbidity Survey replication. *Archives of General Psychiatry, 62,* 593–602.

Kessler, R. C., Chiu, W. T., Dernier, O., & Walters, E. E. (2005). Prevalence, severity, and comorbidity of 12-month *DSM–IV* disorders in the National Comorbidity Survey replication. *Archives of General Psychiatry, 62,* 617–627.

Kessler, R. C., Chiu, W. T., Jin, R., Ruscio, A. M., Shear, K., & Walters, E. E. (2006). The epidemiology of panic attacks, panic disorder, and agoraphobia in the National Comorbidity Survey Replication. *Archives of General Psychiatry, 63,* 415–424.

Kessler, R. C., Demler, O., Frank, R. G., Olfson, M., Pincus, H. A., Walters, E. E., . . . Zaslavsky, A. M. (2005). Prevalence and treatment of mental disorders, 1990 to 2003. *New England Journal of Medicine, 352*(24), 2515–2523.

Kessler, R. C., Petukhova, M., Sampson, N. A., Zaslavsky, A. M., & Wittchen, H.U. (2012). Twelve-month and lifetime prevalence and lifetime morbid risk of anxiety and mood disorders in the United States. *International Journal of Methods in Psychiatric Research, 21*(3), 169–184.

Kessler, R. C., Soukup, J., Davis, R. B., Foster, D. F., Wilkey, S. A., Van Rompay, M. I., & Eisenberg, D. M. (2001). The use of complementary and alternative therapies to treat anxiety and depression in the United States. *American Journal of Psychiatry, 158,* 289–294.

Kessler, R. C., & Üstün, T. B. (Eds.). (2008). *The WHO Mental Health surveys: Global perspectives on the epidemiology of mental health.* Cambridge, England: Cambridge University Press.

Kessler, R. C., & Wang, P. S. (2008). The descriptive epidemiology of commonly occurring mental disorders in the United States. *Annual Reviews of Public Health, 29,* 115–129.

Keuler, D. J., & Safer, M. A. (1998). Memory bias in the assessment and recall of pre-exam anxiety: How anxious was I? *Applied Cognitive Psychology, 12,* S127–S137.

Khalid, N., Atkins, M., Tredget, J., Giles, M., Champney-Smith, K., & Kirov, G. (2008). The effectiveness of electroconvulsive therapy in treatment-resistant depression: A naturalistic study. *The Journal of ECT, 24,* 141–145.

Khalid, R. (1991). Personality and academic achievement: A thematic apperception perspective. *British Journal of Projective Psychology, 36,* 25–34.

Khan, R. M., Luk, C.-H., Flinker, A., Aggarwal, A., Lapid, H., Haddad, R., & Sobel, N. (2007). Predicting odor pleasantness from odorant structure: Pleasantness as a reflection of the physical world. *Journal of Neuroscience, 27,* 10015–10023.

Kiecolt-Glaser, J. K., Garner, W., Speicher, C., Penn, G., & Glaser, R. (1984). Psychosocial modifiers of immunocompetence in medical students. *Psychosomatic Medicine, 46,* 7–14.

Kiefer, H. M. (2004). *Americans unruffled by animal testing.* Retrieved August 8, 2009, from http://www.gallup.com/poll/11767/Americans-Unruffled-Animal-Testing.aspx

Kiefer, M., Schuch, S., Schenk, W., & Fiedler, K. (2007). Mood states modulate activity in semantic brain areas during emotional word encoding. *Cerebral Cortex, 17,* 1516–1530.

Kiehl, K. A., Smith, A. M., Hare, R. D., Mendrek, A., Forster, B. B., Brink, J., & Liddle, P. F. (2001). Limbic abnormalities in affective processing by criminal psychopaths as revealed by functional magnetic resonance imaging. *Biological Psychiatry, 50,* 677–684.

Kihlstrom, J. F. (1985). Hypnosis. *Annual Review of Psychology, 36,* 385–418.

Kihlstrom, J. F. (1987). The cognitive unconscious. *Science, 237,* 1445–1452.

Kihlstrom, J. F., Beer, J. S., & Klein, S. B. (2002). Self and identity as memory. In M. R. Leary & J. P. Tangney (Eds.), *Handbook of self and identity* (pp. 68–90). New York: Guilford Press.

Killingsworth, M. A., & Gilbert, D. T. (2010). A wandering mind is an unhappy mind. *Science, 330,* 932.

Kim, G., Walden, T. A., & Knieps, L. J. (2010). Impact and characteristics of positive and fearful emotional messages during infant social referencing. *Infant Behavior and Development, 33,* 189–195.

Kim, K., & Smith, P. K. (1998). Childhood stress, behavioural symptoms and mother–daughter pubertal development. *Journal of Adolescence, 21,* 231–240.

Kim, U. K., Jorgenson, E., Coon, H., Leppert, M., Risch, N., & Drayna, D. (2003). Positional cloning of the human quantaitive trait locus underlying taste sensitivity to phenylthiocarbamide. *Science, 299,* 1221–1225.

Kinney, D. A. (1993). From nerds to normals—the recovery of identity among adolescents from middle school to high school. *Sociology of Education, 66,* 21–40.

Kirchner, W. H., & Towne, W. F. (1994). The sensory basis of the honeybee's dance language. *Scientific American, 270*(6), 74–80.

Kirsch, I., Cardena, E., Derbyshire, S., Dienes, Z., Heap, M., Kallio, S., . . . Whalley, M. (2011). Definitions of hypnosis and hypnotizability and their relation to suggestion and suggestibility: A consensus statement. *Contemporary Hypnosis and Integrative Therapy, 28,* 107–115.

Kirwan, C. B., Bayley, P. J., Galvan, V. V., & Squire, L. R. (2008). Detailed recollection of remote autobiographical memory after damage to the medial temporal lobe. *Proceedings of the National Academy of Sciences, USA, 105,* 2676–2680.

Kish, S. J., Lerch, J., Furukawa, Y. , Tong, J., McCluskey, T., Wilkins, D., . . . Bioleau, I. (2010). Decreased cerebral cortical serotonin transporter binding in ecstacy users: A positron emission tomography [^{11}c] DASB and structural brain imaging study. *Brain, 133,* 1779–1797.

Kitayama, S., Duffy, S., Kawamura, T., & Larsen, J. T. (2003). Perceiving an object and its context in different cultures: A cultural look at the new look. *Psychological Science, 14,* 201–206.

Kitayama, S., & Uskul, A. K. (2011). Culture, mind, and the brain: Current evidence and future directions. *Annual Review of Psychology, 62*, 419–449.

Klein, C. T. F., & Helweg-Larsen, M. (2002). Perceived control and the optimistic bias: A meta-analytic review. *Psychology and Health, 17*, 437–446.

Klein, S. B. (2004). The cognitive neuroscience of knowing one's self. In M. Gazzaniga (Ed.), *The cognitive neurosciences* (3rd ed., pp. 1007–1089). Cambridge, MA: MIT Press.

Klein, S. B., Robertson, T. E., & Delton, A. W. (2011). The future-orientation of memory: Planning as a key component mediating the high levels of recall found with survival processing. *Memory, 19*, 121–139.

Klein, S. B., & Thorne, B. M. (2007). *Biological psychology.* New York: Worth Publishers.

Klingberg, T. (2010). Training and plasticity of working memory. *Trends in Cognitive Sciences, 14*, 317–324.

Klinger, E. (1975). Consequences of commitment to and disengagement from incentives. *Psychological Review, 82*, 1–25.

Klinger, E. (1977). *Meaning and void.* Minneapolis: University of Minnesota Press.

Klonsky, E. D. (2011). Non-suicidal self-injury in United States adults: Prevalence, sociodemographics, topography, and functions. *Psychological Medicine, 41*, 1981–1986.

Klump, K. L., & Culbert, K. M. (2007). Molecular genetic studies of eating disorders: Current status and future directions. *Current Directions in Psychological Science, 16*(1), 37–41.

Klüver, H., & Bucy, P. C. (1937). "Psychic blindness" and other symptoms following bilateral temporary lobectomy in rhesus monkeys. *American Journal of Physiology, 119*, 352–353.

Knowlton, B. J., Ramus, S. J., & Squire, L. R. (1992). Intact artificial grammar learning in amnesia: Dissociation of classification learning and explicit memory for specific instances. *Psychological Science, 3*, 173–179.

Knutson, B., Adams, C. M., Fong, G. W., & Hommer, D. (2001). Anticipation of increasing monetary reward selectively recruits nucleus accumbens. *The Journal of Neuroscience, 21*, 159.

Knutson, B., Wolkowitz, O. M., Cole, S. W., Chan, T., Moore, E. A., Johnson, R. C., Reus, V. I. (1998). Selective alteration of personality and social behavior by serotonergic intervention. *American Journal of Psychiatry, 155*, 373–379.

Kobasa, S. (1979). Stressful life events, personality, and health: An inquiry into hardiness. *Journal of Personality and Social Psychology, 37*, 1–11.

Koehler, J. J. (1993). The influence of prior beliefs on scientific judgments of evidence quality. *Organizational Behavior and Human Decision Processes, 56*, 28–55.

Koenigs, M., Young, L., Adolphs, R., Tranel, D., Cushman, F., Hauser, M., & Damasio, A. (2007). Damage to the prefrontal cortex increases utilitarian moral judgements. *Nature, 446*, 908–911.

Koffka, K. (1935). *Principles of Gestalt psychology.* New York: Harcourt, Brace and World.

Kohlberg, L. (1958). *The development of modes of thinking and choices in years 10 to 16.* Unpublished doctoral dissertation, University of Chicago.

Kohlberg, L. (1963). Development of children's orientation towards a moral order (Part I). Sequencing in the development of moral thought. *Vita Humana, 6*, 11–36.

Kohlberg, L. (1986). A current statement on some theoretical issues. In S. Modgil & C. Modgil (Eds.), *Lawrence Kohlberg: Concensus and controversy* (pp. 485–546). Philadelphia: Falmer.

Kohler, P. K., Manhart, L. E., & Lafferty, E. (2008). Abstinence-only and comprehensive sex education and the initiation of sexual activity and teen pregnancy. *Journal of Adolescent Health, 42*, 344–351.

Kolb, B., & Whishaw, I. Q. (2003). *Fundamentals of human neuropsychology* (5th ed.). New York: Worth Publishers.

Kolbert, E. (2009, July 20). XXXL. *The New Yorker*, pp. 73–77.

Koller, D. (2011, December 5). Death knell for the lecture: Technology as a passport to personalized education. Retrieved from http://www.nytimes.com/2011/12/06/science/daphne-koller-technology-as-a-passport-to-personalized-education.html?pageswanted=all

Kolotkin, R. L., Meter, K., & Williams, G. R. (2001). Quality of life and obesity. *Obesity Reviews, 2*, 219–229.

Komter, A. (2010). The evolutionary origins of human generosity. *International Sociology, 25*(3), 443–464.

Konen, C. S., & Kastner, S. (2008). Two hierarchically organized neural systems for object information in human visual cortex. *Nature Neuroscience, 11*, 224–231.

Koole, S. L., Dijksterhuis, A., & van Knippenberg, A. (2001). What's in a name: Implicit self-esteem and the automatic self. *Journal of Personality and Social Psychology, 80*, 669–685.

Koss, M. P. (1990). The women's mental health research agenda: Violence against women. *American Psychologist, 45*, 374–380.

Kosslyn, S. M., Alpert, N. M., Thompson, W. L., Chabris, C. F., Rauch, S. L., & Anderson, A. K. (1993). Visual mental imagery activates topographically organized visual cortex: PET investigations. *Journal of Cognitive Neuroscience, 5*, 263–287.

Kosslyn, S. M., Pascual-Leone, A., Felician, O., Camposano, S., Keenan, J. P., Thompson, W. L., . . . Alpert, N. M. (1999). The role of area 17 in visual imagery: Convergent evidence from PET and rTMS. *Science, 284*, 167–170.

Kosslyn, S. M., Thompson, W. L., Constantini-Ferrando, M. F., Alpert, N. M., & Spiegel, D. (2000). Hypnotic visual illusion alters color processing in the brain. *American Journal of Psychiatry, 157*, 1279–1284.

Kounios, J., & Beeman, M. (2009). The Aha! moment. *Current Directions in Psychological Science, 18*, 210–216.

Kounios, J., Fleck, J. L., Green, D. L., Payne, L., Stevenson, J. L., Bowden, E. M., & Jung-Beeman, M. (2008). The origins of insight in resting-state brain activity. *Neuropsychologia, 46*, 281–291.

Kounios, J., Frymiare, J. L., Bowden, E. M., Fleck, J. I., Subramaniam, K., Parrish, T. B., & Jung-Beeman, M. (2006). The prepared mind: Neural activity prior to problem presentation predicts subsequent solution by sudden insight. *Psychological Science, 17*, 882–890.

Kovalevskaya, S. (1978). *A Russian childhood.* New York: Springer-Verlag.

Kraemer, H. C., Shrout, P. E., & Rubio-Stipec, M. (2007). Developing the *Diagnostic and Statistical Manual–V*: What will "statistical" mean in *DSM–V*? *Social Psychiatry and Psychiatric Epidemiology, 42*, 259–267.

Kraepelin, E. (1899). *Psychiatrie.* Leipzig, Germany: Barth.

Krantz, D. S., & McCeney, M. K. (2002). Effects of psychological and social factors on organic disease: A critical assessment of research on coronary heart disease. *Annual Review of Psychology, 53*, 341–369.

Kraus, N., & Chandrasekaran, B. (2010). Music training for the development of auditory skills. *Nature Reviews Neuroscience, 11*, 599–605.

Kravitz, D. J., Saleem, K. S., Baker, C. I., & Mishkin, M. (2011). A new neural framework for visuospatial processing. *Nature Reviews Neuroscience, 12*, 217–230.

Kravitz, D. J., Saleem, K. S., Baker, C. I., Ungerleider, L. G., & Mishkin, M. (2013). The ventral visual pathway: An expanded neural framework for the processing of object quality. *Trends in Cognitive Sciences, 17,* 26–49.

Kravitz, R. L., Epstein, R. M., Feldman, M. D., Franz, C. E., Azari, R., Wilkes, M. S., . . . **Franks, P.** (2005). Influence of patients' requests for direct-to-consumer advertised antidepressants: A randomized controlled trial. *Journal of the American Medical Association, 293,* 1995–2002.

Kreider, T. (2013, January 20). You are going to die. *New York Times.* Retrieved from http://opinionator.blogs.nytimes.com/2013/01/20/you-are-going-to-die/

Kringelbach, M. L., O'Doherty, J., Rolls, E. T., & Andrews, C. (2003). Activation of the human orbitofrontal cortex to a liquid food stimulus is correlated with its subjective pleasantness. *Cerebral Cortex, 13,* 1064–1071.

Krings, T., Topper, R., Foltys, H., Erberich, S., Sparing, R., Willmes, K., & Thron, A. (2000). Cortical activation patterns during complex motor tasks in piano players and control subjects. A functional magnetic resonance imaging study. *Neuroscience Letters, 278,* 189–193.

Krishnan, V., & Nestler, E. J. (2008). The molecular neurobiology of depression. *Nature, 455,* 894–902.

Kristensen, P., & Bjerkedal, T. (2007). Explaining the relation between birth order and intelligence. *Science, 316,* 1717.

Kroeze, W. K., & Roth, B. L. (1998). The molecular biology of serotonin receptors: Therapeutic implications for the interface of mood and psychosis. *Biological Psychiatry, 44,* 1128–1142.

Kruk, M. R., Halasz, J., Meelis, W., & Haller, J. (2004). Fast positive feedback between the adrenocortical stress response and a brain mechanism involved in aggressive behavior. *Behavioral Neuroscience, 118,* 1062–1070.

Kubovy, M. (1981). Concurrent-pitch segregation and the theory of indispensable attributes. In M. Kubovy & J. R. Pomerantz (Eds.), *Perceptual organization* (pp. 55–96). Hillsdale, NJ: Erlbaum.

Kuhl, B. A., Dudukovic, N. M., Kahn, I., & Wagner, A. D. (2007). Decreased demands on cognitive control reveal the neural processing benefits of forgetting. *Nature Neuroscience, 10,* 908–917.

Kuhl, P. K. (2010). Brain mechanisms in early language acquisition. *Neuron, 67,* 713–727.

Kuhl, P. K., & Meltzoff, A. N. (1996). Infant vocalizations in response to speech: Vocal imitation and developmental change. *The Journal of the Acoustical Society of America, 100*(4), 2425. doi:10.1121/1.417951

Kuhl, P., & Rivera-Gaxiola, M. (2008). Neural substrates of language acquisition. *Annual Review of Neuroscience, 31,* 511–534.

Kuhn, S., & Gallinat, J. (2012). The neural correlates of subjective pleasantness. *NeuroImage, 61,* 289–294.

Kunda, Z. (1990). The case for motivated reasoning. *Psychological Bulletin, 108,* 480–498.

Kunda, Z., & Oleson, K. C. (1997). When exceptions prove the rule: How extremity of deviance determines the impact of deviant examples on stereotypes. *Journal of Personality and Social Psychology, 72,* 965–979.

Kunugi, H., Urushibara, T., Murray, R. M., Nanko, S., & Hirose, T. (2003). Prenatal underdevelopment and schizophrenia: A case report of monozygotic twins. *Psychiatry and Clinical Neurosciences, 57,* 271–274.

Kunz, P. R., & Woolcott, M. (1976). Season's greetings: From my status to yours. *Social Science Research, 5,* 269–278.

Kvavilashvili, L., Mirani, J., Schlagman, S., Foley, K., & Kornbrot, D. E. (2009). Consistency of flashbulb memories of September 11 over long delays: Implications for consolidation and wrong time slice hypotheses. *Journal of Memory and Language, 61,* 556–572.

LaBar, K. S., & Phelps, E. A. (1998). Arousal-mediated memory consolidation: Role of the medial temporal lobe in humans. *Psychological Science, 9,* 490–493.

Labrie, V., Pai, S., & Petronis, A. (2012). Epigenetics of major psychosis: Progress, problems, and perspectives. *Trends in Genetics, 28,* 427–435.

Lachman, R., Lachman, J. L., & Butterfield, E. C. (1979). *Cognitive psychology and information processing: An introduction.* Hillsdale, NJ: Erlbaum.

Lackner, J. R., & DiZio, P. (2005). Vestibular, proprioceptive, and haptic contributions to spatial orientation. *Annual Review of Psychology, 56,* 115–147.

LaFraniere, S. (2007, July 4). In Mauritania, seeking to end an overfed ideal. *New York Times.* Retrieved from http://www.nytimes.com/2007/07/04/world/africa/04mauritania.html?pagewanted=all

Lahkan, S. E., & Kirchgessner, A. (2012, March 12). Chronic traumatic encephalopathy: The dangers of getting "dinged." *Springer Plus,* 1:2 doi:10.1186/2193-1801-1-2

Lai, Y., & Siegal, J. (1999). Muscle atonia in REM sleep. In B. Mallick & S. Inoue (Eds.), *Rapid eye movement sleep* (pp. 69–90). New Delhi, India: Narosa Publishing House.

Lake, J. (2009). Natural products used to treat depressed mood as monotherapies and adjuvants to antidepressants: A review of the evidence. *Psychiatric Times, 26,* 1–6.

Lakin, J. M. (2013). Sex differences in reasoning abilities: Surprising evidence that male–female ratios in the tails of the quantitative reasoning distribution have increased. *Intelligence, 41*(4), 263–274. doi:10.1016/j.intell.2013.04.004

Lakshminarayanan, V. R., Chen, M. K., & Santos, L. R. (2011). The evolution of decision-making under risk: Framing effects in monkey risk preferences. *Journal of Experimental Social Psychology, 47*(3), 689–693. doi:10.1016/j.jesp.2010.12.011

Lam, L. L., Emberly, E., Fraser, H. B., Neumann, S. M., Chen, E., Miller, G. E., . . . **Kobor, M. S.** (2012). Factors underlying variable DNA methylation in a human community cohort. *Proceedings of the National Academy of Sciences, USA, 109*(Suppl. 2), 17253–17260.

Lamb, M. E., Sternberg, K. J., & Prodromidis, M. (1992). Nonmaternal care and the security of infant/mother attachment: A reanalysis of the data. *Infant Behavior & Development, 15,* 71–83.

Lamb, M. E., Thompson, R. A., Gardner, W., & Charnov, E. L. (1985). *Infant–mother attachment: The origins and developmental significance of individual differences in Strange Situation behavior.* Hillsdale, NJ: Erlbaum.

Landauer, T. K., & Bjork, R. A. (1978). Optimum rehearsal patterns and name learning. In M. M. Gruneberg, P. E. Morris, & R. N. Sykes (Eds.), *Practical aspects of memory* (pp. 625–632). New York: Academic Press.

Lang, F. R., & Carstensen, L. L. (1994). Close emotional relationships in late life: Further support for proactive aging in the social domain. *Psychology and Aging, 9,* 315–324.

Langer, E. J., & Abelson, R. P. (1974). A patient by any other name . . . .Clinician group difference in labeling bias. *Journal of Consulting and Clinical Psychology, 42,* 4–9.

Langleben, D. D., Loughead, J. W., Bilker, W. B., Ruparel, K., Childress, A. R., Busch, S. I., & Gur, R. C. (2005). Telling truth from lie in individual subjects with fast event-related fMRI. *Human Brain Mapping, 26,* 262–272.

Langlois, J. H., Kalakanis, L., Rubenstein, A. J., Larson, A., Hallam, M., & Smoot, M. (2000). Maxims or myths of beauty? A meta-analytic and theoretical review. *Psychological Bulletin, 126,* 390–423.

Langlois, J. H., Ritter, J. M., Casey, R. J., & Sawin, D. B. (1995). Infant attractiveness predicts maternal behaviors and attitudes. *Developmental Psychology, 31,* 464–472.

LaPierre, S., Boyer, R., Desjardins, S., Dubé, M., Lorrain, D., Préville, M., & Brassard, J. (2012). Daily hassles, physical illness, and sleep problems in older adults with wishes to die. *International Psychogeriatrics, 24,* 243–252.

Lareau, A. (2003). *Unequal childhoods: Class, race, and family life.* Berkeley: University of California Press.

Larrick, R. P., Timmerman, T. A., Carton, A. M., & Abrevaya, J. (2011). Temper, temperature, and temptation: Heat-related retaliation in baseball. *Psychological Science, 22*(4), 423–428. doi:10.1177/0956797611399292

Larsen, S. F. (1992). Potential flashbulbs: Memories of ordinary news as baseline. In E. Winograd & U. Neisser (Eds.), *Affect and accuracy in recall: Studies of "flashbulb memories"* (pp. 32–64). New York: Cambridge University Press.

Larson, R., & Richards, M. H. (1991). Daily companionship in late childhood and early adolescence—changing developmental contexts. *Child Development, 62,* 284–300.

Lashley, K. S. (1960). In search of the engram. In F. A. Beach, D. O. Hebb, C. T. Morgan, & H. W. Nissen (Eds.), *The neuropsychology of Lashley* (pp. 478–505). New York: McGraw-Hill.

Latané, B., & Nida, S. (1981). Ten years of research ongroup size and helping. *Psychological Bulletin, 89*(2), 308–324.

Latané, B., Williams, K., & Harkins, S. (1979). Many hands make light the work: The causes and consequences of social loafing. *Journal of Personality and Social Psychology, 37,* 822–832.

Lattal, K. A. (2010). Delayed reinforcement of operant behavior. *Journal of the Experimental Analysis of Behavior, 93,* 129–139.

Laupa, M., & Turiel, E. (1986). Children's conceptions of adult and peer authority. *Child Development, 57,* 405–412.

Laureys, S., Giacino, J. T., Schiff, N. D., Schabus, M., & Owen, A. M. (2006). How should functional imaging of patients with disorders of consciousness contribute to their clinical rehabilitation needs? *Current Opinion in Neurology, 19,* 520–527.

Lavie, P. (2001). Sleep–wake as a biological rhythm. *Annual Review of Psychology, 52,* 277–303.

Lawrence, N. S., Jollant, F., O'Daly, O., Zelaya, F., & Phillips, M. L. (2009). Distinct roles of prefrontal cortical subregions in the Iowa Gambling Task. *Cerebral Cortex, 19,* 1134–1143.

Lawton, M. P., Kleban, M. H., Rajagopal, D., & Dean, J. (1992). The dimensions of affective experience in three age groups. *Psychology and Aging, 7,* 171–184.

Lazarus, R. S. (1984). On the primacy of cognition. *American Psychologist, 39,* 124–129.

Lazarus, R. S., & Alfert, E. (1964). Short-circuiting of threat by experimentally altering cognitive appraisal. *Journal of Abnormal and Social Psychology, 69,* 195–205.

Lazarus, R. S., & Folkman, S. (1984). *Stress, appraisal, and coping.* New York: Springer.

Leader, T., Mullen, B., & Abrams, D. (2007). Without mercy: The immediate impact of group size on lynch mob atrocity. *Personality and Social Psychology Bulletin, 33*(10), 1340–1352.

Leary, M. R. (1990). Responses to social exclusion: Social anxiety, jealousy, loneliness, depression, and low self-esteem. *Journal of Social and Clinical Psychology, 9,* 221–229.

Leary, M. R. (2010). Affiliation, acceptance, and belonging: The pursuit of interpersonal connection. In S. T. Fiske, D. T. Gilbert, & G. Lindzey (Eds.), *The handbook of social psychology* (5th ed., Vol. 2, pp. 864–897). New York: Wiley.

Leary, M. R., & Baumeister, R. F. (2000). The nature and function of self-esteem: Sociometer theory. In M. P. Zanna (Ed.), *Advances in experimental social psychology* (Vol. 32, pp. 1–62). San Diego: Academic Press.

Leary, M. R., Britt, T. W., Cutlip, W. D., & Templeton, J. L. (1992). Social blushing. *Psychological Bulletin, 112,* 446–460.

Lecky, P. (1945). *Self-consistency: A theory of personality.* New York: Island Press.

Lecrubier, Y., Clerc, G., Didi, R., & Kieser, M. (2002). Efficacy of St. John's wort extract WS 5570 in major depression: A double-blind, placebo-controlled trial. *American Journal of Psychiatry, 159,* 1361–1366.

Lederman, S. J., & Klatzky, R. L. (2009). Haptic perception: A tutorial. *Attention, Perception, & Psychophysics, 71,* 1439–1459.

LeDoux, J. E. (1992). Brain mechanisms of emotion and emotional learning. *Current Opinion in Neurobiology, 2,* 191–197.

LeDoux, J. E. (2000). Emotion circuits in the brain. *Annual Review of Neuroscience, 23,* 155–184.

LeDoux, J. E., Iwata, J., Cicchetti, P., & Reis, D. J. (1988). Different projections of the central amygdaloid nucleus mediate autonomic and behavioral correlates of conditioned fear. *Journal of Neuroscience, 8,* 2517–2529.

Lee, D. N., & Aronson, E. (1974). Visual proprioceptive control of standing in human infants. *Perception & Psychophysics, 15,* 529–532.

Lee, L., Loewenstein, G., Ariely, D., Hong, J., & Young, J. (2008). If I'm not hot, are you hot or not? Physical-attractiveness evaluations and dating preferences as a function of one's own attractiveness. *Psychological Science, 19,* 669–677.

Lee, M. H., Smyser, C. D., & Shimoy, J. S. (2013). Resting-state fMRI: A review of methods and clinical applications. *American Journal of Neuroradiology, 34,* 1866–1872. doi: 10.3174/ajnr.A3263

Lefcourt, H. M. (1982). *Locus of control: Current trends in theory and research* (2nd ed.). Hillsdale, NJ: Erlbaum.

Leichsenring, F., & Rabung, S. (2008). Effectiveness of long-term psychodynamic psychotherapy: A meta-analysis. *Journal of the American Medical Association, 300,* 1551–1565.

Lempert, D. (2007). *Women's increasing wage penalties from being overweight and obese.* Washington, DC: U.S. Bureau of Labor Statistics.

Lenoir, M., Serre, F., Chantin, L., & Ahmed, S. H. (2007). Intense sweetness surpasses cocaine reward. *PLoS ONE, 2,* e698.

Lenton, A. P., & Francesconi, M. (2010). How humans cognitively manage an abundance of mate options. *Psychological Science, 21*(4), 528–533. doi: 10.1177/0956797610364958

Lentz, M. J., Landis, C. A., Rothermel, J., & Shaver, J. L. (1999). Effects of selective slow wave sleep disruption on musculoskeletal pain and fatigue in middle aged women. *Journal of Rheumatology, 26,* 1586–1592.

Leon, D. A., Lawlor, D. A., Clark, H., Batty, G. D., & Macintyre, S. (2009). The association of childhood intelligence with mortality risk from adolescence to middle age: Findings from the Aberdeen children of the 1950s cohort study. *Intelligence, 37*(6), 520–528.

Lepage, M., Ghaffar, O., Nyberg, L., & Tulving, E. (2000). Prefrontal cortex and episodic memory retrieval mode. *Proceedings of the National Academy of Sciences, USA, 97,* 506–511.

LePort, A. K. R., Mattfield, A. T., Dickinson-Anson, H., Fallon, J. H., Stark, C. E. L., Kruggel, F., . . . McGaugh, J. L. (2012). Behavioral and neuroanatomical investigation of highly superior autobiographical memory (HSAM). *Neurobiology of Learning and Memory, 98,* 78–92.

Lepper, M. R., Greene, D., & Nisbett, R. E. (1973). Undermining children's intrinsic interest with extrinsic rewards: A test of the "over-justification" hypothesis. *Journal of Personality and Social Psychology, 28,* 129–137.

Lerman, D. (2006). Consumer politeness and complaining behavior. *Journal of Services Marketing, 20,* 92–100.

Lerman, D. C., & Vorndran, C. M. (2002). On the status of knowledge for using punishment: Implications for treating behavior disorders. *Journal of Applied Behavior Analysis, 35*, 4312–4464.

Leung, A. K.-Y., & Cohen, D. (2011). Within- and between-culture variation: Individual differences and the cultural logics of honor, face, and dignity cultures. *Journal of Personality and Social Psychology, 100*(3), 507–526. doi:10.1037/a0022151

Levelt Committee, Noort Committee, Drenth Committee. (2012, November 28). *Flawed science: The fraudulent research practices of social psychologist Diederik Stapel.* Retrieved from http://www.tilburguniversity.edu/nl/nieuws-en-agenda/finalreportLevelt.pdf

Levenson, J. M., & Sweatt, J. D. (2005). Epigenetic mechanisms in memory formation. *Nature Reviews Neuroscience, 6*, 108–118.

Levenson, R. W., Cartensen, L. L., Friesen, W. V., & Ekman, P. (1991). Emotion physiology, and expression in old age. *Psychology and Aging, 6*, 28–35.

Levenson, R. W., Ekman, P., & Friesen, W. V. (1990). Voluntary facial action generates emotion-specific autonomic nervous system activity. *Psychophysiology, 27*, 363–384.

Levenson, R. W., Ekman, P., Heider, K., & Friesen, W. V. (1992). Emotion and automatic nervous system activity in the Minangkabau of West Sumatra. *Journal of Personality and Social Psychology, 62*, 972–988.

Levin, D. T., & Simons, D. J. (1997). Failure to detect changes to attended objects in motion pictures. *Psychonomic Bulletin & Review, 4*, 501–506.

Levin, R., & Nielsen, T. (2009). Nightmares, bad dreams, and emotion dysregulation: A review and new neurocognitive model of dreaming. *Current Directions in Psychological Science, 18*, 84–88.

Levine, M. (1981). *History and politics of community mental health.* New York: Oxford University Press.

Levine, R. V., Norenzayan, A., & Philbrick, K. (2001). Cross-cultural differences in helping strangers. *Journal of Cross-Cultural Psychology, 32*, 543–560.

Levy, J., Trevarthen, C., & Sperry, R. W. (1972). Perception of bilateral chimeric figures following hemispheric disconnection. *Brain, 95*, 61–78.

Lewin, K. (1936). *Principles of topological psychology.* New York: McGraw-Hill.

Lewin, K. (1951). Behavior and development as a function of the total situation. In K. Lewin (Ed.), *Field theory in social science: Selected theoretical papers* (pp. 791–843). New York: Harper & Row.

Lewis, M., & Brooks-Gunn, J. (1979). *Social cognition and the acquisition of self.* New York: Plenum Press.

Lewis, M. B. (2012). Exploring the positive and negative implications of facial feedback. *Emotion, 12*(4), 852–859.

Lewis, M. D., Hibbeln, J. R., Johnson, J. E., Lin, Y. H., Hyun, D. Y., & Loewke, J. D. (2011). Suicide deaths of active duty U. S. military and omega-3 fatty acid status: A case control comparison. *Journal of Clinical Psychiatry, 72*, 1585–1590.

Lewontin, R., Rose, S., & Kamin, L. J. (1984). *Not in our genes.* New York: Pantheon.

Li, R., Polat, U., Makous, W., & Bavelier, D. (2009). Enhancing the contrast sensitivity function through action video game training. *Nature Neuroscience, 12*, 549–551.

Li, Y. J., Johnson, K. A., Cohen, A. B., Williams, M. J., Knowles, E. D., & Chen, Z. (2012). Fudamental(ist) attribution error: Protestants are dispositionally focused. *Journal of Personality and Social Psychology, 102*(2), 281–290. doi:10.1037/a0026294

Libet, B. (1985). Unconscious cerebral initiative and the role of conscious will in voluntary action. *Behavioral and Brain Sciences, 8*, 529–566.

Liebenluft, E. (1996). Women with bipolar illness: Clinical and research issues. *American Journal of Psychiatry, 153*, 163–173.

Lieberman, M. D., Inagaki, T. K., Tabibnia, G., & Crockett, M. J. (2011). Subjective responses to emotional stimuli during labeling, reappraisal, and distraction. *Emotion, 11*, 468–480.

Lieberman, M. D., & Rosenthal, R. (2001). Why introverts can't always tell who likes them: Multitasking and nonverbal decoding. *Journal of Personality and Social Psychology, 80*, 294–310.

Liebowitz, M. R., Gorman, J. M., Fyer, A. J., Levitt, M., Dillon, D., Levy, G., . . . Davies, S. O. (1985). Lactate provocation of panic attacks: II. Biochemical and physiological findings. *Archives of General Psychiatry, 42*, 709–719.

Lifshitz, M., Aubert Bonn, N., Fischer, A., Kashem, I. R., & Raz, A. (2013). Using suggestion to modulate automatic processes: From Stroop to McGurk and beyond. *Cortex, 49*(2), 463–473. doi:10.1016/j.cortex.2012.08.007

Lilienfeld, S. O. (2007). Psychological treatments that cause harm. *Perspectives on Psychological Science, 2*, 53–70.

Lilienfeld, S. O., Lynn, S. J., & Lohr, J. M. (Eds.). (2003). *Science and pseudoscience in clinical psychology.* New York: Guilford Press.

Lilienfeld, S. O., Wood, J. M., & Garb, H. N. (2000). The scientific status of projective techniques. *Psychological Science in the Public Interest, 1*, 27–66.

Lindenberger, U., & Baltes, P. B. (1994). Sensory functioning and intelligence in old age: A strong connection. *Psychology and Aging, 9*(3), 339–355. doi:10.1037/0882-7974.9.3.339

Lindenberger, U., & Baltes, P. B. (1997). Intellectual functioning in old and very old age: Cross-sectional results from the Berling aging study. *Psychology and Aging, 12*, 410–432.

Lindquist, K., & Barrett, L. F. (2008). Constructing emotion: The experience of fear as a conceptual act. *Psychological Science, 19*, 898–903.

Lindquist, S. I., & McLean, J. P. (2011). Daydreaming and its correlates in an educational environment. *Learning and Individual Differences, 21*, 158–167.

Lindstrom, M. (2005). *Brand sense: How to build powerful brands through touch, taste, smell, sight and sound.* London: Kogan Page.

Liou, A. P., Paziuk, M., Luevano, J.-M., Machineni, S., Turnbaugh, P. J., & Kaplan, L. M. (2013). Conserved shifts in the gut microbiota due to gastric bypass reduce host weight and adiposity. *Science Translational Medicine, 5*(178), 178ra41–178ra41.

Little, B. R. (1983). Personal projects: A rationale and method for investigation. *Environment and Behavior, 15*, 273–309.

Little, B. R. (1993). Personal projects and the distributed self: Aspects of a conative psychology. In J. R. Suls (Ed.), *Psychological perspectives on the self* (Vol. 4, pp. 157–185). Hillsdale, NJ: Erlbaum.

Liu, D., Diorio, J., Tannenbaum, B., Caldji, C., Francis, D., Freedman, A., . . . Meaney, M. J. (1997). Maternal care, hippocampal glucocorticoid receptors, and hypothalamic–pituitary–adrenal responses to stress. *Science, 277*, 1659–1662.

Liu, D., Wellman, H. M., Tardif, T., & Sabbagh, M. A. (2008). Theory of mind development in Chinese children: A meta-analysis of false belief understanding across cultures and languages. *Developmental Psychology, 44*, 523–531.

Livingstone, M., & Hubel, D. (1988). Segregation of form, color, movement, and depth: Anatomy, physiology, and perception. *Science, 240*, 740–749.

Locksley, A., Ortiz, V., & Hepburn, C. (1980). Social categorization and discriminatory behavior: Extinguishing the minimal intergroup discrimination effect. *Journal of Personality and Social Psychology, 39*, 773–783.

Loehlin, J. C. (1973). Blood group genes and Negro–White ability differences. *Behavior Genetics, 3*(3), 263–270.

Loehlin, J. C. (1992). *Genes and environment in personality development.* Newbury Park, CA: Sage.

Loftus, E. F. (1993). The reality of repressed memories. *American Psychologist, 48,* 518–537.

Loftus, E. F. (2003). Make-believe memories. *American Psychologist, 58,* 867–873.

Loftus, E. F., & Ketchum, K. (1994). *The myth of repressed memory.* New York: St. Martin's Press.

Loftus, E. F., & Klinger, M. R. (1992). Is the unconscious smart or dumb? *American Psychologist, 47,* 761–765.

Loftus, E. F., & Pickrell, J. E. (1995). The formation of false memories. *Psychiatric Annals, 25,* 720–725.

Lopes, P. N., Grewal, D., Kadis, J., Gall, M., & Salovey, P. (2006). Emotional intelligence and positive work outcomes. *Psichothema, 18,* 132.

Lord, C. G., Ross, L., & Lepper, M. R. (1979). Biased assimilation and attitude polarization: The effects of prior theories on subsequently considered evidence. *Journal of Personality and Social Psychology, 37,* 2098–2109.

Lorenz, K. (1952). *King Solomon's ring.* New York: Crowell.

Lovaas, O. I. (1987). Behavioral treatment and normal educational and intellectual functioning in young autistic children. *Journal of Consulting and Clinical Psychology, 55,* 3–9.

Low, J., & Watts, J. (2013). Attributing false beliefs about object identity reveals a signature blind spot in humans' efficient mind-reading system. *Psychological Science, 24*(3), 305–311. doi:10.1177/0956797612451469

Lozano, B. E., & Johnson, S. L. (2001). Can personality traits predict increases in manic and depressive symptoms? *Journal of Affective Disorders, 63,* 103–111.

Luborsky, L., Rosenthal, R., Diguer, L., Andrusyna, T. P., Berman, J. S., Levitt, J. T., . . . Krause, E. D. (2002). The dodo bird verdict is alive and well—mostly. *Clinical Psychology: Science and Practice, 9,* 2–12.

Luborsky, L., & Singer, B. (1975). Comparative studies of psychotherapies: Is it true that "everyone has won and all must have prizes"? *Archives of General Psychiatry, 32*(8), 995–1008.

Lucas, R. E., Clark, A. E., Georgellis, Y., & Diener, E. (2003). Reexamining adaptation and the set point model of happiness: Reactions to changes in marital status. *Journal of Personality and Social Psychology, 84,* 527–539.

Ludwig, A. M. (1966). Altered states of consciousness. *Archives of General Psychiatry, 15,* 225–234.

Lykken, D. T. (1995). *The antisocial personalities.* Hillsdale, NJ: Erlbaum.

Lynn, M., & Shurgot, B. A. (1984). Responses to lonely hearts advertisements: Effects of reported physical attractiveness, physique, and coloration. *Personality and Social Psychology Bulletin, 10,* 349–357.

Lynn, R. (2009). What has caused the Flynn effect? Secular increases in the development quotients of infants. *Intelligence, 37*(1), 16–24.

Lynn, R. (2013). Who discovered the Flynn effect? A review of early studies of the secular increase of intelligence. *Intelligence.* Advance online publication. doi:10.1016/j.intell.2013.03.008

Lyons, D. E., Young, A. G., & Keil, F. C. (2007). The hidden structure of overimitation. *Proceedings of the National Academy of Sciences, 104*(50), 19751–19756. doi:10.1073/pnas.0704452104.

Lyubomirsky, S. (2008). *The how of happiness: A scientific approach to getting the life you want.* New York: Penguin.

Lyubomirsky, S., & Lepper, H. S. (1999). A measure of subjective happiness: Preliminary reliability and construct validation. *Social Indicators Research, 46,* 137–155.

MacDonald, S., Uesiliana, K., & Hayne, H. (2000). Cross-cultural and gender differences in childhood amnesia. *Memory, 8,* 365–376.

MacGregor, J. N., Ormerod, T. C., & Chronicle, E. P. (2001). Information processing and insight: A process model of performance on the nine-dot and related problems. *Journal of Experimental Psychology: Learning, Memory, and Cognition, 27,* 176–201.

Mack, A. H., Franklin, J. E., Jr., & Frances, R. J. (2003). Substance use disorders. In R. E. Hales & S. C. Yudofsky (Eds.), *The American Psychiatric Publishing textbook of clinical psychiatry* (4th ed., pp. 309–377). Washington, DC: American Psychiatric Publishing.

Maclean, P. D. (1970). The triune brain, emotion, and scientific bias. In F. O. Schmitt (Ed.), *The neurosciences: A second study program* (pp. 336–349). New York: Rockefeller University Press.

MacLeod, C., & Mathews, A. (2012). Cognitive bias modification approaches to anxiety. *Annual Review of Clinical Psychology, 8,* 189–217.

MacLeod, M. D. (2002). Retrieval-induced forgetting in eyewitness memory: Forgetting as a consequence of remembering. *Applied Cognitive Psychology, 16,* 135–149.

MacLeod, M. D., & Saunders, J. (2008). Retrieval inhibition and memory distortion: Negative consequences of an adaptive process. *Current Directions in Psychological Science, 17,* 26–30.

Macmillan, M. (2000). *An odd kind of fame: Stories of Phineas Gage.* Cambridge, MA: MIT Press.

Macmillan, N. A., & Creelman, C. D. (2005). *Detection theory.* Mahwah, NJ: Erlbaum.

Macrae, C. N., Bodenhausen, G. V., Milne, A. B., & Jetten, J. (1994). Out of mind but back in sight: Stereotypes on the rebound. *Journal of Personality and Social Psychology, 67,* 808–817.

Macrae, C. N., Moran, J. M., Heatherton, T. F., Banfield, J. F., & Kelley, W. M. (2004). Medial prefrontal activity predicts memory for self. *Cerebral Cortex, 14,* 647–654.

Maddi, S. R., Harvey, R. H., Khoshaba, D. M., Fazel, M., & Resurreccion, N. (2009). Hardiness training facilitates performance in college. *The Journal of Positive Psychology, 4,* 566–577.

Maddi, S. R., Kahn, S., & Maddi, K. L. (1998). The effectiveness of hardiness training. *Consulting Psychology Journal: Practice and Research, 50,* 78–86.

Maddux, W. W., Mullen, E., & Galinsky, A. D. (2008). Chameleons bake bigger pies and take bigger pieces: Strategic behavioral mimicry facilitates negotiation outcomes. *Journal of Experimental Social Psychology, 44,* 461–468.

Madigan, S., Atkinson, L., Laurin, K., & Benoit, D. (2013). Attachment and internalizing behavior in early childhood: A meta-analysis. *Developmental Psychology, 49*(4), 672–689. doi:10.1037/a0028793

Maes, M. (1995). Evidence for an immune response in major depression: A review and hypothesis. *Progress in Neuro-Psychopharmacology and Biological Psychiatry, 19,* 11–38.

Maguire, E. A., Woollett, K., & Spiers, H. J. (2006). London taxi drivers and bus drivers: A structural MRI and neuropsychological analysis. *Hippocampus, 16,* 1091–1101.

Mahajan, N., Martinez, M. A., Gutierrez, N. L., Diesendruck, G., Banaji, M. R., & Santos, L. R. (2011). The evolution of intergroup bias: Perceptions and attitudes in rhesus macaques. *Journal of Personality and Social Psychology, 100*(3), 387–405. doi:10.1037/a0022459

Mahon, B. Z., Anzellotti, S., Schwarzbach, J., Zampini, M., & Caramazza, A. (2009). Category-specific organization in the human brain does not require visual experience. *Neuron, 63,* 397–405.

Mahon, B. Z., & Caramazza, A. (2009). Concepts and categories: A cognitive neuropsychological perspective. *Cognitive Neuropsychology, 60,* 27–51.

Mahowald, M., & Schenck, C. (2000). REM sleep parasomnias. In M. Kryger, T. Roth, & W. Dement (Eds.), *Principles and practices of sleep medicine* (3rd ed., pp. 724–741). Philadelphia: Saunders.

Makris, N. , Biederman, J., Monuteaux, M. C., & Seidman, L. J. (2009). Towards conceptualizing a neural systems-based anatomy of attention-deficit/hyperactivity disorder. *Developmental Neuroscience, 31,* 36–49.

Maier, S. F., & Watkins, L. R. (1998). Cytokines for psychologists: Implications of bidirectional immune-to-brain communication for understanding behavior, mood, and cognition. *Psychological Review, 105,* 83–107.

Maier, S. F., & Watkins, L. R. (2000). The immune system as a sensory system: Implications for psychology. *Current Directions in Psychological Science, 9,* 98–102.

Major, B., Mendes, W. B., & Dovidio, J. F. (2013). Intergroup relations and health disparities: A social psychological perspective. *Health Psychology, 32,* 514–524.

Makin, J. E., Fried, P. A., & Watkinson, B. (1991). A comparison of active and passive smoking during pregnancy: Long-term effects. *Neurotoxicology and Teratology, 16,* 5–12.

Malina, R. M., Bouchard, C., & Beunen, G. (1988). Human growth: Selected aspects of current research on well-nourished children. *Annual Review of Anthropology, 17,* 187–219.

Malooly, A. M., Genet, J. J., & Siemer, M. (2013). Individual differences in reappraisal effectiveness: The role of affective flexibility. *Emotion, 13*(2), 302–313. doi:10.1037/a0029980

Mampe, B., Friederici, A. D., Christophe, A., & Wermke, K. (2009). Newborns' cry melody is shaped by their native language. *Current Biology, 19,* 1–4.

Mandel, D. R., & Lehman, D. R. (1998). Integration of contingency information in judgments of cause, covariation, and probability. *Journal of Experimental Psychology: General, 127,* 269–285.

Mandle, C. L., Jacobs, S. C., Arcari, P. M., & Domar, A. D. (1996). The efficacy of relaxation response interventions with adult patients: A review of the literature. *Journal of Cardiovascular Nursing, 10,* 4–26.

Mandler, G. (1967). Organization and memory. In K. W. Spence & J. T. Spence (Eds.), *The psychology of learning and motivation* (Vol. 1, pp. 327–372). New York: Academic Press.

Mankiw, N. G., & Weinzierl, M. (2010). The optimal taxation of height: A case study of utilitarian income redistribution. *American Economic Journal: Economic Policy, 2,* 155–176.

Mann, J. J. (2005). The medical management of depression. *New England Journal of Medicine, 353,* 1819–1834.

Mann, J. J., Apter, A., Bertolote, J., Beautrais, A., Currier, D., Haas, A., . . . Hendin, H. (2005). Suicide prevention strategies: A systematic review. *Journal of the American Medical Association, 294*(16), 2064–2074. doi:10.1001/jama.294.16.2064

Marangell, L. B., Silver, J. M., Goff, D. M., & Yudofsky, S. C. (2003). Psychopharmacology and electroconvulsive therapy. In R. E. Hales & S. C. Yudofsky (Eds.), *The American Psychiatric Publishing textbook of clinical psychiatry* (4th ed., pp. 1047–1149). Washington, DC: American Psychiatric Publishing.

March of Dimes. (2010). *Smoking during pregnancy.* Retrieved July 15, 2010, from http://www.marchofdimes.com/professionals/14332_1171.asp

Marci, C. D., Ham, J., Moran, E., & Orr, S. P. (2007). Physiologic correlates of perceived therapist empathy and social-emotional process during psychotherapy. *Journal of Nervous and Mental Disease, 195,* 103–111.

Marcus, G. (2012, December 3). Neuroscience fiction. *New Yorker.* Retrieved from http://www.newyorker.com/online/blogs/newsdesk/2012/12/what-neuroscicnec-really-teaches-us-and-what-it-doesnt.html

Marcus, G. B. (1986). Stability and change in political attitudes: Observe, recall, and "explain." *Political Behavior, 8,* 21–44.

Markus, H. (1977). Self-schemata and processing information about the self. *Journal of Personality and Social Psychology, 35,* 63–78.

Marlatt, G. A., & Rohsenow, D. (1980). Cognitive processes in alcohol use: Expectancy and the balanced placebo design. In N. K. Mello (Ed.), *Advances in substance abuse: Behavioral and biological research* (pp. 159–199). Greenwich, CT: JAI Press.

Marlatt, G. A., & Witkiewitz, K. (2010). Update on harm reduction policy and intervention research. *Annual Review of Clinical Psychology, 6,* 591–606.

Marmot, M. G., Stansfeld, S., Patel, C., North, F., Head, J., White, L., . . . Feeney, A. (1991). Health inequalities among British civil servants: The Whitehall II study. *Lancet, 337,* 1387–1393.

Marr, D., & Nishihara, H. K. (1978). Representation and recognition of the spatial organization of three-dimensional shapes. *Proceedings of the Royal Society B: Biological Sciences, 200,* 269–294.

Marsolek, C. J. (1995). Abstract visual-form representations in the left cerebral hemispheres. *Journal of Experimental Psychology: Human Perception and Performance, 21,* 375–386.

Martin, A. (2007). The representation of object concepts in the brain. *Annual Review of Psychology, 58,* 25–45.

Martin, A., & Caramazza, A. (2003). Neuropsychological and neuroimaging perspectives on conceptual knowledge: An introduction. *Cognitive Neuropsychology, 20,* 195–212.

Martin, A., & Chao, L. L. (2001). Semantic memory and the brain: Structure and processes. *Current Opinion in Neurobiology, 11,* 194–201.

Martin, K. D., & Hill, R. P. (2012). Life satisfaction, self-determination, and consumption adequacy at the bottom of the pyramid. *Journal of Consumer Research, 38,* 1155–1168.

Martin, N. G., Eaves, L. J., Geath, A. R., Jarding, R., Feingold, L. M., & Eysenck, H. J. (1986). Transmission of social attitudes. *Proceedings of the National Academy of Sciences, USA, 83,* 4364–4368.

Martinez, G., Copen, C. E., & Abma, J. C. (2011). Teenagers in the United States: Sexual activity, contraceptive use, and childbearing, 2006–2010: National Survey of Family Growth. *Vital Health Statistics, 23*(31).

Marucha, P. T., Kiecolt-Glaser, J. K., & Favagehi, M. (1998). Mucosal wound healing is impaired by examination stress. *Psychosomatic Medicine, 60,* 362–365.

Marzuk, P. M., Tardiff, K., Leon, A. C., Hirsch, C., Portera, L., Iqbal, M. I., . . . Hartwell, N. (1998). Ambient temperature and mortality from unintentional cocaine overdose. *Journal of the American Medical Association, 279,* 1795–1800.

Maslach, C. (2003). Job burnout: New directions in research and intervention. *Current Directions in Psychological Science, 12,* 189–192.

Maslach, C., Schaufeli, W. B., & Leiter, M. P. (2001). Job burnout. *Annual Review of Psychology, 52,* 397–422.

Maslow, A. H. (1937). Dominance-feeling, behavior, and status. In R. J. Lowry (Ed.), *Dominance, self-esteem, self-actualization: Germinal papers by A. H. Maslow* (pp. 49–70). Monterey, CA: Brooks-Cole.

Maslow, A. H. (1954). *Motivation and personality.* New York: Harper & Row.

Maslow, A. H. (1970). *Motivation and personality* (2nd ed.). New York: Harper & Row.

Mason, M. F., Magee, J. C., Kuwabara, K., & Nind, L. (2010). Specialization in relational reasoning: The efficiency, accuracy, and neural substrates of social versus nonsocial inferences. *Social Psychological and Personality Science, 1*(4), 318–326. doi:10.1177/1948550610366166

Mason, M. F., Norton, M. I., Van Horn, J. D., Wegner, D. M., Grafton, S. T., & Macrae, C. N. (2007). Wandering minds: The default network and stimulus-independent thought. *Science, 3154*, 393–395.

Masten, A. S. (2004). Family therapy as a treatment for children: A critical review of outcome research. *Family Process, 18*, 323–335.

Masters, W. H., & Johnson, V. E. (1966). *Human sexual response.* Boston: Little, Brown.

Masuda, T., & Nisbett, R. E. (2006). Culture and change blindness. *Cognitive Science, 30*, 381–300.

Mather, M., Canli, T., English, T., Whitfield, S., Wais, P., Ochsner, K., . . . Cartensen, L. L. (2004). Amygdala responses to emotionally valenced stimuli in older and younger adults. *Psychological Science, 15*, 259–263.

Mather, M., & Carstensen, L. L. (2003). Aging and attentional biases for emotional faces. *Psychological Science, 14*, 409–415.

Mather, M., & Carstensen, L. L. (2005). Aging and motivated cognition: The positivity effect in attention and memory. *Trends in Cognitive Sciences, 9*(10), 496–502.

Matsuda, O., & Saito, M. (1998). Crystallized and fluid intelligence in elderly patients with mild dementia of the Alzheimer type. *International Psychogeriatrics, 10*(2), 147–154. doi:10.1017/S1041610298005250

Matsumoto, D., & Willingham, B. (2009). Spontaneous facial expressions of emotion of congenitally and noncongenitally blind individuals. *Journal of Personality and Social Psychology, 96*, 1–10.

Mattar, A. A. G., & Gribble, P. L. (2005). Motor learning by observing. *Neuron, 46*, 153–160.

Matthews, G., & Gilliland, K. (1999). The personality theories of H. J. Eysenck and J. A. Gray: A comparative review. *Personality and Individual Differences, 26*, 583–626.

Matzel, L. D., Han, Y. R., Grossman, H., Karnik, M. S., Patel, D., Scott, N., . . . Gandhi, C. C. (2003). Individual differences in the expression of a general learning ability in mice. *Journal of Neuroscience, 23*(16), 6423–6433.

Maudsley, H. (1886). *Natural causes and supernatural seemings.* London: Kegan Paul, Trench.

Max, A. (2006, September 16). Dutch reach new heights. *USA Today.* Retrieved from http://usatoday30.usatoday.com/news/offbeat/2006-09-16-dutch-tall_x.htm

May, R. (1983). *The discovery of being: Writings in existential psychology.* New York: Norton.

Mayberg, H., Lozano, A., Voon, V., McNeely, H., Seminowicz, D., Hamani, C., . . . Kennedy, S. H. (2005). Deep brain stimulation for treatmentresistant depresssion. *Neuron, 45*, 651–660.

Mayer, J. D., Caruso, D. R., & Salovey, P. (1999). Emotional intelligence meets traditional standards for an intelligence. *Intelligence, 27*, 267.

Mayer, J. D., Caruso, D. R., Zigler, E., & Dreyden, J. I. (1989). Intelligence and intelligence-related personality traits. *Intelligence, 13*(2), 119–133. doi:10.1016/0160-2896(89)90011-1

Mayer, J. D., Roberts, R. D., & Barsade, S. G. (2008). Human abilities: Emotional intelligence. *Annual Review of Psychology, 59*, 507–536.

Maynard-Smith, J. (1965). The evolution of alarm calls. *American Naturalist, 100*, 637–650.

McAdams, D. (1993). *The stories we live by: Personal myths and the making of the self.* New York: Morrow.

McCabe, S. E., Knight, J. R., Teter, C. J., & Wechsler, H. (2005). Nonmedical use of prescription stimulants among U.S. college students: Prevalence and correlates from a national survey. *Addiction, 100*, 96–106.

McCauley, J., Ruggiero, K. J., Resnick, H. S., Conoscenti, L. M., & Kilpatrick, D. G. (2009). Forcible, drug-facilitated, and incapacited rape in relation to substance use problems: Results from a national sample of college women. *Addictive Behaviors, 34*, 458–462.

McClelland, D. C., Atkinson, J. W., Clark, R. A., & Lowell, E. L. (1953). *The achievement motive.* New York: Appleton-Century-Crofts.

McConkey, K. M., Barnier, A. J., & Sheehan, P. W. (1998). Hypnosis and pseudomemory: Understanding the findings and their implications. In S. J. Lynn & K. M. McConkey (Eds.), *Truth in memory* (pp. 227–259). New York: Guilford Press.

McCrae, R. R., & Costa, P. T. (1990). *Personality in adulthood.* New York: Guilford Press.

McCrae, R. R., & Costa, P. T. (1999). A five-factor theory of personality. In L. A. Pervin & O. P. John (Eds.), *Handbook of personality: Theory and research* (pp. 139–153). New York: Guilford Press.

McCrea, S. M., Buxbaum, L. J., & Coslett, H. B. (2006). Illusory conjunctions in simultanagnosia: Coarse coding of visual feature location? *Neuropsychologia, 44*, 1724–1736.

McDougall, W. (1930). The hormic psychology. In C. Murchison (Ed.), *Psychologies of 1930* (pp. 3–36). Worcester, MA: Clark University Press.

McElwain, N. L., Booth-LaForce, C., & Wu, X. (2011). Infant–mother attachment and children's friendship quality: Maternal mental state talk as an intervening mechanism. *Developmental Psychology, 47*(5), 1295–1311. doi:10.1037/a0024094

McEvoy, S. P., Stevenson, M. R., McCartt, A. T., Woodward, M., Haworth, C., Palamara, P., & Circarelli, R. (2005). Role of mobile phones in motor vehicle crashes resulting in hospital attendance: A casecrossover study. *British Medical Journal, 331*, 428–430.

McFall, R. M., & Treat, T. A. (1999). Quantifying the information value of clinical assessments with signal detection theory. *Annual Review of Psychology, 50*, 215–241.

McFarlane, A. H., Norman, G. R., Streiner, D. L., Roy, R., & Scott, D. J. (1980). A longitudinal study of the influence of the psychosocial environment on health status: A preliminary report. *Journal of Health and Social Behavior, 21*, 124–133.

McGarty, C., & Turner, J. C. (1992). The effects of categorization on social judgement. *British Journal of Social Psychology, 31*, 253–268.

McGaugh, J. L. (2000). Memory: A century of consolidation. *Science, 287*, 248–251.

McGaugh, J. L. (2006). Make mild moments memorable: Add a little arousal. *Trends in Cognitive Sciences, 10*, 345–347.

McGowan, P. O., Sasaki, A., D'Alessio, A. D., Dymov, S., Labonté, B., Szyf, M., . . . Meaney, M. J. (2009). Epigenetic regulation of the glucocorticoid receptor in human brain associates with childhood abuse. *Nature Neuroscience, 12*, 342–348.

McGowan, P. O., Suderman, M., Sasaki, A., Huang, T. C. T., Hallett, M., Meaney, J. J., & Szyf, M. (2011). Broad epigenetic signature of maternal care in the brain of adult rats. *PLoS One, 6*(2), e14739. doi:10.1371/journal.pone.0014739

McGrath, J., Saha, S., Chant, D., & Welham, J. (2008). Schizophrenia: A concise overview of incidence, prevalence, and mortality. *Epidemiologic Reviews, 30*, 67–76.

McGue, M., & Bouchard, T. J. (1998). Genetic and environmental influences on human behavioral differences. *Annual Review of Neuroscience, 21*, 1–24.

McGuire, P. K., Shah, G. M., & Murray, R. M. (1993). Increased blood flow in Broca's area during auditory hallucinations in schizophrenia. *Lancet, 342,* 703–706.

McIntyre, S. H., & Munson, J. M. (2008). Exploring cramming: Student behaviors, beliefs, and learning retention in the principles of marketing course. *Journal of Marketing Education, 30,* 226–243.

McKee, A. C., Cantu, R. C., Nowinski, C. J., Hedley-Whyte, E. T., Gavett, B. E., Budson, A. E., . . . Stern, R. A. (2009). Chronic traumatic encephalopathy in athletes: Progressive tauopathy after repetitive head injury. *Journal of Neuropathology and Experimental Neurology, 68,* 709–735.

McKee, A. C., Stein, T. D., Nowinski, C. J., Stern, R. A., Daneshvar, D. H., Alvarez, V. E., . . . Cantu, R. (2012). The spectrum of disease in chronic traumatic encephalopathy. *Brain, 136*(1), 43–64. doi:10.1093/brain/aws307

McKetin, R., Ward, P. B., Catts, S. V., Mattick, R. P., & Bell, J. R. (1999). Changes in auditory selective attention and event-related potentials following oral administration of D-amphetamine in humans. *Neuropsychopharmacology, 21,* 380–390.

McKinney, C. H., Antoni, M. H., Kumar, M., Tims, F. C., & McCabe, P. M. (1997). Effects of guided imagery and music (GIM) therapy on mood and cortisol in healthy adults. *Health Psychology, 16,* 390–400.

McLaughlin, K. A., Nandi, A., Keyes, K. M., Uddin, M., Aiello, A. E., Galea, S., & Koenen, K. C. (2012). Home foreclosure and risk of psychiatric morbidity during the recent financial crisis. *Psychological Medicine, 42,* 1441–1448.

McLean, K. C. (2008). The emergence of narrative identity. *Social and Personality Psychology Compass, 2*(4), 1685–1702.

McNally, R. J. (2003). *Remembering trauma.* Cambridge, MA: Belknap Press of Harvard University Press.

McNally, R. J., & Clancy, S. A. (2005). Sleep paralysis, sexual abuse, and space alien abduction. *Transcultural Psychiatry, 42,* 113–122.

McNally, R. J., & Geraerts, E. (2009). A new solution to the recovered memory debate. *Perspective on Psychological Science, 4,* 126–134.

McNally, R. J., & Steketee, G. S. (1985). Etiology and maintenance of severe animal phobias. *Behavioral Research and Therapy, 23,* 431–435.

McNeilly, A. S., Robinson, I. C., Houston, M. J., & Howie, P. W. (1983). Release of oxytocin and prolactin in response to suckling. *British Medical Journal, 286,* 257–259.

McRae, C., Cherin, E., Yamazaki, G., Diem, G., Vo, A. H., Russell, D., . . . Freed, C. R. (2004). Effects of perceived treatment on quality of life and medical outcomes in a double-blind placebo surgery trial. *Archives of General Psychiatry, 61,* 412–420.

McWilliams, P. (1993). *Ain't nobody's business if you do: The absurdity of consensual crimes in a free society.* Los Angeles: Prelude Press.

Mead, G. H. (1934). *Mind, self, and society.* Chicago: University of Chicago Press.

Mead, M. (1968). *Sex and temperament in three primitive societies.* New York: Dell. (Original work published 1935)

Meaney, M. J., & Ferguson-Smith, A. C. (2010). Epigenetic regulation of the neural transcriptome: The meaning of the marks. *Nature Neuroscience, 13,* 1313–1318.

Mechelli, A., Crinion, J. T., Noppeney, U., O'Doherty, J., Ashburner, J., Frackowiak, R. S., & Price, C. J. (2004). Neurolinguistics: Structural plasticity in the bilingual brain. *Nature, 431,* 757.

Medin, D. L., & Schaffer, M. M. (1978). Context theory of classification learning. *Psychological Review, 85,* 207–238.

Medvec, V. H., Madey, S. F., & Gilovich, T. (1995). When less is more: Counterfactual thinking and satisfaction among Olympic medalists. *Journal of Personality and Social Psychology, 69,* 603–610.

Meeren, H. K. M., van Heijnsbergen, C. C. R. J., & de Gelder, B. (2005). Rapid perceptual integration of facial expression and emotional body language. *Proceedings of the National Academy of Sciences, USA, 102*(45), 16518–16523.

Mehl, M. R., Vazire, S., Ramirez-Esparza, N., Slatcher, R. B., & Pennebaker, J. W. (2009). Are women really more talkative than men? *Science, 317,* 82.

Meindl, J. N., & Casey, L. B. (2012). Increasing the suppressive effect of delayed punishers: A review of basic and applied literature. *Behavioral Interventions, 27,* 129–150.

Meins, E. (2003). Emotional development and attachment relationships. In A. Slater & G. Bremner (Eds.), *An introduction to developmental psychology* (pp. 141–164). Malden, MA: Blackwell.

Meins, E., Fernyhough, C., Fradley, E., & Tuckey, M. (2001). Rethinking maternal sensitivity: Mothers' comments on infants' mental processes predict security of attachment at 12 months. *Journal of Child Psychology & Psychiatry & Allied Disciplines, 42,* 637–648.

Meisel, S. R., Dayan, K. I., Pauzner, H., Chetboun, I., Arbel, Y., & David, D. (1991). Effect of Iraqi missile war on incidence of acute myocardial infarction and sudden death in Israeli citizens. *Lancet, 338,* 660–661.

Mekel-Bobrov, N., Gilbert, S. L., Evans, P. D., Vallender, E. J., Anderson, J. R., Hudson, R. R., . . . Lahn, B. T. (2005). Ongoing adaptive evolution of ASPM, a brain size determinant in *Homo sapiens. Science, 309,* 1720–1722.

Melander, E. (2005). Gender equality and intrastate armed conflict. *International Studies Quarterly, 49*(4), 695–714. doi:10.1111/j.1468-2478.2005.00384.x

Mellon, R. C. (2009). Superstitious perception: Response-independent reinforcement and punishment as determinants of recurring eccentric interpretations. *Behaviour Research and Therapy, 47,* 868–875.

Meltzer, H. Y. (2013). Update on typical and atypical antipsychotic drugs. *Annual Review of Medicine, 64,* 393–406.

Meltzoff, A. N. (1995). Understanding the intentions of others: Re-enactment of intended acts by 18-month-old children. *Developmental Psychology, 31,* 838–850.

Meltzoff, A. N. (2007). "Like me": A foundation for social cognition. *Developmental Science, 10*(1), 126–134. doi:10.1111/j.1467-7687.2007.00574x

Meltzoff, A. N., Kuhl, P. K., Movellan, J., & Sejnowski, T. J. (2009). Foundations for a new science of learning. *Science, 325,* 284–288.

Meltzoff, A. N., & Moore, M. K. (1977). Imitation of facial and manual gestures by human neonates. *Science, 198,* 75–78.

Melzack, R., & Wall, P. D. (1965). Pain mechanisms: A new theory. *Science, 150,* 971–979.

Mendes, W. B., Blascovich, J., Hunter, S. B., Lickel, B., & Jost, J. T. (2007). Threatened by the unexpected: Physiological responses during social interactions with expectancy-violating partners. *Journal of Personality and Social Psychology, 92,* 698–716.

Mendes, W. B., Blascovich, J., Lickel, B., & Hunter, S. (2002). Challenge and threat during social interaction with White and Black men. *Personality & Social Psychology Bulletin, 28,* 939–952.

Mendle, J., Harden, K. P., Brooks-Gunn, J., & Graber, J. A. (2010). Development's tortoise and hare: Pubertal timing, pubertal tempo, and depressive symptoms in boys and girls. *Developmental Psychology, 46*(5), 1341–1353. doi: 10.1037/a0020205

Mendle, J., Turkheimer, E., & Emery, R. E. (2007). Detrimental psychological outcomes associated with early pubertal timing in adolescent girls. *Developmental Review, 27,* 151–171.

Mennella, J. A., Johnson, A., & Beauchamp, G. K. (1995). Garlic ingestion by pregnant women alters the odor of amniotic fluid. *Chemical Senses, 20,* 207–209.

Merikangas, K. R., Wicki, W., & Angst, J. (1994). Heterogeneity of depression: Classification of depressive subtype by longitudinal course. *British Journal of Psychiatry, 164,* 342–348.

Mervis, C. B., & Bertrand, J. (1994). Acquisition of the "Novel Name" Nameless Category (N3C) principle. *Child Development, 65,* 1646–1662.

Merzenich, M. M., Recanzone, G. H., Jenkins, W. M., & Grajski, K. A. (1990). Adaptive mechanisms in cortical networks underlying cortical contributions to learning and nondeclarative memory. *Cold Spring Harbor Symposia on Quantitative Biology, 55,* 873–887.

Messick, D. M., & Cook, K. S. (1983). *Equity theory: Psychological and sociological perspectives.* New York: Praeger.

Meston, C. M., & Buss, D. M. (2007). Why humans have sex. *Archives of Sexual Behavior, 36,* 477–507.

Mestre, J. M., Guil, R., Lopes, P. N., Salovey, P., & Gil-Olarte, P. (2006). Emotional intelligence and social and academic adaptation to school. *Psicothema, 18,* 112.

Mestry, N., Donnelly, N., Meneer, T., & McCarthy, R. A. (2012). Discriminating Thatcherised from typical faces in a case of prosopagnosia. *Neuropsychologia, 50,* 3410–3418.

Metcalfe, J. (2009). Metacognitive judgments and control of study. *Current Directions in Psychological Science, 18,* 159–163.

Metcalfe, J., & Finn, B. (2008). Evidence that judgments of learning are causally related to study choice. *Psychonomic Bulletin & Review, 15,* 174–179.

Metcalfe, J., & Wiebe, D. (1987). Intuition in insight and noninsight problem solving. *Memory & Cognition, 15,* 238–246.

Methven, L., Allen, V. J., Withers, G. A., & Gosney, M. A. (2012). Ageing and taste. *Proceedings of the Nutrition Society, 71,* 556–565.

Meyer-Bahlberg, H. F. L., Ehrhardt, A. A., Rosen, L. R., & Gruen, R. S. (1995). Prenatal estrogens and the development of homosexual orientation. *Developmental Psychology, 31,* 12–21.

Michaela, R., Florian, S., Gert, G. W., & Ulman, L. (2009). Seeking pleasure and seeking pain: Differences in prohedonic and contrahedonic motivation from adolescence to old age. *Psychological Science, 20*(12), 1529–1535.

Michelson, D., Pollack, M., Lydiard, R. D., Tamura, R., Tepner, R., & Tollefson, G. (1999). Continuing treatment of panic disorder after acute responses: Randomized, placebo-controlled trail with fluoxetine. The Fluoxitine Panic Disorder Study Group. *British Journal of Psychiatry, 174,* 213–218.

Mikels, J. A., Maglio, S. J., Reed, A. E., & Kaplowitz, L. J. (2011). Should I go with my gut? Investigating the benefits of emotion-focused decision making. *Emotion, 11*(4), 743–753.

Miklowitz, D. J., & Johnson, S. L. (2006). The psychopathology and treatment of bipolar disorder. *Annual Review of Clinical Psychology, 2,* 199–235.

Milgram, S. (1963). Behavioral study of obedience. *Journal of Abnormal and Social Psychology, 67,* 371–378.

Milgram, S. (1974). *Obedience to authority.* New York: Harper & Row.

Milgram, S., Bickman, L., & Berkowitz, O. (1969). Note on the drawing power of crowds of different size. *Journal of Personality and Social Psychology, 13,* 79–82.

Miller, A. J. (1986). *The obedience experiments: A case study of controversy in social science.* New York: Praeger.

Miller, C., Seckel, E., & Ramachandran, V. S. (2012). Using mirror box therapy to treat phatom pain in Haitian earthquake victims. *Journal of Vision, 12,* article 1323. doi:10.1167/12.9.1323

Miller, D. T., & Prentice, D. A. (1996). The construction of social norms and standards. In E. T. Higgins & A. W. Kruglanski (Ed.), *Social psychology: Handbook of basic principles* (pp. 799–829). New York: Guilford Press.

Miller, D. T., & Ratner, R. K. (1998). The disparity between the actual and assumed power of self-interest. *Journal of Personality and Social Psychology, 74,* 53–62.

Miller, D. T., & Ross, M. (1975). Self-serving biases in the attribution of causality: Fact or fiction? *Psychological Bulletin, 82,* 213–225.

Miller, G. A. (1956). The magical number seven, plus or minus two: Some limits on our capacity for processing information. *Psychological Review, 63,* 81–96.

Miller, K. F., Smith, C. M., & Zhu, J. (1995). Preschool origins of cross-national differences in mathematical competence: The role of number-naming systems. *Psychological Science, 6,* 56–60.

Miller, N. E. (1960). Motivational effects of brain stimulation and drugs. *Federation Proceedings, 19,* 846–854.

Miller, T. W. (Ed.). (1996). *Theory and assessment of stressful life events.* Madison, CT: International Universities Press.

Miller, W. R., & Rollnick, S. (2012). *Motivational interviewing: Helping people change* (3rd ed.). New York: Guilford Press.

Mills, P. J., & Dimsdale, J. E. (1991). Cardiovascular reactivity to psychosocial stressors. A review of the effects of beta-blockade. *Psychosomatics, 32,* 209–220.

Milne, E., & Grafman, J. (2001). Ventromedial prefrontal cortex lesions in humans eliminate implicit gender stereotyping. *Journal of Neuroscience, 21,* 1–6.

Milner, A. D., & Goodale, M. A. (1995). *The visual brain in action.* Oxford, England: Oxford University Press.

Milner, B. (1962). Laterality effects in audition. In V. B. Mountcastle (Ed.), *Interhemispheric relations and cerebral dominance* (pp. 177–195). Baltimore: Johns Hopkins University Press.

Mineka, S., & Cook, M. (1988). Social learning and the acquisition of snake fear in monkeys. In T. Zentall & B. G. Galef, Jr. (Eds.), *Social learning* (pp. 51–73). Hillsdale, NJ: Erlbaum.

Mineka, S., & Ohman, A. (2002). Born to fear: Non-associative vs. associative factors in the etiology of phobia. *Behaviour Research and Therapy, 40,* 173–184.

Mingroni, M. A. (2007). Resolving the IQ paradox: Heterosis as a cause of the Flynn effect and other trends. *Psychological Review, 114,* 806–829.

Minson, J. A., & Mueller, J. S. (2012). The cost of collaboration: Why joint decision making exacerbates rejection of outside information. *Psychological Science, 23*(3), 219–224. doi:10.1177/0956797611429132

Minsky, M. (1986). *The society of mind.* New York: Simon & Schuster.

Miranda, J., Bernal, G., Lau, A., Kihn, L., Hwang, W. C., & LaFramboise, T. (2005). State of the science on psychological interventions for ethnic minorities. *Annual Review of Clinical Psychology, 1,* 113–142.

Mischel, W. (1968). *Personality and assessment.* New York: Wiley.

Mischel, W. (2004). Toward an integrative science of the person. *Annual Review of Psychology, 55,* 1–22.

Mischel, W., Ayduk, O., Baumeister, R. F., & Vohs, K. D. (2004). Willpower in a cognitive-affective processing system: The dynamics of delay of gratification. In *Handbook of self-regulation: Research, theory, and applications* (pp. 99–129). New York: Guilford Press.

Mischel, W., & Shoda, Y. (1999). Integrating dispositions and processing dynamics within a unified theory of personality: The cognitiveaffective personality system. In L. A. Pervin & O. P. John (Eds.), *Handbook of personality: Theory and research.* New York: Guilford Press.

Mischel, W., Shoda, Y., & Rodriguez, M. L. (1989). Delay of gratification in children. *Science, 244,* 933–938.

Mishra, A., & Mishra, H. (2010). Border bias: The belief that state borders can protect against disasters. *Psychological Science, 21*(11), 1582–1586. doi:10.1177/0956797610385950

Mita, T. H., Dermer, M., & Knight, J. (1977). Reversed facial images and the mere-exposure hypothesis. *Journal of Personality and Social Psychology, 35,* 597–601.

Mitchell, J. P. (2006). Mentalizing and Marr: An information processing approach to the study of social cognition. *Brain Research, 1079,* 66–75.

Mitchell, J. P., Heatherton, T. F., & Macrae, C. N. (2002). Distinct neural systems subserve person and object knowledge. *Proceedings of the National Academy of Sciences, USA, 99,* 15238–15243.

Mitchell, K. J., & Johnson, M. K. (2009). Source monitoring 15 years later: What have we learned from fMRI about the neural mechanisms of source memory? *Psychological Bulletin, 135,* 638–677.

Miura, I. T., Okamoto, Y., Kim, C. C., & Chang, C. M. (1994). Comparisons of children's cognitive representation of number: China, France, Japan, Korea, Sweden and the United States. *International Journal of Behavioral Development, 17,* 401–411.

Moffitt, T. E. (1993). Adolescence-limited and life-course-persistent antisocial behavior: A developmental taxonomy. *Psychological Review, 100,* 674–701.

Moffitt, T. E. (2005). Genetic and environmental influences on antisocial behaviors: Evidence from behavioral-genetic research. *Advances in Genetics, 55,* 41–104.

Moghaddam, B., & Bunney, B. S. (1989). Differential effect of cocaine on extracellular dopamine levels in rat medial prefrontal cortex and nucleus accumbens: Comparison to amphetamine. *Synapse, 4,* 156–161.

Mojtabai, R., Olfson, M., Sampson, N. A., Jin, R., Druss, B., Wang, P. S., . . . Kessler, R. C. (2011). Barriers to mental health treatment: Results from the National Comorbidity Survey replication. *Psychological Medicine, 41*(8), 1751–1761.

Molden, D., Lee, A. Y., & Higgins, E. T. (2009). Motivations for promotion and prevention. In J. Shah & W. Gardner (Eds.), *Handbook of motivation science* (pp. 169–187). New York: Guilford Press.

Monahan, J. (1992). Mental disorder and violent behavior: Perceptions and evidence. *American Psychologist, 47,* 511–521.

Monahan, J. L., Murphy, S. T., & Zajonc, R. B. (2000). Subliminal mere exposure: Specific, general, and diffuse effects. *Psychological Science, 11,* 462–466.

Moncrieff, J. (2009). A critique of the dopamine hypothesis of schizophrenia and psychosis. *Harvard Review of Psychiatry, 17,* 214–225.

Montague, C. T., Farooqi, I. S., Whitehead, J. P., Soos, M. A., Rau, H., Wareham, N. J., . . . O'Rahilly, S. (1997). Congenital leptin deficiency is associated with severe early-onset obesity in humans. *Nature, 387*(6636), 903–908.

Monti, M. M. (2012). Cognition in the vegetative state. *Annual Review of Clinical Psychology, 8,* 431–454.

Monti, M. M., Coleman, M. R., & Owen, A. M. (2009). Neuroimaging and the vegetative state: Resolving the behavioral assessment dilemma? *Annals of the New York Academy of Sciences, 1157,* 81–89.

Monti, M. M., Vanhaudenhuyse, A., Coleman, M. R., Boly, M., Pickard, J. D., Tshibanda, L., . . . Laureys, S. (2010). Willful modulation of brain activity in disorders of consciousness. *New England Journal of Medicine, 362,* 579–589.

Mook, D. G. (1983). In defense of external invalidity. *American Psychologist, 38,* 379–387.

Moon, S. M., & Illingworth, A. J. (2005). Exploring the dynamic nature of procrastination: A latent growth curve analysis of academic procrastination. *Personality and Individual Differences, 38,* 297–309.

Moore, D. W. (2003). *Public lukewarm on animal rights.* Retrieved June 22, 2010, from http://www.gallup.com/poll/8461/publiclukewarm-animal-rights.aspx

Moore, E. G. J. (1986). Family socialization and the IQ test performance of traditionally and transracially adopted Black children. *Developmental Psychology, 22,* 317–326.

Moore, K. L. (1977). *The developing human* (2nd ed.). Philadelphia: Saunders.

Moore, L. (2012, August 31). American's future has to be multilingual. *The Washington Diplomat.* Retrieved from http://www.washdiplomat.com/index.php?option=com_content&view=article&id=8549:op-ed-americans-future-has-to-be-multilingual&catid=1492:september-2012&Itemid=504

Moran, P., Klinteberg, B. A., Batty, G. D., & Vågerö, D. (2009). Brief report: Childhood intelligence predicts hospitalization with personality disorder in adulthood: Eveidence from a population-based study in Sweden. *Journal of Personality Disorders, 23*(5), 535–540. doi:10.1521/pedi.2009.23.5.535

Moray, N. (1959). Attention in dichotic listening: Affective cues and the influence of instructions. *Quarterly Journal of Experimental Psychology, 11,* 56–60.

Moreno, S., Marques, C., Santos, A., Santos, M., Castro, S. L., & Besson, M. (2009). Musical training influences linguistic abilities in 8-year-old children: More evidence for brain plasticity. *Cerebral Cortex, 19,* 712–723.

Morewedge, C. K., & Norton, M. I. (2009). When dreaming is believing: The (motivated) interpretation of dreams. *Journal of Personality and Social Psychology, 96,* 249–264.

Morgan, H. (1990). Dostoevsky's epilepsy: A case report and comparison. *Surgical Neurology, 33,* 413–416.

Morgenstern, J., Labouvie, E., McCrady, B. S., Kahler, C. W., & Frey, R. M. (1997). Affiliation with Alcoholics Anonymous after treatment: A study of its therapeutic effects and mechanisms of action. *Journal of Consulting and Clinical Psychology, 65,* 768–777.

Morin, A. (2002). Right hemisphere self-awareness: A critical assessment. *Consciousness & Cognition, 11,* 396–401.

Morin, A. (2006). Levels of consciousness and self-awareness: A comparison of various neurocognitive views. *Consciousness & Cognition, 15,* 358–371.

Morin, C. M., Bélanger, L., LeBlanc, M., Ivers, H., Savard, J., Espie, C. A., . . . Grégoire, J. P. (2009). The natural history of insomnia: A population-based 3-year longitudinal study. *Archives of Internal Medicine, 169,* 447–453.

Morris, C. D., Bransford, J. D., & Franks, J. J. (1977). Levels of processing versus transfer-appropriate processing. *Journal of Verbal Learning and Verbal Behavior, 16,* 519–533.

Morris, R. G., Anderson, E., Lynch, G. S., & Baudry, M. (1986). Selective impairment of learning and blockade of long-term potentiation by an N-methyl-D-aspartate receptor antagonist, AP5. *Nature, 319,* 774–776.

Morris, T. L. (2001). Social phobia. In M. W. Vasey & M. R. Dadds (Eds.), *The developmental psychopathology of anxiety* (pp. 435–458). New York: Oxford University Press.

Morrow, D., Leirer, V., Altiteri, P., & Fitzsimmons, C. (1994). When expertise reduces age differences in performance. *Psychology and Aging, 9,* 134–148.

Moruzzi, G., & Magoun, H. W. (1949). Brain stem reticular formation and activation of the EEG. *Electroencephalography and Clinical Neurophysiology, 1,* 455–473.

Moscovitch, M. (1994). Memory and working-with-memory: Evaluation of a component process model and comparisons with other models. In D. L. Schacter & E. Tulving (Eds.), *Memory systems 1994* (pp. 269–310). Cambridge, MA: MIT Press.

Moscovitch, M., Nadel, L., Winocur, G., Gilboa, A., & Rosenbaum, R. S. (2006). The cognitive neuroscience of remote episodic, semantic and spatial memory. *Current Opinion in Neurobiology, 16,* 179–190.

Moss, D., McGrady, A., Davies, T., & Wickramasekera, I. (Eds.). (2002). *Handbook of mind–body medicine for primary care.* Newbury Park, CA: Sage.

Motley, M. T., & Baars, B. J. (1979). Effects of cognitive set upon laboratory induced verbal (Freudian) slips. *Journal of Speech & Hearing Research, 22,* 421–432.

Moulin, C. J. A., Conway, M. A., Thompson, R. G., James, N., & Jones, R. W. (2005). Disordered memory awareness: Recollective confabulation in two cases of persistent déjà vecu. *Neuropsychologia, 43,* 1362–1378.

Moura, A. C. A. de, & Lee, P. C. (2004). Capuchin stone tool use in Caatinga dry forest. *Science, 306,* 1909.

Mroczek, D. K., & Spiro, A. (2005). Change in life satisfaction during adulthood: Findings from the Veterans Affairs Normative Aging Study. *Journal of Personality and Social Psychology, 88,* 189.

Muehlenkamp, J. J., Claes, L., Havertape, L., & Plener, P. L. (2012). International prevalence of adolescent non-suicidal self-injury and deliberate self-harm. *Child and Adolescent Psychiatry and Mental Health, 6*(10). doi:10.1156/1753-2000-6-10

Mueller, T. E., Gavin, L. E., & Kulkarni, A. (2008). The association between sex education and youth's engagement in sexual intercourse, age at first intercourse, and birth control use at first sex. *The Journal of Adolescent Health, 42*(1), 89–96.

Mueller, T. I., Leon, A. C., Keller, M. B., Solomon, D. A., Endicott, J., Coryell, W., . . . Maser, J. D. (1999). Recurrence after recovery from major depressive disorder during 15 years of observational follow-up. *American Journal of Psychiatry, 156,* 1000–1006.

Muenter, M. D., & Tyce, G. M. (1971). L-dopa therapy of Parkinson's disease: Plasma L-dopa concentration, therapeutic response, and side effects. *Mayo Clinic Proceedings, 46,* 231–239.

Mullen, M. K. (1994). Earliest recollections of childhood: A demographic analysis. *Cognition, 52,* 55–79.

Muller, M. N., & Wrangham, R. W. (2004). Dominance, aggression and testosterone in wild chimpanzees: A test of the "challenge hypothesis." *Animal Behaviour, 67,* 113–123.

Munsey, C. (2008, February). Prescriptive authority in the states. *Monitor on Psychology, 39,* 60.

Murphy, N. A., Hall, J. A., & Colvin, C. R. (2003). Accurate intelligence assessments in social interactions: Mediators and gender effects. *Journal of Personality, 71,* 465–493.

Murray, C. (2002). *IQ and income inequality in a sample of sibling pairs from advantaged family backgrounds.* Paper presented at the 114th Annual Meeting of the American Economic Association.

Murray, C. J., & Lopez, A. D. (1996a). Evidence-based health policy—Lessons from the Global Burden of Disease study. *Science, 274,* 740–743.

Murray, C. J. L., & Lopez, A. D. (1996b). *The Global Burden of Disease: A comprehensive assessment of mortality and disability from diseases, injuries, and risk factors in 1990 and projected to 2020.* Cambridge, MA: Harvard University Press.

Murray, H. A. (1943). *Thematic Apperception Test manual.* Cambridge, MA: Harvard University Press.

Murray, H. A., & Kluckhohn, C. (1953). Outline of a conception of personality. In C. Kluckhohn, H. A. Murray, & D. M. Schneider (Eds.), *Personality in nature, society, and culture* (2nd ed., pp. 3–52). New York: Knopf.

Myers, D. G., & Diener, E. (1995). Who is happy? *Psychological Science, 6,* 10–19.

Myers, D. G., & Lamm, H. (1975). The polarizing effect of group discussion. *American Scientist, 63*(3), 297–303.

Myles, P. S., Leslie, K., McNell, J., Forbes, A., & Chan, M. T. V. (2004). Bispectral index monitoring to prevent awareness during anaesthesia: The B-Aware randomized controlled trial. *Lancet, 363,* 1757–1763.

Nadasdy, A. (1995). Phonetics, phonology, and applied linguistics. *Annual Review of Applied Linguistics, 15,* 68–77.

Nader, K., & Hardt, O. (2009). A single standard for memory: The case of reconsolidation. *Nature Reviews Neuroscience, 10,* 224–234.

Nader, K., Shafe, G., & LeDoux, J. E. (2000). Fear memories require protein synthesis in the amygdala for reconsolidation after retrieval. *Nature, 406,* 722–726.

Nagasako, E. M., Oaklander, A. L., & Dworkin, R. H. (2003). Congenital insensitivity to pain: An update. *Pain, 101,* 213–219.

Nagell, K., Olguin, R. S., & Tomasello, M. (1993). Processes of social learning in the tool use of chimpanzees (*Pan troglodytes*) and human children (*Homo sapiens*). *Journal of Comparative Psychology, 107,* 174–186.

Nahemow, L., & Lawton, M. P. (1975). Similarity and propinquity in friendship formation. *Journal of Personality and Social Psychology, 32,* 205–213.

Nairne, J. S., & Pandeirada, J. N. S. (2008). Adaptive memory: Remembering with a stone age brain. *Current Directions in Psychological Science, 17,* 239–243.

Nairne, J. S., Pandeirada, J. N. S., & Thompson, S. R. (2008). Adaptive memory: The comparative value of survival processing. *Psychological Science, 19,* 176–180.

Nairne, J. S., Thompson, S. R., & Pandeirada, J. N. S. (2007). Adaptive memory: Survival processing enhances retention. *Journal of Experimental Psychology: Learning, Memory, and Cognition, 33,* 263–273.

Nakazato, M., Murakami, N., Date, Y., Kojima, M., Matsuo, H., Kangawa, K., & Matsukura, S. (2001). A role for ghrelin in the central regulation of feeding. *Nature, 409,* 194–198.

Naqvi, N., Shiv, B., & Bechara, A. (2006). The role of emotion in decision making: A cognitive neuroscience perspective. *Current Directions in Psychological Science, 15,* 260–264.

Nathan, P. E., & Gorman, J. M. (2007). *A guide to treatments that work* (3rd ed.). New York: Oxford University Press.

Nathanson, C., Paulhus, D. L., & Williams, K. M. (2006). Personality and misconduct correlates of body modification and other cultural deviance markers. *Journal of Research in Personality, 40,* 779–802.

National Center for Health Statistics. (2004). *Health, United States, 2004* (with chartbook on trends in the health of Americans). Hyattsville, MD: Author.

National Center for Health Statistics. (2012). *Health, United States, 2011* (with special feature on socioeconomic status and health). Hyattsville, MD: Author.

National Research Council. (2003). *The polygraph and lie detection.* Washington, DC: National Academies Press.

Naumann, L. P., Vazire, S., Rentfrow, P. J., & Gosling, S. D. (2009). Personality judgments based on physical appearance. *Personality & Social Psychology Bulletin, 35,* 1661–1671.

Neihart, M. (1999). The impact of giftedness on psychological wellbeing: What does the empirical literature say? *Roeper Review, 22*(1), 10.

Neimark, J. (2004, July/August). The power of coincidence. *Psychology Today,* pp. 47–52.

Neimeyer, R. A., & Mitchell, K. A. (1988). Similarity and attraction: A longitudinal study. *Journal of Social and Personal Relationships, 5,* 131–148.

Neisser, U. (1967). *Cognitive psychology.* New York: Appleton-Century-Crofts.

Neisser, U. (Ed.). (1998). *The rising curve: Long-term gains in IQ and related measures.* Washington, DC: American Psychological Association.

Neisser, U., Boodoo, G., Bouchard, T. J., Jr., Boykin, A. W., Brody, N., Ceci, S. J., . . . Loehlin, J. C. (1996). Intelligence: Knowns and unknowns. *American Psychologist, 51,* 77–101.

Neisser, U., & Harsch, N. (1992). Phantom flashbulbs: False recollections of hearing the news about Challenger. In E. Winograd & U. Neisser (Eds.), *Affect and accuracy in recall: Studies of "flashbulb memories"* (pp. 9–31). Cambridge, England: Cambridge University Press.

Nelson, C. A., Zeanah, C. H., Fox, N. A., Marshall, P. J., Smyke, A. T., & Guthrie, D. (2007). Cognitive recovery in socially deprived young children: The Bucharest early intervention project. *Science, 318,* 1937–1940.

Nemeth, C., & Chiles, C. (1988). Modelling courage: The role of dissent in fostering independence. *European Journal of Social Psychology, 18,* 275–280.

Neuberg, S. L., Kenrick, D. T., & Schaller, M. (2010). Evolutionary social psychology. In S. T. Fiske, D. T. Gilbert, & G. Lindzey (Eds.), *The handbook of social psychology* (5th ed., Vol. 2, pp. 761–796). New York: Wiley.

Neugebauer, R., Hoek, H. W., & Susser, E. (1999). Prenatal exposure to wartime famine and development of antisocial personality in early adulthood. *Journal of the American Medical Association, 282,* 455–462.

Newbold, R. R., Padilla-Banks, E., Snyder, R. J., & Jefferson, W. N. (2005). Developmental exposure to estrogenic compounds and obesity. *Birth Defects Research Part A: Clinical and Molecular Teratology, 73,* 478–480.

Newell, A., Shaw, J. C., & Simon, H. A. (1958). Elements of a theory of human problem solving. *Psychological Review, 65,* 151–166.

Newman, A. J., Bavelier, D., Corina, D., Jezzard, P., & Neville, H. J. (2002). A critical period for right hemisphere recruitment in American Sign Language processing. *Nature Neuroscience, 5,* 76–80.

Newman, J. P., Wolff, W. T., & Hearst, E. (1980). The feature-positive effect in adult human subjects. *Journal of Experimental Psychology: Human Learning and Memory, 6,* 630–650.

Newman, M. G., & Stone, A. A. (1996). Does humor moderate the effects of experimentally induced stress? *Annals of Behavioral Medicine, 18,* 101–109.

Newschaffer, C. J., Croen, L. A., Daniels, J., Giarelli, E., Grether, J. K., Levy, S. E., . . . Windham, G. C. (2007). The epidemiology of autism spectrum disorders. *Annual Review of Public Health, 28,* 235–258.

Newsome, W. T., & Paré, E. B. (1988). A selective impairment of motion perception following lesions of the middle temporal visual area (MT). *Journal of Neuroscience, 8,* 2201–2211.

Neylan, T. C., Metzler, T. J., Best, S. R., Weiss, D. S., Fagan, J. A., Libermans, A., . . . Marmar, C. R. (2002). Critical incident exposure and sleep quality in police officers. *Psychosomatic Medicine, 64,* 345–352.

Niaura, R., Todaro, J. F., Stroud, L., Spiro, A. III, Ward, K. D., & Weiss, S. (2002). Hostility, the metabolic syndrome, and incident coronary heart disease. *Health Psychology, 21,* 588–593.

Nicoladis, E., & Genesee, F. (1997). Language development in preschool bilingual children. *Journal of Speech-Language Pathology & Audiology, 21,* 258–270.

Niedenthal, P. M., Barsalou, L. W., Winkielman, P., Krauth-Gruber, S., & Ric, F. (2005). Embodiment in attitudes, social perception, and emotion. *Personality and Social Psychology Review, 9*(3), 184–211.

Nikles, C. D., II, Brecht, D. L., Klinger, E., & Bursell, A. L. (1998). The effects of current concern- and nonconcern-related waking suggestions on nocturnal dream content. *Journal of Personality and Social Psychology, 75,* 242–255.

Nikula, R., Klinger, E., & Larson-Gutman, M. K. (1993). Current concerns and electrodermal reactivity: Responses to words and thoughts. *Journal of Personality, 61,* 63–84.

Nir, Y., & Tononi, G. (2010). Dreaming and the brain: From phenomenology to neurophysiology. *Trends in Cognitive Sciences, 14*(2), 88–100.

Nisbett, R. E. (2009). *Intelligence and how to get it.* New York: Norton.

Nisbett, R. E., Aronson, J., Blair, C., Dickens, W., Flynn, J., Halpern, D. F., & Turkheimer, E. (2012). Intelligence: New findings and theoretical developments. *American Psychologist, 67*(2), 130–159. doi:10.1037/a0026699

Nisbett, R. E., Caputo, C., Legant, P., & Maracek, J. (1973). Behavior as seen by the actor and as seen by the observer. *Journal of Personality and Social Psychology, 27,* 154–164.

Nisbett, R. E., & Cohen, D. (1996). *Culture of honor: The psychology of violence in the South.* Boulder, CO: Westview Press.

Nisbett, R. E., & Miyamoto, Y. (2005). The influence of culture: Holistic versus analytic perception. *Trends in Cognitive Sciences, 9,* 467–473.

Nissen, M. J., & Bullemer, P. (1987). Attentional requirements of learning: Evidence from performance measures. *Cognitive Psychology, 19,* 1–32.

Nitschke, J. B., Dixon, G. E., Sarianopoulos, I., Short, S. J., Cohen, J. D., Smith, E. E., . . . Davidson, R. J. (2006). Altering expectancy dampens neural response to aversive taste in primary taste cortex. *Neuroscience, 9,* 435–442.

Nock, M. K. (2009). Why do people hurt themselves? New insights into the nature and functions of self-injury. *Current Directions in Psychological Science, 18,* 78–83. doi:10.1111/j.1467-8721.2009.01613.x

Nock, M. K. (2010). Self-injury. *Annual Review of Clinical Psychology, 6,* 339–363. doi: 10.1146/annurev.clinpsy.121208.131258

Nock, M. K., Borges, G., Bromet, E. J., Alonso, J., Angermeyer, M., Beautrais, A., . . . Williams, D. (2008). Cross-national prevalence and risk factors for suicidal ideation, plans, and attempts. *British Journal of Psychiatry, 192,* 98–105.

Nock, M. K., Borges, G., & Ono, Y. (Eds.). (2012). *Suicide: Global perspectives from the WHO World Mental Health Surveys.* New York: Cambridge University Press.

Nock, M. K., Green, J. G., Hwang, I., McLaughlin, K. A., Sampson, N. A., Zaslavsky, A. M., & Kessler, R. C. (2013). Prevalence, correlates and treatment of lifetime suicidal behavior among adolescents: Results from the National Comorbidity Survey Replication–Adolescent Supplement (NCSA–A). *Journal of the American Medical Association Psychiatry, 70*(3), 300–310. doi:10.1001/2013.jamapsychiatry.55

Nock, M. K., Holmberg, E. G., Photos, V. I., & Michel, B. D. (2007). Structured and semi-structured interviews. In M. Hersen & J. C. Thomas (Eds.), *Handbook of clinical interviewing with children* (pp. 30–49). Thousand Oaks, CA: Sage.

Nock, M. K., Kazdin, A. E., Hiripi, E., & Kessler, R. C. (2006). Prevalence, subtypes, and correlates of *DSM–IV* conduct disorder in the National Comorbidity Survey Replication. *Psychological Medicine, 36,* 699–710.

Nolen-Hoeksema, S. (2008). Gender differences in coping with depression across the lifespan. *Depression, 3,* 81–90.

Norcross, J. C., Hedges, M., & Castle, P. H. (2002). Psychologists conducting psychotherapy in 2001: A study of the Division 29 membership. *Psychotherapy: Theory/Research/Practice/Training, 39,* 97–102.

Norrholm, S. D., & Ressler, K. J. (2009). Genetics of anxiety and trauma-related disorders. *Neuroscience, 164,* 272–287.

Norton, M. I., Frost, J. H., & Ariely, D. (2007). Less is more: The lure of ambiguity, or why familiarity breeds contempt. *Journal of Personality and Social Psychology, 92*(1), 97–105. doi:10.1037/0022-3514.92.1.97

Nosanchuk, T. A., & Lightstone, J. (1974). Canned laughter and public and private conformity. *Journal of Personality and Social Psychology, 29,* 153–156.

Nowak, M. A. (2006). Five rules for the evolution of cooperation. *Science, 314,* 1560–1563.

Nuttin, J. M. (1985). Narcissism beyond Gestalt and awareness: The name letter effect. *European Journal of Social Psychology, 15,* 353–361.

Nyborg, H., & Jensen, A. R. (2001). Occupation and income related to psychometric g. *Intelligence, 29,* 45–55.

Oately, K., Keltner, D., & Jenkins, J. M. (2006). *Understanding emotions* (2nd ed.). Malden, MA: Blackwell.

Obama, M. (2013, March 8). Address on childhood obesity presented at the 2nd summit of the Partnership for a Healthier America, George Washington University, Washington, DC.

Ochsner, K. N. (2000). Are affective events richly recollected or simply familiar? The experience and process of recognizing feelings past. *Journal of Experimental Psychology: General, 129,* 242–261.

Ochsner, K. N., Bunge, S. A., Gross, J. J., & Gabrieli, J. D. E. (2002). Rethinking feelings: An fMRI study of the cognitive regulation of emotion. *Journal of Cognitive Neuroscience, 14,* 1215–1229.

Ochsner, K. N., Ray, R. R., Hughes, B., McRae, K., Cooper, J. C., Weber, J., . . . Gross, J. J. (2009). Bottom-up and top-down processes in emotion generation: Common and distinct neural mechanisms. *Psychological Science, 20,* 1322–1331.

O'Connor, T. G., & Rutter, M. (2000). Attachment disorder following early severe deprivation: Extension and longitudinal follow-up. *Journal of the American Academy of Child and Adolescent Psychiatry, 39,* 703–712.

O'Doherty, J. P., Dayan, P., Friston, K., Critchley, H., & Dolan, R. J. (2003). Temporal difference models and reward-related learning in the human brain. *Neuron, 38,* 329–337.

Ofshe, R. J. (1992). Inadvertent hypnosis during interrogation: False confession due to dissociative state, misidentified multiple personality, and the satanic cult hypothesis. *International Journal of Clinical and Experimental Hypnosis, 40,* 125–126.

Ofshe, R., & Watters, E. (1994). *Making monsters: False memories, psychotherapy, and sexual hysteria.* New York: Scribner/Macmillan.

Ohayon, M. M. (2002). Epidemiology of insomnia: What we know and what we still need to learn. *Sleep Medicine, 6,* 97–111.

Ohayon, M. M., Guilleminault, C., & Priest, R. G. (1999). Night terrors, sleepwalking, and confusional arousals in the general population: Their frequency and relationship to other sleep and mental disorders. *Journal of Clinical Psychiatry, 60,* 268–276.

Öhman, A. (1996). Preferential preattentive processing of threat in anxiety: Preparedness and attentional biases. In R. M. Rapee (Ed.), *Current controversies in the anxiety disorders.* New York: Guilford Press.

Öhman, A., Dimberg, U., & Öst, L. G. (1985). Animal and social phobias: Biological constraints on learned fear responses. In S. Reiss & R. Bootzin (Eds.), *Theoretical issues in behavior therapy* (pp. 123–175). New York: Academic Press.

Okagaki, L., & Sternberg, R. J. (1993). Parental beliefs and children's school performance. *Child Development, 64,* 36–56.

Okuda, J., Fujii, T., Ohtake, H., Tsukiura, T., Tanji, K., Suzuki, K., . . . Yamadori, A. (2003). Thinking of the future and the past: The roles of the frontal pole and the medial temporal lobes. *NeuroImage, 19,* 1369–1380.

Okulicz-Kozaryn, A. (2011). Europeans work to live and Americans live to work (Who is happy to work more: Americans or Europeans?) *Journal of Happiness Studies, 12*(2), 225–243.

Olatunji, B. O., & Wolitzky-Taylor, K. B. (2009). Anxiety sensitivity and the anxiety disorders: A meta-analytic review and synthesis. *Psychological Bulletin, 135,* 974–999.

O'Laughlin, M. J., & Malle, B. F. (2002). How people explain actions performed by groups and individuals. *Journal of Personality and Social Psychology, 82,* 33–48.

Olausson, P. O., Haglund, B., Weitoft, G. R., & Cnattingius, S. (2001). Teenage child-bearing and long-term socioeconomic consequences: A case study in Sweden. *Family Planning Perspectives, 33,* 70–74.

Olds, J. (1956, October). Pleasure center in the brain. *Scientific American, 195,* 105–116.

Olds, J., & Fobes, J. I. (1981). The central basis of motivation: Intracranial self-stimulation studies. *Annual Review of Psychology, 32,* 523–574.

Olds, J., & Milner, P. (1954). Positive reinforcement produced by electrical stimulation of septal areas and other regions of rat brains. *Journal of Comparative and Physiological Psychology, 47,* 419–427.

Ollers, D. K., & Eilers, R. E. (1988). The role of audition in infant babbling. *Child Development, 59,* 441–449.

Olofsson, J. K., Bowman, N. E., Khatibi, K., & Gottfried, J. A. (2012). A time-based account of the perception of odor objects and valences. *Psychological Science, 23,* 1224–1232.

Olsson, A., & Phelps, E. A. (2007). Social learning of fear. *Nature Neuroscience, 10,* 1095–1102.

Oltmanns, T. F., Neale, J. M., & Davison, G. C. (1991). *Case studies in abnormal psychology* (3rd ed.). New York: Wiley.

Olton, D. S., & Samuelson, R. J. (1976). Remembrance of places passed: Spatial memory in rats. *Journal of Experimental Psychology: Animal Behavior Processes, 2,* 97–116.

Onishi, K. H., & Baillargeon, R. (2005). Do 15-month-old infants understand false beliefs? *Science, 308,* 255–258.

Ono, K. (1987). Superstitious behavior in humans. *Journal of the Experimental Analysis of Behavior, 47,* 261–271.

Ophir, E., Nass, C., & Wagner, A. D. (2009). Cognitive control in media multitaskers. *Proceedings of the National Academy of Sciences, USA, 106,* 15583–15587.

Orban, P., Lungu, O., & Doyon, J. (2008). Motor sequence learning and developmental dyslexia. *Annals of the New York Academy of Sciences, 1145,* 151–172.

Ormel, J., Petukhova, M., Chatterji, S., Aguilar-Gaxiola, S., Alonso, J., Angermeyer, M. C., . . . Kessler, R. C. (2008). Disability and treatment of specific mental and physical disorders across the world: Results from the WHO World Mental Health Surveys. *British Journal of Psychiatry, 192,* 368–375.

O'Sullivan, L. F., & Allegeier, E. R. (1998). Feigning sexual desire: Consenting to unwanted sexual activity in heterosexual dating relationships. *Journal of Sex Research, 35,* 234–243.

Oswald, L., Taylor, A. M., & Triesman, M. (1960). Discriminative responses to stimulation during human sleep. *Brain, 83,* 440–453.

Otto, M. W., Henin, A., Hirshfeld-Becker, D. R., Pollack, M. H., Biederman, J., & Rosenbaum, J. F. (2007). Posttraumatic stress disorder symptoms following media exposure to tragic events: Impact of 9/11 on children at risk for anxiety disorders. *Journal of Anxiety Disorders, 21,* 888–902.

Owen, A. M., Coleman, M. R., Boly, M., Davis, M. H., Laureys, S., & Pickard, J. D. (2006). Detecting awareness in the vegetative state. *Science, 313,* 1402.

Owens, W. A. (1966). Age and mental abilities: A second adult followup. *Journal of Educational Psychology, 57,* 311–325.

Oztekin, I., Curtis, C. E., & McElree, B. (2009). The medial temporal lobe and left inferior prefrontal cortex jointly support interference resolution in verbal working memory. *Journal of Cognitive Neuroscience, 21,* 1967–1979.

Pagnin, D., de Queiroz, V., Pini, S., & Cassano, G. B. (2008). Efficacy of ECT in depression: A meta-analytic review. *Focus, 6,* 155–162.

Paivio, A. (1971). *Imagery and verbal processes.* New York: Holt, Rinehart and Winston.

Paivio, A. (1986). *Mental representations: A dual coding approach.* New York: Oxford University Press.

Palermo, T. M., Eccleston, C., Lewandowski, A. S., Williams, A. C., & Morley, S. (2011). Randomized controlled trials of psychological therapies for management of chronic pain in children and adolescents: An updated meta-analytic review. *Pain, 148,* 387–397.

Pantev, C., Oostenveld, R., Engelien, A., Ross, B., Roberts, L. E., & Hoke, M. (1998). Increased auditory cortical representation in musicians. *Nature, 392,* 811–814.

Papez, J. W. (1937). A proposed mechanism of emotion. *Archives of Neurology and Pathology, 38,* 725–743.

Parbery-Clark, A., Skoe, E., & Kraus, N. (2009). Musical experience limits the degradative effects of background noise on the neural processing of sound. *Journal of Neuroscience, 11,* 14100–14107.

Parbery-Clark, A., Strait, D. L., Anderson, S., Hittner, E., & Kraus, N. (2011). Musical experience and the aging auditory system: Implications for cognitive abilities and hearing speech in noise. *PLoS One, 6,* e18082.

Parbery-Clark, A., Tierney, A., Strait, D. L., & Kraus, N. (2012). Musicians have fine-tuned neural distinction of speech syllables. *Neuroscience, 219,* 111–119.

Park, B., & Hastie, R. (1987). Perception of variability in category development: Instance- versus abstraction-based stereotypes. *Journal of Personality and Social Psychology, 53*(4), 621–635. doi:10.1037/0022-3514.53.4.621

Park, D. C., & McDonough, I. M. (2013). The dynamic aging mind: Revelations from functional neuroimaging research. *Perspectives on Psychological Science, 8*(1), 62–67. doi:10.1177/1745691612469034

Park, D. C., Polk, T. A., Park, R., Minear, M., Savage, A., & Smith, M. R. (2004). Aging reduces neural specialization in ventral visual cortex. *Proceedings of the National Academy of Sciences, USA, 101*(35), 13091–13095. doi:10.1073/pnas.0405148101

Parker, E. S., Cahill, L. S., & McGaugh, J. L. (2006). A case of unusual autobiographical remembering. *Neurocase, 12,* 35–49.

Parker, G., Gibson, N. A., Brotchie, H., Heruc, G., Rees, A. M., & Hadzi-Pavlovic, D. (2006). Omega-3 fatty acids and mood disorders. *American Journal of Psychiatry, 163,* 969–978.

Parker, H. A., & McNally, R. J. (2008). Repressive coping, emotional adjustment, and cognition in people who have lost loved ones to suicide. *Suicide and Life-Threatening Behavior, 38,* 676–687.

Parkinson, B., & Totterdell, P. (1999). Classifying affect-regulation strategies. *Cognition and Emotion, 13,* 277–303.

Parks, C. D., & Stone, A. B. (2010). The desire to expel unselfish members from the group. *Journal of Personality and Social Psychology, 99*(2), 303–310. doi:10.1037/a0018403

Parrott, A. C. (2001). Human psychopharmacology of Ecstasy (MDMA): A review of 15 years of empirical research. *Human Psychopharmacology, 16,* 557–577.

Parrott, A. C., Morinan, A., Moss, M., & Scholey, A. (2005). *Understanding drugs and behavior.* Chichester, England: Wiley.

Parrott, W. G. (1993). Beyond hedonism: Motives for inhibiting good moods and for maintaining bad moods. In D. M. Wegner & J. W. Pennebaker (Eds.), *Handbook of mental control* (pp. 278–308). Englewood Cliffs, NJ: Prentice Hall.

Parsons, T. (1975). The sick role and the role of the physician reconsidered. *Milbank Memorial Fund Quarterly, Health and Society, 53*(3), 257–278.

Pascual-Ferrá, P., Liu, Y., & Beatty, M. J. (2012). A meta-analytic comparison of the effects of text messaging to substance-induced impairment on driving performance. *Communication Research Reports, 29,* 229–238.

Pascual-Leone, A., Amedi, A., Fregni, F., & Merabet, L. B. (2005). The plastic human brain cortex. *Annual Review of Neuroscience, 28,* 377–401.

Pascual-Leone, A., Houser, C. M., Reese, K., Shotland, L. I., Grafman, J., Sato, S., . . . Cohen, L. G. (1993). Safety of rapid-rate transcranial magnetic stimulation in normal volunteers. *Electroencephalography and Clinical Neurophysiology, 89,* 120–130.

Passini, F. T., & Norman, W. T. (1966). A universal conception of personality structure? *Journal of Personality and Social Psychology, 4,* 44–49.

Pasupathi, M., McLean, K. C., & Weeks, T. (2009). To tell or not to tell: Disclosure and the narrative self. *Journal of Personality, 77,* 1–35.

Patall, E. A., Cooper, H., & Robinson, J. C. (2008). The effects of choice on intrinsic motivation and related outcomes: A meta-analysis of research findings. *Psychological Bulletin, 134*(2), 270–300.

Patrick, C. J., Cuthbert, B. N., & Lang, P. J. (1994). Emotion in the criminal psychopath: Fear image processing. *Journal of Abnormal Psychology, 103,* 523–534.

Patterson, C. J. (1995). Lesbian mothers, gay fathers, and their children. In A. R. D'Augelli & C. J. Patterson (Eds.), *Lesbian, gay and bisexual identities across the lifespan: Psychological perspectives* (pp. 262–290). New York: Oxford University Press.

Pavlidis, I., Eberhardt, N. L., & Levine, J. A. (2002). Human behaviour: Seeing through the face of deception. *Nature, 415,* 35.

Pavlidou, E. V., Williams, J. M., & Kelly, L. M. (2009). Artificial grammar learning in primary school children with and without developmental dyslexia. *Annals of Dyslexia, 59,* 55–77.

Pavlov, I. P. (1923a). New researches on conditioned reflexes. *Science, 58,* 359–361.

Pavlov, I. P. (1923b, July 23). Pavloff. *Time, 1*(21), 20–21.

Pavlov, I. P. (1927). *Conditioned reflexes.* Oxford, England: Oxford University Press.

Payne, J. D., Schacter, D. L., Propper, R., Huang, L., Wamsley, E., Tucker, M. A., . . . Stickgold, R. (2009). The role of sleep in false memory formation. *Neurobiology of Learning and Memory, 92,* 327–334.

Payne, J. D., Stickgold, R., Swanberg, K., & Kensinger, E. A. (2008). Sleep preferentially enhances memory for emotional components of scenes. *Psychological Science, 19,* 781–788.

Pearce, J. M. (1987). A model of stimulus generalization for Pavlovian conditioning. *Psychological Review, 84,* 61–73.

Peck, J., & Shu, S. B. (2009). The effect of mere touch on perceived ownership. *Journal of Consumer Research, 36,* 434–447.

Peelen, M. V., & Kastner, S. (2009). A nonvisual look at the functional organization of visual cortex. *Neuron, 63,* 284–286.

Peissig, J. J., & Tarr, M. J. (2007). Visual object recognition: Do we know more now than we did 20 years ago? *Annual Review of Psychology, 58,* 75–96.

Pelham, B. W. (1985). Self-investment and self-esteem: Evidence for a Jamesian model of self-worth. *Journal of Personality and Social Psychology, 69,* 1141–1150.

Pelham, B. W., Carvallo, M., & Jones, J. T. (2005). Implicit egotism. *Current Directions in Psychological Science, 14,* 106–110.

Pelham, B. W., Mirenberg, M. C., & Jones, J. T. (2002). Why Susie sells seashells by the seashore: Implicit egotism and major life decisions. *Journal of Personality and Social Psychology, 82,* 469–487.

Penfield, W., & Rasmussen, T. (1950). *The cerebral cortex of man: A clinical study of localization of function.* New York: Macmillan.

Pennebaker, J. W. (1980). Perceptual and environmental determinants of coughing. *Basic and Applied Social Psychology, 1,* 83–91.

Pennebaker, J. W. (1989). Confession, inhibition, and disease. *Advances in Experimental Social Psychology, 22,* 211–244.

Pennebaker, J. W., & Chung, C. K. (2007). Expressive writing, emotional upheavals, and health. In H. Friedman & R. Silver (Eds.), *Handbook of health psychology* (pp. 263–284). New York: Oxford University Press.

Pennebaker, J. W., Kiecolt-Glaser, J. K., & Glaser, R. (1988). Disclosure of traumas and immune function: Health implications for psychotherapy. *Journal of Consulting and Clinical Psychology, 56,* 239–245.

Pennebaker, J. W., & Sanders, D. Y. (1976). American graffiti: Effects of authority and reactance arousal. *Personality and Social Psychology Bulletin, 2,* 264–267.

Penner, L. A., Albrecht, T. L., Orom, H., Coleman, D. K., & Underwood, W. (2010). Health and health care disparities. In J. F. Dovidio, M. Hewstone, P. Glick, & V. M. Esses (Eds.), *The Sage handbook of prejudice, stereotyping and discrimination* (pp. 472–489). Thousand Oaks, CA: Sage.

Perenin, M.-T., & Vighetto, A. (1988). Optic ataxia: A specific disruption in visuomotor mechanisms. I. Different aspects of the deficit in reaching for objects. *Brain, 111,* 643–674.

Perilloux, H. K., Webster, G. D., & Gaulin, S. J. C. (2010). Signals of genetic quality and maternal investment capacity: The dynamic effects of fluctuating asymmetry and waist-to-hip ratio on men's ratings of women's attractiveness. *Social Psychological and Personality Science, 1*(1), 34–42. doi:10.1177/1948550609349514

Perkins, D. N., & Grotzer, T. A. (1997). Teaching intelligence. *American Psychologist, 52,* 1125–1133.

Perlmutter, J. S., & Mink, J. W. (2006). Deep brain stimulation. *Annual Review of Neuroscience, 29,* 229–257.

Perloff, L. S., & Fetzer, B. K. (1986). Self-other judgments and perceived vulnerability to victimization. *Journal of Personality and Social Psychology, 50,* 502–510.

Perls, F. S., Hefferkine, R., & Goodman, P. (1951). *Gestalt therapy: Excitement and growth in the human personality.* New York: Julian Press.

Perrett, D. I., Burt, D. M., Penton-Voak, I. S., Lee, K. J., Rowland, D. A., & Edwards, R. (1999). Symmetry and human facial attractiveness. *Evolution and Human Behavior, 20,* 295–307.

Perrett, D. I., Rolls, E. T., & Caan, W. (1982). Visual neurones responsive to faces in the monkey temporal cortex. *Experimental Brain Research, 47,* 329–342.

Perry, R., & Sibley, C. G. (2012). Big Five personality prospectively predicts social dominance orientation and right wing authoritarianism. *Personality and Individual Differences, 52,* 3–8.

Persons, J. B. (1986). The advantages of studying psychological phenomena rather than psychiatric diagnoses. *American Psychologist, 41,* 1252–1260.

Pessiglione, M., Seymour, B., Flandin, G., Dolan, R. J., & Frith, C. D. (2006). Dopamine-dependent prediction errors underpin reward-seeking behavior in humans. *Nature, 442,* 1042–1045.

Petersen, A. C., & Grockett, L. (1985). Pubertal timing and grade effects on adjustment. *Journal of Youth and Adolescence, 14,* 191–206.

Petersen, J. L., & Hyde, J. S. (2010). A meta-analytic review of research on gender differences in sexuality, 1993–2007. *Psychological Bulletin, 136*(1), 21–38. doi:10.1037/a0017504

Peterson, C., & Siegal, M. (1999). Representing inner worlds: Theory of mind in autistic, deaf and normal hearing children. *Psychological Science, 10,* 126–129.

Peterson, C., Wang, Q., & Hou, Y. (2009). "When I was little": Childhood recollections in Chinese and European Canadian grade school children. *Child Development, 80,* 506–518.

Peterson, G. B. (2004). A day of great illumination: B. F. Skinner's discovery of shaping. *Journal of the Experimental Analysis of Behavior, 82,* 317–328.

Peterson, L. R., & Peterson, M. J. (1959). Short-term retention of individual verbal items. *Journal of Experimental Psychology, 58,* 193–198.

Peterson, S. E., Fox, P. T., Posner, M. I., Mintun, M. A., & Raichle, M. E. (1989). Positron emission tomographic studies of the processing of single words. *Journal of Cognitive Neuroscience, 1,* 154–170.

Petersson, K. M., Forkstam, C., & Ingvar, M. (2004). Artificial syntactic violations activate Broca's region. *Cognitive Science, 28,* 383–407.

Petitto, L. A., & Marentette, P. F. (1991). Babbling in the manual mode: Evidence for the ontogeny of language. *Science, 251,* 1493–1496.

Petrie, K. P., Booth, R. J., & Pennebaker, J. W. (1998). The immunological effects of thought suppression. *Journal of Personality and Social Psychology, 75,* 1264–1272.

Petry, N. M., Alessi, S. M., & Rash, C. J. (2013). Contingency management treatments decrease psychiatric symptoms. *Journal of Consulting and Clinical Psychology, 81*(5), 926–931. doi:10.1037/a0032499

Petty, R. E., & Cacioppo, J. T. (1986). The elaboration likelihood model of persuasion. In L. Berkowitz (Ed.), *Advances in experimental social psychology* (Vol. 19, pp. 123–205). New York: Academic Press.

Petty, R. E., Cacioppo, J. T., & Goldman, R. (1981). Personal involvement as a determinant of argument-based persuasion. *Journal of Personality and Social Psychology, 41,* 847–855.

Petty, R. E., & Wegener, D. T. (1998). Attitude change: Multiple roles for persuasion variables. In D. T. Gilbert, S. T. Fiske, & G. Lindzey (Eds.), *The handbook of social psychology* (4th ed., Vol. 1, pp. 323–390). Boston: McGraw-Hill.

Pew Research Center for People & the Press. (1997). *Motherhood today: A tougher job, less ably done.* Washington, DC: Author.

Pew Research Center for People & the Press. (2009). *Growing old in America: Expectations vs. reality.* Retrieved May 3, 2010, from http://pewsocialtrends.org/pubs/736/getting-old-in-america

Pham, M. T., Lee, L., & Stephen, A. T. (2012). Feeling the future: The emotional oracle effect. *Journal of Consumer Research, 39*(3), 461–477.

Phelan, J., Link, B., Stueve, A., & Pescosolido, B. (1997, August). *Public conceptions of mental illness in 1950 in 1996: Has sophistication increased? Has stigma declined?* Paper presented at the American Sociological Association, Toronto, Ontario.

Phelps, E. A. (2006). Emotion and cognition: Insights from studies of the human amygdala. *Annual Review of Psychology, 24,* 27–53.

Phelps, E. A., & LeDoux, J. L. (2005). Contributions of the amygdala to emotion processing: From animal models to human behavior. *Neuron, 48,* 175–187.

Phillips, F. (2002, January 24). Jump in cigarette sales tied to Sept. 11 attacks. *Boston Globe,* p. B1.

Phills, C. E., Kawakami, K., Tabi, E., Nadolny, D., & Inzlicht, M. (2011). Mind the gap: Increasing associations between the self and Blacks with approach behaviors. *Journal of Personality and Social Psychology, 100*(2), 197–210. doi:10.1037/a0022159

Piaget, J. (1954). *The child's conception of number.* New York: Norton.

Piaget, J. (1965). *The moral judgment of the child.* New York: Free Press. (Original work published 1932)

Piaget, J. (1977). The first year of life of the child. In H. E. Gruber & J. J. Voneche (Eds.), *The essential Piaget: An interpretative reference and guide* (pp. 198–214). New York: Basic Books. (Original work published 1927)

Piaget, J., & Inhelder, B. (1969). *The psychology of the child* (H. Weaver, Trans.). New York: Basic Books.

Piazza, J. R., Charles, S. T., Sliwinski, M. J., Mogle, J., & Almeida, D. M. (2013). Affective reactivity to daily stressors and long-term risk of reporting a chronic physical health condition. *Annals of Behavioral Medicine, 45,* 110–120.

Pinel, J. P. J., Assanand, S., & Lehman, D. R. (2000). Hunger, eating, and ill health. *American Psychologist, 55,* 1105–1116.

Pines, A. M. (1993). Burnout: An existential perspective. In W. B. Schaufeli, C. Maslach, & T. Marek (Eds.), *Professional burnout: Recent developments in theory and research* (pp. 33–51). Washington, DC: Taylor & Francis.

Pinker, S. (1994). *The language instinct.* New York: Morrow.

Pinker, S. (1997a). Evolutionary psychology: An exchange. *New York Review of Books, 44,* 55–58.

Pinker, S. (1997b). *How the mind works.* New York: Norton.

Pinker, S. (2003). *The blank slate: The modern denial of human nature.* New York: Viking.

Pinker, S. (2007, March 19). A history of violence. *The New Republic Online.*

Pinker, S., & Bloom, P. (1990). Natural language and natural selection. *Behavioral and Brain Sciences, 13,* 707–784.

Pitcher, D., Garrido, L., Walsh, V., & Duchaine, B. C. (2008). Transcranial magnetic stimulation disrupts the perception and embodiment of facial expressions. *Journal of Neuroscience, 28*(36), 8929–8933.

Plassman, H., O'Doherty, J., Shiv, B., & Rangel, A. (2008). Marketing actions can modulate neural representations of experienced pleasantness. *Proceedings of the National Academy of Sciences, USA, 105,* 1050–1054.

Platek, S. M., Critton, S. R., Myers, T. E., & Gallup, G. G., Jr. (2003). Contagious yawning: The role of self-awareness and mental state attribution. *Cognitive Brain Research, 17,* 223–227.

Plato. (1956). *Protagoras* (O. Jowett, Trans.). New York: Prentice Hall. (Original work circa 380 BCE)

Pleis, J. R., Lucas, J. W., & Ward, B. W. (2009). Summary of health statistics for U.S. adults: National health interview survey, 2008, *Vital Health Stat 10*(242). National Center for Health Statistics.

Plomin, R., & Caspi, A. (1999). Behavioral genetics and personality. In L. A. Pervin & O. P. John (Eds.), *Handbook of personality: Theory and research* (Vol. 2, pp. 251–276). New York: Guilford Press.

Plomin, R., DeFries, J. C., McClearn, G. E., & Rutter, M. (1997). *Behavioral genetics* (3rd ed.). New York: W. H. Freeman and Company.

Plomin, R., DeFries, J. C., McClearn, G. E., & McGuffin, P. (2001). *Behavioral genetics* (4th ed.). New York: W. H. Freeman and Company.

Plomin, R., Haworth, C. M. A., Meaburn, E. L., Price, T. S., Wellcome Trust Case Control Consortium 2, & Davis, O. S. P. (2013). Common DNA markers can account for more than half of the genetic influence on cognitive abilities. *Psychological Science, 24*(4), 562–568. doi:10.1177/0956797612457952

Plomin, R., Scheier, M. F., Bergeman, C. S., Pedersen, N. L., Nesselroade, J. R., & McClearn, G. E. (1992). Optimism, pessimism, and mental health: A twin/adoption analysis. *Personality and Individual Differences, 13,* 921–930.

Plomin, R., & Spinath, F. M. (2004). Intelligence: Genetics, genes, and genomics. *Journal of Personality and Social Psychology, 86,* 112–129.

Plotnik, J. M., de Waal, F. B. M., & Reiss, D. (2006). Self-recognition in an Asian elephant. *Proceedings of the National Academy of Sciences, USA, 103,* 17053–17057.

Poliak, S., & Pelas, E. (2003). The local differentiation of myelinated axons at nodes of Ranvier. *Nature Reviews Neuroscience, 4,* 968–980.

Polivy, J., & Herman, C. P. (1992). Undieting: A program to help people stop dieting. *International Journal of Eating Disorders, 11,* 261–268.

Polivy, J., & Herman, C. P. (2002). If at first you don't succeed. False hopes of self-change. *American Psychologist, 57,* 677–689.

Polzanczyk, G., de Lima, M. S., Horta, B. L., Biederman, J., & Rohde, L. A. (2007). The worldwide prevalence of ADHD: A systematic review and metaregression analysis. *American Journal of Psychiatry, 164,* 942–948.

Pond, R. S., DeWall, C. N., Lambert, N. M., Deckman, T., Bonser, I. M., & Fincham, F. D. (2012). Repulsed by violence: Disgust sensitivity buffers trait, behavioral, and daily aggression. *Journal of Personality and Social Psychology, 102*(1), 175–188. doi:10.1037/a0024296

Poole, D. A., Lindsay, S. D., Memon, A., & Bull, R. (1995). Psychotherapy and the recovery of memories of childhood sexual abuse: U.S. and British practitioners' opinions, practices, and experiences. *Journal of Consulting and Clinical Psychology, 63,* 426–487.

Poon, S. H., Sim, K., Sum, M. Y., Kuswanto, C. N., & Baldessarini, R. J. (2012). Evidence-based options for treatment-resistant adult bipolar disorder patients. *Bipolar Disorders, 14,* 573–584.

Pope, A. W., & Bierman, K. L. (1999). Predicting adolescent peer problems and antisocial activities: The relative roles of aggression and dysregulation. *Developmental Psychology, 35,* 335–346.

Porter, S., & ten Brinke, L. (2008). Reading between the lies: Identifying concealed and falsified emotions in universal facial expressions. *Psychological Science, 19,* 508–514.

Portocarrero, J. S., Burright, R. G., & Donovick, P. J. (2007). Vocabulary and verbal fluency of bilingual and monolingual college students. *Archives of Clinical Neuropsychology, 22,* 415–422.

Posner, M. I., & Raichle, M. E. (1994). *Images of mind.* New York: W. H. Freeman and Company.

Post, R. M., Frye, M. A., Denicoff, G. S., Leverich, G. S., Dunn, R. T., Osuch, E. A., . . . Jajodia, K. (2008). Emerging trends in the treatment of rapid cycling bipolar disorder: A selected review. *Bipolar Disorders, 2,* 305–315.

Posthuma, D., & de Geus, E. J. C. (2006). Progress in the molecular-largenetic study of intelligence. *Current Directions in Psychological Science, 15,* 151–155.

Postman, L., & Underwood, B. J. (1973). Critical issues in interference theory. *Memory & Cognition, 1,* 19–40.

Postmes, T., & Spears, R. (1998). Deindividuation and anti-normative behavior: A meta-analysis. *Psychological Bulletin, 123,* 238–259.

Powell, R. A., Symbaluk, D. G., MacDonald, S. E., & Honey, P. L. (2009). *Introduction to learning and behavior* (3rd ed.). Belmont, CA: Wadsworth Cengage Learning.

Power, M. L., & Schulkin, J. (2009). *The evolution of obesity.* Baltimore, MD: Johns Hopkins University Press.

Prasada, S., & Pinker, S. (1993). Generalizations of regular and irregular morphology. *Language and Cognitive Processes, 8,* 1–56.

Pratkanis, A. R. (1992). The cargo-cult science of subliminal persuasion. *Skeptical Inquirer, 16,* 260–272.

Pressman, S. D., Cohen, S., Miller, G. E., Barkin, A., Rabin, B. S., & Treanor, J. J. (2005). Loneliness, social network size, and immune response to influenza vaccination in college freshmen. *Health Psychology, 24,* 297–306.

Price, J. L., & Davis, B. (2008). *The woman who can't forget: The extraordinary story of living with the most remarkable memory known to science.* New York: Free Press.

Prior, H., Schwartz, A., & Güntürkün, O. (2008). Mirror-induced behavior in the magpie (*Pica pica*): Evidence of self-recognition. *PLoS Biology, 6,* e202.

Prochaska, J. J., & Sallis, J. F. (2004). A randomized controlled trial of single versus multiple health behavior change: Promoting physical activity and nutrition among adolescents. *Health Psychology, 23,* 314–318.

Procopio, M., & Marriott, P. (2007). Intrauterine hormonal environment and risk of developing anorexia nervosa. *Archives of General Psychiatry, 64*(12), 1402–1407.

Protzko, J., Aronson, J., & Blair, C. (2013). How to make a young child smarter: Evidence from the database of raising intelligence. *Perspectives on Psychological Science, 8*(1), 25–40. doi:10.1177/1745691612462585

Provine, R. R. (2000). *Laughter: A scientific investigation.* New York: Viking.

Pruitt, D. G. (1998). Social conflict. In D. T. Gilbert, S. T. Fiske, & G. Lindzey (Eds.), *The handbook of social psychology* (4th ed., Vol. 2, pp. 470–503). New York: McGraw-Hill.

Punjabi, N. M. (2008). The epidemiology of adult obstructive sleep apnea. *Proceedings of the American Thoracic Society, 5,* 136–143.

Puterman, E., Lin, J., Blackburn, E. H., O'Donovan, A., Adler, N., & Epel, E. (2010). The power of exercise: Buffering the effect of chronic stress on telomere length. *PLoS ONE, 5,* e10837.

Pyc, M. A., & Rawson, K. A. (2009). Testing the retrieval effort hypothesis: Does greater difficulty correctly recalling information lead to higher levels of memory? *Journal of Memory and Language, 60,* 437–447.

Pyers, J. E., & Senghas, A. (2009). Language promotes false-belief understanding: Evidence from learners of a new sign language. *Psychological Science, 20*(7), 805–812.

Pyers, J. E., Shusterman, A., Senghas, A., Spelke, E. S., & Emmorey, K. (2010). Evidence from an emerging sign language reveals that language supports spatial cognition. *Proceedings of the National Academy of Sciences, USA,107,* 12116–12120.

Pyszczynski, T., Holt, J., & Greenberg, J. (1987). Depression, self-focused attention, and expectancy for positive and negative future life events for self and others. *Journal of Personality and Social Psychology, 52,* 994–1001.

Quattrone, G. A. (1982). Behavioral consequences of attributional bias. *Social Cognition, 1,* 358–378.

Querleu, D., Lefebvre, C., Titran, M., Renard, X., Morillon, M., & Crepin, G. (1984). Réactivité de nouveau-né de moins de deux heures de vie á la voix maternelle [Reactivity of a newborn at less than two hours of life to the mother's voice]. *Journal de Gynécologie Obstétrique et de Biologie de la Reproduction, 13,* 125–134.

Quiroga, R. Q., Reddy, L., Kreiman, G., Koch, C., & Fried, I. (2005). Invariant visual representation by single neurons in the human brain. *Nature, 435,* 1102–1107.

Quoidbach, J., Gilbert, D. T., & Wilson, T. D. (2013). The end of history illusion. *Science, 339,* 96–98.

Qureshi, A., & Lee-Chiong, T. (2004). Medications and their effects on sleep. *Medical Clinics of North America, 88,* 751–766.

Rabbitt, P., Diggle, P., Holland, F., & McInnes, L. (2004). Practice and drop-out effects during a 17-year longitudinal study of cognitive aging. *Journal of Gerontology: Psychological Sciences and Social Sciences, 59*(2), 84–97.

Race, E., Kcanc, M. M., & Verfaellie, M. (2011). Medial temporal lobe damage causes deficits in episodic memory and episodic future thinking not attributable to deficits in narrative construction. *Journal of Neuroscience, 31,* 10262–10269.

Radford, E., & Radford, M. A. (1949). *Encyclopedia of superstitions.* New York: Philosophical Library.

Rahe, R. H., Meyer, M., Smith, M., Klaer, G., & Holmes, T. H. (1964). Social stress and illness onset. *Journal of Psychosomatic Research, 8,* 35–44.

Raichle, M. E., & Mintun, M. A. (2006). Brain work and brain imaging. *Annual Review of Neuroscience, 29,* 449–476.

Rajaram, S. (2011). Collaboration both hurts and helps memory: A cognitive perspective. *Current Directions in Psychological Science, 20,* 76–81.

Rajaram, S., & Pereira-Pasarin, L. P. (2010). Collaborative memory: Cognitive research and theory. *Perspectives on Psychological Science, 6,* 649–663.

Ramachandran, V. S., & Altschuler, E. L. (2009). The use of visual feedback, in particular mirror visual feedback, in restoring brain function. *Brain, 132,* 1693–1710.

Ramachandran, V. S., & Blakeslee, S. (1998). *Phantoms in the brain: Probing the mysteries of the human mind.* New York: Morrow.

Ramachandran, V. S., Brang, D., & McGeoch, P. D. (2010). Dynamic reorganization of referred sensations by movements of phantom limbs. *NeuroReport, 21,* 727–730.

Ramachandran, V. S., Rodgers-Ramachandran, D., & Stewart, M. (1992). Perceptual correlates of massive cortical reorganization. *Science, 258,* 1159–1160.

Ramirez-Esparza, N., Gosling, S. D., Benet-Martinez, V., & Potter, J. P. (2004). Do bilinguals have two personalities? A special case of cultural frame-switching. *Journal of Research in Personality, 40,* 99–120.

Randall, A. (2012, May 5). Black women and fat. *New York Times.* Retrieved from http:// www.nytimes.com/2012/05/06/opinion/sunday/why-black-women-are-fat.html?_r=0

Rapaport, D. (1946). *Diagnostic psychological testing: The theory, statistical evaluation, and diagnostic application of a battery of tests.* Chicago: Year Book Publishers.

Rapoport, J., Chavez, A., Greenstein, D., Addington, A., & Gogtay, N. (2009). Autism-spectrum disorders and childhood onset schizophrenia: Clinical and biological contributions to a relationship revisited. *Journal of the American Academy of Child and Adolescent Psychiatry, 48,* 10–18.

Rappoport, J. L. (1990). Obsessive-compulsive disorder and basal ganglia dysfunction. *Psychological Medicine, 20,* 465–469.

Rauschecker, J. P., & Scott, S. K. (2009). Maps and streams in the auditory cortex: Nonhuman primates illuminate human speech processing. *Nature Neuroscience, 12,* 718–724.

Raz, A., Fan, J., & Posner, M. I. (2005). Hypnotic suggestion reduces conflict in the brain. *Proceedings of the National Academy of Sciences, 102,* 9978–9983.

Raz, A., Shapiro, T., Fan, J., & Posner, M. I. (2002). Hypnotic suggestion and the modulation of Stroop interference. *Archives of General Psychiatry, 59,* 1155–1161.

Raz, N. (2000). Aging of the brain and its impact on cognitive performance: Integration of structural and functional findings. In F. I. M. Craik & T. A. Salthouse (Eds.), *The handbook of aging and cognition* (pp. 1–90). Mahwah, NJ: Erlbaum.

Read, K. E. (1965). *The high valley.* London: Allen and Unwin.

Reason, J., & Mycielska, K. (1982). *Absent-minded?: The psychology of mental lapses and everyday errors.* Englewood Cliffs, NJ: Prentice-Hall.

Reber, A. S. (1967). Implicit learning of artificial grammars. *Journal of Verbal Learning and Verbal Behavior, 6,* 855–863.

Reber, A. S. (1996). *Implicit learning and tacit knowledge: An essay on the cognitive unconscious.* New York: Oxford University Press.

Reber, A. S., & Allen, R. (2000). Individual differences in implicit learning. In R. G. Kunzendorf & B. Wallace (Eds.), *Individual differences in conscious experience* (pp. 227–247). Philadelphia: John Benjamins.

Reber, A. S., Walkenfeld, F. F., & Hernstadt, R. (1991). Implicit learning: Individual differences and IQ. *Journal of Experimental Psychology: Learning, Memory, and Cognition, 17,* 888–896.

Reber, P. J., Gitelman, D. R., Parrish, T. B., & Mesulam, M. M. (2003). Dissociating explicit and implicit category knowledge with fMRI. *Journal of Cognitive Neuroscience, 15,* 574–583.

Recanzone, G. H., & Sutter, M. L. (2008). The biological basis of audition. *Annual Review of Psychology, 59,* 119–142.

Rechsthaffen, A., Gilliland, M. A., Bergmann, B. M., & Winter, J. B. (1983). Physiological correlates of prolonged sleep deprivation in rats. *Science, 221,* 182–184.

Redick, T. S., Shipstead, Z., Harrison, T. L., Hicks, K. L., Fried, D. E., Hambrick, D. Z., . . . Engle, R. W. (2013). No evidence of intelligence improvement after working memory training: A randomized, placebo-controlled study. *Journal of Experimental Psychology: General, 142,* 359–379. doi:10.1037/a002908

Reed, C. L., Klatzky, R. L., & Halgren, E. (2005). What vs. where in touch: An fMRI study. *NeuroImage, 25,* 718–726.

Reed, D. R. (2008). Birth of a new breed of supertaster. *Chemical Senses, 33,* 489–491.

Reed, G. (1988). *The psychology of anomalous experience* (rev. ed.). Buffalo, NY: Prometheus Books.

Regan, P. C. (1998). What if you can't get what you want? Willingness to compromise ideal mate selection standards as a function of sex, mate value, and relationship context. *Personality and Social Psychology Bulletin, 24,* 1294–1303.

Regier, T., & Kay, P. (2009). Language, thought, and color: Whorf was half right. *Trends in Cognitive Sciences, 13,* 439–446.

Reichbach, G. L. (2012, May 16). A judge's plea for pot [op-ed article]. *New York Times,* p. A27.

Reis, H. T., Maniaci, M. R., Caprariello, P. S., Eastwick, P. W., & Finkel, E. J. (2011). Familiarity does indeed promote attraction in live interaction. *Journal of Personality and Social Psychology, 101*(3), 557–570. doi:10.1037/a0022885

Reiss, D., & Marino, L. (2001). Mirror self-recognition in the bottlenose dolphin: A case of cognitive convergence. *Proceedings of the National Academy of Sciences, USA, 98,* 5937–5942.

Reissland, N. (1988). Neonatal imitation in the first hour of life: Observations in rural Nepal. *Developmental Psychology, 24,* 464–469.

Renner, K. E. (1964). Delay of reinforcement: A historical review. *Psychological Review, 61,* 341–361.

Renner, M. J., & Mackin, R. (1998). A life stress instrument for classroom use. *Teaching of Psychology, 25,* 46–48.

Rensink, R. A. (2002). Change detection. *Annual Review of Psychology, 53,* 245–277.

Rensink, R. A., O'Regan, J. K., & Clark, J. J. (1997). To see or not to see: The need for attention to perceive changes in scenes. *Psychological Science, 8,* 368–373.

Repacholi, B. M., & Gopnik, A. (1997). Early reasoning about desires: Evidence from 14- and 18-month-olds. *Developmental Psychology, 33,* 12–21.

Rescorla, R. A. (2006). Stimulus generalization of excitation and inhibition. *Quarterly Journal of Experimental Psychology, 59,* 53–67.

Rescorla, R. A., & Wagner, A. R. (1972). A theory of Pavlovian conditioning: Variations in effectiveness of reinforcement and nonreinforcement. In A. Black & W. F. Prokasky, Jr. (Eds.), *Classical conditioning II* (pp. 64–99). New York: Appleton-Century-Crofts.

Ressler, K. J., & Mayberg, H. S. (2007). Targeting abnormal neural circuits in mood and anxiety disorders: From the laboratory to the clinic. *Nature Neuroscience, 10,* 1116–1124.

Ressler, K. J., & Nemeroff, C. B. (1999). Role of norepinephrine in the pathophysiology and treatment of mood disorders. *Biological Psychiatry, 46,* 1219–1233.

Rice, K. G., Richardson, C. M. E., & Clark, D. (2012). Perfectionism, procrastination, and psychological distress. *Journal of Counsiling Psychology, 39,* 288–302.

Richards, M., Black, S., Mishra, G., Gale, C. R., Deary, I. J., & Batty, D. G. (2009). IQ in childhood and the metabolic syndrome in middle age: Extended follow-up of the 1946 British birth cohort study. *Intelligence, 37*(6), 567–572.

Richards, M. H., Crowe, P. A., Larson, R., & Swarr, A. (1998). Developmental patterns and gender differences in the experience of peer companionship during adolescence. *Child Development, 69,* 154–163.

Richert, E. S. (1997). Excellence with equity in identification and programming. In N. Colangelo & G. A. Davis (Eds.), *Handbook of gifted education* (2nd ed., pp. 75–88). Boston: Allyn & Bacon.

Richters, J., de Visser, R., Rissel, C., & Smith, A. (2006). Sexual practices at last heterosexual encounter and occurrence of orgasm in a national survey. *Journal of Sex Research, 43,* 217–226.

Ridenour, T. A., & Howard, M. O. (2012). Inhalants abuse: Status of etiology and intervention. In J. C. Verster, K. Brady, M. Galanter, & P. Conrod (Eds.), *Drug abuse and addiction in medical illness: Causes, consequences, and treatment* (pp. 189–199). New York: Springer.

Rieber, R. W. (Ed.). (1980). *Wilhelm Wundt and the making of scientific psychology.* New York: Plenum Press.

Riefer, D. M., Kevari, M. K., & Kramer, D. L. F. (1995). Name that tune: Eliciting the tip-of-the-tongue experience using auditory stimuli. *Psychological Reports, 77,* 1379–1390.

Rimer, J., Dwan, K., Lawlor, D. A., Greig, C. A., McMurdo, M., Morley, W., & Mead, G. E. (2012). Exercise for depression. *Cochrane Database of Systematic Reviews, 7,* CD004366.

Ringach, D. L., & Jentsch, J. D. (2009). We must face the threats. *The Journal of Neuroscience, 29,* 11417–11418.

Risko, E. F., Anderson, N., Sarwal, A., Engelhardt, M., & Kingstone, A. (2012). Every attention: Variation in mind wandering and memory in a lecture. *Applied Cognitive Psychology, 26,* 234–242.

Risman, J. E., Coyle, J. T., Green, R. W., Javitt, D. C., Benes, F. M., Heckers, S., & Grace, A. A. (2008). Circuit-based framework for understanding neurotransmitter and risk gene interactions in schizophrenia. *Trends in Neurosciences, 31,* 234–242.

Rizzolatti, G. (2004). The mirror-neuron system and imitation. In S. Hurley & N. Chater (Eds.), *Perspectives on imitation: From mirror neurons to memes* (pp. 55–76). Cambridge, MA: MIT Press.

Rizzolatti, G., & Craighero, L. (2004). The mirror-neuron system. *Annual Review of Neuroscience, 27,* 169–192.

Rizzolatti, G., Fabbri-Destro, M., & Cattaneo, L. (2009). Mirror neurons and their clinical relevance. *Nature Clinical Practice Neurology, 5,* 24–34.

Rizzolatti, G., & Sinigaglia, C. (2012). The functional role of the parieto-frontal mirror circuit. *Nature Reviews Neuroscience, 11,* 264–274.

Roberson, D., Davidoff, J., Davies, I. R. L., & Shapiro, L. R. (2004). The development of color categories in two languages: A longitudinal study. *Journal of Experimental Psychology: General, 133,* 554–571.

Roberts, G. A. (1991). Delusional belief and meaning in life: A preferred reality? *British Journal of Psychiatry, 159,* 20–29.

Roberts, G. A., & McGrady, A. (1996). Racial and gender effects on the relaxation response: Implications for the development of hypertension. *Biofeedback and Self-Regulation, 21,* 51–62.

Robertson, L. C. (1999). What can spatial deficits teach us about feature binding and spatial maps? *Visual Cognition, 6,* 409–430.

Robertson, L. C. (2003). Binding, spatial attention and perceptual awareness. *Nature Reviews Neuroscience, 4,* 93–102.

Robins, L. N., Helzer, J. E., Hesselbrock, M., & Wish, E. (1980). Vietnam veterans three years after Vietnam. In L. Brill & C. Winick (Eds.), *The yearbook of substance use and abuse* (Vol. 11). New York: Human Sciences Press.

Robins, R. W., Fraley, R. C., & Krueger, R. F. (Eds.). (2007). *Handbook of research methods in personality psychology*. New York: Guilford Press.

Robinson, A., & Clinkenbeard, P. R. (1998). Giftedness: An exceptionality examined. *Annual Review of Psychology, 49,* 117–139.

Robinson, D. N. (1995). *An intellectual history of psychology*. Madison: University of Wisconsin Press.

Rodieck, R. W. (1998). *The first steps in seeing*. Sunderland, MA: Sinauer.

Roediger, H. L., III. (2000). Why retrieval is the key process to understanding human memory. In E. Tulving (Ed.), *Memory, consciousness, and the brain: The Tallinn conference* (pp. 52–75). Philadelphia: Psychology Press.

Roediger, H. L., III, & Karpicke, J. D. (2006). Test-enhanced learning: Taking memory tests improves long-term retention. *Psychological Science, 17,* 249–255.

Roediger, H. L., III, & McDermott, K. B. (1995). Creating false memories: Remembering words not presented in lists. *Journal of Experimental Psychology: Learning, Memory, and Cognition, 21,* 803–814.

Roediger, H. L., III, & McDermott, K. B. (2000). Tricks of memory. *Current Directions in Psychological Science, 9,* 123–127.

Roediger, H. L., III, Weldon, M. S., & Challis, B. H. (1989). Explaining dissociations between implicit and explicit measures of retention: A processing account. In H. L. Roediger, III & F. I. M. Craik (Eds.), *Varieties of memory and consciousness: Essays in honor of Endel Tulving* (pp. 3–41). Hillsdale, NJ: Erlbaum.

Rogers, C. R. (1951). *Client-centered therapy: Its current practice, implications, and theory*. Boston: Houghton Mifflin.

Rogers, T. B., Kuiper, N. A., & Kirker, W. S. (1977). Self-reference and the encoding of personal information. *Journal of Personality and Social Psychology, 35,* 677–688.

Roig, M., Skriver, K., Lundbye-Jensen, J., Kiens, B., & Nielsen, J. B. (2012). A single bout of exercise improves motor memory. *PLoS One, 7,* e44594. doi:10.1371/journal.pone.0044594

Romero-Corral, A., Montori, V. M., Somers, V. K., Korinek, J., Thomas, R. J., Allison, T. G., . . . Lopez-Jiminez, F. (2006). Association of body weight with total mortality and with cardiovascular events in coronary artery disease: A systematic review of cohort studies. *Lancet, 368*(9536), 666–678.

Ronay, R., & Galinsky, A. D. (2011). Lex talionis: Testosterone and the law of retaliation. *Journal of Experimental Social Psychology, 47*(3), 702–705. doi:10.1016/j.jesp.2010.11.009

Rosch, E. H. (1973). Natural categories. *Cognitive Psychology, 4,* 328–350.

Rosch, E. H. (1975). Cognitive representations of semantic categories. *Journal of Experimental Psychology: General, 104,* 192–233.

Rosch, E. H., & Mervis, C. B. (1975). Family resemblances: Studies in the internal structure of categories. *Cognitive Psychology, 7,* 573–605.

Rose, S. P. R. (2002). Smart drugs: Do they work? Are they ethical? Will they be legal? *Nature Reviews Neuroscience, 3,* 975–979.

Roseman, I. J. (1984). Cognitive determinants of emotion: A structural theory. *Review of Personality and Social Psychology, 5,* 11–36.

Roseman, I. J., & Smith, C. A. (2001). Appraisal theory: Overview, assumptions, varieties and controversies. In K. R. Scherer, A. Schorr, & T. Johnstone (Eds.), *Appraisal processes in emotion: Theory, methods, research* (pp. 3–19). New York: Oxford University Press.

Rosenbaum, J. E. (2009). Patient teenagers? A comparison of the sexual behavior of virginity pledgers and matched nonpledgers. *Pediatrics, 123*(1), e110–e120.

Rosenberg, T. (2013, March 27). The destructive influence of imaginary peers. *New York Times*. Retrieved from http://opinionator.blogs.nytimes.com/2013/03/27/the-destructive-influence-of-imaginary-peers/

Rosenhan, D. (1973). On being sane in insane places. *Science, 179,* 250–258.

Rosenkranz, K., Williamon, A., & Rothwell, J. C. (2007). Motorcortical excitability and synaptic plasticity is enhanced in professional musicians. *The Journal of Neuroscience, 27,* 5200–5206.

Rosenstein, M. J., Milazzo-Sayre, L. J., & Manderscheid, R. W. (1990). Characteristics of persons using specifically inpatient, outpatient, and partial care programs in 1986. In M. A. Sonnenschein (Ed.), *Mental health in the United States* (pp. 139–172). Washington, DC: U.S. Government Printing Office.

Rosenthal, R., & Fode, K. L. (1963). The effect of experimenter bias on the performance of the albino rat. *Behavioral Science, 8,* 183–189.

Ross, L. (1977). The intuitive psychologist and his shortcomings: Distortions in the attribution process. *Advances in Experimental Social Psychology, 10,* 173–220.

Ross, L., Amabile, T. M., & Steinmetz, J. L. (1977). Social roles, social control, and biases in social-perception processes. *Journal of Personality and Social Psychology, 35,* 485–494.

Ross, L., & Nisbett, R. E. (1991). *The person and the situation*. New York: McGraw-Hill.

Ross, M., Blatz, C. W., & Schryer, E. (2008). Social memory processes. In H. L. Roediger III (Ed.), *Learning and memory: A comprehensive reference* (Vol. 2, pp. 911–926). Oxford, England: Elsevier.

Rossano, F., Carpenter, M., & Tomasello, M. (2012). One-year-old infants follow others' voice direction. *Psychological Science, 23*(11), 1298–1302. doi:10.1177/0956797612450032

Rosvall, M., & Bergstrom, C. T. (2008). Maps of random walks on complex networks reveal community structure. *Proceedings of the National Academy of Sciences, USA, 105,* 1118–1123.

Roth, H. P., & Caron, H. S. (1978). Accuracy of doctors' estimates and patients' statements on adherence to a drug regimen. *Clinical Pharmacology and Therapeutics, 23,* 361–370.

Rothbart, M. K., & Bates, J. E. (1998). Temperament. In W. Damon (Series Ed.) & N. Eisenberg (Vol. Ed.), *Handbook of child psychology: Vol. 3. Social, emotional and personality development* (5th ed., pp. 105–176). New York: Wiley.

Rothbaum, B. O., & Schwartz, A. C. (2002). Exposure therapy for posttraumatic stress disorder. *American Journal of Psychotherapy, 56,* 59–75.

Rotter, J. B. (1966). Generalized expectancies for internal versus external locus of control of reinforcement. *Psychological Monographs: General and Applied, 80,* 1–28.

Rotton, L. (1992). Trait humor and longevity: Do comics have the last laugh? *Health Psychology, 11,* 262–266.

Roy-Byrne, P. P., & Cowley, D. (1998). *Pharmacological treatment of panic, generalized anxiety, and phobic disorders.* New York: Oxford University Press.

Roy-Byrne, P. P., & Cowley, D. S. (2002). Pharmacological treatments for panic disorder, generalized anxiety disorder, specific phobia, and social anxiety disorder. In P. E. Nathan & J. M. Gorman (Eds.), *A guide to treatments that work* (2nd ed., pp. 337–365). New York: Oxford University Press.

Rozenblit, L., & Keil, F. C. (2002). The misunderstood limits of folk science: An illusion of explanatory depth. *Cognitive Science, 26,* 521–562.

Rozin, P. (1968). Are carbohydrate and protein intakes separately regulated? *Journal of Comparative and Physiological Psychology, 65,* 23–29.

Rozin, P., Bauer, R., & Catanese, D. (2003). Food and life, pleasure and worry, among American college students: Gender differences and regional similarities. *Journal of Personality and Social Psychology, 85,* 132–141.

Rozin, P., Dow, S., Moscovitch, M., & Rajaram, S. (1998). What causes humans to begin and end a meal? A role for memory for what has been eaten, as evidenced by a study of multiple meal eating in amnesic patients. *Psychological Science, 9,* 392–396.

Rozin, P., Kabnick, K., Pete, E., Fischler, C., & Shields, C. (2003). The ecology of eating: Smaller portion size in France than in the United States helps to explain the French paradox. *Psychological Science, 14,* 450–454.

Rozin, P., & Kalat, J. W. (1971). Specific hungers and poison avoidance as adaptive specializations of learning. *Psychological Review, 78,* 459–486.

Rozin, P., Scott, S., Dingley, M., Urbanek, J. K., Jiang, H., & Kaltenbach, M. (2011). Nudge to nobesity: I. Minor changes in accessibility decrease food intake. *Judgment and Decision Making, 6,* 323–332.

Rozin, P., Trachtenberg, S., & Cohen, A. B. (2001). Stability of body image and body image dissatisfaction in American college students over about the last 15 years. *Appetite, 37,* 245–248.

Rubin, M., & Badea, C. (2012). They're all the same! . . . but for several different reasons: A review of the multicausal nature of perceived group variability. *Current Directions in Psychological Science, 21*(6), 367–372. doi:10.1177/0963721412457363

Rubin, Z. (1973). *Liking and loving.* New York: Holt, Rinehart & Winston.

Rubin-Fernandez, P., & Geurts, B. (2012). How to pass the false-belief task before your fourth birthday. *Psychological Science, 24*(1), 27–33. doi:10.1177/0956797612447819

Rudman, L. A., Ashmore, R. D., & Gary, M. L. (2001). "Unlearning" automatic biases: The malleability of implicit prejudice and stereotypes. *Journal of Personality and Social Psychology, 81,* 856–868.

Rusbult, C. E. (1983). A longitudinal test of the investment model: The development (and deterioration) of satisfaction and commitment in heterosexual involvements. *Journal of Personality and Social Psychology, 45,* 101–117.

Rusbult, C. E., & Van Lange, P. A. M. (2003). Interdependence, interaction and relationships. *Annual Review of Psychology, 54,* 351–375.

Rusbult, C. E., Verette, J., Whitney, G. A., & Slovik, L. F. (1991). Accommodation processes in close relationships: Theory and preliminary empirical evidence. *Journal of Personality and Social Psychology, 60,* 53–78.

Ruscio, A. M., Stein, D. J., Chiu, W. T., Kessler, R. C. (2010). The epidemiology of obsessive-compulsive disorder in the National Comorbidity Survey Replication. *Molecular Psychiatry, 15,* 53–63.

Rushton, J. P. (1995). Asian achievement, brain size, and evolution: Comment on A. H. Yee. *Educational Psychology Review, 7,* 373–380.

Rushton, J. P., & Templer, D. I. (2009). National differences in intelligence, crime, income, and skin color. *Intelligence, 37*(4), 341–346.

Russell, B. (1945). *A history of Western philosophy.* New York: Simon & Schuster.

Russell, J., Gee, B., & Bullard, C. (2012). Why do young children hide by closing their eyes? Self-visibility and the developing concept of self. *Journal of Cognition and Development, 13*(4), 550–576. doi:10.108 0/15248372.2011.594826

Russell, J. A. (1980). A circumplex model of affect. *Journal of Personality and Social Psychology, 39,* 1161–1178.

Rutledge, R. B., Lazzaro, S. C., Lau, B., Myers, C. E., Gluck, M. A., & Glimcher, P. W. (2009). Dopaminergic drugs modulate learning rates and perseveration in Parkinson's patients in a dynamic foraging task. *Journal of Neuroscience, 29,* 15104–15114.

Rutter, M., O'Connor, T. G., & the English and Romanian Adoptees Study Team. (2004). Are there biological programming effects for psychological development? Findings from a study of Romanian adoptees. *Developmental Psychology, 40,* 81–94.

Rutter, M., & Silberg, J. (2002). Gene–environment interplay in relation to emotional and behavioral disturbance. *Annual Review of Psychology, 53,* 463–490.

Ryan, R. M., & Deci, E. L. (2000). Self-determination theory and the facilitation of intrinsic motivation, social development, and wellbeing. *American Psychologist, 55,* 68–78.

Ryle, G. (1949). *The Concept of Mind,* Hutchinson, London.

Sachs, J. S. (1967). Recognition of semantic, syntactic, and lexical changes in sentences. *Psychonomic Bulletin & Review, 1,* 17–18.

Sacks, O. (1995). *An anthropologist on Mars.* New York: Knopf.

Sacks, O. (1996). *An anthropologist on Mars* (ppbk). Visalia, CA: Vintage.

Saks, E. R. (2013, January 25). Successful and schizophrenic. *New York Times.* Retrieved from http://www.nytimes.com/2013/01/27 /opinion/sunday/schizophrenic-not-stupid.html

Saffran, J. R., Aslin, R. N., & Newport, E. I. (1996). Statistical learning by 8-month-old infants. *Science, 274,* 1926–1928.

Sahakian, B., & Morein-Zamir, S. (2007). Professor's little helper. *Nature, 450*(7173), 1157–1159.

Sakuraba, S., Sakai, S., Yamanaka, M., Yokosawa, Y., & Hirayama, K. (2012). Does the human dorsal stream really process a category for tools? *Journal of Neuroscience, 32,* 3949–3953.

Sallet, J., Mars, R. B., Noonan, M. P., Andersson, J. L., O'Reilly, J. X., Jbabdi, S., . . . Rushworth, M. F. S. (2011). Social network size affects neural circuits in macaques. *Science, 334*(6056), 697–700. doi:10.1126/science.1210027

Salmon, D. P., & Bondi, M. W. (2009). Neuropsychological assessment of dementia. *Annual Review of Psychology, 60*, 257–282.

Salovey, P., & Grewal, D. (2005). The science of emotional intelligence. *Current Directions in Psychological Science, 14*(6), 281–285.

Salthouse, T. A. (1984). Effects of age and skill in typing. *Journal of Experimental Psychology: General, 113*, 345–371.

Salthouse, T. A. (1987). Age, experience, and compensation. In C. Schooler & K. W. Schaie (Eds.), *Cognitive functioning and social structure over the life course* (pp. 142–150). Norwood, NJ: Ablex.

Salthouse, T. A. (1996a). General and specific mediation of adult age differences in memory. *Journal of Gerontology: Series B: Psychological Sciences and Social Sciences, 51B*, P30–P42.

Salthouse, T. A. (1996b). The processing-speed theory of adult age differences in cognition. *Psychological Review, 103*, 403–428.

Salthouse, T. A. (2000). Pressing issues in cognitive aging. In D. Park & N. Schwartz (Eds.), *Cognitive aging: A primer* (pp. 43–54). Philadelphia: Psychology Press.

Salthouse, T. A. (2001). Structural models of the relations between age and measures of cognitive functioning. *Intelligence, 29*, 93–115.

Salthouse, T. A. (2006). Mental exercise and mental aging. *Perspectives on Psychological Science, 1*(1), 68–87.

Salvatore, J. E., Kuo, S. I.-C., Steele, R. D., Simpson, J. A., & Collins, W. A. (2011). Recovering from conflict in romantic relationships: A developmental perspective. *Psychological Science, 22*(3), 376–383. doi:10.1177/0956797610397055

Sampson, R. J., & Laub, J. H. (1995). Understanding variability in lives through time: Contributions of life-course criminology. *Studies of Crime Prevention, 4*, 143–158.

Sandin, R. H., Enlund, G., Samuelsson, P., & Lenmarken, C. (2000). Awareness during anesthesia: A prospective case study. *Lancet, 355*, 707–711.

Sapolsky, R. M., & Share, L. J. (2004). A pacific culture among wild baboons: Its emergence and transmission. *PLoS Biology, 2*, e106.

Sara, S. J. (2000). Retrieval and reconsolidation: Toward a neurobiology of remembering. *Learning & Memory, 7*, 73–84.

Sarris, V. (1989). Max Wertheimer on seen motion: Theory and evidence. *Psychological Research, 51*, 58–68.

Sarter, M. (2006). Preclinical research into cognition enhancers. *Trends in Pharmacological Sciences, 27*, 602–608.

Sasanuma, S. (1975). Kana and kanji processing in Japanese aphasics. *Brain and Language, 2*, 369–383.

Satcher, D. (2001). *The Surgeon General's call to action to promote sexual health and responsible sexual behavior.* Washington, DC: U.S. Government Printing Office.

Satterwhite, C. L., Torrone, E., Meites, E., Dunne, E. F., Mahajan, R., Ocfernia, M. C., . . . Weinstock, H. (2013). Sexually transmitted infections among U. S. women and men: Prevalence and incidence estimates, 2008. *Sexually Transmitted Diseases, 40*(3), 187–193.

Savage, C. R., Deckersbach, T., Heckers, S., Wagner, A. D., Schacter, D. L., Alpert, N. M., . . . Rauch, S. L. (2001). Prefrontal regions supporting spontaneous and directed application of verbal learning strategies: Evidence from PET. *Brain, 124*, 219–231.

Savage-Rumbaugh, S., & Lewin, R. (1996). *Kanzi: The ape on the brink of the human mind.* New York: Wiley.

Savage-Rumbaugh, S., Shanker, G., & Taylor, T. J. (1998). *Apes, language, and the human mind.* Oxford, England: Oxford University Press.

Savic, I., Berglund, H., & Lindstrom, P. (2005). Brain response to putative pheromones in homosexual men. *Proceedings of the National Academy of Sciences, USA, 102*, 7356–7361.

Savic, I., & Lindstrom, P. (2008). PET and MRI show differences in cerebral asymmetry and functional connectivity between homo- and heterosexual subjects. *Proceedings of the National Academy of Sciences, USA, 105*(27), 9403–9408.

Sawa, A., & Snyder, S. H. (2002). Schizophrenia: Diverse approaches to a complex disease. *Science, 295*, 692–695.

Sawyer, T. F. (2000). Francis Cecil Sumner: His views and influence on African American higher education. *History of Psychology, 3*(2), 122–141.

Scarborough, E., & Furumoto, L. (1987). *Untold lives: The first generation of American women psychologists.* New York: Columbia University Press.

Scarr, S., Pakstis, A. J., Katz, S. H., & Barker, W. B. (1977). Absence of a relationship between degree of White ancestry and intellectual skills within a Black population. *Human Genetics, 39*(1), 69–86.

Schachter, S. (1982). Recidivism and self-cure of smoking and obesity. *American Psychologist, 37*, 436–444.

Schachter, S., & Singer, J. E. (1962). Cognitive, social, and psychological determinants of emotional state. *Physiological Review, 69*, 379–399.

Schacter, D. L. (1987). Implicit memory: History and current status. *Journal of Experimental Psychology: Learning, Memory, and Cognition, 13*, 501–518.

Schacter, D. L. (1996). *Searching for memory: The brain, the mind, and the past.* New York: Basic Books.

Schacter, D. L. (1999). The seven sins of memory: Insights from psychology and cognitive neuroscience. *American Psychologist, 54*(3), 182–203.

Schacter, D. L. (2001a). *Forgotten ideas, neglected pioneers: Richard Semon and the story of memory.* Philadelphia: Psychology Press.

Schacter, D. L. (2001b). *The seven sins of memory: How the mind forgets and remembers.* Boston: Houghton Mifflin.

Schacter, D. L. (2012). Adaptive constructive processes and the future of memory. *American Psychologist, 67*, 603–613.

Schacter, D. L., & Addis, D. R. (2007). The cognitive neuroscience of constructive memory: Remembering the past and imagining the future. *Philosophical Transactions of the Royal Society of London. Series B: Biological Sciences, 362*, 773–786.

Schacter, D. L., Addis, D. R., & Buckner, R. L. (2008). Episodic simulation of future events: Concepts, data, and applications. *Annals of the New York Academy of Sciences, 1124*, 39–60.

Schacter, D. L., Addis, D. R., Hassabis, D., Martin, V. C., Spreng, R. N., & Szpunar, K. K. (2012). The future of memory: Remembering, imagining, and the brain. *Neuron, 16*, 582–583.

Schacter, D. L., Alpert, N. M., Savage, C. R., Rauch, S. L., & Albert, M. S. (1996). Conscious recollection and the human hippocampal formation: Evidence from positron emission tomography. *Proceedings of the National Academy of Sciences, USA, 93*, 321–325.

Schacter, D. L., & Buckner, R. L. (1998). Priming and the brain. *Neuron, 20*, 185–195.

Schacter, D. L., & Curran, T. (2000). Memory without remembering and remembering without memory: Implicit and false memories. In M. S. Gazzaniga (Ed.), *The new cognitive neurosciences* (2nd ed., pp. 829–840). Cambridge, MA: MIT Press.

Schacter, D. L., Dobbins, I. G., & Schnyer, D. M. (2004). Specificity of priming: A cognitive neuroscience perspective. *Nature Reviews Neuroscience, 5*, 853–862.

Schacter, D. L., Gaesser, B., & Addis, D. R. (2012). Remembering the past and imagining the future in the elderly. *Gerontologist, 59*(2), 143–151. doi:10.1159/000342198

Schacter, D. L., Guerin, S. A., & St. Jacques, P. L. (2011). Memory distortion: An adaptive perspective. *Trends in Cognitive Sciences, 15*, 467–474.

Schacter, D. L., Harbluk, J. L., & McLachlan, D. R. (1984). Retrieval without recollection: An experimental analysis of source amnesia. *Journal of Verbal Learning and Verbal Behavior, 23*, 593–611.

Schacter, D. L., Israel, L., & Racine, C. A. (1999). Suppressing false recognition in younger and older adults: The distinctiveness heuristic. *Journal of Memory and Language, 40*, 1–24.

Schacter, D. L., & Loftus, E. F. (2013). Memory and law: What can cognitive neuroscience contribute? *Nature Neuroscience, 16*, 119–123.

Schacter, D. L., Reiman, E., Curran, T., Yun, L. S., Bandy, D., McDermott, K. B., & Roediger, H. L., III. (1996). Neuroanatomical correlates of veridical and illusory recognition memory: Evidence from positron emission tomography. *Neuron, 17*, 267–274.

Schacter, D. L., & Tulving, E. (1994). *Memory systems 1994.* Cambridge, MA: MIT Press.

Schacter, D. L., Wagner, A. D., & Buckner, R. L. (2000). Memory systems of 1999. In E. Tulving & F. I. M. Craik (Eds.), *The Oxford handbook of memory* (pp. 627–643). New York: Oxford University Press.

Schacter, D. L., Wig, G. S., & Stevens, W. D. (2007). Reductions in cortical activity during priming. *Current Opinion in Neurobiology, 17*, 171–176.

Schafer, R. B., & Keith, P. M. (1980). Equity and depression among married couples. *Social Psychology Quarterly, 43*, 430–435.

Schaie, K. W. (1996). *Intellectual development in adulthood: The Seattle Longitudinal Study.* New York: Cambridge University Press.

Schaie, K. W. (2005). *Developmental influences on adult intelligence: The Seattle Longitudinal Study.* New York: Oxford University Press.

Schapira, A. H. V., Emre, M., Jenner, P., & Poewe, W. (2009). Levodopa in the treatment of Parkinson's disease. *European Journal of Neurology, 16*, 982–989.

Schatzberg, A. F., Cole, J. O., & DeBattista, C. (2003). *Manual of clinical psychopharmacology* (4th ed.). Washington, DC: American Psychiatric Publishing.

Schenk, T., Ellison, A., Rice, N., & Milner, A. D. (2005). The role of V5/MT+ in the control of catching movements: An rTMS study. *Neuropsychologia, 43*, 189–198.

Scherer, K. R. (1999). Appraisal theory. In T. Dalgleish & M. Power (Eds.), *Handbook of cognition and emotion* (pp. 637–663). New York: Wiley.

Scherer, K. R. (2001). The nature and study of appraisal: A review of the issues. In K. R. Scherer, A. Schorr, & T. Johnstone (Eds.), *Appraisal processes in emotion: Theory, methods, research* (pp. 369–391). New York: Oxford University Press.

Schiff, M., Duyme, M., Stewart, J., Tomkiewicz, S., & Feingold, J. (1978). Intellectual status of working class children adopted early in upper middle class families. *Science, 200*, 1503–1504.

Schildkraut, J. J. (1965). The catecholamine hypothesis of affective disorders: A review of supporting evidence. *American Journal of Psychiatry, 122*, 509–522.

Schiller, D., Monfils, M. H., Raio, C. M., Johnson, D. C., LeDoux, J. E., & Phelps, E. A. (2010). Preventing the return of fear in humans using reconsolidation update mechanisms. *Nature, 463*, 49–54.

Schilling, O. K., Wahl, H.-W., & Wiegering, S. (2013). Affective development in advanced old age: Analyses of terminal change in positive and negative affect. *Developmental Psychology, 49*(5), 1011–1020. doi:10.1037/a0028775

Schlegel, A., & Barry, H., III. (1991). *Adolescence: An anthropological inquiry.* New York: Free Press.

Schlesinger, J. *The insanity hoax: Exposing the myth of the mad genius.* Ardsley-on-Hudson, NY: Shrinktunes Media.

Schmader, T., Johns, M., & Forbes, C. (2008). An integrated process model of stereotype threat effects on performance. *Psychological Review, 115*, 336–356.

Schmidt, F. L., & Hunter, J. E. (1998). The validity and utility of selection methods in personnel psychology: Practical and theoretical implications of 85 years of research findings. *Psychological Bulletin, 124*, 262–274.

Schmitt, D. P., Jonason, P. K., Byerley, G. J., Flores, S. D., Illbeck, B. E., O'Leary, K. N., & Qudrat, A. (2012). A reexamination of sex differences in sexuality: New studies reveal old truths. *Current Directions in Psychological Science, 21*(2), 135–139. doi:10.1177/0963721412436808

Schmitt, D. P., Realo, A., Voracek, M., & Allik, J. (2008). Why can't a man be more like a woman? Sex differences in personality traits across 55 cultures. *Journal of Personality and Social Psychology, 94*, 168–182.

Schneider, B. H., Atkinson, L., & Tardif, C. (2001). Child–parent attachment and children's peer relations: A quantitative review. *Developmental Psychology, 37*, 86–100.

Schnorr, J. A., & Atkinson, R. C. (1969). Repetition versus imagery instructions in the short- and long-term retention of paired associates. *Psychonomic Science, 15*, 183–184.

Schoenemann, P. T., Sheenan, M. J., & Glotzer, L. D. (2005). Prefrontal white matter volume is disproportionately larger in humans than in other primates. *Nature Neuroscience, 8*, 242–252.

Schonberg, T., O'Doherty, J. P., Joel, D., Inzelberg, R., Segev, Y., & Daw, N. D. (2009). Selective impairment of prediction error signaling in human dorsolateral but not ventral striatum in Parkinson's disease patients: Evidence from a model-based fMRI study. *NeuroImage, 49*, 772–781.

Schott, B. J., Henson, R. N., Richardson-Klavehn, A., Becker, C., Thoma, V., Heinze, H. J., & Duzel, E. (2005). Redefining implicit and explicit memory: The functional neuroanatomy of priming, remembering, and control of retrieval. *Proceedings of the National Academy of Sciences, USA, 102*, 1257–1262.

Schouwenburg, H. C. (1995). Academic procrastination: Theoretical notions, measurement, and research. In J. R. Ferrari, J. L. Johnson, & W. G. McCown (Eds.), *Procrastination and task avoidance: Theory, research, and treatment* (pp. 71–96). New York: Plenum Press.

Schreiner, C. E., Read, H. L., & Sutter, M. L. (2000). Modular organization of frequency integration in primary auditory cortex. *Annual Review of Neuroscience, 23*, 501–529.

Schreiner, C. E., & Winer, J. A. (2007). Auditory cortex mapmaking: Principles, projections, and plasticity. *Neuron, 56*, 356–365.

Schubert, T. W., & Koole, S. L. (2009). The embodied self: Making a fist enhances men's power-related self-conceptions. *Journal of Experimental Social Psychology, 45*, 828–834.

Schultz, D., Izard, C. E., & Bear, G. (2004). Children's emotion processing: Relations to emotionality and aggression. *Development and Psychopathology, 16*(2), 371–387.

Schultz, D. P., & Schultz, S. E. (1987). *A history of modern psychology* (4th ed.). San Diego: Harcourt Brace Jovanovich.

Schultz, W. (2006). Behavioral theories and the neurophysiology of reward. *Annual Review of Psychology, 57*, 87–115.

Schultz, W. (2007). Behavioral dopamine signals. *Trends in Neurosciences, 30*, 203–210.

Schultz, W., Dayan, P., & Montague, P. R. (1997). A neural substrate of prediction and reward. *Science, 275*, 1593–1599.

Schwartz, B. L. (2002). *Tip-of-the-tongue states: Phenomenology, mechanisms, and lexical retrieval.* Mahwah, NJ: Erlbaum.

Schwartz, C. E., Wright, C. I., Shin, L. M., Kagan, J., & Rauch, S. L. (2003). Inhibited and uninhibited infants "grown up": Adult amygdalar response to novelty. *Science, 300,* 1952–1953.

Schwartz, J. H., & Westbrook, G. L. (2000). The cytology of neurons. In E. R. Kandel, G. H. Schwartz, & T. M. Jessell (Eds.), *Principles of neural science* (pp. 67–104). New York: McGraw-Hill.

Schwartz, S., & Maquet, P. (2002). Sleep imaging and the neuropsychological assessment of dreams. *Trends in Cognitive Sciences, 6,* 23–30.

Schwartzman, A. E., Gold, D., & Andres, D. (1987). Stability of intelligence: A 40-year follow-up. *Canadian Journal of Psychology, 41,* 244–256.

Schwarz, N., & Clore, G. L. (1983). Mood, misattribution, and judgments of well-being: Informative and directive functions of affective states. *Journal of Personality and Social Psychology, 45,* 513–523.

Schwarz, N., Mannheim, Z., & Clore, G. L. (1988). How do I feel about it? The informative function of affective states. In K. Fiedler & J. Forgas (Eds.), *Affect cognition and social behavior: New evidence and integrative attempts* (pp. 44–62). Toronto: C. J. Hogrefe.

Schweizer, T. A., Ware, J., Fischer, C. E., Craik, F. I. M., & Bialystok, E. (2012). Bilingualism as a contributor to cognitive reserve: Evidence from brain atrophy in Alzheimer's disease. *Cortex, 48,* 991–996.

Scoville, W. B., & Milner, B. (1957). Loss of recent memory after bilateral hippocampal lesions. *Journal of Neurology, Neurosurgery, and Psychiatry, 20,* 11–21.

Scribner, S. (1975). Recall of classical syllogisms: A cross-cultural investigation of errors on logical problems. In R. J. Falmagne (Ed.), *Reasoning: Representation and process in children and adults* (pp. 153–173). Hillsdale, NJ: Erlbaum.

Scribner, S. (1984). Studying working intelligence. In B. Rogoff & J. Lave (Eds.), *Everyday cognition: Its development in social context* (pp. 9–40). Cambridge, MA: Harvard University Press.

Sedlmeier, P., Eberth, J., Schwarz, M., Zimmermann, D., Haarig, F., Jaeger, S., & Kunze, S. (2012). The psychological effects of meditation: A meta-analysis. *Psychological Bulletin, 138,* 1139–1171.

Seeman, T. E., Dubin, L. F., & Seeman, M. (2003). Religiosity/spirituality and health: A critical review of the evidence for biological pathways. *American Psychologist, 58,* 53–63.

Segall, M. H., Lonner, W. J., & Berry, J. W. (1998). Cross-cultural psychology as a scholarly discipline: On the flowering of culture in behavioral research. *American Psychologist, 53*(10), 1101–1110.

Seidman, G. (2013). Self-presentation and belonging on Facebook: How personality influences social media use and motivations. *Personality and Individual Differences, 54,* 402–407.

Seligman, M. E. P. (1971). Phobias and preparedness. *Behavior Therapy, 2,* 307–320.

Seligman, M. E. P. (1995). The effectiveness of psychotherapy: The consumer reports study. *American Psychologist, 48,* 966–971.

Selikoff, I. J., Robitzek, E. H., & Ornstein, G. G. (1952). Toxicity of hydrazine derivatives of isonicotinic acid in the chemotherapy of human tuberculosis. *Quarterly Bulletin of SeaView Hospital, 13,* 17–26.

Selye, H., & Fortier, C. (1950). Adaptive reaction to stress. *Psychosomatic Medicine, 12,* 149–157.

Semenza, C. (2009). The neuropsychology of proper names. *Mind & Language, 24,* 347–369.

Semenza, C., & Zettin, M. (1989). Evidence from aphasia from proper names as pure referring expressions. *Nature, 342,* 678–679.

Senghas, A., Kita, S., & Ozyurek, A. (2004). Children create core properties of language: Evidence from an emerging sign language in Nicaragua. *Science, 305,* 1782.

Senior, J. (2014). *All joy and no fun: The paradox of modern parenthood.* New York: Harper-Collins.

Senju, A., Maeda, M., Kikuchi, Y., Hasegawa, T., Tojo, Y., & Osanai, H. (2007). Absence of contagious yawning in children with autism spectrum disorder. *Biology Letters, 3*(6), 706–708.

Senju, A., Southgate, V., Snape, C., Leonard, M., & Csibra, G. (2011). Do 18-month-olds really attribute mental states to others?: A critical test. *Psychological Science, 22*(7), 878–880. doi:10.1177/0956797611411584

Senju, A., Southgate, V., White, S., & Frith, U. (2009). Mindblind eyes: An absence of spontaneous theory of mind in Asperger syndrome. *Science, 325,* 883–885.

Serpell, R. (1974). Aspects of intelligence in a developing country. *African Social Research, 17,* 578–596.

Seybold, K. S., & Hill, P. C. (2001). The role of religion and spirituality in mental and physical health. *Current Directions in Psychological Science, 10,* 21–23.

Seymour, K., Clifford, C. W. G., Logothetis, N. K., & Bartels, A. (2010). Coding and binding of color and form in visual cortex. *Cerebral Cortex.* doi:10.1093/cercor/bhp265

Shafritz, K. M., Gore, J. C., & Marois, R. (2002). The role of the parietal cortex in visual feature binding. *Proceedings of the National Academy of Sciences, USA, 99,* 10917–10922.

Shah, J. Y., Higgins, E. T., & Friedman, R. S. (1998). Performance incentives and means: How regulatory focus influences goal attainment. *Journal of Personality and Social Psychology, 74,* 285–293.

Shallcross, A. J., Ford, B. Q., Floerke, V. A., & Mauss, I. B. (2013). Getting better with age: The relationship between age, acceptance, and negative affect. *Journal of Personality and Social Psychology, 104*(4), 734–749. doi:10.1037/a0031180

Shallice, T., Fletcher, P., Frith, C. D., Grasby, P., Frackowiak, R. S. J., & Dolan, R. J. (1994). Brain regions associated with acquisition and retrieval of verbal episodic memory. *Nature, 368,* 633–635.

Shariff, A. F., & Tracy, J. L. (2011). What are emotion expressions for? *Current Directions in Psychological Science, 20*(6), 395–399.

Sharot, T. (2011). *The optimism bias: A tour of the irrationally positive brain.* New York: Pantheon Books.

Shaw, J. S., Bjork, R. A., & Handal, A. (1995). Retrieval-induced forgetting in an eyewitness paradigm. *Psychonomic Bulletin & Review, 13,* 1023–1027.

Shedler, J. (2010). The efficacy of psychodynamic psychotherapy. *American Psychologist, 65,* 98–109.

Shedler, J., & Block, J. (1990). Adolescent drug use and psychological health: A longitudinal inquiry. *American Psychologist, 45,* 612–630.

Sheehan, P. (1979). Hypnosis and the process of imagination. In E. Fromm & R. S. Shor (Eds.), *Hypnosis: Developments in research and new perspectives* (pp. 293–319). Chicago: Aldine.

Sheese, B. E., & Graziano, W. G. (2005). Deciding to defect: The effects of video-game violence on cooperative behavior. *Psychological Science, 16,* 354–357.

Shen, H., Wan, F., & Wyer, R. S. (2011). Cross-cultural differences in the refusal to accept a small gift: The differential influence of reciprocity norms on Asians and North Americans. *Journal of Personality and Social Psychology, 100*(2), 271–281. doi:10.1037/a0021201

Shenton, M. E., Dickey, C. C., Frumin, M., & McCarley, R. W. (2001). A review of MRI findings in schizophrenia. *Schizophrenia Research, 49,* 1–52.

Shepherd, G. M. (1988). *Neurobiology.* New York: Oxford University Press.

Shepperd, J., Malone, W., & Sweeny, K. (2008). Exploring the causes of the self-serving bias. *Social and Personality Psychology Compass, 2*(2), 895–908.

Sherry, D. F., & Schacter, D. L. (1987). The evolution of multiple memory systems. *Psychological Review, 94,* 439–454.

Sherry, S. B., & Hall, P. A. (2009). The perfectionism model of binge eating: Tests of an integrative model. *Journal of Personality and Social Psychology, 96*(3), 690–709.

Shiffman, S., Gnys, M., Richards, T. J., Paty, J. A., & Hickcox, M. (1996). Temptations to smoke after quitting: A comparison of lapsers and maintainers. *Health Psychology, 15,* 455–461.

Shih, M., Pittinsky, T. L., & Ambady, N. (1999). Stereotype susceptibility: Identity salience and shifts in quantitative performance. *Psychological Science, 10,* 80–83.

Shimamura, A. P., & Squire, L. R. (1987). A neuropsychological study of fact memory and source amnesia. *Journal of Experimental Psychology: Learning, Memory, and Cognition, 13,* 464–473.

Shin, L. M., Rauch, S. L., & Pitman, R. K. (2006). Amygdale, medial prefrontal cortex, and hippocampal function in PTSD. *Annals of the New York Academy of Science, 1071,* 67–79.

Shinskey, J. L., & Munakata, Y. (2005). Familiarity breeds searching. *Psychological Science, 16*(8), 596–600.

Shipstead, Z., Redick, T. S., & Engle, R. W. (2012). Is working memory training effective? *Psychological Bulletin, 138,* 628–654.

Shiv, B., Loewenstein, G., Bechara, A., Damasio, H., & Damasio, A. R. (2005). Investment behavior and the negative side of emotion. *Psychological Science, 16,* 435–439.

Shomstein, S., & Yantis, S. (2004). Control of attention shifts between vision and audition in human cortex. *Journal of Neuroscience, 24,* 10702–10706.

Shore, C. (1986). Combinatorial play: Conceptual development and early multiword speech. *Developmental Psychology, 22,* 184–190.

Shultz, S., & Dunbar, R. (2012). Encephalization is not a universal macroevolutionary phenomenon in mammals but is associated with sociality. *Proceedings of the National Academy of Sciences, 107,* 21582–21586.

Shweder, R. A. (1991). *Thinking through cultures: Expeditions in cultural psychology.* Cambridge, MA: Harvard University Press.

Shweder, R. A., & Sullivan, M. A. (1993). Cultural psychology: Who needs it? *Annual Review of Psychology, 44,* 497–523.

Siegel, A., Roeling, T. A. P., Gregg, T. R., & Kruk, M. R. (1999). Neuropharmacology of brain-stimulation-evoked aggression. *Neuroscience and Biobehavioral Reviews, 23,* 359–389.

Siegel, S. (1976). Morphine analgesia tolerance: Its situational specificity supports a Pavlovian conditioning model. *Science, 193,* 323–325.

Siegel, S. (1984). Pavlovian conditioning and heroin overdose: Reports by overdose victims. *Bulletin of the Psychonomic Society, 22,* 428–430.

Siegel, S. (2005). Drug tolerance, drug addiction, and drug anticipation. *Current Directions in Psychological Science, 14,* 296–300.

Siegel, S., Baptista, M. A. S., Kim, J. A., McDonald, R. V., & Weise- Kelly, L. (2000). Pavlovian psychopharmacology: The associative basis of tolerance. *Experimental and Clinical Psychopharmacology, 8,* 276–293.

Siegler, R. S. (1992). The other Alfred Binet. *Developmental Psychology, 28*(2), 179–190. doi:10.1037/0012-1649.28.2.179

Sigman, M., Spence, S. J., & Wang, T. (2006). Autism from developmental and neuropsychological perspectives. *Annual Review of Clinical Psychology, 2,* 327–355.

Sigurdsson, T., Doyere, V., Cain, C. K., & LeDoux, J. E. (2007). Longterm potentiation in the amygdala: A cellular mechanism of fear learning and memory. *Neuropharmacology, 52,* 215–227.

Silver, N. (2013, March 26). How opinion on same-sex marriage is changing, and what it means. *New York Times.* Retrieved from http://fivethirtyeightblogs.nytimes.com/2013/03/26/how-opinion-on-same-sex-marriage-is-changing-and-what-it-means/

Silver, R. L., Boon, C., & Stones, M. H. (1983). Searching for meaning in misfortune: Making sense of incest. *Journal of Social Issues, 39,* 81–102.

Simon, L. (1998). *Genuine reality: A life of William James.* New York: Harcourt Brace.

Simon, R. W. (2008). The joys of parenthood reconsidered. *Contexts, 7,* 40–45.

Simons, D. J., & Chabris, C. F. (1999). Gorillas in our midst: Sustained inattentional blindness for dynamic events. *Perception, 28,* 1059–1074.

Simons, D. J., & Levin, D. T. (1998). Failure to detect changes to people during a real-world interaction. *Psychonomic Bulletin & Review, 5,* 644–649.

Simons, D. J., & Rensink, R. A. (2005). Change blindness: Past, present, and future. *Trends in Cognitive Sciences, 9,* 16–20.

Simpson, A., & Riggs, K. J. (2011). Three- and 4-year-olds encode modeled actions in two ways leading to immediate imitation and delayed emulation. *Developmental Psychology, 47*(3), 834–840. doi:10.1037/a0023270

Simpson, E. L. (1974). Moral development research: A case study of scientific cultural bias. *Human Development, 17,* 81–106.

Simpson, J. A., Campbell, B., & Berscheid, E. (1986). The association between romantic love and marriage: Kephart (1967) twice revisited. *Personality and Social Psychology Bulletin, 12,* 363–372.

Simpson, J. A., Collins, W. A., & Salvatore, J. E. (2011). The impact of early interpersonal experience on adult romantic relationship functioning: Recent findings from the Minnesota Longitudinal Study of Risk and Adaptation. *Current Directions in Psychological Science, 20*(6), 355–359. doi:10.1177/0963721411418468

Simpson, J. A., Collins, W. A., Tran, S., & Haydon, K. C. (2007). Attachment and the experience and expression of emotions in romantic relationships: A developmental perspective. *Journal of Personality and Social Psychology, 92*(2), 355–367. doi:10.1037/0022-3514.92.2.355

Singer, P. (1975). *Animal liberation: A new ethics for our treatment of animals.* New York: Random House.

Singer, T., Seymour, B., O'Doherty, J., Kaube, H., Dolan, R. J., & Frith, C. D. (2004). Empathy for pain involves the affective but not sensory components of pain. *Science, 303,* 1157–1162.

Singh, D. (1993). Adaptive significance of female physical attractiveness: Role of waist-to-hip ratio. *Journal of Personality and Social Psychology, 65,* 293–307.

Skinner, B. F. (1938). *The behavior of organisms: An experimental analysis.* New York: Appleton-Century-Crofts.

Skinner, B. F. (1948). "Superstition" in the pigeon. *Journal of Experimental Psychology, 38,* 168–172.

Skinner, B. F. (1950). Are theories of learning necessary? *Psychological Review, 57,* 193–216.

Skinner, B. F. (1953). *Science and human behavior.* New York: Macmillan.

Skinner, B. F. (1957). *Verbal behavior.* New York: Appleton-Century-Crofts.

Skinner, B. F. (1958). Teaching machines. *Science, 129,* 969–977.

Skinner, B. F. (1971). *Beyond freedom and dignity.* New York: Bantam Books.

Skinner, B. F. (1972). The operational analysis of psychological terms. In B. F. Skinner, *Cumulative record* (3rd ed., pp. 370–384). New York: Appleton-Century-Crofts. (Original work published 1945.)

Skinner, B. F. (1979). *The shaping of a behaviorist: Part two of an auto-biography.* New York: Knopf.

Skinner, B. F. (1986). *Walden II.* Englewood Cliffs, NJ: Prentice Hall. (Original work published 1948)

Skoe, E., & Kraus, N. (2012). A little goes a long way: How the adult brain is shaped by musical training in adulthood. *Journal of Neuroscience, 32,* 11507–11510.

Skotko, B. G., Levine, S. P., & Goldstein, R. (2011). Self-perceptions from people with Down syndrome. *American Journal of Medical Genetics Part A, 155*(10), 2360–2369. doi:10.1002/ajmg.a.34235

Slagter, H. A. (2012). Conventional working memory training may not improve intelligence. *Trends in Cognitive Sciences, 16,* 582–583.

Slater, A., Morison, V., & Somers, M. (1988). Orientation discrimination and cortical function in the human newborn. *Perception, 17,* 597–602.

Slotnick, S. D., & Schacter, D. L. (2004). A sensory signature that distinguished true from false memories. *Nature Neuroscience, 7,* 664–672.

Smart, E., Smart, L, & Morton, L. (2003). *Bringing Elizabeth home: A journey of faith and hope.* New York: Doubleday.

Smetacek, V. (2002). Balance: Mind-grasping gravity. *Nature, 415,* 481.

Smetana, J. G. (1981). Preschool children's conceptions of moral and social rules. *Child Development, 52,* 1333–1336.

Smetana, J. G., & Braeges, J. L. (1990). The development of toddlers' moral and conventional judgments. *Merrill-Palmer Quarterly, 36,* 329–346.

Smith, A. R., Seid, M. A., Jimanez, L. C., & Wcislo, W. T. (2010). Socially induced brain development in a facultatively eusocial sweat bee *Megalopta genalis* (Halictidae). *Proceedings of the Royal Society B: Biological Sciences.*

Smith, E. E., & Jonides, J. (1997). Working memory: A view from neuroimaging. *Cognitive Psychology, 33,* 5–42.

Smith, M. L., Glass, G. V., & Miller, T. I. (1980). *The benefits of psychotherapy.* Baltimore: Johns Hopkins University Press.

Smith, N., & Tsimpli, I.-M. (1995). *The mind of a savant.* Oxford, England: Oxford University Press.

Snedeker, J., Geren, J., & Shafto, C. (2007). Starting over: International adoption as a natural experiment in language development. *Psychological Science, 18,* 79–87.

Snedeker, J., Geren, J., & Shafto, C. (2012). Disentangling the effects of cognitive development and linguistic expertise: A longitudinal study of the acquisition of English in internationally adopted children. *Cognitive Psychology, 65,* 39–76.

Solomon, J., & George, C. (1999). The measurement of attachment security in infancy and childhood. In J. Cassidy & P. R. Shaver (Eds.), *Handbook of attachment: Theory, research and clinical applications* (pp. 287–316). New York: Guilford Press.

Solomon, S., Greenberg, J., & Pyszczynski, T. (1991). A terror management theory of social behavior: The psychological functions of self-esteem and cultural worldviews. In M. P. Zanna (Ed.), *Advances in experimental social psychology* (Vol. 24, pp. 93–159). New York: Academic Press.

Solomon, S., Greenberg, J., Pyszczynski, T., Greenberg, J., Koole, S. L., & Pyszczynski, T. (2004). The cultural animal: Twenty years of terror management theory and research. In J. Greenberg, S. L. Koole, & T. Pyszczynski (Eds.), *Handbook of experimental existential psychology* (pp. 13–34). New York: Guilford Press.

Son, L. K., & Metcalfe, J. (2000). Metacognitive and control strategies in study-time allocation. *Journal of Experimental Psychology: Learning, Memory, and Cognition, 26,* 204–221.

Sonnby-Borgstrom, M., Jonsson, P., & Svensson, O. (2003). Emotional empathy as related to mimicry reactions at different levels of information processing. *Journal of Nonverbal Behavior, 27,* 3–23.

Southgate, V., Senju, A., & Csibra, G. (2007). Action anticipation through attribution of false belief by two-year-olds. *Psychological Science, 18,* 587–592.

Sparrow, B., Liu, J., & Wegner, D. M. (2011). Google effects on memory: Cognitive consequence of having information at our fingertips. *Science, 333,* 776–778.

Spearman, C. (1904). "General intelligence," objectively determined and measured. *American Journal of Psychology, 15,* 201–293.

Speisman, J. C., Lazarus, R. S., Moddkoff, A., & Davison, L. (1964). Experimental reduction of stress based on ego-defense theory. *Journal of Abnormal and Social Psychology, 68,* 367–380.

Spelke, E. S. (2005). Sex differences in intrinsic aptitude for mathematics and science: A critical review. *The American Psychologist, 60*(9), 950–958. doi:10.1037/0003-066X.60.9.950

Spellman, B. A. (1996). Acting as intuitive scientists: Contingency judgments are made while controlling for alternative potential causes. *Psychological Science, 7,* 337–342.

Spencer, L. G. (1929). *Illustrated phenomenology: The science and art of teaching how to read character—A manual of mental science.* London: Fowler.

Sperling, G. (1960). The information available in brief visual presentations. *Psychological Monographs, 74* (Whole No. 48).

Sperry, R. W. (1964). The great cerebral commissure. *Scientific American, 210,* 42–52.

Spinoza, B. (1982). *The ethics and selected letters* (S. Feldman, Ed., & S. Shirley, Trans.). Indianapolis, IN: Hackett. (Original work published 1677)

Spiro, H. M., McCrea Curnan, M. G., Peschel, E., & St. James, D. (1994). *Empathy and the practice of medicine: Beyond pills and the scalpel.* New Haven, CT: Yale University Press.

Spitz, R. A. (1949). Motherless infants. *Child Development, 20,* 145–155.

Sprecher, S. (1999). "I love you more today than yesterday": Romantic partners' perceptions of changes in love and related affect over time. *Journal of Personality and Social Psychology, 76,* 46–53.

Squire, L. R. (1992). Memory and the hippocampus: A synthesis from findings with rats, monkeys, and humans. *Psychological Review, 99,* 195–231.

Squire, L. R. (2009). The legacy of patient HM for neuroscience. *Neuron, 61,* 6–9.

Squire, L. R., & Kandel, E. R. (1999). *Memory: From mind to molecules.* New York: Scientific American Library.

Squire, L. R., Knowlton, B., & Musen, G. (1993). The structure and organization of memory. *Annual Review of Psychology, 44,* 453–495.

Squire, L. R., & Wixted, J. T. (2011). The cognitive neuroscience of memory since HM. *Annual Review of Neuroscience, 34,* 259–288.

Srivistava, S., John, O. P., Gosling, S. D., & Potter, J. (2003). Development of personality in early and middle adulthood: Set like plaster or persistent change? *Journal of Personality and Social Psychology, 84,* 1041–1053.

Sroufe, L. A., Egeland, B., & Kruetzer, T. (1990). The fate of early experience following developmental change: Longitudinal approaches to individual adaptation in childhood. *Child Development, 61,* 1363–1373.

Staddon, J. E. R., & Simmelhag, V. L. (1971). The "superstition" experiment: A reexamination of its implications for the principles of adaptive behavior. *Psychological Review, 78,* 3–43.

Stanovich, K. E. (2009). *What intelligence tests miss: The psychology of rational thought.* New Haven, CT: Yale University Press.

Starkey, P., Spelke, E. S., & Gelman, R. (1983). Detection of intermodal numerical correspondences by human infants. *Science, 222,* 179–181.

Starkey, P., Spelke, E. S., & Gelman, R. (1990). Numerical abstraction by human infants. *Cognition, 36,* 97–127.

Staw, B. M., & Hoang, H. (1995). Sunk costs in the NBA: Why draft order affects playing time and survival in professional basketball. *Administrative Science Quarterly, 40,* 474–494.

Steele, C. M., & Aronson, J. (1995). Stereotype threat and the intellectual test performance of African Americans. *Journal of Personality and Social Psychology, 69,* 797–811.

Steele, C. M., & Josephs, R. A. (1990). Alcohol myopia: Its prized and dangerous effects. *American Psychologist, 45,* 921–933.

Steele, H., Steele, M., Croft, C., & Fonagy, P. (1999). Infant-mother attachment at one year predicts children's understanding of mixed emotions at six years. *Social Development, 8,* 161–178.

Stein, D. J., Phillips, K. A., Bolton, D., Fulford, K. W. M., Sadler, J. Z., & Kendler, K. S. (2010). What is a mental/psychiatric disorder? From *DSM–IV* to *DSM–V. Psychological Medicine, 40*(11), 1759–1765. doi:10.1017/S0033291709992261.

Stein, M., Federspiel, A., Koenig, T., Wirth, M., Lehmann, C., Wiest, . . . Dierks, T. (2009). Reduced frontal activation with increasing second language proficiency. *Neuropsychologia,47,* 2712–2720.

Stein, M. B. (1998). Neurobiological perspectives on social phobia: From affiliation to zoology. *Biological Psychiatry, 44,* 1277–1285.

Stein, M. B., Chavira, D. A., & Jang, K. L. (2001). Bringing up bashful baby: Developmental pathways to social phobia. *Psychiatric Clinics of North America, 24,* 661–675.

Stein, Z., Susser, M., Saenger, G., & Marolla, F. (1975). *Famine and development: The Dutch hunger winter of 1944–1945.* Oxford, England: Oxford University Press.

Steinbaum, E. A., & Miller, N. E. (1965). Obesity from eating elicited by daily stimulation of hypothalamus. *American Journal of Physiology, 208,* 1–5.

Steinberg, L. (1999). *Adolescence* (5th ed.). Boston: McGraw-Hill.

Steinberg, L. (2007). Risk taking in adolescence: New perspectives from brain and behavioral science. *Current Directions in Psychological Science, 16*(2), 55–59. doi:10.1111/j.1467-8721.2007.00475x

Steinberg, L., & Monahan, K. C. (2007). Age differences in resistance to peer influence. *Developmental Psychology, 43,* 1531–1543.

Steinberg, L., & Morris, A. S. (2001). Adolescent development. *Annual Review of Psychology, 52,* 83–110.

Steiner, F. (1986). Differentiating smiles. In E. Branniger-Huber & F. Steiner (Eds.), *FACS in psychotherapy research* (pp.139–148). Zurich: Universität Zürich, Department of Clinical Psychology.

Steiner, J. E. (1973). The gustofacial response: Observation on normal and anencephalic newborn infants. In J. F. Bosma (Ed.), *Fourth symposium on oral sensation and perception: Development in the fetus and infant* (DHEW 73–546; pp. 254–278). Bethesda, MD: U.S. Department of Heath, Education, and Welfare.

Steiner, J. E. (1979). Human facial expressions in response to taste and smell stimulation. *Advances in Child Development and Behavior, 13,* 257–295.

Stellar, J. R., Kelley, A. E., & Corbett, D. (1983). Effects of peripheral and central dopamine blockade on lateral hypothalamic self-stimulation: Evidence for both reward and motor deficits. *Pharmacology, Biochemistry, and Behavior, 18,* 433–442.

Stellar, J. R., & Stellar, E. (1985). *The neurobiology of motivation and reward.* New York: Springer-Verlag.

Stelmack, R. M. (1990). Biological bases of extraversion: Psychophysiological evidence. *Journal of Personality, 58,* 293–311.

Stephens, R. S. (1999). Cannabis and hallucinogens. In B. S. McCrady & E. E. Epstein (Eds.), *Addictions: A comprehensive guidebook* (pp. 121–140). New York: Oxford University Press.

Sterelny, K., & Griffiths, P. E. (1999). *Sex and death: An introduction to philosophy of biology.* Chicago: University of Chicago Press.

Stern, J. A., Brown, M., Ulett, A., & Sletten, I. (1977). A comparison of hypnosis, acupuncture, morphine, Valium, aspirin, and placebo in the management of experimentally induced pain. In W. E. Edmonston (Ed.), *Conceptual and investigative approaches to hypnosis and hypnotic phenomena* (Vol. 296, pp. 175–193). New York: Annals of the New York Academy of Sciences.

Stern, W. (1914). *The psychological methods of testing intelligence* (G. M. Whipple, Trans.). Baltimore: Warwick & York.

Sternberg, R. J. (1986). A triangular theory of love. *Psychological Review, 93,* 119–135.

Sternberg, R. J. (1999). The theory of successful intelligence. *Review of General Psychology, 3*(4), 292–316. doi:10.1037/1089-2680.3.4.292

Stevens, G., & Gardner, S. (1982). *The women of psychology* (Vol. 1). Rochester: Schenkman Books.

Stevens, J. (1988). An activity approach to practical memory. In M. M. Gruneberg, P. E. Morris, & R. N. Sykes (Eds.), *Practical aspects of memory: Current research and issues* (Vol. 1, pp. 335–341). New York: Wiley.

Stevens, L. A. (1971). *Explorers of the brain.* New York: Knopf.

Stevenson, R. J., & Boakes, R. A. (2003). A mnemonic theory of odor perception. *Psychological Review, 110,* 340–364.

Stevenson, R. J., & Wilson, D. A. (2007). Odour perception: An object-recognition approach. *Perception, 36,* 1821–1833.

Stewart-Williams, S. (2004). The placebo puzzle: Putting together the pieces. *Health Psychology, 23,* 198–206.

Stickgold, R., Hobson, J. A., Fosse, R., & Fosse, M. (2001). Sleep, learning, and dreams: Off-line memory reprocessing. *Science, 294,* 1052–1057.

Stickgold, R., Malia, A., Maguire, D., Roddenberry, D., & O'Connor, M. (2000). Replaying the game: Hypnagogic images in normals and anmesics. *Science, 290,* 350–353.

Stigler, J. W., Shweder, R., & Herdt, G. (Eds.). (1990). *Cultural psychology: Essays on comparative human development.* Cambridge, England: Cambridge University Press.

St. Jacques, P. L., & Schacter, D. L. (2013). Modifying memory: Selectively enhancing and updating personal memories for a museum tour by reactivating them. *Psychological Science, 24,* 537–543.

Stone, A. A., Schwartz, J. E., Broderick, J. E., & Deaton, A. (2010). A snapshot of the age distribution of psychological well-being in the United States. *Proceedings of the National Academy of Sciences, USA, 107*(22), 9985–9990. doi:10.1073/pnas.1003744107

Stone, J., Perry, Z. W., & Darley, J. M. (1997). "White men can't jump": Evidence for the perceptual confirmation of racial stereotypes following a basketball game. *Basic and Applied Social Psychology, 19,* 291–306.

Stoodley, C. J., Ray, N., J., Jack, A., & Stein, J. F. (2008). Implicit learning in control, dyslexic, and garden-variety poor readers. *Annals of the New York Academy of Sciences, 1145,* 173–183.

Storm, B. C., Bjork, E. L., Bjork, R. A., & Nestojko, J. F. (2006). Is retrieval success a necessary condition for retrieval-induced forgetting? *Psychonomic Bulletin & Review, 2,* 249–253.

Storms, M. D. (1973). Videotape and the attribution process: Reversing actors' and observers' points of view. *Journal of Personality and Social Psychology, 27,* 165–175.

Strack, F., Martin, L. L., & Stepper, S. (1988). Inhibiting and facilitating conditions of the human smile: A nonobtrusive test of the facial feedback hypothesis. *Journal of Personality and Social Psychology, 54,* 768–777.

Strayer, D. L., Drews, F. A., & Johnston, W. A. (2003). Cell phone induced failures of visual attention during simulated driving. *Journal of Experimental Psychology: Applied, 9,* 23–32.

Streissguth, A. P., Barr, H. M., Bookstein, F. L., Sampson, P. D., & Carmichael Olson, H. (1999). The long-term neurocognitive consequences of prenatal alcohol exposure: A 14-year study. *Psychological Science, 10,* 186–190.

Striano, T., & Reid, V. M. (2006). Social cognition in the first year. *Trends in Cognitive Sciences, 10*(10), 471–476.

Strickland, L. H. (1991). Russian and Soviet social psychology. *Canadian Psychology, 32,* 580–595.

Striegel-Moore, R. H., & Bulik, C. M. (2007). Risk factors for eating disorders. *American Psychologist, 62,* 181–198.

Strohmetz, D. B., Rind, B., Fisher, R., & Lynn, M. (2002). Sweetening the till: The use of candy to increase restaurant tipping. *Journal of Applied Social Psychology, 32,* 300–309.

Stroop, J. P. (1935). Studies of interference in serial verbal reactions. *Journal of Experimental Psychology, 18,* 643–661.

Strueber, D., Lueck, M., & Roth, G. (2006). The violent brain. *Scientific American Mind, 17,* 20–27.

Stuss, D. T., & Benson, D. F. (1986). *The frontal lobes.* New York: Raven Press.

Subramaniam, K., Kounios, J., Parrish, T. B., & Jung-Beeman, M. (2009). A brain mechanism for facilitation of insight by positive affect. *Journal of Cognitive Neuroscience, 21,* 415–432.

Substance Abuse and Mental Health Services Administration. (2005). *Results from the 2004 National Survey on Drug Use and Health: National findings* (DHHS Publication No. SMA 05–4062, NSDUH Series H-28). Rockville, MD: U. S. Department of Health and Human Services.

Suchman, A. L., Markakis, K., Beckman, H. B., & Frankel, R. (1997). A model of empathic communication in the medical interview. *Journal of the American Medical Association, 277,* 678–682.

Suddendorf, T., & Corballis, M. C. (2007). The evolution of foresight: What is mental time travel and is it unique to humans? *Behavioral and Brain Sciences, 30,* 299–313.

Suderman, M., McGowan, P. O., Sasaki, A., Huang, T. C. T., Hallett, M. T., Meaney, M. J., . . . Szyf, M. (2012). Conserved epigenetic sensitivity to early life experiences in the rat and human hippocampus. *Proceedings of the National Academy of Sciences, USA, 109*(Suppl. 2), 17266–17272.

Sulloway, F. J. (1992). *Freud, biologist of the mind.* Cambridge, MA: Harvard University Press.

Sundet, J. M., Eriksen, W., & Tambs, K. (2008). Intelligence correlations between brothers decrease with increasing age difference: Evidence for shared environmental effects in young adults. *Psychological Science, 19,* 843–847.

Susman, S., Dent, C., McAdams, L., Stacy, A., Burton, D., & Flay, B. (1994). Group self-identification and adolescent cigarette smoking: A 1-year prospective study. *Journal of Abnormal Psychology, 103,* 576–580.

Susser, E. B., Brown, A., & Matte, T. D. (1999). Prenatal factors and adult mental and physical health. *Canadian Journal of Psychiatry, 44*(4), 326–334.

Suthana, N., & Fried, I. (2012). Percepts to recollections: Insights from single neuron recordings in the human brain. *Trends in Cognitive Sciences, 16,* 427–436.

Suzuki, L. A., & Valencia, R. R. (1997). Race-ethnicity and measured intelligence: Educational implications. *American Psychologist, 52,* 1103–1114.

Swann, W. B., Jr. (1983). Self-verification: Bringing social reality into harmony with the self. In J. M. Suls & A. G. Greenwald (Ed.), *Psychological perspectives on the self* (Vol. 2, pp. 33–66). Hillsdale, NJ: Erlbaum.

Swann, W. B., Jr. (2012). Self-verification theory. In P. Van Lang, A. Kruglanski, & E. T. Higgins (Eds.), *Handbook of theories of social psychology* (pp. 23–42). London: Sage.

Swann, W. B., Jr., & Rentfrow, P. J. (2001). Blirtatiousness: Cognitive, behavioral, and physiological consequences of rapid responding, *Journal of Personality and Social Psychology, 181*(6), 1160–1175.

Swayze, V. W., II. (1995). Frontal leukotomy and related psychosurgical procedures before antipsychotics (1935–1954): A historical overview. *American Journal of Psychiatry, 152,* 505–515.

Swednsen, J., Hammen, C., Heller, T., & Gitlin, M. (1995). Correlates of stress reactivity in patients with bipolar disorder. *American Journal of Psychiatry, 152,* 795–797.

Swets, J. A., Dawes, R. M., & Monahan, J. (2000). Psychological science can improve diagnostic decisions. *Psychological Science in the Public Interest, 1,* 1–26.

Swinkels, A. (2003). An effective exercise for teaching cognitive heuristics. *Teaching of Psychology, 30,* 120–122.

Szasz, T. S. (1987). *Insanity.* New York: Wiley.

Szechtman, H., & Woody, E. Z. (2006). Obsessive-compulsive disorder as a disturbance of security motivation: Constraints on comorbidity. *Neurotoxicity Research, 10,* 103–112.

Szpunar, K. K. (2010). Episodic future thought: An emerging concept. *Perspectives on Psychological Science, 5,* 142–162.

Szpunar, K. K., Khan, N. Y., & Schacter, D. L. (2013). Interpolated memory tests reduce mind wandering and improve learning of online lectures. *Proceedings of the National Academy of Sciences, USA, 110,* 6313–6317.

Szpunar, K. K., Watson, J. M., & McDermott, K. B. (2007). Neural substrates of envisioning the future. *Proceedings of the National Academy of Sciences, USA, 104,* 642–647.

Tajfel, H., Billig, M. G., Bundy, R. P., & Flament, C. (1971). Social categorization and intergroup behaviour. *European Journal of Social Psychology, 1,* 149–178.

Tajfel, H., & Turner, J. C. (1986). The social identity theory of intergroup behavior. In S. Worchel & W. G. Austin (Eds.), *Psychology of intergroup relations* (pp. 7–24). Chicago: Nelson.

Tajfel, H., & Wilkes, A. L. (1963). Classification and quantitative judgement. *British Journal of Psychology, 54,* 101–114.

Takahashi, K. (1986). Examining the Strange Situation procedure with Japanese mothers and 12-month-old infants. *Developmental Psychology, 22,* 265–270.

Tamir, M., & Ford, B. Q. (2012). Should people pursue feelings that feel good or feelings that do good? Emotional preferences and well-being. *Emotion, 12,* 1061–1070.

Tamis-LeMonda, C. S., Adolph, K. E., Lobo, S. A., Karasik, L. B., Ishak, S., & Dimitropoulou, K. A. (2008). When infants take mothers' advice: 18-month-olds integrate perceptual and social information to guide motor action. *Developmental Psychology, 44,* 734–746.

Tamminga, C. A., Nemeroff, C. B., Blakely, R. D., Brady, L., Carter, C. S., Davis, K. L., . . . Suppes, T. (2002). Developing novel treatments for mood disorders: Accelerating discovery. *Biological Psychiatry, 52,* 589–609.

Tanaka, F., Cicourel, A., & Movellan, J. R. (2007). Socialization between toddlers and robots at an early childhood education center. *Proceedings of the National Academy of Sciences, USA, 104*(46), 17954–17958.

Tang, Y.-P., Shimizu, E., Dube, G. R., Rampon, C., Kerchner, G. A., Zhuo, M., . . . Tsien, J. Z. (1999). Genetic enhancement of learning and memory in mice. *Nature, 401,* 63–69.

Tang, Y. Y., Lu, Q., Fan, M., Yang, Y., & Posner, M. I. (2012). Mechanisms of white matter changes induced by meditation. *Proceedings of the National Academy of Sciences,109,* 10570–10574.

Tarr, M. J., & Vuong, Q. C. (2002). Visual object recognition. In S. Yantis & H. Pashler (Eds.), *Stevens' handbook of experimental psychology: Vol. 1. Sensation and perception* (3rd ed., pp. 287–314). New York: Wiley.

Tart, C. T. (Ed.). (1969). *Altered states of consciousness.* New York: Wiley.

Task Force on Promotion and Dissemination of Psychological Procedures. (1995). Training in and dissemination of empirically validated psychological treatments: Report and recommendations. *Clinical Psychologist, 48,* 3–23.

Taylor, D., & Lambert, W. (1990). *Language and culture in the lives of immigrants and refugees.* Austin, TX: Hogg Foundation for Mental Health.

Taylor, E. (2001). *William James on consciousness beyond the margin.* Princeton, NJ: Princeton University Press.

Taylor, S. E. (1986). *Health psychology.* New York: Random House.

Taylor, S. E. (1989). *Positive illusions.* New York: Basic Books.

Taylor, S. E. (2002). *The tending instinct: How nurturing is essential to who we are and how we live.* New York: Times Books.

Taylor, S. E., & Brown, J. D. (1988). Illusion and well-being: A social psychological perspective on mental health. *Psychological Bulletin, 103,* 193–210.

Taylor, S. E., & Fiske, S. T. (1975). Point-of-view and perceptions of causality. *Journal of Personality and Social Psychology, 32,* 439–445.

Taylor, S. E., & Fiske, S. T. (1978). Salience, attention, and attribution: Top of the head phenomena. In L. Berkowitz (Ed.), *Advances in experimental social psychology* (Vol. 11, pp. 249–288). New York: Academic Press.

Teasdale, J. D., Segal, Z. V., & Williams, J. M. G. (2000). Prevention of relapse/recurrence in major depression by mindfulness-based cognitive therapy. *Journal of Consulting and Clinical Psychology, 68,* 615–623.

Telch, M. J., Lucas, J. A., & Nelson, P. (1989). Non-clinical panic in college students: An investigation of prevalence and symptomology. *Journal of Abnormal Psychology, 98,* 300–306.

Tellegen, A., & Atkinson, G. (1974). Openness to absorbing and self-altering experiences ("absorption"), a trait related to hypnotic susceptibility. *Journal of Abnormal Psychology, 83,* 268–277.

Tellegen, A., Lykken, D. T., Bouchard, T. J., Wilcox, K., Segal, N., & Rich, A. (1988). Personality similarity in twins reared together and apart. *Journal of Personality and Social Psychology, 54,* 1031–1039.

Temerlin, M. K., & Trousdale, W. W. (1969). The social psychology of clinical diagnosis. *Psychotherapy: Theory, Research & Practice, 6,* 24–29.

Terman, L. M. (1916). *The measurement of intelligence.* Boston: Houghton Mifflin.

Terman, L. M., & Oden, M. H. (1959). *Genetic studies of genius: Vol. 5. The gifted group at mid-life.* Stanford, CA: Stanford University Press.

Tesser, A. (1991). Emotion in social comparison and reflection processes. In J. Suls & T. A. Wills (Ed.), *Social comparison: Contemporary theory and research* (pp. 117–148). Hillsdale, NJ: Erlbaum.

Teyler, T. J., & DiScenna, P. (1986). The hippocampal memory indexing theory. *Behavioral Neuroscience, 100,* 147–154.

Thaker, G. K. (2002). Current progress in schizophrenia research. Search for genes of schizophrenia: Back to defining valid phenes. *Journal of Nervous and Mental Disease, 190,* 411–412.

Thaler, K., Delivuk, M., Chapman, A., Gaynes, B. N., Kaminski, A., & Gartlehner, G. (2011). Second-generation antidepressants for seasonal affective disorder. *Cochrane Database of Systematic Reviews,* CD008591.

Thaler, R. H. (1988). The ultimatum game. *Journal of Economic Perspectives, 2,* 195–206.

Thase, M. E., & Howland, R. H. (1995). Biological processes in depression: An updated review and integration. In E. E. Beckham & W. R. Leber (Eds.), *Handbook of depression* (2nd ed., pp. 213–279). New York: Guilford Press.

Thelen, E., Corbetta, D., Kamm, K., Spencer, J. P., Schneider, K., & Zernicke, R. F. (1993). The transition to reaching: Mapping intention and intrinsic dynamics. *Child Development, 64,* 1058–1098.

Thibaut, J. W., & Kelley, H. H. (1959). *The social psychology of groups.* New Brunswick, NJ: Transaction Publishers.

Thoma, S. J., Narvaez, D., Rest, J., & Derryberry, P. (1999). Does moral judgment development reduce to political attitudes or verbal ability? Evidence using the defining issues test. *Educational Psychology Review, 11,* 325–341.

Thomaes, S., Bushman, B. J., Stegge, H., & Olthof, T. (2008). Trumping shame by blasts of noise: Narcissism, self-esteem, shame, and aggression in young adolescents. *Child Development, 79*(6), 1792–1801.

Thomas, A., & Chess, S. (1977). *Temperament and development.* New York: Brunner/Mazel.

Thomason, M., & Thompson, P. M. (2011). Diffusion imaging, white matter, and psychopathology. *Annual Review of Clinical Psychology, 7,* 63–85.

Thompson, B., Coronado, G., Chen, L., Thompson, L. A., Halperin, A., Jaffe, R., . . . Zbikowski, S. M. (2007). Prevalence and characteristics of smokers at 30 Pacific Northwest colleges and universities. *Nicotine & Tobacco Research, 9,* 429–438.

Thompson, C. P., Skowronski, J., Larsen, S. F., & Betz, A. (1996). *Autobiographical memory: Remembering what and remembering when.* Mahwah, NJ: Erlbaum.

Thompson, P. M., Giedd, J. N., Woods, R. P., MacDonald, D., Evans, A. C., & Toga, A. W. (2000). Growth patterns in the developing brain detected by using continuum mechanical tensor maps. *Nature, 404,* 190–193.

Thompson, P. M., Vidal, C., Giedd, J. N., Gochman, P., Blumenthal, J., Nicolson, R., . . . Rapoport, J. L. (2001). Accelerated gray matter loss in very early-onset schizophrenia. *Proceedings of the National Academy of Sciences, USA, 98,* 11650–11655.

Thompson, R. F. (2005). In search of memory traces. *Annual Review of Psychology, 56,* 1–23.

Thomson, D. M. (1988). Context and false recognition. In G. M. Davies & D. M. Thomson (Eds.), *Memory in context: Context in memory* (pp. 285–304). Chichester, England: Wiley.

Thorndike, E. L. (1898). Animal intelligence: An experimental study of associative processes in animals. *Psychological Review Monograph Supplements, 2,* 4–160.

Thornhill, R., & Gangestad, S. W. (1993). Human facial beauty: Averageness, symmetry, and parasite resistance. *Human Nature, 4,* 237–269.

Thornhill, R., & Gangestad, S. W. (1999). The scent of symmetry: A human sex pheromone that signals fitness? *Evolution and Human Behavior, 20,* 175–201.

Thurber, J. (1956). *Further fables of our time*. New York: Simon & Schuster.

Thurstone, L. L. (1938). *Primary mental abilities*. Chicago: University of Chicago Press.

Tice, D. M., & Baumeister, R. F. (1997). Longitudinal study of procrastination, performance, stress, and health: The costs and benefits of dawdling. *Psychological Science, 8*(6), 454–458.

Tienari, P., Wynne, L. C., Sorri, A., Lahti, I., Läksy, K., Moring, J., . . . Wahlberg, K. E. (2004). Genotype–environment interaction in schizophreniaspectrum disorder: Long-term follow-up study of Finnish adoptees. *British Journal of Psychiatry, 184*, 216–222.

Timmerman, T. A. (2007). "It was a thought pitch": Personal, situational, and target influences on hit-by-pitch events across time. *Journal of Applied Psychology, 92*, 876–884.

Tittle, P. (Ed.). (2004). *Should parents be licensed?: Debating the issues*. New York: Prometheus Books.

Todd, A. R., Bodenhausen, G. V., Richeson, J. A., & Galinsky, A. D. (2011). Perspective taking combats automatic expressions of racial bias. *Journal of Personality and Social Psychology, 100*(6), 1027–1042. doi:10.1037/a0022308

Todd, J. T., & Morris, E. K. (1992). Case histories in the great power of steady misrepresentation. *American Psychologist, 47*(11), 1441–1453.

Toga, A. W., Clark, K. A., Thompson, P. M., Shattuck, D. W., & Van Horn, J. D. (2012). Mapping the human connectome. *Neurosurgery, 71*, 1–5.

Tolman, E. C., & Honzik, C. H. (1930a). "Insight" in rats. *University of California Publications in Psychology, 4*, 215–232.

Tolman, E. C., & Honzik, C. H. (1930b). Introduction and removal of reward and maze performance in rats. *University of California Publications in Psychology, 4*, 257–275.

Tolman, E. C., Ritchie, B. F., & Kalish, D. (1946). Studies in spatial learning: I: Orientation and short cut. *Journal of Experimental Psychology, 36*, 13–24.

Tomasello, M., & Call, J. (2004). The role of humans in the cognitive development of apes revisited. *Animal Cognition, 7*, 213–215.

Tomasello, M., Davis-Dasilva, M., Camak, L., & Bard, K. (1987). Observational learning of tool use by young chimpanzees. *Human Evolution, 2*, 175–183.

Tomasello, M., Savage-Rumbaugh, S., & Kruger, A. C. (1993). Imitative learning of actions on objects by children, chimpanzees, and enculturated chimpanzees. *Child Development, 64*, 1688–1705.

Tomkins, S. S. (1981). The role of facial response in the experience of emotion. *Journal of Personality and Social Psychology, 40*, 351–357.

Tooby, J., & Cosmides, L. (2000). Mapping the evolved functional organization of mind and brain. In M. S. Gazzaniga (Ed.), *The cognitive neurosciences* (pp. 1185–1198). Cambridge, MA: MIT Press.

Tootell, R. B. H., Reppas, J. B., Dale, A. M., Look, R. B., Sereno, M. I., Malach, R., . . . Rosen, B. R. (1995). Visual-motion aftereffect in human cortical area MT revealed by functional magnetic resonance imaging. *Nature, 375*, 139–141.

Torgensen, S. (1986). Childhood and family characteristics in panic and generalized anxiety disorder. *American Journal of Psychiatry, 143*, 630–639.

Torrey, E. F., Bower, A. E., Taylor, E. H., & Gottesman, I. I. (1994). *Schizophrenia and manic-depressive disorder: The biological roots of mental illness as revealed by the landmark study of identical twins*. New York: Basic Books.

Tracy, J. L., & Beall, A. T. (2011). Happy guys finish last: The impact of emotion expressions on sexual attraction. *Emotion, 11*(6), 1379–1387. doi:10.1037/a0022902

Tracy, J. L., Shariff, A. F., Zhao, W., & Henrich, J. (2013). Cross-cultural evidence that the noverbal expression of pride is an automatic status signal. *Journal of Experimental Psychology: General, 142*(1), 163–180.

Trebach, A. S., & Zeese, K. B. (Eds.). (1992). *Friedman and Szasz on liberty and drugs: Essays on the free market and prohibition*. Washington, DC: Drug Policy Foundation Press.

Treede, R. D., Kenshalo, D. R., Gracely, R. H., & Jones, A. K. (1999). The cortical representation of pain. *Pain, 79*, 105–111.

Treisman, A. (1998). Feature binding, attention and object perception. *Philosophical Transactions of the Royal Society (B), 353*, 1295–1306.

Treisman, A. (2006). How the deployment of attention determines what we see. *Visual Cognition, 14*, 411–443.

Treisman, A., & Gelade, G. (1980). A feature integration theory of attention. *Cognitive Psychology, 12*, 97–136.

Treisman, A., & Schmidt, H. (1982). Illusory conjunctions in the perception of objects. *Cognitive Psychology, 14*, 107–141.

Trivers, R. L. (1972). Parental investment and sexual selection. In B. Campbell (Ed.), *Sexual selection and the descent of man, 1871–1971* (pp. 139–179). Chicago: Aldine.

Trompeter, S. E., Bettencourt, R., & Barrett-Connor, E. (2012). Sexual activity and satisfaction in healthy community-dwelling older women. *American Journal of Medicine, 125*(1), 37–43. doi:10.1016/j.amjmed.2011.07.036

Trull, T. J., & Durrett, C. A. (2005). Categorical and dimensional models of personality disorder. *Annual Review of Clinical Psychology, 1*, 355–380.

Tucker, E. (2003, June 25). Move over, Fido! Chickens are becoming hip suburban pets. *USA Today*. Retrieved from http://usatoday30.usatoday.com/money/2003-06-25-pet-chickens_x.htm

Tucker-Drob, E. M., Rhemtulla, M., Harden, K. P., Turkheimer, E., & Fask, D. (2010). Emergence of a Gene × Socioeconomic Status interaction on infant mental ability between 10 months and 2 years. *Psychological Science, 22*(1), 125–133. doi:10.1177/0956797610392926

Tuerlinckx, F., De Boeck, P., & Lens, W. (2002). Measuring needs with the Thematic Apperception Test: A psychometric study. *Journal of Personality and Social Psychology, 82*, 448–461.

Tulving, E. (1972). Episodic and semantic memory. In E. Tulving & W. Donaldson (Eds.), *Organization of memory* (pp. 381–403). New York: Academic Press.

Tulving, E. (1983). *Elements of episodic memory*. Oxford, England: Clarendon Press.

Tulving, E. (1985). Memory and consciousness. *Canadian Psychologist, 25*, 1–12.

Tulving, E. (1998). Neurocognitive processes of human memory. In C. von Euler, I. Lundberg, & R. Llins (Eds.), *Basic mechanisms in cognition and language* (pp. 261–281). Amsterdam: Elsevier.

Tulving, E., Kapur, S., Craik, F. I. M., Moscovitch, M., & Houle, S. (1994). Hemispheric encoding/retrieval asymmetry in episodic memory: Positron emission tomography findings. *Proceedings of the National Academy of Sciences, USA, 91*, 2016–2020.

Tulving, E., & Pearlstone, Z. (1966). Availability versus accessibility of information in memory for words. *Journal of Verbal Learning and Verbal Behavior, 5*, 381–391.

Tulving, E., & Schacter, D. L. (1990). Priming and human memory systems. *Science, 247*, 301–306.

Tulving, E., Schacter, D. L., & Stark, H. (1982). Priming effects in wordfragment completion are independent of recognition memory. *Journal of Experimental Psychology: Learning, Memory, and Cognition, 8*, 336–342.

Tulving, E., & Thompson, D. M. (1973). Encoding specificity and retrieval processes in episodic memory. *Psychological Review, 80,* 352–373.

Turiel, E. (1998). The development of morality. In N. Eisenberg (Ed.), *Handbook of child psychology: Vol. 3. Social, emotional and personality development* (pp. 863–932). New York: Wiley.

Turkheimer, E. (2000). Three laws of behavior genetics and what they mean. *Current Directions in Psychological Science, 9,* 160–164.

Turkheimer, E., Haley, A., Waldron, M., D'Onofrio, B., & Gottesman, I. I. (2003). Socioeconomic status modifies heritability of IQ in young children. *Psychological Science, 14,* 623–628.

Turkheimer, E., & Waldron, M. (2000). Nonshared environment: A theoretical, methodological, and quantitative review. *Psychological Bulletin, 126,* 78–108.

Turner, D. C., Robbins, T. W., Clark, L., Aron, A. R., Dowson, J., & Sahakian, B. J. (2003). Cognitive enhancing effects of modafinil in healthy volunteers. *Psychopharmacology, 165,* 260–269.

Turner, D. C., & Sahakian, B. J. (2006). Neuroethics of cognitive enhancement. *BioSocieties, 1,* 113–123.

Turner, M. E., & Pratkanis, A. R. (1998). Twenty-five years of groupthink theory and research: Lessons from the evaluation of a theory. *Organizational Behavior and Human Decision Processes, 73*(2–3), 105–115. doi:10.1006/obhd.1998.2756

Tversky, A., & Kahneman, D. (1973). Availability: A heuristic for judging frequency and probability. *Cognitive Psychology, 5,* 207–232.

Tversky, A., & Kahneman, D. (1974). Judgment under uncertainty: Heuristics and biases. *Science, 185,* 1124–1131.

Tversky, A., & Kahneman, D. (1981). The framing of decisions and the psychology of choice. *Science, 211,* 453–458.

Tversky, A., & Kahneman, D. (1983). Extensional versus intuitive reasoning: The conjunction fallacy in probability judgment. *Psychological Review, 90,* 293–315.

Tversky, A., & Kahneman, D. (1992). Advances in prospect theory: Cumulative representation of uncertainty. *Journal of Risk and Uncertainty, 5,* 297–323.

Twenge, J. M., Campbell, W. K., & Foster, C. A. (2003). Parenthood and marital satisfaction: A meta-analytic review. *Journal of Marriage and Family, 65,* 574–583.

Tyler, T. R. (1990). *Why people obey the law.* New Haven, CT: Yale University Press.

Umberson, D., Williams, K., Powers, D. A., Liu, H., & Needham, B. (2006). You make me sick: Marital quality and health over the life course. *Journal of Health and Social Behavior, 47,* 1–16.

Uncapher, M. R., & Rugg, M. D. (2008). Fractionation of the component processes underlying successful episodic encoding: A combined fMRI and divided-attention study. *Journal of Cognitive Neuroscience, 20,* 240–254.

Ungerleider, L. G., & Mishkin, M. (1982). Two cortical visual systems. In D. J. Ingle, M. A. Goodale, & R. J. W. Mansfield (Eds.), *Analysis of visual behavior* (pp. 549–586). Cambridge, MA: MIT Press.

Urban, N. B. L., Girgis, R. R., Talbot, P. S., Kegeles, L. S., Xu, X., Frankie, W. G., . . . Laruelle, M. (2012). Sustained recreational use of ecstasy is associated with altered pre- and postsynaptic markers of serotonin transmission in neocortical areas: A PET study with [11c] DASB and [11c] MDL 100907. *Neuropsychopharmacology, 37,* 1465–1473.

Ursano, R. J., & Silberman, E. K. (2003). Psychoanalysis, psychoanalytic psychotherapy, and supportive psychotherapy. In R. E. Hales & S. C. Yudofsky (Eds.), *The American Psychiatric Publishing textbook of clinical psychiatry* (4th ed., pp. 1177–1203). Washington, DC: American Psychiatric Publishing.

U.S. Census Bureau. (2012). *The 2012 statistical abstract: National data book.* Washington, DC: Author.

U. S. Department of Health and Human Services. (1979). *Ethical principles and guidelines for the protection of human subjects of research.* Retrieved from http://www.hhs.gov/ohrp/humansubjects/guidance/belmont.html

U.S. Department of State. (2013, January). *FY 2012 annual report on intercountry adoption.* Washington, DC: Bureau of Consular Affairs, Office of Children's Issues. Retrieved from http://adoption.state.gov/content/pdf/fy2012_annual_report.pdf

Vacha, E., & McBride, M. (1993). Cramming: A barrier to student success, a way to beat the system, or an effective strategy? *College Student Journal, 27,* 2–11.

Valentine, T., Brennen, T., & Brédart, S. (1996). *The cognitive psychology of proper names: On the importance of being Ernest.* London: Routledge.

Valins, S. (1966). Cognitive effects of false heart-rate feedback. *Journal of Personality and Social Psychology, 4,* 400–408.

Vallacher, R. R., & Wegner, D. M. (1985). *A theory of action identification.* Hillsdale, NJ: Erlbaum.

Vallacher, R. R., & Wegner, D. M. (1987). What do people think they're doing? Action identification and human behavior. *Psychological Review, 94,* 3–15.

Vallender, E. J., Mekel-Bobrov, N., & Lahn, B. T. (2008). Genetic basis of human brain evolution. *Trends in Neurosciences, 31,* 637–644.

Vance, E. B., & Wagner, N. N. (1976). Written descriptions of orgasm: A study of sex differences. *Archives of Sexual Behavior, 5,* 87–98.

van den Boom, D. C. (1994). The influence of temperament and mothering on attachment and exploration: An experimental manipulation of sensitive responsiveness among lower-class mothers with irritable infants. *Child Development, 65,* 1457–1477.

van den Boom, D. C. (1995). Do first year intervention effects endure? Follow-up during toddlerhood of a sample of Dutch irritable infants. *Child Development, 66,* 1798–1816.

van Dis, I., Kromhout, D., Geleijnse, J. M., Boer, J. M. A., & Verschuren, W. M. M. (2009). Body mass index and waist circumference predict both 10-year nonfatal and fatal cardiovascular disease risk: Study conducted in 20,000 Dutch men and women aged 20–65 years. *European Journal of Cardiovascular Prevention & Rehabilitation, 16*(6), 729–734.

Van Dongen, E. V., Thielen, J.-W., Takashima, A., Barth, M., & Fernandez, G. (2012). Sleep supports selective retention of associative memories based on relevance for future utilization. *PLoS One, 7,* e43426. doi:10.1371/journal.pone.0043426

van Honk, J., & Schutter, D. J. L. G. (2007). Testosterone reduces conscious detection of signals serving social correction: Implications for antisocial behavior. *Psychological Science, 18,* 663–667.

van Ijzendoorn, M. H. (1995). Adult attachment representations, parental responsiveness, and infant attachment: A meta-analysis on the predictive validity of the Adult Attachment Interview. *Psychological Bulletin, 117,* 387–403.

van Ijzendoorn, M. H., Juffer, F., & Klein Poelhuis, C. W. (2005). Adoption and cognitive development: A meta-analytic comparison of adopted and nonadopted children's IQ and school performance. *Psychological Bulletin, 131,* 301–316.

van Ijzendoorn, M. H., & Kroonenberg, P. M. (1988). Cross-cultural patterns of attachment: A meta-analysis of the strange situation. *Child Development, 59,* 147–156.

van Ijzendoorn, M. H., & Sagi, A. (1999). Cross-cultural patterns of attachment: Universal and contextual dimensions. In J. Cassidy & P. R.

Shaver (Eds.), *Handbook of attachment: Theory, research and clinical applications* (pp. 713–734). New York: Guilford Press.

van Ittersum, K., & Wansink, B. (2012). Plate size and color suggestibility: The Delboeuf illusion's bias on serving and eating behavior. *Journal of Consumer Research, 39,* 121–130.

van Praag, H. (2009). Exercise and the brain: Something to chew on. *Trends in Neuroscience, 32,* 283–290.

van Stegeren, A. H., Everaerd, W., Cahill, L., McGaugh, J. L., & Gooren, L. J. G. (1998). Memory for emotional events: Differential effects of centrally versus peripherally acting blocking agents. *Psychopharmacology, 138,* 305–310.

Van Vliet, I. M., van Well, E. P., Bruggeman, R., Campo, J. A., Hijman, R., Van Megen, H. J., . . . Van Rijen, P. C. (2013). An evaluation of irreversible psychosurgical treatment of patients with obsessive-compulsive disorder in the Netherlands, 2001–2008. *Journal of Nervous and Mental Disease, 201,* 226–228.

Vargha-Khadem, F., Gadian, D. G., Copp, A., & Mishkin, M. (2005). FOXP2 and the neuroanatomy of speech and language. *Nature Reviews Neuroscience, 6,* 131–138.

Vargha-Khadem, F., Gadian, D. G., Watkins, K. E., Connelly, A., Van Paesschen, W., & Mishkin, M. (1997). Differential effects of early hippocampal pathology on episodic and semantic memory. *Science, 277,* 376–380.

Vazire, S., & Mehl, M. R. (2008). Knowing me, knowing you: The relative accuracy and unique predictive validity of self ratings and otherratings of daily behavior. *Journal of Personality and Social Psychology, 95,* 1202–1216.

Veldhuizen, M. G., Douglas, D., Aschenbrenner, K., Gitelman, D. R., & Small, D. M. (2011). The anterior insular cortex represents breaches of taste identity expectation. *Journal of Neuroscience, 31,* 14735–14744.

Vinter, A., & Perruchet, P. (2002). Implicit motor learning through observational training in adults and children. *Memory & Cognition, 30,* 256–261.

Vitkus, J. (1999). *Casebook in abnormal psychology* (4th ed.). New York: McGraw-Hill.

Vondra, J. I., Shaw, D. S., Swearingen, L., Cohen, M., & Owens, E. B. (2001). Attachment stability and emotional and behavioral regulation from infancy to preschool age. *Development and Psychopathology, 13,* 13–33.

Von Frisch, K. (1974). Decoding the language of the bee. *Science, 185,* 663–668.

Voon, V., Pessiglione, M., Brezing, C., Gallea, C., Fernandez, H. H., Dolan, R. J., & Hallett, M. (2011). Mechanisms underlying dopamine-mediated reward bias in compulsive behaviors. *Neuron, 65,* 135–142.

Vortac, O. U., Edwards, M. B., & Manning, C. A. (1995). Functions of external cues in prospective memory. *Memory, 3,* 201–219.

Vrij, A., Granhag, P. A., Mann, S., & Leal, S. (2011). Outsmarting the liars: Toward a cognitive lie detection approach. *Current Directions in Psychological Science, 20*(1), 28–32.

Vygotsky, L. S. (1978). *Mind in society: The development of higher psychological processes.* Cambridge, MA: Harvard University Press.

Wade, N. J. (2005). *Perception and illusion: Historical perspectives.* New York: Springer.

Wade, S. E., Trathen, W., & Schraw, G. (1990). An analysis of spontaneous study strategies. *Reading Research Quarterly, 25,* 147–166.

Wadhwa, P. D., Sandman, C. A., & Garite, T. J. (2001). The neurobiology of stress in human pregnancy: Implications for prematurity and development of the fetal central nervous system. *Progress in Brain Research, 133,* 131–142.

Wager, T. D., Rilling, J., K., Smith, E. E., Sokolik, A., Casey, K. L., Davidson, R. J., . . . Cohen, J. D. (2004). Placebo-induced changes in fMRI in the anticipation and experience of pain. *Science, 303,* 1162–1167.

Wagner, A. D., Schacter, D. L., Rotte, M., Koustaal, W., Maril, A., Dale, A. M., . . . Buckner, R. L. (1998). Remembering and forgetting of verbal experiences as predicted by brain activity. *Science, 281,* 1188–1190.

Wagner, G., & Morris, E. (1987). Superstitious behavior in children. *Psychological Record, 37,* 471–488.

Wai, J., Putallaz, M., & Makel, M. C. (2012). Studying intellectual outliers: Are there sex differences, and are the smart getting smarter? *Current Directions in Psychological Science, 21*(6), 382–390. doi:10.1177/0963721412455052

Waite, L. J. (1995). Does marriage matter? *Demography, 32,* 483–507.

Wakefield, J.C. (2007). The concept of mental disorder: Diagnostic implications of the harmful dysfunction analysis. *World Psychiatry, 6,* 149-56.

Walden, T. A., & Ogan, T. A. (1988). The development of social referencing. *Child Development, 59,* 1230–1240.

Waldfogel, S. (1948). The frequency and affective character of childhood memories. *Psychological Monographs, 62* (Whole No. 291).

Waldmann, M. R. (2000). Competition among causes but not effects in predictive and diagnostic learning. *Journal of Experimental Psychology: Learning, Memory, and Cognition, 26,* 53–76.

Walker, C. (1977). Some variations in marital satisfaction. In R. C. J. Peel (Ed.), *Equalities and inequalities in family life* (pp. 127–139). London: Academic Press.

Walker, L. J. (1988). The development of moral reasoning. *Annals of Child Development, 55,* 677–691.

Walker, N. P., McConville, P. M., Hunter, D., Deary, I. J., & Whalley, L. J. (2002). Childhood mental ability and lifetime psychiatric contact. *Intelligence, 30*(3), 233–245. doi:10.1016/S0160-2896(01)00098-8

Wallace, J., Schnieder, T., & McGuffin, P. (2002). Genetics of depression. In I. H. Gottlieb & C. L. Hammen (Eds.), *Handbook of depression* (pp. 169–191). New York: Guilford Press.

Wallbott, H. G. (1998). Bodily expression of emotion. *European Journal of Social Psychology, 28,* 879–896.

Walster, E., Aronson, V., Abrahams, D., & Rottmann, L. (1966). Importance of physical attractiveness in dating behavior. *Journal of Personality and Social Psychology, 4,* 508–516.

Walster, E., Walster, G. W., & Berscheid, E. (1978). *Equity: Theory and research.* Boston: Allyn & Bacon.

Walton, D. N. (1990). What is reasoning? What is an argument? *Journal of Philosophy, 87,* 399–419.

Walton, G. M., & Spencer, S. J. (2009). Latent ability: Grades and test scores systematically underestimate the intellectual ability of negatively stereotyped students. *Psychological Science, 20,* 1132–1139.

Waltzman, S. B. (2006). Cochlear implants: Current status. *Expert Review of Medical Devices, 3,* 647–655.

Wamsley, E. J., & Stickgold, R. (2011). Memory, sleep, and dreaming: Experiencing consolidation. *Sleep Medicine Clinics, 6,* 97–108.

Wang, J. L., Jackson, L. A., Zhang, D. J., & Su, Z. Q. (2012). The relationships among the Big Five personality factors, self-esteem, narcissism, and sensation seeking to Chinese university students' uses of social networking sites (SNSs). *Computers in Human Behavior, 28,* 2313–2319.

Wang, L. H., McCarthy, G., Song, A. W., & LaBar, K. S. (2005). Amygdala activation to sad pictures during high-field (4 tesla) functional magnetic resonance imaging. *Emotion, 5,* 12–22.

Wang, P. S., Aguilar-Gaxiola, S., Alonso, J., Angermeyer, M. C., Borges, G., Bromet, E. J., . . . Wells, J. E. (2007). Use of mental health services for anxiety, mood, and substance disorders in 17 countries in the WHO World Mental Health Surveys. *Lancet, 370*, 841–850.

Wang, P. S., Berglund, P. A., Olfson, M., & Kessler, R. C. (2004). Delays in initial treatment contact after first onset of a mental disorder. *Health Services Research, 39*, 393–415.

Wang, P. S., Berglund, P., Olfson, M., Pincus, H. A., Wells, K. B., & Kessler, R. C. (2005). Failure and delay ininitial treatment contact after first onset of mental disorders in the National Comorbidity Survey Replication. *Archives of General Psychiatry, 62*(6), 629–640.

Wang, P. S., Demler, O., & Kessler, R. C. (2002). Adequacy of treatment for serious mental illness in the United States. *American Journal of Public Health, 92*, 92–98.

Wang, S.-H., & Baillargeon, R. (2008). Detecting impossible changes in infancy: A three-system account. *Trends in Cognitive Sciences, 12*(1), 17–23.

Wansink, B., & Linder, L. R. (2003). Interactions between forms of fat consumption and restaurant bread consumption. *International Journal of Obesity, 27*, 866–868.

Wansink, B., Painter, J. E., & North, J. (2005). Bottomless bowls: Why visual cues of portion size may influence intake. *Obesity Research, 13*, 93–100.

Wansink, B., & Wansink, C. S. (2010). The largest last supper: Depictions of food portions and plate size increased over the millennium. *International Journal of Obesity, 34*, 943–944.

Ward, J., Parkin, A. J., Powell, G., Squires, E. J., Townshend, J., & Bradley, V. (1999). False recognition of unfamiliar people: "Seeing film stars everywhere." *Cognitive Neuropsychology, 16*, 293–315.

Warneken, F., & Tomasello, M. (2009). Varieties of altruism in children and chimpanzees. *Trends in Cognitive Sciences, 13*, 397–402.

Warnock, M. (2003). *Making babies: Is there a right to have children?* Oxford, England: Oxford University Press.

Warren, K. R., & Hewitt, B. G. (2009). Fetal alcohol spectrum disorders: When science, medicine, public policy, and laws collide. *Developmental Disabilities Research Reviews, 15*, 170–175.

Warrington, E. K., & McCarthy, R. A. (1983). Category specific access dysphasia. *Brain, 106*, 859–878.

Warrington, E. K., & Shallice, T. (1984). Category specific semantic impairments. *Brain, 107*, 829–854.

Watanabe, S., Sakamoto, J., & Wakita, M. (1995). Pigeons' discrimination of painting by Monet and Picasso. *Journal of the Experimental Analysis of Behavior, 63*, 165–174.

Watkins, L. R., & Maier, S. F. (2005). Immune regulation of central nervous system functions: From sickness responses to pathological pain. *Journal of Internal Medicine, 257*, 139–155.

Watson, D., & Pennebaker, J. W. (1989). Health complaints, stress, and distress: Exploring the central role of negative affectivity. *Psychological Review, 96*, 234–254.

Watson, D., & Tellegen, A. (1985). Toward a consensual structure of mood. *Psychological Bulletin, 98*, 219–235.

Watson, J. B. (1913). Psychology as the behaviorist views it. *Psychological Review, 20*, 158–177.

Watson, J. B. (1924). *Behaviorism.* New York: People's Institute.

Watson, J. B. (1928). *Psychological care of infant and child.* New York: Norton.

Watson, J. B., & Rayner, R. (1920). Conditioned emotional reactions. *Journal of Experimental Psychology, 3*, 1–14.

Watson, R. I. (1978). *The great psychologists.* New York: Lippincott.

Watt, H. J. (1905). Experimentelle Beitraege zu einer Theorie des Denkens [Experimental contributions to a theory of thinking]. *Archiv fuer die gesamte Psychologie, 4*, 289–436.

Watzke, B., Rüddel, H., Jürgensen, R., Koch, U., Kristen, L., Grothgar, B., & Schulz, H. (2012). Longer term outcome of cognitive-behavioural and psychodynamic psychotherapy in routine mental health care: Randomised controlled trial. *Behaviour Research and Therapy, 50*, 580–387.

Weaver, I. C. G., Cervoni, N., Champagne, F. A., D'Alessio, A. C., Sharma, S., Seckl, J. R., . . . Meaney, M. J. (2004). Epigenetic programming by maternal behavior. *Nature Neuroscience, 7*, 847–854.

Webb, T. L., Miles, E., & Sheeran, P. (2012). Dealing with feeling: A meta-analysis of the effectiveness of strategies derived from the process model of emotion regulation. *Psychological Bulletin, 138*(4), 775–808.

Weber, R., & Crocker, J. (1983). Cognitive processes in the revision of stereotypic beliefs. *Journal of Personality and Social Psychology, 45*, 961–977.

Webster Marketon, J. I., & Glaser, R. (2008). Stress hormones and immune function. *Cellular Immunology, 252*, 16–26.

Wechsler, H., & Nelson, T. F. (2001). Binge drinking and the American college students: What's five drinks? *Psychology of Addictive Behaviors, 15*(4), 287–291. doi:10.1037/0893-164X.15.4.287

Wegner, D. M. (1989). *White bears and other unwanted thoughts.* New York: Viking.

Wegner, D. M. (1994a). Ironic processes of mental control. *Psychological Review, 101*, 34–52.

Wegner, D. M. (1994b). *White bears and other unwanted thoughts: Suppression, obsession, and the psychology of mental control.* New York: Guilford Press.

Wegner, D. M. (1997). Why the mind wanders. In J. D. Cohen & J. W. Schooler (Eds.), *Scientific approaches to consciousness* (pp. 295–315). Mahwah, NJ: Erlbaum.

Wegner, D. M. (2002). *The illusion of conscious will.* Cambridge, MA: MIT Press.

Wegner, D. M. (2009). How to think, say, or do precisely the worst thing for any occasion. *Science, 325*, 48–51.

Wegner, D. M., Ansfield, M., & Pilloff, D. (1998). The putt and the pendulum: Ironic effects of the mental control of action. *Psychological Science, 9*, 196–199.

Wegner, D. M., Broome, A., & Blumberg, S. J. (1997). Ironic effects of trying to relax under stress. *Behavior Research and Therapy, 35*, 11–21.

Wegner, D. M., Erber, R., & Raymond, P. (1991). Transactive memory in close relationships. *Journal of Personality and Social Psychology, 61*, 923–929.

Wegner, D. M., Erber, R. E., & Zanakos, S. (1993). Ironic processes in the mental control of mood and mood-related thought. *Journal of Personality and Social Psychology, 65*, 1093–1104.

Wegner, D. M., & Gilbert, D. T. (2000). Social psychology: The science of human experience. In H. Bless & J. Forgas (Eds.), *The message within: Subjective experience in social cognition and behavior* (pp. 1–9). Philadelphia: Psychology Press.

Wegner, D. M., Schneider, D. J., Carter, S. R., & White, T. L. (1987). Paradoxical effects of thought suppression. *Journal of Personality and Social Psychology, 53*, 5–13.

Wegner, D. M., Vallacher, R. R., Macomber, G., Wood, R., & Arps, K. (1984). The emergence of action. *Journal of Personality and Social Psychology, 46*, 269–279.

Wegner, D. M., & Wenzlaff, R. M. (1996). Mental control. In E. T. Higgins & A. Kruglanski (Eds.), *Social psychology: Handbook of basic mechanisms and processes* (pp. 466–492). New York: Guilford Press.

Wegner, D. M., Wenzlaff, R. M., & Kozak, M. (2004). Dream rebound: The return of suppressed thoughts in dreams. *Psychological Science, 15,* 232–236.

Wegner, D. M., & Zanakos, S. (1994). Chronic thought suppression. *Journal of Personality, 62,* 615–640.

Weinstein, N. D. (1980). Unrealistic optimism about future life events. *Journal of Personality and Social Psychology, 39,* 806–820.

Weintraub, D., Papay, K., & Siderowf, A. (2013). Screening for impulse control symptoms in patients with de novo Parkinson disease: A case-control study. *Neurology, 80,* 176–180.

Weir, C., Toland, C., King, R. A., & Martin, L. M. (2005). Infant contingency/extinction performance after observing partial reinforcement. *Infancy, 8,* 63–80.

Weiser, M., Zarka, S., Werbeloff, N., Kravitz, E., & Lubin, G. (2010). Cognitive test scores in male adolescent cigarette smokers compared to non-smokers: A population-based study. *Addiction, 105*(2), 358–363. doi:10.1111/j.1360-0443.2009.02740.x

Weisfeld, G. (1999). *Evolutionary principles of human adolescence.* New York: Basic Books.

Weissenborn, R. (2000). State-dependent effects of alcohol on explicit memory: The role of semantic associations. *Psychopharmacology, 149,* 98–106.

Weissman, M. M., Markowitz, J. C., & Klerman, G. L. (2000). *Comprehensive guide to interpersonal psychotherapy.* New York: Basic Books.

Weldon, M. S. (2001). Remembering as a social process. In D. L. Medin (Ed.), *The psychology of learning and motivation: Advances in research and theory* (Vol. 40, pp. 67–120). San Diego, CA: Academic Press.

Wenzlaff, R. M., & Wegner, D. M. (2000). Thought suppression. In S. T. Fiske (Ed.), *Annual review of psychology* (Vol. 51, pp. 51–91). Palo Alto, CA: Annual Reviews.

Wernicke, K. (1874). *Der Aphasische Symptomenkomplex* [The aphasic symptom complex]. Breslau: Cohn and Weigart.

Wertheimer, M. (1982). *Productive thinking.* Chicago: University of Chicago Press. (Originally published 1945)

Wesch, N. N., Law, B., & Hall, C. R. (2007). The use of observational learning by athletes. *Journal of Sport Behavior, 30,* 219–231.

Westrin, A., & Lam, R. W. (2007). Seasonal affective disorder: A clinical update. *Journal of Clinical Psychiatry, 19,* 239–246.

Wexler, K. (1999). Maturation and growth of grammar. In W. C. Ritchie & T. K. Bhatia (Eds.), *Handbook of child language acquisition* (pp. 55–110). San Diego: Academic Press.

Whalen, P. J., Rauch, S. L., Etcoff, N. L., McInerney, S. C., Lee, M. B., & Jenike, M. A. (1998). Masked presentations of emotional facial expressions modulate amygdala activity without explicit knowledge. *The Journal of Neuroscience, 18,* 411–418.

Whalley, L. J., & Deary, I. J. (2001). Longitudinal cohort study of childhood IQ and survival up to age 76. *British Medical Journal, 322,* 1–5.

Wheatley, T., & Haidt, J. (2005). Hypnotic disgust makes moral judgments more severe. *Psychological Science, 16,* 780–784.

Wheeler, M. A., Petersen, S. E., & Buckner, R. L. (2000). Memory's echo: Vivid recollection activates modality-specific cortex. *Proceedings of the National Academy of Sciences, USA, 97,* 11125–11129.

White, B. L., & Held, R. (1966). Plasticity of motor development in the human infant. In J. F. Rosenblith & W. Allinsmith (Eds.), *The cause of behavior* (pp. 60–70). Boston: Allyn & Bacon.

White, F. J. (1996). Synaptic regulation of mesocorticolimbic dopamine neurons. *Annual Review of Neuroscience, 19,* 405–436.

White, G. M., & Kirkpatrick, J. (Eds.). (1985). *Person, self, and experience: Exploring pacific ethnopsychologies.* Berkeley: University of California Press.

White, N. M., & Milner, P. M. (1992). The psychobiology of reinforcers. *Annual Review of Psychology, 41,* 443–471.

Whitney, D., Ellison, A., Rice, N. J., Arnold, D., Goodale, M., Walsh, V., & Milner, D. (2007). Visually guided reaching depends on motion area MT+. *Cerebral Cortex, 17,* 2644–2649.

Whorf, B. (1956). *Language, thought, and reality.* Cambridge, MA: The MIT Press.

Whybrow, P. C. (1997). *A mood apart.* New York: Basic Books.

Wicker, B., Keysers, C., Plailly, J., Royet, J.-P., Gallese, V., & Rizzolatti, G. (2003). Both of us disgusted in *my* insula: The common neural basis of seeing and feeling disgust. *Neuron, 40,* 655–664.

Wicklund, R. (1975). Objective self-awareness. In L. Berkowitz (Ed.), *Advances in experimental social psychology* (Vol. 8, pp. 233–275). New York: Academic Press.

Wiederman, M. W. (1997). Pretending orgasm during sexual intercourse: Correlates in a sample of young adult women. *Journal of Sex & Marital Therapy, 23,* 131–139.

Wiener, D. N. (1996). *B. F. Skinner: Benign anarchist.* Boston: Allyn & Bacon.

Wiesenthal, D. L., Austrom, D., & Silverman, I. (1983). Diffusion of responsibility in charitable donations. *Basic and Applied Social Psychology, 4,* 17–27.

Wig, G. S., Buckner, R. L., & Schacter, D. L. (2009). Repetition priming influences distinct brain systems: Evidence from task-evoked data and resting-state correlations. *Journal of Neurophysiology, 101,* 2632–2648.

Wiggs, C. L., & Martin, A. (1998). Properties and mechanisms of perceptual priming. *Current Opinion in Neurobiology, 8,* 227–233.

Wilcoxon, H. C., Dragoin, W. B., & Kral, P. A. (1971). Illness-induced aversions in rats and quail: Relative salience of visual and gustatory cues. *Science, 171,* 826–828.

Wiley, J. L. (1999). Cannabis: Discrimination of "internal bliss"? *Pharmacology, Biochemistry, & Behavior, 64,* 257–260.

Wilhelm, I., Dieckelmann, S., Molzow, I., Ayoub, A., Molle, M., & Born, J. (2011). Sleep selectively enhances memories expected to be of future relevance. *Journal of Neuroscience, 31,* 1563–1569.

Wilkinson, L., Teo, J. T., Obeso, I., Rothwell, J. C., & Jahanshahi, M. (2010). The contribution of primary motor cortex is essential for probabilistic implicit sequence learning: Evidence from theta burst magnetic stimulation. *Journal of Cognitive Neuroscience, 22,* 427–436.

Williams, A. C. (2002). Facial expression of pain: An evolutionary account. *Behavioral and Brain Sciences, 25,* 439–488.

Williams, C. M., & Kirkham, T. C. (1999). Anandamide induces overeating: Mediation by central cannabinoid (CB1) receptors. *Psychopharmacology, 143,* 315–317.

Williams, K. D., Nida, S. A., Baca, L. D., & Latané, B. (1989). Social loafing and swimming: Effects of identifiability on individual and relay performance of intercollegiate swimmers. *Basic and Applied Social Psychology, 10,* 73–81.

Willingham, D. T. (2007). Critical thinking: Why is it so hard to teach? *American Educator, 31*(2), 8–19.

Wilson, K., & Korn, J. H. (2007). Attention during lectures: Beyond ten minutes. *Teaching of Psychology, 34,* 85–89.

Wilson, T. D. (2002). *Strangers to ourselves: Discovering the adaptive unconscious.* Cambridge, MA: Harvard University Press.

Wilson, T. D. (2009). Know thyself. *Perspectives on Psychological Science, 4,* 384–389.

Wilson, T. D. (2012, July 12). Stop bullying the "soft" sciences. *Los Angeles Times*. Available from http://articles.latimes.com/2012/jul/12/opinion/la-oe-wilson-social-sciences-20120712

Wilson, T. D., & Lassiter, G. D. (1982). Increasing intrinsic interest with superfluous extrinsic constraints. *Journal of Personality and Social Psychology, 42,* 811–819.

Wilson, T. D., Meyers, J., & Gilbert, D. T. (2003). "How happy was I, anyway?" A retrospective impact bias. *Social Cognition, 21,* 421–446.

Wimber, M., Rutschmann, R. N., Greenlee, M. W., & Bauml, K.-H. (2009). Retrieval from episodic memory: Neural mechanisms of interference resolution. *Journal of Cognitive Neuroscience, 21,* 538–549.

Wimmer, H., & Perner, J. (1983). Beliefs about beliefs: Representations and constraining function of wrong beliefs in young children's understanding of deception. *Cognition, 13,* 103–128.

Winawer, J., Witthoft, N., Frank, M. C., Wu, L., Wade, A. R., & Boroditsky, L. (2007). Russian blues reveal effects of language on color discrimination. *Proceedings of the National Academy of Sciences, USA, 104,* 7780–7785.

Windeler, J., & Kobberling, J. (1986). Empirische Untersuchung zur Einschatzung diagnostischer Verfahren am Beispiel des Haemoccult-Tests [An empirical study of the value of diagnostic procedures using the example of the hemoccult test]. *Klinische Wochenscrhrift, 64,* 1106–1112.

Windham, G. C., Eaton, A., & Hopkins, B. (1999). Evidence for an association between environmental tobacco smoke exposure and birthweight: A meta-analysis and new data. *Pediatrics and Perinatal Epidemiology, 13,* 35–57.

Winner, E. (2000). The origins and ends of giftedness. *American Psychologist, 55,* 159–169.

Winocur, G., Moscovitch, M., & Bontempi, B. (2010). Memory formation and long-term retention in humans and animals: Convergence towards a transformation account of hippocampal–neocortical interactions. *Neuropsychologia, 48,* 2339–2356.

Winter, L., & Uleman, J. S. (1984). When are social judgments made? Evidence for the spontaneousness of trait inferences. *Journal of Personality and Social Psychology, 47,* 237–252.

Winterer, G., & Weinberger, D. R. (2004). Genes, dopamine and cortical signal-to-noise ratio in schizophrenia. *Trends in Neuroscience, 27,* 683–690.

Wise, R. A. (1989). Brain dopamine and reward. *Annual Review of Psychology, 40,* 191–225.

Wise, R. A. (2005). Forebrain substrates of reward and motivation. *Journal of Comparative Neurology, 493,* 115–121.

Wittchen, H., Knauper, B., & Kessler, R. C. (1994). Lifetime risk of depression. *British Journal of Psychiatry, 165,* 16–22.

Wittgenstein, L. (1999). *Philosophical investigations.* Upper Saddle River, NJ: Prentice Hall. (Originally published 1953)

Wixted, J. T., & Ebbensen, E. (1991). On the form of forgetting. *Psychological Science, 2,* 409–415.

Wolf, J. (2003, May 18). Through the looking glass. *The New York Times Magazine,* p. 120.

Wolf, J. R., Arkes, H. R., & Muhanna, W. A. (2008). The power of touch: An examination of the effect of duration of physical contact on the valuation of objects. *Judgment and Decision Making, 3,* 476–482.

Wolff, P., & Holmes, K. J. (2011). Linguistic relativity. *WIRES Cognitive Science, 2,* 253–265.

Wong, D. T., Bymaster, F. P., & Engleman, E. A. (1995). Prozac (fluoxetine, Lilly 110140), the first selective serotonin uptake inhibitor and an antidepressant drug: Twenty years since its first publication. *Life Sciences, 57,* 411–441.

Wood, J. M., & Bootzin, R. R. (1990). Prevalence of nightmares and their independence from anxiety. *Journal of Abnormal Psychology, 99,* 64–68.

Wood, J. M., Bootzin, R. R., Rosenhan, D., Nolen-Hoeksema, S., & Jourden, F. (1992). Effects of the 1989 San Francisco earthquake on frequency and content of nightmares. *Journal of Abnormal Psychology, 101,* 219–224.

Woodley, M. A., te Nijenhuis, J., & Murphy, R. (2013). Were the Victorians cleverer than us? The decline in general intelligence estimated from a meta-analysis of the slowing of simple reaction time. *Intelligence.* Advance online publication. doi:10.1016/j.intell.2013.04.006

Woods, S. C., Seeley, R. J., Porte, D., Jr., & Schwartz, M. W. (1998). Signals that regulate food intake and energy homeostasis. *Science, 280,* 1378–1383.

Woody, S. R., & Nosen, E. (2008). Psychological models of phobic disorders and panic. In M. M. Anthony & M. B. Stein (Eds.), *Oxford handbook of anxiety and related disorders* (pp. 209–224). New York: Oxford University Press.

Woody, S. R., & Sanderson, W. C. (1998). Manuals for empirically supported treatments: 1998 update. *Clinical Psychologist, 51,* 17–21.

World Health Organization (WHO). (2004). *Global mortality and burden of disease estimates for WHO member states in 2002* (Data file). Geneva, Switzerland: Author. Retrieved from www.who.int/healthinfo/statistics/bodgbddeathdalyestimates.xls

Wrangham, R., & Peterson, D. (1997). *Demonic males: Apes and the origin of human violence.* New York: Mariner.

Wren, A. M., Seal, L. J., Cohen, M. A., Brynes, A. E., Frost, G. S., Murphy, K. G., . . . Bloom, S. R. (2001). Ghrelin enhances appetite and increases food intake in humans. *Journal of Clinical Endocrinology and Metabolism, 86,* 5992–5995.

Wrenn, C. C., Turchi, J. N., Schlosser, S., Dreiling, J. L., Stephenson, D. A., & Crawley, J. N. (2006). Performance of galanin transgenic mice in the 5-choice serial reaction time attentional task. *Pharmacology Biochemistry and Behavior, 83,* 428–440.

Wulf, S. (1994, March 14). Err Jordan. *Sports Illustrated.*

Wundt, W. (1900–1920). *Völkerpsychologie. Eine untersuchung der entwicklungsgesetze von sprache, mythos und sitte* [Völkerpsychologie: An examination of the developmental laws of language, myth, and custom]. Leipzig, Germany: Engelmann & Kroner.

Yamaguchi, S. (1998). Basic properties of umami and its effects in humans. *Physiology and Behavior, 49,* 833–841.

Yang, S., & Sternberg, R. J. (1997). Conceptions of intelligence in ancient Chinese philosophy. *Journal of Theoretical and Philosophical Psychology, 17,* 101–119.

Yeo, B. T. T., Krienen, F. M., Sepulcre, J., Sabuncu, M. R., Lashkari, D., Hollinshead, M., . . . Buckner, R. L. (2011). The organization of the human cerebral cortex estimated by intrinsic functional connectivity. *Journal of Neurophysiology, 106,* 1125–1165.

Yeshurun, Y., & Sobel, N. (2010). An odor is not worth a thousand words: From multidimensional odors to unidimensional odor objects. *Annual Review of Psychology, 61,* 219–241.

Yik, M., Russell, J. A., & Steiger, J. H. (2011). A 12-point circumplex structure of core affect. *Emotion, 11*(4), 705–731.

Young, R. M. (1990). *Mind, brain, and adaptation in the nineteenth century: Cerebral localization and its biological context from Gall to Ferrier.* New York: Oxford University Press.

Yucha, C., & Gilbert, C. D. (2004). *Evidence-based practice in biofeedback and neurofeedback.* Colorado Springs, CO: Association for Applied Psychophysiology and Biofeedback.

Yuill, N., & Perner, J. (1988). Intentionality and knowledge in children's judgments of actor's responsibility and recipient's emotional reaction. *Developmental Psychology, 24,* 358–365.

Yzerbyt, V., & Demoulin, S. (2010). Intergroup relations. In S. T. Fiske, D. T. Gilbert, & G. Lindzey (Eds.), *The handbook of social psychology* (5th ed., Vol. 2, pp. 1024–1083). New York: Wiley.

Zahn-Waxler, C., Radke-Yarrow, M., Wagner, E., & Chapman, M. (1992). Development of concern for others. *Developmental Psychology, 28,* 126–136.

Zajonc, R. B. (1968). Attitudinal effects of mere exposure. *Journal of Personality and Social Psychology, 9,* 1–27.

Zajonc, R. B. (1989). Feeling the facial efference: Implications of the vascular theory of emotion. *Psychological Review, 96,* 395–416.

Zebrowitz, L. A., Hall, J. A., Murphy, N. A., & Rhodes, G. (2002). Looking smart and looking good: Facial cues to intelligence and their origins. *Personality and Social Psychology Bulletin, 28,* 238–249.

Zebrowitz, L. A., & Montepare, J. M. (1992). Impressions of baby-faced individuals across the life span. *Developmental Psychology, 28,* 1143–1152.

Zeki, S. (1993). *A vision of the brain.* London: Blackwell Scientific.

Zeki, S. (2001). Localization and globalization in conscious vision. *Annual Review of Neuroscience, 24,* 57–86.

Zentall, T. R., Sutton, J. E., & Sherburne, L. M. (1996). True imitative learning in pigeons. *Psychological Science, 7,* 343–346.

Zentner, M., & Mitura, K. (2012). Stepping out of the caveman's shadow: Nations' gender gap predicts degree of sex differentiation in mate preferences. *Psychological Science, 23*(10), 1176–1185. doi:10.1177/0956797612441004

Zernike, K. (2012, August 25). After gay son's suicide, mother finds blame in herself and in her church. *New York Times, p. A14.*

Zhang, T. Y., & Meaney, M. J. (2010). Epigenetics and the environmental regulation of the genome and its function. *Annual Review of Psychology, 61,* 439–466.

Zhong, C.-B., Bohns, V. K., & Gino, F. (2010). Good lamps are the best police: Darkness increases dishonesty and self-interested behavior. *Psychological Science, 21*(3), 311–314. doi:10.1177/0956797609360754

Zihl, J., von Cramon, D., & Mai, N. (1983). Selective disturbance of movement vision after bilateral brain damage. *Brain, 106,* 313–340.

Zillmann, D., Katcher, A. H., & Milavsky, B. (1972). Excitation transfer from physical exercise to subsequent aggressive behavior. *Journal of Experimental Psychology, 8,* 247–259.

Zimprich, D., & Martin, M. (2002). Can longitudinal changes in processing speed explain longitudinal age changes in fluid intelligence? *Psychology and Aging, 17,* 690–695.

Zuckerman, M., DePaulo, B. M., & Rosenthal, R. (1981). Verbal and nonverbal communication of deception. In L. Berkowitz (Ed.), *Advances in experimental social psychology* (Vol. 14, pp. 1–59). New York: Academic Press.

Zuckerman, M., & Driver, R. E. (1985). Telling lies: Verbal and nonverbal correlates of deception. In W. Seigman & S. Feldstein (Eds.), *Multichannel integrations of nonverbal behavior* (pp. 129–147). Hillsdale, NJ: Erlbaum.

Name Index

Subject Index

Note: Page numbers followed by f indicate figures; those followed by t indicate tables.